S0-CFL-931

Discovering Psychology

Discovering Psychology

Bernard Weiner, *University of California, Los Angeles*
Willard Runquist, *University of Alberta*
Peggy A. Runquist, *University of Alberta*
Bertram H. Raven, *University of California, Los Angeles*
William J. Meyer, *Syracuse University*
Arnold Leiman, *University of California, Berkeley*
Charles L. Kutscher, *Syracuse University*
Benjamin Kleinmuntz, *University of Illinois, Chicago Circle*
Ralph Norman Haber, *University of Rochester*

S R A SCIENCE RESEARCH ASSOCIATES, INC.
Chicago, Palo Alto, Toronto, Henley-on-Thames, Sydney, Paris, Stuttgart
A Subsidiary of IBM

LIBRARY OF CONGRESS CATALOGING IN PUBLICATION DATA

Main entry under title:

Discovering psychology.

Includes bibliographies and indexes.
1. Psychology. I. Weiner, Bernard. [DNLM:
1. Psychology. BF139 D611]
BF121.D56 150 76-30320
ISBN 0-574-17935-6

Acknowledgments We wish to thank the following for permission to reprint, abridge, or adapt:

Earlier versions of Chapters 16 and 17 appeared in ESSENTIALS OF ABNORMAL PSYCHOLOGY. Copyright © 1974 by Benjamin Kleinmuntz. By permission of Harper & Row, Publishers.

Page 312 Excerpted from *Remembering: A Study in Experimental and Social Psychology* by F. C. Bartlett. © 1932 Cambridge University Press. Used by permission of the publisher. **461–63** Excerpted from "Behavior therapy in the home: Amelioration of problem parent-child relations with the parent in a therapeutic role" by R. P. Hawkins, R. F. Peterson, E. Schweid, and S. W. Bijou in *Journal of Experimental Child Psychology,* 1966, 4:99–107. © 1966 Academic Press, Inc. Used by permission of the publisher and R. P. Hawkins. **475** Reprinted with permission from T. H. Holmes and R. H. Rahe, "The social readjustment rating scale," *Journal of Psychosomatic Research,* 1967, 11:213–18. ©1967, Pergamon Press Ltd. **487–88** Reprinted from THE COMPLETE INTRODUCTORY LECTURES ON PSYCHOANALYSIS by Sigmund Freud. Translated and Edited by James Strachey. By permission of W. W. Norton & Company, Inc. Copyright © 1966 by W. W. Norton & Company, Inc. Copyright © 1965, 1964, 1963 by James Strachey. Copyright 1933 by Sigmund Freud. Copyright Renewed 1961 by W. J. H. Sprott. Copyright 1920, 1935 by Edward L. Bernays. **504, 506, 520, 521, 526** Earlier versions of these case reports appeared in ESSENTIALS OF ABNORMAL PSYCHOLOGY. Copyright © 1974 by Benjamin Kleinmuntz. By permission of Harper & Row, Publishers. **556** Reprinted with the permission of Farrar, Straus & Giroux, Inc. from LISTENING WITH THE THIRD EAR. Copyright 1948 by Theodor Reik, Copyright © by Arthur Reik. **561** Reprinted from *The Science of Living* by K. A. Adler. Copyright 1929, 1957, by Dr. Kurt Adler. Used by permission of Sanford J. Greenburger Associates. **563–64** Carl R. Rogers, CLIENT-CENTERED THERAPY. Copyright © 1951. Used by permission of Houghton Mifflin Company. **572–73** Reprinted from "Behavior modification in adult psychiatric patients" by Edward S. Sulzer in L. B. Ullmann and L. Krasner (eds.) *Case Studies in Behavior Modification,* 1965. © 1965 by Holt, Rinehart and Winston, Inc. Used by permission of B. Sulzer-Azaroff.

Tables 3A•1, 3A•2 Adapted from "Physical maturing among boys as related to behavior" by M. C. Jones and N. Bayley in *Journal of Educational Psychology,* 1950, 41:129–48. *Copyright 1958 by the American Psychological Association. Reprinted by permission.*

Table 4•2 Adapted from *Biological Foundations of Language* by E. H. Lenneberg. © 1967 John Wiley & Sons, Inc. Used by permission of the publisher. **4•3** Adapted from "An investigation of the development of the sentence and the extent of vocabulary in young children" by M. E. Smith in *University of Iowa Studies in Child Welfare,* 1926, 3(5). © 1926 University of Iowa. Used by permission of the publisher. **4•4** Modified and reproduced by permission. Copyright © 1969 by The Psychological Corporation, New York, N.Y. All rights reserved.

Table 5•3 Adapted from "Sex, age, and state as determinants of mother-infant interaction" by H. Moss in *Merrill-Palmer Quarterly,* 1967, 13:19–36. © 1967 The Merrill-Palmer Institute. Used by permission of the publisher and author. **5•5** Adapted from "Sex-Role stereotypes: A current appraisal" by I. K. Broverman, S. R. Vogel, D. K. Broverman, F. E. Clarkson, and P. S. Rosenkrantz in *Journal of Social Issues,* 1972, 28:63. © 1972 Society for the Psychological Study of Social Issues. Used by permission of the publisher and I. K. Broverman. **5•9** Adapted from "Parental power legitimation and its effects on the adolescent" by Glen H. Elder, Jr., in *Sociometry,* 1963, 26:50–65. © 1963 American Sociological Association. Used by permission of the publisher.

Table 6•1 Adapted from "The differentiative effects of age upon human learning" by F. L. Ruch in *Journal of General Psychology,* 1934, 11:261–85. © 1934 The Journal Press. Used by permission of the publisher and author. **6•2** Adapted from Botwinick, *Aging and Behavior.* Copyright © 1973 by Springer Publishing Company, New York. Used by permission. **6•3** Adapted from "Children's perceptions of the elderly" by T. Hickey, L. Hickey, and R. Kalish in *Journal of Genetic Psychology,* 1968, 112:227–35. © 1965 The Journal Press. Used by permission of the publisher and authors. **6•4** Adapted from "Age norms, age constraints and adult socialization" by B. L. Neugarten, J. W. Moore, and J. C. Lowe in *American Journal of Sociology,* 1965, 70:710–17. © 1965 The University of Chicago Press. Used by permission of the publisher. **6•5** Adapted from "A social psychological perspective on aging" by R. I. Havighurst in *Gerontologist,* 1968, 8(2):67–71. **6•6** Adapted from "Physiological effects of social environments" by S. Kiritz and R. Moos in *Psychosomatic Medicine,* 1974, 36:96–114 © 1974 American Psychosomatic Society. Used by permission of American Elsevier Publishing Co.

Table 7•1 From NEW DIRECTIONS IN PSYCHOLOGY I. Copyright © 1962 by Holt, Rinehart and Winston, Inc. Reprinted by permission of Holt, Rinehart and Winston. **7•2** Adapted from *Introduction to Psychology,* 6th ed., by E. R. Hilgard, R. C. Atkinson, and R. L. Atkinson. © 1975 Harcourt Brace Jovanovich, Inc. Used by permission of the publisher.

Table 13•1 Adapted from "The measurement and reinforcement of behavior of psychotics" by T. Ayllón and N. H. Azrin in *Journal of the Experimental Analysis of Behavior,* 1965, 8:357–8.3. Copyright 1965 by the Society for the Experimental Analysis of Behavior, Inc. Used by permission of the publisher and T. Ayllón. **13•2, 13•3, 13•4** Nicholas S. DiCaprio. *Personality Theories: Guides to Living.* Philadelphia: W. B. Saunders Company, 1974. © 1974 W. B. Saunders Company. Used by permission of the publisher and author.

Tables 14•2, 14•3 Reprinted from *Personality: Strategies for the Study of Man* by R. M. Liebert and M. D. Spiegler. © 1974 The Dorsey Press. Used by permission of the publisher. **14•4** Donn Bryne, AN INTRODUCTION TO PERSONALITY: Research, Theory, and Applications, 2nd ed., © 1974, pp. 279–280. Adapted by permission of Prentice-Hall, Inc., Englewood Cliffs, New Jersey.

(continued on page 878)

Contents

Preface

During the last decade relevance became a prime requisite in education, especially at the college level. Students expected instant success, and we as teachers were held accountable in many cases for instant expertise on the part of the students. Many academicians predicted that this approach would soon wear thin. This prophecy has come about.

Today many students realize that what counts in the long run is quality. Not all knowledge can be instantly acquired and applied to the problems of everyday life, but knowledge is nonetheless valuable for other reasons—or even for its own sake.

Discovering Psychology is based on the premise that knowledge, presented in a coherent and well-written manner, is the cornerstone of our educational system. As the authors of this textbook, we have tried to present psychology the way we know it—as a science that asks more questions than it answers.

The writing of this book was a learning experience for each of us. We met numerous times as a group, agreed on a detailed outline for each section, read each other's chapters, and made critical comments as necessary. The result is a textbook that presents psychology as an ever-changing science. We have tried to convey in the book the excitement we feel that our discipline has to offer.

In providing a thorough overview of the field of psychology, we have given the instructor a wide range of choices about which areas to cover in depth and which to cover lightly or to omit. To help you structure a course that fits your particular situation, we have put together three alternate arrangements in the chapters (Table A).

After taking an introductory psychology course, many students decide to take other courses in psychology and may even decide to become psychology majors. This is the kind of interest and enthusiasm that an instructor hopes to arouse and maintain, perhaps by the way he or she structures the course or because of the text used. We feel that this text is inspiring and informative not only for those students who go on afterwards for further in-depth study, but also for the students who take an introductory psychology course in order to broaden their perspectives on life.

We want to call to your attention several aspects of the book that we hope will facilitate your use of it. The material that we have chosen to put in the colored boxes throughout the chapters is often controversial. You will find in many of these boxes reports of theories, studies, and experiments that may be at

Table A Alternate Arrangements of Chapters

BIOLOGICAL-EXPERIMENTAL ORIENTATION		PERSONALITY-SOCIAL ORIENTATION		SHORTER GENERAL COURSE	
1	Paths to Psychology	**2**	Research Methods of Psychology	**2**	Research Methods of Psychology
2	Research Methods of Psychology	**3**	The Nature of Developmental Psychology	**3**	The Nature of Developmental Psychology
7	Sensory Processes	**4**	The Development of Cognitive Competence	**4**	The Development of Cognitive Competence
8	Visual Perception: The Active Perceiver	**5**	Social Development	**5**	Social Development
23	Genetics and Behavior	**6**	The Psychology of Aging	**8**	Visual Perception: The Active Perceiver
9	Memory	**12**	Motivation	**9**	Memory
10	Basic Learning Processes	**13**	Theories of Personality	**10**	Basic Learning Processes
11	Cognition	**14**	The Assessment of Personality	**11**	Cognition
12	Motivation	**15**	The Dynamics of Personality: Stress, Conflict, Inhibition, and Frustration	**12**	Motivation
24	Communication in the Brain	**16**	Behavior Pathology	**13**	Theories of Personality
25	Behavioral Biology	**17**	Behavior Change	**15**	The Dynamics of Personality: Stress, Conflict, Inhibition, and Frustration
21	Two Approaches to Animal Behavior: Ethology and Psychology	**18**	Person Perception and Interpersonal Evaluation	**16**	Behavior Pathology
22	Brain Evolution and Behavior Evolution	**19**	The Psychological Dynamics of Inter-personal Influence	**17**	Behavior Change
3	The Nature of Developmental Psychology	**20**	The Dynamics of Interaction Between Individual and Group	**18**	Person Perception and Interpersonal Evaluation
4	The Development of Cognitive Competence			**19**	The Psychological Dynamics of Inter-personal Influence
5	Social Development			**21**	Two Approaches to Animal Behavior: Ethology and Psychology
6	The Psychology of Aging			**23**	Genetics and Behavior

NOTE: Instructors who prefer a briefer introduction to psychology than the one supplied by the complete text can abridge the text either by not using certain chapters (probably those that most overlap other chapters or courses as, for example, the short course organization suggested in this table omits Chapters 1, 6, 7, 14, 20, and 22) or by not using various groupings of chapters (as, for example, the organization suggested in this table omits the whole unit on biological psychology). Instructors may simply omit those chapters or units that they ordinarily do not include in their course.

the cutting edge of our discipline—and then again they may prove to lead nowhere. Throughout the text you will also find that certain words appear in boldface. Definitions of these terms can be found in the glossary, which has been incorporated into the index. You will also find at the back of the book two appendixes—one on statistics and one on the metric system of measurement. Refer to these as necessary to enhance your understanding of the textual material.

A text such as this cannot be written without the help of many people—more than we can name here. However, we would like especially to thank the reviewers listed below, whose comments were invaluable:

Peter A. Fried, Carleton University
Robert Goodale, Boston State College
Barry R. Haimson, Southeastern Massachusetts University
James W. Hall, Northwestern University
Charles C. Hodge, St. Lawrence University
Walter Mink, Macalester College
Herbert L. Mirels, Ohio State University
Peter E. Nathan, Rutgers—The State University of New Jersey
Stephen E. Palmer, University of California, Berkeley
Alexander Rosen, University of Illinois, Chicago Circle
Robert M. Rosenbaum, Erindale College, University of Toronto
Joseph Stokes, University of Illinois, Chicago Circle
Stanley Sue, University of Washington
Larry Till, Cerritos College
Keith T. Wescourt, Stanford University
David Wood, University of Arkansas
Zakhour Youssef, Eastern Michigan University

We express appreciation also to the editors who worked on various chapters—Lionel Gambill, Carol King, and Alice Rosendall—and to Ben Dawson for his work on the biological chapters. The staff at Science Research Associates was invaluable, and we would like especially to mention Michael Zamczyk, who brought us all together, and Gretchen Hargis, who somehow managed to survive the ordeal of working with nine authors on one book. Without her patience and dedication this book would never have been published.

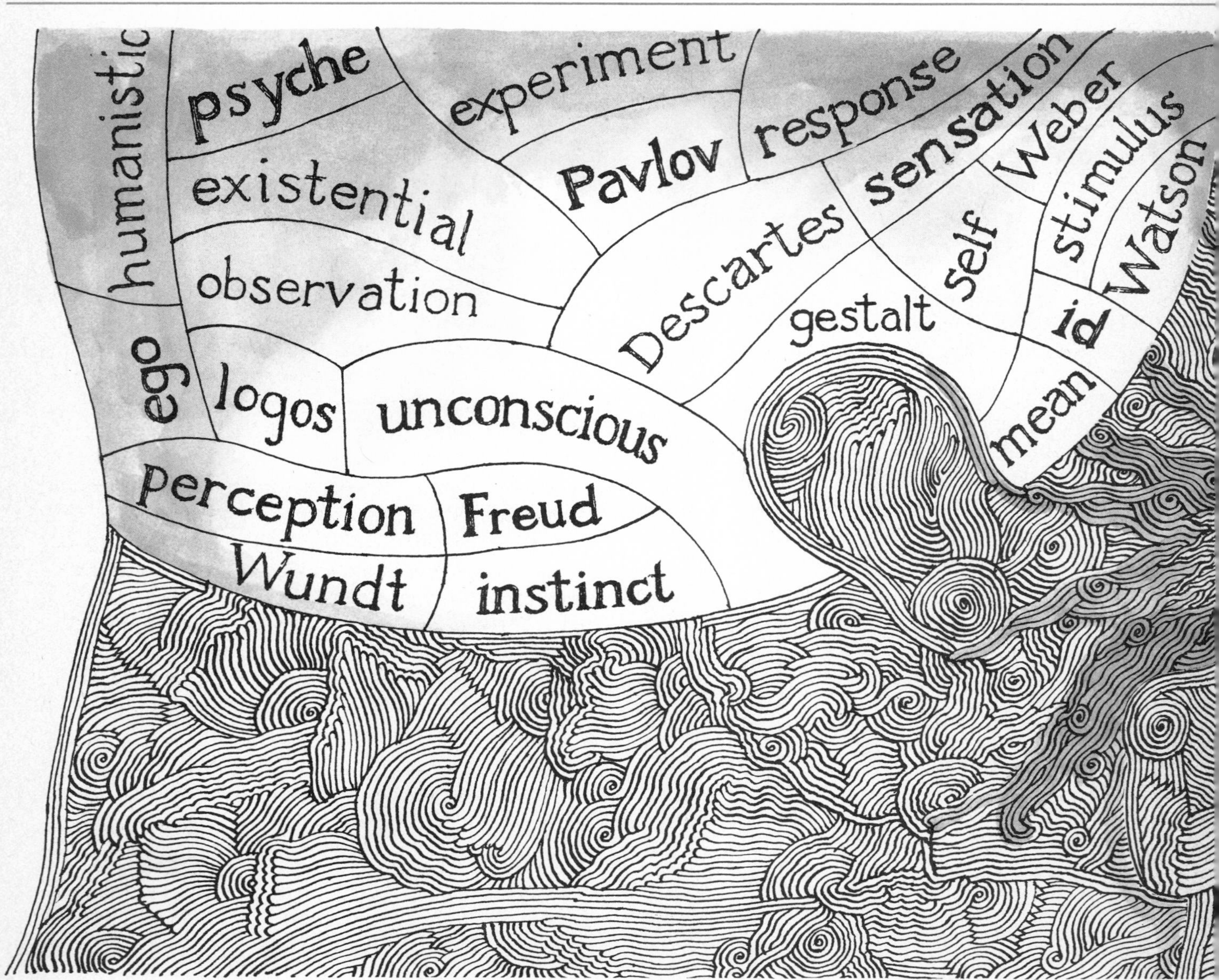
humanistic
psyche
experiment
response
sensation
Weber
stimulus
Watson
existential
Pavlov
observation
Descartes
self
gestalt
id
ego
logos
unconscious
mean
perception
Freud
Wundt
instinct

Psychology: The Science of Behavior

I What is psychology and what makes it a science? Psychology is as old as the observation of behavior—whether another person's behavior or one's own. In a sense, the observation of behavior became a science when individuals began comparing their observations and devising systems to accumulate observations and to evaluate conflicting explanations.

As we shall see in Chapter 1, attempts to understand and explain behavior have been made for centuries. Current explanations still conflict at times, even though methods of observation and recording have improved. The basic assumptions underlying competing theories can sometimes be as untestable in psychology today as they were centuries ago—and as they continue to be in all fields of inquiry, from mathematics to religion.

Chapter 2 introduces some of the methods psychologists have developed in order to increase the reliability (replicability) of their findings and to extend these findings with some validity to similar situations or organisms. Even these methods, however, have their origins in competing assumptions about human behavior. Despite what the popular press may say when reporting a scientific discovery, behavioral scientists recognize that "proof" is not necessarily infallible.

Psychology is ultimately whatever behaviors psychologists choose to study, and the science of psychology is whatever methods they choose to convince other psychologists of the validity of their findings.

Paths to Psychology

1 There are many paths to modern psychology. If we tried to go back over them all we would find that they eventually become lost in the prehistoric past when all natural events, including human behavior, were explained as magic or the workings of good and evil spirits.

A great-man theory of history would lead us to philosophers like Plato and Aristotle, theologians like Thomas Aquinas, and scientists like Darwin. A *zeitgeist* (spirit of the times) theory would lead us to demonology, the birth of science, global expansion, and space exploration. All of these influences have helped to define human behavior, which is the chief subject matter of this book.

The historical record indicates that humans have always tried to understand themselves and others, but only for a little more than a century have the rules of science been applied to human behavior. Prior to that, the scientific method was applied only to physics, biology, and chemistry. In order to understand where psychology stands now, we must go back to these scientific ancestors and to physiology and medicine. With these we shall begin tracing the divergent paths that lead to modern-day psychology.

Psychology As the Science of the Mind

1·1 One of the early milestones on one path to psychology was the work of Ernst Weber (1795–1878), a physiologist interested in touch and the muscle senses. Experimenting on the muscle sense Weber phrased what would be considered today a psychological question: Given two weights, what is the smallest difference between them that can reliably be discriminated when they are lifted? Using different weights, Weber found that the *just-noticeable difference* (jnd) tended to be a constant ratio. In other words, if one ounce had to be added to a 40-ounce weight before the weight lifter felt it as heavier, two ounces would have to be added to an 80-ounce weight.

Constant ratios were found also for just-noticeable differences in pitch and in the lengths of lines. On the basis of these findings, Weber formulated the relationship $\triangle I/I = k$, where $\triangle I$ is the smallest detectable change in stimulus intensity, I is the intensity of the stimulus, and k is a constant. Weber was a physiologist, but he was asking something about how the mind works.

Gustav Fechner (1801–1887), a German physicist, extended Weber's research by comparing the physical magnitude of lights or tones at each jnd level. Fechner found a logarithmic relation between these magnitudes and their psychological sensations (Figure 1·1) and formulated a law of psychophysics known as the *Weber-Fechner law:* As psychological or mental sensations increase arithmetically, corresponding physical magnitudes increase geometrically. Or, $S = k \log R$, where S is the mental sensation, k the Weber constant, and R the physical magnitude. Fechner, publishing his findings in 1860, believed he had found a way to measure the relationship between the senses and the mind, or as he put it, between mind and body.

Structuralism: Investigating Conscious Experience In 1858 a German physiologist, Wilhelm Wundt (1832–1920) published a book on sensory **perception** that included a review of Weber's work on touch, as well as other psychologists' contributions on vision. This book showed the beginnings of a physiological psychology. More interesting, the preface contained a direct appeal for an experimental and a social psychology: Psychology must use the empirical methods applied to the physical sciences, Wundt said, in order to analyze conscious experience.

In 1875, Wundt became professor of philosophy at the University of Leipzig (there were no chairs of psychology at that time). There he supplemented his lectures on physiological psychology with laboratory demonstrations. By 1879 these demonstrations had become so important to the course that the room as-

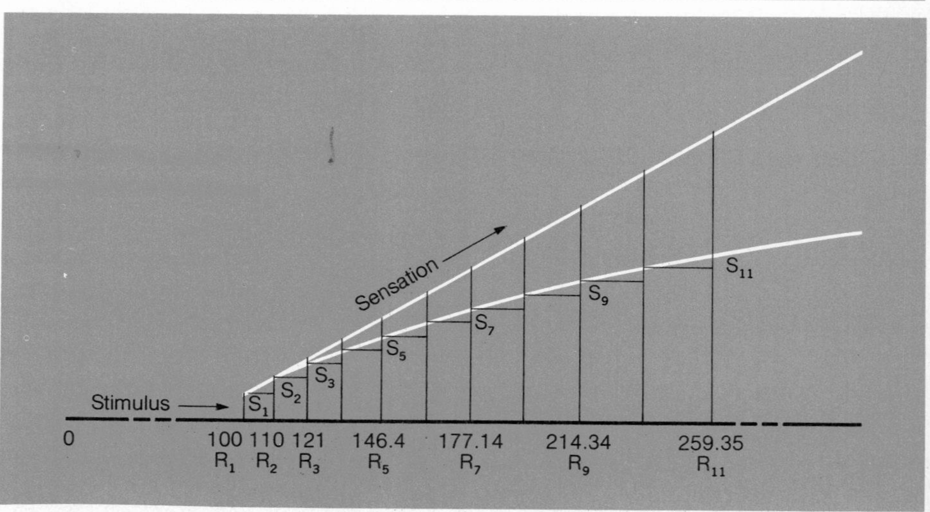

Fig. 1·1 The relation between increases in the intensity of the stimulus and increases in the intensity of the sensation as described by the Weber-Fechner law. (From Garrett, 1951)

signed for them took on the aspects of an experimental laboratory, and scientific psychology was born. Wundt and his followers, known as structuralists, relied on *introspection*, in which each experimental subject systematically looked inward and described his own mental processes and experiences.

In its first formal definition, then, psychology was the scientific investigation of conscious experience. The investigations that flowed from Wundt's laboratory included further exploration of the studies initiated by Weber and Fechner on the smallest amounts of physical energy detectable by the senses (absolute threshold) and the smallest amount of change in above-threshold physical energy detectable by the senses (differential threshold). Other studies included an examination of conscious activity when complex reactions are called for (for example, respond to the red light but not to the green), the span of attention, and the contents of mind during word-association tasks or during the experience of musical tones. In each experiment the subjects (graduate students) examined and described the contents of their consciousness when a stimulus was presented.

For the next forty years graduate students from around the world flocked to Leipzig to learn Wundt's method (controlled introspection) and share his ideas. From there they moved on to found new laboratories. Wundt had established a science whose time had come, but the paths it took thereafter were anything but his. Almost every major school of psychology after Wundt focused on something he had neglected or endorsed something he had rejected. Those schools became known as functionalism, gestaltism, psychodynamic psychology, behaviorism, and humanistic psychology.

Mind As a Survival Mechanism The American philosopher and psychologist William James (1842–1910) made the point that only descriptions of static conscious elements were coming from Wundt's laboratory. Such an approach was artificial and ill-founded, James said, because consciousness flows. In addition to flowing in various states and relations, said James, consciousness survived the evolutionary process and therefore must serve an adaptive function. It was this stress on the adaptive aspects of mind that gave James's brand of psychology its name: functionalism.

James's emphasis on the survival value of mind became the stimulus for a practical turn in psychology (Watson, 1971), and soon psychologists in the United States were studying learning, intelligence, child development, animals, mental health, and personality. German psychology continued within the confines of Wundt's direction for a time, but very soon other German schools were established, and German psychology began to move away from Wundt's search for conscious elements.

Imageless Thought At Würzburg, Germany, Oswald Külpe (1862–1915), a former assistant of Wundt's, began the experimental investigation of thought. To examine the process of making judgments, Külpe's students gave each other a simple and easily controlled task: lift two weights and state which is heavier. Usually the difference between the two weights was large enough to be easily distinguished. When the subjects were asked to describe the mental sensations and feelings corresponding to their correct judgments, the results were rather shocking. The students found plenty of sensations and feelings—some corresponding to the experience of lifting the weights and others that were unrelated to the task at hand, but none that could be linked reliably to the judgment itself in spite of its accuracy. Külpe was startled. Ever since Aristotle, judgment was presumed to follow a set of logical and definite rules. Instead, the Würzburg school found that an irrational chain of sensations and feelings led to a rational conclusion unerringly drawn, with nothing present in the mind to explain how it did so.

In trying to analyze other thought processes, the students gave subjects instructions such as "Add the following numbers. . ." or "When I say a word, respond with the first other word that comes to mind." The subjects were thus prepared to carry out a particular thought process. The experimenters thought that this readiness to respond in a particular way (also called a *set* or *determining tendency*) might be allied with a particular set of sensations or feelings. However, no such alliance was found, even though the subjects' answers showed that thoughtful activity had taken place. For example, when the subjects were asked to add, they never subtracted instead of adding.

Gestaltism: Phenomena As the Data of Psychology Max Wertheimer (1880–1945) was a student of Külpe's at Würzburg. Familiar with the studies on imageless thought, Wertheimer became interested in a phenomenon of vision called *apparent motion.* Alternate the flash of two similar lights placed side by side, and when the time interval between their flashing reaches a critical point, the two lights are experienced as a single light swinging back and forth. You can observe this phenomenon on theater marquees where pulsating lights give an illusion of movement along the edges of the marquee. Wundt had explained apparent motion as due to muscle sensations present when the eyes focus on the alternating impulses.

Wertheimer rigged an apparatus in which apparent motion was observed when two lines simultaneously moved in opposite directions. Since the two eyes could not move in opposite directions at the same time, Wertheimer held that Wundt's explanation was inadequate. Instead, Wertheimer took the position that perception deals with wholes (**gestalts**) not parts. The German word *gestalt* has no English equivalent, but it is variously translated as *whole, form, pattern,* or *configuration.*

Fig. 1·2 Different experiences emerge from the rearrangement of four identical lines.

Wertheimer proceeded to look for laws of perceptual organization. He and other Gestalt psychologists argued that perceptual organization is imposed by the brain and determines the form of the parts. For example, four lines by themselves are simply four lines; but move them around a bit and different experiences emerge (Figure 1·2). Emergent phenomena such as these signaled to Gestalt psychologists that psychology should be the study of holistic mental phenomena, for to take any conscious experience and analyze it into constituent parts was to describe conscious experience as something it was not.

Psychology As the Study of Dynamic Unconsciousness

1·2 During the nineteenth century, progress in neurology was considerable in France and much was known concerning diseases of the nervous system. In spite of advances, however, the waiting rooms in neurology clinics were crowded with patients who complained that their nerves were gone. Jean Charcot (1825–1895) a neurologist at Salpêtrière in Paris, identified a syndrome he labeled **hysteria.** The major symptoms included such things as paralysis of the limbs, being unable to straighten up, or anesthesia in some area of the body. Examination of these cases showed no underlying neural pathology.

Charcot, who had studied hypnosis, observed that hysteric patients were capable of reaching deep stages of hypnosis, and that their symptoms could be modified by his suggestion. He believed that the hysteria and the ability to be hypnotized were related and that both were due to an undiscovered organic pathology. Other views of hypnosis were also current, especially the views of Ambroise-Auguste Liébault (1823–1904) and Hippolyte Bernheim (1844–1919). Both had used hypnosis to treat medical problems, especially "nerves." Contrary to Charcot, Liébault and Bernheim took the position that hypnosis was not an organic pathology but a willingness to accept new attitudes and beliefs while in a sleep-like trance.

In 1882 Sigmund Freud (1856–1939) began private practice in neurological therapy in association with Joseph Breuer (1842–1925). Breuer had been treating hysterics with hypnosis, and Freud had occasion to notice that psychological con-

Jean Charcot lecturing on hypnosis at Salpêtrière, the famous neurological clinic in Paris, where Freud went to study the use of hypnosis in treating hysteria. (The Bettman Archive)

Psychologists and Psychiatrists

Sigmund Freud was a psychiatrist, not a psychologist, and although the two professions may share enough similarities to confuse the layman, they have distinct differences.

Psychiatrists are medical doctors. They receive their training in medicine and then specialize in the treatment of patients with behavior problems. Psychiatrists who specialize in the diagnostic and treatment methods of Freud are called psychoanalysts. Not all psychiatrists are psychoanalysts.

Psychologists receive their early training in courses dealing with not only the design and analysis of experiments, but also personality, learning and cognition, human growth and development, and sensation and perception, as well as social, abnormal, comparative, and physiological psychology. Some go on to receive a Ph.D. in clinical psychology, in which they specialize in the assessment and treatment of behavior disorders. Clinical psychologists work in such settings as probation offices, mental hospitals, community mental health centers, and prisons, as well as in private practice.

Psychiatrists often give neurological examinations and prescribe medicine and drugs as part of their treatment. Clinical psychologists are not licensed to provide those services.

Not all psychologists are clincial psychologists. Table 1A·1 shows the many divisions of psychology that psychologists work in, and Figure 1A·1 shows the relative percentages of psychologists in the United States who specialize within various subfields.

Experimental psychologists specialize in research, although psychologists in other subfields do research also. In fact, the Ph.D. is a research degree, and all professional psychologists make a research contribution to their profession as part of their indentification with science.

School psychologists work with children and school staff in evaluating behavioral handicaps to learning and

Table 1A·1 Current Divisions of the American Psychological Association.

1.	General psychology	**19.**	Military psychology
2.	Teaching of psychology	**20.**	Adult development and aging
3.	Experimental psychology	**21.**	Society of Engineering Psychologists
5.	Evaluation and measurement	**22.**	Psychological aspects of disability
6.	Physiological and comparative psychology	**23.**	Consumer psychology
7.	Developmental psychology	**24.**	Philosophical psychology
8.	Personality and social psychology	**25.**	Experimental analysis of behavior
9.	Society for the Psychological Study of Social Issues	**26.**	History of psychology
10.	Psychology and the arts	**27.**	Community psychology
12.	Clinical psychology	**28.**	Psychopharmacology
13.	Consulting psychology	**29.**	Psychotherapy
14.	Industrial and organizational psychology	**30.**	Psychological hypnosis
15.	Educational psychology	**31.**	State psychological association affairs
16.	School psychology	**32.**	Humanistic psychology
17.	Counseling psychology	**33.**	Mental retardation
18.	Psychologists in public service	**34.**	Population psychology
		35.	Psychology of women
		36.	Psychologists interested in religious issues

flicts repressed (kept from conscious awareness) in the waking state were often expressed under hypnosis. Freud journeyed to France to study hypnosis and hysteria under Charcot and Liébault. Upon his return to Vienna, Freud combined his knowledge of hypnosis and hysteria with a "talking cure" practiced by Breuer in which a patient was encouraged to express repressed memories while under hypnosis. Gradually, Freud modified his own use of hypnosis in

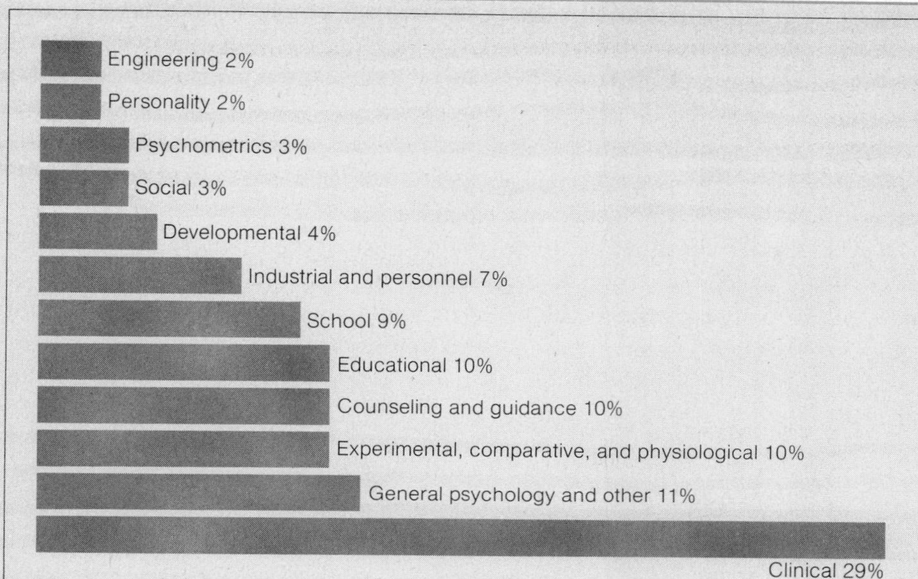

Fig. 1A·1 Subfields within psychology. (After Cates, 1970)

school adjustment. They also administer and interpret a variety of psychological tests and consult with parents and teachers about psychological variables in school settings.

Developmental psychologists study human development, from birth to old age, while educational psychologists specialize in research on the learning and teaching process. Social psychologists are concerned with the behavior of individuals in groups; they often focus on the development of attitudes, opinions, and prejudices in the group setting.

The counseling psychologist deals with many of the same emotional and adjustment problems that the clinical psychologist does, although typically the problems involve normal adjustment and career guidance. Physiological psychologists study the relation between behavior and the physiology of the body; typical areas of research include investigation of the biological bases of learning and memory, and physiological drive states and behavior. Comparative psychologists study the behavior of lower organisms as an area of interest in its own right, and also for behavioral analogs in humans. Industrial and engineering psychologists are involved in employee selection and morale and in testing and designing equipment so as to minimize human error and obtain the maximal interface between the capabilities and limitations of humans and technology.

Psychologists are becoming more and more visible outside mental health settings. They are called upon to testify before congressional committees as to the advisability of proposed legislation dealing with, for example, infant day care, alcoholism, and programs for the aged. In court, psychologists are sometimes asked to testify on the psychological dynamics of defendants. Psychologists also act as consultants to medicine and dentistry in relation to problems such as psychological barriers to the acceptance of health care programs by the general public. Psychologists are active in advertising, in nursing, and in industrial settings as facilitators of group dynamics and also of intrapersonal dynamics related to stresses on the job.

favor of having the patient lie on a couch and express his train of thinking (**free association**).

The discovery of **unconsciousness** was not new with Freud; intuitive conceptions had been available for centuries. From his observations of neurotic patients, Freud proposed the theory that unconsciousness is not a static state in which ideas repose when not in consciousness. Instead, unconscious wishes, and especially sexual and

Sigmund Freud (1856–1939). Freud introduced not only a method of dealing with certain types of mental illness, but also a theory of the organization of the mind.

aggressive impulses, press for fulfillment, but the images and feelings accompanying these drives are disguised or held in unconsciousness to protect the self from feeling sinful or embarrassed. Freud saw evidence for unconscious dynamics not only in the clinic where mental conflict between a patient's impulses and inhibitions could result in physical paralysis and anesthesia (as in the case of hysteria), but also in ordinary slips of the tongue or pen, dream content, forgetting, accidents of various kinds, and other poorly disguised expressions of unconscious wishes.

Freud's original contribution to psychology was recognition of the dynamic aspect of the unconscious and its implications for understanding mental illness. As Freud elaborated his theory, he based its underpinnings on evolution and the biology of the body. Later he also saw its implications for child development, creativity, civilization, and religion, to name a few of the areas on which he touched.

For many years the tie between psychodynamic psychology and academic psychology was not strong because **psychoanalysis** began in neurology and medicine, and academic psychology was concerned with scientific method. Freud's approach to understanding human behavior was through **naturalistic observation** (Shakow and Rapaport, 1964), which made psychoanalysis appear as "bad" science when compared with the laboratory methods of academicians. Eventually, of course, Freudian theory was applied to everything in psychology from children to advertising, and academic psychologists were forced to consider unconscious dynamics as well as conscious experience.

Psychology Without Mind

1·3 After the publication of Darwin's book, *Origin of Species* (1859), people began not only to see animals as related to humans, but also to investigate animal behavior as revealing evolutionary traces remaining in humans. G. J. Romanes (1848–1894) a British biologist and friend of Darwin, collected popular and scientific observations on animals, and published them in *Animal Intelligence* (1882). In this book Romanes presented evidence for three levels of ideas: simple (sensations, perceptions, and memories), complex (combinations of simple ideas), and notional (symbolic and abstract). All animals shared the first level, some animals and humans shared the second, but only humans possessed the third (Capretta, 1967). Romanes went on to suggest that the mental development of human newborns recapitulates the simple-to-complex pattern found in lower animals (Table 1·1).

Romanes's views stirred immediate controversy because much of his evidence was anecdotal, and his observations anthropomorphic (attributing human characteristics of thinking and feeling to nonhumans). Zoologist C. Lloyd Morgan (1852–1936) suggested that pitfalls such as these should be avoided by adopting a *law of parsimony:* In no case may we interpret an action as the outcome of the exercise of a higher psychical faculty if it can be interpreted as the exercise of one that stands lower on the psychical scale (Morgan, 1894).

Table 1·1 Romanes's Comparison of the Human Embryo with That of Various Animal Species

SEQUENCE	PRODUCTS OF INTELLECTUAL DEVELOPMENT	PSYCHOLOGICAL SCALE	PSYCHOGENESIS OF HUMAN
28	Indefinite morality	Anthropoid apes, dog	15 months
27	Use of tools	Monkeys, elephant	12 months
26	Understanding of mechanisms	Carnivores, rodents, ruminants	10 months
25	Recognition of pictures; understanding of words; dreaming	Birds	8 months
24	Communication of ideas	Hymenoptera	5 months
23	Recognition of persons	Reptiles, cephalopods	4 months
22	Reason	Higher crustaceans	14 weeks
21	Association by similarity	Fish, batrachians	12 weeks
20	Recognition of offspring; secondary instincts	Insects, spiders	10 weeks
19	Association by contiguity	Mollusks	7 weeks
18	Primary instincts	Larvae of insects, annelids	3 weeks
17	Memory	Echinoderms	1 week
16	Pleasures, pains		Birth
15, 14, 13	Nervous adjustments	Coelenterates	Embryo
12, 11, 10, 9	Partly nervous adjustments	Unknown animals, probably coelenterates, perhaps extinct	Embryo
8, 7, 6, 5	Non-nervous adjustments	Unicellular organisms	Embryo
4, 3, 2, 1	Protoplasmic movements	Protoplasmic organisms	Ovum and spermatozoa

(Vertical label "Consciousness" spans sequences 13–28 in the Psychological Scale column.)

(Adapted from Romanes, 1882)

At about the same time, Edward Lee Thorndike (1874–1949) began the experimental investigation of animal learning by placing kittens in a puzzle box and recording how long it took them to get out. In his interpretation of the efforts he observed, Thorndike appealed to a simple process of trial and error—accidental success rather than intelligent inference. Thorndike said that a response becomes

Three Viewpoints: Structuralist, Gestaltist, Behaviorist

The differences in approach between the structuralists, the gestaltists, and the behaviorists can be seen in the examples that follow.

Titchener was an ardent disciple of Wundt's. In his college text, *An Outline of Psychology* (1896), Titchener speculated on the number of sensation qualities available to account for human psychological experiences:

Eye	32,820
Ear (audition)	11,600
Nose	?
Tongue	4
Skin	4
Muscle	2
Tendon	1
Joint	1
Alimentary canal	3?
Blood vessels	?
Lungs	1?
Sex organs	1
Ear (static sense)	1
More than	44,435

Each one of these forty thousand qualities is a *conscious element,* distinct from all the rest, and altogether simple and unanalyzable. Each one may be blended or connected with others in various ways, to form *perceptions* and *ideas.* A large part of psychology is taken up with the determination of the laws and conditions which govern the formation of these sensation complexes.

The above list represents the full resources of the normal mind. It must not be supposed, however, that every normal individual has had experience of all the qualities enumerated. It is safe to say that no one, not even the most experienced psychologist, has seen all the possible visual qualities, heard all the possible tones, smelled all the possible scents, and so on. The list is a summary of the results obtained by many observers in the course of minute investigations of our capacity of discrimination in the various fields of sense.

Apart from this, a slight abnormality is much more common than is ordinarily supposed. Very many people are more or less color-blind: they confuse red with green, or have a shortened spectrum, that is, do not see the full number of red and violet qualities. Very many are partially tone-deaf, have a defective sense of smell, and so forth. But when all allowances are made, the average number of conscious elements must run into the tens of thousands.

As a gestaltist, Wertheimer (1923) criticized the attempt by structuralists to analyze wholes into artificial elements:

> I stand at the window and see a house, trees, sky.
>
> And I could, then, on theoretical grounds, try to sum up: there are 327 brightnesses (and tones of color).
>
> (Have I "327"? No: sky, house, trees; and no one can realize the having of the "327" as such.)
>
> Let there be, in this particular calculation, about 120 for the house, 90 for the trees, and 117 for the sky; in any case I have *this* togetherness and *this* distribution, not 127 and 100 and 100, or 150 and 177.

connected to the stimulus that initiates it, and when random responses lead to success (escape from the box in this instance), repeated successes stamp in the connection between stimulus and response. Thorndike had gone beyond Morgan. There was no need to postulate ideas in animals; their response to a stimulus was muscular and therefore lower on the psychical scale than the mental response that humans are capable of making.

Meanwhile, in Russia, Ivan Pavlov (1849–1936) was turning from his work on the digestive glands (which won him a Nobel Prize in 1904) to the investigation of psychic secretions. Ivan Sechenov (1829–1905), a Russian physiologist had performed experiments on the relationship between reflexes and the brain. Sechenov reached the conclusion in 1863 that mind was simply the working brain and nervous system, and that thinking represented inhibited reflexes. According to Sechenov, reflexes are either innate or learned (by association), and thinking is merely reflex activity with the response phase unexpressed (Watson, 1971).

Pavlov was familiar with Sechenov's work, and in his own work on the digestive glands he had studied the saliva flow stimulated by placing meat in a dog's mouth.

I *see* it in specific togetherness and specific distribution; and the manner of unity and separation [togetherness and distribution] in which I see it is not determined simply by my whim. It is quite certain that I cannot actualize another desired kind of coherence according to the dictates of my whim.

(And what a remarkable process, when suddenly something of that sort is attained! What astonishment when, after staring at a window for a long time, making many vain attempts, and in a bemused mood, I discover that the pieces of a dark frame and a bare branch combine to form a [Roman] N.)

Or take two faces cheek to cheek.

I see one (with, if one wishes, "57" brightnesses) and the other (with its "49"), but not in the division 66 plus 40 or 6 plus 100.

Theories that would suggest that I see "106" there remain on paper; it is two faces that I see.

At a seminar with his students in the Russian Military Medical Academy in Leningrad in 1934, Pavlov criticized gestalt phenomenology:

The gestaltists adhere to the point of view that an isolated feature should by no means be studied; they prove this in splendid fashion by stating that if a single feature of the face is exposed, and the rest of the face is covered, nothing will come out of it. This is self-evident. Separate features assume different importance in the entire whole; some of them stand out in bold relief, others are disguised, recede into the background, and so on. That is quite obvious. But the features must be identified. In the end, when one analyzes a face, one must on the basis of definite features depict it as quiet, calm, willful, very tender, and the like. Of course, without analyzing the constituent parts one cannot comprehend anything. The same thing applies to the human character. If one takes isolated traits and analyzes each of them separately, naturally it will be impossible to determine the given character; for this purpose it is necessary to take a system of traits and to establish which of the traits in this system are more prominent, which are hardly visible, and so on.

The author adds that human and animal organisms are a "gestalt." But nobody doubts their integrity. At the same time, however, nothing prevents the decomposition of this system into its component systems of blood circulation and digestion, as well as the decomposition of the latter into the stomach, intestines, gastric glands, and the like. This is simply forcing an open door.

Further, it is said that our behavior is not a mere sum of reflexes. Again, what a truth! That is a commonplace. But they picture the matter in such a way as if a system were a sort of a sack filled pell-mell with potatoes, apples, cucumbers, and other such. Nobody has ever expressed such an idea.

Sooner or later saliva began to flow when the feeding attendant simply approached a dog. Eventually, the sound of the attendant approaching, but still out of the dog's sight, would initiate saliva flow. The sound of the attendant's footsteps had become a **conditioned stimulus.** As a physiologist Pavlov was reluctant to get involved in mental processes, but finally he decided to go ahead in the manner of Sechenov—he described his findings without reference to mentalistic concepts such as ideas or expectancies. The **conditioned responses** he observed were the result of a complex interaction between **excitation** and **inhibition** processes in the brain, and required no higher psychical processes than those already available in neurophysiology (Bruno, 1972).

Behaviorism In 1910 psychologists in the United States were under the impression that Wundt's methods had failed at Würzburg (Boring, 1957). The psychology journals contained argument and counterargument on the possibility of imageless thought; what had begun as a science of conscious elements was looking more and more like a religious debate.

To put a stop to the squabbling, John B. Watson (1878–1958) suggested in 1913 that psychology reject introspection as a method because of its unreliability among observers and begin again, this time with a focus on behavior. Watson argued that behavior alone is objectively observable and by itself includes no presumptions about mental images, thinking, or mind. He argued for a doctrine of parsimony, and although he did not deny the possibility of consciousness, he asked psychologists to ignore it and to use only the more objective and reliable data of behavior (Boring, 1957). So great was the need for an objective science of the mind that by 1915 in America, psychology became defined as the scientific investigation of behavior. Subjective and mentalistic concepts such as mind, consciousness, ideas, self, and **instinct** fell to the behaviorist's ax.

With behaviorism a new vocabulary emerged. For example, **sensation** was redefined as **discrimination** behavior, *meaning* was redefined as what an organism does in a situation, **learning** came to mean number of trials to reach an acceptable level of success established by the experimenter, *thinking* became electrical activity recorded from muscles, and *awareness* was redefined as the verbalization of a rule or difference. Psychology journals were filled with charts and tables, and though debate continued over various assumptions and interpretations, all psychologists were observing the same responses. The change in method and data became known as **behaviorism,** and the direction of psychology in the United States became resolutely altered from its Wundtian beginnings.

Humanistic and Existential Psychology

1·4 There is in psychology a contemporary path that also began with a rejection of Wundt's assumption that scientific methods appropriate to the physical sciences are directly applicable to humans. In addition to rejecting the methods of physics, the new school called **humanistic psychology,** rejected the methods of behaviorism because the human experiences of growth and fulfillment appear to lie outside behaviorism's psychology without mind. Humanistic psychology rejects also the Freudian assumption that psychological faculties are in service to the body. Humanistic psychologists want psychology to define itself as the science of human experience and to pay attention to the forces of fulfillment found in growing, loving, sharing, coping, and knowing.

According to Abraham Maslow (1916–1970) and Carl Rogers (1902–   ), humans are unique in the animal kingdom because they have *metaneeds* (psychological needs beyond the biological needs of the body): needs for security, love, self-esteem, aesthetics, self-expression, and **self-actualization.** Humanistic psychology takes the position that humans are inherently good and that the selfish and defensive dynamics observed by Freud are an effect of society and not a cause. Humanistic psychologists feel that validity for their view of human nature is found in personal experience, feelings of nonstriving when coping well, feelings of being loved, and the joy of expressing positive regard for others.

Table 1·2 Some Differences between Behavioristic, Psychoanalytic, and Existential Approaches

ITEM FOR COMPARISON	BEHAVIORISM	PSYCHOANALYSIS	EXISTENTIALISM
Model of person	Mechanistic	Biological-mechanistic	Social-anthropological
Concept of personality	Materialistic	Biological-materialistic	Nonmaterialistic
Orientation	Empirical	Intuitive-analytic	Being (attempts to be)
Primary relationship	Scientist-object	Physician-patient	Person-person (encounter)

(Adapted from Correnti, 1965)

Related to humanistic psychology is **existential psychology.** Both espouse a personal-fulfillment model of the human race, and both focus on feelings of congruence between perceived self and ideal self. However, existentialists stress that life is the fulfillment of personal choices rather than the fulfillment of innately human metaneeds. Each individual must establish his or her own feelings of identity and being-in-the-world, or face a feeling of nothingness and alienation from the world, say the existentialists.

Table 1·2 summarizes a few of the differences between the behavioristic, psychoanalytic, and existential approaches to describing the nature of human beings.

Paths to the Psyche

1·5 The definition of *mind* has changed many times and with each change in definition have come different implications for the function of the mind and for the human being.

In Homer's *Iliad, psyche* (the ancient Greek word for soul, self, or mind from which psychology takes its name) was used in the modern sense of breath. Breath was a sign of life. Gradually *psyche* came to mean life, and later the principle of life. Socrates (c. 470 B.C.) and Plato (427–347 B.C.), divided psyche into a rational part that could unravel the meaning of life and apprehend ideal forms and an irrational part that participated in the imperfect forms presented to our senses. Death was a release from the bonds of the flesh. After several incarnations, the rational soul could rise to participate in absolute perfection (Watson, 1971).

For Aristotle (384–323 B.C.), a student of Plato's, *psyche* simply meant the principle of life—the quality or essence that distinguishes living from nonliving matter. Aristotle taught there were three different levels of psyche: vegetative, animal, and rational. Vegetative souls characterized the plants, having only the qualities of nutrition, growth, and reproduction. Animal souls had the vegetative qualities plus movement and sensation. Rational souls had the vegetative and animal qualities plus reason and will. Only the human had a rational soul. It was Aristotle's hierarchy that Galen (a second century Greek physician) acknowledged in his description of spirits in the blood.

According to Galen, the principles of life are certain spirits that dwell in the blood. Blood is formed in the liver and there charged with natural spirits. Upon reaching the heart, Galen taught incorrectly, some blood seeps through pores in the septum into the left ventricle, where it is mixed with air from the lungs to form vital spirits. These spirits are distributed by the arteries, some of which go to the brain. In the brain, these vital spirits become animal spirits, which are then distributed throughout the body by the hollow nerves.

Centuries later, it was the difference between Plato's and Aristotle's definition of *psyche* that the Catholic philosopher Thomas Aquinas (1225–1274) struggled to reconcile. In his study of Aristotle, Aquinas found the view that the ability to comprehend transpersonal and universal knowledge (knowledge of such concepts as freedom and justice) is a function of the psyche and is immortal, while the kind of practical knowledge and memory that comes from our jobs and personal experience decays with the body (Bruno, 1972). By finding immortality in Aristotle's concept of psyche, Aquinas made Aristotle compatible with Plato and the church.

In Greco-Roman mythology, Psyche was the personification of the human soul and (as in Platonic philosophy) was loved by Eros. The term *psyche* has long been used in trying to describe the relationship between the rational and the irrational and between the physical and the nonphysical in a person. (The Bettmann Archive)

In his own teachings Aquinas followed much of Aristotle, teaching that the rational soul and body are united in humans and that plants and animals participate on another level. Aquinas also ascribed an inner sense to animals that was not given them by Aristotle; this sense corresponded to what later ages named **instinct.** According to Aquinas, birds select nesting materials with the aid of this estimative power, and animals rely on it to flee from natural predators (Watson, 1971). Aquinas taught that humans have this inner sense also, but in humans it is under the control of reason.

According to Aquinas, the human soul has the vegetative power (as Aristotle described it) and the sensitive power (or faculty), which included the five senses, the estimative power, memory, imagination, and a so-called common sense that accounted for the perception of qualities (such as wetness) that are not the province of a single sense modality (such as vision). Humans experience the emotions of love, desire, and joy, or alternatively, hatred, avoidance, and grief. Aquinas called these emotions concupiscible appetites because they were triggered by stimuli presented to the senses. The forces behind these emotions (hope, courage, despair, fear, and anger) were called the irascible appetites, and their function was to mobilize the individual when stimuli were attractive or foreboding.

At the rational level, which humans alone possessed, were will and intellect. Free will is known to us through those activities in which we perceive a choice. The intellect includes an active intellect that acts upon sensations to form meanings and concepts, and a passive intellect that is more akin to conscious awareness. It was Aquinas's description of the rational soul that the French philosopher René Descartes (1596–1650) accepted (as the average person does today) as distinguishing mind from body. Under Descartes's dualism, mind remained immaterial and free, while body was made material and mechanical.

A hundred years later the French physician-philosopher Julien de la Mettrie (1707–1751) argued, as Sechenov and Pavlov would, that mind and body are both machines—that thought is nothing more than the mechanical action of the brain and nervous system. Toward the end of the eighteenth century Franz Joseph Gall (1758–1828), an anatomist, combined the concept of mental faculties with la Mettrie's materialism and introduced the thesis that the strength of mental faculties can be assessed by measuring the amount of cortical tissue present under the bumps and hollows of the skull (*phrenology*).

In the centuries during which human behavior has been examined, various methods have been applied to obtain knowledge of the psyche: dogma, introspection, tradition, revelation, classification, faith, naturalistic observation, phenomenology, legislation, experiment, and skepticism, to name a few. The story of psychology follows these many paths, and old questions are often re-examined, using new methods that lead to new findings. The content that psychologists are trying to define has been around for a long time; the questions that modern psychologists ask change after each new answer.

Summary

The paths to modern psychology are several, from ancient philosophy and religion to the physiology and physics of 125 years ago. Ernst Weber and Gustav Fechner initiated the modern period by asking psychological questions about sensory processes. Wundt began to lecture on physiological psychology. Eventually he called for a science of psychology and established a laboratory.

Wundt defined psychology as the scientific investigation of conscious experience, but nearly every school of psychology after him rejected that beginning. The functionalists, who said Wundt's analyses made consciousness too static, preferred to investigate consciousness in terms of its use. Because psychologists at Würzburg could find no conscious experiences corresponding to the psychological processes of judgment and set, they moved away from Wundt's definition. Max Wertheimer found evidence contradictory to Wundt's explanation of apparent movement, and argued that conscious experiences are organized as gestalts and should not be analyzed as parts.

Freud drew attention to unconscious dynamics in normal and abnormal behavior, making the analysis of conscious experience simply the analysis of the tip of an iceberg.

Behaviorism questioned the need for a concept of either consciousness or unconsciousness and suggested that psychology would be better served by the study of behavior. Humanistic and existential psychology saw psychology as already misguided when Wundt applied a model of studying the physical sciences to a study of the mind. Behaviorism and psychoanalysis compounded the problem, humanistic psychologists argue, by leaving out what is uniquely human (in the case of behaviorism) and characterizing humans as selfish and manipulative (in the case of psychoanalysis). People have unique metaneeds to fulfill, argue humanistic psychologists, and in so doing they experience the positive feelings of growing and loving heretofore ignored by psychology. Existentialists agree that each individual has a life to fulfill, but see that fulfillment as stemming from personal choices rather than from innate destiny.

A brief look at psychological concepts examined by the ancients shows that varied paths to the psychological definition of humans are not new inventions, and variety may even be necessary to forestall simple definitions of a complex organism.

Suggested Readings

The following works are the standard introductions to the history of psychology. Watson spends more time on the ancient Greeks and medieval thought, but aside from that major difference, all three are complementary.

Boring, Edwin, G. 1957. *A history of experimental psychology*, 2d ed. New York: Appleton-Century-Crofts.

Murphy, Gardner, and Joseph Korach. 1972. *Historical introduction to modern psychology*. 3d ed. New York: Harcourt, Brace, Jovanovich.

Watson, Robert I. 1971. *The great psychologists*. 3d ed. Philadelphia: Lippincott.

The foundations of humanistic and existential psychology are more completely traced in:

Bühler, Charlotte, and Melanie Allen. 1972. *Introduction to humanistic psychology*. Monterey, California: Brooks/Cole.

van Kaam, Adrian. 1969. *Existential foundations of psychology*. Garden City, New York: Image Books.

Research Methods of Psychology

2 Does violence on television and in movies lead to violent crimes because of suggestion and imitation? Are women as capable as men of functioning under pressure in jobs that cause stress? Does the forced integration of schools brought about by busing result in better education and equal opportunity for black students? Does sex education in elementary school help young people to form satisfactory heterosexual relationships and avoid the problems of venereal disease and unwanted pregnancies? Does habitual use of marijuana undermine an individual's motivation to achieve?

All of these questions have aroused controversies in the United States within the recent past. While the general public debates such issues in city halls and school auditoriums, psychologists try to design studies that lead to empirical answers and solutions based on facts, rather than on biases and emotion. As you may have noted, the questions pertain to aggression, stress, learning, sexuality, and motivation, all of which are embraced within the study of psychology.

Aggression and motivation are *constructs;* they are concepts about unobservable processes that affect outward, observable behavior. No one has ever seen motivation, but the term has been defined and accepted among psychologists because it provides a logical explanation for certain aspects of behavior. Even though it is a construct, rather than a physical object, motivation can be measured. Test scores are one kind of measurement. Psychologists have devised tests on which high scores indicate a high level of achievement motivation. When the first of these tests were designed, the experimenters postulated that a subject with a great desire to achieve would try much harder to do well on a test than the subject who was indifferent.

In studying animals, an investigator might deprive a rat of food for a period of time in order to increase the animal's motivation to obtain food by running through a maze. Motivation can be measured in terms of the number of seconds in which the rat runs the maze and obtains the food reward. When the first of these tests were designed, the experimenters postulated that fast action on the part of the hungry rat indicates a high level of motivation. A *postulate* is an underlying principle that the scientist assumes to be true. A postulate begins to look like a fact when many experimenters have conducted the same kind of study and arrived at the same results.

Hypothesis Testing

2·1 Probably you have heard someone claim that pornography causes an increase in the number of sex crimes. At the present time, such a claim is just a **hypothesis.** In fact, there is another hypothesis that asserts that pornographic films and literature decrease the number of sex offenses by providing an outlet for sexual impulses. A hypothesis is just an educated guess until some scientist designs a procedure to measure the behavior in question. One of the major objectives in establishing a science of psychology was to employ scientific methods in the testing of hypotheses.

Another current hypothesis states that children learn better in an open classroom than in a traditional classroom. A problem arises in testing this hypothesis because the meaning of the term *open,* as applied to classrooms, is broad and ambiguous. The term suggests that the children are participating in many activities rather than sitting quietly at their desks and listening to the teacher. But it is not clear what implications the term has for program activities; *open* can be defined in different ways by different program directors. What is needed to test the hypothesis is a set of specific program characteristics that are directly observable. The distinguishing features of one program can then be compared with the significant characteristics of another program. At the end of the school year the children can be tested to determine how much learning has occurred in each program.

Variables Suppose that in one classroom (program A) each child is allowed to choose activities from a list provided by the teacher. In another classroom (program B) all children take part in the same activities. Notice how these two programs vary: Activity choice is a distinguishing characteristic of program A and assigned activity is a distinguishing characteristic of program B. The distinction between self-chosen and teacher-assigned activity is a *variable.* If the two programs and the two groups of pupils were alike except for this one variable, the school psychologist could use the test results to infer whether children derive more benefit from guidance and structure provided by the teacher or from helping to plan their own curricula.

The Operational Definition In everyday conversation all of us understand the meaning of the word *learn.* If you say to a friend, "I learned the multiplication tables in the third grade," chances are your friend will accept your statement without asking whether you learned the tables through "times twelve" or only through "times ten," or whether you can quickly multiply any two single-digit numbers, or how many errors you might make in solving a hundred multiplication problems. Unlike casual conversation, scientific communication requires precision in the use of words. The psychologist tries to devise definitions in terms of behaviors, or operations, that can be observed and, preferably, measured.

An *operational definition* defines a word, such as *learning,* in terms of specific operations performed by the experimenter or by the subject. The following are operational definitions of learning:

The subject has learned the response when ten consecutive errorless trials occur.

Learning has occurred when the subject has made ten errorless trials in a five-minute time period.

Learning has occurred when the experimenter has counted ten correct responses over twelve consecutive trials.

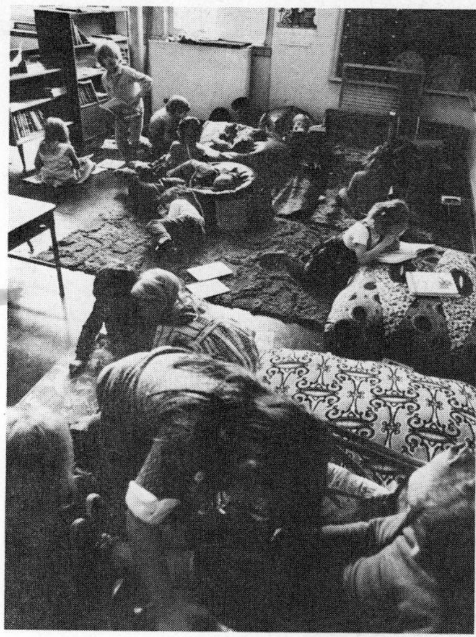

To test the hypothesis that children learn better in an open classroom than in a traditional classroom, we might control the type of teacher-pupil interaction as opposed to the types of materials used or the arrangement of the room. (Environmental Psychology Program, City University of New York)

Each of these definitions limits the word *learning.* Operationism can be criticized on the grounds that it is too narrow, but operational definitions enable psychologists to communicate with precision and to *replicate* (repeat) experiments. If the results of a study are valid, an experiment conducted in one laboratory can be replicated with the same results in any other laboratory. Confirmation is essential to scientific research.

The operational definition also helps to eliminate *observer bias,* which is any personal tendency on the part of the experimenter that affects the empirical data and the results of the experiment. In research, precautions must be taken so that the expectations of the investigators do not alter the results of the study. Precautions are especially important in behavioral sciences like psychology, which often deal with constructs. In studying aggression in preschool children, for example, two observers might disagree about what constitutes an aggressive act. If Child A punches Child B, one observer might say that the child who received the punch deserved it, and the second observer might contend that the child doing the punching didn't really mean it. When operational definitions are used, however, observers have a list of behaviors that must be recorded as aggression, regardless of the circumstances under which the acts occur. The experiment can be replicated because there is no disagreement about what constitutes aggression.

Theories

2·2 Theories are used by psychologists to organize their thinking about a particular problem, to help them conceptualize empirical relationships, and to provide direction as to what aspects of behavior seem likely to prove productive in further research efforts. Some, like the theories of Clark Hull and Sigmund Freud, are very broad and encompassing, while others are more modest in scope.

There are no right or wrong theories in an absolute sense, but there are good and bad theories. One important criterion for judging the quality of a theory is whether or not its postulates can be tested. Many postulates inherent in certain theories are impossible to test or are included in the theory as absolute givens and thus are not testable. Good theories tend to be structurally unified in that postulates relate to each other in a systematic and meaningful way, and these relationships can be specified and tested.

Most theories develop through an inductive process whereby established empirical facts are related by means of a concept. *Induction* is a process of reasoning in which the general is derived from the particular. For example, Freud made specific observations about his patients, began to see relationships between these observations, and gradually developed psychoanalytic theory, which he applied not only to neurotic patients but to all human beings.

A second type of theory emerges from the hypothetico-deductive method introduced by Hull and later expanded by Kenneth Spence (1957). *Deduction* is a process of reasoning in which a conclusion follows necessarily from premises that have been presented; the conclusion cannot be false if the premises are true. Hull's premises were seventeen postulates about the process of learning. The postulates are interrelated, and they relate to the basic concept, or theory. When he died in 1952, Hull had deduced 133 statements about the learning process that could be tested empirically.

A theory is continually modified as new data become available or as certain predictions or hypotheses prove to be incorrect (Figure 2·1). As a general criterion, however, theories in any scientific field become important or lose significance, depending on the amount of research they generate. Theories developed by Freud, Piaget, and Hull and Spence have generated an enormous number of studies and for that reason must be considered important and influential. We will discuss Freud's theories in detail in Chapters 3, 13, and 17, and Piaget's theory in Chapters 3 and 4.

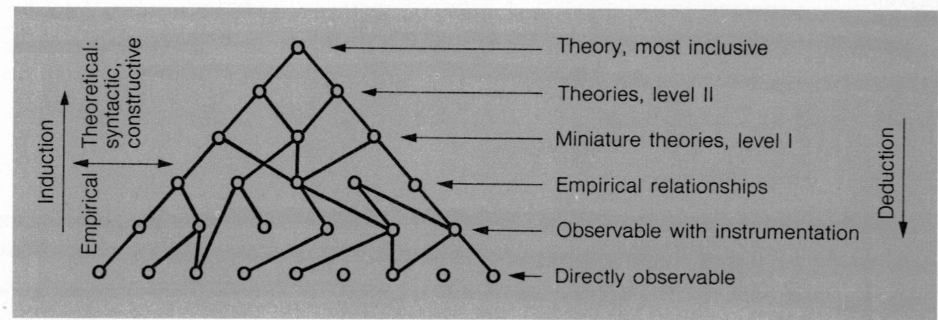

Fig. 2·1 A schematic representation of the multiple relationships that lead to theory construction and theory usage. Fruitful theories help to integrate known empirical relationships and to direct the scientist to new observations and further theoretical elaborations.
(From Thompson, 1962)

Descriptive Research

2·3 Psychological research is concerned either with demonstrating that a particular behavior can be predicted or with describing a behavior and the variables associated with it. The experimental method is best suited to developing the knowledge necessary for prediction, but many of the questions psychologists ask cannot be answered experimentally. Some experiments would be impractical, unethical, or both if human subjects were used. When laboratory research is impossible, psychologists use **descriptive research** to describe behaviors and the contexts within which specific behaviors occur.

Suppose that a psychologist is interested in the effects of punishment on the social and emotional development of children. The most direct way to study this problem is first to assign parents randomly to two groups. One group of parents would use punishment with no rewards in rearing their children, and the second group of parents would use a reward system with no punishment. After ten years, ratings of the children would be obtained from their teachers, peers, and psychologists. If differences emerged between the two groups of children, the experimenter could reasonably conclude that punishment affects social and emotional development. The manipulation of human subjects in this manner is obviously unethical because of long-range effects upon the children and indirectly upon society as well.

The effect of discipline has been studied extensively by means of descriptive procedures. The experimenter obtains a sample of parents who are willing to cooperate and observes the disciplinary practices used by the parents with their children. The parents' behaviors and the child's behaviors are described by trained observers. The experimenter then examines the data for relationships between the two sets of behaviors. This observation is less precise than a laboratory experiment because the sample of subjects is biased when only volunteers are used and because the observers cannot control the variables. In disciplining children, for example, very few parents use any one practice consistently. Despite these difficulties, a considerable amount of information has been accumulated using descriptive procedures.

One type of descriptive research involves studying animals in their natural habitat. Here Dr. David Horr is shown observing orangutans in a Borneo jungle. (Irven DeVore, Anthro-Photo)

In some instances, descriptive research is a source of hypotheses for further work in the laboratory, where an effort can be made to identify the precise variables causing the observed behaviors. Good descriptive research provides an important source of data from which it is possible to construct theories. Unlike the laboratory experiment, which is artificial, the descriptive approach conducted in natural settings is directly related to real-life situations. Ethologists (scientists who study animals in their natural habitats) have demonstrated that good descriptive research can contribute significantly to an understanding of the interaction of organisms and their environment (Lorenz, 1965).

Observation of children in their homes, or chimpanzees on the African game preserves, are called field studies. The *field-study method* is a research technique in which the investigator observes subjects in their usual environments without attempting to control conditions. Often the subjects are unaware that they are being observed. Using the *life-history method*, psychologists compile a detailed description of the development of various forms of behavior throughout the life of an individual or a group. In clinical psychology such a description is called a *case history* and is used to identify the causes of emotional or social adjustment problems. A third technique of descriptive research is the *survey method* in which data are obtained from a selected group by means of questionnaires or interviews. The Gallup and Harris polls are among the most familiar examples of survey research. All of these methods enable psychologists to compile descriptive data.

The Correlational Method When psychologists have identified a behavior and described the context in which it occurs, they attempt to discover whether there is a relationship between the behavior and the context. In some situations where descriptive research is used, investigators look for the relationship between behavioral change and time. In the most common situation, psychologists focus on multiple behaviors and generate questions about the relationship between these behaviors. Correlation is concerned with the degree of relationship between two or more variables.

A *correlation coefficient* is a number used as a statistical index to show the relationship between two sets of measurements (see Appendix A). The two sets of measurements might be, for example, reading test scores and IQ test scores for a group of students. If people with high IQs are better readers, then the two sets of scores are positively correlated: A student with a high IQ score will also have a high score on the reading test. The magnitude of correlation coefficients can range from ±1.00 to zero. A perfect positive correlation is expressed as +1.00. A correlation of −1.00 (perfect negative) means that high performance on one test is accompanied by low performance on the other. Perfect correlations rarely occur.

A psychologist might seek to find out whether a relationship exists between a child's aggressive behavior and the context in which it occurs. (Elizabeth Hamlin, Stock, Boston)

Typical correlations are between .35 and .70. The correlational statistic indicates the degree to which a change in one variable is accompanied by a change in the other.

Although a correlation indicates the degree of relationship between two sets of behaviors, it does not show a cause-and-effect relationship. If the school psychologist sees a group of unruly, aggressive pupils in a classroom with an angry, punitive teacher, the psychologist infers that there is a positive correlation between the hostility of the teacher and the aggression of the pupils, but it is impossible to infer which behavior is the cause and which is the effect.

Despite the limitations of the correlational method, it permits investigators to discover relationships that might otherwise go undetected. It also allows investigators to examine variables that otherwise would be beyond the scope of laboratory experimentation.

Experimental Research

2·4 The **experimental method,** which is particularly suitable for testing hypotheses, is the strongest available method for developing and understanding psychological concepts. If the results of the experiment are to be valid, however, particular care must be taken in designing the experiment. *Experimental design* can be divided into five steps (Kirk, 1968):

1. State the statistical hypothesis. A statistical hypothesis restates a research hypothesis in a way that enables the experimenter to make accurate measurements: If *x*, then *y*, holding all other conditions constant.
2. State rules for carrying out the experimental procedure and collecting the data. Any accidental variable might alter the outcome and make the results invalid.
3. Specify the apparatus and instruments to be used in the experiment.
4. State rules for analyzing the data. Analysis of the data involves describing the results of the experiment by statistically analyzing the measurements (raw scores) and making inferences from the statistics. One of the most useful statistics is also one of the simplest: the mean, which is the arithmetic average.
5. State rules for decision making.

Suppose that our research hypothesis is that motivation can be studied by manipulating the number of hours of food deprivation for a group of rats. Our statistical hypothesis might then be that if the rats are hungry (*x*), they will run through the maze faster (*y*), provided that no accidental variables are allowed to intervene.

We can obtain a precise measurement for *x* by depriving the rats of food for a specific period of time, and a precise measurement for *y* by timing the rats as they run through the maze and recording the measurement after each trial. In order to hold all other conditions constant, we can make certain that the rats (1) have not had previous experience with maze learning, (2) are healthy, and (3) are of the

Two Approaches to Animal Intelligence: Description and Experimentation

Both description and experimentation have long been used to gather data that are important in psychology. Darwin and Freud, for example, used observation and description, whereas Pavlov and Skinner obtained their discoveries primarily by means of experimentation.

Although both methods can present problems in the collection and interpretation of data, description is perhaps more likely to prove unreliable. The researcher can fall into the trap of merely telling anecdotes that seem to prove a point. Even Darwin lapsed into this mode when he studied the development of his own child (1877).

Compare the descriptive approach used by George J. Romanes with the experimental approach used by Edward L. Thorndike. Both worked with data about how a cat learns to open a door and from these data both drew conclusions about animal intelligence. In his book *Animal Intelligence* (1882), Romanes presents hearsay evidence to help support his view that in opening the door the cat displays the ability not only to imitate observable human behavior but also to reason.

> Of course in all such cases the cats must have previously observed that the doors are opened by persons placing their hands upon the handles, and having observed this, the animals forthwith act by what may be strictly termed rational imitation. But it should be observed that the process as a whole is something more than imitative. For not only would observation alone be scarcely enough (within any limits of thoughtful reflection that it would be reasonable to ascribe to an animal) to enable a cat upon the ground to distinguish that the essential part of the process as performed by the human hand consists, not in grasping the handle, but in depressing the latch; but the cat certainly never saw anyone, after having depressed the latch, pushing the doorposts with his legs. That this pushing action is due to an originally deliberate intention of opening the door, and not to have accidentally found this action to assist the process, is shown by one of the cases communicated to me (by Mr. Henry A. Gaphaus). For in this case, my correspondent says, "the door was not a loose-fitting one by any means, and I was surprised that by the force of one hind leg she should have been able to push it open after unlatching it." Hence we can only conclude that the cats in such cases have a very definite idea as to the mechanical properties of a door. They know that to make it open, even when unlatched, it requires to be *pushed*—a very different thing from trying to imitate any particular action which they may see to be performed for the same purpose by man.
>
> The whole psychological process, therefore, implied by the fact of a cat opening a door in this way is really most complex. First the animal must have observed that the door is opened by the hand grasping the handle and moving the latch. Next it must reason, by "the logic of feelings"—if a hand can do it, why not a paw? Then, strongly moved by this idea, it makes the first trial. The steps which follow have not been observed, so we cannot certainly say whether it learns by a succession of trials that depression of the thumb-piece constitutes the essential part of the process, or perhaps more probably, that her initial observations supplied it with the idea of clicking the thumb-piece. But, however this may be, it is certain that the pushing with the hind feet after depressing the latch must be due to adaptive reasoning unassisted by observation; and only by the concerted action of all its limbs in the performance of a highly complex and most unnatural movement is its final purpose attained.

same age and the same strain. If some of the rats are sick, for example, their performance in the maze cannot be compared to the performance of healthy rats.

For apparatus we might use a T-maze, which is a pathway built in the shape of a T with the starting box at the base of the T; goal boxes, where food will be presented to the rat, are at either end of the cross piece. The food is the **stimulus** in this case because it causes the rat to run through the maze. This action is called the **response.** We need an instrument with which to time each rat's response.

The raw scores we obtain will be for the speed of running through the maze for each rat on each trial. To make these scores meaningful, we might compare the

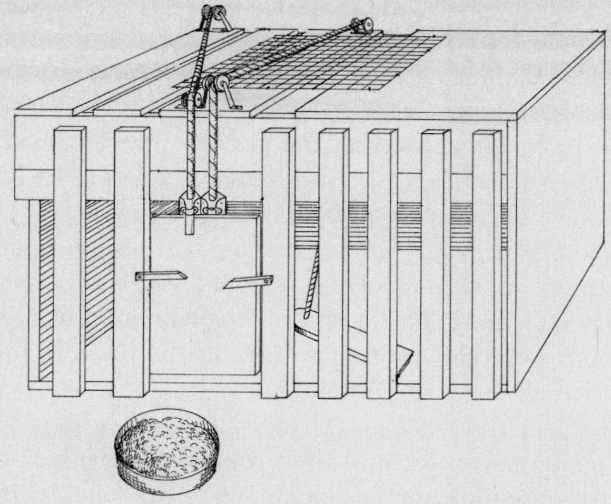

Unlike Romanes, Thorndike conducted experiments using apparatus he had built himself (Figure 2B•1) and recorded the amount of time it took the cat to get out of the box on each successive trial (Figure 2B•2). On the basis of these data Thorndike concluded that the cat gradually learned the solution through trial and error—a finding that turned out to be in accord with the results of later experiments by behaviorists such as Skinner.

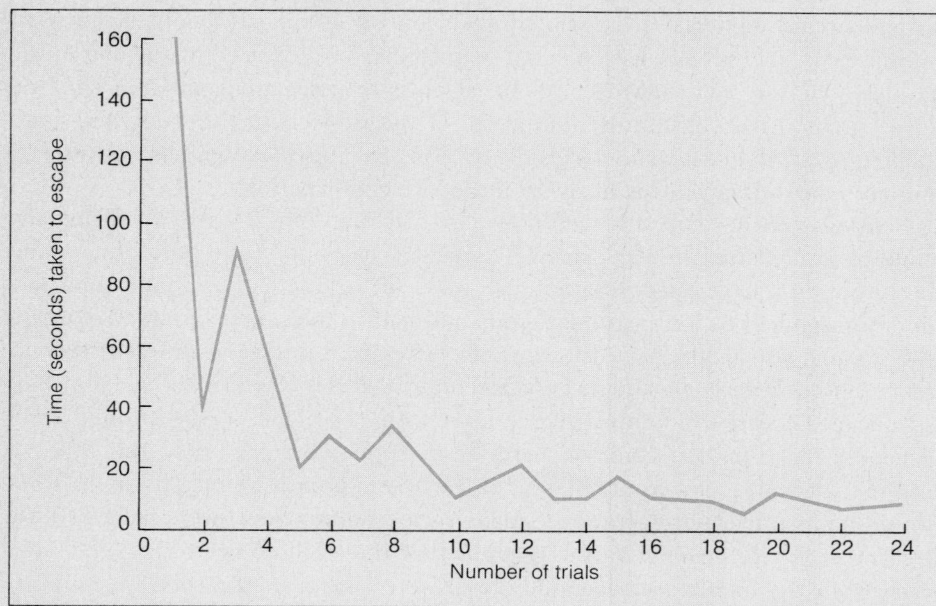

Fig. 2A•1 A Thorndike puzzle box. In order to free itself and gain access to food placed outside the box, the hungry cat had to learn to push a pedal. Similar boxes required the cat to learn to open the door by pulling a loop or turning a latch. (Adapted from Garrett, 1951)

Fig. 2A•2 Learning curve of a cat. (From Thorndike, 1911)

average speed of running through the maze for rats deprived of food for ten hours with the average for rats deprived for six hours.

Based on the outcome of the experiment, we will make a decision about the truth or falsity of our research hypothesis.

Treatment and Control Groups Often the experimental design calls for the random assignment of subjects to two groups: the treatment group and the control group. The subjects might be people, animals, or things—almost anything that an investigator wants to test. Half the subjects are assigned to the experimental group,

In contrast to the rat on the right (from the control group), the rat on the left shows the effects of overeating as a result of surgical treatment of its ventromedial hypothalamus (thought to be the appetite regulator). (Time-Life Picture Agency)

which is called the *treatment group* because these are the subjects who will receive the treatment involved in the experiment (for example, food deprivation in the study of maze learning in rats). Half the subjects are placed in the *control group*, which does not receive the treatment. After the treatment has been administered, the experimenter measures the performance of the subjects in both groups to determine whether there is any difference between the two groups. If all other conditions have been held constant, any difference in the performance of the two groups can be attributed to the treatment. If hungry rats (the treatment group) run the maze faster than rats fed on demand (the control group), the difference in running speed is considered a result of experimental manipulation. Without a control group for comparison, it would not be possible to state that the treatment was responsible for the difference.

The experimental method can be expanded to include more than one treatment group and more than one control group, but the same principles are involved.

One of the most important methods employed by psychologists is the random assignment of subjects to treatment and control groups. *Random assignment* means that every subject has an equal opportunity to be placed in any one of the groups. One way of achieving randomization is to pull names out of a hat. Another method is to arbitrarily number all of the subjects in the study and use a table of random numbers to assign the subjects to groups. Assignment of subjects on any nonrandom basis is likely to invalidate the experiment.

Suppose you developed a technique for teaching long division to fifth-grade children and wanted to verify its effectiveness. The appropriate procedure would be to obtain a large enough sample (say, 200 fifth-grade children) and then randomly assign half to the treatment group and half to the control group. To obtain the sample, you might have to use subjects from a number of different schools representing both high and low socioeconomic levels. Socioeconomic status is significant because it is known that children from the higher socioeconomic levels generally make higher scores on math tests. Remember that only the children in the treatment group would be taught the new approach to long division. What would happen if children from the lower socioeconomic level were placed in the treatment group (possibly on the grounds that the children need help), and children from the higher socioeconomic level were placed in the control group? It might appear that the new method of teaching long division had failed because the two groups were nearly identical in test scores at the conclusion of the experiment.

Independent and Dependent Variables Although researchers use the word *variable* to refer to any condition that varies, it is important to make a distinction between the **independent variable** and the **dependent variable.** To avoid confusion of terms, it may be helpful to think of an experiment in terms of treatment and outcome. The independent variable is the treatment variable, and the dependent variable is the outcome variable. The treatment variable is independent because the experimenter can control it at will, providing that such manipulations are part of the experimental design. The outcome variable is not controlled by the experimenter; it is dependent because it depends on the result of the experimenter's manipulations. In other words, the dependent variable changes as a result of changes in the independent variable.

An independent variable is a variable that is manipulated or varied over groups in the experiment. In a study of the effects of motivation on rate of learning in white rats, the independent variable manipulated might be the number of hours of food deprivation. The experimenter might allow one group of animals to go without food for ten hours, another group for seven hours, and another group for three hours. A control group would be fed on demand. The independent variable is the variable that the experimenter manipulates because there is reason to believe that the manipulation will influence behavior. The manipulation can be defined accurately and repeated by another experimenter.

The conditions measured as the consequences of manipulations are called dependent variables. Stated simply, these are the outcome variables that tell the experimenter whether the experiment has worked. In many psychological experiments, measuring dependent variables is relatively easy. In learning experiments, for example, a dependent variable might be the number of correct responses made by the subjects in treatment and control groups after a fixed number of trials. Another measure of learning is a test score. Still another measure is number of trials to reach the *criterion,* which might be defined as ten consecutive correct responses. Decisions about criteria are made on the basis of **probability.** Since ten out of ten correct responses is a low-probability event, it is reasonable to believe that the behavior did not occur by chance. As the criterion slips to nine out of ten, the probability of a chance occurrence increases.

Self-concept may be described as the image one has of oneself as a result of experiences and the interpretation of them. This construct is difficult to measure in an experiment, perhaps because its meaning is elusive. (Eileen Christelow, Jeroboam)

In some psychological studies the dependent variable is more difficult to measure. At present there is considerable interest in designing experimental manipulations to improve the **self-concept** of children. The difficulty of measuring a construct like self-concept is reflected in the unsatisfactory outcomes of such experiments. The inconsistent results suggest that either there is no general agreement about the meaning of self-concept, or the measures have been poorly developed.

Alternative Designs A design that involves both single or multiple treatments and a control group can be expanded by including more than one independent variable and measuring more than one dependent variable. Another alternative is a design in which no control group is needed. The investigator might be interested in comparing the effects of two or more treatments, but not in comparing the treatment effects with the effect of no treatment at all.

In an experimental model involving a single experimental group, the investigator might be interested in learning how an independent variable influences a measure (such as reaction time) in an individual subject. The investigator determines the normal rate of response, or the *base rate,* for each subject, possibly by asking the subject to push a button in response to a stimulus. After obtaining the base rate over a period of time, the experimenter introduces the independent variable and

It appears that nuisance variables are being controlled in the housing and feeding of these pigeons. (Ken Heyman)

notes changes in the subject's performance. The independent variable is maintained for a fixed period of time until the behavior appears to be stable, or reliable, showing that the manipulation is effective. In the next step, the investigator withdraws the independent variable, anticipating that the subject's behavior will return to its original base rate. The change in behavior upon withdrawal, called *extinction*, demonstrates that the change in base rate is in fact caused by the independent variable and not by some extraneous factor. Such an experiment might be used to study the effects of alcohol, or some other drug, on reaction time in drivers of motor vehicles.

One of the major advantages of the individual-subject approach is that each subject serves as his or her own control, so that his or her characteristics are taken into account. If the results for a number of subjects are similar, the investigator can conclude that the manipulations have the same general effect for all subjects, regardless of their particular individual characteristics. Research of this kind underlies the **behavior modification** approach to teaching techniques (Chapter 10) and to psychotherapy (Chapter 17).

Finally, there is a group of psychologists whose research involves only the use of single subjects. These investigators, following the lead of B. F. Skinner (1953), are primarily interested in discovering the basic laws of learning. Through the manipulation of many variables with only one subject, they assume they can best determine how these laws operate. What appear to be verifiable and replicable are certain basic procedures for controlling the behavior of human beings and animals (Skinner, 1948, 1971). One feature of the single-subject design is that it accounts for variation between individuals.

Control of Nuisance Variables In addition to independent and dependent variables, all experiments include *nuisance variables*, or undesired sources of variation. Unless they are controlled, nuisance variables can bias the outcome of the experiment. A *bias* is any factor in an experiment that systematically introduces error or systematically distorts a set of data.

Bias might be introduced by the experimenter or by the subject. We have already considered observer bias as it might apply to judging acts of aggression among preschool children, and the bias that might result from the use of diseased animals in the laboratory. Physical conditions are another source of bias.

Suppose that we use scraps of wood to build a T-maze in which to train white rats to turn into the right alley to obtain a reward (a pellet of a new rat chow). The wood we use for the right alley has previously been painted gray, but the wood for the left alley has never been painted, and the floor texture is different in the two alleys. We paint the maze flat black. If our experiment is more successful than similar studies reported in the literature, must we attribute this finding to the use of a new rat chow? Could the experiment be biased by a difference in brightness and floor texture in the two alleys? What is the effect of making all the animals turn right? Some animals learn faster turning to the left. It is possible to account for directional preferences by first determining the preference and then training the animal to turn in the opposite direction, or by assigning the animals at random to one or the other alley.

The above example is contrived so that the nuisance variables are obvious. The difficulty of identifying nuisance variables under actual conditions is illustrated by an experiment in which a psychologist was testing a technique for reducing anxiety in human subjects. Using the electrocardiograph, the investigator recorded the subject's heart rate as an index of anxiety; the heartbeat is faster when anxiety is increased and slower when anxiety is reduced. To eliminate nuisance variables, the experimenter tried to maintain constant temperature and humidity and to eliminate extraneous noise in the laboratory room. Nevertheless, the subjects' heart rates fluctuated erratically in a way that was not related to experimental manipulations. The fluctuations were finally explained by the discovery that the electrocardiograph was not controlled by the subject's heart rate, but by electrical current generated by an elevator in a shaft next to the laboratory.

Reliability *Reliability* refers to the degree to which the results are consistent upon repetition of the experiment. The investigator cannot simply assume that a test, a questionnaire, or even a laboratory experiment is reliable. Procedures for determining reliability must be formulated before the experiment is conducted. The scientific method presumes that the experimental manipulation will be administered to all subjects in precisely the same manner and that the dependent variable will be measured in precisely the same way. Consistency is necessary in order to ensure the reliability of the dependent variable measure.

When a subject responds in a particular way, it is assumed that the same response will occur on the next occasion. But sometimes an experiment requires that the subject make only a single response. A single-response score is often unreliable, and its reliability is impossible to estimate. A very large sample of subjects may be used when it is not possible to obtain repeated measures. Replication of the experiment becomes extremely important when the single-response method is used.

Measuring the Sample

2·5 A psychologist formulates a hypothesis about human behavior in the belief that the hypothesis applies to a large group of people or to human beings in general. If the psychologist states that anxiety affects performance on college examinations, such a statement might apply to every college student in the world. Since it would be impossible to study all the college students in the world (or even all the college students in Rhode Island), the psychologist must choose a sample of students in order to examine the relationship of anxiety to test performance. A **sample** is a small group that is observed or tested experimentally as representative of the total group.

The total group is called the *population*. A population includes all the members of a specific identifiable group, which may be human or animal. Populations have

Sampling Older Subjects

One of the important objectives of gerontologists is to describe the characteristics of the intellectual functioning of older people, but obtaining a representative sample of this population is not easy. It would be convenient to draw on the elderly who are in institutions or on the members of "Golden Age" clubs and other social organizations for the aging. However, the people in these two groups probably represent extremes of the general population of old people. One group cannot function adequately without constant supervision, and the other is able presumably to participate in group activities.

Harold Jones and Herbert Conrad (1933) conducted a pioneering study on the growth and decline of mental abilities in persons between ages 10 and 55. They used as subjects the inhabitants of nineteen villages in Massachusetts, New Hampshire, and Vermont. To recruit participants, they showed a "free" movie at the local town hall. Even families living on farms some distance away came.

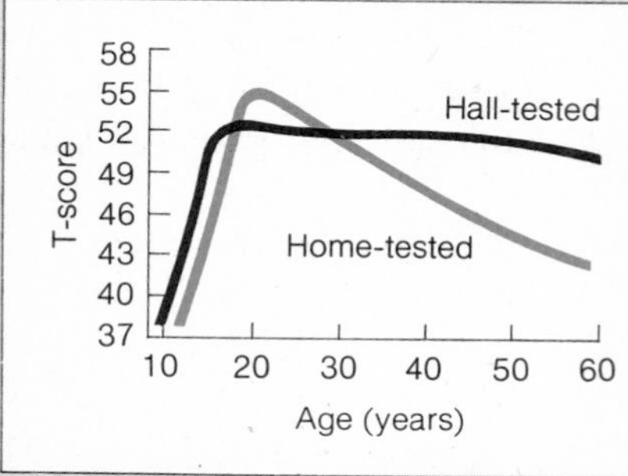

Fig. 2B·1 Growth and decline of ability on the Army Alpha test for hall-tested and home-tested subjects (Jones and Conrad, 1933)

After all, there was a serious depression at the time and anything free was eagerly accepted. The investigators asked only that the viewers also participate in the testing program they were conducting. These people constituted only part of the sample, however. In addition, the investigators conducted their tests on a house-to-house (farm-to-farm) basis. In these ways they were able to obtain a representative sample of people of all ages, including the ill and the reluctant.

Figure 2B·1 compares the growth and decline of performance for subjects who came to the town hall for testing with that of subjects who were intensively sought out and tested at home. The intensively sought subjects performed less well even at the younger age levels (except at age 20, for reasons that are unclear). After their peak score, decline set in immediately and was rather steep.

The results of this aspect of the study demonstrate that researchers must be very cautious about making generalizations regarding the population of old people, and that we must also be cautious in basing policies on research.

characteristics that make them unique in terms of their learning, social structures, and many behaviors of interest to psychologists. The total group can be divided into subpopulations, such as males, females, age groups, or socioeconomic classes. Samples are chosen to reflect the characteristics of populations. The more adequate (or less biased) the sample is, the better the approximation of the population will be.

One of the major techniques used by psychologists, particularly in work with human subjects, is the *representative sample*. Representative samples are selected in terms of the percentage of types of people represented in that particular population. If one were interested in studying verbal learning among 35-year-old subjects, for example, it would be possible to determine from census data the characteristics of almost all 35-year-olds in the United States. Perhaps 55 percent of this population is female, 45 percent is black, 10 percent is retarded, and so on. If the investigator who had sufficient funds thought that such expensive procedures were worthwhile for the validity of a study, it would be possible to obtain samples from these categories in proportions directly related to the population proportions. This procedure is used by pollsters.

Unfortunately, middle-class white children and college students are most typically used as subjects in psychological investigations. Such groups are available and cooperative but they hardly constitute a representative sample. Generalizations drawn from such samples are necessarily restricted. Rats are frequently used in animal studies because they are more economical to obtain and maintain—although the rats used by psychologists are not representative of the rat population. Primate research is very important because monkeys and apes are more closely related to humans on the phylogenetic scale, but such research is extremely expensive.

On some occasions psychologists use *biased samples* because it is convenient to test certain variables on samples that are not representative. Many psychologists have used retarded children, children born with brain injury, or children who have suffered brain injury in accidents (Reitan, 1971). Studies using retarded children have been used to demonstrate basic learning processes (Zeaman and House, 1963) and social reinforcement among institutionalized children (Zigler and Harter, 1969).

The characteristics of the sample should be described carefully as scientific communication. If human subjects are used, their ages ought to be included with an indication of the age range of the sample, the number of males and females, and other salient features, such as socioeconomic status. If animals are used, it is important to specify the species. "White rats" is not adequate; a complete statement should describe the strain, the age, and sex of the rats as well as other important features, such as whether the animals have been used in other experiments. The investigator should report the number of subjects in the experimental and control groups, or the total number of subjects observed and the amount of observation time for each of the subjects. The more subjects there are in the study, the more likely it is that the generalization made from the sample to the population will be accurate.

Measurements and Scales The object of both descriptive research and experimental research is to measure a sample in order to make inferences about the population that the sample represents. The measurement may be as simple as a yes-or-no answer on a questionnaire, or it may be as complex as measuring the behavioral responses (the dependent variable) of hundreds of subjects in experimental research. Measurement is the indispensable component of research because it provides the means to quantify observations. In psychology, measurements are organized in number systems called scales, and several kinds of scales are used.

All types of scales involve certain properties related to their units of measurement, the distances separating points on a scale. We know, for example, that on a weight scale the unit distance between 80 and 90 pounds is equal to the unit distance between 140 and 150 pounds. Most psychological scales, however, can be

Age can be used as a scale in various ways. For example:

Mike is four years old (nominal).
Mike is older than Marie (ordinal).
The difference between Mike's age and Marie's age is the same as that between Marie's age and Juan's age (interval).
Mike is twice as old as Marie (ratio).

However, the growth that a year represents varies greatly over the entire lifespan as well as from person to person at the same age. (Zoe Pearson)

characterized by the fact that their unit distances are unequal. S. S. Stevens (1951) summarized the properties of four types of scales, including the kinds of inferences permitted by each.

Nominal Scales Nominal scales are not true scales. They simply name categories of measurement. They neither require numbers nor imply a comparison between the categories named. For example, a nominal scale used to measure test responses might name two categories: true or false. This type of scale is sufficient when the psychologist is interested in measuring only the frequency of data occurring in each category.

Ordinal Scales Ordinal scales are composed of ranked measures. For example, the alphabetical grades given in schools are ordinal measures. The psychologist can infer that one measure on an ordinal scale is comparatively greater or lesser than another measure on the scale. For example, a grade of "B" is always higher than a "C" and lower than an "A." Because the distances between measures on an ordinal scale are not necessarily equal, however, no inferences can be drawn as to how much greater or lesser a particular measure may be.

Ordinal scales predominate among psychological scales, even though some successful work has been reported in establishing interval scales. Therefore, most psychological research permits little more than rank-ordering of data. This has not seriously impeded research, however, because statistical methods and research designs have been developed for use with ordinal scales. Nevertheless, statements about absolute differences among subjects or data should be viewed with caution.

Interval Scale Interval scales are composed of ranked measures also. Unlike ordinal scales, however, interval scales begin with zero points from which measures are marked at equal intervals throughout. The zero points on interval scales are not absolute zeros; rather they are assumed or derived. For example, both the centigrade and Fahrenheit temperature scales are interval. Zero on the centigrade scale is defined arbitrarily as the point at which water freezes. On the Fahrenheit scale, it is the temperature produced by combining equal weights of snow and salt, a point thirty-two intervals or degrees below the freezing point of water.

A problem with psychological scales is how to define a reasonable zero point. Thurstone (1955) measured the growth of different abilities using an interval scale. He defined the zero point of his growth scale as the point at which his subjects showed no variation in performance on tests of ability.

Because interval scales have equal units of measurement, the psychologist can infer how much greater or lesser one measure is than another. For example, each interval or degree on the Fahrenheit thermometer represents an equal expansion of mercury. Therefore, 70°F is always ten degrees greater than 60°F, and five degrees less than 75°F. The psychologist also can compare differences between measures at different points on an interval scale. For example, it is accurate to infer that the difference between 0°F and 50°F is equal to the difference between 50°F and 100°F. Because interval scales do not have true zero points, however, it is inaccurate to infer that the absolute value of one measure is a multiple or ratio of another. For example, it is inaccurate to say that 100°F is twice as hot as 50°F.

Ratio Scales Ratio scales are interval scales based on true or absolute zero points, points at which the quality being measured no longer exists. For example, the zero point on a weight scale is the point at which a mass becomes weightless. The absolute values of all measures on a ratio scale can be compared using all mathematical functions, including multiples and ratios. For example, it is accurate to infer that 100 pounds is twice as heavy as 50 pounds, and that the ratio of 50 pounds to 100 pounds is equal to the ratio of 25 pounds to 50 pounds.

Because the determination of an absolute psychological zero is impossible, ratio scales to measure psychological data can be approximated only.

Statistics

2•6 Psychological research is a way of testing hypotheses by gathering relevant information, or data. We have observed how data are derived from test scores, survey answers, or measurements made in the laboratory. Whatever the research method, the result is a mass of scores that must be reduced to a manageable form that can be understood and interpreted. *Statistics* is the science that deals with collecting, ordering, and interpreting data.

Descriptive Statistics Descriptive statistics are statistical measurements that describe, organize, and summarize sets of data obtained from a sample of individuals. These measurements provide three major types of information.

1. Measures of central tendency: What is the average score?
2. Variability: How much do the other scores differ from the average score?
3. Correlation: What is the degree of relatedness between two or more variables represented by two different sets of scores?

Measures of Central Tendency A measure of central tendency is a number that represents the average subject in the sample. This measure can also be an estimate of the average individual in the population. The average summarizes information about the sample, even though it may not exist within the sample; for example, the arithmetic average of babies born in the United States to married couples in the 20- to 25-year age group is 1.8. An average does not represent the characteristics of all members of a population; for example, it is possible to determine the average income for any group of people even though some of the people are currently unemployed and some are millionaires.

There are three measures of central tendency. The **mode** is the score that occurs most frequently in a set of scores. This statistic is seldom used because it lacks stability. A change in performance of one subject can substantially change the mode and distort the characteristic of the group. A second index of central tendency is the **median,** or the fiftieth percentile. Fifty percent of the cases fall below the median and 50 percent fall above it. The median is used when the data come from an ordinal scale, rather than from an equal-interval scale. The median is useful also when the scores tend to pile up, with an unusually large number of high or low scores. The **mean** is the measure of central tendency most frequently used in psychological research. The mean is the arithmetic average, the sum of all the scores divided by the number of scores.

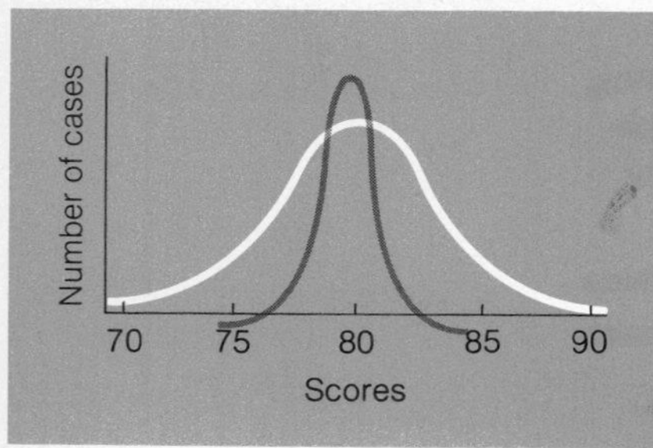

Fig. 2·2 Two different distributions: the gray line shows a distribution with low variability (a range of 10), and the white line shows a higher variability (a range of 20). The mean is the same (80) for both distributions.

Variability The average score is not adequate to describe the characteristics of a sample. Populations are also characterized by a degree of variation. In evaluating a subject within a sample, it is useful to note the individual's position in the *distribution,* which is the range of scores from lowest to highest. Suppose that the two curves in Figure 2·2 represent the distribution of scores on two final exams, and your score is 85 on each of these two examinations. How would variability affect your grade on each exam? If variability is high (that is, there is a wide range of scores), the subject's score must be extremely high or low before it is noteworthy. If variability is low, then a minor deviation from the average may be significant.

The most frequently used index of variability is called the **standard deviation** (see Appendix A). When large amounts of data are plotted on a graph, they often fall into a symmetrical distribution curve shaped somewhat like a bell (Figure 2·3). The mean is indicated by the high point at the center of the bell because most cases fall near the mean. Above and below the mean the curve tapers off sharply because few scores are very high or very low. IQ scores for the entire population fall into the normal distribution curve, and so do the results of chance events, such as rolling dice or tossing pennies. Figure 2·3 shows a normal distribution represented by the bell-shaped curve, with standard deviations indicated along

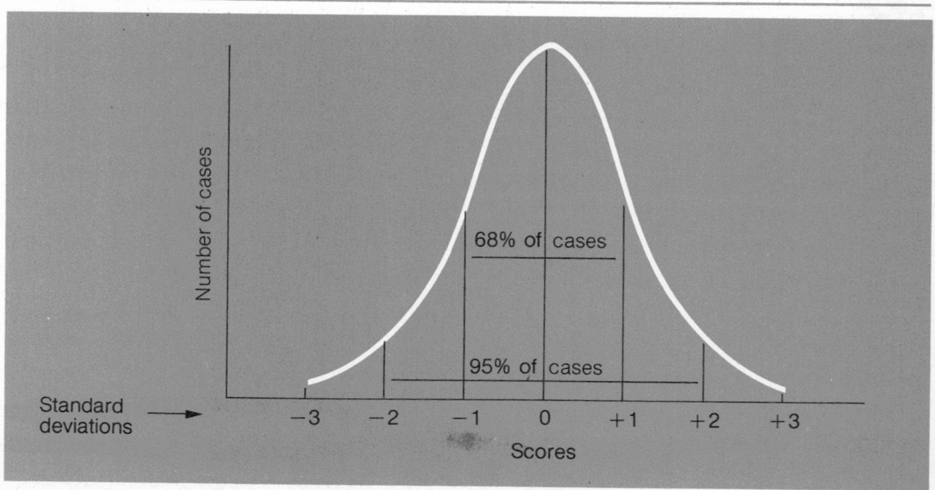

Fig. 2·3 Bell-shaped curve indicating a normal distribution.

Interpreting Age-criteria Data

The palmar reflex—a grasping reaction of the fingers (but not the thumb) to stimulation of the palm of the hand—begins on the average at four months of age and continues until approximately eight months of age. This is a type of age-criteria data that developmental psychologists have found from studying various behaviors, including reading readiness (which generally occurs at six and a half years of mental age) and walking (which the typical child does at age twelve months).

These data provide a descriptive picture of development and can be useful guidelines for both professionals and parents. However, they can be misused, as when parents use the data as a basis for putting pressure on a child to improve performance on a particular skill.

Two concepts are involved in understanding the proper use of age-criteria data (or any kind of normative data): the *average,* which refers to an index that best represents the group and the amount of variation around the average. The index most often used is the *mean,* the arithmetic average—a representation of the "typical" individual, who almost never exists in a sample. Other indexes that may be used are the median (the middle-most measure in a set of measures) and the mode (the measure that occurs most frequently).

Suppose that both a one-week-old baby and a one-year-old child are four pounds underweight. Even though the deficit is the same in each case, we recognize the far greater cause for alarm in the former case because the average weight for week-old infants is only seven to eight pounds.

The same principles hold when interpreting an individual's performance on any other measure, physical or psychological. How much variation is there in the population, above and below the average? Where does the individual stand relative to that variation around the average? Failure to take both indices into account leads to many unwarranted decisions about children and to needless anxiety among parents.

the base line. Sixty-eight percent of the cases tend to fall between plus one and minus one standard deviation of the mean; 95 percent of the cases fall between plus two and minus two standard deviations.

Correlation A correlation shows the degree of relatedness between two sets of scores. Table 2•1 shows scores for eight individuals on two different tests. In Figure 2•4 the scores for each individual on both tests are plotted on a graph called a scatterplot. This particular scatterplot indicates a positive correlation between

Table 2•1 Scores for Eight Individuals on Two Tests

INDIVIDUAL	TEST A	TEST B
1	22	19
2	21	17
3	20	18
4	19	16
5	23	20
6	24	22
7	22	21
8	25	23

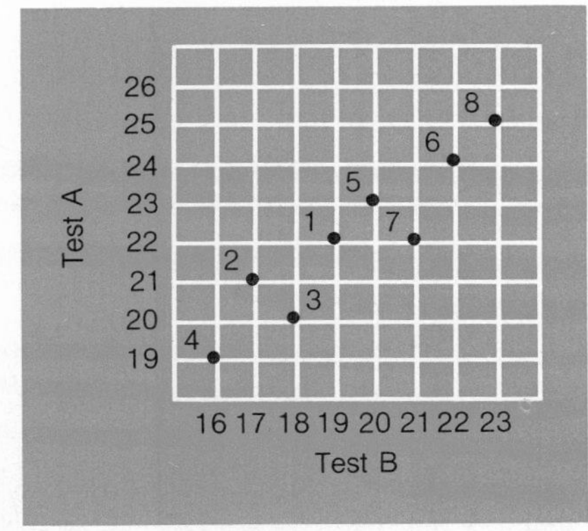

Fig. 2•4 Scatterplot showing a positive correlation between scores on two different tests.

the two measures: people who scored high on Test A usually scored high on Test B, and people who scored low on Test A usually scored low on Test B.

The scatterplots in Figure 2•5 show how three measures—reading, self-concept, and color concepts—might correlate with IQ scores. Assuming that people with high IQs are good readers, the first plot shows a perfect correlation, or a correlation coefficient of +1.00. The self-concept measure also correlates positively with IQ, but the correlation coefficient is only +.40. The third plot shows zero correlation between IQ and color concepts.

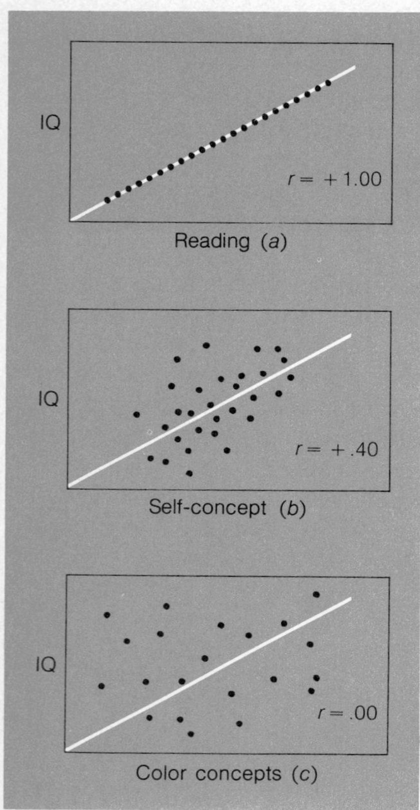

Fig. 2•5 Scatterplots showing (a) perfect correlation, (b) positive correlation, and (c) zero correlation.

One of the major advances in statistical analysis occurred with the development of **factor analysis,** a procedure for further analyzing correlation coefficients. Suppose we administer a battery of fifty tests to a group of college freshmen in order to develop measures of personality and interests, as well as verbal and mathematical abilities. When the testing is completed, we correlate all the measures with each other. This procedure results in an intercorrelation *matrix,* a table of numbers consisting of fifty rows and fifty columns. Through factor analysis it is possible to reduce the number of tests into clusters by grouping tests that measure essentially the same thing. Now instead of having to examine all fifty scores, we might need only ten scores. Factor analysis, then, is a data reduction procedure for reducing intercorrelations into tests that go together.

Inferential Statistics Descriptive statistics describe measurements obtained from a sample of individuals, rather than from the entire population. Inferential statistics use descriptive statistics to estimate the probability that measurements made on a sample would be the same if made on the whole population. At the conclusion of an experiment, it is possible to compute the mean and the standard deviation of the scores obtained by the experimental group and the control group. If there is a difference between the means, the investigator must determine whether the difference is sufficiently large that it is unlikely that it occurred by chance. If the difference occurred by chance, the results are invalid, and the experiment cannot be replicated. Statistical inference enables the investigator to make a judgment about the truth or falsity of the research hypothesis.

Summary

The objective of scientific psychology is the acquisition of knowledge about behavior through the testing of hypotheses. Observations made either in natural settings or in the laboratory enable psychologists to gather data and make predictions about the behavior of humans and other organisms. Two major procedures for gathering and interpreting data are the correlational method and the experimental method.

The correlational method involves making observations and using a statistical index called the correlation coefficient to examine the relationships between two or more variables, such as a behavior and the environmental context in which it occurs.

There are various experimental designs in which a treatment (the independent variable) is administered to a group of subjects, and the outcome (the dependent variable) is measured. A common design involves the use of a control group, which does not receive the treatment but is used for comparison. A change in the experimental group that does not occur also in the control group is assumed to be the result of treatment.

Generally it would be impossible to test the entire population identified in a research hypothesis. It is customary to draw a sample from the population, measure the sample, compute one or more descriptive statistics from the measurements, and use the descriptive statistics to make inferences about the population. Statistical inference enables the researcher to determine that the outcome of the experiment occurred as a result of the treatment, not by chance. The hypothesis is considered true when the findings have been replicated by other experimenters.

Suggested Readings

Arnoult, M. D. 1976. *Fundamentals of scientific method in psychology.* 2d ed. Dubuque, Iowa: Wm. C. Brown.

This volume provides a more sophisticated treatment of the rules and methods of science as applied to psychology.

Dethier, V. G. 1962. *To know a fly.* San Francisco: Holden-Day.

A light-hearted but serious account of the development of a research program applied to a single species and the numerous ways that obstacles were overcome.

McCain, G. and Erwin, M. Segal. 1969. *The game of science.* Belmont, Cal.: Brooks/Cole.

A relatively simple introduction to the rules of science and methods of scientific inquiry.

Developmental Psychology

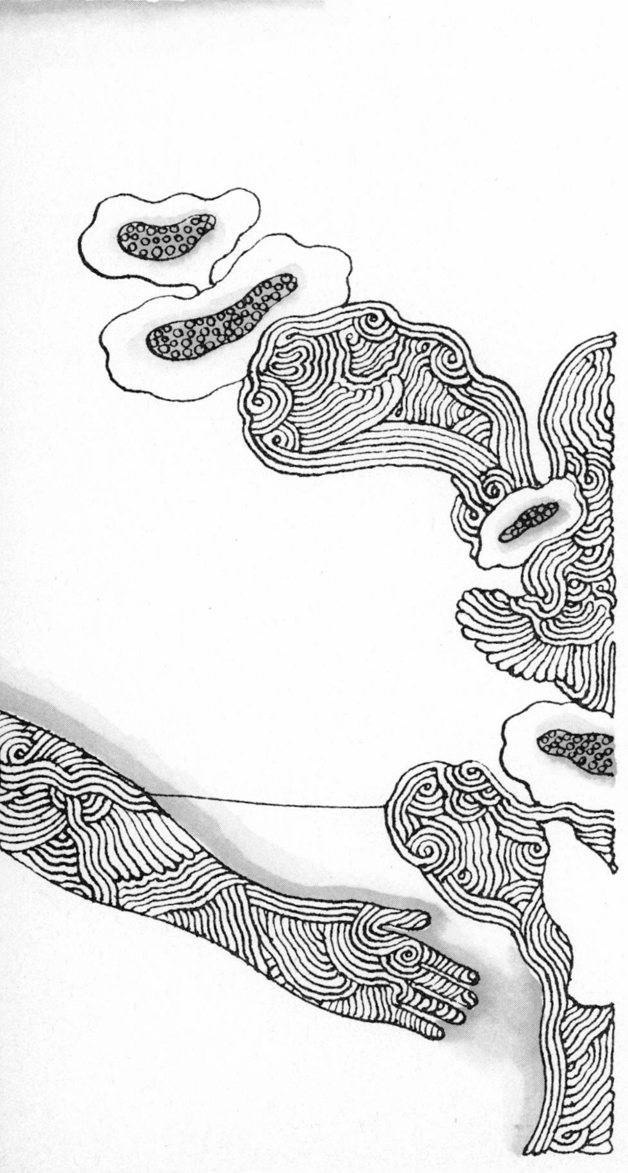

II Developmental psychology includes the study of perception, learning, motivation, personality, social psychology, biopsychology, and psychogenetics—topics that you will encounter in other sections of this book. This section on developmental psychology provides a preview of the subjects to come and introduces some basic psychological concepts.

Most students and many psychologists equate developmental psychology with the study of children and adolescents. True, a considerable amount of research has been devoted to childhood and adolescence, but actually developmental change does not cease at age eighteen or twenty. It slows down and is not so noticeable until the accumulated effects of age and disease begin to take their toll. Nevertheless, more and more developmental psychologists are studying aging, because we need to know about this process and how people can sustain a sense of importance and dignity throughout life.

This section describes a broad array of issues. Do babies have preferences for certain stimuli and, if so, what kinds of stimuli do they prefer? How do the processes of acquiring knowledge function, and how are they influenced? How do child-reading practices affect behavior? What developmental changes occur during the adolescent period? What happens to the intellectual abilities of elderly people—do they become childlike, or do some abilities decline and others increase or remain stable?

Chapter 3 provides an overview of developmental psychology, its basic research methods and theories. Chapters 4 and 5 examine the development of learning and of social abilities, respectively. Chapter 6 discusses the effects of aging on learning, and the psychological and social consequences of aging.

The Nature of Developmental Psychology

3 Developmental psychology encompasses a broad range of study. It is concerned with the biological, intellectual, emotional, and social development of the individual throughout the entire lifespan. Indeed, it overlaps most other areas of psychology.

Developmental psychologists seek to answer questions such as: How do babies perceive the world? How does puberty affect personality? Do the aged really tend to become childlike? Developmentalists believe that at least partial answers to these kinds of questions can be found by studying *processes* (the ways behavioral responses are organized). These processes are thought to change in an orderly manner as the individual develops from conception to death. By studying the relationship between changes in process and broad concepts such as cognitive development, socialization, and aging, developmental psychologists hope to create a comprehensive theory that will predict, explain, or describe changes in behavior at every level of development.

In light of the fact that prediction, explanation, and description of changes in behavior are within the scope of learning research (see Chapter 10), the need for a separate and broad-ranging developmental psychology has been questioned. In summarizing the issues surrounding this question, Edward Zigler (1963) observed that learning research focuses on changes in the strength or accuracy of behavioral responses over relatively short periods of time. Developmental research, on the other hand, is concerned with changes in the form or organization of responses over much broader periods. Langer (1969) concludes further that although learning mechanisms determine some aspects of behavioral change, other aspects must be considered. Broader and qualitatively different concepts, such as those used by developmentalists, are required to describe and explain the dramatic behavioral changes that occur over periods as long as a lifespan.

Developmental psychology concerns not only the early stages of life, when growth is perhaps most dramatic, but the whole lifespan. (Zoe Pearson)

In their attempts to formulate and explain such broad concepts of behavior change, theorists stress the interaction between *heredity* and *environment*. Traditional developmental theorists tend to emphasize the importance of biological maturation and notions about behavior sequence and adaptation. Other theorists refuse to believe that such genetically based concepts can explain the complex behavior changes that occur during development. Such theorists emphasize the importance of environmental influences on behavior. They tend to explain behavioral development in terms of the association of environmental events with behavioral responses followed by rewards or punishments. Wherever the emphasis is placed ultimately, a comprehensive theory of human development must include both heredity and environmental factors.

The data on which developmentalists base their theories have been gathered through a variety of research methods. Some early researchers simply observed and described the development of their own children. As experimental methods have become available, however, researchers have sought more control over what they observe. Because development is associated with age-related concepts, some researchers have tried to use chronological age or some other measure of time as an independent variable (see Chapter 2). Results of such studies tend to produce circular reasoning: for example, the fifteen-month-old child walks because it is fifteen months old. Merely the passage of time cannot explain the fact that the average fifteen-month-old walks but the average ten-month-old does not. Rather, the change results from behavioral events during that time period. The task of the developmental researcher is to identify, control, and explain such behavioral events. This task is extremely difficult when the range of time being studied is months, years, lifespans, or even generations.

Because developmental psychology is concerned with answering broad questions concerning human behavior, it is often difficult to test developmental concepts and theories with the precision that can be required in some other areas of psychology. However, pressing human problems require broad answers, and developmental theory appears to be a valuable source for practical solutions to many such problems.

Applying Developmental Principles

3·1 An understanding of development is essential for parents, teachers, physicians, and others whose jobs require direct intervention in human lives. The significance of developmental psychology reaches all people, especially those of us who, as wage earners and taxpayers, support public programs in education, medical and mental health care, and nutrition. The findings of developmental researchers are being applied to urgent, controversial, and highly publicized issues, such as how to make up for presumed cultural deficiencies in preschool and school-age children, how best to rear children, and how to care for the aging.

Compensatory Education Programs Children from low-income families tend to perform poorly in school. Assuming that this poor performance is due to inadequate or inappropriate stimulation in the home, compensatory education programs seek to meet the specific needs of culturally disadvantaged children. Among the better known such programs that grew out of the war on poverty in the 1960s are Project Head Start, Project Follow Through, and the day-care programs.

Project Head Start is designed to give preschool children from disadvantaged backgrounds the kinds of experiences that middle-class children have, in order to increase their readiness for kindergarten and first grade. Evaluation studies suggest that the program is not meeting these expectations. Some people argue that the children in the program are incapable of learning (essentially a biological-genetic orientation), whereas others believe that the programs are inadequate for the needs of the children. It may be that we simply do not know enough about learning principles, cognition, and teaching techniques to be able to generate the kinds of programs the children need or perhaps we do not understand well enough the characteristics of the population for whom compensatory education programs are designed. Most educators possess limited knowledge of the environments from which these children come and therefore tend to view them as stereotypes.

Project Follow Through extends from kindergarten through third grade. While attempting to use learning materials designed to make up for the presumed deficiencies in the children's environments, the developers of this project varied the kinds of programs children received. Some programs are highly structured. Some emphasize language development. Some are based on Piaget's description of the mental evolution of the child. Educators hope to determine what kinds of programs work best with different kinds of children.

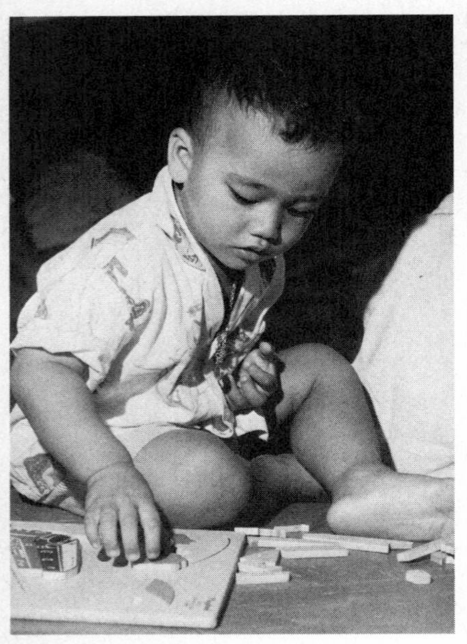

Day-care centers exist throughout the world. Thailand, for example, launched a day-care program in 1961 that is now being assisted by several UN agencies. (UNICEF Photo by Prathana Konsupto)

Now Project Follow Through is being evaluated to see whether it is helping children increase their knowledge. Preliminary data suggest that the more structured programs are the most effective with children in kindergarten and first grade, but by the third grade, children from the less structured programs begin to catch up. Even though the different kinds of programs produce similar results at the end of third grade, social and emotional development may be differentially influenced by these programs and their influence should be more carefully examined.

Day-care programs, designed for children from infancy through preschool, were developed so that the children of mothers who work full time can receive care that is beneficial both emotionally and educationally. No systematic evaluation of day care has yet been completed, but already opponents argue that the child who is taken care of by various people other than the mother will later demonstrate symptoms of disturbed emotional development and unsatisfactory social relationships. Considerably more research is needed to clarify the importance of the mother-child relationship and the developmental effects of inadequate mothering.

Child-rearing Practices The behaviorist John B. Watson proclaimed that children are products of their environments. True, the home and the parents are usually the immediate and consistent environmental contacts of children. But how influential are parents in the cognitive, social, and emotional development of their children? What difference does it make in a child's development if the father is the primary care giver, or if the father is absent altogether (because of divorce or death, for exampıe), or if the child is reared primarily by persons other than the parents?

In trying to determine the effects of varous child-rearing practices, developmentalists have not conducted (and probably never will) carefully controlled experiments in which children are randomly assigned to parents. Much of the research in the area of child-rearing practices does not allow even tentative conclusions to be made and rarely warrants recommending one child-rearing practice over another—despite claims in magazine articles on how to rear a child or how to be a good parent.

Some studies indicate that children's behavior has an effect on the way parents treat children. In one such study (Osofosky and O'Connell, 1972) parents' behaviors were observed in the laboratory while their teen-age daughters behaved in a dependent or independent way on certain tasks. It was found that the parents tended to be more controlling of their daughters' behaviors when the daughters behaved in a dependent way. The investigators also observed that the mothers used encouragement with their daughters on the tasks, whereas the fathers tended to help directly with the tasks.

Some research indicates that the more child-centered and democratic child-rearing practices tend to be associated with children who are brighter, socially and emotionally more mature, and more positively viewed by their teachers. But, as we shall see in Chapter 5, the parents of these children are above average in

Preschool Programs and Social and Emotional Development

In the United States preschool programs have long been used to enhance the cognitive development of children. What effects do these programs have when they are used to foster the social and emotional development of children?

In one experiment (Thompson, 1944) four-year-old children were equated and randomly assigned to two treatment groups—twelve to treatment A, where the teachers adopted an impersonal attitude toward the children, and eleven to treatment B, where the teachers were warmly and closely involved with the children. In treatment B personal guidance was the primary aim of the curriculum. The materials available to the teachers and children in both groups were equivalent.

On the basis of observations, the following social and emotional areas of behavior were examined: ascendancy (attempts to dominate peers), social participation, leadership, constructiveness (when faced with possible failure), and number of nervous habits. At the beginning of the experiment there were no differences between the two groups on any of these behavior categories. At the end of the experiment the children in treatment B were more ascendant and constructive, and evidenced greater social participation and leadership. There were no differences in nervous habits.

education and income. It may be that the concept of the best child-rearing practice is relative to various factors such as the characteristics of the parents themselves.

Care for the Aging The scientific study of aging, **gerontology,** crosses many fields, including psychology, sociology, social work, nutrition, and medicine. The modern study of aging probably was triggered by G. Stanley Hall in his book *Senescence, the Last Half of Life* (1922), but until recently social scientists showed little interest in the problems of people over sixty-five. The aging process was viewed simply as a reversal of childhood and adolescent development, accompanied by physiological and degenerative problems of greater interest to medical science than to social science.

Gerontology did not grow as a scientific discipline as long as the number of people over sixty-five was relatively small and the elderly were part of the nuclear family. Today longevity is increasing, and grandparents typically do not live with their children and grandchildren. Increased life expectancy (accompanied by sustained vigor and health) and the change in the concept of the nuclear family have raised important questions of social policy with respect to a substantially increased, and apparently increasing, aging population.

Perhaps the most pervasive problem of the elderly involves income. The average annual income of the typical married couple between ages twenty and sixty-four is slightly over $10,000. At retirement, this income drops 50 percent. Because retirement income usually comes from a fixed pension program and from social security, it cannot keep up with inflation. Therefore the real income of retired persons probably drops more than 50 percent. This reduction places severe limitations on the choices people have after retirement about how to spend their time and money. The finances and the living arrangements of older people are further affected by the fact that, on the average, women can expect to outlive their husbands by seven to ten years.

Today several universities in the United States offer graduate programs on various aspects of aging. The National Institute on Aging and the Administration on Aging are attempting to provide funds for research on the psychological and physiological processes of aging and to develop programs that will meet the needs of older people. To evaluate such programs, we must first have some knowledge of the aging process. We will deal with theories of aging later in this chapter and in Chapter 6.

Major Developmental Theories

3•2 Theories of developmental psychology generally rely on the concept of maturation to explain behavioral development. Maturation refers to genetically based biological processes of growth. The child becomes an adult, growing older and older, regardless of environmental factors, but these factors can affect the rate of development.

Most theories of development assume that, as new levels of behavior emerge, each level is built on and dependent on the immediately preceding level, and that the order in which the levels emerge is identical in all cultures.

Some theorists also assume that behaviors or sequences of behavior, that appear in all cultures are genetically transmitted from generation to generation because of their adaptive value. This assumption is rooted in the "survival of the fittest" notion of Darwin's theory of evolution. For example, D. G. Freedman (1964) argues that smiling in young infants is a universal, unlearned behavior that has survival value: it helps the child win acceptance in a potentially lethal environment.

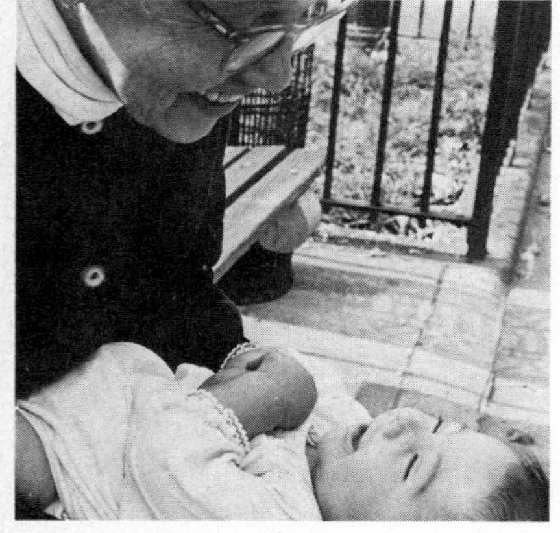

Is smiling in young infants a universal, unlearned behavior that is perpetuated because of its survival value? (Anna Kaufman Moon, Stock, Boston)

Theories such as those of Freud, Piaget, and Bruner, classify the course of human development into segments or stages. The behavioral processes associated with each stage are said to be qualitatively distinct (different in kind). Other theorists view development as continuous. They believe that developmental differences are simply changes in the complexity or diversity (quantitative differences) of behavior.

Theories of Cognitive Development As an aspect of learning, cognition refers to the processes involved in using information, concepts. and language. Rather than always simply responding to a stimulus, we sometimes restructure or interpret our perceptions and thoughts. One way we are able to learn is by seeing relations between objects and events, thoughts and ideas.

We shall deal with the specific nature of cognition in Chapter 11, but here (and in Chapter 4) we want to discuss the development of cognitive processes—the different ways of knowing and forms of knowledge that occur throughout life. All three theories of cognitive development that we shall consider are stage theories. They also share the viewpoint that cognitive development proceeds from rather primitive reflex responses (largely stimulus-bound) to ever-increasing representations and abstractions. Each of these theoretical models recognizes not only the biological antecedents of behavior but also the necessity for appropriate environmental stimulation.

Piaget: The Child As Active Learner Jean Piaget, a Swiss psychologist who was interested in the nature of knowledge, attempted to explain how people acquire an adult knowledge, or understanding, of the world. He used the term *structure* to represent the organization of knowledge and focused on the formation of structures and their interactions with the environment (1950).

Piaget assumed that the child is an active learner rather than a passive reactor to environmental input. Even at the beginning of life, the child is acting on the environment, using responses that are reflexive, (spontaneous and unlearned). The child's primitive structures are formed through the interplay of action and perception.

According to Piaget, two processes are basic to the development of new knowledge or structures: *accommodation*, modification of knowledge of the environment to incorporate new objects or experiences, and *assimilation*, incorporation of a new object or experience into an existing structure. These two processes modify existing structures and therefore modify knowledge.

According to Piaget, the child moves progressively from relying on perception and direct contact with objects to using symbols and ideas. Beginning with rudimentary reflex responses, the child moves through four stages: sensorimotor intelligence, preconcrete operations, concrete operations, and formal operations. We will examine each of these stages in detail in the next chapter.

Jean Piaget (1896–). According to Piaget, cognitive development proceeds in stages that always follow the same order, each stage being a self-consistent whole and not simply more of whatever came before.

Bruner: From Reflexes to Symbols Jerome S. Bruner's theory of cognitive development consists of three stages (1964):

1. The enactive stage: The child forms primitive schemata (organized patterns of behavior) based on repetitive motor activities involving various objects.
2. The iconic stage: The child begins to function more and more with images, which are free from the motor acts associated with objects.
3. The symbolic stage: The child's knowledge is reflected in language, the abstract system that is furthest removed in psychological distance from the actual object or its associated motor acts.

Like Piaget, Bruner sees the general cognitive development as going from simple reflexive and associative actions to ever-increasing symbolic representations of the world. Unlike Piaget, however, Bruner emphasizes the ways in which culture affects a child's development of knowledge of the world. Bruner also views language as symbolic representation, whereas for Piaget symbolic representation is a prerequisite for language and language development.

Werner: Orthogenesis In evolutionary theory the term *orthogenesis* applies to the phenomenon in which a progressive change in living beings appears to occur

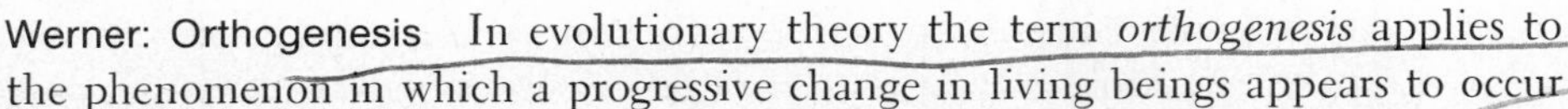

along definite lines of development, independently of external factors. The term is also applied to a theory that social evolution proceeds in the same direction and through the same stages in every culture, despite differing external conditions. Heinz Werner (1948, 1957) applied the term orthogenesis to developmental changes in mental organization. He specified two fundamental characteristics of the processes underlying mental activities (rather than the content of these activities):

Being able to tie shoes is one aspect of hierarchic integration involved in the development of manual control. This level of dexterity grew out of increasing co-ordination at grosser tasks and will in turn lead to more precise control, as is needed in writing, for example. (Elizabeth Crews, Jeroboam)

1. Differentiation: Primitive and generalized action systems (the mental processes employed by an organism) become successively more differentiated, but at the same time they fuse with other systems to form a more integrated means of action.
2. Hierarchic integration: As more advanced integrated systems emerge, they take over less developmentally sophisticated systems. Each level of development, though dependent on the previous level, is nevertheless qualitatively distinct from it and takes over the governing of its behaviors.

Hierarchic integration is not linear and does not occur overnight. Werner therefore postulated the genetic principle of spirality: As the organism advances toward some ultimate state of maturity, it will at times retreat temporarily to its original level before resuming its inexorable growth.

The concept of hierarchic integration is similar to Piaget's notion of hierarchic structures. It may well represent a more explicit description of the phenomenon. That these models overlap would appear to be a consequence of shared philosophical positions. We will meet the concept of orthogenesis again in Chapter 4 when we discuss the acquisition of walking behavior.

Theories of Personality Development and Socialization The work of Freud and Erikson is typically identified with personality development. The work of Kohlberg on moral development and the development of sex-role concepts, and the work of Bandura on social learning are more often identified with processes of socialization. According to Bandura, socialization involves the acquisition of behaviors through imitation (observational learning) and reinforcement.

The theories of Freud, Erikson, and Kohlberg share the same philosophical view of human beings as do the theories of Piaget, Bruner, and Werner. All of these theorists explicitly recognize the biological origins of humans, the internal sources of energy for development, and the interrelationships among physiological and psychological structures. Bandura's approach, however, involves an adaptation of several basic principles of **stimulus-response (S-R) theory.** In other words, his view is that behavioral change occurs through the association of a stimulus and a response followed by reinforcement. The work of these four theorists will be described in more detail in Chapter 5.

Freud: Psychosexual Stages After treating many patients and observing the frequency of problems related to sex, Sigmund Freud came to believe that th-

Freud at various stages in his life: at age eight with his father, at age sixteen with his mother, and at age sixty-six with his grandson. (Left and middle: Austrian Information Service, New York; right: Snark International)

energy underlying all human behavior comes from an instinctive drive called the libido, which is sexual in nature. Freud used the word *sexual*, however, in a very broad sense to refer to any kind of activity that gives physical pleasure. The libido, then, includes all urges to satisfy the body and the senses (1923).

The basic personality structures proposed by Freud are the id, the superego, and the ego. Personality consists of the interaction of these structures and the external world. Briefly, the *id* is the source of all instinctive energy. The *superego* is postulated as being the conscience; it defines and attempts to maintain the moral and ethical values of the culture. The id and the superego work in opposition to each other and are therefore in basic conflict. The *ego* serves to mediate between these two opposing structures. In effect, the ego represents the rational processes and maintains an adjustment between the id, the superego, and the external world. (These concepts will come up again in Chapter 13 when we discuss theories of personality.)

According to Freud's theory, there are three stages of personality growth: oral, anal, and genital. In each of these psychosexual stages the child attempts to achieve pleasure in ways that focus on different parts of the body.

Table 3•1 presents these stages, the behaviors that typically accompany each stage, the objects commonly chosen to satisfy the sexual impulses at each stage, and the approximate age range at which each stage occurs. Freud believed that all children go through these stages in the same sequence.

The effects of early stages of psychosexual development persist throughout later stages and even into adulthood, particularly if a fixation (an attachment to an object of infancy or childhood) has been formed. Especially at the early psychosexual stages, before the ego and the superego have had a chance to develop, fixations are most likely to occur because parents either permit excessive grat-

Table 3·1 The Theoretically Normal Development of Children According to Freud's Hypotheses of Psychosexual Development

PERIODS AND STAGES	MODE OF FINDING PLEASURE	OBJECT CHOICE	APPROXIMATE AGE RANGE
Infancy Period			
Oral Stage			Birth to 1 year
Early	Sucking, swallowing (incorporating)	Self	
Late	Biting, devouring (destroying)		
Anal Stage			1 to 3 years
Early	Expelling (rejecting, destroying)	Self	
Late	Retaining (controlling, possessing)		
Early Genital Stage (phallic)	Touching, rubbing, exhibiting and looking at genitalia, investigating, comparing, questioning, fantasizing (tender affection)	Parent (Oedipal fantasies)	3 to 5 years
Latency Period (no new zone)	Affectional trends	Development of social feelings	5 to 12 years
Adolescent Period			12 to 19 years
Late Genital Stage	Reactivation of modes of infancy period Emergence of adult mode of finding pleasure	Revival of Oedipal fantasies Homosexual Heterosexual	

(Adapted from Healy, Bronner, and Bowers, 1930, 1958)

ification of the child's sexual impulses or excessively frustrate gratification, or alternate between these two practices. For example, a fixation may occur at the early oral stage because the child's sucking needs are not satisfied. (One reason why breast-feeding becomes modish from time to time may be that it is thought to be superior to bottle-feeding as a means of meeting a baby's sucking needs.) Later fixations may occur when the ego (rationality) is unable to mediate between the id (needs) and the superego (moral values).

Freud observed among his patients that, depending on the stage at which a fixation occurred and the reasons for it, specific personality traits tended to result. For example, a person fixated at the early oral stage because of unusual deprivation was likely to be passive, pessimistic, and dependent. Fixation at the late anal stage may result in obstinacy (perhaps to the point of defiance and vindictiveness), orderliness, and overconcern for details.

According to Freud, a crucial aspect of personality development is the resolution of the Oedipal conflict. The Oedipal conflict occurs during the genital stage when the child, who has previously been self-absorbed, develops an erotic attachment toward the parent of the opposite sex; this attachment is accompanied by feelings of rivalry toward the parent of the same sex. Resolution cannot occur directly since few, if any, cultures permit incest. Freud developed a complex theoretical account of the resolution process. According to this theory, negative feelings toward the same-sex parent become a source of guilt. The child becomes overwhelmed with anxiety because of guilt feelings and the fear of being punished by the same-sex parent. (Freud interpreted a boy's fear as the fear of castration. The girl's fear is defined in less specific terms.) Freud said that the child wants to ease anxiety by removing the source of threat, the same-sex parent, but the parent is too powerful to be removed by physical force.

To ease anxiety, the child identifies with the same-sex parent. The process that Freud called identification has two significant results. The superego emerges when the child adopts the same-sex parent's values, which represent the rules of society. By copying the behavior of the same-sex parent, the child develops an appropriate sex identity and sex role. Successful resolution of the Oedipal conflict enables the individual to move toward a fully functioning adult sexuality. The person does not remember the Oedipal conflict because it is repressed, or buried in the unconscious.

Freud believed that unresolved conflicts at any of the psychosexual stages could result in neuroses, which we will discuss in Chapter 16 on behavior pathology.

Erik H. Erikson (1902–). Erikson suggested that throughout life the individual confronts a series of crises, the outcomes of which can have either positive or negative effects on personal growth.

Erikson: Psychosocial Stages Erik Erikson (1963, 1968) has expanded the psychoanalytic position to allow a more central role for environmental demands. Erikson's theory is a stage theory, but the stages reflect the interaction of the maturing organism with constantly changing environmental demands. Changes in the environment are correlated with the maturational level of the child.

Each of Erikson's eight stages represents a psychosocial crisis that must be resolved in a satisfactory manner before the individual can advance to the next psychosocial stage. Here again we see the fundamental attribute of developmental theory, namely the hierarchical organization and reliance of one stage on another.

> The human personality in principle develops according to steps predetermined in the growing person's readiness to be driven toward, to be aware of, and to interact with a widening social radius; and . . . society, in principle, tends to be so constituted as to meet and invite the succession of potentialities for interaction, and attempts to safeguard and to encourage the proper rate and the proper sequence of their unfolding. This is the "maintenance of the human world." (Erikson, 1950, p. 270)

Kohlberg: Moral Development Lawrence Kohlberg has adapted Piaget's principles to the study of moral concepts (1964) and sex-role behaviors (1966). Kohlberg asserts (1) that progressive developmental changes reflect changes in level (stages) of cognitive functioning and (2) that cognitive and affective development occur simultaneously but represent different substantive components of structural change. Like Erikson, Kohlberg believes that social development is, in essence, the restructuring of the concept of self, in its relationship to concepts of other people, conceived as being in a common social world with social standards (1966).

Adjustment and Rate of Physical Maturation

Several researchers have examined the effects of early and late physical maturation on self-concept, peer relationships, and general adjustment. The data reported here come from a study of Mary Cover Jones and Nancy Bayley (1950). Their report is based on data from the longitudinal study at the Institute of Child Development, University of California.

Two groups of sixteen boys each were identified as early and late maturers on the basis of several measures of skeletal age, a measure of bone development that is frequently used to assess physical maturity. These groups had maintained their differences over a period of approximately four and a half years. On the average, the two groups were separated in skeletal age by two years.

Table 3A·1 Mean Standard Scores for Sixteen-Year-Old Boys on Various Reputation Traits

TRAIT	EARLY-MATURING	LATE-MATURING
Attention-getting	48.1	52.2
Restlessness	45.3	52.9
Talkativeness	47.9	53.0
Bossiness	47.1	52.6
Assurance in class	45.6	50.0
Popularity	54.0	50.7
Leadership	51.3	47.5
Humor (about self)	53.5	48.7
Having older friends	56.2	42.3
Good appearance	54.4	49.3

(From Jones and Bayley, 1950)

Table 3A·2 Mean Standard Scores for Sixteen-Year-Old Boys on Various Observed Traits

TRAIT	EARLY-MATURING	LATE-MATURING	SIGNIFICANCE OF DIFFERENCE
Attractiveness of physique	60.6	45.0	1%
Grooming	54.6	49.8	5
Animation	49.6	61.2	
Eagerness	47.9	59.3	5
Uninhibitedness	52.5	60.2	
Matter-of-factness	60.5	43.6	2
Unaffectedness	60.7	46.2	5
Relaxation	61.1	40.6	1

NOTE: Significance of difference is a statistical concept referring to the probability that the differences occurred by chance.
(From Jones and Bayley, 1950)

Kohlberg's model of the growth of moral understanding is a stage model that is sequential and presumably does not vary from one culture to another.

Bandura: Social Learning Theory In Albert Bandura's social learning theory (1969b), imitation is viewed as an important source of learning socially acceptable (or unacceptable) behaviors. The kinds of behaviors that are learned are only coincidentally associated with chronological age. As the child matures chronologically, the behavioral expectations of society change and behaviors relevant to those demands become more important to the child.

This theory has generated an enormous amount of empirical data. The variables that affect imitation can be manipulated easily in an experiment. The child must have a model to imitate, but the model might be the same sex as the child or the opposite sex; the model might be the same age as the child or older or younger; the model might be reinforced, punished, or ignored for performing a specific behavior. All of these manipulations were used by Bandura to show that modeling

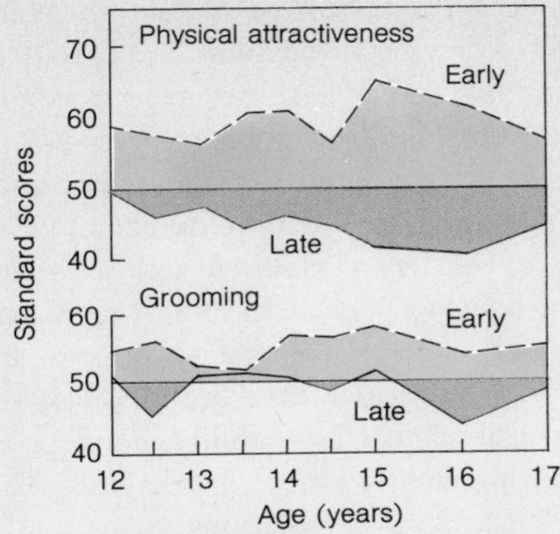

Fig. 3A·1 Mean standard scores for early- and late-maturing boys in physical appearance. (From Jones and Bayley, 1950)

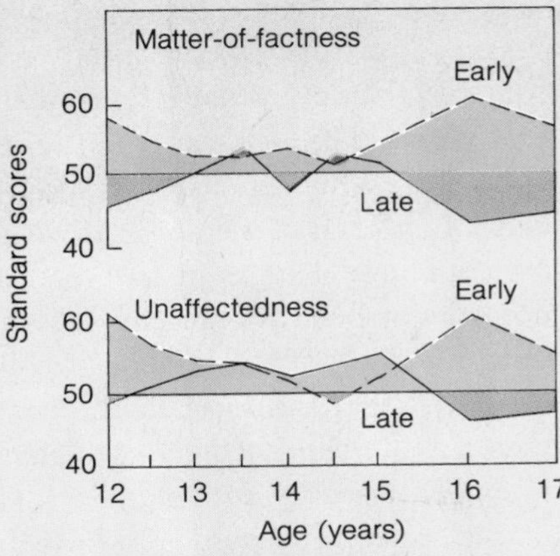

Fig. 3A·2 Mean standard scores of early- and late-maturing boys in attention-seeking behavior. (From Jones and Bayley, 1950)

On the basis of each boy's reputation as defined by his classmates, the two groups were compared on various social behaviors such as restlessness, talkativeness, and popularity (Table 3A·1). Observational data were also collected on traits such as physical attractiveness and unaffectedness (Table 3A·2). Both the reputation data and the observational data suggest that the early-maturing boys display more mature patterns of behavior and superior levels of adjustment than their late-maturing peers.

In order to provide a developmental perspective, Jones and Bayley plotted the means for each group at each six age levels for appearance (Figure 3A·1) and attention-seeking behavior (Figure 3A·2). These graphs show that early maturers are rated as superior in physical attractiveness and grooming. Although the differences are not large, it appears that at the ages of sixteen and seventeen the early maturing are judged to be relatively unaffected and matter-of-fact in contrast with the late-maturing boys.

One might argue that these findings reflect an overall psychological superiority inherent in the early-maturing boys. It is equally plausible that because of their advanced physical status, cultural expectations demand more mature social behaviors. Superior grooming, for example, may be a response to societal expectations—adults are expected to be neat and clean. When the late-maturing boys catch up, the same social demands will be made on them, which in turn will generate behavior that is more mature. This latter interpretation is consistent with the findings that by the age of twenty-one, differences between the two groups are essentially nonexistent.

is indeed an important aspect of the socialization process. He and his co-workers have shown, for example, that a child will imitate aggressive acts that have been observed either in real life or on film—and is even more likely to do so when the model has been rewarded for aggression.

Psychoanalytic theorists see imitation as the preface to the process of identification. Bandura and other behavioral theorists do not, however, distinguish between imitation and identification as Freud defined it because there are no observable differences between them. Since Freud did not name the specific variables that influence identification, this concept cannot be tested experimentally; however, the research on imitation has resulted in valuable insight into the environmental factors that affect identification.

Although the laboratory research generated by social learning theory is impressive, it seems to ignore developmental changes in the competencies of children. During the course of development, the child approaches the multitude of appropriate behaviors that society expects from adults and encounters situations that are unique. In spite of some anxiety about not knowing how to respond, the child makes an approximately appropriate response. The socialized adult is able to deal with a broad variety of situations, including many that have never been experienced before. Through earlier experiences, no doubt including imitation and modeling, the adult has acquired a set of rules that are applied to new situations.

This interpretation is consistent with Kohlberg's cognitive-developmental view, which combines changes in the cognitive capabilities of children with a variety of domains of behavior—in this case social behavior. Social learning theory can account for many of the actions of children at relatively young ages, prior to approximately eight years, when the child's cognitive capabilities are relatively restricted. As the child achieves a higher level of cognitive capability, however, it is no longer necessary to depend entirely on previously observed behaviors. The adult can generate responses to both familiar and novel situations.

Theories of Aging Theorists have been more successful in describing the aging process than in explaining it. Clearly, disease is the main cause of death during later life. The data in Table 3•2 show a continuing rise in death rates per 100,000 population with each decade of life, and dramatic increases from age fifty-five onward. Cardiovascular diseases are the major cause of death at all age levels, especially after age seventy-five. Of course, these data do not explain why disease processes should have such devastating effects among older people.

Although biological variables, including disease, play an important role, medical models simply do not provide a complete picture of the aging person. Successful aging is related to psychological as well as biological variables. Unfortunately, there has been relatively little interest in this problem. Even though he was a prolific theoretician, Freud paid little or no attention to the processes of aging because he viewed personality and personality development as something that stabilized after adolescence. At this point we must be content with a number of minitheories, which leave much to be desired.

Table 3•2 Death Rates per 100,000 Population in the United States During 1969

	AGE (YEARS)						
CAUSE OF DEATH	15–24	25–34	35–44	45–54	55–64	65–74	75 and over
Major cardiovascular diseases	4.4	16.8	86.3	293.5	816.9	2155.5	6752.7
Malignant neoplasms (tumors)	7.7	16.5	62.0	180.4	420.2	770.3	1171.2
Influenza and pneumonia	2.7	4.1	9.4	18.2	40.5	106.9	429.6
Diabetes mellitus	0.7	2.1	5.4	12.2	38.7	93.1	190.8
Bronchitis, emphysema, and asthma	0.5	0.6	2.6	9.9	38.0	89.4	138.4

SOURCE: Table G, Monthly Vital Statistics Report of the U.S.P.H.S., 1970, 18, No. 13, pp. 6–7.

Counterpart Theory Like many developmental theories we have discussed so far, counterpart theory (Birren, 1964) makes use of evolutionary concepts. Specifically, it outlines the genetic mechanisms that control aging and longevity.

The basic logic underlying counterpart theory is as follows:

1. Since aging and longevity are postreproductive features of a species, neither of these features is directly subject to natural selection.
2. If these features are genetically determined, they must occur in association with counterpart characteristics of development that were (earlier in the organism's life) subject to natural selection.
3. If some process of this kind were not operating, the characteristics of aging and longevity would vary randomly among individuals, and aging would consist simply of random changes over time.

Suppose a man wanted to select a wife who would contribute to a very long life for his children. He therefore chose a mate and waited to see how long she would live. By the time he was satisfied that she would probably produce long-lived offspring, she could no longer reproduce. In other words, the genetic features influencing aging and longevity cannot be selected during mating because they cannot be identified until reproductive capability is no longer present. Nevertheless, counterpart theory postulates that some system of natural selection is operating via links to other characteristics of development. That is to say, genes that are important in aging are also important in earlier developmental states.

An older person may tend to withdraw from social activity, though disengagement is not necessarily part of the aging process for every person. (Julie O'Neil, Stock, Boston)

Disengagement Several investigators have noted that many older people withdraw from active social engagement. People in their seventies and eighties become more involved with themselves and less with other people and outside events. E. Cumming and W. Henry (1961) view this disengagement as a normal process, though not as an inevitable developmental outcome uninfluenced by external events. Instead, Cumming and Henry attempt to determine the early antecedents of adjustment to later life, and they often refer to age roles and age expectations. From their point of view, the degree of disengagement varies among individuals depending on earlier experiences, societal attitudes, and the social opportunities available within the community.

Life History Bernice Neugarten and her students (Neugarten and Datan, 1973) have worked out a theory that integrates both biological development and gross environmental events within a sociological framework. According to this view, people of different generations reflect different life histories, which in turn influence behavior. For example, a woman in her seventies and a college-age woman will experience the Women's Liberation Movement very differently, partly because their life histories are very different.

Data developed by this group of investigators demonstrate how age norms in the United States have changed over the past 100 years. Behavioral expectations of people also have changed: people marry later, live longer, and so on. These changes delineate the age strata in our society in terms of characteristics such as religious behavior, marital status, leisure-time activity, and consumer behavior.

Although this work is related to recent conceptualizations of intergenerational differences, it is also a way of conceptualizing a portion of the aging process.

> Many of the punctuation marks of the life cycle are . . . social rather than biological in nature, and their timing is socially regulated. These concepts point to one way of structuring the passage of time in the lifespan of the individual; and in delineating a social time clock that can be superimposed upon the biological clock, these concepts are helpful in comprehending the life cycle. (Neugarten and Datan, 1973)

Research Methods

3·3 Early studies of developmental change were concerned primarily with description. In 1877 Charles Darwin reported in detail his observations of changes in a developing infant. His report is representative of numerous infant biographies that have attempted to describe changes during the beginning stages of life. These early reports did not make it clear under what conditions the infants were observed, however, and their objectivity must be questioned because the subject infants typically were children of the observers.

Piaget's studies were criticized on similar grounds: he used only three subjects, all of whom were his own children. Because Piaget had not established standard procedures, psychologists were unable to duplicate his study in order to verify his observations. Lack of systematic replication was a serious drawback in the early 1930s when psychology was moving rapidly away from traditional descriptive methods.

At that time behavioristic scientists favored the use of artificial laboratory studies as a means of *explaining* observed phenomena. They thought that effects could be studied experimentally by using animals. Some of the earliest studies of physical and motor maturation used salamanders as subjects (Carmichael, 1926). These animals were anesthetized for a period of time while a control group continued normal activity. Results of these studies demonstrated that the structures required for swimming behavior continue to develop without practice. Other well-known examples of the experimental use of animals for the study of developmental problems are Riesen's study of a chimpanzee reared in darkness (1947) and Harlow's work on monkeys reared with surrogate (substitute) mothers (1959).

Many studies were made using classical experimental methods with children, rather than animals or adults, as subjects (Reese and Lipsitt, 1970). Although these studies were methodologically sophisticated and substantiated the basic principles of behaviorism, they did not particularly contribute to our knowledge of developmental change.

Around 1960 there was a shift away from strict adherence to behaviorism. Piaget's work was "discovered," and methods were devised for testing his theory.

Subsequent research has produced evidence that generally supports his views, although his age norms for behavior changes appear to be incorrect.

As you can see, some of the problems in the study of developmental psychology require the development of special research designs and techniques.

Gesell's photographic dome provides the observer with controlled conditions under which to observe and record infant behavior. A movable camera is mounted in the upper left section of the dome. (Gesell Institute of Child Development)

Overcoming Difficulties in Studying Infants and Children Problems are involved in research with particular age groups, especially the very young. Even with children up to the age of seven years, investigators cannot rely on verbal instructions or verbal responses. They must develop other techniques that are relatively standardized and objective, techniques from which reliable estimates of behavior can be obtained.

Observational Methods Developmental psychologists have developed sophisticated procedures for observing the behavior of children in a variety of settings, including the home, the classroom, and the laboratory. Some of these procedures help simply to increase the objectivity of the observer; others allow the observer to have more control over the conditions in which the observations are made and thus they verge on being experimental.

Among the first type of improvement of observational procedures is the use of film or tape to record behaviors. Arnold Gesell, one of the leaders in the use of observational techniques, developed a so-called photographic dome from which to photograph the behavior of babies and toddlers. These devices reduce the possibility of missing important events during the actual observation session and permit the investigator afterward to examine behaviors repeatedly in extraordinary detail.

When the purpose of a study is to examine a particular behavior such as aggression or dependency (rather than a broad spectrum of behaviors) or a set of highly specific variables, the following procédure (largely a modification of basic experimental procedure) can be used:

1. Define the particular behavior to be observed and the behavioral attributes that will be counted as instances of the behavior.
2. Develop checklists or other procedures for observers to use in recording events.
3. Establish procedures for determining reliability. One way is to have two or more observers record behaviors independently. The minimum acceptable level of observer agreement is approximately 90 percent, but most investigators strive to achieve at least 95 percent agreement.
4. Establish the minimum time required to obtain stable estimates of behavioral attributes. Investigators have not yet determined how much time should be allocated, but probably a single hour of observation is not enough.
5. Establish the time-sampling techniques that will be used to obtain observations of behavior at different periods of time while the child is in the setting under consideration. One would not plan, for example, to make all nursery

school observations twenty minutes before or after lunch, because then hyperactivity or calmness might appear to be typical behaviors of the children.

One time-sampling technique that might be used is to divide the day into a number of time units and sample them randomly, making observations throughout each unit of time. Another technique is to observe the children for an extended period, such as one hour, but record observations every three minutes or every five minutes, for a total of twelve to twenty observations. If the one-hour period is randomly selected over all possible one-hour segments, a rather complete picture of an individual child's activities can be obtained.

6. Conduct pilot studies and on the basis of these modify and improve the techniques.

This procedure allows one to collect a considerable amount of data showing how children interact with significant features of their environments, including adults. Most of this work has been done in day-care centers, preschools, and the primary and elementary grades. Considerably more observational work is needed in the home to understand the characteristics of parent-child interactions. Although laboratory studies are convenient for experimenters, the results may not fully represent the quality of interaction that occurs between children and their care givers in the everyday environment.

An observational-laboratory procedure that concerns the attachment of mother and baby (Ainsworth, 1972), however, has been widely used, primarily with older infants (nine to fourteen months old), and has contributed important new information about attachment. The mother is present with the baby when a stranger enters the room. After a few minutes the mother leaves the room, and observations are made of the baby's reactions to the stranger. Recent work suggests the existence of individual differences in strength of attachment, which may have important implications for subsequent patterns of social and cognitive development. We will discuss attachment in more detail in Chapter 5.

Experimental Methods Investigators often devise experimental techniques for use with subjects of varying ages. One of the earliest experiments of this kind was conducted by M. Kuenne (1946) with young children. This experiment involved **discrimination learning,** in which the subject is rewarded for responding to the correct stimulus but is not rewarded (or is punished) for responding to the incorrect stimulus. (Use of rewards is called reinforcement because they strengthen behavior.)

Kuenne designed a transposition experiment in which the subject must learn to see a certain relationship between two objects (in this particular case that one object is smaller than the other) and apply it to pairs of other objects (in this particular case always selecting the smaller object). After learning to select the correct stimulus (usually ten out of ten correct choices), the subject is presented with a pair of stimuli, of which one is the originally correct stimulus and the other is a smaller stimulus (now the correct stimulus). This is called a near transposition test because the sizes of the stimuli are somewhat similar to those in the training test. Next a far transposition test is given: again the smaller stimulus is to be selected, but both of the stimuli are substantially smaller than any used previously.

Assume that children can guess the correct response 50 percent of the time without actual discrimination. The data in Table 3•3 indicate that children between three and five years of mental age tend to choose the correct stimulus at a level better than chance on the near transposition test, but at chance level on the far transposition test. In the case of children whose mental age is seven years and above, selection of the correct stimulus on both the near and far transposition tests is almost identical to their performance on the training stimuli. In the next chapter we shall consider explanations for this difference in performance; we shall also discuss mental age in more detail in Chapter 4 when we discuss intelligence tests.

Teaching machines are sometimes used with children not only to present information clearly but also to involve the child in the learning process. The child is "taught" in the sense of being reinforced for engaging in appropriate behaviors. (Fred Kaplan, Black Star)

Behavior Modification Out of B. F. Skinner's behaviorism grew behavior modification, the application of principles of conditioning in order to change behavior. Although this widely publicized work is not developmental, it has provided a successful technology for changing the behavior of children. Perhaps one of the best known programs is the so-called teaching machine, which uses programmed materials to minimize children's errors in learning and to maximize reinforcement for learning. Students are rewarded by immediate feedback that tells them which answers are correct. The materials increase in difficulty, requiring more and more complex skills.

Behavior modification has been used mainly with children either to increase certain wanted behaviors (such as cooperation) or to reduce certain unwanted behaviors (such as aggression or dependency). At first the child and the care giver are observed for a period of time in order to establish (1) whether the wanted (or unwanted) behavior is indeed occurring or it is misperception on the part of the care giver; (2) the rate at which the wanted (or unwanted) behavior is occurring (base rate); and (3) the frequency with which the care giver reinforces the wanted (or unwanted) behavior. Presumably the wanted behavior is not being reinforced (or at least not enough), and the unwanted behavior is being reinforced.

Table 3•3 Near and Far Transposition at Different Age Levels

MEAN CHRONOLOGICAL AGE (MCA) (MONTHS)	MEAN MENTAL AGE (MMA) (MONTHS)	NUMBER OF CORRECT RESPONSES IN 10 TRIALS	
		Near Test	Far Test
37.6	40.7	9.3	5.0
44.4	56.2	7.4	6.5
64.2	66.7	10.0	7.8
65.0	76.6	10.0	9.9

(Adapted from Kuenne, 1946)

Behavior modification involves increasing the frequency of reinforcement for the wanted behavior or decreasing the frequency of reinforcement for the unwanted behavior. The ideal in this procedure is to reward immediately all instances of the wanted behavior but to ignore all instances of the unwanted behavior (because even recognition can act as a reinforcer). This procedure makes use of the principle of extinction: a behavior will stop eventually if it is not reinforced. Unwanted behavior that is dangerous, however, such as throwing blocks, is interrupted immediately, and thereafter the child is observed carefully to prevent further occurrences. Some unwanted behaviors, such as temper tantrums, are typically treated by physically removing the child from the environment (until the behavior ceases) and letting the child act out the behavior without an audience of peers or care givers.

We will meet the subject of behavior modification again in Chapter 10 on learning and in Chapter 17 on behavior change.

Chronological Age As an Independent Variable Because developmental psychology evolved from an interest in describing behavioral change, chronological age (or some other index of time such as mental age or skeletal age, the degree to which cartilage has been replaced by bone) became a natural index against which to assess such changes. Two methods that developmentalists have used to study correlations between chronological age and other developmental variables are the cross-sectional method and the longitudinal method. The former compares average scores or measurements of subjects of different age groups. The latter compares the scores or measurements of the same group of subjects as they develop from one age level to the next.

Cross-sectional Method Suppose we are collecting data on height for boys and girls from age six through age nineteen. Using the cross-sectional method, we would proceed as follows:

1. Select subjects at the various age levels needed. To avoid distortions in the data and consequent errors of interpretation with respect to age trends, samples at each age level must be drawn from essentially the same populations. Careful selection within age groups is also important.
2. Measure or test the subjects at each age level. Measurements of each child are taken on only one occasion, thus making it possible to collect data for several developmental points (such as height and weight) in a single day's testing.
3. Compute averages for each age group, and draw conclusions.

On the basis of the height data presented in Figure 3•1, one conclusion is that the average boy is eventually taller than the average girl. Another conclusion is that the rate of growth is relatively constant for both sexes until the approach of maximum height. This conclusion, however, is incorrect. From other data we know that between the ages of twelve and sixteen a significant growth spurt takes place,

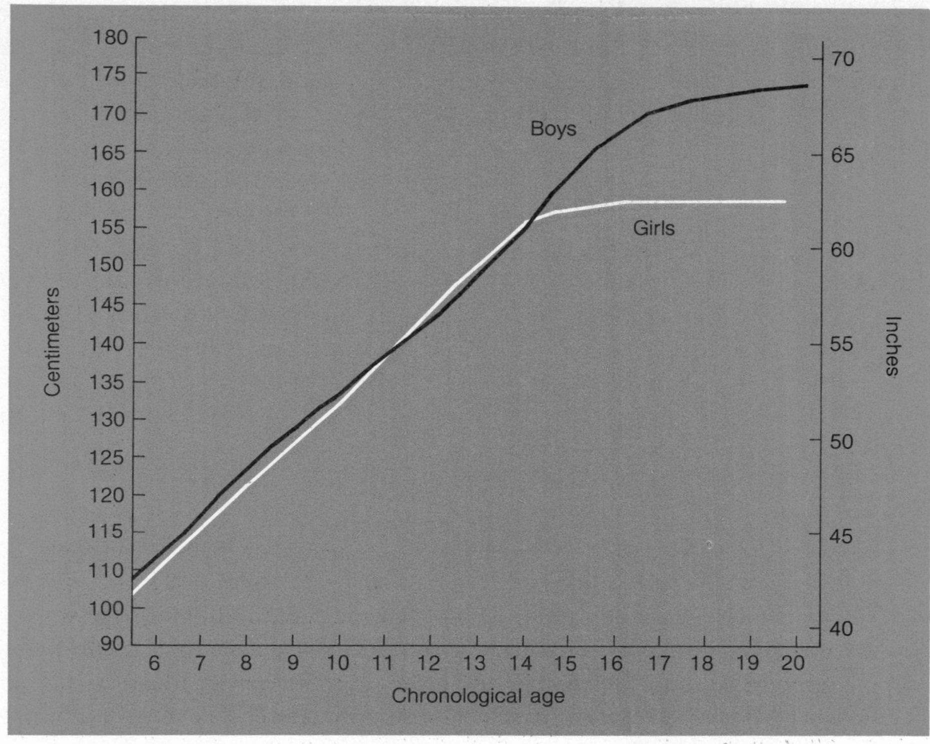

Fig. 3•1 Average growth trends in standing height of a sample of 1458 boys and girls. The data are from the Harvard Growth Study, which involved two overlapping samples—one cross-sectional and the other longitudinal. (From Shuttleworth, 1939)

indicating the onset of puberty. In our representative sample, some children have already achieved the growth spurt, some have not started it, and the others are somewhere in the midst of it. The curve in Figure 3•1 does not reflect this phenomenon because averaging distorts the results.

To present a more accurate description of height development, we could plot increments of growth (average gains from year to year) against age (Figure 3•2). When this technique is used, the typical growth spurt is revealed.

Suppose that a group of eighty-year-olds and a group of forty-year-olds are being compared in learning ability. Cross-sectional data may lead to the conclusion that age causes a decline in this ability. We know, however, that the average educational level of eighty-year-old people is substantially lower than that of today's forty-year-old subjects. This confusion occurs because the data do not reflect the life experiences of the subjects. They do not take into account the status of the older subjects when they were the same age as the younger subjects in the sample.

Longitudinal Method Perhaps a more accurate method for describing the course of development is the longitudinal method—the systematic and comprehensive study of the same people over an extended period of time. The Berkeley Growth Study, initiated in 1929, is still gathering data as subjects approach age fifty and their children marry and produce offspring. Other well-known longitudinal studies

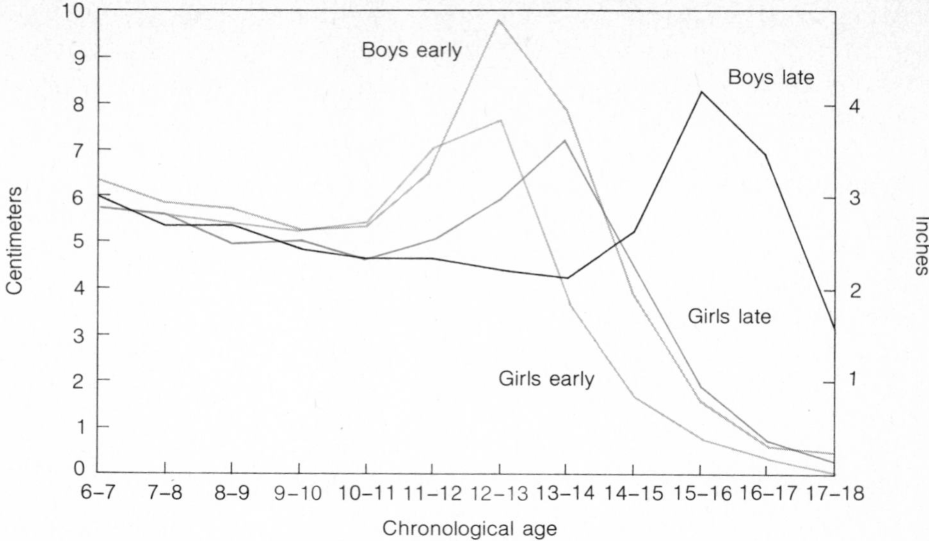

Fig. 3•2 Average yearly increments of growth in standing height for early as compared to late maturing boys and girls. Late and early categories have been determined by age at maximum growth. (Adapted from Shuttleworth, 1939, by Horrocks, 1962)

are the Harvard Growth Study and the Fels Growth Studies. All three studies have generated large amounts of information with respect to age changes, and hypotheses concerning the causes of change that go beyond the concept of physiological maturation. A major advantage of the longitudinal method is that it provides continuous data on the same subjects over time; this makes it possible to determine relationships not only between earlier and later events, but also between different aspects of behavior (such as personality and intelligence), and to examine how these relationships are affected by time.

The growth curves in Figure 3•3 are from longitudinal data based on individuals in the Harvard Growth Study (Shuttleworth, 1939). These curves reflect the variation in heights that can occur for a particular chronological age. The curves also show that adolescent girls vary in the velocity of their growth.

A disadvantage of the longitudinal method, in addition to the time required to collect a meaningful amount of data is that subjects lose interest, cannot be located, or die. Losses that result from failure to cooperate or from death cannot be assumed to be random. In longitudinal studies using college students, for example, increases could be expected each year in the average aptitude test score because the students with initially lower scores had dropped out or failed. Another problem with the longitudinal method is that the investigator may learn too late that more measures should have been made at an earlier time if unforeseen results are to be explained. Careful planning is required to maximize the usefulness of longitudinal data.

In the longitudinal method, when individuals are tested over a long period of time, the data do not reflect the cultural changes that affect the individual. Since the quality of life generally changes over time, each age group matures in a cultural environment that is unique and may well influence the course of development.

Because the effects of environmental changes are not included in the performance measure, the longitudinal method tends to reduce the effects of aging. Other environmental events such as wars may affect the nature of the longitudinal data in ways that are unique to a particular generation.

Distinguishing Genetic and Environmental Influences One of the experimental designs unique to developmental psychology involves the use of twins—usually identical (twins who derive from a single fertilized ovum) rather than fraternal (twins who result from the fertilization of two ova by two sperms). At infancy, identical twins can be distinguished from fraternal twins by means of several physical measures. Studies of identical twins in particular have generated important findings and continue to be one of the better techniques in the study of genetic contributions to behavior.

Studies of sensory deprivation involve the restriction of a particular sensory system such as vision, hearing, or touch. These studies are important because they show whether or not environmental stimulation is necessary for the normal de-

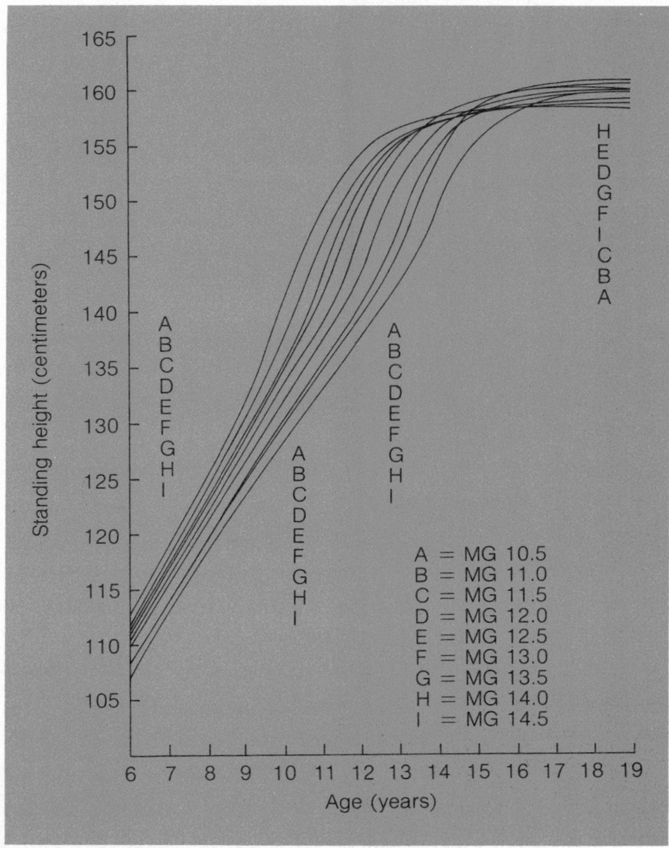

Fig. 3·3 Growth trends as related to age at maximum growth (girls). (After Shuttleworth, 1939. From Greulich, 1944)

Age Changes in Vocabulary

When different age groups are compared on measures of intellectual development, almost all of the tests that are used include vocabulary as an important component of performance. Regardless of whether the cross-sectional or longitudinal method is used in this research, it is assumed that the difficulty level of the words is constant for all age groups. A word that was the appropriate difficulty level for a twenty-year-old in 1960 should still be at the appropriate level for a twenty-year-old in 1980.

On the Stanford-Binet intelligence test, for example, there are fifty words that a child might be asked to define. The order in which the words appear was derived from data indicating the percentage of children at each of several age levels who were able to define the words correctly. From the composite of these data, the words were arranged from easiest to hardest. On the 1960 revision of the text, the word *Mars* was at approximately the nine-year-old level of difficulty. But since 1960 Mars has been televised frequently because of space exploration, and so through increased familiarity it may have become an easier word. This example illustrates how cultural events can influence test performance.

Rolf Monge and Eric Gardner (1972) attempted to develop an "age-fair" vocabulary test. Their basic idea was to use words that have high frequency of usage in several generations and to administer these words to appropriate age groups. They selected their words from various topical areas that seemed likely to reflect generational changes in vocabulary—transportation, diseases, finance, and slang, to name a few. Each of the vocabulary tests was administered to samples of subjects ranging in age from twenty through eighty years old. Usually items that had been familiar to the older subjects when they were younger were answered more accurately than were more modern items. For example:

A two-door electrically driven sedan is called a

1. brougham
2. herdic
3. tourister
4. Gibson
5. jaunting car

Toy racing cars operated by remote control are called

1. minicars
2. slot cars
3. handcars
4. relay cars
5. speedsters

More of the subjects in the 50- to 60-year bracket knew the answer (brougham) to the first sample item whereas more subjects in the 20- to 30-year bracket responded correctly (slot cars) to the second sample item.

This study shows that performance on tests is influenced by generational differences, which in turn are probably caused by environmental differences.

velopment of perceptual processes and what consequences occur if external stimulation is lacking. These studies are more commonly used with animals than with human beings.

The Co-twin Control Design In the co-twin control design, one twin serves as the control while the other twin undergoes various experimental manipulations, depending on the purpose of the experiment.

Myrtle McGraw (1935) used a set of fraternal twins to study various developmental processes. In her study Johnny (the experimental twin) received systematic training, but Jimmy (the control twin) did not. The work of Arnold Gesell (1954) and his colleagues at the Yale Clinic of Child Development involved a pair of identical twins known as twins T (for trained) and C (for control). These twins were given different environmental experiences. Since they were identical, any differences in the initial onset of behavior indicated that the specific behavior under consideration is controlled by environmental circumstances rather than by genetic and biological determinants.

Johnny (the twin whom McGraw trained) is shown here as he puts together boxes to use in reaching a hanging object. This exercise makes use of various behaviors, including grasping, walking, and climbing. (Myrtle B. McGraw)

In both studies the twins were taken from their homes and were cared for in a day-care center located on the Yale campus. The experimental twin received special training in creeping, crawling, walking, grasping, climbing, and other normal behaviors. McGraw labeled these behaviors phylogenetic because they are common to all normal members of the human species. She found that training had no significant effects on the timing or sequence of these behaviors. Gesell later interpreted these results as showing that human development is largely governed by a strict genetic timetable.

McGraw identified a second set of behaviors (such as roller skating, skiing, and swimming) as ontogenetic—skills that can be learned but are not common to all

At twenty-one months Johnny (shown here) skated with a rhythmical movement rather than just pushing with one foot as did Jimmy (the untrained twin) at twenty-six months. (Myrtle B. McGraw)

people. McGraw did not begin training Johnny in these skills until she had seen signs of readiness. The ability to walk, for example, would be considered one of the signs of readiness for training in roller skating.

In teaching Johnny to skate, McGraw used a technique called successive approximations, in which learning occurs in a series of stages. She gradually moved Johnny from skating with high friction skates on a thick mat to using skates with ball bearings on a hard, smooth surface. Whenever Johnny fell, she and her associates were supportive and saw to it that he got up immediately and attempted the behavior again. When Johnny was twenty months old, for example, he was skating at the top of a steep cement incline when suddenly he found himself coasting down backward. With the experimenter's approval, he continued to practice this behavior. At twenty-four months of age he was able to go down the decline backwards by stooping over and placing his hands on his feet in order to see between his legs and steer more effectively.

Jimmy received no training in the ontogenetic activities and was unable to keep up with his brother. McGraw's work thus demonstrated that when the neuromuscular structures are developed sufficiently, unusual gains in behavior are possible if appropriate learning techniques are used. This work served as the basis for the concept of reading readiness. It remains to be seen whether this particular competency, presumed to be largely phylogenetic, can be improved with training.

Sensory Deprivation To study visual deprivation, Riesen (1947) reared a chimpanzee who was fitted with goggles that produced diffused light (light that prevented atrophy of the retinal nerve fibers but by which it was impossible to discern forms). When the lenses were removed and the chimpanzee was placed in a normal environment, the initial visual processes were very primitive and normal discriminatory responses were absent for some time.

Fig. 3•4 Rob's sitting position, cylinders in place. (After Nissen, Chow, and Semmes, 1951)

To study tactile deprivation, Nissen, Chow, and Semmes (1951) reared a chimpanzee, Rob, beginning at age five weeks in such a way that he was unable to receive touch sensations through his hands and feet Figure 3•4. He was tested periodically, and after the materials were removed at the age of thirty-one months, his behavior was tested against that of chimps reared under normal conditions. Rob developed normally in terms of walking and visual discrimination even though he did not have the tactual-kinesthetic sensations the other chimps had.

On tests of tactual-motor coordinations, Rob demonstrated a number of deficiencies. When his trunk or head was stimulated, for example, he did not bring his fingers to that region as did the other chimps. He did not show grooming behavior or cling to the attendant who carried him. Although Rob eventually learned to bring his fingers to a given place with great speed and accuracy, other so-called instinctive behaviors such as grooming never did appear.

Such studies suggest that sensory deprivation can have permanent negative consequences, and that the environment plays an important role in development. In other words, the genetic potential of an organism requires environmental stimulation for emergence and development.

Summary

Although developmental psychology includes many aspects of general psychology, it emphasizes changes in fundamental processes over time. Rooted in Darwinian theory, developmental psychology views behavioral change as being a consequence of the interaction of biological structures and environmental stimulation. Behaviors that are adaptive to the environment are maintained, but other behaviors disappear.

Developmentalists are involved in helping to solve current social problems. Psychologists have contributed to the development of compensatory programs for children, including Head Start, Follow Through, and day-care services. Results of their studies may also change our ideas about the effects of various child-rearing practices. Developmental psychologists are also helping to develop more responsive environments for the aging.

Particularly important to developmental psychology are the theories of cognitive development formulated by Piaget, Bruner, and Werner, who emphasize stages of development. Piaget believes that the sequence of these stages never varies. Personality and socialization theories include those of Freud, Erikson, Kohlberg, and Bandura. With the exception of Bandura, these theorists also rely on stages and sequences; Bandura stresses imitation of the behavior of models. Biological theories of aging emphasize either genetics or the cumulative effects of disease. Sociological theories show that elderly are relegated to a lower status in our society.

Research methods employed by developmental psychologists are similar to those used by psychologists in other areas, but special techniques have been devised to measure behavior change over extended periods of time: the cross-sectional and the longitudinal methods. Both methods have specific strengths and weaknesses that must be weighed in terms of intended outcomes. The co-twin control method is widely used to determine the relative effects of practice on development. Co-twin studies by Gesell and McGraw show that practice effects are minimal, although external stimuli do play a role in development. Sensory deprivation studies using animals have shown that stimuli play a role in development, and that sensory deprivation has serious, long-term negative effects.

Suggested Readings

Friedrich, D. 1972. *A primer for developmental methodology.* Minneapolis, Minn.: Burgess.

A carefully condensed discussion of the major methodological issues involving research in developmental psychology.

Goulet, L. R., and P. B. Baltes, eds. 1970. *Life-span developmental psychology: Research and theory.* New York: Academic Press.

This is the definitive volume in terms of current research trends in developmental psychology. The materials cover both theoretical and methodological detail.

Mussen, P., ed. 1970. *Carmichael's manual of child psychology.* 2 vols. New York: Wiley.

Almost all known scientific and theoretical concepts about children can be found in these two volumes. Research methods associated with each topical area are examined.

Muuss, R. E. 1975. *Theories of adolescence.* 3d ed. New York: Random House.

All of the important theories of adolescence are included in this book. The concise, readable discussions include Freud, C. S. Hall, Erikson, and Piaget.

Wohlwill, J. F. 1973. *The study of behavioral development.* New York: Academic Press.

Technical problems involved in developmental research are described, and solutions are discussed.

The Development of Cognitive Competence

4 A major concern of developmental psychologists is changes in cognitive abilities (ways of knowing about the environment) during the course of life. At birth a human being has a broad repertoire of perceptual and motor abilities, and seeks knowledge about the environment through certain kinds of behaviors. After following an orderly sequence of many kinds of behavior, the individual reaches a plateau of cognitive competence at about twenty years of age. We will examine these stages of cognitive development from a structuralist point of view.

The structuralist is primarily concerned with *competence,* whereas the behaviorist investigates learning or *performance.* Competence can be inferred from behavior, but performance on a specific behavioral attribute does not necessarily provide evidence of competence to perform similar behaviors in which the stimulus is changed but the same rules must be followed. The structuralist believes that the individual has an innate ability not only to learn behaviors, but also to generate rules that are logically consistent. We will meet this distinction again when we discuss learning in Chapter 10.

Interest in cognitive abilities increased in the early years of this century because of the development of intelligence tests that provide convenient techniques for measuring components of cognitive competency. The assessment of intellectual ability described in this chapter has enabled psychologists to formulate hypotheses about **cognition** that encompass the entire lifespan.

Early Perceptual Development

4·1 According to structuralist theories, the source of energy (or motivation) for learning is derived from the organism, rather than from the environment. This position can be verified in very young infants, who search their environments even though their normal physiological needs have been met

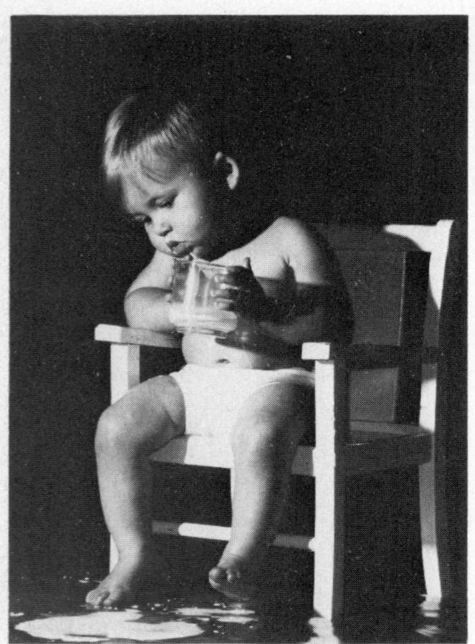

The child is attending to one stimulus (the milk puddle) in place of the stimulus (the glass of milk) that had occupied him. (Jeanne Thwaites, BBM Associates)

and they have not been taught to expect a specific reinforcement. Through searching behavior, inputs from the senses are stored for use on later occasions. According to several theorists, searching behavior produces the human infant's earliest learning about his or her environment. Even babies two to three days old show preferences for certain kinds of stimuli. Research on the visual sense suggests that (1) preferences for particular visual stimuli are innate, and (2) these early preferences have adaptive significance for later development.

Not all psychologists share this view of innate pattern preferences. Some believe that the sensory input to the newborn baby is meaningless and that preferences are formed only after considerable experience with various kinds of stimuli and reinforcement from the environment. A purely structuralist position does not completely explain these early phenomena. Perhaps we can safely say that for the very young infant, the world is not a blooming mass of confusion, as William James suggested, but that considerable experience is required before stimulus attributes become integrated and meaningful.

The Orienting Reflex The orienting reflex is an unlearned response that concentrates the full attention of the organism on the nature and characteristics of the stimuli (Pavlov, 1927). Recent research indicates that the orienting reflex is accompanied by involuntary physiological responses. One of the most thoroughly studied responses is cardiac deceleration, a slowing of the heart (Steinschneider, 1967). Other physiological manifestations of this reflex include a general decrease in motor activity, dilation of the pupils, and changes in the galvanic skin response (GSR), which is the electrical conduction of the skin.

The orienting reflex is similar to what is currently called *attentional behavior*, which can be demonstrated in the laboratory when at least two contrasting stimuli are presented and the subject's preference for each of the stimuli is measured as a function, for example, of the duration of visual fixations on each one. Perhaps the distinction between the two terms is that the orienting reflex represents primarily the physiological aspects of attention, whereas attending behavior represents primarily the psychological aspects. One can argue that a child can be attending to a particular stimulus without analyzing it in a psychological or cognitive sense, but it seems reasonable to assume that if the child changes attention from object A to object B, some attribute of the newly viewed object is being processed in a psychological sense.

Habituation If the child continued to attend to all novel stimuli, he or she would be unable to function because of the inability to discriminate important from unimportant aspects of the environment. Fortunately, with repeated exposure to a particular stimulus object or class of objects, the child gives less and less attention to it. This process of **habituation** both limits the stimuli to which orienting reactions occur and helps the child to determine which aspects of the environment are most useful for efficient functioning.

According to structuralist theory, habituation indicates that the person has established a relatively permanent structure, or representation, of a stimulus or class of stimuli. During early infancy, more orienting responses and longer periods of habituation are appropriate because so much of the world is new. As the child matures, the structures of the more common stimuli in the child's world become established. With maturity, orienting responses are fewer, but habituation to broader classes of stimuli is more rapid. Through orienting behavior the child learns about the environment by forming structures that represent the world. The process of ferreting out the most important aspects of the world appears to be a learning phenomenon because children are reinforced differently when they respond to appropriate rather than inappropriate stimuli.

Wendell Jeffrey (1968) has developed a more detailed conceptualization of habituation, which he refers to as the *serial habituation hypothesis.* Like the orienting reflex and attention, he contends, habituation is crucial for continued structure development and subsequent problem solving. When cues that were initially most salient to the baby have habituated, less salient cues are permitted to generate attending responses. With stimulus repetition, the infant develops a continuous, orderly sequence of attending responses to the stimulus. Eventually this behavioral sequence ceases, and the infant attends only to the most salient of the stimulus. "It is both the integration of a pattern of attending responses and the discontinuity of that pattern with other attending responses or patterns that define an object percept [the impression of an object obtained through the senses] or what we shall call more generally a *schema*" (Jeffrey, 1968, p. 325).

Up to this point we have focused on the major theories about early cognitive development. These observations have been well documented in studies concerning visual and auditory perception. In these studies psychologists observe fixation time (the period during which the infant directs attention to a particular stimulus).

Studying Attention and Habituation There are two methods for measuring attention and habituation:

1. A single stimulus is presented and fixation time is recorded over successive trials.
2. Two stimuli are presented and fixation time for each is recorded so that comparisons can be made.

In a variation on these two methods, a single stimulus (such as a tone) is presented until habituation occurs, and then a second stimulus on the same dimension (for example, two tones) is introduced; the experimenter looks for recovery of attending responses.

Perhaps the best known studies of pattern (form) perception in children were reported by R. Fantz (1961, 1963), who used the paired-stimulus method. He developed the looking chamber, where the infant lying in a crib can see two objects hanging from the ceiling. Through a peephole the experimenter observes the

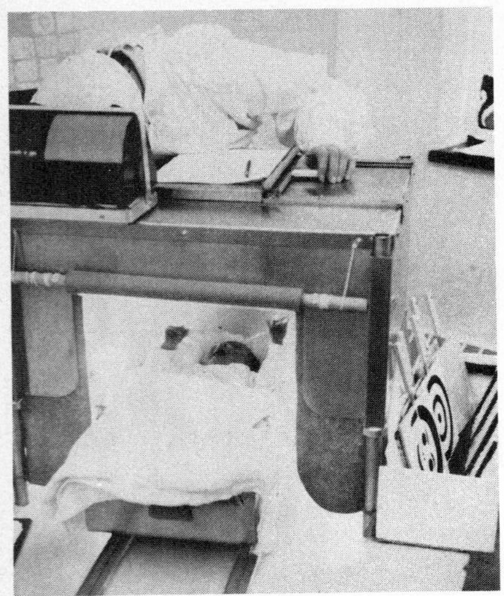

The looking chamber developed by Fantz to observe and record the preferences of infants for certain kinds of visual stimuli. (Fantz, 1963. Courtesy of Dr. Robert Fantz)

infant's eye fixations and movements and determines which of the two stimuli is being examined. On the basis of duration of fixations for each stimulus, inferences are made about the infant's stimulus preference.

The kinds of stimuli that were used are shown in Figure 4•1 along with data for a sample of infants between two and three months of age and for infants older than three months. Regardless of age level, fixation time was greatest for the picture of the face and lowest for the plain colored circles. Numerous hypotheses have been offered to explain this preference, including that babies tend to show a greater interest in more complex stimuli.

What stimulus features determine attractiveness? In a methodologically sophisticated study, Salapatek and Kessen (1966) found that when young infants attended to a triangle they were in fact fixating primarily on the angles and paid little attention to the other features. Evidence indicates that with maturity the eye-movement patterns of children shift from a fixation on a single feature of the stimulus to a more integrative pattern. As the schema for a stimulus becomes firmly established, almost no eye movements are required before the stimulus can be identified. This developmental shift is consistent with the serial habituation hypothesis.

Representative eye-movement patterns are shown in Figure 4•2, where the task was for young children and college-age subjects to identify a fire hydrant in a

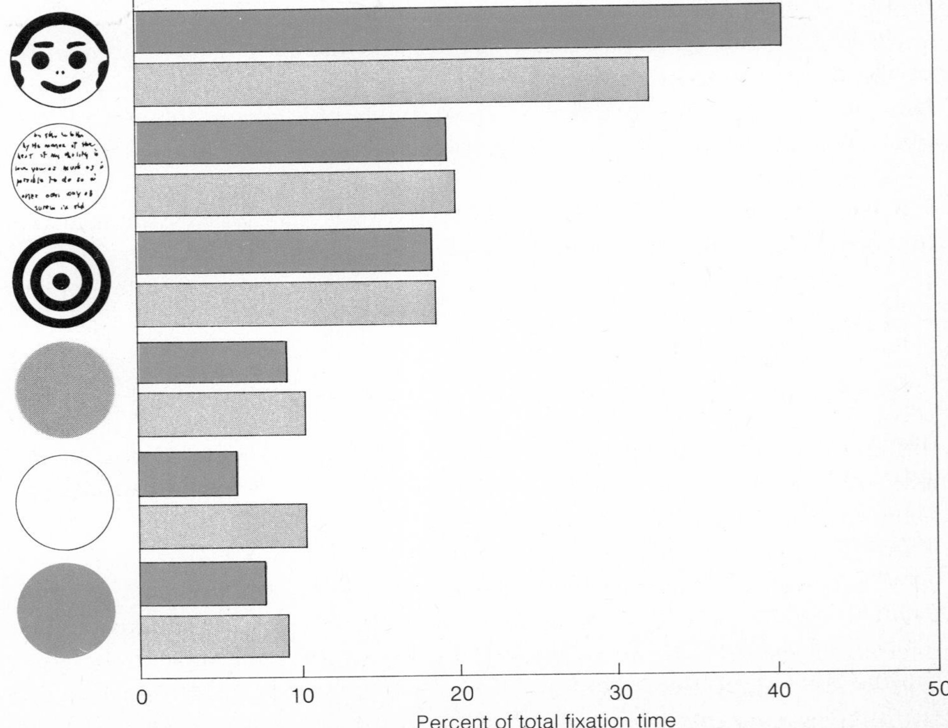

Fig. 4•1 Importance of pattern rather than color or brightness was illustrated by the response of infants to a face, a piece of printed matter, a bull's-eye, and plain red, white, and yellow disks. Even the youngest infants preferred patterns. Upper bars show the results for infants from two to three months old; lower bars, for infants more than three months old. (Fantz, 1961)

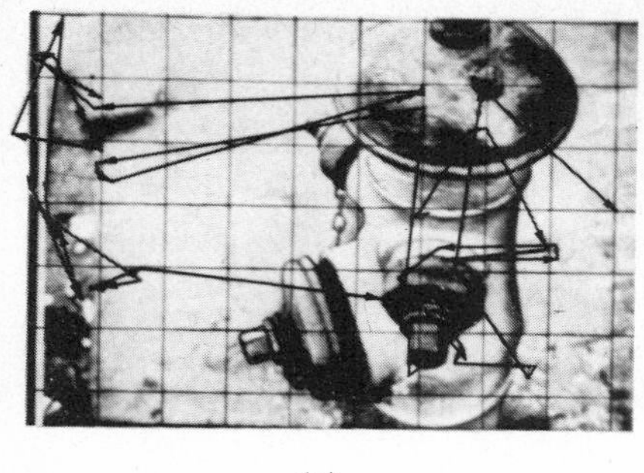

(a)

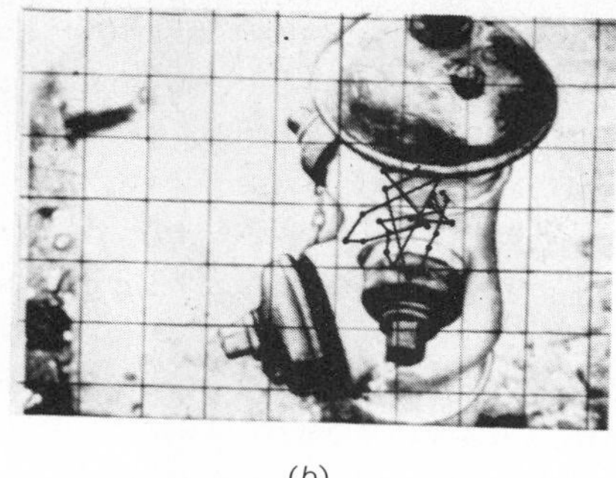

(b)

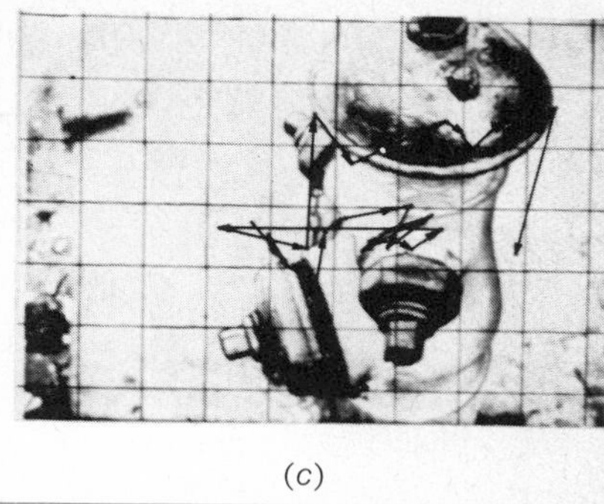

(c)

Fig. 4•2 Eye-movement patterns over a flat surface for an adult (*a*), a six-year-old (*b*), and another six-year-old (*c*). Compared to the adult, the children tend to cover less of the object and to fixate on a detail—not necessarily one that would provide information necessary for identifying the object, since they have not scanned the entire object for important features. (Mackworth and Bruner, 1970)

photograph (Mackworth and Bruner, 1970). Figure 4•3 shows representative eye-movement patterns for four-year-old and seven-year-old children who were asked to examine a nonsense figure (which could not be labeled) in order to identify it later when it was embedded in a set of other nonsense figures (Zaporozhets, 1965). In both instances (which involved perception of flat surfaces rather than of depth), the older groups very rapidly located features along the perimeter of the stimuli that would be useful for identification. The younger children made more eye movements and tended not to fixate on the perimeter that distinguished the stimulus from the other stimuli.

In addition to complexity, *familiarity* and *discrepancy* affect fixation time. In an experiment using pictures of human faces (Haaf and Bell, 1967), the infants fixated longest on the most realistic face and least on the figure with the least amount of detail (Figure 4•4). These data suggest that to infants below the age of four months, another compelling feature of stimuli is their meaning or familiarity. In Figure 4•4, the second face-like figure, which is not as discrepant as the fourth figure, is second in terms of fixation time. The third figure is apparently too simple to be of interest.

Beyond the age of four months, infants appear to be increasingly attracted to stimuli that are moderately different from the more familiar stimulus. Kagan, Henker, Hen-Tov, Levine, and Lewis (1966) demonstrated developmental changes in the attention paid to normal and distorted faces. The subjects were four-month-olds and eight-month-olds. Among the four-month-olds, the normal face generated more attention, but the distorted face was more effective for the older group. These authors concluded: "Fixation time is apt to be low to very familiar and very novel patterns but equally high for a band of stimuli representing recently formed schemata as well as moderate violations of these schemata" (Kagan, Henker, Hen-Tov, Levine, and Lewis, 1966).

These results are consistent with J. McV. Hunt's (1961) hypothesis of the match, which proposes that there is an optimal degree of discrepancy between the organism's familiarity (or schema) in a particular circumstance and the ability to cope with that discrepancy. If the discrepancy is too great, then the organism becomes overwhelmed or frightened and avoids the particular stimulus circumstance. If the stimulus represents a perfect match with an already existing schema, then the

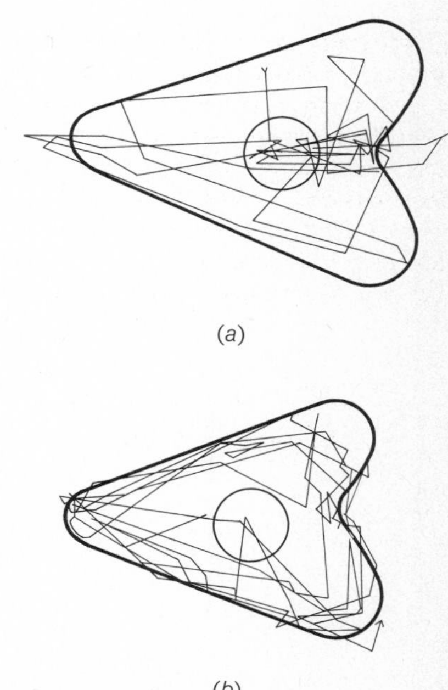

(a)

(b)

Fig. 4•3 Eye-movement patterns over a flat surface for a young child (*a*) and an older child (*b*). (Zaporozhets, 1965)

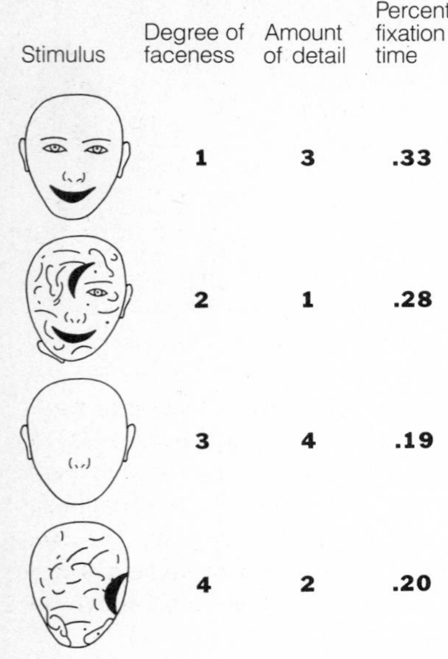

Fig. 4·4 Differences in fixation time for four different facial stimuli. (Haaf and Bell, 1967)

organism demonstrates boredom (relatively few, if any, fixations). Hunt suggests that when the optimal discrepancy occurs, the organism's self-generated attempts to incorporate the discrepancy into an already existing schema afford pleasure. Therefore, one way to maintain curiosity in children may be to provide numerous opportunities for incorporating discrepancies into already existing schemata; the environment should neither understimulate nor overstimulate.

Hunt points out that Myrtle McGraw (whose work with Johnny and Jimmy we examined in Chapter 3) capitalized on the concept of the match with respect to **ontogenetic** activities. Recall that she started Johnny on roller skating and swimming, among other activities, at points when he first evidenced the capabilities to begin these more advanced motor activities.

Auditory experience has been observed in a few studies of the orienting reflex in infants. A study (Bronshtein and Petrova, 1952) of infants ranging in age from approximately two hours to eight days used a pacifier with a rubber pipe attached to one end, which in turn was attached to a recorder so that a recording could be made whenever the baby sucked the pacifier. This device made it possible to record when an auditory stimulus was presented and terminated, and to observe changes in the sucking rate (Figure 4·5). A variety of stimuli were used including organ pipes, a harmonica, and a whistle, but the basic stimuli were musical tones in the 60 to 70 decibel range. From our earlier discussion of the orienting reflex, we know that the rate of sucking should diminish substantially upon introduction of a novel stimulus. Indeed, the data presented in the results of this study, and other habituation studies (Eisenberg, Coursin, and Rupp, 1966) support the conclusion that discrimination and habituation to auditory stimuli occur in young infants, though with greater regularity among the older children.

Motor Behaviors Visual and auditory processes form the basis for the young infant's early representations of the environment. These representations come to play an important role in learning, but infants do not learn about their environment exclusively through perceptual processes. From birth on, motor behaviors are directly involved in the formation of environmental representations.

From the first day of life, the motor behavior patterns of the infant are systematic. They reflect the symmetries of bodily parts that will become a total action system. The newborn baby has the physical structures necessary for survival, but some are not yet functional. The major task is to integrate the motor behaviors associated with physical development. Because the central nervous system is not completely developed, the integration, inhibition, and control of motor responses are quite primitive.

Newborn babies evidence earlier control of the upper extremities (the head or the arms) than of the lower extremities. This developmental pattern is called *cephalocaudal development*. There is also a horizontal trend; that is, there is control of structures closest to the midline (the shoulders) compared to the outer extremities (the fingers). This pattern is called *proximodistal development*. Even though the human being is able to gain control of arm movements rather rapidly,

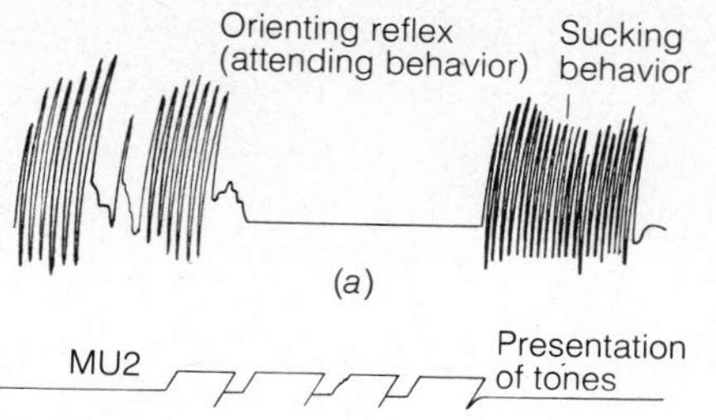

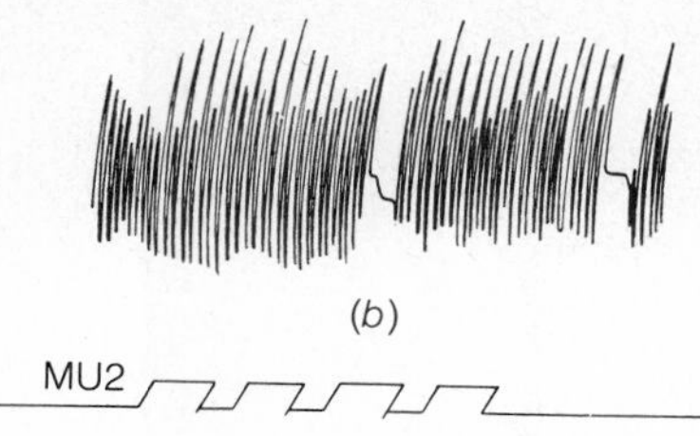

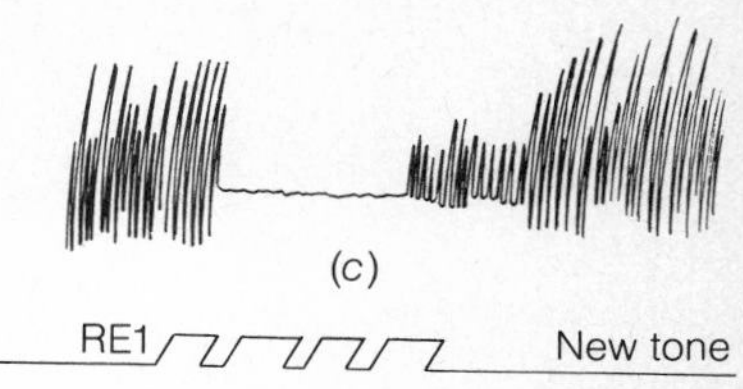

Fig. 4·5 Differentiation of musical tones by a child 4 hours and 25 minutes after birth. (*a*) The child is attending to the tones as they are first presented. (*b*) Nine tone presentations later, the child has habituated to the tones, as evidenced by the continued sucking. (*c*) The orienting reflex recurs when a different tone is presented. (Bronshtein and Petrova, 1952)

it takes a number of years to gain control of the fine motor movements required, for example, in writing.

Newborn babies display a set of reflexes that weaken with age and eventually disappear. For example, if one stimulates the newborn's palm, the fingers reflexively close into a fist. This response is called the **palmar** (or grasp) **reflex.** If there is an object to grasp, the infant holds that object until fatigue of the muscles eventually terminates the response. In one of Halverson's samples, approximately 27 percent of the infants under the age of twenty-four weeks were able to support their own weight by means of this involuntary grasp reflex. The thumb is not involved in any functional way. Thumb-forefinger prehension, which is uniquely human, is not present at birth; it can take as long as a year to emerge and become part of a smooth integrated act of grasping (Halverson, 1937).

Another reflex that is present in the newborn but eventually disappears is called the **plantar reflex.** If one stimulates the sole of the newborn's foot (the plantar surface), the toes fan out. This reflex is sometimes tested among adults to determine whether brain damage has occurred. Approximately six months after birth the response to the same stimulation of the plantar surface is a curling of the toes. This curling is called the *Babinski response,* named for the man who initially discovered the relationship in adults. Among the other reflexes that make up the behavioral repertoire of the newborn infant is the *Moro reflex,* or startle response. When the infant is startled by a sudden loud noise or a blow to the surface of the crib mattress, the response is outstretching of the arms, extension of the legs, and throwing back of the head.

An early swimming reflex can be generated by placing the baby on its stomach, from which position it will make characteristic swimming movements. These movements are sufficiently vigorous to propel the infant through water (McGraw, 1935). McGraw realized that this reflexive response represents both a phylogenetic and an ontogenetic behavior. It is phylogenetic in that it appears as a reflex in all normal human infants; it is also ontogenetic because, as the reflex weakens over time, systematic learning experiences in swimming can be introduced.

Here again is a clear example of McGraw's use of the term *readiness.* As the swimming reflex response weakened, either by appearing only sporadically, by losing its vigor, or by lasting only a short time, she recognized a transition period, indicating that the child was ready for formal instruction.

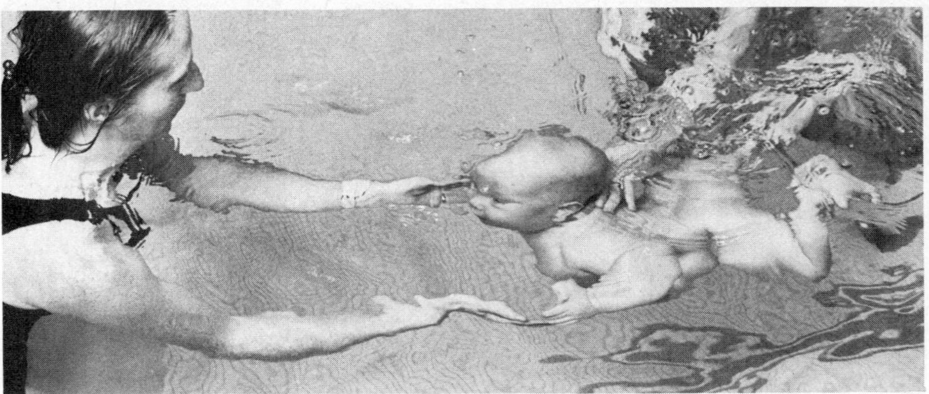

The weakening of the swimming reflex was used by McGraw as an indicator of readiness for formal instruction. (Leo Choplin, Black Star)

Early infant behavior is probably not controlled at the highest cerebral levels but at a subcortical level. Furthermore, evidence suggests that mature control of behavior is impossible because the *myelinization* process is incomplete. Myelin, a fatty sheath that surrounds nerve fibers, apparently continues to develop until as late as eighteen years of age. In addition to its importance in acquiring voluntary control of initially involuntary responses, myelin is also related to the speed with which nerve impulses are transmitted. This subject will be discussed further in Chapter 24.

Many important studies have described the developmental stages in the acquisition of erect locomotion, with considerable agreement in results despite differences in the observational procedures and in the samples of children used by the investigators. Ames (1937) described fourteen stages in learning to walk (Figure 4•6), which are similar to the nine stages identified by Myrtle McGraw (1941). There is considerable agreement also between Shirley (1931) and Bayley (1935), as shown in Figure 4•7.

In general, it appears that through a process of maturational change called individuation, the child becomes capable of separately moving and controlling the various bodily parts, such as arms, trunk, and legs. Neuromuscular maturation is rapid, and as the bodily parts become functional they also become coordinated. This process has been called reciprocal interweaving (Gesell, 1954): the child's structural growth and increasing repertoire of motor behaviors work together to bring about the proper integration of opposing muscle groups. Finally, the child acquires enough physical maturation and experience to make movements in three-dimensional space.

The typical child progresses from making relatively primitive, although coordinated, reflex actions to the extremely complex and integrated act of walking in approximately thirteen to fifteen months, although some children walk as early as ten months and others as late as eighteen months. Even the child that walks at thirteen months is likely to fall frequently or to encounter difficulties with spatial relations. Probably not until after five or six months of experience does locomotor ability become smooth and integrated.

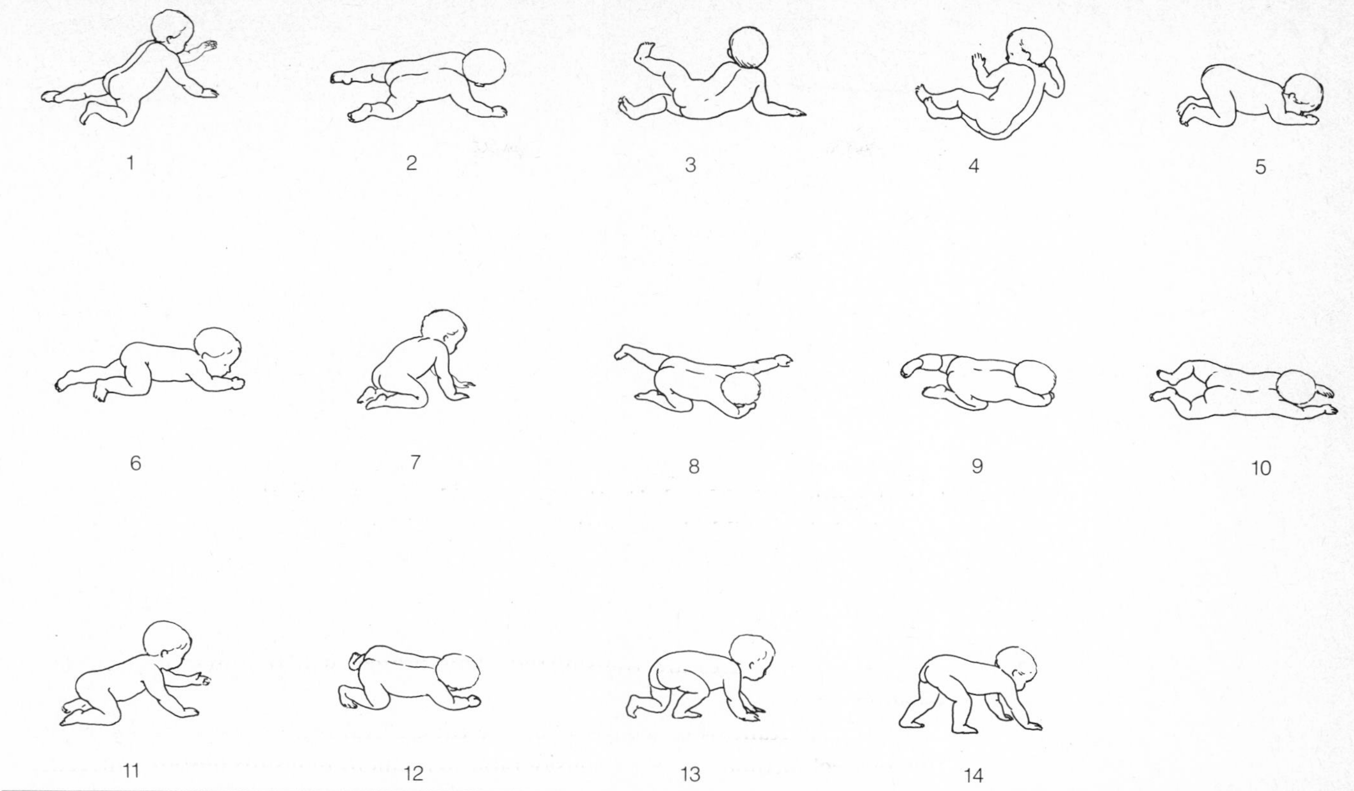

Fig. 4·6 The fourteen stages of prone progression described by Ames (1937).

Gesell's concept of reciprocal interweaving is similar to Werner's principle of orthogenesis, which we discussed in Chapter 3. As the child advances toward walking, differentiation and hierarchic integration occur. It seems reasonably certain that, with respect to walking, Werner and Gesell are correct in their conceptualization of sequential patterning and hierarchical organization. These principles may also be relevant to other aspects of development, including cognition.

Discrimination Learning Although we are examining cognitive competency from the structuralist viewpoint, important contributions from behaviorist research studies complement the discussion. They reflect age differences and show performance outcomes of the competencies acquired during early development. Behaviorists use experimental methods, rather than descriptive techniques, and they assume that all behavior results from the association of a stimulus (S) and a response (R). The association of S and R results from *conditioned learning.*

Behaviorists distinguish between reflex behavior, which is involuntary, and operant behavior, which is felt to be under the control of the individual. Operant conditioning occurs when a stimulus becomes associated with a response and the response recurs because of reinforcement, which is usually a reward of some kind.

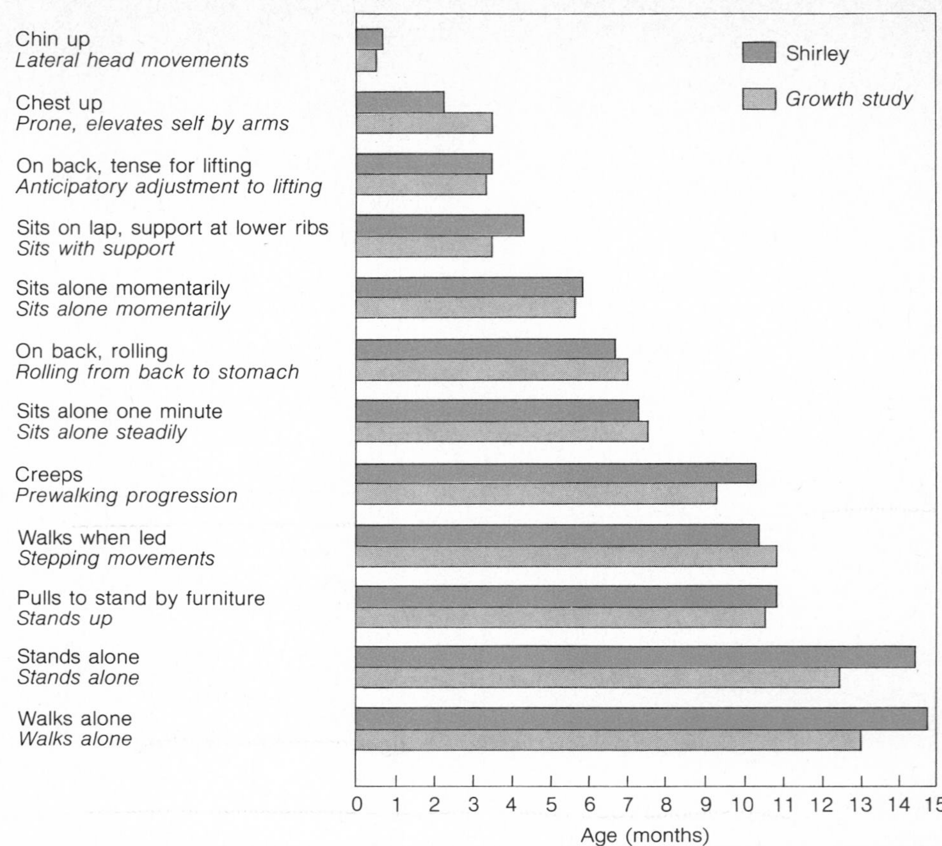

Fig. 4·7 Norms for certain anti-gravity and locomotion skills obtained with 61 white infants by Bayley and 25 white infants by Shirley. (Bayley, 1935)

Classical conditioning involves paired stimuli. A reflex response becomes conditioned to a new stimulus that initially did not elicit this response. A common example occurs when an infant touches a hot stove for the first time. Withdrawal of the hand from the stove is a reflex action, a response that does not have to be learned. In other words, the child is responding to an unconditioned stimulus (US), the heat from the stove. Until additional learning takes place, however, the infant may be afraid of the stove whether the stove is hot or cold. In this case, the stove has become a conditioned stimulus (CS) and withdrawal from the stove itself, rather than from heat, is a conditioned response (CR). The second stimulus (the stove) causes no response until it has been paired, or presented simultaneously, with the first stimulus (heat). Eventually, as a result of conditioning, both stimuli result in the same response.

Visual Discrimination In a visual discrimination learning experiment, the infant must both discriminate between stimuli (usually on the basis of form and color) and associate a response with a stimulus. This technique is known as the free operant procedure and has been used successfully with young children. A stimulus

Prenatal Conditioning

Is it possible to condition an unborn child? This question cannot yet be answered because of the procedural difficulties involved in conducting the crucial experiments. Nevertheless, interest in this phenomenon persists, if for no other reason than to determine when conditioned learning can be started successfully with human beings.

One of the best known studies that attempted to demonstrate prenatal conditioning was reported by Spelt (1948). The subjects were sixteen human fetuses, all but two at or beyond the seventh month of gestation. Spelt had discovered that a loud sound made just outside the mother's body caused the fetus to move, but a vibrator applied to the mother's abdomen did not. The loud noise, made by an oak clapper, was the unconditioned stimulus (US). Fetal movements were recorded by means of tambours taped to the mother's abdomen.

During the learning trials the vibrator was applied to the mother's abdomen for five seconds and the loud sound was produced as vibration ended. After fewer than a hundred paired presentations of vibrator and sound, the fetuses moved in response to the vibrator alone. The vibrator had become a conditioned stimulus (CS). The number of trials required to produce the conditioned response varied considerably, however. In some instances as few as fifteen paired presentations apparently resulted in conditioning.

Lipsitt (1963) studied conditioning during the first year of life. In reviewing Spelt's study, Lipsitt shows that it is necessary to test for *pseudoconditioning,* or sensitization, by using a control group. Pseudoconditioning occurs when the US alone induces a predisposition to respond to other previously neutral stimuli. In the Spelt study it is possible that this phenomenon occurred with the fetuses, the mothers, or both. Spelt was not insensitive to the possibility of pseudoconditioning in the mothers; he did use three nonpregnant controls. But Lipsitt contends that these controls were given too few trials to test for pseudoconditioning adequately. Lipsitt makes the following observation:

> The questions raised by this study, notwithstanding Spelt's apparent success in establishing fetal conditioning, when considered in light of difficulties . . . encountered by researchers with full-term neonates, indicates that fetal conditioning should be explored more fully. Methods might be used in such further work to eliminate the mother's perception of the loud-sound US. This could be accomplished by subjecting her to a loud continuous masking noise through earphones while the infant is subjected to the US. Also, control [subjects] who receive the CS and US in the same number and intensity as experimental [subjects], but at non-conditioning intervals from one another, might be utilized profitably. (Lipsitt, 1963).

display is presented to the subject who is free to select in some way, such as pushing a panel, any of the stimuli. Selection of the correct stimulus is followed by a reward. With extremely young infants, this reward may be a nutritive solution delivered through a bottle. Among older infants, a novel stimulus serves as an effective reinforcer.

The physical arrangements for a color discrimination learning experiment are shown in Figure 4•8 (Lipsitt, 1963). The infants were eight months old, and the reinforcing stimulus for pushing the correct panel was a buzzer. Half the subjects were reinforced for choosing the red stimulus and the other half for choosing the blue stimulus. Three panels were available to the infant even though the discrimination involved only two colors. (When only two panels were used in this experiment, the babies frequently pressed both panels at one time, thus ensuring a reinforcer—and confounding the results of the experiment!) With the three-panel arrangement, the middle panel could be pressed but it never led to a reinforcer. The equipment was also designed so that if two panels were pressed simultaneously, no reinforcers were delivered. The results of the study (Figure 4•9) showed that infants can make a discrimination between red and blue and can also learn to associate the stimulus with a specific response.

Although children can learn a variety of visual discriminations, some dimensions, such as color and form, are learned more readily than others; children seem to acquire stimulus preferences related in some way to chronological age. With respect to form and color, there is a shift from form to color preference sometime between three and four years of age and then a return to form preference (Brian and Goodenough, 1929; Suchman and Trabasso, 1966). Relatively few studies have examined size and number preferences. Recent evidence discovered by Smiley (1972) suggests that form is preferred by older children and college students. Although the rate of learning a discrimination problem results from reinforcement, a preferred stimulus is learned more rapidly.

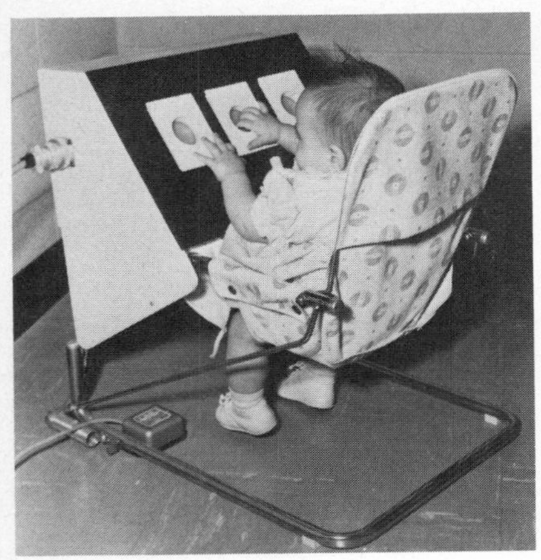

Fig. 4•8 Three-panel apparatus for study of operant discrimination in young children. Colors appear in windows on panels. Pressing "correct" panel produces buzzer sound. (From Lipsitt, 1963. Courtesy of Lewis P. Lipsitt)

Auditory Discrimination Relatively few studies of auditory discrimination have been undertaken. In a series of studies that produced improved methods of studying infants, E. Siqueland and L. Lipsitt (1966) performed an auditory discrimination experiment using two groups of eight infants each, ranging in age from 48 to 116 hours. The procedure made use of the infant reflex that occurs

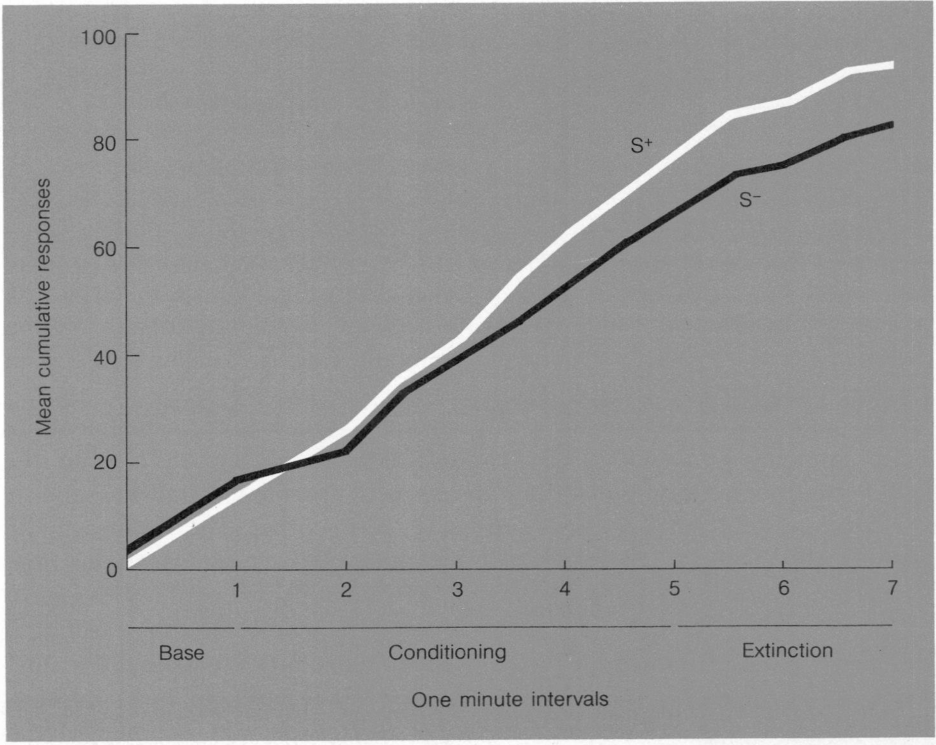

Fig. 4•9 Mean cumulative responses to positive stimulus (S+) and negative stimulus (S−). (From Lipsitt, 1963)

when one strokes an infant's cheek: the head turns toward the tactile stimulation. In the study an auditory stimulus (either a tone or a buzzer) was sounded, and two seconds later the infant's cheek was stimulated for five seconds. Reinforcement (by means of a dextrose solution) followed head turns in the appropriate direction (to the right or left as established during training) in response to the auditory stimulus. Control subjects received the same stimuli applied to either the left or right cheek, but reinforcement was given eight to ten seconds after the pairing of the auditory-tactile stimulation.

The physical apparatus that was used to measure head movements is shown in Figure 4•10. The results, summarized in Figure 4•11, showed that it is possible to produce an acquired auditory discrimination during the first few days of life. In a second phase of this experiment, the correct head-turn response was reversed; that is, after thirty trials babies trained to turn left were reinforced for turning right and the opposite reversal was made for those initially trained to turn left. The reversal data lend support to the conclusion that the head-turn behavior was a function of the reinforcement.

Conditioned head turning was shown in another major series of studies by H. Papoušek (1967a, 1967b). The conditioned stimulus was a bell presented for ten seconds. Each left head-turn response (a minimum head turn of thirty degrees) made within ten seconds was reinforced. After the left head turn was established, a buzzer was introduced. The infants were now required to make a right head turn to the buzzer. The data in Figure 4•12 indicate that babies are capable of learning

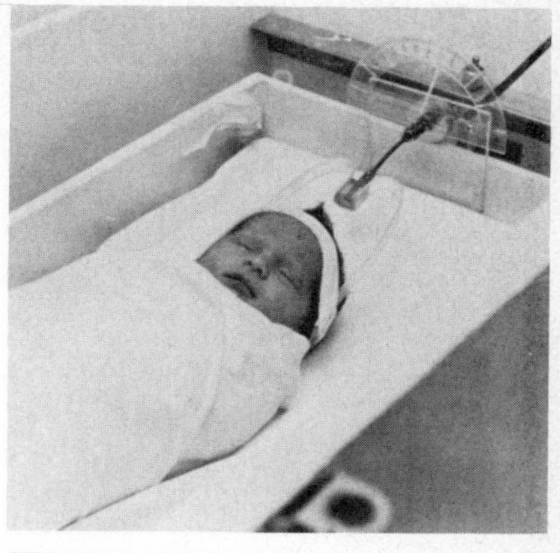

Fig. 4•10 Newborn with headpiece attached for recording head-turning responses. (From Siqueland and Lipsitt, 1966. Courtesy of Lewis P. Lipsitt)

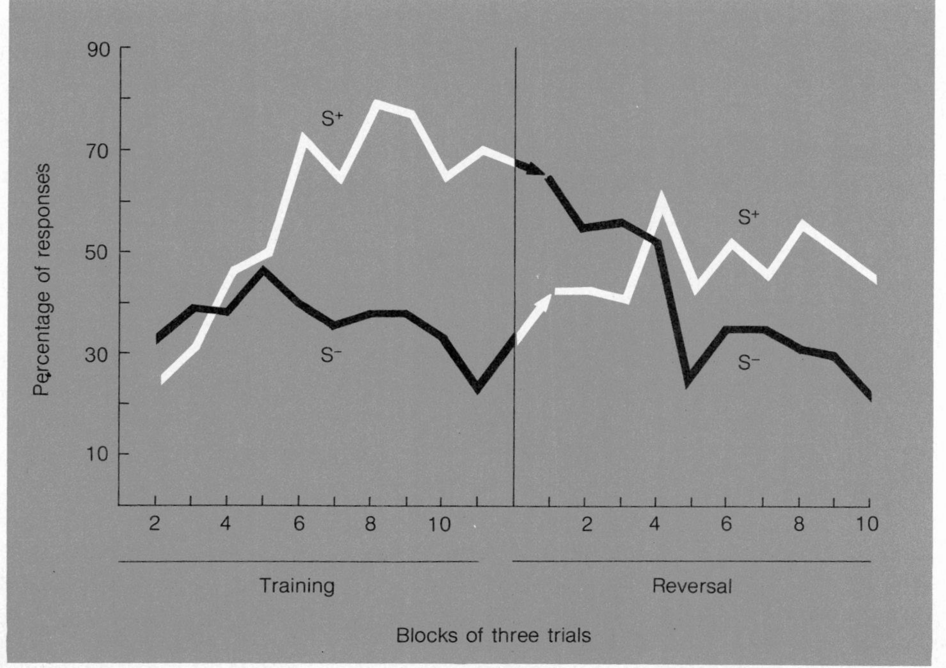

Fig. 4•11 Comparison of percentage of responses to auditory stimulus (positive) and tactile stimulus (negative) during training and reversal trials. (From Siqueland and Lipsitt, 1966)

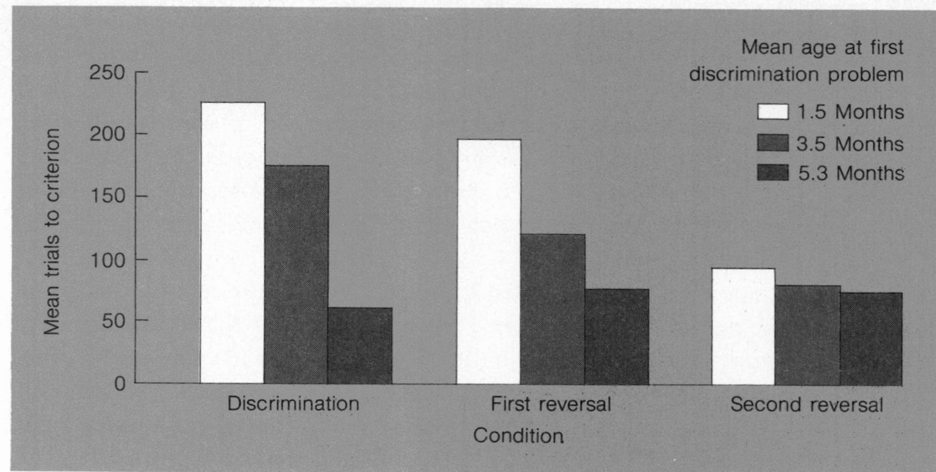

Fig. 4·12 Comparison of three age groups on mean number of trials to criterion on original discrimination problem and subsequent reversal problems. (Adapted from Papoušek, 1967b)

conditioned responses shortly after birth, but that the learning rate is positively influenced by maturation.

Gustatory and Olfactory Discriminations Because the infant is equipped with a large number of taste buds, a baby is probably capable of distinguishing tastes, but evidence to support that conclusion is not available. The infant cannot say whether one substance tastes different from another, and current experimental instruments are not sensitive enough to detect such differences. The development of better instrumentation should lead to the discovery of taste preferences among infants (Reese and Lipsitt, 1970).

Similar problems have limited the study of olfactory discrimination among infants. Engen, Lipsitt, and Kaye (1963), using Engen's habituation procedure, were able to detect differences in responses of infants to odors at two days of age. Essentially this procedure involved placing the infant on a stabilimeter (a device that is sensitive to the movements of the infant) and placing a pneumograph around the infant's abdomen to record changes in breathing rate. In each of ten consecutive trials, a cotton swab saturated with an odorant (the experimental stimulus—in this case acetic acid, phenylethyl alcohol, asafetida, or anise oil) was placed 5 millimeters beneath an infant's nostrils for ten seconds. Then a non-odorous dilutant (the control stimulus) was presented in a similar way. Changes in activity and breathing were recorded throughout the procedure. If there was no response to the control stimulus, the behavioral changes were attributed to the odorous stimulus.

Initial responses to each of the four odors were different. Acetic acid, for example, at first generated between 80 and 100 percent responses, whereas phenylethyl alcohol initially elicited responses on only 10 to 25 percent of the trials. Over trials, however, the responses of the infants decreased dramatically. The investigators interpreted these results as a function of a decrease in novelty, rather than as sensory adaptation. After several presentations, the stimulus was no longer unique. If sensory adaptation had occurred, the infants would have been unable to distinguish the odorant from the dilutant.

Dimensional Discrimination Learning The conditioning of discriminations in infants is very difficult. One reason for this is the incomplete development of basic neurological structures. Also, infant behavior is sensitive to state variables, including hunger, fatigue, or general excitability. With increasing neurological maturation, children become more readily conditionable until approximately six years of age. G. Razran (1933) observed that after that age, children become more resistant to conditioning.

Sheldon White (1965) contends that children older than six process information through the use of hypotheses, which interfere with conditioning because conditioning is largely automatic. According to White, a transition in processing information occurs between the ages of five and seven years. This transition period involves a change from an associative level of learning to one that is cognitive. *Associative learning* is characterized by a rapid rate of responding, in which the child responds automatically. As the child matures and learns numerous associations, information processing becomes increasingly more abstract and deliberate.

What is the evidence in support of White? We have already examined one key study—the transposition study (Kuenne, 1946) in Chapter 3. In that study children were trained to respond to the smaller of two stimuli. In the near transposition test, the smaller of the training stimuli (the originally positive stimulus) became the larger of the two. In the far transposition test, a new pair of stimuli were used but the size relationship was maintained. The results of that study indicated that on the test using stimuli near (similar to) those used in training, children below the age of five years picked the smaller (correct) stimulus; on the test using stimuli far (different) from those used in training, these children chose the two stimuli equally. Older children selected the smaller stimulus on both types of tests.

During the course of this experiment, the older children often spontaneously verbalized the solution to the problem: "It is always the smaller of the two." These verbal behaviors were regarded as significant clues affecting transposition behavior —the ability to see a relationship between objects and apply it in other situations. The child who verbalized "smaller than" appeared to be responding to the relative sizes of the stimuli rather than to their individual characteristics.

From this experiment a number of others developed, including one known as the reversal and nonreversal shift (Kendler and Kendler, 1962). One method of using this experiment is shown in Figure 4•13. In the *reversal shift* the child selects the previously incorrect stimulus, whereas in the *nonreversal shift* the child selects an attribute (black or white) that was not previously relevant. The reversal shift was easier for the older children, and the nonreversal shift was easier for the younger children. It was observed that regardless of age, children who spontaneously verbalized about the size dimension performed better on the reversal shift.

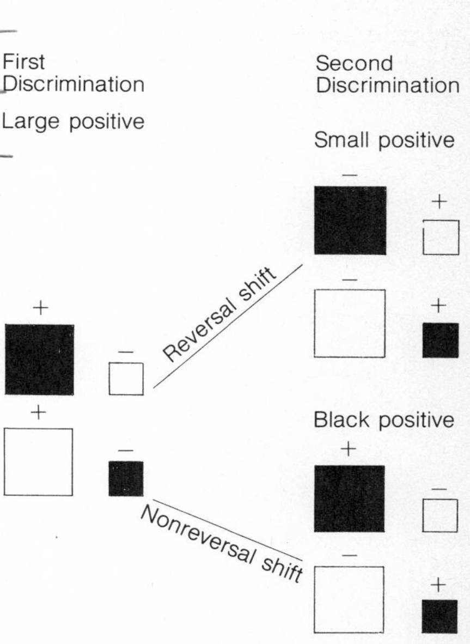

Fig. 4•13 First, one group of children learn (ten correct choices in ten trials) to select the larger of two stimuli. Then the group is shown the same pair of stimuli, but half are now rewarded for choosing the smaller of the pair (the reversal shift). The remaining children are rewarded for selecting either the large or the small black stimulus (the nonreversal shift). (From Kendler and Kendler, 1962)

These results were interpreted by Tracy and Howard Kendler as evidence for a mediation theory: Stimuli initiate not behavior but internal responses, including muscle reactions and implicit verbal reactions. One of the primary mediational cues is language—perhaps a single word such as *larger* or *smaller*, for example. The Kendlers hypothesized that the older (and presumably more verbal) children learn that the first discrimination is based on relative size, and then on this basis they associate a mediational cue with the stimuli; the younger, less articulate children do not have a mediational cue that would interfere with learning a new discrimination (such as one based on color rather than on relative size). Furthermore, in the nonreversal shift one of the new correct responses (large black box) has been reinforced, but in the reversal shift the new correct responses (small boxes) never have been reinforced.

The results of this study and others suggested that if the children were given verbal training, or in some way were provided with a mediational cue, they would perform better on the reversal-shift problem than children not receiving such training. But when children were taught to verbalize the mediator, they did not use it during the actual experiment. Hayne Reese (1962) suggested that children's inability to apply a verbal statement is evidence for mediational deficiency: Although they can verbalize a concept, their verbalizations do not control their behavior.

L. Tighe and T. J. Tighe (1965) performed a reversal- and nonreversal-shift experiment that cast additional doubts on the validity of the mediational hypothesis. In their experiment, the subjects were overtrained on the initial discrimination learning task. *Overtraining* means that even after meeting the criterion set by the experimenter in the training trials (such as ten correct responses in ten attempts), the subject is given extra trials on the original learning task. Nothing in mediational theory predicts the outcome of this manipulation. The high percentage of reversal shifts among children three to five years of age has led to the *attentional hypothesis*, which suggests that between five and seven years the child's ability to attend to the dimensions of the task improves.

This hypothesis assumes that two processes operate in a discrimination learning task:

1. Scanning the stimuli to determine the dimensions defining the stimulus characteristics. For example, in the reversal and nonreversal shift experiment, the subject would determine that the stimuli differ in size and brightness.
2. Determining which dimension is correct and which value—large or small, light or dark—is correct. If the initial choice is incorrect, the subject might try another value on the same dimension or switch dimensions completely.

This model was developed by Zeaman and House (1963), who viewed attention as mediating between the stimuli and the choice response. Jeffrey (1968), you will recall, developed a theory explaining how children become aware of the stimulus dimensions and how they determine the probability that one dimension is more likely than another to be correct.

White describes an additional eighteen behaviors for which there is research evidence demonstrating qualitative changes in learning between the ages of five and seven years. At present we are only beginning to approach an understanding of how these changes occur, what their implications are for designing academic programs for young children, or how they relate to adult mental processes.

> The data on temporal contingencies in learning, and the material on the various shifts in the 5–7 age period, may define something about the structure of adult mental processes. Adults may have available an "associative level," laid down early in development, relatively fast acting, following conventional associative principles, and in the normal adult relatively often existing as a potential, but inhibited, determinant of behavior. The "cognitive layer," laid down after the associative mode of response, is taken to be relatively slower in action and to process information in ways which are only beginning to be understood. (White, 1965, pp. 215–16)

Piaget's Theory of Cognitive Development

4·2 The most influential conception of cognitive development is that of Jean Piaget (1950), a Swiss psychologist who believes that children acquire cognitive abilities in a series of four stages that do not vary from child to child or from culture to culture. Piaget's theory has been criticized because of this assumption of invariance. His methods have been questioned because he observed relatively few children, and his objectivity has been doubted because the subjects he observed most extensively were his own children. Most developmental psychologists, however, see Piaget as an extremely astute observer and his theory as a highly integrated conceptual model.

In Piaget's view, the infant is an active, seeking organism that acquires knowledge by interacting with the environment. The child is operating upon the environment, and the environment in turn is operating upon the child. This continuous interplay, over the course of time, generates knowledge and sets of information-processing rules that are more or less consistent with the expectations of the child's society. What is important to Piaget is not the substance of the child's knowledge but the processes by which these rules are acquired.

Equilibration *Equilibration* is a balance that exists when the world and the child's cognitive structures are in harmony. Piaget explained that the child's current structures, or representations of the world, are imposed on the environment even though they may or may not accurately reflect the environment. The environment provides the child with some form of feedback indicating the accuracy of these perceptions. Disequilibration exists when the child experiences a mismatch between his existing structure and the feedback from the environment (Hunt, 1961).

To explain how modification of existing structures occurs, Piaget describes two complementary processes: accommodation and assimilation. *Accommodation* involves the modification of structures to fit environmental demands. The child modifies existing structures through perceptions that result from new experience. The responses of the child become more adaptive through accommodation. *As-*

Conceptual Tempo and Information Processing

Cognitive style refers to the behaviors a person employs during the solution of a problem. Styles vary from one age level to another and within age levels. Differences among individuals at a specific age level involve the degree to which a person is analytic or impulsive in approaching a cognitive task. Jerome Kagan has labeled the analytic-impulsive dichotomy *conceptual tempo.*

The measurement of conceptual tempo is done on a relatively difficult task that requires time for processing information. Kagan developed such a task, known as Matching Familiar Figures. The subject is shown a particular figure (called the standard) and then must find among six similar figures the one that matches the standard (Figure 4A·1). The scoring procedure involves both the number of errors (wrong choices) made on each task and the speed with which the subject makes an initial response. On the basis of this task, four groups of subjects were identified: fast-responders/high errors; fast-responders/low errors; slow-responders/high errors; and slow-responders/low errors. Two of these groups have received major attention —fast-responders/high errors and slow-responders/low errors. They are called, respectively, impulsives and reflectives.

In school, the reflective child is usually viewed more positively than the impulsive child. Kagan (1965) examined the reading performance of impulsive and reflective children. His hypothesis that impulsives make more reading errors than do reflectives was confirmed. In many other studies reflective children outperform impulsive children on achievement tests and other measures that require careful consideration of alternatives.

Fig. 4A·1 Sample item from Matching Familiar Figures task. The top center figure (the standard) is examined by the subject. With the standard still present, the subject is given six choices and asked to find the identical figure among them. The subject who fails to note a minor change in even just one line is likely to make a wrong choice. The subject responds until making either a correct choice or six wrong ones, whichever comes first. (From Kagan, 1965)

What causes these differences in cognitive style? Many psychologists are convinced that environmental variables are primarily responsible, because it has been observed that many parents are models of impulsive behavior and advise their children to respond rapidly. Furthermore, the results of studies in which efforts were made to make the impulsive child more reflective have been inconsistent. In some instances the behavior has been changed, but the change has not generalized to other situations or has not been proven to be permanent.

John Wright (1974) contends that both reflectivity and impulsivity, as well as the styles ignored by investigators, are adaptive but for different situations. There are certain motor coordination tasks, for example, where speed and accuracy are positively correlated. In these instances rapid responding is a positive attribute. Wright proposes a model in which speed and efficiency are the key measures. In some situations speed is important and the most efficient means of information processing. In other situations, the task demands more deliberate behavior. He states: "After all, our long-range goal is still to give each child the widest possible range of information-processing skills and to teach him when to use each of them, while simultaneously preserving the uniqueness and individuality of each child's intellectual development" (Wright, 1974).

similation is the process whereby the child attempts (1) to impose already existing structures on an environmental event and (2) to translate environmental events in such a way that they are consistent with current perceptions. Assimilation and accommodation, which are constantly functioning, enable the child to develop toward higher levels of adaptation.

Piaget's Developmental Stages Piaget's four stages are levels of cognitive processes that reflect the qualitative changes he observed in children's development (Table 4•1). The transitions from one stage to another are gradual and do not necessarily occur simultaneously with respect to all features of the child's functioning.

Table 4•1 Achievements and Characteristics of Piaget's Stages of Intellectual Development

STAGE	APPROXIMATE AGE RANGE (YEARS)	MAJOR ACHIEVEMENTS	MAJOR CHARACTERISTICS
Sensorimotor period	0–2	Infant differentiates self from objects; attains concept of object permanence. Beginnings of imitation of absent, complex nonhuman stimuli; imaginative play and symbolic thought.	Infant seeks stimulation and makes interesting spectacles last. Primitive understanding of causality, time, and space; means-end relationships.
Preoperational period	2–6	Development of the symbolic function; symbolic use of language. Beginnings of attainment of conservation of number and ability to think in classes and see relationships.	Intuitive problem solving. Thinking characterized by irreversibility, centration, and egocentricity.
Period of concrete operations	6 or 7 through 11 or 12	Logical thinking involving concrete operations of the immediate world, classification, and seriation. Attains conservation of mass, length, weight, and volume.	Thinking characterized by reversibility, decentration, and ability to take role of others.
Period of formal operations	11 or 12 on	Flexibility, abstraction, mental hypotheses testing.	Considers possible alternatives in complex reasoning and problem solving.

(Adapted from Hetherington and Parke, 1975)

Within each stage there occurs both a vertical development that brings the child closer to a new stage and a horizontal development whereby the child incorporates a broader range of behaviors.

The age levels associated with each stage are approximations. Although Piaget does not assert that all children reach each new stage at the same age, he believes that all children proceed through these stages in the same order.

The Sensorimotor Period As an active, seeking organism learning about the environment through attentional behaviors, the infant from birth can call upon a broad repertoire of perceptual and motor abilities. During the first substage, called *reflexive* (0–2 months), the infant's behavior is largely governed by reflexes, but gradually the behavior becomes more efficient. In the second substage, *primary circular reactions* (2–4 months), behavior continues to be reflexive, but under certain conditions the infant repeats actions. (Piaget uses the term *circular reactions* to describe repetition of behavior.) These actions involve the infant's own body—moving the hand in front of the eyes or making a fist—but do not include objects because the infant is not yet aware that its own being is separate from the objects.

During the third substage, *secondary circular reactions* (4–8 months), the child manipulates objects, but only when the objects are touched by chance and the objects remain in view as a consequence of these actions. In the early part of this stage the child does not realize that when an object is out of sight it still exists. This phenomenon, called **object permanence,** begins to develop during these four months, as does also some intentionality of behavior. Now the child moves from accidentally but repeatedly shaking a rattle to the awareness that his or her action on the rattle is causing the sound. There is dramatic improvement in the child's ability to coordinate looking at an object, grasping it, and manipulating it.

During the fourth substage, *coordination of secondary reactions* (8–12 months), the infant begins to coordinate already acquired behavior patterns and use them to achieve new ends. The act of hitting an object, for example, now evolves into a means for moving an obstacle to obtain another object. Perhaps the most important characteristic of substage 4 is the increased flexibility that enables the child to develop new means-end relationships based on the existence of the structures developed during substage 3.

During substage 5, *tertiary circular reactions* (12–18 months), object permanence becomes clearly established. If one takes a toy that the child is watching and puts it behind a screen, the child will quickly reach behind the screen to locate the toy. It is no longer necessary for some portion of the toy to remain visible before the child will search for it. The achievement of object permanence is important because it indicates a more abstract level of functioning. The child continues to elaborate and develop new means-end relationships using already familiar objects in endlessly different ways. The child seems to focus attention on the properties of objects and to ask, "What will happen if I do this?" Dropping objects from the crib or high chair is a newly discovered act that produces a great deal of joy in the baby, if not in the parent. In addition to active experimentation to determine new means-end relationships, the child applies familiar means to new situations.

In the sixth and final substage, *internalized abstract representation* (18–24 months), the child is determining new means of achieving ends through the mechanisms of mental coordinations.

The Preoperational Period (2–7 years) Piaget views the shift to more representational processes as a critical transition in cognitive development and has set that event off as the point of transition to the preoperational stage. This stage is subdivided into the *preoperational phase* (2–4 years) and the *intuitive phase* (4–7 years). The most dramatic occurrence during the preoperational phase is the onset of language, a major achievement in the symbolic use of representational skills. For Piaget, language is an event that occurs coincidentally with the onset of the preoperational period, probably as the result of neurophysiological maturation. Unlike J. B. Watson, who said that thought processes are actually motor habits in the larynx, Piaget asserts that language is a symbolic system: it communicates concepts but does not embody them.

Another important aspect of this phase is the child's increasing engagement in fantasy play, as when an ordinary block becomes a tank. During this period the child acquires idiosyncratic concepts and symbols. Highly egocentric thinking leads to difficulties when the child tries to communicate ideas to others with different representational and symbolic systems. Play helps the child to modify and expand existing structures and to deal with the potentially overwhelming demands of reality. Observations of children indicate that both a great deal of what they have assimilated in the first two to four years of their lives, and new representations that are being assimilated, are reflected in their highly imaginative and symbolic role-playing. More systematic observations of the toddlers' play behavior might

In the second of Piaget's four developmental stages, a child is likely to engage in imaginative and symbolic role-playing. (David Powers, Jeroboam)

demonstrate how they perceive the world and how, through their play behavior, modifications in existing schemata occur.

Piaget and his associates developed a set of tasks designed to study the mental operations of children at different developmental stages. Among these tasks are the famous conservation problems (Figure 4•14). These problems are useful for understanding the characteristics of children in the intuitive phase, when they typically have difficulty seeing the constancy of certain attributes throughout various physical rearrangements. In the conservation of liquids problem, the child must recognize several principles: (1) no water is added or taken away during the operation of pouring the liquid from one container into another; (2) the wideness of one beaker compensates for the tallness of the other; (3) pouring the water from one beaker into another is equivalent to pouring it in the opposite direction (the concept of *reversibility*); and (4) there are two dimensions to the task, height and width, and they vary together in a constant relationship. The child must attend to the two dimensions simultaneously. The phenomenon of attending to only a single dimension or attribute, which occurs in other kinds of problems at this age level, is referred to as **centration.**

Centration has been demonstrated in an imaginative study by K. G. O'Bryan and F. J. Boersma (1971), who recorded the eye movements of children performing the conservation of fluid task. The technique permitted O'Bryan and Boersma to film the beakers and also the eye fixations and sequence of eye fixations of children in the intuitive phase who failed to conserve, and of older children who did conserve. The younger children tended to place more of their eye fixations on a single

(*a*) CONSERVATION OF LENGTH

1. Two sticks are aligned in front of the subject, who admits their equality.

2. One of the sticks is moved to the right. The subject is asked whether they are still the same length.

(*b*) CONSERVATION OF NUMBER

1. Two rows of counters are placed in one-to-one correspondence. The subject admits their equality.

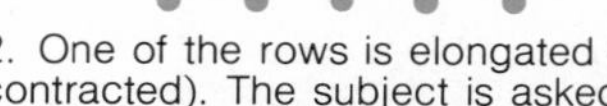

2. One of the rows is elongated (or contracted). The subject is asked whether each row still has the same number.

(*c*) CONSERVATION OF LIQUIDS

1. Two beakers are filled to the same level with water. The subject sees that they are equal.

2. The liquid of one container is poured into a tall tube (or a flat dish). The subject is asked whether each contains the same amount.

Factors Influencing Children's Memory Performance

Why does the memory ability of children improve with age? Three relevant factors change as children mature:

1. Use of rehearsal. Older children review material during test trials, whereas younger children do not.
2. Attachment of verbal labels to stimuli. As children mature, they increasingly use symbols to represent actual objects. Perhaps, in the process of verbal labeling, the child pays more attention to the stimuli, or a verbal label may simply be a more efficient (less complex) stimulus to recall.
3. Categories for grouping items. In general, grouping items makes it easier to recall specific ones, but the type of categorization can further facilitate memory. There is some evidence that children with a mental age of two months use rhyming (*hit-sit*); functional categories (*apple-eat*) are likely to be used at a mental age of three years; and at a mental age of five years more inclusive categorizations (*dog-cat*) are employed. An inclusive categorization can more readily handle more items and is therefore more efficient.

In general, children are capable of rehearsing, attaching verbal labels, and grouping items, whatever their age. When younger children are specifically instructed and trained to rehearse, for example, their performance improves markedly, often attaining the same level as that of the older children. It is the spontaneous use of the three abilities that differentiates older children. The lack of this spontaneity is called production deficiency; it seems especially important in understanding age differences in performance on memory tasks.

attribute, typically the height of the taller beaker, whereas the older children's eye fixations showed that they were using both dimensions to determine their equality.

David Elkind (1969) has extensively examined the phenomenon of centration in terms of perceptual and cognitive integration. Elkind developed tasks that assess children's ability to integrate identifiable parts into wholes (Figure 4•15). An important feature of integrative behavior is that it shows the ability to perform multiple classification and to coordinate parts into meaningful wholes. Elkind's data suggest that intuitive-phase children are less likely to demonstrate integrative behavior than are older children.

Perhaps the outstanding characteristic of children in the intuitive phase, in contrast to children in the preconceptual phase, is that they possess a much more adaptive intelligence. John Flavell makes the following observation:

> The child becomes noticeably more testable in formal experiments from age four or five on. He is much more able to address himself to a specified task and to apply adapted intelligence to it rather than simply to assimilate it to some egocentric play schema. It is no accident that the lower age limit in most Piaget experiments is about four years. And not only does the child become testable *per se* in the late preoperational years, he also becomes capable of reasoning about progressively more complex and extended experimental problems of displays in the testing situation. (Flavell, 1963, pp. 162–63)

In effect, the intuitive child is in a transitional stage leading toward concrete operations. The children evidence more mature behaviors in certain areas on occasion, but each day seems to bring forth more evidence of maturity.

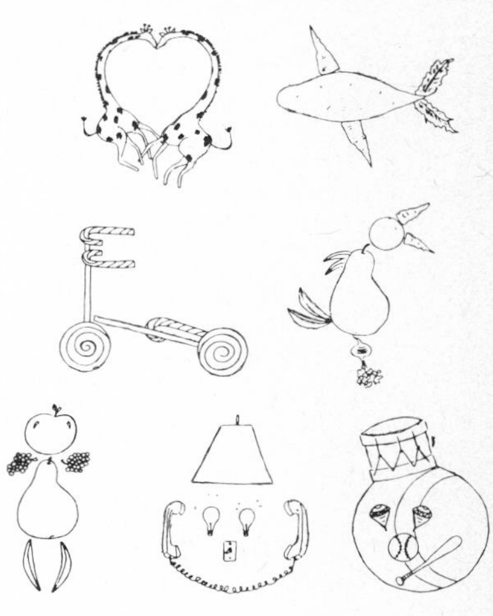

Fig. 4•15 Items used in the Picture Integration Test. In describing each picture, the child can either name the individual parts or integrate them into a whole figure, or both. (From Elkind, 1969)

Maternal Teaching Styles and Cognitive Development

R. D. Hess and V. Shipman (1967) extensively studied the variations in the behaviors of mothers toward their children on learning tasks. One hypothesis they examined was that observed differences in learning among children from families of different income levels are, at least in part, related to the teaching styles of the mothers.

In a study concerning this hypothesis, all the mothers in the sample were shown how to use a toy for copying linear designs: turning one dial caused the line to move vertically whereas turning the other dial caused the line to move horizontally. The mothers were then asked to copy five designs while they controlled one dial and their child controlled the other dial. They were also told that they would be allowed to tell the children anything during the task, including providing directions and showing the child various model designs by way of explanation.

The study showed that the mothers differed in the type and amount of direction and explanation they gave. The typical middle-class mother guided her child with specific directions during the task. Most lower-class mothers told the child only to turn the knob and became more specific only after an error had been made. Middle-class mothers also used the models substantially more often than did lower-class mothers. Indeed, the nature of the task almost necessitated using these models in helping the child comprehend the purpose of the mother's directions.

According to Hess and Shipman, when a mother does not give specific directions, the child can basically only guess about what is wanted—at least until he gets more information through maternal praise or disapproval for each response. The child also has difficulty making meaningful responses when the mother does not provide a goal (as by showing the child a model). The child cannot know in advance how to respond or how the mother in turn will respond unless the mother explains the sequence and pattern of responses. These are all aspects of communication between the mother and child.

The intuitive phase is characterized by substantial growth in the quality of mental operations, but the operations are still limited. The children can deal with only a single dimension, thus, they are unable to cope with multiple classification tasks. They do not possess a concept of reversibility, which is essential to fairly simple arithmetic functions, and they are unable to generalize available mental operations from one set of tasks to another.

Concrete Operations Period (7–11 years) During the stage of concrete operations the child achieves an understanding of the conservation of mass, weight, and volume and has achieved a highly flexible set of processes with which to respond to environmental demands. The assimilatory and accommodatory processes are coming closer to equilibrium. In addition to multiple classification, reversibility, and equality, children acquire the ability to perform seriation tasks—to arrange stimuli in graduated hierarchical arrangements. Somewhat later, the child becomes capable of handling problems of transitivity: If John is taller than Bill, and Bill is taller than Dan, who is taller, John or Dan? The transitivity problem derives from the seriation problem because it involves ordered differences among stimuli. But in the transitivity problem there is the additional requirement of a mental transformation in the form of *greater than* and *less than* as the basis of ordering the stimuli.

The Formal Operations Period (11+ years) The child is nearing the stage of abstract thinking and conceptualization and the capacity for hypothesis testing. There is now some question whether all people achieve formal operations, and even whether these processes are necessary to all people. Piaget (1972) himself has suggested that perhaps this stage is limited to people whose mental activities require logical thought, such as mathematicians and physicists. Klaus Riegel (1973) examined Piagetian conceptualizations in terms of the interactions of the individual and society and concluded that the attainment of formal operations is not a necessary terminal point. He suggests, however, that if such demands are made, the individual can develop the capability to cope with them.

More than any of the other stages in Piaget's model, the stage of formal operations is probably susceptible to environmental influence. Among the leading critics of Piaget's insistence on the concept of invariance are psychologists who believe that logical concepts may be a function of environmental quality. Other critics are the experimenters who have trained children in specific tasks to accelerate the appearance of concrete operations. Many investigators have used conservation and seriation tasks to show that children can be trained in these competencies during earlier stages of development (Gelman, 1969; Kingsley and Hall, 1967).

Language Development

4•3 Scientists who accept a structural view of language development, including Chomsky (1957), Lenneberg (1967), Brown (1970), and McNeill (1970), are called *psycholinguists.* These scientists argue that human beings are neurologically constructed in such a way that language acquisition can occur and all the rules necessary for grammar can be generated. In other words, language development is a function of a highly specialized logic system unique to human beings. Indeed, children learn a large number of rules of grammatical structure in such a short time that it does not seem plausible they could do so if they depended entirely on associative or imitative learning.

The assumption about rule generation is demonstrated when the child, in forming the plural of an irregular word such as *mouse,* says "mouses." Because children are seldom exposed to that incorrect plural, it is unlikely that they learn it by imitation and reinforcement. What the response *mouses* seems to indicate is that the child is following the rule for the formation of a plural, even though the rule does not apply in this instance.

In an interesting experiment, Jean Berko (1958) studied children's use of word endings. Unfinished sentences were read aloud, and the children were expected to complete them with the properly inflected words (Figure 4•16). What makes this study unique and important is that Berko used nonsense syllables so that the children's responses could not be influenced by previous experience with the actual words themselves. The children were applying their rules for forming plurals and were doing it well.

Fig. 4·16 A sample stimulus from Berko's experiment. The correct response ("wugs") was made by 76 percent of the preschool children tested and by 97 percent of the first-grade children tested. (From Berko, 1958)

In keeping with the structural view of language developments, Lenneberg (1967) hypothesized that every normal child acquires a language system primarily as a function of maturation. To buttress his argument for maturation, he developed the material in Table 4·2, which shows that the maturational sequence of motor development parallels the emergence of vocalization and language.

The most important issue that the psycholinguists have developed is the relationship between semantics and cognitive development.

Table 4·2 Developmental Milestones in Motor and Language Development

AT THE COMPLETION OF	MOTOR DEVELOPMENT	VOCALIZATION AND LANGUAGE
12 weeks	Supports head when in prone position; weight is on elbows; hands mostly open; no grasp reflex	Markedly less crying than at 8 weeks; when talked to and nodded at, smiles, followed by squealing-gurgling sounds usually called *cooing,* which is vowel-like and pitch-modulated; sustains cooing for 15 to 20 seconds.
16 weeks	Plays with a rattle placed in his hands (by shaking it and staring at it), head self-supported; tonic neck reflex subsiding	Responds to human sounds more definitely; turns head; eyes seem to search for speaker; occasionally some chuckling sounds
20 weeks	Sits with props	The vowel-like cooing sounds begin to be interspersed with more consonantal sounds; acoustically, all vocalizations are very different from the sounds of the mature language of the environment
6 months	While sitting, bends forward and uses hands for support; can bear weight when put into standing position, but cannot yet stand with holding on; reaching is unilateral; no thumb apposition yet; releases cube when given another	Cooing changes into babbling resembling one-syllable utterances; neither vowels nor consonants have very fixed recurrences; most common utterances sound somewhat like *ma, mu, da,* or *di*
8 months	Stands holding on; grasps with thumb apposition; picks up pellet with thumb and fingertips	Reduplication (or more continuous repetitions) becomes frequent; intonation patterns become distinct; utterances can signal emphasis and emotions
10 months	Creeps efficiently; takes side steps, holding on; pulls to standing position	Vocalizations are mixed with sound-play such as gurgling or bubble-blowing; appears to wish to imitate sounds, but the imitations are never quite successful; beginning to differentiate between words heard by making differential adjustment

(From Lenneberg, 1967)

Vocabulary Development Among the earliest and most extensively studied phenomena is the growth of the child's vocabulary. Madorah Smith (1926) traced the development of oral vocabulary from approximately 8 months to 72 months of age. The results of that study (Table 4•3) show that the increments of growth are especially great around three and four years of age, but these data underestimate the functional vocabulary that children possess. The receptive vocabulary of children is much greater than the expressive vocabulary, as evidenced by the fact that they can understand spoken language before they can use it.

A related aspect of vocabulary development is the development of sentence length. At approximately 18 months the child's sentence consists of, on the average, one or two words. Thereafter, the length of sentences improves rapidly, achieving the adult level—six or seven words—probably around age seven or eight. Figure 4•17 shows the growth in use of morphemes by three children. A morpheme is the smallest unit of meaning in a given language and is frequently synonymous with a word. However, it is a more sensitive measure of sentence length because it permits the investigator to give credit for the use of plurals, prefixes, and suffixes.

Children's initial utterances are single words. McNeill has suggested that these first single-word utterances may represent not mere labeling of objects but one-word sentences expressing an idea. The term used for this interpretation of single-word utterances is *holophrastic speech*, which means that children are limited phonologically to uttering single words at the beginning of language acquisition, even though they are capable of conceiving of something like full sentences (McNeill, 1970). McNeill suggests that holophrastic speech can express the child's emotional

Table 4•3 Average Size of Oral Vocabularies of Children (Adapted from Smith, 1926)

YEARS MONTHS	NUMBER OF WORDS	GAIN
8	0	
10	1	1
1- 0	3	2
1- 3	19	16
1- 6	22	3
1- 9	118	96
2- 0	272	154
2- 6	446	174
3- 0	896	450
3- 6	1222	326
4- 0	1540	318
4- 6	1870	330
5- 0	2072	202
5- 6	2289	219
6- 0	2562	273

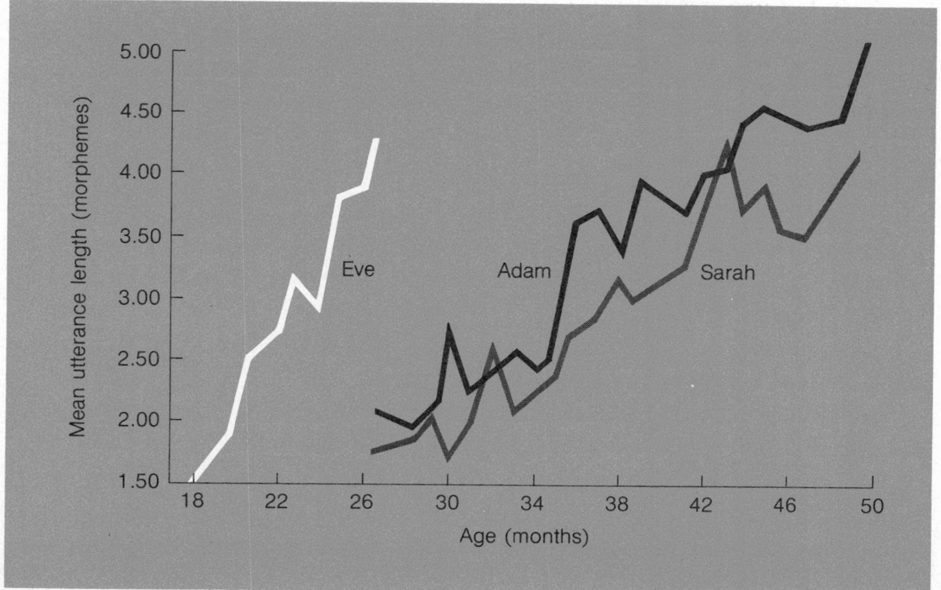

Fig. 4•17 Mean utterance length for each of three children. Morphemes (meaningful segments) are plotted rather than words in order to give credit for the use of inflections such as plural word endings. (After Brown, 1970. From Ruch and Zimbardo, 1971)

state, represent an idea, or name an object. In order to understand holophrases one must know about the context in which they occur.

The Development of Grammar At approximately 18 months of age, the child begins to use grammar by putting two or more words together. One of the earliest grammars used by children was described by Braine (1963) as consisting of sequences of pivot words and open words. There are a few pivot words and many open words. In the pivot-open construction the child uses the pivot word, for example *pretty*, in conjunction with a number of open words to form sequences, such as *pretty boy*, *pretty shoe*, *pretty baby*. In this two-word sequence a pivot word can be in either position, but never in both. *It* is a pivot word that always appears last, as in *fix it*. Complex grammatical rules involving subjects, objects, nouns, adjectives, adverbs, and verbs evolve from this primitive beginning. Great strides are made between 22 and 32 months, and speech acquires adultlike properties around 48 months (Brown and Bellugi, 1964). From an infinity of combinations of structures that might be developed, children learn the rules that apply to their own language and eliminate those that would lead to incorrect utterances.

Chomsky's (1957, 1968) view of language acquisition proposes that a child learns the rules that allow production and comprehension of an unlimited number of grammatical variations. His theory, known as transformational grammar, makes a distinction between surface structure and deep structure. *Surface structure* refers to the spoken and written words themselves. The meanings ascribed to the surface materials are the *deep structures*, which are not directly observable. In the sentences, "David made a touchdown" or "The touchdown was made by David," the surface structures are different, yet they have the same meaning; the surface and deep structures are identical. However, despite identical surface structure in both cases, the sentence "The heat is on" can have at least two different meanings, depending on the context and manner in which it is said. One use might refer to an actual heating system, whereas another might refer to psychological pressure or even to a race.

Semantics and Cognition The relationship between semantics (meaning) and cognition is beginning to capture the interest of psychologists and psycholinguists alike. The major concern of L. Bloom (1970) and Roger Brown (1973) is that focusing on the structure of language has turned interest away from the relationship between language and meaning. The pivot-open sequence and the early grammatical constructions of children represent sequences of words, but do not contribute to our understanding of the child's meaning.

Bloom's work has amply demonstrated the need to examine the semantic properties of children's developing speech. One of the major findings is that understanding a child's utterance requires a knowledge of the context within which it occurred. The language of children, like their thought processes, is ambiguous. A small child who says "more up high" may want someone to push the playground swing or to reach for a cookie on the top shelf. Such utterances require contextual stimuli for precise comprehension.

Bloom argues for more intensive observational research emphasizing language in a context. She further suggests that longitudinal studies are more likely to unravel the parallelisms between cognitive growth and the refinement of grammar. She comments, "Children learn language as a means of representing or coding information that they have already acquired about objects, events, and relations in the world. Language development, in this view, follows from and depends upon conceptual development in a logical way" (Bloom, 1970).

The Multiple Meanings of Intelligence

4•4 Intelligence is an abstraction that can be measured only through specific behaviors; it does not exist in some specific region of the head. Intelligence can be also defined simply as what an intelligence test measures. Some makers of intelligence tests believe that intelligence is a single trait, whereas others believe that it is made up of various traits. Accordingly, there are a variety of tests that measure a variety of different attributes, but the high correlation of their scores shows that they are measuring the same thing, which we take to be human intellectual capability.

The content of these tests varies with the age of the subject. For example, we do not ask three-month-old infants to define words, but we may involve them in psychomotor tasks, such as grasping objects or following objects with their eyes. As children mature, the tests begin to emphasize the important verbal aspects of cognitive development and become increasingly abstract.

Types of Tests Among the many infant tests available, the three best known were developed by Gesell (1928), Bayley (1969), and Cattell (1940). Although these tests differ in format and emphasis, they overlap more than they differ. The demands of the items become more complex over time, as you can see by the sample in Table 4•4. The development of these infant scales relies heavily on careful observation, especially of the average age at which particular behaviors occur. Although these tests are often used to determine whether an infant is normal, their predictive power is negligible. They provide information about the acquisition of a variety of psychomotor capabilities and the early onset of language, and they identify grossly abnormal children—but usually the status of such children is obvious.

Table 4•4 Sample Items from the Bayley Infant Scales

ITEM	AGE PLACEMENT (MONTHS)
Coordinates horizontally eyes	0.5
Vocalizes once or twice	0.9
Visually recognizes mother	2.0
Carries ring to mouth	3.8
Looks for fallen spoon	6.0
Imitates words	12.5
Says two words	14.2
Attains toy with stick	17.0
Names five pictures	25.0

(Bayley, 1969)

One of the earliest intelligence tests was developed in France by Alfred Binet and Théophile Simon (1908) to identify children who would be unable to benefit from an elementary education program. This early test consisted primarily of psychomotor tasks (such as copying a circle or a square and stringing beads) that seemed most appropriate for preschool children. In the United States the test items were translated, revised, and standardized by Lewis Terman, who was then a professor

Is the IQ Constant?

Is it possible to make a long-range prediction about an individual on the basis of IQ test performance? From a biological-genetic viewpoint, it is plausible to assume that IQ is fixed at conception. Adoption agencies act on that assumption when they attempt to match IQ scores of infants and preschool children with those of the adoptive parents. But several important studies have raised the question: "Is the IQ really constant?"

Honzik, Macfarlane, and Allen (1948) administered individual tests to more than 150 children over a period of sixteen years as part of a longitudinal study conducted at the University of California at Berkeley. Although the sample was selected as being representative of the general population, it became clear as the study progressed that the children were above average in ability. The mean IQ score at age eight was 118, and it had increased to 123 by age fifteen. For the age period from six to eighteen years, 60 percent of the children evidenced IQ changes of 15 or more points, and one-third of the group changed by 20 or more points. Some children showed consistent gains over time while other children showed consistent losses over time.

Kagan, Sontag, Baker, and Nelson (1958) postulated that (1) in order to perform well on IQ tests, children must have both the skills and the motivation to perform well; and (2) children who show consistent gains in IQ over a long period of time will evidence high achievement needs, competitive strivings, and curiosity. Using longitudinal data from the Fels Study, Kagan and his colleagues selected subjects who had shown either consistent IQ gains (an average of 17 points from age six to age ten) or consistent decreases (an average of minus 5 points over the same period of time). At age six, the two groups had approximately equivalent mean IQ scores, 119 for the gainers and 116 for the losers. The measures of need achievement were obtained from the Thematic Apperception Test, and aggression was assessed using the Rorschach (ink-blot) Test.

In one study of intelligence (Sherman and Key, 1932), the IQs of rural mountain children and of mountain village children were found to decline as the children grew older—indicating that intelligence is not constant. (Earl Dotter, BBM Associates)

On the basis of the tests the children who consistently gained in IQ test performance proved to be more achievement oriented, more aggressive, and more curious. There were significant sex differences, with boys showing more aggression and achievement orientation. In the sample of IQ gainers, there were twice as many boys and girls. The authors point out that achievement strivings, aggression, and curiosity are much more likely to occur in a social environment that values these attributes and rewards the child for developing them.

Sherman and Key (1932) examined the IQ performance of children from the isolated mountain regions of Virginia and West Virginia. They compared the test performance of 102 children from rural mountain areas against 81 children from a mountain village. Examination of the performance of the two groups on the Pintner-Cunningham Primary Mental Test showed a steady decline in performance with increasing age. In the case of the mountain children, the IQ decline was from 84 at seven years to 53 at eleven years. This decline would have changed their mental category from low average to retarded. Over the same period the IQs of the village children also declined (from 94 to 76) but not as drastically.

As the children grew older, the discrepancy between the demands of their environments and those of the urban middle-class (which are presumably reflected in the kinds of questions asked on IQ tests) increasingly diverged. This study demonstrates that intellectual growth will, within limits, develop to a level commensurate with environmental demands.

On the basis of these studies and others, the conclusion is warranted that the IQ is not constant.

at Stanford University—hence the name Stanford-Binet Intelligence Test, which has since become one of the most widely used intelligence tests in the United States. Originally published by Terman in 1916, the test has undergone several revisions, the latest in 1960.

In his expansion of the Stanford-Binet test, Terman emphasized test items that measure abstract reasoning ability and the use of abstract symbols. He added items on vocabulary (What is an orange? What is an envelope?), general reasoning, analogies, and arithmetic problems that have to be solved mentally. Terman's concept of intelligence was similar to the one proposed by Charles Spearman (1927), who suggested that intelligence is a unitary trait called psychical energy or *g* (for general intelligence). Spearman defined *g* as a general factor of mental energy possessed by all individuals in varying degrees and operating in all mental activities in amounts that differ according to the demands of the task.

The view that intelligence is comprised of a number of relatively independent abilities was developed primarily by L. L. Thurstone (1946). Using the mathematical procedure known as **factor analysis**, Thurstone identified primary factors (which vary from one age level to another) and designed the Primary Mental Abilities Test to measure them. The following are some examples of these tests:

1. Verbal Comprehension (V): measures verbal abilities, such as vocabulary.
2. Reasoning Ability (R): measures the ability to reason abstractly and symbolically.
3. Numerical Ability (N): measures the ability to do numerical calculations rapidly and accurately.
4. Space Relations (S): measures visual-form relationships, or the ability to visualize spatial relations.
5. Word Fluency (W): measures the ability to think of words rapidly in response to cues, such as the initial letters of the words. (Thurstone and Thurstone, 1950).

David Wechsler (1955) also disagreed with Terman's definition of intelligence but did not go as far as Thurstone in developing independent factors. Wechsler's argument was that there is a verbal component and a nonverbal (or performance) component to intellectual ability. His tests are the Wechsler Adult Intelligence Scale (WAIS) and the Wechsler Intelligence Scale for Children (WISC).

The verbal scale consists of six subtests, all requiring abstract reasoning ability:

1. General Information (This subtest is based on the assumption that brighter people will be better informed about a variety of subjects than are average people.)
2. Comprehension
3. Arithmetic
4. Similarities
5. Digit Span (an index of short-term memory)
6. Vocabulary

(a)

(b)

Items similar to those contained in two of the five performance subtests of the Wechsler Adult Intelligence Scale: Picture Completion (*a*) and Object Assembly (*b*). (The Psychological Corporation)

The performance tests consist of five subtests, which vary somewhat in the degree of abstract reasoning required:

1. Digit Symbol Substitution: requires the subject to learn a code and substitute the code for numbers.
2. Picture Completion: requires the subject to examine a picture and tell the examiner what is missing.
3. Block Design: requires the subject to use nine colored blocks in reproducing a set of designs. This test is quite difficult and correlates highly with performance on the vocabulary subtest of the verbal scale.
4. Picture Arrangement: requires the subject to arrange a series of pictures (presented in random order) so that they make a sensible story.
5. Object Assembly: requires the subject to assemble a set of pieces (much like a jigsaw puzzle) so that they make a meaningful figure.

All subtests of the performance group are timed.

The Intelligence Quotient (IQ) and Mental Age (MA) The **intelligence quotient (IQ)** is one of psychology's best known and perhaps least understood concepts. It is not a direct measure of inherent intellectual capacities, but rather an indirectly derived measure of relative mental development among children.

The IQ is associated with the Stanford-Binet Intelligence Test designed for children through age eighteen. The test is composed of numerous tests that have been age-graded according to the chronological levels at which most children pass them. A child's **mental age (MA)** is computed on the basis of the number of tests passed. The IQ relates the MA score to the child's chronological age (CA).

IQ scores for all Stanford-Binet tests until the 1960 revision were computed using the following equation, which is designed to yield only whole numbers.

$$IQ = \frac{MA}{CA} \times 100$$

If a child's MA score is equal to the child's chronological age, the IQ score will be 100. The tests are designed so that this figure will be the mean score. Children passing the tests at advanced age levels will have IQs higher than 100. Children who fail tests that most same-age children pass have IQs lower than 100.

One problem with the scores derived from this equation is that they have different meanings when the total distribution of IQs is different at different age levels. For example, if a larger proportion of five-year-olds than six-year-olds have IQs below 116, a five-year-old child with that IQ is relatively more intelligent than the six-year-old child with the same IQ.

To avoid this problem, the 1960 revision of the Stanford-Binet equated the **standard deviations** of IQ distributions at each age level. This method of deriving comparable scores was also used successfully in the original version of the WAIS and in the WISC. On the revised Stanford-Binet all IQs are standard scores that are proportional to the true scores and that can be plotted on a normal curve with a mean of 100 and a standard deviation of 16 (Figure 4·18). The equation for determining standardized IQs is as follows:

$$\text{standard IQ} = \frac{X - M}{SD} \times 16 + 100$$

where X is IQ as determined by the earlier equation; M is the mean IQ for the particular age level; and SD is the standard deviation for that age. Standard IQ and IQ are identical when M equals 100 and SD equals 16. This is the case at all age levels except two and one-half years, six years, and twelve years.

IQ scores are most significant in terms of their probability of occurrence. For example, a person who obtains an IQ of 70 on the Stanford-Binet test equals or exceeds only 3 percent of the population, whereas someone with an IQ of 136 equals or exceeds 99 percent of the population. Once an IQ score moves beyond 136, the person can be defined as exceptional. A child with an IQ of 152 is equalled or excelled by only 8 out of 10,000 children; a child with an IQ of 160 is equalled or excelled by only 1 child out of 10,000. In his monumental studies of genius, Terman (1925) included children with IQs of 140 and above.

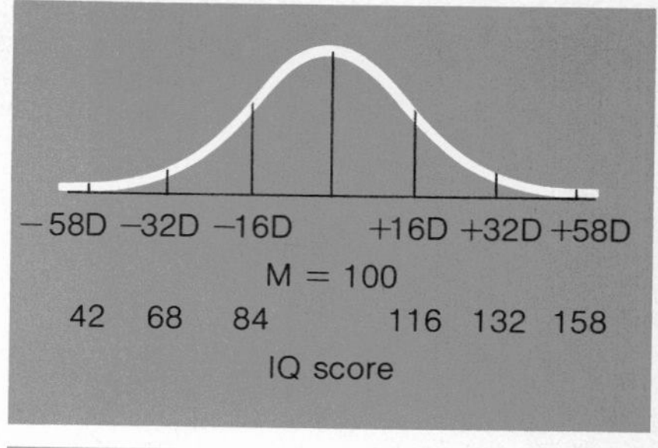

Fig. 4·18 Deviation IQ scores: 68 percent of IQ scores fall within one standard deviation of the mean, 95 percent within two standard deviations, and 99.7 percent within three standard deviations.

The Concepts of Reliability and Validity **Reliability** can be defined as the degree of consistency (between 0 and 1.0) in responses if the test is repeated. Perfect reliability (1.0) is seldom obtained for many reasons. The emotional state of a person taking the test can be affected by unavoidable variations in testing conditions, such as extraneous noise, unusually high or low temperature, or even the manner in which the test is introduced by the examiner. The items themselves on a test can affect reliability if they are pitched at the wrong level of difficulty or if the wording is ambiguous. If the task is too simple, a change of one or two points will substantially alter the relative position of individuals within the group of test-takers, and this effect will lower reliability. Maximum reliability can be expected when there is maximum variability among subjects.

In the *split-half technique* for obtaining an estimate of a test's reliability, either the odd and even items on the test are correlated with each other, or the items in the first half of the test are correlated with those in the second half. This technique is advantageous because data need be gathered during only one administration of the test and the correlations are easy to do. However, it tends to overestimate reliability because the single administration maintains constant testing conditions; a test-taker who feels sick at the beginning of the test is not likely to feel any better at the end. Furthermore, even items are as likely as odd items to be ambiguously written. Constant irrelevant conditions such as these interfere with the assessment of a test's reliability because they make it impossible to determine whether performance is influenced by problems inherent in the test or by the irrelevant conditions.

In the *test-retest technique,* the same subjects receive the same test on two occasions separated by some period of time. If the test is repeated too soon after the original administration, the subjects may remember how they responded on the previous occasion, and repetition of remembered responses will inflate the reliability. If the period of separation is too long, changes may occur in the subjects, and performance may change as a consequence. In this case the reliability of the test will be underestimated.

Another technique for estimating the reliability of a test involves the use of *equivalent tests*—two or more forms (often designated by letters) that measure the same thing and have the same mean and the same variability. Prior to the 1960 revision of the Stanford-Binet, for example, there were two equivalent forms of the test. For the most part, the development of equivalent forms is so difficult that they rarely are used. However, when they are, administering the different forms on different days provides the best estimate of reliability.

What level of reliability should an IQ test have? The answer depends on how the test results are to be used. According to the American Psychological Association, if the test results will affect the placement of a child or an adult in a special education program or an institution, the test should have a reliability of at least .90, and be an individually administered test given by a certified psychometrician. Tests that are individually administered include the Stanford-Binet and the WAIS, whereas the Primary Mental Abilities Test is intended to be administered in groups. If the IQ test is being used as a screening device, as is likely in the administration of group tests, then the association recommends that the reliability be at least .85. Although group tests allow one rapidly and at modest expense to obtain IQ estimates on large numbers of people, reliabilities on these tests are usually lower than those on individually administered tests.

Do intelligence tests measure what they purport to measure? Can they predict anything of functional significance? Most research in the area of test **validity** has been done with school children. Although the results indicate that IQ tests predict performance in school at better than a chance level, there is still a considerable degree of error. Part of the problem, of course, is that instructional systems differ and, more important, that children are differentially motivated to perform well in school. Nevertheless, for any one individual there is apt to be considerable error of prediction. This finding has prompted many parent groups to argue that IQ tests should not be given at all.

Research on Intelligence and Intelligence Tests Extensive research has failed to show whether intelligence is a single trait, on the order of Spearman's *g*, or a number of traits, such as those defined by Thurstone and Wechsler. One technique for investigating what the various intelligence tests are measuring uses factor analysis, which attempts to find the underlying relationships in a series of correlations. Tests with high correlations can be grouped together as representing one factor.

In order to gain a clear perspective on cognitive development, Thurstone (1955) published developmental data for each of seven primary mental abilities: verbal comprehension, reasoning ability, numerical ability, space relations, word fluency, perceptual speed, and immediate memory. One of Thurstone's major achievements in this study was to develop an interval scale with a hypothetical zero point. As we noted in Chapter 2, most psychological scales have no known, or even assumed, zero point. Thurstone, however, extrapolated the amount of variation from age five downward (without stating where on a time scale zero occurred) and then developed scale units from this arbitrary zero point.

Results of the study (Figure 4•19) indicate that the perceptual speed factor and the space relations factor emerge earliest and achieve the highest level of all factors. It is unlikely, however, that either factor is particularly important to higher level cognitive abstract performance. The verbal comprehension factor emerges relatively late and at the age of nineteen is still below the other factors. The word fluency factor, which represents the most complex and the highest level of achievement, appears to take longest to develop. This finding is consistent with the general observation that species higher on the phylogenetic scale take longer to develop in terms of all aspects of behavior.

W. J. Meyer and A. W. Bendig (1961) administered the Primary Mental Abilities Test to 100 eighth-grade children and to the same 100 children four years later. They found two factors: factor 1 was comprised of the Vocabulary, Reasoning, and Numerical Ability tests, and factor 2 was comprised of the Spatial Ability test. (The Word Fluency test proved to be unreliable and was dropped from the analyses.) Having factor-analyzed the data, these investigators reported the possibility of a single binding unitary factor like *g*.

P. R. Hofstaetter (1954) performed a factor analysis of IQ test data derived from the Berkeley Longitudinal Study from infancy through eighteen years. (Hofstaetter's findings do not generalize to all tests because he used only the

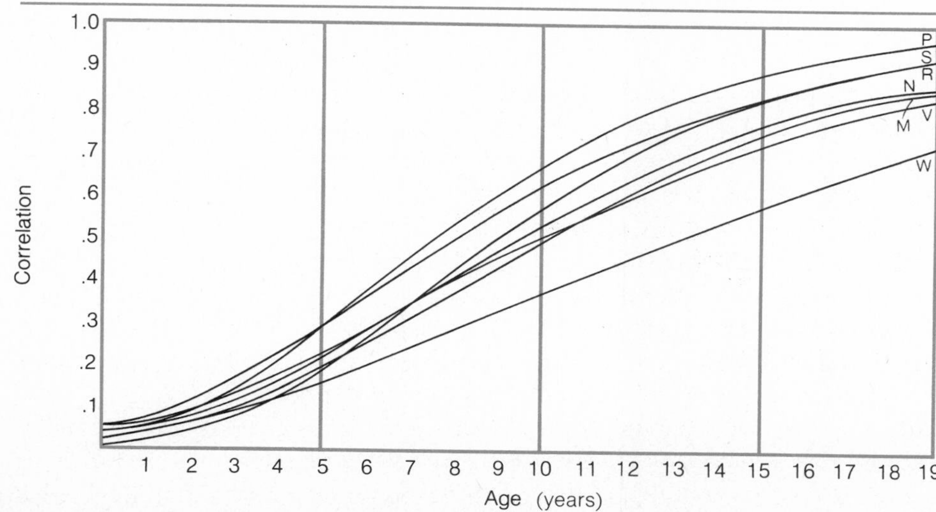

Fig. 4•19 Mental growth curves for seven primary mental abilities: perceptual speed (P), space relations (S), reasoning ability (R), numerical ability (N), immediate memory (M), verbal comprehension (V), and word fluency (W). In this scale Thurstone arbitrarily defined zero as that point where there is no longer any variation among subjects. (Thurstone, 1955)

Stanford-Binet for subjects from age two on.) Three factors emerged at successive stages of development: (1) initially, sensorimotor alertness; (2) for two- and three-year-olds, persistence; (3) sometime after age four and becoming more potent thereafter, a general intellective factor considered to be very much like Spearman's *g*. This finding is consistent with Sheldon White's position (1965) that human beings begin to demonstrate abstract reasoning abilities sometime during the age period from five to seven years.

Perhaps the most plausible model of intelligence was suggested by Phillip Vernon (1960). His model postulates a hierarchical ordering of traits or abilities, at the top of which is *g* (Figure 4•20). Derived from *g* are two major group factors that he considers to be a verbal-educational factor (v:ed) and a practical-mechanical factor (k:m). The v:ed factor consists of tests such as vocabulary, analogies, and reasoning and mathematical problems. The k:m factor might consist of tests of spatial relations and manual dexterity. The major factors divide into more numerous minor group factors, which are subdivisions of the major group factors. Vernon's model seems consistent with most of the data and incorporates the thinking of the major theoretical positions.

Identifying Deviant Development Although most developmental psychologists are primarily interested in normal development, their work has implications for the identification of deviant development. Data for identifying mentally retarded children have been compiled over many years as a result of the use of mental ability tests. More recently many theories have been formulated to explain the behavior of learning-disabled children—children who have difficulty learning but are not retarded. The work of the developmentalists with respect to perceptual-motor development has contributed to an understanding of the problems encountered by these children. We now believe that these children are not different in an absolute sense but rather that their development follows the normal course at a slower rate.

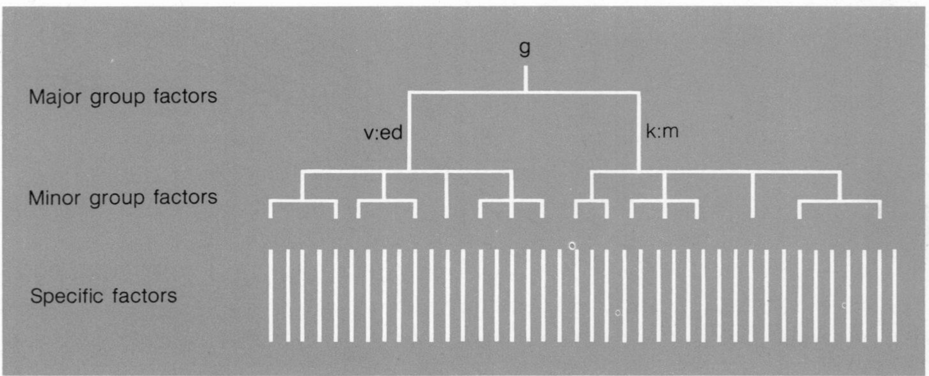

Fig. 4•20 Diagram illustrating hierarchical theory of human abilities. (From Vernon, 1960)

Genetics and Intelligence

4•5 Aptitude and intelligence tests are used to make very important decisions affecting human lives: whether to place a child in a school for normal children or for retarded children, or in a program for educable retarded children or for trainable retarded children; whether to place someone in an accelerated program in a public school or college; whether to admit an applicant to a university, graduate school, or professional school.

Perhaps more time, money, and research have been devoted to the assessment of mental ability than to any other area of psychology. Despite this research, IQ testing is under attack by groups concerned that the tests are a means of systematic discrimination against racial minorities. The content of the tests has been described as relevant to middle-class white people but insensitive to the experiences of other groups. Do IQ tests measure the innate mental ability of the individual? To what degree does environment affect performance on the tests?

Data Supporting a Genetic View A furor over the race issue was generated by Arthur Jensen (1969) in a monograph considering possible reasons for the presumed failure of compensatory educational programs, such as Project Head Start and Project Follow Through. Jensen cited evidence that, on the average, black children score approximately 15 IQ points lower than white children. Jensen interpreted IQ difference as being 80 percent attributable to genetic factors, leaving environmental variables only a negligible role. All of the research that Jensen cited, however, was conducted with middle-class white children. These data suggest that there is a strong genetic component influencing performance on IQ tests.

The major research findings related to the question of genetic endowment (nature) versus environmental variables (nurture) are summarized in Figure 4•21. When the IQ scores of randomly paired individuals are correlated, the median correlation is zero and there is only a slight difference as a function of being reared apart or reared together. Of particular importance is the comparison of monozygotic twins (who are genetically identical because they develop from a single fertilized egg) and dizygotic twins (who are no more similar than other siblings because they develop from two fertilized eggs). The median correlations for the monozygotic twins (approximately .78 and .90) are generally higher than for the dizygotic (fraternal) twins; the dizygotic twin correlations (approximately .50) are similar to those reported for siblings and for parent and child. This difference is generally taken to be the major evidence in support of genetic determination.

The major criticisms of these studies is that among twins one would ordinarily expect greater similarity of environment and therefore a greater similarity in performance on IQ tests. There is, in fact, some evidence to support that position; the median correlations for twins or siblings reared together are higher than for twins reared apart. Even in those situations where identical twins are reared apart, it should not be inferred that the environments of the twins are radically different. Because state laws and social work procedures try to match the families of the twins

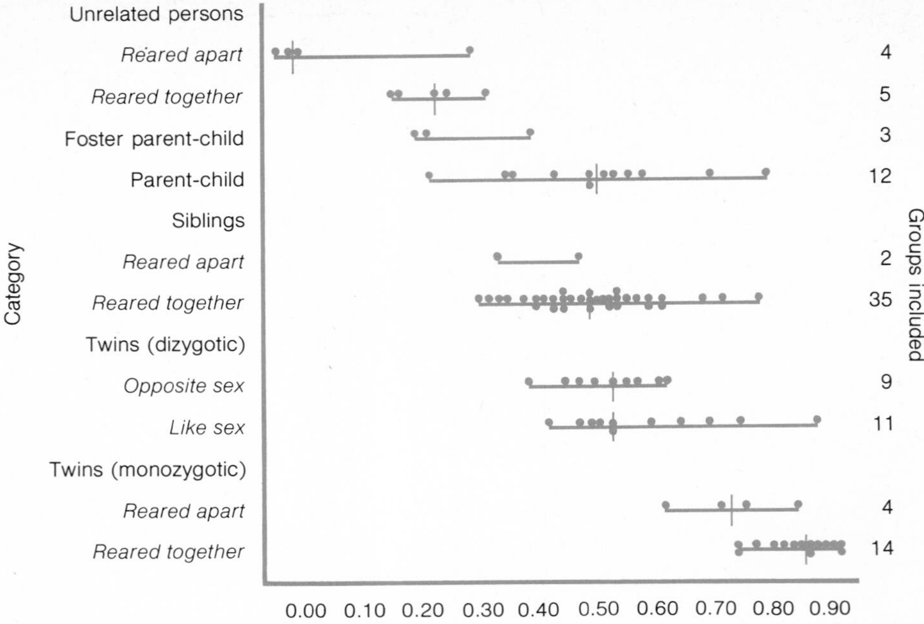

Fig. 4·21 Summary of major research findings on correlations of genetic-based and nongenetic-based pairings. The degree of relatedness between the pairs increases from top (unrelated persons) to bottom (monozygotic twins reared together). (From Erlenmeyer-Kimling and Jarvik, 1963)

as closely as possible, the data on twins reared apart may overestimate the contribution of genetics.

A second and more critical problem is that these studies were conducted with middle-class white children. The heritability estimates are applicable only to that population. When environment is held relatively constant, variation in IQ test performance is probably attributable to genetics. There is no evidence that the heritability estimates developed for middle-class white children apply to black children or that the environments of black children are as constant as those of the white middle classes.

Other methods for studying the nature-nurture question involve comparing foster parent-child and true parent-child correlations. In this method the environmental position predicts that the foster parent-child correlations should be higher than the true parent-child correlations. If the genetic position is correct, then one would expect the opposite. The data suggest that the correlations between the true parent and child are higher than between the foster parent and child (Honzik, 1957). But these results have been questioned by a series of extremely important studies by Marie Skodak and Harold Skeels (1949) and Skeels (1966). In 1949 these investigators followed up 100 adopted children and found that their IQs averaged approximately 20 points higher than those of their true mothers. This finding occurred even though the data, like that of Honzig, indicated a higher correlation between true parent and child than between foster parent and child.

These data demonstrate another principle: high correlations between sets of data do not necessarily mean that the differences between the means for the same set

Culture-fair Intelligence Tests

Not all children can be tested with the Stanford-Binet Intelligence Test or the Wechsler Intelligence Scale for Children. Some children do not understand the language used in these tests, some have a severe hearing loss, and for some the content is inappropriate or irrelevant. In these and other circumstances, various other tests can provide a more accurate estimate of the child's intellectual potential. These tests are said to be culture fair because they are designed to reduce the bias common to more culturally defined tests.

Originally developed by Florence Goodenough (1926), the Draw-a-Person test requires the child to draw a picture of a complete person. This test is presumed to be culture fair for all children except the visually handicapped, because most children have the opportunity to observe other people. In estimating intellectual ability from this measure, artistic ability is of no concern. The norms that have been developed for this test demonstrate that as children progress developmentally they are better able to represent human beings in two dimensions, and pay more attention to detail, proportion, and sex differentiation (Figure 4B·1).

Fig. 4B·1 Man and woman drawn by a retarded boy (*a*) and by a girl of high-average ability (*b*). (Harris, 1963)

of data are equivalent. Remember that correlations indicate the degree of relationship, or relative position, on two variables. A person can be very high on one variable compared to a norm group, and low on the second variable compared to a norm group but be the highest person on both variables within the sample group. These data strongly suggest that there is a genetic component to intellectual development but that it is quite susceptible to environmental variation—an implicit substantiation of the interaction hypothesis.

Data Supporting an Environmental View In Skeels's 1966 report, children who had been given special treatment in an orphanage were compared with a control group for whom no special arrangements had been made. There were 13 children in the experimental group and 12 children in the control group. The mean pretest IQ of the experimental group was 64. They were placed in the special program in the 1930s. The mean pretest IQ of the control group was 84. This group was identified after completion of the experiment from existing records at the orphanage.

The children in the experimental group were transferred from an orphanage nursery to an institution for the mentally retarded. The crucial feature of the treatment program was the fact that the other children in the wards were older, brighter girls. Only two babies were placed in each of these wards. This meant that each baby received attention from the thirty girls in addition to a head matron and her assistant. Skeels describes the situation as follows:

> The children received constant attention and were the recipients of gifts; they were taken on excursions and were exposed to special opportunities of all kinds. For example, it was the policy of the matron in charge of the girls' school division to single out certain children who she felt were in need of special individualization and to permit them to spend some time each day visiting her office. This furnished new experiences, such as being singled out, receiving special attention and affection, new play materials, additional language stimulation, and meeting other office callers. (Skeels, 1966).

The experimental environment was in stark contrast to the meager desolate environment of the orphanage.

Posttest comparisons were made over a period from 21 months to 53 months for the experimental group and from 20 months to 57 months for the control group. It was found that the experimental group gained approximately 31 points whereas the contrast group lost approximately 21 points. In the followup showing what happened to these children in adulthood, it is impressive to note that the subjects in the experimental group were living self-sufficient lives whereas the control-group subjects were almost uniformly dependent on society.

Summary

The term *cognition* refers to the process of knowing about the environment. From a structuralist point of view, the young infant is an active seeker of knowledge, rather than a passive organism. This assumption has been demonstrated by work on early perceptual preference of infants, on the orienting reflex, and on the process of habituation. Infants have a preference for slightly novel stimuli, rather than stimuli that are either very familiar or totally unknown to them.

The development of cognition requires that the child interact with various aspects of the environment. Research on motor development shows that the baby is born with a number of reflexes, such as the palmar or grasp reflex, which eventually are replaced by other responses. Such changes in reflexes, along with changes in the organization of motor responses, are signs of neuromuscular development, which in turn is related to the emergence of new cognitive representations of the world.

Experiments derived from stimulus-response (S-R) behavior theory demonstrate the infant's competencies with respect to sensory discrimination; for example, normal young infants have adequate visual, auditory, olfactory, and gustatory discriminations.

After the dramatic changes that occur in the first two years of life, changes during the next three years are somewhat less obvious. Research related to dimensional discrimination learning has demonstrated another series of changes in the qualitative performance of children that begins at approximately five years of age. White provides evidence for a transition during this period from an associate level of learning to a cognitive strategy.

Piaget believes that in order for cognitive development to occur, the organism must interact with the environment. He explains these interactions in terms of equilibration, accommodation, and assimilation. Piaget describes cognitive development in a series of four invariant stages: the sensorimotor period, the preoperational period, concrete operations period, and formal operations period.

The measurement of mental ability is related to varous concepts of intelligence, and tests have been designed consistent with these varying concepts. A test is considered reliable if the responses are consistent when the test is repeated. The validity of IQ tests has been questioned because, although they predict school performance at better than a chance level, there is a considerable degree of error. There is insufficient evidence to show how genetic and environmental factors affect the performance of individuals.

Suggested Readings

Bower, T. G. R. 1974. *Development in infancy.* San Francisco: W. H. Freeman.
Numerous innovative experiments are described demonstrating the importance of the psychological environment in early development. The coverage of perceptual development is especially interesting.

Ginsberg, H. 1972. *The myth of the deprived child.* Englewood Cliffs, N.J.: Prentice-Hall.

This paperback examines the public schools, IQ tests, and compensatory education programs to demonstrate how they contribute to the problems of lower-class children. A persuasive case is made for change in the system to accommodate all children.

Phillips, John L., Jr. 1975. *The origins of intellect.* 2d ed. San Francisco: W. H. Freeman.

A highly readable condensation of Piaget's theory of cognitive development. The stages are clearly described, and the supporting experiments are clearly illustrated.

Reese, H, and Lipsitt, L, eds. 1970. *Experimental child psychology.* New York: Academic Press.

A complete examination of the research literature on children from an experimental viewpoint. Each chapter is written by a scholar in a particular area.

Slobin, D. I., ed. 1971. *The ontogenesis of grammar.* New York: Academic Press.

This book covers the major theories of language acquisition.

Social Development

5 Suppose you are looking at forty babies through the window of a hospital nursery and that one of the babies belongs to you. Chances are you could not pick out your own child. Yet these babies will eventually become recognizably unique individuals in terms of intellectual capability and personal characteristics. They will vary in their attitudes and responses to themselves as persons and to the social demands of their environment. Even later in life, despite the biological and social potential for enormous variation in personal and social attributes, human beings show more similarities than differences in behavior. Psychologists must try to explain both the development of differences and the development of similarities.

This chapter examines factors associated with differences and similarities in behavior. How do parents respond to their children? How do child-rearing practices affect personality and behavior? How do children form moral judgments? How do biological differences affect the behavior of boys and girls? How do children learn the sex roles prescribed by society? What are the adjustment problems of adolescents? Why are peer relationships important? Is there a generation gap? The main consideration is the consequences of parental behaviors on the adaptiveness of children to the changing demands of society.

Parent-Child Relations

5·1 The attitudes and behaviors of parents toward their children have powerful effects in determining the child's social development, emotional development, and general personality characteristics. John B. Watson, the founder of behaviorism, asserted that with selective child-rearing practices, one could develop a physician, a lawyer, or a derelict. Others have raised serious questions about unidirectionality (the assumption that children are molded by their parents) and have stressed the significance of interaction between parent and child. Some have even suggested that the parent is molded by the child.

Attachment Behavior H. R. Schaffer and G. E. Emerson (1964) defined **attachment** as the tendency of the young to seek the proximity of other members of the species, particularly the mother. This behavior was identified through the naturalistic observations of John Bowlby (1958), 1969, 1973), who contends that attachment behavior has a biological basis in that it enables the young to survive.

Bowlby proposed five species-specific behaviors that increase the probability of survival. Clinging, sucking, and following provide contact maintenance for the infant, typically from the mother. Crying and smiling are instrumental in bringing adult members, again typically the mother, into contact with the infant. Initially, according to Bowlby, these behaviors are not directed toward the mother, but she is the one who responds. The behaviors then become integrated and focused on the mother and form the basis for attachment to her. Attachment develops as an active process on the part of the infant. Bowlby believes that attachment is more important than breast-feeding in preventing emotional disturbances:

> My impression in taking the histories of many children is that there is little if any relationship between form and degree of disturbance and whether or not the child has been breast-fed. The association which constantly impresses itself upon me is that between form and degree of disturbance and the extent to which the mother has permitted clinging and following, and all the behavior associated with them, or has refused them. In my experience a mother's acceptance of clinging and following is consistent with favorable development in the absence of breast-feeding, while rejection of clinging and following is apt to lead to emotional disturbance even in the presence of breast-feeding. (Bowlby, 1958, p. 370)

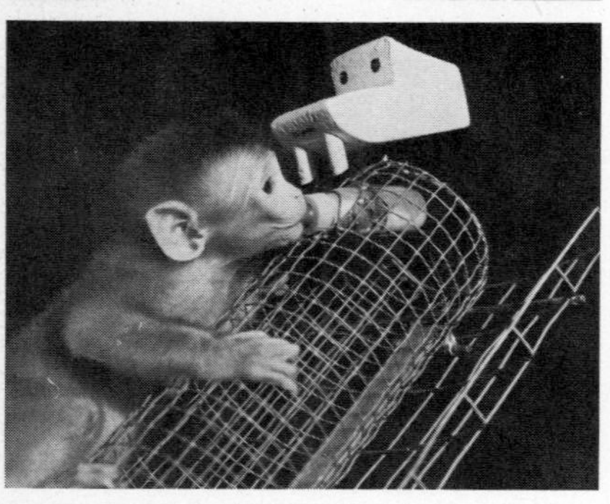

Cloth and wire surrogate mothers were used in Harlow's experiment on the nature of attachment in infant monkeys. (H. F. Harlow, University of Wisconsin Primate Laboratory)

Harlow's Monkey Experiments Attachment behavior was demonstrated in the now famous experiments of Harry Harlow on the development of love in infant monkeys (Harlow, 1959; Harlow and Harlow, 1966). Monkeys were raised with two types of artificial surrogate mothers: one made entirely of wire and the other made of wire with a terry cloth covering. Half of the monkeys were fed from the wire mother, and half from the cloth-covered mother. According to learning theory, each monkey should have formed an attachment to the mother by which it was fed. But the monkeys would stay with the wire surrogate mother only long enough to satisfy their hunger need. Otherwise it was clear that the wire-fed monkeys preferred to sit on, play with, and maintain contact with the cloth-covered mother. Those monkeys that were fed by the cloth-covered mother almost never made contact or spent time with the wire mother.

An experiment was designed to generate fear in the infant monkeys in order to observe their responses. A mechanical teddy bear that moved forward beating a drum caused uncontrollable fear in almost all the monkeys. The data

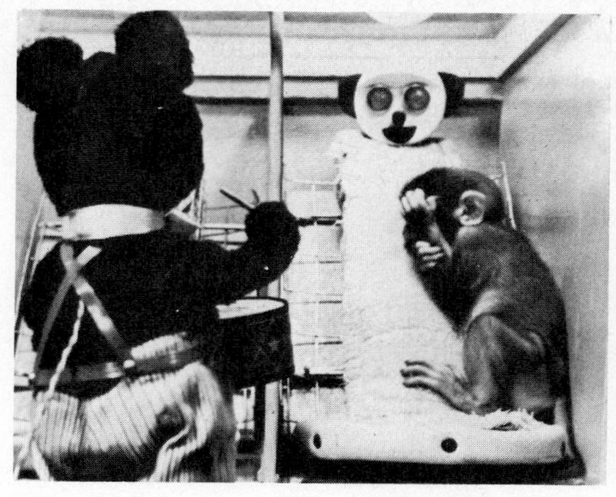

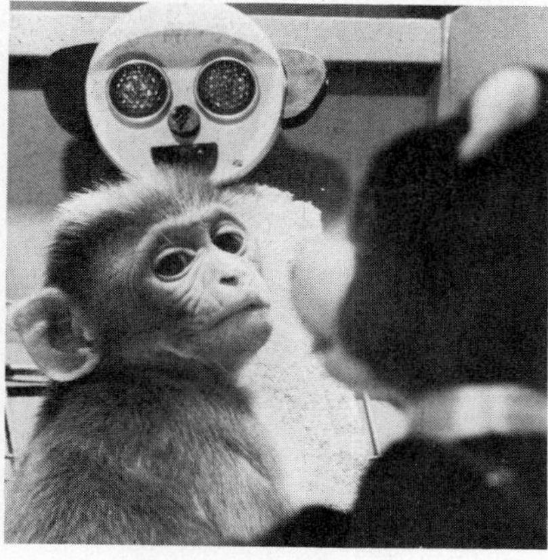

When a mechanical teddy bear was used to arouse fear in the monkeys, they would first cling to the cloth mother and then look at the strange object. (H. F. Harlow, University of Wisconsin Primate Laboratory)

demonstrate dramatically that regardless of which artificial mother had fed the monkeys, most of them sought protection from the cloth one (Figure 5•1).

In another test of the effects of being reared by the different mothers, the investigators placed the monkeys in a room far larger than their cages. This open field contained a number of unfamiliar objects, including a small artificial tree, a crumpled piece of paper, a folded gauze diaper, a wooden block, and a doorknob. The dependent variable was the degree to which the animal explored the room or showed fear by clinging to the surrogate mother's body. The results of this experiment show that the animals reared with the cloth mother evidenced little or no fear behavior when the cloth mother was present (Figure 5•2). Those reared with the wire mother were, on the contrary, quite fearful.

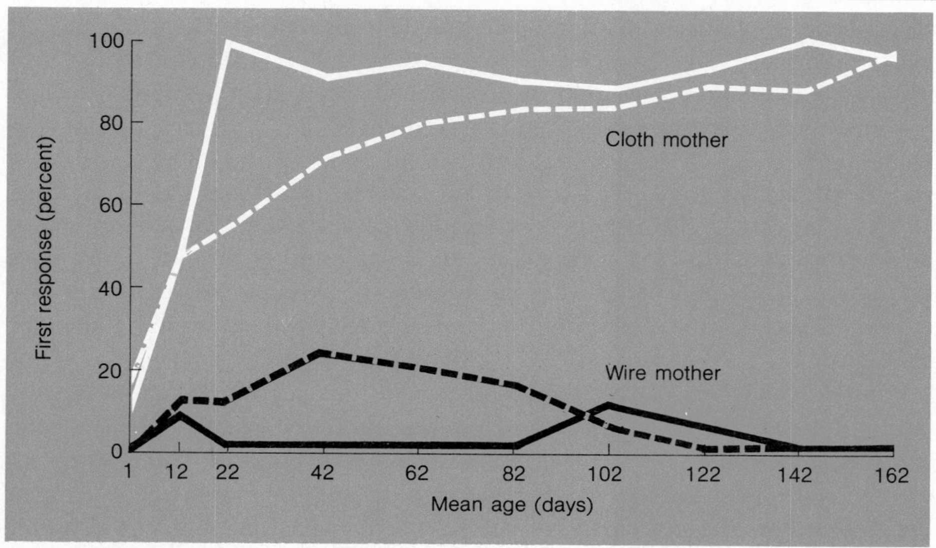

Fig. 5•1 When confronted by a strange object, even the infant monkeys who had been fed on the wire mother (broken lines) tended to seek reassurance from the cloth mother rather than from the wire mother. (Data from Harlow, 1959)

Fig. 5•2 In the open-field test, all infant monkeys familiar with the cloth mother were much less disturbed when she was present (color) than when no mother was present (white); scores under 2 indicate unfrightened behavior. Infants that had known only the wire mother were greatly disturbed, whether she was present (black) or not (white). (Data from Harlow, 1959)

In the open-field test, only the cloth-covered mother could give the monkeys confidence to explore the unfamiliar room. (H. F. Harlow, University of Wisconsin Primate Laboratory)

Even though Harlow and Harlow were working with monkeys and used laboratory procedures, their conclusions about their results are surprisingly similar to Bowlby's statement: "Above and beyond demonstration of the surprising importance of contact comfort as a prime requisite in the formation of the infant's love for its mother—and the discovery of the unimportant or nonexistent role of the breast and active nursing—our investigations have established a secure experimental approach to this realm of dramatic and subtle relationships" (Harlow, 1959).

Attachment Behavior in Human Infants In a longitudinal study, Schaffer and Emerson (1964) investigated the age of onset, the intensity, and the objects of attachments in human infants. Their sample consisted of 31 males and 29 females, ranging in age from 5 to 23 weeks. Each infant was followed up until the age of 18 months. Situations were designed to elicit attachment behavior: the infant was left alone in a room with strangers, in a carriage outside the house, in a carriage outside shops, in a crib at night; the infant was put down after being held in the adult's arms or lap; and the infant was passed by while in a crib or chair. When mothers were interviewed during regular home visits, investigators asked the following questions: What forms of protest, if any, does the infant display and under what circumstances? Does protest occur regularly or only at certain times? At whom is protest directed? How would you judge its intensity?

Prior to six months of age, the infants sought contact and attention equally from strangers and familiar people; they also protested equally when anyone left them. Protest occurred to a specific individual, typically the mother, increasingly after six months, peaking between 12 and 18 months. The data in Figure 5•3 show the percentage of the sample for which attachment behavior was elicited by four situations involving the loss of visually maintained contact. These are average scores, and there is considerable variation around these means.

In summarizing their results, Schaeffer and Emerson proposed three stages in the attachment process:

1. *Asocial stage*: The baby seeks optimal arousal indiscriminately from all aspects of its environment. This stage terminates at approximately seven months of age.
2. *Prosocial stage:* Begins when a single person is identified as a particularly satisfying attachment object. Approximately 65 percent of the subjects selected the mother. For the remainder of the infants, the father was likely to be the first attachment choice. During this phase the infant actively seeks out people for stimulation.
3. *Social stage*: Begins at about eight months of age and is characterized by an attachment to specific objects or persons. One might speculate that the child should protest much less about separation from familiar persons after 18 months of age, when object permanence has been established as a cognitive competence.

Mary Ainsworth and her colleagues used a laboratory setting to observe a series of planned mother-child separations and reunions and a sequence of behaviors involving the infant and a stranger (Table 5•1). Exploratory behaviors, proximity behaviors, contact-seeking behaviors, and contact-maintaining behaviors of the infants were recorded in a setting similar to Harlow's open-field situation. The 56 infants, 49 to 65 weeks old, actively played and explored when their mothers were present, but active behavior decreased dramatically when a stranger entered the room (episode 3). Before the mother left the room, contact seeking and maintaining were weak. Upon the first reunion (episode 5)

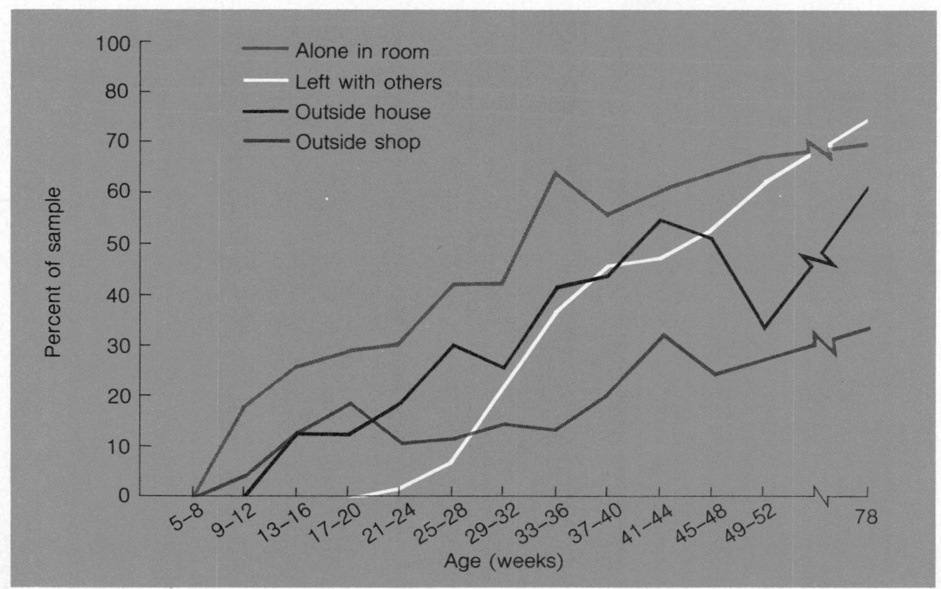

Fig. 5•3 Percentage of infants who obtained attachment scores in four situations where they lost visual contact with their mothers. (From Schaffer and Emerson, 1964)

Table 5·1 Design for Observing Attachment Behavior in Human Infants

EPISODE	TIME (MINUTES)
1. Mother carries baby into strange room, accompanied by an observer who leaves.	3
2. Mother places baby on floor, and then sits in a chair.	3
3. Stranger enters, sits quietly for one minute, talks with the mother for one minute, then slowly approaches the baby.	3
Three minutes later the mother leaves.	3
4. Stranger and baby are alone.	3
5. Mother returns and stranger leaves; mother and baby are alone.	3
6. Mother leaves; baby is alone.	3
7. Stranger returns; stranger and baby are alone.	3
8. Mother returns and stranger leaves; session terminates.	

contact maintaining was very high, and it increased even more during the second reunion (Ainsworth, Bell, and Slayton, 1971; Ainsworth and Wittig, 1969). These findings, along with reports by Schaffer and Emerson, and Harlow and Harlow, support the proposition that attachment behavior is a normal phenomenon occurring sometime after the sixth month and reaching its peak at approximately 12 months of age. Although data from other cultures is lacking, it seems that attachment behavior is normal for children everywhere.

Not all mothers are equally receptive or sensitive to the attachment needs of their children. Bowlby suggests that when the mother is not available or cannot provide fulfillment for the child's attachment needs, the child's social and emotional development may be impaired. In the extreme case, Bowlby believes **separation anxiety** eventually leads to withdrawal from the environment and produces an asocial human being who is mostly interested in material things. Bowlby's descriptions are based primarily on clinical cases.

Ainsworth noted considerable variation among the children in her study and attempted to explain these differences by classifying the children and their mothers into three groups:

1. Group A children showed very little desire for contact or proximity to the mother and very little reaction when she left the room or returned. Ainsworth described these women as openly rejecting mothers.
2. Group B children followed the typical attachment pattern. Mother-child interactions were the most satisfactory for this group.
3. Group C children reacted violently when separated from their mothers. Although these mothers were not openly rejecting, the mother-child interactions were not very harmonious, according to Ainsworth.

Bowlby (1973) suggests that the A and C children may well grow up with less self-reliance and trust of others than the infants in the B group.

The observations by Ainsworth and Bowlby, however, can be interpreted from another point of view: Possibly the behaviors of the A, B, and C mothers were in part caused by the children. Willard Hartup and J. Lempers (1973) state, "We would like to propose that attachment be recorded as characteristic of neither the mother nor the infant, but as a structural property of mother-child interaction." The need for more research is evident. With the exception of the clinical observation of Bowlby, there are no longitudinal studies demonstrating the long-term effects of variations in attachment behavior.

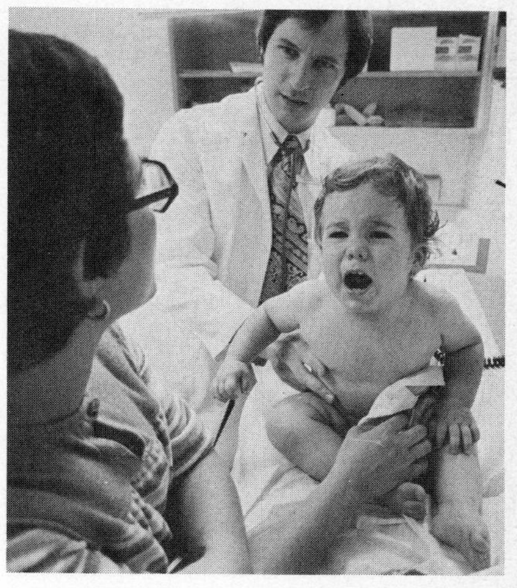

At the age of six to eight months, children typically begin to show anxiety over separation from their mothers. (Robert V. Eckert, Jr.)

Home Atmospheres The impact of parental behavior on infants has been recognized only recently, but there have been a number of important and well-conducted studies showing the relationships between parental behavior and the behavior of preschool and school children. Many studies have investigated the frequency and nature of disciplinary techniques ranging from physical punishment, threat of punishment, and withdrawal of privileges to the use of rewards for good behavior. Parents employ both positive and negative responses to their children's behavior, but in varying degrees. Discipline is only one of the features that affect the quality of parent-child interactions. Many studies concerned with the quality of interactions have attempted to rate the entire home atmosphere.

One method of rating parent behaviors and evaluating their effects on children can be illustrated by a major study by A. Baldwin, J. Kalhorn, and F. H. Breese (1945, 1949). This work was part of the Fels Research Institute program, and the observers used the Fels Parent Behavior Rating Scales, originally developed by H. Champney, 1941, consisting of thirty items:

1. Home adjustment
2. Home active
3. Home nondiscord
4. Family sociable
5. Coordination
6. Child-centered
7. Contact duration
8. Intense contact
9. Nonrestrictive
10. Nonenforcement
11. Nonseverity
12. Justification
13. Democracy
14. Clarity policy
15. Effectiveness
16. Nonfriction
17. Nonsuggestion
18. Noncoercive
19. Accelerational
20. Babying
21. Protectiveness
22. Noncriticism
23. Favorable criticism
24. Explanation
25. Solicitous
26. Acceptance
27. Understanding
28. Nonemotional
29. Affectionate
30. Rapport

When used by trained observers, these scales have high inter-observer agreement, and the description of the home environment on different occasions tends to be very stable.

On the basis of data obtained by using these scales, Baldwin and his co-workers identified three major home atmospheres: democratic, rejectant, and indulgent (Table 5•2). In democratic homes parents attempt to provide their children with information so that the children can learn to make their own decisions.

Table 5·2 Three Types of Home Environments

HOME ENVIRONMENT	PARENTS' PERSONALITY	ATTITUDE TOWARD CHILD	BEHAVIOR TOWARD CHILD	CHILD (AT SCHOOL AGE)
Democratic	Well-adjusted, vital, outgoing	Objective and yet warmly involved Patient, understanding	Enjoy child as a child and as an individual Allow child to participate in family decisions	Tends to be liked by peers May have talent for leadership and organization
Rejectant	Aggressive, dominant, self-centered	Want child to be quiet and unobtrusive Assume that child will do something irritating or contrary to home standards	Impose rigid standards of behavior Meet immediate situations with arbitrary demands	Stubbornly resistant to adult authority Confused about what behavior is acceptable
Indulgent	Narrow-minded, concerned about morals and social graces	See child as a new and more attractive version of self	Gratify any of child's wishes with which they can identify	Self-centered; manages parents

(From Baldwin, Kalhorn, and Breese, 1945)

In rejectant homes the parents use coercive or autocratic measures. Indulgent homes are characterized by permissiveness.

Because the Fels study is longitudinal, it was possible to examine the long-range effects of these three variations in child-rearing practices. The children from democratic homes were described by their preschool teachers as highly active, curious, and aggressive. Because many middle-class adults see aggressiveness as a negative trait, it is not surprising that children from democratic homes were viewed as below average in sociability and friendliness. Children in the rejectant group were generally regarded as normal, which means they were not aggressive or unduly active, but conformed to the wishes and expectations of their teachers. Apparently behaviors instilled in the home were reinforced at school and thus maintained. The children from indulgent homes were viewed as highly active and curious, but also as highly social and less aggressive than children from democratic homes.

Examination of the same children at school age reveals a very different picture. Children from democratic homes were rated, in general, as highly social and friendly with a maintenance of high curiosity but with more control over activity rates. The aggressiveness that seemed problematical in the preschool years is transformed into assertiveness, meaning that these children make their presence known and achieve their goals through what might be called socially accepted aggression. The children from rejectant homes are now regarded as quarrelsome, aggressive (in a negative sense), and less socially adaptive. The children from indulgent homes became more shy and less sociable, probably as a result of learning that their demands were not necessarily accepted outside the home. Thus we see a developmental picture showing the impact of three kinds of home atmospheres at two levels.

Three dimensions are necessary to describe parental behavior according to Becker (1964), who based his model on data from a wide range of studies, including the Fels studies: restrictiveness versus permissiveness, warmth versus hostility, and anxious-emotional involvement versus calm detachment. Becker defined these opposites in behavioral terms; for example, warmth is characterized by acceptance, approval, positive response to dependency behavior, high use of praise and discipline, and low use of physical punishment. Restrictiveness is defined by enforced demands for modesty, table manners, orderliness, toilet training, and control of noise and aggression (toward siblings, peers, and parents). Both the democratic and the indulgent parent are high on warmth and permissiveness (the upper right-hand quadrant of Figure 5•4), but the indulgent parent is also high on emotional involvement while the democratic parent is high on calm detachment.

One might speculate that the parent who is anxiously and emotionally involved with the child tries to protect the child from possible unpleasant events, and thus deprives the youngster of important learning experiences. With adults who are not emotionally involved, the child may not know how to respond. The calm, detached parent permits the child to make mistakes and to learn from them through the parent's use of explanation. Many research studies provide evidence for the psychological advantages of rearing children in a warm, democratic home atmosphere. This approach is seldom easy, however, because society is generally critical of permissiveness in child-rearing, and because many parents are not emotionally and intellectually prepared to rear children in this way. Parents who are more confortable with the authoritarian approach may revert to punitive behaviors at the first sign of distress. It is probably better

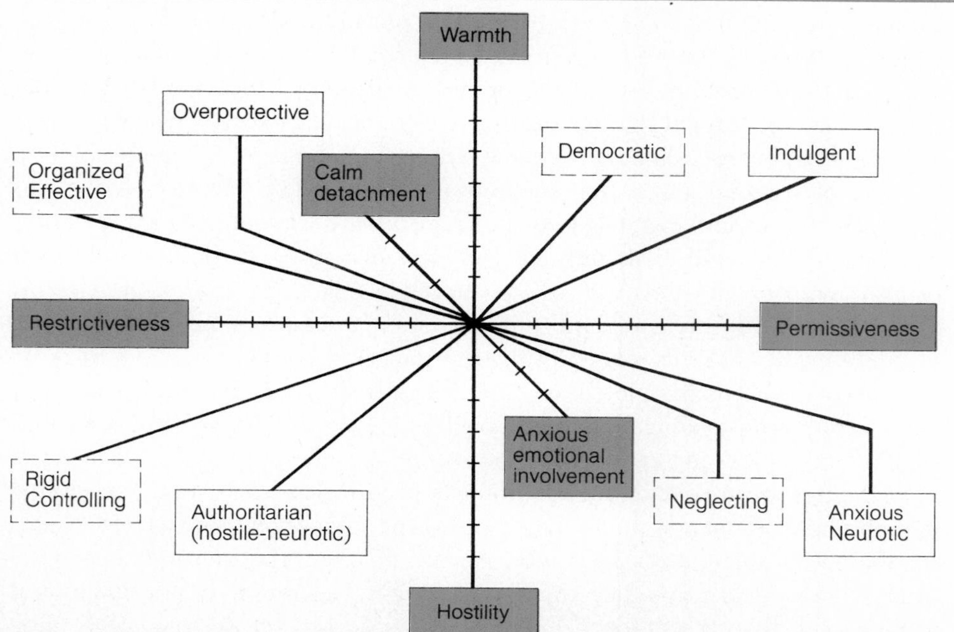

Fig. 5•4 Becker's hypothetical model for parental behavior. (From Becker, 1964)

Adults such as parents and teachers can make some learning experiences unpleasant when they assert their power. (Cary Wolinsky, Stock, Boston)

to be consistent in managing the child than to develop an artificial home atmosphere that is inconsistent with one's own values.

Punishment As a Disciplinary Technique Power assertion, love withdrawal, and induction are the three forms of punishment identified by M. L. Hoffman and H. D. Salzstein (1967), who tried to determine the effects of each form on child development. Power assertion is the use of physical punishment, withdrawal of privileges, or the threat of either of these. The parent is more powerful both physically and psychologically and uses this power to control the child's behavior. Psychologically, power assertion is similar to **avoidance conditioning**, in which the subject is taught to approach one stimulus by being punished for approaching a second stimulus, or is taught not to make any responses whatsoever. When punishment is used, parents rarely provide the children with an alternative response that is acceptable. Some evidence (Estes, 1944) suggests that punishment reduces the strength or the frequency of a response, but when the response has been weakened, the effects of punishment begin to fade. When these effects are extinguished, the punished response becomes stronger and may reappear. When a child forgoes an attractive activity viewed as dangerous by the parent, the use of punishment is not likely to be effective unless the parent provides an equally attractive alternative.

We have seen that children from rejectant homes where punishment is used frequently, exhibit conformity in the preschool years but aggression and resistance to authority during the school-age years. These children appear to be less socialized and less able to cope with social demands and expectations, possibly because they never learn for themselves what behaviors are appropriate in different situations. They are dependent on adult direction. Physical punishment is most effective in preventing transgressions when the adult is present, or when the probability of getting caught is high. In other words, the child learns "don't get caught" rather than an acceptable alternative behavior.

As a disciplinary technique, love withdrawal is defined as nonphysical expression of parental anger and disapproval of the child's behavior. Using this approach, the parent might ignore the child, isolate the child, or even express a dislike for the child. This technique induces fear through the implicit threat of abandonment and direct attack on the child's ego. Love withdrawal seems to generate guilt in the child and thus becomes a pervasive and continuing form of punishment. (The advantage of physical punishment, if there is one, may be that when the act is completed and the hurt subsides, the punishment is over.) Love withdrawal probably results in fewer transgressions on the part of the child, whether an adult is present or not—because guilt is always present.

In the third technique, induction, the parent provides explanations concerning appropriate and inappropriate behavior. Using induction, the parent might, for example, explain to a child why the use of physical aggression is inappropriate. Parents who spank their children use physical aggression to punish physical aggression. Unlike the other techniques, induction appears to be neither phys-

Teaching Styles and Socialization of Children

A considerable amount of research has been done on teacher-child interaction, especially teachers' use of praise and reproof and the variables that influence teachers' reactions to children.

Most teachers have been taught that reward is a more effective technique for changing behavior than is punishment. Nevertheless, the research evidence (Thompson, 1962) indicates that, from preschool through at least senior high school, the predominant form of evaluative feedback to children is verbal punishment. Teachers continue to use it, even though it does not change the children's behavior. Furthermore, verbal reproof is not given out equally. Many children are essentially ignored—they receive little reproof or praise. Less intelligent, lower achieving, and less well-adjusted children receive more reproof than do other children. Boys receive more reproof than girls. These data suggest that disruptive, threatening (to the teacher's integrity or success) behaviors are most likely to elicit negative behavior from the teacher.

Recently it has been argued that a teacher's behavior may result in a less intelligent child's continuing to perform at a low level. That is, knowing that a child has below-average ability, the teacher treats the child in such a way that success is almost impossible for the child to achieve. This phenomenon is known as a self-fulfilling prophecy. According to some studies, however, teachers can and do identify the less intelligent child without the aid of tests or the observations of other teachers. This evidence suggests that the child's behavior may itself be the major determinant of teacher behaviors and perceptions (Dusek, 1975).

ical nor emotional. Its effectiveness depends on the child's cognitive ability to understand the behavior required in specific situations. Induction becomes more effective as the child grows older and is able to formulate rules on the basis of parental explanations.

The Role of Fathers In a study by Marian Radke (1946) of disciplinary techniques, the children perceived their mothers as more influential authorities in their lives than their fathers. Although home-atmosphere data and punishment data primarily reflect the responsibility of the mother, it would be unwise to conclude that fathers have no effect on child-rearing practices and the consequent development of their offspring. Unfortunately, there is very little data available with which to assess the impact of the father, partly because fathers are more difficult to involve in research projects.

G. R. Bach (1946) compared the father fantasies of twenty children whose fathers were absent from home with the fantasies of twenty control children whose fathers were at home (Figure 5•5). One of the major findings is that the father-absent group portrayed their fathers as extremely affectionate, whereas the fantasies of the children whose fathers were present indicated more aggression. The data seem consistent with the hypothesis that fathers play a major role in the sex-role identification of both sons and daughters. Radke found that mothers tended to differentiate aggressive behavior in their sons and daughters to a lesser degree than fathers. Fathers permitted more aggression among their sons than among their daughters. Hoffman (1970) has suggested that "the father's role is

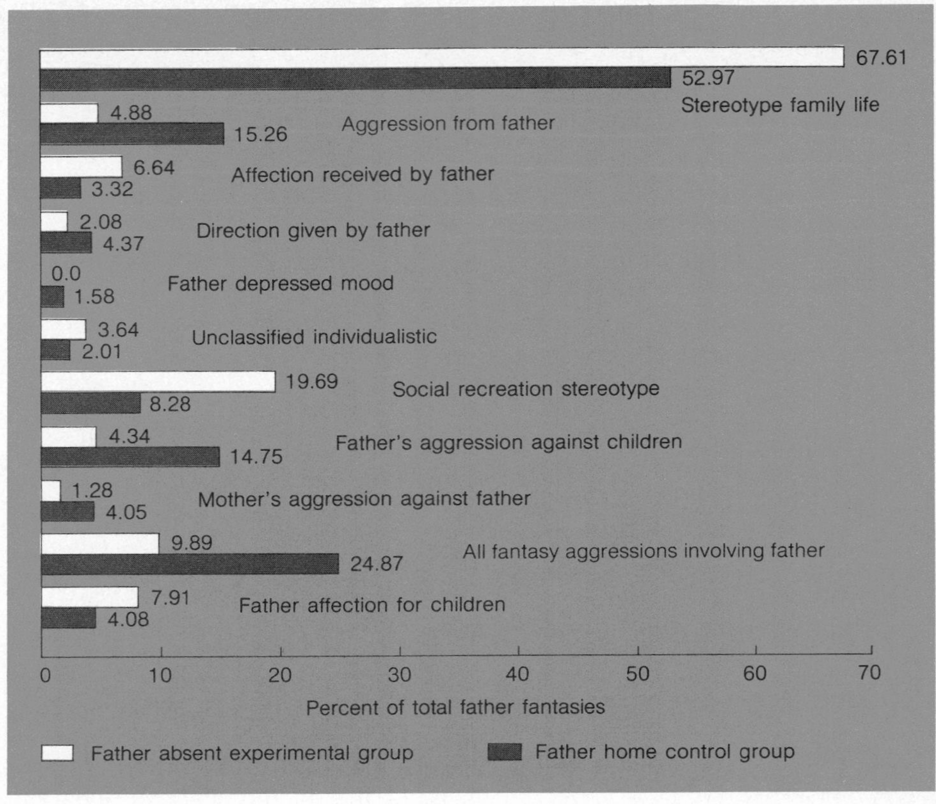

Fig. 5·5 The father fantasies of twenty children whose fathers were at home and of twenty children whose fathers were absent from home. Note the larger amounts of father aggression in the fantasies of the father-home group. (From Bach, 1946)

ordinarily latent in its effects and becomes manifest only under exceptional circumstances such as those often associated with delinquency. . . . the father's importance may lie mainly in providing an adequate role model that operates in the background as a necessary supporting factor."

The Role of the Infant Does the behavior of the parent cause the behavior of the child? The studies we have reviewed suggest that it does. But remember that correlations do not permit cause-and-effect interpretations; they only indicate the degree of relationship between sets of variables. It would be equally logical to infer that the parent's behavior is caused by the child's behavior. Parents react one way to an infant who smiles, coos, and sleeps soundly and another way to a baby whose irritability and sleeplessness disrupt routine. An outside observer would probably conclude that the fatigue and anxiety of the parents are the cause, rather than the result, of the baby's irritability. But as every parent knows, babies are not all alike. There is evidence that personality traits are inherited and that emotionality is one of these hereditary characteristics.

The degree to which emotionality is inherited was studied by H. Jost and L. W. Sontag (1944). The subjects included identical twins, fraternal twins, and random pairings of children. To measure emotionality, the investigators used the galvanic skin response (**GSR**) by measuring the perspiration level in the palm of the hand, which changes as a result of emotional reactivity. When various stimuli were presented to the children, there was a significant correlation in the reactions of identical twins. Similarities were substantially smaller among siblings, and there was no correlation whatsoever among unrelated pairs.

That maternal behavior is partly dictated by infant behavior was demonstrated by Howard Moss (1967), who found that male infants are more irritable than female infants, and consequently boys get more attention from their mothers (Table 5•3). Specifically, it seems that male babies are consistently more demand-

Table 5•3 Mean Frequency of Maternal and Infant Behavior at Three Weeks and Three Months

BEHAVIOR	THREE-WEEK OBSERVATION		THREE-MONTH OBSERVATION	
	Males ($N = 14$)	Females ($N = 15$)	Males ($N = 13$)	Females ($N = 12$)
Maternal variables				
Holds infant close	121.4	99.2	77.4	58.6
Holds infant distant	32.2	18.3	26.7	27.2
Total holds	131.3	105.5	86.9	73.4
Attends infant	61.7	44.2	93.0	81.8
Maternal contact (holds and attends)	171.1	134.5	158.8	133.8
Feeds infant	60.8	60.7	46.6	41.4
Stimulates feeding	10.1	14.0	1.6	3.6
Burps infant	39.0	25.9	20.9	15.3
Affectionate contact	19.9	15.9	32.8	22.7
Rocks infant	35.1	20.7	20.0	23.9
Stresses musculature	11.7	3.3	25.8	16.6
Stimulates/arouses infant	23.1	10.6	38.9	26.1
Imitates infant	1.9	2.9	5.3	7.6
Looks at infant	182.8	148.1	179.5	161.9
Talks to infant	104.1	82.2	117.5	116.1
Smiles at infant	23.2	18.6	45.9	46.4
Infant variables				
Cry	43.6	30.2	28.5	16.9
Fuss	65.7	44.0	59.0	36.0
Irritable (cry and fuss)	78.7	56.8	67.3	42.9
Awake active	79.6	55.1	115.8	85.6
Awake passive	190.0	138.6	257.8	241.1
Drowsy	74.3	74.7	27.8	11.1
Sleep	261.7	322.1	194.3	235.6
Supine	133.7	59.3	152.7	134.8
Eyes on mother	72.3	49.0	91.0	90.6
Vocalizes	152.3	179.3	207.2	207.4
Infant smiles	11.1	11.7	32.1	35.3
Mouths	36.8	30.6	61.2	116.2

(From Moss, 1967)

ing. They have higher frequencies of crying and fussing and are awake more of the time than females. Because the baby's cry instigates maternal intervention, crying behavior accounts in part for the structure of the mother-infant relationship. These conclusions are based on home observations of infants at three weeks and at three months of age, and the inter-rater reliability is high (.97).

It is possible that the highly irritable and demanding baby, whether male or female, is more likely to receive negative reactions from the mother than the baby who is nondisruptive and adaptive. In our culture, articles in popular magazines insist that the baby's behavior reflects the adequacy of mothering. A mother is admired when her baby is calm, adaptive, and generally well-behaved. The irritable baby probably represents a threat to the mother, especially when she is unable to mollify the child's demands. Consistent threat of this kind could eventually lead to hostile and rejecting behavior on the part of the mother as suggested in a study by Joy Osofosky and Edward O'Connell (1972) and in an earlier study by Barbara Merrill (1946).

Moral Behavior and Judgment

5·2 How do parent-child relationships and patterns of child-rearing affect the development of moral behavior? The term *moral behavior* is used here in its broadest meaning to include the acquisition and understanding of the rules that govern the behavior of people in any specific society. There are numerous conceptual models concerned with moral development, and each model has generated a large amount of research (Kohlberg, 1969, and Hoffman, 1970, 1975). We will present here the highlights of psychoanalytic theory, social learning theory, Piagetian theory, and in somewhat greater detail, Kohlberg's cognitive-developmental theory.

A useful theory of moral development must take into account two phenomena: (1) the number of social situations in which there is both an appropriate and an inappropriate behavior is probably infinite; and (2) most people obey the rules of their particular society even when the probability of being apprehended for minor transgressions is negligible. The first condition implies that it is impossible to expect children to learn the appropriate response to every situation that will confront them in the course of a lifetime. Yet most people are capable of making an appropriate response in a situation they have not previously experienced or observed. The second aspect of moral theories implies that people will behave in a moral and ethical manner even though they would be the only ones to know about their transgressions. The first instance questions how moral rules are learned, and the second is concerned with how moral behavior is sustained.

Psychoanalytic Theory In **psychoanalytic theory,** the rules for behaving morally are relegated to the conscience, or **superego,** of the individual. Freud said that human beings are born amoral, with no inhibitions against their pleasure-seeking impulses. At first the parents dominate the child's behavior by granting affection or by threatening punishment. In the normal course of development each child begins to play the role of the person he or she would like to be: a boy imitates his father, and a girl imitates her mother. While playing this make-believe role, Freud said, the child competes with the parent of the same sex for the affection and attention of the other parent. This competition is the so-called **Oedipal relationship** in the case of males, and the **Electra complex** in females. It leads to feelings of guilt and the fear of being punished by the same-sex parent.

To reduce the anxiety associated with the threat of physical harm from the same-sex parent, the child identifies with that parent and, through the mechanism of the superego, internalizes that parent's standards and values. If **identification** with the same-sex parent is satisfactory, the child will completely incorporate the rules of society as represented by that parent. What is left somewhat vague in this formulation is how identification occurs and whether the Oedipal (Electra) conflict must be postulated as the basis for identification and internalization.

Piagetian Theory Piaget (1932) was concerned with the child's development of a sense of justice and respect for the rules of society. In order to examine conformity to social rules, Piaget set up a contrived situation. He gave some children marbles and asked them how the game was played, whether new rules could be made up, and whether these rules could be fair. Responses to the question of fairness represented the children's understanding of the nature of rules (Flavell, 1963).

On the basis of this study, Piaget developed a stage theory of children's conformity and understanding of rules. Children begin playing marbles in what appears to be a haphazard fashion. At stage 4, which coincides with formal operations, children are able either to alter rules to fit unique situations or to invent new rules to cover special circumstances.

The development of a sense of justice was investigated by telling children stories about persons who engaged in various wrongdoings. The children were then asked why the acts were wrong, or which of two acts was more wrong, and why they thought so (the moral dilemma). For example, children were asked which of two girls was guiltier: one who stole a roll to give to a poor, hungry friend, or one who stole a (less costly) ribbon for herself. Piaget derived a number of these situations from his analyses of the children's responses. He found that they used retributive justice in two ways. Younger children employed what Piaget called expiatory punishment, the punishment that fits the crime; that is, the severity of punishment should be in proportion to the seriousness of the offense. Older children employed what Piaget called punishment by reciprocity, which is the demonstration of the consequences of an act through punishment logically related to the misdeed. An example from Flavell (1963) may clarify this concept. Suppose a child fails to bring food home from the supermarket after being requested to do so. Reducing the size of the child's meal or refusing to do a favor for the child would be examples of punishment by reciprocity, the former because there is now less food available, and the latter because the child refused to do a favor.

When Piaget published his theory of the emergence of moral judgment in 1932, he described two broad stages of moral development. In the first stage, which he termed the *morality of constraint* or moral realism, children obey rules because rules are rigid and unalterable. Behavior is either right or wrong: people will be punished for their misdeeds (he termed this *imminent justice*). The second stage Piaget labeled *morality of cooperation* or reciprocity. At this level of development children regard rules as being relative, or without absolute rights and wrongs. Furthermore, their concept of justice includes considerations of intentionality, and following moral rules is considered essential to the successful functioning of society. Finally, in this stage punishment is viewed as a reciprocal action on the part of society.

Hoffman (1970) expanded on Piaget's theme that emerging concepts of morality depend to a large degree on peer interactions, as opposed to parent-child interactions. Hoffman argues that by sharing in decision making with peers, children gain confidence in their ability to apply rules to different situations and to make decisions about altering rules. The rules can then be viewed as the result of agreement and cooperation between individuals sharing a common goal. Through peer interactions, children become aware that their thoughts and feelings are similar to those of their peers and therefore reciprocal. In this way everyone realizes that rules can benefit the entire group. Because of the reciprocal nature of these interactions, children learn a great deal about how to live in a rule-governed society.

Adult-child interactions, which tend to be one-sided or authoritative, prevent the child from testing alternatives in a neutral, nonpunitive setting. Perhaps children from democratic home atmospheres are more sociable and more adaptive to new situations because in those homes the quality of interactions between child and parent are more reciprocal than authoritative. Under those conditions, children may feel more comfortable in testing their ideas in spite of the risk of failure.

Kohlberg's Theory A conception of moral development that follows the principles of Piaget and bridges the areas of cognition and socialization is found in the work of Lawrence Kohlberg (1963, 1964, 1969). Kohlberg is not particularly interested in the content of moral responses, nor with variation in moral behavior. He begins with the assumption that children have a morality that is distinct and different from adult morality and sets as his objective an understanding of the psychological processes underlying moral judgments at each of several developmental stages.

Kohlberg's stage model of moral development was based on interviews with a large number of boys and girls ranging from six to sixteen years of age. During the interviews the children heard ten stories, each posing a moral dilemma. The following stories are representative:

1. Joe's father promised he could go to camp if he earned the $50 for it, then changed his mind and said Joe could go to camp if he gave him the money

he had earned. Joe lied and said he had earned $10, not $50, then went to camp using the other $40 he had made. Before he went, he told his younger brother Alex about the money and about lying to their father. Should Alex have told their father?

2. In Europe a woman was near death from a rare form of cancer. There was one drug that doctors thought might save her. It was a form of radium that a druggist in the same town had recently discovered. The drug was expensive to make, but the druggist was charging ten times what the drug cost him to make. He paid $200 for the radium and charged $2000 for a small dose of the drug. The sick woman's husband, Heinz, went to everyone he knew to borrow money, but he could get together only about $1000. He told the druggist that his wife was dying and asked him to sell the drug cheaper or let him pay later. But the druggist said: "No, I discovered the drug, and I'm going to make money from it." So Heinz got desperate and broke into the man's store to steal the drug for his wife. Should the husband have done that?

Kohlberg was not particularly interested in the children's yes or no, but rather in their reasoning for each response they gave. Using some thirty aspects of morality, Kohlberg was able to fit these responses into three levels of moral development, with each level divided into two stages (Table 5•4).

The Premoral Level At the premoral level of development, good and bad or right and wrong are determined by authority figures. Children anticipate the physical consequences resulting from their actions and obey rules in order to gain rewards and avoid punishments.

In stage 1, the child's fear of punishment results in complete deference to the attitudes and values of the authority figure. A concept of manipulative self-serving emerges in stage 2 from an immature reciprocity based on "You do favors for me and I'll do favors for you." Reciprocity is not yet based on justice.

Table 5•4 Kohlberg's Levels and Stages of Moral Development

LEVEL	STAGE
I Premoral	**1.** Punishment and obedience orientation
	2. Naive instrumental hedonism
II Conventional role conformity	**3.** Good-child morality of maintaining good relations, approval of others
	4. Authority-maintaining morality
III Self-accepted moral principles	**5.** Morality of contract, of individual rights, and of democratically accepted law
	6. Morality of individual principles of conscience

(Kohlberg, 1964)

Conventional Role Conformity At the second level, conventional role conformity, children begin to incorporate the rules of others and respect their judgment. The child is not yet independent from the values of immediate authority figures; behavior is guided by anticipated praise or blame. But there is also evidence that the immediate consequences (praise and blame) are becoming less important than the desire to maintain the accepted social order and live up to the expectations of others.

Stage 3 is composed of a sort of good-child morality—good and bad are defined by what pleases others. While conforming to cultural stereotypes, the child begins to judge the behavior of others by considering intentions as well as actions. Stage 4 is a law-and-order orientation, characterized by a respect for authority and a motive to maintain the social order for its own sake. Physical consequences appear to play a less important role at this stage than in the previous stages.

Self-accepted Moral Principles At the third level, self-accepted moral principles, children begin to define morality in a more individualistic way. They are moving away from the authority of unspecified social groups and from identification with any particular group or authority figure. Children now recognize the possibility of conflict between several socially accepted standards.

Stage 5 emphasizes a legalistic viewpoint. Morality is defined in terms of mutually agreed-upon standards of conduct. These young people know that laws are formed on a rational basis and can, therefore, be changed to fit fluid social situations. Along with increased development of one's personal moral code, there is an understanding that morality is relative, and conflict between personal opinions can be resolved by means of a set of agreed-upon procedures. In stage 6 moral judgments and explanations are governed by a set of abstract universal ethical principles. The universal principles of justice, equality, and human rights govern individuals in their day-to-day affairs.

Kohlberg uses the term *universal* in describing stage 6 because he believes that all children can attain this level of moral development. Failure of a child to attain the highest stage can be explained in terms of environmental variations. The development of morality requires the interaction of the child in an environment that supplies appropriate information. As the child attains each new stage, the preceding stage is displaced in the same progression that occurs in the development of cognition. The child shows evidence of some aspect of a more advanced stage and will occasionally evidence judgments from a preceding stage. Perhaps the following quote from Kohlberg (1964) best summarizes his position:

> Such an interpretation of the direction of development of moral judgment implies that development is in many ways the same, regardless of the child's nation (in Western culture), social class, peer group, or sex. While such a belief flies in the face of prevalent notions of limited cultural relativism, it is somewhat supported by empirical evidence.

The Research Evidence On the question of universality, Kohlberg (1969) has reported data for ten-, thirteen-, and sixteen-year-olds in the United States,

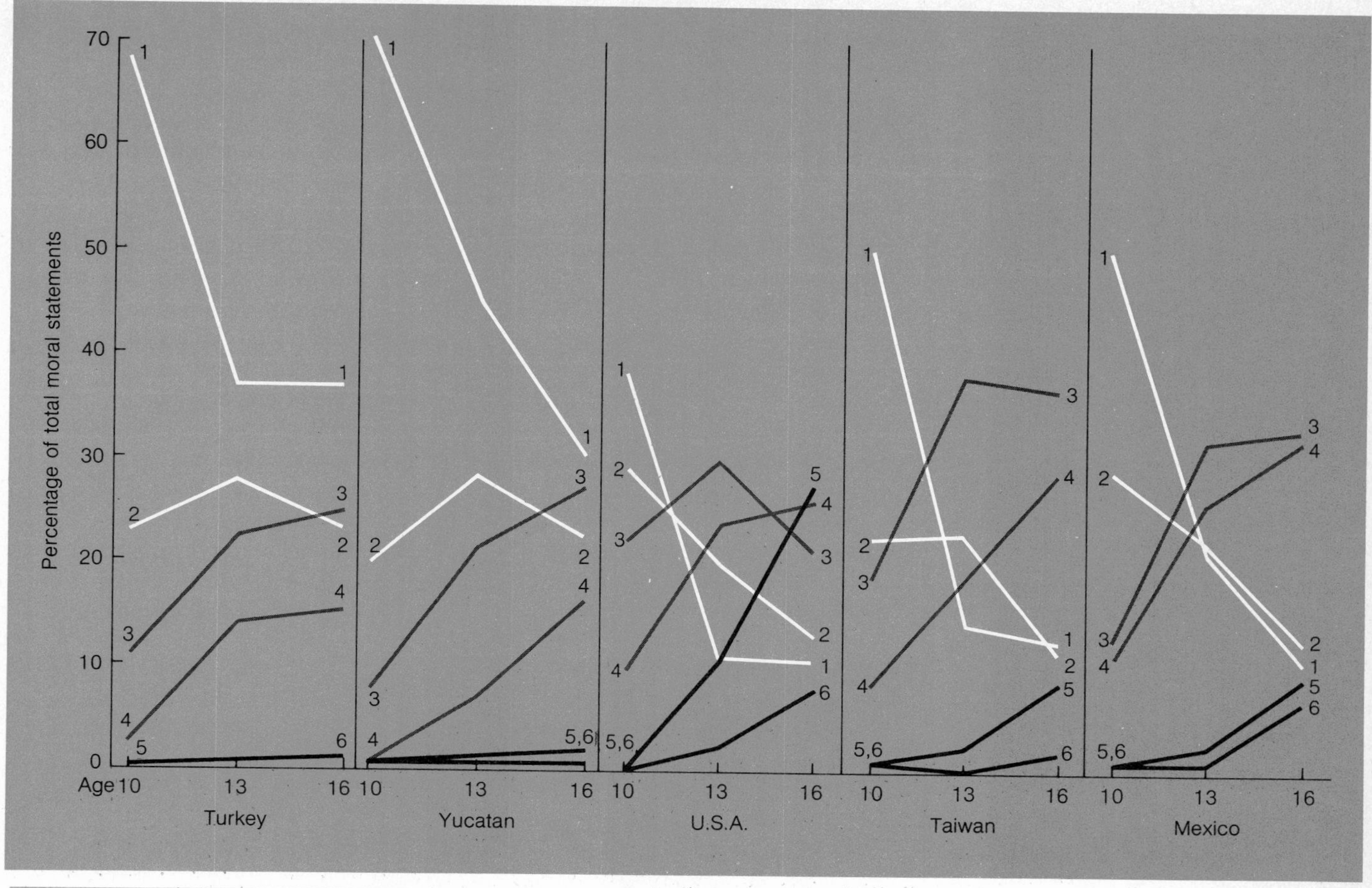

Taiwan, Mexico, Turkey, and the Yucatan. He has also studied seven other cultures. Percentages of moral statements made by the children at each of the three age levels within each of the five cultures were plotted for the six stages (Figure 5•6). At age ten in each of the cultures, the order of stages is entirely consistent with the hypothesized order (Table 5•4). Among the children in the United States, the developmental trend is toward the increasing use of judgments based on stages 3, 4, and 5 with a relatively infrequent use of stage 6. In the other cultures, stages 5 and 6 are not used very often, suggesting that either the cultures do not provide environmental input for the development of these stages or that the children in these cultures simply develop more slowly than do children in the United States.

Fig. 5•6 Age trends in moral judgment in isolated village boys in Turkey and Yucatan and middle-class urban boys in the United States, Taiwan, and Mexico. In general, the percentage of total moral statements at the premoral level (stages 1 and 2) declines with age in each of the five countries, whereas the percentage at the level of conventional role conformity (stages 3 and 4) increases. The increases at the level of self-accepted moral principles (stages 5 and 6), however, are much more pronounced among the middle-class urban boys. (Kohlberg, 1969)

Two of Kohlberg's hypotheses are supported by data from the experiments of E. Turiel (Turiel, 1966; Turiel and Rothman, 1972):

1. An individual can assimilate concepts one stage above his current level of functioning more readily than concepts two stages above. Apparently, moral development progresses in successive stages, and the skipping of stages is unlikely.

Children's Fears

The behaviorist John B. Watson thought that (1) children are born with three primary emotions—fear, rage, and love; (2) specific stimuli elicit each of these emotions; and (3) each emotion has a characteristic response pattern. Subsequent research failed to substantiate Watson's assertions and generated a very different theory. Essentially, infants are now viewed as possessing the physiology necessary for a broad range of emotional reactions. At birth, emotional reactions are diffuse and cannot be distinguished from each other. No one stimulus is consistently responsible for a particular emotional response; any stimulus can have either a calming or an upsetting effect. As the infant matures, emotional behaviors become more specific and identifiable. Two of the earliest emotions that differentiate are fear and anger. More subtle emotions emerge with further learning.

Fears develop in two ways: through conditioning and through cognition. Conditioned fears usually occur first by accident, as when a child accidentally touches a hot stove and then becomes afraid to touch the stove at all. Similarly, a child who is accidentally knocked down by a dog may avoid all dogs for fear of being hurt again. These are direct forms of conditioning. Conditioned fear responses can also occur indirectly. In a famous study conducted by Watson with an eleven-month-old boy named Albert, a steel bar was struck just as Albert touched a white rat. Previously, Albert had not shown any fear of the rat, but he did not like the loud noise. After the noise was regularly combined with touching the rat, Albert exhibited extreme fear of rats. Furthermore, the original conditioning situation generalized to a broad variety of similar stimuli—including a white rabbit, a fur coat, and the experimenter's hair.

Conditioning, however, cannot account for all fears. Several experiments have shown that fears can also develop through cognition. D. O. Hebb (1949) conducted an experiment in which chimpanzees of different ages, from infancy through maturity, were shown models of chimpanzee heads separated from their bodies. The young infants showed little if any agitation to the stimulus, the middle group showed distinct agitation, and the mature group was clearly in panic. On the basis of these results, Hebb suggested that novel objects generate fear but not at all age levels; the animal must be sufficiently mature to recognize the incongruity of the stimulus.

The same pattern emerges with human fears. A. Jersild (1954) found that over time some fears that children have increase whereas

2. Each new stage represents a reorganization of preceding stages, rather than a simple addition to the preceding stage. The reorganization does not, however, prevent children from occasionally accepting rationalizations at a lower stage than their current level of functioning.

The Turiel and Rothman study is one of the few that attempted to demonstrate a relationship between behavior and the level of moral reasoning. These experimenters found a relationship at stage 4 but not at stages 2 and 3. From a developmental view, there may be a progressive integration of reasoning and behavior. Through social-learning techniques, Turiel and Rothman were able to change the level of moral reasoning used by children in the immediate situation, but the changes were not maintained. This finding suggests that although the effects of imitation can be demonstrated in the laboratory, the child's level of moral reasoning may remain unchanged. Perhaps these social-learning studies modified behavioral choices rather than the cognitive processes postulated by Kohlberg to underlie moral reasoning.

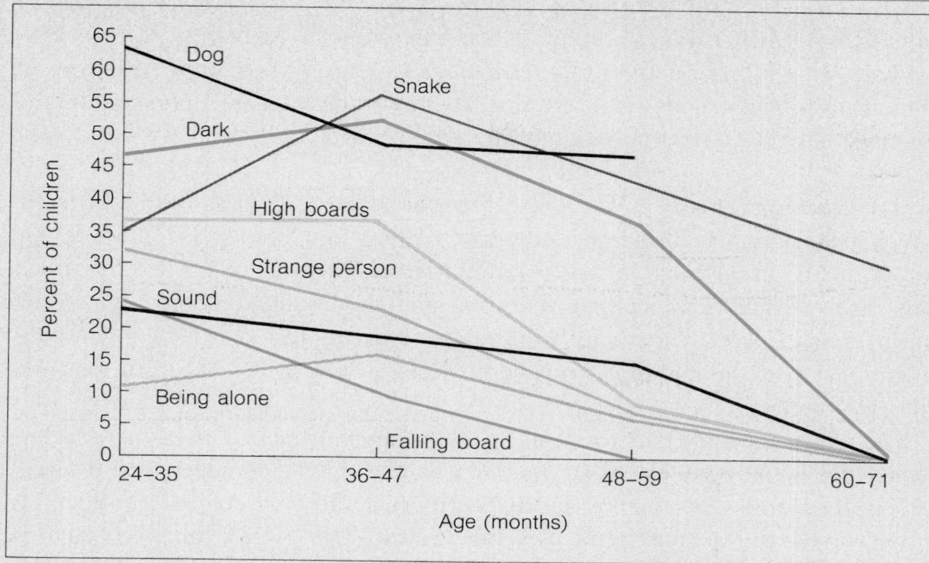

Fig. 5A·1 The percentage of children at various age levels who showed fear in response to several experimental situations designed to induce a fearful response. (From Jersild, 1954)

others decline (Figure 5A·1). Fears of snakes, for example, increase until around ages three to four and decline thereafter. To explain these age trends in terms of conditioning would require too many assumptions about environmental events, such as types of movies or television programs seen. Data such as these can be explained, however, in terms of cognitive development.

J. P. Zubek and P. A. Solberg (1954) summarized the existing literature on age differences in three types of fear: fears of concrete events (animals, falling, accidents), personal inadequacies (personal failure, loss of friends or property), and imaginative fears (supernatural events). The data indicate that 80 percent of fears up to eight years of age are concrete. These fears decline between ages eight and twelve to roughly 50 percent and remain at that level throughout adulthood. Fears of personal inadequacies, which are almost totally absent prior to twelve years of age, show a large increase after that age and continue to increase into adulthood, especially among males. Imaginative fears are infrequent prior to age five but show an increase between five and twelve years of age, declining sharply during adolescence and continuing to decline during adulthood.

Kohlberg (1969) has argued that his stages of moral development are more highly related to chronological age than to Piaget's stages of cognitive development. But the parallels in the cognitive and moral theories have been demonstrated by Lee Lee (1971), who studied 195 middle-class boys, 15 from each class from kindergarten through twelfth grade (ages 5½ to 17 years). Lee first determined the stage of cognitive development of each child by administering Piaget's series of conceptual tasks. Lee then administered Kohlberg's levels of moral reasoning. Cognitive level, independent of age, correlated highly with level of moral reasoning. A child who demonstrated concrete operational thought, for example, was more likely to demonstrate level 4 moral reasoning. Thus, the ability to employ increasingly abstract modes of moral reasoning is related to the ability to handle abstraction in other behavioral domains.

Kohlberg's model of moral development is not universally accepted. His claim that the model applies to all cultures has been criticized because the data are derived from only twelve cultures, and because the conceptual framework, measurement techniques, or scoring procedures may have been unsuitable in cultures with different requirements for thinking and problem solving. Kohlberg himself contends that morality is culturally defined; that is, morality develops through the interaction of the child and the particular environment. At present there is little evidence that scores on the moral judgment scale are reflected in behavior. Although Kohlberg's model is interesting, its importance to our understanding of morality has yet to be amply demonstrated.

Social Learning Theory According to **social learning theory,** the child learns which behaviors are considered moral or correct by experiencing rewards and punishments, by instruction, and by imitating the actions of others. Identification is a continuing process of acquiring and modifying responses as a result of direct and indirect experience with parents and other models. The moral judgments that begin in childhood can be modified at any age by intervention from the environment.

The major contributions to social learning theory as related to moral development have been made by Albert Bandura (1969a, 1969b; Bandura and Walters, 1963). Bandura's approach is behavioristic and therefore places considerable emphasis on the general principles that govern the acquisition of behaviors. Through observation, the child not only learns most social behaviors but also acquires behaviors indicative of identification with a model.

Response facilitation occurs when the child sees the model perform a positive act, such as helping others. When this occurs, children typically show a higher incidence of helpful behaviors. Apparently children have an understanding of appropriate and inappropriate behavior but require a releaser stimulus to perform positive behaviors. In the case of negative behaviors, children need to observe the consequences before deciding on a course of action.

Several experiments have demonstrated the inhibition effect that a model can have on behavior: children who observed peers being punished for playing with toys intended for others displayed fewer approach responses to those toys. Chil-

According to social learning theory, a child's imitation of the behavior of others has important effects on moral development and sex-role learning. (Jeffrey Blankfort, BBM Associates)

dren who did not observe their peers being punished played freely with the toys (Parke and Walters, 1967; Walters, Parke, and Cane, 1965; Walters, Leat, and Mezei, 1963). Bandura (1965) designed a situation in which an adult model was either rewarded or ignored for aggressive behavior in a controlled laboratory situation. More aggressive behavior was later demonstrated by children who saw the model rewarded. This study is an example of the disinhibition effect that a model can have on behavior.

The degree to which behavior will be modeled is a function of the characteristics of the child, the model, and incentive conditions. If the model is of the same sex as the child and is perceived as a positive person, more imitation will occur. Imitation is also more likely to occur when the child is offered incentives (such as candy) for behaving like the model.

Social learning theory does not account for the age-related trend in the level of moral judgments that is reflected by Kohlberg's data. A strict interpretation of the imitation position suggests that children's moral judgments should be comparable to those of their models, regardless of age. In addition, imitation theory does not provide an explanation for the changes that occur in the levels of children's moral judgments. Despite these problems, Bandura has provided excellent data on the variables that influence the moral behaviors of children. What is needed now is a model that blends the behavioral and cognitive aspects of moral development.

Sex-role Learning

5·3 Sex-role stereotypes are a subject of much debate today because of the secondary position given to women in our culture. At an early age most children hear injunctions such as "Boys don't play with dolls" or "Girls don't fight." Researchers have attempted to learn whether nurturance (represented by doll play) and aggression (represented by fighting) are related to biological variables, such as sex hormones, or whether these and many other assumed sex differences are culturally derived.

Sex-role learning starts when children, usually before the age of four, identify themselves as either boys or girls and learn that their gender is constant (the concept of *gender constancy*). The child then recognizes other members of the same sex and begins to observe their behavior.

Both the psychoanalytic psychologists and the social learning theorists stress imitation as important to sex-role learning. According to social learning theory, boys imitate their fathers and other males, girls imitate their mothers and other females. Both sexes copy peer models as well as adults. When children are rewarded for copying sex-appropriate behaviors, the behaviors are reinforced. Sex-inappropriate behaviors are punished and thereby extinguished. To Freud's followers, however, imitation is just one step toward identification; along with the formation of the superego, sex-role identity emerges when the Oedipus (Electra) complex is resolved.

One of the beliefs about sex differences that is unsupported by experimental data is that girls are more social than boys. (Michelle Vignes, BBM Associates)

We will examine the evidence with respect to sex differences and attempt to find out how **sex-role typing** occurs. In seeking to answer the question "How do males and females come to view themselves, to behave, and to feel in certain ways that are defined by their culture?" We will emphasize the cognitive-developmental view.

The Sex Hormones and Behavior The sex hormones are hormones that have some bearing on sexual development and function. Those that are more abundantly produced by the male are androgens, and those that are more abundantly produced by the female are estrogens. The male hormone has the effect of masculinizing the growing individual of either sex. Genetic females of many species when given high levels of androgens become masculinized both physically and behaviorally. When *testosterone* (a male hormone) is injected into female rats, there is an increase in their fighting behavior in adulthood. Studies of highly aggressive male animals indicate that they have higher levels of androgen than less aggressive males. Conversely, when abnormal levels of female hormones are present in genetic males, their behavior is characterized by lower aggression and passivity. Thus the experimental evidence at the animal level (Beach, 1958) and the evidence at the human level (Money and Ehrhardt, 1972) indicate that sex hormones have consistent and specifiable effects on behavior.

Sex Differences in Behavior Eleanor Maccoby, in her monumental review of the literature on sex differences, provides nineteen summary points. She classified these differences as unfounded beliefs, fairly well established differences, and ambiguous findings. The unfounded beliefs about sex differences include the following:

1. *Girls are more social than boys.* The data indicate that the sexes are equally interested in social interactions and that they are equally motivated by social rewards to achieve. There appear to be no differences in terms of empathy. Boys and girls spend approximately the same amount of time interacting with their playmates.
2. *Girls are more suggestible than boys.* On such measures as spontaneous imitation, susceptibility to peer pressure, and susceptibility to other social influence situations, there appear to be no sex differences.
3. *Girls have lower self-esteem.* There are no data to support this position in either childhood or in adolescence. Little or no information exists for adulthood. The only sex differences in self-esteem are that girls have greater self-confidence in the area of social competency, and boys more confidently view themselves as strong, powerful, dominant, and potent.
4. *Girls are better at rote learning and simple repetitive tasks. Boys are better at tasks that require higher-level cognitive processing and the inhibition of previously learned responses.* Negative evidence was derived when girls and boys performed tasks involving simple **conditioning, paired-associate learning, discrimination learning,** and **reversal shift.**

5. *Girls are less analytic.* On a broad variety of perceptual-cognitive tasks, there are no consistent sex differences in problem solving.
6. *Girls are more affected by heredity, boys by environment.* If there is any tendency in the data, it is in fact in the opposite direction. Male identical twins are more alike than female identical twins, but both sexes show similar resemblance to their parents.
7. *Girls lack achievement motivation.* In the pioneering studies of **achievement motivation,** girls score higher than boys in achievement imagery under neutral conditions. Boys need to be challenged by appeals to the ego or competitive motivation to bring their achievement imagery up to the level of girls. Boys' achievement motivation does appear to be more responsive to competitive arousal than girls', but this does not imply a generally higher level. In fact, observational studies of achievement striving either have found no sex difference or have found girls to be superior (Maccoby and Jacklin, 1974).
8. *Girls are auditory, boys visual.* At no period in life from infancy through late childhood is there any evidence to support this assertion.

One sex difference that is well established is that boys excel in visual-spatial ability—at least during adolescence and adulthood. (Robert Foothorap, Jeroboam)

Certain sex differences, however, are fairly well established:

1. *Girls have greater verbal ability than boys.* This is one of the better known sex differences. Girls show a more rapid development of language than boys. From preschool to early adolescence, verbal abilities for the sexes are fairly similar. Female superiority begins around age eleven and increases throughout high school, for both receptive and productive language as well as for highly abstract verbal tasks.
2. *Boys excel in visual-spatial ability.* This difference is typically found in adolescence and adulthood but not in childhood.
3. *Boys excel in mathematical ability.* Since many people believe that the differences in mathematical ability are exclusively a function of societal attitudes, we quote Maccoby and Jacklin's summary in its entirety:

> The two sexes are similar in their early acquisition of quantitative concepts, and their mastery of arithmetic during the grade-school years. Beginning at about twelve–thirteen, boys' mathematical skills increase faster than girls'. The greater rate of improvement appears to be not entirely a function of the number of math courses taken, although the question has not been extensively studied. The magnitude of the sex differences varies greatly from one population to another, and is probably not so great as the difference in spatial ability. Both visual-spatial and verbal processes are sometimes involved in the solution of mathematical problems; some math problems can probably be solved in either way, while others cannot, a fact that may help to explain the variation in degree of sex difference from one measure to another. (Maccoby and Jacklin, 1974, p. 352)

4. *Males are more aggressive.* We have already seen that the male sex hormone is apparently correlated with aggressiveness. The data indicate that boys are more aggressive both physically and verbally. These differences appear as early as two years of age.

Most people assume that girls exhibit more nurturance and maternal behavior than boys and that boys have a higher activity level. The data are ambiguous, however. Maccoby and Jacklin found that in these areas individuals vary in response to different situations. Data were inconclusive in the following categories also: tactile sensitivity; fear, timidity, and anxiety; competitiveness (most of the research has involved situations in which competitive behavior is maladaptive); dominance (evidence indicates that boys make more dominant attempts, but they are dominant toward each other and not toward girls); and compliance.

The Social Learning View Representing the social learning views, Walter Mischel (1966) indicates that the sex-typing process begins when the individual learns to discriminate sex-appropriate behaviors. The subject learns appropriate behaviors in situations that are unique during the second phase of sex-type learning, through generalization from the specific learning setting to different settings. Behaviors learned in the home, for example, are generalized when they are adapted for use on the playground or in school. Children acquire these sex-appropriate behaviors not only through their own experiences but also by imitating a model when they observe that the behavior of the model is rewarded. Of particular importance is the degree to which a particular behavior is rewarded, or reinforced, by both peers and authority figures.

Research Findings The data show that society has differential expectations that define appropriate masculine behavior and appropriate feminine behavior. Society's notions about appropriate or inappropriate behavior are less flexible for males than for females. Although tomboyishness is not particularly acceptable female behavior, it is tolerated more than so-called sissy behavior on the part of boys. Stereotypic sex-role behaviors are summarized in Table 5•5.

Sex-typed shaping Many behaviors are so complex that the child will not imitate them correctly on the first attempt. If the initial attempt is rewarded, and if each subsequent attempt that is closer to the desired behavior is rewarded, the child may eventually perform the complex behavior correctly. This process of rewarding successive approximations is known as shaping. Sex-appropriate behaviors can be learned through intentional or unintentional shaping on the part of the parent. The strongest evidence of shaping applies to the discouragement of sex-inappropriate behavior in boys. Parents encourage their children to adopt sex-appropriate behavior, but they do so more intensely whenever there is the slightest suggestion of sexually deviant behavior (**homosexuality,** for example). The intensity of parental reaction to seemingly deviant behavior is much greater for sons than it is for daughters.

Otherwise, Maccoby and Jacklin (1974) found that parents treat girls and boys in much the same way. Regarding the hypothesis that sex-appropriate behavior is rewarded and sex-inappropriate behavior is punished, they reported:

Table 5·5 Stereotypic Sex-role Items

Competency cluster: masculine pole is more desirable

FEMININE	MASCULINE
Not at all aggressive	Very aggressive
Not at all independent	Very independent
Very emotional	Not at all emotional
Does not hide emotions at all	Almost always hides emotions
Very subjective	Very objective
Very easily influenced	Not at all easily influenced
Very submissive	Very dominant
Dislikes math and science very much	Likes math and science very much
Very excitable in a minor crisis	Not at all excitable in a minor crisis
Very passive	Very active
Not at all competitive	Very competitive
Very illogical	Very logical
Very home-oriented	Very worldly
Not at all skilled in business	Very skilled in business
Very sneaky	Very direct
Does not know the way of the world	Knows the way of the world
Feelings easily hurt	Feelings not easily hurt
Not at all adventurous	Very adventurous
Has difficulty making decisions	Can make decisions easily
Cries very easily	Never cries
Almost never acts as a leader	Almost always acts as a leader
Not at all self-confident	Very self-confident
Very uncomfortable about being aggressive	Not at all uncomfortable about being aggressive
Not at all ambitious	Very ambitious
Unable to separate feelings from ideas	Easily able to separate feelings from ideas
Very dependent	Not at all dependent
Very conceited about appearance	Never conceited about appearance
Thinks women are always superior to men	Thinks men are always superior to women
Does not talk freely about sex, with men	Talks freely about sex with men

Warmth-expressiveness cluster: feminine pole is more desirable

FEMININE	MASCULINE
Doesn't use harsh language at all	Uses very harsh language
Very talkative	Not at all talkative
Very tactful	Very blunt
Very gentle	Very rough
Very aware of feelings of others	Not at all aware of feelings of others
Very religious	Not at all religious
Very interested in own appearance	Not at all interested in own appearance
Very neat in habits	Very sloppy in habits
Very quiet	Very loud
Very strong need for security	Very little need for security
Enjoys art and literature	Does not enjoy art and literature at all
Easily expresses tender feelings	Does not express tender feelings at all easily

NOTE: Responses were obtained from 74 college men and 80 college women.
(Broverman, Vogel, Broverman, Clarkson, and Rosenkrantz, 1972)

> We must summarize our analyses of this hypothesis with the conclusion that we have been able to find very little evidence to support it, in relation to behaviors other than sex typing as very narrowly defined (e.g., toy preference). The reinforcement contingencies for the two sexes appear to be remarkably similar (Maccoby and Jacklin, 1974).

Different eliciting qualities of boys and girls Do the different biological tendencies of males and females interact with parental behavior to shape the behavior of the parents? This hypothesis suggests a circular process of reciprocal behavior modification leading to a harmonious balance. An example is the study conducted by Moss showing that sons get more maternal attention than daughters during infancy because boys are more demanding. The data show, however, that initial biological differences between the sexes are not powerful enough to elicit consistently different reactions from caretakers.

Cross-sex and same-sex effects How does the interaction of sex of parent and sex of child affect child-rearing practices? Maccoby and Jacklin found that fathers are more tolerant of aggression by their daughters, whereas mothers are more tolerant of aggression by their sons—a contradiction with Radke's finding that fathers are less accepting of aggression by their daughters than by their sons, and that mothers tend to be equally nonaccepting of aggression by both sons and daughters. Obviously more evidence is needed to clarify this particular interaction. Research involving fathers has been so limited that very little is known about their role in the socialization of sons and daughters. Johnson (1963) suggested that fathers are much more sensitive to the appropriateness of sex-role behaviors than are mothers. In view of the current interest in sex-typed behaviors, the necessary methodology should be developed to specify the father's contribution in this important aspect of human growth and development.

The Cognitive-Developmental View Within the framework of cognitive development, sex roles are learned as part of the process by which the child tries to structure or organize the world through assimilation and accommodation. The major contributor to this view is Kohlberg (1966; Kohlberg and Zigler, 1967). According to Kohlberg, sex-role learning starts when children learn to identify themselves as males or females and further learn that their gender is constant. The child then recognizes that there are other members of society with the same sex, whose behavior he or she observes. Sex-typed behavior is not dependent on imitation; rather it results from the child's ability to induce organized rules consistent with one sex role or the other.

After the child has made a consistent gender identity from a set of rules, the engagement in sex-appropriate behaviors and the imitation of same-sex models becomes rewarding. (By contrast, in the social learning and imitation view it is assumed that sex identity comes from engaging in sex-appropriate behavior.) The meaning of *masculinity* or *femininity* changes with increasing cognitive development. As the concept becomes more sophisticated, the kinds of behaviors that are viewed as sex-appropriate expand. But at any point in the child's development, behaviors are consistent with the child's current conceptions of masculinity or femininity.

Related Research Kohlberg and Zigler (1967) administered a number of measures of sex-typing: two projective indices of sex-typing, a measure of sex-typing preferences for other children, verbal expression of dependency, an index of relative attachment to mother and father, and imitation of adults (Table 5•6). These measures were administered in two series (a year apart) to a sample consisting of two groups of middle-class children, ages four to ten. One group was gifted (mean IQ 132) and the other was average (mean IQ 104). On the last three measures, the sex-role attitudes of the children varied more as a function of mental age than chronological age.

For example, on the dependency measure, girls between ages four and eight did not change their sex-role orientations, but the bright group and the average group maintained opposing orientations. A more complex reversal (on the same dependency measure) showed up in boys at the same age levels. Figure 5•7 diagrams the mean percentage of dependency displayed toward the male experimenter by boys at ages four to ten. The cross-sectional data (designated by the long curve) show that bright four-year-olds have a preference for adult males, whereas their average peers have a preference for adult females. Among the brighter

Table 5•6 Summary of Trends from Ages Four to Eight Found on Measures of Sex-role Attitudes

MEASURES	BOYS Average	Bright	GIRLS Average	Bright
It scale, picture test, and peer preferences	All boys become more same-sex oriented until age six (then less so for peer preferences).		All girls become less same-sex oriented with age on It scale and peer preferences, but slight increase on picture test.	
Verbal expression of dependency	Change from opposite-sex orientation at age four to same-sex orientation at age seven.	Change from same-sex orientation at age four to opposite-sex orientation at age seven.	Remain slightly same-sex oriented.	Remain slightly opposite-sex oriented.
Parent attachment, imitation of adults	Become more father-oriented with age.	Do not change their initial father orientation.	Initially mother-oriented; become more father-oriented with age.	Do not change their initial neutrality of choice.

(Adapted from Kohlberg and Zigler, 1967)

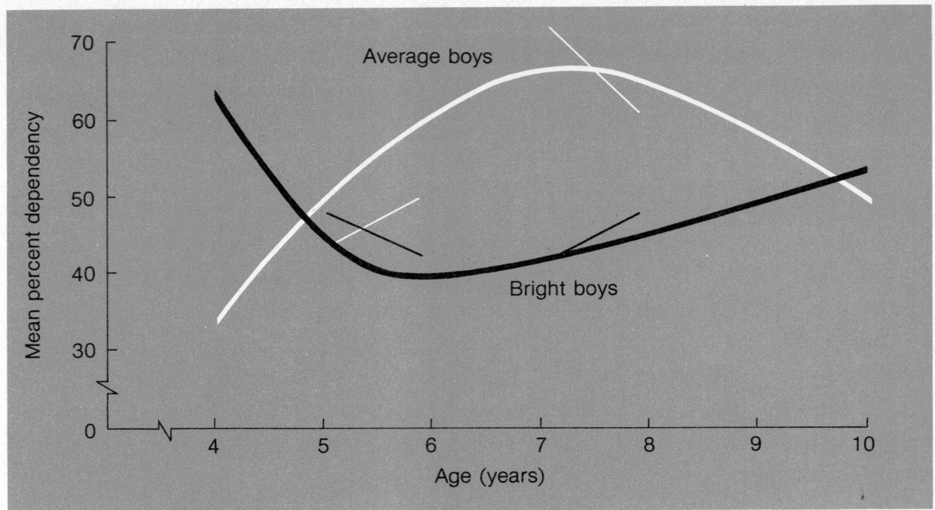

Fig. 5·7 Mean percentage of dependency displayed toward male experimenter by boys at six ages. (Kohlberg, 1966)

boys, after age four there is a shift toward preference for females and then, after age seven, a shift toward a more neutral orientation. The longitudinal data (designated by the short straight lines) indicate that between ages five and six the average boy shows an increased preference for males, whereas the bright boy shows a decreased preference.

> Such reversals, timed in terms of mental rather than chronological age, suggest that cognitive development involves conceptual reorganization of social attitudes, and that intellectual development initiates new social attitudes and developmental tasks, rather than simply facilitating learning or adaptation to tasks imposed by the social environment or by body maturation. Were the latter the case, the chronological age of the developmental reversals should be the same for bright and average groups, with only the rate of acceleration in the new trend more advanced for the bright children. (Kohlberg, 1966, pp. 150–51)

The Kohlberg and Zigler model provides an explanation of role typing that is more encompassing than social learning theory and imitation models, because it incorporates cognitive development along with social reinforcement and imitation variables. Cognitive development to some extent affects the course of the child's sex-role orientation. The importance of the environment is implicit in the Kohlberg-Zigler model. In order for sex-typed behavior to develop over time, the child must have the opportunity to interact with and observe models.

Adolescence

5·4 G. Stanley Hall (1916) was one of the first people to identify a psychology of adolescence and to employ scientific methods in the study of this stage. Hall saw the biological changes that occur at pubescence (around the age of thirteen) as the beginning of a stage that is discontinuous from childhood and is characterized by storm and stress. In Hall's view, this period of turmoil results from changes in the structure and function of organs, along with an intensification of the sex drive, but with little if any influence from the environment.

Hall assumed that the period of intense storm and stress is universal. In his view, every adolescent must learn to live with the sex drive and adjust to physical changes that include a taller and heavier body as well as reproductive capacity and the appearance of secondary sexual characteristics. But more recent writers have shown that there are groups of teen-agers (especially in other cultures) who do not demonstrate the behavioral manifestations of adolescent storm and stress.

Among certain tribes in the New Hebrides, one of the rites associated with becoming a man involves leaping from a tower; vines attached to the ankles arrest the fall just above the ground. (Film Study Center, Peabody Museum, Harvard University)

Cultural Theories Two books by Margaret Mead, *Coming of Age in Samoa* (1950) and *Growing Up in New Guinea* (1953), brought into serious question the assumption that storm and stress are universal characteristics of adolescence. Among the people Mead observed, there was no term for adolescence, nor were there any particular discontinuities from childhood into the period following pubescence.

The work of Ruth Benedict (1954) provides a developmental theory from a cultural anthropological point of view: continuities or discontinuities in the transition from childhood to adolescence or adolescence to adulthood can depend on cultural factors. Among certain cultures examined by Benedict, the transition from childhood to adulthood is gradual and continuous because it is based on the increasing capability of a child to assume more and more independence and adult responsibility. Where the transition is more discontinuous and abrupt, greater problems of adjustment can occur.

In the United States the adolescent stage seems to have grown out of cultural change and economic necessity (Campbell, 1969). Sixty or seventy years ago, most boys and girls were expected to leave school between the sixth and eighth grades and seek gainful employment. Employment was available to the unskilled, and it was economically important for the growth of the country that such jobs be filled. Since that time, the need for unskilled factory and agricultural workers has dwindled, while advances in technology have increased the demand for highly skilled labor. Laws that keep children in school until they are at least fourteen years of age (more often sixteen) have been created. Today young people, and high school dropouts in particular, represent the highest unemployment rate in the nation. By extending the period of dependency upon childhood, this cultural change has provided us with a population of adolescents.

As Kurt Lewin (1948) has suggested, the adolescent in the United States is considered neither a child nor an adult. Because the definition of age-appropriate behavior is unclear, adolescents experience a conflict of attitudes, values, and life-styles.

Erikson's Theory of Identity Development For Erikson, adolescence is a period in which each person must answer the question, "Who am I?" When Erikson talks about **identity development,** he implies that adolescents must determine where they came from, who they are, and what will become of them. This identity crisis is not resolved through maturation, but through sustained and intensive consideration of these existential questions.

Although he begins from Freud's position, Erikson acknowledges the importance of environmental support in the form of both warm and accepting parents and identification with a peer group. Peers are important in establishing one's personal identity because their perceptions of the individual are based on a contemporary culture, while parents and other adults represent authority and another generation. Feedback that the adolescent receives from the peer group is significant because adolescents "are sometimes morbidly, often curiously, preoccupied with what they appear to be in the eyes of others as compared with what they feel they are and with the question of how to connect earlier cultivated roles and skills with the ideal prototypes of the day" (Erikson, 1959).

The danger, as Erikson sees it, is that if the adolescent fails to achieve a sense of personal identity, role diffusion and identity confusion occur, and delinquency or potential psychotic personality disorganization may result. But once the identity crisis is resolved, said Erikson, quoting Freud, the individual is able "to love and to work."

Adjustment Problems Adolescence is a period in which the individual must adjust to new social roles. As Erikson noted, adjustment is most likely to occur in an atmosphere in which failure does not have long-term consequences. On the basis of observation and research evidence, the four areas that seem most representative of the kinds of problems faced by the adolescent are independence seeking, self-concept, sexual behavior, and generational conflict.

Striving for Independence One of the roles of the adolescent is that of practicing independence from parents (McCandless, 1970). The adolescent should have the opportunity to learn to behave in ways that are independent from the family unit and that will be successful and effective within the broader cultural context. This striving for independence often creates conflict with parents and others on whom the individual has relied. The parents are required to make an adjustment in the form of letting go so that the young person can achieve independence. Striving for independence is not a problem within the family unit if the adolescent and parent match in terms of the degree of independence desired and deserved and the degree of independence the parents are willing to allow. On the other hand, when there is a mismatch, the result is conflict, which can have serious consequences. Thus, the properties of the parent-child relationship continue to be important throughout adolescence.

Striving for independence begins with making personal decisions and eventually leads to economic independence from parents (Douvan and Adelson, 1966; Elder, 1968). Chronological age, sex, and degree of physical maturity are factors related to parental attitudes toward independence. The older the children, the more willing parents are to give them independence. M. Gold and E. Douvan (1969) investigated independence behavior in girls ranging in age from eleven to eighteen years. The data summarized in Table 5•7 show that there is growth in terms of behavior and emotional independence from the family as a function of age. Douvan and Adelson found that boys were more interested in establishing independence from parental control, sought more responsibility for their own behaviors, and were more preoccupied with this issue than girls. Girls experienced less difficulty concerning independence because their views were in greater harmony with the views of their parents.

The effects of child-rearing practices on adolescents' perceptions of their parents have been investigated by G. H. Elder (1962, 1963, 1968, 1971), who studied approximately 7350 adolescents varying in socioeconomic status. Students in grades seven through twelve were asked to rate their parents on characteristics such as legitimacy in the use of authority (whether the rationale for demanding a certain behavior is given) and communication patterns between parent and offspring. In the 1962 study, Elder identified seven types of child-rearing techniques from the adolescents' ratings: autocratic, authoritarian, democratic, equalitarian, permissive, laissez-faire, and ignoring (Table 5•8). One of the questions that Elder examined was the degree to which adolescents felt wanted or unwanted as a result of each type of child-rearing practice. The data summarized in Table 5•8 show that autocratic, laissez-faire, and ignoring parents tend to produce feelings of unwantedness among their adolescent offspring. Elder concluded that adolescents who are allowed to participate in self-direction feel that they are wanted by their parents.

Elder (1963) examined parental types as they relate to adolescent strivings for independence. Each parent type was further analyzed into those parents who explained the rules they used in determining allowable behavior and those who did not provide explanations. It was Elder's position that parents who do not explain are viewed as coercive. When parents provide reasons that the adolescents view as legitimate, there is greater likelihood of a positive parent-child relationship

Table 5•7 Indices of Behavioral and Emotional Independence for Adolescent Girls

ITEM	GIRLS AGE 11 (*N* = 206)	GIRLS AGE 18 (*N* = 148)
Behavioral Independence		
Dates or goes steady	4%	94%
Has job outside home	34	60
Spends most of free time with friends	22	46
Spends most of free time with family	68	44
Emotional Independence		
Thinks friendships can be as close as family relationships	53	71
Chooses adult ideals outside family	22	48
Chooses adult ideals within family	66	52
Chooses a friend as confidant	5	33
Chooses one or both parents as confidant(s)	67	36

(Adapted from Gold and Douvan, 1969)

Table 5·8 Seven Types of Child-rearing Techniques and the Degree to Which Adolescents Reared by Them Feel Unwanted

CHILD-REARING TECHNIQUE	DESCRIPTION	PERCENT OF ADOLESCENTS WHO FEEL UNWANTED	
		By Mother	By Father
Autocratic	Parents tell adolescent what to do and allow little initiation or assertiveness.	41.7	40.1
Authoritarian	Parents tell adolescent what to do but listen to adolescent's point of view.	25.7	17.6
Democratic	Parents allow ample opportunity for adolescent to make own decisions but retain final authority.	10.9	8.4
Equalitarian	Parents and adolescent are involved equally in making decisions about adolescent's behavior.	11.0	11.1
Permissive	Adolescent makes own decisions, but parents like to be heard and make input.	11.1	11.0
Laissez-faire	Adolescent makes own decisions and need not listen to parents.	56.8 (Laissez-faire and Ignoring combined)	58.0 (Laissez-faire and Ignoring combined)
Ignoring	Adolescent makes own decisions, and parents do not care what the decisions are.		

(Adapted from Elder, 1962)

characterized by reciprocity of attitudes. This interactional pattern leads to independence and autonomy. Elder hypothesized that independence would be most evident in adolescents with permissive, less autocratic parents who explained the reasons for their rules of conduct.

Elder obtained indices of the individuals' confidence in their own values and of their perceived degree of independence (Table 5·9). Independence was highest among adolescents whose parents explained rules and were perceived as being democratic and permissive. Autocratic parents, or those who infrequently gave explanations, tended to have youngsters with lower degrees of self-confidence and independence. Similar findings for adolescents have been reported by Coopersmith (1967) and Rosenberg (1965). Parents can generate in their children feelings of self-confidence, or they can undermine their children, who then feel unwanted and uncertain, with consequent identity diffusion. Furthermore, parents can fail to provide opportunities for their children to test views and behaviors as well as age-related experiences in behaving independently. These children are unlikely to grow up capable of autonomous and independent functioning.

Is There a Generation Gap? Cultures rarely remain sufficiently static so that the values and attitudes of one generation of young people will be identical to those experienced by the previous generation when they were of comparable age. Indeed, such a state would seem undesirable because it would suggest that no social prog-

Table 5·9 Levels of Parental Power and Frequency of Explanation in Relation to Types of Adolescent Dependence-Independence Behavior

LEVEL OF PARENTAL POWER	PARENTAL EXPLANATIONS	*N*	TYPES OF ADOLESCENT DEPENDENCE-INDEPENDENCE BEHAVIOR[a] Lack of Confidence		Confidence		*Total Percent*
			Dependent	*Independent*	*Dependent*	*Independent*	
Autocratic	Frequent	139	27.3	6.5	37.4	28.8	100
	Infrequent	231	34.2	14.7	20.3	30.3	100
Democratic	Frequent	1233	10.5	6.7	37.6	45.2	100
	Infrequent	194	22.7	9.8	35.6	31.9	100
Permissive	Frequent	729	13.2	7.2	29.8	49.8	100
	Infrequent	177	28.2	13.6	24.9	33.3	100

[a]The degree of self-confidence in personal ideas and values was measured by the following item: How confident are you that your own ideas and opinions about what you should do and believe are right and best for you? [Lack of confidence] (1) Not at all confident, (2) Not very confident, (3) I'm a little confident. [Confidence] (4) I'm quite confident, (5) I'm completely confident. Self-reliance in problem-solving and decision making was measured by the following item: When you have a really important decision to make, about yourself and your future, do you make it on your own, or do you like to get help on it? [Dependent] (1) I'd rather let someone else decide for me, (2) I depend a lot upon other people's advice, (3) I like to get some help. [Independent] (4) Get other ideas then make up my own mind, (5) Make up my own mind without any help.
(From Elder, 1963)

ress had occurred. Recently, however, a number of events have suggested that the gap between generations is widening. These events have involved young people in behaviors such as mass protests, use of hard drugs and alcohol, and relaxation of sexual mores. Some investigators (Conger, 1973; Munns, 1971) argue that the issue is better described as a cultural generation gap resulting from rapid changes in life style. These changes are associated with new values and interests very different from those of previous generations.

The essential question is whether a generation gap exists and, if so, how extensive it is. The answer seems to be that a cultural generation gap exists, but it is neither as large nor as extensive as the popular media would have us believe. W. W. Meissner (1965) reported for thirteen- to eighteen-year-old boys that 89 percent were happy in their homes, and 84 percent spent more than half of their leisure time at home; 74 percent were proud of their parents and did not hesitate to have them meet their friends. Douvan and Adelson, in their sample of fourteen- and eighteen-year-olds, found that there were relatively few, if any, serious disagreements between parents and their adolescents on a number of socially relevant issues.

In a more recent study, M. M. Meisels and F. M. Cantor (1971–72) asked a sample of 225 college students a series of questions related to such issues as religion, sexual freedom, music, and dress. They found that the students' views were more closely aligned with the perceived views of their parents than with the perceived views of their peers. There were no sex differences in this behavior. D. Yankelovich (1969) reports that approximately 67 percent of the adolescents in his sample and 70 percent of the parents expressed the opinion that a generation gap exists but that it is not nearly as large as has been suggested. About 25 percent of both parents and adolescents felt that there is a relatively large generation gap.

The values of adolescent political activists have been found to differ not only from those of older generations but also from those of their peers. (Thelma Shumsky, Jeroboam)

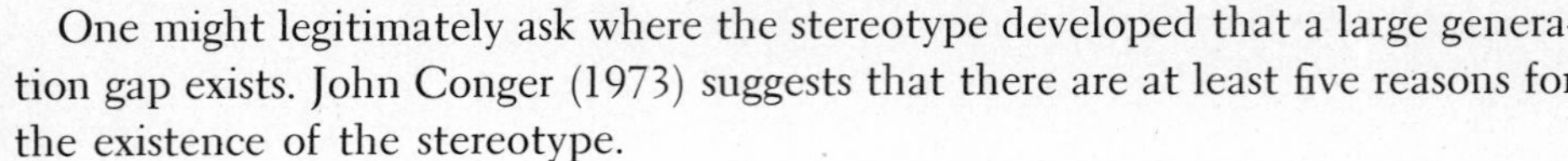

One might legitimately ask where the stereotype developed that a large generation gap exists. John Conger (1973) suggests that there are at least five reasons for the existence of the stereotype.

1. Some of the research concerned with intergenerational differences involves highly selective samples of adolescents, ranging from campus activists to cultural dropouts whose values are considerably different from those of the parent generation but are also different from those of the average adolescent.
2. Variations among values held by adolescents and among values held by adults are greater than the variations between the two groups. In this case we would expect to find that the adolescent-parent gap is no greater than the variation in opinions within a group of adolescents.
3. Parents and their adolescents traditionally have differences of opinions because they have experienced different environmental influences. The parents' world when they were sixteen was very different from the world experienced by their sixteen-year-olds.
4. There is an underemphasis on the ability of adolescents and their parents to understand, be sympathetic, and even support each other's views, especially when there is good or adequate communication between parents and adolescents.
5. Research evidence has focused on differences between generations instead of on similarities. Apparently similarities in parent and child attitudes occur with sufficient frequency to offset any conclusion that there is a wide, overwhelming generation gap.

Peer Relationships Because of the recognized importance of satisfactory peer relationships, considerable research has been devoted to such subjects as the effects of proximity and socioeconomic status on social groupings, the relation of character traits like introversion and extroversion to popularity and social acceptability, the stability of adolescent friendships, and dating behavior and heterosexual relationships.

During early adolescence, social groups are similar to the groups found among younger children in that they are typically composed of same-sex members from a restricted geographic region. The more popular members tend to be those who are brighter and better adjusted, come from a higher socioeconomic status, and perform well in school (Thompson, 1962). In early adolescence members of a group begin to be drawn from a wider geographic region. Not surprisingly, the unisexual nature of the group begins to change in such a way that both males and females find themselves members of two somewhat overlapping groups, a unisexual group and a heterosexual group (Meyer, 1959; Dunphy, 1963). According to W. J. Meyer, unisexual groupings are maintained by environmental settings such as work and recreation. In social circumstances, heterosexual relationships are clearly sanctioned. However, these situations occur with more frequency as one progresses through the adolescent period.

Correlates of Popularity among School-age Children

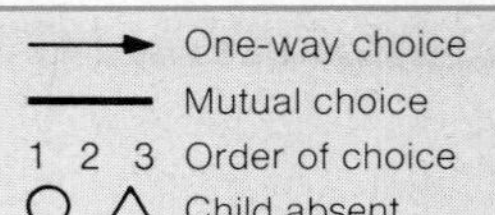

Jacob Moreno (1953) introduced a technique, called sociometry, for assessing interaction structures among members of groups. This technique involves asking group members to select three other members of the group as preferred partners for a particular activity. The choices that each group member makes provide information about the structure of the group and about the popularity of individuals within it.

Figure 5B•1, called a sociogram, presents the pattern of choices among the children in a sample classroom. In this social structure, Janet Toll appears to be a very popular child around whom subgroups revolve. Mary Jokin, however, was not chosen by anyone. This does not necessarily mean that she is isolated in actual daily interactions, since other children may settle for Mary's companionship when their preferred choices are not available.

Research using sociometry to study children's groups, particularly in the classroom, has yielded several interesting findings:

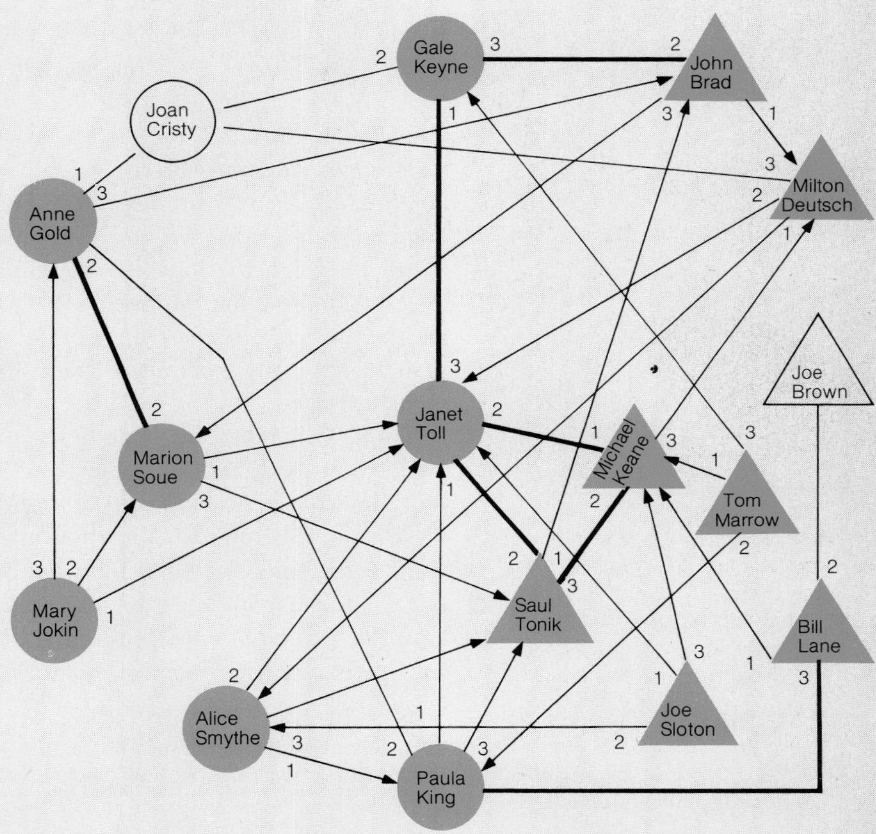

Fig. 5B•1 The social structure of one classroom. The data for this sociogram were obtained by asking each child in the class to make first, second, and third choices among classmates for a particular social activity. (From Jennings, 1948)

1. Compared to less popular children, popular children are higher achievers, as well as being brighter, better adjusted, and physically attractive.
2. Children's friendships are based on compatibility of interests and social backgrounds. For example, the friendships that form among primary-grade children are usually among children who live in the immediate neighborhood or ride the same school bus. Among older children, groups tend to form less on the basis of geography and more in terms of interests.
3. Some groups of children are cohesive whereas others consist of a number of smaller groups or cliques. Among younger children, for example, groups tend to form along unisexual lines with subgroups within each sex. Among older children, preteen-agers, and teen-agers, group structures are less determined by sex, although same-sex preferences prevail.

To define popularity and social groupings, Raymond Kuhlen and Beatrice Lee (1943) conducted a study in which they attempted to determine what behavioral traits were associated with social acceptability for males and females in grades six, nine, and twelve. The sample consisted of 700 people, evenly divided with respect to sex and grade level. Summarized in Table 5•10 are the traits having the highest and the lowest association with acceptability for grades six, nine, and twelve. At the twelfth-grade level, more than at the sixth-grade level, the highly accepted adolescent tends to be active, socially aggressive, and extroverted. At all grade levels and for both sexes, the more popular youngsters are those judged to be good-looking, enthusiastic, able to initiate games and activities, and good-humored. At all ages children who are highly accepted by their own sex are also highly accepted by the opposite sex. These findings have been replicated to a remarkable degree (Mussen, Conger, and Kagan, 1974).

Friendship fluctuations were examined in two studies (Horrocks and Thompson, 1946; Thompson and Horrocks, 1947) of 965 urban and 905 rural children, ages eleven through eighteen years. For both sexes and for both the rural and the urban groups, there was a definitive trend toward greater stability in friendships with increasing age.

During the adolescent period interest in dating increases. Douvan and Adelson make the case that dating behavior, like other peer interactions, is extremely important to the development of interpersonal skills necessary for satisfactory and healthy adult heterosexual relationships. Dating, which typically starts for girls at around age fourteen and for most boys between ages fourteen and fifteen, is more prevalent among middle-class adolescents than among lower-class adolescents. One aspect of socioeconomic status is that little dating occurs between social class levels largely because such friendships are formed early on the basis of geographic con-

Table 5•10 Differences between Percentage of Socially Accepted and Socially Unaccepted Children in Three Grades Who Were Thought by Their Classmates to Possess Various Traits

	BOYS IN GRADES			GIRLS IN GRADES		
TRAITS	6	9	12	6	9	12
Restless	−28*	0	+19	−31*	−14	+25*
Talkative	−4	+14	+50	−3	+23	+31*
Acts older than age	+12	+20	+4	+17	+17	−25
Good looking	+80*	+50*	+54*	+73*	+53*	+42*
Enthusiastic	+92*	+76	+77*	+80*	+60*	+69*
Active in games	+76*	+50*	+38*	+45*	+40*	+52*
Bosses others	0	+3	+19	0	+17	+31
Enjoys jokes	+44*	+47*	+50*	+42*	+53*	+65*
Enjoys joke on self	+76*	+50*	+62*	+65*	+37*	+62*
Number of cases in each extreme group	25	30	26	29	30	29

*Differences larger than two times their standard error.

NOTE: Minus differences show traits that are more characteristic of unaccepted children, whereas plus differences show traits that characterize accepted children.
(Kuhlen and Lee, 1943)

siderations—street, neighborhood, and school. These findings are supported by the assumption of Eric Gardner and George Thompson (1956) that the attractiveness of individuals for each other is based on mutual reinforcement of social needs. If values, attitudes, and behaviors are part of the reinforcement, different social groupings will have different reinforcement hierarchies.

Fears and Anxieties Adolescents are affected by vocational, social, and educational problems, as well as by an inordinate concern about physical inadequacies (Bonar, 1942; Mooney, 1942). Concerns about physical appearance emerge earlier for girls but become more important for both sexes with increasing age. In our culture, according to the data, one's physical appearance is at least as important as one's general intellectual ability. There are sex differences with respect to adolescent anxieties. Girls feel more self-conscious than boys, but boys show earlier and greater concerns about money. Both boys and girls at all age levels included show a high degree of anxiety with respect to examinations. Concerns about heterosexual relationships emerge around age fifteen, are maintained for two or three years, and then show a decline as adolescents gain more experience with this area of life.

Summary

The attitudes and behavior of parents have powerful effects in determining the social and emotional development and personality characteristics of their children. Research studies involving children of all ages have revealed the importance of parental acceptance of the child. Attachment has been demonstrated, both in human infants and in monkeys, by experimenters who have shown that the young benefit from being allowed to follow and cling to their caretakers. Children from democratic homes are social and assertive at school age and are more likely to achieve their goals. Parents who are willing to explain behavioral rules teach their children to make independent judgments that can be generalized to a wide range of social situations.

Moral behavior has been examined from a cognitive viewpoint by Piaget and from a chronological approach by Kohlberg. Both Piaget and Kohlberg explained the development of moral judgment in stage theories that progress from behavior controlled by fear of punishment at the lowest level to individualistic understanding of abstract ethical principles at the mature level.

The examination of sex roles has assumed increasing importance in recent years as attention has been directed to discrimination against women. One of the tasks of developmental psychology has been to distinguish biological sex differences from sex-typing decreed by society. A review of the literature by Maccoby and Jacklin pointed to many misconceptions and some genuine sex differences, for example, that males are more aggressive and that females excel in verbal competency.

Adolescence has been described as the period in which the individual strives for independence. Successful adjustment is found in families in which there is a match between the adolescent's desire for independence and the parents' willingness to grant it. Researchers have found that agreement between parents and adolescents is extensive enough to bring into question the assumption that a serious generation gap exists. Apparently the generation gap is a cultural phenomenon that affects a minority of families. But even in the presence of warm and open family ties, the adolescent needs to develop peer relationships to facilitate the transition to adulthood.

Suggested Readings

Baltes, P., and Schaie, K. W., eds. 1973. *Lifespan developmental psychology: Personality and socialization.* New York: Academic Press.

A group of fourteen authors examine different aspects of socialization. Some topics included are sex roles, moral development, and intergenerational relations.

Ginott, H. 1965. *Between parent and child.* New York: Macmillan.

This bestseller states in understandable terms how parents can improve relationships with their children. Numerous anecdotes from therapy sessions add to the fascination of the material.

Goslin, D. A., ed. 1969. *Handbook of socialization theory and research.* New York: Rand McNally.

The editor included every phase of childhood and adolescent socialization. A critical reference for further study of socialization.

Lynn, D. B. 1974. *The father: His role in child development.* Monterey, Cal.: Brooks/Cole.

The almost forgotten role of fathers is examined in terms of the available research. This is a most timely and useful book.

Osofosky, H. J. 1968. *The pregnant teenager.* Springfield, Ill.: Charles C. Thomas.

A review of the social, medical, and educational problems of the pregnant teen-ager.

Roiphe, A. R. 1970. *Up the sandbox.* Greenwich, Conn.: Fawcett.

A perceptive view of women's roles in American society and why so many resist breaking tradition.

Sears, R.; Maccoby, E. E.; and Levin, H. 1957. *Patterns of child rearing.* Evanston, Ill.: Row, Peterson.

A research report based on interviews with parents who use different child-rearing practices.

The Psychology of Aging

6 If you were very old, what would your most crucial problems be? How would you go about solving them? How might you live most effectively and with least damage to your ideals and standards? In old age, one must rely on others. When this time arrives for you, what kind of people would you like to deal with? If you were to face death in the near future, what would matter most? What circumstances would make death acceptable? Would any condition or events make you feel that you might be better off dead?

Your answers to these questions may be far more significant than you think. Several researchers have suggested that our youthful attitudes toward aging may actually help to determine the kind of people we will be when we ourselves are old. While this may or may not be true, we know that attitudes toward aging are becoming more important because the number of old people is increasing rapidly in the United States. The lengthening of human life has resulted in social and political issues that affect young and old alike.

A person can be defined as old in terms of the physical and mental capacity of the individual, but in general the population thought of as elderly in the United States consists of people who are sixty-five or older. In 1940 only 6.8 percent of the population was sixty-five or older, but by 1970 the percentage had risen to 9.9. A recent projection indicates that the percentage will be 10.2 by 1980 but will hold relatively constant thereafter.

Our experience with underprivileged children has taught us that, in order to design effective programs, we need solid knowledge about the target population: no single program can be recommended for all members of a population. Similarly, we need knowledge about the characteristics of the elderly as policies affecting them are proposed, debated, and legislated.

The study of aging is called **gerontology**. **Geriatrics**, the medical specialty that deals with the process of aging, is devoted to the diagnosis and treatment of the diseases of old people. Gerontologists are not exclusively psychologists but include members of other disciplines, such as sociology, biology, architecture, and political science. The work described in this chapter is primarily psychological but includes a number of studies developed from a sociological point of view. In emphasizing the cognitive characteristics of the aging and how people treat the aging, we are building on data described in previous chapters. Developmental psychology embraces the entire lifespan and recognizes that there is continuity in growth.

Studies of Learning and Cognition

6·1 Although there is increasing interest in the characteristics of aging, investigators have encountered many methodological problems, beginning with the difficulty of finding a suitable sample of subjects to study. A psychologist can easily find a representative sample of children, because children of all ethnic, racial, and socioeconomic groups are brought together in schools. Samples of the young adult population can be found in colleges. But there is no single location where a psychologist can find a representative sample of the aging. Organizations specifically designed for the elderly attract those who are socially active and in comparatively good health and consequently do not represent the entire population. Studies of Senior Citizen groups thus result in a biased sample.

Investigators have discovered another source of bias: individuals who are superior in learning and cognition are likely to live longer than other people. In a longitudinal study in which the same people were tested once every five years, the subjects who began the study with the lowest test scores either died at relatively early ages or lost interest and refused to cooperate with the experimenters (Riegel, Riegel, and Meyer, 1967). The same bias was reported by Baltes, Schaie, and Nardi (1971), who tested their subjects once every seven years. Because of the successively increasing bias of the samples with age, the effects of aging on cognitive behaviors are underestimated.

A second sampling problem results because the experiences of different age groups are not comparable; for example, older people tend to have less education. In laboratory research, if one is comparing three different age groups—a young group in their twenties, a middle-age group in their forties, and an older group in their sixties—the data on learning and cognition will probably show progressive decline with increasing age. It is plausible that the age differences result from experiential differences rather than from aging. To the degree that years of education influence performance on cognitive tasks, the results of any study not controlling for education will be biased.

There are other problems that bias results in working with the aging. For example, whereas it is relatively easy to gain the cooperation of young children and teen-agers, (including college sophomores), it is not easy to obtain the cooperation of old people. Most laboratory tasks, such as learning nonsense syllables, seem irrelevant and trivial to the elderly. In some instances, noncooperative behavior may also be a psychological rationalization to camouflage fear of failure.

Motivation Jack Botwinick (1973) contends that motivation of elderly subjects does not necessarily involve overcoming a lack of physiological or emotional involvement, but rather channeling their involvement toward tasks that seem relevant to them. He presents evidence that the older subject is at least as motivated as the younger subject, if not more so. Thus the distinction is that older subjects are motivated in some task situations and not in others.

In order to study cognition among the aging, psychologists must use tasks for which the subjects are unlikely to know the correct answers. D. Arenberg (1968) developed a highly complex task to measure problem-solving ability among aging subjects. The task proved to be overwhelmingly difficult and therefore of little value. He then analyzed his task into the required cognitive skills and developed a test that contained more meaningful material. Making the task more relevant substantially improved the performance of the subjects. By making the concepts more familiar and less abstract, Arenberg may have altered the difficulty level of the task, or even changed the entire task.

Nevertheless, the study serves to illustrate how task relevance influences the performance of older people. A similar kind of task manipulation was made by I. M. Hulicka (1967), and again the results indicated that performance of elderly subjects improves considerably when tasks are meaningful. But the performance of the older subjects under the meaningful conditions was not as good as the performance of the younger control subjects.

At 168 years of age, this resident of the Soviet republic of Georgia in the Caucasus still works in his garden. (Tass from Sovfoto)

Cautiousness Although cautiousness is a possible explanation for the performance decrement among older subjects, cautiousness at any age level (especially among older people) can be intelligent and adaptive behavior. Specifically, studies of the capacities of the aging consistently show a decrement in hearing, vision, and other sensory systems, as well as a slowing of reaction time. Cautiousness is a realistic response to the limits imposed by age. But cautiousness may also result from failure-anxiety, which is a partial explanation of the poorer performance of older subjects relative to younger subjects. Several early studies led to this interpretation, but Floyd Ruch's (1934) is a classic because it specified the kinds of tasks that aging affects most.

Ruch was interested in determining the degree of learning-ability loss with age. Three different age groups of forty subjects each were involved in the study: 12 to 17 years, 34 to 59 years, and 60 to 85 years. Ruch used two motor-learning tasks and three verbal-learning tasks that required subjects to change their existing habit patterns. The motor-learning tasks consisted of establishing a simple eye-hand coordination response. The verbal-learning tasks were much more difficult because they involved vision. These tasks consisted of paired associates that were relatively simple because they had high association values (man-boy), a series of nonsense equations ($E \times Z = G$) that represented new materials, and a false multiplication task ($3 \times 5 = 25$) that interfered with established habit patterns. Using the performance of the young group as the base rate, Ruch compared the percentage

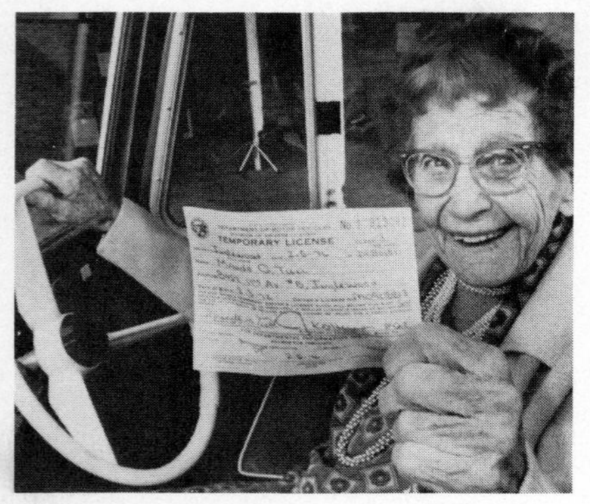

Although reaction time typically slows down as one ages, this woman learned to drive at age 91 and was able to renew her license at age 104. (Wide World Photos)

performance of the middle-age and old-age groups against the base rate (Table 6•1). Regardless of the type of task—easy or difficult, new or old—the old subjects scored lower than the middle-age subjects. The old subjects' performance was most seriously affected on tasks that conflicted with habit patterns.

S. Korchin and L. Basowitz (1957), using the paired-associate procedure, varied the complexity of the task. They reported essentially the same results as Ruch, but a detailed examination of their data showed that the older subjects made more errors of omission than of commission, even though they had been instructed to guess. The investigators interpreted this finding as indicative of greater cautiousness. Although cautiousness is one reason for performance decrement among older subjects, if this fear of responding incorrectly were overcome, the performance of the old subjects probably would not match that of the middle-age or younger subjects. This conclusion stems from numerous studies showing that manipulations designed to improve the performance of the elderly also improve the performance of younger people.

Reaction Time *Reaction time* (RT) is different from cautiousness and motivation because RT is both a dependent variable and an explanation for performance decline on behaviors that involve the **central nervous system.** Reaction time can be measured and is sensitive to a variety of experimental conditions. In this context it is a dependent variable. But in the study of aging, it is also used as an explanation for performance decrements.

One of the most straightforward experiments in psychology is the reaction-time experiment in which the subject is asked to press a button upon presentation of a stimulus. The task can be made more complex by instructing the subject to press one button upon presentation of stimulus A and another button upon presentation of stimulus B. As the task becomes more complex, reaction time is extended to allow the subject to process the information and make the appropriate response. There are three identifiable components involved in RT behavior: signal detection, signal processing, and responding (pressing the button).

Table 6•1 Average Proficiency of Three Age Groups in Various Learning Tests of More or Less Congruence with Established Habits

TEST	YOUNG (12–17)	MIDDLE AGE (34–59)	OLD (60–85)
Motor learning			
Direct vision	100%	98%	84%
Mirror vision	100	96	54
Verbal learning			
Paired associates	100	90	82
Nonsense equations	100	80	48
False multiplications	100	72	47

NOTE: Results are expressed as percentages of the averages for the youngest group.

(Adapted from Ruch, 1934)

The Interaction of Age and Speed with Verbal Learning

In the paired-associate learning task the subject is first presented with pairs of words (often one pair at a time, which may be presented on a screen as first one member and then both members). After such learning trials, the person is shown only one member of a pair and is asked to provide the word with which it was previously paired.

The difficulty of the task can be manipulated in terms of the difficulty of association between member pairs (*chair-table* is easier than *chair-motor*), the number of pairs used, and the timing of the two stages in the task. The time between presentation of one member of a pair (*chair*, for example) and the other member (*table*) is the anticipation interval. The amount of time given the subject to examine the pair (*chair-table*) is the inspection interval. During the anticipation interval the subject makes a verbal response, and during the inspection interval the subject learns the correct answer. Each of these intervals can be increased or decreased.

The paired-associate learning task is widely used by psychologists to study the effects of certain variables on verbal learning. The task is well suited for this purpose because it permits the investigator to control many important variables that might confound experiments conducted outside the laboratory. From these experiments there is considerable evidence that the shorter the anticipation interval, the more serious the effects on the elderly person's performance compared to that of a younger person. These results indicate that elderly people require more time to prepare for a problem.

Given sufficient time, can the elderly person process a problem rapidly? In a paired-associate learning task using 162 adult males of various ages, Rolf Monge and David Hultsch (1971) used three different inspection intervals (2.2, 4.4, and 6.6 seconds) and three different anticipation intervals (2.2, 4.4 and 6.6 seconds) in order to investigate the effects of these variables as a function of age. The average age of the young males was 28.28 years and 49.40 for the older males. Eighteen subjects, nine young and nine old, were randomly assigned to each of the nine experimental groups.

Ten pairs of words were used: *ticket-angry, factory-ready, market-unusual, attention-normal, kitchen-certain, insurance-pleasant, diamond-simple, stranger-favorite, habit-delicate,* and *lawyer-empty*. The words in this list possess high recognition, but the association levels are moderately difficult. The dependent variable is the verbal response made during the anticipation interval.

The results showed that age affected performance when the anticipation interval was varied but not when the inspection interval was varied. The longer the inspection interval, the better was performance at all age levels. The most important finding of this study is that anticipation interval and inspection interval did not jointly interact with age. The total time available per item does not differentially influence different age groups. This study makes clear that it is the anticipation interval that causes performance decrement among older subjects and not the time required to process the information.

In one RT experiment, Birren and Botwinick (1955) asked two age groups of subjects (19 to 36 years of age and 61 to 91 years) to judge which of two vertical bars was shorter. They varied the difficulty of the discrimination by varying the difference in the height of the two bars from 1 percent to 50 percent. The longest reaction time for both groups was for the smallest height differences, but the older subjects were more adversely affected by these difficult discriminations than the younger subjects. Botwinick (1971) conducted another study to find out whether the slowing reaction time in older subjects was due to decreased sensory acuity. One group of subjects ranged in age from 17 to 22 years, the other group from 64 to 91 years. This time Botwinick used a tone as the stimulus and adjusted the intensity of the tone to each individual. With this control, any differences in reaction time could not be attributed to differences in sensory acuity. The results of this work did not alter the conclusion that RT is adversely influenced by aging.

The effects of aging on reaction time are apparently even more extreme when task complexity is increased by the use of multiple responses. In a study reported by Goldfarb (1941), five different age groups responded to two levels of complexity: a two-choice task and a five-choice task. Results indicated that the effects of increasing task complexity were significantly greater for the oldest group than for the younger groups.

Some gerontologists believe that "age-related deficits in cognitive and perceptual abilities are a result of the slowing with age or, at least, share a common antecedent with it" (Botwinick, 1973). In other words, the commonly observed decline in cognitive and perceptual functioning is thought to reflect deterioration of the central nervous system (CNS). RT is considered to be a direct measure of CNS functioning, which is not affected by cultural variation or educational level. This hypothesis can be tested only with correlational data because it is impossible ethically to change the CNS of human beings. If the hypothesis is true, speed tests should correlate with the results of cognitive tests.

In one of the major studies (Botwinick and Storandt, 1973), a series of speed tests did not correlate with such untimed cognitive tests as vocabulary or comprehension. An interesting finding, however, was that the speed tests did correlate significantly (between .58 and .66) with tests developed to diagnose brain damage. These tests employ measures that require new organization of old materials and the learning of new materials. Since these tests are designed to be sensitive to central nervous system dysfunction, moderate correlations with the speed tests seem plausible.

Qualitative Change Research shows that older people learn more slowly and experience memory deficits, in addition to the increase in reaction time. These effects of aging on learning and cognition are changes in quantity. There is little evidence to support the belief that performance changes in quality as a result of age. It takes the older person longer to complete the processing of information, but the process remains the same in healthy individuals. Both *cerebrovascular* disease (commonly called a stroke) and *cardiovascular* (heart) diseases may be severe enough to retard cognitive functions. But the normal process of aging does not cause a person to regress toward a second childhood. In Piaget's terms, such a regression would turn back from formal operations to concrete operations to sensorimotor operations. There are studies in which old people could not handle some of the concrete operations tasks, but if these subjects were functioning at a preconcrete operational level, they could not handle the routine matters of living. The older person who cannot handle some of the concrete operations tasks may be overly cautious or lack the motivation to tackle them.

A further case against the regression position can be developed from the data on intellectual abilities. Typically, older people differ from younger people, but the difference is in terms of efficiency. There is evidence that on vocabulary tests, older people actually perform better. It is possible that the common practice of forced retirement at 65 is, in a majority of cases, inappropriate because it wastes human potential by removing experienced workers from business and the professions.

Assessing Mental Ability From infancy through early adolescence, cognitive competence and learning ability increase rapidly. Thereafter until the ages of 50 to 55, there are few changes in capabilities except that people become more proficient in the use of abstract verbal symbols.

The results of three classic studies of age changes in IQ test performance are presented in Figure 6•1. The three curves are approximately parallel. This similarity is significant for two reasons: (1) the sampling method in all three studies is cross-sectional (different subjects at each of the age points), and (2) each study used a different test. The Army Alpha study (Jones and Conrad, 1933) was conducted in New England; the Otis (Miles and Miles, 1932) in two communities in California; and the Wechsler (1955) study was conducted in New York City. Regardless of the content of the test or the nature of the sample, the results show mental growth until roughly age 20 and then a gradual decline until age 60.

Reaction time declines only slightly until age 55, then shows a greater decline thereafter. If performance on intelligence tests declines after age 20, can this decline be attributed to reaction time? To answer this question, it is necessary to examine the subtests of the **WAIS**, particularly the performance items, which are uniformly timed. When difficulty levels of the eleven subtests are ranked (Table 6•2), a rank of 11 represents the best score and a rank of 1, the poorest score. Without exception, the highest ranking subtests are from the Verbal Scale, which is not timed, and the lowest ranking subtests are from the Performance Scale—once again showing the strong effects of speed on performance among the aging. Superiority on verbal items as opposed to performance items has been so pervasive that Botwinick (1973) refers to it as "the classic aging pattern." Indeed, Carl Eisdorfer,

Table 6•2 Difficulty Levels of WAIS Among the Elderly

SUBTEST	RANK
Information	1 (easiest)
Vocabulary	2
Comprehension	3
Arithmetic	4
Similarities	5
Digit Span	6
Picture Completion	7
Object Assembly	8
Block Design	9
Picture Arrangement	10
Digit Symbol	11 (hardest)

(Adapted from Botwinick, 1973)

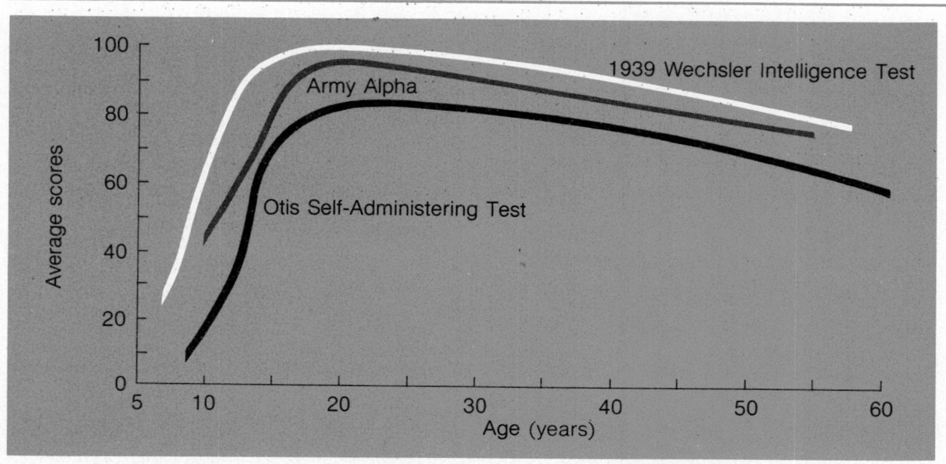

Fig. 6•1 Average scores obtained by three different researchers, each using a different test and a different sample population. (From Pressey and Kuhlen, 1957)

The Creative Years in Science and Literature

Is there a decline in intellectual capacity with age? Performance on tests of intellectual aptitude and on a variety of other tasks suggests not only that there is, but also that the decline starts slowly and becomes progressively more serious. Although it is not easy to refute these data, it seems reasonable to explore their functional significance. The data do not mean, for example, that the knowledge and skills developed during the younger years disappear. Instead the learning of new materials may become more difficult.

To what degree do age-related factors influence the quantity and quality of work done by scientists and literary scholars? Harvey Lehman (1936) conducted extensive research studies on the productivity of chemists, mathematicians, physicists, astronomers, inventors, short-story writers, and poets. The procedure involved finding out from source books the noteworthy contributions of these individuals, their birth and death dates, and the date of production of each work. Corrections were made to allow for the fact that death reduces the number of workers at successively higher age levels.

The data for science and literature are presented in Figure 6A·1. These

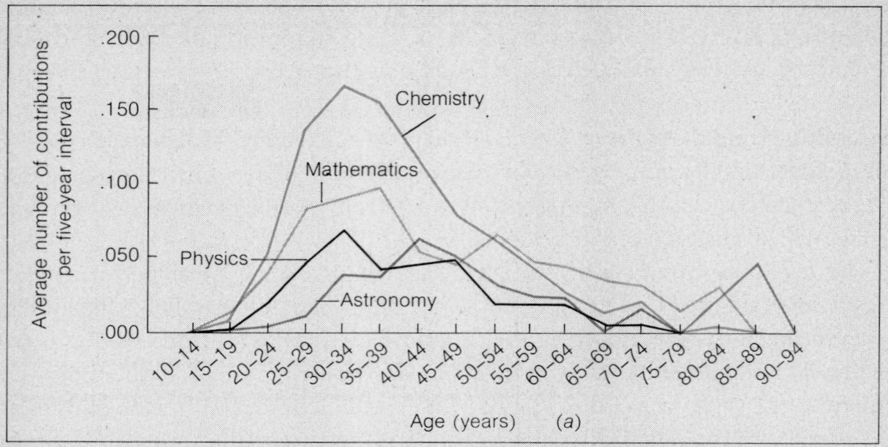

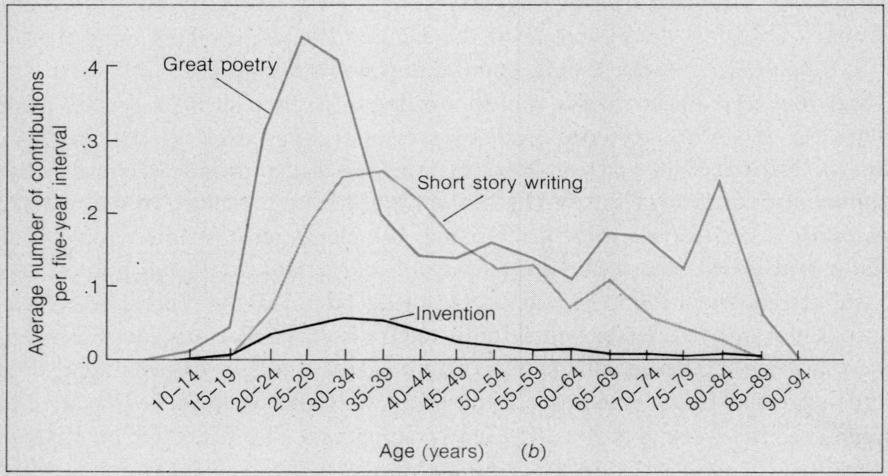

Fig. 6A·1 Age trends in productivity in various areas of science (*a*) and literature (*b*). (Lehman, 1936)

data show that productivity is differentially influenced by age, depending on the person's area of endeavor. Lehman concluded that the decrement in productivity does not necessarily indicate a concomitant decrement in creative ability. He believes that the decrement is attributable to multiple factors that have yet to be identified. Probably one factor is motivation; the established older person does not need to publicly demonstrate ability as much as does the younger person. Possibly the older person also becomes more selective about what is published.

Ewald Busse, and L. D. Cohen (1959) report that this aging pattern holds for blacks and whites; all socioeconomic levels; dull, average, and bright individuals; and people in the community as well as those in mental hospitals.

The effects of age on an individual's ability to solve logical problems are tested at the Gerontology Research Center, National Institute on Aging, in Baltimore. (NIA Gerontology Photo)

Other researchers have pointed out, however, that the performance subtests are qualitatively different from the verbal subtests. In a study by J. E. Doppelt and W. L. Wallace (1955) the performance part of the WAIS was given with and without time limits and, surprisingly from the point of view of the reaction time interpretation, the results were essentially the same. The major factor contributing to the decline on performance subtests with aging may be that they require perceptual functioning and, more important, the ability to process new information. The verbal subtests, on the other hand, mainly tap well rehearsed and overlearned behaviors. W. Owens (1963), in a longitudinal study of age and mental abilities, found that over a thirty-year age period (from 19 years to 49 years) the verbal performance of his subjects actually increased, so that at the later age the average score of the subjects was higher than it had been at age 19.

In recognition of this classic aging pattern Raymond Cattell (1963) postulated an organization pattern of crystallized intelligence and fluid intelligence. According to Cattell, *crystallized intelligence* is learned and is therefore subject to environmental variations. In developmental studies using the longitudinal method, crystallized intelligence shows little decline—perhaps because the level of environmental stimulation changes little for adults, especially from the middle years on. Crystallized intelligence shows a sharp decline in cross-sectional studies, however. For example, young people (on the average) have more education today than do their parents and certainly their grandparents. With more opportunities to learn more, they perform better on tests of vocabulary and general information (which are good tests for assessing crystallized intelligence) than do the older generations.

Fluid intelligence is less influenced by environmental differences but is influenced by genetic and physiological factors. Perhaps because of the increase in reaction time with age and the assumed deterioration of central nervous system functioning, fluid intelligence shows decline in longitudinal studies but not in cross-sectional studies. Physiological functions are assumed to hold up relatively well until serious illness occurs or until extreme old age. It is also reasonable that physiological adequacy is relatively constant across generations.

Cattell's conceptual division of intelligence into crystallized and fluid suggests that people who achieve a high level of education may show less performance decline on IQ tests as a result of aging. In a study by J. Birren and D. Morris (1961) both the age level (between 25 and 64 years) and the educational level of the subjects were included in the data analyses. It was found that educational level was more important than age in determining general intellectual level.

The most likely explanation for the observed decline in cognitive performance is that biological functioning deteriorates. A sharp drop in cognitive performance often signals impending death. Decline in IQ may be a result of cardiovascular and cerebrovascular disease (Baer, 1972; Eisdorfer and Wilkie, 1973).

The Social Adjustments of Aging

6•2 As yet, no one has formulated a theory to organize what is known about the developmental stage known as aging. But it is possible to examine social aspects of aging (including social interactions, socialization, and personality change) from the viewpoint of Erik Erikson, who described the eight stages of psychosocial development. Erikson said that each stage must be achieved successfully in order to avoid some form of personality dysfunction and to attain the next higher stage.

The objective of Erikson's eighth and last stage is "acquiring a sense of integrity and avoiding a sense of despair." Preparation for the later adult years begins in stage 7, middle age, when the purpose is achieving "a sense of generativity and avoiding a sense of self-absorption." The major objective is to provide a firm foundation for the satisfactory physical and psychological development of one's children. The adult who displays generativity accepts the responsibility for assuring that the new generation develops a strong sense of trust. When adults reject this challenge and turn away from their children and the community, they have become self-absorbed.

Erikson's final stage is a direct consequence of stage 7 because having been successful in the development of the new generation, the individual can sense the fullest meaning of trust. A sense of integrity serves to counteract an opposing sense of despair and disgust generated by the fear of impending death as the end to an unfulfilled life. As Erikson views it, the person who is successful in this final stage achieves wisdom and derives from this wisdom the integrity not to fear death. Erikson (1950) states, "Healthy children will not fear life, if their parents have integrity enough not to fear death."

Socialization of the Aging Socialization, an important topic in the study of children and adolescents, is equally important in the study of aging. We have learned how chronological age, sex, and cultural values influence behavior. One aspect of this socialization process occurs in terms of age-defined codes of behavior and dress. Comments like "Act your age" or "Those clothes are too young for you" are common examples of how people of all ages, including older people, exert this socialization pressure. There are many ways in which elderly people are defined by the attitudes of others.

Attitudes Toward the Aging How do younger people perceive elderly people? The answer to this question suggests how young and middle-age people view their own forthcoming old age.

T. Hickey, L. Hickey, and R. Kalish (1968) asked 208 third graders in parochial and public schools to write an essay about an old person. These children came from both wealthy and working-class homes. Many of them were Americans of Mexican descent. Their essays most frequently mentioned physical characteristics and social characteristics of the elderly and these two major categories included several subclassifications (Table 6•3). The data suggest that children view older people as feeble and most different from themselves with respect to ambulatory

Table 6·3 Children's Perceptions of Physical and Social Characteristics of Older People

CHARACTERISTIC	HIGH INCOME (N = 118) Number of responses	Percent of responses	Percent of respondents	LOW INCOME (N = 90) Number of responses	Percent of responses	Percent of respondents
Physical						
Ambulatory differences	21	27.6	17.8	9	40.9	10.0
Visual and auditory differences	4	5.3	3.4	1	4.5	1.1
Hair and beard differences	10	13.2	8.5	6	27.3	6.7
Skin deterioration	11	14.5	9.3	2	9.1	2.2
General feebleness	30	39.5	25.4	4	18.1	4.4
Social						
Kindness	98	51.6	83.1	53	53.0	58.9
Meanness	29	15.3	24.6	24	24.0	26.7
Poverty	2	1.1	1.7	2	2.0	2.2
Loneliness	18	9.5	15.3	1	1.0	1.1
Leisure time	31	16.3	26.3	8	8.0	8.9
Eccentricity and/or senility	12	6.3	10.2	12	12.0	13.3

NOTE: The percentage of respondents does not total 100, since the number of responses per respondent was unlimited.
(Adapted from Hickey, Hickey, and Kalish, 1968)

behaviors. Although most of the children in the study viewed older people as kind or friendly, a sizable percentage viewed older people as mean. In considering the results of their study, the authors conclude:

> If childhood attitudes toward roles do, indeed, influence their behavior when they eventually achieve those roles, and to the extent that children's essays are valid indicators of their perceptions of the roles of the elderly, the following picture emerges: the wealthy children anticipate having considerable leisure time, but being lonely, perhaps relatively isolated from their family; they will be kind and friendly, and eventually become generally feeble, but not indulge in eccentric behavior. Children from poorer homes do not anticipate loneliness, and are less likely to think about future leisure; however, senility and generally peculiar behavior are to be expected, with a suggestion of mean and unfriendly behavior. (Hickey, Hickey, and Kalish, 1968, p. 233)

In a similar study (Hickey and Kalish, 1968), high school and college students had less positive views of elderly people than did the children. Even well-educated young adults hold a generally negative view of old people—which suggests how these young people might approach their own old age. More recently, Kalish (1975) has suggested that attitudes toward elderly people may be changing because of sympathetic presentations in magazines and on television.

How do the elderly perceive themselves? Are their perceptions related to those of other generations? I. Ahammer and Paul Baltes (1972) had groups of adolescents, adults, and elderly people evaluate the desirability of the personality dimensions

By expecting an aging person to behave in certain ways, many people may restrict the opportunities available to the aging. (Norman Hurst, Stock, Boston)

of affiliation, achievement, autonomy, and nurturance. The major findings of this study is that adolescents and adults place greater value on nurturing behavior than do the elderly. The younger people also felt that the elderly should not value autonomy, at least to the degree that the elderly persons in this study did. It appears that young people attempt to mold the elderly into a stereotype that elderly people resist. Apparently cultural pressure to conform to a set of highly specified behaviors occurs during aging, more than at any other stage in life. Yet there is no logical reason, and as we shall see soon, no empirical evidence to justify greater conformity at this age level.

Age Status Structure Age norms represent a system of social control that Bernice Neugarten refers to as *age status structure* (Neugarten and Datan, 1973). In a study by Neugarten, Moore, and Lowe (1965), 50 middle-age men and 43 middle-age women, all middle-class, assigned an appropriate age for a series of descriptive statements (Table 6•4). A very high percentage of respondents agreed to these particular age categories: the lowest percentage is 64, and the median is approximately 88. Analysis of the data indicates that the age-norm system influences the middle-aged and the old more than the young.

Because the sample in Neugarten's study is small and is comprised exclusively of middle-class individuals we cannot say for sure whether these findings apply to all age groups and all economic levels. But if you were reared in the culture that helped define these categories, probably nothing in the data will surprise you. Neugarten and Datan (1973) summarize their results in the following way:

> Many of the major punctuation marks of the life cycle are social rather than biological in nature, and their timing is socially regulated. These concepts point to one way of structuring the passage of time in the life span of the individual, and in delineating a social time clock that can be superimposed upon the biological clock, these concepts are helpful in comprehending the life cycle.

Younger people have many ways of identifying themselves. In the United States, teen-agers have a definable culture. Adults identify themselves by profession or occupation and also by sex roles, such as wife and mother or husband and father. Such identities are lost by the elderly when a spouse dies or when retirement is mandatory at age 65. People may be reluctant to identify with a group called *the aging* because it represents a loss of prestige. G. Streib (1965) found that the aged do not identify with an aging group, nor do they have a definable culture. As Kalish (1975) points out, being elderly is a roleless role: being old is defined in terms of what one is not, rather than what one is.

Disengagement *Disengagement* is a tendency for older people to withdraw from activities. Cumming and Henry (1961) interviewed and tested two samples of adult subjects, one ranging in age between 48 and 68 years, and the other between 70 and 80 years. On the basis of their data, they put forward the concept of disengagement, which they originally ascribed to biological forces. Later studies, however, pointed to extremely powerful social forces that generate and encourage disengagement. Cumming and Henry also postulated that disengagement is a positive adaptive approach to successful aging, a position that has been seriously questioned.

Table 6·4 Consensus in a Middle-Class Middle-Age Sample Regarding Various Age-Related Characteristics

AGE-RELATED CHARACTERISTICS	AGE RANGE DESIGNATED AS APPROPRIATE OR EXPECTED	PERCENT WHO CONCUR	
		Men (N = 50)	Women (N = 43)
Best age for a man to marry	20–25	80	90
Best age for a woman to marry	19–24	85	90
When most people should become grandparents	45–50	84	79
Best age for most people to finish school and go to work	20–22	86	82
When most men should be settled on a career	24–26	74	64
When most men hold their top jobs	45–50	71	58
When most people should be ready to retire	60–65	83	86
A young man	18–22	84	83
A middle-age man	40–50	86	75
An old man	65–75	75	57
A young woman	18–24	89	88
A middle-age woman	40–50	87	77
An old woman	60–75	83	87
When a man has the most responsibilities	35–50	79	75
When a man accomplishes most	40–50	82	71
The prime of life for a man	35–50	86	80
When a woman has the most responsibilities	25–40	93	91
When a woman accomplishes most	30–45	94	92
A good-looking woman	20–35	92	82

(Neugarten, Moore, and Lowe, 1965)

G. Maddox (1963), in a study of 250 older people, showed that morale levels were directly related to activity levels: increasing activity levels were indicative of increasing morale, and decreasing activity levels were associated with decreasing morale. The hypothesis that disengagement universally leads to successful aging seems to be incorrect.

Robert Havighurst, Bernice Neugarten, and Sheldon Tobin (1968) showed that no one theory is adequate to account for successful adaptation to old age. These investigators found many exceptions to the assertion that activity is associated with life satisfaction. Although the active elderly person was more likely to have higher life satisfaction, a sufficient number of exceptions made this rule very weak. Many people who were disengaged reported general life satisfaction.

Because a theory based entirely on activity or disengagement is inadequate to account for the variation in aging patterns, Neugarten, Havighurst, and Tobin (1968) attempted to study differences in personality. They took the viewpoint that disengagement is adaptive for some people but not for others. Conversely, high levels of activity may generate high life satisfaction for some people and not for others. To test these hypotheses, they developed three sets of data: (1) personality classification based on 45 different traits; (2) social role activity as measured by the frequency and intensity of activity as a parent, spouse, grandparent, kin-group member, worker, homemaker, citizen, friend, neighbor, club and association member, and church member; and (3) life satisfaction based on taking pleasure in daily activities, regarding life as meaningful and accepting what life has been, feeling successful in having achieved major goals, having a positive self-image, and maintaining happy and optimistic attitudes and moods. The investigators used a small sample, 59 men and women, ages 70 to 79.

As with any age group, a common interest and purpose can draw together older people, and the satisfaction each person derives from group activity may differ. (Action, Vetter)

Their analyses revealed four major personality types (integrated, armored-defended, passive-dependent, and unintegrated) and several subdivisions (based on role activity scores and life-satisfaction ratings) for a total of eight patterns (Table 6•5). There are three subgroups within the integrated personality type, each with a different level of activity.

1. The *reorganizers*. These people may be considered the optimal group according to the American cultural tradition that says, "Stay young, stay active, and refuse to grow old."
2. The *focused*. These people have integrated personalities and perceive themselves as having high life satisfaction, but their level of activity is average. In adjusting to old age, these people become selective in their activities.
3. The *disengaged*. These people have integrated personalities and high life satisfaction, but low activity. They are generally described as self-directed persons.

The three patterns show that neither activity level nor disengagement adequately defines life satisfactions and dissatisfactions among the aging. High-satisfaction people often demonstrate high role activity, but the numbers within this overall category are not large enough to correlate satisfaction and activity.

People labeled armored-defended are achievement-oriented and defensive against anxiety, and need to impose tight controls over their impulses. Within this personality group the authors found two personality patterns, one labeled holding-on and the other labeled constricted. Aging is threatening to these people. They cope

Table 6•5 Personality Type in Relation to Role Activity and Life Satisfaction (Age 70–79; *N* = 59)

PERSONALITY TYPE	ROLE ACTIVITY	LIFE SATISFACTION High	Medium	Low	Pattern
	High	9	2		A
Integrated	Medium	5			B
	Low	3			C
	High	5			D
Armored-defended	Medium	6	1		E
	Low	2	1	1	
	High		1		F
Passive-dependent	Medium	1	4		
	Low	2	3	2	G
	High		2	1	
Unintegrated	Medium				
	Low	1	2	5	H
	Total	34	16	9	

NOTE: A = reorganizer, B = focused, C = disengaged, D = holding on, E = constricted, F = succorance-seeker, G = apathetic, H = disorganized.
(Neugarten, Havighurst, and Tobin, 1968)

with this threat by clinging to middle-age patterns. The remaining personality types and patterns represent less satisfactory adjustments to aging, at least as defined by our culture: succorance-seeker, apathetic, and disorganized. Neugarten and her colleagues summarized their data as follows:

Investigators have found that an aging person who has a close friend with whom to talk tends to be more satisfied with life in general. (Frank Siteman, Stock, Boston)

> We regard personality as the pivotal dimension in describing patterns of aging and in predicting relationships between level of social activity and life satisfaction. There is considerable evidence that, in normal men and women, there is no sharp discontinuity of personality with age, but instead an increase in consistency. Those characteristics that have been central to the personality seem to become even more clearly delineated, and those values the individual has been cherishing become even more salient. In the personality that remains integrated—and in an environment that permits—patterns of overt behavior are likely to become increasingly consonant with the individual's underlying personality needs and desires. (Neugarten, Havighurst, and Tobin, 1968, p. 177)

Another aspect of life satisfaction is worth noting. M. F. Lowenthal and C. Haven (1968) found that for some people the availability of a confidant appears to be sufficient for general life satisfaction. The confidant is someone with whom a person feels free to discuss personal matters, someone who is able to understand problems without extended explanations. Usually the elderly prefer to discuss personal matters with someone their own age, since generational similarity increases the ability to understand. Apparently elderly people do not need many friends, but it is crucial to have someone who will listen.

Family Relationships After reviewing research literature on living arrangements among the elderly, Lillian Troll (1971) concluded that older people prefer to maintain their own households. Their reluctance to live with their children is based in part on a desire to permit younger people to live their own lives. More important, independence allows the elderly to maintain competency and self-determination. Often the elderly person is unable to maintain a household because of the death of a spouse, chronic ill health, or financial considerations. When this happens, psychological burdens are placed on both old and young. For the older person, moving to the home of a child means lower status, a change in role, and to some degree at least, a loss of independence.

According to the available data, most elderly people in the United States live in their own homes. Despite the geographic distance that ordinarily exists between children and their elderly parents, the elderly parent is not abandoned by the adult children (Shanas, Townsend, Wedderburn, Friis, Millhof, and Stehouwer, 1968; Streib, 1958; and Sussman, 1965). Patterns vary with financial circumstances, but in general active contacts and relationships are maintained between parents and their adult children.

Loss of Spouse Perhaps the most serious crisis that faces an elderly person is the loss of a spouse. It is far more likely that women will lose their husbands than that husbands will lose their wives both because women usually marry men older than themsleves and because men tend to die younger. Loss of a spouse results

Psychological Factors in Marital Happiness

One of the earliest systematic studies about the psychological factors involved in successful marriages was conducted by Lewis M. Terman (1938). The data were secured from a questionnaire administered to 792 couples. The questions focused on three general areas: personality factors, familial and other background variables, and factors associated with sexual adjustments in the marriage. A score for each factor was computed.

The personality factor can be viewed as an index of temperamental predisposition to find happiness rather than unhappiness in marriage. It correlated .46 with the overall index of marital happiness. Among both husbands and wives, those people prone to be unhappy were more likely, in general, to be touchy and critical, to lose their tempers easily, to rebel against orders or direction, to lack self-confidence, to show little interest in children and old people, and to have great shifts in mood.

Nine background factors were most predictive of marital happiness: parents with happy marriages; childhood happiness; harmonious relationship with mother; firm, but not harsh, home discipline; strong identification with father; little or no conflict with father; parental openness regarding sex; infrequent and moderate childhood punishments; and positive premarital attitudes toward sex.

Among the sex factors contributing to overall happiness, two variables stand out: wife's orgasm adequacy, and differences in strength of sex drive of husband and wife.

Orgasm frequency of the wife contributed significantly to the overall happiness score of both the wife and the husband. Women who reported experiencing orgasms regularly, and their husband's as well, had higher happiness scores than did women who reported never (or sometimes) experiencing orgasm. The frequency of orgasm of the husbands had the same effects on the happiness scores as was found for the wives. With regard to strength of sex drive, the preferred status was that both partners have roughly equivalent sex drives.

Terman concluded that the data do not confirm the notion, then prevalent, that the key to marital happiness is sexual compatibility. Sex contributes no more than do the personality and background factors.

in intense bereavement, often accompanied by guilt, loss of companionship and sexual satisfactions, and changes in friendship patterns. Some people experience intense and prolonged bereavement, whereas others recover more rapidly. Marriage satisfaction and depth of attachment are not related to successful recovery. Probably some women go through a kind of rehearsal for widowhood, realizing that they are likely to become widows. Loss of a spouse is a major cause of the lack of life satisfaction often expressed by elderly people.

Retirement For people with adequate incomes, retirement may bring opportunities for a variety of new activities, but leisure is accompanied by a decline in responsibility, status, and self-identity that reduces life satisfaction. Adjustment to retirement is influenced by health status, alternative sources of satisfaction, and financial security (Streib, 1956). Regardless of socioeconomic status, where work is not only a source of income, but also a source of considerable satisfaction, forced retirement is perceived as a negative event.

Like men, career women undergo an abrupt change of status upon retirement. For women who are homemakers, a form of retirement occurs when their children leave home. The general belief is that when middle-age women no longer have children to care for, they become bored and unhappy. There is apparently little or no evidence to substantiate this belief. Indeed, there are some studies suggesting that parents are relieved when their children no longer are dependent on them and do not consume their time and energies.

Menopause At approximately the time when children are leaving home, women enter the physiological period called **menopause**. The "change of life" usually occurs between ages 46 and 50, when menstruation gradually ceases and the child-bearing function comes to an end. Many women experience physical discomforts, such as hot flashes, headaches, dizziness, or pains in the joints. The degree to which these reactions are disruptive varies considerably within samples of women and has been estimated to be as low as 10 percent. The departure of children from the home at this time has clouded the psychological consequences of menopause. The woman's role may change abruptly from active mother to someone with very few responsibilities. Marital stress is common also during this period. The husband may be extremely busy with his career, now at its peak, or he may be experiencing a period of readjustment caused by a discrepancy between his achievements and the goals that he set for himself earlier in life. Women who perceive their lives as happy and meaningful are less likely to report serious adverse effects during the menopause.

A questionnaire was used to elicit attitudes toward menopause among women in four age groups: 21 to 30, 31 to 44, 45 to 55, and 56 to 65 (Neugarten, Wood, Kraines, and Loomis, 1968). The evidence shows a strong age difference in the perception of menopause. More younger women than older women viewed menopause as a significant event. Neugarten and her associates ascribe this difference to a lack of concern among older women about the loss of reproductive capacity. Their data show that a generally positive attitude toward life helps to minimize adverse effects of menopause.

Personality Changes Throughout our discussions of social and personality development, we have shown that personality changes are usually not a function of chronological age. The notion that adolescence, for example, is characterized by considerable emotional stress was rejected on the grounds that such stress is not universal, and individual problems can be explained in terms of specific environmental events. A central theme, then, has been the consistency of personality across the life span, including the aging period.

Nevertheless, many scholarly discussions of aging have preserved the notion that personality characteristics are tied to biological age as opposed to cultural forces. We think that on the basis of accumulated evidence, personality characteristics of the aging are much more a function of cultural expectations than of biological changes. Unfortunately, the evidence in this area focuses on a very limited number of personality variables. We will explore some of these variables to determine whether the adjectives that are so readily applied to the elderly (such as *introverted* and *rigid*) have any basis in fact.

Introversion Like disengagement, **introversion** refers to a kind of inwardness and a reticence to engage in activity with others. Relationships between introversion and age have been established mainly with personality tests designed to measure introversion and extroversion. Results of a study (Gutman, 1966) in which subjects aged 17 through 94 were tested for introversion-extroversion suggested that there is an increase in the tendency toward introversion with age. Similar findings have been reported by others, but the correlations are extremely small.

Rigidity **Rigidity** has many meanings in psychology. The word *rigid* may be applied to a person who repeats a response even though it is incorrect or inappropriate, or to attitudes and value systems that are very narrow and unyielding.

Else Frenkel-Brunswik (1949) developed a life-style conceptualization by defining rigidity as intolerance of ambiguity. People who are unable to tolerate ambiguity attempt to impose a structure on the world by viewing things in black and white, interpreting situations prematurely and usually inaccurately, or by taking extreme positions on issues. Ambiguous situations are especially anxiety-producing for these people. In order to control or reduce anxiety, they try to organize their lives to conform with their narrow, unyielding views. Frenkel-Brunswik associated such behavior tendencies with conservatism, prejudice, dogmatism, and the avoidance of new experiences. Furthermore, she assumed that all of these behaviors are associated with increasing adult age.

Raymond Kuhlen (Pressey and Kuhlen, 1957) analyzed a national sample of 9000 college graduates whose attitudes on a number of issues were obtained through written verbal statements. He predicted that older individuals would be more prejudiced and would more frequently fail to respond to questions that they considered ambiguous. Both hypotheses were supported, but the results may reflect different generations rather than different chronological ages.

Studies demonstrating increasing rigidity in later life are confounded by differences in learning ability between older and younger subjects. The rigidity that is observed experimentally or clinically in older people may be a consequence of reduced learning ability. Research in which learning ability is controlled is needed but very difficult to achieve.

The Self-Concept **Self-concept,** the image that people have of themselves, reflects both their actual experiences and their interpretations of these experiences. The effect of aging on self-concept is uncertain. Some studies show an increase in positive self-concept with age, some show no change in positive self-concept with age, and others show a decrease in positive self-concept. H. Kaplan and A. Pokorny (1970) suggested that there is likely to be a more positive self-concept among people whose standard of living is consistent with their expectations. They also suggest that self-concept does not suddenly emerge in the later years as positive or negative (or somewhere in between), but continues the trend of previous years of experience.

In one of the very few lifespan studies of self-concept, Rolf Monge (1976) asked more than 2000 adolescents in grades 9 through 12, plus an additional sample of

1894 people ranging in age from 20 through 89, to rate the concept *my characteristic self* using 21 polar adjective pairs. The data were analyzed for both age differences and sex differences. On the basis of a factor analysis of the intercorrelations of the items, Monge found four component factors:

Throughout his life Rembrandt painted many self-portraits. At the time of this particular one, he was in his sixties—having suffered the decline in popularity of his painting style and the loss of most of his work and other possessions in bankruptcy proceedings. (Alinari-Art Reference Bureau)

1. The achievement-leadership factor is defined positively by adjectives such as *superior, smart, successful, valuable, sharp, confident, steady,* and *strong.* A person who has positive ratings on this component perceives himself or herself as being capable and intelligent, a front-runner. Negative ratings convey self-acceptance by the individual as a loser.
2. The congeniality-sociability factor is defined by *kind, nice, friendly, good,* and *stable.* People who attain positive ratings on this factor tend to view themselves as open and responsive to social stimulation.
3. Adjustment is defined by the positive adjectives *refreshed, relaxed, satisfied, healthy,* and *happy,* versus the negative adjectives *tired, nervous, dissatisfied, sick,* and *sad.* Monge viewed these adjectives as conveying the self-image of a person comfortably accommodated to the environment and making adequate adjustments to both positive and negative immediate situations. These people probably approximate Erikson's notion of integrity.
4. The masculinity-femininity factors showed that males and females view the essential structure of the factors similarly but disagree about whether a particular adjective is positive or negative. Monge reports that males view *ruggedness* and *hardness* as positive, for example, whereas females view *delicate, soft,* and *weak* as positive.

The data showing age trends for each sex (Figure 6•2) indicate that for both sexes there is a sharp rise from adolescence into young adulthood in viewing oneself positively on the achievement-leadership factor. This rise continues for males until the age group 35 to 49 years, at which time there is a slight but consistent decline. For females the decline occurs after age 34, and the low self-concept on this factor is maintained until the last age level. Monge speculates that the increase after 65 for women may be due to their adaptation to their husbands' retirement or death by means of leading a more active life and taking a more direct role in managing their own affairs.

The age trend for congeniality-sociability factor is essentially flat but rises significantly in the post-retirement years for both sexes. Monge is probably correct in suspecting that this age effect is a function of the sample: subjects were selected from Senior Citizen centers and social clubs. These settings attract congenial and sociable people, rather than the alienated and incapacitated.

With respect to the third factor, adjustment, there is a decline from the adolescent period to early adulthood and then a consistent increase until the mid-sixties, when self-perceived adjustment declines slightly. The readjustments that occur in marriage, child rearing, and adaptation to the stresses of adult life are followed by the decline during post-retirement years.

The fourth factor, masculinity-femininity, is unique. Apparently adolescent males need to perceive themselves as real men while they establish a sense of identity. A parallel trend occurs for females. Once this sense of identity is established, there is a relaxation in role playing, and the sexes view the polar adjectives less rigidly. Monge's data showing that adults become less concerned about their masculinity or femininity are consistent with research by Lewis Terman and Catherine Cox Miles (1936), who found that the interests and attitudes of men and women become more similar with age.

Monge's research suggests that an overall interpretation of self-concept and aging must take into account both the specific situation of the individuals in the study and the kinds of self-concepts being assessed. What is needed now is a series of short-term (ten to twenty years) longitudinal studies using Monge's sophisticated methods to determine to what degree the observed effects can be attributed to aging.

Mental Illness It is difficult to determine whether certain forms of mental illness are natural consequences of aging or correlates of aging, or whether psychopathology in the aged is somehow related to a deficiency in biological functioning (Gurland, 1973). Among the aging there is a higher incidence of psychopathology related to biological dysfunction, especially cerebrovascular disease. In the more severe cases of organic psychosis caused by chronic brain dysfunction, the person requires

Male and female roles tend to become less rigidly defined as a person ages. (Bruce Davidson, Magnum)

institutionalization. Although such cases are relatively few, a larger category includes general psychological states that are probably not directly related to the effects of aging but are correlates of aging.

Many of the losses we have already examined affect the person's psychological adjustment: spouse, close friends, relatives, job, social status, general health, and cognitive abilities. The least surprising form of mental illness that occurs among elderly people is a chronic state of **depression**. Perhaps only an exceptional person would be able to withstand not only the frequent losses but also the physical lim-

Fig. 6·2 Age trends for each sex on four component factors derived from data on the concept *my characteristic self*: achievement-leadership, congeniality-sociability, adjustment, and masculinity-femininity. (Monge, 1976)

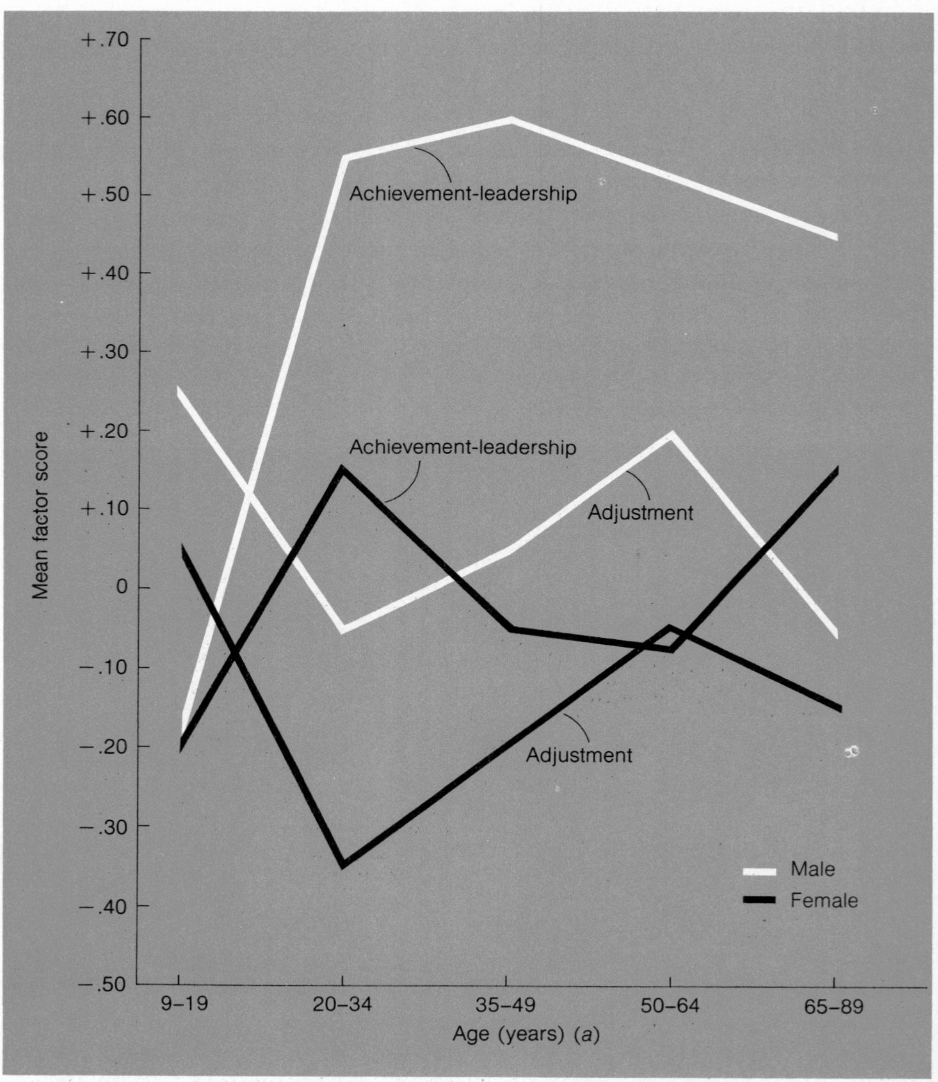

itations that accompany old age. Depression could be considered a normal response to aging. That depression is a frequently occurring form of adjustment has been documented by N. E. Zinberg and I. Kaufman (1963) and by E. Busse and J. B. Reckless (1961).

The mildly depressed elderly person who is not physically ill can be treated through environmental changes involving social activity (Botwinick, 1973). Programs involving social engagements enable the person to gain gratification from interactions with a broad variety of people (Busse and Pfeiffer, 1969). Botwinick

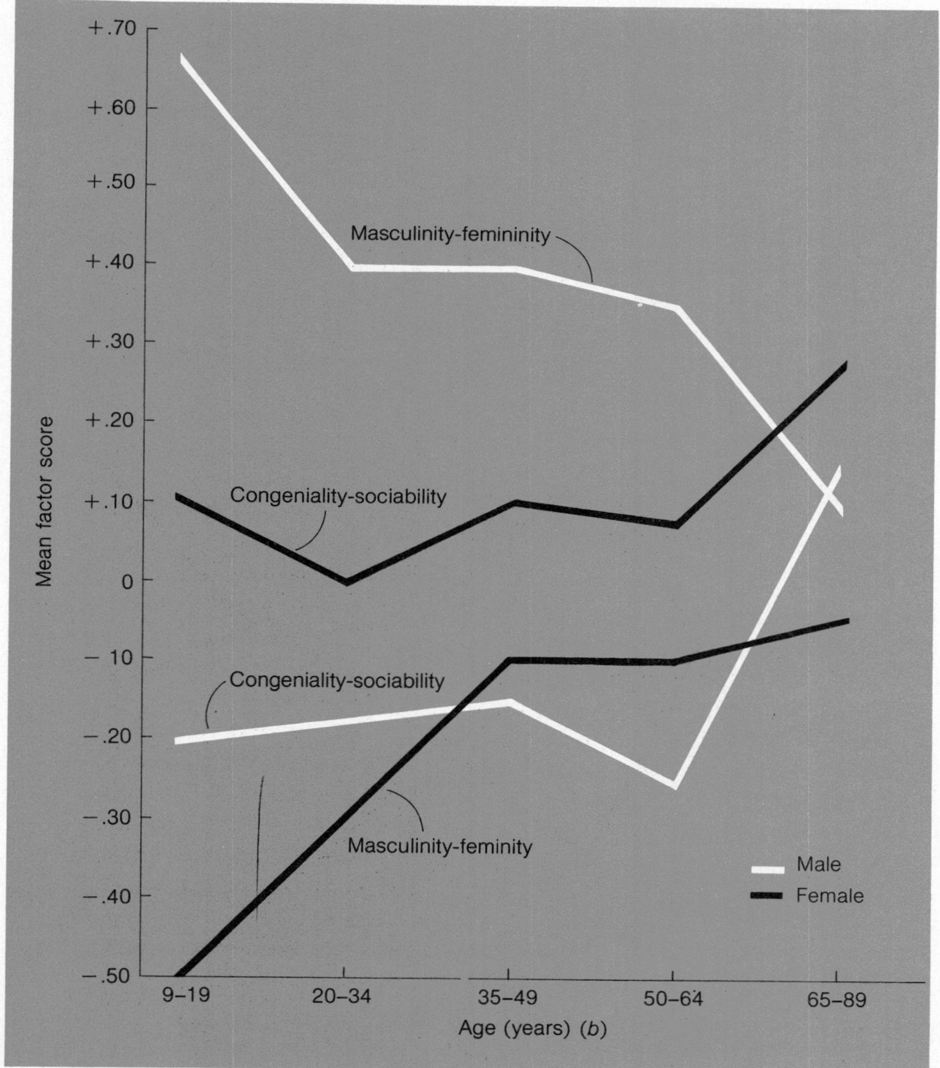

Fig. 6·2 continued

Personality and Coronary Heart Disease

There is a general consensus that a person who smokes, has a family history of coronary disease, and frequently eats cholesterol-rich foods is a strong candidate for a heart attack. There is now research evidence to suggest that personality predispositions may also be related to the incidence of heart disease.

The most extensive program of research attempting to link behavioral variables to coronary heart disease has been undertaken by M. Friedman and R. Rosenman (Friedman, 1969). These investigators have found that coronary-prone individuals display a certain behavior pattern (Type A):

1. Highly competitive
2. Involved in many activities that have time pressures
3. Extraordinarily alert
4. Like to set own work pace
5. Tend to be impatient with slowness (even to the point of hurrying conversations or supplying words for persons with whom they are talking)
6. Appear restless, and engage in fist clenching, grimaces, and explosive speech

People who are characterized by Type B behavior (essentially the opposite of Type A) are easy-going. They rely on their creative energy and reasoning ability in coping with demands made on them. They do not use hostility, are not prone to hurry, and do not become tense over time pressures.

The ideal experimental procedure for determining the relationship between these two behavior patterns and the incidence of heart disease would be to take a random selection of people and make some of them Type A's and the others Type B's and then look for differences in rate of heart disease. Obviously, this is not feasible. We are therefore left with correlational data.

Friedman and Rosenman developed a scale to assess a person's type of behavior pattern. Positive answers to questions such as the following indicate a Type A person:

> "Do you drive harder to accomplish things than most of your associates?"
>
> "Do you have the impression that time is passing too fast for the things you'd like to get done?"
>
> "If a car in your lane is going too slowly for you, what do you do about it?"
>
> "When you play a game with persons of your own age, do you play mainly to win?"

Using questions such as these with over 3500 men (ages 35 through 59) who were free of clinical heart disease, the Western Collaborative Group Study (WCGS) found a 50 percent incidence of Type A persons. Compared to Type B's, Type A's showed the following:

1. Approximately three times greater incidence of heart disease
2. Larger increases in serum cholesterol, triglycerides, and Beta-lipoproteins.
3. Smaller whole blood clotting times
4. Several other warning signals associated with impending heart conditions.

During the first five years of the study up to six times more Type A than Type B men died because of heart disease. Furthermore, the coronary vasculature of deceased Type A men (whether they died from heart disease or some other cause) showed twice as much basic atherosclerosis as that of the deceased Type B men.

Rosenman and Friedman believe that the Type A pattern of behavior is related to environmental factors. They assert that the pattern emerges when the environment arouses particular facets of an individual's personality. In a recent speech reported in the newspaper, Dr. Friedman speculated that the incidence of Type A persons may be rising to 70 percent because of several environmental factors. Young people are leaving the hippie movement (which he believes to be counter to Type A behavior) and returning to more traditional societal expectations (competing for grades and jobs). He also says that although women typically show a lower incidence of Type A behavior than men, women's increasing participation in business and the professions will add to the number of Type A's.

These statements are clearly speculative. It does seem clear, however, that self-imposed stress (such as is found among Type A's) is associated with heart disease.

suggests that in many cases depression results from an unwillingness to give up familiar life patterns and adopt new ones more in accordance with current capabilities. An object of therapy would be to help the aging person modify goals.

Another form of seemingly maladaptive behavior that occurs with great frequency among the elderly is *hypochondriasis*, an exaggerated concern about one's health. This behavior is also a correlate of aging because the probability of disease increases with age. Hypochondriasis may also be part of the disengagement process. Preoccupation with ill health is a mechanism that the elderly person can use to avoid confronting the realities of psychological and physical decrement and to avoid situations in which failure is likely.

Other emotional problems occur among the elderly less frequently than depression and hypochondriasis. After middle age suicide rates increase for men but decrease for women. Alcoholism is less prevalent among the aging than among younger age groups. In terms of other forms of functional disease, the elderly are not very different from younger people.

Death and Dying Robert Kastenbaum and Ruth Aisenberg (1972) have examined in detail the philosophical, personal and social implications of death. Although elderly people might be expected to fear death more than the young, Kastenbaum concludes that most old people are not afraid of death. People who achieve the eighth stage of development described by Erikson do not express fear but accept the inevitability of death and have no regret about their lives. Death is feared most by young people who feel that they have a right to live to old age. To some extent death is feared by normal human beings regardless of age, but Kastenbaum's data suggest that concern with death and hostility toward death are more prevalent among young people.

The research literature on death and dying is relatively sparse, and Kastenbaum and Aisenberg suggest some questions that should be examined:

> How does aversion (and other responses) to death develop? What stages does it pass through? What are the critical factors which influence its scope, particularity, and intensity? How does the development of death responses interweave with other aspects of personality growth? . . . From what standpoint can we say that one orientation toward death—fearing, sorrowing, overcoming, participating—is "better" than another? Our own assumptions about the meaning of human life must be examined, as well as the death attitudes and attitude-correlates of our subjects. (Kastenbaum and Aisenberg, 1972, pp. 107–108)

Environmental Adaptations for the Aging

6•3 Elderly people, like middle-age people and young people, cannot be readily categorized. Individuality is maintained until death. But certain aspects of the aging process increase the difficulties of adapting to environmental demands. The greatest handicap of aging is the decline of physical capability. Because of sensory losses, a decrease in available energy, and a decline in physical agility, even ordinary

This man lives in the tenant wing of an urban hotel—another housing alternative but probably not one that many elderly people would choose. (Nikki Arai, BBM Associates)

behaviors can become burdensome. Consequently, questions arise about appropriate housing for the elderly. Keeping in mind that old people prefer their own housing arrangements, how should housing be designed for the elderly? What other environmental features would make a meaningful difference in permitting a comfortable old age as opposed to a stressful one?

Housing Alternatives Several housing possibilities are available to elderly people. Among planned communities for elderly people there are some that do not permit children and even have minimum age requirements. Many people find these communities satisfactory, but others feel that such communities cut the elderly person off from contemporary society. Conceivably this is why such arrangements are successful; contemporary society may represent a threat to some elderly people. Other planned communities include younger families with children in one area somewhat separated from the older people, so that children and younger adults are present but not forced on the elderly person. Communities of this kind are usually expensive, perhaps beyond the financial means of most elderly people.

Federal and state housing programs have been largely unsuccessful in relieving the housing problems of the elderly. Most of the low-rent, high-rise apartments have been designed for the entire low-rent group, rather than for the elderly. One consequence is that the elderly experience increased loneliness and isolation in a living environment designed with younger people in mind. Private builders have been reluctant to enter this market because the profit level is too low.

High-rise apartments that have been constructed for and rented only to elderly people have been more successful. Many elderly people find these developments attractive. Yet other people choose to remain in their own homes, if possible. There is simply no one answer to what living arrangements are best for elderly people.

State and Federal Programs As the population of people sixty-five years of age and over increases, and as the cost of maintaining the typical person in that age category outstrips their savings and retirement funds because of inflation, state and federal governments have enacted legislation for a variety of programs. The major federal agency for these programs is the Administration on Aging, which has offices in major cities throughout the United States. One responsibility of these offices is to provide elderly people with information concerning various issues relevant to their lives.

The effectiveness of federal and state programs has not been systematically examined. Some of these programs include Meals-on-Wheels, which provides food for nonambulatory people; centers that offer many programs, including continuing education and health services; day-care facilities in which the individual can receive outpatient medical services, such as physical therapy, and other kinds of services; a foster grandparent program in which low-income elderly people are paid a nominal fee for working and playing with institutionalized children; the Retired Senior

The foster grandparent shown here built the doll house for the girl he works with at a state hospital and training school. (Action, Vetter)

Volunteer program, in which elderly people develop and provide community services, but without compensation; and transportation services specifically designed for elderly people.

Environments for the Aged It is possible to develop environments for the aged in terms of both the physical demands of the environment and its psychological attributes. A. Schwartz (1975) has written an excellent description of a model based chiefly on the work of H. Proshansky, W. Ittelson, and A. Rivlin (1970) of the Environmental Psychology Program of the City University of New York. In this model the optimal environment for the aged is seen as providing necessary and appropriate cues, stimulation, and support (Table 6•6). The older person may need help in the form of environmental cues for activities such as locating spaces and finding one's way. The environment can also provide stimulation for the person as a whole, including social and intellectual interests. Finally, environments that are supportive of elderly persons meet many specific needs as well as providing options such as allowing for a person's desire for privacy (a luxury that is simply not available in the typical institutional setting). Schwartz makes many concrete suggestions for developing environments in which the individual continues to control his or her own life and is able to maintain self-esteem. In summarizing his position, Schwartz (1975) states:

> Spaces and places are improperly designed not only in physical terms but because designs also overlook human needs for privacy, territoriality, and freedom of choice, and often conceive of the individual as a simple machine man. Unintended consequences are often ignored and no attempt is made to evaluate just how well

Table 6·6 Sample Functions and Their Implementation for Three Design Elements in Artificial Environments for the Aged

DESIGN ELEMENTS	FUNCTIONS	IMPLEMENTATION
Environmental Cues	To identify spaces (private or public)	Signs with letters or recognizable symbols, good contrast, easily read from walking or wheelchair eye-level
	To show way through space	Additional reinforcing signs at frequent intervals
	To warn of hazards	Texture effects for hazard zones
	To locate service areas	Color-themed suites or areas
Environmental Stimulation	To use all senses	Bright, intense colors; maximum contrast for color and music; nonbland foods, wines; textured surfaces
	To maintain appropriate degree of variety	Pictures, plants, flowers, mobiles that can be changed; varying levels of music (while keeping sound levels and quality compatible with elderly listeners)
	To challenge with activities that have intrinsic value or meaningful outcomes	TV, radio, tape-recordings, records, large-print books and newspapers for entertainment, information, discussion; ready availability of pets for observing, stroking, or care-taking; frequent contact options with babies, children, young adults
Environmental Support	To provide appropriately designed furnishings	Oversize knobs, handles; controls with extensions that allow control by arm or leg pressure; detachable head, shoulder, or arm supports for wheelchairs, sitting chairs
	To facilitate communication	In-house phone system; ready access to reading lights, large print, magnifying glasses, radio-TV earphones
	To provide privacy options	Entering a room only when invited; providing locks for doors
	To foster individualization	Encourage personalizing rooms; some personal items through living areas; maximum flexibility to accommodate individual eating tastes, habits, and rhythm

(Adapted from Kiritz and Moos, 1974)

This woman appears to have arranged her environment so that she can easily maintain her interests. Perhaps, her look of well-being also comes partly from having a place to do with as she wishes. (Department of Housing and Urban Development)

the setting actually works. The danger is that the person will adjust at the price of continuing erosion of the properties that make him distinctly human.

Increasing population is a problem that involves social policy and is, therefore, necessarily political. The data, however, are clear: we can no longer ignore the impact of the environment on human beings.

Summary

In conducting studies among the aging, psychologists have been handicapped by lack of access to a suitable population of elderly people for testing. Devising learning tests for mature people is difficult because the test must reflect the subject's current ability to learn rather than the effects of prior learning. Nonsense learning tasks, which are used successfully with children and young people, are often rejected by elderly subjects who are more cautious and see such tasks as trivial. Cross-sectional studies of learning are biased because today's young adults, on the average, have accumulated more years of formal education than their grandparents.

Studies show that learning ability and cognitive competence increase rapidly from infancy to about age twenty, then decline only slightly until about age fifty-five. After fifty-five there is a marked decline in all tasks except verbal tasks, in which performance continues to increase. Decline in intellectual ability during old age has been attributed variously to a slowing of reaction time, loss of sensory acuity (especially vision and hearing), and physical debilitation caused by cerebrovascular and cardiovascular diseases.

Our youthful views of the aging may help to determine what kind of people we will become when we ourselves are old. When young and old are asked to describe the characteristics of aging, considerable agreement results; but old people value autonomy far more than our society expects them to. The elderly do not identify with a group called the aging, and, unlike teen-agers, do not have a definable culture.

Disengagement, the tendency to withdraw from activity, can be interpreted as a positive adaptive approach to the physical limitations of aging, or as a maladaptive approach that deprives the individual of the gratification possible through social interaction. Although activity is associated with greater life satisfaction among the elderly, many happy but inactive individuals are exceptions to the rule. Individuality is maintained until death, and successful aging can be defined only in relation to specific personality types. Personalities do not change radically as people grow older but tend to become more consistent.

Two factors that decrease life satisfaction among the aging are loss of spouse and forced retirement, both of which necessitate radical changes in life style and alterations of self-concept. Although financial security tends to offset the adverse effects of retirement, many males experience a decline in self-concept after age 65. The trend is reversed in women, possibly because married women have greater freedom after their husbands retire, and widows have a more direct role in managing their own affairs.

Depression and hypochondriasis are the two psychological states most frequently associated with aging. Both can be described as correlates of aging, rather than results of aging, because depression is a normal reaction to losses, such as death of spouse or friends, and concern about ill health is realistic during old age.

As the number of people over sixty-five increases, there is a greater need for retirement communities and also for the kind of services that enable the elderly to remain in their own homes despite the physical limitations of aging. Most people prefer independence and tend to remain in their homes. Programs for the aging are now being devised with state and federal funding, but it is too soon to assess their effectiveness.

Suggested Readings

Birren, J., ed. 1959. *Handbook of aging and the individual.* Chicago: University of Chicago Press.

A comprehensive review of all aspects of aging. An excellent reference resource.

Eisdorfer, C., and Lawton, M. P., eds. 1973. *The psychology of adult development and aging.* Washington, D. C.: American Psychological Association.

This outstanding volume discusses learning, psychophysiology pathology, and socialization as they relate to aging.

Hardy, R. E., and Cull, J. A., eds. 1973. *The neglected older American: Social and rehabilitative services.* Springfield, Ill.: Charles C. Thomas

The health, transportation, housing, and financial needs of older Americans are described. Their needs are great.

Kalish, R. A. 1975. *Late adulthood: Perspectives on human development.* Monterey, Ca.: Brooks/Cole.

Kalish's book provides a clear description of the methodological problems in studying old people and incisive definitions of important problems. His humanistic analysis of aging provides numerous insights into the problems confronting this group in our society.

Kübler-Ross, E. 1969. *On death and dying.* New York: Macmillan.

A readable scholarly analysis of the issues associated with death and dying. An original conceptualization of the victim's changing reactions to impending death is presented.

Miller, A. 1951. *Death of a salesman.* New York: Bantam.

A play depicting the adaptive mechanisms of an unsuccessful salesman in the middle years.

Basic Processes

III That psychology should begin by examining the senses was not an accident, for ever since Plato and Aristotle the senses had been considered the path to the mind. Plato held that we know an imperfect world but that by looking inward, the mind can apprehend another world of perfect forms. Aristotle saw mind as knowing only its own cumulative experiences, and believed that universals are nothing more than generic images.

By the time of Weber and Fechner, British philosophers such as Locke, Hume, and Berkeley had essentially endorsed Aristotle's position and were concerned with describing the process by which simple and complex ideas are formed from stimuli impinging on the senses. Meanwhile, the German philosopher Immanuel Kant was asking how the structure of the mind itself organized incoming sensations. Soon Hermann Ebbinghaus began the scientific investigation of memory, looking for laws inherent in the ideas of Locke, Hume, and Berkeley.

More than any other areas of psychology, sensation, perception, memory, learning, cognition, and motivation stand in direct relation to ancient philosophical questions. Sensation and perception ask: How do we know? Memory, learning, and cognition ask: How do we retain what we know and how is knowledge transformed with experience? Motivation asks: What makes organisms active, and what makes one activity dominant over another?

For some rather surprising answers to these questions already in hand, we turn to the consideration of basic processes.

Sensory Processes

7 The study of **sensation** and **perception** is the oldest area in the discipline of psychology; it is also a science in its own right and a part of philosophy. Many scholars still consider it to be the central core of psychology, for they believe that to understand sensation is to understand the basis of all human knowledge. Those who do not take such an extreme view still acknowledge that sensation and perception form the principal basis on which we maintain contact with the world. Some philosophers contend that perception is a window to reality: what we see is what really is.

Without concerning ourselves with whether reality exists if we are not there to perceive it, we can attend to how our perceptions are reported. When an eyewitness to a crime later identifies one of the participants from among suspects in a lineup, is that identification infallible? Experiments have shown that mistakes in identification are easily made, especially if the circumstances of the original perception were hurried, confused, or highly emotional. What does it mean, then, to say that what we see or remember seeing may not be what really was?

We need a way to separate the parts of our perceptual experience that come from direct stimulation of receptors from the parts that are somehow added, distorted, or otherwise changed by the perceiver. This chapter will concern the first aspect of this separation. The second aspect will be discussed in the next chapter, where we shall see that the perceiver is an active participant in the perceptual process and not simply a passive recipient of stimulation.

How many senses are there? The traditional five are vision, audition, smell, taste, and touch—all tying us to the outer world. Two other senses are concerned with our inner environment: one for sensing our body parts, and the other for sensing balance and equilibrium. Each of these seven senses can be identified by its particular sensory surfaces. These specialized **receptors** transduce (convert) some form of energy from the outer environment or from inside us into *neural signals*, which are then transmitted through the nervous system. In this chapter we shall look at the kinds of environmental energies to which we are sensitive and at the receptor mechanisms that transduce these energies.

Measuring Sensations: Psychophysics

7·1 Sensory systems (such as vision, audition, smell, taste, and touch) respond to energy and transduce it into neural signals that are sent to the brain for processing (selection, identification, awareness, storage, and so forth) and response (immediate or delayed). The energy itself can be measured by means of certain physical instruments. A photometer, for example, measures the number of quanta of electromagnetic radiation that form light, thereby indicating the light's intensity. This is a physical measurement, not a sensation. To say that the light appears bright, however, reports a sensation. To say that the more intense the light (as measured by a photometer) the brighter it appears, states a *psychophysical* relationship—a relationship between sensation (psychology) and energy (physics).

In general, psychophysical relationships exist for all the senses, but they vary with measurement conditions and are rarely linear. That is, an increase in sensation may not be equal to a corresponding increase in energy. Doubling the energy of a light, for example, does not necessarily make the light appear to be twice as bright.

Although a few persons have the equivalent of perfect pitch for the different kinds of energy that are picked up by our senses, most of us cannot say that a light is one million quanta, a tone 82 decibels, a taste 33 parts per million, a touch 0.003 gram per square centimeter, and so forth. Perceivers do not perceive in terms of physical measurement scales; and (for complicated reasons) even if they did, these measurements would not be useful. Lights are bright or dim or various shades in between. How do we report these shades so that a psychophysicist can determine the psychophysical relationship between the brightness of the light and the intensity of the stimulation?

Aspects of Stimulation To Be Measured **Psychophysics** is usually concerned with the following four aspects of the impact of energy on a perceiver:

1. *Minimal detection*: the smallest amount of energy required in a given situation to enable the perceiver to detect that something has happened (I smell something).
2. *Discrimination*: the ability to detect that a change in stimulation has occurred even in the midst of other stimuli (the smell is different from what I smelled just before the oven was turned on).
3. *Recognition and identification*: the ability to recognize the pattern of change as a familiar one (we had that for dinner once before) and to assign it to a specific labeled category (I smell duck for dinner).
4. *Scaling*: the ability to measure the amount of sensation (that duck smells gamier than the one we had last week).

In France professional wine tasters are employed to make discriminations among various wines that may lead to the discovery of a wine fraud. (© Gilles Peress, Magnum Photos, Inc.)

Each of these aspects requires the perceiver to make some kind of response with respect to what he has perceived. The psychophysicist's concern is that the perceiver be able to use his response to measure or specify the psychophysical relationship between stimulus energy on the one hand and response, or sensation, on the other.

Detection In 1860, Gustav Theodor Fechner published a monumental treatise on psychophysical methods which is still useful today. We have already noted in Chapter 1 that Fechner extended Weber's law into the more general formulation that physical stimulus magnitudes are logarithmically related to their psychological sensations ($S = \text{k} \log R$). He also investigated the minimal amount of energy needed to produce an affirmative **detection** response 50 percent of the time.

Suppose you are in a lightproof cave trying to determine the minimal amount of light that can be detected. A friend standing 5 feet away strikes ten matches in succession and each time asks whether you can see the light from the match. If you can, then the light energy of the matches is not at threshold but well above it, because you detected its presence 100 percent of the time. Next, your friend moves to 10 feet away from you and repeats the experiment; he continues this process until he finds a distance at which you are able to see the light from the matches only five times out of ten, or 50 percent of the time. The amount of energy needed to produce this 50-percent detection response constitutes the **sensory threshold.**

Although you might wish to try this experiment, it would be impractical to do so because your friend would have to stand nearly 40 kilometers (25 miles) away from you under optimal conditions before you would fail to detect even a single match. The eye is much more sensitive than any photometer designed or constructed so far. In order for a light to be detected under optimal conditions, only five of the 127 million photoreceptors in either eye must absorb a single quantum of light energy, the minimal indivisible unit of electromagnetic energy. Thus, the visual system could scarcely be more sensitive than it is.

Most detection experiments are designed to determine the lowest energy value at which an observer is able to detect a stimulus—the **absolute threshold** (also called the **detection threshold**). This value indicates the maximal sensitivity of a particular receptor to a particular type of energy. As you can see from the values for each **sense modality** listed in Table 7•1, the human senses are incredibly sensitive.

Sense detection is, strictly speaking, not determined by the sensitivity of our sense receptors alone. At minimal intensity levels we are not always certain we detected the stimulus when it was presented. Perhaps our senses were fooling us or we were not attending as acutely as we can.

Discrimination In everyday life, we need to discriminate one stimulus from another rather than from the absence of stimulation. How intense does a sound have to be in order to be heard on a busy street corner at the rush hour? As the level of background sound increases, so must the sound level of the stimulus if it is to be heard. This psychophysical relationship is different from the one for detection. It concerns how much change in energy over the background level is needed for the stimulus to be noticed.

In 1843 Ernst Weber discovered that the psychophysical relationship between stimuli contained a constant term for each sense modality he tested. To test for discriminating differences between weights, Weber had his subject lift a standard weight in one hand and another weight that varied slightly from the standard in the other hand. The two weights looked the same, and so the subject had to pick the heavier or the lighter weight by feel alone. How small could the extra weight be and still be noticed as different? Weber found that whatever the weight

Table 7•1 Some Approximate Absolute Thresholds

SENSE MODALITY	STIMULUS	ABSOLUTE THRESHOLD
Vision		
Brightness	Candle flame	48 kilometers (30 miles) distant (on a dark clear night)
Audition		
Loudness	Tick of a watch	6 meters (20 feet) distant (under quiet conditions)
Taste		
Sweet solution	1 teaspoon sugar	8 liters (2 gallons) water
Smell	1 drop perfume	Diffused throughout six-room apartment
Touch	Wing of fly on cheek	Falling from distance of 1 centimeter (0.4 inch)

(Adapted from Galanter, 1962)

Decision Processes in Psychophysics

Psychophysical tasks are always difficult to judge. The subject must strain to hear a quiet sound, see a dim light, feel a light touch, and so forth. Sometimes the subject is certain that a stimulus was present, and sometimes the same subject may be equally certain that he or she saw, heard, or felt nothing. However, at other times, the subject may be unsure about whether an apparent sensation was due to a stimulus or to the subject's imagination.

Some persons are very cautious—before they will say that they detected something, they have to feel confident. If they attribute their sensation to imagination rather than to a stimulus, they will say that they detected nothing. Other persons are willing to take risks and will say that they detected the stimulus even when in doubt. A "cautious" subject usually shows a high threshold, and a "risk-taking" subject, a lower threshold. Therefore, simply measuring the number of times a subject says yes does not provide enough evidence from which to determine the subject's threshold.

Decision theory suggests a way of scoring the answers in a psychophysical experiment that separates the subject's sensitivity to the stimulus intensity from the effect of confidence or caution on the responses made (Swets, Tanner, and Birdsall, 1961). The four possible outcomes of this scoring procedure are shown in Figure 7A·1. "Hit" refers to a yes response to the presentation of the stimulus, and "miss" refers to a no response to the stimulus. "False alarm" refers to a yes response to the presentation of a blank when no stimulus was presented, and "correct reject" refers to a no response to a blank.

		PRESENTATION	
		Stimulus	Blank
RESPONSE	Yes	Hit	False alarm
	No	Miss	Correct reject

Fig. 7A·1 Four possible outcomes for use in scoring a psychophysical experiment.

In a decision-method experiment, the subject may be told that on half of the trials, stimuli of intensity 35 will be presented and on the other half, stimuli of intensity 0 (a blank trial). Each time a presentation is made, the subject must reply yes or no to indicate whether or not the stimulus was detected.

Let's say the subject is given 200 trials, 100 of which are all of a moderate stimulus intensity, and 100 of which are blank. A cautious subject, being uncertain, may say yes to the stimulus fewer than 50 times—perhaps only 40 times, resulting in a hit rate of 40/100 and a miss rate of 60/100. Because of such a subject's caution, he or she will rarely say yes to a blank, resulting in a false alarm rate of, for example, only 5/100, and a correct reject rate of 95/100.

The subject who likes to take risks, however, may reply yes to perhaps 70 of the 100 times the stimulus is presented, resulting in a hit rate of 70/100 and a miss rate of only 30/100. Such a subject's false alarm rate will also be high, because he or she will reply yes (the stimulus was present) on a high percentage of blank trials. It is quite possible for such a subject to have a false alarm rate of, for example, 20/100.

The ideal would be to have a high hit rate and simultaneously a low false alarm rate. Although the mathematics of decision theory are much more complex than indicated here, comparing the hit rate to the false alarm rate allows the experimenter to determine how many of each subject's responses result from his or her sensitivity to sounds and how many responses result from caution or from risk-taking.

of the standard, the variable weight had to differ by only 2 percent to be just noticeably different. Thus, for a 100-gram standard, the variable had to weigh at least 102 (or at most 98) grams; for a 50-gram standard, the variable had to weigh 51 (or 49) grams; for a 1500-gram standard, the variable had to weigh 1530 (or 1470) grams; and so forth. On the basis of this finding, Weber formulated the relationship $\Delta I/I = k$, where ΔI is the smallest detectable change in stimulus intensity, I is the intensity of the stimulus already present, and k is a constant.

Table 7·2 Weber's Constants

SENSE MODALITY	WEBER'S CONSTANT
Vision	
Brightness	1/60
Audition	
Loudness of a tone	1/10
Pitch of a tone	1/333
Taste	
Saline solution	1/5
Skin senses	
Surface pressure	1/7
Deep pressure	1/80
Lifted weights	1/50

NOTE: Data are approximate, from various determinations. The smaller the fraction, the greater the differential sensitivity. (Adapted from Hilgard, Atkinson, and Atkinson, 1975)

Table 7·2 gives **Weber's constants** for several sense modalities. You can see that the modality most sensitive to change is audition, in which we can discriminate a change in pitch if the physical change in frequency is 0.3 percent. Although not listed in the table, the sense of smell is least sensitive to change.

The Weber constants do not hold at the extreme ranges of standard values, however. If you had to lift a standard weight of 50,000 grams (about 100 pounds), what would be the just-noticeable difference (jnd) for the variable? It would actually be much greater than 1000 grams, because 100 pounds is almost beyond our capacity to make discriminations. What is the jnd for a 1 gram weight (about 1/30 ounce)? Many persons would not be able to tell that the 1 gram weight was in one hand, and so would not feel the difference of a 1.02 gram weight in the other hand. In fact, you might need to hold a 3 or 4 gram weight in order to detect the sensation of weight at all.

Recognition and Identification It may be less important to see a sign at night than to be able to read the sign. Identification of a stimulus occurs when the perceiver can label it or place it in an appropriate category or classification.

It is possible to study the psychophysical relationships between the physical measures of a stimulus and the psychological responses of recognition and identification. However, these relationships have not been important in themselves because recognition and identification depend on the perceiver's prior experience with the stimulus, on the expectation of what might be presented, and on motivation for the task. Because the physical stimulus itself is of less importance in that case, the topics of recognition and identification will be postponed until the next chapter, when we deal more fully with the perceiver.

Scaling We often want to scale, or order, stimuli that are clearly different and yet related to each other. For example, if I have four lights, each double the physical intensity of the previous one, I may want to know whether each appears to be double the brightness of the previous one—that is, whether the psychophysical relationship is linear. I can determine the amount of difference between the appearance of the lights by having a perceiver assign numbers to his sensations.

We use this scaling technique unconsciously in everyday life but not in a way that is useful psychophysically. "Today is twice as hot as yesterday" implies a scale of heat sensations. If today is 26°C, does that mean that yesterday was 13°C? Probably not, although we can't tell from the statement.

Let us consider a typical scaling task in the laboratory. A number of lights, all of the same wavelength but differing in intensity (the number of quanta they emit) and all well above absolute threshold, are shown one at a time to a perceiver, who is asked to assign a number to each light as it is presented to indicate its relative brightness. The perceiver first assigns an arbitrary *anchor* value to the first light, so that the relative brightness of each subsequent light can be described with an appropriate number. The series might be presented several times in different orders. If the perceiver gives different numbers for the same light, his scale value for this light would be the average of these numbers. This procedure is called *magnitude estimation.*

The curve labeled brightness in Figure 7•1 shows the results of a typical psychophysical procedure. When the physical energy is low, small energy changes produce large differences in appearance. However, when the physical energy is high, further changes produce little discriminable change in appearance. If the experiment were repeated with lines instead of lights and if the perceiver were asked to assign numbers representing the appearance of the line lengths, the results would look like the curve labeled length in Figure 7•1.

Both of these functions, as well as most psychophysical scaling tasks like these, can be described as a *power* or *exponential function* in the form $S = kI^n$ (S. Smith Stevens' power law), where S is the value of the sensation as assigned by the perceiver, I is the physical intensity of the stimulus as measured by some physical measuring instrument, k is a constant that is different for each sense modality and experimental condition, and n is an exponent. In Figure 7•1, n is less than

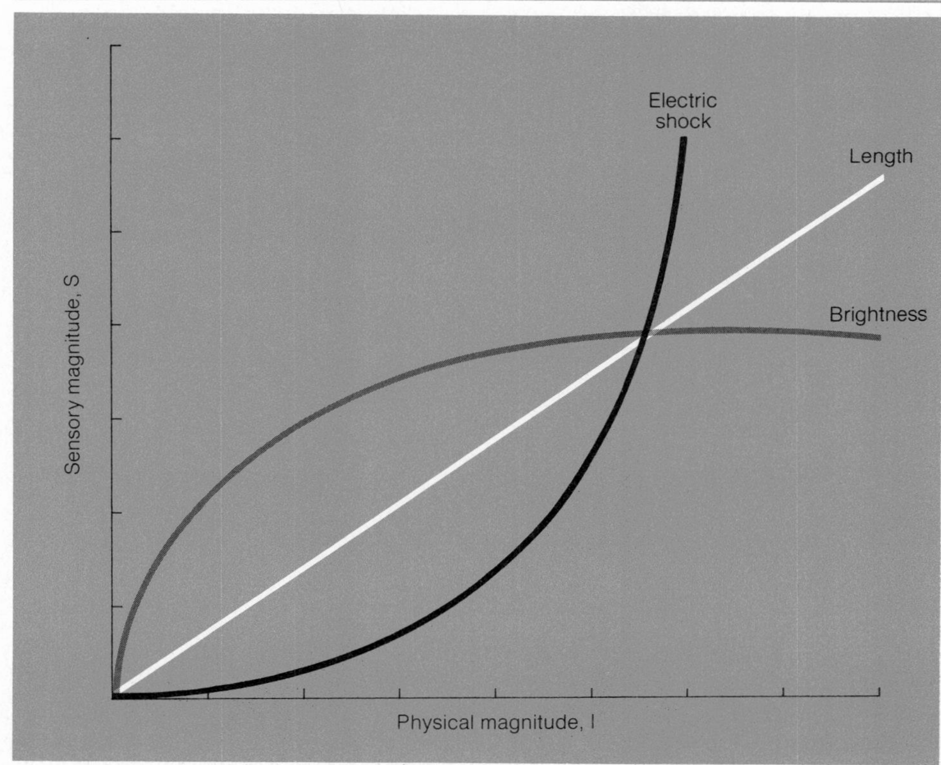

Fig. 7•1 Sensory-magnitude-estimation functions for brightness (light intensity), length, and electric shock (pain). (From Haber and Hershenson, 1973)

1 for the brightness curve, whereas n is equal to 1 for the length curve. For other modalities, such as scaling the strength of electric shock, the value of n is greater than 1: small shocks are perceived as close together; but as the shock level increases, the same physical differences are felt to be much larger.

We have been discussing psychophysical scales in which the physical dimension is independently specified, as when readings are given by a meter. What about scaling dimensions that have no physical counterpart, or ones that we do not know how to measure? Can you assign numbers to all of the Presidential hopefuls to represent their liberalness, using a middle-of-the-roader as an anchor value of 10? Or can you assign numbers to all of the men in a class as a function of their handsomeness, using some average-looking man as 10? Such scaling procedures can be done, even though there are no known physical dimensions underlying their scales.

Summary Psychophysics is defined as a study of the relationship between the physical energy of a stimulus and its psychological appearance to a perceiver. This relationship has to be studied because a one-to-one linear function between physics and psychology cannot be assumed, and is in fact rare.

Four different psychophysical questions are important:

1. How much energy is needed for a perceiver to be able to detect its presence in the absence of interfering background energy?
2. How much change in energy is needed to discriminate that energy from a background energy level?
3. What is the relationship between physical changes in a stimulus and our ability to recognize or identify that stimulus?
4. What is the shape of a psychophysical relationship between changes in energy and changes in sensation?

For each of these questions, different procedures are needed, ranging from experiments in which the detection threshold is measured to those in which the perceiver assigns numbers to sensations.

In these determinations, three laws are also important:

1. Weber-Fechner law ($S = k \log R$). The intensity of the perception (that is, its sensation) is proportional to the log of the intensity of the stimulus.
2. Weber's law ($\Delta I / I = k$). The smallest detectable change in stimulus intensity is proportional to the intensity of the stimulus already present.
3. Stevens' power law ($S = kI^n$). The intensity of the perception is proportional to the physical intensity raised to a given power.

7·2 Humans are highly dependent on visual stimulation for information both to survive and to enjoy life.

The Visual System

Stimuli for Vision The human body has evolved biological receptors for certain parts of the spectrum of electromagnetic radiation. The photoreceptors in each eye respond to a narrow band of radiation. We cannot see wavelengths shorter than about 400 nanometers, such as ultraviolet rays, because the outer covering of our eyes absorbs them rather than allowing them to pass through to the photoreceptors. At sufficient intensities, these potentially harmful ultraviolet rays can burn our eyes severely. We do not see wavelengths longer than about 700 nanometers because they are too weak to stimulate and excite the photoreceptors, but special skin receptors do respond to infrared radiation.

The intensity of the electromagnetic radiation called light is determined by the number of light quanta, or *photons*, that are radiated in a given direction by a source over some unit of time. When a stream of photons encounters a surface, some are *reflected*, some are *refracted* (or bent) because of the different densities of the mediums, such as air and water, through which the photons are passing, and some may be absorbed by the surface and changed into another form of energy, such as heat. The characteristics of a particular surface determine the fate of the photons that strike it. Black surfaces absorb photons; shiny surfaces reflect them. Photons have visual significance only if they are reflected from an object into our eyes through the pupils and are then absorbed by the photoreceptors of the retinas.

In addition to intensity, light also varies in duration, extent, and wavelength. The duration of stimulation is measured by the number of seconds or fractions of a second that a stimulus lasts. There is no lower limit on time—that is, there is no duration of a flash of light too brief to be seen if it is sufficiently intense. Light intensity can be increased and duration reduced by equal amounts without altering its visual effect. Some electronic photoflash units emit light for no more than one millionth of a second, but appear very bright because they are very intense.

The physical extent of light involves how the size of an object reflecting light to the eye is represented on the retina. When an object is close to our eyes, it reflects many photons into our retinas; when an object is far away, fewer of the reflected photons reach our eyes, and the area the photons cover is relatively small. As an object of constant size moves away from our eyes, its projected size on the retina decreases in direct proportion to the increase in distance. If we know the object's physical size and either its distance from us or the angle subtended by photons reflected from the object's extremities (the *visual angle*), we can calculate the object's projected size by applying the equations in Figure 7·2. As the figure indicates, when an object moves close to our eyes, the visual angle subtended by its extremities increases, and the object's projected size also increases.

To determine the smallest width of a black line that can be detected against a

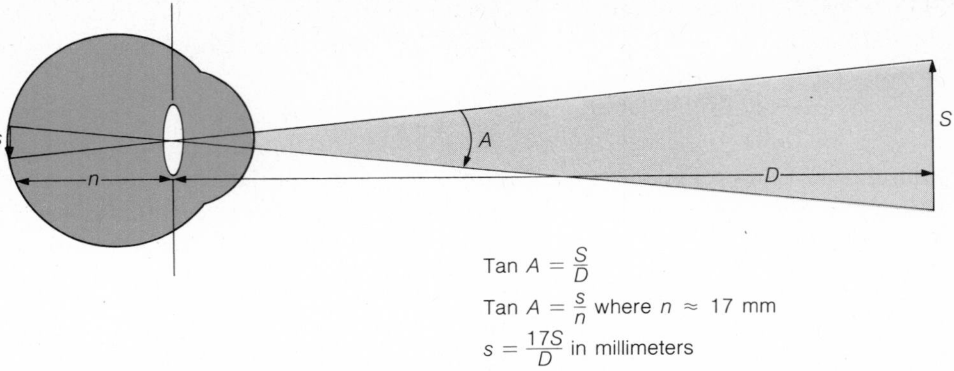

Fig. 7•2 Schematic representation of the relationships among the physical size of an object (S) at a distance (D) from the eye, the visual angle (A) formed by rays of photons reflected from the object's extremities, and the size of the retinal projections (s). The distance from the lens to the retina, n, is 17 millimeters in the average adult human eye. (From Haber and Hershenson, 1973)

white background, we must know its visual angle and its distance from us. As it turns out, the line must have 1/2 second of arc, or 1/7200 degree of visual angle (60 seconds in a minute, 60 minutes in a degree, and 360 degrees in a complete circle). Table 7•3 lists some visual angles for common objects at specified distances.

Because variations in the wavelengths of visible light provide the stimulation for our perception of color, we shall discuss wavelength later when we discuss color. We can now turn to how energy from a visual stimulus is received.

Receptors for Vision Figure 7•3 represents the anatomy of an adult human eye. The *sclera,* or outer white surface, is opaque and does not transmit light. The only opening in the sclera is in the front of the eye and is covered by the *cornea,* a transparent curved protective coat. The cornea functions primarily to keep foreign particles out of the eye and to absorb unwanted radiation (especially ultraviolet light). It also begins the process of focusing the light rays.

Behind the cornea is the *iris,* a diaphragm that opens and closes in response to the intensity of the light reaching the eye. You can watch your iris close if you look into a mirror where the light level is low and then increase the light level.

Table 7•3 Some Visual Angles of Common Objects at Specified Distances from a Perceiver

OBJECT	VIEWING DISTANCE	VISUAL ANGLE
Thumbnail	Arm's length	1.5°–2°
Letter of alphabet 1.6 mm wide (0.05 mm on retina)	50 centimeters	12 minutes of arc
Sun or moon		30 minutes of arc
Quarter	Arm's length 85 meters 5 kilometers	2° 1 minute 1 second

NOTE: Fovea is about 2° in diameter.

The pigmentation in our irises gives us our distinctive eye color. The opening in the iris is called the *pupil,* which appears black because it opens into a dark chamber from which virtually no light is reflected.

Behind the iris is the *lens.* In a camera the lens can be moved nearer to or farther from the photoreceptor surface (the film) to adjust the focus. In the adult human eye, however, the distance from the lens to the retina, which contains the photoreceptors, is fixed at about 17 millimeters (mm). The lens changes its shape in order to focus light rays on the retina. Several sets of muscles around the lens cause it to thicken (become more convex) for focusing on near objects and to become less thick (concave) for far ones.

The center of the eye is filled with fluids that maintain the eye's shape. The *retina,* a network of densely packed receptor cells, covers about 200° around the curved inside back surface of the eye. At the rear of the eye in the retina is a small opening called the *optic disc,* where nerve fibers from the photoreceptors exit to the brain through the *optic nerve* and where the blood supply enters to these photoreceptors and to other neural units inside the eye. Because it contains no receptors, the optic disc is often called the blind spot. Figure 7•4 tells you how to locate your own blind spot.

Three sets of muscles are attached around the outside of the eyeball to move the eye in its socket. One set moves the eye back and forth, another set moves it up and down, and a third set rotates it in its socket as we tip our heads.

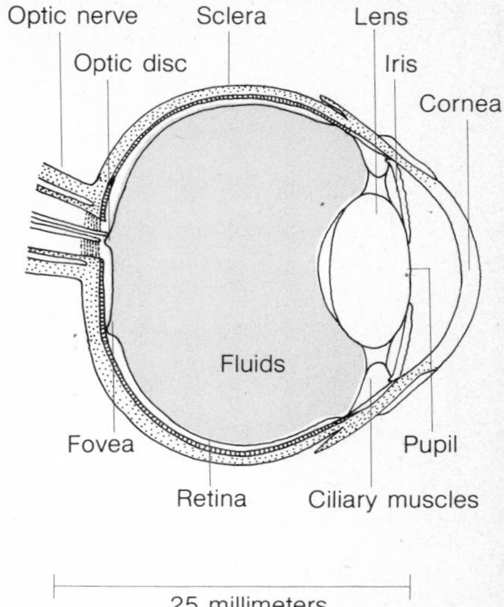

Fig. 7•3 Horizontal cross section of a typical human eye. Photoreceptors in the retina convert light into nerve impulses that are carried to the brain by the optic nerve.

Photoreceptors in the Retina: Rods and Cones The photoreceptors in the retina are called **rods** and **cones** (Figure 7•5). The retina contains about 120 million rods and 7 million cones. These 127 million photoreceptors are very closely packed together on the inside of the eye, which if flattened would form a circle less than 5 centimeters in diameter. The tip of a sharp pin is larger than the area covered by 500 photoreceptors at their densest point.

The two types of photoreceptors can be distinguished by their location, structure, and function. Cones are found everywhere in the retina but are most densely packed

A B

C D

To locate your blind spot in your right eye, close your left eye and with your right eye look at *A.* Move the book closer or farther away until *B* disappears. It is now projected on your blind spot. To find your blind spot in the left eye, reverse this procedure.

While you have *A* projected on the blind spot in your left eye, shift your gaze from *B* to *D. A* will not reappear as *C* disappears. In this way eye movements shift objects on our retina.

Fig. 7•4 Directions for finding your blind spot. (Adapted from Haber and Fried, 1975)

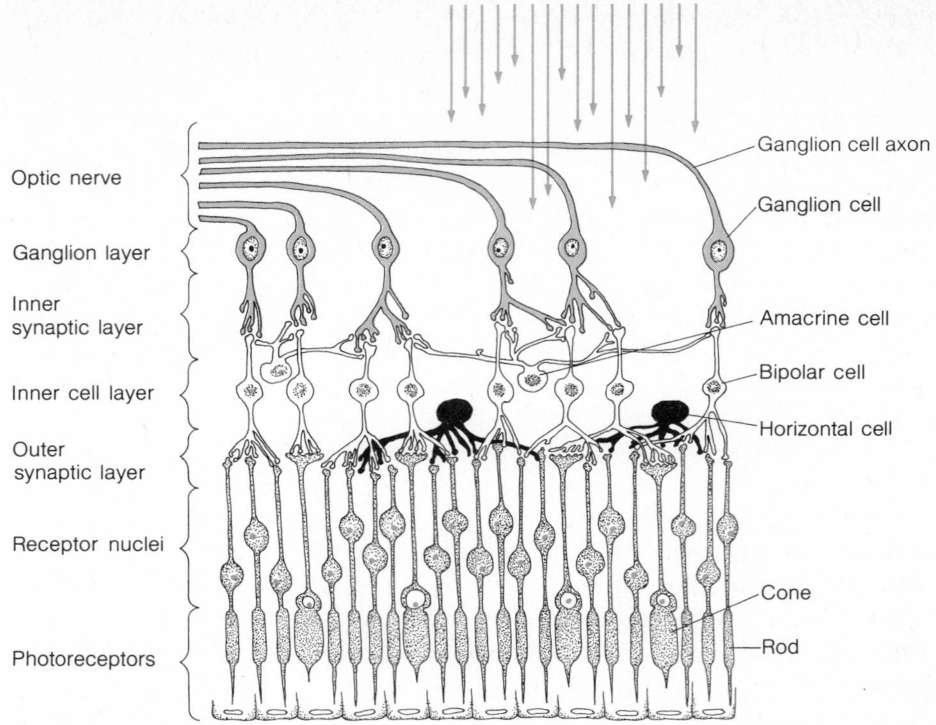

Fig. 7·5 Cross section of the retina, showing the main neural components. Light passes through most of the retina before it gets to the receptor layer, where it fires the rods and cones. (Adapted from Dowling and Boycott, 1966)

in the small area called the **fovea**, which is located almost directly behind the pupil when the eye is looking straight ahead. The density of the cones decreases as their distance from the fovea increases. The rods, however, are found everywhere except in the fovea.

The rods are primarily responsible for the low detection thresholds for light. The cones, however, cannot respond to low light levels such as are found outdoors during twilight or at night. Rods, therefore, are used for night vision, whereas both rods and cones are used for vision in normal or high light levels.

If each photoreceptor had its own private link to the brain, there would have to be 127 million fibers in the optic nerve leaving the eye. In fact, however, there are slightly less than one million such fibers. Therefore, a number of receptors converge on one fiber. More than 10 thousand rods can be connected to the same optic nerve fiber. Because that fiber then has no way of specifying which one of the 10 thousand rods is active, the specific location of photon absorption on the retina is not very well coded. The cones, however, especially those located in the center of the fovea, enjoy more private pipelines to the brain. Nearly half of the one million fibers in the optic nerve serve only one cone each and privately feed information to the brain about the activity levels of the foveal cones.

Rods, with their great ability to converge, are sensitive detectors of stimuli. Cones, however, because of their lower sensitivity, catch photons only when the light is more intense. The cones, then, are better able than the rods to discriminate a pattern made up of small details. This ability is called **visual acuity**.

All of the 120 million rods have the same sensitivity to varying wavelengths, responding most strongly to wavelengths around 500 nanometers and less strongly to longer or shorter ones. Rods are color-blind, and all light (regardless of wavelength) produces only variations in intensity—that is, shades of gray from black to white. Cones occur in three different subtypes, one of which is most sensitive to long wavelength light, one to medium, and one to short. Stimulation arising from these three types of cones allows us to see colors.

Neural Units in the Retina Each photoreceptor (rod or cone) is connected to a neural unit called a *bipolar cell*, which in turn is connected to a different kind of neuron called a *ganglion cell*. The very long end of a ganglion cell is called an *axon*; the ganglion cell axons are the fibers of the *optic nerve*. Between some of the bipolar cells are interconnecting neural units called *horizontal cells*; similar ones called *amacrine cells* interconnect some of the ganglion cells (Figure 7•5). These cells represent all of the neural elements inside each eye.

The neural mass, along with most of the capillaries carrying the blood supply, is located in front of the photoreceptors, that is, directly in the path of the incoming light. Why this strange arrangement should have occurred is not clear, but it does result in some streams of photons being absorbed or reflected before they reach the photoreceptors. The foveal photoreceptors are more accessible to photons because the neural units and capillaries are to the side of the fovea.

Neural Signals in the Retina If all transmission were simply excitatory, a photoreceptor, if sufficiently excited by absorbed photons, could excite the bipolar cell connected to it. If the bipolar cell were sufficiently excited by its converging photoreceptors, that bipolar cell could then excite the ganglion cell connected to it, thus providing a signal across the optic nerve to the brain. Because each cone must absorb many photons before it can excite a bipolar cell, and because each bipolar cell (especially those in the fovea) has only one or a few cones connected to it, a bipolar cell will not become active until each foveal cone has absorbed a great many photons. The rods, however, do not need to absorb many photons to become active, and in addition, many rods converge on each bipolar cell. Thus, a few photons spread thinly over converging rods are enough to arouse the bipolar and ganglion cells located there.

Not all transmission, however, is excitatory. In fact, when light levels are at normal room illumination or above, excitatory effects interact with inhibitory ones to permit some very sophisticated sensory coding of information by the simple neural network in the retina.

Visual scientists have suspected for over a century that inhibitory processes might be present in the visual system, but not until the 1940s were these directly measured by H. K. Hartline, who received the Nobel Prize for his work. Hartline could not work with a primate eye because its photoreceptors and neural units are too small for the recording electrodes then available. Under the assumption that neural processes are similar in most eyes, he studied *Limulus*, a horseshoe crab living along the Atlantic coast, which has large and easily accessible photoreceptors and ganglion cells.

In a typical experiment, Hartline (1949) placed an electrode on the axon of a ganglion cell (optic nerve fiber) so that whenever the nerve fiber was active, its impulses could be amplified and recorded. He then directed a normal beam of light onto one photoreceptor at a time, moving the beam around until it struck a photoreceptor that was connected to the ganglion cell attached to the electrode. Hartline first discovered that the output of the ganglion cell was directly proportional to the intensity of the light. He then directed a second beam of light onto a photoreceptor neighboring the first one. If the intensity of the two light beams was very low, shining a second beam nearby increased the output of the ganglion cell connected to the amplifier, showing an excitatory effect. However, if the intensity of each beam was high, shining the second beam decreased the activity of the ganglion cell, indicating that the output of one photoreceptor was inhibiting the activity of the ganglion cell fed by the other stimulated photoreceptor.

Of what advantage is such inhibition? Consider what the brain really needs to know about what is happening at the retina. If the entire retina were uniformly and intensely illuminated, such as when it is stimulated by an illuminated white wall or a clear sky, a purely excitatory coding system would send many impulses to every fiber of the optic nerve, but the message on each would be the same. However, a single fiber can convey the same message by simply saying "uniform" and by using its activity level to convey the intensity of the stimulus. In an inhibitory system, the stimulated ganglion cells inhibit each other and neighboring ganglion cells. If all photoreceptors were equally stimulated, any area of uniform stimulation on the retina would signal lower than normal excitation to the brain.

Discontinuity in the intensity of light reaching different parts of the retina occurs when surfaces of objects or direct photon sources reflect varying numbers of photons into the eye. A white wall with a black stripe on it, for example, reflects many photons from the white part but few from the black part. This nonuniform pattern is projected onto the retina, where all but a stripe of receptors will absorb many photons (Figure 7•6). How can the brain be informed of this stimulus pattern in the most efficient way so that the edges of the black stripe will be identified?

As Figure 7•6 shows, this information is coded by a combination of excitation and inhibition among the neural units. There are basically four different types of responses, depending on where the ganglion cells are located in relation to the incoming photons:

1. Ganglion cells located at the sides of the retina where the light intensity is high inhibit each other and therefore send fewer impulses to the brain than usual.
2. Ganglion cells located at the edge of the white area nearest the black stripe receive much excitation from the white area and little inhibition from the black area, and therefore have a large output.

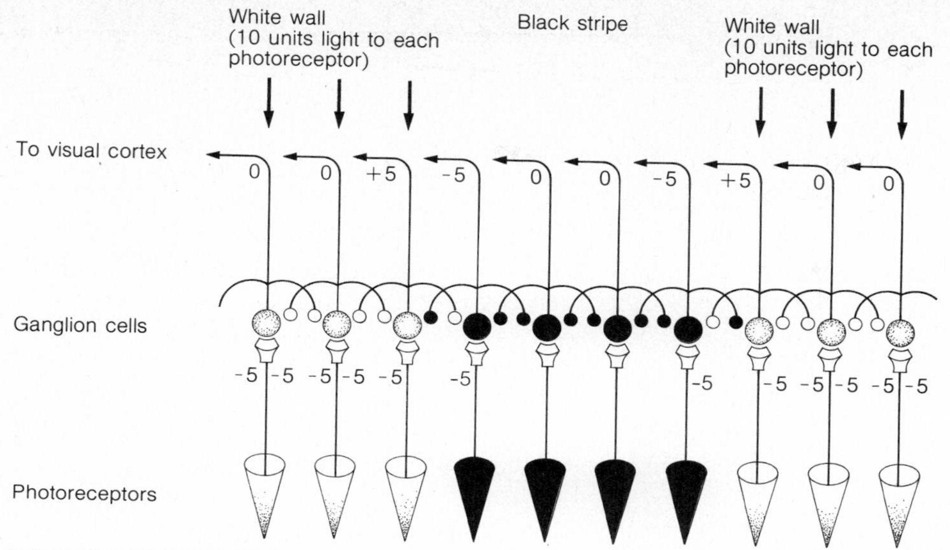

Fig. 7·6 Lateral inhibition can produce an intensification of edges. Assume that each of the side photoreceptors receives 10 units of excitation and that each stimulated ganglion cell provides −5 units of inhibition to its two neighbors. The resulting excitation (the numbers where the nerve fibers lead to the visual cortex) shows that only the edge of the stripe is coded and sent to the brain. (Adapted from Haber and Fried, 1975)

3. Ganglion cells located along the edge of the black stripe receive little excitation from the black area and much inhibition from the white area. Consequently, they produce much less excitation than they would normally.
4. Ganglion cells located in the middle of the black stripe are little excited and little inhibited. Their response is therefore low, although it is higher than the response of the ganglion cells at the edge of the black stripe.

The result of this nonuniformity is that the brain receives an enhanced response from the intense side of an edge and a reduced response from the dim side. This combination of excitation and inhibition causes the edge itself to stand out much more than it would in a solely excitatory system.

Although the combination of excitation and inhibition permits discontinuities in light falling on the retina to be enhanced as they are represented in the brain, the inhibitory properties of this system are effective only if light levels are moderate or high. When the light is feeble, the task of the visual system is to detect its presence rather than to notice and enhance details. For this reason we cannot notice fine details at night.

Transmission of Information from Eye to Brain As with the retina, the interconnection of the neurons in the eye with those of the brain (Figure 7·7) is more than simply a matter of direct wire-and-switch connections. The optic fibers from each eye meet at a point called the *optic chiasma*, where they divide uniquely so that the fibers from receptors on the nasal (nose) side of each eye terminate in the brain hemisphere opposite the eye. Thus, receptors from the nasal side of the right eye terminate in the left brain hemisphere, while those from the nasal side of the left eye terminate in the right brain hemisphere. Fibers from the temporal

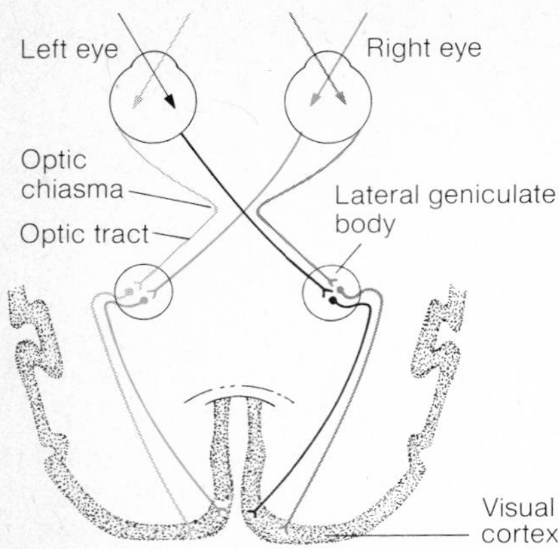

Fig. 7·7 Schematic representation of the visual pathways from each eye to the visual cortex via the optic chiasma. The parts of the visual field are represented at each level by numbers and can be traced through the system by following the corresponding lines. (Adapted from Gardner, 1975)

(temple) side of each eye do not cross over but terminate in the same hemisphere as the eye from which they originate.

If the eyes are looking straight ahead, an object located to the left will reflect light to the nasal side of the left eye and to the temporal side of the right eye. Receptors from both of these areas terminate in the right hemisphere of the visual cortex, so that objects to the left of center are represented in the right hemisphere. The converse is true for objects to the right of straight ahead. If the object is located straight ahead, it will reflect light onto both sides of each retina and will project into both hemispheres.

These structural connections account for how objects are represented, but the mechanism of image projection is more complex. In the fovea, where there is almost a one-to-one convergence between cones and ganglion cells, each foveal photoreceptor corresponds to a single cortical cell in the primary visual cortex. Outside the fovea, however, a large number of receptors converge on each primary cortical cell.

There is no isomorphic map of the retina in the cortex; if you could look into the visual cortex and if each cell glowed when it was activated, the pattern of glowing in the cortex would not resemble the pattern on the retina. There are, however, connections in the primary visual cortex that correspond to the location of the retinal photoreceptors.

The two eyes are structurally interrelated, so that each of the optic nerve fibers representing a particular cone in one eye has a counterpart in the other eye. These corresponding points are important in depth perception, which will be discussed in the next chapter.

Receptive Field Coding in the Visual System We have already discussed how the combination of the excitatory and inhibitory connections among neural units in the retina permits efficient coding of sensory information, so that the brain is not bombarded with more signals than it needs. Similar coding occurs between the eye and the visual cortex to further increase the efficiency of information transmission.

Let's say that you want a ganglion cell to tell the brain that there is a small, round spot of light illuminating an area of the retina, covering perhaps a thousand receptors. This single ganglion cell should increase in activity when that spot is present but should not activate if the spot is too big or not round or somewhere else on the retina. This is a simple coding problem.

Imagine a doughnut-shaped area of receptors in some part of the retina, not necessarily near the fovea, as shown in Figure 7·8. The whole area covers about a thousand receptors; about half of them are in the inner area, and the rest are in the outer ring. They all converge onto a single ganglion cell. If the bipolar cell for each inner-area receptor has an excitatory connection to every other bipolar cell serving inner-area receptors and if all these bipolar cells have excitatory connections to our ganglion cell, then if a spot of light falls anywhere in the inner area, a large output will occur at our ganglion cell. If the bipolar cells in the outer area have excitatory connections with each other but an inhibitory connection with our ganglion cell, then if the spot is large enough to cover both inner and outer receptors, our ganglion cell will be excited by the inner area and inhibited by the outer area so that it will not activate. If the spot falls only on the outer area, the ganglion cell will be inhibited only, so that it will be suppressed to a level even lower than if no light at all were present.

What has been described is called an *on-center, off-surround concentric receptive field,* or a *spot detector.* The activity level of a single ganglion cell can tell the brain about the presence, shape, and location of a particular spot. The receptive field of a ganglion cell is the area of the retina over which light can affect that ganglion cell. This type of receptive field for ganglion cells is now known to be a basic coding device in most mammalian visual systems.

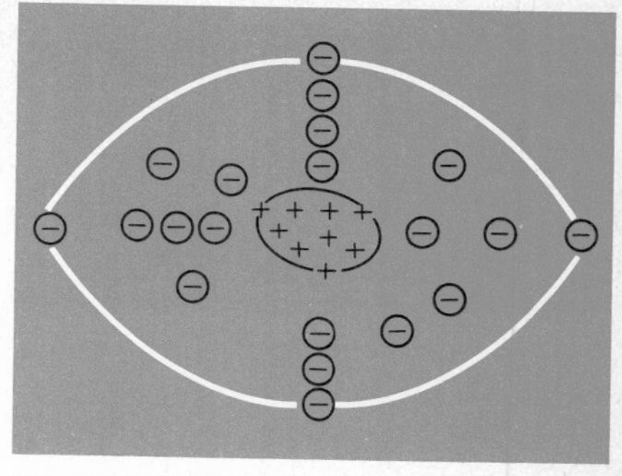

Fig. 7·8 Schematic drawing of an on-center, off-surround concentric receptive field at the ganglion-cell level. Plus signs indicate that an elevation in cell activity is found when light falls on that portion of the receptive field, and minus signs indicate a decrease in activity. (From Haber and Hershenson, 1973)

The concentric receptive fields of the ganglion cells are apparently combined so that several ganglion cells are connected to a single cell in the visual cortex to permit very high-order coding. For example, imagine a group of overlapping concentric receptive fields aligned over part of the retina, such as in Figure 7·9. If a line of light no wider than the center of each concentric field fell across the centers, that line would stimulate the centers but not much of the surrounding area in each receptive field. If all the ganglion cells had excitatory connections to a single cortical cell, then that cortical cell would become much more active than usual. If the line were wider than the centers, more of the surrounding areas in each receptive field would be stimulated, thereby inhibiting the ganglion cells and cancelling the cortical response. This same type of coding would also occur if the line on the retina were oriented slightly differently from the concentric receptive fields; a single cortical cell would signal the presence, location, width, and orientation of the particular line, as before. This type of cortical cell is called a *line detector.*

There are coding systems in the visual system not only for spots and lines, but also for movement velocity, acceleration, curves, wavelength combinations defining colors, stereoscopic depth, and probably for others not yet discovered. In each case, one or a few cortical cells can represent the coding of thousands of receptors in the retina—a coding that reduces visual stimulation to a small number of visual features.

Factors that Affect Visual Reception and Processing In our discussion of psychophysics we suggested that it is reasonable to expect an increase in sensation proportional to increases in intensity. However, this expectation is rarely fulfilled.

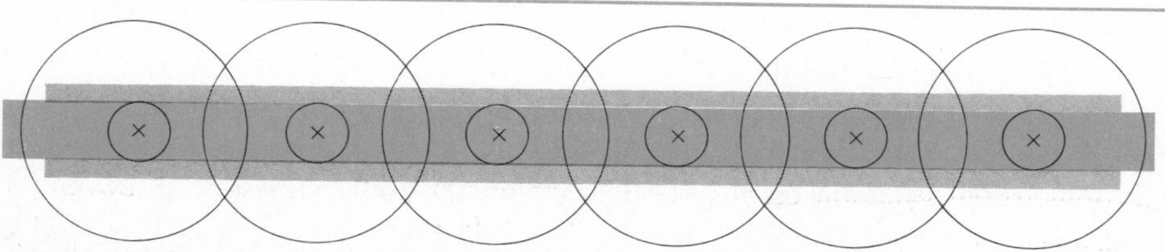

Fig. 7·9 Overlapping concentric receptive fields of several ganglion cells aligned on the retina and connected to a single cortical cell (line detector).

How to Locate and Map a Receptive Field

Much of the research on visual receptive fields has been done using primates, which have visual systems so similar to those of human beings that experimental results can be generalized with confidence from one species to the other. However, because of the far greater expense and difficulty in testing and maintaining primates, cats are often used as experimental subjects. Although greater care must be used in generalizing the results of such experiments to human beings, much is known about the differences between the two visual systems, and so we can learn a great deal about the visual receptive fields of human beings by studying cats.

In a receptive-field mapping procedure, a neural unit in the level of the visual system to be studied is isolated and connected to a recording electrode. If, for example, a ganglion cell is to be mapped, its axon must first be separated from other fibers in the optic nerve, and then the electrode is attached to it at a point just behind the eye. If a cortical cell is to be mapped, the recording electrode is placed in the visual cortex.

A recording electrode is a very fine needle that is electrically insulated except for its tip. When the tip is placed next to or in neural tissue, any changes in the electrical potential of that tissue are picked up by very sensitive amplifiers, recorded by computer, and displayed continuously on a monitor, so that the experimenter can see what is happening (Figure 7B•1). The experimenter's goal is to find all of the visual stimuli that

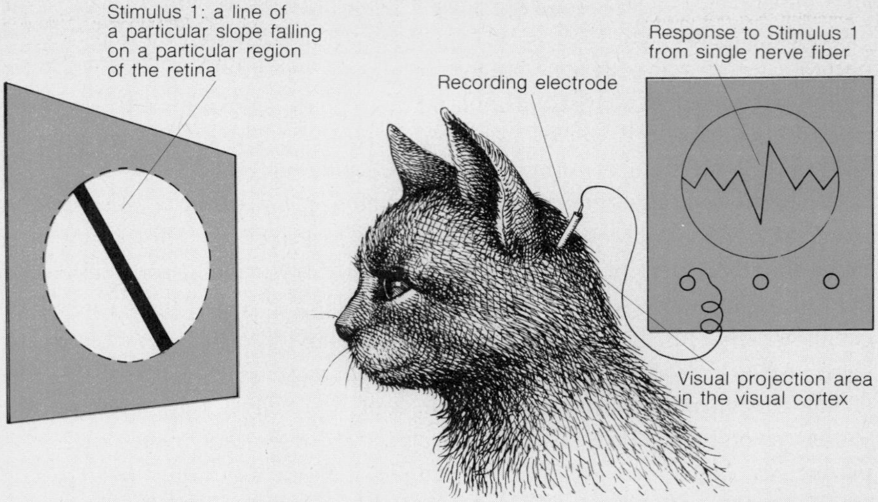

Fig. 7B•1 Schematic representation of the procedure for mapping the receptive field of a cortical cell. (From Haber and Hershenson, 1973)

Several important factors, in addition to the intensity of light, determine the magnitude of sensation. Most significant of these is the adaptation state of the eye—that is, its adjustment to the prevailing level of light intensity.

Adaptation If we walk into a dark theater from a bright street, we probably will not be able to see the aisle or the seats for several minutes; similarly, when we walk out of a darkened theater into a bright street, we are momentarily dazzled and blinded. Each of these situations is an example of the slow adjustment of sensitivity when the stimulation intensity suddenly shifts substantially. These adjustments are called **adaptation**—*dark adaptation* when we adjust to the dark, and *light adaptation* when we adjust to the light. The two processes are not mirror images of each other, and each process reveals important properties of the visual system.

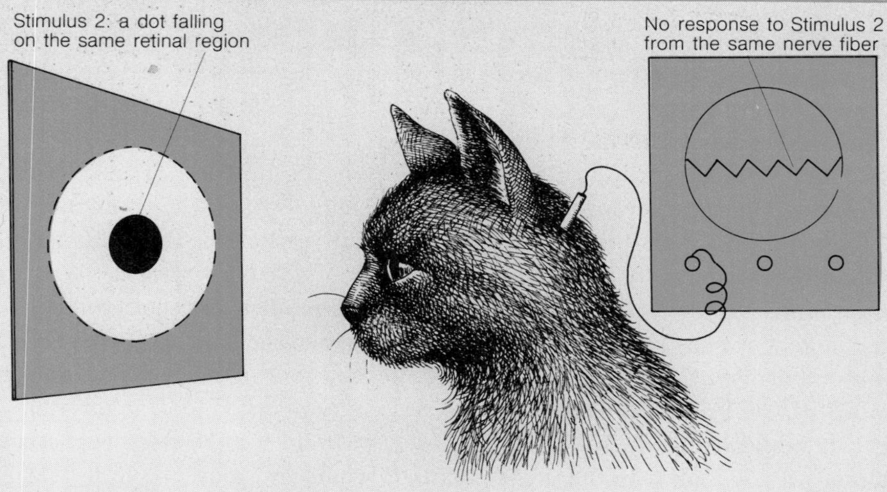

Fig. 7B·1 continued

will produce a change in the electrical activity of the particular neural unit being measured.

During the experimental procedure, the animal is held so that his eyes are looking directly at a screen on which stimuli are projected and moved about. Each particular location on the screen corresponds to a specific place on the animal's retinas; the center of the screen corresponds to the animal's foveas.

If a ganglion cell is being mapped, the first stimulus presented is usually a small spot of light, which is moved over the screen (and therefore the retina) until a change is noted in the pattern on the monitor. The spot is then moved over the screen close to the stimulus location that produced the observed change, thus making a *grid* of the retina showing where the electrical activity of the cell increased or decreased. This grid is a map of the ganglion cell's receptive field for the specific light stimulus presented (in this case, a small spot of light).

This process is then repeated for spots of varying sizes and intensities. Stimuli of different shapes can be presented (for example, a white bar of light of a given length, width, and intensity). In the course of an experimental session many different stimuli can be studied, each one of which will result in a unique receptive field. By comparing these maps, the experimenter can determine the shape of the receptive fields of the particular ganglion cell being studied and the nature of the stimuli it codes.

The same procedure is followed for mapping cortical cells, except that greater varieties of stimuli are usually presented. Some cortical cells respond only if the stimulus is moving, and so mapping cortical receptive fields can become very complex. However, the basic procedures for receptive-field mapping are the same for all neural units.

Dark Adaptation The visual system can function easily at any given moment when the light intensities in a scene differ by a ratio of no more than about 100 to 1. If, under a single light source, some objects reflect nearly all of the light falling on them (say, 90 percent) and others reflect virtually none (say, less than 10 percent), then the intensity ratio is about 10 to 1, and we have no trouble perceiving the scene. When the ratio exceeds 100 to 1, however, we can see the details in a dark object but not those in the lightest object in our field of vision, or vice versa. The same problem occurs with photographic film. If the contrast ratios in a scene are greater than the film can resolve, a photographer may get either detailed clouds over a uniformly black landscape, or uniformly white clouds and sky over a detailed landscape.

One way to study dark adaptation is to flood a perceiver's eyes for a few minutes with a quantity of light equivalent to bright daylight and then shut the light out completely. The perceiver is then shown a small spot of light and asked to try to detect it. In essence, the subject's detection threshold for the spot of light is being measured. At first the threshold is very high because the eyes have little sensitivity to low light levels after exposure to intense light. As time passes, the sensitivity of the eyes increases and the threshold drops.

In Figure 7•10 this drop in threshold is plotted as a function of time. Notice that the dark adaptation function has two segments—one for the cones and one for the rods. The cones begin to gain in sensitivity as soon as the lights go out and improve by a factor of 10 within the first two minutes. No matter how long the subject remains in the dark after about the first four minutes, the cones will not become more sensitive. The rods do not begin to adapt to the dark until after several minutes, but then their sensitivity improves beyond that of the cones by a factor of 1000. If you leave a well-lighted room and go outdoors to look at the stars at night, it would be nearly 30 minutes before you could see the stars clearly (and then only if you looked to the side so that you would use your rods to see them).

Light Adaptation When you walk out of a darkened theater, you may be uncomfortable and have to squint; but a few seconds later your eyes can function normally, even though the light levels may have been suddenly increased 10,000 fold. The process by which sensitivity to light is reduced as we move from low to high light levels occurs very rapidly. Most of the change takes place in less than one second, and all of the adjustment is made within a minute or so.

The time course of light adaptation is measured by a detection threshold task using a small spot of light. Each time the light is turned on, the perceiver adapts so rapidly that the lights must be turned off to let the perceiver dark adapt before another lights-on trial can be run. The level of response to intensity is therefore partially dependent on the adaptation state of the eye.

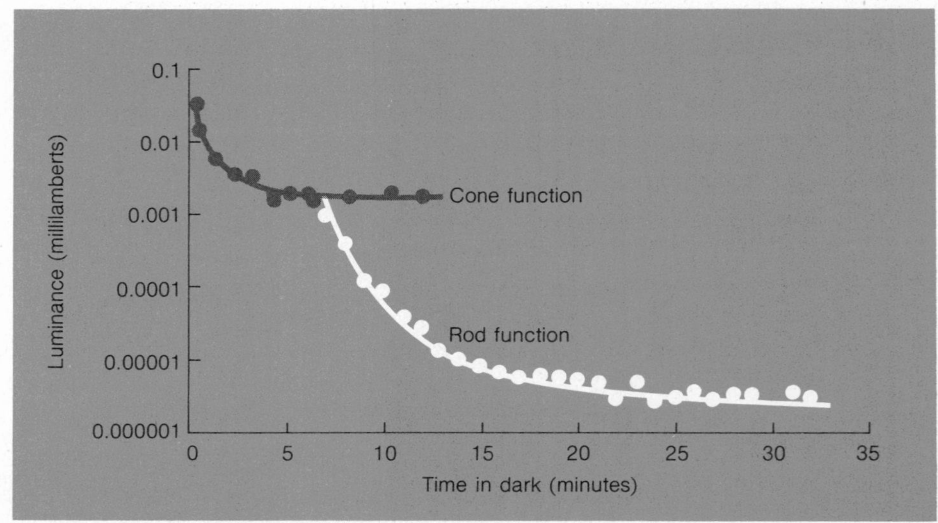

Fig. 7•10 The time course of dark adaptation as shown by the decrease in luminance threshold as a function of time after the exposure of a human eye to an intense light. (From Hecht, 1934)

Contrast A second factor that affects how bright a particular light intensity will appear is the level of the surrounding light intensities. The four gray patches in Figure 7•11 reflect the same amount of light intensity to the eyes, but they appear to be different in brightness because of the variation among the light intensities of their surrounding areas. As a general rule, the brightness of a surface will appear to increase as the intensity of its surrounding area decreases, and vice versa. This effect, called *simultaneous brightness contrast*, occurs even though the physical energy from the surface itself does not change.

Contrast effect can also appear when the surface and a surrounding area are viewed successively rather than together. If you look at a bright wall and then at a gray patch, the patch will appear darker than it would if you looked first at a dark wall.

Brightness contrast effects occur in part as a result of inhibitory connections among adjacent neural units. In the case of simultaneous contrast, the receptors that are stimulated by an intense surrounding area excite ganglion cells, which have inhibitory connections to other ganglion cells, some of which in turn are connected to the receptors under the gray patch. Because they are inhibited by the ganglion cells under the intense surroundings, the intensity of their response to the gray patch will not result in as much net excitation as if there had been no surrounding area, or if the surrounding area had been less intense.

The simultaneous contrast effect works two ways. The gray patch makes the more intense surrounding area appear brighter than if the gray patch had been more intense; at the same time, the intense surrounding area makes the gray appear less bright. The contrast effect, therefore, pushes the two areas farther apart in apparent brightness than they actually are. Which area exerts the greater effect depends on its relative size, but a surrounding area will generally affect the inside area to a greater degree than an inside area will affect its surroundings.

Successive contrast works in the same way as simultaneous contrast except that the effects of inhibition occur over time as well as over space. If you look first at an intense surface, the neural activity created by the absorption of photons, including the inhibition generated, persists. When a second stimulus is presented, the activity it generates is reduced by the amount of the inhibition left over from the first stimulus. Because our eyes rarely look at total darkness, there is always some accumulated inhibition, but it varies from moment to moment, depending on the intensity of the most recent stimulus. Therefore, contrast effects, along with adap-

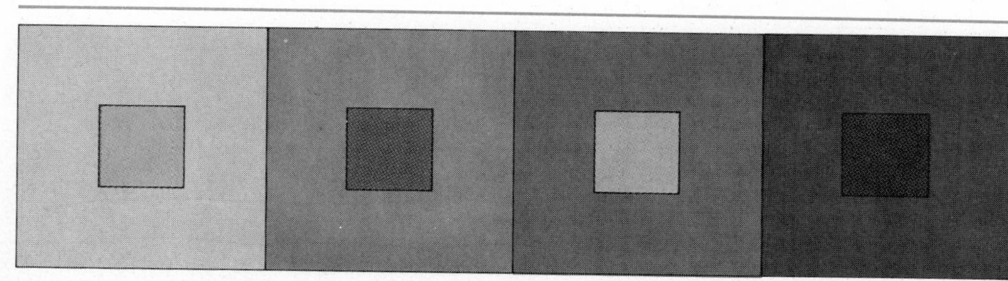

Fig. 7•11 An example of simultaneous brightness contrast when looking at a gray square against backgrounds that differ in reflectance. (From Haber and Hershenson, 1973)

tation, decrease the possibility that a simple proportional psychophysical relationship exists between intensity and brightness.

The Movable Eye Our discussion so far has almost ignored the fact that human beings are *binocular perceivers*: we have two eyes located in the front of our heads such that the fields of view picked up by each eye overlap substantially. Furthermore, each of our eyes moves in its socket relative to our head and to the other eye. These movements greatly increase the power of our perceptual abilities but pose some complications to understanding how vision works.

To say that we are looking at something implies that we are pointing our foveas at it. If an object is far away, the lines of sight of the two eyes (a hypothetical line drawn from the center of each fovea through the center of the pupil opening onto the object out in space) will be parallel. If the object is quite close, say at arm's length, then the lines of sight of the eyes will converge on the object.

Large Eye Movements Two groups of eye movements can be distinguished by their magnitudes. The larger movements are of two kinds—those made when you search for something (called *saccadic movements*, after the French word for *jerky*), and those made when you visually pursue an object moving relative to your head (called smooth or *pursuit movements*).

Ask a friend to let you watch her eyes while she reads a book (peer over the top of the page as close to her as you can). You will see her eyes move jerkily across the line of print, stop at one fixation point, move quickly to a new one, and so forth. The same pattern occurs in any visual task in which you are picking up information around you, such as when you search for a friend in a crowd or look through a windshield while driving. Using precise measuring instruments, experimenters have shown saccadic movements to be very rapid; the eye generally moves from one point of fixation to the next in 0.025 to 0.1 second, depending on the distance traveled by the eye. The fixations between each movement may last for only 0.2 second; they are typically around 0.25 to 0.3 second for reading and may last as long as 1 second for some types of searching such as examining small objects.

Pursuit movements are smooth rather than jerky and occur only when you have a moving target to look at. If you hold your head still and watch a bird in flight across your visual field, your eyes will move smoothly in their sockets, keeping the target located over your foveas. Your eyes will also swing smoothly in their sockets when you fixate on a stationary object as you turn your head.

It is impossible to make smooth eye movements if there is no moving object or if your head is not moving. Smooth eye movements are therefore quite different from saccadic movements. In fact, evidence suggests that different brain control systems subserve each type of movement.

Small Eye Movements One type of small eye movement we have already mentioned is *convergence*, where the two eyes move relative to each other as they both orient toward a fixed object.

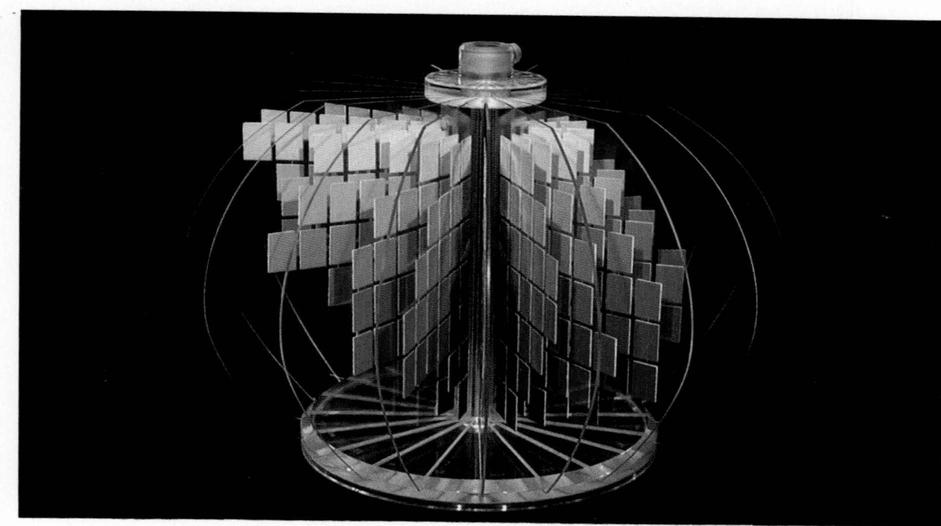

Fig. 7·14 A color solid showing the three dimensions of color sensitivity—brightness, saturation, and hue. There is a gradual change in brightness from black to white along the central axis. (From Munsinger, 1971)

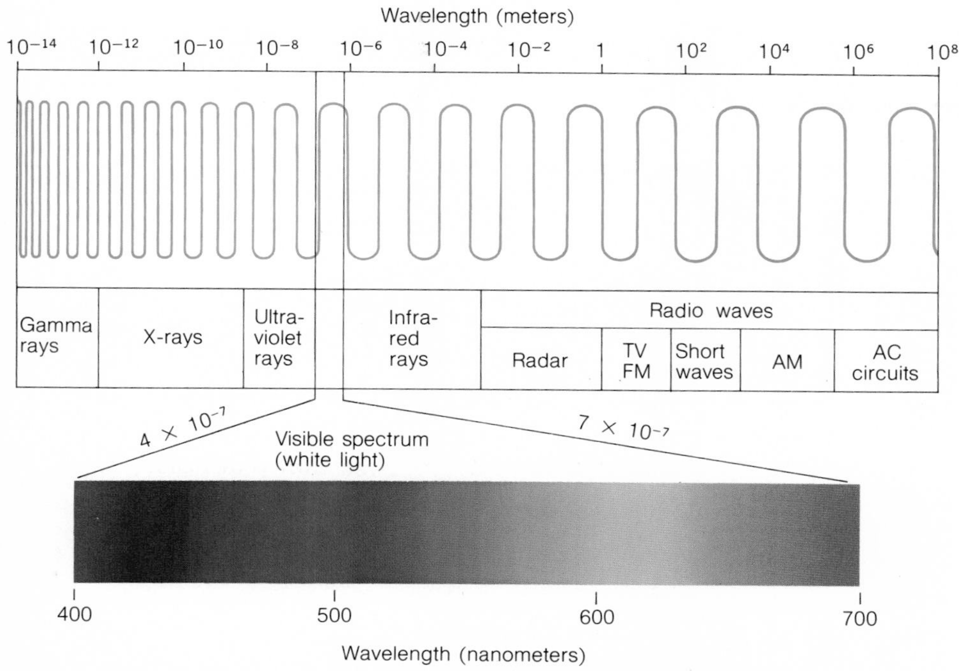

Fig. 7·15 The full spectrum of electromagnetic radiation, of which the human eye can see only the narrow band extending from about 4×10^{-7} to about 7×10^{-7} meters (400 to 700 nanometers) in wavelength. (Adapted from Bourne and Ekstrand, 1973, and McConnell, 1974).

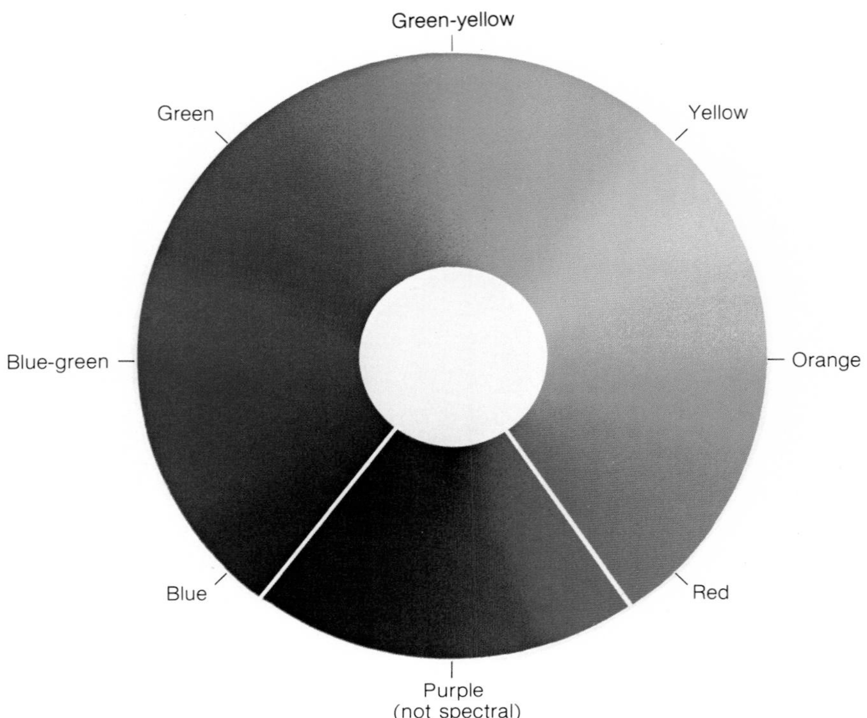

Fig. 7·16 Circular cross section of a conical color solid showing the spectral colors.

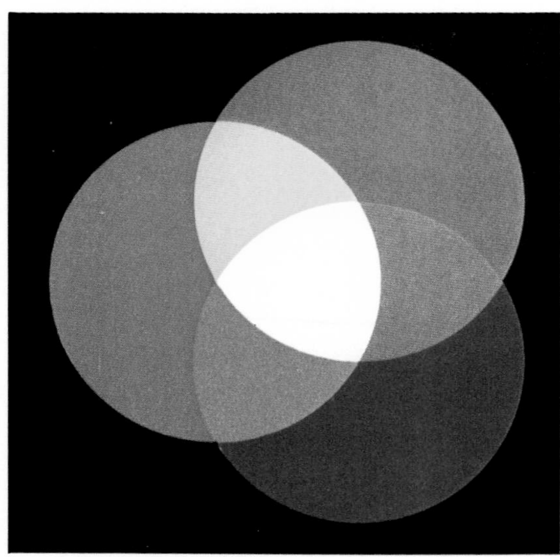

Fig. 7·17 An additive color mixture, where lights interact to form other colors. In this example the principal additive primary lights are red, green, and blue. When mixed in appropriate amounts as beams of light, they produce white light. Yellow, magenta, and cyan result where each pair of additive primaries (red, green, and blue) overlap. Where they all overlap, white results. Color television is an example of this type of color mixing. (Inmont Corporation)

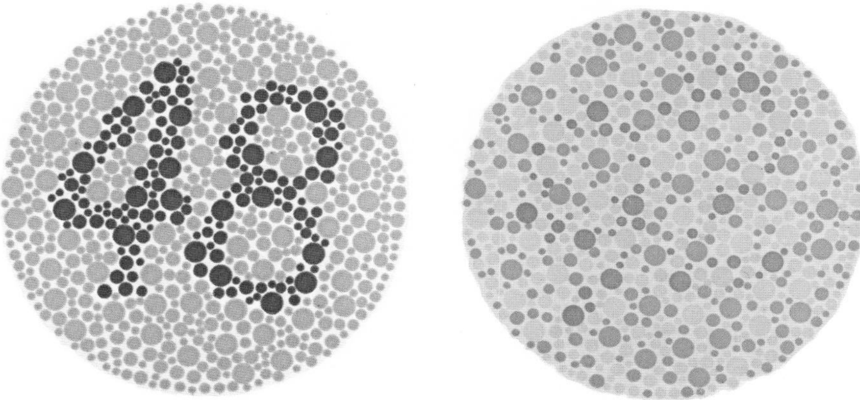

Fig. 7·18a These two illustrations are from a series of color-blindness tests. Persons with normal vision see a number 48 in the left plate; those with red-green color blindness do not. Persons with normal vision see a number 92 in the right plate; those with red-green color blindness may see one number or none. These examples are representative of the fifteen charts necessary for a complete color recognition examination. [Reproduced by permission of the author of the Dvorine Pseudo-Isochromatic Plates, distributed by Harcourt Brace Jovanovich, New York, N.Y. (Reproductions may not be exact. Original plates must be used for accurate testing.)]

Fig. 7·18b Many color-blind people cannot distinguish the colors red and green. To them they look like nearly identical grays, as shown on the right half of this representation. (Inmont Corporation)

Fig. 7·19 Simultaneous contrast stripe effect (*a*). The blue areas in the pattern are printed with exactly the same color ink, but they appear different against a nonuniform background. To observe heightened effects, tilt the design or look at it from a distance.

Simultaneous contrast (*b*). Although this ring is all the same shade of gray, you can change its apparent color by placing your finger or a pencil along the line separating the red and blue backgrounds. (Inmont Corporation)

(*a*)

(*b*)

Fig. 7·20 Stare at the center of this flag for about 30 seconds. Then look at a white wall or a white sheet of paper. You will see a negative afterimage in the colors complementary to those shown here. (From Haber and Fried, 1975)

Another type of small eye movement is called *drift,* in which the orientation of the eye slowly drifts off a fixated target. Although the distance moved during a drift is very small, it is sufficient to misalign your eyes so that you no longer look where you started to or where you intended.

To correct a drift, the eye will make a *microsaccade* to bring the point of fixation back to its approximate original position. Figure 7•12 shows a sequence of drifts and microsaccades over a one-second viewing period. The microsaccades are very fast. No matter how careful and attentive you are, it is virtually impossible, except after prolonged feedback training, to prevent drifts and microsaccades from occurring.

The importance of drifts and microsaccades is related to the sensory coding effects of inhibition discussed earlier, when we learned that there is little information to the brain when the stimulation over a given area of the retina is unchanging. If your eyes were absolutely stationary and were looking at a scene that did not move, the brain would receive no further information about the scene after the initial signals. It is therefore necessary for the scene to drift slightly over the retina from time to time in order to initiate new bursts of signals to the brain and to maintain vision.

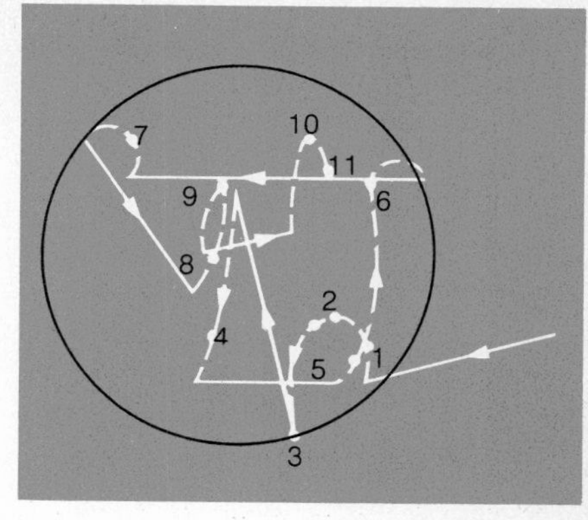

Fig. 7•12 Displacements of the retinal projection of a point source of light caused by a brief sequence of drifts and microsaccades as well as tremors (slight movements resulting from tension created by opposing sets of muscles pulling each eye). (From Ditchburn, 1955)

Temporal Coding in Vision Vision is primarily a spatial sense. It provides information about the relative positions of objects (where they are and how far away) and about their relative sizes, shapes, and so forth. Vision also provides information about changes in time. How long did something last? In what order did a series of visual events occur? Did two events occur simultaneously or did one follow the other? Each of these questions reflects different aspects of the precision with which time is coded in the visual system.

Time is coded poorly within the visual modality compared to audition, which is primarily a temporal rather than a spatial sense. In vision the major emphasis is on coding the location of a stimulus and the kinds of spatial discontinuities present in its pattern on the retina. This emphasis seems to be at the expense of doing as precise a job of coding time as of coding space.

Temporal Summation As we already know, the rods in the retina converge onto bipolar cells, which in turn converge onto ganglion cells. When energy levels are low, the connections between these neural units are primarily excitatory. The rod receptors are therefore superb detectors of minimal light energy. Another device for detecting minimal amounts of light energy is known as **temporal summation**—the accumulation of excitation over time in order to increase the chances of there being enough energy to excite the next neural unit. Temporal summation was first noted by Robert Wilhelm Bunsen (who is credited with inventing the Bunsen burner) and has since been worked out quite precisely as an intensity–time trade-off.

When the intensity of a brief flash of light is controlled so that it is just at detection threshold, flash intensity may be increased in proportion to a decrease in flash duration and the light stimulus will still be at threshold level. This relation-

What Happens to Vision When the Eye is Stabilized

Every second, our eyes make as many as four saccades and a number of microsaccades to correct drifts that occur between saccades. Each of these movements shifts the position of our eyes relative to the visual world and affects how we code visual stimuli. But how would our visual system function if our eyes did not make saccades, microsaccades, and drifts?

Because it is virtually impossible to prevent small eye movements, experiments have been devised to neutralize their effects by moving the visual scene projected on the retina by exactly the same amount as our eyes move. One such technique involves fitting the subject's eyes with a contact lens that is so snug it cannot move over the cornea. (The other eye is covered with a black eye patch.) A mirror is attached to the contact lens off to one side of the pupil opening so that the mirror will move whenever the eyes move. A narrow beam of light is projected onto the mirror, from which it is reflected to a screen in front of the subject. Whenever the subject moves his or her eyes (and thereby the mirror), the image on the screen moves in exact synchrony with the subject's eye movements. The retinal projection is therefore always in a fixed relationship to the movement of the subject's eyes, and the effect of naturally occurring small eye movements is effectively counteracted.

The results of the many studies using this technique have been consistent. When the picture is first projected onto the screen, the subject can see it and describe it normally. Within a few seconds, however, parts of the picture appear to fade; within 5 to 20 seconds, the subject reports that the entire picture has faded and the screen looks blank.

The parts of the picture falling on the fovea usually persist longer than those falling on the periphery of the retina, and sharp contours persist longer than blurry or indistinct ones. If the contact lens slips, some parts of the picture may reappear briefly and then fade again. Such slippage allows the projected image to move suddenly across the retina and to produce a new burst of electrical activity.

ship can be written as $I \times D = k$, where I is intensity, D is duration, and k is a constant. Thus, if the intensity of the light is below threshold, the visual system can still detect it if the duration of the light is extended. Of course, then precise detection of duration is sacrificed to increase the chances of detecting intensity.

In spite of the assistance given to the detection of low light intensities by temporal summation, you cannot see a very dim star even if you stare at it for hours. The summation effect lasts for only about 0.1 second, and so at night the visual system cannot tell the difference between an intense flash lasting 0.001 second and a flash 1/100 as intense lasting 100 times longer. These differences could be distinguished if the summation effects were to last longer than 0.1 second, but 0.1 second is a long time, compared to the auditory system's ability to detect time differences of 0.000001 (one-millionth) second.

In the daytime when light levels are much higher than at night, the visual system does not need to detect minimal amounts of light energy and can therefore focus on finer discrimination of both spatial and temporal details. Excitatory connections are replaced by inhibitory ones, so that spatial and temporal summations occur less frequently than at night. In high intensity ranges the $I \times D = k$ relationship holds only for summation times up to 0.01 second.

Visual Acuity How thin can a black line be and still be noticed against a white background? How small can a black spot, such as an airplane, be and still be noticed against a background such as a bright sky?

The processes underlying pattern perception depend on our being able to detect detail—that is, to resolve discontinuities in energy falling on the retina. These discontinuities occur when there are differences in the energy being reflected from two parts of one surface or from two surfaces. Detecting discontinuity therefore provides a means to perceive details or a pattern. The minimal size of a detail that a visual system can detect determines its visual acuity.

Probably the most familiar visual acuity task is the Snellen eye chart (Figure 7•13). This eye chart is standardized for reading letters or symbols at a distance of 20 feet. At this distance, the smallest letters the average person can read are those whose stroke width is 1 minute of arc (20/20 visual acuity). If you must stand 20 feet away to read letters that the standard observer can read at 40 feet (letters 2 minutes of arc wide), your acuity is 20/40. If you can read at 20 feet what the average observer would have to stand at 10 feet to see distinctly, your acuity is 20/10, which is about the best score that any human being can make on this kind of recognition task; it represents an ability to resolve details down to 1/2 minute of arc.

If your unaided visual acuity is below 20/40, you are not allowed to drive a car in most states unless you wear corrective lenses. If your visual acuity is 20/400, you are usually considered legally blind. The typical letter size for book print when viewed at 50 centimeters (about 20 inches) is 15 minutes of arc—30 times larger than the lower limit of acuity.

Another type of visual acuity test involves detection. How narrow a black line can you detect against an intense background? This type of test can detect finer acuity than the Snellen test because you need only to perceive an intensity discontinuity. The limit of this test is about 0.5 second of arc—60 times finer than the lower limit of the recognition acuity test and about 35 times smaller than the width of a single foveal cone. Although we do not know much about the visual acuity of other animals, human beings probably have the best visual acuity of any biological visual system, with some exceptions for very specialized forms.

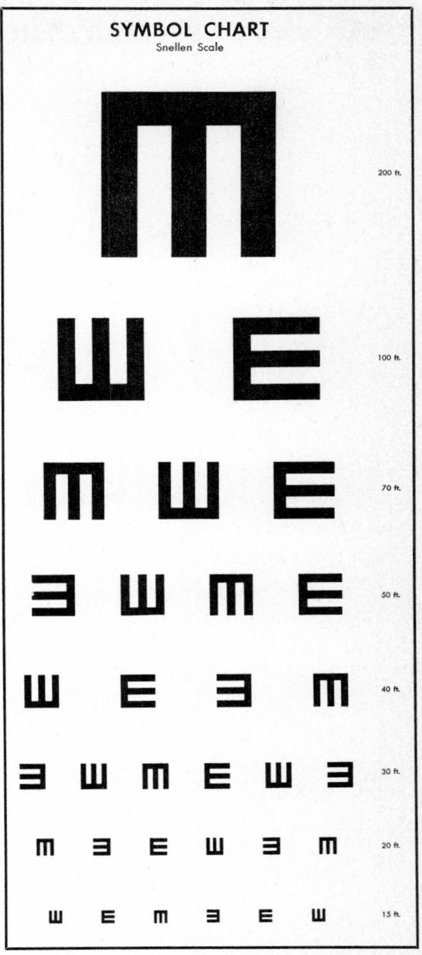

Fig. 7•13 Snellen eye chart. (Courtesy of the National Society for the Prevention of Blindness, Inc., New York)

The Perception of Color Color accounts for most of the affective connotations surrounding vision. It is important in sensuality, pleasure, and fear, and in signaling danger. It is virtually indiscriminable from normal perceptual experience. It is also one of the most complex aspects of vision.

Description of Color The word *color* connotes a sensation. Just as intensity is the physical dimension underlying the psychological dimension of brightness, so are there physical dimensions underlying the sensation or appearance of colors. The three most important of these physical dimensions are *intensity, wavelength,* and *purity,* all of which affect respectively the psychological dimensions of *brightness, hue,* and *saturation.*

When we speak of shades of gray or of lights of varying wavelength, we usually assume that brightness remains constant. Generally, brightness increases as the number of photons in a light increase, but because light intensity varies as a function of its wavelength, some variation in brightness occurs when wavelength changes.

Hue refers to the color of a light—for example, blue, green, or red. The physical dimension underlying hue is its light wavelength; each wavelength has a unique hue.

Saturation of light is commonly called depth of color. Red is a deeper color than pink, although both may be of the same hue (wavelength). The saturation of light depends on how much white light is added before hue disappears completely. The physical dimension underlying saturation is the quantity of white light contained in the light beam. Because white light contains all wavelengths of the visible light spectrum in equal quantities, adding white light dilutes any hue without changing the hue itself.

All three psychological dimensions of color—brightness, saturation, and hue—can be used together to describe the appearance of light. These are often combined and represented in a color solid (Figure 7•14). (Figures 7•14 through 7•20 are in the color section.) As you can see, each patch of color differs from each other one simultaneously in brightness, saturation, and hue. Brightness varies from top to bottom (as from white to black), saturation increases from the center to the outer edge, and the hues are arranged around the perimeter of the solid. Figure 7•15 shows the hues spread out as a function of wavelength.

Mixing Lights of Different Hues The different hues in Figure 7•14 are represented around the circumference of the conical color solid. A circular cross section of this solid is represented in Figure 7•16, which shows all the spectral colors (those produced by unique wavelengths) plus the purples, which are various mixtures of long (red) and short (blue) wavelength light. The hues that are directly opposite each other on the circle are called *complementary* because when any such pair of colored lights is mixed in equal amounts, the resulting combination appears white. For example, if you place a red filter over one projector and a green filter over another, and then focus the filtered light from each projector onto the same surface, the surface will appear white (that is, have no hue).

If the intensities of the two lights in each complementary pair are not equal, the resulting hue will be the hue of the more intense light, only less saturated—that is, it will look as though some white light had been added to it. How a mixture of complementary hues will look can be worked out along a line drawn between the hues on the perimeter (the line will pass through white). The mixture will be proportional to the intensities of each light. For example, if twice as much red is used as green, the mixture will be a red saturated halfway between white and the maximally saturated red on the perimeter of the color circle.

The Coding of Hue Brightness is perceived from variations in the number of photons absorbed by the photoreceptors. Hue is perceived from variations in the

Color Mixing

We can use a **color circle** to determine which hue and how much saturation a light mixture will have.

Suppose that we are mixing complementary lights of equal intensity. We know that every point on the surface of the color circle represents a particular hue and a particular saturation. If we draw a line between the two complementary hues that we are mixing, the midpoint of the line will fall on white. We therefore know that white light will be produced. If the lights are of unequal intensity, the light produced will be the hue of the more intense light with its saturation reduced.

Suppose that we are mixing two noncomplementary lights. A line drawn between the two noncomplementary hues on the color circle will contain a variety of hues and saturations. If we mix yellow and greenish blue, for example, the resultant hue can be found on the connecting line in the color circle at some point *x*, whose location will be determined by the relative quantities of the two noncomplementary lights in the mixture. Drawing another line from white through *x* to the circumference of the circle allows us to identify the hue by name and by wavelength. The hue's saturation will be a function of *x*'s proximity to white. In Figure 7C·1, yellow and greenish blue were mixed in equal proportions; the resulting hue is an approximately quarter-saturated yellowish green.

Suppose that we are mixing three noncomplementary lights, each from a different part of the spectrum. (In other words, the triangle formed by the three respective hues on the circumference of the color circle contains within it the point for white.) We can combine two of the three lights at a time, making three pairs—blue and yellowish green, blue and red, and red and yellowish green, for example (Figure 7C·2). By adjusting each light's intensity, we can produce all of the hues (including the nonspectral purples) between any two of the three hues. We can therefore produce any hue and any saturation contained within the triangle formed by the three hues on the circumference of the color circle. Although any hue can be made by mixing three lights and suitably balancing their intensities, there is an upper limit to the saturation obtainable, since some saturation points in the circle will fall outside the triangle.

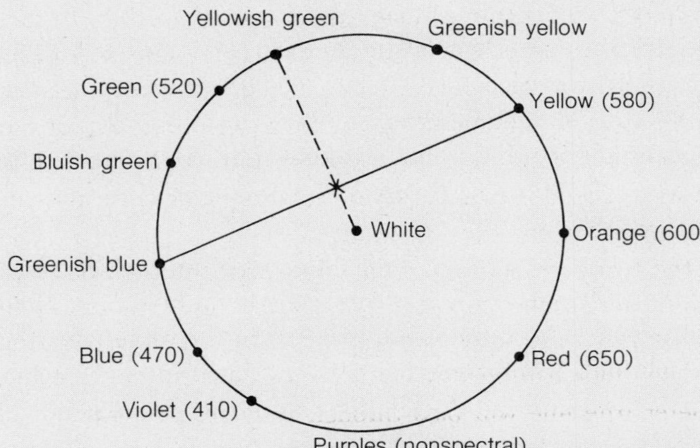

Fig. 7C·1 Using a color circle to determine the hue and saturation that will result from combining two noncomplementary lights.

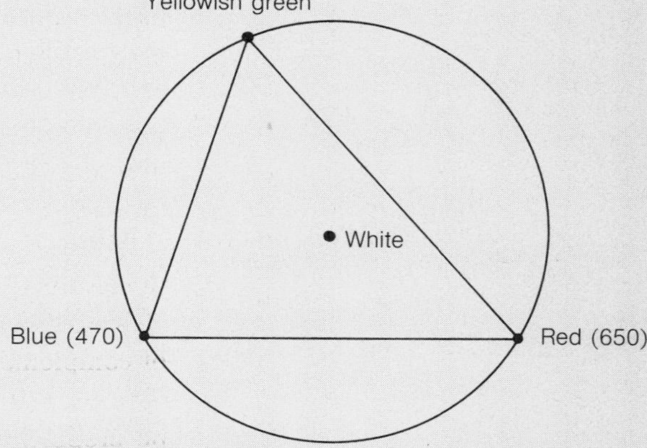

Fig. 7C·2 Combining three noncomplementary lights can produce any hue and any saturation within the triangle.

wavelength of the electromagnetic radiation of the photons. We know that visible electromagnetic radiation varies in wavelength between 400 and 700 nanometers. When the light entering our eyes is primarily from the short-wavelength end of the spectrum (that is, 400 nanometers), we experience blue light. When the light is primarily from the long-wavelength end of the spectrum, we experience red. This relationship was discovered about 1670 by Isaac Newton, who showed that sunlight is composed of all the visible wavelengths of light and can be separated with a prism into the spectral colors. When light passes from air into a prism, it is refracted, because glass has a different density than air. The amount of refraction is inversely proportional to the wavelength of the light, and so the short-wavelength beams are bent more than the long-wavelength ones. The prism separates the wavelengths of white light in a rainbow effect and each hue can be seen separately.

How does the visual system respond to different wavelengths and code them for the brain? This question is being answered as techniques are developed to record electrical activity from single neural units in the visual system and to generate and measure electromagnetic radiation precisely. However, the basic concept behind the present theory of color vision and its neural processes is nearly two centuries old, having been worked out from known facts by intuition and careful deduction.

Following Newton's work, the major theory of color vision was that there must be some kind of receptor in the eye for each wavelength. Thus, if we can see and distinguish 20 hues, there must be 20 different kinds of receptors, each sensitive to its unique wavelength. Because we can see each hue wherever it falls on the eye, these 20 types of receptors must be repeated all over the retina.This theory ran into trouble when careful observers noticed that although we have only seven names for the rainbow colors, we experience many more hues than that. In fact, while an adult might reliably use and recognize only 20 to 30 color names, he or she can reliably discriminate (scale) between 100,000 and 250,000 different fractional wavelengths within the 400 to 700 nanometer range. Even in the eighteenth century, long before the magnitude of this number was known, it was thought to be much larger than 20 or even 100. Thus, the theory of the unique receptor for each wavelength seemed unreasonable.

Before 1800 it was known that if you take three different beams of light, each from a different part of the electromagnetic spectrum, mix them by shining them on the same white surface, and make suitable adjustments in their relative intensities, you can produce any hue. If the three lights are of equal intensity, white light is produced (Figure 7•17). However, the relationship of this phenomenon to the sensation of color was not then understood.

Additive Coding Theory Around 1800 Thomas Young proposed a new explanation of how hues are coded based on how lights are mixed physically to make any hue from only three wavelengths. He arrived at his theory primarily by deduction, but when direct measurements were taken 150 years later to test his ideas, Young's theory turned out to be nearly correct.

Young postulated that there are only three receptors—one sensitive to long-wavelength light, one sensitive to middle-wavelength light, and one sensitive to short-wavelength light—and that the excitations of these three receptors mix together in the brain to enable us to see all hues in the same way that all hues can be produced by mixing three beams of light. According to Young, long-wavelength light stimulates the long-wavelength cone (the "red" cone) a great deal, and the "green" and "blue" cones very little; when the output of the three cones is mixed together, red is seen. Light nearer the middle of the spectrum stimulates the red and green cones but not the blue cone; when the output of the three cones is mixed together, yellow is seen. According to this theory, white is the simultaneous stimulation of all three receptors, black is the absence of stimulation, and gray is a simultaneous response of smaller magnitude from the three receptors.

No one during Young's time knew much about the receptors in the retina nor had anyone seen them, although the presence of some kind of photosensitive receptors in the back of the eye was assumed. We now know that Young was right in postulating only three types of receptors repeated over the retinal surface. Three distinct types of cones have been identified, each maximally sensitive to a different region of the electromagnetic spectrum. Thus, only the long-wavelength cone will absorb many of the photons from a long-wavelength light stimulus, and the other two types of cones will not be affected very much.

Young was wrong, however, in postulating that the output from the three types of cones combine in their transmission to the brain in the same way that the three beams of light combine. We now know that the bipolar cells serving the three types of cones have not only excitatory (adding or combining) connections to the ganglion cells, but also inhibitory connections. Therefore, the coding of wavelength information is much more complex than Young imagined.

Opponent-Coding Theory From inferences about how inhibition in the nervous system must function, Ewald Hering (1870) proposed an alternative to Young's color-coding theory. In his **opponent-coding theory**, Hering postulated that the activity level of the three types of cones is not simply coded as excitation, and also that only two ganglion cells are needed to signal wavelength to the brain—one for red/green and one for yellow/blue.

One of these ganglion cells transmits a red/green code by becoming more active when there is a predominance of long-wavelength red light on the retina and less active when there is a predominance of medium-wavelength green light on the retina. The red cones are connected to these ganglion cells with an excitatory **synapse**; the green cones have an inhibitory synapse. When the eye has been stimulated by green light for some time, the green cones become less sensitive, inhibit the ganglion cells less, and allow the long-wavelength light to stimulate the red cones; therefore white light looks reddish. The sensation coded by the yellow/blue type of ganglion cell looks yellow if the ganglion cell is more active than usual, and blue when it is less active. When the combinations of these two types of ganglion cells arrive at the brain, any color can be sensed.

Although some of the color-mixing information that Young used in his original theory is inherent in Hering's opponent-coding theory, Hering's theory is consistent with the manifestations of color blindness and color contrast that confused Young. Let's look briefly at each of these phenomena.

Color Blindness About 10 percent of all human beings, 9 out of 10 of whom are males, suffer from some type of *color blindness*—the inability to make all the discriminations among hues that a normal perceiver can make. The most common type of this visual defect is a red/green discrimination loss, in which the perceiver cannot tell the difference between a red and a green light by hue alone. He may be able to tell them apart if one wavelength is more intense than the other or if they are in different familiar positions (such as in a traffic light), but he cannot discriminate them by the sensation of hue (Figure 7•18).

A rarer type of color blindness is a yellow/blue discrimination loss, in which wavelengths from these two spectral regions produce the same sensation if their intensities are equal. The third and most rare type involves the total absence of hue discrimination—all wavelength stimulation produces shades of gray differing only in brightness.

The explanation of color blindness posed a problem for Young. If colors are coded by combining the outputs from the three types of cones, as Young thought, then a red/green color-blind person must be deficient in long-wavelength cones, so that light longer than wavelengths producing green must be coded by the green cone. But if that is the case, how can such a perceiver discriminate yellow (something a red/green color-blind person can easily do)? Young said that the sensation of yellow is a result of equal activity of the red and green cones, just as yellow light is produced by adding red and green light together—a theory clearly inconsistent with the manifestations of color blindness. A similar problem is posed by yellow/blue color blindness. If yellow is made from green and red, and blue is made from blue, how could yellow and blue ever be confused? Young tried unsuccessfully to figure out these problems, which Hering's theory explains satisfactorily.

Color Contrast We already know that the brightness of a surface is not simply a function of the intensity of light reflected from it, but is in part determined by the intensities reflected from the surrounding surfaces. Color contrast is related to brightness contrast. Both simultaneous and successive hue contrast of a surface are affected by the wavelengths of a light reflected not only from that surface, but also from surrounding surfaces (Figure 7•19).

If you stare for half a minute or so at long-wavelength light (red) and then look at a gray surface, the surface will have a green tinge, or *afterimage* of red. The reverse is also true; if you stare at green and then at gray, the gray looks red (afterimage of green). The same is true for yellow (blue afterimage) and blue (yellow afterimage). In fact, every hue has an afterimage hue, or complementary color, that will be seen if you stare at the first hue for a while and then look at a white surface (Figure 7•20).

If you stare at middle-wavelength light for a while, the green cones will be stimulated much more than the red and blue cones. Because of temporal inhibition, further stimulation will result in decreased sensitivity of the green cones (just as prolonged light stimulation will result in a lowering of receptor sensitivity). If you then look at white, which contains equal quantities of all visible light wavelengths, the blue and red cones will absorb more photons than the green cones will, and you will perceive a hue containing much blue and red and little green. According to Young's theory, this stimulus condition should make the gray look purple, but in fact, it looks red, as Hering's theory predicts.

Red, green, and blue are called *primary colors* because any color can be made from the mixture of their wavelengths. Therefore, according to Young, yellow must be a derived color resulting from a mixture of equal parts of red and green without blue. However, the sensation of yellow is that of a pure color. It is easy to see that orange is a mixture of red and yellow, but yellow doesn't look like a mixture of red and green, and so it is considered a primary color. This is an objection that Hering noted.

Summary Our eyes are especially adapted to the range of electromagnetic radiation between 400 and 700 nanometers that is commonly called light. Light varies in intensity, wavelength, duration, and extent.

The photoreceptors on the retina, which change light energy into neural signals, are the rods and cones. Rods are more numerous than cones and are primarily responsible for the detection of light at low energy values. Cones are most densely packed in the fovea, and although they require higher light levels to detect a stimulus than rods do, cones have better visual acuity—that is, they are better able than rods to signal visual patterns made up of small details.

Between the lens of the eye and the retina are a variety of neural cells that integrate neural signals initiated at the photoreceptors. A single optic nerve fiber leading from this intervening neural mass to the brain may be connected to more than 10,000 rods, while more than half of the foveal cones enjoy a private pipeline to the brain.

Not all transmission of information in the visual system is excitatory. At normal room illuminations and above, inhibitory effects interact with excitatory ones to permit rather sophisticated sensory coding even at the level of the retina. The combination of excitatory and inhibitory connections among neural units in the retina permits efficient coding of sensory information so that the brain is not bombarded with more signals than it needs. Similar coding occurs between the eye and the visual cortex to increase further the efficiency of information transmission. There are coding systems in the visual system for spots, lines, movement velocity, acceleration, curves, colors, and depth, and in each case one or a few cortical cells can represent the coding of thousands of receptors—a coding that reduces visual stimulation to a small number of visual features.

Factors other than the intensity of light help to determine the magnitude of our sensations. Dark- and light-adaptation processes, and simultaneous and successive brightness contrasts indicate that the relationship between the intensity of a light and perceived brightness is not a simple one.

Eye movements play a role in visual perception. Small eye movements misalign the eyes so that they no longer look at the point of original fixation. To correct such a drift, a microsaccade is made to bring the point of fixation back to its original position. The importance of drifts and microsaccades is related to the coding effects of inhibition. If the eyes were absolutely stationary and were looking at a scene that did not move, the brain would receive no further information about the scene after the initial signals. As the scene drifts slightly over the retina from time to time, new bursts of signals are sent to the brain and perception of the visual scene is maintained.

In general, time is coded poorly within the visual modality, whose major emphasis is on coding the location of a stimulus and the spatial discontinuities of its pattern on the retina. This general principle is borne out by experiments on temporal summation.

The minimal size of a detail that a visual system can detect is called its visual acuity. The Snellen eye chart is a familiar test of this ability. Other discrimination tests measure visual acuity sharp enough to detect intensity discontinuities smaller than the width of a single foveal cone.

Color accounts for most of the affective connotations of vision. The three most important physical dimensions underlying the sensation or appearance of colors are intensity, wavelength, and purity, corresponding respectively to the psychological dimensions of brightness, hue, and saturation. Brightness refers to shades of gray and is familiar in the visual patterns that show up on black-and-white television. Hue is popularly referred to as the color of a light, and saturation as the dimension that distinguishes a pink from a deep red.

It is possible to distribute hues around the circumference of a circle so that hues directly opposite each other, when mixed in amounts of equal intensity, appear white (complementary hues). If the amounts are not equal, the resulting hue is a less saturated version of the more intense hue. The relationship between wavelength and hue was discovered by Isaac Newton when he used a prism to separate sunlight into the spectral colors ranging from red (700 nanometers) to blue (400 nanometers).

The fact that suitable mixtures of three lights from different parts of the electromagnetic spectrum can generate all other hues led Thomas Young to propose a theory of color vision based on the assumption that the retina contained only three kinds of cones, one sensitive to long wavelengths, one to short wavelengths, and one to wavelengths in the middle range of the spectrum. Three types of color receptors have been found, but rather than simply mixing their transmissions to the brain in the way that lights can be combined, inhibitory connections have also been found. The opponent-coding theory proposed by Ewald Hering is consistent with the integration of excitatory and inhibitory processes found in ganglion cells serving the three types of cones. This theory also accounts for certain color-blindness and color-contrast phenomena unsuccessfully handled by Young.

Most of the next chapter will deal with more complex aspects of vision. We shall now briefly discuss the auditory system and the other five senses.

The Auditory System

7•3 Like vision, audition provides contact with the world. Therefore, we must be particularly concerned with the means by which auditory stimuli arise and travel in the environment before they reach and affect the auditory receptor surfaces.

Stimuli for Hearing The stimuli for audition are mechanical vibrations, as compared to electromagnetic vibrations for light stimuli. When an object is struck, it is set in oscillatory motion, which gradually dies down. If the object is surrounded by any substance, or *medium*, the molecules in that substance are alternately compressed and expanded as the object vibrates back and forth (*oscillates*). The larger the distance traveled by each vibration, the greater the compression and expansion of surrounding molecules. The faster the object vibrates, the greater the frequency with which compression and expansion movements alternate.

Figure 7•21 illustrates expansion and contraction of the molecules of a surrounding medium (air) induced by a mechanical vibration. The waveform thus induced is a *sound wave*, the stimulus for hearing. Sound waves have two components: *frequency* (the rate at which contractions and expansions occur per unit of time—usually seconds) and *amplitude* (the amount of contraction or expansion that occurs in each wave). A string on a piano that sounds middle C vibrates at the rate of 262 cycles (times) per second (now called hertz, or Hz, after the German physicist Heinrich Rudolf Hertz). The frequency of a wave is determined by the rate at which the object vibrates, which in turn is determined by the object's size

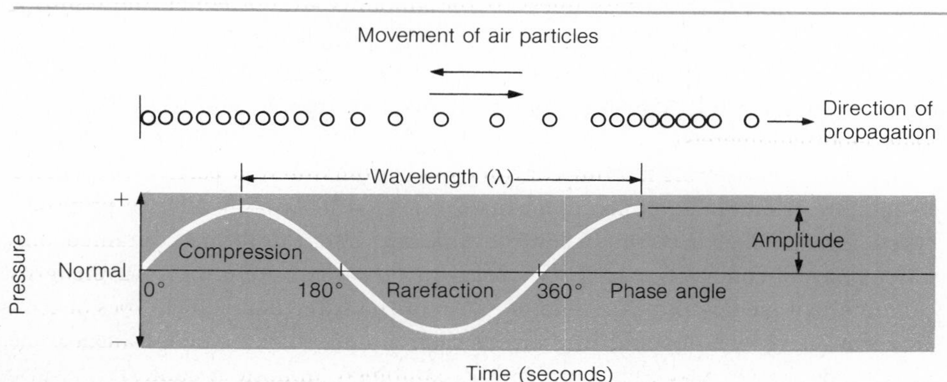

Fig. 7•21 A graphical representation of the instantaneous pressure changes in a simple acoustic wave as a function of time. (Corso, 1967)

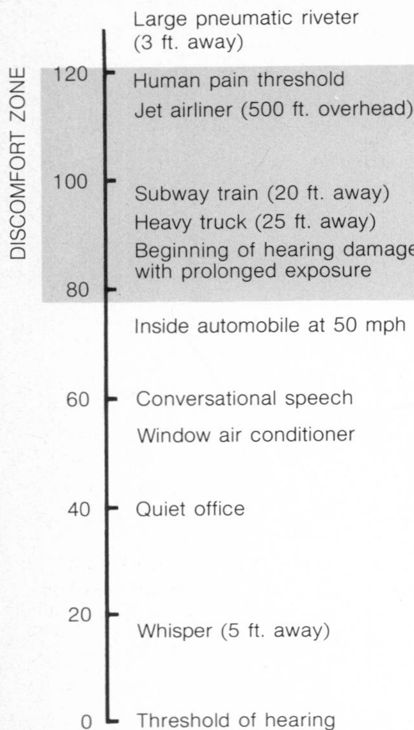

Fig. 7•22 The amplitude of various common sounds scaled in decibels. (Hilgard, Atkinson, and Atkinson, 1975)

and shape, but not by how hard it is struck. A short string or wire or tuning fork vibrates more rapidly than a long one; and a thin one, more rapidly than a thick one. But a middle C string always has the same frequency regardless of whether it is struck softly or vigorously, or is strummed in the same way as a banjo or guitar string.

Amplitude (intensity), however, depends directly upon how much the object is deflected when it is set to vibrating. The amplitudes of sounds are measured in decibels, or db (named after Alexander Graham Bell). Figure 7•22 gives amplitude values for some typical sounds. The zero point is set at the absolute threshold for detecting 1000 Hz in a sound-deadened testing room.

What we have said so far applies only to pure tones—those that occur only when a single object vibrates in a homogeneous medium. The frequency given off under these special conditions is called the *fundamental frequency* of that tone. But a vibrating object will give off several additional frequencies, which are called *overtones*. Overtones occur because the object—a string, a wire, a rod, or something else—vibrates both as a whole and in sections of one-half, one-third, one-fourth, and so on. Each section produces a frequency that is a multiple of the fundamental—two times, three times, four times, and so forth. Each of the overtones is at a successively lower amplitude and so will not be as loud as the fundamental frequency.

The pattern of overtones determines the *timbre* of the sound. Because vibrating bodies differ in the way in which their overtones are generated, some are suppressed while other are emphasized. The characteristic pattern of overtone suppression and emphasis makes a flute sound different from a piano or a voice producing the same fundamental frequency.

What happens when a sound has overtones? Instead of the pure *sine wave* in Figure 7•21, a much more ragged wave pattern is formed (Figure 7•23). The instrument that produced this waveform can be identified by observing where the peaks and valleys occur in the spectrogram.

What happens when two objects are set in vibratory motion? The sound waves generated by each object interact, because both vibrating bodies are compressing and expanding the same molecules. If the objects are vibrating at the same frequency and exactly in phase (each wave of each object beginning together), the resulting frequency will be the same, but the amplitude will be doubled. If they are perfectly out of phase, they will cancel each other because one compression will offset an expansion, and vice versa. The amplitude will be zero and you will hear nothing. Such an occurrence is not typical, however; usually the pattern of interaction is more chaotic.

If two sounds differ somewhat in frequency, their peaks and valleys will sometimes match, sometimes be opposite, and sometimes be in between. When they match, the resulting sound is strong; when they are opposite, the sound is weak. If the difference in frequency is small, then both the in-phase and out-of-phase oscillations will occur repeatedly and we will hear a throbbing, called *beats*. If the frequencies are far apart, we will not hear the beats because there will be fewer occasions when the two oscillations are either perfectly in phase or perfectly out of phase.

Harmony among different sounds is said to occur when there is an absence of beats—that is, when the sounds combine in such a way that the fundamentals and overtones are sufficiently close, or when the close tones are not strong enough in amplitude to set up beats. Of course, what is considered harmonious differs from person to person, from culture to culture, and from time to time, and so there can be no physical definition of harmony, in spite of attempts since Pythagoras to make one up.

The speed with which sound travels depends primarily upon the density of the surrounding medium. In a perfect vacuum, such as outer space or on the moon, it cannot travel at all because of the absence of molecules. It travels about 330 meters per second in air at sea level, about 1520 meters per second in water, and about 6000 meters per second in steel. Therefore, you can hear the approach of a railroad train nearly 20 times farther away by putting your ear to the rail than by waiting for the sound to arrive through the air.

Noise is a combination of sounds in which many different frequencies are mixed together. *White noise* comprises all frequencies at roughly equal amplitudes. Radio static or a bathroom shower most closely resembles the sound of white noise.

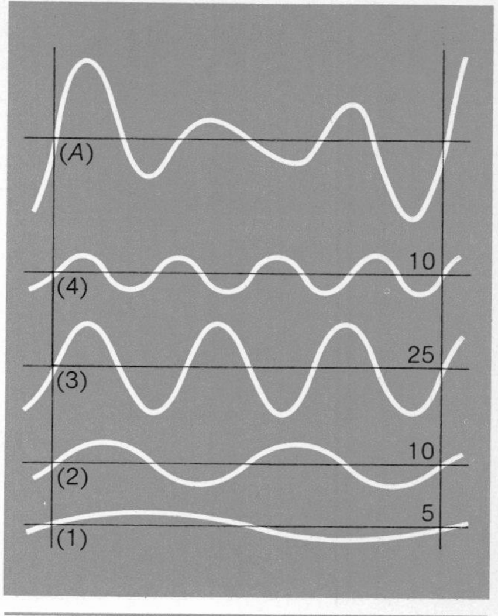

Fig. 7·23 Analysis of a complex wave. The irregular curve (A) may be analyzed into four regular ones, each with the relative amplitude shown at the right. (From Beasley, 1931)

Receptors for Audition Because sound begins with mechanical vibration, the initial reception process must transduce the vibration of molecules in the medium (usually air) into a vibratory process in the body that must in turn generate neural signals to reflect the frequency, amplitude, and mixture of sound waves present in the mechanical vibration stimulus.

Mechanical Reception of Sound Figure 7·24 shows a sketch of the ear including the *auricle*—a sound-collecting funnel that is visible outside the head—and the most important parts of the inner ear. The auricle is not essential for hearing in

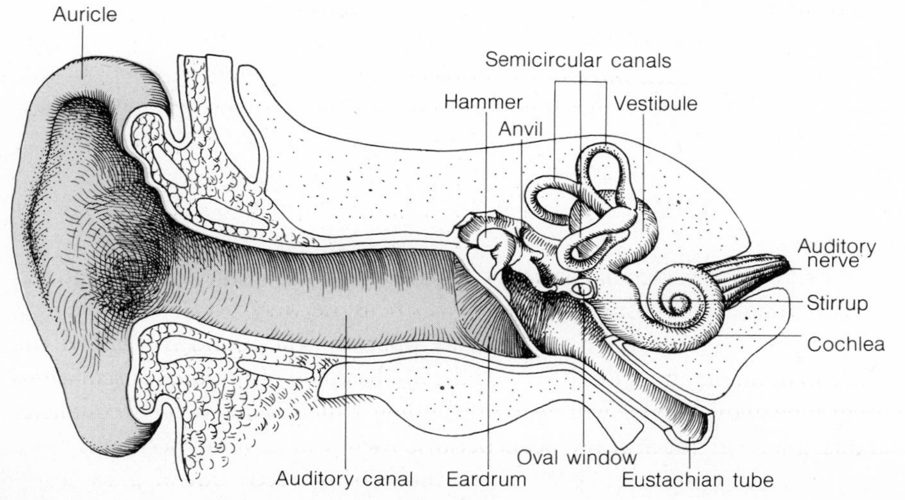

Fig. 7·24 Sound pounds on the eardrum (external ear), which moves the three bones of the middle ear. The last of the three bones, the stirrup, vibrates the surface of the inner ear, which transmits the mechanical force to the fluid inside. (From Brown and Herrnstein, 1975)

humans, although it helps sounds to find their way down the *auditory canal* to the *eardrum*. When air molecules vibrate against it, the eardrum is set in vibratory motion. In youth its vibration frequency is the same as that of air up to about 20,000 Hz, then it drops to half that frequency as the eardrum stiffens with age. In order for us to hear a sound, its pressure must move the eardrum only one billionth of a centimeter—a distance smaller than the diameter of the smallest atom. The auricle, auditory canal, and eardrum comprise the outer ear.

The middle ear is filled with air and contains three tiny bones that transmit vibrations from the eardrum to the liquid-filled tube in which the auditory receptors are located. These bones are named for their shapes: *hammer*, *anvil*, and *stirrup*. They multiply the magnitude of vibration from the eardrum at the outer ear to the oval window at the inner ear by about twenty-five-fold.

Translation of vibrations into neural signals occurs in the inner ear, which consists of two parts. The first part contains the three *semicircular canals* and the *vestibular sacs*, which control and regulate balance and equilibrium. The second part is a snaillike tube called the *cochlea*, which is filled with fluid and receptors. Figure 7·25 shows a cochlea and an uncoiled cochlear section.

When the stirrup pushes inward on the oval window of the cochlea, it exerts pressure on the fluids there. The force exerted travels down the vestibular canal and back up the tympanic canal to the round window, which bulges and contracts to equalize the pressure. Between the two canals, the *basilar membrane* stretches the length of the cochlea. On it rests the *organ of Corti*, in which tiny hair cells are activated by the pressure of the moving fluids, thus stimulating the neurons at the beginning of the auditory nerve to send neural impulses to the brain.

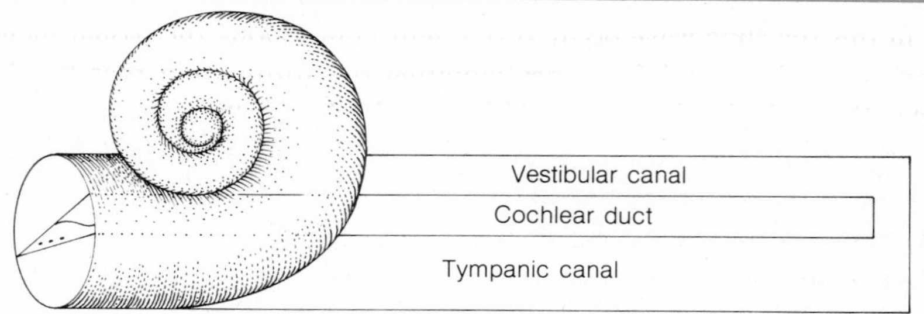

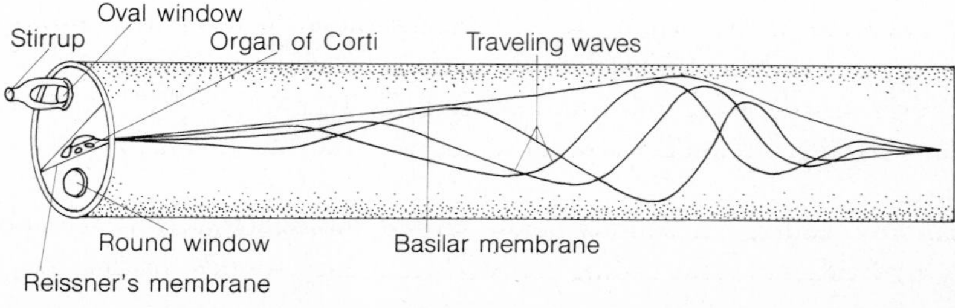

Fig. 7·25 The cochlea. The unrolled cochlear section shows how the stirrup pumps on the oval window. The force travels down the vestibular canal and back up the tympanic canal to the round window, swinging the basilar membrane up and down and creating bulges. The traveling wave is the track of the largest bulge at each location on the membrane for a sound of a particular frequency. Perched on the basilar membrane inside the cochlear duct is the organ of Corti, the structure from which the neurons of the auditory nerve originate. (From Brown and Herrnstein, 1975)

Neural Signals in the Cochlea In the middle of the nineteenth century, Hermann von Helmholtz worked out a theory of auditory coding for sound frequency that was nearly correct. He postulated that the hair cells along the organ of Corti act as resonators set for different frequencies. Therefore, just as a tuning fork of a given frequency can be set into vibration by surrounding air vibrating at that frequency, so can the resonators in the organ of Corti be made to vibrate. A 1000 Hz tone, for example, sets only the 1000 Hz hairs to resonating. Thus, the frequency of a particular sound is translated into a location in the cochlea. If each set of hair cells is connected to a different fiber in the auditory nerve, then the pattern of activity in the auditory nerve will match the frequency of the sounds arriving at the ear.

It took nearly a hundred years to work out the details of this theory and repair its errors. This work was done primarily by Georg von Békésy, who in 1961 received the Nobel prize in medicine and physiology for his work on the physical mechanism of stimulation within the cochlea. Although von Békésy's model of hearing is not complete, there is sufficient reason to believe that two separate processes are involved—one for low frequency sounds (below about 4000 Hz), and the other for high frequency sounds (those above 4000 Hz).

Von Békésy (1960) showed that Helmholtz's theory was right for the higher frequencies. When the stirrup pushes in on the oval window, the pressure generated travels down one canal in the cochlea and back through the other canal and pushes outward on the round window. When the stirrup pulls in, the pressure travels in the reverse direction. These pressures are transmitted almost instantaneously, but in addition a slow traveling wave is set up along the basilar membrane separating the two canals. This wave does not travel back and forth but only outward, in much the same way that small waves spread out from a stone dropped into water. Von Békésy discovered that the location and sharpness of the maximum bulge in this traveling wave occur at different points along the basilar membrane, depending on the sound frequency vibrating the stirrup, and that this location provides the code for frequency. Although the hair cells are not resonators, as Helmholtz thought, the coding system does translate frequency into a location in the cochlea—the key to Helmholtz's theory.

This accounts for the coding of high frequency vibrations. When the vibrations are below several thousand hertz, however, the lump in the traveling wave is quite broad and nearly always occurs at the same location in the far end of the cochlea, regardless of the specific frequency of the sound stimulus. Therefore, low frequencies are not very well coded. Theorists other than von Békésy, notably Wever, have shown that when the stimulus frequency is low, the neurons in the auditory nerve fire directly in synchrony with the frequency. Thus, a 100 Hz tone excites the auditory nerve 100 times per second. This frequency code would not work for very high frequencies because the auditory nerve could not follow so rapidly.

Apparently, coding for sounds below several thousand hertz is accomplished directly by frequency; and coding for high frequency sounds, by the location in the cochlea where the traveling wave makes its maximum bulge. For tones in the middle frequencies, both coding mechanisms are used, together.

Amplitude coding appears to be much simpler than frequency coding. Regardless of frequency, the greater the amplitude—that is, the harder the stirrup pushes on the oval window—the more neurons are activated and the more rapidly they fire.

Transmission of Information from Ear to Brain It is not yet known how the movements of the hair cells in the organ of Corti give rise to neural signals in the fibers of the auditory nerve, but somehow they induce activity in the 25,000 or so neurons leaving the cochlea in each ear. There are four nerve junctions between the cochlea of each ear and the auditory cortex of each hemisphere (Figure 7•26). All the way through, the neurons are bundled and separated by frequency; and so whatever frequency of sound is presented, only a portion of the neurons are active. At each junction there is a "map" of frequencies similar to the coding along the basilar membrane.

As in the visual system, some of the nerve fibers in each ear cross to the opposite hemisphere of the brain, while others project into the hemisphere on the same

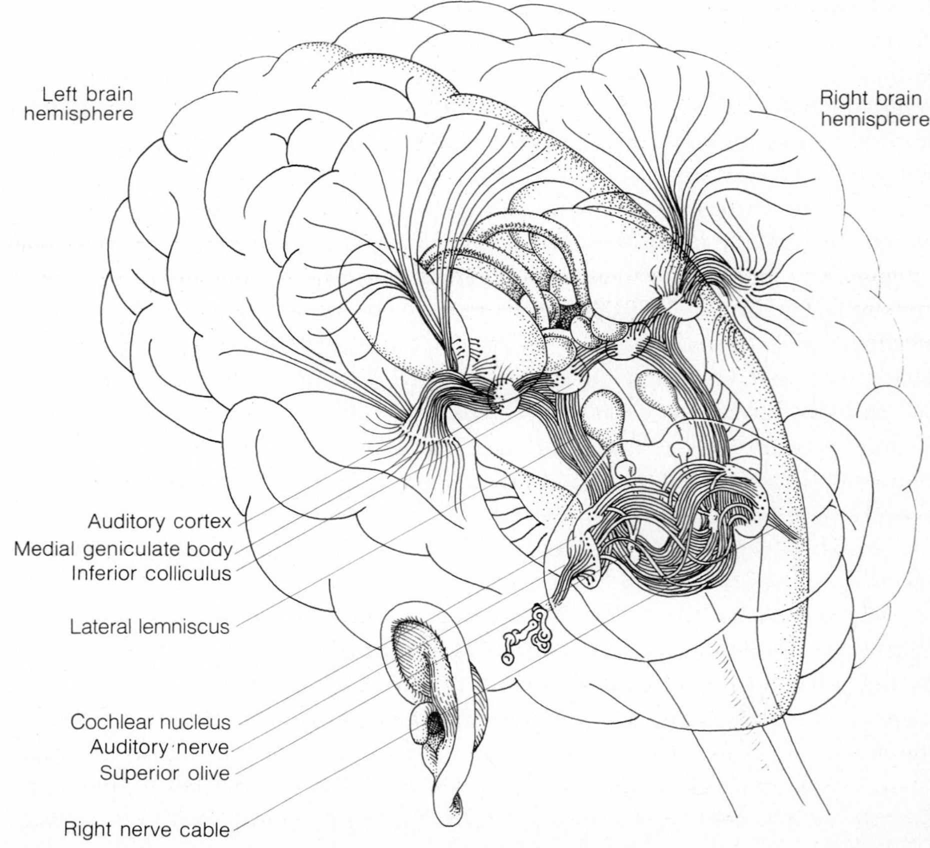

Fig. 7•26 The neurons arising in the organ of Corti form the two branches of the auditory nerve, one for each ear. The auditory nerve goes as far as the cochlear nucleus, where the next set of neurons originates. Several more relay stations intervene—at the superior olive, the inferior colliculus, and the medial geniculate—before the message is delivered to the auditory cortex on the outer layer of the brain. Along the way, nerve fibers cross from left and right and otherwise shape the neural representation of the sound. (From Brown and Herrnstein, 1975)

side. The extent of switching is not known in as much detail as it is for vision, but it is clear that more fibers cross than stay on the same side of the brain.

Factors that Affect Auditory Reception and Processing Although space does not permit detailed coverage of these factors here, we shall discuss a few specific topics.

Absolute Threshold for Audition Because we are almost never in a sound-free environment, the intensity of sound stimuli has to be measured on a relative scale. The decibel scale is usually used to measure sound intensity. It represents the intensity of sound pressure relative to a standard level. The standard commonly used is the amount of sound pressure needed to be detected at an absolute threshold of 0.0002 dyne per square centimeter by a typical observer. A dyne is a unit of force that will impart an acceleration of one centimeter per second per second (or per second squared) to a mass weighing one gram. The *force pressure* is applied over an area of one square centimeter. The quantity 0.0002 dyne is very small and corresponds to the force needed to deflect the center of an eardrum one billionth of a centimeter.

An absolute threshold of 0.0002 dyne per square centimeter is the average value for typical young adults. This value increases substantially with age, and a fifty-year-old person may require 100 times as much sound pressure to detect the same stimulus. This loss of sensitivity is due to decreasing resiliency in the eardrum and growing inflexibility of the mechanical linkages in the middle ear—inevitable concomitants of aging.

We are most sensitive to sound frequencies between 1500 and 4000 Hz—that is, we need far less pressure to hear those frequencies than higher or lower ones (Figure 7•27). Because decibels are on a logarithmic scale, a difference of 50 decibels between 100 Hz and 3000 Hz means that 10,000 times more sound pressure is needed to detect the former frequency than to detect the latter one. We cannot hear sounds below about 20 Hz, but we can often feel them if they are sufficiently intense. The lowest frequency that a pipe organ can produce is about 10 Hz.

Because of loss in flexibility of the mechanical processes, aging affects sensitivity to frequency as well as to amplitude. We gradually lose our ability to hear the higher frequencies. A young child can hear up to 20,000 Hz, a young adult to about 15,000 Hz, a middle-aged adult to 10,000 Hz, and a senior citizen no more than 7000 or 8000 Hz.

Some animals are sensitive to frequencies far above the upper limit of our auditory system (20,000 Hz). Mice and bats can hear up to 100,000 Hz, and bats and porpoises use very high frequency sounds to echo-locate. In general, the bigger the animal, the lower the upper-frequency sounds they can produce and hear, although porpoises may be an exception. Human beings excel in their sensitivity to amplitude for the frequencies they hear best and in ability to distinguish among frequencies. Some animals can hear particular types of sound better than humans

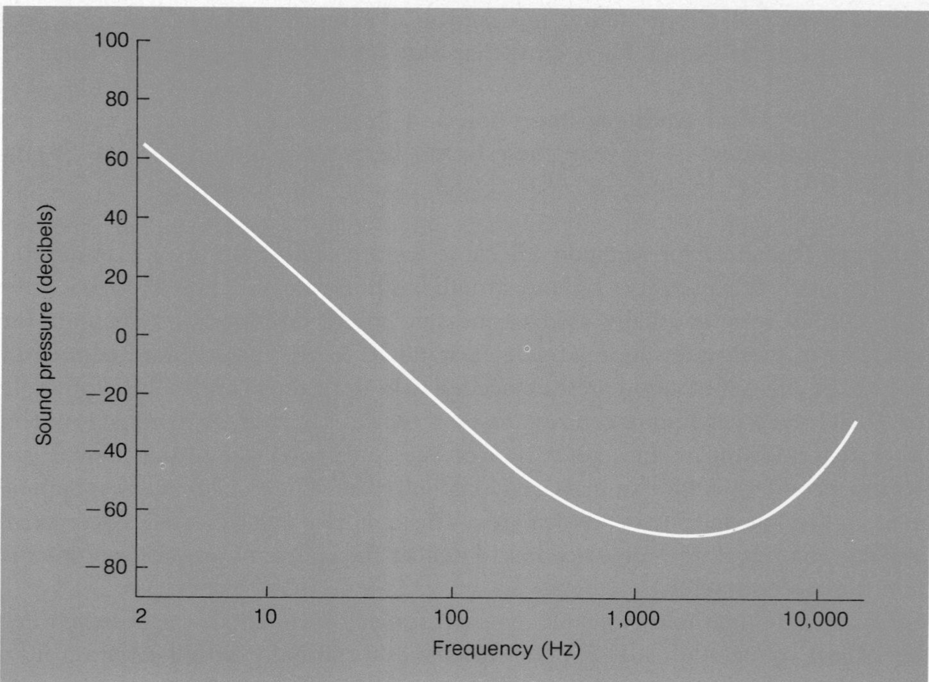

Fig. 7·27 The curve shows the detection threshold of hearing. It traces the lowest audible intensity on the *Y*-axis against frequency along the *X*-axis. Intensity is measured in decibels; frequency is on a logarithmic scale to compress the higher frequencies and stretch out the lower ones.

can, but this ability is due to a specific pattern of sound recognition rather than to its absolute level.

Sensitivity to Differences among Sounds How much of a change has to be made in the intensity of a tone at a constant frequency for you to detect the change? How much change has to be made in the frequency of a tone at a constant intensity for you to notice the change? Both of these questions relate to Weber's law, which states that the amount of change needed for discrimination in a sensory dimension is a constant proportion of the standard value.

We are most sensitive to intensity changes when the frequency is within the range of our greatest frequency sensitivity. The Weber fraction for a 4000 Hz tone is 1/20; therefore, an increase or decrease in sound pressure of only 5 percent would be detected as different. The Weber fraction for a 10,000 or 1000 Hz tone is 1/5, or 20 percent; and it becomes even larger for the higher frequencies. The Weber fractions are constant for all values of intensity except very quiet tones. Greater change is needed for quiet tones to be detected, a requirement corresponding to the discrimination of low-intensity visual stimuli.

The auditory system is much more sensitive to changes in frequency than to changes in intensity. In the range of mild or high intensities, the ear can detect a frequency change when the change is no more than 0.3 percent, or 1/333. This is the smallest Weber fraction for any human sense modality. Weber fractions are larger for less intense tones, approaching 1 percent for very quiet ones, but these measurements still represent very great sensitivity. Sensitivity is less at very low frequencies (below 500 Hz) or at very high ones (above 12,000 Hz), because you cannot hear those frequencies well.

If you listen to a 100 Hz tone and a 4000 Hz tone of equal physical intensity, the 4000 Hz tone will sound much louder because the auditory system is more sensitive to sounds of that frequency. The psychophysical relationship between intensity and loudness must therefore take frequency into account. If a 100 Hz tone is increased in intensity, it will decrease slightly in apparent pitch. A 6000 Hz tone, however, will increase in apparent pitch as its intensity is increased. In the region of greatest sensitivity, 1500 to 4000 Hz, pitch remains relatively constant as intensity changes. As you can readily see, the psychophysical relationships between frequency and pitch and between intensity and loudness are as complicated as the relationships involved in the sensation of vision.

Spatial Coding of Audition How can we identify the location of a sound? As we noted earlier, vision is a spatial sense, ideally adapted to provide information about the layout of space. Audition functions better as a temporal sense, giving information about the order and sequence of events. However, we can tell where a sound came from and where it is going relative to us.

Movement of Sound Sources The approach or departure of a train or jet plane is easily perceived because the intensity of the sound changes inversely with the distance from the perceiver. This **Doppler effect** leads to a perceived frequency change. Compared to a retreating sound, an approaching sound appears to increase in frequency as well as in intensity as it gets closer. In this way, physical changes in both intensity and frequency give substantial information about movement toward us or away from us. If the movement is lateral and does not result in a substantial change in distance, the change in localization information over time is used to perceive the movement.

Localization of a Sound If you blindfold an observer, and ask him or her to point to a sound source, you will find that the pointing error is probably very small. Our accuracy in locating a sound in space is incredibly good, especially for sounds that are to the side.

At low frequencies (below about 1500 Hz), we locate a sound by the difference between the times the sound arrives at our two ears. Under optimal conditions, we can discriminate a difference in arrival time of 1/30,000 second, or 0.000033 second. Compare that ability to the accuracy of the visual system to discriminate time differences.

As sound frequencies increase, the two ears cannot very well discriminate differences in time of arrival, so that this source of information disappears. However, above about 3000 Hz, the difference in intensity between the sound reaching the nearer ear and the sound reaching the farther ear is detectable and provides another source of information. Since most sounds in the natural environment are made up of many frequencies, both sources of information are available.

Any sound directly ahead, overhead, behind, or under us will reach both ears at the same time and with the same intensity. It is therefore not surprising that we often think a sound comes from behind when it comes from in front. We are not entirely at the mercy of chance, however, because some information comes from the sound shadows cast by our bodies. These sound shadows are slightly different for sounds ahead of us than for sounds behind us, and they help us to locate the source of a sound by providing different background patterns for the stimulus.

Our accuracy of localization for all sources of sound is increased manyfold if we move our heads. Because the movement is self-produced, the brain knows how much we move, probably by keeping track of the afferent signal issued to the neck muscles that produce the movement. After the movement is completed, both time-of-arrival and intensity differences for the sound will have changed. If the sound source is stationary and the amount of change in these two sources of information is exactly equal to the amount we move our head, then we acquire another sample of the time-of-arrival and intensity differences with which to locate the direction of the sound. If the sound was originally in front of us, the movement will now put it to one side; if it was behind us, the movement will now put it to the other side. Therefore, head movements immediately clarify the source of sounds that originally were in a plane passing vertically through the head.

Head movements also help locate moving sounds, especially if their distance from us does not change. Each movement produces a new sample of information, which changes with the movement of both the sound source and the head. We can use the additional samples to compute the sound's location by subtracting the effect produced by head movement alone; the differences are due to the movement of the sound. In the next chapter, we shall see the power of this type of comparison for the visual system when we consider eye movements as a source of visual information about the visual movement of objects in space.

Summary The stimuli for audition are the expansion and contraction of air molecules caused by mechanical vibrations. The sound waves thus induced vary in frequency (hertz) and amplitude (decibels). Frequency and amplitude are physical components and correspond respectively to the sensations of pitch and loudness. Vibrating objects give off overtones that are multiples of the fundamental frequency and correspond to the sensation of timbre, or tone quality. Timbre accounts for the differences we hear among musical instruments when they play the same note. Phase differences between two or more sound waves of the same frequency may interact to affect the amplitude of the sound, and sound waves that differ slightly in frequency generate beats. Harmony occurs when beats are absent. Noise is random combinations of sounds of many different frequencies.

Sound travels faster in steel than in air; it cannot travel at all in the absence of a medium. Sound traverses the outer ear from the auricle, through the auditory canal, and to the eardrum. Vibrations of the eardrum are amplified in the middle ear by the hammer, anvil, and stirrup, and are translated into neural impulses inside the cochlea of the inner ear. Tiny hair cells in the organ of Corti sense high frequencies, which are coded by the location of the maximum bulge along the oscillating basilar membrane. For sounds below about 4000 Hz, the neurons in the auditory nerve fire in synchrony with the stimulus frequency. Amplitude coding is simpler than frequency coding and relies directly on the extent to which the stirrup pushes on the oval window.

Between each cochlea and the auditory cortex of each hemisphere are four neural junctions bundled and separated by frequency. Some of the nerve fibers in each ear cross to the opposite brain hemisphere, but the extent of switching is not completely known.

Sound intensity is measured in decibels. The threshold of hearing in the average young adult is 0 decibels; the threshold of auditory pain is 120 decibels. We are most sensitive to sound frequencies between 1500 and 4000 Hz, although the range of hearing in young adults is between 20 and 20,000 Hz. With advanced age, frequencies higher than 7000 or 8000 Hz and intensities in the lower decibel range are not perceived. We are more sensitive to changes in frequency than to changes in intensity, and we are most sensitive to changes in intensity within the range of our greatest sensitivity to frequency.

At frequencies below about 1500 Hz, the location of a sound to the side is discriminated by time differences in the sound's arrival at the two ears. At higher frequencies, intensity differences between the two ears provide cues for sound location. Sounds directly over, under, ahead, and behind are located less easily than sounds to the side; but if we move our heads, we increase our ability to locate stationary and moving sound sources.

The Other Senses

7·4 Although vision and audition are probably the senses most relevant to psychology, our other senses are also important. They include taste, olfaction, the skin senses, the equilibrium senses, and kinesthesis. We shall discuss each of them briefly.

Taste From the plainest soup to a gourmet's delight, the qualities of food that influence taste are simply four: sweet, sour, salty, and bitter. What distinguishes appetizers from desserts are the combinations and proportions of these qualities along with properties such as odor, texture, solubility, and temperature. For example, if you are blindfolded and you hold your nose while tasting slices of apple and of onion, you will be unable to distinguish between the two types of slices.

The taste receptors (taste buds) are a small group of *gustatory* (taste) cells clustered like orange sections in small egg-shaped projections called *papillae* (Figure 7·28). At the top of each cell are *fibrils* (slender, hairlike fibers) that project into the *gustatory pore* (a minute opening on the surface where the taste bud is lo-

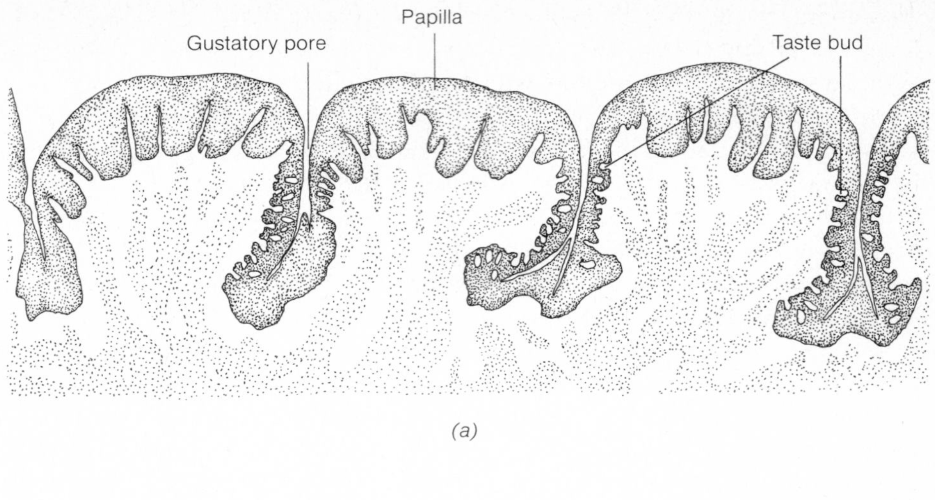

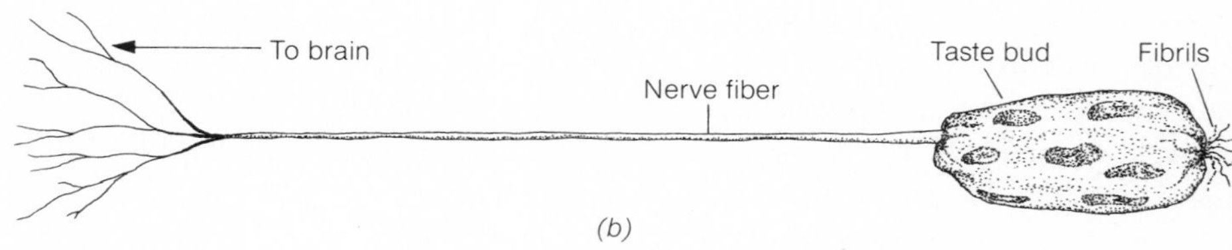

Fig. 7·28 (*a*) Papillae, each containing many taste buds. (*b*) An individual taste bud with its nerve fiber.

cated). Taste buds are distributed over the tip, sides, and rear of the upper surface of the tongue; they are also found on the palate, tonsils, epiglottis, pharynx, underside of the tongue, floor of the mouth, and mucosa of the lips and cheeks (Börnstein, 1940).

All food substances are somewhat soluble in water, and as these substances mix with saliva and flow into the gustatory pores, an electrical impulse is triggered in the nerve fibers interwoven at the base of the taste buds. These nerve fibers carry impulses from the taste receptors to the brain along at least three different neural pathways, which also carry information from the touch receptors and thereby supply patterns of feeling along with taste information. Taste in human beings is represented in an area of the brain close to the areas for touch sensations of the mouth, tongue, and pharynx. Speculation about the odor component of taste experience has led some investigators to conclude that the cortical areas for taste and smell lie in close proximity, but in fact they are quite separate.

In search for the basis of the four taste qualities, the chemical composition of food substances has been studied, but no simple relationships have yet emerged. For example, it was once thought that the taste of common table salt (sodium chloride) was due to either the sodium ion or the chloride ion; however, when one of these ions is combined in a substance without the other ion, a salty taste is not perceived. Furthermore, substances that taste salty do not always produce the same taste quality at all concentrations (Dzendolet and Meiselman, 1967).

Sensitivity to the four qualities is distributed unevenly on the tongue; sensitivity to sweetness is greatest at the tip of the tongue, sourness along the sides, bitterness at the back, and saltiness over the entire surface. Attempts to relate each papilla to a specific taste quality have been hindered by the difficulty of isolating these tiny receptors for experimental purposes; but careful experiments conducted by von Békésy (1964, 1966) suggest that an individual papilla is specialized for signaling one taste quality, which is mediated by all of the gustatory cells within that papilla.

Taste intensity is influenced by the amount of surface area stimulated; small surface areas therefore require stronger concentrations of a substance in order to signal the same intensity as a larger area. Studies by C. Pfaffmann (1960) show that individual gustatory fibers in the cat signal intensity differences by varying the firing rate of the stimulated fiber. Application of a stimulus substance to an area of the tongue mediated by a single fiber results in an initial burst of impulses and then a smooth decline in firing frequency. Increases in stimulus intensity are signaled by increases in firing rate and the recruitment of additional fibers. Sensitivity to changes in taste intensity vary with both subject and substance, but a Weber fraction of 1/5 is an average value for human beings.

Taste differences among species are observable as well as measurable. Guinea pigs and hamsters respond to sugar strongly, dogs and raccoons moderately, and cats not at all (Beidler, 1961).

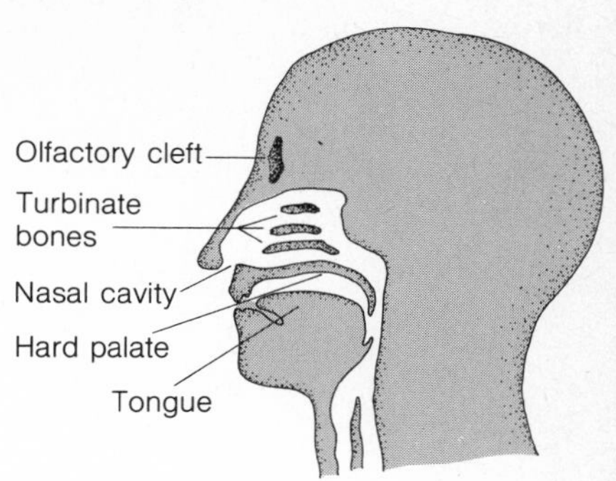

Fig. 7•29 The nasal passages. Odor reception depends largely on the ability of air currents to carry odorous particles to the olfactory cleft from both the nasal cavity and the mouth cavity. (Adapted from Pfaffmann, 1948)

Olfaction Contrary to popular belief, the property of food most responsible for a gourmet's delight is odor rather than taste. As we have seen, taste quality is limited to combinations of sweet, sour, salty, and bitter, and holding our noses while the medicine goes down is a popular relief from distasteful substances. As with taste, the stimuli for smell are chemical molecules; however, the two senses differ widely in sensitivity. Our noses are sensitive to relatively minute quantities of airborne substances, while our taste buds require comparatively larger amounts of stimuli for detection (Table 7•1).

Most of the air inhaled during ordinary breathing passes directly to the throat and lungs, but some particles escape from the main air current and reach the receptors in the olfactory cleft, which is located high in the nasal cavity (Figure 7•29). During chewing and swallowing, movements of the palate and throat create air currents that carry odorous particles to the olfactory cleft from the back of the mouth cavity.

The olfactory receptors are long bipolar cells that project through the tissue lining the top and sides of the olfactory cleft. The receptor nerve endings (axons) collect in the olfactory bulb to form the olfactory nerve pathways to the brain. Secondary cells carry neural impulses directly to the cortex. The olfactory system is therefore the simplest of our senses: it has only two junctions between the receptor cells and cortex. These cortical areas are not well known, however, and research is still being done on them.

Because the olfactory cleft is inaccessible, it is difficult to study using current laboratory techniques. However, methods for determining threshold levels have discovered that the nose is capable of detecting one molecule of *mercaptan* (an odoriferous chemical that smells like rotten eggs) in 50 trillion molecules of air (Moncrieff, 1944). Although measurements such as these suggest that the nose is indeed sensitive, the range of its sensitivity to various odors is wide. For example, ether must be 100,000 times more concentrated than artificial musk in order to be detected.

Another factor in determining the absolute threshold for an odorant is its rate of flow. During normal breathing an estimated 5 to 10 percent of the total flow of air passes to the olfactory cleft; sniffing increases that amount to 20 percent or more. For example, one molecule of mercaptan in 50 trillion molecules of air is detectable, but one sniff delivers about 10 trillion molecules to the olfactory cleft, thereby greatly increasing the possibility of detection.

Compared to its detection sensitivity for odorants, the ability of the human olfactory apparatus to discriminate differences in concentration is poor. T. Engen (1961, 1964) and his colleagues have shown that increasing the concentration of certain odorants a hundredfold above the detection threshold only doubles the odorant's reported strength. This relative insensitivity to concentration differences has led to speculation that two sets of receptors are present in the olfactory cleft—one for detection and one for identification of the stimulus.

Attempts have been made to identify the physical properties of odorants that result in our characteristic perceptions of them. One theory proposes that the relative ease with which substances evaporate at ordinary temperatures is an index of detectability, but this relationship does not always hold. For example, musk is a powerful odorant that is used in the manufacture of perfume; however, it does not evaporate readily. Pure water evaporates relatively easily, but it is odorless.

Other theories suggest solubility criteria and refractive indices as indicative of odorant qualities, but the relationships between these properties and odorant characteristics do not always hold. Probably the most promising theory of smell is by J. G. Amoore (1970), who identified relationships between the shape and configuration of odorant molecules and their perceived smell. Amoore postulated seven classes of odorants, including spherical camphoraceous molecules, disc-shaped musk molecules, and wedge-shaped mint molecules. Presumably these molecules fit corresponding receptor sites in the olfactory cleft, thereby stimulating their specialized receptors and giving rise to their characteristic smells. Other investigators have suggested modifications of Amoore's hypothesis, and research on the stimuli for olfaction continues.

Skin Senses The stimulus for the sensation of touch is not the pressure exerted on the skin receptors, but the *gradient* between areas of greater and lesser pressure (Meissner, 1859; von Frey and Kiesow, 1899). For example, if you stand absolutely still in a bathtub half full of water and attend to the experience of water pressure on your legs, you will sense pressure only at the point where the surface of the water touches your legs. Pressure sensations also result whenever a sufficiently steep mechanical deformation of the skin occurs, such as when the skin is pulled during the removal of adhesive tape from around a wound.

In addition to touch, skin receptors also mediate sensations of heat, cold, and pain. Traditionally these four sensations were thought to be generated by different types of receptors: touch by Pacinian and Meissner's corpuscles, cold by Krause end bulbs, warmth by Ruffini endings, and pain by free nerve endings (Figure 7•30). However, the cornea of the eye, which contains only free nerve endings, is capable of yielding all four sensations; and sensitivity to touch is found in hairy areas of the body that do not contain Pacinian or Meissner's corpuscles. Recent research on Meissner's corpuscles, Ruffini endings, and Krause end bulbs has discovered similarities among these three forms indicating that they probably represent different developmental stages of a single receptor type.

Although attempts to assign specific functions to specific nerve endings have been unsuccessful, some regularities have been found. For example, free nerve endings, which are apparently involved in pain reception, are distributed over the entire body. Pacinian corpuscles (touch) are found throughout the body in the deeper layers of the skin, especially around muscles and in certain membranes. Pacinian corpuscles are sensitive to small displacements of their onionlike surface, but they do not respond to temperature changes.

Adaptation to pressure occurs quickly—for example, as much as 80 percent of the original pressure in three seconds; by the time we are ready to put on our hat, we have already adapted to the weight of our coat. Adaptation to pain, such as

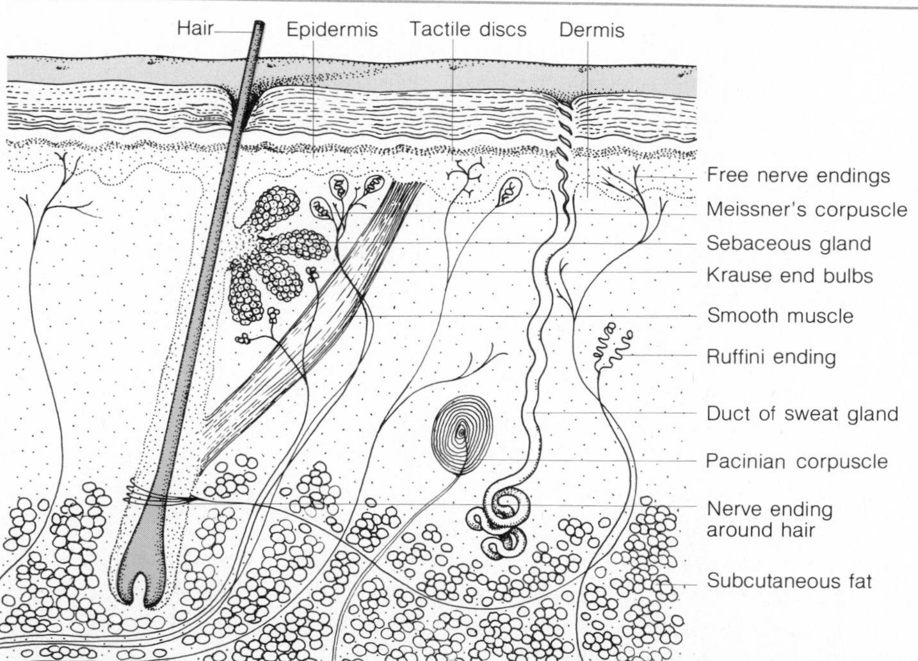

Fig. 7•30 Composite diagram of the skin in cross section. In the epidermis are free nerve endings; in the dermis are Meissner corpuscles, Krause end bulbs, and Ruffini endings. The subcutaneous tissue is chiefly fatty and vascular but contains Pacinian corpuscles, the largest of the specialized endings. (From Gardner, 1975, after Woollard, Weddell, and Harpman, 1940)

occurs when a needle is injected, takes as long as five minutes and can be complete. The time required for temperature adaptation depends on the difference between the temperature of the stimulus and our normal skin temperature; in general, we adapt more quickly to cold than to heat.

Using hairs of graduated stiffness and measuring how much pressure it took to bend them, M. von Frey (1899) found that the absolute threshold for the detection of touch varies, depending on the part of the body being stimulated. The fingertips and tongue are especially sensitive to touch; by comparison, the soles of our feet are impervious. The determination of thresholds for pain showed the cornea of the eye to be extremely sensitive, while the fingertips are relatively insensitive. Determining the thresholds for temperature change is a very complex process and depends on skin temperature, on whether the rate of change in the stimulus temperature is gradual enough to permit adaptation, and on the size of the skin area being stimulated.

Equilibrium Senses In a normal person, information about the orientation of the head and the movement of the body as a whole is always available. The vestibular apparatus of the inner ear (Figure 7•31) senses the movement of the entire body. The part of the system that mediates this information comprises three fluid-filled *semicircular canals* located at right angles to each other and each having its own *bulbous ampulla* lined with hair cells. As a person moves in any direction, the fluid in one or in some combination of the canals is set in motion, thus moving the hairs in the ampullae and creating a neural signal.

The part of the system that mediates information on the orientation of the head comprises the vestibular sacs—the *utriculus* (utricle) and the *sacculus*

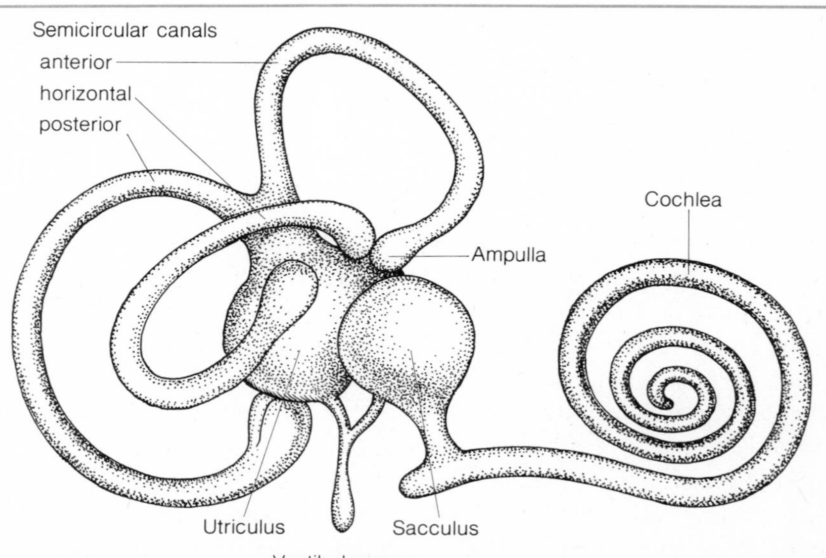

Fig. 7•31 The vestibular mechanism of the inner ear, which conveys information to the brain about the movement of the body. (Johnson et al., 1972)

(saccule)—which are also fluid filled and lined with hair cells. The utricle contains nerve endings necessary to the maintenance of normal posture. The relationship to equilibrium or to locomotion of the nerve endings in the saccule has not yet been discovered.

The stimuli for the vestibular-canal receptors are changes in the rate of bodily motion but not the motions themselves. When we are carried along in an airplane at a constant rate, we are hardly aware that we are moving.

Damage to the vestibular apparatus on one side of the head results in nausea, vomiting, disorientation, and distress when the head is moved; these symptoms usually disappear in a few days or weeks. Damage to the vestibular apparatus on both sides causes none of these symptoms. (The vestibular apparatus has been strongly implicated in motion sickness.) Electrical stimulation of the vestibular apparatus on one side of the head produces nausea and vomiting, but deaf individuals whose vestibular apparatus has been impaired bilaterally do not exhibit motion sickness.

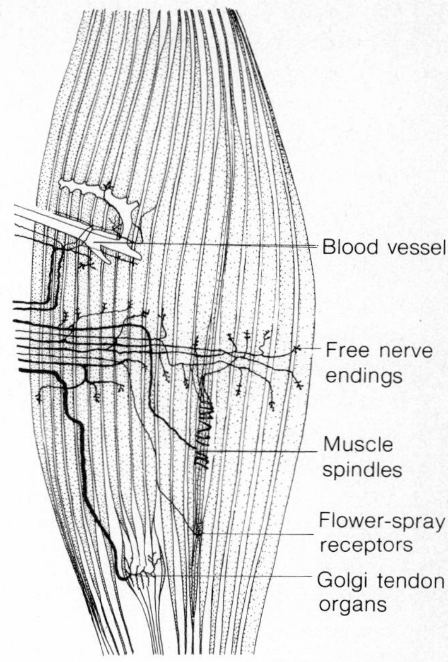

Fig. 7•32 Nerve endings in muscle, three of which subserve kinesthesis: muscle spindles, flower-spray receptors, and Golgi tendon organs. (From Creed et al., 1972)

Kinesthesis Kinesthetic receptors are located in the joints between the bones, and in the muscles and tendons. They signal the changing positions of all our body parts and underlie our ability to make coordinated and skilled bodily movements.

Several receptors for sensing movement have been identified (Figure 7•32). *Muscle spindles* are intertwined among the muscle fibers; these nerve endings fire when the muscle is stretched, but not when it contracts. *Flower-spray* receptors on muscle spindles are sensitive to passive muscle stretch and apparently provide feedback on body posture. *Golgi tendon organs* are excited by intense stretching of the tendon and cause muscles to relax, thereby sometimes acting as a safety valve. Free nerve endings are distributed widely throughout muscles, tendons, ligaments, and joints, and are apparently responsible for pain sensations in these areas as well as for temperature regulation.

Summary Our senses other than vision and audition include taste, smell, the skin senses, equilibrium, and kinesthesis. Taste is restricted to the four qualities sweet, sour, salty, and bitter, but our sense of smell makes food seem flavorful. The chemical composition of food substances is believed to account for the four taste qualities, but these relationships have not yet been identified.

The receptors for olfaction are located in the olfactory cleft high in the nasal cavity. These receptors are extremely sensitive to minute quantities of airborne substances. Theories proposed to explain the perception of particular odors attempt to relate stimulus intensity to the evaporation rates, solubility, refractive indices and molecular configurations of the odorant substances. The last theory forms the basis of much current research on odorants.

There are four skin senses: touch, pain, heat, and cold. Attempts to relate a single fiber type to each skin sensation have not been successful.

Extrasensory Perception

ESP includes several phenomena. *Mental telepathy* is the ability to transfer thoughts from one person to another or to influence what someone else is thinking. *Clairvoyance* is the perception of physical events by other than sensory means, such as knowing who is telephoning before you pick up the receiver, or knowing what number is on a card in a sealed envelope before the envelope is opened. *Precognition* is the correct perception of a future event. *Psychokinesis* involves the ability to influence a physical event mentally, such as willing a particular number to turn up on a die. These abilities involve extrasensory perception only if they occur without normal sensory information or if they could not reasonably have been predicted. (Knowing that a ringing telephone signals a call from your husband is not clairvoyant if he always calls at that same time every day.)

Attempts have been made to study ESP using psychophysical procedures similar to those used in experiments on the traditional sensory systems, and controlled tests have been used to demonstrate that certain persons can reliably perform acts of mental telepathy or clairvoyance. In the latter type of test, the main technique is to have the subject predict the next card in a deck of cards. This is a test of mental telepathy if another person present has seen the card, and a test of clairvoyance if no one has seen the card. If a twenty-five-card deck contains five identical sets of five different symbols, then correct predictions by chance would be 20 percent. A few subjects have scored as high as 30 percent correct even after many trials and repeated testing. Obtaining such accuracy repeatedly cannot be attributed to chance alone but must have some nonchance cause, which in this case was attributed to ESP.

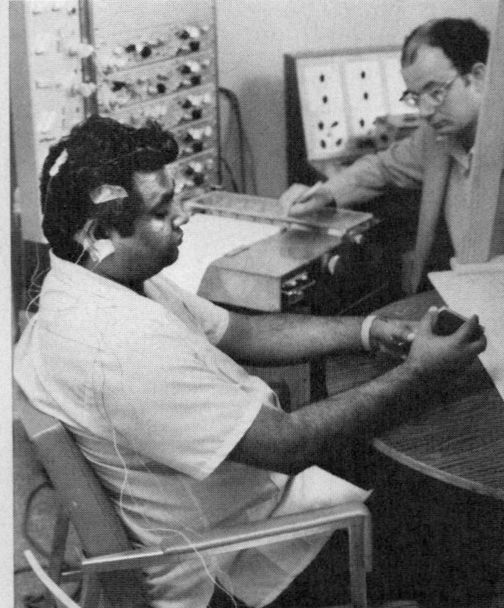

In an ESP experiment at the Institute for Parapsychology, Durham, North Carolina, a researcher studies the brain wave patterns made as a Trinidadian clairvoyant tries to restore the cards to an order known to the researcher. (Henry Groskinsky, Time-Life Picture Agency, © Time Inc.)

Many scientists are not comfortable with either the research on ESP or the questionable practices surrounding demonstrations of ESP. In many instances inappropriate procedures, deception, or faulty statistical assumptions or techniques have been used; and many psychics, mediums, and mentalists have been exposed as fakes. Circumstances such as these make it difficult to believe the results of honest endeavors in ESP research.

Some scientists object that no evidence has been presented on how ESP functions. What are its receptor processes? How does transfer occur? What circumstances affect performance? Why are there such wide variations in ability among persons? Without theoretical orderliness and a scientific approach to these questions, the study of ESP will continue to lack scientific respectability, despite the several respectable and prestigious scientists who study it.

The vestibular apparatus of the inner ear monitors movement of the body (the semicircular canals) and orientation of the head (the vestibular sacs). Unilateral damage to the vestibular apparatus results in temporary nausea and distress, but bilateral damage causes no major postural problems.

Kinesthetic receptors are located in the muscles, tendons, and joints. They mediate knowledge of the position of our limbs and provide the feedback necessary for skilled and coordinated movement. Receptors responsible for providing this information are the muscle spindles, flower-spray receptors, and Golgi tendon organs. The free nerve endings found among the muscles and joints apparently mediate pain at these locations.

Interrelationships among the Senses

7·5 Human beings are continually surrounded by a flow of energy that impinges on specialized receptors that send neural signals to the brain. The brain has little trouble in identifying the sense modality or receptor site from which a particular signal came because the neural pathways for each modality terminate in different cortical areas.

But do our senses interact with each other? Do they enhance each other, so that we hear a sound better if lights are flashing at the same time? Does information from one sense transfer to the other senses, so that we will recognize an object visually if we have previously held it but not seen it? Can we retrain a sensory system to take over the function of a sense that is deficient—for example, can a blind person learn to read by using just the fingers.

The answer to all of these questions is yes. These interactions are possible because of interconnections among the different sensory receptor areas in the brain. Thus, although the neural pathways from the eyes terminate in the visual cortex and those from the ears in the auditory cortex, both sensory systems stimulate lower brain centers, which in turn affect other parts of the cortex. Furthermore, there are interconnecting nerve pathways between the auditory and the visual cortexes, for example, and between the vestibular apparatus and the part of the brain that regulates postural reflexes. Therefore, while we have examined each sensory modality separately, we should remember that the object of study in psychology is the behavior of the integrated person, and the purpose of analyzing the parts is to clarify the whole.

Suggested Readings

Christman, R. J. 1971. *Sensory experience.* Scranton: Intext.

Geldard, F. A. 1972. *The human senses.* 2d ed. New York: Wiley.

Readable accounts of all the senses.

Haber, Ralph N., and Hershenson, Maurice. 1973. *The psychology of visual perception.* New York: Holt, Rinehart & Winston.

Chapters 1 through 6 of this textbook on visual perception cover the same topics as are in this chapter, but at a more advanced level.

Held, Richard, and Richards, Whitman. 1972 *Perception: Mechanisms and models (Readings from Scientific American).* San Francisco: W. H. Freeman.

A fine collection of papers on basic mechanisms.

Kling, John, and Riggs, Lorin, eds. 1971. *Experimental psychology.* 3d ed. New York: Holt, Rinehart & Winston.

A handbook with a number of very specialized chapters on all of the senses, each written by an expert in his field.

Moncrieff, R. W. 1967. *The chemical senses.* 3d ed. London: Leonard Hill.

Pfaffman, Carl, ed. 1969. *Olfaction and taste.* New York: Rockefeller University Press.

The most technical accounts of olfaction and taste.

Visual Perception: The Active Perceiver

8 In the previous chapter, our focus was on (1) the reception of energy for each sensory modality, (2) the receptors responsible for the transduction of that energy into neural signals, and (3) some of the factors that affect the psychophysical relationships between physical stimuli and psychological perceptions. In this chapter, the perceiver will be treated as an active agent in the perceptual process. We shall see that perception is determined by more than the energy patterns splashed on the retinal surface or battering the eardrum, and we shall consider what our senses do for us—how we use information about the physical dimensions of energy to perceive the world.

Visual stimulation comes from features such as edges, lines, widths, orientations, angles, curves, and movements; but our perceptions are those of chairs, faces, rooms, and landscapes. In order to translate visual features into a perception, we use certain techniques, or *perceptual strategies.* These strategies include (1) separating some features in a scene from others, depending on their distance from us and their position in visual space, (2) identifying features specific to each particular object or form, and (3) acquiring information by moving our eyes to different fixation points. These strategies are interdependent and reinforce each other, and are used simultaneously rather than serially. They represent the most elaborate interaction that occurs in psychology: processing information from the senses integrated with knowledge and prior experience.

As we saw in the previous chapter, optical information is transmitted from the retina to the brain by a sequence of abstract codes which reconstruct in the visual cortex the properties of the objective scene. In this chapter we shall examine four properties of these constructions.

1. The depth and spatial arrangements of the objective visual scene are preserved by the information about the scene's three-dimensionality.

2. The description of the scene itself is preserved, and not simply the ever-changing stimulation on our retinas.
3. The panoramic quality of scenes is preserved. Each *fixation* (place our eyes look) represents only part of the scene clearly; the rest is either off to one side, or too close or too far away to be in focus. Despite these momentary fragmentations, the perception that results from the integration of many glances is more panoramic, complete, clear, and detailed than any single fixation can provide.
4. Our expectations of what a scene contains influence our construction.

Perceptual Strategies to Segregate Visual Features into a Three-Dimensional Scene

8•1 The information contained in the projections on our retinas enables us to make three-dimensional constructions of our visual world. From this information, we can perceive some objects as being closer than others, or more solid, rectangular, or upright, and so forth. Some information is inherent in the visual scene; additional information is acquired as we move about.

The Stationary Perceiver and the Discrimination of Space Retinal images are influenced by two important factors: (1) the light rays that illuminate the objects in front of our eyes and that are reflected from them onto our retinas, and (2) the shapes, sizes, and textures of the surfaces of these objects and of the features they contain.

Information from Projective Size Figure 8•1 shows light reflected from objects into a perceiver's eyes. Only the rays reflected from the objects' extremes are shown, but in fact rays are reflected from every point on an object, through the lens and onto the retinal surface. The two sticks shown on the field are identical in size but located at different distances from the perceiver. Although the objective size of the far stick has not changed, its projective size on the retina is smaller than that of the near stick. Projective size is a function of the visual angle (the angle

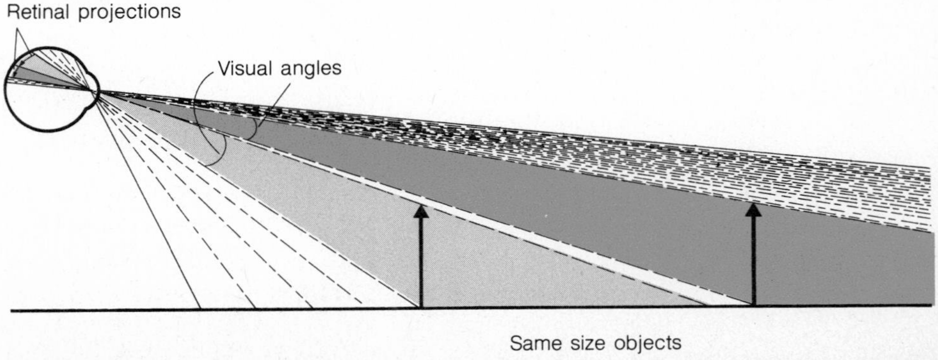

Fig. 8•1 As their distance from the perceiver increases, objects of equal size project smaller images onto the retina and equidistant stripes are projected as closer together. (Adapted from Gibson, 1950)

formed at the lens of the eye by the rays of light reflected from the extremes of an object), which decreases as objective distance increases; therefore, the farther away an object is, the smaller its projective size.

The objective distance between each stripe on the field in Figure 8•1 is the same, but the projective distances between stripes farther away from the perceiver are smaller than the projective distances between stripes closer to the perceiver. Thus, while the objective field is a uniform pattern of equidistant stripes, the retinal projection represents the near stripes as farther apart and the far stripes as progressively closer together. This relationship makes objectively parallel lines such as railroad tracks appear progressively closer together (and therefore not parallel) as their distance from the perceiver increases, until the tracks at the horizon appear to meet.

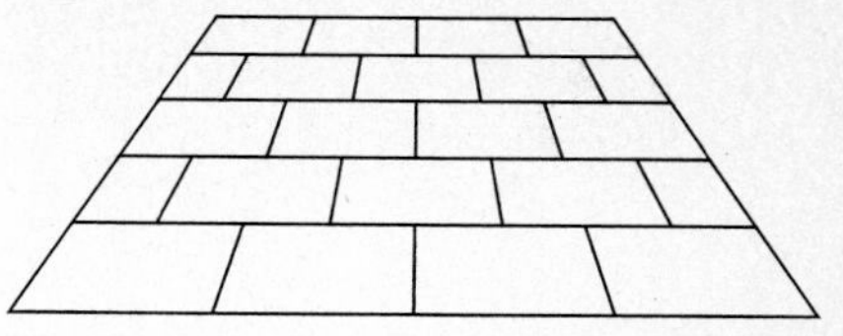

Fig. 8•2 The projective images of tiles on a floor become progressively smaller and more dense as the objective distance between the perceiver and the tiles increases. A horizontal surface such as a tile floor has a constant gradient (rate at which projective density changes).

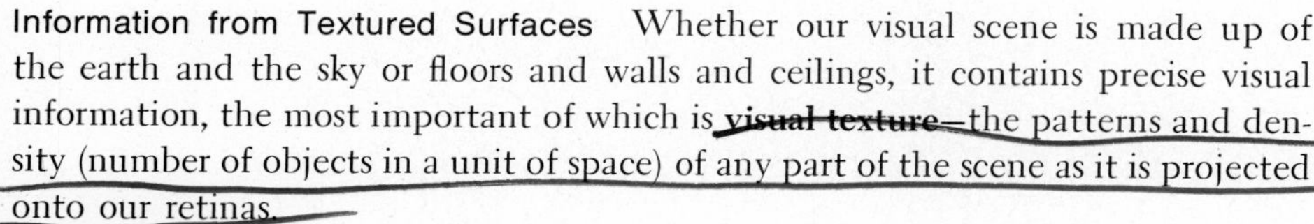

Information from Textured Surfaces Whether our visual scene is made up of the earth and the sky or floors and walls and ceilings, it contains precise visual information, the most important of which is **visual texture**—the patterns and density (number of objects in a unit of space) of any part of the scene as it is projected onto our retinas.

Objective texture is relatively uniform for each surface in a scene. For example, the density of the grass or of the yard markers on a football field is about the same over the entire field, and the size of the tiles in a floor does not vary. However, these elements of texture are not projected uniformly to the eye. Rather, the retinal projection has a **texture gradient**—a rate of change in projective texture that is a function of the distance of each objective surface point from the eye (Figure 8•2).

No matter where we stand or in which direction we look, texture densities increase as objective distances increase. These densities remain constant only when our eyes are equidistant from all parts of the objective surface. For example, if we sit in the center of a planetarium and look upward, all parts of the inside surface of the surrounding sphere will be equidistant from our eyes. Most perceivers have difficulty discriminating the depth or distance of such a spherical surface, and so the "sky" in a planetarium seems to be infinitely far away.

Texture density would also appear to remain constant if a surface were specially constructed so that the physical size of each objective point increased in exact proportion to the distance of those points from the eyes. Density–distance relationships such as these, however, occur only in the psychologist's laboratory or in a special place such as a planetarium.

Scaling Visual Space For nearly all normal viewing, the objects in the visual scene are either on the surface where we are standing or on an adjacent surface. The texture gradients of these surfaces provide a scale of the visual space around us. For example, if the texture of the surface stretching away from our feet suddenly changes to a finer texture whose density increases at the same rate as the nearer texture gradient, the surface must have dropped at the point of discontinuity but remained parallel to the near surface (Figure 8•3a). If the texture density increases from the discontinuity at a faster rate than the near texture gradient, the surface must have sloped uphill relative to the near flat surface (Figure 8•3b).

The ground does not have to be continuously in view for texture gradients to provide a scale of distance. On a golf course, for example, the ground might be level, then slope out of sight into a gully and become visible again on the other side. If the grass surface on the other side of the gully is parallel to the near surface, its texture will have the same rate of change (gradient) as the near ground, but it will be much finer. The difference in the absolute amount of texture provides a scale of information about the width of the gully.

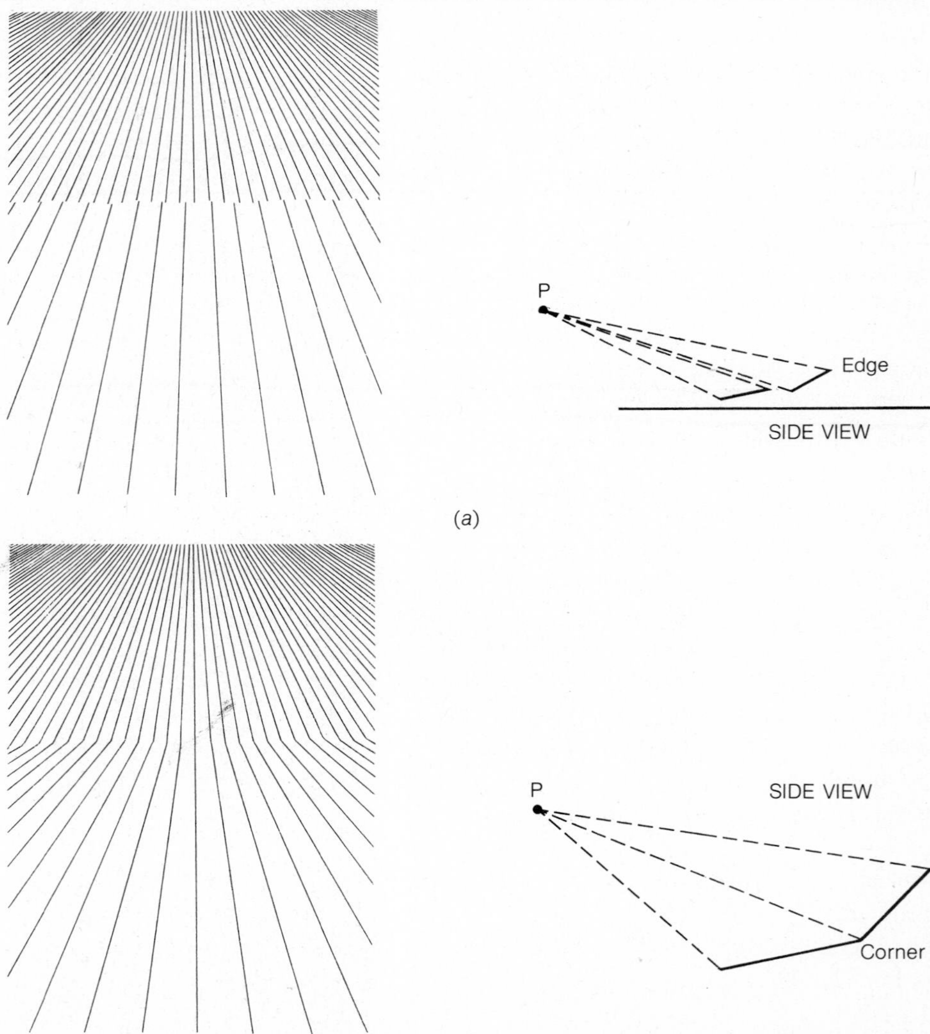

Fig. 8•3 (*a*) View of the visual texture gradients provided by two parallel surfaces, with the far surface below the near one. This discontinuity produces the perception of an edge. (*b*) View of the visual texture gradients provided by a surface changing its direction. This discontinuity produces the perception of a corner. (From Haber and Hershenson, 1973)

The visual scale of space that is defined by texture gradients is always present. It is available in a single glance or in repeated viewings, and permits us to interrelate parts of the scene not continuously in view. As we turn our heads around, the scale of the scene in front of us is the same as the one that was behind us but is now visible. Thus, we can perceive whether an object behind us is as far away as one in front of us even though we cannot see both of them at the same time.

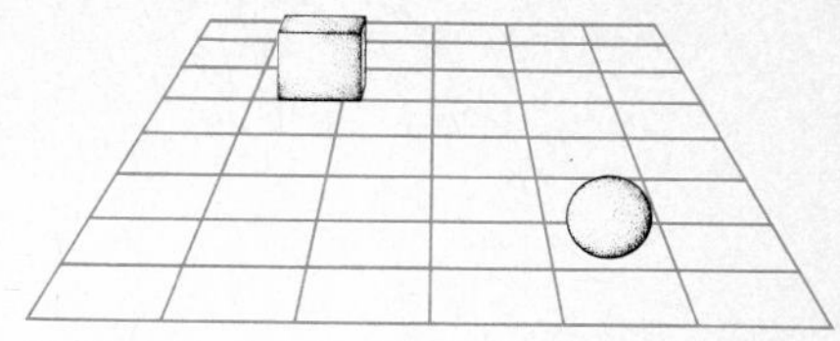

Fig. 8•4 Projective texture densities enable us to locate objects in visual space and to determine their relative sizes.

Locating Objects in Visual Space How can we perceive an object's distance from us or from another object? Because objects rest on the ground or are seen against the ground in some way, texture densities provide a scale of distance. Where a near object intersects the ground, the texture of the ground is coarser than it is around a far object (Figure 8•4). Furthermore, the objects themselves have texture, and these textures appear increasingly fine the farther the objects are from the viewer. We know that the box in Figure 8•4 is farther from us than the ball, not only because the ground has a finer texture where the box intersects it than where the ball intersects it, but also because the box's texture is finer than the ball's. We also know that the box is larger than the ball because it covers up many more units of texture.

How can we tell whether an object is vertical, at a slant, or lying flat? This problem is depicted in Figure 8•5a where the checkerboards are one texture, the surface another texture. We know that the checkerboards are the same distance away because they all intersect the ground at the same level on the texture gradient. However, we perceive them as being at different angles, from the upright one on the left to the flat-lying one on the right. Four related sources of information form this unambiguous perception.

1. The texture gradients among the checkerboards vary. The texture of checkerboard *A* has no gradient; therefore, all parts of this checkerboard must be equidistant from the observer, and the checkerboard must be upright, or vertical, with respect to the line of sight. Each successive checkerboard to the right has a greater texture gradient, with the greatest density at the top (the part farthest from the observer). The checkerboards must therefore lie progressively more flat, tipping away from the observer.
2. The texture gradients of the checkerboards vary with respect to the ground. Only the gradient of checkerboard *E* equals (has the same rate as) the gradient of the ground. Therefore, this checkerboard must lie either on the ground or parallel to it.
3. The angle formed between the face of the checkerboards and the ground increases as the difference between the texture gradients of the checkerboards and the ground decreases (Figure 8•5b). Checkerboard *A* forms a 90° angle with the ground and has no gradient. Checkerboard *E* lies flat on the ground and therefore forms a 180° angle with it; its gradient is equal to the ground.
4. The projective shapes of the checkerboards change with slant. If the checkerboards are all objectively square, then as they slant away from the perceiver,

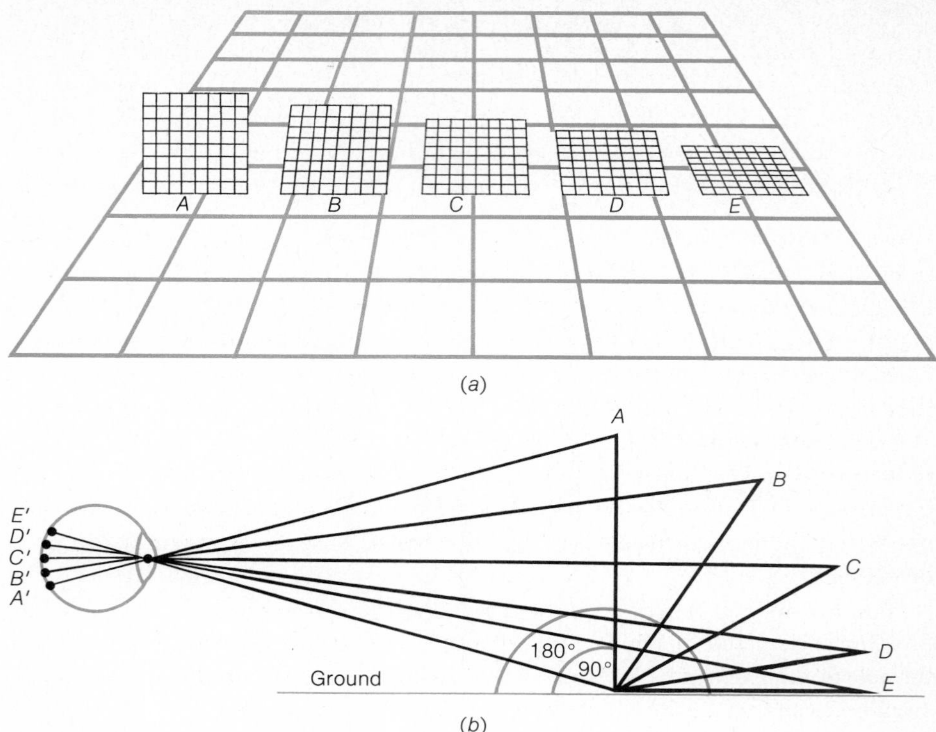

Fig. 8•5 (*a*) Textured shapes on a textured ground. (*b*) As the checkerboards slant away from the perceiver, the angles they form with the ground between them and the perceiver increase. (From Haber and Hershenson, 1973)

their projective shapes become increasingly trapezoidal. The projective shapes of the units within each checkerboard provide additional information about slant.

If texture is partially defined by internal detail such as the tiles in a floor or the bricks in a wall, the projective shape of each textural unit will provide information about the slant of the surface. The gradient and the projective shape of an object's units (for example, bricks) will agree exactly with the gradient in the surface of the object itself (wall).

When we face a brick wall, for example, its parts appear progressively farther away as they extend away from our eyes because the bricks' projective shapes become increasingly trapezoidal in all directions from our line of vision (Figure 8•6). The gradient in the wall is constant, telling us that the wall is flat rather than dished or curved.

Occlusion Another source of information in retinal projections of visual scenes is the manner in which near objects *occlude*, or visually block, objects behind them. For example, we interpret one side of the top and bottom displays in Figure 8•7 as being closer than the other side. The edge that occlusion creates between near and far objects and between objects and the ground almost always defines a texture discontinuity that helps to articulate the relative locations of objects.

There are usually other cues to help us find these edges (such as differences in color between two objects), but the changes that occlusion creates in visual textures effectively define edges. Although occlusion is not a texture, the information it provides always agrees with the texture-gradient information we obtain by scaling space.

Lighting Effects Lighting, shadowing, haziness, and brightness provide additional sources of information. For example, the objects in Figure 8•8 are defined by their shadows, which result from the direction of light. If the picture is inverted, the lighting direction is reversed, so that all the objects in the picture are reversed in depth—that is, what stood out before is now a hole.

If all objects are illuminated with a light of the same intensity, the near objects appear brighter and more distinct than the far ones. When far objects are illuminated with a light of lower intensity than the light illuminating near objects, the far objects appear to be more distant than they do when they are illuminated with the same intensity light as near objects. Mountains therefore appear to be closer on clear days than on hazy days.

We do not know whether these sources of information are used by themselves or whether they provide information by affecting texture. It is possible that haze or decreased brightness makes texture appear finer, and consequently surfaces appear to be farther away.

The Moving Perceiver and the Organization of Space We have seen that the retinal projection contains many sources of information, all perfectly correlated

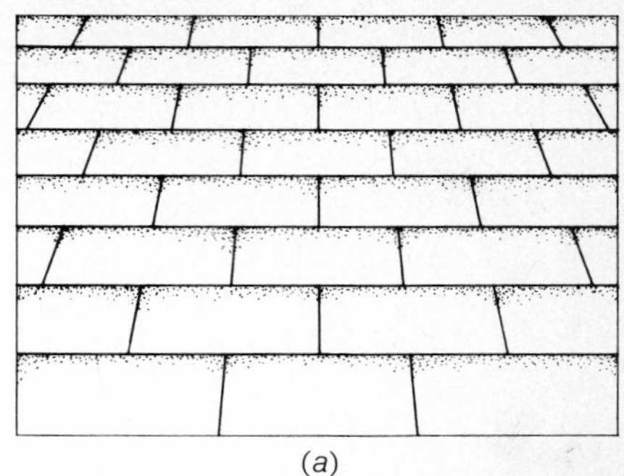

(*a*)

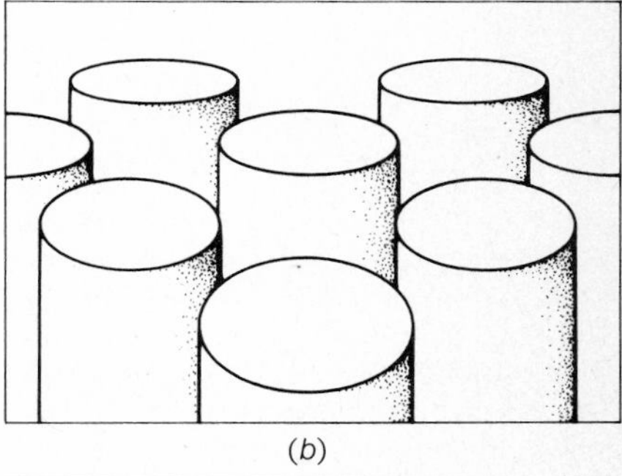

(*b*)

Fig. 8•6 (*a*) Bricks project trapezoidal images on our retinas. As we move farther away from the bricks, the images they project become smaller and more trapezoidal. (*b*) Objectively circular objects project elliptical images.

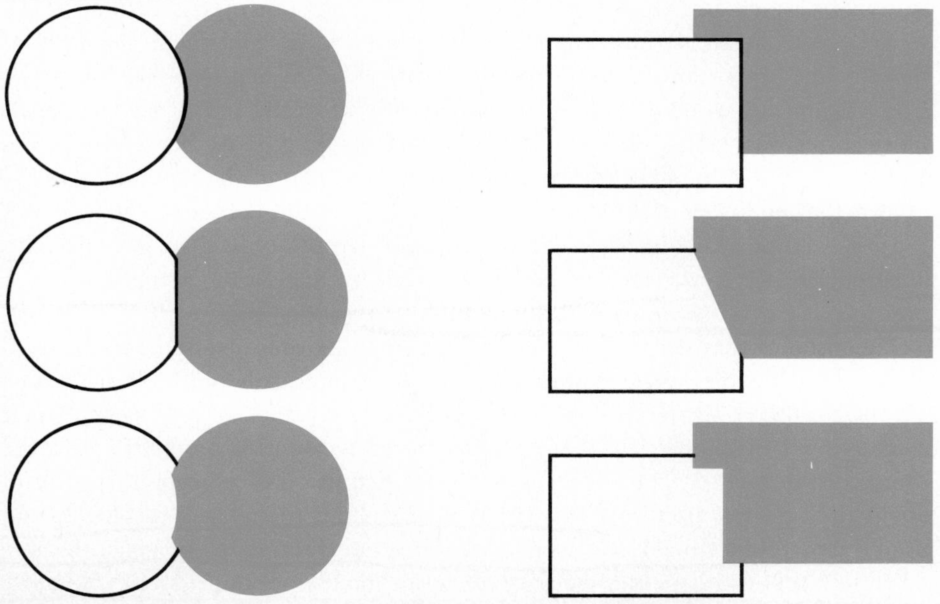

Fig. 8•7 An object with a continuous outline is perceived to be in front of an object whose outline is discontinuous. (From Haber and Hershenson, 1973)

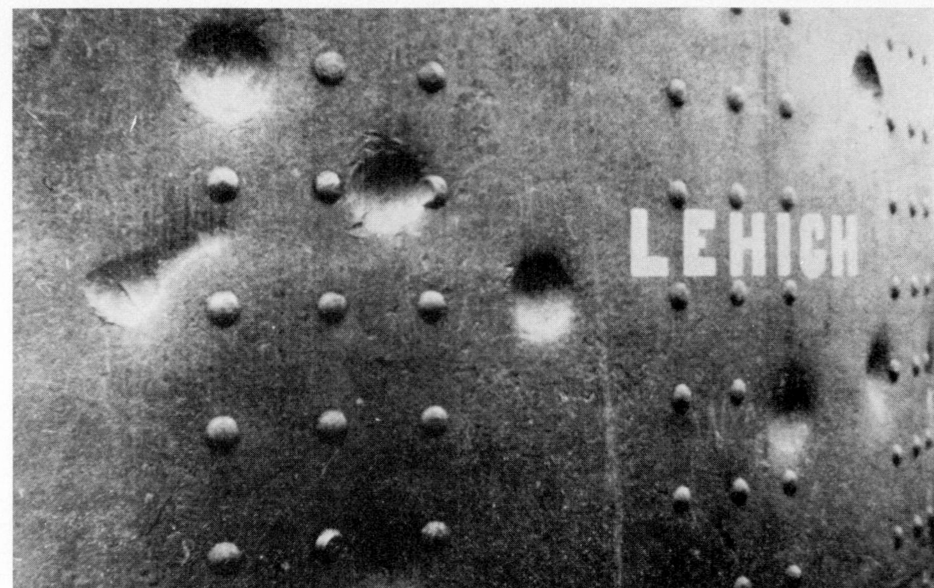

Fig. 8·8 The effect of the direction of light on the appearance of objects. When the picture is turned upside down, the shapes are inverted. (C. H. Stoelting Co.)

with each other, but so far we have concentrated only on what we can see without moving our eyes or heads. These two kinds of movements greatly simplify our task of perceiving.

Motion Parallax When we move only our eyes and keep our heads and bodies stationary, we change the orientation of our eyes but not their location. When we move our heads, we move our eyes to a new location in space: this kind of movement is important in perceiving the visual scene. When we move our heads from side to side while fixating on an object in front of us, we can see far objects move in relation to the object on which we are fixating. If we move our bodies and our heads to the right, for example, we can see around the right side of near objects that no longer occlude other objects or the ground behind them; however, the left side of near objects occludes previously visible objects or ground. This apparent change in the relative position of objects, due to the actual change of position of the observer, is termed *parallax.*

The distance that near and far objects appear to move is inversely proportional to their distance from us. For example, if we move our heads and bodies laterally, an object 10 feet away from us will uncover twice as much of an object 20 feet away as it will of an object 15 feet away. Thus we have another perfectly correlated source of information about the location and definition of objects in space and about their relative positions. If we are not sure about the relative distances from us of the parts of a visual scene, we can resolve our uncertainty by moving sideways: far objects will travel shorter distances over our moving retinas than near objects.

This process is called **motion parallax** and is illustrated in Figure 8•9. Percept A shows how the man, the house, and the tree appear to a perceiver standing at point 1 and fixating on the house. As the perceiver moves from points 1 to 5, the relative positions of the three objects shift, and the objects cover up and uncover each other. The objects nearer to the perceiver than the one he is fixating on will move in a direction relative to the fixated object that is opposite to the perceiver's direction of motion. All objects farther away than the fixated object will move in the same direction as the perceiver. Thus, the man appears to move to the right and the tree to the left, as the perceiver moves to the left while fixating on the house. If the perceiver had been looking at the tree, then both the house and the man would have appeared to shift opposite to the perceiver's direction of motion.

The specification of the relative positions of objects by motion parallax provides an important source of information about the scaling of space and corresponds to information derived from texture gradients. Thus, the two sources of information perfectly complement each other. (Motion parallax does not help perceptions of flat scenes such as paintings, movies, or photographs because all objects in these visual fields are the same distance from the eye, and movement cannot alter their relative positions.)

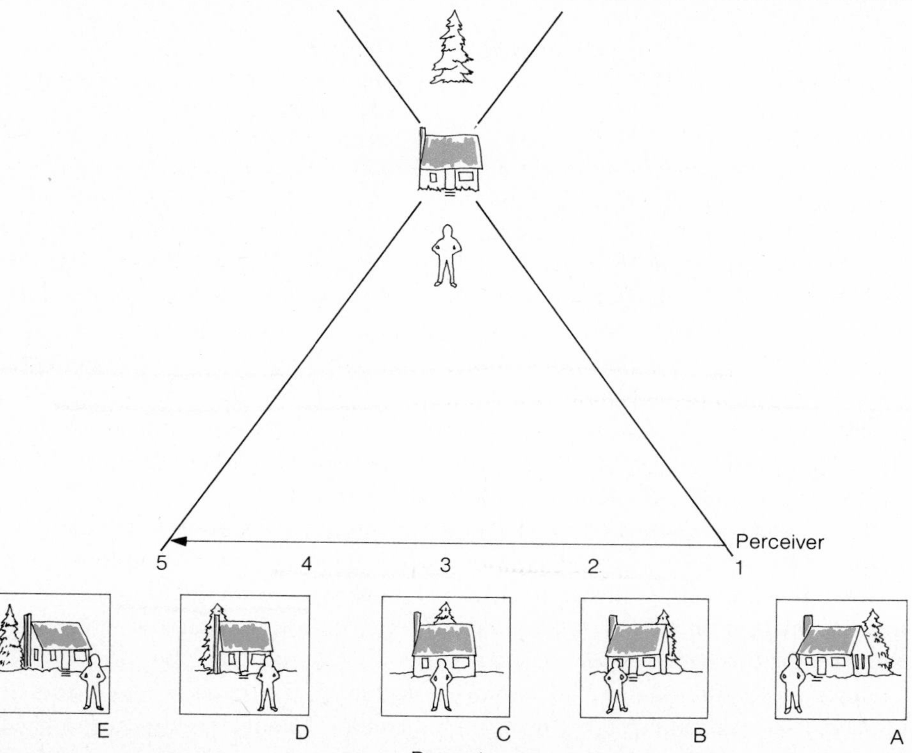

Fig. 8•9 The transformations on the retina when moving through a sequence of positions and fixating on a point of intermediate distance. (From Haber and Hershenson, 1973)

Afferent and Efferent Interactions in Motion Perception

Over one hundred years ago, H. von Helmholtz performed a simple experiment that was later repeated in greater detail by von Holst (1954), with the same results.

The subject was first given a drug that temporarily enervated the eye muscles so that the eyes could not be moved voluntarily. The experimenter then moved the subject's eyes until the subject reported looking at a target directly ahead. The experimenter then asked the subject to look at another target a few degrees to the right. Of course, although the subject's brain sent instructions (*efferent impulses*) to the eye muscles, nothing happened. However, the subject reported that the visual scene appeared to shift to the right by the same amount as the subject had tried to move the eyes to the right. On the basis of the efferent instructions it had issued, the subject's brain expected there to be an eye movement to the right. The visual cortex interpreted the lack of change in the retinal projection as due to the visual world having moved the same amount and in the same direction as the efferent instructions dictated.

Next, the experimenter told the subject to look at the target straight ahead while the experimenter moved the subject's eyes to the target on the right. The subject reported that the visual world appeared to move to the left by about the same amount as the experimenter had moved the subject's eyes. Apparently movements of the retinal projection, in the absence of efferent instructions from the brain to the eye muscles, are interpreted as movements of the visual scene. When the eyes were turned to the right, the projection was displaced to the left, and so the subject reported that the visual field appeared to move to the left.

In the last condition, the subject was told to move the eyes to the target on the right; at the same time, the experimenter moved the subject's eyes to that target. This time the subject reported that there was no movement of the visual field. Apparently the change in the retinal projection (afferent information) was exactly equal to the instruction to move the eyes (efferent information).

After the drug wore off, the subject was asked to look at the target straight ahead, and then to move the eyes to the target on the right. The subject reported no movement of the visual field, presumably for the same reason that none was seen in the last condition: the instruction to move and the visual results of the movement were equal.

This group of experiments shows that stable perception results from a comparison being made between two sources of information when we move our eyes: the afferent information from the changes on the retinal projection, and the efferent instruction from the brain to the eye muscles. When these two sources agree perfectly, we see the visual world as stable; when they disagree, we attribute the difference between them to movement of the visual world.

Accommodation In viewing any three-dimensional scene, we continually shift the **accommodation** of our eyes—that is, how far into the scene we focus. A near object on which we focus is sharply defined, but objects farther away are fuzzy. If we focus on far objects or on the distant horizon, all parts of the visual scene except very near objects appear sharply defined and clear.

The information about depth that accommodation provides is less precise than scaling space from texture gradients or motion parallax, but it complements the latter strategies. If either of the space scales is unclear, accommodation may provide the information needed to specify exactly the location and relative positions of the parts of the scene.

Shifts in accommodation do not occur instantly. To transfer focus from the horizon to a near object takes nearly 0.5 second. Although we are not normally aware of the gradients of clarity that shift from far to near as this accommodation is made, it seems likely that the gradient itself is a useful source of information about the relative positions of objects.

Are Two Eyes Better Than One? Everything we have said so far applies to perception requiring only one eye—that is, all sources of information are available to each eye separately. Actually, two eyes are not necessary either for perceiving the three-dimensionality of space or for articulating objects in a visual scene. You can easily verify this fact by covering one of your eyes with a patch and observing what you see as you walk around. However, human beings are binocular—that is, we have two eyes. Because our eyes point forward from the front part of our heads, our visual fields overlap almost completely. The slight discrepancy between the views received by each eye is accounted for by the distance between the two eyes (about 6.5 centimeters in an average adult). We shall first consider the optics, and then the perceptual consequences, of having two eyes.

The Optics of Having Two Eyes As Figure 7•7 in the previous chapter showed all photoreceptors on the nasal side of the right eye and the temporal side of the left eye have neural connections to the left hemisphere of the visual cortex. Thus, points 7 through 11 in Figure 8•10 (and all points to the right of center in a visual scene) are represented visually only in the left half of the brain. Similarly, points 1 through 5 (and all points to the left of center in a visual scene) are represented visually only in the right half of the brain. This division occurs at the center of each fovea (fixation point 6 in Figure 8•10).

These connections are quite precise and specifiable. For example, the points numbered 1 on the two retinas shown in Figure 8•10 are called *corresponding points* because each of them is in the same spatial relationship to their respective foveas (the same distance to the right of each fovea). The ganglion cells (whose axons are the optic nerve fibers) that carry signals from the photoreceptors for these corresponding points terminate in the same hemisphere by converging on the same cortical cell. This system of connections is the same for every location on the retina: for each ganglion cell leaving one eye, there is a corresponding ganglion cell leaving the other eye; both receive signals from the corresponding points on the two retinas and converge on the same cortical cell in the visual cortex of the appropriate brain hemisphere.

Perceptual Consequences of Having Two Eyes Look again at Figure 8•10. Point 7, or any other point on the visual surface, reflects light to its corresponding points on each retina. Because these points are connected to the same cortical cell, the information coming from the left retina agrees perfectly with the information coming from the right retina. This process occurs whenever the scene has no depth. In other words, whenever the correspondence between the two retinas is perfect, the visual scene must be flat.

If the scene is not flat (one object is closer to the perceiver than another, as in Figures 8•9 and 8•11) and if you fixate on the middle object so that it projects

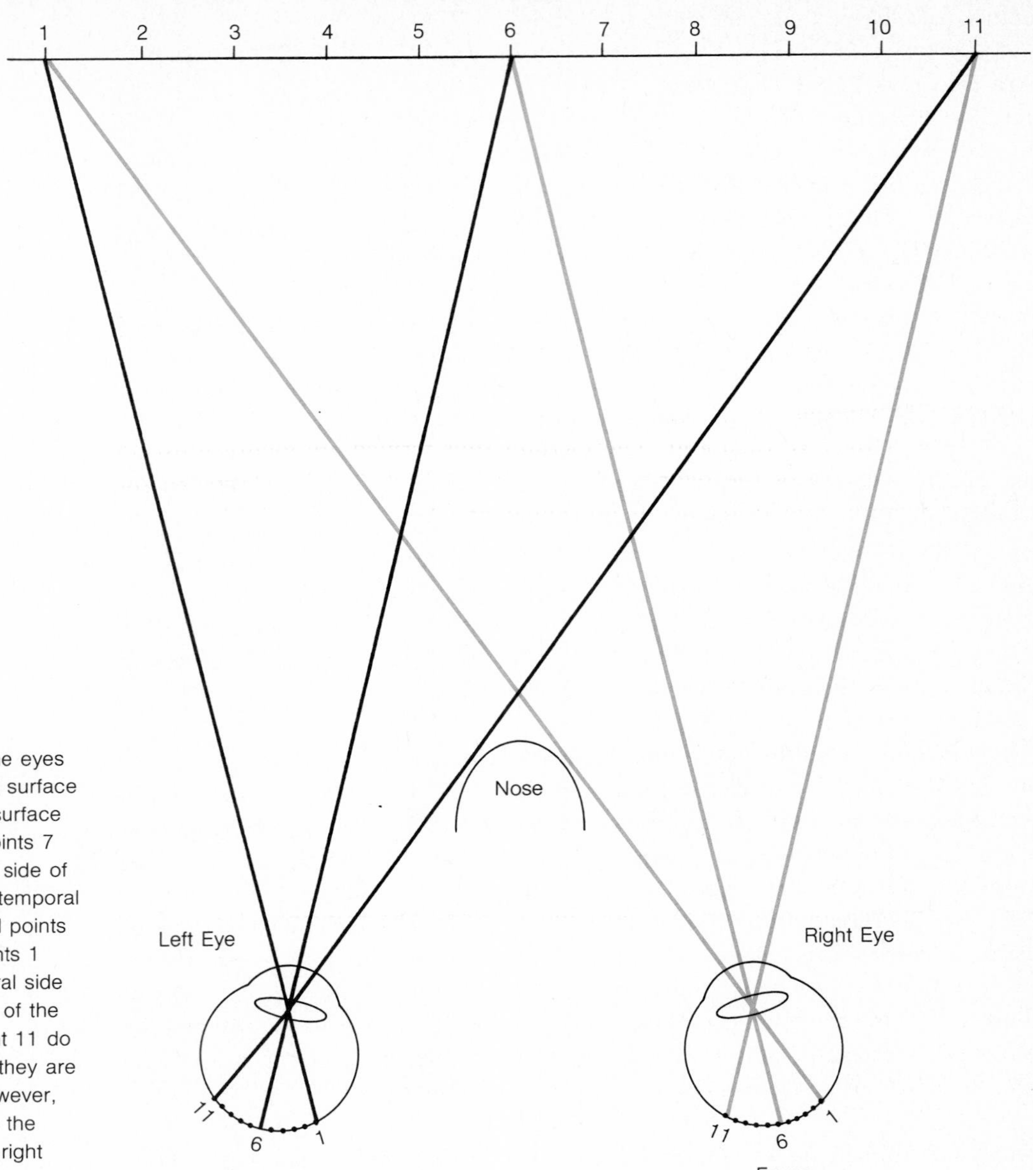

Fig. 8·10 Binocular perception. The eyes are looking at point 6 on the visual surface in front of them. All points on the surface to the right of the fixation point (points 7 through 11) project onto the nasal side of the retina of the right eye and the temporal side of the retina of the left eye; all points to the left of the fixation point (points 1 through 5) project onto the temporal side of the right eye and the nasal side of the left eye. (Points to the right of point 11 do not reflect to the left eye because they are blocked by the nose; they can, however, be seen by the right eye. Points to the left of point 1 do not reflect to the right eye but can be seen by the left eye.)

to corresponding points on both foveas, then the far object projects to the nasal side of both retinas rather than to corresponding points; the near object projects to the temporal side of both retinas. Whenever objects are at different distances from the head, they stimulate *noncorresponding points*; the difference in the distance between the objects determines the degree of noncorrespondence. Noncorresponding stimulation therefore provides a direct source of information about *depth* in a visual scene that cannot be obtained from one eye alone.

Around 140 years ago Sir Charles Wheatstone (1838) invented the stereoscope—a device for simultaneously viewing two pictures of the same object but each drawn from a slightly different point of view. That is, in a stereoscope the scene viewed by the left eye has been drawn (or photographed) from a perspective slightly to the left of the scene viewed by the right eye (Figure 8•12). In this way, the stereoscope creates the noncorrespondence or disparity that is necessary for perceiving depth.

Some recent experiments have shown how powerful **stereoscopic depth** is, and more important, that it results solely from disparity between noncorresponding points. For example, Bela Julesz (1964) devised a way of making pairs of pictures to be viewed stereoscopically in which noncorrespondence provides the only source of information about depth. The Julesz pair shown in Figure 8•13 was created by randomly inserting either a black or a white spot into each of the 1,000,000 locations in a 1000 × 1000 grid. The pictures thus formed are identical except that the center area of the right-hand picture is shifted slightly relative to the left-hand picture. This difference is not apparent when you view both pictures with both or one of your eyes, but if you look at the right-hand picture with your right eye and the left-hand one with your left eye, the center portions will not reflect to corresponding locations in your two eyes. The center will then appear to be at a different distance relative to the rest of the surface—either as a hole in the page or as a platform in front of the page.

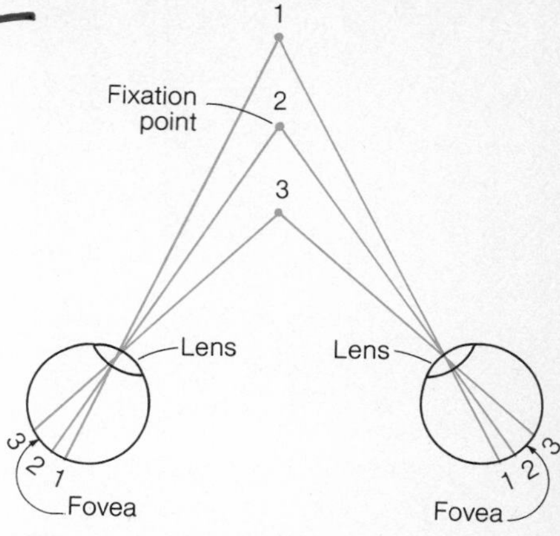

Fig. 8•11 Looking at three objects in a row and fixating on the middle one. (From Brown and Herrnstein, 1975)

The Stability of Space Perception: Perceptual Constancy To be truly useful, our visual perception of the environment must remain unchanged by our orientation, our distance from particular objects, our motion while viewing a scene, or the amount of illumination present. In fact, none of these variables affects the way we organize visual space—a phenomenon called *perceptual constancy.* Its aspects include constancy of size, shape, color, and motion. The principles for each of these are similar.

Size Constancy When we view an object, information about its relative size is available from the relationship of its texture to the texture of the ground at the point where the object rests, the shape of its outline in relation to the amount of ground the object occludes, and so forth. If the object is moved farther away, the relationship of its texture to the texture of the ground at the farther point is the same as before because both textures are correspondingly finer. Further, the amount of ground the object covers up relative to the object's size is the same as before. In fact, every source of information that defines the scale of space and the articulation of objects in space remains constant, thereby establishing that the size of a particular object does not change when its distance from the perceiver changes. A five-foot-tall woman appears to be five feet tall, whether we are talking with her at arm's length, or viewing her from across the room or from the end of the block. Although size constancy can be destroyed in the laboratory by system-

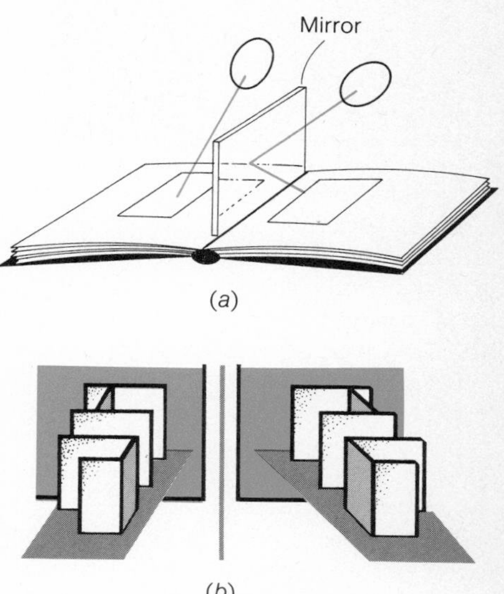

Fig. 8•12 A simplified stereoscope (*a*) can be created by placing a small mirror on the gray center line in the double image (*b*). Adjust the mirror until the reflection appears to be on the same plane as the picture on the page. If you focus on the picture in the mirror with one eye and on the other picture with the other eye, a stereo effect will develop. (Adapted from Hochberg, 1964, and Haber and Fried, 1975)

atically removing the normal sources of information, it holds in the natural environment.

Fig. 8•13 Basic random stereo pair. (From Julesz, 1964)

Shape Constancy The projective outline of a door or window is not rectangular unless the door or window is viewed head-on. Viewed from different perspectives, however, these objects are still perceived as rectangular because of shape constancy. We already know that the texture gradient of a surface provides direct information about the rate at which the surface slopes away from us. Any object that is at the same slant as the ground on which it rests has the same texture gradient as the ground, and its projective outline will change similarly to the projective outlines of the units of texture in the ground.

Imagine looking at a brick wall in which there is a door (Figure 8•14a). If you are directly in front of the door, its projective outline will be rectangular. The texture of the door will not have a gradient because each part of the door is the same distance from your eyes. The texture of the wall adjacent to the door will have no gradient, but the parts of the wall away from the door will have the same gradient in all directions.

If you continue to fixate on the same objective point but move to the side of the door (Figure 8•14b), a substantial gradient will be produced in the retinal projection of the visual scene. At the near edge the texture of the door will be coarser and the outline wider; the texture of the bricks in the wall will be coarser the nearer they are to you, and the projective outline of the wall will be larger at the nearer edge. But the important point is that every one of these gradients will be equal—the projective outline of the door changes in shape at the same rate as its texture and the outline and texture of the wall. This visual information therefore lets you preserve the shape and location of the door with respect to the wall.

If the door is partly open (Figure 8•14c), it occludes part of the wall and casts shadows on the ground and on the wall. Thus, it provides added visual information about its slant in relation to the wall and about its true shape.

Motion Constancy As we move about in the visual world, projections slide over our retinas, but we do not perceive the world as moving. We perceive instead that the world is continuously stable and that our heads or bodies have moved. We do not become confused because we know that we have initiated the movement. If we look at a stationary scene and hold our eyes, head, and body motionless, a particular pattern of stimulation is projected to the retina. We shall consider this pattern as a base line and compare other patterns to it.

First, let us consider a change in which the entire pattern shifts to the right; the extreme right-hand edge of the visual scene disappears, and a new part of the visual world comes into view at the left. Only one circumstance can produce this change: an eye movement to the left without a change in either the position of our head or body, or in the visual scene itself. Since only this particular natural circumstance can produce this transformation in the projective pattern on the

Fig. 8·14 Shape constancy. Our perception of the door changes either as we change with respect to it or as the position of the door changes. (Photographs by Stephen J. Potter; drawing adapted from Gibson, 1950)

retina, visual information alone should be adequate to tell us that it was our eyes and not the world that moved.

But what if only part of the visual scene is displaced to the right? Only one circumstance can produce such a change: an object in motion relative to an otherwise stationary visual world. This information is conveyed as a relative displacement of part of the pattern of stimulation on the retina.

Suppose that the visual scene shifts to the right but that its components shift at different rates, so that some components are occluded more than others. Only one circumstance can produce this change: viewing a stationary scene while the head is moving laterally to the left. This circumstance occurs when we look, without our moving our eyes, head, or body, at a stationary scene through the window of a train that is moving laterally to the left, or when we walk or run ahead while looking at a 90° angle to our path of motion. When we fixate on a near object, such as a spot on the train window, trees near the track flash across our stationary retina at a high rate, while distant hills are displaced slowly.

We can complicate the previous condition by moving our eyes, head, or body. The perceptual details become more complex, but the principle remains the same. Each particular type of motion—whether of specific objects, the entire visual scene, our eyes, head, or body, or any combination of these—produces a unique pattern of change in the retinal pattern of stimulation. Specific visual information is always correlated with the change perceived in the visual world. The information available in the transformations that occur within the retinal projection, in addition to displacements across the retina, enable perceivers to distinguish between their own motions and those of the visual scene.

The perceptual constancies are critical for adaptive living. Even though retinal projections change in many respects, those changes preserve a relationship among all the sources of information. This constancy, along with the various scales of space, enables us to determine that the properties of objects in the visual scene do not change. Therefore, the constructions we make from retinal projections remain the same, although our objective distance or our orientation changes as we move. We are therefore able to perceive the objects in a scene independently of the momentary changes in the retinal projection of light coming from those objects.

Summary Objective images projected on the retina contain texture gradients (changes in density) that are functions of the object's distance from the perceiver. We perceive the blades of grass on a field immediately before us; but as the field stretches away from us, the blades become crowded together so that we no longer perceive them individually. Discontinuities in texture densities and differences between the gradients of a continuous ground before us and a discontinuous surface beyond allow us to discriminate hills and valleys. Near objects in a visual field intersect the ground where the texture density is coarser than where far objects intersect it, and objects' surface textures become increasingly fine (more dense) the farther the objects are from our eyes. Texture helps us to perceive size because larger objects cover more units of texture than do smaller objects that intersect the ground at the same place. Manipulating texture gradients creates illusions such as the "sky" in a planetarium or the experience of distance in a psychologist's laboratory.

When several objects lying at different angles to a flat surface (ground) intersect the surface at the same point, constant densities (no gradient) are reflected from objects at right angles to the surface, while gradients equal to the gradient of the ground are reflected by objects lying on or parallel to the ground. Furthermore, the projective shapes of rectangular objects slanting away from us become more trapezoidal (or elliptical, in the case of circular objects) as objective slant increases.

Other depth cues are provided by occlusion (near objects occlude more objects behind them than far objects do) and by lighting effects (near objects are brighter and clearer than far objects when the amount of light falling on the objects is of equal intensity). Furthermore, near objects create larger texture discontinuities between their edges and the adjacent surface than far objects do.

When we move our heads from side to side while looking at a fixation point, near objects move farther to the side than far objects do, and we can see slightly more of the near objects' sides than we can of the far objects' sides. This phenomenon is called *motion parallax* and provides another cue for depth perception.

Accommodation, or shifting the focal point of our eyes, changes the relative clarity of near and far objects, complementing exactly the information we receive from motion parallax and texture characteristics.

Having two eyes set slightly apart provides information about depth that cannot be obtained from one eye alone. When the eyes are focused on a flat scene such as a photograph, corresponding points on the two retinas are stimulated. When the eyes view a three-dimensional scene, the two retinas see a slightly different version of the visual field, resulting in the perception of depth. Binocular vision can be imitated by using prisms to make slightly disparate pairs of flat pictures yield a perception of depth, as in a 3-D viewer.

Perceptual constancies enhance the usefulness of our visual perceptions. For example, information about the relative size of an object is available from the relationship between the object's texture and the texture of its surroundings. Moving the object nearer to us or farther away changes that relationship by a constant proportion, and so the perceived size of the object remains the same. Similar principles hold for shape, color, and motion. Perceivers are not troubled by retinal changes in these dimensions because the visual information projected preserves a relationship among all the sources of visual information and because the various scales of space are still present.

Panoramic Perception: Integration of Successive Glances

8·2 When we move around, retinal projections continually change; new parts of the visual scene sweep into view on one side of the retina while parts on the other side are occluded and disappear. When we make saccadic (rapid, discontinuous) eye movements, retinal projections are successively displaced four or five times every second. However, we perceive neither the flow of the retinal stimulation nor the disjunction of the successive glances; and although the retinal projection is represented in fine detail at the fovea and less sharply outside it, we perceive a continuously clear and distinct panorama of the visual world.

How does the visual system integrate successive glances into a continuous scene that is larger and more uniformly clear than any one glance at any single instant could provide? Apparently, perception involves a cognitive construction of the visual scene in addition to the neural translation of stimulation on the retina. Suppose that a camera takes several pictures of a scene, each from a different vantage point, and that these pictures are pasted together to represent the entire scene. This pasting together process is somewhat analogous to our process of visual integration. Although we do not yet understand how this process works, we do have some idea of several mechanisms that may be involved. We shall consider four of these mechanisms: motion perspective, saccadic suppression, expectancy guidance, and sensorimotor integration.

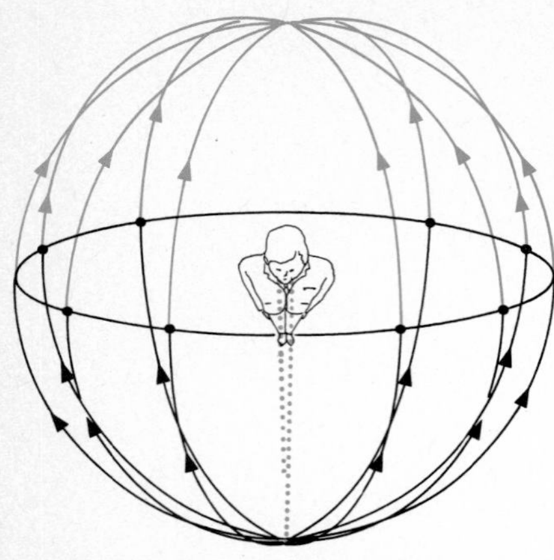

Fig. 8·15 Transformations in the visual field flow in a spherical pattern past the observer's head as the person moves. (From Gibson, 1950)

Motion Perspective We already know that as we move, the changes in the retinal projection provide important sources of information about the layout of visual space. When we shift from one position to another, the momentary stationary array on the retina changes to another pattern. When we move continuously through space, the retinal projections flow across the retina according to systematic rules.

The direction of the flow for an observer walking forward is illustrated in Figure 8·15. The transformations in the visual field of this observer are represented as projections on a spherical surface surrounding the head. The horizon and the sky or stars in the field of view above do not move. However, the ground below and the visual scene to the side flow past in a continuous stream. No matter which way the observer looks, the flow decreases upward through the visual field and vanishes into the horizon. In this sense the flow has a perspective. The rate at which the perceptual element flows when the perceiver's locomotion rate is constant, is inversely proportional to its physical distance from the observer—that is, the flow decreases as the objective distance increases. In this sense, flow produces a gradient.

As the perceiver changes the field of view by moving from one place to another, new kinds of transformations are introduced that specify more complex changes in the environment. The successive transformations in the retinal projection of a person approaching a doorway are illustrated in Figure 8·16. This sequence of pictures shows the relationship between the movement of the observer and the changes in the retinal projection. As the observer moves forward, objects appear to emerge from behind the aperture within the door frame; the objects in the far room become less occluded and their texture densities decrease as their textural units increase in size. Our ability to perceive openings in the visual scene as correlating directly with the properties of the retinal projection permits locomotion without collision.

Motion perspective provides information about the layout of space and integrates the entire visual scene, binding it together and giving it a continuity that a single glance cannot provide.

Saccadic Suppression Saccadic eye movements could be useful in providing motion perspective information, but they are so fast they produce blur, which interferes with maintaining an integrated panoramic view. However, the visual system has a blur-reducing device called *saccadic suppression* that momentarily lowers the sensitivity of the visual system during a saccade. In a demonstration of this phenomenon, P. L. Latour (1962) asked a perceiver to look at a cross projected on a screen. Occasionally the cross would disappear, and then reappear somewhere else. At its reappearance, the perceiver was to move his eyes to the new location as quickly as he could (make a saccadic eye movement). He was also told that from time to time a small spot of light would flash on the screen and that he was to try to detect its presence (a detection threshold task). The detection threshold (the ability to detect the spot 50 percent of the time) was determined for times when the perceiver had been fixating on a particular cross for a while, and when he was

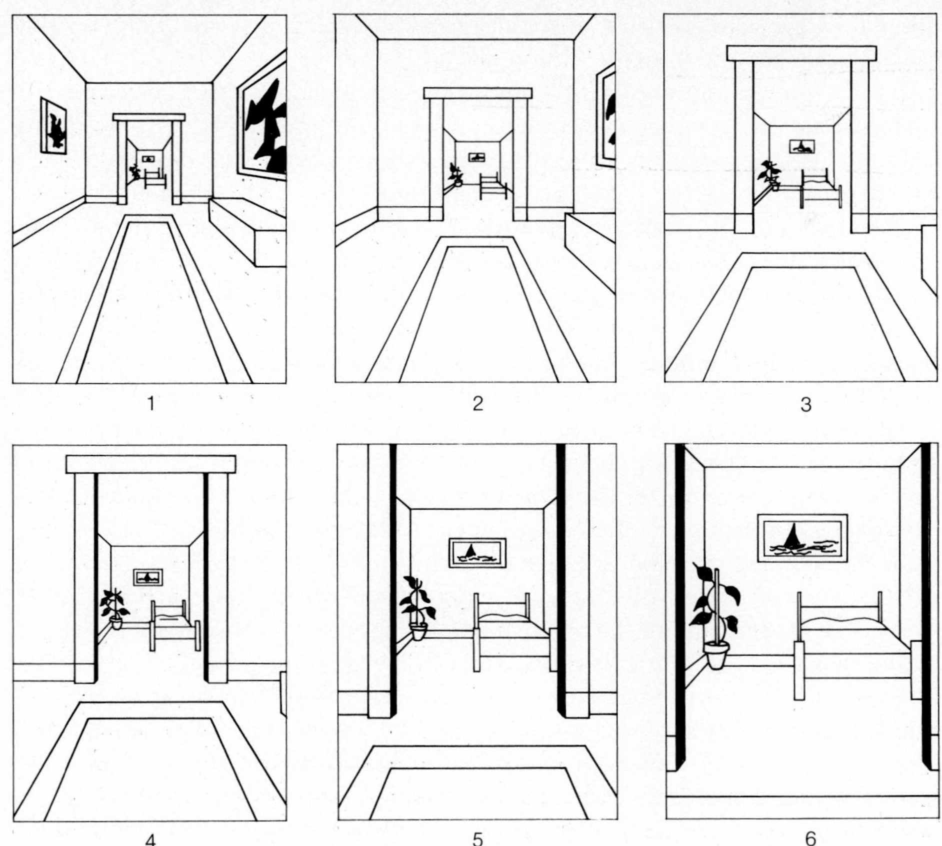

Fig. 8•16 The optical transitions that occur when a perceiver moves through a visual scene. (From Gibson, 1966)

moving his eyes. The results of the experiment showed that detection sensitivity drops significantly when a saccadic eye movement is made (Figure 8•17). Although the drop in sensitivity is not enough to produce momentary blindness, it does reduce the details of perception that would have created blur from a projection sliding across the retina at a high rate of speed. Saccadic suppression is therefore another technique that helps integration across fixations.

Expectancy Guidance Try a simple experiment. Keep your eyes fixed on some point in a complex visual scene and attend to the parts of the scene to the side of the fixation point. Because your eyes are not moving, the side areas of the scene will be fuzzy and unclear. However, you will have some idea of what the side area looks like from the general information in the less blurry parts of the retinal projection as well as from both your memory of what you saw when you looked previously and your knowledge of the visual world. From the blur and from prior information, you can create simple predictions or visual expectations about what you would see if you turned your head or moved your eyes. These expectations are not always perfectly true, but they make it easier for you to see the new scene

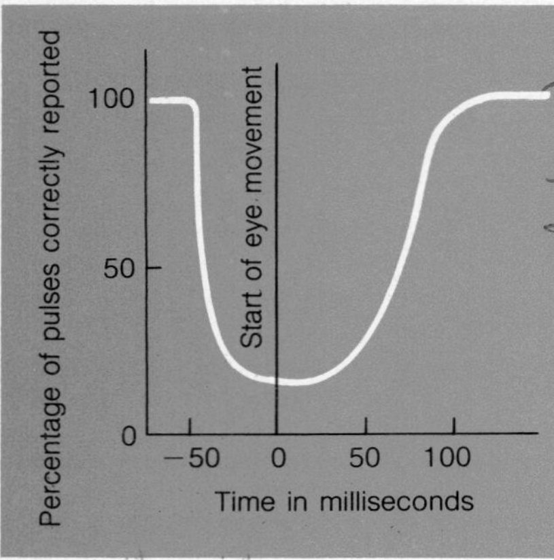

Fig. 8•17 Percentage of light pulses detected in relation to saccadic eye movements. (From Latour, 1962)

after you move your gaze to it. They also make it easier for you to perceive a continuity between your current fixation and the next one.

Try the preceding experiment several times. Although you are now aware of what you are doing, visual expectations such as these apparently occur automatically and without awareness. Our expectation before we move our eyes contributes to our perception of the panorama of the visual scene. The panorama may not be clear over our retinas at any one instant, but we can construct its details from our expectations. The more experience we have had and the more we look over a scene, the more helpful our expectations and the more panoramic our perception.

Sensorimotor Integration The last technique to be discussed that helps us construct an integrated panorama of the visual scene concerns the interrelationship of our bodily movements and our visual-perception processes. If you reach out to touch an object you see, is the sight of your hand moving toward that object necessary to the accuracy of the touching? How is the *afferent* visual information (flowing from receptors to the brain) related to the *efferent* instructions (flowing from the brain to muscles) to move the hand?

If you move your eyes to the right, you will not "see" the retinal projection slide across the retina to the left. You attribute the change in the retinal projection to the movement of your eyes rather than to the movement of the visual scene. Now instead of moving your eyes by an instruction from your brain to your eye muscles, poke the side of one eyeball gently with your finger. The visual world jumps, even though the change in the retinal projection is similar to that produced when you move your eyes with your eye muscles. In one case, a specific motor instruction is given. In the other case, the eye is moved by an external force; the visual system itself has no way of knowing the eye moved, and so it attributes the movement it perceives to the scene and perceives the scene as being in motion.

The correlation between visual information and motor instruction has been of interest to psychologists for well over a hundred years. In the 1890s one technique used to study this phenomenon was to have a perceiver subject wear special glasses that altered the normal optical patterns on the retinas, thereby disturbing the correlation between visual experience and motor instructions to the eyes. Since then many such experiments have been done, the most dramatic of which were Ivo Köhler's. In one study, Köhler (1964) wore mirrors in front of his eyes that inverted the retinal projections (Figure 8•18). In the top of his visual field Köhler saw his feet and the floor; in the bottom of his view was the ceiling.

When Köhler first put the mirrors on, he could not walk without help and was very dizzy. These difficulties lasted only a few days; within a week, he was skiing again, driving a car, writing, and performing all of his normal tasks, with little apparent loss of precision or skill. Even more important, he reported that after the second or third day, he perceived the visual world as right side up. It was not that he had learned to reach down for an object he saw as up, but that he actually perceived the object as down where it really was. He called this process *perceptual adaptation.*

Köhler wore the mirrors for several months. No matter how he tested himself, his perceptions were exactly as they had been before he put the mirrors on, even though the retinal projection was inverted from its normal orientation. The critical test came when he took the mirrors off. If he had made a conscious learning adjustment to the inversion, he would be able to return to normal within only a few minutes because he would still know how to perform all of the familiar visual–motor skills. However, when he took the mirrors off, Köhler had as much difficulty as when he first put them on. He could not ski, drive, walk, or do anything requiring visual–motor coordination. It took him nearly as long to return to normal as it had taken him to adapt to the mirrors.

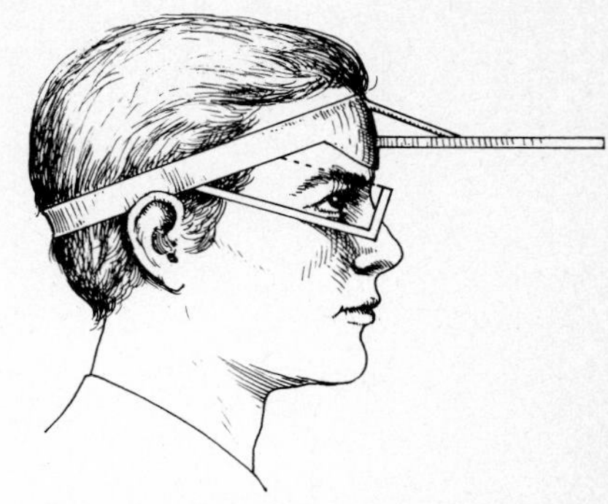

Fig. 8·18 The mirror headgear used by Ivo Köhler to produce up-down inversion of vision. (Smith and Smith, 1962)

Köhler and others repeated this and related experiments a number of times. In addition to mirrors that invert the visual world, the experimenters tried mirrors and prisms that reverse right and left, invert and reverse the visual scene, displace everything to one side or another, and even displace the top half of the visual field but leave the lower half straight ahead. In every case, perceptual adaptation occurred.

These and other experiments demonstrate the importance of correlations between visual input and self-initiated movement. In experiments where the perceiver was moved around in a wheelchair (Held and Hein, 1958), no perceptual adaptation occurred; the visual world continued to look as confused as it did when the prisms, lenses, or mirrors were first put on. Only when the perceiver initiated his own movements—that is, when he issued *efferent* instructions to his muscles—did he adapt to seeing the world normally.

Presumably perceivers continually build up correlations between their perceptions and the movements that produce those perceptions. These correlations change, especially in early life as body size changes, arms get longer, and eyes get farther from the ground. It is critical, at least for the first fifteen years or so of life, that we be capable of adjusting these correlations. Apparently, we continue to be able to make these adjustments for years after we stop growing, as the preceding experiments show.

Summary The human visual system integrates many successive glances at a visual scene into a clear, continuous panorama. Mechanisms apparently involved in the integration process include motion perspective, saccadic suppression, expectancy guidance, and sensorimotor integration.

When an observer moves through space, projections of visual images flow over the retina according to systematic rules. The rates at which these projections flow are inversely proportional to the distance of the object from the observer, so that a flow gradient is produced. Moving through space also integrates the cues provided by apertures in the visual world (doors, windows, and spaces between objects) as they open into textural patterns that become less dense as we approach them, thus unifying visual space and providing it with continuity.

Saccadic eye movements would produce some blurring between fixations in a scene were it not for saccadic suppression, which momentarily lowers visual sensitivity during each saccade and therefore helps integrate successive fixations. Visual continuity is also provided by expectancy guidance, which predicts what we shall see when we look in a new direction. Our expectancies guide where we look and what we construct, and they contribute to our perception of the panorama of a scene.

When we shift our eyes from side to side, we perceive that our eyes, and not the visual world, moved. Efferent instruction from the brain on where to move our eyes is integrated with afferent input from changes produced in the retina; agreement between these two sources of information results in stable perceptions. Interest in this relationship prompted Ivo Köhler to devise special goggles that inverted the visual field. After an initial adaptation period, the normal relationship between visual perception and motor instruction returned. When the goggles were removed after several months, a second adaptation period was required, suggesting that the adaptation was not simply a learned readjustment but a new relationship between visual input and self-initiated movement.

The Role of Experience in Perception

8·3 It seems unlikely that our visual constructions or percepts spring forth without being influenced by our practice at seeing and by our personal experiences and knowledge. In this section we shall consider several aspects of this topic.

The Visual Environment City dwellers live in a carpentered world where most visual scenes contain a preponderance of right angles, straight lines, symmetrical arrangements, vertical walls, and flat surfaces arranged in close formations. Desert nomads, however, live in a visual environment that comprises curved surfaces and generally asymmetric arrangements distributed sparsely over spacious visual scenes where the often unvarying texture reduces some of the discrimination power of the basic scales of space. The visual space of the human inhabitants of a dense rain forest, however, has little extent, as the farthest point in such an environment may be only 10 meters from the perceiver's eyes. Do these three groups of people—city dwellers, desert nomads, and forest inhabitants—have the same feature detectors and the same strategies for constructing a particular visual scene? How is the development of feature detectors and perceptual strategies affected by the visual environment?

In an attempt to discover whether the early visual environment affects the feature detection process, H. V. B. Hirsch and D. N. Spinelli (1970) raised some kittens that wore goggles from birth. Half of the kittens wore goggles that had vertical black stripes painted on them; the other half wore horizontally striped goggles. Their cages were constructed to contain no visible edges or lines, and so half of the kittens saw only horizontal stripes wherever they looked; the other half saw only vertical stripes.

The kittens wore the goggles for several months, until they reached adulthood. Hirsch and Spinelli then tested each grown kitten for feature detectors for horizontal and for vertical lines. They found that the cats had no detectors for the features that had been absent from their environment as they were growing into adulthood. Furthermore, the feature-detector loss persisted even after the cats were exposed to a normal visual environment before testing. When Hirsch and Spinelli raised kittens normally from birth to adulthood and then had them wear striped goggles for several months, they exhibited no loss of detectors for lines. To be effective, the particular deprivation evidently had to occur early in life. This study suggests that early exposure to a feature is necessary for the visual system to develop or to maintain detectors for that feature. While reasearch using kitten subjects may not apply to human beings, Hirsch and Spinelli's results suggest that the characteristics of a particular visual environment may lead to unique feature-extraction capabilities being formed by perceivers who grow up in different environments.

A desert nomad would undoubtedly find New York visually surprising and different. But would such a person be able to detect the lines, angles, and so forth that make up New York's carpentered visual scene? Hirsch and Spinelli's study indicates that whatever trouble such a perceiver might have with the features themselves would probably result from the absence of comparable features in his early visual environment.

Another interesting implication of the Hirsch and Spinelli experiment is that the inability of some young human children to converge their eyes on a single target may impede the development and maintenance of the binocular-disparity detectors necessary for depth perception, and that even if eye-convergence ability is later acquired the binocular-disparity detectors may never develop. This appears to be the case in children for whom the convergence correction is not made until late childhood.

Attempts have been made to test adult human beings who grew up in dissimilar visual environments, but because this research almost always uses flat pictures to test subjects rather than real three-dimensional scenes, we shall discuss these studies in the next section of this chapter. Let us note here only that this research provides more evidence of difficulties in constructing proper scales of space than it does of feature-detector loss, thus implying that although the early visual environment is important, it may not necessarily alter feature-detection processes.

Space Perception in Infants What does a newborn infant see when he first opens his eyes? Answering this question is difficult because of the inability of newborn and very young children to use language to communicate. However, some evidence of infants' abilities to articulate space has been provided by recently developed testing procedures. Some of that research was included in Chapter 4 in relation to perceptual development. We shall lightly review that research in the present context and concentrate on additional findings.

Newborn human beings, as well as neonates of nearly all species, are born with a support reflex that causes them to avoid lack of support and to respond in some way when physical support is absent. Do infants perceive lack of support visually? The answer is clearly yes for virtually every species tested.

Fig. 8•19 The visual cliff apparatus and the reactions of two subjects to the apparent drop-off. (*a*) Although the child patted the glass and thus had tactile evidence of a firm surface, he refused to crawl across it when his mother called to him. (*b*) When pushed out onto clear glass, the baby pig either backed up frantically or froze in fear. (Al Fenn, Time-Life Picture Agency, © Time Inc.)

One technique for measuring space perception in infants has been the use of a visual cliff (Figure 8•19). The infant is placed on a solid plank that lies across the middle of a very large glass plate. The glass on one side of the plank rests on a table covered with a checkered tablecloth. On the other side of the plank, the checkered tablecloth is three feet below the glass. If the infant can perceive the relative depths of each side, then it should perceive one side as safe to crawl on, while the other side should appear to entail lack of support and a consequent fall.

During the testing procedure, the infant is put on the plank and called by the mother, first from one side and then from the other. Nearly all human infants refuse to come to their mothers across the cliff side. The glass feels the same on both sides of the plank, and so the infant must perceive the depth of the cliff side visually. Apparently the infant receives the most important source of information about the cliff by moving its head to help articulate the depth of the cliff side in the layout of space.

Animals have been tested on the visual cliff as soon as they were old enough to move around, and kittens were tested on the first day they opened their eyes. The results of these experiments were the same as those using human infants of crawling age (about four to six months).

The perceptions of human infants not yet able to crawl have been tested using the procedures described in Chapter 4 to identify where in the visual scene the newborn infant fixates. The results of this research are dramatic. Although William James (1890) described the newborn infant's initial perceptions as no more than "a blooming, buzzing confusion," we now know that even at a few minutes of age, human infants possess and use important perceptual abilities.

The infants tested exhibited a consistent preference for one part of a scene over another. For example, when offered a triangle to look at, the infant's eyes fixated at one of the triangle's corners (Figure 8•20a). When the infant's field of view was empty, the eyes looked randomly across a horizontal sweep (Figure 8•20b).

During the first few weeks of life, infants generally look at sharp edges or at any division between high and low light intensities. Their eyes seem to be captured by these features, so that once directly fixated, the eyes cannot break away. These capturing features are large and are generally on the perimeter of figures. Even large internal features are not fixated on.

These effects decrease over the first month of life, so that the infant is able to explore the environment visually more than before, looking away and then back, perusing an entire figure rather than locking onto a single feature, and selecting and visually capturing features. Toward the end of the second month, the infant is more likely to fixate on internal rather than external features. Meanwhile detection, visual acuity, eye-movement control, accommodation, and most other visual abilities are developing. Not until about age two months, however, are infants able to construct a percept that extends beyond each single retinal projection or that involves active or creative effort.

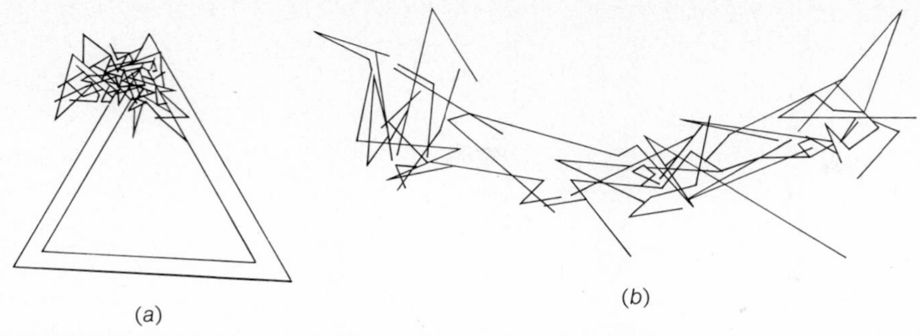

Fig. 8·20 Visual scanning patterns of a human newborn looking at a large, black equilateral triangle (*a*) and a blank field (*b*). Each dot represents one eye-orientation time sample. (From Salapatek and Kessen, 1966)

Marshall Haith (1976) measured where infants fixated on real faces in front of them and on two-dimensional faces on a TV screen. The infants younger than about two months fixated on bold features on the perimeter of the face (for example, the hair–skin boundary on a dark-haired, light-skinned person). As the infants grew older, they began to explore and fixate on a variety of features, gradually attending more and more to internal ones such as noses, lips, eyes, and moles. When most of the infants reached about two months of age, their fixation patterns drastically changed, so that they attended primarily to the observed person's eyes, shifting to the mouth only when it moved. As the person continued to talk, the infants' fixation patterns flitted back and forth between the mouth and the eyes.

Haith's findings imply that the crying response to strange faces that begins around two months of age (Spitz and Wolf, 1946) represents an early construction of a percept. A two-month-old infant apparently can organize the jungle of separate facial features into a meaningful and integrated face. It seems unreasonable that an infant would cry at the sight of a stranger if he has not previously constructed a representation of "familiar" that exists independent of lighting, hair combed or mussed, makeup on or off, and so forth. (However, changing hair style or color may lead to a new construction.)

Because of their special motivational significance and their high occurrence as visual objects, faces are quite naturally one of the early constructions that infants make. However, by the time they are two or three months old, infants are able to construct other percepts (Bower, 1975). In each of his experiments, T. G. R. Bower tested infants on different aspects of perceptual constancies. An infant looking at a box may perceive only the retinal projection (features on the retina), so that every change in orientation, distance, or lighting produces a different projection and thus a different percept. If an infant is able to construct a percept of the box (its shape, size, color, and so forth), he or she will be able to select the familiar box irrespective of the changes in distance, slant, orientation, and lighting that alter the retinal projection. Such infants are apparently able to perceive more than individual retinal features, and are able to construct a percept of an object in the visual scene by scaling space and using motion parallax and the other processes discussed earlier in this chapter.

Testing for Size Constancy in Two-month-old Infants

T. G. R. Bower (1964) used a conditioning procedure to demonstrate the presence of size constancy in two-month-old infants. The subject was placed in a raised cradle with the head propped firmly so that the infant could see down the table (Figure 8A·1). Under the pillow against one ear was a silent but sensitive switch that recorded when the infant turned his head to that side. On another table in front of the infant was a stand to hold a cube, which was turned enough to be visible as a cube and not merely as a flat square. As soon as the cube was placed on its stand, the session began.

Whenever the infant turned his head enough to close the switch, the experimenter, who was until then hidden from view, would pop up, smile, and say "peek-a-boo." (It was previously determined, based on each infant's response, that this was a positive reinforcement.) The experimenter then disappeared, to reappear only when a head-turning response occurred. The infant received no reinforcement for head turning unless the cube was in place. The criterion for a conditioning response to the sight of the cube was met when the infant always made a head-turning response within a fixed amount of time when the cube was in place, but did not make one within that time when the cube was absent.

To answer the critical question of what aspect of the cube constituted the conditioned stimulus for the conditioned response, Bower ran four testing conditions, each with a different group of infants. The four groups differed in how the cube was presented during testing (Table 8A·1).

Fig. 8A·1 Arrangements for T. G. R. Bower's (1964) experiment on size constancy in infants.

Bower's experiments are too imprecise to define the details of the construction process in infants, and further studies of this subject are needed. How much variation in the retinal projection can infants accept before they will construct a new percept? And, more important, what effect does experience with early-environment objects such as faces have on the ease of learning to make constructions?

Expectancy Guidance Revisited The preceding discussion covered perceptual processes during the first few months of life but did not take into account what the perceiver expected to see—that is, the ability to anticipate visually on the basis of present knowledge and prior experiences. Although little is known about perceptual expectancies for very young infants, we do know that expectancy guidance is an important part of the construction processes in adult human beings.

One characteristic of visual perception is that we can construct a stable articulation of a scene without having seen all parts of it. We can fill in gaps and perceive parts of objects that are not immediately visible. We know what the scene will look like if we move to the right, even before we move. Being able to do this

Table 8A·1 Characteristics of Stimuli Used in Bower's Experiment on Size Constancy in Infants

GROUP	DISTANCE FROM CUBE (meters)	REAL SIZE OF CUBE (meters on a side)	PROJECTIVE SIZE OF CUBE (meters on retina)
Training			
All groups	1	0.3	0.0051
Testing			
Group 1	1	0.3	0.0051
Group 2	3	0.3	0.0017
Group 3	1	0.9	0.0153
Group 4	3	0.9	0.0051

The original training was with a cube that measured 0.3 meter on a side and was placed 1 meter away. However, from that information alone, we cannot determine whether the infant was seeing a 0.3 meter cube (a response that presumes size constancy), any object 1 meter away, or any object with a projective size of 0.0051 meter on the retina. (See Figure 7·2 on calculating projective size.)

After the conditioning criterion was met, no further reinforcements were given, and testing began. In group 1, the distance, the real size, and the projective size were the same as in testing. In group 2, the distance was tripled to 3 meters, reducing the projective size although the cube stayed the same size. In group 3, the distance was the same as in testing (1 meter), but a much larger cube was used so that both real size and projective size increased. In group 4, the larger cube was used but the distance was 3 meters, and so only the projective size was the same as in training. Each of these four conditions differs from the others on two of the three factors to which the infant might have been responding.

The results were clear. The infants in groups 1 and 2 gave the most conditioned responses, and the two groups did not differ from each other. The infants in groups 3 and 4 gave substantially fewer responses. Because group 1 was identical to training conditions, it was used as the base line. The only group that was as responsive as group 1 was the group in which the physical object was the same size as the object with which the infants were trained. Therefore, the infants must have been able to construct a representation of that size. In other words, they had size constancy. It did not matter to the infants in group 2 that the distance was changed, or that the projective size was changed.

depends on our having visual expectancies of what we shall see if we move our eyes, or if we follow a line that we expect to change in one direction but not another.

These visual expectancies are particularly useful in guiding the sampling of the visual scene and in using those samples to construct complete percepts. Our expectations direct where our eyes move, where our attention falls within each glance, and what features we notice. If our expectations of what we shall see are strong, they can even fill in parts of the scene we do not look at directly—we simply construct those parts by hypothesis.

Several experiments have examined eye movements to determine what accounts for where we look in a visual scene. Figure 8·21 shows the results of one such study (Mackworth and Morandi, 1967). Over 80 percent of all fixations on a typical picture occur over less than 20 percent of the scene. Vast regions are never looked at, while others are examined repeatedly. When different areas of the pictures are rated separately for their informativeness or predictability, it is found that the high concentrations of fixations always coincide with areas that present a great

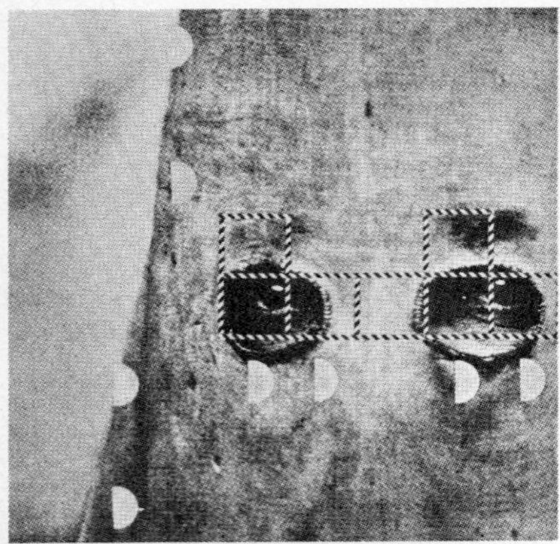

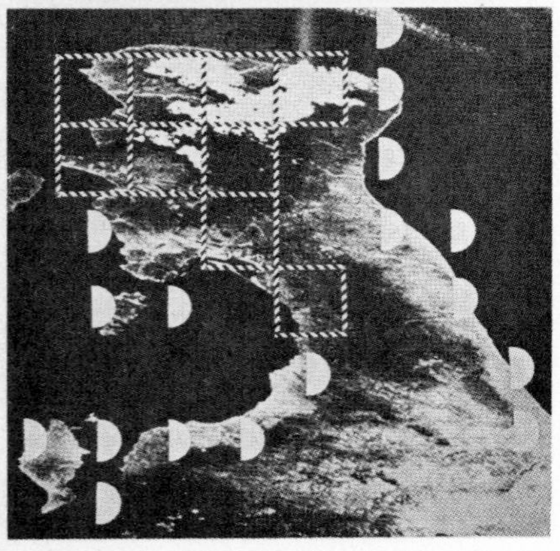

Fig. 8•21 Eye fixations made while looking at a map picture. (From Mackworth and Morandi, 1967)

deal of information and about which predictions cannot easily be made. Perceivers rarely, if ever, look at areas they can predict. Further, the pattern is apparent after the initial glance. Perceivers do not glance everywhere to gain an overall view and then begin to concentrate on certain locations in the visual scene; rather, their first fixation tells them where to look next and what can be ignored.

What happens if a scene contains objects that are unfamiliar? Are they harder to see? If constructions are based on expectations, then unfamiliar, unusual, or unpredictable components of a visual scene should be more difficult for us to construct. This hypothesis is supported by perception research: unfamiliar objects take longer to see or to find; they have a higher threshold; they are more likely to be overlooked than are familiar objects; and they are more likely to be misperceived as something familiar.

One type of study (Solomon and Postman, 1952, for example) has examined the visual identification threshold for perceiving words, some of which are very familiar to most perceivers and some of which are generally unfamiliar (rarely seen in print or heard in speech). Virtually every study of this type found higher thresholds for unfamiliar words. Longer exposure times, higher intensities, more presentations, and higher contrasts were needed to produce an identification accuracy equivalent to that for familiar words. We shall return to an aspect of this phenomenon at the end of this chapter when we consider reading processes.

Another type of study has focused on what happens when a picture is internally incongruous. The natural visual environment does not usually contain incongruous scenes; but even when it does, we usually are not aware of the incongruities because we simply do not see them. For example, J. S. Bruner and L. Postman (1949) asked perceivers to identify playing cards, in some of which the suits (hearts, spades, diamonds, clubs) did not agree with their traditional (red or black) colors. They found that the subjects usually misperceived the cards, calling a red spade a red heart (or occasionally a black spade). Some perceivers reported a "compromise" perception, in which a red spade was called a purple spade.

There are some dramatic though contrived situations in which we ignore our experiential expectations in arriving at a perception. A number of experimental arrangements have been devised in which the source of information about space was deliberately reversed. In one of the more famous demonstrations Adelbert Ames (1955) built a room in which, from a particular vantage point, the walls, floor, and ceiling appeared to form right angles (Figure 8•22a). Actually, most of the angles did not contain 90 degrees, and the right end of the far wall was much closer to the perceiver than the left end. Consequently, when each of two persons stood in opposite corners of the far wall, they appeared to the perceiver to be the same distance away; in fact, the person on the left was twice as far away as the person on the right (Figure 8•22b). In this situation if the person on the left is the same height as the near person, the visual angle of his height will be one-half the visual angle of the near person.

Two sets of visual expectations conflict with each other in the Ames room: expectations about the shapes of rooms, and expectations about the sizes of people.

(a)

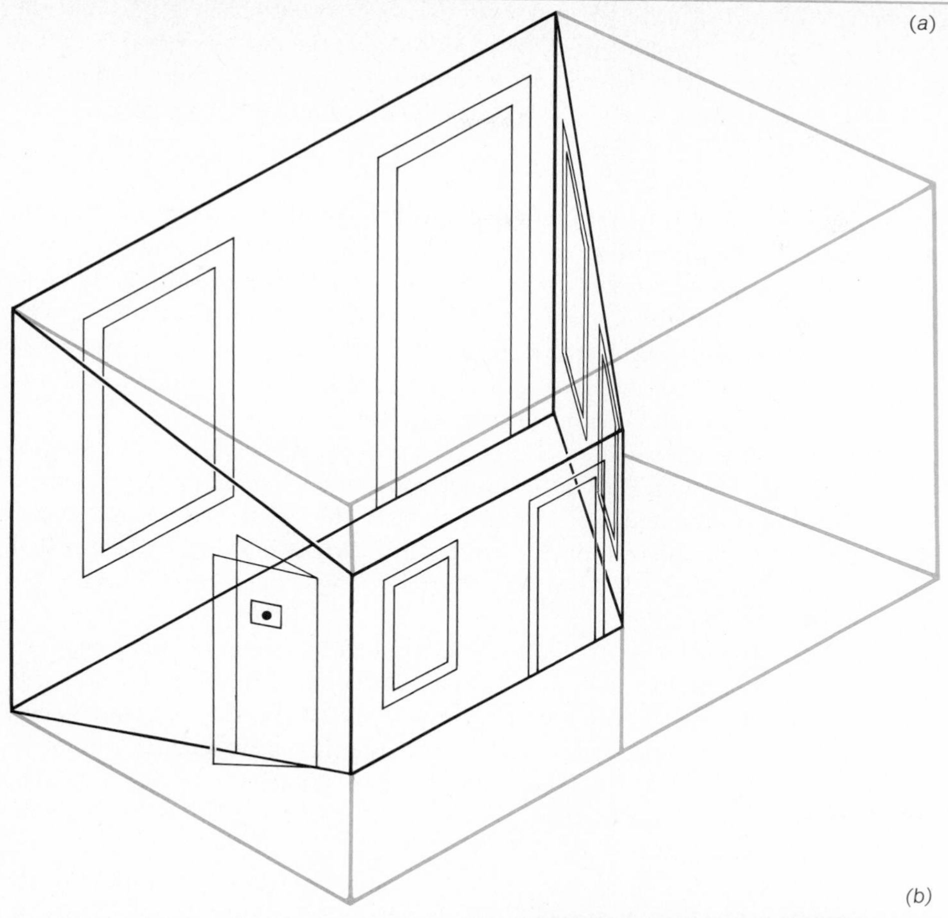

(b)

Fig. 8·22 (*a*) The Ames room. The ceiling of the room sloped down to the right, the floor sloped up, and the windows and doors (which varied in size) were not rectangular in every case. The color lines show how the perceivers constructed the shape of the room as normal. (From Ittelson, 1952) (*b*) Two girls (actually not very different in height) in the Ames room, seen from a certain vantage point. The girl who appears larger is actually the nearer one. (Peter Vilms, Jeroboam)

Virtually every perceiver tested perceived the room as normal (it is not) and the people as distorted (they are not). This room is one of the most powerful examples of how easily we can be induced to misconstruct perceptions from deliberately distorted sources of information, even to the point of misperceiving peoples' sizes (one of our most familiar perceptions).

Momentary and Dispositional Differences in Perception In discussing the role of experience, we have considered three topics related to the differences in perceivers' constructions that result from (1) the early visual environment, (2) developmental changes in early life, and (3) expectancies based on past experience. We shall now discuss how constructions are affected by motivational or instructional processes influencing the perceiver while a scene or picture is being viewed and by the perceiver's own temperament and character.

One of the most pervasive aspects of perception is its selectivity. We do not notice most of the components of the visual world, and we are not aware of having seen them after the scene passes. Yet everything in the visual scene is represented in the pattern of stimulation on the retina, and current evidence indicates that this pattern is completely coded and transmitted to the visual cortex. Where, then, does selectivity operate?

Most of the selective acts of vision are determined by where we orient our eyes. We choose to look at one object and not at another, and so we do not perceive the other object. We can even select within a single glance, so that some aspects of the visual world are processed while others are not. If you are reading, you might not notice the typeface, smudges on the page, underlining done by a prior reader, or even the misprints on the page—yet all of these features reflect different intensities onto the retina and are coded.

How aware or conscious we are of the content of visual scenes varies greatly from moment to moment, both as a function of our internal state and as a function of the various stimuli in the scenes. But most experimental psychologists are wary of discussing concepts of consciousness, even when the term is used to mean awareness of perceptual events. Rather than saying "being conscious of" or "being aware of," they usually use the more neutral words "attending to." Whatever the term, however, the concept is important but confusing. There has not been enough research on the process of *being aware* to identify what determines when we become aware. Can we turn awareness on and off? Can we be unaware of something and yet react or respond to it in some way? These questions have all been considered, and some of them constitute a large body of research literature—but we still do not know the answers.

We do know that human beings take in, process, and respond to stimuli of which they are unaware. Nearly all of our automatic motor skills function in this way. Once you know how to drive an automobile well, you are capable of responding to a vast range of stimuli without being aware of them. These stimuli must have been extensively processed because the scene we view through the windshield has to be fully constructed in three dimensions, with all objects properly segregated and correctly placed relative to each other. Such a construction cannot be made from passively treating the visual features of separate glances, but only from constructing the continuous sequence of glances we make as we drive.

One concept of awareness implies that the perceiver fully constructs the scene in front of the eyes but does not retain that construction (or remember what was seen). If, for example, you were asked whether you saw a red car parked at the curb, you would answer yes only if the red car were still in your visual field. This concept implies that we construct representations of everything in the scenes before us but save only the aspects of our constructions that have importance or meaning, or in some way hold our attention. It also implies that perceptual selectivity occurs after constructions have been made—that is, our memories do the selecting. We remember what we attend to and forget the rest, but initially we saw everything.

William Hogarth (1697–1764) captioned this engraving as follows: "Whoever makes a design without the knowledge of perspective will be liable to such absurdities as are shown in this frontispiece." (Courtesy of the Trustees of the British Museum)

Although this interpretation must be carefully tested experimentally, it is at least partially inconsistent with one aspect of the everyday experience of most perceivers. There seem to be many instances in which we actually fail to perceive something—we are unaware of some of the objects in view. Therefore the concept of the construction of a percept may be synonymous with the awareness of the scene being constructed; otherwise, we would always be aware of what we constructed, at least at the time.

These problems will continue to plague the study of visual perception for some time, and we shall meet them again in this chapter.

Instructional Selectivity: Searching for a Target We look at scenes for pleasure, for information, for vigilance, because we are told to look, or simply because our eyes happen to be open. Do these different task demands affect what we see and the way in which we construct percepts of the visual scene? The answer is clearly yes.

In one study, A. L. Yarbus (1967) showed that perceivers change their pattern of fixation while looking at a picture as a result of the instructions given to them. Figure 8•23 shows six sets of eye movement patterns over the same picture, each for a different instruction. For example, a perceiver will concentrate on different areas when you ask how many people are in the picture than when you ask whether the scene is a happy one. Apparently the perceiver makes different constructions of a scene depending upon what he or she wants to see.

Another way to study the effects of task demands is to study how perceivers search visually. How do we find a familiar face in a crowd? If someone tells you that he saw your name in the paper, how do you find it from among all the words on every page? These are problems of visual search—looking for a particular target from among a large number of irrelevant objects.

How much do you have to process an irrelevant object before you know that it is not the one you are looking for? The answer is "not much." In fact, after having searched through something, perceivers usually have little memory of the irrelevant items or objects. Those apparently do not have to be identified in order for them to be rejected.

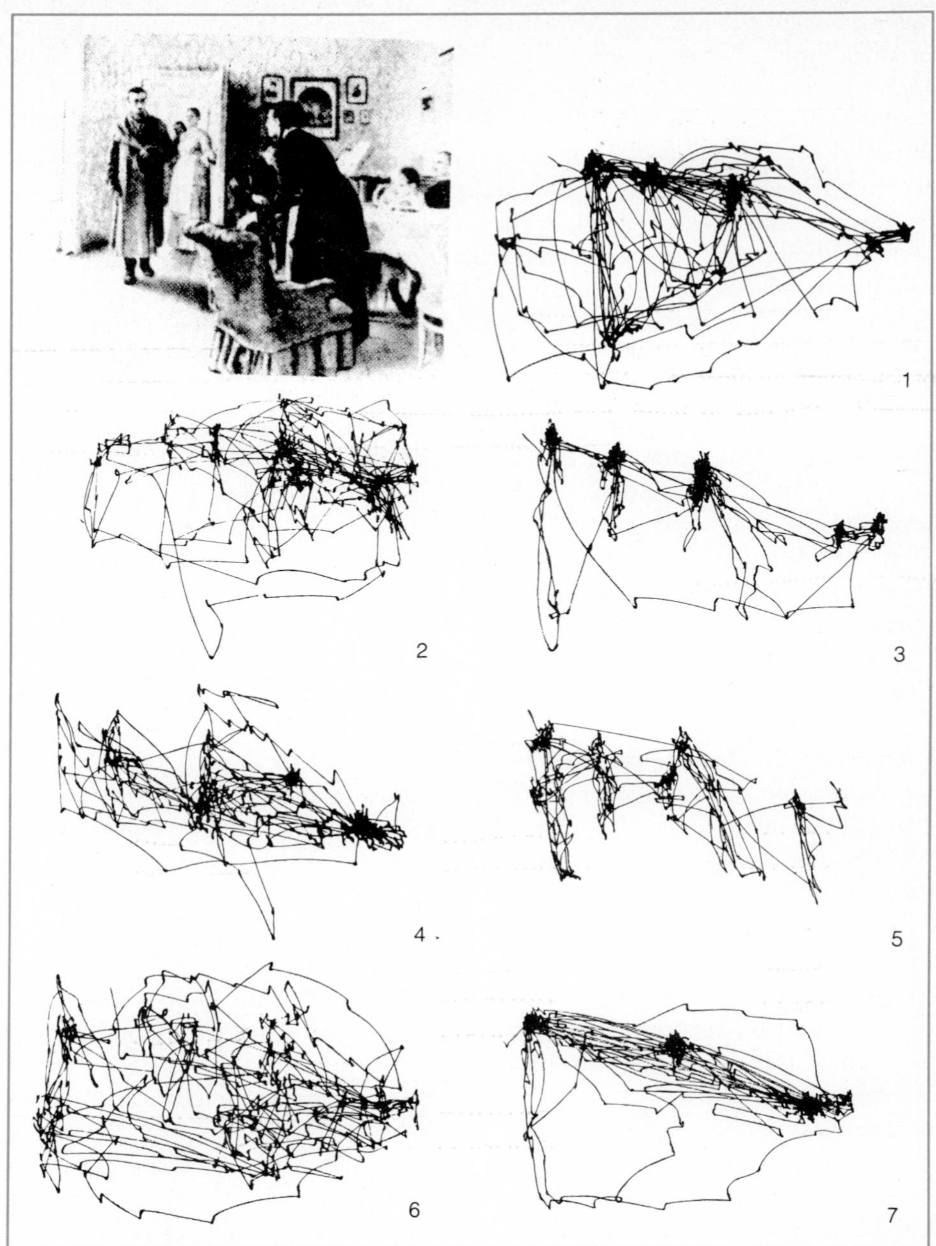

Fig. 8·23 Six sets of eye movement patterns over the same picture, each for a different instruction. (From Yarbus, 1967)

One technique that has been used to study task demands (Neisser, 1963) is to ask perceivers to search as quickly as possible a list of letters to find, for example, the line that contains the letter *K* (Figure 8·24, list 1). As soon as he finds the letter, the subject presses a button. The total search time divided by the number of lines from the top of the list to the line containing the target gives the amount of time needed to search the letters on each line. One of the most interesting findings from this research is that the visual features of the letter alone are often sufficient for the search task. Contrast the ease of finding Z in list 2 with that of finding Z in list 3. In each case in Ulric Neisser's experiments, the differences are almost two to one. When the visual features of the target differ substantially, the speeds are so fast that the searcher could not have identified the nontarget items, but apparently searches only for visual features—straight lines among curves, for example.

The importance of Neisser's findings is that under appropriate conditions we can select how much to perceive, and construct no more than that. This kind of selectivity involves the ability to carry out only the stimulation processing necessary for the task at hand. For example, when we drive a car, only a small part of the visual scenes flowing by are relevant for driving. All other stimuli can be ignored. Even the relevant items (such as traffic signals, curves, and potential hazards) need not be processed beyond what is necessary for the immediate task. You do not need to know the make or color of a car in order to determine whether you can change lanes.

EHYP	ODUGQR	IVMXEW
SWIQ	QCDUGO	EWVMIX
CFCJ	CQOGRD	EXWMVI
WBYH	QUGCDR	IXEMWV
OGTX	URDGQO	VXWEMI
GWVX	GRUQDO	MXVEWI
TWLN	DUZGRO	XVWMEI
XJBU	UCGROD	MWXVIE
UDXI	DQRCGU	VIMEXW
HSFP	QDOCGU	EXVWIM
XSCQ	CGUROQ	VWMIEX
SDJU	OCDURQ	VMWIEX
PODC	UOCGQD	XVWMEI
ZVBP	RGQCOU	WBVEMI
PEVZ	GRUDQO	XMEWIV
SLRA	GODUCQ	MXIVEW
JCEN	QCURDO	VEWMIX
ZLRD	DUCOQG	EMVXWI
XBOD	CGRBQU	IVWMEX
PHMU	UDRCOQ	IEVMWX
ZHFK	GQCORU	WVZMXE
PNJW	GOQUCD	XEMIWV
CQXT	GDQUOC	WXIMEV
GHNR	URDCGO	EMWIVX
IXYD	GODRQC	IVEMXW

Fig. 8·24 Abbreviated examples of lists used in visual search tasks. The target letter is *K* in list 1, and *Z* in lists 2 and 3. (From Neisser, 1963)

Another important characteristic of visual search is the interplay of the features picked up by the high acuity areas of the fovea and by the rest of the retina. If a target is small and finely detailed (as in Figure 8•24), it is usually necessary to look directly at it in order to identify it. Does this mean that the rest of the retina is not needed? Quite the contrary. There is a close interplay between the kinds of information coded by the high- and low-acuity areas of the retina. At each glance, the surrounding part of the retina picks up the general information about large details that is needed by the visual system for determining the most likely place to look next. The fovea concentrates on the item being looked at to determine whether it is the target. If it is not, then the eye shifts to a new item—not randomly, but following the information picked up by the retinal surroundings of the previous fixation.

Motivated Selectivity: Perceptual Defense and Vigilance The same kind of selectivity that we use when searching for a particular target can be produced by our motivational state. For example, if we are very hungry when driving, we are more likely to notice (construct more fully) restaurants, grocery stores, and so forth than if we are not hungry.

Psychologists have been particularly interested in this subject, and there is a large body of experimental literature concerning it. Research shows that whether you are aware of it or not, your internal motivational state selects how much processing you carry out on the visual scene in the same way that target-search instructions do. Apparently, however, motivational variables have a smaller effect than do explicit search instructions.

Some personality theories, especially the psychoanalytic theories of Freud (see Chapter 13), hypothesize that stimulation capable of making the perceiver anxious or fearful will be blocked from awareness (not selected for complete processing). This phenomenon is called *perceptual defense*. Furthermore, according to Freud, stimulation that signals immediate danger is selected for processing—a phenomenon called *perceptual vigilance*. Therefore, only those unpleasant stimuli where danger is not immediate would be perceptually avoided.

Freud's idea has been difficult to test. One study used a word-identification task in which words were flashed very briefly or dimly on a screen, and the subject was required to identify each one. If naming a particular word to the experimenter made the subject uncomfortable, then the duration or intensity of the flash needed for the perceiver to be able to identify the word would be higher—illustrating perceptual defense. This effect was not very large in the laboratory tests, but the evidence suggests that anxiety can affect what is processed for identification and what is not. At least in a word-identification task, anxiety apparently slows the perceiver's response and results in more stimulus energy being required for the perceiver to complete an identification.

Theories about perceptual defense create a paradox—how can we process something sufficiently to know it is anxiety-provoking, and at the same time block it sufficiently so that we are not made anxious by it? One theoretical solution to the paradox separates the processes of stimulus-content construction from the processes of awareness or consciousness. Whether we become aware of a scene's content or whether we remember it depends on factors different from those that enable us to construct the scene. This theoretical distinction has been particularly useful in research because we are not yet able to devise experimental operations to measure percept construction independent of awareness or consciousness.

Another theory involves the concept of *multiple levels of perceptual processing* (Erdelyi, 1974). We have already stated that a perceiver who is visually searching can learn enough about an object to know it is *not* what is sought and can reject it, without processing it to the point of identification. Matthew Erdelyi suggests that, as in the target-search task, the amount of processing carried out depends on the tasks and what they mean to the perceiver. Just as a perceiver may stop processing a target as soon as its irrelevance is determined, so may a perceiver stop processing an anxiety-producing or upsetting stimulus.

Erdelyi coupled the levels-of-processing concept with the theory of *selective bias.* At times, a great deal of information is needed before its meaning or implication is perceived; at other times, conclusions can be reached from a single item. This variation is often caused by how consonant the information is with the perceiver's expectation. If the expectation is confirmed, the perceiver is biased to accept the information without looking further. If the information is unexpected, the perceiver will look further before reaching a conclusion.

Another determinant of how much information we need is its importance to us. If something is potentially dangerous, only a few cues may put us on the alert even before we identify the danger. If the stimulus is neutral, we can afford to take the time for more processing. Thus, the amount of evidence we need (how much we process a stimulus) can vary both as a function of our expectation about what we are seeing, and as a function of the importance or meaning the stimulus has for us.

Using both of these concepts—levels of processing and selective bias—Erdelyi suggests how the paradox of perceptual defense is avoided. The word *who-e,* in which the fourth letter is absent or indistinct, will usually be perceived as *whose* rather than *whore* simply because expectation tells us that the latter word occurs comparatively seldom in print. If the word really is *whore,* however, partial processing may tell the perceiver that the stimulus is capable of producing anxiety, and he or she may therefore stop processing. Because processing was not completed, the word was not identified but only classed as "upsetting." This process raises the threshold for the "dirty word." When we feel upset or uneasy without knowing why, we have probably processed enough information to discover that the stimulus is upsetting, but we have stopped processing before we have exactly identified the stimulus.

Individual Differences in Perception: Cognitive Style The final aspect of motivated selectivity we shall discuss is related to personality and to individual differences in our perceptual processes. It seems quite reasonable to expect different perceivers to select and concentrate on different aspects of the visual world and to differ in what they ignore. Research on individual differences has been linked closely to research on cognitive style that involves certain personality variables. However, in spite of much work, the linkage, while plausible, has not been firmly demonstrated experimentally.

Many of the personality variables have been studied by dividing each one into two essentially opposite parts—for example, *field dependent* and *field independent*. This variable concerns how sensitive a perceiver is to context or surroundings when perceiving a stimulus or making decisions. A field-dependent person is able to perceive a scene comprising interrelated parts but is poor at identifying an incongruity. A field-independent person can ignore irrelevant information and concentrate only on the relevant stimulus; such a perceiver is aware of changes in scenes because he or she does not depend on context.

A second personality dichotomy with presumed perceptual consequences is called *impulsive–reflective*. Some persons need little information in order to arrive at conclusions or take action; others do not act until all aspects are considered. Perceptually, these characteristics imply that impulsive persons search a scene hurriedly and unsystematically, are likely to miss the target object, and are apt to accept superficial similarities as identifications because all of the relevant details are not carefully looked at. Such a person might allow expectancies to guide his or her constructions so strongly that not enough weight is given to the visual features present in the retinal projection. The reflective person, on the other hand, searches visual stimuli more thoroughly, carefully, and efficiently, and makes fewer errors.

These and other personality effects are reasonable examples of different kinds of motivational selectivity, but the relationship between personality or motivation and perceptual selectivity is not yet well understood. Researchers hope that further work will clarify this interesting subject.

Summary Studies of the role of experience in visual perception suggest that early exposure to a particular visual feature is necessary for a perceiver to be able to detect its presence as an adult, but that such deprivation is not likely to cause many perceptual differences in humans. Experiments with human infants indicate that feature-detection processes are functioning at birth, but that features are not constructed into integrated percepts until the infant reaches the age of two or three months. At that age, infants are able to construct faces and use scales of space to identify objects.

Our expectancies about a scene direct where we look, what features we notice, and what we ignore. Unfamiliar objects have a higher threshold than familiar objects and are more likely to be overlooked or misperceived. We usually unconsciously ignore incongruities, but the deliberately distorted sources of information presented by the Ames room lead us to ignore our expectations and to misperceive familiar objects such as the sizes of people and the shape of a room.

Our constructions are affected by our motivation, by instructions given to us, and by our own temperament. When we perform a task, we choose where to look and what to process; and although we may at least partly construct everything we see, we apparently select what we will perceive and remember, and are unaware of or forget irrelevant stimuli. When we search for a target object, we process only enough of the features of objects to know that they are not what we seek; the process of target search is assisted by the interplay between the high- and low-acuity areas of the retina.

Anxiety-provoking stimuli may be blocked or processed differently from neutral stimuli; stimuli signaling danger may be processed at a faster rate and from fewer cues than neutral stimuli require. Our perceptions are also affected by how dependent we are on the context of a stimulus and by personality traits such as impulsiveness.

Perceiving Flat Pictures

8·4 Our discussion so far has focused on the perception and discrimination of objects in visual space. Scenes that are drawn or photographed are represented on flat surfaces and do not contain the same information about depth that our three-dimensional world gives us. However, we usually have little trouble perceiving either the objects in pictures or their proper depth relationships.

Research on pictures is actually older than research on real scenes. Early scientists felt that the latter were too complicated and that the best way to study them would be to start with the apparently more simple processes involved in perceiving flat, two-dimensional drawings, and then to generalize their findings to three-dimensional scenes. However, the analysis presented in this chapter suggests that three-dimensional perception (1) uses a set of principles that may not apply to flat pictures and (2) is in no sense derived or secondary.

Given that we can perceive pictures, it is reasonable to ask how we do it. What are our constructions of internal representations of pictures like? How is it that we perceive pictures so easily? Is this ability learned, or can we correctly perceive the first picture we ever see?

In looking at this building, we do not see what we expect to see. We have to sort out which windows and walls actually exist. (Owen Franken, Stock, Boston)

The best treatise on the articulation of depth in flat pictures comes from the notebooks of Leonardo da Vinci. His interest was in the reverse process—not how to perceive a picture, but how to draw it. Western artists prior to about the fifteenth century did not use the laws of perspective. Objectively parallel lines were not drawn to converge in the distance, far objects were not drawn smaller, less distinct, or more desaturated in color than near ones, nor were they placed higher in the picture plane. Leonardo was able to reverse the normal depth perception process so as to use these sources of information to make flat drawings more realistic.

Organization in Pictures: Principles of Grouping. Nearly seventy years ago a group of psychologists began a program of research on how the parts of a flat visual display are organized to produce certain perceptions. These so-called *Gestalt* psychologists (after the German word for form or organization) used two-dimensional line drawings for their research because relationships could easily be specified and studied without the presence of confounding details. They were not interested in scales of space, and in fact said very little about three-dimensional organization. Their focus was entirely on identifying the properties in the retinal projection that lead the perceiver to construct one type of percept rather than another. Gestalt psychologists proposed a set of principles that describe these properties.

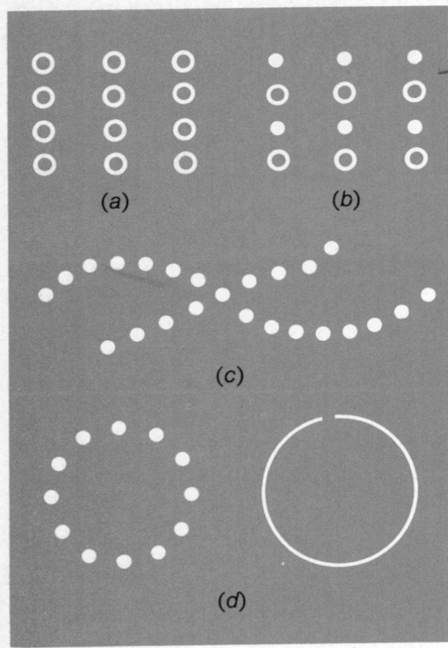

Fig. 8•25 Examples of gestalt laws of perceptual organization. (From Haber and Hershenson, 1973)

1. *Principle of proximity:* Elements in a drawing that are near each other tend to be organized together. For example, the 12 dots in Figure 8•25a can be constructed as three columns, four rows, or a matrix. However, because the dots are closer together vertically than horizontally, nearly all perceivers organize this drawing as three columns.
2. *Principle of Similarity:* Visually similar elements tend to be organized together. In Figure 8•25b the organization is seen as four horizontal rows because the elements in each of these rows are similar to each other. Although proximity is also evident in this particular example, similarity dominates.
3. *Principle of common fate* (a derivative of similarity): Elements that change or move as a group become organized together by their common fate. For example, if the middle column in Figure 8•25b were gradually moved higher, the 12 dots would be organized as columns rather than rows. This principle explains why we can see patterns in dancing; when several dancers move together, they are seen as a group. This is an example of similarity of movement rather than of shape.
4. *Principle of continuity:* Elements that form interesting patterns tend to be organized as a continuous figure rather than as disconnected units. In Figure 8•25c the dots are seen as two continuous lines rather than as four separate lines or two V-shaped objects touching at their points.
5. *Principle of closure:* Gaps between elements of a continuous pattern are filled in perceptually. Both examples shown in Figure 8•25d are therefore seen as circles.
6. *Principle of good figure:* Some organizations are more stable, more complete, or more satisfying than others. According to this principle, circles are better figures than ellipses, and so a figure has to be quite elliptical before it is seen not as a circle. This is perhaps the most controversial principle because of the absence of any independent definition of what is good. For most applications, what is good is what is seen, and the principle therefore becomes circular.

Pattern Recognition and Identification Both recognition and identification imply that a current percept is compared to a memory (reconstruction of a previous percept). Most theories of pattern recognition and identification have therefore focused on the nature of the stored representation and particularly on the comparison process.

One important set of patterns comprises the alphabetic characters, which become highly familiar with experience. Apparently whatever we store about them helps us to identify each letter we see. One theory (an eighteenth century approach not typically identified with any one person or school) proposes that we construct an exact visual representation, or *template*, for each character and that as we read, we compare each successive character to the 26 templates until a match occurs; we then give the name of the matching template to the stimulus letter. This process is somewhat analogous to the system used by banks to "read" the digit codes on the bottom of bank checks. However, such an explanation seems inapplicable to our recognition processes because 26 templates are not enough to identify an English alphabet that appears in hundreds of different typefaces, type styles, and type sizes, and in almost infinitely varied handwriting styles. It seems most unlikely that we have a template for each variation of each character of the alphabet.

Another theory is that we represent a familiar pattern as a set of features. Using this hypothesis, Eleanor J. Gibson (1969) selected 12 features (vertical, horizontal, and diagonal lines, open and closed curves, and so on to represent the 26 letters of the English alphabet. These features change slightly according to typeface; for example, for one typeface of capital letters, an *A* is two diagonal lines and one horizontal line. No other letter has these features regardless of the arrangement.

The feature-list approach is more plausible than the template theory, and it has survived a number of tests. For example, experiments have shown that two letters are more likely to be visually confused if their respective feature lists are similar; and the more features needed to discriminate the feature pattern of a particular letter, the longer it will take to learn the features and to identify the pattern when it appears.

A deficiency of the feature-list approach to pattern identification is its failure to consider the relative importance of features and their interrelationships. Sometimes a small feature is unimportant—for example, whether the ninth capital letter is printed I or I. But consider O and Q, or R and P; a small feature change makes a big difference in these cases and completely changes the identification. Furthermore, a single-feature list makes no provision for ignoring visual noise. Consider Θ, Ø, -O, and Q. The first three are O with a stray line; the last is the letter Q.

Current evidence suggests that human beings use some kind of feature storage rather than templates. The exact form in which these features are stored is not yet clear, however, because we do not know how we interrelate the features.

Visual Illusions We are all familiar with line drawings that fool the eye—for example, two lines appear unequal in length, but when measured with a ruler, they are found to be exactly equal. Even when the perceiver understands the principle or draws the lines himself, he is still fooled. These visual illusions are different from momentary misperceptions such as thinking that a face is familiar and then discovering that you never saw the person before. Once examined, misperceptions disappear; however, we are almost always fooled by illusory drawings such as those in Figure 8•26.

These and other two-dimensional visual illusions are not always the result of the same perceptual-confusion technique. For example, the log-and-railroad-track

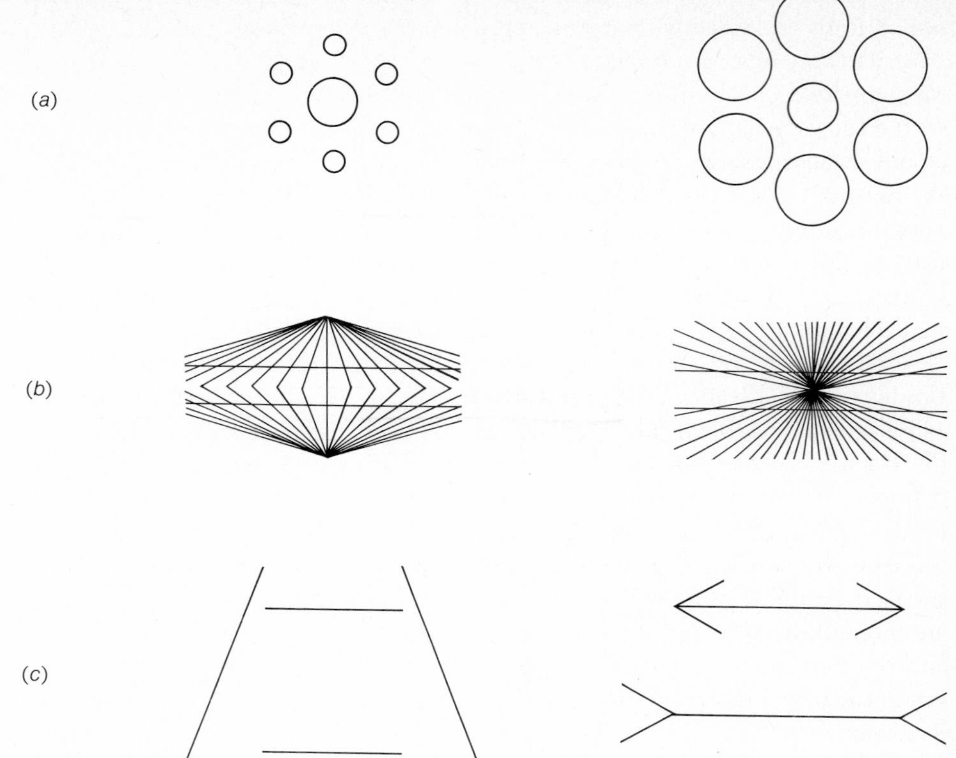

Fig. 8•26 Visual illusions. (*a*) The center circles are the same size, but the one to the left looks larger because of its size in relation to the surrounding circles. (*b*) The horizontal lines are parallel but they appear curved because of the intersecting lines. (*c*) In each case the two horizontal lines are the same length, but the upper one appears shorter because of the position of the surrounding lines.

drawing in Figure 8•27 is illusory because it contains conflicting perspective cues. As railroad tracks stretch away into the distance, their parallel parts appear to converge and their horizontal crossbars appear progressively shorter. If logs of equal physical length are drawn horizontally across the railroad tracks, the log drawn closer to the convergence point of the tracks appears to be larger than the log drawn in the nearer (lower) part of the picture. This illusion works because we interpret converging lines as representing parallel lines stretching away in the distance.

Not all illusions can be explained as simply as the one in Figure 8•27, and some illusions cannot yet be explained at all. However, it seems likely that in each illusion, the confusion results from problems we have in extracting the proper information from contradictory and incomplete perceptual cues.

Besides being fun to look at, visual illusions are important because they can help us to understand normal perception. There are only a few instances in which the natural environment creates illusions. Probably the most dramatic of these is the illusion of the relative sizes of the moon and the sun. Other examples include mirages over deserts or over warm, open, flat surfaces, and the moon racing through the clouds (rather than the clouds racing past the moon). The visual confusion

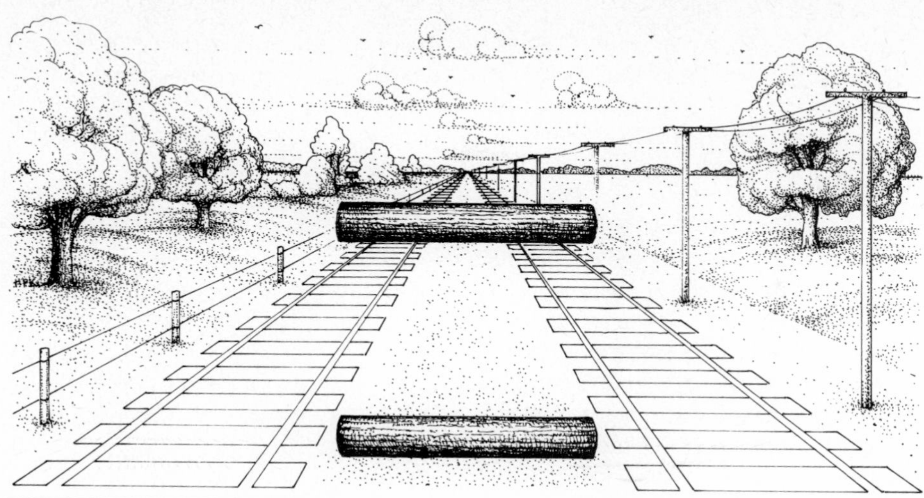

Fig. 8•27 Which log would you rather lift?

created by the two-dimensional drawings of illusory shapes and by the few natural illusions depends on some combination of conflicting spatial information, along with the absence of most of the information needed to discriminate the scene fully.

The Role of Experience in Perceiving Pictures Is being able to perceive pictures something that we have to learn to do, or is it independent of specific practice? The evidence on this subject is scant and somewhat contradictory.

In a dramatic study, Julian Hochberg and Virginia Brooks (1962) examined what happens to a child's ability to perceive pictures when that child has never before seen a picture. The Hochbergs raised one of their children in such a way that he saw no two-dimensional representations—no pictures on the wall, no cereal boxes, no TV, no billboards, and so forth. When the child reached the age of about eighteen months, he was tested for his ability to recognize familiar three-dimensional objects represented in two-dimensional drawings. First, he was asked to name different objects, such as shoe, cat, and chair. He was later given a picture of each object he named correctly and asked to name the object depicted. The child gave the correct name to nearly every picture, despite the fact that he had no experience either in seeing pictures or in naming an object from its picture. Apparently the ability to perceive objects in pictures is substantially unlearned.

Other work, however, suggests that experience does play a role in picture perception. Many experiments have been done with members of cultures where virtually no two-dimensional representations are seen in an entire lifetime. In one such study (Deregowski, 1972), perceivers were asked to describe objects and their spatial relationships in pictures (Figure 8•28). The subjects had no trouble recognizing the objects depicted (thus confirming that object perception in two-dimensional representations is unlearned), but they often had great difficulty in perceiving the placement of objects in space. Thus, the subjects' perceptions of

The Changing Sizes of the Moon—A Natural Visual Illusion

Two thousand years ago, Ptolemy made the first recorded speculation on why the moon appears larger when it is near the earth's horizon than when it is overhead. Since then many theories have been proposed, but none has yet survived critical tests. The explanation outlined here seems to have the greatest support at the moment.

The physical size of the moon does not change as it traverses the sky, nor does its distance from the earth change significantly. Thus, the size of the projection of the moon on our retina is constant, and the apparent size changes are illusory. This illusion affects virtually all perceivers, and it persists despite the perceiver's knowledge of careful measurements or analysis to the contrary. It does not matter whether you know why the illusion occurs—the moon still seems to be larger when it is near the horizon.

Very far away objects of unknown size, such as the sun, moon, and stars, are interpreted to be at some far but finite distance. We have no way to perceive how far away these objects are because the sky contains no ground upon which a scale of space can be constructed, and so we treat all objects in the sky similarly. Although the sun is nearly 400 times farther away than the moon is, they both seem to be the same distance away. When the moon is seen near the horizon, a scale of space stretches away from us toward it. However, no matter how far we can see along that scale, the moon is beyond the end of the scale. Therefore, when the moon or sun is near the horizon, we misinterpret its distance away as being farther than its distance when it is overhead.

If two objects subtending equal visual angles appear to be at different distances from the perceiver, then he or she will interpret the objects' sizes as being different. If the overhead moon is perceived as nearer than the horizon moon, then even though the retinal sizes projected by both moons are identical, the overhead moon will be visually constructed as smaller than the horizon moon.

Several tests of this explanation have been tried so far, with mixed results. When perceivers are asked about when the moon looks closer—at the horizon or overhead—they usually *but not always* say it looks closer when it is overhead. If perceivers are tested where a horizon is absent (such as looking horizontally from a high-flying plane at night when the ground is invisible), they judge the straight-ahead and overhead moons to be about *but not exactly* the same size. In the former test, the illusion does not completely persist; in the latter case, it does not completely disappear. Therefore, the explanation we have proposed here may not constitute the complete answer to why the moon's size appears to change at the horizon.

the size of the elephant and of the antelope were usually determined by the objective size of the animals drawn rather than by their real-life sizes. Apparently, neither the perspective information in the drawing nor knowledge from past experience that elephants are larger than antelopes, was utilized. Therefore, some of the strategies used for perceiving depth in two-dimensional pictures must not be available to perceivers who have had no experience in viewing such pictures.

Further work needs to be done on the role of experience in perceiving pictures in order to determine which strategies about depth are learned and how rapidly the learning process takes place.

Memory for the Content of Pictures In one experiment (Standing, Conezio, and Haber, 1970), college students were briefly shown over 2500 candid photographs taken by amateur photographers. Some students had ten seconds to look at each picture, while others had only one second. The students were later shown photographic pairs, each of which contained one photograph from the set they had seen, and one photograph they had not seen before. The students were able to pick out the familiar photograph from each of many hundreds of pairs more than 90 percent of the time; for some students, this number was 98 percent. They were able to recognize the familiar photographs regardless of whether they were tested on the same day that they saw the last of the 2500 photographs or on the following day, whether they had originally been given one second or ten seconds to look at each photograph, and even whether they saw the familiar photograph in its original or in its mirror-imaged orientation.

Fig. 8•28 Two examples of drawings used to test for the importance of experience in perceiving flat pictures. (From Deregowski, 1972)

Perhaps the students were able to recognize so many pictures because photographs of real objects or scenes have an internal organization and a coherence that provide many highly correlated sources of information upon which recognition can be based. To test this theory, Joan Freedman and Ralph Haber (1974), showed their subjects drawings such as those in Figure 8•29. The subjects saw each drawing for five seconds. For each drawing presented, some subjects saw a face and some did not. When a picture was viewed more than once by the same subject, sometimes a face was seen and sometimes not. The drawings themselves did not change, and so the change in perception must have occurred in the perceiver, who had sometimes organized a percept and sometimes not.

The subjects were then shown a larger set of drawings that contained all of the original ones plus an equal number they had never seen. They were asked to indicate for each one whether they saw a face, and whether the drawing was familiar. For the drawings in which they could see a face, the subjects were accurate in reporting whether it was new or old; but if they could not see a face in the drawing, then they were at chance level (50–50) in being able to tell whether it was new or old. Recognition memory was excellent for the drawings the perceiver had been able to organize, but the same drawing perceived as a random assortment of blobs was not remembered at all.

These findings suggest that the organizational process in perception is critically important for an initial coherent perception and for a memory of what was seen previously. This experiment does not explain why picture memory is excellent; but because this area of research is an active one, answers are likely to be forthcoming.

Fig. 8•29 Two examples of faces shown only in highlights. (From Mooney, 1957)

Summary Three-dimensional perception uses principles not applicable to flat pictures, although early researchers hoped to apply the results of studying simple pictures to the perception of the real world. Leonardo da Vinci analyzed natural depth perception and applied the principles he discovered to his artistic work. Four centuries later, Gestalt psychologists analyzed how two-dimensional displays are organized, or grouped, to produce certain perceptions. Among the laws of organization they identified are the principles of proximity, similarity, common fate, continuity, closure, and good figure.

Theories of pattern recognition and identification have focused on the nature of the stored representation and on the comparison process. The theory of template matching between a visual stimulus and stored experience requires an infinite store and is therefore implausible. The theory of feature analysis postulates fewer

How Much Do You See in a Single Flash?

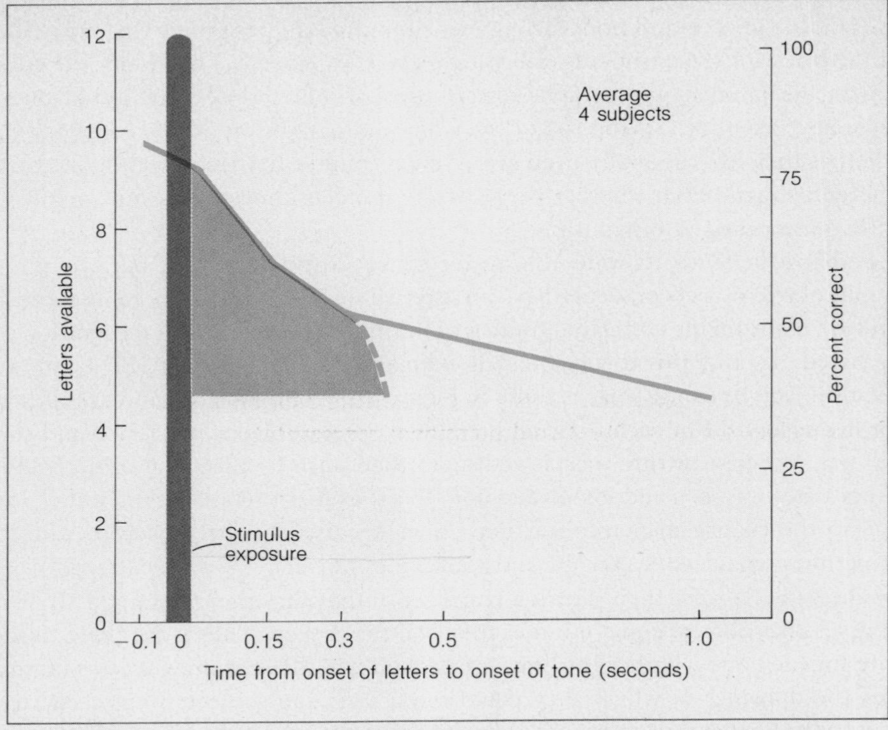

Fig. 8B·1 Number of letters correctly reported as a function of the delay of the tone afterward. (From Sperling, 1960)

Have you ever viewed a bunch of random objects for only a second or two and then tried to name as many of them as you could? Typically, recall is much less than perfect in this situation. Was there not enough time even to see the features of all the objects, or does the loss come in processing the information?

George Sperling (1960) devised an experimental technique to answer these questions and to gain some knowledge about the properties of iconic information storage. He arranged letters into 3 rows of 4 letters each with no repeating letters. The subject was told that he would be shown such 12-letter arrays, and that he should report all the letters he could remember. Each exposure duration was 0.05 second. The average number of letters correct was between 4 and 5, or between 35 and 40 percent. When only one row of 4 letters was presented, the subjects averaged 3.5 letters correct. (This number of 4 to 5 does not change no matter how many letters are presented.)

Sperling changed the task to one where the subject was told to report only one row of 4 letters each time, rather than all 12 letters. The row to be reported would be indicated by a tone: a high pitch for the top row, a low pitch for the bottom row, and a medium pitch for the middle row. The tone would sound just before, during, or after the 0.05 second flash of the array of letters.

When the tone began just as the flash ended, the subject had no prior knowledge of which row he would be expected to report, and so the subject had to preserve the features of all 12 letters in the array after their flash terminated. On this particular task, Sperling's subjects averaged about 3.3 correct out of 4 or 83 percent—about the same as if only one row had been presented. Therefore the subjects must have had available virtually all the features of all 12 letters (83 percent of 12 is 10, or 3.3 letters per row).

In this experiment, Sperling varied the time between the end of the flash and the tone. The data presented in Figure 8B·1 suggest that as long as the tone sounds within about 0.3 second after the flash ends, not many features of the display are lost. Apparently for this period of time, there is some storage of information about the letters (shown in the figure by the shaded area).

This experiment provided knowledge about two aspects of iconic storage. First, nearly all of the features of the stimulus are contained in the store immediately after a visual presentation, regardless of how few of them are used by the perceiver to report a letter. Second, storage persists for less than 0.5 second.

elements in storage and has gained some support, but how the feature relationships are stored in such a model is not yet understood.

Visual illusions in flat drawings have attracted psychologists' attention because they seem to be based on a manipulation of cues that causes us to misinterpret the scene. Not all visual illusions can yet be explained, but most seem to result from a combination of conflicting spatial information and an absence of the information needed to resolve the conflict.

Experiments designed to determine which depth-perception strategies used for two-dimensional pictures are learned and how rapidly such learning takes place have not been conclusive. However, research on memory for the content of pictures shows that human beings are remarkably good at recognizing photographs they have seen before only briefly. Recent experiments using incomplete drawings of human faces suggest that facility in recognizing pictures may be related to how the perceiver organizes the two-dimensional representation.

The Information-Processing Approach to Perception

8•5 The concept of perception as a *system of processing information* currently guides a great deal of perceptual research on the stages, or stores, through which the perceiver progresses while constructing a percept of a visible object or scene. As yet, we do not know enough about either the nature of the stages or the neural organization of the brain to locate the specific cortical centers responsible for each stage, and until these stages are identified neurophysiologically and related to specific brain centers and neural mechanisms, we are limited to an information-processing model of perception. In this context, *processing* means changing, translating, refining, reducing, or otherwise altering information so that it becomes more useful and can be better saved, better retrieved, or better related to previously processed information. *Information* means the content of the visual scene, of the retinal projection, or of any of the processing stages; it is changed and represented differently at each stage and must be processed before it can be transferred from one stage to the next.

Perception is not immediate. It takes time for processing to occur, and that time is divided among the separate stages which contain information as (1) a pattern of light energies distributed over the retina, (2) a set of visual features extracted from the retinal projection, (3) a constructed percept that interprets features from sequences of retinal projections, (4) a verbal description (name of the percept or of the separate objects it contains), and (5) a conceptual understanding of what has been seen. The interrelationships among these and the other stages are shown in the flow diagram in Figure 8•30. Each box corresponds to a stage, and each arrow to a process or set of operations.

We have already discussed how the information on the retinal projection (the first stage) is coded into visual features (the first process) and sent to the primary visual cortex. In this part we shall discuss the four stages that have drawn the greatest attention from researchers.

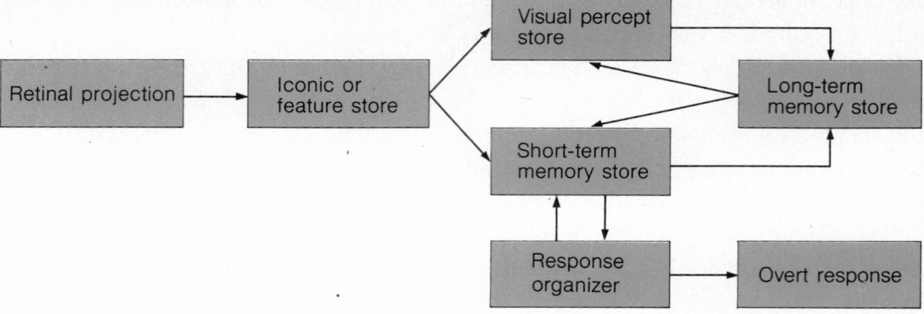

Fig. 8·30 An information-processing model illustrating the more important stores and processes of the visual system.

Iconic Store The second stage is called the *iconic store;* it contains a set of features (lines, angles, curves, colors, movements, and so forth) from a retinal projection and is the first representation of information in the visual cortex. The *icon* contains the features of the entire retinal projection, including those from the fovea and the less distinct features from the retinal areas surrounding the fovea. The coding of the icon is visual, automatic, and independent of higher-level knowledge, past experience, or expectations. Although the latter three variables determine how the icon is processed for transfer to the next stage and strongly influence what is represented there, they do not affect the content of the icon itself.

Features stay in the iconic store long enough to be completely processed, but they must be transferred to the third stage before a new set of features arrives from the first stage (the retinal projection). Otherwise, features from one fixation could become confused with features from a subsequent fixation. Once a retinal stimulation is coded on the icon, processing can continue to completion even if the stimulation terminates. Processing in iconic store can safely persist for 0.2 second because only one saccadic eye movement can occur in that time interval.

In a study of iconic store processing time, Ralph Haber and Lionel Standing (1969) showed a subject a series of light flashes, each lasting 0.01 second. The subject was asked whether the flash completely disappeared after it was presented. If the answer was yes, then the time interval between each flash was shortened; if the answer was no, then the interval between flashes was increased. By varying this interval, a time value was reached for which the subject said the flash just faded. This value was close to 0.2 second for all subjects tested. Because the flash itself lasted for only 0.01 second, the difference of 0.19 second must have been due to persistence of the coding of the flash in the visual cortex.

These results seem consistent with visual displays in normal viewing, where each pattern of stimulation lasts about 0.2 second and is then replaced by another pattern as the eye makes a saccade. Other experiments indicate that saccadic suppression discretely separates the features of one fixation from those of the next. These studies suggest that if, during the 0.2-second persistence interval, the perceiver does not completely code or process the icon for transfer to the next store, then all information from that fixation is lost when the next set of features arrives at the iconic store from the subsequent fixation.

The short persistence of features in the iconic store represents an important aspect of selectivity in perception. The iconic store is probably synchronized to the duration of each fixation that the eyes make, so that at any given time it contains only the features of one retinal projection.

The information in the iconic store can have four different fates. First, features may not be processed and therefore they become lost. Second, features may be compared with each other but not processed further. They will therefore be replaced when the features of the next retinal projection arrive. For example, the visual-search experiments by Ulric Neisser (1963) suggest that when a round letter is sought from among angular ones, the searcher attends only to the feature of curving and does not process the features into letter names or remember them. This strategy probably occurs only when the task demands are so specific that the feature shapes alone provide sufficient information.

The third and fourth fates that iconic features can have involve further processing, and storing the resulting information in subsequent stages.

Visual Percept Store Iconic features are processed for transfer into the *visual percept store* according to the expectations, past experience, learning strategies, and knowledge of the perceiver. The process of constructing a visual percept was implied in our discussion of how we construct a panoramic representation of the three-dimensional visual world by coding the information in the retinal projection and transmitting it to the visual cortex. When we process information about texture densities, gradients, and discontinuities, for example, we are transferring information from the iconic store to the visual percept store.

The visual percept store puts together information from successive iconic stores (from different fixations). The visual percept therefore represents the entire visual world and is larger, more complete, clearer, and longer lasting than any single fixation.

An important aspect of percepts is that they can be re-created from prior stimulation. If we are asked to imagine the face of someone very familiar, such as a close relative or friend, we will "see" an image of that face. The percept is not usually so vivid or clear as a percept of the same face when it is immediately before our eyes, but it is something we see—it is not merely an idea or a concept: This special kind of remembering is uniquely visual.

Look again at Figure 8•30. The arrows pointing into the visual percept from both short-term and long-term memory (two stages we shall discuss shortly) imply that we can construct a percept not only from ongoing stimulation, but also from prior stimulation stored in the more permanent stages. Although fewer studies have been made of the process of re-creating percepts (imagery) than of creating percepts from current stimulation, more research on this interesting topic will undoubtedly be done.

Short-term Memory Store When a perceiver wishes to attach names or labels to the objects in his visual field, he processes the visual features differently than if he merely wishes to construct a percept of them. We know relatively little about how this processing is done for the names of objects, but much has been learned about naming letters and words—a task adults do with great facility whenever they read print. Research on the latter process shows that perceivers use a number of different strategies, some of which depend heavily on the task and on how meaningful the reading material is.

In one study, George Sperling (1963) asked perceivers to report the letters they saw arrayed in a flash; each trial contained between two and six randomly chosen letters that did not spell anything. Because Sperling was interested only in the transfer of information from iconic store to short-term memory store, he decided to limit the time the features would be available for processing in the iconic store. He therefore followed each presentation with a flash of visual noise—in this case, a pattern of random squiggles—to either replace the letter features in the iconic store or obliterate them. The time between the onset of the letter-array flash and the onset of the visual-noise flash represented all the processing time that is available to a perceiver.

The results of Sperling's experiment are shown in Figure 8•31. If the subjects had processing times of 0.02 second or less, they could not correctly report any letter, no matter how many were presented. If they had 0.03 second, the subjects could report one letter (usually the leftmost one in the array); if 0.04 second, two letters; and so forth. Apparently, about 0.01 second was required for the features of each letter to be processed into short-term memory store, and each letter was processed successively, starting with the leftmost letter.

Sperling's study is important because it measured the time required for transferring information from iconic store to short-term memory store. It also identified another important characteristic of the short-term memory store—its limited capacity, illustrated by the fact that the most letters correctly reported was five, even from arrays of six letters. Only about four or five unrelated letters were held in short-term memory at any one time.

If Sperling had allowed a processing time of 0.1 second, would the subjects have been able to report correctly arrays nine letters long? We know from the work of Sperling and of many other researchers that the subjects could not have done so. Research evidence suggests that although all the features from the entire retinal projection are represented in the iconic store, the short-term memory store can hold only a few names or labels at a time; and others are lost.

What happens if the letters in an array spell a word, so that the letter sequences are predictable? For example, if the language used is English and if the initial letter is *t*, the second letter must be *h, r, w, y,* or a vowel. Apparently knowledge of permissible letter sequences such as these enable perceivers to scan the features of an icon rapidly, and after they identify the initial letter in this example as *t*, then they must compare the features of the second letter against only the nine permissible letters rather than against all 26 letters of the alphabet. Therefore,

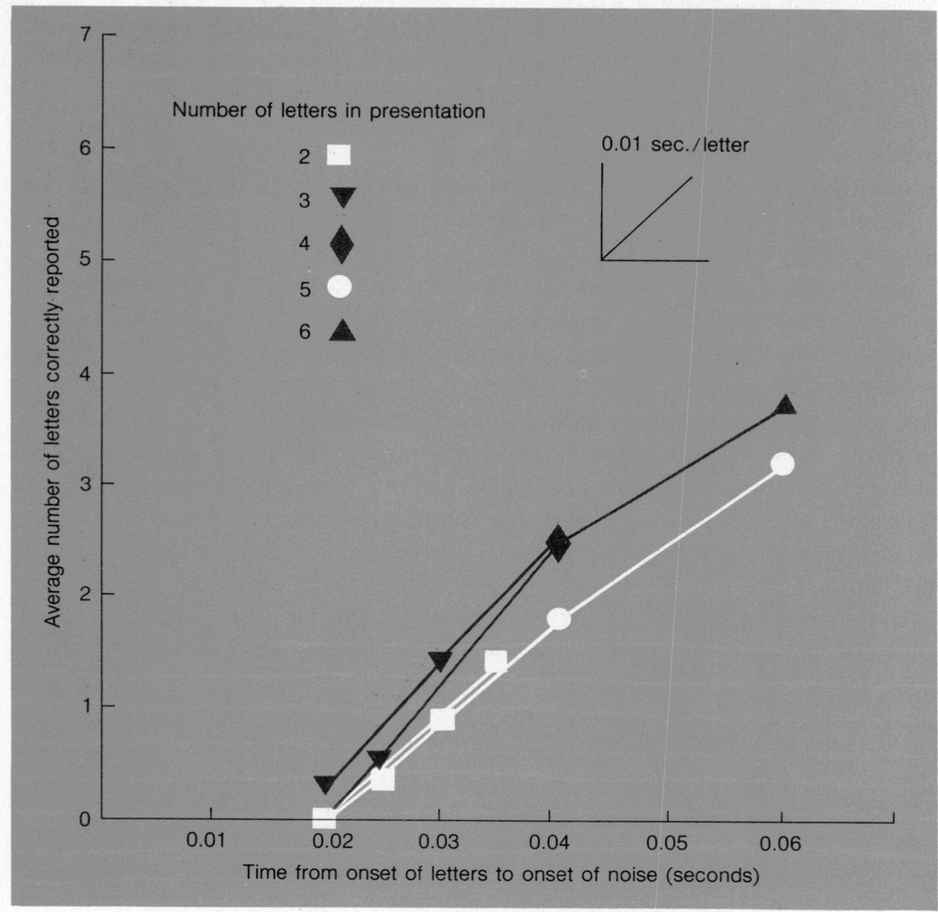

Fig. 8·31 The average number of letters correctly reported as a function of the time allowed for processing. (From Sperling, 1963)

processing times for letter arrays that spell words are much shorter than they are for random-letter arrays. However, even this suggestion is too simple.

Research evidence suggests that words are processed as a *chunk*, or unit, rather than letter by letter or even from left to right. Perceivers must therefore be able to use the features from all the letters simultaneously, while applying their knowledge of the shape of the entire word rather than of each letter. Furthermore, as we need not completely process each letter in order to identify the word it contains, so we need not completely process every word in a sentence in order to read. (We shall consider reading as a visual-information-processing task later in this chapter.)

The concept of a chunk was introduced by George Miller (1956) to describe the nature of the limit on how much information can be held in short-term memory at any one time. Miller's experiments showed that this limit was about seven single, unrelated items (such as a letter, a word, or a number), and that the number varied for different kinds of tasks. Miller further suggested that if we could combine, or *recode*, several related items to form a new larger unit (a chunk), no more space would be taken up in short-term memory than was occupied by any one of the chunk's components. For example, each letter of Sperling's random arrays constituted a single item, and Sperling's subjects could hold no more than four or five of these letters in short-term memory store at any one time. However, according to Miller, if the letters in an array spell a word, the perceiver will code them as a word rather than as separate letters (chunk the letters together into a single item). A perceiver should therefore be able to store four or five separate words as easily as four or five unrelated letters.

Recoding may occur as features are processed into the short-term memory store, or after the named items are already in short-term memory. Apparently chunking letters into words occurs during feature processing of the icon, which explains why neither the number of letters nor the left-to-right sequence that characterizes processing arrays of unrelated letters is manifested in the processing of real words. However, chunking of unrelated words may occur later—as in anagram solving, where each letter must be named separately and later organized into a chunk. (The study of chunking that occurs after items have been named is usually part of research on verbal learning rather than on perception and will be covered further in Chapter 11.)

An important aspect of short-term memory, in addition to its limited capacity, is its relatively brief life span. While items held there persist longer than features in the iconic store do, persistence time is usually in seconds. Can you hold a telephone number you just looked up for as long as ten seconds without forgetting any of the digits? But we can remember telephone numbers and the names of items we perceive longer than ten seconds. When we do this, two related processes are involved:

1. We can rehearse (repeat as a group) the items in the short-term memory store. For reasons we do not yet entirely understand, this repetition process either reduces the chances that we will forget any of the items, or it extends the time limit within which we can remember all the items.
2. We can transfer the item held in short-term memory to a more permanent store, which considers the meanings of the names or items rather than trying to remember isolated units. This technique also involves rehearsal, but it is fundamentally a process that transforms information from names (short-term memory) into concepts or meanings (long-term memory).

Long-term Memory Store If perceivers use their knowledge and past experience to process current stimulation, that knowledge must be stored and maintained somewhere. That store is usually called long-term memory, a term implying that its capacity is large (perhaps even infinite) and that its contents persist for a long time (perhaps even a lifetime). Although we know something about the capacity and content persistence of this store, we know very little about how images or percepts and labels are processed into meanings. We know that additional steps

The late Arturo Toscanini (1867–1957) was known for his ability to conduct without having a score to refer to. Presumably the information he needed was stored in long-term memory. (NBC)

for these processes must exist because we find losses in the literal memory of percepts or words but few losses in the conceptual memory of their meaning. After a delay, a perceiver will accept a synonym in place of the original word, and a substitute picture with the same content and organization as the one he was shown earlier.

Although research on the processing, or transfer, of information from short-term to long-term memory has traditionally been the province of psychologists studying verbal learning rather than perception, such studies are relevant to both fields and should therefore foster an exchange of information among the scientists concerned with this topic.

Summary Visual perception can be considered as an information-processing system wherein information in one form is changed, translated, refined, reduced, or otherwise altered to become more useful and better saved, retrieved, or related to previously processed information. Information in visual perception refers to the content of the visual scene, of the retinal projection, or of any of the processing stages. It takes time for processing to occur, and that time is believed to be divided into separate stages, each of which contains different information. As yet not enough is known about the neurophysiology involved to specify the cortical centers involved at each stage, and so research has focused instead on the steps that perceivers go through in order to perceive and to know what is in the visual field.

The iconic store stores features such as lines, angles, curves, hues, and movement independently of higher-level knowledge, past experience, or expectations. The latter aspects become operative at later stages. Evidence for the iconic store comes from experiments in which subjects reported the fading time of lights briefly flashed on the retina and from experiments on the duration of saccadic suppressions. The information contained in the icon will be replaced by the next retinal projection and lost unless it is processed for transfer to the next store. Sometimes processing at the iconic store stage involves simple feature comparisons, such as when we search for a letter among different shapes.

Does Memory Always Get Worse?

A typical experiment in memory recall presents some material to be learned and then, after learning has occurred, tests for how much can be recalled. Recall is poorer if the learners are tested a day later than it is when they are tested immediately after learning. The trend is downward: the longer the delay between learning and recall, the less is recalled. The experimental literature is replete with such facts, which agree with most everyday experience.

A number of recent experiments show that under some conditions, however, memory improves over time. Matthew Erdelyi and Joan Becker (1974) presented two groups of subjects with 60 items: one group saw 60 simple sketches of single objects, while the other group saw the 60 words that described each object. The subjects were asked to recall as many as they could, and to guess at any they could not recall. Each group of subjects had three recall trials. Half of the subjects in each group made the three recall attempts one right after the other. The other half had a few minutes between each attempt during which they were to think about the stimuli (words or pictures) they had just seen.

As can be seen from Figure 8C·1, reported recall of pictures gets better, while it changes little for words. Furthermore, thinking about the stimuli between recall attempts helps for pictures, but not for words. Erdelyi has shown this same pattern of results in several other studies with different experimental designs.

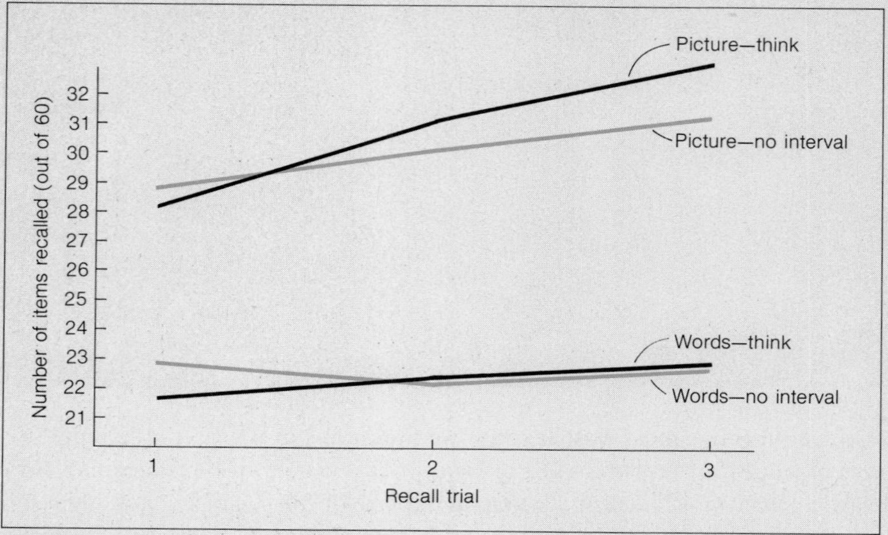

Fig. 8C·1 Recall improves with successive trials, for pictures but not for words.

What is it about pictures that makes it possible for us to remember more of them over time rather than less? Erdelyi proposes several explanations, one of which is that pictures permit a greater mental imagery (internal visualization of the stimuli) than normally occurs with words. This imagination process helps recall. In fact, a few of the subjects from the word group reported after testing that they had tried to visualize, or form mental images of, the words. These few subjects demonstrated improved memory for words even though the word group as a whole did not improve in recall.

Recognition memory for pictures is superior to that for words. Erdelyi therefore suggests that if all the pictures are in storage and if the subject is motivated to devote enough time and attention to recalling them, he or she could perhaps recall them all. In a recent study, Erdelyi (1976) showed that with repeated recall attempts over a week's time, subjects recalled virtually all the pictures they saw, but word recall did not improve.

These results are intriguing because of the light they shed on some of the special characteristics of perception and memory for pictures.

At the visual percept stage, information is put together from successive iconic stores according to our expectations, experience, learning strategies, and knowledge. This process occurs in panoramic perception, in which a percept is constructed from successive visual fixations. The visual percept stage can also reconstruct prior stimulation, such as images of an object that is no longer in the visual scene.

At the short-term memory stage, the perceiver gives names or labels to the features present in the visual field. Research by Sperling suggests that the time course for transferring the features of letters from the iconic store to the short-term memory store is about 0.01 second per letter, up to about four or five unrelated letters. Words are processed individually in a single chunk at a faster rate than that required to identify each of the letters the word contains. Research by Miller shows that short-term memory is limited to four or five items regardless of whether those items are unrelated letters or whole words. Items held in short-term memory persist longer than features held in iconic store, and rehearsing the content of short-term memory helps to transform that information into a more permanent form.

The long-term memory store is exceedingly large and long lasting. How material in long-term memory is transformed from units to concepts is not well understood, but it is known that items may be lost from long-term memory without a consequent loss of meaning.

Reading As Visual Processing

8•6 Reading is one of the most complex and important visual tasks. In spite of nearly one hundred years of research, we do not yet fully understand the reading process or how its visual and cognitive components interact—but reading illustrates this interplay perhaps better than any other task we have yet discussed.

Eye Movements in Reading Our eyes move over texts in regular patterns (Figure 8•32). Every second, a literate adult makes three or four saccades, each lasting between 0.02 and 0.03 second; the fixations between saccades last from 0.25 to 0.3 second. Saccades are usually to the right along the line (for reading most languages), but leftward regressive eye movements do occur.

Reading speed is usually stated in units of the number of words read in one minute. An average college student can read an easy novel at the rate of about 300 words per minute. To read a difficult textbook, the student might have to slow to a rate of 100 words or less per minute. In addition to the text's difficulty, reading speed is affected by the reader's comprehension skills (ability to understand and paraphrase the text, and to identify new words). Persons who comprehend well usually read relatively quickly, but the relationship between comprehension and reading speed is neither linear nor constant among readers. Some persons, either self-taught or taught in a speed-reading course, can read easy material at speeds of

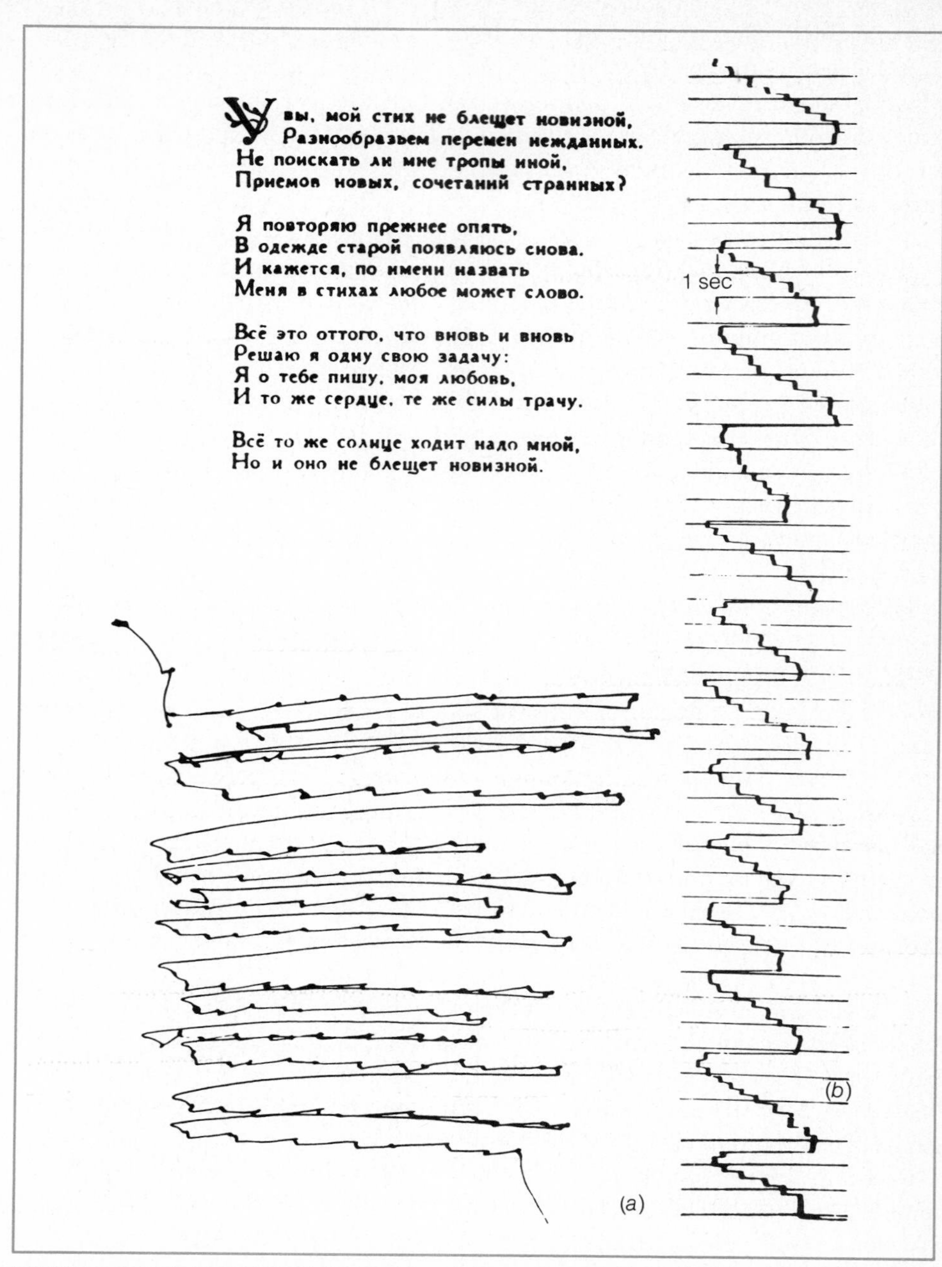

Fig. 8·32 Two different recordings of eye movements made while a perceiver is reading a Russian poem. (From Yarbus, 1967)

1000 to 5000 words per minute; a few persons can read faster than 10,000 words per minute.

Duration of fixation and saccade speeds are about the same for both easy and difficult texts, and for good readers and poor ones. However, if the text is easy, we move our eyes farther during each saccade so that we make fewer fixations per line, thus saving time and increasing reading speed. We also make fewer regressions on easy text; a typical college student reading easy material makes less than one regression for every ten eye movements. For difficult material such as a foreign language grammar, this ratio can increase to five regressions for every ten eye movements—that is, every other eye movement goes back over something that was read before.

The human eye makes an average of 3.5 fixations per second, or 210 fixations per minute. If the average word on the page you are now reading contains 6 character spaces (including the space following each word) and you read at the rate of 300 words per minute (1800 character spaces per minute), each fixation will cover about 1.4 words (8.5 character spaces). However, if you read this page at a rate of 105 words per minute, then each word is looked at twice because each fixation covers only half a word. Thus, only at speeds greater than 300 words per minute is the eye skipping more than an occasional word. At 2000 words per minute, the eye lands on about every tenth word; most lines are therefore fixated only once.

Extraction of Meaning Knowing what the eye is doing does not help us to understand how we comprehend the text or extract its meaning. How meaning is represented in language will be discussed in Chapter 11, but perceptual research suggests some clear hypotheses about how meaning is extracted from what we read. We know that comprehending what is read is an active process; the reader has to pursue perceptual strategies of construction in order to extract meaning from a text.

Some older theories of reading comprehension suggest that reading is a stepwise progression of increasingly higher levels of processing, the lowest step of which is the coding of the graphic shapes on the page into visual features. These features are then named as letters, the letters are combined into a word, the word is combined with other constructed words into a complete sentence, and so forth. This theory is appealing because it is simple; but it is wrong, for several reasons:

1. Good readers are able to read faster than this process would permit.
2. We frequently fail to notice misspellings, typographical errors, and even incorrect words. If we progressed from letters to words to sentences, we should always notice letter combinations that make no sense or are incorrect or misplaced.
3. Nearly all words in English have more than one meaning, but most sentences are unambiguous. This lack of ambiguity occurs because the meaning of a sentence is specified by its syntactic context, which we grasp before we comprehend the specific meaning of each word the sentence contains.

Apparently, readers begin to construct the meaning of a sentence from a hypothesis about what they are going to read. This hypothesis is constructed from what they have read up to that point, including the previous sentences, their general knowledge of the topic, and what they have abstracted from the author's style and point of view. The constructions, or hypotheses, are primarily about meaning, and only secondarily about specific words.

The first task for the reader is not to identify letters or even individual words, but rather the structure of the sentence. Some cues about sentence structure are provided by the distribution of word lengths in the sentence. Articles and prepositions are short, pronouns are short compared to the nouns they stand for, prepositional phrases have a characteristic structure defined by the lengths of the words they contain, and so forth. A single fixation allows us to see the distribution of word lengths for several words on either side of the fixated word without processing the side words. The same fixation also provides information about the shapes of several words off to each side. The most frequently occurring of the many three-letter words in English have different shapes (*the* does not resemble *was*).

The information provided by the shape of words and their lengths enables us to make hypotheses about words as well as about sentence structure. We use this information along with the features of the letters the words contain to verify or revise our hypotheses. Therefore, we do not need to process all the letters of a word to identify it, and we may not notice a typographical error, especially if it occurs as a letter we need not identify in order to construct the word it is part of.

Ask a friend to read a newspaper story aloud to you as accurately but as rapidly as possible and tape-record the reading. If you then carefully compare the tape recording to the original text, you will find many discrepancies. Most of the errors will be substitutions of a synonym. Occasionally changing one word will throw the syntax off, necessitating that several more words be changed in order for the reading to be grammatical. In the majority of such cases, the reader does not pause and is not often aware of the substitutions because they are consistent with the reader's hypotheses about the meaning of the text, even though the words may not be literally the same as those in the text. Several literal versions of a story can be derived from its meaning, depending on what parts of the text's sentences the reader actually constructed.

This view of reading is similar to that described for looking at scenes and pictures. The end product in both cases is a construct: for reading, it is a meaning; for scenes and pictures, it is a percept. In both cases the perceiver's construction is based on the visual features and on the expectation about how these quantities should be organized together to make a coherent result.

Experiments have been devised to test the theory that hypotheses about meaning guide reading. In one such study (Haber, Haber, and Rosenberg, 1976) college students were asked to read a series of brief stories. Each story began with only a few sentences, ending randomly in the middle of a sentence. The reader had to read the story from the beginning and, when the end was reached, to guess the next word. As soon as the missing word was correctly guessed, that word and some more of the story appeared. The reader continued as before, reading to an end and guessing the missing word, until the entire story had been presented and read.

When the stories were difficult, the correct word was guessed about 20 percent of the time. This is in itself a surprisingly high percentage, for it implies that of the thousands of possible words, the reader's uncertainty is only one word among the five words that would be appropriate to the story at that point. When the stories were easy, the guessing accuracy increased to about 40 percent. In both conditions, the readers were constructing hypotheses about what was to come based on what they had already read.

In another facet of this experiment, the reader was given the number of letters or the outline of the word to be guessed. This cue doubled the accuracy of guessing to well over 80 percent for easy stories, clearly demonstrating that readers use information about word length and word shape in extracting meaning from text.

The theory of reading presented here is not new, but only in the last few years has it been taken seriously enough by experimenters to be rigorously tested. So far, it appears to be not only plausible but correct. This theory is a dramatic departure from the serial-decoding theory of reading, but it is consistent with the other aspects of visual perception discussed in this chapter.

Summary The interplay between visual and cognitive components in visual information processing is reflected in the reading process. Our eyes make three or four saccadic movements per second as they move over text. How far each saccade takes our eyes affects the speed with which we read. Reading rates for easy material are faster than they are for difficult texts because our eyes make fewer regressions on easy material. In general, readers who comprehend well read quickly.

Perceptual research has shown that extracting meaning from material is not a simple feature-building process. We have expectancies about what we are going to read based on what we have read previously. We modify our expectancies as reading progresses according to the meaning of the text, the shapes of words, and the distribution of word lengths. A letter or two in one or two words is usually sufficient to maintain the story line. This view of reading is similar to that described earlier for looking at scenes and pictures. The end product in reading is a meaning, while for scenes and pictures it is a percept.

Summary

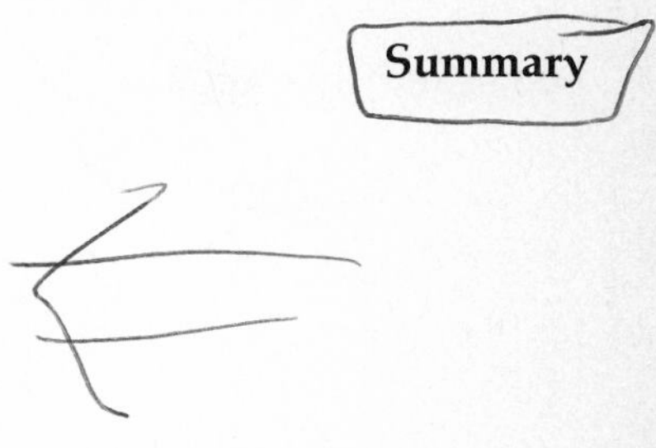

In this chapter we have seen how perceivers actively participate in the processes of visual perception. We use information from surface textures, densities, texture gradients, and projective shape to scale space and to discriminate objects. In moving through the visual scene, we integrate cues from occlusion, lighting effects, motion parallax, and accommodation in constructing percepts of objects in depth. No matter where we move or in what orientation we place ourselves, our perceptual strategies correlate with and reinforce each other.

We use several techniques to construct a single panoramic perception from the many successive fixations we make in a scene. As we move through space, we use the rates at which projections flow across our retinas, the apertures that open onto changing texture densities, saccadic suppression, and our expectancies about what we shall see to unify the visual world. We correlate efferent instructions from our brain to our eye muscles with afferent input from our retinas to our brain; if this relationship is temporarily disturbed, we can restore it by adaptation.

Experience plays an important part in our perceptions and influences our expectancies about the visual scene. It affects where we look, what we notice, what we process, and the extent of our processing. Our perceptions are also influenced by our motivation for a task, our feelings about a stimulus, and our unique temperament.

We are able to organize and perceive two-dimensional representations of real objects and scenes, usually without prior experience. We probably recognize and identify objects from their characteristic features. Visual illusions fool us, however, even when we understand the reasons why they work.

According to the information-processing theory of perception, we process information from the retinal projection through successive stores, or stages. We can stop processing at any stage; if we fail to process features in the iconic store, they will be lost after about 0.2 second when information from the next retinal projection arrives at the visual cortex. We integrate separate sources of information in the visual percept store according to our expectations, experience, and knowledge, and we can re-create images from prior stimulation. When we attach names or labels to percepts in order to identify them, they enter the short-term memory store, which can hold only a few items at a time. By processing stimuli in chunks or recoding existing items, we can hold more information in short-term memory. Information in the long-term memory store has meaning and permanence, and can be retrieved and processed back to the short-term memory and visual percept stores for further use.

When we read, we use both visual and cognitive strategies to process visual information. We make hypotheses concerning what we are about to read from what we have read before and from retinal projections of the shapes and distributions of words to either side of the fixated word. Reading is a vital perceptual process, requiring us to participate actively in extracting meaning from what we read.

Suggested Readings

Gregory, Richard. 1973. *Eye and brain: The psychology of seeing*. 2d ed. New York: McGraw-Hill.

——— 1970. *The intelligent eye.* New York: McGraw-Hill.

Two excellent paperback books covering basic topics in visual perception and applying them to art, painting, design, and nature.

Haber, Ralph N., and Hershenson, Maurice. 1973. *The psychology of visual perception.* New York: Holt, Rinehart & Winston.

Chapters 7 through 15 of this textbook on visual perception cover the same topics as are in this chapter, but at a more advanced level.

Zakia, Richard. 1975. *Perception and photography.* Englewood Cliffs, N.J.: Prentice-Hall.

A fine application of principles of perception to photography and to photographers.

Memory

9 Like many terms in psychology, **memory** is part of our everyday vocabulary, and it is important to see how the technical term is related to commonly used meanings of the word. Three of these meanings have psychological implications. First, memory is the ability to retain or reactivate past thoughts, images, or ideas (as in "I am losing my memory" or "Willie has a terrible memory"). Second, it is the content of a particular memory, either all of what one remembers (as in "Amnesia patients have no memory of their previous lives") or a memory of a specific event (such as "Peggy's memory of the lecture was accurate"). Third and most important as a psychological meaning, it is the act or process of remembering.

A superb description of memory as a process was written in 1885 by Hermann Ebbinghaus, a German psychologist who did the first experiments on memory.

> Mental states of every kind—sensations, feelings, ideas—which were at one time present in consciousness and then have disappeared from it, have not with their disappearance absolutely ceased to exist. Although the inwardly turned look may no longer be able to find them, nevertheless they have not been utterly destroyed and annulled, but in a certain manner they continue to exist stored up, so to speak, in the memory.
>
> We cannot, of course, directly observe their present existence but it is revealed by the effects which come to our knowledge with a certainty like that with which we infer the existence of the stars below the horizon.
>
> These effects are of several kinds. In the first group of cases we can call back into consciousness by an exertion of the will directed to this purpose, the seemingly lost states—that is, we can reproduce them voluntarily. During attempts of this sort—that is, attempts to recollect—all sorts of images toward which our aim was not directed accompany the desired images to the light of consciousness. Often indeed the latter entirely miss the goal, but as a general thing among the representations is found the one which we sought and it is immediately recognized as something formerly experienced. It is absurd to

suppose that our will has created it anew, as it were, out of nothing. It must have been present somehow or somewhere. The will, so to speak, has only discovered it and brought it to us again.

Ebbinghaus went on to consider spontaneous as opposed to intentional recall, but this brief passage captures the essence of what it means to remember. In somewhat more modern terms, memory refers to the processes involved in the storage and retrieval of information.

Psychologists may use the term *memory* to refer either to the ability to store and retrieve, to the content (the information stored and retrieved), or to the processes involved. It is important therefore to understand just what is being referred to when someone talks about memory. For the most part, this chapter will concentrate on the processes involved in the storage and retrieval of information.

How Memory Works

9·1 Information can be remembered only if it is put into the memory system (storage) and later got out of the memory system (retrieval).

Storage Storage involves two processes: **rehearsal** (attending to or keeping information in mind) and **coding** (putting information into a form different from that in which it was presented).

Hermann Ebbinghaus (1850–1909). Ebbinghaus showed that scientific methods could be used to study what was then considered one of the domains of philosophy—the thought processes involved in memory.

Rehearsal Rehearsal can itself be a form of memory, since you retain information as long as you are thinking about it. For example, you may look up a telephone number and say it over and over to yourself until you reach the telephone to dial it. Going over the information repeatedly is also an effective way to store information permanently. You are rehearsing when you memorize a poem or repeat French vocabulary words over and over.

Rehearsal maintains information for more or less immediate use, as in our example of looking up a telephone number. If your rehearsal of the number is disrupted before you dial it, the number will be mostly forgotten. If you get a busy signal, you will probably have to look up the number again before dialing. But if you repeatedly get a busy signal (and therefore repeatedly dial), you may eventually remember the number, even though you made no attempt to memorize it.

These effects can be seen in a traditional experiment on **memory span,** in which the subject is read a string of digits and asked to repeat them immediately. Most people have difficulty remembering a string of nine or more digits and will make mistakes when asked to repeat the string. If the subject is given a series of nine-digit strings to repeat and the same string occurs every third time, recall will gradually improve for the repeated string but not for the others. Merely rehearsing a string long enough to maintain it momentarily produces a permanent residue that accumulates with repeated practice (Figure 9·1).

Thus information that is not rehearsed or committed to more permanent storage is lost. The maximum duration of this nonrehearsed information appears to be about twenty seconds.

Our capacity for rehearsal appears to be limited. The average number of items an adult can keep in memory is about seven—exactly the number of digits in a telephone number. Without using special tricks some people can hold nine or ten items, and almost every adult can retain at least five. Children have a smaller memory capacity.

Rehearsal is believed to be essentially verbal. That is, information must be coded into verbal form in order to be rehearsed. We have some evidence, however, that items such as pictures may be rehearsable as images.

Although the most important function of rehearsal seems to be maintaining information for immediate use, it may have another valuable function: holding information while it is being coded for more permanent storage. There is evidence that the longer information is rehearsed, the more likely it is to be permanently retained. The relationship is not perfect, however, and it is obviously not just the repetition of the information that is important. For example, attention to a word's formal properties, such as its sound, produces less effective later retrieval than attention to its meaning. Thus accessibility is determined not only by the time spent rehearsing but also by the kind of coding that takes place during that time.

Coding Coding is perhaps the most important memory function. It can be either *selective* or *elaborative*. When you see a stray dog, for example, you may remember that it was light brown but not that it was a light brown collie. Your attention was directed only to part of the information presented. At other times you may add to the information presented, as when you remember a word in terms of its meaning or in terms of an image of what the word refers to.

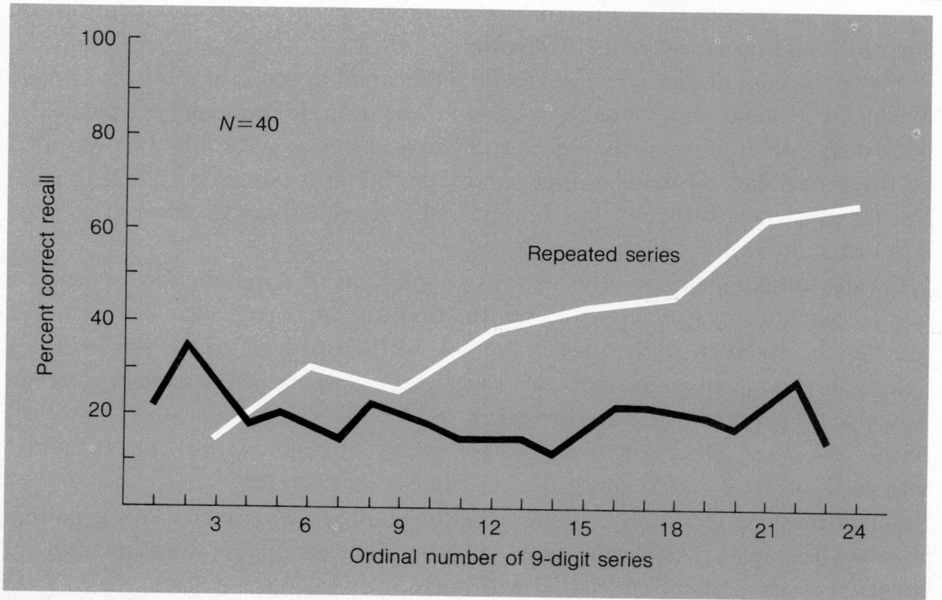

Fig. 9·1 This graph shows the correct recall of nine-digit number strings recalled immediately after presentation. The repeated series is a specific nine-digit sequence occurring in the 3rd, 6th, 9th . . . 24th position in the series of tests. Each of the other points is a nonrepeated nine-digit number. (Hebb, 1961)

Since telephone numbers have seven digits, they should be within the memory span of most people. (Andy Mercado)

Coding gives memory tremendous flexibility and power, as we shall see when we discuss mnemonics.

Retrieval Retrieval is remembering. Information that can be retrieved is said to be *accessible* in memory. Information that was once stored but can no longer be retrieved is said to be *lost*. Sometimes information is not immediately accessible but may be retrieved at another time or under somewhat different circumstances. Such information is said to be *available*.

These three aspects of retrieval can be understood in terms of a library analogy in which the books represent the items of information. If you look for a particular book on the shelf where it should be and you find it, it is accessible. If it was filed on the wrong shelf, it may be discovered later, but it is not accessible; it is available. If it has been stolen or has disappeared from the library in some other way, it is lost.

Recall—reproducing the information—is one kind of remembering. It may be *free,* as when all of the accessible information sought is retrieved. For example, you may be asked to study a list of words and then to recall those words in any order you choose. In contrast to this so-called "emptying of the memory," recall may also be *cued,* as when you are asked to remember a specific word in the list. In this case a cue tells you which word is wanted: "It begins with *f*," or "It rhymes with *log*," or "It contains moisture," or "It comes after *dog*."

Sometimes a cue is studied along with the word to be recalled. This is **paired-associate learning,** and it occurs when we try to learn vocabulary words in a foreign language or try to associate names with faces.

The Effectiveness of Retrieval Cues

Although it is well known that adequate cues are necessary for successful retrieval, we know little about what constitutes an adequate cue. Obviously, a cue that leads to successful retrieval is adequate, but can we specify what kinds of cues work and what kinds do not?

Experiments suggest one characteristic that seems to be necessary: an effective retrieval cue must be rehearsed, coded, or otherwise processed along with the to-be-retrieved information when it was being stored.

In one experiment (Tulving and Osler, 1968), people were given a list of 24 words to study with the intention of recalling them later. Each word to be recalled was presented either by itself or with another word that was somewhat but not strongly related to it. For example, *soar* was presented with *eagle,* and *fat* with *mutton.* The learners were told that these words might help them recall the list words later, but were given no further information. After they studied the list, their recall was tested either with or without the cues or "help" words. The people who had no cue word while studying recalled an average of 10.6 of the words when no cue words were present during the test. When the cue words were present, they recalled even fewer words (8.5). Although the cue words were somewhat related to the words to be recalled, they did not aid recall. The people who had the words present during the study period remembered 14.9 words. These results show that the cue words can be helpful, but only if they are presented, and presumably studied, along with the words to be recalled.

What happens when the cue words are strongly related (not weakly related as in the last experiment) to the recalled words? In another experiment (Thomson and Tulving, 1970), people studied a list of words presented either alone, with weak associates (*lamb—stupid*), or with strong associates (*dumb—stupid*) as cue words. They were then tested either without cues, with the weakly associated cues, or with the strongly associated cues. The people who studied without cues recalled 14.1 words when no cues were present at the test. However, these people recalled 19 words when the strongly associated cue words were present at recall. In other words, strongly related cues helped even when they weren't present during study.

Does this finding negate the basic principle that to be effective, a cue must be present at storage? Probably not. A plausible explanation is that strong cues, even when not presented during study, are likely to occur spontaneously. For example, if shown the word *stupid,* people are likely to think of *dumb* even though it isn't presented, while they are not likely to think of *lamb.* Thus the word *dumb* is not really a new cue word for *stupid.* The critical point is what happens when the weak cue word (for example, *lamb*) is presented during study and the strong cue word (*dumb*) is presented on the test. In this case recall drops to 13.9, which is no better than that obtained with no cues at all. Apparently, even a strongly associated cue word doesn't help, if it was blocked during study by the presence of another word.

Another experiment dramatically illustrates the importance of the cue word during study. This experiment (Tulving and Thomson, 1973) begins like the others; a list of words is presented with cue words that are weakly associated. The people who studied the list were then presented with words that would be likely to produce the words on the list as free associates. For example, if one of the words on the first list was *light,* the second list contained the word *dark.* When the people were asked to give associates to these words (that is, to think of words that the words on the second list reminded them of), they thought of 75 percent of the words on the original list. When asked to indicate which of the words were on the original list, however, they identified only 25 percent of them. Thus, in a recognition test without the original cue words, memory for the original list was very poor. After this test, the original cue words were presented and the people were asked to recall the original list. Recall was 63 percent. Recognition, which is typically much better than recall, was much poorer than recall unless the original cue words were present.

In general, all of these experiments make the same point. The effectiveness of a particular cue depends on what happens at storage—how the information to be recalled is coded. Cues are relatively ineffective if they are not involved with the original coding of the information to be recalled—even when the cues are capable of arousing the same memories in a different context.

Another kind of remembering is **recognition.** It is involved if you are asked whether a given word is in a list of words you have studied. This is a yes/no type of recognition. If you were asked to choose the correct word out of several, the recognition process would be multiple choice.

Often information can be neither recalled nor recognized, but its presence in memory can be indicated in another way called relearning or **savings,** which involves studying the same information again. If it takes less study time than it did earlier to reach the same level of recall or recognition, then there must have been some residue in memory even though the information was not accessible. After a given period of study, the number of items that can be retrieved by savings will be greater than the number that can be retrieved by recognition, which in turn will be greater than the number that can be retrieved by recall.

This variation does not, however, simply reflect the fact that recognition is a more sensitive indicator of what is in memory than recall. Rather, it shows that recognition and recall do not demand the same kind of information, a phenomenon well supported by experimental evidence. Some conditions affect recall without affecting recognition, or affect the two differently. For example, a list of words that can be organized into categories such as fruits, animals, sports, and professions is typically easier to recall than a list of unrelated words, but the related words are not usually easier to recognize. Furthermore, a list of uncommon words is usually easier to recognize, but common words are easier to recall. Such differences would not follow merely from recognition's being more sensitive.

Conditions of study also have an effect. Many experienced students report that they study one way for a multiple-choice examination (recognition) and another way for an essay examination (recall).

The value of this strategy has been supported by experiment. S. T. Carey and R. S. Lockhart asked students to memorize several lists of words and then tested them after each list had been presented and studied. Some students were consistently tested for recall, others for recognition. After the last list was presented and studied, the students who had been given recall tests on all previous trials were unexpectedly given a recognition test. These students scored lower on the test than did students who had been given recognition tests on previous trials. If sensitivity had been the only factor involved, the students studying for a recall test would have done *better* than the other students, since recall presumably demands better learning. The implication is that recall and recognition do not demand the same information. What the differences are has not been determined, but experienced students seem to know what is required and study appropriately.

Remembering

9·2 In view of the large amount of information stored in memory, our ability to remember specific items at the appropriate time is miraculous. Assuming that most of the information is available, how do we find what we want in such a huge store?

Organization Once again, the library provides a convenient analogy. You can find the book you want because the books are organized (by general topic, subtopic, and author's name). A book's exact location is also indicated by a code number.

Retrieval of information from memory follows a similar principle. There the organization takes several forms. Material may form into larger units, called **chunks,** with the chunk being coded in some way. Consider, for example, the digit string 176–839–452–461. Each set of three digits has been coded as a single unit, or chunk (for example, 176). Coding chunks in this way is such a powerful method that the same string broken down differently (for example, 17–683–945–24–61) will not even be recognized as the same string. The usual improvement in recallability shown in Figure 9•1 does not occur when the same string is repeated in a different grouping. even when the digits are written down each time they are presented (Bower and Winzenz, 1969).

Meaningful material is commonly dealt with by grouping things that are related in some way. People do this spontaneously even when the material is presented in a disorganized fashion. For example, if words standing for six animals, six fruits, six sports, and six professions are thrown together in random sequence and read to you, you will tend to recall them in groups of words with related meanings. This phenomenon, called **clustering,** may occur on the basis of conceptual categories or associative relations such as light/dark/black, or even in terms of formal properties such as similarities in sound.

Research on the recall of organized lists has shown that clusters function as if they were single units. One researcher, B. H. Cohen, has formulated what he calls the *some-or-none law.* He showed that people could almost always recall several words from a category if they could recall any of the words from that category. Recall failures consisted of omissions of entire categories—for example, all of the professions rather than some animals, some fruits, some sports, and some professions.

Organization in memory goes beyond the mere grouping of related information. More often information is organized into various kinds of *structures,* including *hierarchies* (sometimes called trees). You are probably familiar with the standard outline that organizes a lecture, film, or book chapter into headings and subheadings. Consider the following list of words:

platinum, bronze, limestone, sapphire, silver, ruby, granite, steel, aluminum, copper, gold, diamond, brass, lead, marble, emerald, iron, slate

Now consider the list in Figure 9•2. After three short study periods, people are able to recite the entire list of eighteen words perfectly. In one experiment, four separate sets of words totalling 112 words were arranged in this fashion. After about eleven minutes of study, they were perfectly retained by all of the students involved in the experiment. When presented in a random arrangement, only about one-half of the words could be recalled (Bower, Clark, Lesgold, and Winzenz, 1969).

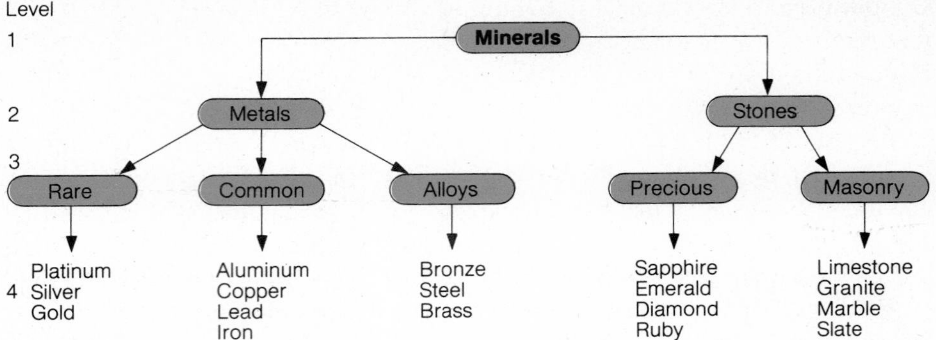

Fig. 9·2 A list of minerals arranged as a hierarchy. The various branch points are called nodes. (Bower, Clark, Lesgold, and Winzenz, 1969)

Many other organizational schemes may also help memory. Even linking ideas into a chain may be helpful. For example, in the chain *soldier, army, navy, ship, sail, canvas, bag, box, carry, truck* each word is related to the next one.

More complex forms of organization can be devised to fit the form of the material to be acquired. Some commercial courses in speed reading devote much of their instruction time to improving comprehension as well as the rate of reading, and the approach to comprehension usually involves teaching ways to devise helpful organizational structures.

Mnemonics Retrieving information from storage also necessitates some means of gaining access to the desired memory. Exactly how retrieval occurs is not well understood, however. We do know that an appropriate retrieval cue must be present, to direct the retrieval process to the information sought, but how the retrieval process itself works is still not known. Using our library analogy again, we can liken this situation to asking a librarian for a book by title and having the librarian obtain the book from a room we have no access to.

Effective retrieval cues, however they work, usually consist of information that either is part of the information sought or is closely associated with it, and that is itself readily accessible. The way to improve retrieval, therefore, is to learn how to code information with potent retrieval cues.

The techniques people use to improve memory by organizing material and by devising retrieval cues are called mnemonic techniques. Mnemonics is simply a matter of using the memory system's natural processes more effectively. It is the basis of most available courses in memory improvement.

Formal mnemonic procedures were used in ancient Greece, where the highly valued art of debate was practiced without benefit of notes. Debaters had to commit formal speeches to memory.

Credit for the first memory system is usually given to Simonides, who lived about 500 B.C. According to hearsay accounts, Simonides attended a banquet and had to leave the room. While he was out, the roof collapsed, crushing the guests beyond recognition. Simonides was able to identify the bodies by remembering where each person sat. He never recorded the memory system he used, but later scholars did describe it. (They taught it as a method of memorizing speeches.) A detailed description of the system appeared in an anonymous work called *Ad Herrenium* (Yates, 1966). In this treatise the author speaks of a *locus* as being an actual architectural space (such as an arch) on which we can place the image of whatever we wish to remember. The loci (or places) should form a sequence that can be remembered in any order. To facilitate memory, this sequence can be marked off at every fifth or tenth place, for example (as by placing the image of a number five or ten there). There should also be some variety to the loci lest their similarity become confusing. When a set of images is no longer used, it fades from memory and the loci can be used again as a device for keeping another set of images.

In this system the places, or loci, provide a set of retrieval cues that easily can be produced to gain access to the information stored with the cues. Information is stored at each place in the form of images selected to be as unique and unlike each other as possible, presumably to avoid interference. (The colloquial metaphor "in the first place" is said to be derived from this system.) These essential elements of Simonides' place system are common to all mnemonic techniques.

In the place system described above the individual makes up his own places and images. In many other organizational schemes, however, a complete and detailed set of retrieval cues is supplied. One early scheme located information on a series of concentric wheels that could be rotated to make different combinations, each producing a different concept. Another system, devised for memorizing dates, coded digits as consonants on the basis of similarities of shape. For example, 1 = *t*, 6 = *d*, 4 = *p*, and 8 = *l*. The trick was to add vowels to the consonants to form a word that you could use as a retrieval cue. In our example, 1648 = tdpl, which is easily expanded to *tadpole*. To retrieve the date, you need only recall the retrieval cue, tadpole, and decode it to obtain 1648.

Another system involved imagining a fifty-room house with fifty locations in each room, each associated with a standard image, an object resembling a numeral

This window of a Turkish antique store resembles the memory boxes that some artists have made—giving specific places to objects that spark many memories, perhaps as though the memories themselves were being stored. However, the author of *Ad Herennium* would probably find the places suggested here too large and the arrangement of images too cluttered and too dimly lighted to be ideal. (Norman Prince)

(for example, 1 = tower of Babel, 6 = horn of plenty). Elaborate rules had to be observed in going from room to room, and there was a numeral-letter coding system like the one described in the previous paragraph. Information was associated with a location by forming compound images with the standard image.

Many of the modern mnemonic schemes are variations on these classic schemes. For example, the place system can be adapted easily to any situation, since it requires only a series of easily organized places. You can imagine walking across campus and use the places in sequence as you come to them, or walk through your house using places in each room. In the stack method, one ingenious version of the place system, different locations on a car are numbered, and information is associated with each location—hood ornament, radiator, bumper, fender, mirror, and so on.

Today the most common mnemonic system is the hook method, launched commercially by Sambrook in 1879, popularized by Dale Carnegie in *Public Speaking and Influencing Men in Business* in 1937, and now sold commercially through newspaper advertisements. This method takes two forms, a rhyme method and a numeral-letter code. The rhyme method involves making a series of standard images accessible by associating each with a rhyming number. For example, one is a bun, two is a shoe, and three is a tree. After the series has been memorized, information is associated with each standard image. Usually one is advised to make the composite image bizarre or unusual, but there is no evidence that this helps. Interactive images—images in which the thing to be recalled is doing something with the standard image—seem to produce better recall.

The theater suggested by Robert Fludd in *Ars Memoriae* (1573) to aid the memory is a place system. (New York Public Library)

The numeral-letter code, like the system described earlier, makes use of formal resemblances between numerals and letters: 1 = *t*, 2 = *n*, and 3 = *p*. Words are then associated with the letters, giving, for example, *t* = tea, *n* = noah, and *p* = post. Once the hook letters are learned, they can be combined to form new hook words; example, 123 = *tnp* = *turnip*. In this case too, one forms images that involve the hook word and the thing to be remembered.

These mnemonic schemes are quite effective; even with minimal instruction, they can improve recall by 50 to 85 percent.

Most of the commercially available mnemonic training courses use images as retrieval cues, but many familiar mnemonic devices are strictly verbal. Usually they take the form of short poems. Many people cannot recall the number of days in a given month without reciting at least the first two lines of the centuries-old verses:

Thirty days hath September,
April, June, and November.
All the rest have thirty-one,
Except February, which has twenty-eight,
Leap year twenty-nine.

And most medical students can recite "On old Olympus' tipmost top, a Finn and German viewed and hopped," even if they cannot recite the names of the twelve cranial nerves having the same initial letters as the words in the poem.

Poem mnemonics can also be used to remember a general principle. Thus a fishing guide in northern Alberta recites, "wind from the east, the fish bite least; wind from the west, the fish bite best."

Powerful as they are, mnemonic devices that use images as retrieval cues are not foolproof. Images too nonspecific to provide accurate decoding can lead to recall failure or erroneous information. For example, *gate* may be used as a retrieval cue for *lamp*, but the image of a gate with a lamp over it may be associated with *light* instead of *lamp*. Furthermore, the association between the hook word and the item to be recalled may be too weak or vague. Then the retrieval cue, even though accessible, can fail to produce the appropriate information.

Forgetting

9·3 Once an item of information is stored in memory, how do you forget it? Why can't any item be retrieved at any time? The task of answering these questions is complicated by two important considerations. First, the notion of forgetting implies that the information was indeed accessible at some earlier time but is not accessible now. We must therefore be careful to exclude situations in which the information was never stored in the first place.

Second, we cannot definitely assert that information, once stored, is never lost from memory. What we do know is that *some* seemingly long-lost memories, even

Theories of Memory

For several years it has been generally agreed that memory has three components: iconic memory, primary memory, and secondary memory. The key property of this system is information flow. Sensory information first goes to the *iconic memory,* where it receives initial processing (as described in Chapter 8). It then enters *primary memory,* which is essentially a rehearsal system. Information can be held in primary memory only as long as it is rehearsed. To be stored more permanently, the information must be coded and stored in *secondary memory,* a relatively permanent, organized storage system.

These three components do not refer to actual places in the brain. When we speak of information as being stored in one of them, we mean that it is remembered and maintained in a certain way. Different kinds of information are also retained in different ways. Although differing in detail, many theories have been built around the conception of memory as a three-component system in which information passes from one state to another.

Many memory phenomena fit this conception quite well. For example, the repetition effect suggests that while a digit system is being held in primary memory for immediate output, the rehearsal involved results in a more permanent trace in secondary memory. Repetition of the same string strengthens the more permanent trace.

The recency effect in free recall has also been offered as one of the clearest examples of a primary-secondary memory distinction. When the items at the end of a list of words are better recalled, these items are presumed to come from primary memory, while those early in the list supposedly come from secondary memory. The fact that the recency effect disappears if recall is delayed for a few seconds represents rapid loss from primary memory. Negative recency occurs because the last few items in the list were not rehearsed enough to get them into secondary memory.

Finally, the existence of anterograde amnesia has long been offered as strong evidence in favor of the theory. The injury to the brain is supposed to leave the secondary memory intact. Primary memory is also intact in that the patient can remember immediate events as long as he attends to or rehearses them. The ability to get information from primary to secondary memory is presumably what is destroyed.

from childhood, are retrieved under special conditions such as senile delirium, hypnosis, or direct stimulation of certain parts of the brain. Obviously these memories were not lost. The only question is whether they indicate the general availability of all early memories or are leftovers from a group of memories most of which are long gone.

In a practical sense, it may not matter. If a library book has been placed on the wrong shelf, no one can ever find it except by searching the entire library, book by book. For all practical purposes the book is not accessible. Whether or not it is in the library has no practical bearing on its accessibility.

Interference Interference occurs when other memories either block retrieval of the information sought or make it difficult for a person to discriminate that information from irrelevant material. Interference by information acquired earlier than the information sought is called **proactive inhibition;** interference by information acquired later is called **retroactive inhibition.** Suppose, for example, that to prepare for a sociology exam and an economics exam on Thursday, you study sociology Wednesday afternoon and economics Wednesday evening. On Thursday

Despite considerable evidence in support of the primary-secondary memory distinction, not all psychologists accept the theory. Most notably, in 1972 two psychologists, Fergus Craik and Robert Lockhart, proposed an alternative, single-system view of memory. They suggested that incoming information is analyzed to different levels depending upon the immediate demands and strategies of the learner. These levels represent different attributes of the incoming information—beginning with simple physical or sensory features, followed by meaning (recognition and identification), and ending with elaboration of the information (associations, images, and the like). Craik and Lockhart call this concept depth of processing. The major factor determining the retention of information is the depth to which it is processed. Thus, information processed at the elaborative level will be more efficiently retained than information processed at the sensory level. Rehearsal may still be used to retain information for immediate use, but does not improve retention unless it is accompanied by further processing.

The major evidence in support of this theory comes from experiments on a phenomenon known as *incidental learning*—learning of material when one is not instructed or motivated to store it. In one such experiment (Craik and Tulving, 1975), people were told that the experiment was a test of their speed of perception. They were first asked a simple question about a word. They were then shown a word for .2 second, and had to answer the question as soon as possible. The questions were designed to induce the person to process the word to different levels, and were of five types: (1) Is there a word present? (2) Is the word in capital letters? (3) Does the word rhyme with______? (4) Does the word belong to the category ______? (5) Will the word fit in the sentence ______? After they had analyzed forty words in this manner, they were given a recognition test for the words. The results were as follows: level 1, 22 percent correct recognitions; level 2, 16 percent correct; level 3, 57 percent; level 4, 78 percent; and level 5, 89 percent. The results clearly indicate the expected relation between depth of processing and memory for the words.

While there are still many questions to be answered, the depth-of-processing concept appears to be a realistic model of the memory system.

the sociology you studied Wednesday afternoon will proactively inhibit the economics you studied Wednesday evening and the economics will retroactively inhibit the sociology.

In the laboratory, retroactive and proactive inhibition have been shown to produce a great deal of forgetting. For example, in one experiment (Runquist, 1957) people learned a list of eight word pairs and were asked to recall the pairs after forty-eight hours. Forgetting was only about 15 percent. However, when another list of word pairs was learned either immediately before or immediately after the list to be recalled, forgetting increased to 50 percent. Effects like these are not restricted to word lists, since retroactive inhibition can occur in almost any kind of learning situation.

The amount of interference is determined by several factors, of which the most important is *similarity*. The more alike two ideas are, the more they will interfere with each other during attempts to recall one of them. When two ideas are extremely similar, however, retention may be enhanced rather than reduced. Instead of interfering, the similar material provides further practice. Thus, as similarity increases, interference first increases, then decreases (Figure 9•3).

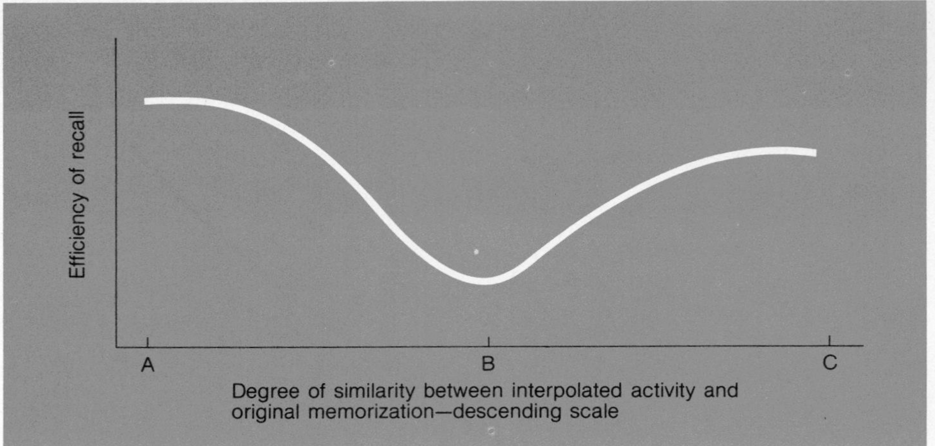

Fig. 9·3 The hypothetical relation between similarity of the interfering material and retention. Note that when similarity approaches identity, recall is best and decreases rapidly to a minimum with moderately high similarity. Thereafter, recall improves as similarity decreases. (From Robinson, 1927)

A second important factor is *time*. Interference increases with time since learning. Immediately after you study, proactive inhibition by material you studied earlier is virtually nonexistent, but it then increases rapidly.

Time spent sleeping does not result in as much forgetting as time spent awake and active. Moreover, sleep that occurs immediately after learning provides more protection against forgetting than sleep that occurs just before the recall test.

Another, rather obvious factor is the amount of potentially interfering material. When only a single list is learned, recall after twenty-four hours may be 70 to 85 percent. As more lists are learned, recall drops off rapidly and may be as low as 10 percent after twenty lists (Figure 9•4).

Interference Reduction In spite of the effects of interference, people are able to acquire large amounts of information and to retrieve specific items with considerable accuracy. What prevents the obliteration of these items by retroactive or proactive inhibition?

One method of reducing interference is *selective coding*—coding the information in terms of characteristics that differentiate it from other information. For example, a person at a conference may avoid confusing the names of new people by focusing on some distinctive feature such as hair style or glasses. Many differentiating factors can be used—the frequency of an event, its location in space or time, its position in a series of events, and so on.

Another method of reducing interference is *intentional forgetting*. There is little evidence that people can actually erase information from memory, but being told to forget something immediately after it is acquired does reduce both its recallability and its potential for creating interference. Being told to forget something may cause a person to classify it as unimportant and thus code it differently from important information. It may also prevent further rehearsing and coding of that information. If the information has not yet been stored, an instruction to forget may prevent storage. Once information has been stored, however, intentional forgetting is seldom complete.

Distortions Sometimes recall is incomplete. For example, someone asked to name the device used to navigate by the sun or stars may repeatedly form words that are close, like *sexton, sextet,* or *secant* but be unable to call up the correct word, *sextant* (Brown and McNeill, 1966).

The tip-of-the-tongue phenomenon is a minor type of distortion: a loss of part of the information needed to produce complete retrieval. Other forms of distortion are much more dramatic, and occur primarily when the information to be remembered is a story, a picture, or a complex series of events such as those happening at the scene of an accident. The most common type of distortion is **leveling,** a loss of detail resulting in recall of only the general pattern of events. Another common type of distortion is **sharpening,** in which some unusual detail may stand out and be remembered regardless of its relevance or lack of relevance to the central event. For example, an accident witness may remember that one of the drivers wore a flowered shirt but be unable to recall any of the details of the accident itself.

A third common type of distortion is **assimilation,** the alteration of memory to fit cultural norms and expectations. For example, a middle-aged man with a crew cut may incorrectly remember that an accident was the fault of the long-haired young driver. He remembers his expectation instead of what he saw.

In one experiment on the assimilation type of distortion, subjects were shown ambiguous line drawings of simple objects such as are shown in the center column

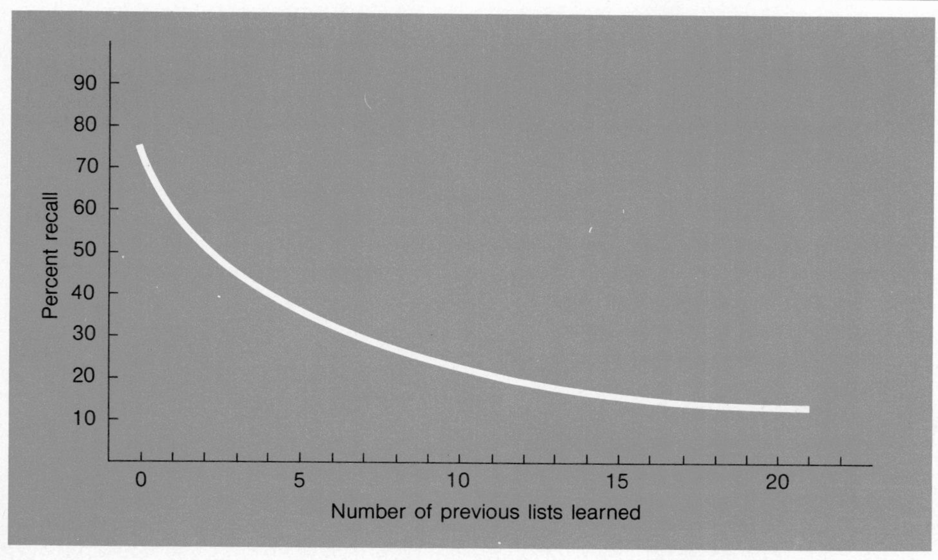

Fig. 9·4 The recall of lists of words 24 hours after learning when different numbers of interfering lists were also learned in the experiment. (From Underwood, 1957)

The War of the Ghosts

Much of what we recall involves reconstructing information (not simply reproducing it), based on whatever parts of it are accessible, plus information from other situations and from general knowledge about the world. This fact was dramatically pointed out by an English psychologist, Sir Frederic Bartlett, in 1932.

Bartlett had students read an unusual story adapted from native North American folklore and then try to recall it. Inevitably, the students distorted the style, content, and manner of the native story to be consistent with their own cultural experiences. Bartlett thought these changes took place during the attempt to recall. Some of them, however, may have been incorporated in the original coding of the material for memory. We are not sure which distortions occur during storage and which during retrieval.

Below you can read the original story and reproductions by two students from the United States.

The Original Story: One night two young men from Egulac went down to the river to hunt seals, and while they were there it became foggy and calm. Then they heard war cries and they thought: "Maybe this is a war party." They escaped to the shore, and hid behind a log. Now canoes came up, and they heard the noise of paddles, and saw one canoe coming up to them. There were five men in the canoe, and they said: "What do you think? We wish to take you along. We are going up the river to make war on the people." One of the young men said: "I have no arrows." "Arrows are in the canoe," they said. "I will not go along. I might be killed. My relatives do not know where I have gone. But you," he said, turning to the other, "may go with them." So one of the young men went, but the other returned home. And the warriors went on up the river to a town on the other side of Kalama. The people came down to the water, and they began to fight, and many were killed. But presently the young man heard one of the warriors say: "Quick, let us go home; that Indian has been hit." Now he thought; "Oh, they are ghosts." He did not feel sick, but they said he had been shot. So the canoes went back to Egulac, and the young man went ashore to his house, and made a fire. And he told everybody and said, "Behold! I accompanied the ghosts and we went to fight. Many of our fellows were killed, and many of those who attacked us were killed. They said I was hit, and I did not feel sick." He told it all, and then he became quiet. When the sun arose he fell down. Something black came out of his mouth. His face became contorted. The people jumped and cried. He was dead.

Reproduction A: Two warriors went out fishing. While they were fishing they saw a canoe come toward them with five warriors in it. Fearing that it might be a war party after them, they went and hid behind some logs. However, the canoe came toward them anyway. When it had come along enough for one of its occupants to speak to the young men, one of the strangers told them to get into the canoe and come along. The speaker said that they were going down the river to fight. One of the young men replied that he had no arrows, but the strangers replied that there were arrows in the canoe. Then one of the young men said that he couldn't go because his people didn't know where he was and that he might get killed. However, he said that his companion might go.

The other young man went with the war party. The six men then went down the river to the predetermined point. When they arrived another group came forth, and they began to fight. Many were killed. Finally one of the original five said that they should go home as the young man they had picked up was hit. When he heard this, the young man concluded that his companions were ghosts, since he didn't feel hurt or sick. The party then returned to the place they had started from and the young man returned to his people and told them of his experience.

Reproduction B: Two Indians were fishing on Egulac one night when they heard shouts and thought them to be from a war party. They hid behind logs and a canoe with five Indians came towards them. The Indians in the canoe asked them to fight with them, but one of the two replied that he had no arrows. The war party said that there were arrows in the boat but he still declined to go because his relatives did not know where he was, but he said his companion could go. They went across the water and started fighting when the Indians said the new companion was hit and they had better leave. He did not feel hurt at all so he decided they must be ghosts.

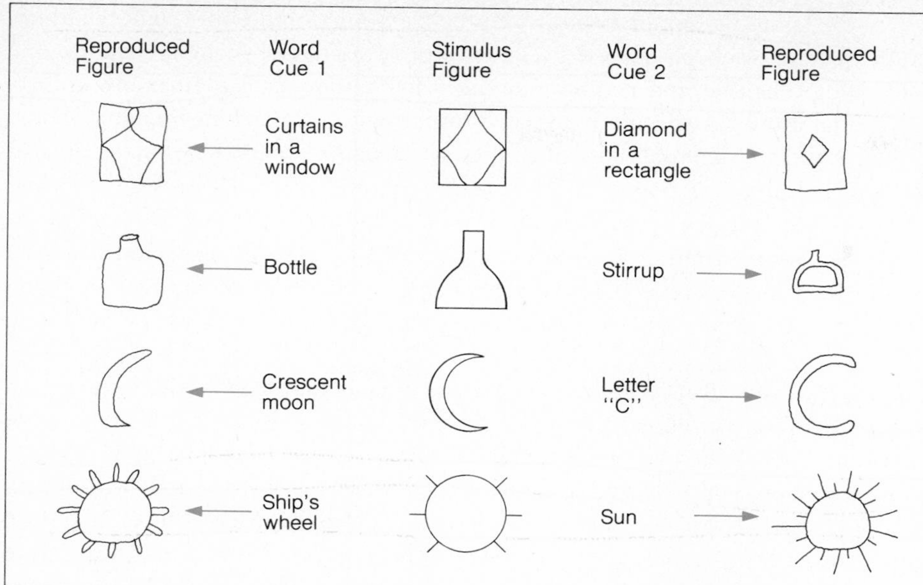

Fig. 9·5 Sample drawings from an experiment on the assimilation type of distortion. In general, the reproductions (outer columns) were distorted to look like the object referred to by name rather than like the actual drawing originally shown (center column). (From Carmichael, Hogan, and Walter, 1932)

of Figure 9•5. When they were given the first set of word cues on the left in the figure, later reproductions resembled those shown in the left column; when they were given the word cues on the right, they drew them to look like those shown in the right column. In other words, the drawings supposedly made from memory matched the labels used by the experimenter more than the drawings seen earlier.

The exact point in the process at which distortions occur is not known. In other words, we don't know whether a person's expectations and mental set distort the perception, the coding process, or the memory, or whether distortion occurs at two or all three of these points. Thus we cannot assert with any finality that assimilative changes take place in memory.

Amnesias Loss of memory is a recurrent theme in popular fiction. Amnesias also happen in real life, as a result of physical damage to the brain, hemorrhage, atherosclerosis, long-term alcohol abuse, concussion, or even intense psychological stress.

Accidents often produce **retrograde amnesia**—loss of memory of events occurring before the injury. The severity of the injury determines how extensive the loss is and how far back in time it goes. Recovery is common and proceeds backward. That is, the events earliest in time are restored to memory first. All general memory functions, such as knowledge of language, are unimpaired.

Anterograde amnesia is an inability to store or code new information. A person having this disorder is able to remember everything that was stored in memory before the disorder occurred but is unable to store new information except by rehearsing it immediately. If rehearsal is disrupted, the memory is virtually wiped out. Since earlier memories are intact and rehearsal maintains information, anterograde amnesia has been offered as evidence of two separate memory systems, one controlling rehearsal and coding and the other serving as a permanent storage.

In some amnesias specific kinds of information are lost from memory. These amnesias include *agnosia* (loss of ability to recognize objects), *apraxia* (loss of movements), *aphasia* (loss of spoken language), and *alexia* (loss of written language). They do not affect information that is presented in other forms. For example, a person suffering from aphasia may still be able to read, and a person unable to recognize objects visually may still recognize them by feeling them. Most of these specific amnesias result from damage to specific parts of the brain.

Cueing Failures Retrieval involves the use of cues that lead to the information sought. It therefore follows that some retrieval failures are due to the absence of important cues. When you have forgotten what you were about to say because of an interruption, you may find it difficult to retrieve the lost thought without recapitulating what you were saying and thinking before the interruption. To obtain the needed cues, you may have to re-create the situation that existed just before the interruption.

Factors Affecting Memory

9·4 The ease or difficulty with which information can be remembered is strongly influenced by the nature of the information, as well as by the way it is presented.

Material Characteristics A word can be packed with meaning or it can be a nonsense word, or it can be somewhere between these two extremes. It can be common or unusual, concrete or abstract, like another word or different from it. Your ability to recall it is influenced by all of these factors.

Meaningfulness Words like *office, army, heaven,* and *doctor* are meaningful in that they are widely used and evoke many associations. Words like *capstan, gamin, ferrule,* and *endive* are less meaningful because their associations are more limited in number and variety. *Gojey, tarop, polef,* and *vorvap* are not meaningful at all, not only because they are not words, but also because they do not even suggest words. Meaningful words are easier to memorize than meaningless words, and the more meaningful a word is, the more effective it is as a retrieval cue.

Meaningfulness is also a quality of strings of words. A sentence like "The economy of Angola is dependent on natural resources" is more meaningful and more easy to remember than "saw the football game will end at midnight in October." Note that "saw the football game will end at midnight in October" has an almost-English quality. It was constructed from overlapping four-word strings, each of which is a meaningful fragment. "Saw the football game," "the football game will," and "football game will end" are meaningful separately even though the entire string makes no sense. A string of randomly chosen words like "byway consequence handsomely financier bent flux cavalry swiftness extent waltz" would be still more difficult to memorize.

Frequency or Familiarity Words like *admiral, comedy,* and *jetty* are as meaningful as *answer, job,* or *friend* but are used less frequently in normal language. They are therefore less familiar, less easily remembered, and less effective as retrieval cues. On the other hand, rarely used words are generally easier to recognize than common words. Just why this is so is not clear.

Concreteness Words like *beaver, piano, barn,* and *clock* are easier to memorize than words like *thing, some, thought,* and *object.* A sentence like "The beaver pushed the frog off the log" is easier to remember than one like "The ideas put forth in the treaty cannot be accurately assessed." The chief difference is that several of the words in the first sentence are concrete: They refer to tangible objects that we can call up as sensory images. The second sentence is full of words that have the opposite quality. Instead of being concrete, they are abstract—they refer to mental constructs, to the world of ideas rather than the world of the senses.

Imagery is such a powerful aid to memory that instructions to use imagery in a recall experiment increase recall by about 25 percent.

Similarity Words can be similar in either of two ways: (1) Formal similarity, as in *rough* and *muff* (similar sounds) or *rough* and *bough* (similar spelling); or (2) semantic (meaning) similarity as in *insane* and *crazy.* A semantic similarity also exists between words that are members of the same conceptual category, such as *football* and *hockey;* words that can be associated, such as *food* and *stomach,* or words that have the same evaluative connotation, such as *war* and *crime.*

Similarity affects memory in complex ways, most often with negative results. As we have already seen, the greater the similarity between items, the greater the proactive and retroactive inhibition—up to a certain point. Similarity among items or among retrieval cues generally results in interference. Nevertheless, if a large amount of material is to be recalled and the order in which it is recalled is not important, similarity among items to be recalled is helpful because it is an important basis for organization.

Furthermore, a single item that differs from all others in a set being memorized is likely to be better retained. For example, if one item in a list is underlined or printed in red, it will be better retained. This is called the *von Restorff* (or isolation) *effect.*

The effects of similarity also depend on the time since study. In a memory span test, a string of words such as *fan, tan, ran, man, can,* and *pan* would be more difficult than a string of unrelated words, but a series of semantically related words like *moose, wolf, bear, skunk, fox,* and *lynx* would not. Generally, the longer the time since study, the more important the semantic effects are.

The Dual-Process Theory of Memory

In the late 1950s, Allan Paivio began to develop a theory of memory that has considerably influenced our understanding of memory processes. He started with two facts: instructions to form images produce substantial increases in one's ability to remember, and memory for concrete as opposed to abstract information consistently differs in a variety of situations. He then proposed a theory based on two distinct memory systems, each designed to perform its own unique memory functions.

According to Paivio, two separate systems are involved in the processing of raw percepts—the imagery system and the verbal system. He suggested that incoming information undergoes three levels of transformations: representational, referential, and associative. *Representational coding* involves coding words as words and objects as images. *Referential processes* enable the image to activate the verbal code, or the word to produce an image. Essentially, we label pictures and form images of the things words represent. *Associative processes* result in more elaborate codes representing associations, composite images, and the like.

Psychological theories typically make use of analogies, and Paivio's theory is no exception. He likens an image of an object or event to a pictorial representation of it except that the picture is in the head. Whether people really "see" images is not his concern. Rather his point is that information is coded as if it were a picture in the head. How an image functions is the critical thing.

The imagery system, according to Paivio, is more suitable for concrete events and can handle much spatially organized information at once. The verbal system resembles a tape recorder. It can deal with information in a linear way (one item at a time) and is more suitable when the original information is presented serially.

Exactly what conditions are best for memory depends on the demands put upon the memory system and on the material being memorized. Images can be used more effectively when the material to be memorized involves concrete ideas, while verbal codes such as sentences or associations are better when the task involves abstract ideas or information presented in sequence.

Paivio's theory is more than a theory of memory, since it includes many other psychological functions. Indeed, the success of the theory can be attributed largely to the fact that it explains many different kinds of phenomena.

Linguistic Factors Memory of an idea is strongly affected in a number of ways by the language forms in which the idea is presented. Some of these effects will be discussed in Chapter 11.

Method of Presentation Memory is also influenced by the way material is presented for study. It may be heard in a lecture or read in a book. It may be studied in a continuous session or a series of sessions interrupted by rest periods. It may be studied in its entirety or as separate bits. It may be studied with or without mnemonic devices. It may also be subject to forgetting, and its retention may be influenced by emotional factors.

Modality Many students report that they cannot learn as well by listening as they can by reading. Research has failed to show any differences in memory for visual versus auditory presentation when the same verbal materials are presented at the same rate. There is one exception. In a memory span task, the last three or so items presented are better recalled when presented in the auditory mode. This effect seems to be due to the persistence of the auditory sensory memory and has little bearing on material in storage.

These findings have a somewhat limited applicability to real-life situations. In the experimental situation the same words were presented at the same rate in both modes. In real life, a lecture cannot be repeated, but written material can be reread until it is grasped. A moment's inattention during a lecture results in some loss of material, and sometimes the cost of reflecting on one idea is not hearing the next idea. Moreover, some materials lend themselves more to one mode than to the other. For these reasons, any comparison of modes is difficult.

Modality affects memory in one more important way. Generally, people are able to remember the mode in which material was presented, and to use this knowledge to reduce interference. Information presented in the auditory mode is less likely to interfere with visually presented information than with other auditory information.

For blind readers of braille, touch substitutes for vision in the task of reading, but presumably memory operates in the same way as in sighted persons. (Karen R. Preuss, Jeroboam)

Spacing of Study Does a given amount of study yield better memorization if it is done in an unbroken stretch or if it is interrupted by several rest periods? Generally, spaced study is beneficial, but the extent of the benefit is determined by several conditions. Spaced study provides the greatest benefits when there is much proactive inhibition and the time between study and recall is relatively long. For short periods of time, however, or when interference is minimal, massed study periods may be more effective.

In planning a study period, bear in mind that in all of the above comparisons, the spacing does not affect the total amount of actual study time. If five hours is all you have in which to study for a test, your wisest move may be to study for the entire five hours with no breaks.

Various factors may contribute to the superiority of spaced study. The rest period may allow rehearsal or coding to occur even surreptitiously. It may also result in more effective coding during the study period by making it easier to hold attention on the material to be memorized.

Part versus Whole Study Generally, a given amount of information is more efficiently memorized by itself than as part of a larger body of information. This does not necessarily mean, however, that learning by parts is more efficient. In the first place, after memorizing the parts one must spend considerable time putting the parts together. Depending on the material, this process may take as long as learning the parts.

In the second place, breaking the material down into parts may destroy the coherence, organization, or structure of the material, making it actually more difficult to memorize. Sometimes the relationship between parts is the most important thing to be learned. Finally, research has shown that people memorizing word lists are handicapped in learning the whole list if they have previously learned

Nonverbal Memory

Most research on memory has been conducted with verbal materials such as lists of words, sentences, and stories. Only recently have psychologists begun to study memory for information presented in other modalities. While many of the characteristics of verbal memory seem also to apply to these other modalities, some interesting differences have been observed.

Picture Memory Memory for visual stimuli, especially faces, is exceptionally good, though why this is so is not clear. In one study (Babrick, Babrick, and Wittlinger, 1975) former students were tested for recognition of photos (taken from yearbooks) of faces of classmates. They found that recognition accuracy was about 90 percent after two months and declined very little over fifteen years.

Sounds Experiments on memory for sounds fall into two categories: those studying memory for natural sounds, and those studying memory for the pitch of a tone. When we hear a sound, we are likely to attach meaning to it by thinking of what it represents. When we hear the sound later, we judge whether we have heard it before by comparing its meaning with the meanings we have in memory; that is, sounds are not remembered in terms of themselves, but are coded into some interpretation of what they are.

To demonstrate the importance of interpretation, Bower and Holyoak (1973) had people listen to a large number of natural sounds (such as jungle insects, heartbeats, and horses trotting), identifying each sound before presenting it. A week later in recognition tests for the sounds, some subjects were given the sounds along with the same labels as before, some were given the sounds with different but equally plausible labels, and some were given the sounds and no labels at all. Recognition was most accurate when the labels were the same, least accurate when different labels were presented, and intermediate when no labels were given. In the unlabeled tests, the person was also asked to supply labels. When he gave the same label as had been given to him at study, he correctly recognized the sound 80 percent of the time. When he gave a different label, he was correct only 45 percent of the time. These data indicate that a sound can be remembered better if it is identified.

Sounds can sometimes, however, be remembered without coding their meaning. If a person is presented with a pure tone and, after a specified time interval, is given another tone to judge as higher or lower in pitch than the original tone, accuracy is seriously affected by other tones placed between the two comparison tones (Massaro, 1970).

Odors It is commonly believed that smells are exceptionally memorable. Many people report noticing that a certain smell is familiar, even when they have not been exposed to it for many years. We have no information on memory for odors over such long periods of time, but some research

part of it, and handicapped in learning part of the list if they have previously learned the whole list. Evidently material that is highly organized as a whole is more easily memorized as a whole, and material that is easily broken down into parts is more easily memorized in parts.

Memory Strategies The coding and retrieval of information are determined in part by the information to be memorized, and in part by the individual and his or her perception of what kind of information will be required at a later date. We have already seen one example of this in the fact that students code one way for recall and another way for recognition.

Coding can be controlled in many ways by the individual—for example, by using the complex mnemonic devices described earlier. There are also strategies that

does indicate that recognition memory for odors is exceptionally good over short periods of time. In one experiment (Engen, Kuisma, and Eimas, 1973), people sniffed a cotton swab containing a common odor (for example, garlic, vanilla, floor wax, various perfumes) and then were tested for recognition by sniffing another swab after intervals of up to thirty seconds. In contrast to results in testing verbal memory, there was virtually no forgetting over the thirty seconds. Even when five different substances were presented during the original study trial, there was no loss over the time interval, though overall memory was not quite as good.

Movements How are we able to reproduce movements? Once we finally make that perfect golf swing, can we remember how we did it so that we can reproduce it?

Once acquired, skilled movements are notably resistant to forgetting. In 1904, E. Swift, practiced juggling balls for forty-two days. In 1910 he attempted the skill again, and it took him only eleven days to reach his former level of proficiency. There are many other instances of similar savings. Such feats actually tell us little about movement memory, since most skills that show remarkable retention are highly overlearned. Consider, for example, the many hours a child spends riding a bicycle compared with the time he spends studying a list of words or reading a single passage. It is no wonder that gross skills are so well retained.

Although not experimentally verified, the memory of an odor can last a long time. Once having smelled a rose, for example, some people easily recognize its scent whenever they are exposed to it. (Karen R. Preuss, Jeroboam)

Recently, psychologists have begun to study memory for simpler movements such as moving a lever a given distance or to a fixed position. Even simple movements such as this show forgetting in short intervals of up to thirty seconds or so; that is, they are less accurately reproduced. They are also susceptible to interference by activities occurring during the retention interval. Making another movement during the interval reduces the accuracy of reproduction, as does also verbal activity. This interference has led some psychologists to consider the possibility that there is some verbal coding as well as memory for the movement itself.

involve only retrieval. When recall occurs immediately after memorizing a long list of words, the last few words on the list are still being rehearsed. If they are recalled first, they are likely to be recalled with considerable accuracy. This effect is called the **recency effect.**

The recency effect in immediate recall is often accompanied by a *negative recency effect* in delayed recall. If you memorize a series of word lists and recall each list immediately after memorizing it, you will show superior recall for the last few items on each list. But if you are then unexpectedly asked to recall all the items in all the lists, you will probably show much poorer recall for those same end-of-the-list items than for all the other items. Presumably you would not have bothered to code and store these items, since doing so was not necessary for immediate recall. Other experiments have shown differences in recall between indi-

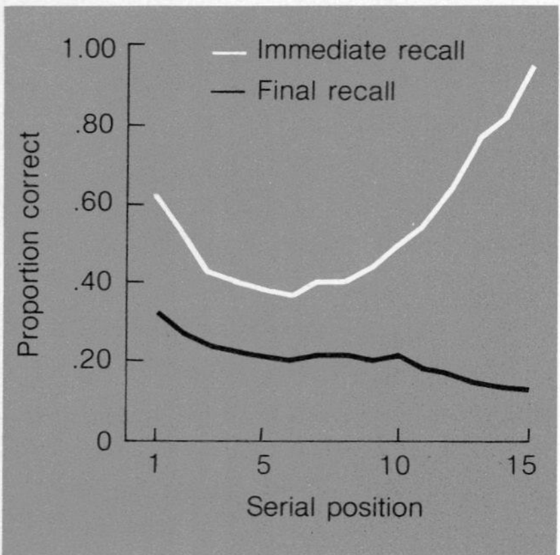

Fig. 9·6 The top line of this graph shows the immediate recall of lists of 15 words according to their position on the list. There is a marked recency effect in that the words in the last five positions are recalled much better than the others. There is also a small primacy effect for words in the first two positions. The lower line shows the recall of items from 10 lists after all of the lists were presented. Note the negative recency effect: items that were better recalled in immediate recall are now recalled more poorly. (Craik, 1970)

viduals who know whether or not they will be tested immediately and individuals who do not (Götz and Jacoby, 1974).

Items at the beginning of a list, though not as easily recalled as those at the end, are more easily recalled than items in the middle. This is the **primacy effect.** Recency, primacy, and negative recency are all apparent in Figure 9·6.

The most important general principle emerging from all these experiments is that both coding and retrieval processes can to some extent be controlled.

Overlearning Most of the factors involved in forgetting that we discussed earlier have little, if any, effect on the rate of forgetting once the information has been acquired. In fact, the most important factor determining how fast material is forgotten is how well it was learned. Even practice beyond the amount needed for perfect recall protects information against forgetting. This is called **overlearning.**

Some students claim that they memorize slowly but retain longer. Careful research has shown, however, that when the amount learned is the same, the forgetting rate is the same, regardless of how long it takes to learn the material. Once again, the real-life situation may differ from the laboratory situation. The amount learned can be equated in the laboratory but probably not in real life. Slow memorizers may in fact do better because by taking more time to learn all the information, they overlearn the easier parts thus reducing forgetting for those parts.

Motivational Factors in Memory Motivation affects memory in numerous ways, three of which we shall examine.

First, trying to learn information is not more effective than merely being exposed to it. Certainly a person who is merely exposed to materials will remember them more poorly than one who is instructed to memorize them. But the intention to learn seems to have nothing to do with this difference. Rather, the coding activities produced by the instruction to learn seem to be the critical factor. For example, people can be given a list of words and asked to rate the words for pleasantness, or to count all the *e*'s and *g*'s in the words, or to record their parts of speech, or to pick a sentence that best fits the word. They are then given a recall test. Although the different activities produce different amounts of recall, the amount of recall is not affected by whether or not the subjects were instructed to learn the words. The results of an experiment of this kind are shown in Figure 9·7. Incidental learning is clearly as effective as intentional learning, provided that the same coding activities are required in both situations.

A second possible effect of motivation on memory is to provide an incentive to rehearse, code, or retrieve more effectively. Research has demonstrated that a reward for correctly remembering items will aid memory if the person is told about the reward before or during the study period.

A third effect is tension. Is it better to be tense and aroused or calm and relaxed when memorizing and recalling information? Generally it is better to be aroused at the time of recall. Whether tension is a help or a hindrance during study depends on the time interval before recall. Tension may make recall immediately

Actors may need to overlearn their parts to ensure that they don't forget them under the stress of a performance. (Kennedy Center Photo by Richard Braaten)

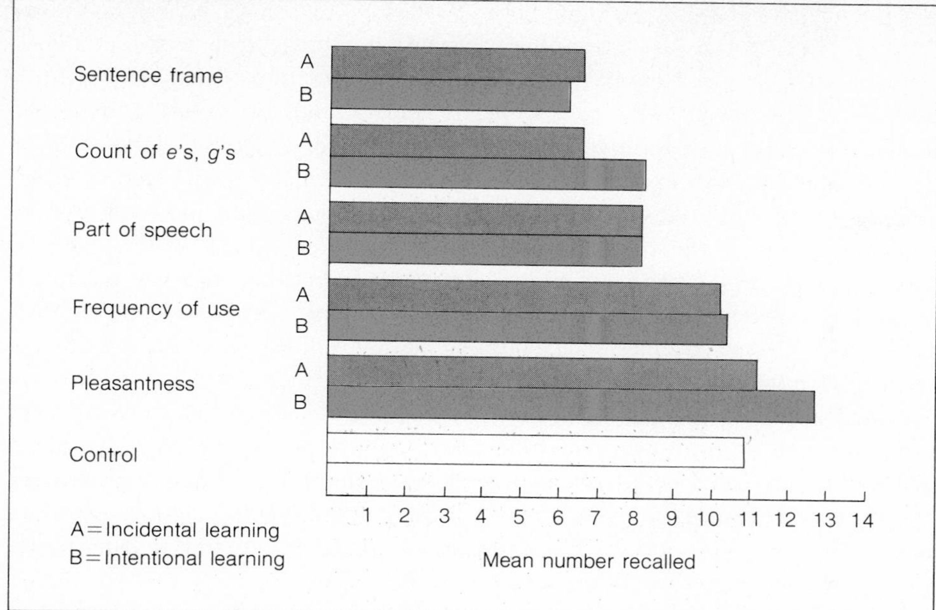

Fig. 9·7 This graph shows the number of words recalled by individuals who performed various operations on a list of words: (1) deciding whether a word fit in the sentence "It is ______"; (2) checking whether the word contained *e* or *g;* (3) determining what part of speech the word was; (4) estimating the frequency with which the word is used in the language; and (5) rating the word for pleasantness. One group of subjects (the intent condition) was also told that they would be asked to recall the words. There were wide variations in recall after the different tasks, but by comparison, differences between those people told about the recall test and those not told were small, and in some cases did not occur. (From Hyde and Jenkins, 1973)

after study poorer, but it may improve recall if recall is delayed by an hour or more. Moreover, the effects of tension vary according to the type of material being memorized. When there is much interference, tension may produce poorer recall. In less confusing circumstances, mild tension may produce better recall. Severe tension or anxiety definitely produces poor retrieval.

Repression On the basis of clinical observations, psychoanalysts have proposed a form of motivated forgetting that they call **repression.** The mechanism of repression is discussed more fully in Chapter 16. The phenomenon itself does resemble the effects of motivation on memory, but the similarity may be more apparent than real. True repression makes unavailable material that has strong emotional content and that may become available only when the emotion is no longer associated with it. Such conditions cannot easily be duplicated in the laboratory; consequently the existence of repression has not been experimentally verified.

Clinical evidence is not fully convincing because the techniques used to produce retrieval of previously unavailable information may do much more for the patient's memory than simply eliminating fears. Severe emotional shock may indeed produce amnesia for the event, but it is not clear whether the emotional reaction precluded effective coding and storage. Moreover, some people are unable to suppress the memory of an unpleasant experience, and instead it becomes, in retrospect, even more traumatic and vivid.

Research on motivational aspects of memory is exceptionally difficult, and many of the results are inconclusive. The generalizations we have cited here should therefore not be accepted with unqualified confidence.

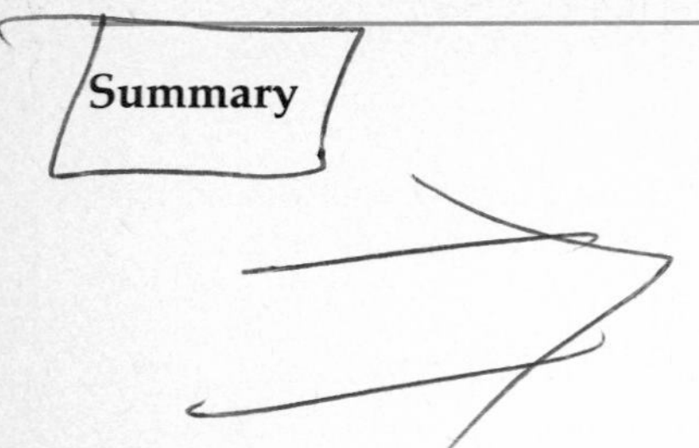

Summary

Memory is the storage and retrieval of information. Storage involves two processes, rehearsal and coding. Rehearsal maintains material for immediate use and occasionally for permanent storage. *Coding* is transforming the information to be stored into a different form by associating, imaging, or otherwise elaborating on the information. *Retrieval* is remembering and is normally manifested as either recognition or recall, but sometimes can be seen as savings (more rapid relearning).

To be retrieved effectively, information must be organized, and it must be coded with retrieval cues that can be used to gain access to the information stored. Memory can generally be improved by using mnemonic schemes to provide such cues. Most of these schemes make considerable use of imagery, which is an exceptionally effective form of coding.

Forgetting can be largely attributed either to failure to provide retrieval cues or to interference from other learning.

Memory is affected by such factors as meaningfulness, familiarity, concreteness, and similarity of material, as well as by spacing of study periods and other conditions of learning. Motivation and stress play a complex role and, depending on the circumstances, may help or hinder learning.

It would be easy to underestimate the role of memory, largely because we are commonly reminded in school that mere memorization of information is not enough, and that understanding, intellectual appreciation, and creativity are the really important psychological functions. As we have seen, though, memory is not a mere rote recording process; it involves a number of rather complex factors. Furthermore, knowledge stored in memory is necessary for the effective performance of complex mental skills, including creative thought.

Suggested Readings

Contemporary psychology: Readings from Scientific American. San Francisco: Freeman, 1971.

The article on short-term memory (by L. R. Peterson, July 1966) and the one on forgetting (by B. J. Underwood, March 1964) are recommended.

Howe, M. J. A. 1970. *Introduction to human memory.* New York: Harper & Row.

A brief and readable but rather theoretical discussion of memory, including a discussion of relevant research and its interpretation.

Lorayne, H., and Lucas, J. 1974. *The memory book.* New York: Ballantine Books.

A do-it-yourself course in memory improvement. It makes use of most of the principles of sound mnemonics, and although rather repetitious, provides specific mnemonics for a number of situations.

Norman, D. A. 1969. *Memory and attention.* New York: Wiley.

Presents an information processing account of memory, including a discussion of the relation between perception and memory.

Yates, F. A. 1966. *The art of memory.* London: Routledge and Kegan Paul.

A complete history and description of mnemonic methods from the Greeks until modern-day commercial methods.

Basic Learning Processes

10

Learning is the ability to modify behavior as a result of experience. This ability, which enables organisms to adapt to changing environmental conditions, is especially important to humans because their capacity to modify their behavior greatly exceeds that of most other animals. Indeed, some psychologists have seriously proposed that all human behavior and knowledge are acquired. Although very few psychologists take this extreme stance today, the significance of learning has led to considerable study of how it occurs and what part it plays in human life.

Learning is usually reflected in relatively permanent changes in behavior resulting from experience. Behaviors that change little during the organism's life are not considered learned because they do not represent change from a previous behavior in the same situation. Some of these unlearned behaviors are simple, such as the reflex withdrawal of a limb from a painful stimulus. Some are complex, such as courtship rituals in various animals. Another kind of behavior that does not reflect learning is temporary behavior changes that result from altered body conditions such as fatigue, disease, and drugs, or from motivational states such as hunger and thirst.

There are two types of permanent changes in behavior that must also be excluded from the definition of learning: those that occur as a result of irreparable damage to the organism such as brain damage, or loss of a limb or sense organ; and those that are part of the normal development of the organism and so do not depend on specific experiences. Birds do not have to learn how to fly. They simply do so when ready.

However, a specific type of behavior is seldom, if ever, solely a result of learning. No matter how much learning is involved in what we do, organic, maturational, and genetic factors are also involved. Sometimes they even determine whether learning can occur at all. As an example of the interaction of maturation with learning, consider the way a child learns to speak. It is generally conceded that a child must have certain intellectual abilities before he can make sense out of the complex pattern of noises emitted by other people. He must also be able to control the tongue, mouth, and larynx to produce the subtle variations in sounds necessary for speech. Neither of these abilities is present at birth, but they normally develop as the child grows older. Until then language learning will not occur.

Because of biological factors, two organisms may learn different things from the same environmental situation. For example, mentally retarded and normal children of the same age will learn to solve simple subtraction problems if they are allowed to try to solve the problems and then are rewarded for correct answers. When given a new set of problems, however, the retarded children cannot obtain correct answers, while the normal children experience no difficulty. Obviously, both groups learned something from their initial training, but the retarded children appear to have memorized the specific answers to each problem while the normal children learned how to subtract.

Properly speaking, the term *learning* defines a process, though not a single process only. That is, it refers to the many ways in which an organism is able permanently to modify what it does in specific situations as a result of its interaction with the environment. This chapter and the next will deal with learning mostly in this sense—how learning takes place and what factors influence it. In this chapter we shall be concerned mainly with forms of learning characteristic of conditioning—forms involving reactions to simple stimuli. In Chapter 11 we shall consider more complicated forms of learning, such as those involved in cognition.

Learning versus Performance

10·1 How does one determine whether learning has occurred? Essentially, the answer to this question is part of our definition of learning. We know learning has occurred when we observe a relatively permanent change in behavior. We know our dog has learned to sit up when we command him to do so and he does. Professors know that their students have learned something when they can answer questions they could not have answered before studying certain material.

Sometimes, however, learning occurs but is not observable. The problem is that we don't know, for example, whether someone has learned a concept if we don't observe any behavior that reflects that learning. All learning can be observed only when we test for it, and what is worse, not all tests show it. The conditions must be appropriate to produce evidence that learning has occurred.

A classic experiment performed in 1929 by Blodgett demonstrates this principle. Blodgett allowed rats to explore a maze that did not have any food at the end. A second group of rats received a piece of food after traversing the maze. As might be expected, the rewarded rats soon learned to get to the end of the maze with few errors, while the nonrewarded rats continued to bumble around showing little improvement. However, when Blodgett gave the nonrewarded rats some food at the end of the maze, they immediately began to perform as well as their continuously rewarded counterparts. In short, they had learned as much as the re-

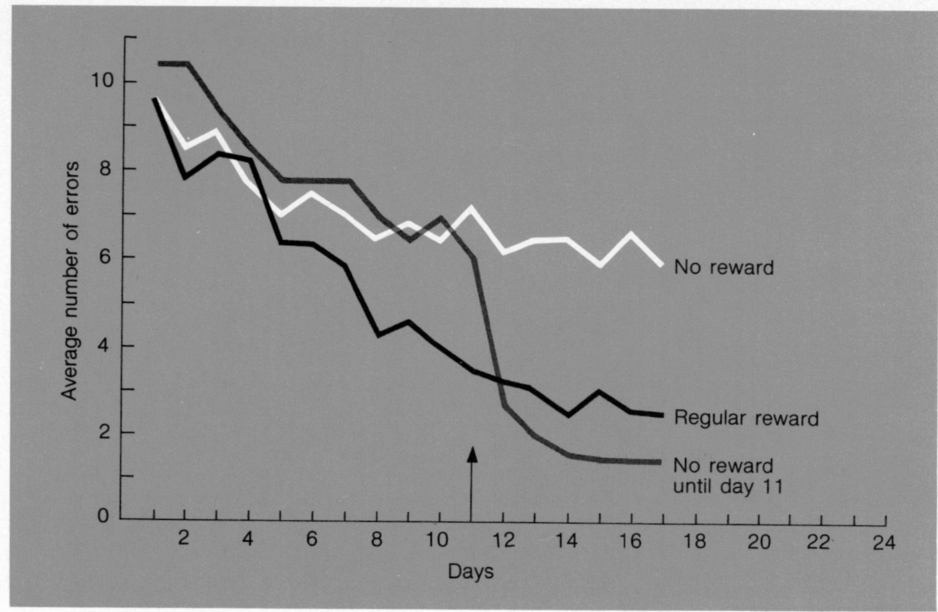

Fig. 10•1 A graph of the results of the Blodgett experiment. It shows the number of errors in traversing a maze for the various groups of rats described in the text. (Blodgett, 1929)

warded rats, but until they too were rewarded, they did not perform as well. (Figure 10•1).

This phenomenon, called **latent learning,** is no stranger to most students. Examinations are supposed to measure the students' knowledge; but if one takes seriously the excuses students give for poor examination scores, it is obvious that they understand that an examination is really a measure of performance rather than knowledge. By using such excuses as "I was so tired I could not think" or "I was not feeling well during the exam" or even "The questions tricked me," the student is arguing that the testing conditions were not appropriate to produce evidence of learning.

Clearly, these students understand the difference between learning and performance. *Learning* is what is in your head. *Performance* is what you do, and a lot of things influence what you do besides what you know. Learning sets limits on performance, but success generally is determined by how what is learned is used.

Primitive Forms of Learning

10•2 Two phenomena that involve permanent behavior changes are so simple that psychologists disagree about whether they should be classified as learning at all.

Habituation Habituation is a decrease in the responsiveness to a particular stimulus as a result of repeated occurrences of that stimulus. For example, people who live near an airport may become oblivious to the constant noise of aircraft taking

These goslings have been imprinted on the woman and follow her as if she were their mother. (Klaus Kalas)

off and landing. After a peaceful vacation in the country they may find the noise difficult to ignore, but will eventually habituate. Unlike sensory **adaptation,** such as increased sensitivity of the eyes to light as time is spent in darkness, each successive habituation occurs with increasing ease. This cumulative effect is what qualifies habituation as a learning process.

Imprinting A second primitive form of behavior change is imprinting, the rapid learning of a species-specific response to a specific stimulus, usually at an early critical age or not at all. For example, when young goslings emerge from their eggs, the first moving object they see is their mother. This initial encounter seems to establish a long-lasting social relationship with the mother. One immediately observable effect is that the goslings swim along behind their mother, but this imprinting also affects later social reactions such as mating behavior. If the first object the goslings see is a human, they will follow that person as if he or she were their mother and will later direct their mating behavior toward humans rather than toward members of their own species.

The critical properties of imprinting that distinguish it from other forms of learning are its species-specificity and its strong dependence on a particular age. Not all animals imprint, nor does imprinted behavior have the same pattern in all animals who do. Whether imprinting occurs in humans is open to question.

Conditioned Responses

10·3 A second class of learning phenomena are processes by which specific stimuli acquire rather precise control over a wide range of specific behaviors. These phenomena are known as classical and instrumental (or operant) conditioning.

Classical conditioning may be described as a process by which a previously neutral stimulus—one that produces no specific reaction—acquires the ability to produce a response previously made to another stimulus. The following story provides a clear example:

> A young man had a romantic interest in the parson's daughter, but the parson had forbidden her to see him. To get even with the parson, the young man "borrowed" the parson's horse one Saturday night. Taking it out to a deserted field, he shouted "whoa," then rather cruelly applied his spurs to the horse's flank, causing the unhappy horse to buck furiously. He repeated this several times. Near dawn, the young man returned the horse to the parson's stable. Sunday morning, as the parson rode up to the church, he shouted "whoa" and the horse bucked him into a large mud puddle.

The horse had been classically conditioned. That is, the word *whoa* had acquired the power to produce bucking, which before had occurred to the stimulus provided by the spurs.

Classical conditioning may be contrasted to **instrumental (or operant) conditioning,** which refers to behavior controlled by rewards and punishment that are contingent upon that behavior. Behavior followed by a reward tends to occur more frequently, and behavior followed by punishment tends to occur less frequently. Scarcely any adult is not aware of this form of learning, since it is undoubtedly the most common method we all use to try to control the behavior of others.

Classical and instrumental conditioning have many similarities and differences, which will be discussed subsequently. For the present, it is sufficient to understand the critical difference between the two procedures. In classical conditioning the only important events are the two stimuli. That is, the occurrence of spurring is dependent only on the occurrence of the word *whoa.* In instrumental conditioning, the important event is the response. That is, the occurrence of a rewarding or punishing stimulus depends on whether a particular response is made. Only if that behavior occurs will the rewarding or punishing stimulus occur. For this reason, some psychologists call classical conditioning *Type S* (for stimulus) and instrumental conditioning *Type R* (for response).

Historically, classical and instrumental conditioning have played varying roles in psychological theory. Because of their simplicity and the ease with which they can be controlled in the laboratory, conditioned responses have at various times been considered the basic unit of behavior, a source of universal principles of learning that apply to all learned behavior, or sometimes just a biologically simple form of learning. Whatever view one chooses, conditioning of both types is an important form of learning.

Classical Conditioning Although informal descriptions of classical conditioning were available for several centuries, it remained for a physiologist to provide the first detailed information about the phenomenon. In the early part of the century,

Ivan Pavlov (1849–1936). Pavlov was awarded the Nobel Prize in 1904, not for his discovery of the conditioned response, but because of his research on digestion.

Ivan Pavlov was doing research on digestive glands. To stimulate the flow of digestive fluids such as saliva, he would provide his experimental animals (dogs) with food. He noticed that the dogs often produced saliva when there was no food in their mouths. Sometimes it was the sight of food, sometimes some extraneous event, such as the experimenter entering the room, that would trigger the flow of saliva. Pavlov at first called these reactions psychic secretions and considered them important enough that he dropped his original research and began to study them in detail.

To study any phenomenon under laboratory conditions, one must first bring it under control, so that it can be produced on demand. Pavlov accomplished this by isolating the dog and carefully controlling all of the stimuli presented to him. The result was the now famous conditioned response experiment. Pavlov would ring a bell and then place some food in the dog's mouth, thus causing him to salivate. After the bell and the food had been paired several times, the presentation of the bell alone would make the dog drool. You can observe a similar preliminary feeding reaction when you are preparing to feed your dog or cat.

Necessary Conditions To illustrate the essential properties of classical conditioning, we shall describe another classic experiment, this one conducted by John Watson and Marjorie Rayner in 1920. In an era in which ethical considerations were probably not as important as they are now, Watson and Rayner developed a conditioned response in a small child named Albert. They showed Albert a white rat and simultaneously produced a loud unpleasant noise by striking a steel bar behind the child's head. The sound caused Albert to cry and fall away from the noise. After several presentations of the rat and the noise, Albert began to cry as soon as he saw the rat.

All of the elements necessary for producing a conditioned response are present in the Watson and Rayner experiment (Figure 10•2). The first necessary element is a stimulus that will reliably produce an immediate reaction. In this case, the sound that resulted from striking the steel bar produced crying and falling back. This stimulus is called the **unconditioned stimulus (US)**, and the response it produces is called the **unconditioned response (UR)**.

The second necessary element is a neutral stimulus, in this case the rat. Actually, few stimuli are ever neutral in the sense that they produce no reaction at all. In fact, if a stimulus produced no reaction, it would be exceptionally difficult to establish a conditioned response to it. The best stimuli produce an *orienting reaction*—clear signs that the organism attends to the stimulus. He may turn toward it, widen his eyes, and so on. On the other hand, if he makes a strong overt reaction to the stimulus, developing a new conditioned response to it will be difficult. This stimulus, which is neutral in the sense that it does not already produce the conditioned response, is called the **conditioned stimulus (CS)**.

The third necessary element for obtaining a conditioned response is that the CS precede the US slightly in time. That is, it is much easier to get a conditioned

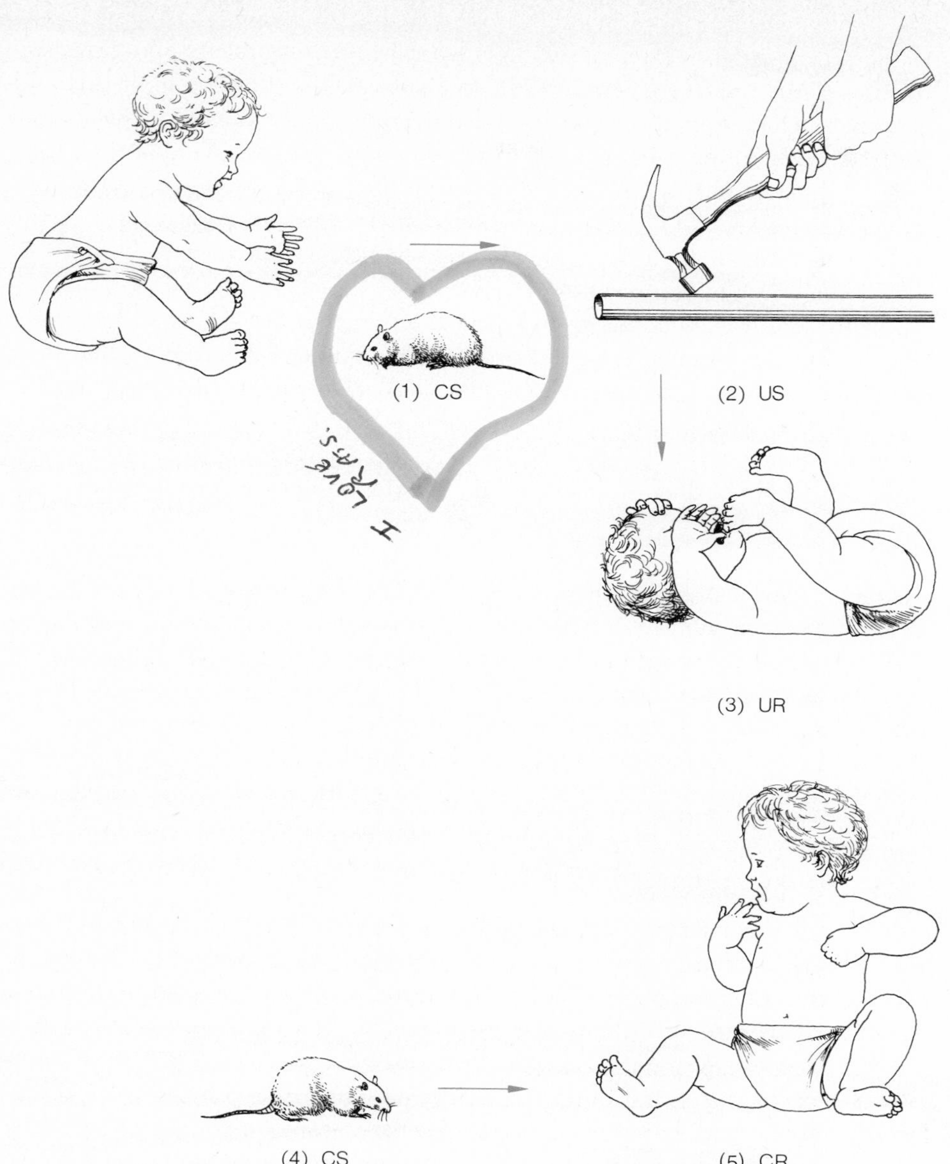

Fig. 10·2 The process of conditioning as exemplified by Watson and Rayner's experiment on the conditioning of an emotional response in a baby named Albert.

response if the rat appears slightly before the noise is heard. The time lag necessary to get the best conditioning varies depending on the response being conditioned, but a zero interval (called *simultaneous conditioning*) is less effective than some delay, and delays longer than about two seconds are less effective than shorter delays. If the US is presented before the CS, conditioning usually does not occur.

A fourth element necessary for conditioning concerns motivation: The US must do more than simply produce a UR; it must also have a positive or negative value to the organism. For example, shining a light into the eye reliably produces contraction of the pupil. Yet it is difficult to condition the contraction of the pupil by using a light as the US. On the other hand, pupil contraction can be more easily conditioned by using a brief shock to the area near the eye (Kimble, 1961).

A light, particularly a dim one, shining into the eye is a relatively neutral stimulus. On the other hand, a shock is likely to be unpleasant or even painful. Pavlov considered such stimuli as having biological significance and recognized that they were more effective as a US.

Finally, it is usually necessary to repeat the presentation of CS and US several times before conditioned responses appear. This is not always true, in that some conditioned reactions become well established after only a single presentation. The critical condition for rapid conditioning is a very strong US. Particularly, if the US is quite painful, emotional reactions such as Albert's response to the loud noise may be quite quickly conditioned. The norm, however, is gradual development with repeated presentations.

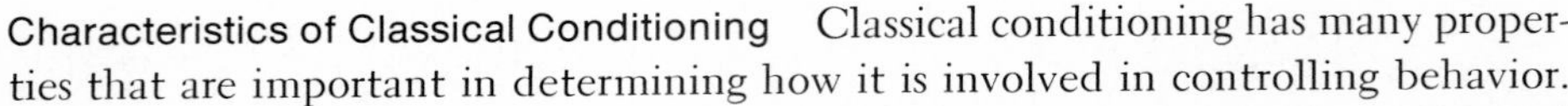

Characteristics of Classical Conditioning Classical conditioning has many properties that are important in determining how it is involved in controlling behavior.

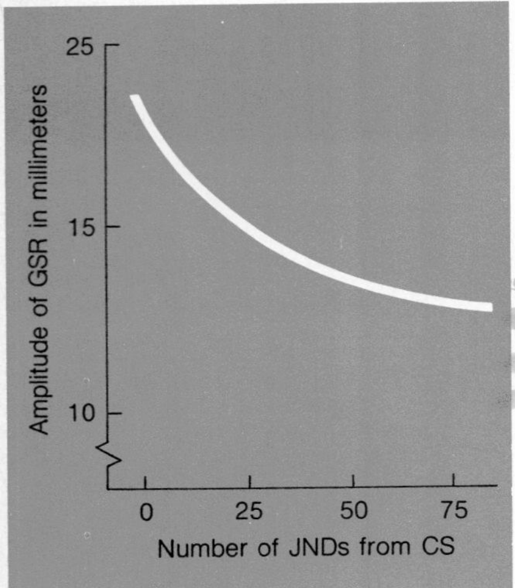

Fig. 10·3 The magnitude of a conditioned reaction to tones of varying frequency after conditioning to a 2000-hertz tone. Note that the test tones differ from one another in units called JND (the smallest detectable difference between two stimuli). The decrease in response as similarity decreases is called a *generalization gradient.* (Hovland, 1937)

Conditioned responses tend to be anticipatory. That is, when a conditioned response is fully developed, it typically precedes the occurrence of the US, or occurs before the US would have been presented. Moreover, it is not simply a replica of the UR, but differs from it in a number of ways. This means that although it is convenient to think of the development of a classically conditioned response as simply substituting the CS for the US, or transferring the UR from the US to the CS, this is not the case. A conditioned response is a particular learned reaction in its own right.

A second characteristic of conditioned responses is that they generalize from one stimulus to another. For example, Albert would cry not only when he saw the rat, but also when he saw any other white furry object such as a fur neckpiece or a Santa Claus mask. Without this phenomenon of **stimulus generalization,** it would be necessary to establish separately a conditioned response to each stimulus. This is uneconomical and downright dangerous. For example, a child who had been burned by sticking his finger into the flame of a red candle in a silver candlestick would treat a green candle or a candle in a gold candlestick as an entirely new stimulus, and he might get burned again.

The major property of stimulus generalization is that the strength of the conditioned response to some stimulus other than the CS depends on its similarity to the CS. This property is illustrated in an experiment by Hovland (1937), who paired a tone of approximately 2000 Hz (hertz) with an electric shock. Shock typically produces a momentary drop in skin resistance to an electric current, an easily measured reaction called the galvanic skin response (GSR). After the GSR had become conditioned to the tone, Hovland presented tones of 1000, 450, and

150 Hz. The greater the difference between the original CS and the test tones, the smaller the magnitude of the conditioned GSR (Figure 10•3).

As generalization enables the organism to respond to stimuli that are almost equivalent, the reciprocal process, **discrimination,** enables the organism to narrow the range of generalization whenever appropriate. This process can be demonstrated by presenting one CS (say a 1000-Hz tone) with the US, and a similar stimulus (say a 500-Hz tone) without the US. The result is that conditioned responses that initially generalize—that is, occur to both stimuli—soon become much more frequent to the CS that is paired with the US (Figure 10•4).

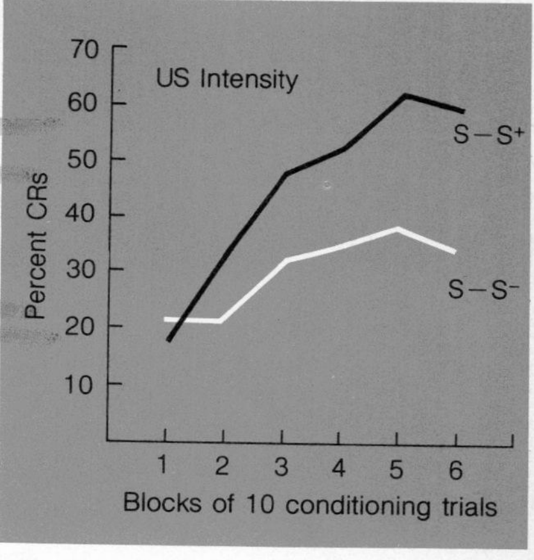

Fig. 10•4 This graph shows the effect of presenting the US with one tone (S+) and not with the other (S−). In this experiment, the US was an air puff to the eye and the CR an anticipating blink to the tone. Note that as conditioning continues, the difference in response to the two stimuli increases. (From Runquist, Spence, and Stubbs, 1958)

It would be a tragedy, at least for Albert, were he to spend the rest of his life crying whenever he saw anything white and furry. Fortunately, conditioned responses are not necessarily permanent. Although they generally do not disappear spontaneously with the passage of time, they may be eliminated by a procedure called **extinction.** This is accomplished by presenting the CS repeatedly without the US. That is, Watson and Rayner could give Albert psychotherapy by presenting the rat to him without the loud noise. Presumably, Albert would at first cry every time the rat was shown to him, but would eventually stop crying. A variation of the extinction procedure, called **desensitization,** would be to show the rat to Albert at a great enough distance that he did not cry. The rat would then be moved progressively closer, in steps small enough not to evoke the crying reaction, until he was able to touch it.

The unfortunate thing about extinction is that it is not permanent. Conditioned responses, once eliminated, often reappear after a time. This phenomenon is called **spontaneous recovery.** Repeated extinction periods, however, tend to prevent spontaneous recovery.

Sensory Preconditioning The principle that a reliable response is necessary for conditioning to occur has one exception: sensory preconditioning, a form of latent learning. Suppose Watson and Rayner had started with two neutral stimuli such as a bell and a flashing light. They could present the bell followed by the light several times and Albert would show very little reaction other than perhaps attending to the two events. The question is whether any association between the two stimuli would have occurred. The test involves two stages. First, the light is presented with a loud noise; then once the conditioned response of crying has been established to the light, Albert can be tested with the bell. If the conditioned response transfers to the bell, we infer that an association was indeed established between light and bell in the first training period. There is no indication that Watson and Rayner actually tried this experiment, but sensory preconditioning has been demonstrated several times. For example, Brogden (1939) presented dogs with 200 pairings of a buzzer and a light. He then conditioned the dogs to lift one leg in response to the light by pairing the light with a shock to the foot. He then tested the dogs with the buzzer, and they lifted the leg in response to the buzzer.

Types of Conditioned Responses A wide variety of conditioned responses has been established in the laboratory with humans and other animals. Generally, conditioned responses can be classified in terms of the nature of the US used and the nature of the response that is conditioned. A US is *appetitive* if it is generally attractive to the organism, or *aversive* if it is a generally unpleasant stimulus such as a loud noise.

Responses may be classified as *skeletal* if they involve the musculature of the body, *organic* if they involve internal organs, or *glandular* if they involve the glands. All of these kinds of conditioning have been established at some time; examples of each type are given in Table 10•1. Three miscellaneous types of conditioned responses do not fit the classification system. *Temporal conditioning* is conditioning to a time interval as a CS. If a US is presented at regular time intervals, a conditioned response may begin to occur at the same time intervals without any external CS being presented. The second type of conditioning, *interoceptive conditioning*, involves application of the CS or the US or both directly to internal organs. The stimuli used may be warm or cold fluids applied to the intestinal lining, distention of the digestive tract or bladder, or mechanical stimulation such as pressure. Most of the work on interoceptive conditioning has been done by Soviet psychologists, much of it on medical patients. The procedure may have some medical value. For example, diuresis (the excessive secretion of urine) has been conditioned in a neutral situation by using excessive fluid intake as a US. Both the urge and the need to urinate are then aroused in that situation.

In the third type of conditioning, called either *voluntary instructed conditioning* or *anticipatory instructed conditioning*, the US is a verbal command to make a voluntary skeletal response. The classic demonstration was performed on young children by A. G. Ivanov-Smolensky in 1933. The children were instructed to press a small rubber bulb on command. In the experiment, the word *press* was preceded by a CS. Bulb-squeezing conditioned responses to the CS soon began to appear.

Implications of Classical Conditioning As you can see, classical conditioning is not simple. It demands certain conditions for its occurrence, and classically conditioned responses have some flexibility. Moreover, the many kinds of responses

Table 10·1 Examples of Typical Conditioned Responses

TYPE OF CONDITIONED RESPONSE	APPETITIVE	AVERSIVE
Skeletal	Swallowing (food or water in mouth)	Eyelid reflex (air puff to cornea)
Organic	Gastrointestinal secretion (food)	Electrodermal—GSR (shock)
Glandular	Salivation (food in mouth)	Salivation (acid in mouth)

NOTE: The typical US is given in parentheses.

and stimuli that can be involved in conditioning suggest that classical conditioning as a form of learning could be involved in a wide variety of behaviors. Certainly, it is not simply a laboratory curiosity, or a way of teaching dogs to drool. In real life, of course, there is no experimenter to present CS and US together until the response develops. Nevertheless, the critical events for the establishment of classically conditioned responses are present in the normal environment of every person. The essence of classical conditioning is that the occurrence of one stimulus (the US) depends on the occurrence of another stimulus (the CS). It is not difficult to think of real-life situations in which this relation holds. A student provided the following example:

> I was standing on a street corner when a bus drove by and blew dust and exhaust fumes in my eye. Now every time I see a bus coming, my eyes water and I close them.

Although this example may seem trivial, the role of classical conditioning in our lives is not trivial. The example is typical of what could be called defensive reflexes—anticipating reactions designed to protect the organism against potentially harmful stimuli. We close our eyes when something seems about to hit us in the face, and we flinch when threatened with a blow. These are other simple examples of such conditioned responses.

Another function served by classical conditioning is to regulate body reactions to external stimuli. Many internal reactions are partially controlled, not by the US that normally produces these reactions but by a wide variety of conditioned stimuli. We salivate when we see food or a picture of food, or sometimes when we merely think of food. We may feel the need to urinate when we hear the sound of running water. We are sexually aroused by a variety of stimuli that are not involved in the sex act at all. Many of these reactions do more than enrich our life. They have functional significance in preparing us for events to come. The heart rate and blood pressure changes, the adrenalin flow and the cold sweat that characterize fear are often aroused by stimuli that are not inherently threatening. In fact, the Watson and Rayner experiment was motivated by a desire to demonstrate that irrational as well as rational fears were established by classical conditioning procedures. Although conditioning is probably not the whole story, there is little doubt that fears often develop in this way. How many children are afraid of dogs because of being knocked down or bitten by a dog when they were younger? And how often does this generalize to other animals?

Instrumental Conditioning At about the same time Pavlov was conducting his research on the classically conditioned response Edward Thorndike, an American psychologist, was demonstrating another type of learning. Thorndike's concern was rather academic. Darwin's arguments about evolutionary continuity among the species of animals had led psychologists to consider whether animals can consciously reason through a problem. In an attempt to answer this question, Thorndike placed a hungry cat in a cage and placed food outside the cage. Depending on the type of cage, the door could be opened from the inside by push-

The Changing Role of Conditioning in Psychology

Since conditioning is such a simple form of learning, a natural question that occurs to the student is "Why have psychologists spent so much time studying the conditioned response, when other kinds of learning seem to be much more important?" To answer this question, it is necessary first to place the conditioned response in historical perspective.

When Pavlov discovered the conditioned response in the early part of the century, he was not interested in it from a psychological point of view. Being a physiologist, he was interested in the workings of the body, not the mind. He saw the conditioned reflex experiment as a technique for revealing how the brain works, particularly what he called "higher cortical functions." The conditioned response was interesting to him not because it was the way learning occurred, but because one could infer from the various effects stimulation produced on the conditioned response just how the brain deals with these stimuli.

However, Pavlov did not entirely ignore the psychological implications of conditioning. As he became more and more involved in the study of the conditioned response, he came to believe that this response was the unit of all learned activity, and that complex learned behavior was simply a compound or chain of conditioned reflexes. The analogy between biology and psychology was simple: as the cell is the unit of life, so the conditioned response is the unit of learned behavior. This idea, combined with the philosophical conviction that except in nonhumans all behavior is due to learning, placed the conditioned response in the forefront of psychological research. As research began to accumulate, it became apparent that this simple notion would not suffice. The picture was complicated by several developments, not the least of which was the detailed analysis of instrumental conditioning and its differences from the Pavlovian variety provided by B. F. Skinner.

These developments did not immediately diminish the importance given to the Pavlovian procedure. Rather, psychologists assumed that conditioning experiments involve all of the essential properties of other learning. Since these situations were obviously better controlled than the practical learning situations in education and other aspects of everyday life, they should be a good source of learning principles. This view is not totally different from Pavlov's original conception of what he was about, but the emphasis has shifted from what conditioning tells us about the functioning of the brain to what it tells us about the psychological processes involved in learning.

Pavlov never studied the brain directly, but inferred what the properties of the brain had to be to produce the conditioning phenomenon. Likewise, psychologists never observed mental learning processes directly, but inferred them from the results of the conditioning experiments. From this point of view, the *facts* of conditioning do not necessarily have general applicability to more complex learning situations. These situations must be analyzed in their own right. The conditioning experiment, because of its simplicity, is intended to reveal the nature of the mind. It is the operation of these abstract principles that one applies to other situations. This position is exemplified most clearly by Clark Hull, an American psychologist who used principles derived from conditioning experiments to explain such diverse phenomena as the primacy and recency effect in serial recall (see Chapter 9) and the occurrence of latent learning and insight in maze learning.

Since the time of Hull and his more active students, this rather grandiose expectation for the conditioned response experiment has been continually eroded. Not the least of the reasons for this has been the difficulty in using conditioning principles to deal with complex human behavior, such as language and problem-solving. Whereas in an earlier day, research on these problems was often conducted within the framework of conditioning, emphasis is now on more complex psychological operations. The simple association between two events demanded by the conditioned response experiment was simply not rich enough to provide a complete picture of the mind.

Nevertheless, conditioning does play an important role in many situations, and its study is still important.

ing a pedal, pulling a loop, or turning a latch. From his observations of how the cat got out of the cage on successive occasions, Thorndike concluded that the cat did not demonstrate true reasoning, but that by a process of trial and error, correct responses were automatically strengthened and incorrect responses weakened.

Whether Thorndike's conclusion was valid or could be generalized to other species is not the point. On the basis of his research, Thorndike formulated a principle called the *law of effect*, which is a general statement about learned behavior.

> Whenever a modifiable connection (between stimulus and response) is made and is followed by a satisfying state of affairs, the strength of the connection is increased.

Thus, Thorndike's cats did not solve the problem, but merely had the successful responses (those that got them out of the cage) strengthened. Eating the food outside the cage was the "satisfying state of affairs." To put it in somewhat less precise terms, rewarded behavior tends to recur and nonrewarded behavior tends to disappear. The law of effect has undergone considerable change, and modern psychologists now speak of the *reinforcement principle*, stated as follows:

> Whenever a response is followed by a reinforcing stimulus, the likelihood of that response occurring will increase.

The fundamental notion here is that behavior can be controlled by its consequences. In other words, we learn to do what results in the occurrence of reinforcing stimuli. This is not exactly the same as saying that rewarded behavior recurs, or that behavior followed by a satisfying state of affairs increases in frequency. Although most things that we call rewards or say are satisfying act as reinforcing stimuli, the reinforcement principle does not say *what* will work. A reinforcing stimulus is simply one that produces learning.

Later we shall consider whether these stimuli have anything in common, but for now it is sufficient to note that such stimuli exist, and that when their occurrence is made to depend on a particular behavior, they are called reinforcing stimuli, and the process is called **reinforcement.** Learning by reinforcement is called instrumental or sometimes operant conditioning.

The Nature of Instrumental Conditioning In contrast to classical conditioning, the most important characteristic of instrumental conditioning is that there is no discrete stimulus that will produce the response to be learned. The response must occur in order to be reinforced. The frequency of a response before reinforcement is called the **operant level.** In any given situation, some responses have a high operant level and some have a low operant level. For example, most cattle in a pasture have a high operant level for grazing and a low operant level for jumping over fences. The operant level is not necessarily innate. It is merely the level of responding before explicit reinforcement, no matter how the behavior originated.

This basic property of instrumental learning makes it seem like an inefficient learning procedure, in which one must wait for the response to occur of its own accord before conditioning it. In this sense, instrumental conditioning is not learning to make a response, but increasing the frequency of a response that is already possible.

For those who are too impatient to wait for a response that has a low operant level, a number of devices can be used to facilitate instrumental conditioning. All of these devices have the same goal: to increase the likelihood that the desired behavior will occur so that it can be reinforced. One simple way is to restrict the environment so that there is little else to do. For example, to teach a rat to press a lever, we put him in a small box with a large lever. He must spend time near the lever because he has no other place to go. A second procedure is exemplified by the method used to teach a pigeon to peck a key for food. The pigeon will peck the key immediately if a few pieces of grain are placed on it. Once the pecking is established, less and less food is placed on the key. Key-pecking will usually continue unabated even after the food has dwindled to nothing.

Shaping is the most flexible and interesting procedure for facilitating instrumental conditioning. It uses the reinforcement principle to establish a series of behaviors that come increasingly close to the desired response. Consider again

The shaping procedure can result in some rather spectacular and unlikely behaviors in animal acts. (Parrots: courtesy of Animal Behavior Enterprises, Inc.; others: Circus World Museum, Baraboo, Wisconsin)

the example of the rat learning to press the lever. At first the desired behavior may have such a low operant level that it never occurs, but as long as the rat moves around the cage (and if he is hungry he probably will do so), you can shape bar pressing by first rewarding him for going near the lever. After he has restricted his behavior to the area near the lever, you can reward him for nearing it with his paws, as when he lifts one or both front paws off the floor. Next, you demand that he rise higher, and eventually you make him touch the lever in order to obtain food. Finally, you reward him only when he presses the lever.

Shaping is not as easy as it sounds, and a great deal of skill is needed in timing the presentation of the reinforcer. Each stage must be reasonably well established before going on to the next. If one stage is too well established, the animal's behavior may become fixated, making it hard to get him to the next stage. If too much is demanded too soon, the lack of reward may cause the animal to go back to earlier responses.

Shaping procedures have enabled animal trainers to produce rather spectacular tricks, such as dogs walking on their hind legs or birds playing table tennis. What the limits of shaping are is not certain. However, behavior that is appropriate for a species is easier to obtain than behavior that is atypical, and species-specific behaviors often interfere with the performance of reinforced behaviors.

An important aspect of shaping and indeed of all reinforcement is that the reinforcing stimulus must immediately follow the desired response. Delays of only a few seconds seriously retard learning. Failure to reinforce a previously reinforced response results in extinction of that response; that is, it decreases in frequency. This is the counterpart of omitting the US in classical conditioning, which also results in a reduction in frequency of the conditioned response. Instrumentally conditioned responses, like classically conditioned responses, also show spontaneous recovery.

Stimulus Control The emphasis in instrumental conditioning is on the relationship between the response and the reinforcing event. Although there is no discrete stimulus that produces the response to be learned, this does not mean that external stimuli are not important. **Stimulus control** refers to the extent to which these stimuli determine the frequency of a response. That is, if we drastically change the environmental conditions and the response does *not* change in frequency, then the response is not being controlled by external stimuli. If we change one aspect of the environment and the response changes in frequency, then that aspect of the environment shows some stimulus control.

Stimulus control is acquired by a procedure called **discrimination training,** in which reinforcement is made contingent not only on a particular response being made, but also on the presence of a particular stimulus. Essentially, the response is reinforced in the presence of one stimulus and not reinforced in the presence of others. The stimulus correlated with reinforcement is called the positive stimulus or **discriminative stimulus.** The stimulus correlated with nonreinforcement is called the negative stimulus.

The Limits of Reinforcement

At one time, psychologists who studied instrumental conditioning were convinced that the reinforcement principle had broad generality. Any response the animal was capable of making could be shaped and brought under the control of a reinforcing stimulus.

Certainly, a large variety of behaviors in both animals and humans are a result of reinforcement applied either intentionally or accidentally. There is also no doubt that deliberate application of instrumental conditioning principles results in successful animal training. These principles have been used in schools, psychological clinics, prisons, and elsewhere to produce desired behaviors.

Yet it is becoming more apparent that the reinforcement principle is not universal and indeed has severe limitations. The first indication of these limits was a phenomenon called *instinctive drift,* as noted by Keller and Marion Breland (1961). This pair of psychologists specializes in producing rather exotic and interesting behaviors in animals for use in circuses, animal shows, television, and motion pictures. The Brelands observed that naturally occurring behaviors often interfered with the development or performance of a particular shaped behavior. For example, a raccoon trained to place nickels in a piggy bank would begin to retain the coins and rub them together. Now, raccoons exhibit an instinctive behavior of this kind with shellfish; the rubbing helps remove the shell. Large birds, such as turkeys, trained to deposit coins in a similar manner, may eat the coins instead. Animals begin gradually to substitute instinctive behavior patterns for those that have been conditioned.

This bear performing in the Moscow Circus may be about to demonstrate instinctive drift—its natural preference for walking on all fours rather than skating upright as it has been trained to do. (Eileen Christelow, Jeroboam)

Instinctive drift is not the only phenomenon that restricts the generality of reinforcement. Rats readily learn to run to a safe place when electric shock to the feet is forthcoming, but they do not readily learn to press a bar to keep from getting shocked (Bolles, 1972). Pigeons have no difficulty learning to peck a key to get food, but it is very difficult to train them to peck a key to avoid punishment.

Not only does reinforcement sometimes fail to work; it also sometimes works when it should not. Animals who eat poisoned food and become ill (but do not die) may acquire an aversion to that food (Revusky and Garcia, 1970). This phenomenon offers the possibility of controlling predator attacks on range animals used for food (for example, cattle and sheep) without killing the predator, thus satisfying ecological needs and at the same time preserving the food supply. From a theoretical point of view, the phenomenon is interesting because the reinforcement (in this case punishment) occurs many hours after the consummatory behavior it controls. This delay violates the principle that reinforcement must be immediate if it is to have any effect.

However, taste aversions are not universal in all species. Predatory birds (hawks) do not succumb to the treatment, and some forms of predators such as ferrets become only partially conditioned—they still kill prey, but do not eat it (Gustavson, Kelly, Sweeny, and Garcia, 1976).

In spite of these exceptions to the principle of reinforcement, instrumental conditioning is a general learning process. Like any other psychological process, its exact way of operating is determined by its interaction with other processes. In this case, the constraints are imposed by various biological properties specific to a given species. Nevertheless, instrumental conditioning is an important process for modifying behavior.

The final result of discrimination training is increased frequency of responding, but only when the discriminative stimulus is present. When the negative stimulus is present, response frequency is low, and sometimes zero. The significance of discrimination training for the control of behavior cannot be overemphasized, for it enables the organism to learn to make particular responses only when appropriate. Were discrimination not possible, reinforced behaviors would occur independently of environmental circumstances, a result that would be truly chaotic. In fact, a good deal of the early social learning of children involves learning such discriminations. For example, certain behaviors may be allowed in children when they are alone with the family but discouraged when company is present.

The concept of stimulus control does not imply perfect discrimination, however. Figure 10•5 shows the results of a typical experiment in the acquisition of stimulus control. A pigeon is reinforced for pecking a key illuminated with a yellow light. Stimulus control is indicated by the fact that changes in the color of the key cause a lower rate of key-pecking. Yet there is still generalization of the response to other stimuli. Just as in the generalization of classically conditioned responses, the more similar the stimuli are, the more frequently the response occurs. Discrimination training can be used to reduce generalization, however. If the pigeon is now reinforced for pecking the yellow key but is not reinforced when the key is orange, the response to the orange key will decrease, resulting in a sharper discrimination than was made originally.

Intermittent Reinforcement So far we have spoken of reinforcement as if it were perfectly correlated with a given response, that is, as if every response of a given

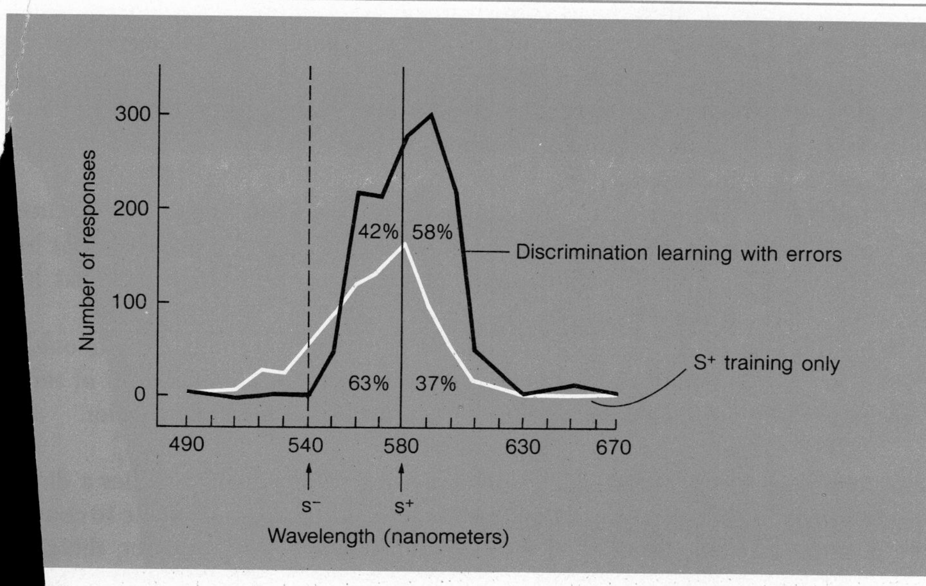

Fig. 10•5 The solid line shows a generalization gradient obtained when a pigeon is trained to peck a key illuminated with a light of 580 nanometers. When the key color is changed, the rate of pecking is reduced. The dotted line shows what happens when, in addition, pecking a key illuminated with a light of 540 nanometers is not reinforced. Note that the gradient is steeper, with responding dropping to zero at 540 nanometers. Note also that response on the other side of the rewarded stimulus increases in frequency. (From Terrace, 1964)

kind were reinforced. In real-life situations, reinforcing stimuli seldom follow every instance of a response. For example, not all telephone calls reach the desired party, not all movies are good ones, and mothers do not feed their children every time they cry. This situation is called intermittent or partial reinforcement.

Typically, intermittent reinforcement is said to be delivered according to a schedule that determines when the reinforcing stimulus will occur. Schedules may be based on time, in which case they are called *interval schedules*, or they may be based on the number of responses, in which case they are called *ratio schedules*. In either case, reinforcement may be *fixed* or *variable*.

In a fixed-interval schedule, reinforcement is provided for the first response that occurs after a specified time interval since the last reinforcement. A fixed-ratio schedule results in reinforcement of the first response after a specified number of responses. Variable-interval and variable-ratio schedules are similar except that the time and number of responses vary from reinforcement to reinforcement. For example, in a variable-ratio schedule the first reinforcement might occur after five, the second after eight, the third after four, and the fourth after seven responses. This would be called VR-6, since the average number of responses between reinforcement is six.

Behavior reinforced by a certain schedule has certain characteristics. For fixed interval schedules the most adaptive behavior would be to wait out the interval, then make the one response that produces reinforcement. The usual pattern, however, is very few responses immediately after reinforcement, with a gradual increase in responding up to the time of reinforcement. Fixed-ratio schedules occur in industry as *piecework pay*—workers are paid by the amount produced. The typical behavior brought about by a fixed-ratio schedule is a high rate of response to complete the ratio requirement, followed by a rest period or break immediately after reinforcement. Both variable-interval and variable-ratio schedules produce regular rates of responding, and that responding is extremely resistant to extinction. The pauses characteristic of fixed schedules are not present, and variable-ratio schedules in particular can produce very high rates of response (Figure 10•6). The most familiar example of variable-ratio schedules are sl[illegible] machines in gambling casinos.

Many intermittent schedules of reinforcement, particularly variable-ratio sc[illegible] ules, produce extremely high resistance to extinction. That is, a response th[illegible] been consistently reinforced extinguishes much more readily than one th[illegible] been reinforced intermittently.

In real life, most reinforcements are not likely to conform consistently [illegible] these schedules in its pure form. There are many complex combination[illegible] four basic schedules, and each produces its own specific type of behav[illegible]

Implications and Applications The principle of reinforcement provi[illegible] means by which manipulation of environmental conditions can be mad[illegible] the behavior of both animals and men. Although, as we shall see lat[illegible]

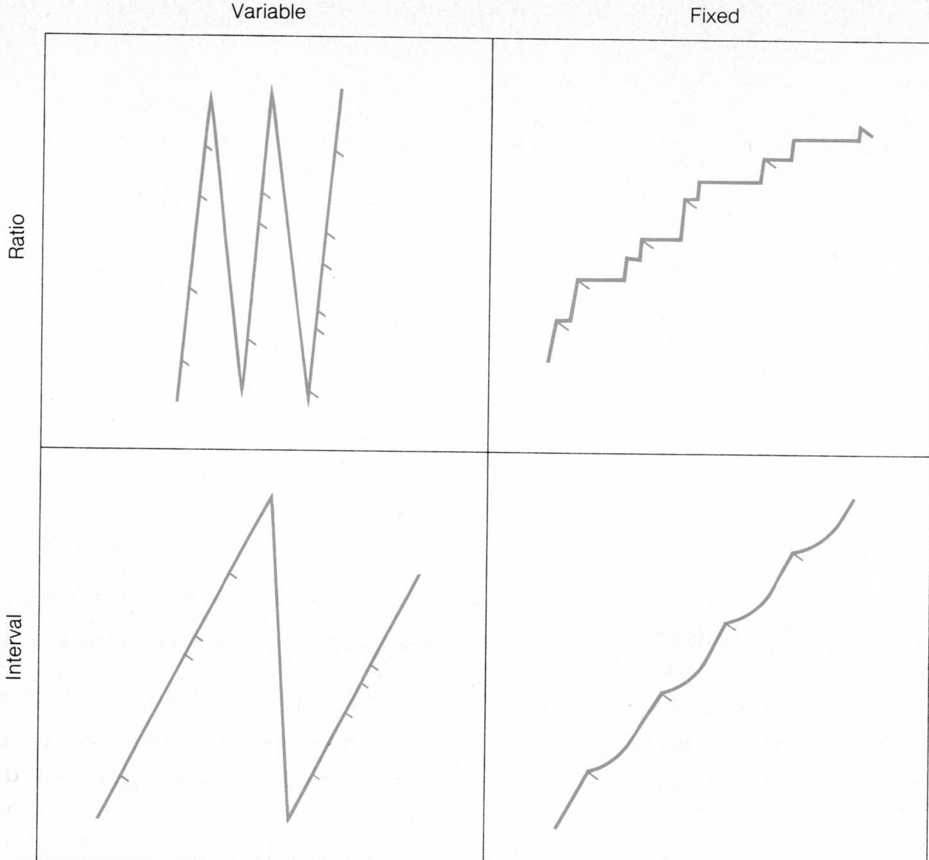

Fig. 10·6 Cumulative records of responding with different reinforcement schedules. Each time the animal responds, the line rises; thus the more rapid the response, the steeper the graph. These kinds of records reflect response rate very clearly. The diagonal slashes represent points where reinforcement was given.

limitations to the principle, it has proved exceptionally valuable in teaching lower animals, young children, and special groups of people, such as the mentally retarded, with whom verbal communication is difficult. The power of the reinforcement principle is so great that a whole technology has developed around it. Its three most common applications are in psychotherapy, education, and animal training.

The use of certain psychotherapeutic procedures called **behavior modification** has steadily increased during the last decade. They have been applied to the treatment of a wide variety of disorders, from emotional disturbances to mental retardation, chronic juvenile delinquency, and psychosis. The purpose of these techniques is to replace socially and personally maladaptive behaviors with acceptable behavior, or to transfer the control of behavior from inappropriate to appropriate discriminative stimuli. The techniques for accomplishing these goals in principle do not involve procedures beyond those described in this chapter. In practice, however, a great deal of skill, ingenuity, and patience is involved in shaping what often prove to be extremely complex behavior patterns. A further discussion of behavior therapy appears in Chapter 17.

Although most teachers are well aware of the effectiveness of praise and encouragement in reinforcing desirable behaviors in the classroom, the formal application of instrumental conditioning principles has been in the development of automatic teaching devices. These devices can be anything from specially designed books to instruction by computer. Most technical aids involve more than just principles of instrumental conditioning, but many of them follow the same format: The student is asked a series of questions; he answers them; and he is immediately informed whether he is correct. The questions are chosen so that wrong answers seldom occur (thus producing almost continuous reinforcement), and lead the student to expand his knowledge and acquire even difficult concepts. This progression in small steps toward final mastery is supposed to be analogous to shaping.

Aversive Learning So far we have considered instrumental conditioning largely within the context of *positive reinforcement*, that is, reinforcement produced by giving the organism something it wants. Informally, these kinds of reinforcement are normally thought of as rewards. However, a great deal of learning depends on the occurrence of unpleasant stimuli. These stimuli are involved in learning in two ways, and it is important to distinguish between the two.

When a particular response can cause the termination of an unpleasant stimulus, the learning is by *negative reinforcement*. It is negative not because of its effects on behavior, but because something is taken away from the organism rather than given to him. Negative reinforcement has the same effect on desired behavior as positive reinforcement: The response increases in frequency.

The training of a pet can entail negative reinforcement in order to reduce the frequency of undesired behaviors such as running away. (Joseph A. Kovacs, Harvard Crimson; Stock, Boston)

The second form of learning involving unpleasant stimuli is called **punishment.** Instead of taking away an unpleasant stimulus when a response has been made, we *present* an unpleasant stimulus when undesired behavior occurs. The general effect, as is well known, is a reduction in the frequency of that response.

Negative Reinforcement There are two forms of aversive learning involving negative reinforcement: (1) **Escape learning** is the learning of a response that will terminate an unpleasant stimulus; (2) **avoidance learning** involves a stimulus signaling that something unpleasant is about to occur. This stimulus gives the organism a chance to make a response that will prevent the occurrence of the unpleasant stimulus. For example, a rat placed in a box with an electric grid floor and a "safe" platform will soon learn to run to the platform when the floor is electrified. If a signal such as a light precedes the occurrence of the shock, the rat will learn to run to the platform when the light goes on, and before the shock occurs.

Simple escape and avoidance behaviors are also part of our everyday repertoire. We soon learn ways of getting away when trapped in an unpleasant social situation; we may even learn behaviors that enable us to avoid those situations when the environment provides signals that one is imminent.

The Pigeon as Pilot

Long after World War II, B. F. Skinner (1960) whimsically recalled an ingenious but bizarre research project in which he was involved during the war.

The problem was the gross inaccuracy of aerial bombardment. Despite elegant and sophisticated instrumentation and much practice, bombardiers were unable to hit specific targets with any regularity. There were too many factors, many of them unknown to the bombardier.

The ideal solution was to have someone in the bomb to steer it (a solution eventually adopted by the Japanese), but the cost of one pilot's life with each bomb was considered too high. Skinner, with typical ingenuity, suggested using pigeons as pilots. Pigeons have one behavioral characteristic that would make them ideal for this function: They can be trained to produce thousands of pecking responses without showing extinction if they are placed under certain reinforcement schedules.

Skinner's idea was simple: Mount the pigeon in the nose of a self-propelled bomb, and train him to peck at an image of the target no matter where it appears on a screen in front of him. (This procedure, in which a pigeon pecks at a specific target as it changes position, has been well researched. It is called *feature positive training.*) A simple electromechanical system, activated by the pigeon's pecking as the image moved away from center, would correct the bomb's course to bring the image back to center. The pigeon would, of course, not survive the ride, but pigeons were considered more expendable than people.

Few technical problems occurred. The pigeon was easily trained to peck at the image of a specific target, such as a certain building, a railroad, or a bridge, and once he acquired the habit, he was uninfluenced by atmospheric pressure, centrifugal force, or external noise.

In January 1944, Skinner presented his device to a committee of distinguished physical scientists. They were impressed with the control system's ability to make course corrections in a laboratory simulation. But when they lifted the top off the control system and saw a pigeon pecking at a screen, they could scarcely contain their laughter. Further funding of the project was refused in favor of other projects with "more immediate promise of combat application."

These rather simple examples of escape and avoidance behavior should not obscure the biological utility of these behaviors. Avoidance learning seems especially important to survival in that it protects the animal from potentially harmful stimuli.

The negative reinforcer for escape learning is obvious, but the reinforcing event for avoidance learning has been more difficult to identify. Since the unpleasant stimulus does not occur, how can it be reinforcing? Furthermore, the fact that the response occurs without the negative reinforcer ought to produce extinction. Some psychologists (for example, Mowrer, 1947) have suggested that avoidance learning has two stages (Figure 10•7). In order to maintain avoidance learning, one must first learn to fear the warning signal. This learning presumably occurs by classical conditioning in which the warning signal is the CS and the unpleasant stimulus the US. Fear then becomes a conditioned reaction to the CS. If a response occurs that prevents the occurrence of the US, it usually also removes the animal from the danger signal and reduces fear. The reduction of fear is presumed to be the reinforcing event.

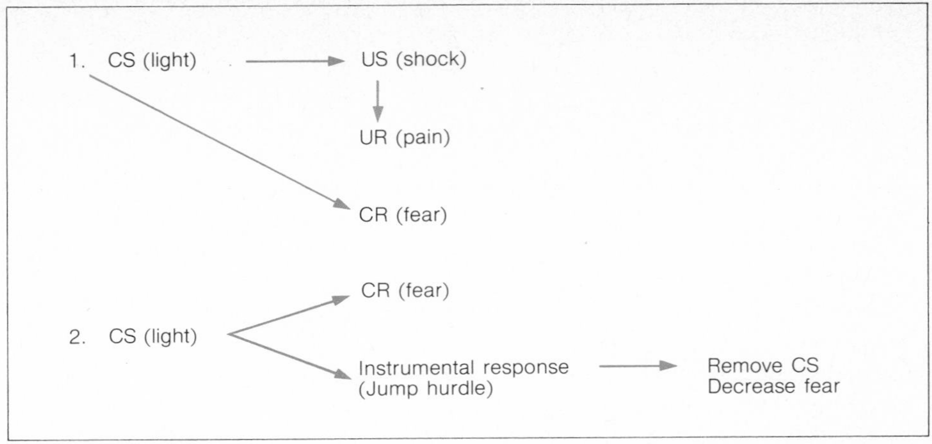

Fig. 10·7 The two stages involved in the two-factor theory of avoidance learning.

This interpretation has been supported by the fact that avoidance responses that cause the warning signal to disappear are learned more readily and remain more stable than those in which the warning signal remains after the response.

Punishment All other considerations aside, punishment of a response effectively reduces its occurrence. To be effective, however, punishment must be used properly. Some peculiar characteristics of punished behavior necessitate a great deal of care in using the procedure to control behavior.

Several characteristics can make a punishing stimulus more effective. First, unpleasant stimuli that have a sudden onset (such as a slap) are much more effective than stimuli whose unpleasantness grows slowly (such as hunger or standing in a corner). Second, a punishing stimulus is more effective if it is delivered immediately after the response has been made rather than after some delay. It may do little good to punish a cat for killing a bird unless it was caught in the act. Third, more intense stimuli are more effective. A hard slap is more effective than a light tap. Finally, in contrast to positive reinforcement, punishment for every response seems to suppress responding better than punishment delivered on an intermittent schedule. Thus, intense stimuli applied suddenly and immediately after every undesired response has occurred produce the most effective suppression.

Once a punished response has been completely suppressed, it is unlikely to return for a long time. This would seem to make punishment an ideal method for eliminating undesirable behaviors. However, a number of other effects on behavior that can or do result from the punishment process complicate the situation.

Responses that are incompletely suppressed or that have received only mild punishment often exhibit recovery. In fact, they may actually show a temporary increase in frequency above their level prior to punishment. This contrast effect seems not to be permanent and may result from a decrease in the intensity of a punishing stimulus as well as from its complete omission.

Perhaps the most important problem engendered by punishment results from

Traumatic Avoidance Learning

In classical conditioning, the presentation of the conditioned stimulus (CS) without the unconditioned stimulus (US) produces extinction of the conditioned response (CR). When the CS signals impending doom, however, the US does not occur as long as the avoidance behavior occurs. Whenever the animal fails to make an avoidance response, the US occurs, thus keeping the CS-fear association intact. If we turn off the US, so that it never occurs even if the animal fails to avoid, does the avoidance response extinguish?

R. L. Solomon, L. J. Kamin, and L. C. Wynne (1953) conducted several experiments that provide at least a partial answer. Their task required dogs to jump over a hurdle from one compartment to another. The CS was a change in illumination plus lowering a door, thus opening the hurdle. They used a very severe shock as a US, and the interval between signal onset and shock was ten seconds. After seven shocks, the dog began avoiding and thereafter for thirty trials never missed, even improving its performance (Figure 10A·1). Actually, the experimenters turned off the shock after ten trials, but the dog did not test reality to see whether there was still any danger. In short, the avoidance behavior was maintained over a long period with no evidence of extinction.

Various procedures were tried in an attempt to see whether the dogs would extinguish the behavior. For example, the experimenters quit opening the gate, so that the dog could not jump over the hurdle, thus forcing it to find out that no danger remained. Or they electrified the floor on the other side of the hurdle so that the dog jumped into a painful situation. In most cases even these severe forms of treatment were to no avail. In fact, one dog at the end of the experiment had made approximately 400 consecutive avoidance responses and was still going strong even though it had received only a few shocks at the start of the experiment.

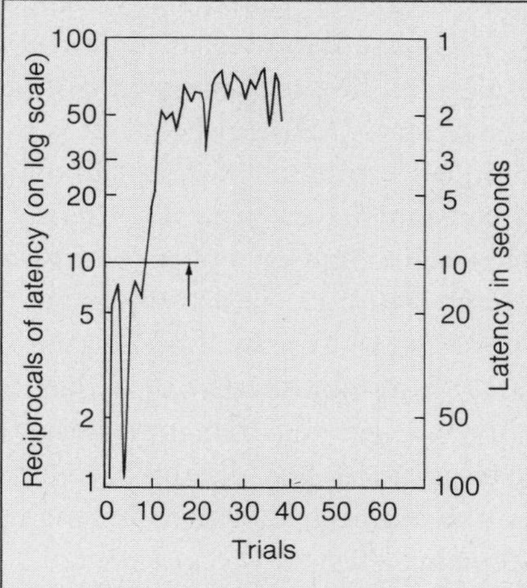

Fig. 10A·1 Performance of a typical dog in avoidance conditioning with traumatic shock as the US. The responses below the horizontal line are escape trials; responses above it are avoidance trials. Shock was turned off permanently at point indicated by arrow. (Solomon, Kamin, and Wynne, 1953)

Why is the behavior so automatic, even when free of its consequences? The investigators suggested two principles that they think characterize avoidance behavior.

The first principle is called *anxiety conservation.* They argue that the behavior in this situation becomes highly automatic and reflexive: The response occurs and removes the dog from the threatening situation even before the conditioned fear reaction (which takes a while to be aroused) can occur. Originally, fear was part of the reaction, but later the reaction occurs automatically and independently of any emotional component, much as an automobile driver reacts to a dangerous situation.

Solomon and his students argue that anxiety is conserved because it is seldom aroused as a response to the CS, and hence is not extinguished. They support their argument with two facts:

1. After a few trials, the dogs show few of the overt characteristics of fear. They simply jump the hurdle.
2. Whenever a particular response shows a long **latency** (the low spots in Figure 10A·1), it is usually followed by a very rapid response on the next occurrence of the CS—as if withholding the response results in an increase in fear.

Even with anxiety conservation, however, the response should eventually extinguish. The principle offered to explain its failure to do so is *partial irreversibility.* Fear never can be completely extinguished, especially if it is established by extremely painful stimuli. The notion that strongly established fears are permanently present has been suggested by many, including psychoanalysts.

Thus, avoidance learning is exceptionally complex, and while negative reinforcement is undoubtedly important, a number of other factors are involved.

associations with the punishing stimulus that may be acquired independently of its aversive properties. Simple discrimination learning can occur with punishing stimuli as well as with reinforcing stimuli. These discriminations are established by punishing a response when a discriminative stimulus is present but not punishing it when the stimulus is not present. Behavior then is suppressed only when the discriminative stimulus is present. This can become a serious problem when the punishing agent becomes the discriminative stimulus. For example, cats are usually punished by their owners for scratching the furniture. Any cat owner will tell you about the difficulty of eliminating furniture scratches by this means. The problem is that the cat is punished only when the owner is present, thus allowing the owner to become a discriminative stimulus for the delivery of punishment. Under these conditions, the cat is likely to learn to suppress furniture scratching only when the owner is visible. In fact, some cats learn to scratch the furniture only after looking to see whether anyone is coming.

The same phenomenon may explain the reported ineffectiveness of punishment in reducing the frequency of unlawful behavior in habitual criminals. Such criminals are punished only when caught, and therefore in the presence of the apprehending party. Unlawful behavior is thus suppressed only when these stimuli are present. Unfortunately, society cannot provide the necessary discriminative stimuli on a constant basis. However, this very principle has been used by at least one undermanned highway police force who attempted to control speeding by parking an empty patrol car in a conspicuous place near a busy highway.

Punishing stimuli can also lose their effectiveness if they come to signal a period of safety from punishment or if they can signal impending reinforcement. It has even been suggested that masochism, an abnormal desire to be physically hurt, may result from this discriminative function of punishing stimuli. In extreme cases, the occurrence of punishment may be accompanied or followed by sexual excitement which serves as a reward.

Several arguments are often given against the willful use of punishment to control the behavior of others. Most of these arguments are based at least in part on fact. One such argument is that punishment can result in chronic general anxiety or other disruptive emotional states. Although the continual occurrence of potentially punishing stimuli can result in persistent emotional disturbance, it seems unlikely that the use of punishment or negative reinforcement is sufficient to produce this effect. Typically, punished animals show signs of increased emotionality only when the punishing stimulus is applied inconsistently or unpredictably. That is, if punishment is not made to depend upon particular responses or does not follow particular stimuli, the animal may develop the symptoms of chronic fear. Animals who have been subjected to a long period of inconsistent punishment often are unable to learn escape or avoidance responses to the same punishing stimulus. Some psychologists have referred to this phenomenon as **learned helplessness.** The lesson to the parent should be clear. Effective punishment must involve a clear-cut contingency between a particular response and the punishing stimulus if unpleasant emotional side effects are to be avoided.

Burrhus Frederic Skinner (1904–)

B. F. Skinner is one of the most celebrated psychologists of our time and probably the most famous experimental psychologist of the century. Strangely enough, however, it is not his contribution as a scientist and teacher of scientists that has enabled him to achieve fame, but rather his controversial social philosophy and its applications and implications. He is better known by the public for *Walden Two,* a novel depicting a utopian society governed by psychological principles, and for *Beyond Freedom and Dignity,* an essay on the state of modern society, than for (a) *The Behavior of Organisms,* his earliest and perhaps most influential scientific work, (b) the massive amount of experimental work performed in his laboratory, or (c) the tremendous number of leading research psychologists who have trained in his laboratory or otherwise been influenced by his ideas.

His contributions to psychology are many. He first clarified the distinction between classical and instrumental conditioning. His emphasis on the role of effects or consequences of behavior in determining what animals (including people) do has led not only to a tremendous amount of research on the results of reinforcing behavior in various ways, but also to the development of technologies based on the reinforcement principle. Skinner's interest in education has led to his involvement in devising teaching machines, textbooks, and curricula using general principles gleaned from research on instrumental behavior.

Unlike many psychologists, Skinner has not tried to explain behavior by postulating various mental processes. Although he has always maintained that behavior is determined by both biological endowment and past experience—a rather conventional view—he has maintained the somewhat radical behaviorist position that mental processes such as thoughts, feelings, perceptions, and sensations do not bear any causal relation to behavior. Thus, he maintains, if we understand the environmental contingencies and the relation of the environment to the behavior of the organism, we know everything we need to know to understand its behavior. To Skinner, explaining behavior consists of being able to specify the conditions under which it occurs.

In his prophetic writing Skinner envisages a behaviorally engineered and controlled society. This view follows directly from the notion that behavior is determined by the environment, particularly by past experience with reinforcing and discriminative stimuli. His basic thesis is that once we discover the relationship between environmental events and behavior, we can use these relations to predict what a person will do, and more important, we can arrange conditions so that the person will be more likely to do what is desirable.

Behavior control is a complex and touchy issue in a democratic society. It may be fair, however, to say that Skinner regards interference with individual freedom as justified if it does the individual some good. Indeed, if we can modify behavior to make a person better, we are even compelled to do so.

It is hard to say whether Skinner's belief in environmental influences on behavior inevitably leads to instrumental conditioning as the model either for psychology or for society. Nevertheless, no one can deny that his views have had considerable influence on the course of psychology, even if sometimes only to provide a foil for theories of behavior that rely on cognitive factors to explain what we do.

A second argument against the use of punishment is that it may result in the appearance of undesirable alternative behaviors. Usually, it is considered a good thing when a punished behavior is replaced by something more desirable. In fact, a very effective program might combine punishment for the undesired response with positive reinforcement for a suitable alternative. Unwanted behaviors do result from punishment, however. These most often involve avoiding the entire situation in which punishment occurred, as in the case of the child punished for certain asocial behavior in the school, who may develop chronic tardiness or even avoid school entirely.

Finally, a frequent reaction to punishment is aggressive behavior. The punishee may attack the punisher, or may displace aggressive reactions to an innocent party. The punished child, for example, may torment the dog, just as the employee who has been rebuked by his boss may take out his anger on a subordinate or even on his wife or children.

Thus, the use of punishment involves a value judgment in which the possible undesirable consequences must be weighed against its demonstrated effectiveness, and consideration must be given to possible alternatives for accomplishing the same ends. As in most cases involving value judgments, psychologists are in no position to make prescriptions; at best they can only describe the consequences.

The Nature of Reinforcement So far we have described the function of reinforcing stimuli in instrumental conditioning, but have sidestepped an important question: What kind of things work as reinforcers? This question does not have a simple answer. It has proved to be virtually impossible to abstract any general property or properties that are common to all reinforcers. Nevertheless, we can describe in a general way some of the things that work.

Reinforcers may be classified as primary or acquired. *Primary reinforcers* are those generally universal among members of a given species; they are usually rooted in a biological need or other organic condition. *Acquired reinforcers* are those resulting from the individual's experience with the environment.

Primary Reinforcers There are three kinds of primary reinforcers. First, substances that are necessary for the survival of the individual or that otherwise return the individual to a normal physiological state are among the most universal and effective reinforcers. Their effectiveness depends, however, on a momentary need. Food, for example, is an effective reinforcer only if the individual is hungry. The reduction of pain or other unpleasant stimulation is an exceptionally effective primary negative reinforcer. The principle involved with this class of reinforcers is that whatever relieves an undesirable condition (pain or hunger) is reinforcing.

The second class of reinforcers are those that increase stimulation. The principle involved here is that whatever turns you on is reinforcing. Food is an effective reinforcer, but tasty foods are better than bland foods. Even sour fruit and pepper are better than oatmeal. Saccharine solution, which has no nutritive value, is more effective than plain water. Most animals learn various responses when reinforced by an interesting or novel happening. For example, rats kept in a dark cage learn to push a switch to make a light go on, and rats kept in a lighted cage learn to turn the light out. Monkeys learn to operate a latch and open a window to see what is outside. Rats learn to go to the side of a maze where there is a striped compartment and to avoid the side where there is only a plain gray compartment.

Under some conditions, they even do this when there is food in the gray compartment. Children learn to cry in order to be kept where there is something going on rather than be isolated somewhere. Adults are entertained by a wide variety of spectator events. The list of examples is endless.

The third class of reinforcing events are not stimuli but behaviors. Certain kinds of strongly motivated behaviors seem to be inherently rewarding, and individuals learn a variety of behaviors in order to be able to indulge in the preferred activity. Sexual behavior, whether or not it culminates in orgasm, is an important reinforcer of this type. Similarly, parents are well aware of the potency of desirable activities as reinforcers, and often use the principle to obtain certain behaviors from their children ("Clean up your room, and you can go out and play").

By learning how to open the window in order to see what's happening outside, this monkey is demonstrating the power of primary reinforcers that increase stimulation. (H. F. Harlow, University of Wisconsin Primate Laboratory)

Many common reinforcers possess more than one of these properties. For example, food reduces a biological need and often tastes good, and eating is a strongly motivated response (which for compulsive eaters may not even be related to hunger or taste). On the other hand, actually eating the food is not always necessary for reinforcement to occur. Animals have learned simple responses when reinforced by milk placed directly in the stomach or sugar fed intravenously. Similarly, sexual behavior certainly increases stimulation as well as being a strongly motivated behavior. However, it does not possess survival value for the individual (regardless of what it does for the species), and before orgasm creates rather than relieves tension. Complexities of this kind have made attempts to isolate a common property of reinforcers unsuccessful.

Reinforcement may also be obtained by directly stimulating certain parts of the **hypothalamus,** a lower brain center. This type of reinforcement has proved an exceptionally effective way of producing instrumental conditioning, but so far its relationship to externally provided reinforcers has remained obscure. A number of differences between behavior controlled by brain stimulation and that controlled by external reinforcers suggest that the external reinforcers do not simply activate a reinforcement center in the brain. For example, brain stimulation does not ever satiate: the animal will go on and on and on making the response until it virtually drops from exhaustion. Furthermore, withdrawal of brain stimulation produces extremely rapid extinction of a response, while extinction from withdrawal of external reinforcers is typically slow and gradual.

Acquired Reinforcers The reinforcers involved in most important human behaviors are, with a few exceptions, most likely to be acquired. Since individual experience is more or less unique, it should not be surprising that the stimuli falling into this class are exceptionally diverse. Indeed, the very fact that stimuli can acquire the ability to reinforce behavior means that almost any conceivable stimulus may be reinforcing for some individual. Our main concern in this section will be not to catalog these reinforcers, but to describe how a stimulus becomes a reinforcer.

Many stimuli become positive reinforcers by being associated with positive primary reinforcers. In a classic experiment, chimpanzees were taught to put poker chips into a vending machine to obtain food. Then they could be taught to make various responses to obtain the poker chips. A reinforcer that acquires its ability in this manner is called a *conditioned*, or *secondary, reinforcer.* This experiment was obviously designed to show how money, which has no inherent value, becomes an effective reinforcer. Presumably, money is reinforcing because it is associated with food.

Stimuli can also acquire negative reinforcing properties. In fact, the explanation of avoidance learning described earlier involves this form of secondary reinforcement. In avoidance learning the warning signal (CS) acquires aversive properties by being associated with an unpleasant US. The disappearance of this CS acts as a reinforcer to maintain the avoidance behavior. Thus, secondary reinforcement can be provided by presenting a stimulus associated with a positive reinforcer, or by withdrawing a stimulus associated with a punishing stimulus. We might also expect that simply presenting a stimulus associated with a punishing stimulus whenever a response occurs would reduce the frequency of that response. It does.

Armed with principles of both positive and negative reinforcement, let us return to the problem of how money acquires its reinforcing value. We can demonstrate by experiment that neutral stimuli can acquire reinforcing properties by association with food. We can also demonstrate that neutral stimuli can acquire negative reinforcing value by being associated with an unpleasant state. For some people, not having money is an unpleasant situation that produces a great deal of anxiety. Moreover, the unpleasantness of not having money may be acquired in the same way as the aversive properties of the warning signal are acquired. Money, then, may be reinforcing not because it has been associated with food, but because it relieves the anxiety associated with poverty.

A lesson can be learned here. We have demonstrated two ways in which we can make a neutral stimulus into a reinforcer. We shall see later that there are others. How did money come to be reinforcing for a particular individual? Experiments showing that money can achieve this power by being associated with the purchase of food or other primary reinforcers do not necessarily mean that for this person it *did* acquire its reinforcing value in that manner. Maybe for this person money is anxiety-reducing. Or maybe it acquired its value in some way we have not yet discovered. The point is that we cannot always explain how a particular behavior came to exist in an individual as long as there are several processes by which it could occur. This does not mean that we do not have general psychological principles. Different stimuli may be reinforcing for different individuals even though the process by which these stimuli acquire their reinforcing value is the same. Conversely, the same stimulus could be reinforcing for two different people, but it could have acquired its reinforcing value for them in different ways.

This limitation is worth remembering in interpreting the present behavior of others when you do not know their personal history.

10·4 Classical and instrumental conditioning represent means by which stimuli come to control behavior rather exactly. In classical conditioning, behavior is controlled by the conditioned stimulus. In instrumental conditioning it is controlled by discriminative and reinforcing stimuli.

It is clear, however, that not all behavior is governed by external stimuli. The effects of environmental stimuli in most animals are modulated by ideas, expectations, and other forms of knowledge. This knowledge has also been learned and is stored in memory. No one has yet been able to define clearly what form knowledge takes, but basically it consists of information about things in the world (concepts) and relations among them. Verbally, we can represent knowledge as a sentence, such as "Caesar is dead" or "It is cold, wet, and windy in Vancouver at Christmas." Knowledge is not necessarily a sentence, but rather the fact represented by the sentence.

One psychologist, D. O. Hebb (1972), has made a distinction between sense-dominated and cognitive behavior. Sense-dominated behavior is that which is completely predictable if the stimulus conditions are known, while cognitive behavior is that governed entirely by knowledge. Whereas some psychologists think that all behavior is controlled by the environment, and others think that all behavior is controlled by cognitions, the truth of the matter is that both kinds of behaviors occur. Indeed, very few interesting things that people do are purely sense-dominated or purely cognitive. Rather there is a gradation of cognitive involvement.

In the remainder of this chapter we consider how cognition affects conditioned responses. In Chapter 11 we shall discuss cognitive processes in more detail.

Cognition and Conditioning Although classically conditioned responses often appear reflexive and automatic, cognitive factors may have a profound effect on the conditioned response. The most important feature of classical conditioning is that the occurrence of the US depends on the appearance of the CS. The most important effects of cognitive factors are those that influence this relationship.

In a procedure analogous to intermittent reinforcement, the CS can sometimes be presented during conditioning without being followed by the US. Suppose we were to present the US paired with the CS half of the time, and the CS by itself half of the time. Moreover, suppose we arrange it so that first there are always two paired presentations, then two of the CS alone, then two more paired presentations, then two more CS alone, and so on. This pattern is called *double alternation* (Figure 10·8). Eventually, the individual gives more conditioned responses when the CS is followed by the US than when it is presented alone. Note that this can occur only if the pattern is learned in some way, since any given CS is distinguishable from any other CS only by its position in the sequence. Responding seldom follows the pattern perfectly, however, even when the individual can predict exactly when the US will occur. This irregularity indicates that knowl-

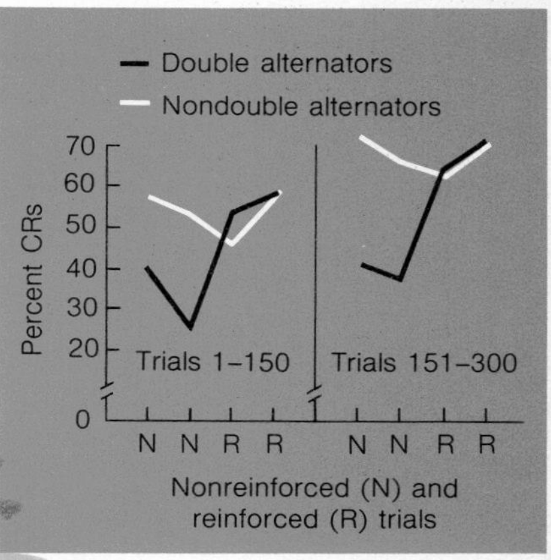

Fig. 10·8 For those people who detect the double alternation of presentation of the CS with the US and the CS alone, the conditioned responses on CS-alone presentations are drastically reduced. (Prokasy, Carlton and Higgins, 1967)

edge of the pattern can only influence, not entirely control, the occurrence of the conditioned response.

Classically conditioned responses can also be easily influenced by verbal instructions about the relationship between the CS and the US. Using a procedure similar to the one Watson and Rayner used with Albert, we can easily condition a variety of emotional reactions; these are usually indicated by such signals as changes in heart rate and blood pressure, sweating of the palms, and increased respiration. After conditioning has taken place, a marked reduction in the conditioned response occurs if the individual is convincingly told that the US will no longer follow the CS. Conditioned responses involving the skeletal muscles can also be reduced by telling the individual not to respond to the CS. Reactions such as increased heart rate are not ordinarily under voluntary control, and so simply telling a person not to respond may have little effect. By using a special instrumental conditioning procedure called **biofeedback**, the individual may be able to learn to control these organic responses.

Verbal instructions can be used not only to reduce conditioned responses, but also to enhance a conditioned response. Most people have a mild emotional reaction to the words "electric shock," particularly if they are sitting in a psychological experiment. In one experiment (Grings, Carlin, and Appley, 1962) people sitting in a darkened room heard words "cool breeze," "green light," "soft music," "dark room," "loud tone," "flickering light," and "finger vibration," each followed by the actual event described. The words "electric shock" produced a much more intense reaction than they normally would, because of a general expectation that the words would be followed by the event they described.

These examples represent only a sample of the numerous ways in which knowledge influences classically conditioned responses. Some of the effects are quite subtle. For example, it is easier to condition a person to blink an eye to the verbal CS "blink" than to the verbal CS "don't blink." Despite these effects, one should not infer that only cognitive factors are involved. Classical conditioning occurs even when the individual is actively involved in some other activity such as performing a problem-solving task or watching a movie (Ross, 1961). The fact that the person being conditioned need not attend to the stimuli in order for conditioning to occur indicates that cognitive involvement is not necessary.

The salient feature of instrumental conditioning is the relationship between the response and the reinforcing stimulus. Cognitive factors can be involved in both components. In some cases, the response that is correlated with reinforcement may be defined only in terms of specific knowledge on the part of the learner. For example, the frequency with which a subject uses words referring to transportation has been increased by reinforcing these words and not reinforcing others. Certainly there is no characteristic that differentiates these words other than the particular function served by their referents. Moreover, verbal instructions about the response desired will, under appropriate motivational conditions, facilitate learning.

Cognitive factors are also involved in determining the effectiveness of the reinforcer. Verbal instructions may again be involved in that they can often be used to convince the person of the value of executing a certain behavior or of obtaining some reinforcing object even when he or she has had no experience with the potential reinforcer. Threat of jail or execution, promise of heaven, and even life insurance are reinforcers largely because we are able to understand their consequences. There is little opportunity for them to acquire reinforcing value directly by secondary reinforcement.

Finally, a phenomenon known as **cognitive dissonance** appears to be involved in many reinforced behaviors. Essentially, cognitive dissonance is a discrepancy between the world you expect and the world you get. Part of our knowledge about the world consists of expectations about the consequences of certain acts and events. When the consequences do not fit our expectations, dissonance results. Behavior that reduces dissonance is reinforced. For example, a student who expects a high grade on a midterm examination but does not receive it may choose any of several alternatives: studying harder to bring the next results more in line with the expectations, quitting school to get away from the dissonance-producing situation, or lowering aspirations to bring expectations into conformity with achievement. All three alternatives lead to a reduction in dissonance and could be reinforced. The important point is that the dissonance is cognitively produced and influences instrumental conditioning.

This chimpanzee has adapted a long blade of dry grass to digging in an anthill for food. His behavior may be evidence that animals can solve problems through seeing a relationship between objects and events. (© National Geographic Society)

Cognitive Learning in Animals Most of our examples of pure classical and instrumental conditioning involved nonhumans and children. Adult behavior is distinctively cognitive, and it is within this domain that the clearest examples of cognitive factors in conditioning and cognitive learning (the acquisition of knowledge) can be found.

This is not to suggest that other animals do not learn in a cognitive manner, or that cognitive factors are not involved in controlling their behavior. Several demonstrations have shown that problem-solving in animals sometimes consists of much more than simply strengthening the correct response by reinforcement. Instead, they seem to solve problems by inventing new behaviors as they see the relationship between various objects and events in their environment. In one classic experiment, W. Köhler (1925) placed a banana outside an ape's cage. When the fruit was too far outside the cage to reach, the ape played with objects in the cage, which included a long stick. Suddenly the ape grasped the stick and used it to rake in the banana. The transformation from stick-as-toy to stick-as-rake was sudden and permanent. From then on, the ape used the stick whenever it was necessary to get food that was outside the cage. However, Thorndike was not necessarily wrong when he characterized his cat's behavior as trial-and-error. Species differences in learning ability are considerable (see Chapters 21 and 22). Yet even nonprimates show insight and knowledge.

The fact remains, however, that the behavior of nonhumans and very young children is controlled more by external stimuli than that of adult humans.

Summary

Learning is the capacity to change behavior as a result of experience, and is reflected in the permanent modification of behavior. Learning is not the change itself, but the process responsible for it; that is, learning may occur but not be immediately observable.

Two primitive forms of learning are *habituation*, the decrease in responsiveness to a stimulus, and *imprinting*, the rapid learning of a species-specific response to specific situations.

The two most important basic forms of learning are classical conditioning and instrumental or operant conditioning. *Classical conditioning* consists of pairing a neutral stimulus with a stimulus that produces a consistent response. The neutral stimulus gradually comes to produce almost the same response. *Instrumental conditioning* is the process by which behaviors followed by reinforcement produce learning. Reinforcers may be classified as positive when presenting them produces learning, or negative when taking them away produces learning. A punishing stimulus is one that suppresses behavior. Reinforcers may also be classified as primary (those that are innate and related to biological needs) and acquired (those that acquire their ability to reinforce through learning).

Cognitive learning refers to the acquisition of facts, that is, information about objects in the world and the relations among them. Cognitive factors are often involved with conditioned responses and either facilitate or inhibit conditioning.

Suggested Readings

DiCara, L. V. Learning in the autonomic nervous system. *Scientific American*, January 1970.

An account of the conditioning of autonomic visceral responses, including the basic principles presumed to underlie biofeedback.

Pavlov, I. P. 1972. *Conditioned reflexes.* London: Oxford University Press.

Pavlov's account of his own research as presented in a series of lectures given in 1924. This book is available from Dover Press in paperback.

Reynolds, G. S. 1975. *A primer of operant conditioning*, 3d ed. Glenview Ill.: Scott, Foresman.

An authoritative and readable review of what is known about instrumental conditioning.

Skinner, B. F. How to teach animals. *Scientific American*, December 1951.

A step-by-step description of training a dog using instrumental conditioning principles.

Skinner, B. F. 1974. *About behaviorism.* New York: Knopf.

Skinner's most recent discussion about behaviorism.

Walker, E. L. 1967. *Conditioning and instrumental learning.* Belmont, Cal.: Brooks/Cole.

A thorough introduction to classical and instrumental conditioning.

Cognition

11 In Chapter 10 we pointed out that learning may involve either conditioning or cognition or, in many instances, a combination of the two. We shall now explore cognitive processes from several different perspectives. First, we shall examine three ways of using information—transfer of training, problem-solving, and creative thinking. Then we shall look at concepts, a form of knowledge that—at least for humans—is especially useful and important. Finally, we shall consider three ways in which language and thought are interrelated.

The study of cognitive processes covers a diverse set of phenomena. It also tends to be highly speculative and theoretical —in contrast to the study of simpler forms of learned behaviors, for which experimental data are easier to gather. By their very nature, cognitive processes do not reflect themselves as directly in observable behaviors as do perceptual processes, memory, and conditioning. As a result, the measures of cognitive activity necessary for definitive research are often biased by extraneous influences and determined by factors that are difficult to control in experiments. Despite these problems, thought and research thus far on cognitive processes can help us understand how people use information, concepts, and language.

Using Information

11·1 Thinking, cognition, and knowledge are names given to one aspect of a system that also includes perception, learning, and memory. The relations between all of these are complex. For example, perception generally involves inputs to the system, but these inputs are considerably modified by learning, memory, and cognition. Memory is primarily the storage part of the system, but it plays a role in the inputs and outputs as well. Cognitive processes are involved primarily in knowing and judging, and thus are responsible for the flexibility in what

A simulation of the real task is often used either for training skills or for doing research. Transfer from such simulations is assumed to be positive. The flight simulator here is of a twin-engine Cessna 421C. (Courtesy of Cessna Aircraft Company)

you do with the information you have perceived, learned, or remembered. As with both knowledge and judgment, cognition operates in perception, modifying sensory inputs. It also plays a part in learning and memory. Its effects are most easily seen, however, in various outputs—the application of old learning to new situations, the solving of problems, and creative thought.

Transfer of Training Shortly after World War II several test pilots lost their lives in identical crashes while testing a new jet fighter plane. The pilots were all veteran fighter pilots, and no evidence could be found that the planes were defective in any way. Yet each time, after a flawless test flight, the plane would suddenly nose down and crash during its landing approach. Finally one pilot landed safely and emerged from the cockpit with the answer to the puzzle. The design engineers had placed the switch that released and inflated the life raft in the same location as the switch used to lower the wing flaps on a common World War II fighter plane. The pilot, intent on the demanding task of landing a high-performance airplane, would revert to an earlier but now inappropriate response. The life raft (placed behind the pilot) would rapidly inflate, forcing the pilot against both the stick and the control panel. The pilot who survived had grabbed his pocket knife and stabbed the life raft, deflating it before it could immobilize him.

This story illustrates **transfer of training,** the effect of previous learning on the learning or performance of a new task. Transfer may be *positive* when learning or performance is helped by previous learning, or it may be *negative,* as in the example given, when previous learning hinders or disrupts performance on the new task. If there is no effect, transfer is said to be zero.

Both practically and theoretically, transfer is one of the most important psychological concerns. It would be hard to imagine any learning, even in very young children, that is not influenced by what is already known. Many of the factors that influence learning and memory do so because of earlier learning. Formal education and training programs are in fact predicated on the assumption that what is learned in the formal setting will transfer positively to a wide variety of other tasks. Indeed, curricula and various specific training programs are usually based on particular facts or theory about the nature of transfer.

Educators at one time subscribed to what has been called *formal discipline.* The basic proposition of this belief is that various specific mental abilities can be trained by formal studies that require those abilities. Thus, courses in Latin were believed to strengthen memory, and geometry was believed to improve reasoning. About 1900, two psychologists, Edward Thorndike (the same Thorndike who observed how cats learn to get out of a cage) and Robert Woodworth, performed a series of experiments specifically examining the amount of transfer from one activity to another, and found no evidence to support formal discipline. Over the years, similar research has failed to refute Thorndike and Woodworth. Even transfer of rate of memorizing from one kind of material to something very different is almost negligible, and sometimes negative.

Thorndike and Woodworth concluded that the positive transfer that did appear in their experiments was determined by what they called identical elements—including parts, operations, aims, methods, and approaches, as well as general principles and rules, and perhaps even attitudes. Thus, practice in addition transfers to multiplication because addition is identical to one operation in multiplying. As a result of this research, more emphasis has been placed on direct training for educational objectives instead of simply assuming that transfer is broad and automatic.

The general point of view represented by the theory of identical elements also led to the discovery of various specific principles by which transfer occurs. Perhaps the most important of these is similarity. Transfer is greatest when the new learning conditions are highly similar to the conditions under which the original training occurred. For this reason, pilot training often involves a simulation of the actual airplane cockpit and various situations are programmed onto the instruments so that the prospective pilot has to learn to react appropriately. Often such devices simulate only certain aspects of the real situation.

Specific stimulus and response relations are also important determiners of transfer whenever the learning situation involves clear-cut stimulus-response reactions. In tasks that involve learning to make the same response to a new stimulus, positive transfer is greatest when the stimuli are most similar. Stimulus generalization (described in Chapter 10) is one example of the operation of this principle, but it also operates in situations other than conditioning. One of these involves memorizing word lists when cue words (stimuli) are similar and words to be recalled (responses) are the same. For example, after having learned that the Spanish *cinco* means "five," one can more easily learn that the French *cinq* means "five" than that the Cree *niyaanan* means "five" (situation A in Figure 11•1).

On the response side, the facts of transfer are somewhat more complicated. When a new response to the same stimulus is required, transfer is typically negative. Our test pilots were essentially victims of this principle when they inflated the life raft instead of lowering the flaps in a situation (the stimulus) that demanded landing the plane. The principle may also operate in learning verbal associations, although negative transfer is typically less frequent in such situations than when a specific skilled response is involved. Theoretically, it should be more difficult to learn that the Cree word for "five" is *niyaanan* after having learned the French *cinq* (situation B in Figure 11•1). When the word to be recalled is similar to the original word, transfer may be positive; that is after learning *cinq*, it should be easier to learn *cinco*. Often, however, any advantage due to similarity is wiped out by confusion over which word is French and which Spanish.

Negative transfer also occurs if stimulus and response elements are re-paired, that is, if you have to learn that what was correct for A is now correct for B and vice versa. Imagine the chaos that would result if the clutch in a car were placed on the right and the brake on the left! On some farm machinery and other heavy mobile equipment the throttle is operated with the hands and the hydraulic system that regulates the machine's function is operated with the feet. Many naive

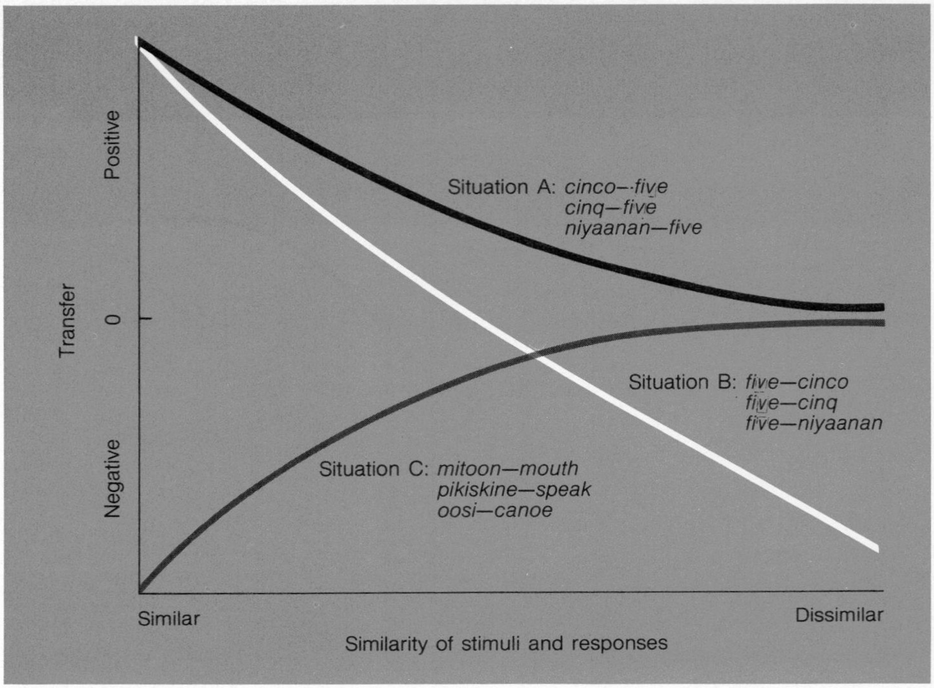

Fig. 11·1 The amount and direction of transfer in three situations where the similarity of both cue stimuli and to-be-recalled items is varied.

A. Cue stimuli vary from similar to dissimilar (*cinco, cinq, niyaanan*); to-be-recalled items identical (*five*).
B. Cue stimuli identical (*five*); to-be-recalled items vary from similar to dissimilar (*cinco, cinq, niyaanan*).
C. Cue stimuli different (*mitoon, pikiskive, oosi*); to-be-recalled items vary from similar to dissimilar (*mouth, speak, canoe*).

(Adapted from Underwood, 1949, p. 303)

operators have difficulty at first, because of the tendency to react with the feet for desired speed changes. Re-pairing verbal associations also may produce negative transfer.

Generally speaking, there is an important relation between transfer and interference in memory (see Chapter 9). The amount of forgetting produced by a prior task or an interpolated task depends upon the amount and direction of transfer. The greater the negative transfer, the more extensive will be the retroactive and proactive inhibition. When transfer is positive, interference—if it exists at all—is slight. In one experiment (Barnes and Underwood, 1959), people learned to associate several nonsense words with two-syllable adjectives (for example, JOV = insane) so that they could recall the adjectives when given the nonsense words. They then memorized a second set of words in which the nonsense words were the same but the adjectives different. After learning the second set, they were asked to recall the adjectives from the first set. When the second adjective was unrelated to the first one (for example, JOV = peaceful), a situation that produces negative transfer, 51 percent of the first list of adjectives could be recalled. When the second adjective was a synonym of the first list (for example, JOV = crazy), a situation that produces positive transfer, 86 percent of the adjectives could be recalled.

Transfer of specific stimulus-response relations is not necessarily direct, but may be mediated by a network of associative linkages between elements. For example, once we have learned that Mike is in Moose Jaw, and that Moose Jaw is in Saskatchewan, it is a relatively simple matter to learn that Mike is in Saskatchewan. Note that having learned that Mike is in Moose Jaw, you *should* find it harder to learn that Mike is in Saskatchewan because you are essentially learning a new association to a previous stimulus. Positive transfer is made possible by the existence of the mediating association between Moose Jaw and Saskatchewan.

Many forms of transfer do not involve the transfer of specific stimulus-response relations. One extremely important class of transfer phenomena has been labeled **learning sets** or learning-to-learn. People and other animals generally are better at learning tasks when they have had more experience in learning tasks of the same type. For example, if people are required to learn lists of words in the laboratory, they improve from list to list even though there are no words repeated in the various lists. Monkeys learn to solve a simple problem—such as determining which object conceals some food—more efficiently when they have had several problems of the same kind previously, even when the actual objects change from problem to problem. The defining characteristic of learning sets is that no similarities exist among the actual stimuli or responses that can produce the transfer.

Exactly what one learns in acquiring a learning set is not well understood. Whatever is involved, the particular skills learners acquire exist at several different levels. For example, practice learning of lists of word pairs produces more transfer to learning different pairs than to learning a serial string. Moreover, transfer is greater from word lists to other word lists than to lists of nonsensical letter combinations. However, general learning skills are also acquired, since there is some positive transfer even across tasks.

Whereas in some cases learning sets seem to involve learning skills or special techniques, such as learning to image more effectively or learning to use available study time more effectively, they also involve learning specific rules or general principles that can be applied to a variety of learning materials. You may recall the differences in transfer to new problems between retardates who learned to solve simple subtraction problems by memorizing the answers and students who learned the principles of subtraction. Effects of this kind have been demonstrated in many cases. Primarily because of its greater transferability, learning by understanding is superior to learning by rote memorization.

This rabbit is doing tasks similar to tasks it has done before. It was first trained to turn the wheel in the "Charlie Chance" act. Then it was easily transferred to the task of twirling the Easter egg after pawing in the finger paint. These two behaviors use the food-getting behavior of the rabbit—the rapid, repetitive scratching with which a rabbit digs up roots and the like. (Animal Behavior Enterprises, Inc.)

Problem-solving A problem situation exists whenever a person is trying to attain some goal that his immediate reaction does not accomplish and several courses of action are possible. A hungry rat searching for food in a maze, a student working out the intricacies of registration, a mechanic trying to diagnose and correct a malfunction in a car, and a politician trying to devise a scheme for relieving poverty or preventing a war—all are engaged in problem-solving.

Problem-solving, strictly speaking, is not a form of learning because a person who has learned the solution to a problem can readily repeat it the next time the problem occurs. Nevertheless, learning is involved in problem-solving because previous learning plays an important part in the process and may largely determine how and when the problem is solved. Problem-solving is largely a problem in transfer of training, and many of the things that happen when people try to solve problems illustrate the principles of transfer we have just described.

When he needed some protection from the sun, this man found another use for a newspaper besides the standard one of reading it. (© Elizabeth Hamlin, 1976; Stock, Boston)

The most dramatic and noticeable transfer effects in problem-solving are negative—that is, situations in which knowledge acquired in similar situations is now inapplicable but dominates attempts to solve the present problem. Such negative transfer may take several forms.

Some problems can be solved by simply performing a series of steps or operations, called *algorithms*. For example, the solution to a quadratic equation can be obtained by simply using the appropriate formula and plugging in the coefficients. A series of problems all solvable by the same algorithm may lead a person to apply this algorithm automatically, without thinking about each problem. As long as the algorithm works, this behavior is adaptive, but if the nature of the problems changes, the person may experience great difficulty in abandoning the algorithm and finding a new solution. In simple mathematics problems, a student may try an inappropriate algorithm over and over, as if not believing that it does not work. Students also persist in using a complex and tedious solution to a problem even though a simple and direct one is possible, if they have successfully used the long solution in the past. Although usually helpful, algorithms are not always a good thing, since they may block the emergence of an appropriate or more efficient solution.

A second and similar source of negative transfer in problem-solving is called *functional fixedness*, the tendency to see an object's uses in terms of only the customary ones. For example, an electrical switch is commonly used only to switch electrical devices on or off; and so a person using the weight property of a switch to solve the problem of papers blowing away must have overcome the tendency to see the switch only as a switching device.

There has been a great deal of research on functional fixedness, and several facts about its negative transfer effects on problem-solving have emerged:

1. The negative effect of functional fixedness occurs only when an unusual use of an object is essential to solving a problem. When the solution involves the normal use of an object, interference with the solution does not occur.
2. Training in unusual uses for objects reduces the negative effect.
3. The negative effect is more serious when the common use for an object is emphasized. For example, a small cardboard box can be fastened to a wall with a thumbtack and used as a shelf; people more readily see the box as a shelf if it is given to them empty than if it is given to them with something in it (Glucksberg, 1962).

Transfer from previous learning is a major cause of difficulty in solving problems. The type of solution attempted in a problem-solving task obviously depends upon the problem-solver's assessment of what the problem is. (Note that we said *type* of solution. A problem-solver never tries all possible solutions, but instead restricts his attempts to solutions that seem appropriate.) The assessment of the problem

Problem-solving:
Algorithms and Heuristics

In general, all problems involve a number of possible actions, only one or a few of which are appropriate. Many problems also involve subgoals. In these cases, a single response does not solve the problem, but puts the solver in a better position to proceed. Thus, solving a problem often involves two processes: selecting subgoals, and selecting responses to meet the subgoals.

Problem-solving procedures fall into two broad categories, *algorithms* and *heuristics.* An algorithm is a fixed procedure that, if applied to a given problem, always generates a solution. Examples of algorithms come largely from mathematics. The procedure for solving quadratic equations, the determinant method for solving simultaneous equations, the procedure for extracting the square root, and the binomial theorem for computing the probabilities of events are all algorithms. To arrive at a solution, one need only follow a set procedure.

Algorithms may appear in any situation in which following a specified set of rules will produce a given outcome. A recipe for bread is an algorithm for baking bread. The owner's manual gives an algorithm for starting a tractor, or for computing a sum on an electronic calculator. Algorithms need not be efficient. One algorithm for solving anagrams (words with the letters scrambled) would be to systematically generate every possible letter arrangement and check it to see whether it is a word. The inefficiency comes from the fact that some possibilities (for example, *sbn*) cannot exist, and hence are wrong regardless of where the other letters might be.

In Go, which originated in China perhaps forty-two centuries ago but has flourished in Japan in more recent centuries, each player seeks to control as many of the 361 positions as possible. With each turn a player must decide where best to place a stone so as to enclose territory or to stop the opponent from enclosing territory. (Mark Chester)

Most human problem-solving is characterized not by algorithms, but by heuristics. Although an exact definition is difficult, essentially a heuristic is a rule that reduces the number of possible solutions to a problem that must be considered. For example, in chess there are 10^{120} alternative patterns of response through the board. An algorithm that tries to provide a fixed rule for responding in every situation is clearly hopeless. With that many possibilities it would be equally hopeless to consider the consequences of every potential move. Consequently, heuristic principles essentially determine chess decisions, as when a player considers only moves that do not place a piece in danger of being captured.

A heuristic does not guarantee a solution; often it does not provide a solution at all. Heuristics do have one advantage over algorithms: A given heuristic can be applied to a broader variety of situations, whereas an algorithm may be quite specific. Heuristics can, for example, narrow alternatives, define subgoals, control the sequence of hypotheses examined, and select a part of the problem to begin on.

type, however, can only be made in terms of the solver's familiarity with similar problems. In other words, the problem is initially classified on the basis of familiar elements.

What often makes a problem a problem is that certain elements, because of their familiarity, are identified as critical to its solution but are actually irrelevant;

and so any attempts to solve the problem by manipulating these elements will fail. Repeated failures to solve a problem by applying a stereotyped approach should (but unfortunately often do not) force the solver to reassess the problem—to look for crucial differences between the present problem and those it seems to resemble, to question initial assumptions about the properties and uses of the elements in the problem situation, and to combine these elements in less obvious ways that might lead to a solution. Hints provided by someone who already knows the solution or who perceives different critical elements in the problem can also make the solver reassess the problem situation and redirect his efforts at solving it.

In sum, freeing oneself from familiar, often stereotyped, patterns of thinking is a necessary condition for successfully solving many problems. Only if we are able to overlook the obvious, will we be able to find a less salient characteristic, an unusual function, or a subtle relationship on which the solution might depend.

Creative Thinking Problem-solving often demands the ability to produce extremely rare or completely novel responses in familiar situations. This ability, the thing we call originality, is the main ingredient in creative accomplishments.

Originality is not the only element of **creativity,** however. By our definition, an original idea is simply an unusual one for a given setting, and it may be unusual for reasons that have nothing to do with creativity. It is well known, for example, that mental patients typically give many unusual responses when asked to free-associate with common English words. Yet few if any of these people would be considered creative. A rare response may mean no more than that an individual is

---

An ingenious invention—but one wonders about its usefulness in any age. (From *Absolutely Mad Inventions,* compiled from the records of the U.S. Patent Office by A. E. Brown and H. A. Jeffcott, Jr.)

DEVICE FOR PRODUCING DIMPLES.

No. 560,351. Patented May 19, 1896.

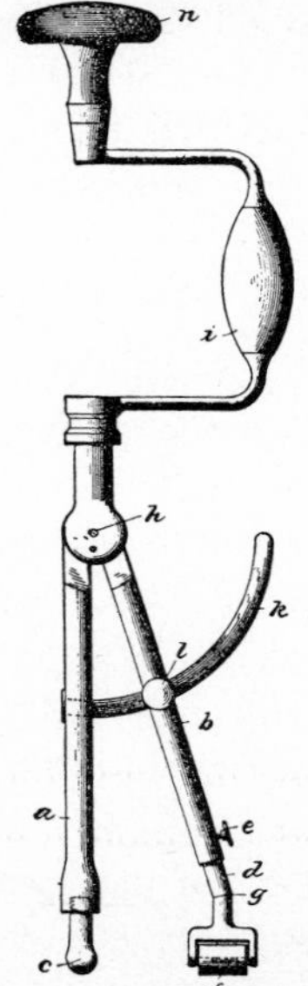

. . . The present invention consists of a device which serves either to produce dimples on the human body or to nurture and maintain dimples already existing.

When it is desired to use the device for the production of dimples, the knob or pearl c of the arm a must be set on the selected spot on the body, the extension d, together with the cylinder f, put in position, then while holding the knob n with one hand the brace i must be made to revolve on the axis x. The cylinder f serves to mass and make the skin surrounding the spot where the dimple is to be produced malleable. . . .

not completely attending to the task at hand. An unusual response can also occur simply because of a failure in communication of the instructions, resulting in an inappropriate response. Such responses can also occur by intent, perhaps because of an unwillingness to cooperate or a wish to appear different. Would you think your friend creative if you asked "What time is it?" and got the response "When death tolls the dumb, the hour will come"?

If originality is not the only criterion for judging creativity, then what other factors must be taken into consideration? In his book on thinking, D. M. Johnson (1972) listed several factors. One, of course, is *appropriateness* to the situation. Even artistic accomplishments are judged by this criterion: a new style of writing or painting, for example, must be appropriate to the content one wishes to communicate. A second factor is the *usefulness* of the accomplishment. Usefulness in this instance does not mean immediate or direct practical utility, but rather meeting some emotional or intellectual need. Other, less general, criteria include *ingenuity* (the creative act involves cleverness rather than systematic, logical, or plodding routine) and *breadth* (creative works or ideas cover a wider scope of human experience or have a wider range of applications or implications than noncreative ones). Even more specific criteria might also be included; for example, an original idea or work is more likely to be judged creative if its originator already has a reputation for creativity. The more specific the criterion, however, the greater the restriction to particular classes of creative achievements.

Note that these criteria are almost entirely subjective, and there can be much disagreement in deciding how creative, useful, or ingenious a particular innovation is, depending not only on who is judging, but also on when the judgments are made. Judgments of the usefulness and breadth of an accomplishment, for example, are sometimes made only in retrospect. Difficulties such as these have made direct study of the creative process impossible. At present two main lines of research are being pursued: (1) developing **objective tests** for assessing creativity and (2) discovering the common characteristics of people who are generally recognized as highly creative. We shall briefly examine each of these approaches.

Attempts to assess creativity have focused primarily on originality—the ability to produce unusual or very rare responses. A wide variety of paper-and-pencil tests have been devised to assess this ability. Many of these tests specifically instruct the subject to produce unusual but appropriate responses, and typically, as many of these responses as possible. One test, for example, requires subjects to list as many uncommon uses as they can for familiar objects such as a newspaper. Other tests are not so direct. S. Mednick, in 1962, devised a very different type of test, known as the **Remote Associates Test,** which consists of several sets of three words each. The subject's task is to think of a fourth word that is related to each of the three members of a set. The word *party*, for example, would be an appropriate associate to *surprise, line,* and *birthday*, as would *cheese* for the triad *rat, blue,* and *cottage*. Obviously the more remote the relationship between the desired fourth word and the stimulus triad, the greater the requirement for thinking of rare or infrequent associations.

Tests such as these are always constructed with a particular view of creativity in mind. An obvious assumption of the first type of test, for example, is that there are quantitative as well as qualitative differences between the creative and noncreative thinkers; more specifically, the creative thinker should be able to produce more unusual responses than the noncreative thinker. The rationale of the Remote Associates Test is more specific. It presumably differentiates between the creative thinker and the noncreative thinker on the basis of the strength of specific associations to various stimuli. Noncreative thinkers are assumed to have a very strong tendency to give the common stereotyped responses to a stimulus and only a weak tendency, at best, to give rare responses; hence the curve (Figure 11·2) showing their associative response strength as steep. Creative thinkers, in contrast, are less likely to give the common stereotyped responses and more likely to give the more remote, unusual ones; the curve of their response strength tends to be flatter.

The second main approach in the investigation of creative thinking has been to study people who are generally recognized as creative to discover whether they possess common characteristics or patterns of characteristics. If they do, then these characteristics can be used as a diagnostic tool to identify potentially creative people for further study. Ideally, to gather this type of information, one would give an identical battery of tests that would assess all possible personality and motivational characteristics as well as intellectual abilities of creative individuals from a wide variety of fields.

Obviously, such a project is too broad to be practical. Existing research has typically involved creative thinkers from only one field at a time and used only a

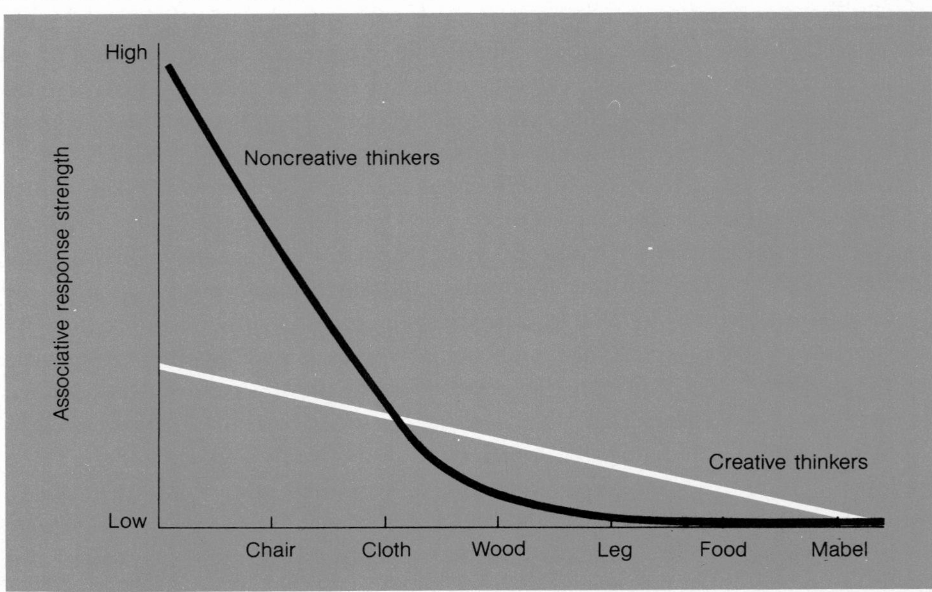

Fig. 11·2 Hypothetical associative distributions for the stimulus word *table*. (From Mednick, 1962)

Karl Duncker on Problem-solving

One of the most thorough experimental studies of problem-solving was conducted by Karl Duncker (1945), who was concerned with the solution of practical problems. The best known of these problems is how to apply X rays, high intensities of which destroy organic tissues, to cure a tumor within the body (for example, in the stomach).

To trace the thinking process during the solution period, Duncker would present the problem, then ask the person to think aloud. Duncker hoped that through examining the protocols generated, he would be able to describe the steps involved in solution. There are, of course, limitations to this procedure largely because forced verbalization might interact with the thought process. For example, speech might be unable to keep up with thinking and thus slow the thought process, or the speech requirement might demand that the thought process be more orderly than it normally is.

After examining the protocols, Duncker concluded that solving a problem involves analysis of the problem situation and analysis of the goal. In essence, the first step is to look over the situation and determine where the trouble lies. The second is to determine what has to be done to achieve a solution. Clearly, these processes fall into the class of heuristics.

Solutions achieved by analyzing the situation are considered "good" or rational, as opposed to solutions obtained by what Duncker calls *resonance,* or reference to past experience. A solution by means of resonance is strongly dependent on identical or similar problems encountered in the past.

Rational problem-solving depends upon reformulating the elements of the problem, using objects in new ways, or reorganizing the elements of the problem. Consider, for example, the two-string problem shown in Figure 11A•1: To solve the problem, a person must see pliers as a weight to be used to make a pendulum out of the string. Neither of these properties is normally part of either strings or pliers. Duncker calls this process recentering.

Despite his assignment of a lesser role to solutions obtained by past experience, Duncker considers past experience important in determining the ease with which unique functions for an object are discovered or unusual properties seen. If a person has no experience with wrenches as wrenches, for example, he may more readily see a wrench as a weight.

Also important in producing recentering are hints. A hint may be more than simply a verbal suggestion. For example, in the pendulum problem the experimenter may brush against one of the strings and set it swinging, thus suggesting the pendulum principle to the solver.

Duncker's thinking has been extremely influential. His emphasis on recentering or restructuring and analyzing the problem has formed the basis for several theories of problem-solving based on heuristics.

Fig. 11A•1 Two-string problem: How to tie the two strings together. Solution: Attach a weight to one string, and then swing it enough to catch it while holding the other string.

limited battery of tests, which unfortunately, frequently differ from one study to another. Included among the groups of creative thinkers studied, for example, are architects (reported by D. W. MacKinnon in 1962), creative writers (Barron, 1957, 1965), and research scientists (Taylor and Barron, 1963). In spite of the limitations of this research, some apparent commonalities have been identified. The tentative and obviously incomplete picture we have of the creative thinker shows a person of superior intelligence, with high aspirations, who is enthusiastic and industrious, independent and nonconforming, but also uncooperative, unsympathetic, and unreliable in his dealings with others—not an altogether flattering picture. Clearly a great deal of research remains to be done.

Concepts

11·2 People usually respond to stimuli not as single unique objects or events but rather as instances of a particular class of stimuli whose members show some similarity. This ability to classify and categorize stimuli brings order and hence predictability into our world. Imagine what life would be like without the ability to identify a new stimulus as an animal, a plant, a machine, or whatever. How would you respond to it? Should you approach it? Pick it up? Eat it? Run from it? Without the ability to identify an object as at least a potential member of some class, you have no way of knowing how to respond to it.

To identify objects, events, or relationships as members of a class, you have to have a **concept** of that class—knowledge of some shared property or common relationship. Although the stimuli may differ in several other respects, the shared attributes separate them from other stimuli. Any common property or similarity is sufficient to define a class of events, that is, to distinguish exemplars from nonexemplars. It could be one or more common physical features, such as shape, color, weight, or texture; it could be a common function, such as cutting, writing, throwing, or eating. It could be a common cause or effect.

Obviously, one stimulus can belong to many classes, each class being defined by different characteristics. A tree is a member of the class of living things, the class of shade-providing objects, the class of fuel sources, the class of tall things, and so on. Which class-defining property you notice depends on the prominence of the property; on your own mental set, needs, and experience; and on the circumstances of the moment. For example, if you are sweating under a hot sun, you are more likely to notice a tree's shade-providing function than its fuel function.

Assessing Concepts Concepts are knowledge about the way the world can be partitioned. With this knowledge an individual can behave in ways that would not be possible without it. A person who knows how to distinguish harmless from poisonous mushrooms can collect them freely in the woods; people lacking this knowledge must buy their mushrooms at the store.

There are, as we have seen, two ways of knowing whether someone knows a concept:

1. The person can correctly identify new instances of the concept.
2. The person can specify the characteristics that define the concept.

The second criterion is much more difficult to meet. Most people can identify a dog when they see one, but few can say what characteristics make an animal a dog. Some of the problems in using this method of assessment will become apparent as we look at different types of concepts.

Types of Concepts Concepts basically partition the world into two classes of things: members or exemplars of the concept and nonmembers or nonexemplars of the concept. Exemplars by definition share one or more characteristics not possessed by nonexemplars. These characteristics are known as the *relevant attributes* of concept definition. The simplest partitioning of stimuli can be done on the basis of a single relevant attribute; for example, we can distinguish red from nonred things, broken from whole things, and hard from soft things simply by the presence or absence of one distinguishing characteristic. Usually, this kind of partitioning produces large classes of stimuli that differ vastly in most other respects.

The more specific the concept, the more relevant attributes we need to define it. In most cases, not only the presence or absence of individual attributes is important, but also particular combinations or patterns of the presence or absence of the relevant attributes. These patterns, called rules, are necessary in defining more complex concepts.

These rules are of several kinds. *Conjunctive rules* require that all of the relevant attributes be present before a given stimulus can be considered an exemplar of the concept. A lie, for example, is distinguished from a nonlie on two relevant attributes: whether or not the statement is false, and whether or not there is intent to mislead. Only statements that are both false and intended to mislead are lies. False statements without this intent, and true statements regardless of intent, are not lies.

Inclusive disjunctive rules do not require the presence of all relevant attributes. An eligible voter in most municipalities is a resident or a property owner in that municipality. Either or both characteristics could be possessed by an exemplar.

Other concepts are constructed from combinations of conjunctive and disjunctive rules. For example, a strike in baseball is a pitched ball that is fairly delivered but not struck at, struck at but missed, or struck at but hit foul (except on the third strike).

In other concepts the relationship between attributes, rather than their mere presence or absence, distinguishes exemplars from nonexemplars. Isosceles triangles, for example, are distinguished from other triangles by having two sides of equal length. Similarly we can classify married couples into three categories on the basis of a dominance relationship: husband dominating, wife dominating, and neither dominating. Notice that the same attributes are present for each class; only the relationship differentiates them. Almost any relationship, no matter how abstract, can form the basis of such concepts. What is the common relationship

Learning words to describe objects, events, and relationships is an important part of education at every level. (National Education Association Communications Services, Joe Di Dio)

in the number pairs 1, 1; 4, 16; and 9, 81? Or between the letters *d*, *h*, *l*, and *p*? By detecting the relationship you can use that relationship to predict other members of the class.

Learning Concepts A concept may be acquired in either of two general ways. One procedure is to be shown instances along with their concept names. That is, a person watching a hockey game for the first time may not understand the concept of "offside." If he is watching on Canadian television (where the relevant attributes are seldom specified by the commentator), he can acquire the concept only by trying to abstract the relevant attributes and rules from instances of offside and nonoffside as they occur. Obviously, this procedure could be quite inefficient, since the instances necessary to provide a clear differentiation between exemplars and nonexemplars may not occur.

A much more efficient procedure for acquiring a concept would be to test hypotheses about the attributes and rules defining a concept by repeatedly selecting an object or event on the basis of these hypotheses and inquiring whether or not it meets the test. Whereas in the first case the person must be content with whatever information comes to him, in the second case he actively controls the flow of information. The problem of discovering a cure for cancer may be likened to discovering the attributes and rules for a cure. Thus, research is essentially a problem in concept-learning. Good researchers test hypotheses about which attributes are necessary for a cure to occur; that is, they select a particular combination of attributes and test to see whether that combination produces the desired effect.

Psychologists have studied the learning of concepts by combining simple attributes such as shape, size, and color and requiring people to try to discover the concept. This research has shown that the particular instances selected for test are seldom chosen at random but are based on information obtained from previous tests that have led one to hypothesize about the concept. The different ways in which people consider and test hypotheses in solving concept-learning problems are sometimes called strategies (Bruner, Goodnow, and Austin, 1956).

There are two broad strategies: *focusing*, which deals with hypotheses about individual attributes, and *scanning*, which deals with hypotheses about the total concept. In an experimental situation using *conservative focusing*, a positive instance of the attribute that is to be identified is presented. The person being tested is then given instances that differ in only one attribute from the original instance. If a tested instance is also said to be positive, the person knows that the distinguishing attribute is irrelevant; if the test is negative, he knows it is relevant. Suppose the initial positive instance is a large white triangle, and the first tested instance is a large white circle. (Figure 11•3). If this instance is also said to be positive, then shape cannot be relevant. If it is negative, then shape must be relevant. The process continues until only relevant attributes are left. In *focus gambling*, the same general procedure is followed except that more than one attribute at a time are changed. In this strategy a successful (positive) test indicates

What is a nerd?

○ is not a nerd
△ is a nerd
● is not a nerd
○ is not a nerd
▲ is not a nerd
● is not a nerd
▲ is a nerd
△ is not a nerd

Fig. 11·3 A typical arbitrary concept (using size, shape, and color as attributes in this case) composed for a laboratory experiment on concept learning. Can you decide which attributes and rule define a nerd?

that all of the changed attributes are irrelevant and so one has made some progress toward determining which of the attributes is relevant.

Scanning strategies follow a similar breakdown. The person may use successive scanning, in which one hypothesis at a time is tested, or *simultaneous scanning*, in which more than one hypothesis at a time is tested. If the concept is complex, scanning procedures put a burden on the person, since much information must be handled at once. Despite this inefficiency, most people, if given a choice, tend to use a scanning strategy. There is some evidence of a shift toward conservative focusing as one acquires more experience with solving these kinds of problems.

The number of attributes necessary to define a concept and their saliency also affect its rate of acquisition. The more attributes there are, the more combinations that could occur to define the concept and, hence, the harder the problem is to solve. Apparently, some attributes are more likely than others to be selected first. When those attributes are relevant, the concept may be readily identified. Saliency is not a fixed characteristic of an attribute, but may vary from person to person and may also depend on the context and other factors.

Finally, the particular rule that defines the relation among attributes also affects acquisition. Generally, conjunctive concepts are more readily acquired than disjunctive concepts.

Certain presentation conditions are also important. For example, positive instances usually produce more rapid learning than negative instances. This is true for most types of concepts, even when the amount of information to be obtained from a given instance is equated. There are a few kinds of concepts (such as disjunctive concepts), however, for which negative instances appear to be more important. The timing of presentations is also relevant, but not in the way one might think on the basis of the reinforcement principle. The time between occurrence and the presentation of information about whether it is a positive or negative instance is not nearly as important as the time between the presentation of the information and the next occurrence. Apparently, the learner must have time to assess the information provided by the previous instance and to modify his hypothesis to account for it.

If all concepts had to be acquired inductively—that is, by abstracting relevant attributes and relationships from many specific stimulus instances that embody the concept—we would probably have few concepts.

Luckily, humans have the capacity to communicate their concepts through language, thus reducing the need for each of us to search systematically for regularities in the environment. Concept learning via language tends to be deductive rather than inductive. That is, learners are usually told the relevant attributes or the relationship that defines the concept, or both, and then tested for understanding by being required to apply the description to identify a specific instance. The description of the concept is often a formal definition that outlines commonalities with other experiences and gives criteria for distinguishing exemplars of the concept. This aspect of dictionary definition can be seen in the following:

The Impact of the Computer on the Study of Cognitive Processes

Recent advances in the study of cognition can be attributed almost entirely to the advent of the electronic computer, which has provided a new way of theorizing about cognitive processes as well as new ways of testing such theories.

The basis for this new approach lies in an analogy between human beings and computers as similar information-processing systems. Both are capable of receiving information from external sources; both represent information in a form different from the way it appears in the environment; both are capable of integrating newly received information with other information previously stored in the system; both are capable of manipulating information in a variety of ways and of performing operations on it that will lead to desired states; and finally, both are capable of communicating the outcome of these operations and of returning new information to the environment.

The computer can perform such activities only when it is specifically programmed to do so. It must be instructed in great detail exactly what operations to perform on what aspects of the data and in what order. Even a seemingly unimportant change or omission in the instructions could make a problem unsolvable. The analogy between human and computer is thus clearly based on the similarities between the mental operations performed by a person and the operations prescribed by the computer program.

Whenever a human and a computer are capable of solving the same problem, are they using identical operations? Clearly, arriving at the same answer does not prove that they arrived there in the same way. However, the steps in a computer program may suggest hypotheses, which can be subjected to experimental test, about the steps a human might follow in handling similar problems, as well as the ordering of such steps. Conversely, knowledge and hypotheses about the ways in which humans solve problems can be written into a computer program to see whether these operations are sufficient in and of themselves to guarantee solution. In essence, the computer program seems to be an extremely valuable tool for determining how humans process information in a wide variety of tasks.

There have been several attempts to use the computer to model or simulate human behavior in essentially cognitive tasks. Probably the best known of these models is the General Problem Solver (GPS), described by Allen Newell and Herbert Simon in 1963. This model attempts to simulate a wide variety of human cognitive behaviors; it incorporates many of the concepts, heuristics, and other strategies that are believed to underlie such behavior. The general strategy of GPS in attacking a problem is as follows:

1. Examine the situation to see whether there is a discrepancy between the present state (the problem) and some desired state (the goal). If there is no difference, there is no problem and no further operations are needed.
2. If there are discrepancies, identify their exact nature and formulate a plan to eliminate them. GPS removes discrepancies by applying a series of operations, each of which alters some features of the situation but leaves others unchanged. These operations are applied one at a time; after each, the two states are again compared to see whether discrepancies still exist. If they do, then further transformation is applied until these differences too have been eliminated.
3. In many cases, a chosen operation cannot be applied directly to the current state. When this happens, GPS establishes a subgoal or a series of subgoals that alter the state so that a desired operation can be applied. Only after these subproblems have been solved can the original problem be tackled.

To make this process a bit more concrete, we shall consider a description of a human thinking (Newell, Simon, and Shaw, 1960).

> "I want to take my son to nursery school. What's the difference between what I have and what I want? One of distance. What changes distance? My

In the movie *2001: A Space Odyssey* (1968), a computer named Hal has been programmed not only to supervise a journey to Jupiter but also to feel human emotions such as paranoia, humiliation, and vengeance. The astronauts are as prisoners in their spacecraft, spied on by Hal. (MGM)

> automobile won't work. What's needed to make it work? A new battery. What has new batteries? An auto repair shop. I want the repair shop to put in a new battery; but the shop doesn't know I need one. What is the difficulty? One of communication. What allows communication? A telephone . . ." (p. 259).

Clearly, even from this incomplete description, GPS seems to mimic some of the basic analysis humans perform in solving problems.

How does one judge the adequacy of a computer simulation model? Probably the most frequently used procedure is to compare the protocol of a human subject with the trace (a print-out of the results of each step) of the computer's approach to the same problem. The subject is required to think aloud as he works through the problem. This provides a reasonable description not only of what the subject did at different stages in solution but also a verbal report of why he did it. This protocol can then be compared line by line with the computer output to look for similarities in processing operations.

Using essentially this approach in evaluating GPS, Newell and Simon (1963) concluded that "if the mechanism of the program (or something essentially similar to it) were not operating, it would be hard to explain why the subject uttered the remarks that he did." A variation of this procedure is to have an independent judge compare the machine trace and a human protocol. If he cannot identify which represents the human and which represents the computer, the simulation must be considered quite good.

We cannot yet say what the final impact of computer technology will be on the study of cognitive processes, but it has almost totally refocused studies of cognitive processes. Instead of determining what factors influence the ability of humans to solve specific problems, we are trying to determine the actual processes involved in solving or attempting to solve such problems. A complete understanding of thought must depend upon such an analysis.

Umiak an open boat used by the Eskimos, about thirty feet long and eight feet wide, consisting of a wooden frame covered with skins and propelled usually with a broad paddle.

Now you know what a umiak is, but to know that you must already have several other concepts (boat, Eskimo, frame, propelled, and so on).

Much of our formal education consists of introducing new concepts in this way. Who does not remember being given a description of the major parts of speech and then spending what seemed to be endless hours identifying nouns, verbs, adjectives, and adverbs? Verbal definition is the only way some concepts can be acquired. This is particularly true of such abstract concepts as gravity, or mathematical concepts such as those described earlier. These concepts are too far removed from concrete experience to be learned inductively.

Formal definitions are not the only way concepts can be acquired through language. Simply seeing or hearing a new term in a variety of verbal contexts may provide the meaning of that term. For example, in one experiment (Werner and Kaplan, 1950) children discovered what a corplum was by being given the following information:

A corplum may be used for support.
Corplums may be used to close off an open space.
A wet corplum doesn't burn.
You can make a corplum smooth with sandpaper.

Basically, as with definitions, each statement describes a relevant attribute that distinguishes corplums from noncorplums.

An important distinction should be made here. Although many words in our language provide labels for concepts, words are not the same as concepts. In many cases, the same word can designate more than one concept, as do the very familiar words *red, grass, wolf,* and *poker.* Often no single word adequately distinguishes one concept from another. One must then add words to define the concept.

Obviously, the role of language in communicating concepts is an important one. We shall next examine this unique human quality in more detail.

Language

11·3 In any discussion of knowledge from a psychological point of view language must be considered an integral part of knowledge. Language is important for two reasons. First, it is a vehicle for the communication of most knowledge. Information about ideas, concepts, and relationships is conveyed from one person (a speaker or writer) to another (a listener or reader). Second, it is an example of a highly complex rule-governed system of knowledge that all but the most mentally deficient humans can master.

The basic communication process consists of three steps:

1. The speaker (or writer) wishes to communicate an idea to another person.

2. He or she encodes and expresses the idea in a linguistic message, either as a sequence of sounds (speech) or as a sequence of written symbols (writing).
3. The listener (or reader) attending to the message decodes it from its linguistic form back into an idea. Hopefully, it is the same idea the originator of the message meant to convey.

The success of the communication process obviously demands that the originator and the receiver of the message share a knowledge of a common language system. Failure of communication can occur either because the originator fails to encode the idea appropriately or because the receiver fails to decode it correctly.

Before considering how language functions both in communication and as a system involved in thought, we shall examine the aspects of the linguistic system shared by most speakers and listeners.

Generally, the users of a language possess three kinds of knowledge about that language: *phonemic* information, *morphemic* information, and *syntactic* information.

Phonemes The basic speech sounds of any language are called phonemes. Phonemic information is the minimal information necessary to distinguish one utterance from another. For example, the initial phonemes (designated with slashes) /p/ and /b/ are all that distinguish the spoken words *pat* and *bat*, and the middle phonemes /š/ and /ž/ which correspond to the letters *c* and *z*, distinguish the words *glacier* and *glazier*.

Differences in phonemes do not always correspond to spelling differences, nor does phonemic identity mean that words are necessarily spelled alike. Consider the words *thigh* and *thy*. The *th* sound is different in the two words, but the *igh* and *y* are pronounced the same.

There are forty-six phonemes in English, each produced by an elementary sound characteristically called a distinctive feature. These features are qualities such as *voicing* (whether the vocal cords are activated, as in /p/ and /b/), *stopping* (whether the nasal passage is open or closed, as in /s/ and /t/), and *acuteness* (whether or not the sound is forward in the mouth, as in /b/ and /d/). There are several other distinctive features, but these examples should suffice to indicate the structure of the phoneme system.

No language contains phonemes representing all combinations of features, and most phonemes differ from one another in more than one way, thus slight variations in sound are not critical to the identification of a phoneme, and confusion is minimized. Generally speaking, the fewer the distinguishing features, the greater the chances of confusion, particularly when there is little other information available with which to make the distinction. For example, telephone operators may have more trouble distinguishing between *Rudy* and *Ruby* than between *Dave* and *Dale*.

Besides being able to recognize and produce individual phonemes, one must also know how they can be combined into longer sequences. Although few people could verbalize the rules that determine such permissible sound sequences, or are even consciously aware of them, most speakers know these rules intuitively, or they would not be able to construct sequences. For example, when pluralizing nouns in English, voiced consonants must be followed by the voiced /z/ and unvoiced consonants by the unvoiced /s/. Similarly, any speaker knows that English words cannot start with *sb*, *sd*, or *sg*, but *st*, *sp*, and *sk* are allowed.

Morphemes A morpheme is a minimal sound, or sound combination, that conveys meaning within a language. Thus, while phonemes are just sounds, morphemes are meaningful sounds. *Boy*, *coy*, and *joy* are morphemes, but *doy*, *loy*, and *moy* are not.

Words are not synonymous with morphemes, but rather are constructions of (usually) two or more morphemes. The words *boys*, *coyly*, and *joyous* all consist of two morphemes, the roots *boy*, *coy*, and *joy* plus the affixes *-s*, *-ly*, and *-ous*. The affixes are not words, since they cannot stand alone, but they do have meaning and hence are morphemes. The morphemic structure of a sequence follows certain rules and conveys information to a listener who knows the rules. For example, -ly added to an adjective produces an adverb, and -ous added to a noun root results in an adjective.

Syntax Syntax is the system by which morphemes and morpheme constructions are integrated into meaningful utterances or sentences. The phrase rather than the single word seems to be the basic unit of analysis for sentences, and the *phrase structure* of the sentence indicates how words within a phrase and phrases within a sentence are organized.

The importance of phrase structure for understanding a sentence is shown by the following example:

They are frying chickens.

Does the word *they* refer to chickens that are to be fried rather than roasted, or does it refer to people who are cooking the chickens? This sentence is an example of syntactic ambiguity arising because it is unclear whether the word *frying* is part of the verb phrase *are frying* or part of the noun phrase *frying chickens*. Thus knowledge of the phrase structure of an utterance may be necessary in order to understand its meaning, especially in written English. Note that in *spoken* English the ambiguity illustrated could be prevented by differences in stress: *fry*ing chickens as opposed to frying *chick*ens.

Phrase structure is not the only psychologically important aspect of the syntax of a sentence. Consider the following sentences:

The book was found by a little boy.
The book was found by a rotten log.

On the surface, these two sentences are identical. That is, if we were to break the sentence down into phrases, they would be perfectly alike except for the ter-

The Phrase Structure of Sentences

Modern linguists typically represent the underlying structure of a sentence as a *tree diagram* that partitions the sentence into phrases, subphrases, and words. The steps involved in formally specifying the structure of a sentence are called *rewrite rules.* These structures have a number of implications for understanding what a speaker and a hearer know about their language.

Consider the simple sentence *The snow buried the car.* The levels of analysis for this sentence are as follows:

1. sentence (s) ⟶ noun phrase (np) + verb phrase (vp)
2a. noun phrase (np) ⟶ determiner (d) + noun (n)
2b. verb phrase (vp) ⟶ verb (v) + noun phrase (np)
3. determiner ⟶ *The*
noun ⟶ *snow, car*
verb ⟶ *buried*

The tree structure generated by these rewrite rules is shown in Figure 11B·1. This simple example indicates the procedure involved and the kind of result obtained, although rewrite rules can be exceptionally complicated since they must apply to any sentence.

You may think that trees such as in Figure 11B·1 are little different from the sentence diagrams many of us had to learn in school to represent grammatical rules. Such diagrams, however, are based on superficial relations of the parts of a sentence and are somewhat arbitrary, whereas phrase-structure trees are generated by the rewrite rules. It is these rules that some psychologists (for example, Deese, 1970) think constitute our knowledge about syntax.

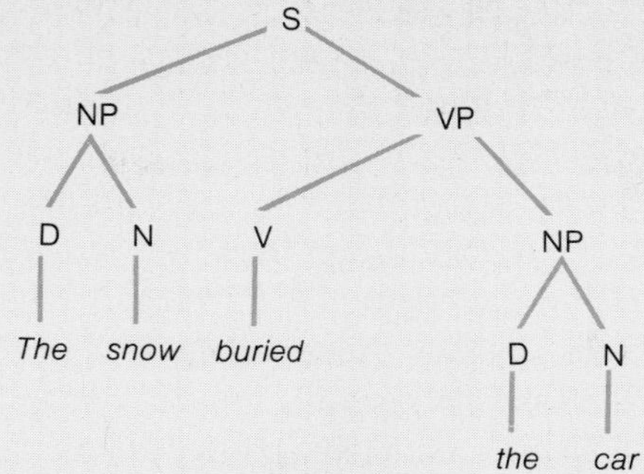

Fig. 11B·1 Tree diagram for the sentence *The snow buried the car.*

At some level people understand a string of words in a fashion that does not proceed from left to right. Otherwise, they could not distinguish the meaning of an ambiguous sentence such as *They are frying chickens.* From a linguistic point of view, the two interpretations of this sentence lead to different trees produced by different rules (Figure 11B·2), and these rules provide a convenient way of characterizing the difference in meaning.

Whether differences in meaning are characterized psychologically by differences in structure has yet to be determined. We know from several experiments that phrase structure has some psychological counterpart. For example, to memorize sentences, people seem to organize, or "chunk," sentences by phrases. They tend to recall or forget entire phrases rather than words within phrases.

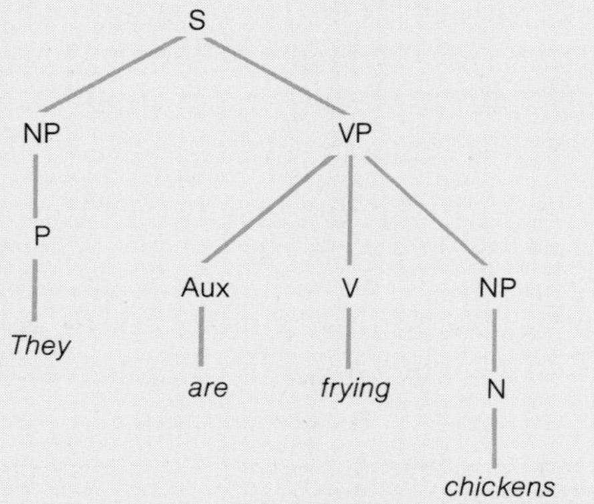

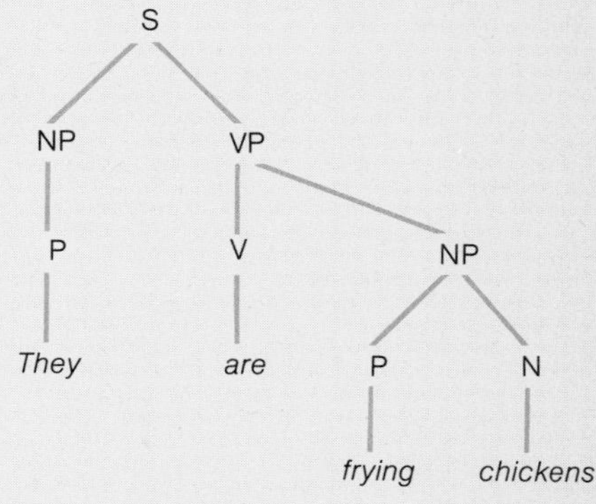

Fig. 11B·2 Two tree diagrams showing different interpretations of the sentence *They are frying chickens.*

minal phrase. Nevertheless, despite identical phrase structure, there are real differences between the sentences. The differences can be clearly seen by changing the form of the sentence from passive to active voice.

A little boy found the book.
Someone found the book by a rotten log.

In the first sentence the final phrase becomes the subject of the transformed sentence. In the second sentence, this transformation would not make sense *(The rotten log found the book)*. Thus, the interpretation of a sentence also involves a knowledge of *transformation rules,* which allow one to change the surface phrase structure of a sentence from one form to another with few, if any, changes of meaning. Thus, in addition to *surface structure* (the sound level of language), sentences have an underlying *deep structure* (the meaning level of language), which is not always apparent from surface structure alone.

Transformation rules specify not only the relations among different sentence types, such as active, passive, negative, affirmative, and interrogative, but also changes in tense. These rules enable the speaker or listener to go from one form of a sentence to another. As conveyed in a sentence, a simple idea can usually be represented by a relationship between subject, verb, and object. Applying transformation rules, a speaker can emphasize or call into question the different aspects of the relationship, as can be seen in Table 11•1.

Having examined the general knowledge a speaker and listener must share about their language, we can look at some of the psychological factors involved in the production and comprehension of a verbal utterance, and at the role of language in various cognitive tasks.

Factors Affecting Production and Comprehension Memory, context, and vocabulary are among the factors that affect our use of language.

Memory Although in theory, any person who knows the rules of his language should be capable of producing or comprehending any grammatical sentence generated by those rules, there are limitations. Suppose someone read you the following sentence, and then asked you to recall it:

The prize that the ring that the jeweler that the man that she liked visited made won was given at the fair.

Could you repeat the sentence exactly or even paraphrase it? Most people could not. This sentence was created by repeatedly applying a familiar transformation

Table 11·1 Four types of Transformation and Sample Sentences

TYPE OF TRANSFORMATION	SENTENCE TO BE TRANSFORMED	TRANSFORMED SENTENCE
Deletion	You go home. The girl whom I saw left.	Go home. The girl I saw left.
Addition	Bernie left.	Did Bernie leave?
Displacement	Bill picked up the bottle.	Bill picked the bottle up.
Substitution	Judy greatly admires Judy.	Judy greatly admires herself.

rule—the rule for "self-embedding relative clauses." Consider variations on the same sentence that use from none to three embeddings.

None: *She liked the man that visited the jeweler that made the ring that won the prize that was given at the fair.*
One: *The man that she liked visited the jeweler that made the ring that won the prize that was given at the fair.*
Two: *The jeweler that the man that she liked visited made the ring that won the prize that was given at the fair.*
Three: *The ring that the jeweler that the man that she liked visited made won the prize that was given at the fair.*

Clearly, as the number of embeddings increases, the sentence becomes less and less immediately comprehensible. What makes it so difficult? If you examine each sentence, you will see that as the degree of self-embedding increases, the nouns occurring early in the sentence become increasingly distant from the verbs they are related to, thus placing a tremendous burden on immediate memory. With the written sentence in front of you and with a little effort, you could work out the meaning of even a fourth-degree embedded sentence; if the sentence were spoken, you would not be able to remember enough to determine the sentence structure, particularly which verb goes with which noun.

The added burden to immediate memory is not restricted to self-embedded sentences. In general, the addition of any transformation increases the memory load and makes a sentence more difficult to understand. This increase in difficulty can be seen even in simple memory tasks in which people are given sentences containing one or more transformations and asked to recall them. In one experiment (Mehler, 1963) declarative sentences were recalled best. Passive sentences were not remembered as well as active, since they involve a transformation, but were remembered better than passive questions, which involve two transformations. Interestingly enough, what appears to be forgotten is the particular transformation. Passive sentences were often remembered as active, negatives as affirmatives, and questions as declaratives. The inverse seldom happened, that is, actives were almost never recalled as passives.

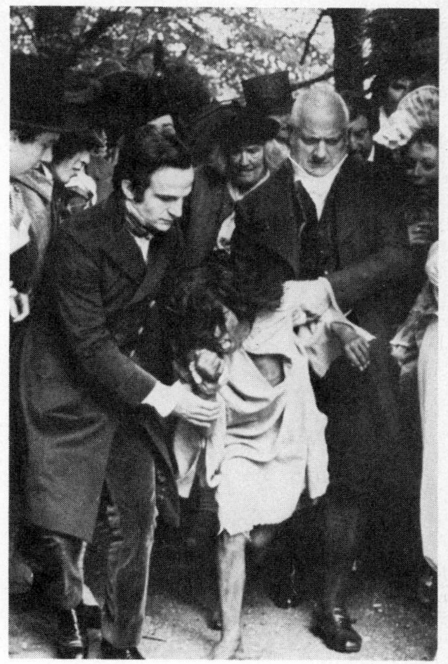

The civilizing of a child who had grown up in the wild was undertaken by Dr. Jean Itard in 1798, and in 1969 Francois Truffaut made a film based on the doctor's account of the process. The doctor believed that the child was not a deaf and dumb idiot who had been abandoned, but a normal child who could not speak or reason because he had been deprived of human contact. (United Artists)

Context A second factor of paramount importance in comprehending verbal utterances is the context in which an utterance appears. Statements that in isolation are ambiguous are clearly comprehensible when they are made in the appropriate context. For example, the meaning of the statement "They are frying chickens" becomes readily apparent as an answer to the question "Where are the Smiths?" A nonsensical statement such as "She seems to like dirt best" is more meaningful when it is made by a mother in a soap commercial who is explaining how her small daughter's clothes get dirty: "She plays on the grass, in a sandbox, and on a big dirt pile behind the house. She seems to like dirt best."

An unintelligible comment such as "Tom likes him but he likes him better than he likes Tom" can be meaningful if accompanied by pointing to the people referred to. It could then be translated as "Tom likes *Gene* best, but *Gene* likes *Al* better than *Gene* likes *Tom*."

To gauge the importance of context, try listening to someone carrying on a telephone conversation. When you can hear only one person talking, you lose the context provided by the other person, and the statements you do hear are often incomprehensible.

Vocabulary Shared concepts and vocabulary are obvious requirements for conveying information. How meaningful would the concepts *intermittent primary positive reinforcement* or *continuous secondary negative reinforcement* be to your parents if you were trying to tell them how to control the behavior of your younger brothers or sisters? Yet the same terms used among psychology students can communicate effectively.

Some Aspects of Meaning Meaning is not inherent in an utterance. Instead it is assigned by the originator and also by the receiver. Different people are likely to assign somewhat different meanings, especially when general and abstract words are used. Concepts and the words used to represent them, as well as information about how one concept is related to another, are part of **semantic memory.** How is all this information represented and organized?

One possibility is that concepts are organized in networks of associations. These networks can be observed directly by giving a person a word and asking him to give the first word he thinks of—the classic free-association experiment. This is not to say that the relation of one word to another is a direct one-directional connection from A to B to C, and so on, but that concepts are related according to their distance from one another in a complex associative structure. Consider a simple four-word structure comprised of the words *moth, insect, wings,* and *bird. Moth* produces *insect* and *wings* as associations; *insect* produces only moth; *wings* produces only *bird;* and *bird* produces only *wings.* The structure of this small group of words would be indicated thus:

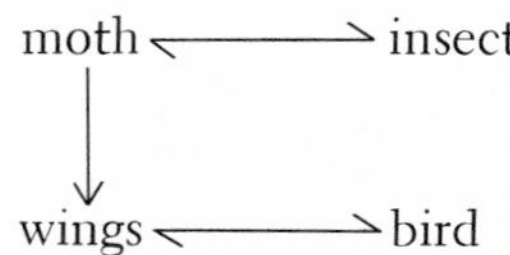

In other words, *moth* and *insect* are directly related to each other, while *moth* and *bird* are less closely related, since the relation is mediated by the common associate *wings.* Strength of association can also be a factor, since *bird* occurs about half the time in association with *wings,* but *wings* occurs with *moth* only about 4 percent of the time. Some psychologists (for example, Deese, 1962) have argued that the associations we get in the free-association test do not directly represent the way concepts are related but only indicate this relationship. By looking at the particular words that group together in the free-association test, we can determine a common underlying property. For example, *wings* is related to both *moth* and *bird* (part-whole), but *insect* is a class of which *moth* is a member (whole-part).

The ultimate extension of this approach to meaning is to analyze each concept in terms of its attributes. A. R. Quillian proposed a scheme of this kind. A given word, such as *canary*, has a configuration of associations (node) with other words such as *bird;* in this case these class properties include "has wings," "can fly," and "has feathers." Only information about canaries that is not shared by the more general class *bird* is associated directly with *canary:* "it is yellow" and "it can sing." This feature distinguishes Quillian's scheme from one based on pure associations. An example of the kind of structure generated is shown in Figure 11•4.

To determine whether information might be organized this way, Collins and Quillian (1969) asked people simple questions about various concepts. They reasoned that it would take a person longer to answer a question such as "Do canaries fly?" which demands information from two nodes, than to answer a question such as "Can canaries sing?" which involves only a single node. The results showed that this was indeed true. Two-level questions took almost 1.4 seconds to answer, while one-level questions took 1.3 seconds. The differences are small but consistent.

Relationships among concepts are not always determined by concrete attributes. C. E. Osgood (1952) asked people to use certain pairs of adjectives, opposite in meaning, to rate a series of concepts. For example, is the concept *mother* good or

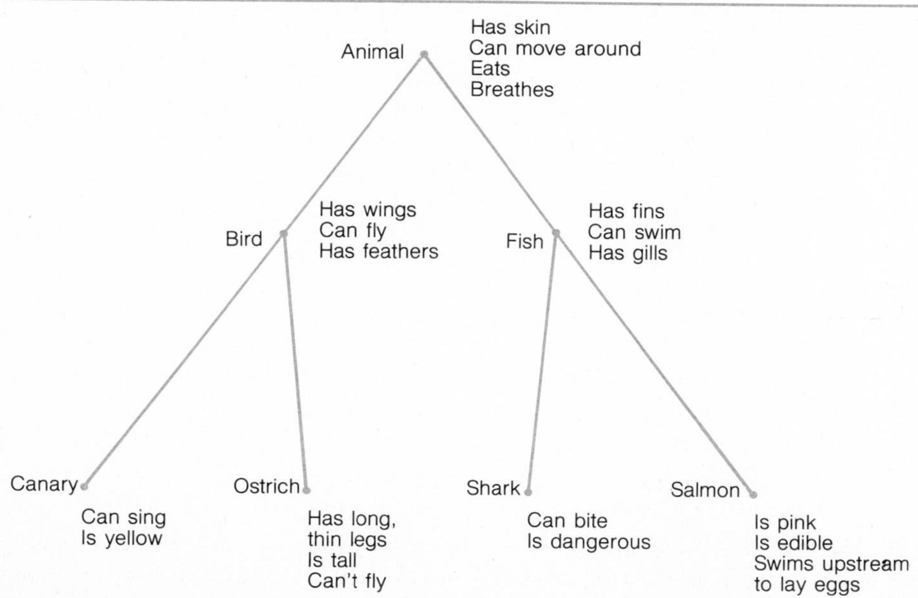

Fig. 11·4 A simple structure relating several birds and fish. (From Collins and Quillian, 1969)

bad, strong or weak, active or passive, rough or smooth? From these ratings, any concept seemed to be describable in terms of three abstract attributes: evaluation (good-bad), activity (active-passive), and potency (strong-weak). For example, *war* is bad, active, and strong; *friendship* is good and strong, but relatively neutral with respect to activity; *sleep* is good but passive; and so on.

These attempts to deal with meaning are largely concerned with concepts represented by single words. As we noted earlier, knowledge that is expressed in a sentence is not actually the sentence itself, but the information represented by the sentence. Clearly, this information consists of more than just single objects, since sentences can be complex. To understand them, we need to know not only the meaning of individual concepts but also the relation between them.

If we do not remember knowledge as sentences, how do we remember it? No one really knows, but the scheme suggested by John Anderson and Gordon Bower (1973) is typical of current attempts to characterize semantic memory. In their scheme the unit of information is called a *proposition*, which merely specifies the key ideas and characterizes the relation between them. Once again we turn to the branching outline, which by now ought to be familiar to you.

We shall start with a simple example (Figure 11•5a): *Sam roped a calf.* This sentence has three units: *Sam* (actor), *roped* (verb), and *calf* (object). One branch of the proposition contains the actor (subject), and the other the predicate, including the verb and the object. This analysis is similar to parsing sentences, except that it is based more on information content than on rules of grammar.

Such structures can represent more complex information than subject-verb-object sentences. For example, we can include context information, such as location of the event in time or space, and qualifying information about the subject or the object. An example of structures for these kinds of sentences is given in Figure 11•5b.

According to the theory, each idea is independent but is linked to other ideas in the proposition by the relations specified by the connections between nodes. Not all psychologists agree with this part of the theory, for it means that we gain access to an idea only by going through other nodes. Rather, it has been suggested that in some manner a combined idea is created from individual ideas; for example, *Sam-ropes* may be represented as *cowboy,* thus providing a more flexible structure.

As another alternative, A. Paivio has suggested that at least some knowledge exists as images (see Chapter 10).

Much research remains to be done before we can claim any understanding of the process of meaning.

Thought As Implicit Speech Perhaps the most extreme view was presented by John B. Watson (1924b). He held that thinking consists of actual but unobservable movements (behavior). Thus verbal thought is the actual movement of talking reduced to a level at which it cannot be observed by ordinary means, while

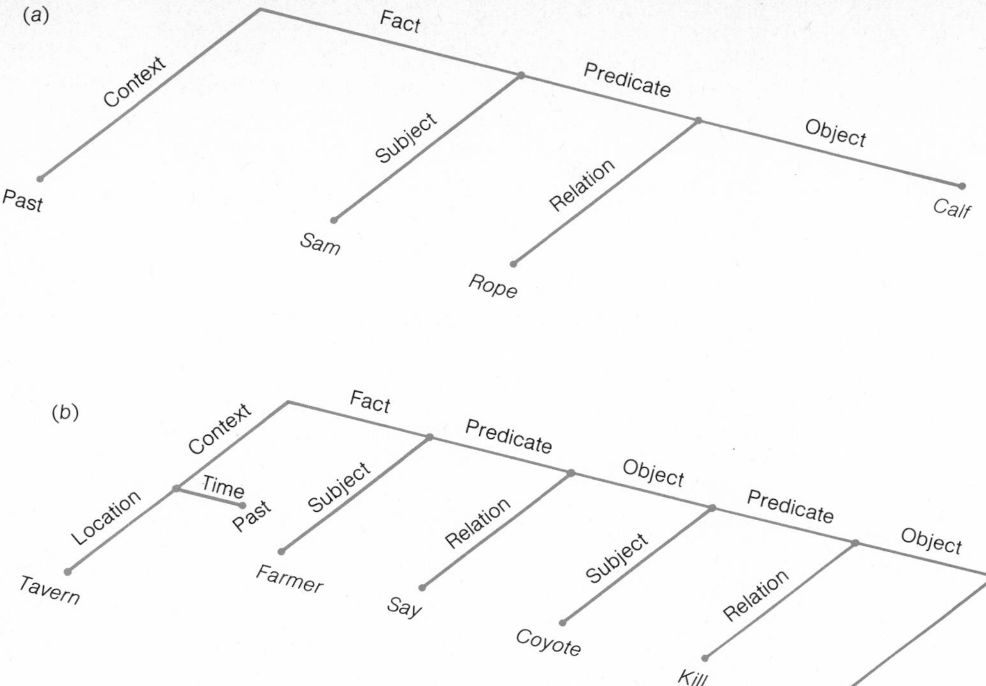

Fig. 11·5 Meaningful structures as conceived by Anderson and Bower. (a) *Sam ropes the calf.* (b) *In the tavern, the farmer said the coyote killed the lamb.*

nonverbal thought (such as thinking about a movement) is covert activity in the appropriate part of the skeletal musculature.

This view was made more credible when appropriately sensitive equipment was able to detect electrical activity in the muscular system at the appropriate site. Although this muscular activity could be activated by the thought rather than actually being the thought, we may yet learn for sure that implicit muscular activity plays a role in thinking. It appears that the small movements of the speech musculature (eyes, tongue, and larynx) that sometimes occur during reading may enhance comprehension, particularly when the material being read is difficult.

Language As a Determiner of Thought According to the **linguistic relativity** principle or Whorfian hypothesis (after its originator, Benjamin Lee Whorf, 1956), the structure of language determines how a person perceives the world. The speakers of different languages thus view the world differently. As Whorf said, "we dissect nature along lines laid down by our native languages." Whorf drew most of his supporting evidence from correlations between linguistic structure and the perception of external events by people speaking different languages.

From his study of American Indian languages, especially Hopi, Whorf came to think that languages can lead to various models of reality. For example, where the subject-predicate grammar of English forces us to supply verbs with subjects, Hopi allows subjectless verbs. We say, "The light flashed." A Hopi says "*rehpi*": *flash* (*occurred*). Whorf hypothesized that without this subject-predicate distinction in their language, the Hopi tend not to postulate a doer for every action, as we do.

Similarly, Whorf claimed that the tenses in the Hopi language cannot be understood purely in terms of our concepts of past, present, and future; for the Hopi the past and the future are manifest in the present. Time, according to Whorf, is seen by the Hopi as duration, as a continuous "getting later," not as the unraveling of bits or chunks such as hours and days.

As yet, no research has either supported or refuted the Whorfian hypothesis. It seems likely, however, that the differences in the structure of language reflect differences in the importance of certain discriminations in a particular culture rather than differences in perception. Thus, Arabians have more words for *camel* and Eskimos more words for *snow* because differences within these classes of objects play a more important role in their lives than they do in ours, not because they think about camels and snow in ways that we who have only one word cannot. Having different words to distinguish a small, tawny-beige, long-haired, shaggy, female camel from a large, tawny-beige, long-haired, shaggy, female camel simply facilitates thinking about or communicating information about these animals.

Language As a Tool for Thought Much of our experience seems to be encoded and stored in memory in linguistic form. It may then be recalled in this form and decoded so that the information can be used to perform a variety of cognitive tasks.

Several facts about memory for nonverbal events seem to result from the use of these so-called verbal loops (Glanzer and Clark, 1963). You may remember from Chapter 9 that objects seen and then later labeled as they are studied tend to be perceived in memory as the object labeled rather than as the object originally seen. Even simple colors show this effect. A blue-green that is labeled *green* tends to be remembered as more greenish, while if it is labeled *blue* it tends to be remembered as more bluish.

Verbal labeling performs several other functions. In solving problems, labels given to various components necessary to solve the problem may direct the solver's attention to a unique function of a component necessary to solve the problem. For example, in the box-candle problem described earlier when the tacks are placed in the box, the problem is solved more quickly if the tacks and box are labeled separately.

Verbal labeling is also involved in learning to discriminate among objects. Learning separate names for a set of objects that are highly similar in appearance helps us tell them apart, while learning common labels for them hinders this discrimination. It is not clear, however, just how the label is involved in this process. Perhaps it is not involved at all, and having to learn different labels merely forces us to attend to the distinguishing characteristics of objects.

Much of our experience cannot be labeled by single words. In fact, most descriptions of objects, events, or relationships require some sort of distinguishing modifier. Generally, the fewer words used to describe a stimulus, the better the stimulus can be remembered. Here again we see the usefulness of having a single word to represent a given concept. If part of a long descriptive label—such as that for a particular type of camel—is lost, the concept is not accurately specified. Some terms in technical jargon, for example, have the advantage of allowing their users to avoid long descriptive labels, part of which might be forgotten.

The syntax of the language used to encode information may also determine how well it is remembered. We have already seen an example of this in the greater difficulty of remembering passive or interrogatory sentences. Because a sentence tends to be recalled in chunks defined by phrase boundaries, a sentence's phrase structure is also an important determiner of how easily it is recalled. If one word of a phrase is recalled, the whole phrase is recalled, and we tend to forget whole phrases rather than words within phrases.

The underlying structural characteristics of a sentence may also affect its retention. Sentences of identical phrase structure such as *canoes are made by natives* and *canoes are made by hand* are remembered differently despite their sameness. Again we see the importance of transformation rules in language.

The forms in which ideas are expressed affect not only how well they are remembered, but also how reasonable they are. Reasoning involves reaching a conclusion from a set of premises or propositions. For example:

All people are fallible.
All psychologists are people.
Therefore psychologists are fallible.

This type of formal argument is called a *syllogism.* While it is presented here somewhat artificially, it is actually a general form of verbal reasoning.

Syllogistic reasoning can be difficult even for intelligent persons, and a number of factors (some of them linguistic) can lead to false conclusions. Consider:

All Newfoundlanders are slow-witted.
Ted is a Newfoundlander.
Therefore Ted is slow-witted.

This conclusion is logical, but it is not true as long as there is at least one Newfoundlander who is not slow-witted. In other words, the premise may not be true.

If we have information such as

Some politicians live in Ottawa.
Pierre lives in Ottawa.

it is fallacious to conclude that *Pierre is a politician.* If we were to presuppose that

All Albertans are friendly.
All oil executives are friendly.

Learning to call the different shapes by their names may help these children complete the complex task in front of them—lining up identical shapes in a row. (Wycliffe Bible Translators, Inc.)

Is Language a Uniquely Human Characteristic?

In the last half-century, several attempts have been made to teach humanlike language to chimpanzees. The earliest attempts were not notably successful. In the 1930s, Winthrop and Luella Kellogg raised Gua, a female chimpanzee, as a companion to their infant son. Although Gua was not given special language training, she was raised in a normal verbal environment. During this time, she acquired a vocabulary of about 100 words to which she would respond with appropriate behaviors. However, she never learned to produce any of the words.

The second attempt was made by Kathy and Keith Hayes in the late forties. Their chimpanzee also was able to learn to follow verbal requests. Despite considerable formal training, the chimpanzee learned to say only "Mama," "Papa," and "cup," but not to use these words consistently with their specific referents.

These early attempts led to the conclusion that the ability to learn language is distinctly human, but more recent attempts have suggested otherwise. Among non-human primates, the chimpanzee has demonstrated extraordinary conceptual ability and seems a suitable candidate for learning the complex symbolic system that typifies human language. It is generally recognized, however, that the vocal apparatus of the chimpanzee is not well-adapted for the production of speech. Based on this premise, Allen and Beatrice Gardner have trained an infant chimpanzee, Washoe, to use the American sign language commonly employed by the deaf. They kept the chimp in an intellectually stimulating, homelike social environment, but did not allow human vocalization in her presence. They taught Washoe the signs by ordinary shaping procedures, and by taking advantage of the natural imitative tendencies of the chimp to model the trainer's signs.

After four years, she had an expressive vocabulary of 132 signs. She also could combine these signs appropriately into two-and three-word "utterances," and answer who, what, where, why, and when types of questions. Her sentences did not necessarily follow normal English word order or any consistent order, but word order is not normally important in sign language. One of the most significant features of her language was her ability to generalize to vastly different situations signs learned in a specific context. For example, she learned the sign for *more* to indicate "more tickling," but she later used the sign spontaneously to ask for other services such as brushing or for second helpings of food or drink, and eventually for repeated performances such as imitations. The sign *open* was taught her so that she would learn to open three specific doors. As soon as she mastered this usage, she asked for other objects to be opened, including containers such as bottles and briefcases, and even a water faucet.

Recently the Gardners adopted two-day-old chimpanzees and started training immediately. These chimps learned much more rapidly, acquiring thirteen to fifteen signs by age six months whereas Washoe had learned only two.

A somewhat different approach to the problem has been attempted by David Premack. His chimpanzee, Sarah, has been trained to communicate by using different shaped, colored plastic pieces each referring to a different concept. Premack has concentrated on teaching Sarah to communicate in sentences constructed by placing the plastic symbols in a specific order. She acquired a vocabulary of about 130 symbols, which represent the names of specific things, such as *apple* and *Mary,* as well as names for classes of things, such as *fruit* and *human.* In order to create sentences, Sarah also learned verbs, adjectives, relational terms such as *same* and *different,* conditionals such as *if* and *then,* and symbols to indicate a question or negation.

it would be just as fallacious to assume that *all Albertans are oil executives.* Yet intelligent adults would be more likely to accept this conclusion because the word *all,* appears in both premises and in the conclusion. This phenomenon, called the atmosphere effect, has other manifestations. For example, when premises are

The language was initially acquired by instrumental conditioning procedures. The names of objects were taught by demanding that she present the correct symbol in order to obtain the object. To learn relations like *on* or *under,* she was shown two objects exemplifying the relation and had to provide the correct symbol for the relation. At first, single symbols were sufficient, but soon she had to string two symbols together, such as *give banana,* and eventually longer strings were required. The correct order of the symbols was always as important as the use of the correct symbol.

Eventually, Sarah learned symbols to stand for abstract concepts such as *name of.* Once she understood this concept, she could be taught the name of new objects by showing her the symbol for *name of* in the presence of the new object and its symbol. In essence, she was using language to learn language.

Like Washoe, Sarah shows some interesting capabilities that go beyond the context of specific sentences. For example, she can follow a command such as *Sarah insert apple pail banana dish.* She will place each object in its appropriate container. To do this, she must understand the grammatical rules that make *pail* refer to *apple, dish* to *banana, insert* to both of these objects, and *Sarah* to herself as the implied actor who must carry out both actions. These behaviors show that she is not simply chaining words together or learning specific responses to specific stimuli, but can interpret the structure of the symbol system as well as its individual elements.

The most recent attempt to teach a language to a chimpanzee was carried out at the Yerkes Primate Research Center by Dwane Rumbaugh, Timothy Gill, and Ernst Von Glasersfeld. Their chimp, Lana, communicates by means of a computer console, on which she punches out requests by striking keys containing specific symbols. As in Sarah's language, the order of the symbols is critical in determining the meaning of a given "utterance" and the computer will not respond to Lana's commands if they are not grammatical. She has also learned to correct ungrammatical sentences given her by the computer.

This chimpanzee's "reading" of the concepts denoted by the plastic pieces on the language board result in her handing the apple to her trainer. (David Premack)

Does this research demonstrate that chimpanzees can be taught human language? Despite some obvious similarities between what they have acquired and human language, there is little agreement as to whether they have really learned a language. There are two problems. One is largely a matter of definition. What is and what is not a language? Clearly, the chimpanzee is capable of learning to communicate by manipulating symbols according to a prescribed set of semantic and syntactic rules. To the extent that this defines a language, the chimps have indeed learned one. However, natural human language and artificial chimpanzee language differ in complexity and flexibility, and the chimps have not yet demonstrated that they can acquire a system as complex and flexible as the human.

The second question is whether chimpanzees can use language in the same ways that humans do. The chimps are able to ask and answer questions, and to make requests. Humans, however, can encode novel experiences and then communicate them. We do not know whether chimpanzees can do this.

Furthermore, there is some question about whether the capacity to deal with abstract concepts such as *justice* and *destiny* depends on linguistic competence. If so, would chimpanzees, having acquired a language, be more capable of using abstract concepts?

written in negative form (*No grain is grown in Sudbury*), false conclusions in a similar form are accepted more often than false conclusions written in a positive form.

Other cognitions also affect reasoning of this type. Reasoned judgments about controversial or emotionally loaded issues about which people have strong preconceptions are more difficult to make than about neutral topics. Thus, students make more errors like this:

Creating a shortage will increase prices.
Oil prices have increased.
Therefore oil companies have created a shortage.

than like this:

Flowers grow better when fertilized.
Those flowers are growing well.
Therefore they were fertilized.

Note, however, that the *form* of the argument is the same in each case.

Problems other than syllogistic reasoning are susceptible to the effects of linguistic forms. Consider a problem such as this:

Alberta is not as cold as Manitoba.
Alberta is colder than Ontario.
(Then where is it coldest?)

These are called three-term series problems. You may note that there are alternative ways of phrasing the same set of relations among the three provinces. For example, we could state that

Manitoba is colder than Alberta.
Alberta is colder than Ontario.

Even though the same information is carried by the two sets of sentences, the earlier set takes longer to solve. In this case, the example illustrates a finding common to nearly all cognitive tasks: negatively stated information is more difficult to work with. Just why this is the case is not clear.

Summary

Transfer of training is the influence of previous learning on new learning or on the performance of a different behavior. It may be positive (beneficial), negative (a hindrance), or zero (nonexistent). Basically, the amount and direction of transfer depend upon the similarity between the two tasks.

Solving problems always involves transfer. Often such transfer is negative, in that previous knowledge interferes with the emergence of the correct solution. Creative thinking generally involves two factors—uniqueness or novelty, and value. Tests for assessing creativity have been only partially successful.

A concept represents a class of objects or events that have some property or properties (attributes) in common. Concepts are generally acquired by testing hypotheses to find out whether a given stimulus is or is not an instance of the concept. Concepts are also learned by verbal communication.

Language is both a vehicle for communication and a cognitive system in its own right. Essentially, a language consists of phonemes (sounds), morphemes (meaningful units), and syntax (grammatical rules). Many factors are involved in speech production and comprehension; these include memory, context, and meaning.

Language has occasionally been considered to determine thought, but its function as a tool for thinking and reasoning has been more thoroughly studied.

Suggested Readings

Bourne, L.; Ekstrand, B.; and Dominowski, R. 1971. The psychology of thinking. Englewood Cliffs, N.J.: Prentice-Hall.

A comprehensive textbook which covers virtually all aspects of problem solving and concept learning.

Carroll, J. B. 1964. *Language and thought.* Englewood Cliffs, N.J.: Prentice-Hall.

A complete general description of the role of language in a variety of psychological situations.

Deese, J. 1970. *Psycholinguistics.* Boston: Allyn & Bacon.

An introduction to the study of language. It includes a good description of the nature of language from a linguistic point of view.

Gardner, R. A., and Gardner, B. T. 1969. Teaching sign language to a chimpanzee. *Science* 165:664–672.

The story of Washoe, the hand-talking chimp.

Polya, G. 1945. *How to solve it.* Garden City, Doubleday Anchor.

A readable lesson in the heuristics of geometry problems from a mathematics professor who cares.

Wason, P. C., and Johnson-Laird, P. N. 1968. *Thinking and reasoning.* Middlesex: Penguin Books.

A collection of some of the basic papers published in the problem-solving, cognition area.

Motivation

12 The study of **motivation** attempts to answer the broadest *why* question in psychology: Why do organisms behave as they do? The question could be phrased another way: What moves an individual to act? The word *motive* can be traced to the Latin verb *movere,* to move. Answering the question involves a search for the causes of action, also labeled the determinants of behavior.

People who are not professional psychologists may have little trouble explaining motivation. Some actions such as eating or even fighting we may consider the result of innate drives. To explain individual differences in motivation, we may say, for example, that a person who refuses to work is lazy whereas someone who works hard is concerned with achievement and success. But such explanations are greatly oversimplified.

Behavior is influenced by many factors. Some determinants are temporary, as deprivation may be in the case of hunger, and some are stable, such as the trait of gluttony. In addition, environmental factors affect behavior: the amount or attractiveness of food, for example, may determine whether a person eats or not. Motivational psychologists examine the effects of many factors that may influence a behavioral sequence from start to finish, including how long the behavior persists and how vigorous it is.

Two dominant conceptions of motivation have vied for acceptance and popularity: either motivated behavior is mechanical or it is cognitive. The mechanistic theory focuses on the energy needed to run the human machine and the determinants of the input-output connections (**habits**) that direct the machine's activities. In contrast, a rationalistic or cognitive approach assumes that organisms are self-directing and that higher mental processes partly determine motivated behavior. These two orientations are part of what is known as the mind-body problem.

The Mind-Body Problem

12·1 How does thought (the mind) influence action (the body)? Many hypotheses have been formed to explain how mental and bodily processes are related, but they can be grouped into two basic categories.

1. Mind and body are independent: they have distinct and parallel functions but do not interact (Figure 12·1a). A person may think about food and experience an intention to obtain it, but the thought and the intention do not bring about action. Thought and action occur simultaneously, without any causal relationship. Mechanists frequently accept this dualist position, which separates the mind and body.
2. Mind and body interact. One group of interactionists contends that thoughts are the product of action (Figure 12·1b). For example:

   "I am eating a great deal; I must be hungry."
   "I just argued for the passage of this controversial bill; I must be in favor of it."
   "I am running; I must be afraid." (Bem, 1972)

   In these examples thoughts are behavioral by-products, not causes. This conception also is consistent with a mechanistic view of motivation.

   Another group of interactionists, called cognitive motivational theorists, says that thoughts partly determine actions (Figure 12·1c).

   "I am in favor of this bill; I will argue for it."
   "I am afraid; I will run."

   In general, cognitivists also recognize that some behaviors (for example, **reflex** actions) are not motivated by thoughts, that some determinants of behavior (for example, hormonal influences) do not have a conscious representation, and that behaviors may influence thought processes.

In the formative years of the experimental study of motivation, around 1930–55, most motivational psychologists did not accept the cognitive point of view. Rather,

Fig. 12·1 Three types of organization for mind and body.

(*a*) **Independent**

```
Thought   A . . . . . . . . B . . . . . . . . C
 Action   A′ . . . . . . . . B′ . . . . . . . . C′
```

(*b*) **Interacting: Thought follows action**

```
Thought   A . . . . . . . . B . . . . . . . . C
          ↑                 ↑                 ↑
 Action   A′ . . . . . . . . B′ . . . . . . . . C′
```

(*c*) **Interacting: Mutual influence of thoughts and actions**

```
Thought   A . . . . . . . →B . . . . . . . →C
          ↓                 ↓                 ↓
 Action   A′ . . . . . . . . B′ . . . . . . . . C′
```
(with arrows from A′ to B and from B′ to C)

they contended that behavior can be explained primarily in terms of drive, stimulus, and response. The person was conceptualized as a machine; the task of the psychologist was to understand the structure and the function of the machine. Because machines do not think, there was no need for cognitive constructs. But since the late 1950s the cognitive point of view has repeatedly proven more effective than the mechanistic one. It has therefore gained ascendancy in the field of motivation.

An Approach to Developing Laws of Motivation

12·2 Identifying the determinants of behavior and precisely stating their effects have been among the main goals of the study of motivation. Let us see how these goals work out in the investigation of a particular type of motivation—hunger.

One research method for studying motivation proceeds as follows:

1. Create a mathematical model of the determinants appropriate to the behavior being studied.
2. Determine how to measure the behavior determinants in actual experiments.
3. Make theoretical predictions based on the model.
4. Gather data.
5. Compare the data with the results projected on the basis of the model.
6. Accept, reject, or modify the model as needed.

Consider a problem of hunger motivation: What is the force of attraction of a child toward food when the child is called to dinner? Among the indicators of motivational strength that we can measure are how soon she starts to come to the dinner table (the latency of the response or time it takes before the response is initiated) and the speed with which she moves to eat (the intensity or magnitude of the response). We might then hypothesize that the latency and speed of the response will depend on several factors: the time since the child last ate, the strength of her personality disposition to take pleasure in eating, whether she knows and likes what is being served for dinner, and the distance between the food and her.

If we wanted to predict the force of attraction between two inanimate objects, we would need to know not only the mass of each object (a stable characteristic), but also the distance between them. Through empirical tests we could then determine that the force of attraction between the objects is directly related to their masses and inversely related to the square of their distance from each other:

$$\text{Force} = \frac{\text{Mass of object 1} \times \text{Mass of object 2}}{(\text{Distance between objects 1 and 2})^2}$$

We can borrow these physical relationships and also express the strength of hunger motivation as an equation, such as

Many factors can enter into eating behavior besides hunger, including the availability and attractiveness of food. (Culver Pictures)

$$\text{Hunger motivation} = \frac{(\text{Hunger} + \text{Gluttony}) \times \text{Incentive}}{\text{Distance}}$$

To test whether the proposed model is correct, we must link the determinants of behavior in the model to measurable operations in the real world. Clearly, we can measure hours of deprivation and the distance from the food. In addition, we can determine the disposition toward gluttony by asking the child about her feelings toward food or actually observing how much food she consumes at a meal or during an entire day, and we can ascertain how much she likes the food to be served. We can also use the speed of approach toward food to measure the strength of attraction. In other words, we can determine whether the data fit the theoretical predictions—our model of the way certain experimental variables should relate to each other.

Consider the three situations outlined in Table 12•1, where a numerical value (from one to three units) has been assigned to each of the four variables. Of course, determining, for example, that 24 hours of deprivation are equivalent in numerical value to the attractiveness of a steak is very difficult. But if we accept the values given in the table and apply the theoretical model, we find that we can expect greatest motivation to be aroused in condition 3, second-most in condition 2, and least in condition 1. Note that the most gluttonous individual (3) is expected to exhibit the least hunger motivation (condition 1). This paradox occurs because an observed behavior (such as eating) does not necessarily indicate the strength of a personality trait (such as gluttony): many other behavior determinants are at work.

Now we are ready to conduct our experiments. Using infrahumans (lower organisms) as subjects, we will vary the hours of deprivation, the gluttony of the

Table 12·1 A Model of Action Applied to Hunger Motivation

VARIABLES	CONDITION 1	CONDITION 2	CONDITION 3
Deprivation time	24 hours (3)*	12 hours (2)	2 hours (1)
Trait of gluttony	high (3)	low (1)	medium (2)
Food object	spinach (1)	steak (3)	chicken (2)
Distance from food	one mile (3)	one block (2)	one foot (1)

$$\text{Hunger motivation} = \frac{(\text{Deprivation} + \text{Gluttony}) \times \text{Incentive}}{\text{Distance}}$$

$$\text{Condition 1} = \frac{(3 + 3) \times 1}{3} = 2$$

$$\text{Condition 2} = \frac{(2 + 1) \times 3}{2} = 4.5$$

$$\text{Condition 3} = \frac{(1 + 2) \times 2}{1} = 6$$

*Indicates the numerical value assigned to the variable.

subjects, the attractiveness of the goal, and the distance from it. If the data confirm our expectation that speed of approach to food is fastest in condition 3 and slowest in condition 1, then we can have confidence in our model. If the data are not in accord with our model, then we will have to modify or maybe even discard it. We might decide, however, that our measurement techniques were inadequate or that we did not conduct the experiments properly. In that case, we probably would not reject the model but only hold it with somewhat less confidence.

The Mechanistic (Drive) Theory of Motivation

12•3 In the early 1900s many psychologists relied on the word **instinct** to explain many kinds of behavior. Each instinct was believed to have a cognitive (mental), affective (emotional), and conative (motivational) component. If a person recognized some kind of danger, showed signs of fear, and began to run, such actions were attributed to the "instinct" to escape. One psychologist (Holt, 1931) summarized the pervasive and misleading use of the concept of instinct in the following way:

> If he goes with his fellows, it is the "herd instinct" which activates him; if he walks alone, it is the "antisocial instinct"; . . . if he twiddles his thumbs, it is the "thumb-twiddling instinct"; if he does not twiddle his thumbs; it is the "thumb-not-twiddling instinct." Thus everything is explained with the facility of magic—word magic.

In the late 1920s the concept of **drive** began to replace instinct as an explanatory principle of motivation (Beach, 1955). It was suggested that psychological needs cause the organism to undertake behaviors that offset the need state. That is, drives are a product of need states and result from physiological imbalance. Needs thus generate the energy required for action.

Clark Hull, with the aid of colleagues such as Kenneth Spence, formulated a theory of motivation based on the concept of drive. Hull stated that there are two essential determinants of behavior: drive and habit. Drive provides the "motor" or energy for action, while habits (stimulus-response connections) guide the organism. Furthermore, drive and habit were assumed to relate multiplicatively. In its simplest form, Hull's theory of motivation (1945, 1951) was:

Behavior = Drive × Habit

Empirical Support for Drive Theory Typically, investigators attempting to support drive theory first train infrahumans, frequently rats, to engage in some behavior such as pressing a bar for food. The number of reinforced responses (habit strength) is manipulated, so that prior to the crucial test trials some groups have high habit strength for bar pressing while others have low habit strength. Immediately before the test trials half of the animals at each level of habit strength are deprived of food for differing amounts of time, so drive strength is varied. During the subsequent test the experimenter measures some indicator of motivation for

Clark L. Hull

Clark L. Hull, born in New York in 1884, grew up on a farm in Michigan where he attended a one-room rural school. Hull, who was dedicated to his work, completed his fifth book just prior to his death in 1952.

Hull played a dominant role in academic psychology, although he is little known among the lay public. He is second only to Freud in the number of literature citations from other psychologists. During the 1940s close to 70 percent of the published experimental articles in the two leading journals in the fields of learning and motivation cited his name.

Hull had three relatively independent careers in psychology. He first studied aptitude testing and statistical procedures. Then he turned to hypnosis and conducted classic experiments on suggestibility. During this period Hull was concerned also with robots (he had majored in engineering as an undergraduate), and his behavioristic thinking may have grown from this interest.

Hull's main contributions came from the study of learning and motivation. He adhered to a *hypothetico-deductive* method of science, constructing a theory with postulates and then testing deductions from these postulates in carefully controlled laboratory settings. Hull spent the major portion of his academic life at Yale University, where he provided the theoretical underpinnings for the Institute of Human Relations. People from all fields worked at this institute, and under Hull's influence, one of the most fruitful periods of collaborative research in the history of the social sciences occurred.

food such as resistance to extinction (how long the animals persist in pressing the bar for food when that response is no longer reinforced).

A typical research finding is depicted in Figure 12•2, which shows that (1) the greater the habit strength, the greater the persistence of the bar-pressing response;

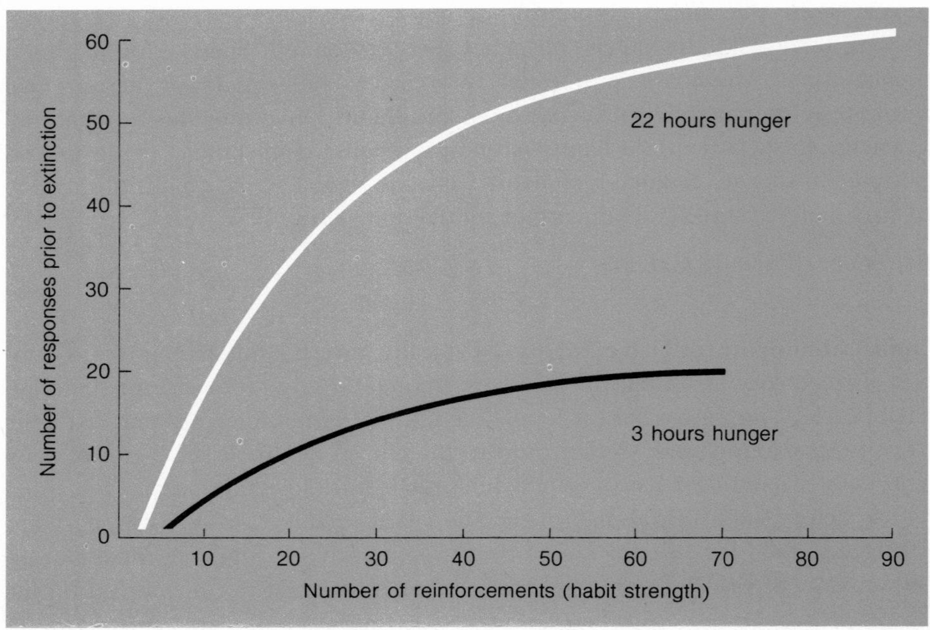

Fig. 12·2 The combined effects of two levels of drive (hours of deprivation) and habit (number of reinforced trials) on resistance to extinction. (Adapted from Perin, 1942)

(2) the greater the level of drive, the greater the persistence; and (3) drive and habit multiply (as specified by Hull). If drive and habit were related additively, then the curves representing the two deprivation groups would be parallel rather than diverging as habit strength increases.

Empirical support for Hull's theory was derived not only from animal experimentation but also from investigations with human subjects, usually involving **aversive conditioning.** In these experiments, drive level is manipulated by presenting various intensities of an **aversive stimulus,** such as a puff of air to the eye. (Aversive stimuli impel the subject to return to a state of equilibrium in order to prevent damage to oneself.) Prior to the aversive puff of air, a tone or some other stimulus is presented. The experimenter then measures the speed of acquisition of the conditioned eye-blink response. This defensive reaction is elicited by the tone (the conditioned stimulus) prior to the onset of the air puff (the unconditioned stimulus).

One representative experiment (Spence, 1958) showed that the greater the intensity of the aversive air puff and the greater the number of conditioning trials (habit strength), the greater the likelihood of responding with eye closure to the preceding tone. As shown in Figure 12·3, the learning curves diverge, demonstrating a multiplicative relationship between drive and habit.

Additive versus Multiplicative Relationships

A simple illustration shows that parallel lines reveal an additive relationship between two variables while diverging lines indicate a multiplicative relationship.

Let us give drive and habit each the arbitrary values 1 and 2. Table 12A·1 shows the totals of these values when drive and habit are related in an additive manner. When these totals are plotted (Figure 12A·1), the lines are parallel. On the other hand, when drive and habit are related multiplicatively, Table 12A·2 results, and the lines based on these data diverge (Figure 12A·2).

Thus, parallel lines indicate additive relations, and diverging lines indicate a multiplicative relationship between variables.

Additive Relation of Drive and Habit

Habit strength	Drive strength 1	Drive strength 2
1	2	3
2	3	4

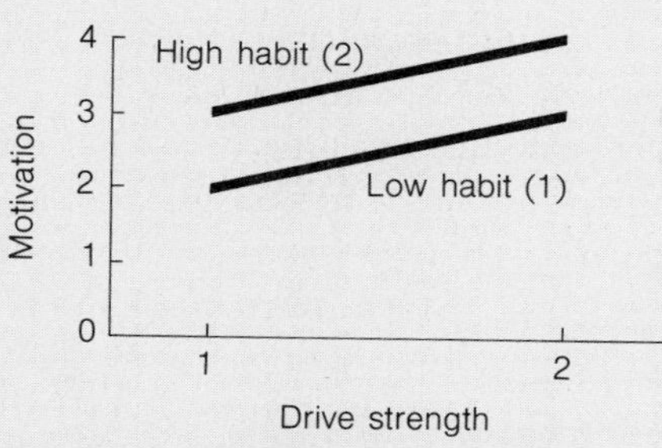

Fig. 12A·1 Parallel lines indicate an additive relationship between drive and habit.

Multiplicative Relation of Drive and Habit

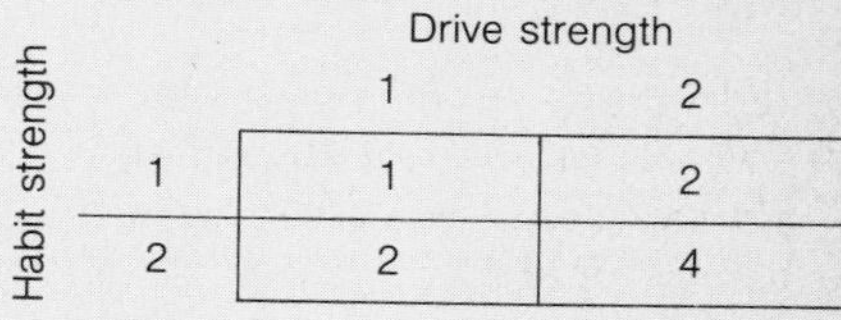

Habit strength	Drive strength 1	Drive strength 2
1	1	2
2	2	4

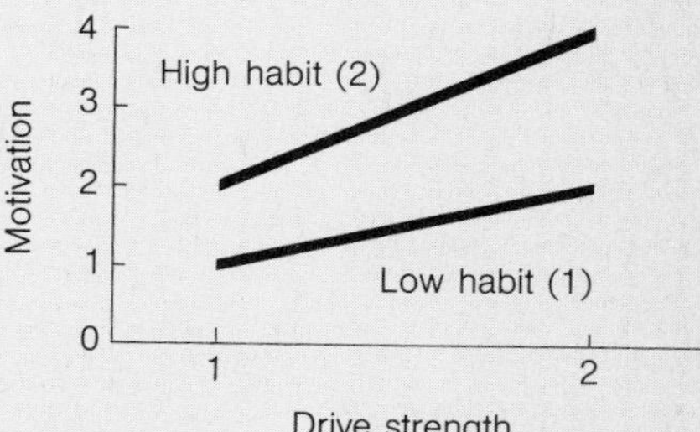

Fig. 12A·2 Diverging lines indicate a multiplicative relationship between drive and habit.

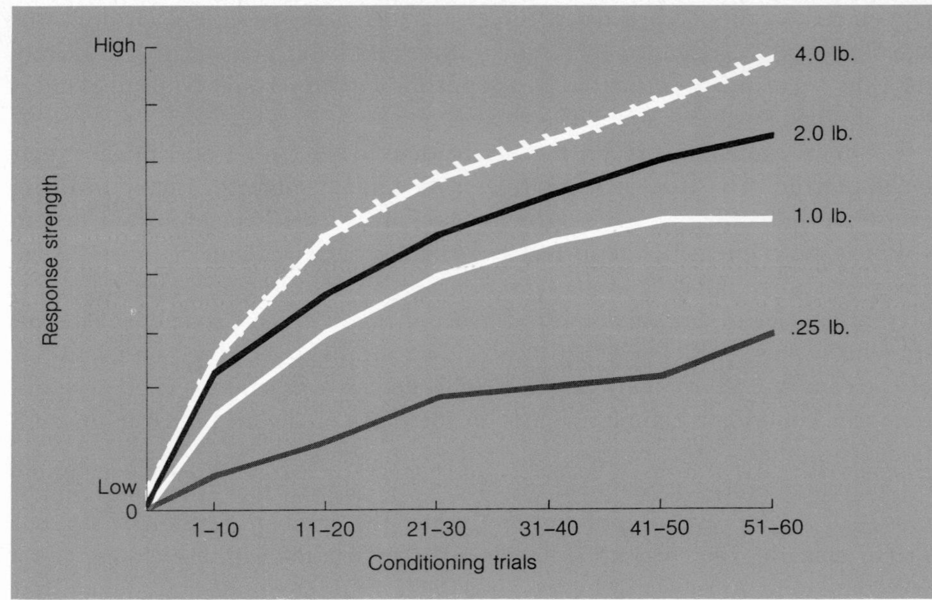

Fig. 12·3 Performance during acquisition of eyelid conditioned responses as a function of the intensity of the unconditioned stimulus (in pounds of air pressure) and habit strength (increasing trials). (Adapted from Spence, 1958)

Fear (Anxiety) As a Learned Drive One of the most significant contributions of Hull's drive theory is the notion that fear, or anxiety, is a learned drive. To demonstrate the drive properties of fear, Neal Miller (1948) placed rats in a shuttle box with two compartments, one white and the other black, each separated by a door. When placed in the white compartment, the rats received an electric shock, but they could escape from it by running through the door into the black compartment. On the first few trials when they received the shock, the rats showed signs of fear and pain such as urination and squealing, and made the escape response only after a relatively long latency. With more and more trials, the response latency became shorter and shorter, until the rats ran into the black compartment before the shock was even turned on. That is, they avoided, rather than escaped from, the shock.

The experimental procedure then was slightly modified so that, in addition to the shock not being turned on, the door remained closed when the rats tried to go through it. To open the door, they had to learn a new response, such as turning a wheel. In this situation some of the rats discovered the new response, and over time they made this response with shorter and shorter latency. This experimental sequence is shown in Figure 12•4.

This demonstration led Hull to conclude that when neutral stimuli are paired with the onset of a drive, the stimuli themselves become the occasion for the onset of a secondary, or learned, drive. Miller (1951, p. 436) stated:

> Fear is called *learnable* because it can be learned as a response to previously neutral cues; it is called a *drive* because it can motivate learning and performance of new responses in the same way as hunger, thirst, or other drives.

The idea that fear is a drive state that activates habits was later incorporated by some personality and clinical psychologists into their attempts to understand neurotic behavior.

Individual Differences and Drive Theory The most relevant applications of drive theory have been demonstrated in experiments measuring individual differences in drive strength. Drive theorists such as Spence have argued that, given the same magnitude of an aversive stimulus, some individuals react more intensely than others. That is, there are individual differences in emotional or drive reactivity.

To measure individual differences in drive level, Janet Taylor (1953) developed the *Manifest Anxiety* (MA) *Scale,* a self-report, true-false inventory containing fifty items that are indicators of high anxiety (for example, I cry easily; I work under a great deal of stress). Persons scoring high on the MA scale have been found to condition faster in the aversive air puff situation described previously than individuals scoring low on the scale.

Paired-Associate Learning Drive theory also has been applied to human behavior in the learning of paired associates. The paired-associates task used by drive theorists requires the learning of a list of word pairs, so that the second word of the pair will be anticipated from the appearance of the first word. These lists vary in

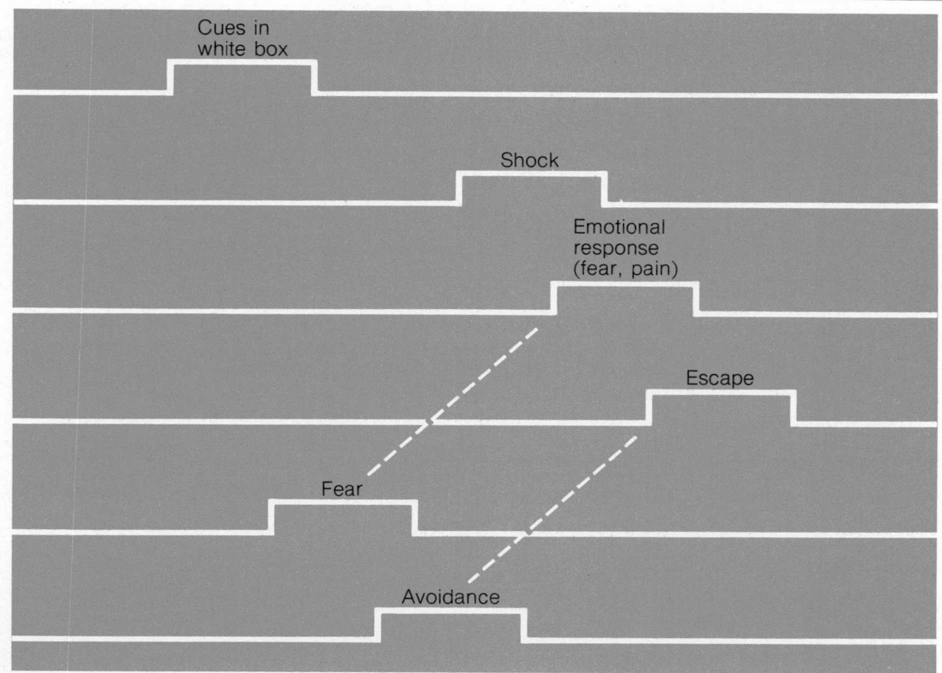

Fig. 12·4 Schematic representation of the temporal sequence in the fear-as-an-acquired-drive paradigm. The fear response, which initially follows shock, moves forward in the temporal sequence and is elicited by cues in the white box prior to the onset of the shock. Similarly, the instrumental escape response, which removes the organism from the aversive situation, is emitted prior to the onset of shock, thus becoming an avoidance response. (From Weiner, 1972)

difficulty. An easy list contains word pairs with high pre-experimental associations, such as synonyms, so that even prior to the experiment the subject is likely to give the correct response to the word presented. Examples of such pairs are *roving-nomad, tranquil-quiet,* and *pious-devout.* On a difficult word list, the dominant, pre-experimental associations are incorrect, as in *quiet-double* and *serene-head-strong.*

Drive theorists have hypothesized that subjects classified as high in drive will perform relatively better on simple tasks but relatively worse on difficult tasks than subjects classified as low in drive. To understand the model on which this hypothesis is based, let us assume that a stimulus word can elicit only two responses —one correct (C), the other incorrect (I)—and that we can separate subjects into those with high drive (D_H) and those with low drive (D_L). We can then assign numerical values to the strength of each response tendency ($C = 2$, $I = 1$) and to the drive level ($D_H = 2$, $D_L = 1$). According to Hull's model, an increase in drive level (D) increases the difference ($C - I$) between the tendency to make a correct response and the tendency to make an incorrect response.

High-Drive Group	**Low-Drive Group**
$C = D_H \times 2$	$C = D_L \times 2$
$= 2 \times 2 = 4$	$= 1 \times 2 = 2$
$I = D_H \times 1$	$I = D_L \times 1$
$= 2 \times 1 = 2$	$= 1 \times 1 = 1$
$C - I = 4 - 2 = 2$	$C - I = 2 - 1 - 1$

Thus, the difference in response strength between correct and incorrect answers is greater among high-drive than among low-drive persons. This model leads to a prediction that has been confirmed: subjects scoring high on the MA scale learn easy paired-associates lists faster than do subjects scoring low on the MA scale (Spence, Farber, and McFann, 1956). If the dominant habit had been incorrect, as on a difficult task, then heightened drive (anxiety) would be expected to interfere with learning. This hypothesis also has been confirmed.

Cognitive Approaches to Motivation

12·4 Mechanists such as Skinner and Hull see humans as passive organisms who remain at rest until goaded by a stimulus. When the stimulus is turned off, action ceases and the organism returns to a level of equilibrium, where internal stimulation is zero. Cognitivists, on the other hand, conceive of humans as active, information-processing organisms who seek stimulation and knowledge, mastery of the environment, and fulfillment of their potential. They regard zero-level stimulation as an aversive state to be avoided.

The need for varied stimulation was dramatically illustrated by Donald Hebb and his colleagues in what is known as the study of **sensory deprivation.** In one such procedure, the subject lies alone in a white room, wearing goggles that evenly distribute the light, and with arms (and sometimes legs) padded to minimize tactile stimulation. College students placed in this situation of severely limited external input reported an inability to think. Some even reported having hallucinations. Few of the subjects could remain in this setting for more than eight hours, although they were well paid. All reported that the experience was extremely unpleasant.

Of course, we may not need experimental subjects to confirm the unpleasantness of sensory deprivation. Similar feelings are experienced by a child forced to remain in his or her room or by a prisoner in solitary confinement. Indeed, the reader has probably experienced the agitation and lack of focus that often accompany boredom or other states of minimal input from the external world.

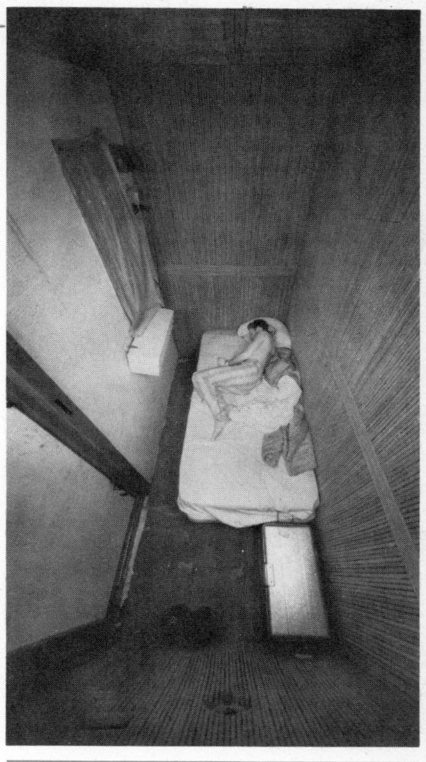

The student in this experiment is cut off from most normal environmental stimulation. (Yale Joel, Time-Life Picture Agency © Time Inc.)

Stimulus Complexity and Motivation Even though lack of stimulation is unpleasant, there is evidence that people are disturbed also by high input from overstimulating environments. Daniel Berlyne (1960), guided in part by findings in sensory deprivation experiments, hypothesized that people will approach and explore an environmental stimulus if it is at a level of intermediate complexity. If the originality of a complex abstract painting startles us but we are not motivated to examine the work of art in detail, its complexity may be described as above the optimal level. Art objects that are too simple or obvious may not attract many people either. Apparently there is an intermediate level of stimulus complexity that is most attractive (Figure 12•5).

Of course, the optimal level of complexity depends on the viewer. The abstract painting might not seem overly complex to someone who has studied abstract art or viewed many different kinds of art. As we have said repeatedly, behavior depends on the characteristics of both the person and the environment.

The Rewarding Effects of Increasing Stimulation The hypothesis that there is an optimal level of stimulus input implies that organisms often act to increase external stimulation. During one sensory deprivation experiment the subjects repeatedly chose to push a button that let them hear the same stock market report. Infrahumans as well as humans are seekers of stimulation. Rats will press a light to change their level of visual stimulation; monkeys will engage in puzzle manipulations for endless periods of time—pressing a button for the puzzle, solving it, pressing for another puzzle, and so on.

These intrinsically regulated motivations may be adversely affected by extrinsic **incentives,** such as food rewards (Harlow, 1953). In experimental studies food was given to a monkey after each puzzle was solved. When the food was later withheld following the correct puzzle solution, the monkey ceased to push the button for the puzzles. The intrinsic attractiveness of the puzzles was no longer sufficient to instigate behavior. Numerous experiments with human subjects have convincingly demonstrated the same phenomenon (Deci, 1975).

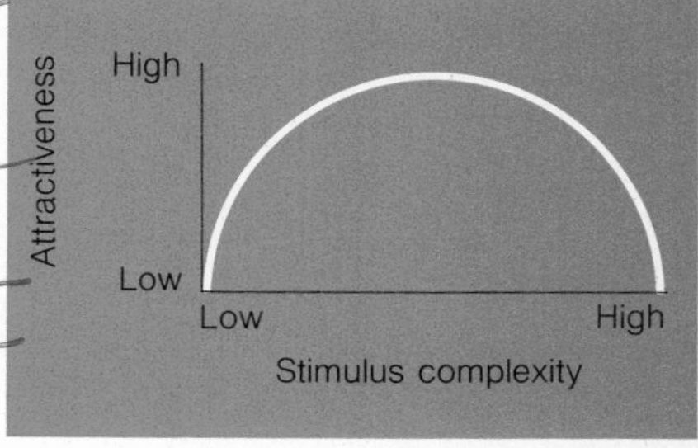

Fig. 12•5 The relationship between attractiveness and stimulus complexity.

We can conclude that the Skinnerian belief that external rewards increase the likelihood of repeating the rewarded behavior often is not true. Just as some students will not study for the sake of the intrinsic rewards of knowledge, neither will some other students study to obtain the high grades offered as an extrinsic incentive to perform well. The analysis of motivation has repeatedly shown that no single concept, such as need or reinforcement, is sufficient to explain the complexities of behavior.

Boredom can result from lack of stimulation. In spite of the revelations that came out of the Senate Watergate hearings and their significance, the lengthy testimony and questioning could sometimes result in boredom for members of the investigating committee. (Wide World Photos)

Cognitive Dissonance and Consonance The motivational significance of a cognition is determined not only by its content and complexity, but also by its relationship or "fit" with other cognitions. Cognitions that are inconsistent with each other may create an imbalance that has motivational consequences. According to Leon Festinger (1957), if the implications of two or more cognitions are mutually exclusive, then **cognitive dissonance** arises. Festinger also maintains that because dissonance is unpleasant, the individual is motivated to reduce it. Apparently, when cognitions are not in harmony, processes are instigated to help bring them into balance, or consonance.

A woman who smokes even though she has read that smoking causes lung cancer is likely to experience cognitive dissonance, since these elements of knowledge do not fit together well. One way to reduce this dissonance is to stop smoking, difficult though that may be. Another way is to alter cognitions, such as by choosing to believe that lung cancer is not caused by smoking. A survey asking respondents whether they thought the link between smoking and lung cancer had not been sufficiently proven revealed that the greater the smoking habit, the greater the percentage of individuals who do not believe that smoking causes lung cancer (Table 12•2). To bolster consonant beliefs about smoking, a smoker might seek data indicating that smoking does not cause lung cancer, affiliate with others who smoke, ignore articles that discuss the smoking-cancer link, or remember the 100-year-old who smokes a cigar a day.

Table 12•2 Relation between Lack of Belief in the Carcinogenic Effects of Smoking and the Degree of Smoking Habit

SMOKING HABIT	PERCENTAGE BELIEVING SMOKING-CANCER LINK IS NOT PROVEN
Nonsmoker	55%
Light smoker	68%
Medium smoker	75%
Heavy smoker	86%

Experimental Studies of Cognitive Dissonance A few experimental methodologies have been used extensively to demonstrate the motivating effects of cognitive dissonance. The experiments are often intriguing as well as novel. In one well-known procedure (Festinger and Carlsmith, 1959), subjects in a dissonance-arousing experimental condition were given a small reward ($1) to perform a task that was inconsistent with their beliefs: recruit subjects for an experiment that they knew to be boring but that they were asked to describe as interesting. Subjects in a second experimental condition were given a large reward ($20) to do the same task. The experimenters reasoned that lying for a small reward produces more dissonance than does lying for a large reward, and so the subjects who were to receive $1 would be more motivated to reduce the dissonance. One way they might do this would be to perceive the experiment for which they were recruiting subjects as more interesting than it really was. If the experiment were perceived as interesting, then the recruiters would not be lying and their behavior would

Does this smoker believe that smoking may be dangerous to his health? If so, he may resolve this cognitive dissonance by believing that drinking is a greater health hazard and that smoking helps him cut down on his drinking. (Andy Mercado, Jeroboam)

be consistent with the small reward. The data on this controversial study revealed that subjects in the $1 condition rated the experiment as more interesting than did subjects in the $20 condition. That is, attitudes toward the task were inversely related to the reward given for participation.

In a similar series of experiments more closely related to traditional motivational phenomena, subjects were asked to refrain from eating or drinking for a period of time (Brehm, 1962). When the subjects reported back to the experimenter, they were requested to undergo further deprivation. Some subjects were given reasonable pay for their discomfort, while others were asked to comply without reward. No reward, coupled with the knowledge of continued hunger or thirst, theoretically creates a state of cognitive dissonance. One way to reduce the dissonance is to perceive the deprivation as not particularly aversive. To test this notion, the subjects were given an opportunity to eat or drink before leaving the experimental room. Those in the dissonance-producing (no-compensation) condition ate and drank less than did subjects in the no-dissonance (reward) condition. The dissonance-aroused subjects evidently believed that they were not very hungry or thirsty.

One final experiment is reported here to indicate the type of data that have been gathered by dissonance theorists. In this experiment, female subjects were permitted to volunteer to participate in a supposedly frank discussion of sex (Aronson and Mills, 1959). Before the discussion they were required to undergo an interview. In one condition the interview was embarrassing, with the subjects required to repeat "dirty" words. In the second experimental condition, a typical interview was conducted. All of the subjects then heard a boring and intellectualized discussion of sex. It is dissonant to undergo a difficult initiation and then participate in a poor discussion. One way to reduce this dissonance is to perceive the boring discussion as interesting, so that the embarrassment of the initial interview would be considered worthwhile. The data supported this hypothesis; the females given the embarrassing interview liked the discussion more than females given the typical interview.

In sum, dissonance research has demonstrated that relationships between cognitions have motivational implications. In addition, some of the data suggest that *perceptions* of internal states, whether accurate or not, control behavior. Of course, this is the position championed by cognitive psychologists and is antithetical to the arguments of the drive theorists.

Expectancy-Value Theory

12·5 The alternative model to Hull's drive theory proposed by cognitive psychologists is labeled **expectancy-value theory:**

> Motivated behavior is determined by the subjective expectancy of goal attainment and by the anticipated incentive value of the goal.

An *expectancy* is a belief that *A* leads to *B*. It has an if-then logic: "If I turn left, then I will reach food" or "If I dress well, then I will attract new friends." Thus, an expectancy can be considered a subjective probability regarding the efficacy of certain behaviors, or a perceived link between a behavior and goal attainment. The *incentive value* of a goal refers to its perceived attractiveness, and is influenced by factors such as quantity and quality.

Expectancy-value theory is in accord with a common sense view of motivation, which affirms that what we do depends on the likelihood of getting something and just how good that something is. Decision theorists use the same fundamental rule to explain choice in gambling situations: the bet selected in part depends upon the odds given and the amount of the payoff. Kurt Lewin, Edward Tolman, Julian Rotter, and John Atkinson are among the prominent motivational psychologists who have formulated expectancy-value theories of behavior.

Lewin's Field Theory Like others trained in Gestalt psychology, Kurt Lewin used concepts borrowed from physics (such as *field, force,* and *tension*) to account for perceptual phenomena. He then adapted these terms to explain motivated behavior.

Interaction of the Person and the Environment According to Lewin, a motivated sequence proceeds as follows:

1. A need arises and produces *tension.*
2. The tension permits an environmental object to acquire a *valence,* or attractiveness.
3. The valence induces a *force* on the person to approach the object.
4. The object is approached, and the goal is attained.
5. The need is satisfied, and tension dissipates.
6. The environmental object loses its valence.
7. There is no longer a force acting on the person.
8. Behavior ceases.

In this sequence behavior is jointly influenced by the person and the environment.

In Lewin's terminology, psychological environment is not the same as the physical environment. To illustrate this point, Lewin cites the story of a horseback rider who, lost in a snowstorm, saw a light in the distance and rode directly toward it. Arriving there, he learned that he had just crossed a barely frozen lake. The rider's behavior certainly would have been different if the danger in crossing the lake had been a psychological, as well as a physical, reality.

Tension The person and the environment are subdivided into "regions." The regions within the person can be considered containers or vessels with walls, which sometimes hold tension. (Imagine tension as being a fluid contained in these regions.) In Lewin's terminology, a region can be in a "state of tension," which is brought about by an unfulfilled need; forces are then instigated to return the region to a nontense state.

Valence When an inner-personal region is in a state of tension, an appropriate object in the environment acquires a valence. For example, food becomes attractive when a person is hungry. As hunger increases, tension increases and typically spreads across the regions. Eventually, an object that has the properties necessary to acquire a positive valence may coordinate with these regions. In a situation of great deprivation, even a shoe may be attractive as food.

Valence varies as a function of both the intensity of a need and the properties of the goal object. As hunger increases, so does the positive valence of food; similarly, some kinds of food have greater positive valence than others for a hungry person.

Force The strength of the force (motivation) acting on the person to approach a goal depends partly on the valence of the goal and partly on the position of the person relative to the goal. Lewin stated that force usually increases as the *psychological distance* between the person and the goal object decreases, but not always. Faraway countries appear especially attractive, for example, and so may potential mates who "play hard to get."

The determinants of the force on the person toward the goal are conceptualized as:

$$\text{Force} = \frac{\text{Valence of the goal}}{\text{Psychological distance}}$$

or

$$\text{Force} = \frac{\text{Needs of the person; properties of the goal}}{\text{Psychological distance}}$$

Thus, force (motivation) is greatest when the need is maximum, when the incentive or goal object is most attractive, and when the object is closest.

When the desired goal is attained, the tension dissipates, which in turn decreases the valence of the environmental object. For example, to a sated person food is not attractive. Because valence decreases, the force acting on the person to approach the goal decreases, and action ceases.

Substitution Substitute activity refers to goal-related behaviors that occur in place of the desired goal activity. There are two key questions concerning such behaviors. First, do they originate because the first goal has not been attained? For example, did Michelangelo and da Vinci engage in creative artistic expression because of unfulfilled sexual desires, as Freud suggested? Second, after substitute goal attainment, does the desire for the original goal decrease? For example, did the creative expressions of Michelangelo and da Vinci actually satisfy their sexual needs and decrease the strength of their unfulfilled sexual desires? This question concerns the value, rather than the origin, of substitute activities.

Studies attempting to demonstrate substitute value were devised by Lewin and his students. Lewin noticed that when subjects are interrupted at a task, they tend to resume that task when given the opportunity. We can observe this tendency in ourselves too: if some interesting activity we are engaged in is interrupted by a telephone call, we generally return to that activity after the call. Lewin reasoned that if the tendency to return to a prior task is diminished because of some intervening activity, then that activity has substitute value.

In one pertinent experiment conducted by Lewin and his students, children were interrupted while making a clay figure (Lewin, 1935). Some of the children were then allowed to complete a different figure. Subsequent spontaneous resumption of the first figure task provided an index of the substitute value of the second figure task. It was found that the greater the similarity between the first and the second figures, and the greater the difficulty of making the second figure, the less the children tended to complete the interrupted figure task. Later experimentation also indicated that the more a second activity is liked, the greater its substitute value (Henle, 1944).

It thus appears that goals may have substitute value and can decrease previously unfulfilled or unsatisfied desires. Unfortunately, the experimental study of substitution has examined only achievement-related motivations and has used only the interrupted task experimental paradigm.

Catharsis It is but a short step from the study of substitute value to investigations of the effects of fantasy activity on goal strivings. In one of the investigations examining task resumption, for example, the reality of the intervening task was varied. Some subjects only thought about completing the interrupted figure task, other subjects talked through the completion, and still others actually finished the initial task. Substitute value varied directly with the degree of reality of the intervening activity. The more real the intervening activity, the less the tendency to resume the initial figure task. However, unreal or fantasy completions also had some substitute value (Lewin, 1935).

It has long been held that fantasy activity can have substitute value. Aristotle, for example, stated that one function of witnessing tragedy in a drama is that the observer is purged of passions. This purging is called a **catharsis** of the emotions. Psychologists have conducted many investigations guided by the notion of catharsis. The research closest to the Aristotelian conception examines the general hypothesis that observing motivated behavior in others reduces one's own motivations. This so-called catharsis hypothesis leads to concrete predictions such as: watching one's hero hit a home run reduces achievement strivings, sexual desires are reduced after reading or viewing pornography, and watching a powerful leader reduces one's desire for power.

Do viewers of violence, such as in *Bonnie and Clyde,* experience a release of hostility that might otherwise compel them to act, or do they learn from such a movie ways to express their hostility? (Warner Bros.)

Most of the experimental study of catharsis has concerned aggression, specifically whether observing an aggressive act reduces the viewer's aggressive tendencies. The practical implications of this question extend to the violence depicted on television. Some parents fear that their children will become more aggressive because of such programming, but the notion of catharsis suggests that watching violent acts on television should reduce a person's aggressive tendencies. Can psychologists resolve this controversy?

There is no simple yes or no answer to the question of whether viewing violent programs increases or decreases tendencies toward violence. Many factors are involved. We know that viewing can lead to imitation, and so the depiction of violence on television may teach aggressive behaviors. The hijacking of airplanes, for example, did not emerge as a threat until after this form of kidnapping was portrayed in a television program. Another factor is that when one sees social rules being violated successfully, avoidance tendencies generated by fear and guilt may be reduced.

Because many processes and structures may be affected by the same external input (Feshbach, 1964), it is difficult to test the catharsis notion. However, most psychological investigations report an increase in aggressive expression after the viewing of hostile actions, and most psychologists do not accept the catharsis hypothesis.

Atkinson's Theory of Achievement Motivation An expectancy-value theory of motivation related to Lewin's has been formulated by John Atkinson (1964), who has focused his attention on achievement-related behavior. According to

Atkinson, the motivation to approach an achievement-related goal is determined by three factors: the *motive for success* (Ms), which is considered to be a relatively stable individual difference and is often labeled the need for achievement; the *expectancy of success,* which is the subjective probability (Ps) of reaching the goal and can vary in magnitude from zero to one; and the *incentive value of success* (Is), or the amount of pride that one anticipates given a successful accomplishment.

Atkinson assumes that these three motivational determinants relate to one another multiplicatively:

$$\text{Approach motivation} = \text{Ms} \times \text{Ps} \times \text{Is}$$

In achievement-related contexts, incentive value and subjective probability have a special relationship:

$$\text{Is} = 1 - \text{Ps}$$

That is, the easier the task, the less the pride that comes with success; the more difficult the task, the greater the feelings of accomplishment, given success.

The motivational models proposed by Lewin and Atkinson are similar in many respects. Both propose that behavior is a function of properties of the person (tension or motive), properties of the environment (the incentive of the goal), and the perceived distance between the person and the goal. But for Atkinson the personal determinants are relatively enduring individual differences, rather than temporary tense states, and the incentive value is not independent of the expectancy of success.

In Table 12•3 values are assigned to the three determinants of achievement approach behavior to illustrate the effects of these variables on strength of motivation. There is a systematic relationship between Ps and the strength of motivation, with motivation to achieve success maximal at the level of intermediate task difficulty (Ps = .50). One is not attracted to easy tasks because winning has little incentive value, and one tends not to undertake overly difficult tasks because winning is too infrequent. When the need for achievement increases, as shown in the right half of Table 12•3, the relative motivation to undertake intermediate difficulty tasks grows in strength. The difference between .18 and .50, which is .32, is greater than .16: the preference for intermediate risk increases as Ms in-

Table 12•3 Strength of Approach Motivation in Achievement-Related Contexts

	LOW Ms (Ms = 1)	HIGH Ms (Ms = 2)
TASK	Ms Ps Is	Ms Ps Is
Easy (Ps = .90)	1 × .90 × .10 = .09	2 × .90 × .10 = .18
Intermediate (Ps = .50)	1 × .50 × .50 = .25	2 × .50 × .50 = .50
Difficult (Ps = .10)	1 × .10 × .90 = .09	2 × .10 × .90 = .18

NOTE: Ms = need for achievement; Ps = probability of success; and is = incentive value of success.

creases. In theory, then, individuals highest in their achievement desires are most attracted to intermediate difficulty activities.

Many risk-preference experiments have been conducted to test Atkinson's model. In these investigations the subjects typically are given a number of tasks that vary in difficulty level and are asked to perform any of them. The data resulting from their choices indicate that:

1. Individuals high in achievement needs exhibit a predominant preference for tasks of intermediate difficulty.
2. Individuals low in achievement needs typically display either no clear task preferences or a moderate preference for tasks of intermediate difficulty.
3. Individuals high in achievement needs often exhibit a greater preference for tasks of intermediate difficulty than do individuals low in achievement needs.

In sum, there is a general preference for intermediate difficulty tasks, although this preference appears stronger among individuals highly motivated to achieve success. These data provide support for Atkinson's theory.

Achievement Needs and Economic Development One of the most interesting extensions of the study of achievement motivation has been the work of David McClelland (1961) relating achievement needs to economic growth. Initially his analysis was influenced by (1) child-rearing data reporting a relationship between early independence training (such as allowing the child to make his or her own decisions) and the development of achievement needs and (2) Max Weber's speculations that capitalism arose as one consequence of the Reformation, which emphasized self-reliance and productivity. Since Protestant beliefs would not allow individuals to spend the results of their labors self-indulgently, profits were reinvested and further prosperity resulted. With these two factors in mind, McClelland suggested that Protestant values produce early independence training which, in turn, promotes need for achievement and economic development.

Protestantism ↘ Early independence training ⟶ Need achievement in a culture ↗ Economic development

McClelland has examined these four relationships: (1) Protestantism and early independence training, (2) early independence training and need for achievement, (3) need for achievement and economic growth, and (4) Protestantism and economic growth. Of these, the third relationship has produced the most extensive, novel, and controversial data.

To determine the amount of achievement motivation in a culture, McClelland examines written materials such as speeches, folktales, songs, and children's readers. These writings are scored for achievement needs and related to available indexes of economic activity in a society, such as the consumption of electrical power, the amount of coal imports, and the number of independent artisans. Data from a wide array of cultures and times, including contemporary America, Tudor England, and ancient Greece, provide evidence that increases in need for achievement precede economic development, while decreases in need for achievement precede economic decline.

One such relationship is shown in Figure 12•6: The number of patents in the United States, one indicator of achievement expression, rises after an increase in need for achievement and declines after a drop in achievement scores. According to these data, the level of achievement motivation in our culture is dramatically decreasing.

Attribution Theory Attribution theory was first introduced by Fritz Heider (1958) and is currently very influential among psychologists. According to this theory, people behave as they do because of their perceptions of causality (the reasons why an event occurs).

Assume, for example, that while riding the subway someone steps on your toes. If you believe that the event was accidental, you might smile and exchange comments about the transportation system. But if you perceive the action as intentional, you might respond with hostility, move to a different place, or even seek the help of others.

The effects of causal ascription on aggressive retaliation have been well documented in experimental studies. In one investigation subjects were given electric shocks by another subject (a confederate of the experimenter) supposedly to facilitate learning (Nickel, 1974). The confederate was perceived as free to determine the level of shock administered. The subjects in one experimental condition were led to believe that the confederate intended to administer a small amount

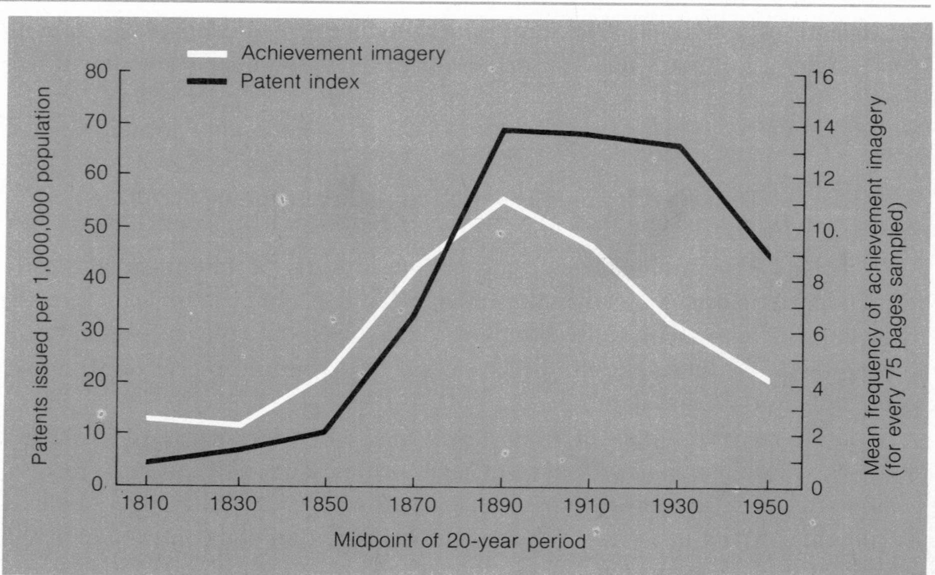

Fig. 12•6 Mean frequency of achievement imagery in children's readers and the patent index in the United States, 1800–1950. (Adapted from de Charms and Moeller, 1962)

Fritz Heider

Fritz Heider was born in Austria in 1896 and received his Ph.D. from the University of Graz in 1920. From Graz he moved to Berlin, where he came under the influence of the Gestalt psychologists, particularly Kurt Lewin and Max Wertheimer. Heider came to the school for the deaf at Smith College for a year-long visit, and he established permanent residency in the United States after his marriage to another now-prominent psychologist, Grace Moore Heider. In the late 1940s Heider left Smith for the University of Kansas, where he has remained.

His insights concerning interpersonal relations and common sense psychology were neglected by psychologists until publication of his book *The Psychology of Interpersonal Relations* (1958). Heider is responsible for two seminal contributions to psychology: *balance theory,* which gave rise to other theories of cognitive organization, including cognitive dissonance; and the study of attribution processes, currently the most popular topic in social psychology.

Heider's writings are sparked with warmth and wit. He is perhaps unique among academic psychologists in drawing heavily on works of literature for his scientific insights. He exemplifies the scholar-humanist-scientist ideal.

of shock, but because the apparatus was poorly labeled, a large amount of shock was given by mistake. In a second condition no excuse was given for the large shock that was administered. In both conditions the actual amount of shock received was identical. The roles were then reversed and the subjects were allowed to shock the confederate during the learning task. As anticipated, a much greater level of shock was given in the control or intentional condition than in the misinformed condition.

Determinants of Causal Judgments Inasmuch as behavior is significantly influenced by causal ascriptions, it is important to reach correct inferences about causes. Harold Kelley (1967) has systematically related various sources of information to causal inferences. He states that if the behaviors observed are consistent with social **norms** (all toes are being stepped upon), and the action is inconsistent with the usual behavior of the person (he or she does not step on your toes in other situations), then the action is likely to be ascribed to the environment (the crowded subway). On the other hand, if the action is inconsistent with social norms (only your own toes are being stepped on), and the behavior is consistent for the person (he or she does this even when the subway is less crowded), then the behavior will be ascribed to the actor. In a similar manner, if a student succeeds at an exam that most others fail, and this student has succeeded at past exams also, then the success is ascribed to the person (he or she is perceived as being smart). On the other hand, if a student who usually fails succeeds when others also succeed, then the recent success is perceived as due to the ease of the task, an environmental cause.

In addition to specific informational cues, there are a number of other interesting determinants of causal ascriptions. Some evidence (Jones and Nisbett, 1971) suggests that we tend to ascribe behaviors of others to personality traits ("He hit me because he is aggressive"), but our own behavior to situational factors ("I hit him because I was provoked"). Ego-enhancing and ego-defensive influences on causal

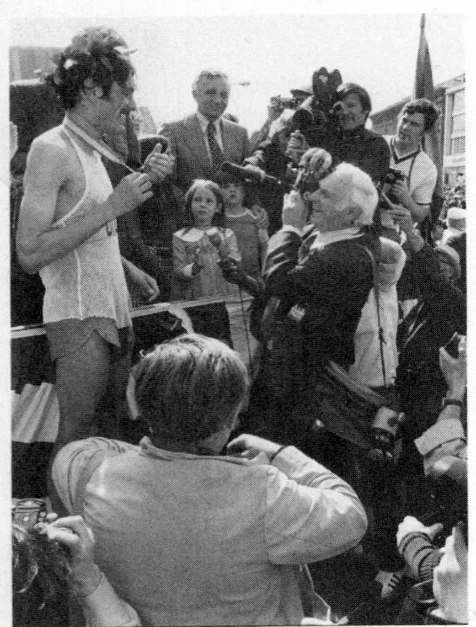

Would the victor in the race be so happy if he had won because of some external factor, such as an unfit opponent, rather than his own skill? (Donald C. Dietz, Stock, Boston)

ascriptions have also been demonstrated. For example, there is a general bias to ascribe to oneself success more than failure. Some investigators have reported that teachers take credit when the performance of their students is increasing, but blame the students when their performance is deteriorating (Beckman, 1970).

Consequences of Causal Attributions Like expectancy-value theory, attribution theory has examined expectancy and affect. The relationships between causal ascriptions and affect and between causal ascriptions and expectancy have been most clearly demonstrated in achievement-related contexts. For example, success ascribed to personal ability or effort produces greater pride in accomplishment than do attributions of success to the ease of the task or to good luck. In general, outcomes attributed to the self (internal locus of control) magnify affective reactions in achievement-related contexts, while outcomes ascribed to the environment (external locus of control) minimize affective reactions of pride and shame.

Expectancy changes are related to a "stability" dimension of causality. If failure is ascribed to low ability, or to the difficulty of the task, then there is a heightened expectancy of future failure when the task is again attempted. But if the failure is attributed to bad luck, or to a lack of effort, then the expectancy of future failure is moderated. In sum, if causes are subject to change, then the outcome is perceived as changeable. But if the causes of an event are perceived as relatively stable, then the outcomes are expected to remain unchanged. When a student with a poor record wants to be admitted to a graduate program, the student usually ascribes the past performance to a lack of effort because of personal difficulties and anticipates doing well in the future. But frequently the evaluator ascribes the performance to a stable disposition, such as low ability or laziness, and refuses admission because the poor performance is expected to continue.

There also is evidence documenting a maladaptive state called **learned helplessness.** A person in this state believes that he or she can do nothing to gain rewards or avoid punishments, but in reality the person can. When a person assumes that causes are not subject to change and expects past outcomes to recur, the person gives up rather than continuing to strive toward a goal (Seligman, 1975). It has been suggested that learned helplessness may be an important cause of depression.

Because causal ascriptions influence affect and expectancy, if the attribution process can be altered, subsequent or contingent actions also should change. In one study demonstrating such a cognitive control of action, external causal ascriptions as well as repeated failures were induced among individuals classified as high or low in achievement needs (Weiner and Sierad, 1975). Subjects in one experimental condition were given a placebo pill that allegedly caused failure at a task by interfering with hand-eye coordination. When failure could be ascribed to the pill, individuals low in achievement needs performed better. Such individuals typically ascribe failure to low ability, which produces negative affect (shame) and inhibits performance. But in the pill-attribution condition the failures could be externalized, or rationalized, thus minimizing negative affect and enhancing

Causal Attributions And Evaluative Judgments

The experiment we will describe demonstrates the effects of causal attributions on the evaluation of others (Weiner and Kukla, 1970).

In this investigation, subjects pretended that they were teachers dispensing performance feedback to their pupils on the basis of level of ability (high or low), expenditure of effort (high or low), and their outcome on an exam (clear success, moderate success, borderline, moderate failure, and clear failure). All twenty combinations of these evaluative factors (2 levels of ability × 2 levels of effort × 5 levels of outcome) were either rewarded with gold stars (from one to five) or punished with red stars (from one to five). For example, a subject might use one red star to evaluate a pupil high in ability, low in effort, and borderline in performance. A mixture of reward and punishment, or gold stars and red stars, could not be given.

The results of one representative experiment using this simulation paradigm are given in Figure 12B•1, where the no ability-effort group (–AE) is uppermost and the ability-no effort group (A–E) is the bottom curve. From these data we can conclude that:

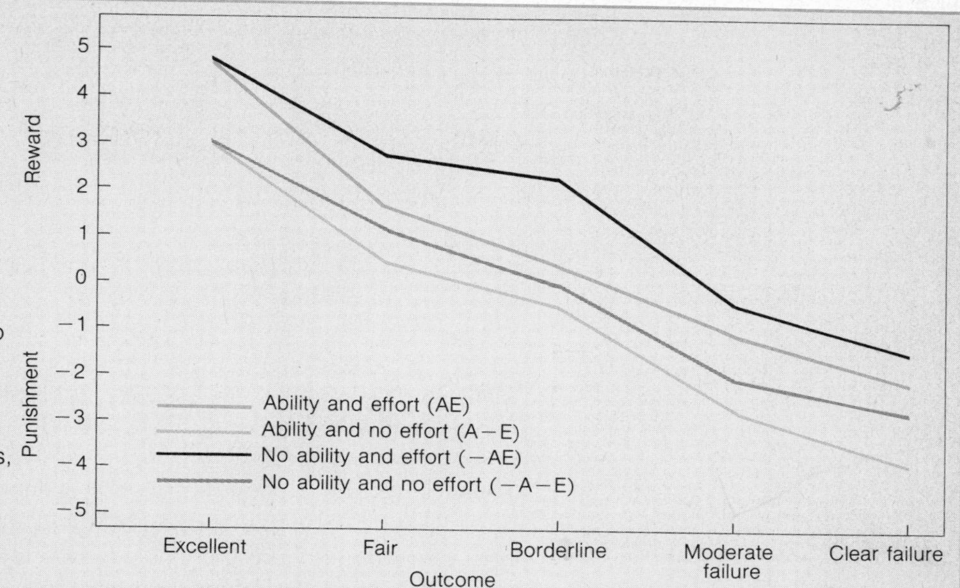

Fig. 12B•1 The effects of outcome, ability level, and effort expenditure on rewards and punishments. (From Weiner and Kukla, 1970)

1. Outcome is the most important evaluative factor: success is rewarded while failure is relatively punished.
2. Effort is an important evaluative determinant: trying is rewarded while the absence of effort is punished.
3. Lack of ability is positively appraised: individuals without ability are rewarded more and punished less than those perceived as having ability.

When considered in conjunction with outcome and effort, lack of ability often emerges as a beneficial attribute, for failure attributed to lack of ability is not severely punished, while success in spite of low ability is highly rewarded. We can probably all think of individuals who have been given great publicity and admiration for overcoming a physical handicap to perform a difficult feat, such as completing a marathon race or doing well in school. On the other hand, the baseball player who has great skills but refuses to practice and does not perform well, or the intelligent student who does not study and receives a poor grade, elicits social disapproval.

performance. This study also found that external ascriptions for failure hinder the performance of persons highly motivated to achieve success. Apparently, these individuals perform best when taking personal responsibility for their actions.

In sum, an attributional model of achievement motivation takes the form depicted in Figure 12•7, which indicates various factors that influence causal inferences. The causal antecedents in achievement settings include specific information

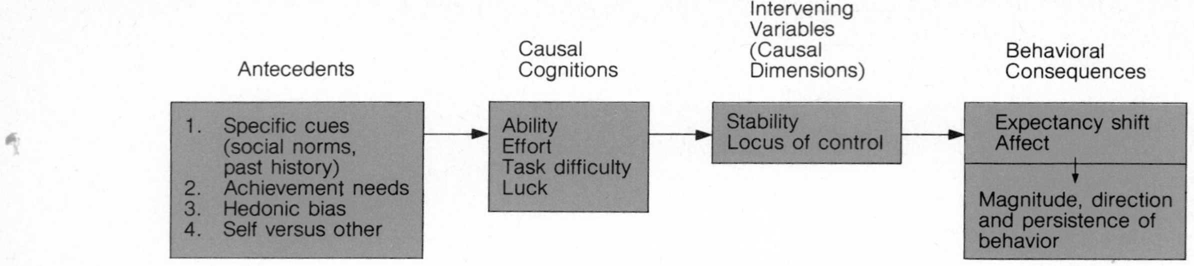

Fig. 12·7 An attributional model of motivation.

(such as social norms and past performance history), individual differences in achievement needs, hedonic biases, and self versus other judgments. The perceived causes of success and failure primarily are ability, effort, task difficulty, and luck. These causes can be placed within dimensions of causality, such as locus of control (internal versus external) and causal stability (stable versus unstable). The dimensions, in turn, influence the affective reactions (pride and shame) to success and failure, as well as the subjective expectancy of success. Affect and expectancy in part determine subsequent action. In this attributional model cognition and motivation cannot be meaningfully separated.

Summary

Motivation is concerned with the general question of "Why do organisms behave as they do?" Motivational psychologists have answered this question by identifying the determinants of action and specifying their mathematical relationships.

There have been two principal approaches to the study of motivation—mechanistic and cognitive. The mechanistic viewpoint assumes either that thoughts do not influence action or that actions lead to thoughts. The model formulated by Hull, which states that Behavior = Drive × Habit, has been the most influential of the mechanistic models. It has been able to predict the behavior of infrahumans under varying degrees of deprivation as well as the behavior of humans in aversive conditioning and paired-associates learning situations.

The cognitive approach to motivation assumes that thoughts influence action. The mental processes of greatest significance in most cognitive theories of motivation are expectancy and anticipated value. The cognitivists contend motivation is influenced by (1) forward-looking beliefs concerning the likelihood that a particular behavior (or set of behaviors) will reach a particular goal and (2) the anticipated value of the goal.

Lewin's field theory is one example of an expectancy-value approach to motivation. Lewin postulated that the force acting on a person is directly related to the intensity of a need (tension) and the quality of the goal object, and inversely related to the distance from the goal. Tension can be reduced either by attaining the goal or by reaching goals that have substitute value. Observations of others engaged in goal-directed activity may have substitute value (catharsis), but this hypothesis has yet to be clearly documented.

A model of achievement-related behavior developed by Atkinson also exemplifies the expectancy-value orientation. In his model achievement motivation is determined by the motive for success as well as by the probabilities and incentive values of success; furthermore, probability and incentive value are inversely related in achievement contexts. This model leads to the novel prediction that individuals highly motivated to achieve success most desire to undertake tasks of intermediate difficulty. Experimental studies have confirmed the "risk preference" derivation from Atkinson's model.

Attribution theory also fits within the expectancy-value framework. Attribution theorists contend that perceived causality is a key determinant of behavior. Internal versus external perceptions of causality influence affective reactions, while stable versus unstable causal ascriptions influence expectancy of success. Research altering causal attributions has clearly demonstrated that thoughts influence subsequent action.

Suggested Readings

Brown, J. S. 1961. *The motivation of behavior.* New York: McGraw-Hill.

The most complete statement of the drive theory of motivation.

Feshbach, S., and Singer, R. D. 1971. *Television and aggression.* San Francisco: Jossey-Bass.

Description of an experiment controlling what children were allowed to watch on TV.

Jones, E. E.; Kanouse, D.; Kelley, H. H.; Nisbett, R. E.; Valins, S.; and Weiner, B. 1972. *Attribution: Perceiving the causes of behavior.* Morristown, N.J.: General Learning Press.

Original articles describing significant research directions in attribution theory.

McClelland, D. C. 1962. Business drive and national achievement. *Harvard Business Review* 40:99–112.

A summary of the main findings relating achievement motivation to economic growth.

Nebraska symposium on motivation, 1953– . Lincoln, NE.: University of Nebraska Press.

An on-going series that describes current work in the field of motivation.

Weiner, B. 1972. *Theories of motivation: From mechanism to cognition.* Chicago: Rand-McNally.

A detailed analysis of four theories of motivation.

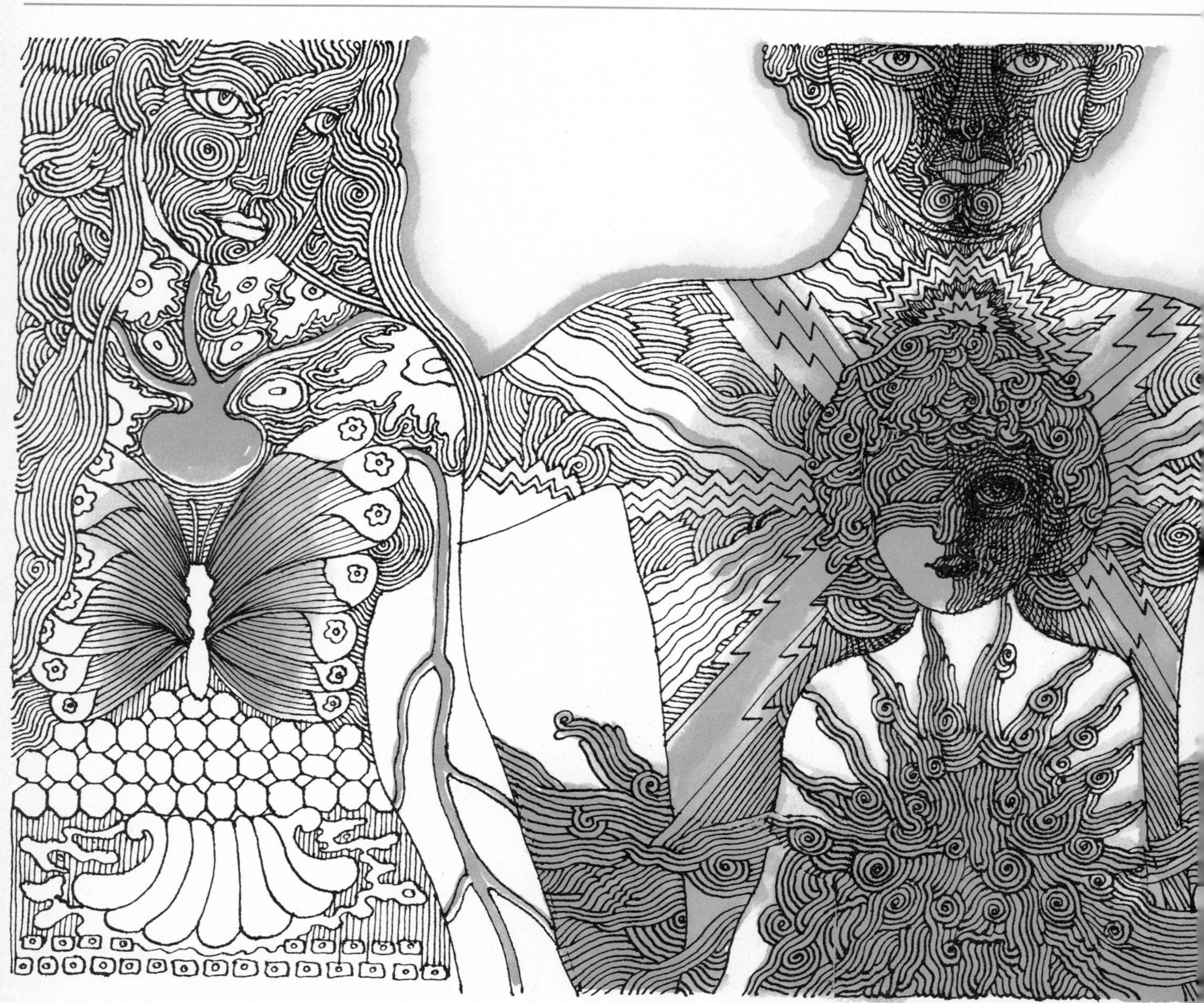

The Person

IV In previous chapters we discussed specific aspects of a person's functioning: perception, the laws of learning, and the determinants of motivation. We now turn to the person as a whole entity—a perceiving, learning, and motivated individual. Chapter 13 examines the fundamental principles that guide human thoughts and behavior. Are we bundles of sexual and aggressive urges? machines? naive scientists? strivers attempting to fulfill our potential? In Chapter 14 we examine how personality is measured and the relationship of assessment to basic beliefs about the person. In Chapter 15 we explore the dynamics of behavior. How can we cope with stress? What determines the resolution of conflicts? What psychological defenses prevent us from acting upon socially unacceptable desires? And what are some consequences of frustration? In sum, this section of the book deals with the theory, measurement, and dynamics of personality.

Theories of Personality

13 To some degree we are all **personality** psychologists. We think about what people are really like. We try to change the behavior of others, as well as our own. We observe childrearing practices and offer our opinions about how children should be raised. Most people even have their own "theories" of personality and behavior: "Fat people are jolly," "People are basically good," or "He is 'a bad seed'," and so forth. From naive insights like these it is possible to derive a scientific framework for the field of personality. This framework will organize some problems of central interest to personality psychologists.

Let us begin with the notion that the person is a whole, or unity. That is to say, we are complete entities. However, although the person functions as a unit, it is useful to conceive of subparts within the person that interact with one another and are interdependent. These subparts are called **traits** or *personality dispositions.* Traits have specific labels, such as introversion, dominance, the need for achievement, impulsivity, and self-control. Such traits are the components of an individual's personality. A trait is sometimes described as a tendency to behave in a particular manner. The aggressive person, for example, tends to abuse others physically or verbally. The affiliative person seeks the company of others.

Traits are important because they influence how the world is perceived, what incentives in the environment serve as reinforcers, and what actions are undertaken (Allport, 1966). A person with a strong affiliative trait might view an invitation to play tennis merely as a pleasant social opportunity. A person highly motivated to achieve success might perceive the same invitation as a challenge from a competitor. Winning is likely to be an important incentive for the achievement-oriented person, who prefers actions that may lead to success rather than activities that, for example, maintain friendships.

Traits are relatively enduring. Unlike feelings of hunger and fatigue, they do not fluctuate from moment to moment. If

I speak with another individual on two successive days or even some months apart, he or she is in some sense the "same" person on these two occasions.

Traits vary *qualitatively* (in quality or kind) from one another. For example, introversion is qualitatively different from the need for achievement. But the strength of any particular trait varies *quantitatively* (in magnitude or degree). In theory, the strengths of the subparts can be measured, and an individual can be characterized as having a certain amount of a particular trait. It might be determined, for example, that an individual is in the upper 10 percent of the population in introversion.

Although the study of personality focuses on the person, it does not neglect the role of the environment. Behavior does not occur in a vacuum. We act in and upon the external world, or what might be called the *psychological field*—the environment as it is perceived by the person. The environment is separate from the person, but the individual and the environment continuously interact and influence one another (Figure 13•1).

The specific situation in which one is placed elicits specific personality characteristics, to a greater or lesser degree. The tendency to strive for success ordinarily is not manifested in a movie theater, for example, but is likely to be exhibited

Fig. 13•1 Schematic representation of the interaction between the person and the environment.

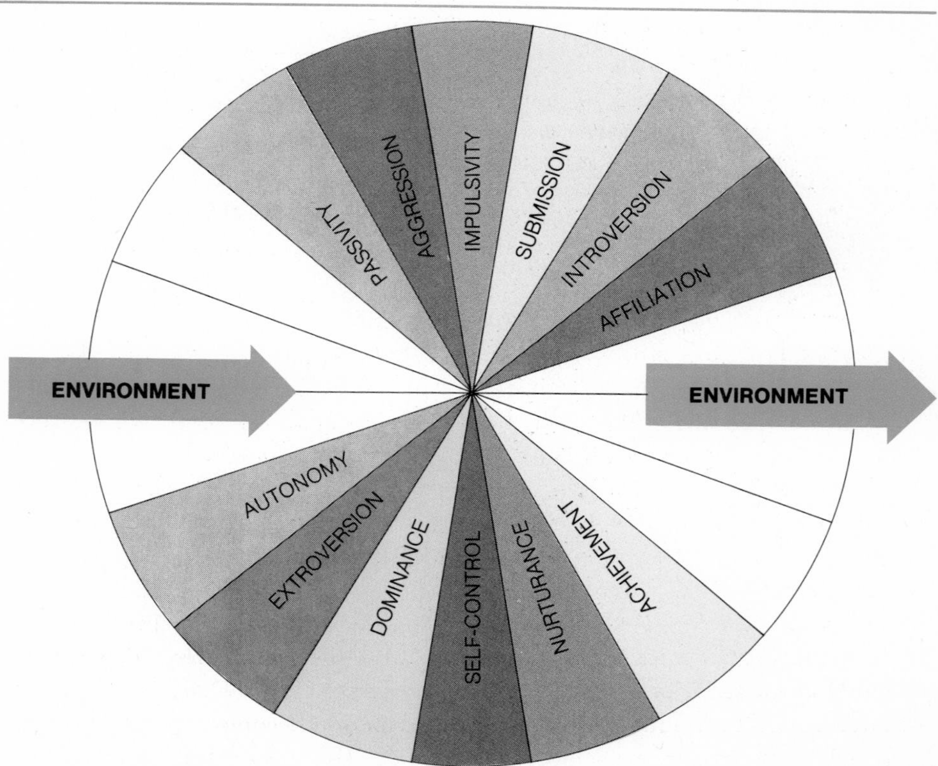

during an academic test or on the athletic field. The tendency to act dominantly is not displayed when reading a book, but is likely to be evident during a political rally or at an organizational meeting. However, a person is not necessarily in an aroused but unexpressed state of achievement or dominance at all times, any more than a soluble chemical is in an aroused but unsatisfied state of solubility at all times. Rather, particular situations are more likely to elicit particular personality dispositions, just as the chemical is more likely to dissolve in particular solutions.

In any specific situation the behaviors observed are in part dependent on the characteristics of the individuals involved. Even if the environment is conducive to achievement-related actions, such behaviors might be exhibited only by individuals with the tendency or desire to succeed in that situation. The environment and the person are intertwined in that the characteristics of each influence behavior.

We must always examine both the internal (personal) and the external (environmental) causes or determinants of behavior. In other words, a person's traits or character cannot be known without a clear and detailed analysis of the situation in which he or she is acting. Similarly, the meaning or influence of the environment can be known only through the behavior of the people acting in that environment.

The Study of Personality

13•1 The four main subdivisions within personality psychology are personality measurement, personality development, psychopathology and personality change, and personality dynamics. The simple theoretical scheme shown in Figure 13•1 gives rise to a number of basic questions about personality.

1. How can personality structure, or the subparts within the person, be measured? This question pertains to *personality assessment*. Should direct self-reports be used? When are indirect, or projective, methods appropriate? What are the properties of a good measure of personality? What do we mean by the reliability and the validity of a personality test? These are some of the questions explored in Chapter 14.
2. How do personality characteristics, or structures, come into being? This question focuses on *personality development*. Is the desire to succeed, for example, influenced by inborn biological factors? Are there genetic determinants of intelligence? Do child-rearing practices influence personality development? Are there particular times in life, such as early infancy, when experiences are particularly important in determining later personality? Do individuals pass through a fixed sequence of developmental stages? Chapters 3 through 6 of this book examine the developmental determinants of personality.
3. How can the subparts, or the personality structures, be altered? This issue is raised in the study of *psychopathology* and *personality change*. Are there any intervention techniques that can help a shy person become more at ease with people or an anxious person feel less fearful? How does group therapy differ

from individual therapy? Does psychotherapy really work? What are some of the techniques used to change personality structure and behavior, and do they apply any of the basic principles of perception and learning? These questions are discussed in Chapters 16 and 17.

4. How do personality structures interact with the environment to influence action? That is, what are the *dynamics* of personality and the laws of motivation? What psychological defenses can help the person cope with stressful environments? What are the psychological consequences of being in an environment that does not provide satisfactions for one's needs? What are the determinants of conflict and conflict resolution? Are there general laws of behavior that precisely specify the mutual influences of personality and the environment on behavior? These are some of the questions explored in Chapters 12 and 15 in which the principles of motivation and psychodynamics are presented.

Although the four areas of measurement, development, personality change, and dynamics constitute separate fields of study, they are interrelated. For example, theories of personality development affect one's choice of approaches to behavioral change. Suppose a therapist assumes that reactions to stress are determined by inborn, unchangeable factors. In order to help a person suffering from overwhelming anxiety, this therapist will attempt to change the person's environment, perhaps by recommending a less demanding job. But the therapist who believes that reactions to stress are changeable might explore the inner (or psychological) determinants of these fear reactions through some form of psychotherapy. Similarly, one's beliefs about the determinants of motivation affect one's choice of personality measures. A therapist who believes that behavior is consciously motivated is more likely to use direct self-report measures of personality than projective assessment devices, which would be more appropriate for the discovery of unconscious motives.

The interrelationships of the various fields of personality are most influenced by the assumptions that the psychologist makes about human nature. Four different assumptions are influential in the field of personality:

1. People strive to reduce inner tensions.
2. People act like machines.
3. People act like scientists.
4. People strive to fulfill their potential.

These conceptions have given rise to psychological theories which, in turn, have affected research and knowledge in personality assessment, development, behavioral change, and psychodynamics. In our examination of these assumptions, we will consider the historical antecedents appropriate to each and the major theories they have spawned.

The Person As Tension Reducer

13•2 The biological and survival model of Charles Darwin is the foundation for the view that human beings strive to reduce inner tensions. From a Darwinian viewpoint, individuals strive to satisfy personal needs within a world of limited and restricted resources. To satisfy these needs, behaviors must be undertaken that will lead to the desired goals. Because virtually all such goals are located in the external world, individuals must adapt to, and function within, the world around them.

Consider a psychological analysis of how behavior is governed by hunger. All organisms have a biological need for food, which makes itself known to the organism by causing discomfort. There is a limited supply of food, and organisms must compete for it. (Humans may compete both with each other and with other species by hunting and gathering, cultivating the land, or obtaining employment and the money that is exchangeable for food.) After the organism has eaten, the internal stimulation that accompanies food deprivation ceases. The organism feels satisfied and remains in an unmotivated state until the onset of hunger again initiates food-related behavior.

Two central concepts guided this analysis of eating behavior: homeostasis and hedonism. **Homeostasis** refers to the tendency to maintain a relatively stable internal environment. That is, the organism tries to remain in a state of internal equilibrium. If food is absent, for example, then disequilibrium exists. The organism initiates the food-related actions that will restore a balance. **Hedonism,** also known as the pleasure principle, is the philosophical doctrine asserting that pleasure and happiness are the chief goals in life. If homeostasis is the governing principle of behavior, then pleasure comes from being in a state of equilibrium, where all one's goals are gratified.

Drive theorists such as Clark Hull extensively used the concepts of homeostasis and hedonism to explain motivated behavior. The most widely known theory of personality, psychoanalytic theory, and its chief architect, Sigmund Freud, also accepted these concepts. We will now examine psychoanalytic theory and its portrayal of humans as tension reducers.

Homeostasis is the process by which the organism satisfies its needs. Since each of a person's needs upsets the equilibrium, the homeostatic process goes on all the time. Even the physiological, social, and emotional needs of a baby can be satisfied only through interaction with the environment. (Jack Ling, UNICEF Photo)

Freud's Psychoanalytic Theory Freud proposed a theory of personality to explain how human behavior typically results from compromises between desires (needs), restrictions in the environment (rationality), and internalized moral values (ideals).

The Structure of Personality According to Freud (1904, 1923), there are three components of personality: **id, ego,** and **superego.** These components are not located somewhere in the brain or in the body. Rather, they are *constructs* that represent interacting, hypothetical structures.

Darwin and Freud: A Comparison

Charles Darwin is one of the most important figures in the history of Western thought. In addition to his influence on Freud, which is discussed in this chapter, Darwin affected the thinking of Karl Marx, Jean Piaget, Ivan Pavlov, and many other key figures in the social sciences.

Unlike the general public, the scientific community was quick to accept Darwin's theory of **evolution.** The prompt approval by other scientists was due to a number of factors. First, the idea of the continuity of the species was in the air. Alfred Wallace proposed a theory almost identical to Darwin's at about the same time, and other biologists were reaching similar conclusions. Furthermore, Darwin amassed a great quantity of carefully documented evidence to support his position, and he communicated these facts to many other scientists. Finally, Darwin was a member of a very respected family. He was a descendent of the Wedgwoods, a cousin of Francis Galton, and grandson of Erasmus Darwin, also a well-known figure.

In contrast to Darwin's conception, Freud's theory was not immediately accepted by the public or by the scientific community. Freud did not openly communicate with other scientists. Furthermore, he did not present carefully accumulated evidence to support his ideas; he gathered his data in a mysterious and secret atmosphere that was closed to all but his patients. And finally, Freud came from an unknown Jewish family at a time of religious discrimination. Thus, the theories of Darwin and Freud initially met with very different receptions by other scientists.

Both Darwin and Freud are part of a continuing trend that relegates humans to a lower status level. First, Copernicus took the Earth and its inhabitants from the center of the universe; then Darwin proved that humans are not unique; finally, Freud contended that individuals are irrational and not even aware of their own motivations. Perhaps the next step, now taking place, is the making of inanimate objects, such as computers, that are more competent than their makers.

The Id As conceived by Freud, the id is intimately related to the biological inheritance of sexual drives (the **libido**) and aggressive drives, which are primarily **unconscious** (Figure 13•2). The id is the reservoir of psychological energy; it responds directly and immediately to bodily needs to discharge internal tension. Hence, it operates according to the doctrine of hedonism. Immediate pleasure is sought through homeostatic processes and tension reduction.

The id accomplishes these goals partly through reflexive processes. A **reflex** is an unlearned response that takes place through the activity of the nervous system. For example, an infant's response to hunger pains is crying; when the infant is nursed or given a bottle, the reflexive behavior of sucking alleviates hunger and leads to a pleasurable state and sleep.

The id can also reduce tension through **primary process thinking,** a mode of thought perhaps most familiar to us as dreaming. Primary process thought is illogical and timeless, and does not distinguish reality from unreality. In the absence of external goal gratification, the id can call upon internal mental acts, such as hallucinations, to fulfill its wishes. According to Freud, one way the infant can reduce the tension of hunger is by imagining ingesting milk. Similarly, we can dream about great accomplishments and temporarily fulfill our desires for achievement.

For survival, organisms must differentiate fantasy from reality—the idea of milk, for example, from milk itself. Since it uses primary process thinking, the id cannot make this distinction. In addition, at times immediate goal gratification will lead to more pain than pleasure, as in the case of sexual or aggressive action that later is punished. Because the id seeks immediate satisfaction, it does not delay gratification. To solve the problem of discrimination and avoid punishment, a new structure is created out of the id that can come to terms with the objective world. This structure is labeled the ego.

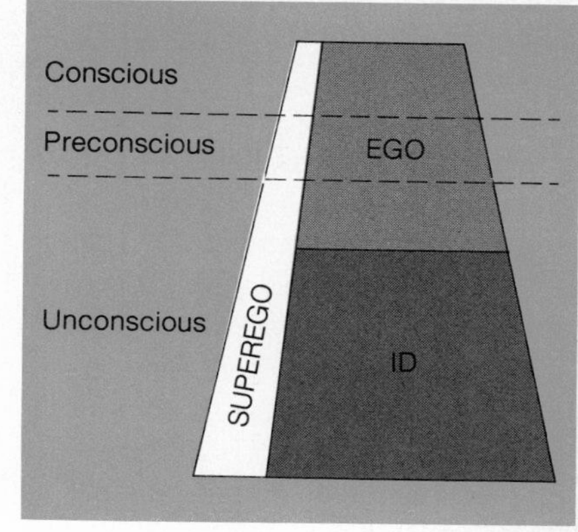

Fig. 13·2 The relationship of the personality structures to the levels of awareness.

The Ego The ego is governed by the **reality principle** rather than the pleasure principle, but this does not mean that hedonism is given up. Rather, the ego serves the id in its pursuit of pleasure and tension reduction, but takes into account the demands of reality. The ego follows the rules of **secondary process thinking,** the typical adult thinking that is characterized by logic, time orientation, and a distinction between reality and unreality. Because the ego also has the tools of memory and attention and the control of motor activity, its existence provides a means for delay of gratification, long-term goal planning, and so on.

The contents of the ego are primarily **conscious** (Figure 13•2) but the person is not aware of all aspects of ego functioning. The ego includes mechanisms of defense, such as repression, that protect one from psychic pain. The defenses typically are not part of the conscious experience of the person. (See Chapter 15 for a discussion of defense mechanisms.)

The Superego According to Freud, the last of the three structures to develop is the superego. It has two main functions, both based on built-in reinforcement processes: (1) to reward individuals for acceptable moral behavior, and (2) to punish actions that are not sanctioned by society, by creating guilt. The superego thus represents the internalization of moral codes and often is called one's conscience. It opposes the expression of unacceptable impulses, rather than merely postponing them, as does the ego.

Freud contended that the development of the superego occurs when the child identifies with the same-sexed parent. Moral values then become internalized, appropriate sex-role behaviors are undertaken, and the conflict with the same-sexed parent for the affection of the opposite-sexed parent (the Oedipal situation) is resolved. The analysis of the resolution of the **Oedipal conflict** led to the detection of the universality of the incest taboo, which is considered to be one of the major discoveries in the social sciences.

Sigmund Freud

Sigmund Freud was born in Frieberg, Moravia on May 6, 1856, and died in London on September 23, 1939. He spent most of his life in Vienna, leaving there only when the Nazis invaded Austria in 1938. After receiving a medical degree from the University of Vienna in 1880, he started his scientific career as a neurologist and quickly established a reputation for his neurological research and medical investigations. He conducted this work despite grave financial difficulties that even prevented his marriage. Academic opportunities were limited because he was a Jew.

During 1885 Freud traveled to Paris to study hypnosis and the treatment of hysteria with Jean Charcot. However, he found hypnosis an unsatisfactory method and began to use a treatment technique developed by Joseph Breuer in which patients were cured by talking about their symptoms. In 1895 Freud and Breuer published *Studies in Hysteria,* which contained Freud's first ideas about the unconscious.

Freud in 1926—at seventy years of age, about to take his first airplane ride. As evidence of the cult that has grown around Freud since his death in 1939, his hat and cane are now among the memorabilia from his life on public display in Vienna. (Top: Snark International; bottom: Austrian Information Service, New York)

The self-report and introspective data that Freud collected led him to concentrate more and more on sexual conflicts as the cause of **hysteria.** After Freud and Breuer parted, Freud worked alone to develop startling and original ideas about **psychosexual development,** the Oedipal complex, dreams, the unconscious, and a wealth of other psychological processes and phenomena.

Freud surrounded himself with a group of disciples from various countries, including Jung from Switzerland and Adler from Austria. But often his interpersonal relationships were stormy and friendships were aborted. His fascinating life story includes his own psychoanalysis, years of addiction to cocaine because of cancer of the jaw, and an invitation to Clark University in 1909 that paved the way for his acceptance after a long period of scientific ostracism. Among his six children is Anna Freud, one of the major contributors to contemporary psychoanalytic theory.

The Integration of Structures Freud was greatly influenced by his training in neurology, where he observed a hierarchical ordering of neural structures. For example, a conflict of excitation and inhibition exists in the nervous system. A stimulus from outside the neuron (nerve cell) can lead to excitation, but other neurons may inhibit the generation of impulses. In a similar manner, Freud conceived the ego to be the executive agency or "highest" structure of the person, responsible for final behavioral decisions. In this capacity it must satisfy the constant demands of the id, be bound by the constraints of reality, and pacify the ideals of the superego (Figure 13•3).

> The ego, driven by the id, confined by the superego, repulsed by reality, struggles to master its economic task of bringing about harmony among the forces and influences working in and upon it; we can understand how it is that so often we cannot suppress a cry: "Life is not easy." (Freud, 1933)

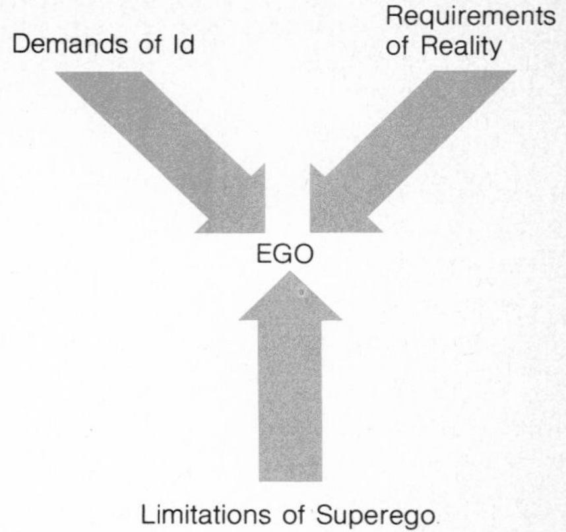

Fig. 13•3 The ego as the mediator of personality.

The Dynamics of Behavior We now turn from the analysis of the structure of personality (the id, ego, and superego) to Freud's theory of behavior. Freud stated that both physical and psychological work require the use of energy. Three energy-related concepts are especially pertinent to his explanation of human behavior:

1. Energy may be either kinetic or potential. *Kinetic energy* is the capacity for doing work that a body in motion possesses. *Potential energy* is the capacity for doing work that a body at rest possesses.
2. *Conservation of energy* means that energy is neither created nor destroyed. A corollary of this law is that energy spent performing one function is unavailable for other functions.
3. *Entropy* is the amount of energy that is not available for doing work.

According to Freud, kinetic energy is cathected, or bound. A **cathexis** involves attachment to an object—longing for the object as well as repeated thoughts, images, and fantasies about it. The binding of energy is unpleasant. It indicates that needs have not been fulfilled, and the energy is not available for other activities. If the desired goal is attained, however, the bound energy is transformed into free (potential) energy that is now available. If all one's desires are fulfilled, then all energy is free. Thus, energy distribution is related to happiness.

Consider how Freud might analyze the situation in which a loved one must go away for a while. Because that person is no longer available as a need satisfier, he or she becomes an object of cathexis. Energy is bound, and the unsatisfied individual may fantasize about being with the loved one, daydream of their reunion, and (because of the conservation of energy) lose interest in friends and hobbies. When the longed-for person returns and needs are again satisfied, the cathected energy is freed to do other work, and there is a state of subjective pleasure.

For Freud, the satisfied person is not in pursuit of stimulation, for activity indicates dissatisfaction. On the contrary, nirvana is a state of complete tension reduction, accompanied by quiescence. One logical extension of this position is Freud's postulation of a **death instinct,** for in death there is an absence of unsatisfied desires. This "instinct" is similar to the alleged wish to return to the womb, where all needs are fulfilled and we are completely under the benevolent care of another.

The Role of Personality Structures in the Dynamics of Behavior The energy needed for behavior resides within the id, which we previously indicated is the reservoir of all psychological energy and is directly responsive to bodily needs. The ego, however, as the "higher" structure, has the power to prevent immediate gratification. If goal attainment will lead to more pain than pleasure, the ego establishes a **counter-cathexis.** This force opposes goal satisfaction and takes the form of a psychological defense, or a **defense mechanism.** The defense might be, for example, **repression,** which banishes the threatening wish from consciousness so that the wish is not directly acted upon by the individual. The defense might be manifested as a neurotic symptom such as hysterical blindness, which also prevents the person from reaching the desired goal. The existence of a conflict between an id cathexis and a counter-cathexis established by the ego is the heart of Freud's model of behavior. Freud viewed the person as in a state of continuous conflict between his or her desires and the demands of society. Such conflicts, according to Freud, provide the foundation for the development of **neuroses.**

Psychological Determinism As Related to Humor, Slips of the Tongue, and Dreams Freud believed that all psychological events are caused, or determined; that is, no behaviors are accidental or haphazard. He applied the principle of determinism to phenomena that had not been subject to systematic psychological analysis before his conception. In particular, Freud analyzed humor, **slips of the tongue,** and dreams. According to him, these three apparently different behaviors serve the same function—to gratify vicariously a forbidden impulse or an unfulfilled wish. That is, they are hidden methods of tension reduction.

Consider, for example, the following joke:

Standing on a golf course green, one golfer is vigorously choking another to death. A third party arrives on the scene and casually says to the aggressor: "Excuse me, but your grip's all wrong."

Freud believed that such a joke evokes laughter because unconscious aggressive urges are being satisfied. Although these desires are typically prevented from expression by the ego, they find an outlet through the socially acceptable form of a joke.

Mental lapses, such as slips of the tongue and forgetting, also have psychological determinants. Freud contended that the famous newspaper error referring to the crown prince as the *clown* prince (now known as a Freudian slip) reflected a hostile feeling that is not ordinarily allowed expression. Similarly, forgetting the date of one's anniversary or an appointment are, according to Freud, manifestations of unconscious wishes.

According to Freud (1900), dreams also are wish fulfillments, or at least attempts at wish fulfillment, and originate in sexual and aggressive impulses. Freud argued that during sleep the ego is weakened or less vigilant, thus allowing for the increased expression of id desires. But the true meaning of the dream, or its **latent**

content, often is masked because of the primary process nature of the dream. The **manifest content** of the dream, or what the dreamer reports, typically is a distortion of the "real" dream contents. With proper analysis, Freud believed, the latent meaning of the dream could be uncovered. He therefore thought that the dream provided the "royal road" to the unconscious. Freud also stated that the vicarious satisfaction provided by the dream has the function of preserving sleep. In the absence of dreams, the unpleasant id impulses would disturb and waken the sleeper.

The dreamlike quality of this painting, *Time Is a River without Banks,* by Marc Chagall arises out of the unusual association of the images, a symbolism as personal as any dreamer's and probably as difficult to penetrate. (Collection, The Museum of Modern Art, New York)

The Formation of Culture Freud conceived of the person as egocentric and naturally selfish, striving to satisfy sexual and aggressive urges and thus reduce biological tensions. Why, Freud asked, should anyone love his or her neighbor? This is an unnatural and unreasonable demand. Individuals are basically antisocial, and civilization is an intrusion, preventing the free expression of instincts.

For organized society to exist, the individual must transform sexual and aggressive urges into expressions that do not harm others or that actually benefit them. For example, Freud believed that great artists such as da Vinci and Michelangelo have unfulfilled sexual urges toward their mothers. These id desires are sublimated and expressed in artistic achievements, but the psychic costs of such transformations are great. Neurosis, Freud claimed, is the price that some must pay for living in society.

Freud and the Scientific Method Freud was well acquainted with the scientific method, having been trained in neurology and medicine. Indeed, he believed that his methods paralleled those of other experimentalists. He would set forth a hypothesis, collect relevant data from observations of his therapeutic patients, and then alter his ideas to fit the new data. Therapeutic sessions were the "microscope" that enabled Freud to uncover pertinent evidence. Freud believed that proper tests of his theory could be conducted only during psychoanalytic treatment; no other validation was needed. But he also accepted observations of hypnotic subjects and his self-analysis and dream interpretations as data to test his theory.

Freud did not test his theory by conducting experiments under controlled laboratory conditions. Rather, his method can be described as primarily dialectic; that is, he arrived at "truth" through a critical and logical examination of the arguments and issues. Freud was unimpressed by the experimental procedures used by psychologists in their search to understand the dynamics of behavior. When an American experimental psychologist apparently demonstrated the existence of repression in a laboratory study, Freud wrote:

> I have examined your experimental studies for the verification of the psychoanalytic assertions with interest. I cannot put much value on these confirmations because the wealth of reliable observations on which these assertions rest make them independent of experimental verification. Still, it [experimental verification] can do no harm.

Current Trends in Freud's Theory Freud's theory was always in flux. Throughout his forty years of active work, and following his death in 1939, his conceptual scheme underwent continual modification. Today the importance of sexual and aggressive drives is still stressed by psychoanalysts, but there is greater emphasis on how one copes with these needs, or adapts to stressful situations (Gill, 1959; White, 1959). The ego and learning processes, rather than the id and instinctual impulses, are focal. But the basic conception of humans as striving to reduce tension has remained, and this assumption still exerts an overriding influence on the psychoanalytic approach to personality.

Implications for the Study of Personality As previously indicated, the basic conception of humans that theorists hold profoundly influences the study of personality assessment, personality development, personality dynamics, and personality change. If the Freudian position that humans are irrational and instinctive is accepted, and if it is believed that the most important determinants of motivation are unconscious, then we have the following implications for the four areas:

1. Personality assessment is conducted with indirect or **projective techniques,** inasmuch as individuals are unaware of their need states or personality structure.
2. Genetic or biological factors are believed to play an essential role in the development of personality. There is a fixed sequence of developmental stages, each characterized by a different bodily zone (oral, anal, genital) as each zone becomes the primary source of the individual's gratification.
3. Conflicts between sexual and aggressive desires, the demands of society, and the prohibitions of the superego form the heart of the study of behavioral dynamics. In addition, the frustration experienced because of unsatisfied desires is directly linked with psychopathology.
4. Personality change must deal with the unconscious and irrational desires of humans. Techniques such as free association and dream analysis are used to permit more direct and interpretable expression of the driving forces.

The Person As Machine

13·3 To what extent are humans, infrahumans, and inanimate objects alike? Both humans and infrahumans appear to be capable of self-induced motion, whereas inanimate objects give the impression of being at rest until acted on by an external force. Even naive observers can readily perceive this difference between animate and inanimate objects. Common-sense distinctions also have been made between humans and infrahumans. Humans are capable of a variety of higher symbolic activities: they anticipate ends, are guided by internalized moral standards, have well-developed linguistic skills, and so on. These mental processes and their behavioral consequences are either completely absent in most infrahumans or are present only in primitive forms.

Some individuals, including the philosopher Descartes, have suggested that infrahumans are more closely linked with inanimate objects than with humans. The mind, Descartes argued, is the seat of the soul. Humans clearly have a soul and a mind, but infrahumans cannot be considered as possessing a soul and, hence, they also have no mind. Descartes thus argued that lower organisms are mere machines, unable to think.

In sum, there is a hierarchical ordering of humans, infrahumans, and inanimate objects. The two poles of this order—humans and inanimate objects—generally are considered to be discontinuous and distinct. Lower organisms at times are coupled with humans, inasmuch as both have the capability of initiating action, while at other times they are linked with inanimate objects, since neither is perceived as having a soul or as capable of complex thoughts.

With the emergence of scientific methodology and systematic observation, these distinctions began to break down. Charles Darwin was primarily responsible for documenting that humans and infrahumans form a genetic and an intellectual continuity. The idea that only humans have a mind and can think is incorrect. Given a human-infrahuman continuity, it is scientifically permissible to study lower organisms and then to generalize the principles of infrahuman behavior to human action.

Why does the tiger leap through the flaming hoop? Behaviorists would probably interpret this act as an automatic response to specific environmental cues. (Circus World Museum, Baraboo, Wisconsin)

The discontinuity between humans and inanimate objects seemed secure, but the advent of **behaviorist psychology** in the 1900s called even this separation into question. Led by John Watson, the behaviorists argued that humans, like inanimate objects, are at rest until acted on by stimuli, or behavioral goads. The introduction of a stimulus arouses the organism to action and *causes* the subsequent behavior. Following the offset of the stimulus, the person is expected to become motionless again. For example, an individual is confronted with an aversive stimulus, such as a shock, which causes the person to engage in activities that remove it. Having escaped from the stimulus, the individual again comes to a state of rest. Neither humans nor inanimate objects are self-initiating actors, according to the behaviorists.

Behaviorists view individuals as being automatically carried along toward a goal rather than as undertaking behavior in order to reach an end state. Thus, humans are like circus animals: the most complicated performances are automatic responses to specific signals. Persons are machines that do not anticipate or think—they merely act. These actions are entirely governed by stimuli that generally reside in the external environment.

The most well-known advocate and contributor to the behaviorist position is B. F. Skinner. Skinner's influence on psychology is probably second only to Freud's. The behavioral engineering outgrowths of Skinner's work, including teaching machines, token economies, behavior modification, and the use of the Skinner box to test everything from the effects of drugs to linguistic development, have influenced the lives of many people.

Skinner's Radical Behaviorism In the Skinnerian approach to personality most of the assumptions, concepts, and inferences are directly based on empirical facts.

Furthermore, the analysis made by the behaviorists is in terms of observable, external events that can be manipulated and controlled. This analysis results in the formulation of unambiguous, empirical laws.

What Is Personality? Behaviorists such as Skinner do not consider personality as a separate and isolated field of study within psychology. Rather, personality and behavior are synonymous. One *is* what one *does;* personality descriptions are merely labels for complex patterns of behavior. A person labeled as dependent, for example, is one who engages in particular types of behavior in relation to other individuals. Thus, a theory of behavior is also a theory of personality.

Behaviorists contend that proven methods of science must be used in the study of personality. **Dream interpretation** and **free association** during **psychotherapy,** the methods used by Freud and his followers, are not considered proper scientific tools as generally used. To understand personality, according to the behaviorists, one must investigate and control the stimulus conditions that precede and determine subsequent action. These conditions reside primarily in the immediate external environment. Discovery of stimulus-response or cause-effect relationships is the scientific goal of the study of personality psychology; the practical goal is to gain control over behavior.

Both psychoanalytic theory and behaviorist psychology assume that behavior is determined and that the laws of behavior can be discovered. But psychoanalytic theory grew from a clinical context and the observation of deviant behavior. Conversely, the Skinnerian approach to personality was an outgrowth of experimental laboratory work and observations of the learning of infrahumans. The scientific context of the behaviorist approach is in part responsible for its advantages over psychoanalytic theory. But the conceptual foundation of the person as a machine makes it difficult for behaviorists to account for the richness and complexity of human personality and behavior.

Consider repression as an example of the two different approaches. According to Freud, wishes that lead to more pain than pleasure are repressed by the ego. Repression is thus a dynamic force, a counter-cathexis. Freud stated that psychological energy is used to prevent the wish from entering consciousness and being acted on. According to Skinner and his followers, verbal or behavioral expression of a forbidden desire was previously punished. In the presence of the stimuli that elicited the punished response, a different response is now made. The prior behavior is "repressed" and its likelihood of entering consciousness has decreased.

Freud and the Skinnerians agree that the memory of the wish is not lost, but unavailable. However, the behaviorists do not use explanatory principles other than punishment, reward, response, and reinforcement. According to them, repressed responses are governed by the same principles of behavior as are other responses, and are not qualitatively different from overt responses.

Personality and Learning According to behaviorists, **learning** is the most important determinant of performance, and behavior can change as a result of experience. Skinner and his followers have focused on operant learning. The term *operant* connotes that an organism operates on the environment or does something to it. Future action is determined by the consequences of the operant behavior. Behaviorists recognize that genetic and biological factors place limitations on the learning and behavior of organisms, but they assume that within the boundaries established by inherited or fixed characteristics, organisms are capable of learning and displaying a wide range of behaviors.

A few basic concepts and procedures introduced in Chapter 10 on learning are extremely relevant to the behaviorist approach to personality.

1. **Reinforcement** is a reward that serves to strengthen the desired response.
2. A **schedule of reinforcement** refers to a rule or a procedure that governs the dispensing of reinforcement.
3. A **discriminative stimulus** is a specific cue that supplies information concerning whether particular behaviors are likely to be reinforced; it sets the stage for operant (rewarded) responses.
4. **Stimulus control** occurs when operant behavior is emitted in the presence of a discriminative stimulus.

Burrhus Frederic Skinner (1904–). According to Skinner, humans are controlled by their environment and therefore must arrange external conditions so that the behaviors they desire are reinforced.

Assume that a rat receives a reward for every (a 100-percent reinforcement schedule) bar-pressing response (operant behavior) made in the presence of a light (discriminative stimulus). After learning has taken place, bar pressing in the presence of the light is considered to be under stimulus control. These simple concepts have far-reaching consequences and play important roles in the behaviorist approach to personality.

One of the basic laws emerging from the study of learning is that behavior is determined by consequences provided by the environment. Behavior that is rewarded tends to be repeated. Rewards modify behavior and increase the frequency of particular responses. This simple principle is the foundation of the behaviorists' approach to personality and psychopathology, for the rate of desirable behaviors theoretically can be increased by appropriate reinforcement. The general finding that behavior is determined by environmental contingencies suggests that one should look to the environment for the essential determinants of action. This, of course, stands in sharp contrast to the detailed intrapsychic principles of behavior formulated by psychoanalytic theorists such as Freud.

Let us take as an example the compulsive gambler, who is subject to psychological analysis by everyone from writers to psychoanalysts. What sort of personality, it is asked, leads to this particular kind of self-destructive behavior? The Skinnerian point of view suggests that this question be changed to "What particular kind of environment and environmental contingencies fosters gambling behavior?"

Gambling typically is reinforced according to a *variable-ratio schedule*. That is, rewards are randomly given, with the wins distributed in an irregular (variable) manner on the basis of the number of responses that have been emitted. This

Learning without Awareness

A controversy in psychology that generated much attention in the late 1950s and 1960s examined whether verbal behavior can be directly manipulated with reinforcement techniques. In a typical experiment, subjects were given a series of cards, each containing a verb and six personal pronouns (Taffel, 1955). The subjects were asked to make up a sentence using the verb and any pronoun. The experimenter then rewarded each sentence starting with *I* or *we* by saying "good" when the sentence was completed. It was found that during the reinforcement phase of this experiment the use of *I* and *we* greatly increased, but, when reinforcement was later withheld, the use of these pronouns decreased. The subjects in the initial investigations reported that they were unaware of the contingency between their response and the reinforcement. It appeared that the learning took place because of the automatic strengthening property of the reinforcer. These research studies were interpreted as supporting both the Skinnerian position and, surprisingly, the Freudian notion of the unconscious.

Subsequent research, however, using more sophisticated, post-experimental interview techniques and indirect assessment procedures, found that only subjects who were aware of the contingency between the response and the reinforcement increased their rate of "correct" responding (see Spielberger, 1962). Subjects who remained unaware of the experimental linkage between *I* or *we* and *good* responded in a random manner. Cognitive psychologists contend that these findings refute the behaviorist belief in mechanical, stimulus-response connections.

Although the *empirical* controversy in the verbal conditioning experiments has been decided, many conceptual issues remain unresolved. To the behaviorist, awareness is nothing other than the verbal report and thus is clearly defined as an observable stimulus. But to the cognitive psychologist awareness is *inferred* from the verbal report and is more than its operational definition (Maltzman, 1966). The ultimate question and controversy between the cognitive and behavioral psychologists is, to what extent does one want to presume that higher mental processes are determinants of behavior?

particular reinforcement schedule leads to great resistance to extinction, and the operant response is maintained at a high and steady rate.

Changing Behavior for the Better Numerous illustrations of apparently deviant or maladaptive behavior are readily understandable from a behaviorist viewpoint. For example, a mother reported that there must be something "wrong" with her child because the child continuously shouted at the parents. Unconscious hostility, unresolved Oedipal wishes, and the like, come to mind as possible explanations, given a psychoanalytic viewpoint. A behaviorist analysis of the situation, which included careful observation and recording of the undesirable behavior and the environmental contingencies, revealed that when the child called to the parents in a normal tone he frequently was ignored, but a loud shout quickly brought a parental response. Speaking moderately had been discouraged over time, while unpleasant yelling was reinforced and the rate of this response increased. The parents were informed of the reinforcement contingencies they were providing and altered their rewarding behavior, attending to moderate tones and ignoring shouts. Soon the disagreeable operant was no longer being emitted.

Reinforcement principles and techniques have also been used in some mental hospitals to change the activities of the patients and increase their rate of positive behaviors. The use of tokens as rewards has given rise to the label of **token economies** for these social experiments.

In one typical investigation, patients who had been hospitalized for an average of sixteen years were placed within a token economy (Ayllon and Azrin, 1965). Operant responses considered desirable by the staff (such as learning a skill, caring for a ward, interacting with people, caring for oneself) were selected for reinforcement. Whenever the attendants observed such behavior, the patient was given one or more tokens, depending on the difficulty or the quality of the job, with a clear statement of why the tokens were given. The patients could save up the tokens and exchange them for a variety of reinforcers, such as leaving the ward, seeing a movie, or having a private talk with the social worker (Table 13·1).

The investigators found that the rate of the rewarded behaviors dramatically increased following the introduction of the token economy. The patients on the ward engaged in more activities, took better care of themselves, and so on. The staff's perception of the capabilities of the patients increased, and the patients' morale improved.

The Preservation of Society In *Beyond Freedom and Dignity* (1971), Skinner contends that we must give up the illusion of freedom and admit that behaviors are under the control of positive reinforcement. Our knowledge of behavioral engineering can then be used to control human behavior for the betterment of

Table 13·1 Examples of Reinforcers Available for Tokens

REINFORCER	NUMBER OF TOKENS	REINFORCER	NUMBER OF TOKENS
Leave from the Ward		*Recreational Opportunities*	
20-min. walk on hospital grounds (with escort)	2	Movie on ward	1
30-min. grounds pass	10	Opportunity to listen to a live band	1
Each additional 30 min.	3	Exclusive use of a radio	1
Trip to town (with escort)	100	Television (choice of program)	3
Social Interaction with Staff		*Commissary Items*	
Private audience with ward staff, ward physician (5 min. free); additional time per min.	1	Consumable items	1–5
Private audience with ward psychologist	20	Toilet articles	1–10
Private audience with social worker	100	Clothing and accessories	12–400
		Reading and writing materials	2–5

(Adapted from Ayllon and Azrin, 1965)

society. But, Skinner states, people refuse to give up the illusion of freedom and the false belief that we are autonomous actors, possessing free will and deserving credit for our actions. If society is to survive, Skinner argues, this conviction must be replaced with the acceptance of external control.

Implications for the Study of Personality If humans are machines, then the study of personality becomes the study of input-output connections, or stimulus-response associations. Personality assessment, development, dynamics, and change are joined and all focus upon these associations.

1. *Personality assessment* is conducted with direct questioning about reactions to certain events, or by means of behavioral analysis in which specific reactions are observed.
2. *Personality development* is the formation and strengthening of particular habits. Learning is stressed, rather than genetic or biological determinants of behavior. There is little reason for a historical analysis of the individual, since recent habits determine behavior. However, one might wish to ascertain how these habits were first acquired.
3. *Behavioral dynamics* involve conflicts between competing habits; that is, different and incompatible responses may be called forth by the same stimulus. The laws of behavior are similar to the laws of learning.
4. *Personality change* is the alteration of stimulus-response connections through the administration of reward and punishment. Techniques are used to guide the individual to emit more adaptive responses and to extinguish responses that are harmful.

The Person As Scientist

13·4 Psychologists who see the person as a machine do not talk about or investigate the mind. But the mind and its processes, such as anticipations and beliefs, are essential to the view of the person as scientist. Because psychology's earliest concern was with the study of the soul and the mind, initially psychology was closely allied to philosophy. Its separation from philosophy began in the late 1800s and was accompanied by the establishment of experimental psychology laboratories by Wilhelm Wundt in Germany and William James in America. In the laboratories, attention was concentrated on mental processes, rather than on such problems as the existence of the soul. To study the mind and consciousness, frequently the *introspective* method was used. Trained subjects would describe their phenomenal experience when viewing a stimulus, such as a color, and attempt to isolate the basic elements that were part of their immediate perception.

But the study of the mind and the use of introspective methodology was soon discarded in experimental research. Psychoanalytic theorists contended that because the important motivators of behavior were unconscious, unguided **introspection** was not adequate to discover the dynamics of behavior. Behaviorists argued that the use of self-report and introspective procedures was not reliable. Different subjects could not agree on the sensations that each was experiencing independently. While one introspectionist maintained that green is neither yellowish nor bluish, another argued that green is a yellow-blue, exactly as blue as it is yellow. With the establishment of more radical behaviorism by John Watson and his followers, the mind was banished from psychological study and replaced by the observation of the movement or the action of organisms. Thus, it is said that psychology first lost its soul and then its mind!

Even after psychology reached its goal and was fully established as an empirical science, psychologists resisted returning to the study of mental processes. But in the 1950s the study of cognitive processes and the mind began to reappear. A number of advances in psychology made it respectable to study higher mental processes. First, computers were devised that were in some ways able to simulate or copy the supposed workings of the mind. It was possible to manipulate the machine programs (their logical rules of operation) as well as the input to the machine, with the goal of better understanding mental processes. The formalization of information-processing languages also helped the study of cognitive processes to become an objective, quantitative science rather than a philosophical endeavor. In addition to these advances, cognitive psychologists were now guided by the sophisticated experimental techniques introduced by the behaviorists. And finally, it had become increasingly evident that the behaviorist approach was limited in scope, unable to grapple with phenomena such as social judgment and social perception, coping strategies, and perceived responsibility.

The significance of cognitive processes within the field of personality increased as cognitions became a more important area of study within general psychology. Psychoanalytic theorists began to give the ego, the seat of cognitive processes and rationality, a more central position in their conception than the id and its drives. These changes were accompanied by systematic research in areas such as self-concept, body image, and ego defenses.

There is no individual comparable in stature to Freud or Skinner who represents the cognitive approach to personality. George Kelly is the most well-known advocate of the cognitive position. His conception of the person as a scientist well illustrates the viewpoint that anticipations, beliefs, and other mental processes are the essential components of a theory of personality.

Kelly's Theory of Personal Constructs Psychologists attempt to explain the behavior of persons, but their theories often are unable to account for their own scientific activity. If persons are impelled by sexual and aggressive instincts, and if all behavior is directed toward the reduction of these primary drives, then why did Freud formulate a theory of personality? Freud contended that higher intellectual activities are derivatives of basic drive-reducing behavior, but his analysis is far from convincing. In a similar manner, if humans are mere machines, as the behaviorists advocate, then how did the new ideas formulated by Skinner originate?

Furthermore, one may ask, why should Skinner read scientific reports, if only the behavior of organisms is believed to be reliable and worthy of consideration? In sum, the Freudian and Skinnerian theories cannot explain the scientific activity of the individual formulating the theory.

George Kelly's theory of personality (1963) can explain scientific endeavors, for Kelly considers the average person to be an intuitive scientist; that is, every person's goal is to predict and understand behavior. To accomplish this aim, the naive person formulates hypotheses about the world, collects data that confirm or disconfirm these hypotheses, and then alters the conception of the world to conform the the new data. The average person operates in the same manner as the professional scientist.

For example, assume that woman *X* believes that man *Y* has strong negative feelings toward her. When *X* meets *Y* at a party, *X* anticipates that *Y* will ignore her, make an insulting remark, or embarrass her in front of her friends. However, assume that to the surprise of *X*, *Y* acts in a friendly manner and seems happy to see her; *X*'s anticipations are incorrect. Assume that this disconfirmation is repeatedly experienced, so that the friendliness at the party cannot be ascribed to a temporary mood or social pressures. On the basis of these data, *X* should reformulate her hypothesis and perceive *Y* as liking her. The new construction more accurately predicts behavior and allows *X* to correctly anticipate her interactions with *Y*.

Many other psychologists in addition to Kelly implicitly accept the conception of the individual as an intuitive scientist. Of great concern to experimental psychologists is the possibility that the subject will infer what the experimenter is trying to prove and then will consciously or unconsciously comply with this hypothesis (Orne, 1962). The demand characteristics of the experiment therefore must be carefully controlled in many psychological investigations, particularly in personality and social psychology. But the very existence of such controls implies that the subjects search for meaning in their environment, formulate hypotheses, and act on the basis of these belief systems. Of course, if the subject were to perceive the experimenter as a nasty or intrusive person, he or she then might try to "ruin" the experiment by disproving the experimenter's hypothesis. This behavior also is in service of the subject's goal and is based on his or her belief systems, as well as on inferences about the purpose of the investigation.

Basic Concepts Kelly believes that behavior is determined by one's perception and interpretation of phenomena, rather than by the physical stimulus itself. Identical external events may give rise to different reactions because of the personal meaning of those events. Refusal by an athlete to argue with the poor decision of a referee might indicate submissiveness to one person but consideration to another. Clearly, there are many ways of viewing the world.

One's manner of construing the world is shaped by prior experiences and by the particular social context where one is (Kelly, 1955). In an investigation pertinent

Are Humans Really Rational?

There is increasing evidence that humans are poor information processors, possessing what has been labeled "bounded rationality." The capacity of the human mind for solving problems is small when compared to the complexity of the problems that are encountered.

A number of convincing experiments demonstrate the limited capacity of humans (see Tversky and Kahneman, 1974). For example, in judgments of the relationship between two variables, people are overly guided by instances of positive relationships. If one knows an individual who smoked marijuana and later dropped out of school, it might be concluded that smoking marijuana and lack of school motivation are correlated, or go together. Students who smoke marijuana and are highly motivated in school, or students who drop out of school but do not use drugs, are ignored in favor of the positive evidence.

Another example of the limits of the mind is illustrated by the principle of "anchoring." A rapid estimation of the product:

$$8 \times 7 \times 6 \times 5 \times 4 \times 3 \times 2 \times 1$$

is typically greater than an estimation of:

$$1 \times 2 \times 3 \times 4 \times 5 \times 6 \times 7 \times 8$$

because of the different starting points of the calculation.

It also has been shown that, when given just a small sample of data, individuals overgeneralize their conclusions and ignore probabilities. Thus, many decisions are "biased," that is, they do not follow the logical rules of mathematics.

to this point, "normals" gained admission to a mental hospital by faking certain symptoms (Rosenhan, 1973). The investigator then examined how long it took the staff to recognize that the pseudopatients were indeed normal. During their stay in the hospital the pseudopatients acted in a normal manner, but their actions were often misinterpreted by the staff. Frequent writing was considered a sign of schizophrenia rather than an intellectual activity; pacing was believed to be an indication of anxiety rather than boredom, and so on. The staff's perception of the individuals in the hospital setting greatly colored their interpretations of the observed behaviors, as well as their reactions to these behaviors.

Construct systems differ in their number of component categories. For example, one individual might categorize other people on a variety of dimensions, such as sincerity-insincerity, introversion-extroversion, and dominance-submission, while another individual uses only one dimension, such as liberalism-conservatism. In addition, constructs have a range and a focus of convenience. The *range of convenience* indicates the breadth of different phenomena to which a construct may be applied. For example, skin color or height might be used to categorize individuals (although these particular classifications might not prove useful in predicting behavior). The *focus of convenience* of a construct refers to the area in which the construct is maximally useful. The tall versus short construct may have its focus of convenience in selecting basketball players.

The range and focus notions frequently are employed by scientists when describing scientific theories. Freudians and Skinnerians argue that the range of convenience of their theories includes a great variety of behaviors; such generalizability is a positive attribute of a theory. But perhaps the focus of convenience of the Freudian model concerns situations involving sexual conflict, whereas the focus of convenience of the Skinnerian conception is infrahuman operant learning.

By structuring the world, persons are better able to anticipate events and to master the environment. Kelly contends that people are motivated to achieve cognitive clarity and that construct systems make the world understandable. There is no conceptual system that is "best" or unmodifiable; individuals can choose between the particular interpretations that they impose on events.

Psychotherapy At times individuals must be aided in their structuring or construal attempts. Psychotherapy, Kelly asserts, is a process in which one's construct system is altered. The therapist must first discover how the client is perceiving the world and then assist the client to reorganize the old system and to find new constructs that are more functional. The therapist might help the client design and implement "experiments" that test particular hypotheses. For example, if an individual perceives a parent or a spouse as "aggressive" or "dominating," then specific behaviors might be suggested to test whether this perception is appropriate.

Role playing and **modeling** frequently are used to help alter construct systems. The therapist might suggest that the client act as if the parent or spouse were not aggressive or dominant in order to test this alternative hypothesis. Or it might be recommended to construe others along a different category, such as friendly-unfriendly. College students often assert that they do not want to leave the university because the people "out there" are not intelligent. They might be advised to apply other relevant constructs, such as helpful-harmful or fun-boring, so that their conceptual system is broadened.

In one social experiment the subjects were teachers who believed the children in their classroom were not learning because the children were lazy (Kelly, 1960). Experimenters suggested that the teachers give the children nothing to do in the classroom and see what happens. Of course, the pupils would not sit without activity. On the basis of this contradictory evidence, the teachers began to consider the school environment and their own inadequacy as causes of poor learning, rather than blaming the problems entirely on the children. The process of construct alteration is not limited to planned change programs or social experiments. It is the essence of adapting to one's environment, and it is always occurring.

Anxiety, Threat, and Guilt **Affects,** or **emotions,** are the main determinants of behavior in virtually all motivational models. But within Kelly's conception, behavior is determined by belief systems and cognitions; affects are consequences of particular construct systems, rather than direct influences on action.

Anxiety, according to Kelly, occurs when one's construct system provides no means for dealing with an experience. For example, interacting with a person that we cannot understand often gives rise to vague feelings of uneasiness. Even greater anxiety is experienced when starting a new job or confronting a new environment. If anxiety reactions to new situations are frequent and severe, then the range of one's constructs must be broadened so that more phenomena can be incorporated. Disconfirmation of a belief also arouses anxiety because it reveals an inadequacy in the construct system. Anxiety is therefore not necessarily bad, for this affective experience is one precondition for construct change.

Kelly distinguishes between threat and anxiety, although both result from defective conceptual systems. *Threat* is experienced when a fundamental change is about to occur in one's construct system. Questioning the purpose of life is threatening, for it may lead to basic conceptual changes. In a similar manner, a deeply involving extra-marital affair may alter one's conception of what it is to be a spouse and parent, and thus engender a threat.

Finally, *guilt* results from a discrepancy between one's ideal self and one's action. If, for example, the ideal self-concept includes honesty, but one cheats, then guilt is experienced. It therefore follows that if a person values deceit, then honest actions should produce feelings of guilt!

International Relations Individuals within a culture share a particular manner of thinking and perceiving. But the disparate life experiences *between* cultures produce different expectations and what might be called national construct systems. For harmonious relationships to exist between cultures, there must be adequate communication and mutual understanding.

The value of Kelly's analysis of national constructs was dramatically revealed in a recent exchange between India and the United States. The Indian government announced that the United States should be honored by the foreign aid it was giving to India. To many Americans this seemed ungrateful, and there was a demand to reduce the foreign aid funds. But in the Indian culture, the bestowal of gifts is one indication that the giver has the necessary means to help others. Thus, gift giving is an honor for the giver, rather than for the receiver. This misunderstanding, which produced great temporary conflict between the two nations, was caused by different perceptions of the psychological meaning of a gift.

Comparison with Psychoanalytic and Behavior Theory Unlike the theories of Freud and Skinner, Kelly's theory offers an intellectual or mentalistic conception of humans. Mechanical determination of any sort is ruled out, and individuals are not slaves to impulses or constrained by biological drives. One has free will, and behavior is determined by cognitions, which are the product of an ever-active, creative process. For Kelly, we are active agents, creators of hypotheses, goal-directed beings, and we can select between different alternatives. Not hedonism and homeostasis, but mastery and perceptual change are the governing principles of action.

Implications for the Study of Personality The conception of the person as a scientist generates a unique approach to personality assessment, development, dynamics, and change.

1. Personality assessment is conducted to understand the individual's construct system. Direct verbal reports are used to determine how the person perceives the world. The assessment does not place the person in an a priori trait category assumed by the assessor.
2. Personality development is relatively neglected. There is a tendency to focus on the present construct system, rather than on how it came into being. The most pertinent developmental work involves the growth of intellectual processes, logical thinking, and conceptual differentiation.
3. Personality dynamics considers the effects of thought upon action and the functional significance of cognitions, as well as the affective consequences of particular construct systems.
4. Personality change, as already discussed, is dependent upon changing construct systems. Methods are used to facilitate the formation of new hypotheses and new expectations.

The Person As Experiencer

13·5 In recent years one branch of psychology has expanded its interests to include not only what the person *is*, but also what the person has the potential to *become*. Those who see the person as an experiencer believe that the individual can overcome harmful effects of childhood training and restrictions imposed by the environment.

Often it is contended that the repressive society of Vienna around the beginning of the twentieth century greatly shaped Freudian theory, with its emphasis on sexual repression, conflict, and neurosis. In America, however, thoughts around 1900 embodied the Darwinian interest in adaptation and function and the optimistic belief that behavior is completely modifiable. John Watson, for example, asserted:

> I wish to draw the conclusion that there is not such a thing as an inheritance of capacity, talent, temperament, mental constitution, and characteristics. These things again depend on training. (Watson, 1924a, p. 74)

The American climate at that time thus nurtured the growth of learning theory, behaviorism, and Skinnerian psychology.

Behaviorism and psychoanalytic psychology were the two important "forces" prior to around 1960, when a third force appeared under the name of **humanistic psychology.** The so-called third force includes **encounter groups** and **sensitivity training, biofeedback** and **altered states of consciousness,** and a broad spectrum of concepts and techniques revolving around the self, subjective experience, and the search for meaning in life. The humanistic movement emerged in a social climate in which individuals, particularly young persons, were questioning traditional values, such as striving for achievement. Public interest in environmental pollution had raised concern about the quality and richness of life. Emphasis upon existential problems naturally gave rise to a more humanistic psychology.

Some human relations groups focus on creativity and growth through exercises to expand awareness or focus on the here and now. (Hap Stewart, Jeroboam)

When the Association of Humanistic Psychology was founded in 1962, four interrelated principles were accepted to guide their scientific pursuits:

1. The experiencing person is of primary interest. Humanistic psychology begins with the study of individuals in real-life circumstances. Humans are subjects (rather than mere objects) of study. Psychological research, humanists contend, cannot be modeled after early physics, in which the objects of study were "out there." The person must be examined and described in terms of personal consciousness, which includes subjective experience and how the individual perceives and values himself or herself. The basic question that humanists grapple with is "Who am I?" Individuals, as travelers in life, must determine where they are and where they wish to go. Humanists follow a holistic approach in which experiences are not broken down into component parts, like "single frames within a film," but the entirety of life is considered.
2. Human choice, creativity, and self-actualization are the preferred topics to investigate. Humanists argue that the study of psychologically crippled people has led to a crippled psychology, while the study of lower organisms has yielded an incomplete psychology devoid of consciousness. The humanists believe that psychologists should study wholesome and healthy individuals, persons who are creative and fully functioning. People have a need to push forward in life, to develop their potentialities and capabilities. These self-actualizing tendencies are of particular significance.

Abraham Maslow (1908–1970). In contrast to Freudianism and behaviorism, which are deterministic, Maslow emphasized human freedom and the capacity for self-actualization.

3. Meaningfulness must precede objectivity in the selection of research problems. Psychological research, according to the humanists, has centered on methods rather than on problems. Often research topics are selected chiefly because objective and convenient methods are available. But research projects should be undertaken because they are significant and pertain to human issues, even if the methods available are weak. Research cannot be value-free; psychologists must study the important issues in peoples' lives.
4. Ultimate value is placed on the dignity of the person. Above all, humans are accepted as unique and noble. Psychologists must understand people, rather than predict or control their behavior. Individuals are believed to have a higher nature with a need for meaningful work, responsibility, and the opportunity for creative expression. The heroic capacity of people is a basic axiom of humanistic psychology.

Prominent spokesmen for humanistic psychology include Gordon Allport, Abraham Maslow, Rollo May, and Carl Rogers. The viewpoints of Maslow and Rogers are examined in greater detail here. Although these theorists are not in complete agreement, and each has unique theoretical ideas that are not incorporated by the other, their conceptions have enough in common to be presented together.

The Humanistic Psychology of Maslow and Rogers According to Maslow and Rogers, the core tendency of a person is to actualize his or her potential. There is an internal, biological pressure to develop fully the capacities and talents that have been inherited. Because the organism has a blueprint to follow and should not suppress basic propensities, the central motivation of the individual is to grow and to enhance the self. In contrast to psychoanalytic theory, humanistic theory asserts that persons are in need of stimulation and strive for higher goals.

Self-actualization

Self-actualization requires an openness to feelings, for subjective states give rise to a sense of personal existence. Recognition of one's own emotions is therefore a key part of the growth process; emotions are generally facilitative rather than something to be avoided.

Although each individual has the potential for self-actualization, this goal may be lost in the process of socialization and development. Rogers and Maslow propose processes that may enhance or interfere with self-actualization.

Positive Self-regard According to Rogers (1959, 1961), as an awareness of the self develops, a need arises for positive regard from others and for positive self-regard. One's **self-concept** is for the most part socially determined. If an individual is accepted totally (*unconditional positive regard*), then *positive self-regard* emerges. But if actions are evaluated rather than the total person and some are judged positively and others negatively (*conditional positive regard*), then *conditions of worth* develop. The person experiences "do" or "do not" as necessary in order to feel appreciated and accepted.

A condition of worth leads to *defensive functioning* and generates discrepancies between the objective and the subjective world, which in turn produce anxiety and threat. Conversely, the *fully functioning* individual is low in anxiety inasmuch as (1) unconditional positive regard is received from others; (2) there is an openness to experience, rather than defensive functioning; and (3) discrepancies between the real and experienced world are minimized. Some of the negative and positive directions of a fully functioning person and traits that characterize the self-actualizing versus the defensive-functioning person are shown in tables 13•2 and 13•3.

Hierarchy of Needs Maslow (1954, 1970) proposes a barrier to self-actualization that is independent of the notion of conditional positive regard. Maslow distinguishes *higher needs*, such as self-actualization, from *lower needs*, such as hunger. The higher the need state, the later it emerges both in the evolutionary scale and within the development of a particular human being.

Table 13•2 Negative and Positive Directions Characteristic of the Fully Functioning Person (Largely derived from statements of clients)

NEGATIVE DIRECTIONS (MOVING AWAY FROM)	POSITIVE DIRECTIONS (MOVING TOWARD)
Away from shells, facades, and fronts	Being in a continual process of change and action
Away from a self that one is not	Trusting intuitions, feelings, emotions, and motives
Away from "oughts" (being less submissive, less compliant in meeting standards set by others)	Being a participant in experience rather than being its boss or controlling it
Away from disliking and being ashamed of self	Letting experience carry one on, floating with a complex stream of experience, moving toward ill-defined goals
Away from doing what is expected, just for that reason alone	Moving toward goals behaviorally, not compulsively planning and choosing them
Away from doing things for the sake of pleasing others at the expense of self	Following paths which feel good
Away from "musts" and "shoulds" as motives for behavior	Living in the moment (existential living); letting experience carry one on
	Possessing greater openness to experience
	Being more authentic, real, genuine
	Moving closer to feelings and self (more willingness to yield to feelings and not to place a screen between feelings and self); journey to the center of self
	Accepting and appreciating the "realness" of self
	Increasing positive self-regard (a genuine liking and sympathy for self)

(From DiCaprio, 1974, p. 371)

Table 13·3 Extremes of a Continuum on the Potentials of Self (as considered by Rogers)

TRAITS OF THE FULLY FUNCTIONING SELF	TRAITS OF THE INCONGRUENT SELF
Self-aware	Out of touch with the self
Creative	Lacks firm sense of identity
Spontaneous	Introjects
Open to experience	Frustrated impulses
Self-determining	Negative emotions
Self-accepting	Antisocial behavior
Free from constraints	Puts forth masks
Lives in his "now"	Unrealistic appraisal of potentials
Allows full outlet of potentials	
Trusts his organism	
Possesses firm sense of identity	
Avoids facades	
Has sense of free choice	
Moves from introjection	
Moves toward self-direction	
Willing-to-be process	
Lives existentially	

(From DiCaprio, 1974)

Maslow maintains that lower needs must be satisfied before the higher needs can seek expression; that is, gratification of lower needs allows the person to progress to the next higher need level. For example, a starving individual cannot be concerned about personal growth. Table 13·4 indicates a hierarchical classification of physiological, safety, love, esteem, and self-actualizing needs, as postulated by Maslow. In addition, the table includes the conditions that give rise to need states, the consequences of need fulfillment, and examples of satisfying experiences.

Promoting Self-actualization Psychotherapy and other, less traditional forms of personality change are designed to enhance personal growth. People are considered not sick, but in need of experiencing the environment with greater openness. If subjective experiences are heightened, then self-actualizing potentialities are more likely to be released. The therapist thus is warm, open, and *self-disclosing*, demonstrating his basic trust and belief in the client. Unconditional positive regard is given. Expression of the client's value and worth should help him or her reorganize the subjective world. In a similar manner, encounter groups and sensitivity training seek to heighten personal experiences and personal awareness by putting the person in touch with his or her feelings. This affective experience theoretically reduces anxiety and therefore frees the growth process.

Culture and Society Humanists believe that individuals in different cultures are basically similar. Need systems and the desire for personal expression are universal, although the particular avenue of expression of needs may differ because of disparate cultural experiences and training. Further, the culture provides a source of gratification, inasmuch as individuals may foster mutual growth. Rather than conceptualizing an environment of limited resources in which individuals compete, and rather than viewing the person as antisocial, humanists contend that people can fully and deeply appreciate one another. Behavior that enhances the self is consistent with enhancing the lives of others, while behavior that is destructive of others also is destructive to the self. Recall that according to Freud, self-gratifica-

Table 13·4 Need Hierarchy and Levels of Personality Functioning

NEED HIERARCHY	CONDITION OF DEFICIENCY	FULFILLMENT	ILLUSTRATION
Physiological ↓	Hunger, thirst Sexual frustration Tension Fatigue Illness Lack of proper shelter	Relaxation Release from tension Experiences of pleasure from senses Physical well-being Comfort	Feeling satisfied after a good meal
Safety ↓	Insecurity Yearning Sense of loss Fear Obsession Compulsion	Security Comfort Balance Poise Calm Tranquility	Being secure in a full-time job
Love ↓	Self-consciousness Feeling of being unwanted Feeling of worthlessness Emptiness Loneliness Isolation Incompleteness	Free expression of emotions Sense of wholeness Sense of warmth Renewed sense of life and strength Sense of growing together	Experiencing total acceptance in a love relationship
Esteem ↓	Feeling of incompetence Negativism Feeling of inferiority	Confidence Sense of mastery Positive self-regard Self-respect Self-extension	Receiving an award for an outstanding performance on some project
Self-Actualization	Alienation Metapathologies Absence of meaning in life Boredom Routine living Limited activities	Healthy curiosity Peak experiences Realization of potentials Work which is pleasurable and embodies values Creative living	Experiencing a profound insight

(From DiCaprio, 1974)

tion and social growth are incompatible and negatively related; as self-gratification increases, cultural growth is deterred, and vice versa. Conversely, according to the humanists, the growth of the self and the social development of culture go hand in hand.

Contrast with Other Conceptions of Personality The humanistic point of view grew out of dissatisfaction with earlier models of personality. In contrast to the Freudian tension-reduction conception, humans are considered basically "good" and in need of stimulation. Attention is centered on the healthy, integrated individual rather than the minimally functioning person. In contrast to the Skinnerian person-as-machine psychology, humanists do not consider the individual as a bundle of potential responses that can be controlled by particular reinforcement contingencies. Rather, individuals are free to respond in various ways and to act spontaneously. The inner world of subjective experience is more significant than external stimuli. The basic human process is consciousness, not rigid stimulus-response couplings that are displayed in particular situations. Finally, in contrast to the cognitive conception of Kelly, affect, emotion, and experience, rather than logic, rationality, and categories of thought, are the central determinants of action.

Scientific Method Many psychologists regard the humanistic approach as anti-science. They contend that there is no such thing as a subjective science, because science follows particular rules, including reliability of observations and established procedures of verification. Certainly private events, such as feelings and subjective experience, differ from public events, such as a ball falling from a tower. Some humanists have gone so far as to contend that their work should be classified as art, rather than science, and that their interests are not amenable to traditional scientific precepts. On the other hand, some humanists have been developing methods that allow for the quantification of subjective experiences. There is a need for new scientific procedures, such as "experiential X rays," that allow more direct access to the study of consciousness and feeling. To be effective and to fulfill its own potential, the humanistic approach must be guided by scientific principles.

Implications for the Study of Personality The humanistic approach to psychology, like other conceptions of personality, generates particular procedures and data in the areas of personality assessment, development, dynamics, and change.

1. Personality assessment requires the gaining of information about private events. The individual's subjective experiences are ascertained through self-report procedures.
2. Personality development is a continual process of positive growth in the direction of higher goals. Of special importance in the pursuit of these goals is the development of a concept of the self and the influence of others on self-regard.
3. Personality dynamics focuses on the role of affect and subjective experience in the expression of the core self-actualizing tendency. Incongruities between

the objective and the subjective world and between the perceived and ideal self are of special significance in determining behavior.

4. Personality change is facilitated by unconditional positive regard from the therapist and through direct exposure to new experiences. The latter approach has been enhanced by the development of a variety of sensitivity and encounter group techniques that supposedly increase self-awareness. Individuals are not "sick" or "well," although people typically are capable of being more than they are.

Summary

Four very different theories of the person have been presented in this chapter. Humans have been described as (1) striving to reduce sexual and aggressive tensions, with social inhibitions producing neurosis; (2) machines with certain inputs automatically producing certain outputs that have been previously rewarded; (3) rational scientists, trying to comprehend the world accurately; and (4) experiencers of the world, seeking to express their basic capacities.

What, then, is the right theory of personality? Clearly none of these theories can be sufficient, for all are correct. Personalities are complex composites of irrational tendencies, reflexive actions, rational capacities, and meaningful experiences. Because we are composites, there is evidence to support each theory. Freudians can point to war, rape, and hysteria; Skinnerians to token reward systems and animal training; Kellians to scientific productivity, problem solving, and beliefs and expectations; and humanists to the search for meaning in life, sensitivity groups, and feelings about oneself. A complete theory of personality will have to incorporate many facets and accept the enormous complexity of personality and behavior.

Suggested Readings

Jones, E. 1953–57. *The life and work of Sigmund Freud*, 3 vols. New York: Basic Books.

Acknowledged as the most complete and accurate biography of Freud.

Liebert, R . M., and Spiegler, M. E. 1975. *Personality: Strategies for the study of man.* Homewood, Ill.: Dorsey Press.

An introductory text comparing various approaches to the study of personality.

Maslow, A. H. July 1968. A theory of metamotivation: The biological rooting of the value-life. *Psychology Today* 2:38–39, 58–62.

A readable overview of Maslow's position.

Nye, R. D. 1975. *Three views of man.* Monterey, Calif.: Brooks-Cole.

Expands the theme of this chapter, summarizing the views of Freud, Skinner, and Rogers.

Shakow, D., and Rapaport, D. 1964. The influence of Freud on American psychology. *Psychological Issues,* no. 13.

Compares Freud and Darwin and their acceptability to scientists.

Skinner, B. F. 1948. *Walden two.* New York: Macmillan.

Skinner's vision of Utopia, founded on behavioristic principles.

Wann, T. W., ed. 1964. *Behaviorism and phenomenology.* Chicago: University of Chicago Press.

An advanced treatment contrasting approaches to personality.

The Assessment of Personality

14 When we talk about someone's personality, perhaps labeling an acquaintance as stingy, hostile, sincere, or friendly, we are engaging in informal assessment. To reach such a judgment, we observe a person's behavior as well as gather information from verbal communications by and about the person. We may have seen a woman leave a small tip in a restaurant, for example, and therefore decided that she is stingy. Such a label may be useful in predicting future behavior. If we are soliciting contributions, we will not count on a large donation from a person we perceive as stingy.

But personality labeling can be dangerous. When we assess others, we tend to overgeneralize from limited observations. Our inferences about people are often based on too little information—or on information that is distorted, especially if the people we are observing are defensive and try to conceal their motives. Incorrect assessment can lead to stereotypes and prejudices.

Psychologists have attempted to replace informal judgment with formal assessment techniques. Many of these techniques seek to quantify individual differences with regard to one or more characteristics. The results of psychological testing are used in various areas, such as educational and vocational planning, diagnosing psychological problems, and marriage counseling. In addition, understanding individual differences is an important aspect of psychology as a science.

Classification by Types and Traits

14·1 No two individuals, not even identical twins, are exactly alike. Because of the great variability from person to person, schemes have been devised to classify individuals according to their similarities and their differences.

One of the earliest classification schemes was devised by

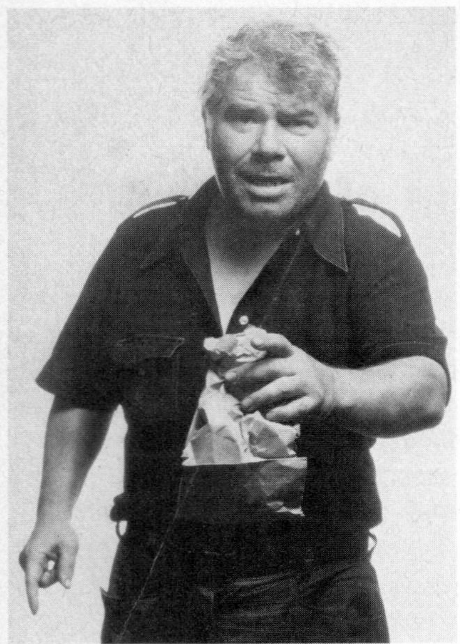

A person's behavior can change greatly from one situation to another, as can our perceptions of the person (Jan Michael)

Hippocrates around 400 B.C. He believed that **temperament** is determined by the relative amount of four fluids in the body:

Dominant Fluid	**Temperament**
Blood	Sanguine (hopeful)
Phlegm	Phlegmatic (nonchalant or calm)
Black bile	Melancholic (sad)
Yellow bile	Choleric (irritable)

Unfortunately, Hippocrates did not have assessment techniques with which to measure either these bodily fluids or these personality variables, and so could not subject his classification system to empirical testing.

Some more current, global views of personality also rely on biological givens to classify individuals. The most well known of these is based on body build. Kretschmer (1925) identified four basic constitutional types: pyknic (short and stocky), athletic (strong and well-proportioned), leptosomic (tall and slender), and dysplastic (a mixture of the other three). Kretschmer, who believed that body build is related to mental disorders, reported that schizophrenics are often leptosomic whereas manic-depressives are typically pyknic.

Somewhat more recently, Sheldon (Sheldon and Stevens, 1942) suggested that there are three fundamental physiques and that each physique is associated with a particular temperament:

Physique	**Temperament**
Endomorphy (soft and round; digestive viscera overdeveloped)	Viscerotonic (relaxed, loves to eat, sociable)
Mesomorphy (muscular, rectangular, strong)	Somatotonic (energetic, assertive, courageous)
Ectomorphy (long and fragile; large brain and sensitive nervous system)	Cerebrotonic (restrained, fearful, introverted, artistic)

Relatively sophisticated rating scales were developed to assess each of these body types, but not much data have been accumulated to support Sheldon's hypothesis.

In general, the type approach to personality assessment failed because it is too simple. Given the complexity of human beings and of their behavior, a person is not likely to fit into only one of a few categories.

The type approach to personality assessment has given way to the search for **traits,** or personality structures. These underlying attitudes or tendencies can only be inferred rather than directly perceived. Assume, for example, that you ask a friend to dinner, but she indicates a desire to be alone that evening. If she has chosen to be alone on many occasions, then you may well infer that she has a relatively stable personality disposition toward introversion. On the other hand, if being alone is an atypical response, then fatigue, pressing work, or a headache may be a more likely explanation than introversion.

In order to arrive at an accurate dispositional label, we must observe more than a consistency of behavior within a person. We must also be able to identify differences between people on the labeled attribute. If all individuals were the same height, then it would not make sense to describe someone as tall or short (except in comparison to infrahumans or inanimate objects). Similarly, if most people responded negatively to a dinner invitation, a negative reply would not be used to infer a personality characteristic.

In sum, we may label someone as having a particular trait if the person responds in the same manner over repeated occasions and other persons respond differently, given the same situations. *Intra-individual consistency* and *inter-individual variability* are essential properties of a trait. These two conditions are expressed in Table 14•1.

Table 14•1 Intra-Individual Consistency and Inter-Individual Variability

	SITUATION 1	
INDIVIDUAL	Time 1	Time 2
A	Response X	Response X
B	Response Y	Response Y
C	Response Z	Response Z

A trait encompasses a variety of apparently diverse behaviors: hitting someone, stealing, or breaking a toy might be considered examples of behavior that an aggressive child engages in. Trait theorists assume that an underlying aggressive structure determines such aggressive expressions. A trait, then, describes a group of correlated behaviors. Because an individual is perceived as having many traits, one can be simultaneously described in a multifaceted manner that incorporates many behaviors. In addition, each trait category is part of a continuous dimension (such as introversion-extroversion), rather than a discrete property that one has or does not have.

Reliability and Validity

14•2 Reliability and validity are basic to assessment. These concepts are interdependent, but each has distinct implications.

The **reliability** of an assessment instrument refers to its precision, or accuracy, as indicated by several features:

1. A reliable assessment instrument gives the same score on different occasions (*test-retest reliability*), assuming that what is being measured remains constant. A reliable measure of intelligence, for example, yields the same score when the same person is tested on two consecutive days, for it is generally accepted that intelligence, like height, does not fluctuate much from day to day.
2. A reliable assessment instrument engenders agreement among observers concerning the behavior that is assessed. The degree of agreement between observers is referred to as *inter-rater reliability*. If three teachers assign three different grades to the same essay, then each teacher's grading method has little inter-rater reliability, and the essays are a poor way of assessing knowledge.
3. A reliable assessment instrument has *internal consistency:* scores on different parts of the instrument are in agreement. If an exam contains only two ques-

The Trait-Situation Controversy

One issue generating a great deal of current interest among psychologists is called the trait-situation controversy (Mischel, 1968, 1969). Opposing emphases on traits versus the environment as the important cause of behavior have produced different types of research and dissimilar theories.

Trait theorists assume that underlying attributes exert a general causal effect on behavior. Personality traits are more important than situational determinants of behavior. As Gordon Allport says, "The same fire that melts the butter hardens the egg." That is, the effects of the situation (fire) depend on the person (butter or egg) in that situation. The trait position is consistent with the approach of psychoanalytic theorists, as well as with that of cognitive and phenomenological psychologists.

Situationists, mostly behaviorist psychologists, take issue with the notion of generalized traits. They argue that behavior varies depending on the situation one is in and that persons act differently in different environments. The earliest empirical study to challenge the trait position assessed the moral character of children across a variety of settings —including cheating on an exam, stealing, and lying. The investigators found little consistency of behavior: being honest in one situation was not strongly related to honesty in other situations. A spate of subsequent research has called into question the alleged generality of traits. Achievement needs might be exhibited in sports but not in academic pursuits, for example, or one might be dominant with family members but not among co-workers.

Trait theorists have responded to this challenge with a mixture of arguments. They contend that what constitutes the same behavior must be broadly defined. For example, sucking one's thumb, smoking a pipe, and obsessive talking are diverse behaviors (**phenotypes**) but might all indicate an oral personality (**genotype**). They also suggest that there are alternate paths of trait expression. A person with high power needs might express this disposition by becoming an officer in a club, while another person might express power concerns by purchasing new, fast cars; but any given individual with high power needs would not necessarily exhibit both of these behaviors.

Another position that has been taken in the trait-situation controversy is that behavior is consistent in the eyes of the observer, but not in reality. Traits are not real, although people do construe the world in a trait-like manner. Support for this argument has been found in evidence that people often perceive their own behavior to be the result of environmental forces, but the behavior of others as due to personality traits (Jones and Nisbett, 1971). Finally, it has been argued that how consistently one acts across different situations is itself an individual difference variable (Bem and Allen, 1974). Some individuals are insensitive to the environment and therefore respond in a consistent manner across many situations. On the other hand, others alter their behavior in different environments.

Most psychologists agree that an interactionist position is reasonable. That is, both the person and the situation interact and modify one another. Both need to be taken into account to predict and to understand behavior.

tions, one fill-in-the-blank and the other multiple-choice, and if the scores received by the students on the two questions are identical, then the test is internally consistent. If the scores have low correspondence, then the questions are measuring different abilities (for example, retention versus recognition of information). In some situations a test with low internal consistency might be desirable.

Factors that influence the assessment instrument but not the attribute being measured are causes of unreliability. On an exam that generates much chance guessing, such as a true-false format, the scores attained are likely to have some unreliability, for luck varies randomly over time. Fatigue, illness, and mood also are causes of unreliability on an exam because they do not uniformly influence the scores over different times or testing sessions.

The ultimate concern of any assessment procedure is **validity:** how well the assessment instrument measures what it is supposed to measure. A reliable instrument might have no validity at all. The length of one's little finger can be assessed with great precision, for example, but it is likely to have low validity as an indicator of intelligence.

Just as there are several types of reliability, there are several kinds of validity. Assessment psychologists (known as **psychometricians**) have distinguished between face, content, concurrent, predictive, and construct validity.

1. *Face validity* means that the assessment instrument logically seems to measure what it purports to measure. For example, a test item such as "Do you worry a lot?" has high face validity within an anxiety scale.
2. *Content validity* is attained when the assessment instrument samples the domain of activities about which inferences are being made. Typing a letter has high content validity in a personnel test for the job of typist, but not necessarily for the job of executive secretary, since typing may be only one facet of such a job.
3. *Concurrent validity* and *predictive validity* pertain to the relationships of the assessment instrument with respect to immediate and future behaviors, respectively. In most instances, these empirical analyses form the heart of the validation procedure.
4. *Construct validity* is involved when the construct that is being measured is part of a broader theory (Cronbach and Meehl, 1955). If the theory is validated, then the measures of the constructs within the theory must also be valid. For example, assume that psychoanalytic theory led to the prediction that ego strength is inversely related to the use of repression. If questions about one's self-concept (ego strength) were found to be related to forgetting, then the scale of ego strength would have some construct validity.

Interdependence of Reliability and Validity Validity is usually bound by reliability. A valid test of knowledge cannot be constructed unless the judges agree on the accuracy of the answers. But sometimes the influence of reliability on validity is negative. A test with high test-retest reliability may be a poor predictor of a fluctuating characteristic, such as mood. Similarly, a test with high internal consistency is likely to be a poor predictor of a complex dependent variable.

At times it is difficult to distinguish reliability from validity. Assume that a question on an assessment instrument asks, "Do you often forget things?" and that the test taker answers yes. Behavioral observations then reveal that indeed the person forgets. It might be contended either that the instrument possesses empirical or predictive validity or that the self-report of forgetting is reliable (it corresponds to other indicators measuring the same thing).

As a general principle, reliability and validity are differentiated on the basis of the similarity of the stimuli that are part of the investigation. Correlations between two similar tests, or between the same test given on multiple occasions, provide evidence for the reliability of the test. But correlations between different responses to different stimuli (for example, intelligence test scores and grades) provide evidence for the validity of the test.

Although assessment psychologists typically attempt to measure traits, or personality structures, many other properties of the person are of interest. Psychoanalytic theorists measure drives or motivation; Skinnerians assess the strength of habits; Kellians ascertain how one perceives or construes the world; and humanists are interested in the intensity of personal experiences and self-concept. In this chapter the discussion of assessment is broadened to include both measurement interests and specific assessment techniques that are associated with the four conceptions of personality outlined in the preceding chapter.

Psychoanalytic Approaches to Assessment

14·3 Psychoanalytic theorists assume that the most important determinants of behavior are unconscious. They have pioneered the development of assessment devices to explore influences on action that are not directly reportable by the person.

The various assessment techniques for tapping unconscious needs, wishes, and conflicts have several common properties.

1. The stimulus material is unstructured or ambiguous, because such stimuli theoretically lead to responses that show the different personalities of the test takers without interference caused by the test itself. Individuals are expected to reveal themselves more fully when external expectations and boundaries are absent.
2. In the testing situations the subjects are not told the purpose of the test.
3. There are no right or wrong answers. The respondents typically are encouraged to give the first thought that comes into their minds. The variety of permissible responses yields an abundance of material.

The indirect assessment procedures listed in Table 14·2 are referred to as **projective techniques.** Allegedly, the respondent interprets the situation and structures the material so that his or her needs, characteristics, and fears are projected onto the stimulus material. Freud considered **projection** to be a defense mechanism in which acceptable as well as unacceptable wishes are attributed externally, rather than to the self. *Paranoia,* for example, is the label applied to a projection of hostile impulses onto others.

Table 14·2 Common Types of Projective Techniques

TYPE OF TASK	STIMULUS MATERIALS	INSTRUCTIONS
Association	Word (e.g., man)	"After hearing each word, say the first word that comes to mind."
Construction	Picture	"Tell a story about the picture."
Completion	Sentence stem (e.g., "I want . . .")	"Complete the sentence."
Expression	Paper and pencil	"Draw a picture of yourself and a person of the opposite sex."
Choice	Photographs of people	Choose the picture you like best and the picture you like least."

(From Liebert and Spiegler, 1974)

The Thematic Apperception Test (TAT) The TAT, which was developed primarily by Henry Murray (1943), can be used in many ways. When it is used by therapists to determine personality traits and conflicts, usually from five to twenty pictures of people in various settings and relationships (Figure 14•1) are shown to the respondent. Allowing about five minutes for each picture, the examiner asks the test taker to relate what went on before the scene in the picture, what is going on now, how the people feel, and what the outcome will be.

How one perceives (imagines) each picture and the stories that one tells are assumed to reflect the person's previous experiences as well as current needs and concerns. The name of the test reflects the belief that personal qualities are projected onto the characters in the pictures; *apperception* means understanding in terms of prior experiences.

Both the content and the structure of the responses are analyzed. Structure includes the length of the story and emotional reactions, such as laughing and crying. In regard to content, the examiner looks for the expression of needs and fears and for areas of conflict and strong emotions. The frequency and intensity of these projections are important clues. With the help of general background information about the respondent, the examiner tries both to determine why the person tells particular stories and what the personality of the storyteller is.

Fig. 14·1 Sample TAT card. (Reprinted by permission of the publishers from Henry A. Murray, *Thematic Apperception Test,* Cambridge, Massachusetts: Harvard University Press, copyright 1943 by The President and Fellows of Harvard College, 1971 by Henry A. Murray.)

Weakness of the TAT Many of the rules concerning the technology of assessment are not met by the TAT. It might make a great difference whether the examiner is male or female, how many pictures are shown and which ones, and how much time is allowed for each story. Because procedures are not fully standardized, norms for the general population cannot be developed. In addition, there typically is poor test-retest reliability, lack of inter-rater agreement, and weak internal consistency. Of greater importance, empirical validity is often absent, with scores not predicting particular behaviors. The best results using the TAT occur when

Clinical versus Statistical Prediction

In the clinical method of predicting behavior, the assessor uses various sources of information, such as the TAT and interview data as well as structured tests. There are no set rules for combining this information, and so judgments are guided by intuition, hypotheses about personality dynamics, and common sense. In the statistical procedure, relationships are established between particular tests and a behavior. Then a formula is uniformly applied to predict individual behavior.

Adherents to the clinical approach describe it as dynamic, global, meaningful, configural, and sensitive, as opposed to mechanical, artificial, academic, static, and oversimplified. On the other hand, advocates of the statistical procedure describe it as verifiable, objective, scientific, precise, and empirical, as opposed to vague, subjective, unscientific, unreliable, and private.

Which procedure in fact has proven more effective in predicting behavior? Carefully conducted research studies using a variety of predictor variables and sources of information have repeatedly found evidence supporting the superiority of the statistical method. In general, the greater the involvement of humans in the assessment process, the less the validity of the prediction.

Critical research studies typically involve predictions of one of three kinds of behavior: grade point average, recidivism (committing criminal acts after release from prison), and recovery from psychoses. In one representative investigation involving predictions of college grade point average (Sarbin, 1942), adherents to the statistical method applied a formula derived from prior studies relating high school rank, aptitude test score, and grade point average. Supporters of the clinical approach interviewed the students and used other kinds of information, such as projective test scores—as well as the high school rank and aptitude scores used in the statistical method. The results of this investigation favored the statistical procedure; predictions were more accurate when based upon the previously derived formula.

Sometimes, however, clinical judgments allow one to take account of data never before used. The following case reported by the noted psychoanalyst, Theodore Reik, illustrates one prediction that could not have been made with a statistical procedure:

> One session at this time took the following course. After a few sentences about the uneventful day, the patient fell into a long silence. She assured me that nothing was in her thoughts. Silence from me. After many minutes she continued about a toothache. She told me that she had been to the dentist yesterday. He had given her an injection and then had pulled a wisdom tooth. The spot was hurting again. New and longer silence. She pointed to my bookcase in the corner and said, "There is a book standing on its head." Without the slightest hesitation and in a reproachful voice I said, "But why did you not tell me you had an abortion" (Meehl, 1954).

a single need, such as the need to achieve or the need for power, aggression, or affiliation, is being measured.

TAT Assessment of Achievement Needs In order to use the TAT as a research tool for measuring **achievement needs,** David McClelland, John Atkinson, and other investigators have adapted it so that it can be administered to groups of individuals not known to the experimenter. In addition, McClelland and his coworkers (1953) have devised a measuring procedure that meets certain reliability standards (especially inter-rater reliability) and a scoring procedure that yields a numerical value representing the strength of the achievement need. This value can be related to other behavioral indicators to determine whether this motivational index is valid.

Measuring Procedure

1. Viewers are asked to construct imaginative stories about the pictures they are to see.
2. A picture is shown on a screen for twenty seconds.
3. Subjects are given four minutes to write their stories on forms with general questions (normally given verbally in the clinical use of the TAT) printed on them at equal intervals:

   What is happening? Who are the persons?

   What has led up to this situation; that is, what has happened in the past?

   What is being thought? What is wanted and by whom?

   What will happen? What will be done?

4. Steps 2 and 3 are repeated until stories have been written for four to eight pictures.

Scoring Procedure The crucial aspect of the content analysis originated by McClelland and his associates is whether a story has achievement imagery. It does if it contains some reference to competition with a standard of excellence. Competition is perhaps most clear when one of the characters is primarily concerned with winning or doing as well as someone else. Competition may also be evident in a character's concern with how well a task is being done, regardless of how well someone else is doing it. Achievement imagery also is scored if a story includes a unique accomplishment (an invention, an artistic act) or a long-term achievement goal (becoming a doctor, being a success in life), or associates strong affect and/or instrumental actions with attaining achievement-related goals.

Using these criteria, we will analyze the following story written in response to a picture that is frequently used for the assessment of achievement needs. (Similar pictures are shown in Figure 14•2.)

> Two inventors are working on a new type of machine. They need this machine in order to complete the work on their new invention, the automobile. This takes place some time ago, and the necessary tools are not available. They are thinking that they will succeed. They want to do a good job and improve transportation. After years of hard work they are successful and feel elated. (McClelland et al., 1953)

This story has achievement imagery because there is pursuit of a unique accomplishment (invention of the automobile) and because there is positive affect (elation) coupled with an unusual amount of instrumental activity (years of hard work). Thus, the figures in the picture are perceived as competing with a standard of excellence.

A story that contains achievement imagery would receive one point and, in addition, would be scored for ten subcategories; it could receive as many as eleven points. Because the particular content to be scored is clearly prescribed, there is very high agreement among the judges. An individual's total achievement score is the sum of his or her scores on the pictures.

Fig. 14·2 Pictures similar to the TAT cards used in the assessment of achievement needs.

When these scores were related to other behavioral indicators, it was found that individuals scoring high on this index are characterized by the following behaviors:

Voluntarily undertaking achievement-related tasks in the absence of other motivation such as monetary rewards and power seeking
Working unusually long and hard at achievement-related activities and engaging in other actions instrumental to fulfilling achievement-related goals (such as selecting achievement-oriented work partners and gathering occupation-relevant information)
Setting realistic goals and preferring tasks of intermediate difficulty
Preferring to receive feedback about the adequacy of their own performance
Oriented toward the future and able to delay gratification
More concerned about winning or doing well than about losing or doing poorly
Experiencing a heightened positive affect, given a successful achievement accomplishment

Conversely, individuals classified as low in need for achievement are described by the following behaviors:

Failing to initiate achievement-related activities in the absence of extrinsic motivation such as monetary rewards and the attainment of power
Working for short periods of time with little intensity at achievement-related tasks, and avoiding behaviors instrumental to the attainment of achievement goals
Setting relatively unrealistic goals that are too easy or too difficult, given their level of ability
Preferring to avoid feedback about the adequacy of personal performance
Oriented to immediate gratification

More concerned about losing or doing poorly than about winning or doing well
Experiencing a dampened positive affect, given a successful achievement accomplishment

Any given individual may display varying degrees of these behaviors.

The TAT appears to have a reasonable amount of validity when assessing a single need and has advanced the psychological understanding of the dynamics of achievement strivings.

Fig. 14•3 Two of the ten inkblots used in the Rorschach test (Hans Huber Publishers, Bern, Switzerland)

The Rorschach Test The Rorschach test is the oldest and perhaps the most used projective instrument. It has been estimated that over one million Rorschach tests are administered each year.

Herman Rorschach (1884–1922) was a Swiss psychiatrist interested in the relationship between personality and perception. He contended that patients with disparate psychiatric disorders differ in their perceptions and thought processes. Initially he examined perceptual processes using geometric forms as stimuli, but later replaced these stimuli with the less structured inkblots.

The inkblots (Figure 14•3) that make up the final Rorschach test were selected because they elicit the widest variety of perceptual reactions. Ten inkblots, printed on 7 × 10 cards, are included in the test. Five of the inkblots are black and gray, two also contain red, and the three others combine a variety of colors. All are bilaterally symmetrical.

The administrator of the test holds up each card and says: "Tell me what this might be." After the interpretations of all the cards have been given, there is an inquiry period when the examiner asks that certain responses be discussed in greater detail.

Various characteristics of the responses are then analyzed (Table 14•3).

1. The *location* of the response refers to the part of the inkblot that gave rise to the **percept** (the whole blot, a portion, a small detail, or the white space).
2. *Determinant* connotes the formal quality of the blot that affects the percept, such as the shape, shading, or color.
3. The *popularity-originality* of the response indicates whether the percept is in agreement with the typical response.
4. The *content* of a percept is the classification of its subject matter, such as human, animal, or nature.
5. *Form level* concerns the correspondence between the percept and the actual inkblot.

Standard scoring procedures for the test have been devised that yield quantitative indexes. Each response category is used to make inferences about personality, and complex relationships between the scoring categories are computed to make global personality judgments. The ratio of human movement responses ("a man dancing") to color ("a red sky"), for example, is thought by some to reveal the relative introversion of the respondent, for movement indicates inner-directedness

Table 14·3 Examples of Scoring of the Rorschach Inkblots

SCORING CHARACTERISTIC	EXAMPLES OF SCORING CATEGORY	SAMPLE RESPONSE
Location	Whole	Entire blot used for concept
	Small usual detail	Small part which is easily marked off from the rest of the blot
Determinant	Form	"The outline looks like a bear"
Popularity-originality	Popular	Response which many people give
	Original	Response which few people give and which fits blot well
Content	Animal figures	"Looks like a house cat"
	Human figures	"It's a man or a woman"
Form-level	High form-level	Concept fits blow well
	Low form-level	Concept is a poor match to blot

(Adapted from Liebert and Spiegler, 1974)

while a color response shows responsiveness to external stimuli. Determinants such as color often are related to emotions. Location responses typically are associated with cognitive traits; for example, a whole response intimates good cognitive organization while a detailed response shows a concern with accuracy. A response such as "This is a bat, but not a very good one" might lead to inferences about obsessiveness and about the use of particular defenses, such as intellectualization. Finally, content is linked with psychological preoccupations, such as sexual identity.

Despite the popularity and fame of this instrument, its reliability and validity are questionable (Jensen, 1964). Many psychometricians believe that there is no evidence to support the Rorschach technique and no justification for its continued use. Clinical psychologists, however, often contend that this test helps them to understand their patients. But it appears now that the popularity of this instrument will decline in the future.

Behavioristic Approaches to Assessment

14·4 The psychoanalytic program of assessment, with its stress on projective measurement, examines general personality structure, as well as dynamic states such as unsatisfied **drives, conflicts,** and **frustrations.** The stimuli used are vague and the tester infers behavioral dispositions that allegedly generalize across all situations. This approach is global and holistic, in that the various facets of an individual are assumed to be interdependent. Test behavior is important only because the responses generate inferences about underlying aspects of the person; that is, the test behavior is considered to indicate the true dynamics of behavior.

The behavioristic approach to personality assessment stands in direct contrast to the psychoanalytic procedure. Selected and carefully defined behaviors are measured, along with the specific stimulus conditions that vary together with the behaviors. Behavior is assumed to vary from situation to situation, and only small aspects of a total personality are examined. Dependence among the various phases of personality and behavior is not assumed. The assessment itself is important because it is a direct sample of the behavior that is of immediate interest. Because no particular instrument, such as the TAT or the Rorschach, is associated with behavioral assessment, a general method will be considered here, rather than a specific measuring device.

A behavioral assessment procedure begins with the selection of a *target behavior*, which is an identifiable event, such as crying, having a tantrum, or disrupting a class. This behavior is then directly observed and recorded. Careful sampling procedures, including a specification of the time intervals in the sample, are followed, and accurate recording methods are devised so that the obtained information will be reliable.

Instead of **naturalistic observation,** controlled laboratory observation may be used to obtain behavioral data. A pertinent object is placed in the individual's environment, for example, and the behavioral responses to it are observed. Data also may be obtained via a *self-report inventory* that asks about specific behaviors, such as whether an anxiety reaction occurs on the job or in school, how frequently the anxiety is experienced, with what intensity, and so on. Although alternative methods are available, every effort is made to measure the target behavior within the environment where it naturally occurs.

The following is a report of a behavioral assessment procedure in a natural environment:

Issue Investigation of the feasibility of treatment in the natural setting (the home) where the child's behavior problem appeared, with the mother serving as the therapeutic agent. The child (C), a four-year-old boy, was brought by his mother (M) to the university clinic because she felt helpless to deal with his frequent tantrums and general disobedience.

Observations Experimenters (Es) observed M and C in the home and noted that many of C's undesirable behaviors appeared to be maintained by attention from the mother. If C behaved objectionably, M would try to explain to him why he shouldn't do something or would try to distract him by offering him toys or food. Observation in the home indicated that the following responses made up a large portion of C's repertory of undesirable behavior: (1) biting his shirt or arm, (2) sticking out his tongue, (3) kicking or biting himself, others, or objects, (4) calling someone or something a derogatory name, (5) removing or threatening to remove his clothing, (6) saying no loudly and vigorously, (7) threatening to damage objects or persons, (8) throwing objects, (9) pushing his sister. These nine responses collectively are called objectionable behavior (OB). The frequency of occurrence is measured by recording, for each ten-second interval, whether or not an OB occurred. Observations are made during one-hour sessions conducted two to three times a week. Two Es are employed as observers on eight occasions and three on one occasion to check the reliability of the response scoring. Reliability is found to range from .70 to 1.00 with an average of .88, indicative of high observer reliability.

Treatment After an initial *baseline period* of sixteen sessions during which C and M interact in their usual way, the *first experimental period* is begun. Every time C emits an OB, M is signalled by E to tell him to stop or to put him in his room by himself and without toys. (This isolation is viewed as a period of "time out" from stimuli associated with positive reinforcement.) When E notices that C is playing in a particularly desirable way, M is signalled to give C attention and approval. During the *second baseline period* M is told to interact with C as she did prior to the experimental period. This is followed by the *second experimental period*, which is the same as in the first except that special attention for desirable play is excluded, save for one accidental instance. Finally, there is a *follow-up period* after twenty-four days without contact between E and M.

Results During the baseline period OB varied between 18 and 113 per session (one hour). During the first experimental period the rate of OB ranged from 1 to 8 per session. Special attention was given ten times. During the second baseline period the rate of OB varied between 2 and 24 per session. M reported that she had trouble responding in her previous way because she now felt more sure of herself. She now gives C firm commands and does not give in after denying a request. She also gives more affection, mostly in response to an increase in affectionate overtures from C. During the second experimental period the rate of OB varied between 2 and 8 per session. The rate of OB remained low after the twenty-four-day interval (follow-up period) and M reports C is well-behaved and less demanding.

Summary The results of this study show that it is possible to observe and treat behavioral problems in the home, with the parent as the therapeutic agent. Since it is widely held that many of the child's problems originate in the home environ-

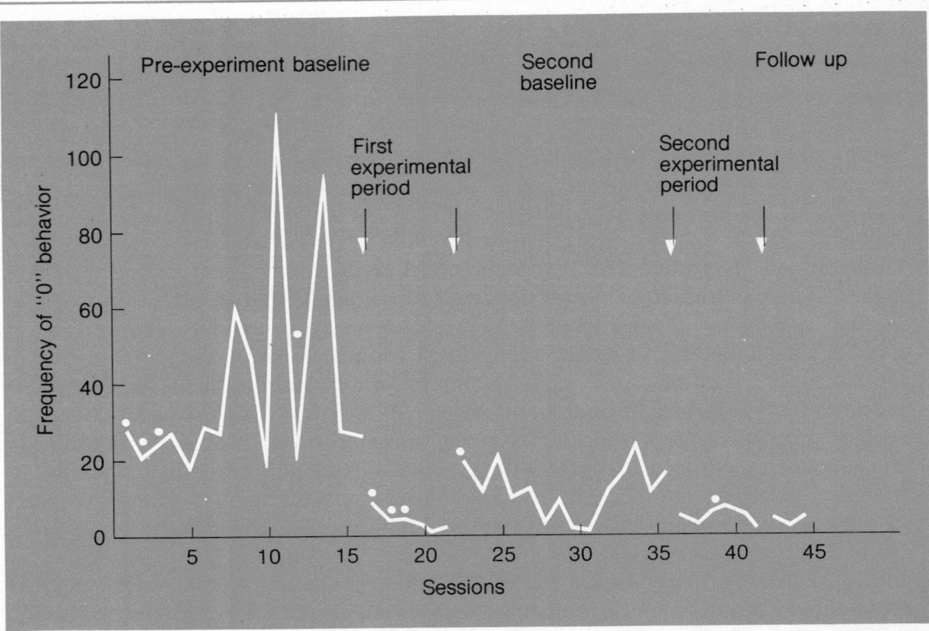

Fig. 14·4 Number of 10-second intervals, per 1-hour session, in which objectionable behavior occurred. Asterisks indicate sessions in which reliability was tested. (From Hawkins, Peterson, Schweid, and Bijou, 1966)

ment, direct modification of this environment (including the behavior of other family members) may arrest the difficulty at its source. (From Hawkins, Peterson, Schweid, and Bijou, 1966)

As shown by this report, there is a close link between the diagnosis of the problem and the treatment. The conditions under which the unwanted behavior occur are identified (diagnosis), and the environment is then changed to alter the behavior (treatment). Furthermore, because there is precise measurement of the target behavior both before and after the treatment, there can be a clear test of the effectiveness of the prescribed treatment. This valuable contribution is most clearly provided by the behavioral approach to personality and assessment.

Assessment of Views of the World

14•5 Because they see the individual as a scientist, whose main goal is to bring about a predictable environment that can be mastered, cognitive psychologists devise tests to measure the individual's view or construction of the world. Some construction processes are conscious while others appear to be unconscious; some are primarily genetically determined while others are influenced by experiential (learning) factors; and some personal constructs are conceived as highly general while others are believed to be relatively specific. Given this diversity, it is not surprising that a large assortment of assessment instruments have been devised to measure the manner in which the world is perceived. But the majority of these instruments are objective tests.

In contrast to the projective techniques exemplified by the TAT and Rorschach tests, the stimuli in objective tests are highly structured. They may be self-appraisal questions, such as "Do you often worry?", or they may be part of a data-gathering procedure in which the subject is asked to give an externally correct response, such as the accurate identification of a geometric form. Self-appraisal questions on a paper-and-pencil test may be structured in any of several ways such as on rating scales, in a true-false format, or in a forced-choice arrangement pitting two or more items. Although objective test formats vary greatly, they minimize the variety of responses possible. In addition, the subjects are tested under identical conditions, and observers can agree on the response that has been given.

Typically, the test behavior observed is used to infer a trait, or an underlying attribute of the person. This attribute is presumed to be common to the population being tested, although individuals supposedly differ on the amount of the attribute that they possess. A single score usually is derived from the assessment instrument, which determines one dimension of personality, such as anxiety, introversion, or need for affiliation. At times a more global assessment is undertaken, however, and there is an attempt to measure the entire personality structure.

Locus of Control Locus of control, or internal versus external control, is conceived as a dimension of personality pertaining to the general beliefs a person

Fun with Personality Tests

Objective personality tests include questions about a wide array of beliefs, feelings, and experiences. At times certain questions may be perceived by the test taker as trivial or inconsequential. The apparent pointlessness of some test items has generated a parlor game of devising personality inventories composed of only facetious queries. One publicized true-false list, in part created by the humorist Art Buchwald, contains the following questions:

1. When I was younger, I used to tease vegetables.
2. Sometimes I am unable to prevent clean thoughts from entering my mind.
3. I am not unwilling to work for a jackass.
4. I would enjoy the work of a chicken flicker.
5. I think beavers work too hard.
6. It is important to wash your hands before washing your hands.
7. It is hard for me to say the right thing when I find myself in a room full of mice.
8. I use shoe polish to excess.
9. The sight of blood no longer excites me.
10. It makes me furious to see an innocent man escape the chair.
11. As a child, I used to wet the ceiling.
12. I am aroused by persons of the opposite sexes.
13. I believe I smell as good as most people.
14. When I was a child, I was an imaginary playmate.

(From *American Psychologist* 20: 1965, p. 990)

holds about the causes of events (Rotter, 1966). Perceived internal control indicates that the person attributes future occurrences and prior happenings to himself or herself, whereas external control indicates that responsibility is attributed to the environment (see the discussion of attribution theory in Chapter 12). For example, an *A* on an exam might be attributed by the receiver of the grade to high ability (internal control) or to the ease of the exam (external control); a win at tennis can be attributed to great exertion (internal control) or to the mistakes of the opponent (external control); and the voracious eating of a meal can be perceived as due to great hunger (internal control) or to the outstanding quality of the food (external control). Locus of control refers to a bias across a wide array of situations that influences the perception of control over the environment and the perceived causes of reward.

There are, of course, situational determinants of perceived control. Chess is generally perceived as under personal control, while roulette typically is not. But some individuals ascribe outcomes at chess to luck, while others perceive winning and losing at roulette as determined by skill. Between these tasks there is a range of events that have both "push" and "pull" components. It must always be remembered that behavior is a function of both the person and the environment. More specifically, there are both situational and personal determinants of the perception of control.

Measurements Locus of control is assessed with a forced-choice, paper-and-pencil questionnaire—the *internal-external (I-E) scale,* which contains twenty-nine items. Six of these items are not scored but serve to disguise the purpose of the test. The scored items have one choice that is an internal response (underlined in the sample items below) while the other choice is an external response. Subjects choose the item they more strongly believe. Some exemplary items are:

1. a. Many people can be described as victims of circumstance.
   b. What happens to people is pretty much of their own making.
2. a. Almost invariably, when I have been sick, it has been because I just happened to be exposed to the disease.
   b. Maintaining good health is largely due to taking care of one's body.
3. a. Going up the ladder of success is pretty much a matter of getting the right breaks in life.
   b. Getting ahead on the job is based on persistence and hard work.

The items on the scale tap various content domains, including academic and social recognition and general life philosophy.

In this scene the drill instructor is likely to be perceived as having internal (personal) control, whereas the recruits may perceive the situation as being beyond their control. (Wide World Photos)

Reliability and Validity The traditional indexes of reliability, intra-test consistency and test-retest stability, are quite sound. Results of the I-E test are significant because perceptions of control influence a wide array of behaviors. For example, individuals scoring high on internality appear more active in their attempts to control and master the environment. They seek out more information relevant to their goals, are less prone to subtle social influence, tend to be better adjusted, and can laugh at themselves in the face of failure, thus exhibiting frustration tolerance and the defenses necessary to cope with stress (Phares, 1972). It has been found, however, that an accurate perception of external control within environments that indeed are oppressive leads to more active attempts to alter those environments. In sum, the manner in which one construes causes has far-reaching implications.

There are other personal constructs besides locus of control, but not all of them can be discovered through direct questioning or through the use of fixed scales. The Role Construct Repertory (Rep) test, which we discuss next, permits inferences to be made about an individual's total construct system, or way of viewing the world.

Role Construct Repertory (Rep) Test Believing that the assessor should not impose particular categories on the test taker, George Kelly devised the Rep test. In this test, the test taker lists the names of people who play fifteen specified roles in his or her life:

1. **Self:** yourself
2. **Mother:** your mother or the person who has played the part of a mother in your life
3. **Father:** your father or the person who has played the part of a father in your life
4. **Brother:** your brother who is nearest your own age or, if you do not have a brother, a boy near your own age who has been most like a brother to you

5. **Sister:** your sister who is nearest your own age or, if you do not have a sister, a girl near your own age who has been most like a sister to you
6. **Spouse:** your wife (or husband) or, if you are not married, your closest present girl (boy) friend
7. **Pal:** your closest present friend of the same sex as yourself
8. **Ex-Pal:** a person of the same sex as yourself whom you once thought was a close friend but in whom you were badly disappointed later
9. **Rejecting Person:** a person with whom you have been associated who, for some unexplained reason, appeared to dislike you
10. **Pitied Person:** the person whom you would most like to help or for whom you feel most sorry
11. **Threatening Person:** the person who threatens you the most or the person who makes you feel the most uncomfortable
12. **Attractive Person:** a person whom you have recently met whom you would like to know better
13. **Accepted Teacher:** the teacher who influenced you most
14. **Rejected Teacher:** the teacher whose point of view you have found most objectionable
15. **Happy Person:** the happiest person whom you know personally (Kelly, 1955)

Of course, one person may play more than one role. For example, one's father may also be the most threatening person.

On the standard Rep grid (Figure 14•5), the three circles in each row designate three roles (a triad) that the subject is to consider together. For each triad the subject determines the construct, such as dominant-submissive or greedy-generous, that links two individuals in the triad and differentiates them from the third member. These constructs represent dimensions along which the significant people in the respondent's life are ordered. In row 1 of the grid, for example, a respondent might perceive the individuals she has identified as the rejecting person and the pitied person as cold and the individual she identified as the attractive person as warm. The respondent then judges the remaining twelve people as having or not having the quality (coldness) and places an X in the appropriate box in row 1 if the characteristic is possessed (father, spouse, and rejected teacher). The respondent completes the remaining fourteen rows in this manner, selecting a construct for each triad.

Using sophisticated mathematical techniques, the tester can reduce the constructs chosen by a respondent to just a few basic ones that the person typically uses in perceiving and classifying others. Even without training, however, one can ascertain which constructs vary together for a particular respondent and thus are not distinct. If a respondent reports that men are cold and women are warm but uses the construct male-female to distinguish the members of a particular triad, we know that the respondent could also have chosen the construct cold-warm for this triad: maleness and coldness are not separate constructs for this person. If all the constructs in a grid are highly interrelated, then the respondent may experience

No.	1 Self	2 Mother	3 Father	4 Brother	5 Sister	6 Spouse	7 Pal	8 Ex-pal	9 Rejecting person	10 Pitied person	11 Threatening person	12 Attractive person	13 Accepted teacher	14 Rejected teacher	15 Happy person	Construct
1			X			X			⊗	⊗		O		X		COLD-WARM
2		O	O	⊗		X		X						X		DEPENDENT-INDEPENDENT
3					O								O		O	
4		O						O					O			
5	O									O		O				
6					O				O					O		
7				O				O			O					
8						O					O				O	
9							O	O				O				
10	O			O	O											
11		O	O								O					
12							O			O					O	
13	O					O	O									
14	O	O	O													
15				O					O					O		

Fig. 14·5 Simplified grid form of the Rep Test.

anxiety because the construct system is too narrow to easily accommodate new situations.

By viewing the circles in the grid vertically rather than horizontally, one can ascertain the perceived similarity between individuals. It might be of interest to discover which parent the respondent perceives as more like himself or herself, or how similar the spouse is to the threatening person. This can be determined by comparing the constructs perceived as describing oneself with the constructs perceived as describing the spouse or the threatening person.

Reliability and Validity Thus far the Rep test has been used sparingly, primarily in clinical rather than research settings. Some reliability studies suggest that grid responses have reasonable test-retest stability, but there has been limited assessment of the test's validity. This research has been conducted almost exclusively in England (Bannister and Fransella, 1971). The Rep test is a promising instrument that illustrates one particularly creative approach to personality assessment.

Field Dependence-Independence Thus far we have examined the assessment of what people think: what they perceive as responsible for events, or what dimensions they use to construe the world. But it is equally important to consider how people perceive and think. This *structural* or information-processing question transcends the particular *content* of thought that might be involved (Harvey, Hunt, and Schroder, 1961).

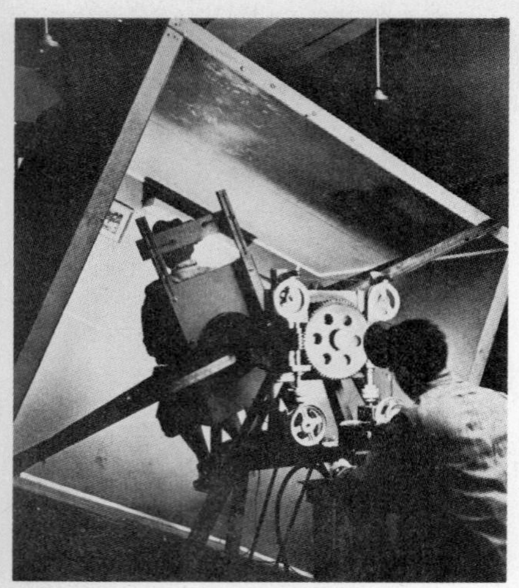

In the tilting-room–tilting-chair test, field-independent individuals tend to perceive the position of their bodies independently of the tilt of the room. (Courtesy of Herman A. Witkin and David Linton, Photographer)

Cognitive differentiation is one structural aspect of thinking that is relevant to the study of personality. We can illustrate this concept as follows. After an hour of interaction with person X, person A says that she likes X because X is friendly and sincere, but person B says that she likes X because X is friendly, sincere, witty, and intelligent. In this evaluation B uses more dimensions than does A. We may further clarify the meaning of cognitive differentiation by noting that humans judge light on the basis of brightness, saturation, and hue, whereas amoebas have only one dimension (brightness) to distinguish light stimuli. Thus, humans have greater cognitive differentiation in the perception of light than do amoebas.

Field dependence-independence is a dimension of personality that reflects cognitive differentiation. An individual labeled as field dependent fuses various aspects of the world and experiences life in a global way. An individual labeled as field independent is characterized as analytical, differentiating incoming information and personal experiences into their component parts.

Research in field dependence-independence has been conducted primarily by Herman Witkin and his colleagues and is part of the general attempt in psychology to relate personality to perceptual processes (Witkin et al., 1962). Three measures have been used successfully to assess field dependence-independence: the tilting-room–tilting-chair test, the rod-and-frame test, and the hidden figures test. Each of these examines the difficulty that a person has in overcoming the influence of the surrounding field when identifying an experience or an external stimulus.

In the tilting-room–tilting-chair test, the person sits on a tilting chair in a darkened room and must determine the position of his or her body. This judgment is complicated by the fact that the surrounding room is independently tilted. Field-dependent individuals are greatly influenced by the immediate visual field when experiencing the position of their own bodies. If the room is tilted, they perceive themselves as tilted, even when they are in an upright position.

In the rod-and-frame test, the subject sits in a darkened room and faces a luminous rod surrounded by a luminous frame. Both the rod and the frame can be rotated independently. Field-dependent individuals in this situation experience a tilted rod as relatively vertical when the frame also is tilted (Figure 14•6). Among field-independent persons, the perception of verticality is less influenced by the position of the frame.

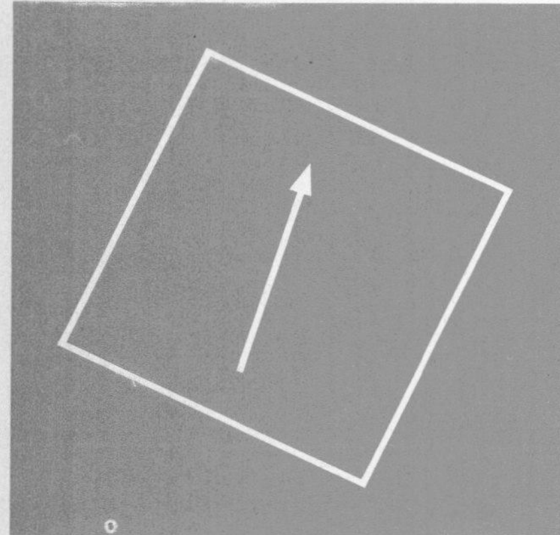

Fig. 14•6 Tilted frame with rod adjusted to "vertical" by field-dependent subject. (From Cartwright, 1974)

In the hidden figures test, the subject must determine which one of five simple figures is embedded in a given, more complex pattern (Figure 14•7). This task is difficult for the field-dependent person.

Unlike paper-and-pencil personality tests, the procedures that measure field dependence-independence have objectively correct answers, which minimize response factors that lower validity, such as withholding information or the desire to present oneself in a socially desirable manner. Many other personality tests also have externally correct answers. Even the IQ test has been used to infer personality dynamics. For example, if an individual has high verbal and high mathematical ability, yet has very little information about the world, then one might infer that repressions and unsatisfied drives are interfering with mental functioning.

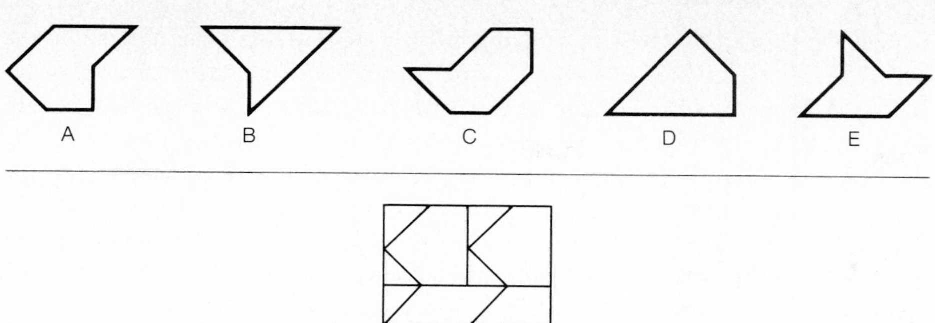

Fig. 14·7 Sample item from Hidden Figures Test. (From Messick, 1962. Copyright 1962 by Educational Testing Service. All rights reserved. Reproduced by permission.)

Reliability and Validity The intra-test reliabilities of the various measures of field dependence-independence are quite high, and they have remarkable stability over time. Their validity has been demonstrated by a consistent pattern of functioning associated with the performance of field-dependent individuals. These persons are prone to change their opinions in the face of influence attempts, pay great attention to others in their environment, and have a weak sense of personal identity. Their general dependency is consistent with the manner in which they view the world. With increasing development, however, there is a trend toward greater differentiation, or field independence, especially among males.

Experiential Approaches to Assessment

14·6 The **phenomenological psychology** of Maslow and Rogers is concerned primarily with subjective experience. The goal of assessment, given this approach, is to gain knowledge about private events. Psychoanalytic theorists attack this difficult problem by using projective techniques, for they assume that the most important private events are unconscious. But phenomenologists and humanists emphasize consciousness and subjective meaning. Their assessment instruments make use of direct self-reports, and the client is aware of the purpose of the test. In addition, a climate of trust is established so that the respondent is ready to share his or her experiences. The focus upon meaning also sets the experiential approach apart from behavioral assessment, inasmuch as the same behavior may have quite different connotations for different individuals, or even for the same individual on different occasions.

The Q-sort The most well-known technique used to assess subjective experience is the **Q-sort** (Stephenson, 1953). This instrument has been especially valuable in the measurement of **self-concept.** In the Q-sort a large number of statements, such as "I am satisfied with myself," are presented to the person (Table 14·4). These descriptive statements are written on separate cards. The test taker then sorts these cards into categories from "least like me" to "most like me." Typically, there are from nine to eleven categories, and each category is assigned a number of points from, say, one to eleven. The respondent is required to place a certain number of cards in each category—for example, a normal distribution of 2, 4, 8, 11, 16, 18, 16, 11, 8, 4, and 2. This procedure permits specific percepts about the self to be quantified. The score of any percept indicates the degree to which the statement agrees with one's self-concept, which in turn can be determined by assigning scores to the positive and negative items.

One valuable use of the Q-sort has been to assess self-concept at various times during psychotherapy. Taking repeated measures can help show whether self-concept changes during treatment. Another practice has been to have the client make two sorts: one for the self and one for the ideal self. Since each statement receives a quantitative score, it is possible to compare (correlate) the perceived self and the ideal self. This correlation has been examined during psychotherapy to test the hypothesis that the discrepancy between the perceived and the ideal self decreases over time. Some support for this hypothesis has been reported (Rogers and Dymond, 1954).

Reliability and Validity As with all approaches to the study of personality, phenomenological instruments must meet scientific standards (Block, 1961). The Q-sort has proven to be an effective procedure, particularly in helping the clinician understand his or her client. Although the accumulation of research evidence

Table 14·4 Q-sort Statements

POSITIVE ITEMS	NEGATIVE ITEMS
I have a warm emotional relationship with others.	I put on a false front.
I am a responsible person.	I often feel humiliated.
I can accept most social values and standards.	I doubt my sexual powers.
Self-control is no problem to me.	I have a feeling of hopelessness.
I usually like people.	I have few values and standards of my own.
I express my emotions freely.	It is difficult to control my aggression.
I can usually live comfortably with the people around me.	I want to give up trying to cope with the world.
I am optimistic.	I tend to be on my guard with people who are somewhat more friendly than I had expected.
I am liked by most people who know me.	I feel helpless.
I am sexually attractive.	My decisions are not my own.
I can usually make up my mind and stick to it.	I am a hostile person.
I am contented.	I am disorganized.
I am poised.	I feel apathetic.
I am a rational person.	I don't trust my emotions.
I am tolerant.	It's pretty tough to be me.
I have an attractive personality.	I have the feeling that I am just not facing things.
I have initiative.	I try not to think about my problems.
I take a positive attitude toward myself.	I am shy.
I am satisfied with myself.	I am no one. Nothing seems to be me.
	I despise myself.

(From Bryne, 1974)

Testing and Public Policy

In recent years psychological testers have been labeled as "brainwatchers" or "snoopers," and have been charged with prying into aspects of one's life that are entirely personal. This charge is supported by the widespread existence of test items that question religious convictions ("I believe in the second coming of Christ"), sexual attitudes ("I am worried about sex matters"), and private thoughts ("Some of my family have habits that bother and annoy me very much"). These sample items were taken from the Minnesota Multiphasic Personality Inventory (MMPI), one of the most widely used and respected assessment instruments. The results and interpretation of such tests may follow an individual throughout his or her life, affecting job opportunities, advancements, and so on.

A congressional hearing concerning psychological testing was held in 1965. This investigation was chaired by Sam Ervin, who later investigated the Watergate scandal. Senator Ervin explained the need for the investigation as follows:

> Investigation by the Constitutional Rights Subcommittee disclosed that psychological test scores and psychiatric evaluations are frequently relied upon by a number of Federal Government departments and agencies in employment situations which radically affect the lives of the individuals involved. We have received numerous complaints that some of the questions contained in the personality inventories relating to sex, religion, family relationships, and many personal aspects of an employee's life constitute an unjustified invasion of privacy. Furthermore, the charge has been made that aside from the invasion of privacy, the procedures surrounding the testing and the use made of the test results present serious due process questions.
>
> As a result the Subcommittee held hearings June 7–10 to examine (a) the content of psychological tests administered by the Government and the extent to which the questions asked constituted an unjustified invasion of the individual's psyche and private life, (b) whether the tests were scientifically valid, and (c) the procedural and due process issues involved in the administration of the tests, including the right to confront his accusers when emotional stability and mental competency are questioned. (Ervin, 1965, p. 880)

The hearings did not uncover any major source of injustice to others. It was pointed out that tests aid in the discovery of unrecognized talent and can assist individuals to attain their civil rights by providing objective evidence of their job qualifications.

We also know that psychological tests can aid in the selection of the right person for the right job, provide information for the diagnosis of mental illness, and predict success in college, among other uses. But at times the use of tests raises ethical questions. Care must be taken and good judgment exercised in weighing the importance of test results.

concerning the reliability and the validity of this instrument has not been great, some validating evidence has been presented, particularly as demonstrated by changes in the self-concept when the person is undergoing psychotherapy. The Q-sort well illustrates that self-perception can be defined operationally and quantified, and that aspects of humanistic psychology can be placed within a testable, scientific framework.

Summary

Personality assessment seeks to differentiate human beings on certain characteristics or behaviors. To reach this objective, measures must be devised that have reliability and validity; that is, assessment instruments must be precise and measure what they are supposed to measure.

Many different types of assessment instruments have been developed. They can be classified as either projective (unstructured) or objective (structured). Projective measures, such as the TAT and the Rorschach, contain ambiguous stimuli that permit a variety of responses. Objective instruments such as the I-E scale and the Q-sort are composed of clearly defined stimuli that limit the possible range of responses. Most objective tests contain self-appraisal items. But some instruments, such as the hidden figures test, include externally correct answers.

Personality assessment is guided by the theory of personality held by the tester. Psychoanalytic theorists typically use projective techniques to tap unconscious structures and states such as drives, conflicts, and frustrations. Behaviorists are concerned with immediate and observable responses, rather than with the alleged underlying dynamics of behavior. They measure overt actions with careful and precise observational techniques. Cognitive psychologists focus upon how the world is perceived and construed. Construction processes are measured with a variety of techniques, ranging from the Rep test to forced-choice questionnaires, such as the I-E scale. Experiential psychologists center their attention on feelings, experiences, and beliefs about the self. These inner states are assessed with self-report techniques that rely upon the trust and the confidence of the test taker.

Clearly, there is a great diversity of assessment instruments. Each test has unique advantages and disadvantages; each has a range and a focus of convenience; and each contributes to our knowledge about the person.

Suggested Readings

American Psychological Association. 1965. *American Psychologist* 20:857–1002.

A special issue examining testing and public policy.

American Psychological Association. 1954. Technical recommendations for psychological tests and diagnostic techniques. *Psychological Bulletin,* 51:part 2.

Outlines appropriate testing procedures and types of validity and reliability.

Buros, O. K. 1972. *Mental measurements yearbook,* 7th ed. Highland Park, N.J.: Gryphon Press.

A complete listing and review of tests in print, published approximately every fourth year since 1938.

Cronbach, L. J. *Essentials of psychological testing.* New York: Harper & Row.

Provides an excellent introduction to the principles of testing.

Jackson, D. N. and Messick, S., eds. 1967. *Problems in human assessment.* New York: McGraw-Hill.

A compendium of relevant topics in the assessment area.

Kelly, E. L. 1967. *Assessment of human characteristics.* Monterey, Calif.: Brooks/Cole.

A very readable introduction to the assessment area.

O.S.S. Staff. 1948. *Assessment of men.* New York: Holt.

An interesting presentation of how agents were selected for the Office of Strategic Services during World War II.

The Dynamics of Personality: Stress, Conflict, Inhibition, and Frustration

15 Dynamics refers to the forces that affect motion and bring about change. **Psychodynamics** is concerned with the forces that produce a change in human thought and action. Often the unconscious determinants of thought and action are emphasized by personality psychologists. In this chapter we will consider the interplay of four active (dynamic) forces that affect behavior: stress, conflict, inhibition, and frustration.

In physics, **stress** is a force that acts upon a body, producing some kind of strain. A psychologically stressful situation produces a strain on the individual. War, slums, fires, and business or school failure are examples of stressful conditions. A person in a state of stress is undergoing emotional difficulty or disturbance.

A **conflict** results whenever more than one response tendency is aroused. A high school graduate who is offered a well-paying job experiences a conflict between the desire for immediate rewards and the desire for long-range benefits that might result from going to college. Aroused motivations are not always displayed in action because there is competition from other motivations and also from inhibitions.

Inhibition is the mental state that prevents an individual from acting on an impulse when the action would be in conflict with the demands of the superego or the social world. When we are angry, we usually do not hit the offender because we feel that violence is wrong and we know that physical aggression leads to unpleasant consequences.

In psychology the word **frustration** has several meanings. It has been defined as interference with an ongoing action, but the word also refers to the condition that the individual experiences as a result of such interference. Psychologists have observed that frustration leads to many consequences, including aggression.

The dynamics of behavior are complex. A decision to act or not to act may cause great stress. Motivations may not be expressed because of conflict and inhibition. Lack of goal gratification is likely to produce an accumulation of frustration. Stress, conflict, inhibition, and frustration are concepts that lie at the heart of psychodynamics.

Stress

15•1 Psychologists use two definitions of stress. One meaning focuses on atypical environmental conditions (**stressor agents**); the other concerns an individual's responses to those situations. The majority of psychological thought has dealt with reactions to stressful environments because, given identical environments, some individuals become quite disturbed while others do not (Lazarus, 1966).

There are several stages in a stress reaction:

1. Alarm and shock result in hormonal and physiological changes, including autonomic excitability, increased heart rate, and a decrease in body temperature (Selye, 1956). These changes are accompanied by emotional reactions, such as feeling threatened and in distress.
2. Defense mechanisms are activated as the individual searches for methods of dealing with the subjectively harmful and aversive situation.
3. If the individual is able to adapt and deal with the environment effectively, the alarm reaction and anxiety state subside.
4. If the mechanisms fail and the stressor continues to control behavior, any number of psychological reactions, including depression, withdrawal, and even suicide, may occur.

Because the consequences of failing to cope adequately with stress can be grave, the organism must develop means of adapting to and dealing with the environment.

The Role of Experience in Dealing with Stress The reader surely has experienced psychological stress reactions upon encountering a subjectively threatening situation, such as the initial ride on a roller coaster, the first job interview, or starting kindergarten. But after repeated experience, riding on the roller coaster is fun, a job interview may be interesting, and kindergarten class is something that most children anticipate happily. Experience clearly aids the individual in adapting to stressor agents.

In one experiment (Epstein and Fenz, 1965), sport parachutists were interviewed before and after a jump and were asked to rate their fears. Half of the parachutists had previously made more than 100 jumps; the other half were inexperienced. The fears reported by the parachutists are shown in Figure 15•1 as a function of the time from the jump.

Experienced parachutists reported becoming, after the decision to jump, less and less fearful as the time of the jump drew near, but naive jumpers became more and more fearful. When action must be taken and danger is confronted, the

The Stress of Change

Any change—even a pleasant one—produces stress (Holmes and Rake, 1967). In order to study the extent of stress produced by change, Thomas Holmes and his colleagues constructed a scale of stress values. They assigned an arbitrary baseline value of 50 life change units (LCU) to the act of marrying and then asked people from several countries to rate other actions and events in terms of it. Using this scale, the researchers found evidence that changes totaling more than 300 LCU within one year could result in serious illness within the next two years (Holmes and Holmes, 1970).

Here are the life events and their scale values (Holmes and Rake, 1967).

Life Event	Scale Value
Death of spouse	100
Divorce	73
Marital separation	65
Jail term	63
Death of close family member	63
Personal injury or illness	53
Marriage	50
Fired from work	47
Marital reconciliation	45
Retirement	45
Change in family member's health	44
Pregnancy	40
Sex difficulties	39
Gain of new family member	39
Business readjustment	39
Change in financial state	38
Death of close friend	37
Career change	36
Change in number of arguments with spouse	35
Mortgage over $10,000	31
Foreclosure of mortgage or loan	30
Change in responsibilities at work	29
Son or daughter leaving home	29
Trouble with in-laws	29
Outstanding personal achievement	28
Spouse begins or stops work	26
Starting or finishing school	26
Change in living conditions	25
Revision of personal habits	24
Trouble with boss	23
Change in work hours or conditions	20
Change in residence	20
Change in schools	20
Change in recreation habits	19
Change in church activities	19
Change in social activities	18
Mortgage or loan less than $10,000	17
Change in sleeping habits	16
Change in number of family gatherings	15
Change in eating habits	15
Vacation	13
Christmas season	12
Minor violations of the law	11

experienced chutist is less likely to experience anxiety that could interfere with performance. It appears that an active, adaptive mechanism is operating, for once the jump is made, the level of fear of the experienced chutist rises again.

Experience as Information Iron rusts because of a chemical process called oxidation, not because of time itself. Similarly, stress decreases with experience, but experience itself is not a cause. Then what process produces the change that accompanies experience?

One possible answer is that experience provides knowledge about the action. We learn just when the roller coaster will plunge, what a job interviewer is likely to ask, and how other kindergarten children act. We now are in a predictable environment and are aware of how our own behavior will affect, and be affected by,

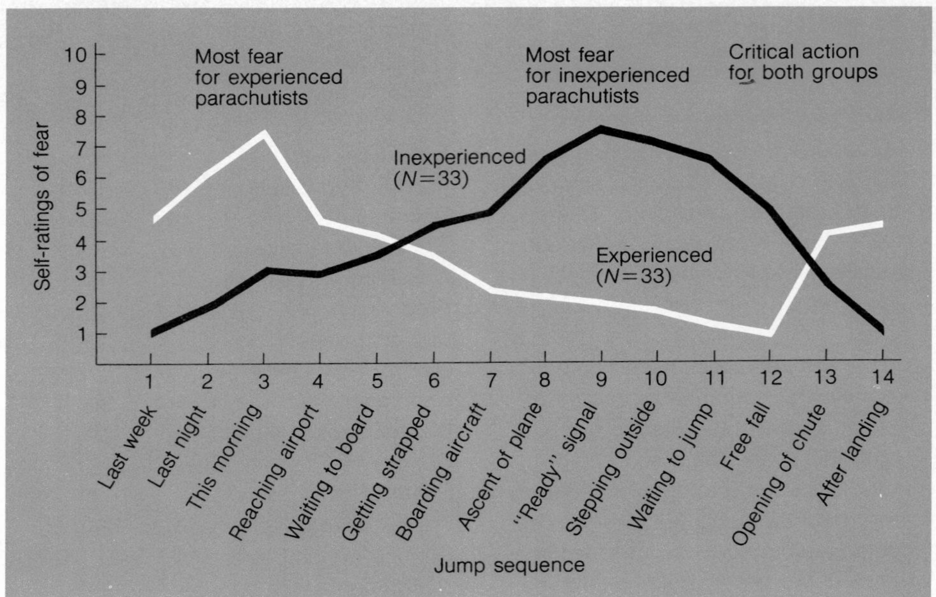

Fig. 15·1 Parachutists' self-ratings of fear experienced before, during, and after a jump. (Adapted from Epstein and Fenz, 1965)

that environment. In addition, we know what behaviors are appropriate. We have learned, for example, that screaming on a roller coaster is natural and not necessarily a sign of cowardice.

Irving Janis, a prominent social psychologist, has extensively studied the effects of information on reactions to stress, particularly in regard to medical operations. Janis (1958) contends that a moderate amount of anticipatory fear facilitates postoperative adjustment and that preparatory information describing the operation and the postoperative pain also aids recovery.

In one experiment supporting this position, conversations were held with patients prior to an operation (Egbert, Battit, Welch, and Bartlett, 1964). One group of patients was given extra operation-relevant information. A second group merely participated in a typical preoperation discussion. After the operation it was found that, compared to the uniformed group, the informed group required less morphine in a post-operative treatment (Figure 15•2) and was released from the hospital an average of three days earlier.

In sum, information aids adaptive reactions to stress. An informed patient who experiences pain will probably think of it as a normal reaction rather than as a sign that the operation was not a success. The latter conclusion would increase fear and emotional disturbance, which might impede improvement. In a similar manner, the experienced parachute jumpers may have learned to deal with their emotions and become aware that these reactions are normal. This attribution would decrease fear and personal feelings of inadequacy. Other mechanisms that control stress, such as repression, denial, and intellectualization, are discussed later in this chapter in the section on defenses.

15·2 If conflict is the result of incompatible responses, then it is apparent that we live in a world of conflict, for many alternatives are open at any one time. Should we study or go out with a friend? If we study, should it be history or psychology? If psychology is chosen, should Chapter 14 be reread or Chapter 15 started? In addition to these conscious choices, conflicts may result from a conscious desire and an unconscious desire that are opposites.

It is obvious that some conflicts produce more stress than others, but what determines the degree or the magnitude of a conflict? This determination is best illustrated by an example involving a relatively simple choice. Assume that it is Saturday night and you want to go to a movie. If there is only one movie in town, and it is precisely the movie that you have been waiting to see, then minimal conflict exists. If there are two movies, a decision must be made, and the potential for increased conflict is present. But suppose one of the movies is the award winner that you have been waiting to see for a year, and the other is *Godzilla Meets the Gorilla,* which you've already seen several times. Little conflict is generated when the attractiveness of one choice far exceeds the attractiveness of the other. But if both the movies in town are award winners that you would like to see, probably some conflict is now produced. A general law may therefore be proposed:

The greater the equality in the attractiveness of the alternatives, the greater the degree of conflict.

What if three attractive movies are being shown? Or a dozen? A second law concerning the magnitude of generated conflict is:

The greater the number of alternatives available, the greater the degree of conflict.

The salesperson who has learned this lesson does not show a customer many different items, because a great number of possible choices might generate a conflict and no sale.

Suppose you were trying to decide which college to attend, which job to accept, or which person to marry. Much greater conflict is aroused in these decisions than in choosing which movie to see. A third general law might be phrased as follows:

The greater the importance of the decision, the greater the degree of conflict.

In sum, the magnitude of conflict is in part determined by the relative equality in the attractiveness of alternatives, the number of possible alternatives, and the importance of the decision:

Conflict = *f* (relative attractiveness of alternatives, number of alternatives, importance of the decision)

A number of taxonomies of conflict have been proposed. We will concentrate on two of them—Brown's and Lewin's.

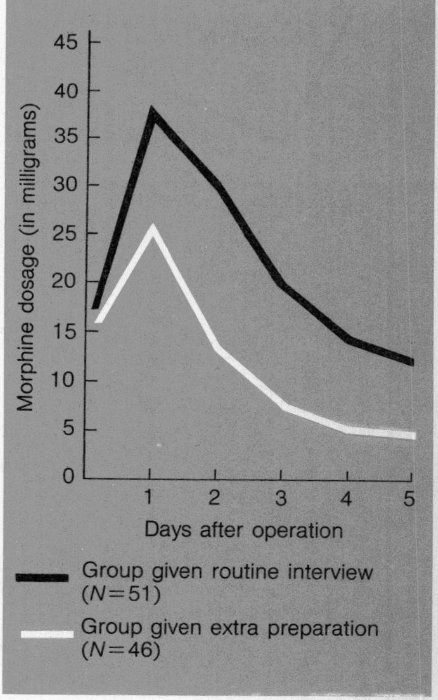

Fig. 15·2 Postoperative narcotic treatment for two groups of surgical patients—those given a special preparatory communication and those given a routine interview. (Adapted from Egbert, Battit, Welch, and Bartlett, 1964)

Conflict: Temporal, Spatial, Discriminative One interesting classification scheme distinguishes between temporal, spatial, and discriminative conflict (Brown, 1957).

1. **Temporal conflict** exists when the attractiveness of alternative choices changes over time. For example, an engaged couple may become more and more uncertain about their decision to marry as the date of the wedding draws near. Job shifts, moving, and other significant changes tend to be perceived with increasing or decreasing favorableness as the time of change approaches.
2. **Spatial conflict** involves a change in physical distance. A teen-ager decides to fight the neighborhood bully, for example, but as he approaches and notices the size of his opponent, he changes his mind. Or a small child at the beach may run toward the water to retrieve a toy, but then run back to escape from an incoming wave.
3. **Discriminative conflict** occurs when one has to choose between two very similar alternatives. For example, among its seafood offerings the restaurant has left only breaded scallops and breaded shrimp. Or the dentist you are considering going to reminds you of both a good dentist and a bad dentist you've been to before.

Discriminative conflicts were first demonstrated by Pavlov. As already indicated in the discussion of Pavlov's conditioning procedure, an unconditioned stimulus (food) is repeatedly paired with a conditioned stimulus (a tone) until the tone itself elicits from the dog the salivation that ordinarily accompanies only the presentation of food. To create a discriminative conflict, Pavlov first instituted a learning period during which a tone of a particular frequency (600 cycles) was paired with the presentation of food; a second tone with a different frequency (800 cycles) also was sounded, but never followed by food. On the conflict trials, a tone half-way between the two prior training tones (700 cycles) was presented, so that the animal was required to discriminate whether this was a "food" or a "no food" tone.

Pavlov reported that in this conflict situation his laboratory dogs exhibited signs of emotionality and disturbance. He compared these behaviors to the "neurotic" actions of humans and suggested that certain mental illnesses might be a result of insoluble discriminative conflicts.

Although this classification scheme is useful, it has many shortcomings. One deficiency is that it is not all-inclusive. Many conflicts do not fit the three conflict types. The conflict between studying history or psychology, for example, is not necessarily spatial, temporal, or discriminative.

Lewin's Classification Scheme A more complete taxonomy of conflict has been proposed by Kurt Lewin, who is often considered to be the founder of the field of experimental psychodynamics, for he was one of the first psychologists to test some of Freud's ideas in controlled laboratory settings (1935, 1936, 1951).

Kurt Lewin

Kurt Lewin was born in Prussia in 1890 and received his doctorate from the University of Berlin in 1914. At Berlin he came under the influence of the **Gestalt psychologists,** particularly Max Wertheimer, Wolfgang Köhler, and Kurt Koffka. At the time of Hitler's rise to power, Lewin was returning to Berlin via Russia after a trip to the United States. He wisely decided that arrival in Germany was unsafe and returned to settle in the United States. After a brief period at Cornell University, Lewin went to the Child Welfare Station at the University of Iowa (1935–1945). In 1945, Lewin became director of the Research Center for Group Dynamics at Massachusetts Institute of Technology. He died of a heart attack in 1947 at age 56.

Lewin's untimely death had been long feared by his colleagues, for his life was filled with activity. He worked on models of motivation as well as the solution of social problems. His applied interests ranged from adolescence and feeblemindedness to national character and food preferences. Working with industrial managers, Lewin initiated the T-group (training group) or encounter movement, which is now a fundamental part of humanistic psychology.

Lewin was a warm person who worked closely with his students and colleagues. Students tell of his coming over late at night, bringing a bottle of wine, and then discussing psychology until dawn. His students include Dorwin Cartwright, Leon Festinger, Harold Kelley, and many others who now dominate the field of social psychology. Lewin strongly identified with America and the American way of life, but he also was a strong supporter of Israel and entertained the idea of settling there.

Lewin differentiated three types of conflict: approach-approach, avoidance-avoidance, and approach-avoidance.

1. **Approach-approach conflicts** occur when there are two or more positive alternatives from which to choose. Examples are the proverbial donkey choosing between two bundles of hay, or a person deciding which of two award-winning movies to see.
2. **Avoidance-avoidance conflicts** are created when a choice is confined to two or more unattractive alternatives, such as a command either to wash the dishes or to vacuum the rug. A decision to read either Chapter 11 or Chapter 12 of this book might be an example of an avoidance-avoidance conflict (but we hope not).
3. **Approach-avoidance conflicts** are aroused when an action has both positive and negative consequences. A malted milk is desired, but it's fattening; a new car is wanted, but it's expensive; success on a forthcoming test is important, but it requires that all social life be suspended for a week. Approach-avoidance conflicts are quite prevalent and characterize most decisions.

Approach-Approach Compared to Avoidance-Avoidance: Unstability and Stability

Lewin contended that approach-approach conflicts are easy to resolve and labeled them *unstable conflicts,* whereas avoidance-avoidance conflicts are difficult to resolve (*stable conflicts*). The reasons for Lewin's presumption can be made clear by a quasi-mathematical model for behavior. Assume that a model for hunger motivation is given by the equation:

$$\text{Hunger motivation} = \frac{\text{Hunger} \times \text{Incentive value}}{\text{Distance from food}}$$

That is, how much one is motivated to attain food depends on how hungry he or she is (the amount of deprivation), the particular kind or amount of food that is available (called the incentive value of the goal), and the distance one is from the food, with increasing distance leading to decreased motivation. One is most motivated to attain food when deprived for a long time, when the food is appealing and readily accessible. (This model also is examined in Chapter 12.)

Now consider an approach-approach conflict in which a donkey stands directly between two bundles of hay. Assume that the donkey's hunger is 2 units of strength, the hay is 6 units of attractiveness, and the donkey is 3 units of distance from each bundle. The conflict is formally conceptualized as follows:

$$\text{Motivation to go left} = \frac{2 \times 6}{3} = 4 \qquad \text{Motivation to go right} = \frac{2 \times 6}{3} = 4$$

The strengths of motivation to go to the bundles of hay on the left and on the right are identical. The animal is caught in a conflict.

How might this conflict be resolved? Assume for the moment that the donkey notices some grass a few steps on his left and moves in that direction. The distance from the hay on the left therefore decreases by, for example, 1 unit. On the other hand, the distance from the hay on the right increases by 1 unit. The altered strengths of motivation are:

$$\text{Motivation to go left} = \frac{2 \times 6}{2} = 6 \qquad \text{Motivation to go right} = \frac{2 \times 6}{4} = 3$$

The strength of motivation to go left now exceeds the strength of motivation to go right. If the assumption is made that the stronger motivational force wins, or determines the direction of behavior, then the donkey will continue to go left. If 1 more unit of distance is traversed, the motivational strengths are:

$$\text{Motivation to go left} = \frac{2 \times 6}{1} = 12 \qquad \text{Motivation to go right} = \frac{2 \times 6}{5} = 2.4$$

There is an increasing difference between the desire to go left and the desire to go right. The donkey therefore approaches the hay on the left; the conflict is resolved. Because of the *growing inequality in the attractiveness of the two choices,* Lewin contended that approach-approach conflicts are easy to resolve.

The conflict cannot be resolved, however, unless the initial equilibrium is altered. The initial shift can be the result of any number of factors, such as new information that alters cognitions and the strength of motivation.

Now consider avoidance-avoidance conflicts. Assume that the conflict again is spatial, involving the aversive consequences of facing the monster Godzilla on the left or the Gorilla on the right. The desire to live is assigned the value of 2 units, the negative incentive or attractiveness of each beast is -6 units, and the individual is 3 units of distance from each monster. The strengths of motivation to flee are:

Motivation to avoid Godzilla (away from left) $= \frac{2 \times -6}{3} = -4$

Motivation to avoid Gorilla (away from right) $= \frac{2 \times -6}{3} = -4$

The force away from either alternative is -4. Thus, a difficult conflict has been established.

Now assume that the equilibrium is broken and the individual decides to go to the left. Perhaps Godzilla is perceived as slower, or less powerful, so that less danger is involved. Again, any new information can result in a change in motivational strengths. If the person goes 1 unit of distance to the left (or 1 unit of distance farther away from the right), then the avoidance motivations are:

$$\text{Motivation away from left} = \frac{2 \times -6}{2} = -6$$

$$\text{Motivation away from right} = \frac{2 \times -6}{4} = -3$$

The motivation to avoid going left now exceeds the motivation to avoid going right. The individual therefore should alter the choice and proceed in the opposite direction or toward the right (away from the left). If 2 units in the direction of the Gorilla happen to be traversed, then the strengths of motivation are:

$$\text{Motivation away from left} = \frac{2 \times -6}{4} = -3$$

$$\text{Motivation away from right} = \frac{2 \times -6}{2} = -6$$

There should again be a shift in choices and a change in direction, for the motivation away from the right now exceeds the motivation away from the left.

In sum, as a decision to go toward one alternative is made, the aversiveness of that alternative increases. On the other hand, the aversiveness of the alternative choice decreases. This imbalance results in a decision shift, and, in theory, a perpetual ambivalence. For this reason, Lewin assumed that avoidance-avoidance conflicts are stable.

Clearly, however, such conflicts eventually are resolved, at least partially. One method of conflict resolution suggested by Lewin is to leave the field, to run away from both Godzilla and Gorilla by going straight ahead. Psychological withdrawal may be considered an extreme example of increasing the distance between unpleasant alternatives. For physical withdrawal to occur, the person must have freedom of movement. For example, there must not be a wall or a lake to the front or rear.

An Experimental Demonstration of Conflict Resolution Difficulty

In theory, avoidance-avoidance conflicts are more difficult to resolve than approach-approach conflicts. With the help of several subjects, the reader can perform a simple experiment to demonstrate this point.

The general experimental procedure requires subjects to select between two possible alternatives (Arkoff, 1957). The instructions are straightforward:

> You will be given a series of questions, each one involving a choice. Two alternatives are given, and you are to select one. For example, you might be asked: "Do you prefer courses in psychology or courses in history?" As soon as you have reached a decision, tell me what it is. I will be timing you, because I also am interested in how long it takes you to reach the decision.

Table 15A·1 Conflict Situations and Order of Presentation for the Study of Approach-approach versus Avoidance-avoidance Conflicts

SITUATIONS	RANDOM ORDERS
Would you rather be (have):	**1.** 3 5 1 4 6 7 2 8
	2. 2 4 1 6 5 7 8 3
1. More attractive or more intelligent?	**3.** 8 4 2 3 1 5 7 6
2. More self-confident or more intelligent?	**4.** 7 3 5 2 1 6 4 8
3. More social poise or more energy?	**5.** 5 4 8 2 3 6 1 7
4. More financial security or a more cheerful disposition?	**6.** 8 3 2 7 4 6 5 1
5. Less attractive or less intelligent?	**7.** 6 7 3 1 8 5 4 2
6. Less self-confident or less intelligent?	**8.** 1 3 7 6 5 8 2 4
7. Less social poise or less energy?	**9.** 4 7 1 2 3 8 6 5
8. Less financial security or a less cheerful disposition?	**10.** 6 8 2 4 3 1 7 5

As the sample items in Table 15A·1 indicate, in half of the conflict situations both alternatives are positive (Would you rather be more intelligent or more attractive?); in the other half both alternatives are negative (Would you rather be less intelligent or less attractive?). A large number of such pairs should be offered, so that any differences in decision time will not be due to the particular content of an item. The reader can change or expand this list, following certain guidelines for proper experimentation.

1. The positive and negative pairings should be identical except for the "more" or "less" qualifiers. This similarity minimizes the likelihood that differences between conflict times will be due to the wording of the questions.

One general implication of this analysis is that aversive situations require blocking off avenues of escape. It is therefore advantageous to create situations in which the positive rather than the negative aspects of the possible choices stand out. If parents say, "Either wash the dishes or vacuum the rug," then hiding must be prevented. But if they say, "You can earn money by doing the dishes or vacuuming the rug," then the parents do not have to erect barriers that prevent hiding.

Approach-Avoidance: Ambivalence Observations of approach-avoidance conflicts reveal what is labeled as *ambivalent behavior.* For example, consider a hungry animal in a runway with food at the opposite end and an electrified grid separating it from the food (Figure 15·3). An approach-avoidance conflict results because running down the alley will have both beneficial and aversive consequences. In this situation, the animal often approaches the food, turns back away from shock, returns to approach the food, and so forth. The behavior oscillates from approach to avoidance. A theory explaining approach-avoidance conflicts is difficult to formulate, for it must account for this vacillation in behavior.

2. The questions should be presented in a different random order. At the bottom of Table 15A·1 ten random orders are given. If the experimenter tests more than ten subjects, the same orders can be used a second time or new random orders can be created either by consulting a random-order table or by randomly selecting numbers from a container. Again, this randomness is necessary in order to avoid outside influences on decision times. For example, if approach-approach conflicts are always given first, then subjects might become bored and take longer than otherwise to decide on the later avoidance-avoidance conflicts.

Table 15A·2 Data Sheet for Conflict Comparisons

SUBJECTS	DECISION TIME								TOTAL TIMES Approach-approach (1+2+3+4)	TOTAL TIMES Avoidance-avoidance (5+6+7+8)
	1.	2.	3.	4.	5.	6.	7.	8.		
1										
2										
3										
4										
5										
6										
7										
8										
9										
10										
Total Times										
Mean Times (Total/N)										

To assess the difficulty of the conflict, measure the time taken to reach a decision. The latency of the response, or the time required to make a decision, is one index of the conflict resolution difficulty.

The data collected can be inserted in Table 15A·2. Mean figures should be computed and the latency times of the two types of conflicts compared. If the decision time of the approach-approach conflicts is less than that of the avoidance-avoidance conflicts, then the hypothesis is substantiated (ignoring here the question of how to test the statistical confidence one can place in the findings).

Prior research indicates that avoidance-avoidance conflict resolution takes almost twice as long as approach-approach conflict resolution.

Miller's Conflict Theory Neal Miller (1944, 1959) has proposed a conceptual framework that explains the dynamics of approach-avoidance conflicts. As a learning theorist with psychoanalytic knowledge, Miller was able to apply experimental training to problems of central importance in human behavior. To correspond to the motivation model introduced in this chapter, Miller's theory is somewhat transformed in the following discussion, but his basic premises and theoretical predictions are accurately presented.

Assume that a rat in the food and shock apparatus shown in Figure 15·3 has 6 units of hunger, the food has a numerical value of 4 units, and at the start of the runway the rat is 6 units away from the food. In addition, assume that the fear of shock has a magnitude of 3 units, the shock intensity has −3 units of negative incentive, and the distance from the shock is 5 units. (Because the shock is in front of the food, the assigned unit of distance is less than 6.) On the basis of the model used in the prior discussion, the strengths of motivation are:

$$\text{Approach motivation} = \frac{6 \times 4}{6} = 4$$

Fig. 15·3 Apparatus to study approach-avoidance conflict.

Start box	Electric grid	Goal object

$$\text{Avoidance motivation} = \frac{3 \times -3}{5} = -1.8$$

The magnitude or strength of the approach motivation (4) is greater than the magnitude of the avoidance motivation (÷1.8) by 2.2 units of strength. The rat therefore should move toward the food (and the shock).

Now consider the hunger and fear of the animal as it moves forward in the runway. The level of hunger, typically determined by the time since last eating, remains relatively constant because the time of deprivation increases only by the short amount of time it takes to move down the runway. In addition, the level of hunger is little affected by the particular environment in which the animal is located. The rat will be just as hungry when it is taken out of the apparatus and returned to its home cage. But what about the intensity of experienced fear? Clearly the rat will not be apprehensive of shock in its home cage. Fear is in large part elicited by information in the environment. One is afraid of falling over a cliff when walking just a few inches from the edge, but that fear quickly subsides when one steps back a yard or two. In a similar manner, the fear that the rat is experiencing will increase as it comes close to the aversive shock and decrease as it moves away from the electrified grid.

Miller therefore proposes that the drive of fear is strongly influenced by situational variables, while the drive of hunger is little affected by external cues. *Distance from the goal has a greater effect upon avoidance than upon approach motivation.*

Let us now apply this principle and derive the implications for the resolution of approach-avoidance conflicts. Recall that at the start of the runway the animal is more motivated to approach the food than to avoid the shock. It therefore begins to go down the runway. Assume for illustrative purposes that the rat goes 1 unit closer to the goal. In this situation, theoretically the desire to eat or the level of hunger remains constant. Conversely, the fear of shock increases. Assume that this increase in fear has the numerical value of 1 unit. Therefore,

$$\text{Approach motivation} = \frac{6 \times 4}{5} = 4.8$$

$$\text{Avoidance motivation} = \frac{4 \times -3}{4} = -3.0$$

The rat should still be motivated to go toward the food, for the approach motivation is greater than the avoidance motivation. However, the inequality between the absolute strengths of motivation is now 1.8 (4.8 minus 3.0). Recall that the difference in motivations prior to the first unit of advance was 2.2 (4.0 minus 1.8).

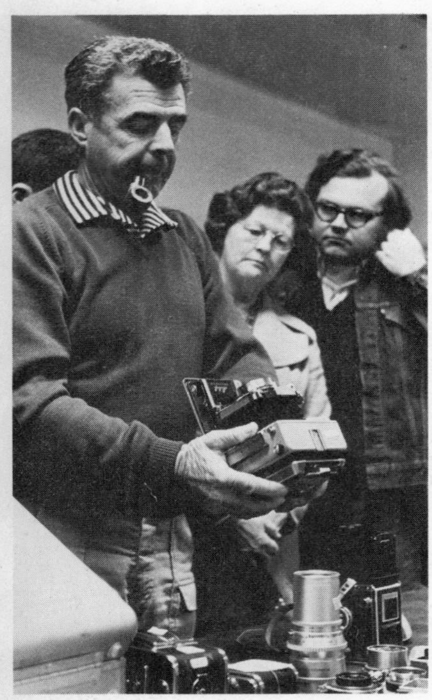

A would-be buyer of an expensive item may experience an approach-avoidance conflict. (Andy Mercado, Jeroboam)

The difference between the approach and avoidance motivational tendencies therefore has decreased as the animal moved toward the positive and negative goals.

As the rat goes another 2 units closer to the desired food and the aversive shock, the motivational strengths become:

$$\text{Approach motivation} = \frac{6 \times 4}{3} = 8$$

$$\text{Avoidance motivation} = \frac{6 \times -3}{2} = -9$$

The absolute strength of avoidance motivation at this point exceeds the strength of approach motivation. The rat should turn around and go back. This analysis is summarized in Table 15•1, which clearly shows that the distance from the goal has a greater effect upon avoidance than upon approach motivation. In this example we would predict that the organism would proceed about 2.5 units toward the food goal and then stop.

A number of theoretical derivations concerning approach-avoidance conflicts have been tested and confirmed in laboratory experiments. One derivation concerns the effects of degree of hunger on conflict resolution. Figure 15•4a essentially repeats the data in Table 15•1, although the curves are flattened and a second approach gradient is added. The two approach gradients differ in magnitude, caused by unequal deprivation levels. The distance between points A and A′ depicts the differential distance of approach to the goal, given two disparate levels of hunger motivation. As the figure shows, the intersection of the approach and avoidance gradients occurs at a point closer to the goal when approach motivation is heightened.

Figure 15•4b includes an additional avoidance gradient. The intersection of the approach and avoidance gradients occurs at a point farther from the goal as

Table 15•1 Changing Strengths of Approach and Avoidance Motivation (as rat traverses runway)

DISTANCE MOVED	APPROACH MOTIVATION	AVOIDANCE MOTIVATION	DIFFERENCE
Start box	$\frac{6 \times 4}{6} = 4$	$\frac{3 \times -3}{5} = -1.8$	2.2
1 unit	$\frac{6 \times 4}{5} = 4.8$	$\frac{4 \times -3}{4} = -3$	1.8
2 units	$\frac{6 \times 4}{4} = 6$	$\frac{5 \times -3}{3} = -5$	1
3 units	$\frac{6 \times 4}{3} = 8$	$\frac{6 \times -3}{2} = -9$	−1

NOTE: It is assumed that (1) hunger is 6 units of strength, (2) the food object has 4 units of attractiveness, (3) the fear of shock has 3 units of strength, (4) the shock level has −3 units of negative value, and (5) the shock is 1 unit in front of the food object, as in Figure 15.3.

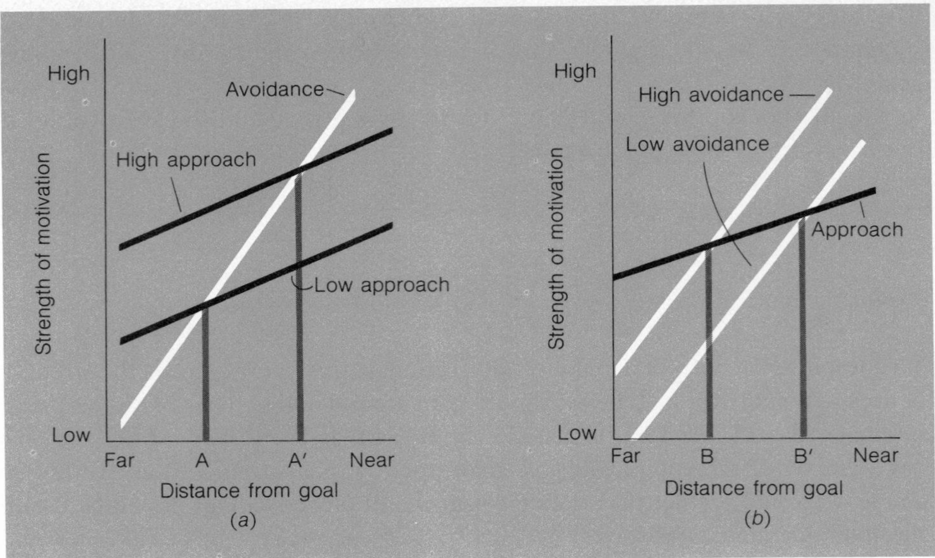

Fig. 15·4 Two examples of approach-avoidance conflicts (*a*) Two degrees of approach motivation; (*b*) Two degrees of avoidance motivation.

the magnitude of avoidance motivation increases; that is, we would expect the animal not to go as close to the goal if, for example, the strength of the anticipated shock increases. The distance between points B and B′ depicts the differential approach to the goal, given two different levels of avoidance motivation.

One method that has been used to get the animals closer to the goal in approach-avoidance situations is to provide some alcoholic beverage before they are placed in the apparatus. Alcohol decreases the amount of experienced fear, thus producing an *increment* in approach behavior.

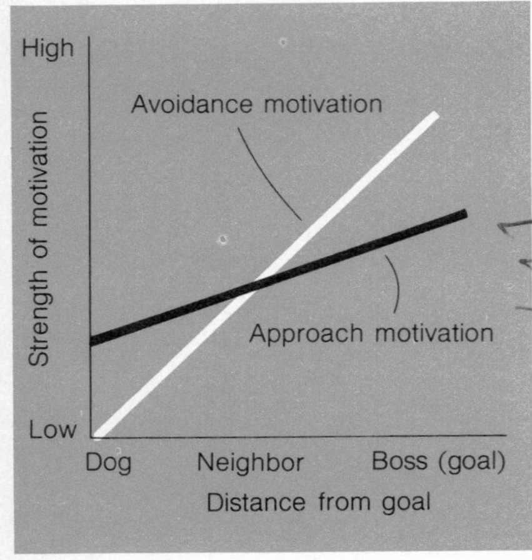

Fig. 15·5 Application of conflict model to displacement.

Conflict and Displacement When one cannot attain a goal because societal rules prevent the behavior, one changes goal objects. This shift is called **displacement.** A frequently cited example of this activity is the worker who cannot express anger at a boss but takes it out on his or her family. In one primitive society, activities for displacing aggression are institutionalized. Outside every hut is a dog; when the male of the household is angry, he may punish this unfortunate animal.

Miller incorporated displacement activity into his conflict model. He reasoned that the aggressive tendency of an angry employee toward a boss, for example, is inhibited by a stronger avoidance tendency. Figure 15·5 depicts this situation. The graph is similar to those in Figure 15·4 except that here distance from the goal is represented by individuals. In theory, a person in this situation would express aggression either at the point of gradient intersection (a neighbor) or where the approach motivation most exceeds the avoidance motivation (the dog). Thus, the aggressive behavior is displaced, or directed toward objects that did not provoke it.

Inhibition, Avoidance, and Defense Mechanisms

15·3 As indicated in our discussion of conflict, inhibition and avoidance are important determinants of behavior. For humans, the fulfillment of desires is often inhibited by rules and norms. We do not, for example, typically hit our fathers or mothers or display physical aggression toward others, even though we may experience such urges. Nor do we generally rape someone when sexually aroused or make sexual advances to members of our immediate families other than spouses. When prohibited aggressive or sexual behaviors are momentarily entertained, psychological mechanisms intervene and inhibit them.

Since much aggression is inhibited, the power of inhibitions is most evident when they break down. Empirical evidence shows that many individuals who engage in extreme acts of violence have previously been overly inhibited in expressing their aggressive feelings. Frequently they are described as model citizens prior to their eruption.

Psychological restraints are believed to be imposed on aggressive desires in part because of the unpleasant or painful consequences that would follow if the desires were acted on. Because the elicited psychological mechanisms have a protective function, they frequently are called *defense mechanisms,* or just defenses.

Some psychological defenses that protect the person from anxiety, punishment, or other unpleasant experiences are obvious, as when a person faints to avoid the sight of blood or the feelings that accompany a serious accident. A person may consciously and rationally derive strategies that enable him or her to cope with stresses and problems, but usually a person is not consciously aware of defenses. In the following discussion we examine some of the unconscious mechanisms stressed by psychologists in the area of psychodynamics—repression, denial, and intellectualization. Fixation and regression are two other defense mechanisms that will be dealt with in regard to frustration.

Repression Freud, who believed that repression is the most significant defense mechanism, described it as follows:

> Every mental process . . . exists to begin with in an unconscious stage or phase and . . . it is only from there that the process passes over into the conscious phase, just as a photographic picture begins as a negative and only becomes a picture after being turned into a positive. Not every negative, however, necessarily becomes a positive; nor is it necessary that every unconscious mental process should turn into a conscious one. This may be advantageously expressed by saying that an individual process belongs to begin with to the system of the unconscious and can then, in certain circumstances, pass over into the system of the conscious.
>
> The crudest idea of these systems is the most convenient for us—a spatial one. Let us therefore compare the system of the unconscious to a large entrance hall, in which the mental impulses jostle one another like separate individuals. Adjoining this entrance hall there is a second, narrower, room—a kind of drawing room—in which consciousness, too, resides. But on the threshold between these two rooms a watchman performs his function: he examines the different mental impulses, acts as a censor, and will not admit them into the drawing room if they displease him. You will see at once that it does not make much difference if the watchman turns away

Defense mech for 4th ques.

a particular impulse at the threshold itself or if he pushes it back across the threshold after it has entered the drawing room. This is merely a question of the degree of his watchfulness and of how early he carries out his act of recognition. If we keep to this picture, we shall be able to extend our nomenclature further. The impulses in the entrance hall of the unconscious are out of sight to the conscious, which is in the other room; to begin with they must remain unconscious. If they have already pushed their way forward to the threshold and have been turned back by the watchman, then they are inadmissible to consciousness; we speak of them as *repressed*. (Freud, 1933)

The defense of repression presumably affects the person by keeping unacceptable ideas, wishes, and feelings out of consciousness. It is assumed that if the wishes remain unconscious, then they will not be directly acted on. Goal seeking is prevented because of the aversive consequences that would follow if the goal were attained. Repression therefore has functional significance: it enables the person to adapt to the environment.

Freud's conception of repression grew from his observations that his patients had amnesia for important memories, but that these memories could be retrieved through special methods, such as **free association** and **dream interpretation.** Freud concluded that their emergence into consciousness was opposed by active inhibitory forces (the "watchman") that must be weakened in order for the memories to reach consciousness.

The Scientific Study of Repression Many different experimental procedures have been used to demonstrate repression in the laboratory, but none has been entirely satisfactory (Weiner, 1966). Because some of the experimental evidence is promising, however, and because of the many clinical observations of repression, the belief in inhibited memories remains strongly entrenched among personality psychologists.

One early technique employed to demonstrate repression was to ask subjects to recall past events and to rate the affect associated with each event. If more pleasant than unpleasant experiences were remembered, it was inferred that repression was operating to interfere with the memory of unpleasant occurrences. This approach is questionable, however, because we may indeed have more pleasant than unpleasant experiences.

A second procedure frequently used in the study of repression is to pair distinctive stimuli, such as digits or words, with pleasant or unpleasant sensations, such as smells, the receipt of money or shocks, and so on. Subjects are later asked to recall the stimuli. When the stimuli paired with the aversive consequences are recalled less often than the stimuli paired with the positive consequences, repression is inferred. This procedure is better than merely asking subjects to recall personal events, because the number of positive and negative experiences is controlled and made equal.

But these studies are also weak. First, the data are not consistent. Sometimes recall of stimuli associated with pleasant experiences is greater and sometimes it isn't. Furthermore, it is difficult to argue that retrieval of the forgotten stimuli is opposed by an active restraining force. The experimental stimuli are far removed from the dangerous sexual and aggressive urges discussed by Freud.

A third research procedure used to study repression examines the recall of successful and failed achievement activities. If it is ego-protective to forget failures, repressive forces should impede remembrance of prior poor performances. Subjects in these experiments typically are given a number of tasks to solve. Because half of the tasks are too long to solve within the time allotted, the subjects experience success on half of them and failure on the other half. They then are asked to recall the tasks on which they worked. Again, however, the findings are inconsistent. At times there is greater recall of the incompleted tasks and at times better recall of the completed tasks.

Finally, a fourth experimental procedure to study repression involves the recall of *complex-related words.* The notion of a complex-related word was first advanced by Carl Gustav Jung, the Swiss psychoanalyst. Jung would read subjects a list of words and ask them to respond with the first word that came to mind. In using this *word-association* technique, Jung noted that unusually long pauses preceded some responses. He inferred that in these instances the stimulus words were related to a *personality complex,* or an area of emotional disturbance associated with repressed, conflict-arousing material. Because of this association, the immediate responses were likely to meet with censorship, resulting in a longer time period before the appearance of the verbalized response. Some convincing experimental demonstrations of repression use complex-related words and find less recall of these words during controlled experimentation.

Denial and Intellectualization Two additional mechanisms of defense identified by Sigmund Freud, and later elaborated on by his daughter, Anna Freud, are denial and intellectualization. **Denial** refers to a refusal to accept consciously the existence of a threatening situation. Children often use this primitive defense mechanism. For example, after walking past the yak cage at the zoo, a father casually asked his son, who had acted extremely afraid of the yaks on previous visits to the zoo, "Did you see the yaks?" His son answered, "What yaks? They don't live here any more."

Intellectualization, or isolation, occurs when an idea and its emotional accompaniment become detached. That is, an emotional event is dealt with in an overly intellectual manner, thus neutralizing its affective significance. The doctor coolly performing an autopsy is a good illustration of the power of intellectualization.

The existence of the defenses of denial and intellectualization has been best demonstrated by their effects on stress reactions. Richard Lazarus (1966, 1968) has conducted a systematic program of research on stress reactions in which denial and intellectualization are experimentally manipulated. The general experimental procedure is to record various measures of autonomic arousal, such as heart rate

An Experimental Demonstration of Repression

Table 15B·1 Outline of Experiment Using Complex-Related Words and Hypnosis to Demonstrate Repression

STAGE	CONTROL CONDITION	EXPERIMENTAL CONDITION
1	Determine conflict-related and neutral words	
2	Nothing	Hypnosis
3	Learn selected conflict-related and neutral words	
4	Nothing	Instructions to later recall only ten words
5	Recall #1, waking state	Recall #1, waking state
6	Nothing	Lift posthypnotic suggestion
7	Recall #2	Recall #2

Some convincing experimental demonstrations of repression make use of complex-related words. In one study, association reaction times were first ascertained to a series of words. Some days later the subjects were given a list of words to learn that contained nine normal-latency (neutral) words and nine long-latency (complex-related) words.

Subjects in one of the two experimental conditions learned the list while in a hypnotic state and were told that later, when asked to recall the words in a waking state, they would be able to remember only ten words, no matter how hard they tried (Clemes, 1964). After being asked to recall the words in the waking state, the posthypnotic trance was lifted and a second recall was obtained. Thus, the first recall, but not the second, took place under conditions of active interference. Subjects in a second experimental condition merely learned the list and recalled the words on two occasions, without the posthypnotic interference. This rather complex experimental design is outlined in Table 15B·1.

The words forgotten on the first recall but remembered on the second recall were then analyzed. It was found that only among the hypnotic subjects was there a significantly greater recall of complex-related words on the second, relative to the first, recall period.

Why is this a reasonable demonstration of what is meant by repression? First, the experimental stimuli were considered relevant to each subject and pertinent to their areas of emotional disturbance. This contrasts with investigations using smells or shock, or succeeded and failed tasks. Second, an active inhibiting force was introduced, in this case via an experimental instruction during hypnosis. This force interfered with the emergence of some thoughts into consciousness. And finally, when the active force subsided (removal of the posthypnotic suggestion), more of the emotionally-related words were retrieved. Selective amnesia was demonstrated because the active inhibitory force had little effect upon neutral words. Thus, the procedure is like the therapeutic process in which repressed material supposedly becomes available after the repressive force is weakened.

and galvanic skin response, while subjects view one of two films that typically give rise to stress reactions: a subincision film showing a primitive puberty ritual in which boys have their penises deeply cut, or a safety film depicting workshop accidents. The denial defense is introduced into the experimental condition by means of a sound track indicating, for example, that the subincision operation is not harmful or that the participants in the safety film are actors. Another sound track introduces the intellectualization defense by offering a detached (scholarly in one case, objective in the other) view of the situations. By these means it is ascertained whether emotional reactivity to the films is lowered when the defenses are introduced.

Figure 15•6 shows the results of one study that induced the defensive orientation of denial (Lazarus and Alfert, 1964). The subincision film was used, and the denial theme was introduced either as denial orientation prior to the film or as denial commentary during the film. Skin conduction (changes in the electrical resistance of the skin) was used to measure emotional reaction. The figure shows that (1) the denial defense reduced the degree of reactivity to the *stressor* among subjects in the experimental groups, compared to subjects in a control group that did not receive the defensive sound track; and (2) the reduction of the emotional reactivity is greatest when the defense is introduced in its entirety before the subjects view the film.

Frustration

15•4 Because of conflicts and inhibitions, the goals for which one is striving are not always reached. One of the most prevalent psychological consequences of failure to attain a goal is frustration.

Frustration has a diversity of meanings in psychology. It may refer to an *independent variable,* or experimental manipulation, such as blocking the attainment of a goal, inducing failure, or delivering a personal insult. Performance of the frustrated group is then compared to the performance of a nonfrustrated group to assess the effects of the independent manipulation. Frustration also may refer to a *dependent variable,* as when investigators attempt to measure the amount of frustrated behavior; for example, one might ask whether highly anxious subjects exhibit more frustrated behavior than subjects low in anxiety. Finally, frustration frequently refers to an intervening process that is inferred from observable responses such as aggressive behavior.

It is important also to distinguish frustration as a *product* from frustration as a *process.* An analogy to the field of learning makes this distinction clearer. Learning as a product refers to a change in the organism as a result of experience; learning as a process is an ongoing activity with dynamic qualities. Similarly, frustration is both a product (a result of an event) and a process (a change or dynamic state within the organism).

Many response indicators of frustration as an intervening process have been observed in laboratory situations. These indicators include **aggression, fixation, regression,** and enhanced goal striving.

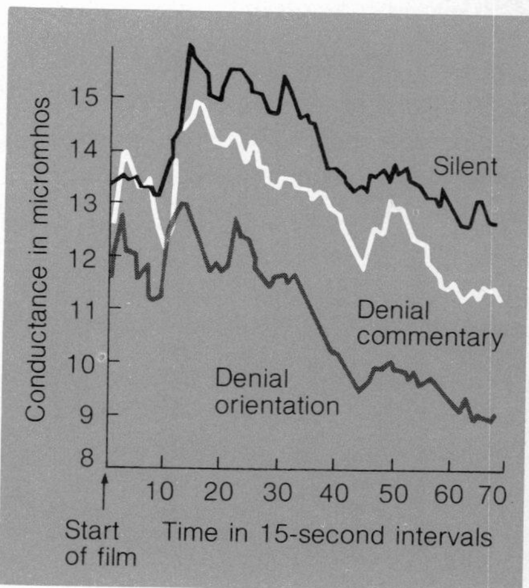

Fig. 15•6 Skin conductance curves during the film period under three experimental conditions. Denial orientation indicates that the sound track was presented in its entirety prior to the film onset. Denial commentary indicates that the denial sound track accompanied, rather than preceded, the film. The control condition is designated as "silent," that is, there is no accompanying sound tract. (Adapted from Lazarus and Alfert, 1964)

Frustration and Aggression The most well-known work on frustration concerns what is called the *frustration-aggression hypothesis.*

In its extreme form, this hypothesis states that aggression always is a consequence of frustration and that the occurrence of aggressive behavior always presupposes the existence of frustration. A number of interesting social experiments have tested these suppositions. In one investigation, (Bettelheim and Janowitz, 1950), veterans of World War II were asked about (1) their occupational status before entering the armed forces and just after returning from service and (2) their attitudes toward Jews. The data, depicted in Figure 15•7, show a relationship between job status alteration and anti-Semitism: Apparently the frustration caused by a negative job situation increases out-group aggression.

In a more direct test of the relationship between frustration and prejudice, children at a day camp were deprived of an expected opportunity to participate in bank night at a local theater (Miller and Bugelski, 1948). Both before and after this frustrating experience the children expressed their attitudes toward Japanese and Mexican boys. The investigation clearly revealed that not being allowed the anticipated fun increased prejudice (aggression) toward groups that were not in any way responsible for the frustration.

Frustration and Fixation Psychologists have long noted what is labeled the *neurotic paradox:* the persistence of responses that apparently result in repeated failure and nonreward. Such responses do not fit traditional learning theories, for negative reinforcement does not appear to decrease behavior.

Norman Maier (1949) conducted a series of experiments demonstrating that frustration can lead to persistent, maladaptive behavior. Maier made use of an apparatus known as the *Lashley jumping stand* (Figure 15•8). An animal, typically

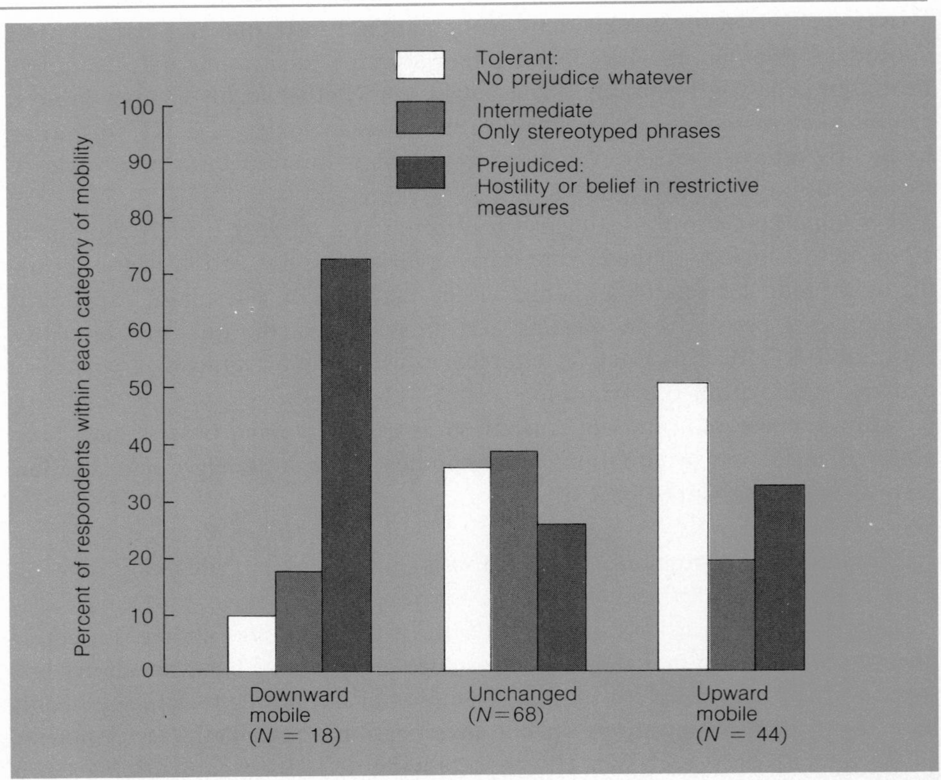

Fig. 15•7 Attitudes toward Jews on the part of veterans in three categories of occupational mobility. (Adapted from Bettelheim and Janowitz, 1950, 1964)

a rat, is placed on the stand facing two cardboard "doors," each marked with a distinctive design. An aversive stimulus forces the rat to jump, striking one of the two cards with its body. If it strikes the door that the experimenter has selected to fall over, the rat lands on a platform, where it receives a food reward. If it strikes the other card, the rat receives a bump and falls into the net below—a rather traumatic punishment. When the reward is randomly assigned to each card and position, many of the animals adopt a stereotyped response and jump to either the left or the right position, regardless of which card design is there. If the *response contingencies* are then altered so that the solution is consistent and the problem is soluble, the animal does not abandon its prior response. Even if the reward is made clearly visible by opening one of the doors, many animals continue to exhibit a position habit.

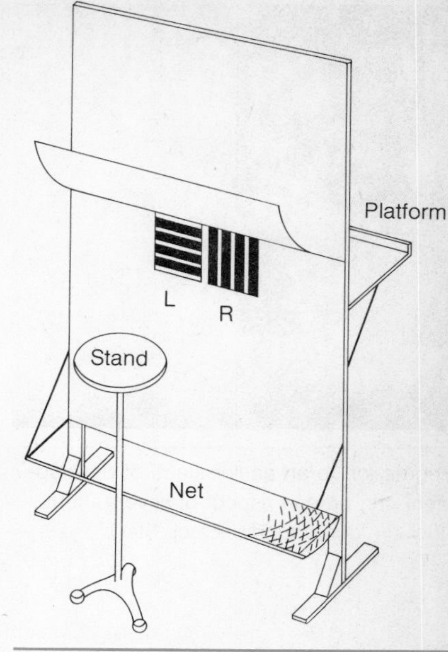

Fig. 15·8 Lashley jumping stand. (From Lashley, 1930)

Maier labels these stereotyped responses as *fixated* inasmuch as the organism seems not to be able to switch to a more adaptive behavior. Fixated responses are quite stable and resistant to change. For example, rats taught to walk to the correct response side will continue to jump to the fixated side when walking and jumping responses are intermixed. To alter a fixated response, guidance is required. During a jump, animals are pushed toward the open door, until gradually they are allowed to make a free choice.

In sum, Maier contends that (1) frustration-instigated behavior is characterized by fixedness and compulsivity; (2) such behavior is not altered by rewards; and (3) fixated behavior can be abandoned only by using the technique of guidance. Based on these facts, Maier argues that frustration-instigated behavior is *qualitatively* different from motivationally-instigated or normal behavior.

Frustration and Regression Freud specified that during childhood the individual selects certain problem solutions with which to cope with conflict and stress and thus reduce the amount of aversive, incoming stimulation. During times of later stress, according to Freud, there is a tendency for the person to repeat these earlier modes of behavior, although they might be inadequate in the present situation. A mild *regression* might be running home to mother in difficult times, while a more extreme form might involve constant thumbsucking.

Kurt Lewin and his colleagues experimentally investigated the Freudian concept of regression by studying the effects of frustration on the constructiveness of play (Barker, Dembo, and Lewin, 1943). It was known that constructiveness of play increases as a function of mental age. Further, it was reasoned that elaborate play activities indicate *future time perspective,* which Lewin believed to be characteristic of later development. Both experimental evidence and a logical analysis of play suggested that an index of constructiveness would reflect regressive tendencies.

In the investigation, children were first brought into an experimental room and allowed to play with attractive toys. Then they were separated from the toys by a partition through which they could see the toys, but could not handle them.

Regression to an earlier stage of development can be one aspect of severe mental illness. (John Laundis, Black Star)

During the separation period, the children could play with other objects located in the room. Throughout the prefrustration and frustration periods the experimenters measured the constructiveness of play. Primitive simple play with little structure (such as examining toys superficially) was described as unconstructive while imaginative and highly developed play (such as using toys as part of an elaborate story) was described as constructive.

The results of the study revealed that the constructiveness of play activities decreased from the prefrustration to the frustration period. During the time of frustration the children's play appeared more primitive and less elaborate. The investigators concluded that frustration can lead to regression.

This research has been criticized because the study did not include a no-frustration control group, and the regressive behaviors might have been due to fatigue or boredom. Nevertheless, the investigation nicely illustrates an attempt to relate frustration and the Freudian defense mechanism of regression.

Frustration and Instigation Frustration has been postulated to be an energizer of behavior. Investigations of the drive properties of frustration have been conducted primarily by psychologists with a behavioristic orientation, among them Abram Amsel.

Amsel (1958) defines frustration as a state resulting from the nonreinforcement of a response that previously had been consistently reinforced. According to Amsel, if an expectancy of a reward has been established, but the response no longer results in a reward, then frustration is experienced. The amount of frustration is directly proportional to the expectancy of the reward.

In one typical investigation demonstrating the motivational properties of frustration (Amsel and Hancock, 1957), two runways were joined so that the goal box of the first runway served as the starting box for the second (Figure 15•9). During the training period of the experiment the animals were fed in both the first and second goal boxes; in the testing phase food was withheld in the first goal box. It was found that, after nonreward in the first goal box, the vigor of performance in the second runway increased above the previous level. This performance increment demonstrates the drive effects of frustration. The immediately augmented response strength after nonattainment of an expected reward is termed the *frustration effect.*

Summary

Stress is an emotional reaction that is displayed in the presence of stressor agents. It can be reduced by experience, in part because prior exposure provides information that abates uncertainty and allows a proper labeling of one's state. In addition, defense mechanisms such as denial and intellectualization enable one to cope with stress reactions.

Conflict exists when multiple responses are aroused simultaneously. Conflict increases as the attractiveness of the alternatives is equalized, as the number of alternatives increases, and as a decision becomes more important. Lewin has identified three types of conflict: approach-approach, avoidance-avoidance, and approach-avoidance. Unlike approach-approach conflicts, avoidance-avoidance conflicts are difficult to resolve because selection of an alternative decreases the desirability of that choice while increasing the desirability of the unselected alternative. In depicting approach-avoidance conflicts, the avoidance gradient (the change in avoidance as a function of distance from the goal) is steeper than the approach gradient, meaning that these conflicts are also difficult to resolve. Displacement activity, or the shifting of responses to a less feared object, can be explained with an approach-avoidance conflict model.

Inhibitions or restraints are imposed on action because at times goal attainment will produce more pain (punishment) than reward. A number of psychological defenses, or defense mechanisms, may be involuntarily invoked to prevent action. Foremost among the defenses is repression, which prevents a forbidden desire from entering consciousness. Denial and intellectualization are other mechanisms of defense. The research evidence bearing upon these defenses is not strong, but a great deal of clinical and anecdotal evidence and some convincing experimental demonstrations support the use of these concepts.

Frustration is one consequence of failure to attain one's goals. Frustration has been demonstrated to produce a variety of reactions, including aggression, fixation, regression, and increased motivation. It is not known under what conditions each of these reactions will be exhibited.

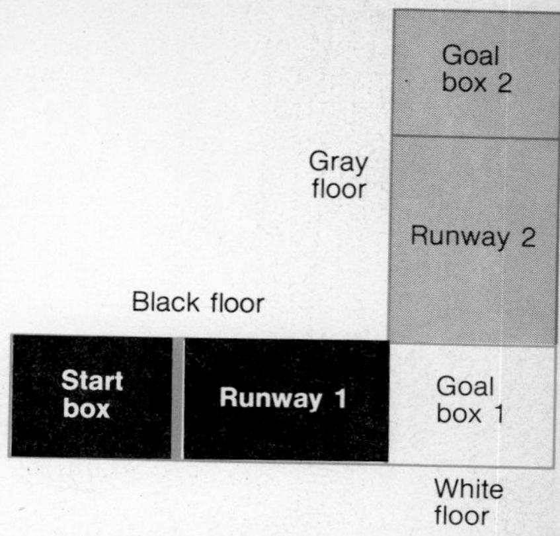

Fig. 15·9 Apparatus for the demonstration of the frustration effect. (From Amsel and Hancock, 1957)

Suggested Readings

Bettelheim, B. 1943. Individual and mass behavior in extreme situations. *Journal of Abnormal and Social Psychology*,38:417–452.

Describes reactions to extreme frustration and stress in a prisoner-of-war camp.

Freud, A. 1967. *The ego and the mechanisms of defense*. Rev. ed. New York: International University Press.

Originally published in 1936, this is a classic discussion of the defense mechanisms by the youngest daughter of Sigmund Freud.

Janis, I. L.; Mahl, G. F.; Kagan, J.; and Holt, R. R. 1969. *Personality*. New York: Harcourt, Brace and World.

A text examining the ramifications of stress, frustration, and conflict with particular case histories.

Lawson, R. 1965. *Frustration*. New York: Macmillan.

Provides an overview and a collection of readings in the study of frustration.

Yates, A. J. 1962. *Frustration and conflict*. London: Methuen.

A critical analysis of theories of frustration and conflict.

Abnormal Behavior

V Abnormal psychology is a subject of keen interest to most people because it touches on many experiences that are part of daily living, and because it seeks to understand the how, the what, and the way of certain feelings and actions. How does anxiety occur? What causes neurosis? Why do people develop ulcers? How do sexual problems arise? Why do some people engage in self-defeating behavior? We are fascinated by abnormal psychology because it deals with us.

Readers who have tried to understand and overcome their own problems in living or who have known people in psychological distress may find this part of the book especially interesting because it describes and inquires into the origins and treatment of our own unusual reactions to the world around and within us. Even the strange and sometimes comical behavior that will be described in Chapter 16 intrigues us because it is often an exaggeration of familiar and normal behavior. Each of us should have little difficulty in recognizing in these pages some of his or her own reactions to the world.

Psychotherapy (Chapter 17) also has a continuity with everyday experience. Most therapies, traditional or radical, institutional or informal, do not rely on esoteric jargon or weird mystiques. They are largely extensions or distillations of common-sense ways of gaining insight, solving problems, increasing awareness, or simply getting more out of life.

Behavior Pathology

16 Humans do not behave always in uniform and predictable ways. This does not mean that there is no rhyme or reason to human behavior or that certain patterns cannot be observed. It does mean that we are exceptional in the diversity (or perversity) of our actions and reactions.

Concepts and Definitions of Abnormality

16•1 Differentiating between normal and abnormal behavior has many practical applications. It may be important to know, for example, how to respond to a family member who is distraught over a seemingly minor matter. It may be necessary to seek professional help for a friend or relative whose thinking and behavior lately have changed in unusual ways; or it may be crucial to consider hospitalization for persons who otherwise might inflict serious injury on themselves or others.

Normality is not easily defined. We shall nevertheless attempt a general definition here by considering three criteria of abnormality: statistical, cultural, and personal.

Statistical Criteria of Abnormality Statistical abnormality is behavior that falls outside the usual or average. Underlying this definition is the assumption that the behavior in question distributes itself symmetrically along the familiar, normal (bell-shaped) curve.

Most biological and psychological traits—for example, height, intelligence, and emotional reactivity—distribute themselves normally in the general population. Since people tend to cluster in the middle of the curve with respect to the behaviors in question, those whose behavior falls to the left or right of this clustering are considered abnormal according to the statistical criterion. However, applying statistics to definitions of abnormality creates certain problems.

First, the statistical definition equates normality with high incidence of a behavior in a population. This is a problem because many undesirable acts (such as violence and bigotry) are normal by this definition. Another problem is where to draw the line between normality and abnormality. Since the selection of this cutoff is usually arbitrary, a person may qualify as normal by one set of standards but abnormal by another. Likewise, shifts in definitions due to changing times, different cultural standards, or even variations in the law from one locale to the next are not taken into account by arbitrarily drawn cutoff points.

Cultural Criteria of Abnormality As we noted above, it is within the societal context that standards of behavioral normality are defined: how to conduct oneself at home and with acquaintances, when to cry and when to laugh, what to wear, how to address certain others, and what is appropriate behavior in various circumstances. In short, society prescribes certain standards of normality, and judges persons abnormal to the degree that they are unable or unwilling to adhere to these standards.

But what if society's prescriptions are faulty or undesirable? The Nazi culture preached racial supremacy and practiced genocide. Did conformity to it constitute normality? In the early seventies, the Watergate mentality condoned lying, cheating, and burglary as a means to a presumed higher end. Similarly, in many criminal subcultures, it is the nonconformist rather than the conformist whose behavior would seem more desirable to most of us.

Furthermore, cultural prescriptions are often irrelevant for certain groups whose history and experience have been radically dissimilar to those of the majority. Black people in America, for example, have found it essential for their survival to develop a profound distrust of whites and of their country. To protect themselves from serious physical and psychological injury, they have had to develop what some psychiatrists have aptly called *cultural paranoia* (Grier and Cobbs, 1968). This form of distrust has become the black norm of appropriate behavior within a hostile environment.

The careless application of cultural criteria can also create problems for innovators. By present cultural standards, for instance, such great historic figures as Moses, Jesus, and Mohammed would, by virtue of their uniqueness and unconventionality, qualify for the label of abnormality, as would Galileo, Lincoln, and Einstein. But it is through the efforts and thinking of such nonconformists, who have dared to chart new courses and defy society's standards, that civilization's greatest achievements have been realized.

Personal Criteria of Abnormality Another criterion of abnormality is personal distress. Most people labeled mentally ill or abnormal are also hurting subjectively. They often have difficulty getting along with those around them. They experience much physical and psychological distress: headaches, nausea, loss of appetite, insomnia, hypochondria, fear of failure, worry, and depression.

Were Jefferson, Lincoln, and Einstein Normal?

This question interested the late Abraham H. Maslow (1970), who preferred to describe mental health rather than mental illness. Maslow embarked on a search for self-actualizing persons, whom he defined as individuals who fully use their talents, skills, and potentialities.

In this search, Maslow studied the lives of persons whom he considered psychologically healthy and self-actualizing, including Jefferson, Lincoln, Einstein, Eleanor Roosevelt, William James, Spinoza, Pablo Casals, Martin Buber, Fritz Kreisler, Adlai Stevenson II, and Martin Luther King, Jr. To him, these persons shared several important attributes: efficient perception of reality and other people; acceptance of self, others, and nature; spontaneity in their thinking and behavior; ability to work within a broad framework of values; detachment from their culture and environment; and a genuine desire to help humankind.

It is difficult to argue about the persons Maslow chose as mentally healthy or about his criteria. However, his investigation relied heavily on the case-study method, which yielded information about a relatively small, select group. Moreover, self-actualization may be out of reach for most persons—as Arnold Buss has commented (1966, p. 3): "If it is a requirement of mental health, then very few persons are mentally healthy. Most segments of society lead a routine life, hemmed in by . . . drudgery of everyday existence. Realizing one's potential requires . . . the motivation and means to break out of . . . the trivial demands of day-to-day living. Few people possess these attributes . . . yet the majority who do not . . . are not maladjusted."

Positive Conceptions of Mental Health

16·2 A common criticism of much psychological theory is that it distorts reality by focusing on the abnormal and pathological. The late Abraham H. Maslow (1954, 1970) tried to correct this imbalance by studying mentally healthy people and attempting to specify the behaviors they had in common. Over the years he collected a great deal of information on the lives and experiences of famous historic and contemporary figures whom he considered healthy, or self-actualized.

Maslow found that these people were able (1) to deal with the world as it is, not as it should be, (2) to accept themselves, others, and nature, and (3) to direct themselves independently of the culture and environment. Furthermore, they experienced more profound interpersonal relations than do most people, had a continuing freshness of appreciation for what went on around them, trusted their own senses and feelings, and were democratic in their attitudes and creative.

Obviously, whatever is said about abnormal behavior is subject to certain reservations, especially in a time of rapidly changing values. We shall try to describe in the following pages the kinds of behavior considered abnormal by most mental health professionals at the time of this writing; it should nevertheless come as no surprise to the reader if many of the concepts and assumptions involved in present models of behavior are swept aside in the next several years by newer insights.

The Neuroses

16·3 A central element of the neuroses is anxiety. Most of us are familiar with a sense of danger or apprehension, in which we experience trembling, a dry mouth, a tremulous voice, profuse sweating, confusion, and sometimes panic. In more extreme instances, urinary and bowel incontinence may result from an overabundance of anxiety. Outwardly, the anxious person seems to be going in several directions at the same time, too confused to settle on a particular course.

According to Freudian, or psychoanalytic, theory, the way one has learned to defend against the anxiety determines the form of the neurosis that develops. In large part this process consists of learning to use one's defenses and it is presumed to be lifelong. The defenses we refer to include **repression** and **displacement,** which we discussed in Chapter 15, as well as **reaction formation, undoing,** and **projection.** All of these are summarized in Table 16·1.

The form of an individual's neurosis, according to most psychoanalytic viewpoints, depends on how he or she defends against anxiety. In the discussion that follows, the neuroses are arranged from least to most successful use of the defenses. Accordingly, we begin our presentation with the anxiety neuroses, in which the person is totally saturated with anxiety.

Anxiety Neurosis Anxiety neurosis occurs when the defenses, especially repression, are functioning inadequately, or not at all. Although no two anxiety attacks are alike, they are generally marked by apprehension and restlessness, and sometimes also by palpitation and sweating, which may be so overwhelming that the individual panics. The panic reaction itself is an intensely frightening experience; it lasts several minutes or more and may recur several times during a day or night.

The current *Diagnostic and Statistical Manual of Mental Disorders* (DSM II)

Table 16·1 Defense Mechanisms Used against Anxiety

TYPE OF DEFENSE	DESCRIPTION
Repression	Unconsciously to deny, ignore, or forget emotionally charged ideas, memories, or desires. Repressed ideas or impulses reappear in various forms, especially when an individual's guard is down.
Displacement	To vent anger and aggression toward a substitute figure (such as a spouse, child, or pet), usually because the original target is too threatening.
Reaction formation	To conceal unacceptable desires and impulses (such as aggression) by behaving in an apparently opposite manner.
Undoing	To perform a ritual over and over in a precise way. If the ritual is not performed correctly, the individual is overwhelmed by anxiety.
Projection	To attribute one's wishes, desires, and impulses to outsiders and thus be rid of them—at least temporarily.

(Adapted from Kleinmuntz, 1974, Table 7·1, p. 159)

To Classify or Not to Classify

The Diagnostic and Statistical Manual of Mental Disorders (DSM II, 1968) is published by the American Psychiatric Association as a guide to psychodiagnosis. It is based on the disease model of mental illness. In this model, persons are said to display behavior *symptoms,* such as depression, anxiety, hallucinations, or delusions; the patterns in which these symptoms cluster are called *syndromes* or diseases; and someone exhibiting a particular pattern is diagnosed as mentally ill. Presumably this psychodiagnosis carries implications about etiology (the origins of the disease), treatment, and prognosis (the course and probable outcome of the disease).

Diagnostic classification of behavior disorders has been criticized on grounds that it stigmatizes people as dangerous and insane (Szasz, 1970) and subjects them against their will to the humiliation of institutionalization. Critics who question whether psychiatric diagnosis is useful for planning treatment have tended to emphasize its unreliability and tenuous relationship to etiology and treatment (Kanfer and Phillips, 1970), as well as its lack of validity (Rosenhan, 1973; Ullmann and Krasner, 1975). Still others assert that the current diagnostic system sensationalizes bizarre behavior and fails to call proper attention to the disorders of everyday life (Millon and Millon, 1974). The severest critics want to throw it out entirely on the grounds that it is irrelevant to understanding the person (Carson, 1969).

It is true that the present state of knowledge does not often permit comprehensive causal or prognostic statements, nor do the diagnostic classifications necessarily carry important treatment implications. Nevertheless, some psychologists defend classification because they believe it has scientific merit (Eysenck, 1960) and that it is needed as a starting point for research into the psychopathologies (Maher, 1970). Others think that the classification scheme may contain much psychological truth that might be overlooked if the scheme were not used (Meehl, 1973). They argue that, rather than decrying and avoiding diagnosis, psychologists should try to improve the classification system because ultimately its use may be justified by yet-to-be-discovered etiological agents and treatment procedures.

Unfortunately, the criticisms will not abate as a result of current work on DSM III (scheduled to be published in 1978). The new version will simply reflect minor shifts in emphasis for current classifications and will classify previously unclassified disorders.

of the American Psychiatric Association (1968) is the classification system we will follow in our discussion. It describes anxiety neurosis as follows (p. 39):

> This neurosis is characterized by anxious overconcern extending to panic and frequently associated with somatic symptoms. Unlike phobic neurosis, anxiety may occur under any circumstances and is not restricted to specific situations or objects. This disorder must be distinguished from normal apprehension or fear, which occurs in realistically dangerous situations.

Case Report 16•1 describes Joseph B.'s symptoms. He used his anxiety attacks, which were almost always precipitated by stressful circumstances such as lecturing before a group or being teased by his fellow workers, to avoid facing his fear of incompetence. His (probably unconscious) reasoning was that as long as he had these attacks he couldn't be held responsible for his poor performance. In other words, his anxiety was a convenient alternative to admitting to himself that he might not pass muster. Ironically, however, in Joseph's case this insanity bit, as he called it, became the occasion for further anxiety.

Case Report 16·1, Anxiety Neurosis

Joseph B., age twenty-six, a laborer at a steel plant, came to a Veterans Administration outpatient clinic because he feared he was losing his mind. Before going into the military he had been having what he called panic attacks, in which he would become dizzy and weak, and then completely immobile. During his two years of army duty he frequently experienced these attacks.

Following his military service, he accepted a laborer's job at the steel mill, and while acknowledging that he was not intellectually challenged by the work, he explained that he would attend college and then seek other employment as soon as he overcame his "insanity bit." However, he found even that job too challenging and he frequently complained that his co-workers teased and harassed him.

One day, while being ridiculed by some of his associates during lunch break, he had his first real anxiety attack at work. He reported that something seemed to snap in his ears, after which everything sounded louder than usual. He held his hands over his ears until he fell to the ground. This anxiety attack lasted about 60 seconds, but thereafter he had a constant fear of a recurrence. He sought help because he was afraid he was losing his mind.

Psychotherapy, conducted twice a week for about six months, disclosed that although his anxiety was of long duration, the immediate precipitants of his military and post-service attacks were related to his marriage before entering the army. His wife was a vivacious young woman who, in sharp contrast to John, was self-confident and outgoing. Therapy was geared to helping him understand the relationship between his anxiety and his lack of self-confidence as a lover, provider, and person. He had to learn also that his apprehension about future attacks was very much related to their actual occurrence. (Adapted from Kleinmuntz, 1974, p. 164)

Anxiety appears on this woman's face, although the situation—she is leaving a circus performance—scarcely seems to warrant such a look of uneasiness. (David Powers, Jeroboam)

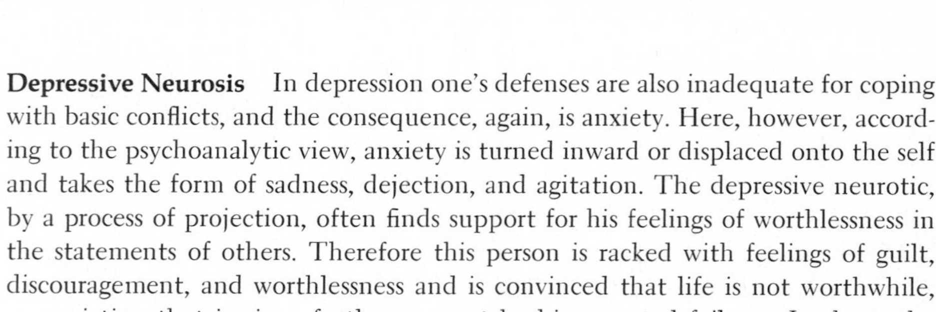

Depressive Neurosis In depression one's defenses are also inadequate for coping with basic conflicts, and the consequence, again, is anxiety. Here, however, according to the psychoanalytic view, anxiety is turned inward or displaced onto the self and takes the form of sadness, dejection, and agitation. The depressive neurotic, by a process of projection, often finds support for his feelings of worthlessness in the statements of others. Therefore this person is racked with feelings of guilt, discouragement, and worthlessness and is convinced that life is not worthwhile, a conviction that is given further support by his repeated failures. In short, the depressive neurotic leads an inert and unhappy existence.

Just as in psychotic depression, which it resembles—except that neurotic depression lacks hallucinations and delusions—the neurotic's depression seems to occur without any identifiable reason, but it is frequently precipitated by a tangible event, such as loss of a job or the death of a close friend or relative. Compared

Depression as Learned Helplessness

In drawing a parallel between clinical depression and helplessness learned in a laboratory, Seligman (1975) suggests that the cause of depression in people is the belief that action is futile. Like an animal or human laboratory subject who learns that outcomes are uncontrollable, depressed people believe that they cannot control those elements of their lives that soothe, gratify, or nurture —in short, depressed people believe they are helpless. Thus, job failure or incompetence at school means that a person's efforts have been in vain, that his responses have failed to achieve valued outcomes; rejection by a loved one means that the person can no longer control this significant source of gratification and support; and physical disease and growing old are equivalent to discovering that one's own responses are ineffective and he or she may be thrown upon the care of others.

Some cases of depression may arise from cultural limitations that make persons feel helpless. (Lyn Gardiner, Stock, Boston)

with the normal person's reaction to these losses, the neurotic's reaction is more than just ordinary grief. His or her feelings of abandonment and hopelessness are out of proportion to the importance of the event.

Obsessive-Compulsive Neurosis *Obsessions* consist of persistent and repetitive intrusions of unwanted thoughts; *compulsions* are either urges or the carrying out of actions or rituals. In many respects the neurotic's obsessive symptoms resemble the unwanted thoughts that most people experience: the irritating TV commercial or jingle that persists in spite of efforts to banish it from memory; the gnawing uncertainty about whether the gas was turned off before leaving home; or the concerned preoccupation with minor details. Compulsive behaviors also plague most people: fussy tidiness; excessive attention to inconsequential matters; or fastidious dress of oneself and one's children. But for most people, these symptoms are transitory and temporary. For the neurotic, they are a constant part of existence, and he or she is persistently burdened with unwanted thoughts and urges.

Paradoxically, if it were not for these symptoms, this person would—according to theory—be extremely anxious anyway because of being forced to confront the real problems he or she is trying to avoid. Yet the intrusion of unacceptable thoughts and the urge to perform undesirable actions makes the obsessive-compulsive neurotic anxious nonetheless. He or she abhors some of the thoughts and is repulsed by some of the urges, but is more often simply annoyed by the silliness of these thoughts and rituals.

Phobic Neurosis In discussing anxiety neurosis, we noted that apprehension seems to be free floating in the sense that it is not attached to, or apparently associated with, any event or object. This is less true in the obsessive-compulsive neuroses, where anxiety does occur, usually because the person is upset over the unacceptable thoughts, impulses, and actions. In the phobic neuroses, anxiety is very much attached to events or objects, so much so that the individual becomes totally preoccupied with avoiding situations that bring him or her into contact with the feared objects.

Although the subjective experiences are similar to those of anxiety neurotics, the phobic's tremulousness, perspiration, nausea, and even panic are associated

Case Report 16·2, Phobic Neurosis

For several months before coming to the student mental health center, Ronald H., an eighteen-year-old freshman at a midwestern university, felt panic whenever he left his dormitory room for his classes. "It would get so bad at times," he told his freshman adviser, "that I thought I would collapse on the way to class. It was frightening and I was afraid to leave the dorm." If he remained in his own room, or not too far from it, however, he felt reasonably comfortable.

It became apparent during the interviews with Ronald that he had experienced similar fear reactions, although not as intensely, since about age thirteen. He also reported other fears, such as becoming contaminated by syphilis and growing prematurely bald. Both of these fears were sufficiently intense and persistent to cause him to compulsively scrub his hands, genitals, and head until these parts became red, and sometimes even bled.

Ronald understood that his fears were unfounded and exaggerated. Sometimes, during the interviews, he could even laugh at his own behavior, but he also felt that many of his precautions and constant worry were necessary to avoid even greater mental anguish and discomfort.

Ronald's history indicated that since he was eight years old he had tended to avoid playing or competing with other children in the neighborhood. Often he chose not to play with them because he could not run as fast or hit a ball as far as they could. His mother strongly rewarded this behavior because she was convinced he would get hurt if he participated in any "rough-housing."

Some years later, at about the age when most boys have reached puberty, Ronald was sent to summer camp against his wishes. This experience was traumatic for him. At camp he began to have serious doubts about his completeness as a boy because, compared to the other boys, he was sexually underdeveloped. He worried a great deal about this and wondered whether he was destined to become a girl. He also had fears that the other boys might attack him sexually.

Although puberty did make a belated appearance and he understood that such things could happen, he continued to worry about his masculinity. He sometimes fantasized that he was a girl and this made him extremely anxious. He seriously considered suicide rather than face the possibility of a future as a homosexual. (Adapted from Kleinmuntz, 1974, p. 168)

with such objects or situations as open spaces (*agoraphobia*), closed spaces (*claustrophobia*), eating in public places, heights (*acrophobia*), airplanes, and germs, to name just a few. The experiences are all alike: an intense and overwhelming fear, which the individual recognizes as irrational ("But why should I be afraid of a mouse?" or "I used to be able to swim; how can I possibly be so frightened of water?") but over which he or she seems to have little or no control.

According to psychoanalytic theory, the phobic neurotic's main defense mechanism is *displacement*, by means of which he or she is able to disconnect the relationship between the actual problem in his or her life and the object that has become symbolic of that conflict. The use of this defense is illustrated in Case Report 16•2, in which Ronald H. was fearful of leaving his dormitory. Although this manifest fear seemed to be his major preoccupation, his phobia may have signified his unwillingness to place himself in a situation in which he might meet someone, male or female, who would make sexual advances toward him. Of course, the precise symbolic meaning of any phobia depends on the individual's earlier experiences and family interactive patterns.

Hypochondriacal Neurosis The hypochondriac's main preoccupation is with presumed diseases, either currently being suffered or about to be contracted. This concern with somatic problems is so intense and so circumscribed that the hypochondriac typically suffers little anxiety about matters not related to his or her organs or health. He or she complains vaguely of multiple aches and pains, or reports localized symptoms such as an aching back, bloated stomach, or pains in the chest radiating down the arms.

A hypochondriac cannot easily be engaged in conversation about anything except his or her somatic functioning. A casual "Hello, how are you?" becomes the occasion for an interminable listing of symptoms. After a doctor has given the hypochondriac a clean bill of health, he or she may be reassured for a while, but soon becomes concerned about the physician's credentials or diagnostic acumen, and shops around to find a sympathetic medical ear.

The Hysterias

16•4 We shall next consider two separate hysterical entities—conversion and dissociative hysteria. **Conversion hysteria** is characterized by sensory and perceptual symptoms that have no traceable somatic or neuronal causes. Thus, someone may have a "glove" paralysis in which he or she feels no pain or has no sense of touch in the area of the hand covered by a glove. There is no organic disorder that can easily cause this form of paralysis; therefore it is apparent that the paralysis is not due to physical causes such as nerve damage. Other sensory and perceptual symptoms include excessive sensitivity (*hyperesthesia*), reduced sensitivity (*hypoesthesia*), the feeling of pins and needles (*paresthesia*), loss of feeling and sensation in one side of the body (*hemianesthesia*), deafness, tunnel vision, and blindness.

Motor symptoms may also be present in conversion hysteria. These include tremors, especially of the hands; tics and twitching; cramps of the voluntary muscles, such as writer's cramp; *aphonia*, or the inability to talk above a whisper; and a feeling of having a lump in the throat. More serious conversion symptoms, at least in terms of their ability to incapacitate, are *hyperplegia* in which the individual is paralyzed on one side of the body and *paraplegia* in which the individual is paralyzed from the waist down.

Dissociative hysteria, as the name indicates, is characterized by a disunity between one part of the individual's personality and another. We shall discuss three major types of dissociation: somnambulism, amnesia, and multiple personality.

In *somnambulism*, or sleepwalking, a person spontaneously gets out of bed and performs various acts, such as leaving the house and going for a short walk, almost as if searching for something specific. On command from an authoritative voice, the sleepwalker will stop what he or she is doing; or he or she may return to bed spontaneously. If questioned closely without being awakened, the person may mumble something that is related to an anticipated or actual anxiety-arousing event.

Amnesia, or loss of memory, is another of the dissociative hysterias. It is defined as the forgetting of one's name, address, or family affiliation, or all of these. In some instances, the complete past is forgotten, although memory for recent events remains intact. Amnesia may last for several minutes or for a month or more.

Massive amnesia, in which an individual's symptoms blot out several unpleasant memories and experiences, is most dramatically manifested in *multiple personality*, the dissociative hysteria in which two or more separate and markedly different

Two of the three faces of Eve, who suffered from a form of dissociative hysteria known as multiple personality. (20th Century Fox)

personalities coexist in the same individual. The most celebrated fictional example of multiple personality is Dr. Jekyll and Mr. Hyde. In one of the earliest scientific descriptions of the disorder, Morton Prince described the case of Miss Beauchamp, a woman he treated, in *Dissociation of a Personality* (1906). More recently, *The Three Faces of Eve* caught the public's fancy as a book (Thigpen and Cleckley, 1954, 1957; Lancaster, 1958) and then a movie.

Like somnambulism and amnesia, multiple personality is an escape reaction from stress or unhappiness. The separate personalities can be quite different from one another, each having its own memories and histories as well as its own identity. Although living in the same household, they may not know of one another's existence. These unique identities protect the individual from confronting some unhappy reality.

Psychophysiological Disorders

16•5 Psychophysiological disorders are described in DSM II (APA, 1968), as follows:

> This group of disorders is characterized by physical symptoms that are caused by emotional factors and involve a single organ system, usually under **autonomic nervous system** innervation. The physiological changes involved are those that normally accompany certain emotional states, but in these disorders the changes are more intense and sustained. The individual may not be consciously aware of this emotional state.

We can clarify this definition by differentiating between psychophysiological symptoms and those of conversion hysteria. Whereas the latter involve peripheral areas (head, limbs, fingers, toes), psychophysiological symptoms affect—among other regions—the organs and tissues of the viscera (heart, stomach, intestines). The physical damage inflicted by the two kinds of ailment also differs. In the psychophysiological disorders there is identifiable organ destruction that may threaten life; in the conversion hysterias, organ involvement and structural changes are minimal and are rarely dangerous.

The many symptoms and disorders that are called psychophysiological are due to the experience of intense and persistent emotional stress that seriously affects various organs and tissues of the body. Sometimes these organic and tissue changes cause irreparable, life-threatening damage. We will limit our discussion to some of the psychophysiological disorders—affecting the skin, the musculature, and the stomach. It must be remembered, however, that not all cases of hives, back pains, stomachaches, and the like are necessarily psychophysiological disorders.

Skin Disorders Among the skin disorders commonly seen are neurodermatitis (eczema) and urticaria (hives). These disorders are psychophysiological in that emotional states cause or aggravate them and they cease or improve with psychotherapy, behavior modification, or hypnosis.

Neurodermatitis is an inflammation of the skin characterized by itching and edema. Often it resembles poison ivy because scratching of the small blisters leads to an oozing sore. If the condition becomes chronic, the skin takes on a thick or horny appearance. Whether its causes are allergic or emotional is still highly controversial. The evidence for its possible allergic origins stems from the observation that it appears in infants in the first several months of life, reaching its height around the ninth month and disappearing in about the second year. As its name seems to imply, its "neuro" or nervous origin is based on evidence of its frequent eruption at times of emotional strain and disappearance under relaxed conditions.

The symptoms of *urticaria* include inflamed blotches over various portions of the body, often accompanied by severe itching. The eruption of these blotches is sudden and general, each lesion lasting a few hours and being succeeded by new ones in other places. The association of some hives with emotional factors has been noted for many years (Deutsch and Nadell, 1946; Saul and Bernstein, 1941), and some psychoanalytically oriented clinicians believe there is a correspondence between them and suppressed weeping. When frustration is followed by weeping, hives presumably do not appear, but they do occur when weeping is inhibited or is not possible for other reasons. This has also been demonstrated in experiments (Kepecs and Robin, 1950), where negative correlations were noted between skin fluid secretion and weeping. The usual experimental procedure is to apply cantharides, a skin irritant that causes a blister. Eight hours later, the experimenter removes the blister top leaving a red oozing surface. The quantity of fluid that accumulates on this surface in one minute is then determined by blotting the surface dry with a previously weighed blotting paper. After a baseline of fluid accumulation is established by observing the subject in a relaxed state, the person is hypnotized and instructed to express various emotions with and without the opportunity to weep.

Musculoskeletal Disorders The most common tension-produced musculoskeletal disorder is a pain in the small of the back, or low back pain. Several stress-interview studies have demonstrated that sustained contraction of the skeletal muscles, such as occurs under emotional strain, plays an important role in the genesis of such backaches. In one of these studies (Holmes and Wolff, 1950), sixty-five patients with backaches were compared with nonbackache patients in situations that threatened their security and engendered apprehension, conflict, and anxiety (all of which were provoked by having an interviewer touch on previously determined sensitive and conflictive topics). Backache patients displayed a significantly greater muscular activity than nonbackache patients, as measured by a muscle-action-potential recorder.

Gastrointestinal Disorders Although the complex cause-and-effect relationships between emotion and gastric disturbances are still not well understood, clinicians have for some time recognized their close ties. Beaumont's direct viewing of digestive changes in men under stress (1833), Pavlov's classic demonstration (1927) of the influence of psychological factors on gastric secretion, and Cannon's classic report (1929) of the influence of emotion on gastric functions are instances of these early observations. More recently, Wolf's (1965), and Wolf and Goodell's studies (1968) on human gastric functions, Alexander's psychoanalytic studies (1950) of patients with ulcers, and Mahl's findings (1953) of increased gastric secretions among students during final examinations have provided additional evidence of the complex interaction of emotion and changes in the digestive system. We shall review one set of animal studies that are particularly suggestive of the way ulcers may form in humans. These are the studies of Brady and his associates (1958) on "executive" monkeys.

In these studies, monkeys were harnessed in restraining chairs so that they could move their hands and limbs but not their bodies. They were then given a series of shocks that might be avoided by pressing a lever every twenty seconds. If a period of twenty seconds elapsed without lever pressing, shock was delivered to their feet.

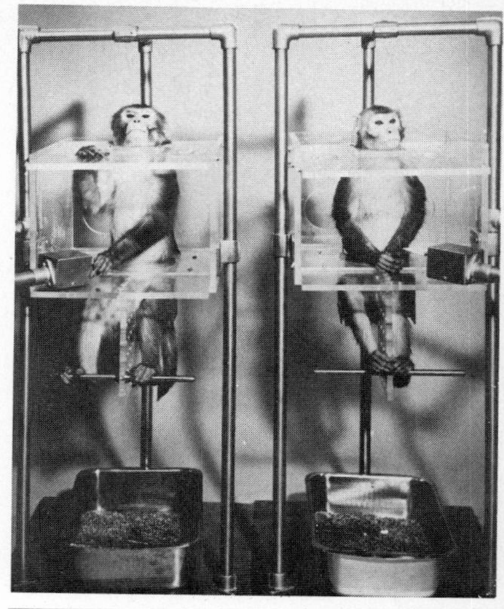

Fig. 16·1 An experimental monkey (left) and a control monkey were restrained in "yoked chairs." Both animals received shocks, but only the experimental, or executive, monkey could press the lever to avoid the shock. (Courtesy Joseph V. Brady; U.S. Army photograph)

This procedure produced ulcers, but it was not clear that the electric shock was the major factor involved. The researchers hypothesized that electric shock was a necessary but not sufficient condition for producing ulcers. To test this hypothesis experimentally, the investigators placed two monkeys in "yoked chairs," as shown in Figure 16·1. Both animals received shocks, but only one could prevent them. The experimental, or executive, monkey as it came to be called, could prevent shocks to itself and to its partner (the control) by working a lever. In this way the number of shocks was the same for both animals, but the executive monkey was also subjected to whatever additional psychological stresses were involved in having to press the lever. The executives developed ulcers while the controls did not.

What factor, then, was responsible for the ulcers? At one point, the experimenters believed that the social interaction between the monkeys was the important variable. To test this possibility the researchers subsequently used soundproofed isolation booths to house each of the restrained animals; once again the executive monkeys developed ulcers. Therefore, they reasoned, something other than social interaction must be the independent variable.

The experimenters then tried increasing the amount of stress on the animals, and they put several monkeys on an eight-hours-on, six-hours-off schedule. After many weeks of this schedule, no gastrointestinal abnormalities were found in these animals even in postmortem examinations. A more strenuous schedule of thirty-minutes-on, thirty-minutes-off also failed to produce ulcers. Then the experimenters stumbled on a "successful" schedule: six hours of rest alternated with six hours of avoidance or shock behavior.

When it became clear that this schedule caused the greatest gastrointestinal destruction, the investigators began to sample the stomach contents and measure the gastric secretions of the animals under various periods of avoidance responding. The results indicated that a one-hour session had no effect on secretion, but that there was a considerable rise in acidity after a three-hour session and an even greater rise after a six-hour session. The most crucial finding was that acid increase occurred at the end of avoidance sessions, reaching a peak several hours later when the animal was resting. These results led them to conclude that emotional stress, if it is to produce ulcers, must be intermittent and have the effect of turning the animal's system on and off.

Subsequent studies, however, have suggested that the way the monkeys were assigned to the executive and control groups may have introduced an extraneous element into the experimental design. All eight monkeys were originally placed on the executive schedule. The first four to start pressing the bar became the executives; the last four became the yoked subjects. It has since been noted in studies using rats, that the more emotional an animal is, the sooner it begins to press the bar when it is shocked (Sines, et al., 1963). This suggests rather strongly that the four most emotional animals became the executives, and the four most phlegmatic or unresponsive became the yoked subjects (Seligman, 1975).

Several studies were conducted by J. M. Weiss (1968, 1970, 1971), who randomly assigned three groups of rats to conditions in which they could and could not control the shocks. These studies showed that the executive animals got fewer and less severe ulcers than the yoked animals. Also the latter lost more weight, defecated more, and drank less than the animals who could control their environments. In other words, the more helpless animals were the more distressed ones. Moreover, Weiss's studies also indicated that the ulceration differences apparently caused by controllability may actually reflect differences in predictability: When an animal engages in an activity to avoid shock, the feedback from bar-pressing predicts safety; the yoked animal cannot control shock, and therefore has no prediction of safety (Seligman, 1975).

The Psychoses

16•6 Psychotic people are considerably more disturbed than either the neurotic or the psychophysiologically ill. Their thinking, actions, and total personalities are more disorganized, and they are less likely to function at home or on the job. In many respects psychotic behavior meets popular expectations of insanity or craziness. Gestures may be bizarre, posture awkward, and speech different, sometimes consisting of words coined at the moment, and their perception of reality is often grossly distorted. The self-perceptions of some psychotics are grandiose, others believe they are being plotted against, and many live in a fantasy world.

DSM II (APA, 1968) lists many types of psychoses: **manic-depressive** illnesses, **paranoid** states, **depression,** and the **schizophrenias.** Only one of these types will be discussed here—the schizophrenias, which are the most frequently seen psychoses. The main difference between the psychoses and the disorders discussed earlier are shown in Table 16•2.

The most recent classification of the American Psychiatric Association lists eleven categories of schizophrenia (simple, hebephrenic, catatonic, paranoid, acute

Table 16·2 Neurotics and Psychophysiologically Ill Compared with Psychotics

ITEM FOR COMPARISON	NEUROTIC OR PSYCHOPHYSIOLOGICALLY ILL	PSYCHOTIC
Attitude toward own illness	Often talks about own symptoms and about former healthiness. Anticipates return to normal self.	Often denies that there is anything wrong and tends to accept own illness as inevitable. Defends own behavior if someone calls attention to it.
Contact with reality	Does not lose contact with reality. If reality testing is at all impaired, it is in the direction of overactivity.	Has lost contact with reality or has tenuous contact with it and substitutes fantasies for it.
Orientation for person, place, and time	Intact	Poor or entirely gone.
Effect of illness on self and others	Complains about falling apart but rarely does so. Continues to function socially and on the job.	Total personality may be disorganized, and lifestyle chaotic. May harm self or others; therefore may require close care or hospitalization.
Prognosis for recovery	Favorable	Sometimes recovery is spontaneous, but usually cures of particular symptoms or behavior are only temporary.

(Adapted from Kleinmuntz, 1974. Table 9·1, p. 227)

schizophrenic episode, latent, residual, schizo-affective, childhood, chronic undifferentiated, and other) and describes their common characteristics—disturbances of thinking, mood, and behavior. The thinking of psychotics, according to DSM II, consists of misinterpretation of reality and difficulties in concept formation. Their mood changes are marked by ambivalence, inappropriate moods, and lack of empathy for others. They may also be withdrawn and behave erratically.

From among the many categories of schizophrenia, we shall discuss the four most frequently seen and differentiated in hospitals: simple, hebephrenic, catatonic, and paranoid. Although the nature and intensity of the symptoms vary from one form of schizophrenia to another, and one patient may have a variety of symptoms, most schizophrenic persons exhibit illogical thinking, bizarre behavior, and withdrawal. The delusions of persecution that many schizophrenics have do not focus on any one person or group: Today's friend may become tomorrow's enemy. These symptoms appear at any age, but they usually appear between the ages of fifteen and twenty-five years. The condition tends to persist, with fluctuations, throughout the person's life.

Simple Schizophrenia This condition develops slowly and insidiously, usually beginning during adolescence. It involves reduction of external attachments and interests, apathy and indifference, a deterioration of interpersonal relations, lower levels of mental functioning, and a lesser ability to cope and function than the individual was capable of before its onset. It is the least dramatic of the four types.

The simple schizophrenic wants to be alone and, in this quest for seclusion, may wander off to strange places, spend nights sleeping in parks or abandoned houses, or even sit in one place for hours. Such behavior becomes especially noticeable if the prepsychotic person was capable of more purposeful activities. When questioned about his or her aimless wandering, or lack of ambition, the person is likely to be vague, evasive, and even perplexed about the condition.

Hallucinations and Delusions

The main symptoms that characterize the psychoses are hallucinations (experiencing things that are not real) and delusions (false but persistent beliefs). The most commonly observed hallucinations and delusions are summarized here, along with their definitions and some examples.

Hallucinations

Auditory Hearing sounds or voices that do not exist. Often the voices are derogatory ("You're an idiot") and instruct the person to perform unwanted acts ("Cut off your left ear").

Visual Seeing nonexistent things, often of a comical sort ("I see a monkey on your shoulder scratching your nose").

Olfactory Smelling odors, frequently offensive and used as proof of a delusion such as persecution ("I smell the unnatural gases that will kill me").

Gustatory Tasting things. Again these may be used to verify a delusion of persecution ("I taste the poison you placed in my food").

Moon man selling moon plots—a delusion of grandeur? (Thelma Shumsky, Jeroboam)

Tactile Sensing crawling creatures or growing things on one's skin. ("Bugs are devouring my outer layer of skin"). These often have a sexual significance for the person ("He fondled my genitals").

Delusions

Persecution The belief that a person or that person's agent is trying to destroy the individual ("This morning I received a signal on the radio that I am to take special heed —my life's in danger").

Grandeur The idea that the individual has been specially appointed to carry out an important mission ("I am speaking to you on behalf of God, whose will I am here to broadcast").

Guilt The conviction that the person is worthless ("I can't stand myself any more"), or has committed an offense ("Arrest me for that crime, I confess it all").

Reference The persistent notion that the individual is the center of attention ("When I got on the bus, all eyes turned on me").

Depersonalization The conviction that one is turning into an inanimate or vegetative object ("My stomach is slowly turning to stone and I am the only witness to the event").

Relatives, especially members of the immediate family, realize that something is wrong when the person does not live up to expectations based on earlier accomplishments. Hallucinations, although rare, are auditory and manifest themselves as a buzzing or ringing in the ears. Delusions are absent. Consequently, these patients are sometimes misclassified as mental retardates, and frequently it is only after brain damage has been ruled out by psychological tests and other examinations that the diagnosis of simple schizophrenia is made.

Hebephrenic Schizophrenia The distinguishing features of the hebephrenic are impulsivity, sudden spontaneous laughing and crying, grotesque grimacing, and silly grinning. Hallucinations are often pornographic ("two cats screwing on your writing pad, Doc"), and delusional thinking is fragmented and inconsistent from one moment to the next. The following transcript, taken during administration of the Wechsler Adult Intelligence Scale to a forty-year-old woman, illustrates a predominantly hebephrenic mood:

EXAMINER *What are the colors in the American flag?*

PATIENT *Well, I think they are red. Let's see now, oh yes, they're quite red, red, red, red.*

EXAMINER *How many months are there in a year?*

PATIENT *Some years have many* (crying) *and some have more. There aren't many more, are there?*

EXAMINER *Why do we wash clothes?*

PATIENT *That's a communist conspiracy.* (Laughs, and then sings some verse she composed.) *The communist powers have perverted our minds with mindless sexism that subverts the sexless mindlessness that sucks the soul.* (Patient doubles up with laughter.)

EXAMINER *Okay, but can you tell me why we wash clothes?*

PATIENT *We don't wash clothes no more.*

EXAMINER *Now, let us try these. How much is four dollars and five dollars?*

PATIENT *Now I remember. . . . Let's see now, well, I had this friend who borrowed, flowered, and sorrowed till she could pay no more, and then she up and died, penniless as a pauper, get it?*

Catatonic Schizophrenia The catatonic patient displays, in addition to some of the other symptoms of schizophrenia, a fluctuation of affect that includes depression, stupor, and excitement. The excitement may occur after long periods of apathy during which the patient may be mute, refuse to eat, be totally unresponsive to surroundings, be incontinent or totally retentive, and maintain one posture for hours or days. At such times, others may have to feed the patient, sometimes intravenously, and attend to his or her physical needs.

Catatonics resemble deeply depressed patients. A distinguishing diagnostic feature, however, is waxy flexibility, which allows them to maintain postures, no matter how uncomfortable. Their experiences are vivid during these periods; after emerging from them, they frequently tell of hearing and experiencing things but being unable to respond because they were convinced that talking would cause something catastrophic to occur.

During the catatonic excitement episode that often follows stupor, the patient is agitated and hyperactive, flails wildly at anyone within range, talks excitedly and incoherently, and may assault someone or mutilate himself or herself severely. Typically such a patient may later report having been completely under the command of "voices" or of having been divinely inspired. Neither the stuporous nor the excited stages are as common now as they were before the advent of the major tranquilizing drugs. The downtrend has been dramatic.

Paranoid Schizophrenia Of all the schizophrenias, the paranoid type is the most common, although some decrease in their incidence has recently been re-

Paranoid schizophrenia can sometimes lead to violent acts. Charles Manson was convicted in 1971 for his part in the 1969 murders of seven people. He apparently suffered from delusions of grandeur (believing that he was both Christ and Satan) and was able to command a group of followers, who were to carry out his scheme (called helter skelter) to start a race war. (Wide World Photos)

ported (Coleman, 1976). This disorder is characterized chiefly by auditory hallucinations and delusions of persecution. Often delusions of grandeur and an excessive religiosity are also evident. The patient's attitude is usually hostile and aggressive, and behavior tends to be consistent with this animosity. DSM II (APA, 1968) differentiates three subtypes of this disorder, depending on the predominant symptoms: hostile, grandiose, or hallucinatory.

The onset of the disorder is usually marked by the moodiness, preoccupation, and suspiciousness characteristic of simple schizophrenia. Gradually, the person's lifestyle becomes more and more chaotic. The person withdraws from social contacts, gives up or loses his job, gets into constant battles with others, accuses others of plotting against him or her, refuses to eat outside the home, questions the contents of food prepared at home, becomes abusive, and assaults others.

In the more advanced stages of paranoid schizophrenia, the person may be frightened of and even attack family members, convinced that they are conspiring against him or her. Speech may be voluble and hoarse because of excited shouting; the person may make strange gestures or utter magical phrases ("bandy-mandy") that have only personal significance. At this active stage of the disorder it is difficult to be in the schizophrenic's presence without becoming a target of delusional thinking: if grandiose, the person may expect to be treated in a manner appropriate to the particular role chosen; if persecuted, the person accuses almost everyone of plotting against him or her.

The following dialogue between a sixty-year-old paranoid schizophrenic man in a state hospital and a clinical psychologist captures the tenor of this form of thinking and behaving:

DOCTOR *Can I get you to join the group therapy session this afternoon? You know, Herbert, you're the only holdout from among the guys on your ward.*

PATIENT *So be it, Doc, so be it. You're not gonna get me in on one of those crazy groups. I got enough troubles keeping away from those guys as is.*

DOCTOR *Why do you want to do that?*

PATIENT *They're fixing to get rid of me.*

DOCTOR *How do you know that?*

PATIENT *Why didn't you see David looking at me funny-like when he passed here before? And you know, they're all spying on me again—through the mirrors that they put around my room at night. Do you like my shave?*

DOCTOR *Your shave?*

PATIENT *Yeah, my shave. That crazy guy came around last night and pasted hair all over my body again. I'll get it off. He's got one of them hair-pasting dingos.*

DOCTOR *Do you think that if you joined the group, maybe that would stop?*

PATIENT *What are you talking about? He'd never tell me it was him. He wouldn't even look at me—they're all in on it.*

DOCTOR *What about Jack? You seem to get along OK with him. He's in the group.*

PATIENT *Jack! He's the worst of the lot.*

DOCTOR *I'd really like to help you get out of here. You've been here more than fifteen years. We've got this resocialization program . . . .*

PATIENT *Oh, I'll get out. Don't you worry. I'll escape out of this crazy place.*

DOCTOR *But you don't have to escape. I can help you get out.*

PATIENT *What? And get on the outside where they can really foul me up? No sir, not me. Besides you need a cure so badly by your method that you want to use me. I'm not gonna be your first cure. No sir, I'll do it my own way.*

This patient has delusions of persecution that include the doctor and several imaginary and real people who spy on him and who cover his body with hair. Because he believes that others are out to get rid of him, he does not participate in some group activities and he finds great significance in other people's gestures and looks. Although he does talk about leaving the hospital, he is ambivalent about the prospects because of his fear of what may happen to him on the outside. At the same time, his delusional thinking is an integrating part of his personality because it allows him to focus on one or two aspects of his environment rather than to show concern about a host of problems.

Note that the kind of "crazy talk" quoted here and on p. 515 is not as random or meaningless as it may seem. The patient is communicating, albeit in an elaborately coded message, significant information about his experience.

Disorders of Childhood and Adolescence

16•7 Childhood and adolescent disorders, unlike those already discussed, are not easily classified for several reasons: children's symptoms do not cluster cohesively, their significance for the overall developed personality is not yet clear, and the criteria of abnormality vary according to the child's stage of development. Bedwetting, for example, is always abnormal for adults but is not considered such for children until they reach a certain age. Behaviors such as tantrums and thumbsucking can be normal or abnormal depending on age.

Childhood Problems We shall discuss childhood disorders that involve disturbances of feeding and eating, disturbances of eliminations, aggression, and withdrawal.

Disturbances of Feeding and Eating The infant's first reflex response is getting food at the mother's breast or from a bottle. This is also the earliest complex social experience, or interaction with another person. From this experience, according to Mussen, Conger, and Kagan (1974), the infant learns two things: first,

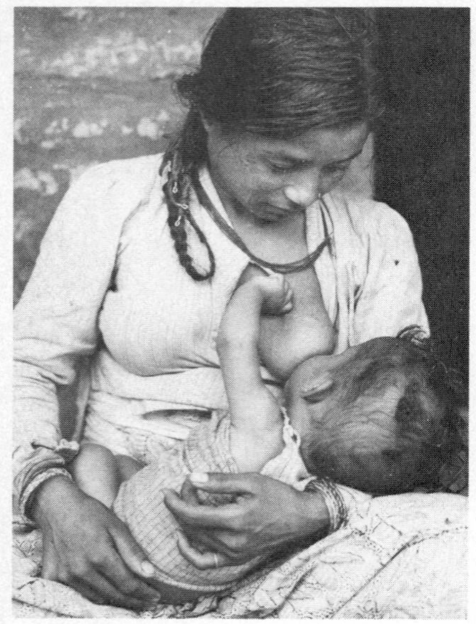

Pathological behavior in children can sometimes develop over problems with feeding or with toilet training. (UNICEF Photo; Eva Demjen, Stock, Boston)

to associate pleasant and comfortable sensations with the visual, tactile, vocal, and auditory stimuli of the mother; and second, to babble, smile, cling, and make body adjustments in response to the person holding him or her. These are important lessons.

If no major difficulties directly associated with feeding crop up, the infant's first trauma occurs when he or she is separated from the mother's (or caretaker's) close contact while being fed. This separation, usually called weaning, corresponds to the time when sucking is relinquished and a new mode of getting food is adopted, which, according to Sears, Maccoby, and Levin (1957, p. 69), "denotes the end of a way of life. The old habits must be replaced by the new; loving nurturance is no longer the inevitable accompaniment of eating; the suckling becomes a child." Weaning usually occurs between the ages of eight and fourteen months, and it is at this time that problems associated with eating become apparent. The infant may be reluctant to relinquish the breast or bottle, may cling to the mother, and may refuse to learn to feed himself or herself. These problems, which become more pronounced with time, manifest themselves in various ways, including refusing food.

There are at least two ways to refuse food. The first and far more frequent way is by dawdling: the child takes two or three bites, holding each one in the mouth for long periods of time without attempting to chew or swallow. This child may not be hungry, may be too busy to eat, may be trying to hold the attention of assembled parents and siblings, or may be trying to avoid what invariably follows the meal—naptime, bedtime, cleaning up, or having to sit on the toilet.

The other form of food refusal, somewhat more serious, is vomiting. Provided that the child is not physically ill, he or she has probably learned that this behavior makes the parents anxious. At first, vomiting may occur accidentally as a consequence of crying or gagging after being forced to eat; but the child notices that this behavior causes parental concern and anxiety and learns to produce it almost at will in order to make the parents anxious or to attract attention.

Problems of Elimination The reflexes to rid oneself of waste matter must be trained. As with feeding, toilet training involves significant social interaction between parent and child, and offers much potential for pathology. Like weaning, toilet training demands that the child change from infantile ways of meeting natural needs to ways that are approved by adults.

The two most clear-cut failures to learn proper forms of elimination are *enuresis* (bedwetting) and *encopresis* (soiling). Enuresis is usually psychogenic, the child failing to learn to control daytime and nighttime urination. Nighttime control is the more difficult to learn because sleep interferes with and blurs the none-too-distinct internal signals that the child must notice in order to exercise sphincter control (Sears, Maccoby, and Levin, 1957). Since enuresis can result from physical malfunctioning, enuretic children are usually examined by physicians to rule out this possibility.

Many psychological factors have been implicated in enuresis. For example, there are cases that result because overtolerant parents were indifferent to bedwetting, never really emphasizing to the child the appropriateness of retaining urine at night; and other cases have been traced to the parents' reassuring the child that the condition is caused by a weak bladder inherited from forebears who had a similar problem. Under these circumstances the child, either as a result of neglect or to uphold the family tradition, may be enuretic for years. There are even some cases reported of males who were inducted into the armed forces and discovered only then that bedwetting was not an acceptable practice.

Enuresis is particularly common among children who must deal with the arrival of a new sibling, separation from family or loved ones, placement in a new home, or a family move to new surroundings. In these cases, the enuresis is almost always accompanied by other signs of emotional upset such as shyness and anxiety; it is short-lived and tends to disappear when the emotional upset subsides.

The most difficult form of nocturnal enuresis to treat is the type that occurs in adults during periods of ordinary stress. Typically these adults have a history of occasional wetting since childhood, and it is associated with daytime anxieties and pressures. Case Report 16•3 illustrates this type.

Encopresis is a rarer and much more serious condition than enuresis. Many children experience occasional relapses to about the age of three and sometimes—for example, during a period of diarrhea—to the age of twelve or later. In the non-retarded and physiologically normal child, encopresis usually involves daytime soiling. It may be an expression of defiance, as in Case Report 16•4, or a mixture of aggression, defiance, and fear.

Case Report 16•3, The Enuretic Football Star

Tom was a 230-pound defensive tackle for a large midwestern university who somewhat reluctantly sought help at the campus counseling center for what he called an embarrassing problem. He explained that ever since he could recall he had been an occasional bedwetter. Tom listed the types of situations that would precipitate his enuresis: overnights away from home, exams, approaching birthdays, and other minor and major occasions that caused apprehension. In high school, Tom explained, he was especially apt to wet his bed on the night before a big football game.

In college, his bedwetting followed a predictable pattern during his freshman year: he would wet the bed the night before a game. He was afraid that, if others in the dorm discovered his enuresis, they'd haze the daylights out of him. During that first year Tom tried desperately to prevent such a confrontation with his peers. He would stay up most of the night before a game. When this worked, he was so tired the next day that he played poorly. If, however, he did get more than just a catnap, he would wet the bed.

Just before he sought help, his enuresis had intensified until it was brought on by the slightest daytime upset. He was especially concerned because his sophomore year of football was about to get under way, and he did not want to face another season of hiding his wet linens and night things. Tom was now seriously considering dropping out of school.

At the insistence of the coach, who was one of the few people to whom Tom spoke about his wetting, he consulted a psychiatrist in the community and was given tranquilizers and short-term psychotherapy, but to no avail. With the cooperation of the coaching staff and the school authorities, a special bed was arranged for Tom in which conditioning procedures could be carried out without drawing undue attention to them. Tom's bedwetting was deconditioned in this way within two weeks. (Adapted from Kleinmuntz, 1974, p. 341)

Childhood Aggression A basic drive, **aggression** is an almost universal characteristic among children. In infancy, it is expressed as rage and anger and consists mainly of crying and random, overall, body movements such as kicking, flailing the arms and legs, arching the back, and twisting the body. At about age one, these random movements become more directed and purposive acts, such as deliberate attacks on someone, usually a parent or sibling, as well as kicking, biting, striking, and screaming.

As the child acquires language, aggression extends to refusing food, name-calling, and arguing. At about eighteen months of age the child deliberately does whatever is forbidden and whatever he or she knows will annoy the parent. By about the third year of life, the child learns that he or she can physically hurt others, and may injure them deliberately. In middle childhood, attacks become less physical and more verbal and include name-calling, swearing, and sarcasm, as well as ridiculing and humiliating others.

The first targets of a child's aggression are usually parents and siblings. The mother is the natural object of aggression because of her role in raising the child; but this aggression is easily displaced onto siblings. Attacks on siblings are somewhat more difficult to control than attacks on parents. The aggression the child learns to express in the home is later easily displaced to other situations.

Withdrawal and Infantile Autism When confronted with threatening or strange people, the young child frequently avoids, flees, or withdraws from the scene. Such **withdrawal** is considered a normal reaction of an inexperienced, small, and generally helpless creature. The child may express withdrawal by hiding his or her face, leaving the room, disappearing behind a sofa or drapes, or—depending on age—by shouting, pulling at or clinging to parents, slamming doors, or doing somersaults. The child may also react passively by being shy, quiet, and unassertive.

Many children display fears, or phobias, as a withdrawal reaction and develop other symptoms such as tics, speech disorders, asthma, excessive masturbation, eating difficulties, and insomnia. When accompanied by these disturbances, withdrawal is viewed as a somewhat more serious sign of personality disorder, but not as serious a sign as infantile **autism.**

Although infantile autism is rare, more has been written about it than about most other disturbances. This is probably due to its rather dramatic symptoms. It is unlike other childhood behavior in that it starts early, usually during the first year of life, and displays a more or less distinctive pattern of symptoms.

Case Report 16·4, Encopresis

Charles was a twelve-year-old boy whose schoolwork was not progressing satisfactorily. His neighborhood acquaintances had all made it to the sixth and seventh grades, but he was still in the fifth grade and not doing well there. One day Charles's homeroom teacher asked to see his mother about a disciplinary matter at school. Charles was to accompany his mother to the teacher's room.

When Charles and his mother arrived, they discovered two or three sets of parents and children ahead of them, and they waited their turn. After a fifteen-minute wait, and just moments before their turn came, Charles's mother hastily took her son by the hand and led him to the nearest toilet. She returned alone shortly thereafter and with some embarrassment explained to the teacher that her son had had a full bowel movement while waiting. The mother said further that this was a long-standing problem between them, that he was always defiant and never did let her toilet train him. His soiling was his way of "shaming" her in front of strangers.

Charles said that his bowel movement was a result of his fear about what the teacher would tell his mother. (Adapted from Kleinmuntz, 1974, p. 343)

Children at an experimental school for autistic children at Rutgers University. Note the characteristic lack of interaction among the children. (Stephen J. Potter)

Before the onset of the disorder, the infant is usually healthy and attractive, even bright and alert. At about four months, however, the child fails to make anticipatory movements and postures prior to being picked up by an adult. Shortly thereafter, more disturbing habits crop up, including prolonged rocking and head-banging, indifference to surroundings, fear of strangers, unusual interest in particular toys or mechanical gadgets, and ritualistic and repetitive play with toys.

Speech is either totally absent or not used for communication; rather the autistic child makes sounds for the sake of self-stimulation and noise. This speech has a parrot-like quality; the child seems not to talk to anyone in particular or to expect a response. Moreover, speech is repetitious and stereotyped; it echoes rather than answering questions. For example, when told "You sit down," the autistic child may or may not obey, but will probably respond with "You sit down."

Adolescent Disorders There are numerous disorders among adolescents, mostly of the neurotic sort, and although many of these disorders closely resemble those found among adults, they have a special quality that makes them typically adolescent.

School Phobia School phobia, which commonly occurs in the lower elementary grades and is usually accompanied by crying, trembling, somatic complaints, and pleas to stay home, takes on a somewhat different form among adolescents. At the younger ages, it is traceable to fears of separation from mother and anxiety about eating in the lunchroom or using strange toilets. For adolescents, school phobia is usually a symptom of a larger neurosis-like personality behavioral pattern and is therefore more resistant to environmental manipulation than the childhood variety.

The adolescent with a school phobia tends to avoid unpleasant situations because he or she lacks skill in coping with them—and school just happens to be one of these situations. Attributing fear of school to any of a variety of precipitating incidents, such a person exaggerates the importance of the incident and uses it to justify irrational behavior. In addition, the adolescent tends to be demanding, especially at home, to pout when crossed, and when disappointed by others, to accuse them of selfishness. This person tends also to be negative, and to seek attention by annoying others and intruding on them.

Miscellaneous Other Adolescent Disorders Some young hypochondriacs use their symptoms aggressively to control or punish parents, to justify their excessive demands and bad temper, and to gain and hold the attention of parents otherwise preoccupied. Others use their somatic concerns to rationalize to themselves or their peers their inability to compete successfully in athletics or schoolwork.

Hysterical symptoms among adolescents also take on a special form, most frequently seen as tics of the head and face. At first these tics are voluntary and serve the purpose of getting hair out of the eyes, loosening a tight-fitting collar, or clearing the throat; but after repetition, they become habitual and involuntary, thus losing their original purpose. Other such symptoms include head-jerking, nodding; blinking; grimacing; throat clicking; coughing; or twitching the shoulders, arms, or fingers.

The special quality of adolescent obsessive-compulsive symptoms, compared with their adult counterparts, is their ritualistic and magical powers, which are closer to the surface of awareness in the younger person. For adolescents, the obsessions and compulsions are conscious and sometimes intentional attempts to solve unresolved conflicts. Paradoxically, adolescents are more resentful than adults of being dominated by these intruding thoughts and rituals, a domination that resembles their experience with their parents.

Anorexia nervosa, almost exclusively restricted to adolescent girls (Bruch, 1970), is characterized by self-starvation: The adolescent severely restricts food intake. This may cause such profound weight loss that life is jeopardized. The physiological changes in advanced stages of anorexia are difficult to treat and sometimes make forced feeding difficult.

Maladaptive Personality Patterns

16•8 The neurotic, psychophysiological, psychotic, and other disorders discussed thus far have captured the exclusive attention of most writers of abnormal psychology textbooks, because of the historical predominance of hospital psychiatry with its focus on the bizarre and the seriously ill (Millon and Millon, 1974). However, contemporary interest is turning more and more to the less severe problems of everyday living. In keeping with this trend, we shall deal with some of the more common but milder personality disorders.

Generally, these disturbances are characterized by maladaptive patterns of behavior that are recognizable by adolescence or earlier. As with childhood and adolescent disorders these personality disorders are an important aspect of abnormal psychology because they may be the bases for understanding the development of more serious disorders.

The DSM II (1968) list of these personality disorders is long. It includes some maladaptive patterns that are clearly milder forms of the neuroses (obsessive-compulsive personality, hysterical personality) and psychoses (paranoid personality, schizoid personality) discussed earlier in this chapter, and some personality types whose labels disclose their behavior patterns (explosive, inadequate, alcoholic, drug-dependent). There are also two personality patterns listed that are not so obvious, the asthenic and passive-aggressive types. *Asthenic* individuals lack enthusiasm, have low energy levels, and seem to be oversensitive to physical and emotional stress. They may appear untroubled and function well in their chosen vocations, but are rather colorless and shy. *Passive-aggressive* personality types also tend to function adequately in most respects, but rather than expressing their assertiveness directly and openly, they tend to be aggressive in an obstructionist, pouting, or procrastinating way.

Two more personality disorders listed in DSM II are of interest to students of abnormal psychology for they pose puzzling etiological and treatment problems: the antisocial personality and sexual deviations.

Antisocial Personality One of the most baffling clinical types confronting the psychologist is the antisocial personality: an individual who exhibits none of the usual neurotic symptoms, is completely rational, shows no psychotic signs, but nonetheless behaves in a clearly maladaptive and disabling way. Paradoxically, this person seems to have insight into others' behavior but not into his or her own. For example, this person may talk of guilt, mistakes, repenting, and starting life all over again, and may sound sincere, but subsequent actions often reveal this as a sham.

Generally, the behavior patterns of the antisocial personality (sometimes also called sociopath or psychopath) become evident by adolescence, and usually follow a predictable course of increasing and unremitting acts against society. These people are described by DSM II as individuals who are basically unsocialized and whose frustration tolerance is low. The characteristics ascribed to the antisocial personalities by several renowned workers in this area (Cleckley, 1959, 1964; Hare, 1970; Karpman, 1961; McCord and McCord, 1964) are summarized in Table 16•3. The main features are inability to form loyal relationships, inability or unwillingness to learn from experience, the tendency to engage in acts that are inadequately motivated, and emotional shallowness. These features are illustrated in Case Reports 16•5, 16•6, and 16•7.

Sexual Deviations Despite liberalization of attitudes toward sex over the past twenty-five years, due in part to the publication of the Kinsey reports (1948, 1953), and in part to changing attitudes toward female sexuality since the introduction of oral contraceptives, sex in American society remains shrouded in prohibitions and misinformation. These taboos and misconceptions—which undoubtedly have their origins in complex patterns of cultural and religious teachings—have taken their toll. The victims include people with clinically recognized sexual disorders, as well as so-called normals whose sexual performance is admittedly maladaptively inadequate.

Drawing the line between abnormal and normal sexual functioning is, of course, difficult. How does one distinguish, for example, between **voyeurism** and a natural curiosity or a normal interest in sex and in the human body; between **fetishism** and a strong attachment to a cherished object; between **satyriasis** (excessive sexual drive in males) or **nymphomania** (insatiable sexual drive in females) and an intense sex drive; or between **masochism** and normally passive sexual behavior? The criteria typically applied in Western societies to make these distinctions are the legal and cultural ones. Both are unsatisfactory, as we shall see.

Table 16·3 Characteristics and Typical Behavior of the Antisocial Personality

CHARACTERISTIC	TYPICAL BEHAVIOR
Inability to form loyal relationships	Treats persons as objects; might marry but desert family.
Lack of insight	Often analyzes the motivations of others, but has no appreciation of own impact on others.
Casual but excessive sexual behavior	Has casual attitude toward sex; sexual contacts are outlandish and erratic.
Pathological lying	Plays many roles—doctor, lawyer, soldier—according to whim; often confused about own accomplishments or identity.
Unreliability and irresponsibility	Unpredictably responsible during some periods, but completely irresponsible during others.
Egocentricity	Behaves parasitically because of an insatiable need to be believed, served, and supported.
Inability to learn from experience, special attention, or punishment	Commits repeated crimes; not deterred by rewards or severe deprivations.
The need to fail	Has no apparent life plan, except perhaps to make a failure of self.
Inadequately motivated antisocial behavior	Impulsively steals and destroys "just for the hell of it."
Impulsiveness	Cannot defer immediate pleasures or tolerate long-term commitments.
Aggressiveness	Reacts to frustration with destructive fury.
Tendency to seek thrills and excitement	Behaves bizarrely and sometimes grotesquely.
Poverty of affect	Incapable of genuine anger or grief.
Inability to feel guilt	Feels no remorse, but can express some other emotions.
Superficial charm and intelligence	Has winning personality and astuteness that seem appropriate for confidence rackets.

(Adapted from Kleinmuntz, 1974. Table 11·1, p. 290)

From a legal standpoint, sexual offenses are sex acts performed visibly or publicly that fall outside the socially acceptable code and hence affront a particular segment of our society; a sexual deviate is any person who breaks a law relating to sexual behavior. In most of the United States and England sexual offenses include oro- and anogenital contacts (in or out of wedlock) and homosexuality, as well as premarital, extramarital, and postmarital intercourse. However, many of the legally (or morally) forbidden acts are common practice in our society (for example, masturbation, orogenital contact, premarital sex, and adultery).

The confusion is compounded when the already close association in the minds of many people between legal and moral prescriptions for proper behavior are

Case Report 16•5, Disloyalty in a Sociopath

A forty-two-year-old sociopath had a criminal record dating back thirty years. He had worked with partners, but only for short periods and for particular crimes. He had a long succession of affairs with women from one end of the United States to the other, and at the time of hospitalization was discovered to have married five women. When confronted with the fact that his marital and extramarital behavior was unusual, he said, "I'm an unusual person with a tremendous capacity to love. Hell, think of all the women I made happy."

Case Report 16•6, Inability to Learn from Punishment

A seventeen-year-old male psychopath, with an IQ of 132 as measured on the Wechsler Adult Intelligence Scale, broke into several gasoline stations along a major highway skirting Pittsburgh. After a night of breaking and entering, he parked his car alongside the highway, leaving his booty of tires, batteries, and automobile parts in clear view of passing cars. When he was later asked to explain his behavior, he shrugged the whole incident off by saying, "You can't win 'em all. Besides a short rest period in the cooler never hurt anybody. I know because I've been in the cooler several times."

Case Report 16•7, A Theft without a Clear Motive

A mother reported that her sixteen-year-old daughter often stole objects from five-and-dime stores, but the last straw was the daughter's theft of some expensive jewelry from some weekend house guests. The mother explained that they were wealthy, that her husband was president of a large and reputable local corporation, and that her daughter had access to anything she wanted just for the asking.

It was evident from the interview with the daughter that she had no particular need for the objects she had stolen, nor was she or any of her close acquaintances addicted to expensive drugs that might provide the motive for the thefts. Rather, she vaguely explained her behavior by saying, "Some people deserve what they get. Besides it is not fair that so few have so much."

Questions about possible altruistic or political motivations yielded even vaguer explanations. The possibility of schizophrenia was also ruled out, since she displayed no psychosis-like symptoms. Further probing disclosed that she often also engaged in "hell-raising" and thefts "just to stir up a little excitement."

(Adapted from Kleinmuntz, 1974, pp. 291, 294)

reinforced by newspaper accounts of sexual crimes in which the sex offender is depicted as an aggressive and dangerous degenerate. But the sex maniac image created by the mass media is inaccurate. As Cameron (1963, p. 660) states, "by far the majority of sex deviants are neither degenerate nor antisocial. Most of them tend to be basically timid . . . and emotionally immature persons whose sexual development has been arrested or distorted early in life."

Hence the legal distinction between acceptable and unacceptable sexual behavior is not satisfactory because it ignores the gradations that lie along the continuum of sexual behavior and tends to equate sexual offenses with sexual disorders.

Cultural definitions of sexual deviations are equally unsatisfactory. The term *deviation* implies the existence of absolute standards of normality from which one might depart, but no such absolute criteria exist, as evidenced by the wide subcultural, cross-cultural, and temporal differences in defining normal sexual behavior and practices. Studies from anthropology and other social sciences have made it abundantly clear that the norms of acceptable sexual behavior vary greatly from culture to culture, to the extent that one culture's acceptable behavior may be a crime punishable by death in another culture. Furthermore, sexual values in one culture vary widely from time to time. Even the legal definitions in our own society reflect this diversity. For example, the age of consent (for a girl) may be 18, 16, 14, 12, 10, or 7, depending on the locale; each state has a different sexual code set down in its laws.

Obviously, any attempt to discuss sexual deviation is fraught with difficulty, but rather than abandon the attempt, we shall concede the changeable and controversial nature of the perceptions and values involved, and arbitrarily classify the sexual deviations into the categories presented in Table 16•4.

Inappropriate Object Choice *Pedophilia* is the selection of a child as the object of an adult's sexual attentions. Pedophiles are especially feared by societies because their acts may result in brutality or murder—actions inspired more by fear of identification and subsequent arrest than by sadistic or homicidal impulses, although such impulses cannot always be ruled out.

Incest, which most commonly occurs between father and daughter, has been considered a violation of a taboo in almost all societies (Ferracuti, 1972; Weiner, 1962; Weinberg, 1955). Its incidence among primitive as well as literate societies

Table 16•4 Categories of Sexual Deviations

INAPPROPRIATE OBJECT CHOICE		DISORDERED SEXUAL FUNCTIONING		MISCELLANEOUS UNACCEPTED MODES OF SEXUAL GRATIFICATION
Animate	Inanimate	Excessive Drive	Diminished Drive	
Zoophilia	Fetishism	Satyriasis	Impotence	Sadism
Pedophilia	Necrophilia	Nymphomania	Frigidity	Masochism
Incest				Voyeurism
Rape				Exhibitionism
Masturbation				
Homosexuality				
Prostitution				

(Adapted from Kleinmuntz, 1974, Table 12•1, p. 312)

Is Homosexuality a Disease?

On December 15, 1973, the Board of Trustees of the American Psychiatric Association (APA) approved a change in its official manual of psychiatric disorders. Homosexuality per se, they voted, should no longer be considered a psychiatric disorder but rather a sexual orientation disturbance. Subsequently, two psychiatrists, Robert Spitzer, a member of APA's committee on nomenclature, and Irving Bieber, chairman of a research committee on homosexuality, addressed the question of whether homosexuality is a psychiatric disorder.

Spitzer first stipulated that to be considered a mental illness, a condition must either regularly cause subjective distress or regularly be associated with some generalized difficulty in social functioning. He therefore argued that homosexuality is not a disorder because many homosexuals are satisfied with their sexual orientation and demonstrate no generalized impairment. After admitting that it is easier to say how it should *not* be characterized than how it *should* be, Spitzer quoted Freud's response to a letter from the mother of a homosexual:

> Homosexuality is assuredly no advantage but it is nothing to be ashamed of. No vice, no degradation. It cannot be classified as an illness. We consider it to be a variation of the sexual function produced by a certain arrest of sexual development.

Although Bieber agreed with Spitzer regarding the difficulty inherent in classifying homosexuality, he argued that the fears that create homosexuality and its psychological inhibitions belong in a psychiatric classification system. If homosexuality is not part of the classification system, it becomes much more difficult to recognize children who are likely to become homosexuals and to treat them and their parents in order to forestall the likelihood of homosexuality.

is rare and has been estimated to be between about one and five per million per year, worldwide. The prohibitions against incest have been variously ascribed to close family habitation from early infancy, which presumably generates an aversion to intrafamilial sexual relationships (Westermarck, 1934), to the expediency of intertribal marriages (Fortune, 1932), to its possible disintegrating effects within the family resulting from sexual rivalries (Malinowski, 1927), and to the need to control erotic impulses within the family in order to promote fuller socialization outside the family circle (Parsons, 1954).

The conditions under which incest occur frequently include alcohol and poor housing, and the act may be accompanied by violence. In one study conducted in Sweden (reported in Ferracuti, 1972), in which 100 cases were investigated, it was found that significant precipitating features were inferior socioeconomic conditions, unstable work records, and obstacles to normal conjugal intercourse. The initiative was taken by the father. The daughter was the mother's replacement in the sexual situation, and the mother tolerated this arrangement.

The average age of the daughter in the cases studied is fifteen years, and this includes many prepubertal girls. According to one source (Weiner, 1962), the daughters who are objects of incest are characteristically precocious in their sex learning and anxious to assume an adult role. They are especially gratified by paternal attention, and they use the incestuous relationship to express their hostility toward the mother. One effect on the daughters is that they frequently become sexually promiscuous afterward.

The statistics on incest can be misleading, since low-income families more often come to the attention of an agency or hospital. In middle-class families, incest is more likely to go unreported. It may be kept a secret or shared only with a family physician or private therapist. Therefore, the picture of the average incest victim presented above may not be an accurate representation of incest in the middle (or upper) classes.

From conversations with private doctors, another image emerges for daughters who are incest victims in these classes: a girl who is not sexually precocious, is forcibly subdued by the father, and sometimes even raped. Frequently these girls are subjected to long-standing but perhaps subtle sexual interactions with their fathers. The girl may not be consciously aware of this relationship with her father until the incest is committed. Such girls usually have sexual attitudes that represent the extremes of the continuum—some being promiscuous and others fearful of, and withdrawn from, sexuality.

Another form of incest, perhaps less frequent than that between father and daughter, is brother-sister incest. Again, because of the nature of the act and society's taboos, statistics are difficult to obtain, but its existence is often disclosed in the confidential relationships of individual or group psychotherapy. This form of incest includes the not-uncommon prepubertal and pubescent explorations and experimentation between brother (usually older) and sister, as well as the more adult brother-sister sexual intercourse that may be initiated by an older brother who feels too inadequate to make advances to someone outside the family. These cases may range from seduction to rape, depending on the personalities of the participants.

Finally, there are instances of incest in which the sexual act of one participant or the other is a symptom of psychopathology. In these cases the father is usually either schizophrenic or brain-damaged, and his judgment about social proprieties is so impaired that sexual intercourse with his daughter is simply one behavioral symptom among a cluster of other deviant acts.

Rape, unlike incest, is considered more a violent attack on women than an attempt at sexual gratification. For example, rapists often use more than necessary force to reach their objectives; and sex may be merely the means they use to humiliate, defile, degrade, and gain mastery. Perhaps this act as a nonsexual, violent, and even political statement is best expressed by a reformed rapist, Eldridge Cleaver, in *Soul on Ice* (1968, pp. 14–15):

> I became a rapist. . . . Rape was an insurrectionary act. It delighted me that I was defying and trampling on the white man's law, on his system of values, and I was defiling his women—and this point, I believe, was the most satisfying to me because I was very resentful over the historical fact of how the white man has used the black woman. I felt I was getting revenge.

But sexual motivation cannot always be omitted from rape. One writer (Astor, 1974, p. 119) reports a case in which a woman who had been raped by an intruder in her bedroom said that, "when he finished, the first time, he just lay there beside

Rape among the Gusii

Among the Gusii of southwestern Kenya, according to Robert LeVine (1959) of the University of Chicago Anthropology Department, the high frequency of rape is a major social problem. An investigation into its causes led LeVine to conclude that rape, at least among the Gusii, has the following causes:

1. Normal sex relations among the Gusii involve male force and female resistance with an emphasis on the pain inflicted on the female. Rape committed by Gusii men can be seen as an extension of this legitimate pattern to illegitimate contexts under the pressure of sexual frustration.
2. The sexual frustration of Gusii young men is due to effectively enforced restrictions on intratribal sex, the sexual inhibitions and provocative behavior of Gusii girls, and economic conditions that force postponement of marriage.
3. If Gusii girls were uninhibited, promiscuity rather than rape would be the consequence.

LeVine proposes that if this analysis is valid, these factors should be found in any society with a high frequency of rape:

1. Severe formal restrictions on the nonmarital sexual relations of females.
2. Moderately strong sexual inhibitions on the part of females.
3. Economic barriers that prolong the celibacy of some males into their late twenties.
4. The absence of physical segregation of the sexes.

This last condition, according to LeVine, distinguishes high rape societies from societies where rape is not feasible (because women are secluded and guarded) and homosexuality may be practiced instead.

me in bed, stroking my body . . . . He asked me how I felt." And another woman recalls that her apartment intruder "seemed to want to talk. He even said that he would like to create some sort of relationship with me." This potential victim then told him that because she was so afraid, he couldn't physically enter her. If he really wanted her she said to the man, "maybe we should go out to dinner. . . . Finally I convinced him that if he would call me, we would make a date and go out. He left, taking my telephone number with him" (Astor, 1974, p. 130).

The impact of rape on the man in the victim's life varies with his closeness to her and the role he is asked to play. Usually the victim's boyfriend or husband feels that she has become a different person—defiled perhaps—and could have resisted, or at least not provoked the attack. Obviously, this does little to abate the already considerable guilt of the victim. The police, who until recently were predominantly male, are often insensitive to the deep sexual humiliation the rape victim experiences. They ask questions that either reflect their prurient interest in the details of the act or betray their suspicion that the victim provoked the rape. Evidently these attitudes have changed somewhat in recent years, according to sociologists who report that victims have increasingly attested to sympathetic treatment by the police. In part, this may be due to more attention being paid to training police and to the use of women interrogators in rape cases. Nevertheless, once the case has been brought to court, some defense attorneys have turned the trial itself into an attack on the victim.

Estimates of the incidence of rape are difficult to obtain because of the reluctance of victims to report these crimes. FBI reports released in 1975 suggest that rape increased by 165 percent in the previous fifteen years. By comparison, murder and aggravated assault rose by about 90 and 140 percent respectively during the same period. Perhaps more revealing about rape patterns is the fact that, according to interviews and information obtained from police blotters, the rapist is often not a total stranger to the victim. Several studies in Philadelphia and Washington (Amir, 1972) have suggested that in about 60 to 65 percent of rapes, victim and offender knew each other previously.

Masturbation is attaining sexual gratification by means of manual or mechanical self-stimulation of the genitals or other erogenous zones for the express purpose of achieving orgasm. Since 93 percent of American males and 62 percent of American females admitted to having masturbated (Kinsey et al., 1948, 1953), masturbation hardly qualifies as an abnormality. It may, however, be considered a deviation when it is practiced in preference to other outlets that are available and reasonably attractive. Furthermore, feeling guilty about masturbating is a cause of personal distress for many because our culture surrounds the act with taboos, and conditions us to associate autoeroticism with defilement.

Disordered Sexual Functioning Disordered sexual functioning can take the form of either excessive or diminished sex drive. *Satyriasis* is an insatiable sexual desire in a male that constantly drives him to pursue sexual gratification. He is so preoccupied with this pursuit that it interferes with all his other activities.

Nymphomania is the female counterpart of satyriasis. The chances of being rejected and perhaps even ostracized by family and acquaintances are, however, greater for the nymphomaniac than the satyr. This reflects our society's double standard. Clinicians have in fact speculated that some females practice promiscuity for the purpose of defying society's sexist moral codes.

The two most common forms of diminished sexual drive are impotence in males and frigidity in females. *Impotence* is the inability of a male to retain an erection long enough for intromission. Masters and Johnson (1970) refer to two forms of impotence: *primary* (in which the male has never become potent) and *secondary*, (in which the male was once potent but has lost his potency). They suggest that impotence is not an absolute condition. Some men may be potent only with prostitutes and impotent with all other women; others may have patterns of potency and impotence that depend on more subtle psychological factors.

Frigidity is sexual unresponsiveness in the female. As in the case of male impotence, there are degrees of frigidity, from slightly diminished sexual drive to a strong aversion to any sexual activity. Also, a woman's frigidity may vary, depending on the particular sexual partner.

Miscellaneous Unaccepted Modes of Sexual Satisfaction All of the following modes are part of the repertoire of behaviors that most people use during foreplay but that when practiced exclusively are considered abnormal. The common ele-

Striptease acts in nightclubs may satisfy the voyeuristic tendencies of some people. (Mitchell Payne, Jeroboam)

ment among them is that they bypass the need for a personal human encounter between the participants.

Sadism is a term derived from the practices of the Marquis de Sade (1740–1814), who attained sexual gratification from fantasizing or inflicting punishment or pain on his sexual partners, and recorded his sadistic fantasies in his novels. The punishment and pain inflicted by the sadist may be either physical or verbal. Physical punishment commonly includes kicking, biting, whipping, and slapping; occasionally this results in the death of the victim. Verbal punishment may take the form of teasing, abusive, or threatening language.

The type and frequency of sadism practiced differ widely from one person to another and, even within the same individual, from one situation to the next. In its least deviant form, mild sadism is expressed when sexual intercourse is accompanied by pinching, biting, or scratching. Some sadists derive pleasure simply from imagining the infliction of pain on the sex object; this is usually a masturbatory fantasy.

A masochist experiences sexual pleasure from having punishment, pain, and humilitation inflicted on him. The term **masochism** can be traced to Count Leopold von Sacher-Masoch (1836–1895), an Austrian writer who sought out women to inflict pain upon him. He obtained sexual satisfaction from the mistreatment he received from them and even derived pleasure from having his sex partners engage in sexual affairs with other men.

Masochism, then, is the counterpart of sadism. Whereas most sadists in our culture are men, masochistic tendencies are found predominantly in women. Undoubtedly the exaggeration of cultural norms for male and female sex behavior plays an important part in determining the formation of these two deviations; that is, a culture that encourages male aggressiveness and female submissiveness can be expected to foster amplifications of these behaviors in deviant sex practices.

The voyeur obtains sexual gratification exclusively by looking at the genitals or some other part of the sex object's body. Occasionally, also, he or she derives erotic pleasure from viewing the sexual activities of others. As in many of the sexual behaviors already mentioned, voyeurism does have a normal excitatory function. To some persons, especially those for whom the usual sex outlets are not available, voyeurism can be considered a normal outlet for sexual needs.

Incidence of Psychopathology

16•9 Although many people who need psychiatric care are never located, because they are either unwilling or unable to gain access to such care, we know that the incidence of psychopathology is high in America. Some glimpse of its prevalence in the general population can be obtained by examining statistics published by the National Institute of Mental Health (NIMH 1973, 1975).

1. Approximately 50 percent of all hospital beds in the United States are occupied by the mentally ill.

2. The incidence of mental illness hospitalization is greater than the combined incidence for all other diseases.
3. About half a million children under the age of eighteen received care in a psychiatric facility in the United States in 1974.
4. Approximately one million people in the noninstitutionalized population were unable to carry on normal daily activities because of mental disorders in 1971.
5. The estimated number of person-years lost in 1971 because of mental illness hospitalization was one million; the estimated person-hours lost during that year in outpatient treatment settings was a staggering 132 million hours.

But as disheartening as these figures may be, some encouraging trends are now evident. The year 1973 represented the eighteenth consecutive year in which the resident population of state and county mental institutions showed a decline (Coleman, 1976). This decline is due to (1) the introduction in 1955 of tranquilizing and antidepressant drugs, (2) greater access to community and other preventive or early treatment settings, and (3) an increased number of halfway houses and other after-care facilities.

Causes of the Behavior Disorders

16•10 By far the most widely accepted explanation for the neuroses and for some of the psychophysiological disorders is that they are of psychological origin and have their roots in the individual's life experiences. Biogenic theories for these disorders have been expounded, but psychogenic theories are much more widely held. In contrast, the main thrust of research on the origins of the schizophrenias has taken a biogenic turn of late. We can only touch on some of the highlights.

The Neuroses and Psychophysiological Disorders Learning theory, particularly the theory of Dollard and Miller (1950), which is a composite of Freudian and Pavlovian concepts, postulates fear or anxiety as the main element in the formation of the neuroses. An illustration of the way Dollard and Miller explain neurotic symptom disturbances is their account of how compulsions are acquired. This theory relies heavily on the anxiety-reducing effects of particular acts such as handwashing or counting objects. They describe how in some cases the rituals produce cues that elicit fear-inhibiting responses, while in other cases they evoke thoughts that are incompatible with the ones eliciting the fear. The following short excerpt from their case of Mrs. A. illustrates their theory (pp. 164–65):

> The primary drive of sex was a constant motivation for sexual thoughts. As soon as she stopped counting, these anxiety-provoking thoughts tended to reappear. Thus she had a compulsion to continue counting whenever she was not completely preoccupied with some other distracting and innocent activity.

Another learning theory approach is that of Skinner. In his account (1953) of the acquisition of hysteria he traces the environmental origins of a neurosis with-

Personality Theories and the Origins of Neuroses

THEORIST AND APPROACH	PERSONALITY THEORIES	ORIGINS OF NEUROSES
Sigmund Freud Psychoanalysis	Infantile sexual complexes develop during various psychosexual stages. Humans are pleasure-seeking organisms who, in their quest for gratification, confront reality and the dictates of a stern society. Unconscious forces and determinants underlie most actions and thoughts.	Anxieties arise because of unresolved infantile sexual attachments. When the ego cannot cope with the anxieties and conflicts brought about by the clash between drives (id) and conscience (superego), it falls back on defense mechanisms. These mechanisms do not eliminate the powerful drives giving rise to anxiety; rather, they seek expression through neurotic symptoms.
Carl G. Jung Analytical psychology	The psyche consists of a number of separate but interacting systems—the ego, the personal unconscious and its complexes, and the collective unconsciousness (the storehouse of latent memory traces from the ancestral past).	The collective unconscious may overshadow the ego and the personal unconscious, thus causing psychopathology. Also, neuroses arise because of incompatible complexes within the person. This incompatibility may be due to repressed or blocked energy discharges, which are stored in the unconscious in highly energized forms. When these unconscious processes break through the repression, they cause irrational behavior.
Alfred Adler Individual psychology	People are motivated primarily by social urges and learn how to cope with the world first in the family, and then in the larger context of living.	The child is engaged in a constant struggle to master the environment. Neuroses come about as a result of real or imagined inferiority feelings and faulty opinions about oneself and the world.
Erich Fromm Ethical psychoanalysis	The person is isolated from self and from society. People have five basic needs: identity, roots, transcendence, relatedness, and a frame of orientation.	People become neurotic because they have not learned to cope with their isolation and have not properly mastered the art of exercising their freedom of choice.

out resort to inner mechanisms (p. 381): "Thus when a solicitous parent supplies an unusual measure of affection and attention to a sick child, any behavior on the part of the child which emphasizes his illness is strongly reinforced." Regarding its treatment, he goes on to say: "One obvious remedial technique for behavior which is the product of excessive reinforcement is to arrange new contingencies in which the behavior will be extinguished."

Yet a third view of the etiology of the neuroses and the psychophysiological dis-

THEORIST AND APPROACH	PERSONALITY THEORIES	ORIGINS OF NEUROSES
Erik Erikson Psychoanalysis	Early infancy lays the foundation for trust or mistrust; subsequent infancy may form the basis for autonomy or doubt; later stages—all the way to late adulthood—may be bases for initiative or guilt, industry or inferiority, ego identity or confusion, integrity or isolation, generativity or stagnation, and integrity or despair.	Neuroses result from the persistence into adulthood of childhood anxieties, which undermine adult security and proper identity.
H. S. Sullivan Interpersonal psychiatry	Personality is the relatively enduring pattern of recurrent interpersonal behaviors.	The neuroses develop because of distortions and complications in interpersonal relationships that have their roots in faulty learning during early developmental stages.
Carl Rogers Self theory	The individual is the only one who can understand his or her experiences and formulate hypotheses about reality on the basis of these experiences.	When the individual is unable to reconcile subjective reality (perceived world) with external reality (the world as it is), then he or she feels threatened and anxious.
Dollard and Miller Respondent-Freudian stimulus-response	The person is born with a range of primary drives that develop, as a consequence of learning, into complex and strong secondary drives. Among the most important of these secondary drives is fear or anxiety.	Strong unconscious conflicts are learned, along with accompanying anxiety, during several critical childhood stages.
B. F. Skinner Operant stimulus-response	All behavior is governed by reinforcement —it is contingent responding.	A stimulus that precedes an aversive or negatively reinforcing situation may evoke strong emotional responses.
A. Bandura Social learning stimulus-response	Adaptive as well as maladaptive behaviors are learned as a result of modeling, as well as classical and operant conditioning.	Maladaptive or neurotic behavior may be acquired because of faulty modeling and inadequate internal and cognitive reinforcements.

orders is Albert Bandura's (1973) **social learning theory,** which emphasizes the importance of **modeling,** or imitation. As we noted in Chapters 3 and 5, a child may form maladaptive habits merely by observing others, without either practicing the responses involved or being reinforced for eliciting them. If, however, the model is reinforced for behaving in certain ways, then the viewer is much more likely to imitate the observed behavior. We shall return to Bandura's theory in Chapter 17, where we discuss its application to behavior therapy; here we shall note only that one can learn (or unlearn) habits by watching a model who is acquiring (or eliminating) such behavior.

Sociocultural variables have also been implicated in the etiology of the neuroses and, not surprisingly, most of the evidence reinforces the idea that neurotic parents foster neurotic individuals (Dohrenwend and Dohrenwend, 1969; Ehrenwald, 1960; Jenkins, 1966). This evidence is based predominantly on statistical surveys or case-history data. The number of possible psychopathogenic familial patterns is infinite; we shall mention only five of them:

1. A parent may displace his or her own hypochondriasis onto a child as, for example in the case of a mother who is overly concerned about her child's health. A typical mother-child interaction in this instance may consist of the mother's going through a checklist of the child's possible symptoms each morning before the child leaves for school. Before long, the child may begin to share the mother's concern. Other neurotic behaviors may be similarly acquired.
2. Parents may promote sibling rivalry inadvertently by favoring one child in the family and ignoring, perhaps even belittling, another.
3. A parent may attempt to have the child live the life that he or she could not, possibly setting unattainable goals for the child. For example, the father who flunked out of law school and became a real estate agent may insist that his son take up where he left off. If the child has other plans or, even worse, if he does not have an aptitude for that line of work, his sense of competence may be seriously undermined by his failures.
4. Parents may use the child as a weapon in their conflicts with each other, and their threats to walk out can be traumatic to the child, causing feelings of insecurity.
5. A child may learn from his parent's frequent marital conflicts that close heterosexual relationships are not gratifying and are to be avoided whenever possible.

The search beyond the family for sociocultural influences indicates that neurosis occurs in all cultures (Eaton and Weil, 1955; Opler, 1959; Plog and Edgerton, 1969; Norbeck et al., 1968), although its symptomatic expression has strong culture-bound features. In one of these studies (Eaton and Weil, 1955) it was found that among the Hutterite sect, the overall incidence of neurosis was lower than for many other cultures, and their symptoms were mild and benign. Moreover, patients in this fundamentalist and isolated sect had chiefly those symptoms that are socially acceptable in their culture. They internalized their tensions as depressive or psychophysiological responses. Phobic and obsessive-compulsive reactions, which would violate strong cultural taboos, were rare.

Cross-cultural research further discloses that gross forms of hysteria, such as hysterical blindness, deafness, convulsions, and paralysis, which are on the decline in Europe and America, are common in such developing countries as India, Lebanon, Egypt, and Tunisia; and that within these countries there is a greater influence of obsessive-compulsive neurosis in urban than in rural areas (Wittkower and Dubreuil, 1968).

Extreme opisthotonic spasm—a drawing from Paul Richer's book on hysteria, *Etudes cliniques sur la grande hysterie,* Paris, 1885. At that time Freud was among the pioneers in the investigation of hysteria through hypnosis. His study led him to believe that hysteria was caused not by organic changes in the nervous system but by emotional disorders that could be relieved by bringing emotionally charged material back into consciousness. (National Library of Medicine)

A common psychoanalytic theme in discussing the origins of the psychophysiological disorders has been that symptoms have symbolic significance. Thus, persons with peptic ulcers are assumed to be symbolizing their internalized aggression against their mothers, persons with ulcerative colitis have deep disturbances in their key object relations, and asthmatics are presumably afraid of losing their mothers or destroying them. Many of these psychoanalytic hypotheses are derived from clinical experiences and are couched in complicated and often nontestable terms. Maher (1966) aptly summarizes this view (which we share) of the main shortcomings of this approach as follows (p. 263):

> It is quite possible that all these observations are true, and useless. Loss of a significant relationship produces grief and general stress. The important ingredient of all these precipitating circumstances may well be simply that they are stressors, not that they specifically involve loss of relationships. The emphasis upon the local characteristics of the stressors may be quite misleading; it certainly has not led to any substantial addition to our knowledge of the mechanisms of psychosomatic illnesses.

A variation on the psychoanalytic theme is Franz Alexander's specific emotion hypothesis (1950), which asserts that for each disorder there is a typical conflict. Alexander stressed, for example, the importance of scratching as an expression of hostile impulses turned inward. Unlike most psychoanalytic theorizing, many of Alexander's theories lend themselves to laboratory tests, and in some instances evidence has been brought to bear on their credibility.

Stress has also been implicated in the psychophysiological disorders. One of the most important contributions to understanding human psychophysiological reactions was made by a University of Montreal endocrinologist, Hans Selye, who introduced the concept of stress into the life sciences. His books *The Physiology and Pathology of Exposure to Stress* (1950) and *The Stress of Life* (1956) were responsible for an unprecedented flurry of research in psychology.

Having observed that most people react to stress by developing nonspecific symptoms, Selye developed his concept of the **general adaptation syndrome** (GAS). According to this concept, various forms of internal and external stress result from injury to tissue, infection from bacterial attacks, fatigue, hunger, and pain, as well as frustration and conflict, and these stressors elicit three reactions: (1) the alarm reaction, in which physiological defenses become active; (2) resistance, in which the organism attempts to meet the challenge of stress; and (3) exhaustion, which occurs if the organism cannot cope with its stressors.

Origins of Schizophrenia In his presidential address to the American Psychological Association, Paul E. Meehl (1962, p. 827) proposed the following wager:

> Suppose that you were required to write down a procedure for selecting an individual from the population who could be diagnosed as schizophrenic by a psychiatric staff; you have to wager $1000 on being right; you may not include in your selection procedure any behavioral fact, such as a symptom or a trait manifested by the individual. What would you write down?

His answer: "There is only one thing you could write down that would give you a better than even chance of winning such a bet—namely, 'find an individual X who has a schizophrenic identical twin.'" More specifically, Meehl's conclusion is: "Schizophrenia, while its content is learned, is fundamentally a neurological disease of genetic origin."

Meehl considers the inherited brain defect as a necessary condition for schizophrenia. He suggests that this neurological defect is most likely to lead to clinical schizophrenia when an individual with it is reared in a stressful environment. In ordinary, nonstressful life situations, according to Meehl, a person with this biochemical defect displays schizotypic behavior, a much milder form of schizophrenia which manifests itself in a tendency to withdrawal and inappropriate emotional expression.

The idea that schizophrenia may be transmitted genetically is supported mainly by twin studies, especially those which show greater incidence of the disorder among identical twins than among fraternal twins, ordinary siblings, or other relatives. Identical twins have the same genetic endowment. They result from the splitting of a single fertilized ovum, and so they are called monozygotic (MZ). Fraternal twins are as similar genetically as any two siblings (except identical twins) born of the same parents. They result from the simultaneous fertilization of two separate ova, and so they are called dizygotic (DZ). Because sex is genetically determined, MZs are always same-sexed, while DZs may be of different sexes.

Twin comparisons presuppose that inherited disorders appear with greater frequency among genetically similar persons. Since MZ twins are of identical heredity, a disorder with a purely genetic origin should show up in both members. DZ twins have different heredities, and so the incidence of a genetic disorder among them should be less than among their MZ counterparts.

These comparisons are usually expressed as a concordance ratio, the percentage of sets of twins in which both members have the schizophrenic disorder. Some of the findings from genetic studies are summarized in Table 16•5, where we see that the average concordance ratio for MZ twins is about 50 percent (with a range from 6 to 69 percent); for same-sex DZ twins it is considerably lower, about 12 percent (with a range from 0 to 19). For opposite-sex DZ twins examined in another study by the same researchers (Gottesman and Shields, 1966), it is still lower, about 5 percent (range: 0 to 11 percent).

There is a significantly greater probability among MZs than among DZs that one twin will have the disorder, if the other twin has it. These findings support the idea that schizophrenia is inherited. However, the lower concordance ratios for opposite-sex DZs than for same-sex DZs suggest that there are strong environmental factors operating. Indeed, opposite-sex siblings usually are treated more differentially than same-sex DZ twins.

Another method for studying possible genetic origins of schizophrenia focuses on people who may be high-risk candidates for the disorder. One supposedly high-risk group that investigators are now studying is normally functioning children who have chronic and severely schizophrenic mothers (Garmezy, 1974). The investigators are searching for preexisting biochemical, physiological, psychological, or life-history features that will reliably differentiate infants who ultimately develop schizophrenia from those who do not (Garmezy, 1974).

Finally, discovering biochemical substances in abnormal persons has always appealed to behavioral scientists because therapy could then be aimed at removing or destroying these substances. A major impetus to this research occurred with the discovery of the psychological effects of hallucinogens (hallucination-producing drugs), among which the best known are mescaline (the active ingredient of peyote) and lysergic acid diethylamide (LSD-25). Experimentation with these drugs, which produced model psychoses (hallucinations and delusions) in normals suggested the possibility that schizophrenics endogenously produce some such substance, which may be responsible for their disorder. Unfortunately, the basic assumption of much of this work—that the mental states produced by hallucinogens are truly comparable to naturally occurring psychoses—and the findings of many other biochemical studies have often been seriously challenged and have not held up under careful replication attempts.

Table 16•5 Concordance Ratios from Eleven Genetic Studies on Monozygotic and Dizygotic Twins

PERCENT/N	
MZ Twins	DZ Twins (same sex)
69/174	11/296
27/95	5/125
65/37	14/58
64/11	15/27
61/41	13/53
60/55	18/11
58/19	0/13
40–50/22	9–10/33
25/38[a]	4–10/90[a]
6–36/16[a]	5–14/20[a]
24–48/21	10–19/41

NOTE: N = number of sets of twins studied.

[a]Male subjects only and without age correction

(Adapted from Gottesman and Shields, 1972, and from Kleinmuntz, 1974. Table 10•2, p. 270)

Causes of Childhood and Adolescent Problems Essentially, the origins of childhood and adolescent disorders resemble those of adult disorders; therefore we shall focus on the causes particularly germane to children.

With the possible exceptions of infantile autism and childhood schizophrenia, for which the most likely explanations are biogenic, the causes of childhood and

Aversive Maternal Control: A Psychogenic Theory of Schizophrenic Development

Alfred B. Heilbrun (1973), professor of psychology at Emory University has proposed an *aversive maternal control* theory of schizophrenia, for which he has collected a modest amount of support (Heilbrun, 1973, p. 251). The child's characteristic mode of responding, this theory holds, is influenced in important ways by his dealings with the mother, the critical socializing agent. If the mother permits the child to assume increasing autonomy while continuing to nurture him affectionately and with trust and respect, then the child will learn to transact effectively with his expanding social environment. If the mother does not communicate love and esteem during this critical period of the child's attaining autonomy, and if the child's sense of worth is further reduced by his perception of maternal rejection, then he may feel unlovable and unworthy of esteem. Thus, sustained maternal control and rejection act together to shape a self-concept that mirrors the mother's disparagement and distrust.

This aversive maternal control, as Heilbrun calls it, introduces circularity into the child's development: initiation of new relationships is deterred by poor self-image, which increases the expectancy of rejection, which in turn entrenches more firmly the very relationship that instigated the problem. The mother, for her part, then comes to regard the child with even greater disapproval as he reaches adolescence, the stage in which more autonomous functioning is expected. The child's fear in forming new and better interpersonal relationships is magnified by the mother's more obvious control and rejection, which derive from her growing realization that her developing child is psychologically deviant.

adolescent abnormalities may be found in family influences. In other words, the kind of family a child is born into determines the sort of person that child will become.

Parents and Home The cause-and-effect linkages between parental (especially maternal) practices and subsequent pathology are very complex. Earlier, predominantly psychoanalytic views tended to oversimplify these relationships. The contemporary approach sees specific parental behaviors simply as indices of large attitude patterns. In determining the personality development of offspring, overall parental attitudes are considered more important than specific child-rearing techniques.

The importance of parental patterns of behavior for shaping personality was noted by Mussen, Conger, and Kagan (1974), who refer to the home-visit studies that Baldwin and his associates (1945, 1949) conducted at the Fels Research Institute. The general findings of this research (as we saw in Chapter 5) suggested that children who grow up in democratic homes, where reasons for regulations are discussed, tend to be active, competitive, outgoing, and nonconforming. Controlled homes, in contrast, provide the opposite type of atmosphere, with very little parent-child interaction and produce children who are not curious, aggressive, or outgoing. Regarding delinquency and aggression specifically, several studies have shown that relationships with parents are critical (Bachman, 1970). Adolescents who get along best with their parents show the least aggression (Bandura, 1973; Mussen et al., 1974).

Intrapsychic and Environmental Variables Of course, an individual's personality is not entirely the product of family interaction patterns. Several additional endogenous (originating from within) and exogenous (originating from without) forces also influence the formation of personality. The child's unique biological and physical endowments play an important role in growing up, as do the extra-familial demands placed on the child by teachers and peers.

As an instance of internal determinants, consider the relation between physical makeup and personality, about which the theorist Alfred Adler had much to say in his early writings. His theory of **organ inferiority,** which originally was intended only to account for psychosomatic symptom selection, was that the individual strives to compensate for this real or perceived inferiority. Adler later extended this view to include any feelings of inferiority, whether they arise from physical or psychological and social disabilities (Adler, 1917, 1927).

Henri de Toulouse-Lautrec (1864–1901). Perhaps his enormous productivity as an artist can be attributed in part to compensation for his stunted growth—the result of breaking both his legs in a fall as a child. (The Bettmann Archive)

Regardless of one's theoretical orientation on this matter, it is difficult to deny the influence of a disability on personality development. One of the more famous examples of compensation is Demosthenes, a stutterer as a child, who became noted for his oratory. Similarly, many Olympic athletes, especially weightlifters and track stars, started on daily physical programs in order to overcome disabilities caused by childhood illnesses.

In addition to endogenous factors, there are many external forces with which the child must cope. These forces, most of which are extra-familial, begin to take on a special significance as the child's social world expands into the neighborhood, nursery school, and elementary school, and beyond. To gain some appreciation of the complexity of these environmental pressures, let us look at what Mussen, Conger, and Kagan (1974) refer to as the adjustment demands of adolescence (p. 556):

> If the adolescent is to become truly adult, and not just physically mature, he must, in the few short years between childhood and nominal adulthood, gradually achieve independence from his family; adjust to his sexual maturation; establish cooperative and workable relationships with his peers, without being dominated by them; and decide on and prepare for a meaningful vocation.

Each of these demands—to become independent, to adjust to sexual changes, to get along with peers, and to make vocational decisions—challenges the adolescent. Establishing true independence from parents requires that the adolescent break the long-standing bonds of parental control. Coming to grips with increased sexual drives and awareness means learning to control a new set of impulses. Getting along with peers and getting the feeling of belonging so vital to self-esteem, sometimes necessitates opposing one's parents. Finally, the problem of deciding on a vocation is a complex one and is subject to parental, subcultural, peer group, and school influences.

Infantile Autism The origin of infantile autism is unknown. Genetic, psychological, and organic determinants have been suggested. The evidence for genetic origins is found in studies showing that concordance for autism is high in both members of monozygotic twins but is rare among dizygotic twins (Ornitz and Ritvo, 1968). Proponents of a genetic hypothesis argue that in all cases the symptomatology is so unique and specific that only a hereditary explanation is plausible.

There is no evidence to suggest that autism is psychogenic. The arguments against a psychological formulation are strong (Kanner and Eisenberg, 1957; Ornitz and Ritvo, 1968; Rimland, 1964) and are based on findings that some clearly autistic children are born of parents who do not fit the supposed autistic parent personality pattern, that most siblings of autistic children are normal, and that autistic children are behaviorally unusual almost from the moment of birth.

The organic hypothesis rests mostly on evidence that autism is closely simulated in children with known brain damage and that autistic children display a cognitive dysfunction that resembles such injury. Rimland, in his book *Infantile Autism* (1964), sets the locus of this damage in the **reticular formation** of the brain and cites as evidence for his hypothesis experimental lesions produced in the brain stems of cats whose subsequent behavior resembled symptoms of children with early infantile autism. These animals became highly inaccessible and undistractable; engaged in ceaseless stereotyped behavior; assumed blank-staring and masklike facial expressions; became mute, unaffectionate, and unresponsive to pain; mouthed many kinds of objects; and became either anorexic or voracious. Rimland (1964, p. 119) concludes that such damage is due to an excess of oxygen in early infancy.

Causes of the Personality Disorders For most personality pattern disturbances, the most plausible explanation seems to be that a combination of inherited mood dispositions and environmental learning mode is responsible for the maladaptive behavior. The most extensive search for determinants has been conducted in relation to biological and psychological factors responsible for sociopathy, or antisocial personality patterns.

Biological Origins of Antisocial Personality The search for biological determinants of sociopathy includes investigations of autonomic reactivity, brain defect, and chromosomal abnormalities. We shall discuss only the first of these.

The clinical observation that the antisocial personality seems devoid of emotional responsivity led one researcher (Lykken, 1957) to compare so-called primary sociopaths (as described in Table 16•3) with secondary sociopaths (clinically similar appearing subtypes such as neurotic sociopaths) and with normals. This study was conducted among two prisoner groups: group I (12 males and 7 females) consisted of prisoners of the primary type; group II (13 males and 7 females) consisted of secondary-type prisoners. A control group (10 males and 5 females) was selected from normal high school and college students matched with the other subjects for age, intelligence, and socioeconomic background.

The experimental hypothesis was that group I subjects (1) would not easily develop anxiety in the laboratory, (2) would show abnormally little anxiety (as measured by the Manifest Anxiety Scale) in real-life situations, and (3) would be relatively incapable of **avoidance learning** in the laboratory. To test the first part of this hypothesis, Lykken took a GSR (galvanic skin response) measure of the blindfolded subjects, who were seated in the lab, while administering to them buzzer (**CS**) and shock (**US**) combinations. He found that group I showed significantly less GSR reactivity to the CS than the other two groups. Of all the tests used, according to Lykken (1957, p. 10), this was the most important one because it showed that if a person "does not produce a GSR to a stimulus, one can be sure that he has not 'reacted emotionally' to that stimulus."

In the avoidance conditioning situation, the results were again that primary psychopaths (group I subjects) showed the least avoidance, and hence the least anxiety; neurotic and other types (group II) showed the most avoidance behavior. These results suggest that primary sociopaths are autonomically less reactive than normals or secondary antisocial types.

Other autonomic reactivity studies (Hare, 1970) have also suggested that primary sociopaths are emotionally underreactive. The findings of these studies taken together, then, suggest that the lack of real-life anxiety displayed by antisocial personality types may be due to a defect in the autonomic nervous system.

Psychological Origins of Antisocial Personality Such a defect, however, if actually supported by other research, does not necessarily attest to hereditary or biochemical origins. This could be learned behavior transmitted by parental or other environmental influences.

One of the more widely accepted formulations of the origins of sociopathy is by Lee Robins, based on her studies described in *Deviant Children Grown Up* (1966). She followed up 524 children who had been seen thirty-two to thirty-seven years earlier in a child guidance clinic. Her findings suggest that the single most reliable predictor of antisocial behavior is a home in which the parents, particularly an alcoholic father, display antisocial behaviors.

Many recent explanations, which are not inconsistent with the above findings, tend to emphasize the role of modeling and socialization in the development of sociopathy. One of these formulations has applicability for all of the personality disorders discussed in this section. For example, according to one source (Buss, 1966), two varieties of parental models may be important in the development of antisocial behavior. One is the parent who is cold and distant, permitting no warm or close relationship to develop. The second model is the parent who is inconsistent in the way he or she provides affection, love, rewards, and punishments. In this instance the child's inconsistent models foster aggression and impulsivity.

Causes of the Sexual Disorders As with the other personality disorders, the origins of the sexual deviations have led to a search for biological as well as psychological determinants. Here we shall focus on psychogenic hypotheses, some of which have already been mentioned.

Ullmann and Krasner (1975, p. 423) observe that, as one moves up the phylo-

Altered Brain States and Sexual Deviation

A number of studies have shown links between brain function and psychosexual behavior among animals (MacLean, 1973) and among human beings (Zitrin et al., 1973). These links are not surprising since we have long known about the connections between **hormones** and sexual behavior. However, investigation of the relationships of altered brain states and sexual psychopathy is relatively recent. Most of the evidence comes from animal research, although some investigators connect clinical observations among human sexual deviates with abnormal brain function.

Arthur Epstein (1973) suggests that sexual deviations such as fetishism, transvestism, transsexualism, exhibitionism, and alterations in sexual drive and potency may be linked to pathological processes affecting the brain's limbic areas (Chapter 24).

A transvestite is someone who adopts the dress or behavior of the opposite sex. In our culture, however, a man who wears a dress is much more likely to be considered a sexual deviate than is a woman who wears pants. (Picatti, Jeroboam)

For example, from his studies of fetishism in two nonhuman primates, Epstein infers the presence of releases from inhibitions that have their center of focus in the **limbic system.** He also reports that in thirteen cases of fetishism or fetishism-transvestism he studied among human epileptic patients, nine displayed abnormal **electroencephalograms (EEG).** From these and other clinical cases cited in the literature of links between epilepsy and fetish behavior, Epstein argues that in the adult fetishist the relationship to the fetish object may be understood as a release from inhibition against approach to a specific object.

Epstein believes that psychopharmacologists and neurosurgeons seeking to devise therapies for the psychosexual disorders should direct their attention to certain areas of the brain. Future studies of sexual psychology and psychopathology may need to take into account the role of the brain, particularly its limbic portions.

genetic scale, the role of instinctual patterns and hormonal control dininishes to such an extent that socialization takes precedence over many physical limitations, even extreme physiological abnormalities.

The effects of social learning are particularly evident among compulsive masturbators who, to take an obvious example, may be driven to their favorite sexual expression whenever they are frustrated by everyday problems. But learning is also apparent in the case of the pedophiles whose preference for children may be a consequence of not having learned how to approach adults for sexual gratification. This person may choose children as sexual objects because of being shy or uneasy in the company of adults; as a throwback to youthful, perhaps pleasant, sexual experiences with peers; or because of an unpleasant experience with an adult sexual partner.

Incest, as we noted earlier, may be due to the person's feelings of inadequacy in approaching another adult, or may be a consequence of the individual's history of repeated rejections by a spouse or lover. It may simply be more expedient, as in the case of father-daughter incest, to seduce someone with whom a close relationship has been cultivated than to begin a new courtship.

The psychodynamics of rape may be more complex, since it is often an act of violence rather than sexually motivated. However, when sex is a motive for rape, the attack may be explained as an exaggeration of society's prescription that males obtain their sex through aggressive and forceful means.

The main etiological factor implicated in the development of satyriasis seems to be the need of some males to prove themselves sexually adequate. What better proof of sexual potency than affairs with many women? These sexual escapades assure a Don Juan that he is wanted and sought after and, perhaps more important, that he is virile. In some satyrs there is also an element of hostile revenge: they vindictively pursue a pattern designed to compensate for the years of sexual deprivation they endured during adolescence. Or the male may simply have an insatiable need for love and attention.

In many respects, the etiology of nymphomania is similar to that of satyriasis. A woman's promiscuous behavior may be a desperate bid for attention and love, and she may be unconsciously fighting a fear that she is sexually inadequate. In this regard, it has been repeatedly mentioned in the literature that many nymphomaniacs come from families lacking emotional warmth and that they are sexually unresponsive (Rosen et al., 1972; Thorpe et al., 1964).

Impotence does not necessarily result from a lack of desire for sexual gratification; it may be due to fear caused by repeated failures with female partners. The belief that he is incapable of doing what is expected of him in a heterosexual relationship may also become a self-fulfilling prophecy: his fear of failure prevents satisfactory coitus, and the failure confirms the fear, establishing the cycle that results in renewed failures.

Impotence may also result from feelings of shame and guilt due to faulty early training, when sexual impulses were associated in the individual's mind with dirt and evil. The corresponding anxiety then makes it physiologically impossible to participate successfully in sexual relations.

Finally, factors implicated in the causes of frigidity are essentially similar to those giving rise to impotence—fear, guilt, and hostility. Fear is perhaps stronger in women than in men because, in addition to the anxiety and shame associated with sex during growing up, women face possible pregnancy. There are instances reported in the clinical literature of women who, although functionally frigid throughout many years of marriage, lost their frigidity after having a hysterectomy or after menopause.

Guilt and hostility play the same role in the etiology of frigidity that they do in impotence. Guilt may be due to faulty training or associations of sex with dirt and evil; hostility may manifest itself in the wife whose affection or love for her husband has waned but who continues to be a dutiful sex partner. Her frigidity thus becomes an expression of animosity toward her husband.

Summary

The differences between normal and abnormal behavior are not self-evident; therefore, statistical, cultural, personal, and other criteria are applied in defining abnormality. Statistical normality is usual or average behavior; deviation from this average defines abnormality. Cultural criteria judge persons abnormal on the basis of their inability or unwillingness to adhere to societal prescriptions. A third criterion of abnormality is to define it in terms of the personal distress experienced by the individual. Finer distinctions separate the disorders into the neurotic, psychophysiological, and psychotic disorders, as well as childhood, adolescent, and other less severe behavior patterns. There are also categories of normal behavior, and these are defined mainly by descriptions of attributes that characterize a select group of exceptionally able people. Abraham H. Maslow found that these people deal with the world realistically, accept themselves and others readily, appreciate their natural environment and culture, and can when necessary, function independently of their surroundings and culture.

According to the psychoanalytic hypothesis and some learning theorists, repression, or unconsciously motivated forgetting, is the main defense mechanism available to the individual for coping with the anxiety of unresolved conflict. The form of the neurosis may be conceptualized according to one's success in dealing with anxiety, of which there are six important types: anxious, depressive, obsessive-compulsive, phobic, hypochondriacal, and hysterical. Anxiety neurosis, which occurs when the defenses are not functioning properly, is characterized by overconcern and apprehension about most situations and events. In depression, the person's anxiety is turned inward, and in the obsessive-compulsive neurosis it manifests itself in unwanted thoughts and urges. The phobic neurotic is overwhelmed by a fear of objects or situations, and the hypochondriacal neurotic is overwhelmed by a fear of having developed a rare disease. The hysterical disorders, which—according to theory—reflect the successful functioning of repression, are marked by sensory, perceptual, and motor symptoms (conversion hysteria) as well as by sleepwalking, loss of memory, and multiple personality (dissociative hysteria).

The psychophysiological disorders are characterized by physical abnormalities that have psychological or emotional bases. In the main, the autonomic nervous system is the mediator between emotion and organic involvement. The tissues and organs involved in these disorders are the skin, muscles, bones, intestines, and cardiovascular system.

Psychotics are more disordered than neurotics, and typically have hallucinations and delusions. Simple schizophrenia develops slowly, usually during adolescence, and is marked by apathy and indifference. Hebephrenic schizophrenia's distinguishing feature is the impulsivity and silliness of persons afflicted by it. Catatonic schizophrenia is characterized by a stupor that is often followed by exaggerated excitement. Of all the schizophrenias discussed here, the paranoid type is the most frequent; its main features include delusions of persecution and auditory hallucinations.

Disorders of childhood and adolescence include disorders of feeding and elimination, aggression, withdrawal, and miscellaneous youthful forms of adult disturbances. The most dramatic among these, although somewhat rare, is so-called infantile autism. It has an early onset, usually at about four months. The infant or child cannot speak with, or relate to and behave normally toward others. The difficulty of classifying the childhood disorders, as we noted, is that the symptoms are not yet well formed.

People diagnosed as suffering from antisocial personality are less severely disturbed than neurotics and psychotics in that they function more adequately in some aspects, but are nonetheless maladaptive and irrational. Their behavior is impulsive and not clearly motivated, and they tend to be undependable, dishonest, disloyal, and generally untrustworthy.

The sexual disorders mentioned were masturbation, pedophilia, incest, rape, satyriasis, nymphomania, impotence, frigidity, sadism, masochism, and voyeurism. With the possible exception of incest and rape, which are often acts of violence rather than sex, drawing the line between abnormal and normal sex is difficult. Nonetheless, legal and cultural distinctions are made, although these are admittedly unsatisfactory.

Psychological theories are more plausible than biological ones for the neurotic, psychophysiological, youthful, and less severe personality patterns. The main thrust of research on the causes of schizophrenia, however, has been biological. Solid evidence has been sparse for either psychogenic or biogenic explanations, and the weight of the arguments seems to favor a combination of hereditary and environmental effects on behavior. Isolating the relative contribution of either of these seems to be the main difficulty.

Suggested Readings

Cleckley, H. 1964. *The mask of sanity.* 4th ed. St. Louis: Mosby.

This difficult-to-find book contains many fascinating case descriptions of antisocial personalities.

Glass, C. D., and Singer, J. E. 1972. *Urban stress: Experiments on noise and social stressors.* New York: Academic.

Awarded the American Association for the Advancement of Science Sociopsychological prize for 1971, this is a report on how to study the effects on human beings of noise, electric shock, harassment, and discrimination.

Kaplan, B., ed. 1964. *The inner world of mental illness.* New York: Harper & Row.

Contains personal accounts of what it is like to be mentally ill.

Kleinmuntz, B. 1974. *Essentials of abnormal psychology.* New York: Harper & Row.

One of this book's distinguishing features is its emphasis on psychopathology among blacks in America.

Laing, R. D. 1967. *The politics of experience.* New York: Ballantine.

The tone of this book by a British psychiatrist is set by the following statement:

"Given the conditions of contemporary civilization, how can one claim that the 'normal' man is sane?"

Millon, T., and Millon, R. 1974. *Abnormal behavior and personality: A biosocial learning approach.* Philadelphia: W. B. Saunders.

In addition to covering the traditional abnormalities, this book, unlike many others, discusses the personality pattern disturbances—the more common but milder personality disorders characterized by maladaptive patterns of behavior.

Seligman, M. E. P. 1975. *Helplessness: On development and death.* San Francisco: W. H. Freeman.

On the basis of extensive animal and human research on the causes of depression, the author formulates a theory of its development that postulates loss of control and unpredictability as central concepts.

Selye, H. 1974. *Stress without distress.* Philadelphia: J. B. Lippincott.

An excellent summary of this pioneer researcher's life work on the physiological and psychological effects of stress and how to avoid it.

Ullmann, L. P., and Krasner, L. 1975. *A psychological approach to abnormal behavior.* 2d ed. Englewood Cliffs, N.J.: Prentice Hall.

This book is distinguished by its behavioral approach to the abnormalities, their causes and cures.

Zubin, J., and Money, J., eds. 1973. *Contemporary sexual behavior: Critical issues in the 1970s.* Baltimore: Johns Hopkins.

Articles in this book cover topics from animal to human sex research and from abortion to zoophilia.

Behavior Change

17 All psychotherapies begin with an inquiry into the nature of a problem and then strive, usually by means of verbal give and take, to produce beneficial changes in behavior or personality. The precise techniques used by the therapist, and the course and length of the relationship, depend on his or her training and orientation. Freudian therapists, for instance, because of their emphasis on unconscious motives, tend to rely chiefly on free association and dream analysis. Adlerians are more oriented toward promoting sound social relationships and therefore stress goal-setting and social striving. Rogerians value creative growth and self-actualization and hence favor nondirective therapeutic strategies designed to permit self-discovery.

Varieties of Psychotherapy

17·1 Some therapists play a passive or nondirective role during psychotherapy, thus placing on the client the major responsibility for change. Others are more directive during sessions and may even tell the patient how best to conduct himself or herself in everyday dealings. Still others, especially among the more behaviorally oriented therapists, use direct methods of manipulation. But there are some commonalities worth noting among the verbal psychotherapies.

Commonalities among Various Psychotherapies The psychotherapies are similar to each other in four ways:

1. The therapist always accepts the person. Regardless of the therapist's biases and standards, and no matter what the patient says or claims to have done, the therapist does not make moral judgments.
2. There is, with few exceptions, an emphasis on verbal communication as a means of establishing connections between the patient's inner and outer worlds. The therapist needs excellent listening skills and the ability to facilitate free expression.

Therapy demands more than just listening and responding, however; it also requires the ability to grasp meanings from minimal cues. Theodor Reik (1948, p. 145), a Freudian psychoanalyst, describes this ability as "receiving, recording, and decoding these 'asides,' which are whispered between sentences and without sentences," or "listening with a third ear." Such sensitivity facilitates understanding. The feeling of being understood is a powerful motivator for a troubled client, often encouraging him or her to communicate without constraint.

3. Each participant performs according to an agreement. The therapist agrees to assume responsibility for the client's psychological well-being; in return, the client or patient is expected to be completely honest, insofar as possible, about his or her feelings and actions and is committed to changing himself or herself.

   The unique relationship between therapist and patient has been called a *contract* by some (Menninger, 1958) and a *partnership* by others (Sundberg et al., 1973). It often requires that the therapist take an objective and perhaps detached view of the patient and his or her problems, lest the therapist become emotionally involved and hence render himself or herself unable to help.

4. Psychotherapy aims to provide the patient with insight, or understanding, about himself or herself in relation to others. Whether the individual is able to apply the insights gained in therapy to everyday affairs may depend largely on the skill of the therapist.

Scope and Range of Psychotherapy Goals In addition to the commonalities discussed above, the psychotherapies share a variety of aims. Common overriding goals are to help people cope competently with everyday affairs, to make people aware of the significance and consequences of what they are doing, and to help them take responsibility for their own dealings and actions. Specific objectives may include removing maladaptive responses; curing phobias, tics, or bedwetting; restructuring personality; resolving real or imagined conflicts; alleviating anxiety; improving interpersonal skills; and facilitating the acquisition of greater self-understanding.

These aims are sometimes difficult to attain because our reactions to the world around us are often firmly fixed as a result of lifelong patterns of behaving. Furthermore, it is not unusual for people to stoutly defend even their most unrewarding behaviors. Nor is it easy to gain new insights about oneself, even under the most favorable therapeutic conditions. In other words, for most of us, it has taken a lot of learning to become what we are, and it may take a lot of time to unlearn old habits and acquire new ones.

The Setting Psychotherapy may occur in an inpatient setting such as a mental or general hospital, or it may take place in a variety of outpatient places. Typically, with the more disturbed and disrupted people, psychotherapy is conducted in the hospital because it is deemed necessary to remove the individual from the home environment that contributed to the problem. But hospitalization no longer necessarily means commitment to an institution. It now includes many kinds of care in part-time hospital settings.

When it is not important to hospitalize an individual, psychotherapy takes place in any of several outpatient facilities. The traditional outpatient care center is the so-called mental health or mental hygiene clinic, but this has given way of late to the easily accessible walk-in or store-front clinics, crisis intervention centers, hot-line telephone numbers, and growth centers.

The Patient or Client Until perhaps the mid 1960s almost the only people to consult mental health professionals were severely disturbed and chronically anxious individuals. With the greater accessibility of mental health care and growth centers, and because of the public's increased awareness of possible gains to be realized from psychotherapy, many people are now seeing therapists or attending group sessions whenever they sense that their current modes of coping are unsatisfactory, or whenever they feel they are not getting what they want out of life.

Clients may be seen individually on a one-to-one basis, or they may be seen as a couple, a family, or a group. When a client is seen individually, the therapist may recommend that a spouse or some other family member also seek consultations either with the same therapist or with someone else. It is quite common for a husband and wife to be seen by the same therapist, either sequentially or together. When it is apparent that the problem involves other members of the immediate or extended family, the therapist may also want to see them. Again, they need not all see the same therapist, but it is essential that the therapeutic efforts be coordinated.

Group therapy, as we shall see later in this chapter, can be carried out in addition to individual psychotherapy or by itself. There are many types of groups, ranging from the traditional psychoanalytic variety to encounter groups typical of growth centers, where the group leader is known as a trainer or facilitator rather than a doctor.

The Therapist Traditionally, the three professionals that dealt with clients were the *psychiatrist*, *clinical psychologist*, and *psychiatric social worker*. The first of these is an M.D. This person's medical training and biological orientation equip him or her especially well for the somatic treatments. The clinical psychologist, a Ph.D. with graduate training in psychology, is especially well qualified for psychological assessment and research methodology. The social worker's unique contribution, no doubt an outgrowth of the history of that profession, is the collecting of extensive family history and home environment information about clients.

This traditional separation of roles breaks down, however, as far as verbal psychotherapy is concerned. All three types of professionals conduct diagnostic and therapeutic interview sessions with clients. Their success in bringing about behavior or personality change is related more to their individual skills and experience than to the credentials they hold.

In addition to these traditional mental health workers, there are others involved in treatment. In the hospitals, of course, there are the psychiatric nurses and aides who, in well-run inpatient facilities at least, are sympathetic and important participants in the patient's well-being. More recently, lay persons called paraprofessionals have been trained to deliver mental health care services on a paid or volunteer basis. In some hospital programs everyone—patients and staff alike—assumes both the therapist's role and the patient's role.

Perhaps the most time-honored tradition in using paraprofessionals is the use of parents as therapists. Among the first such uses was Freud's analysis of a phobia in a five-year-old boy (Little Hans) via the boy's father. Characteristically, *filial therapy*, as it is called, is conducted by the parents after they have been trained by therapists. Much of the training involves teaching parents to listen more closely to what their children are saying, verbally and nonverbally. This is often best accomplished, especially when young children are involved, by having the parents conduct action-oriented play sessions with their offspring.

College students have also undertaken peer counseling. The so-called *peer-help centers* that have sprung up on college campuses became popular in the late 1960s and early 1970s because of radical changes of lifestyles among many college students. As a result of these changes, which in many instances polarized into conflicts between school personnel and students, some counselors and students realized that it might be helpful for some students to talk to their peers about their problems rather than to someone having drastically different values or perceptions, with whom they might not be able to communicate easily.

More recently the *hot-line* approach to conducting therapy has come into popular use in communities and colleges. Hot-lines are widely advertised in newspapers and other media and invite people to call on the telephone to discuss their problems, particularly if crises have suddenly arisen. The hot-line at the University of Illinois in Chicago, for example, is attended around the clock by volunteer students who have been trained by the school's counseling personnel. Recent tabulations have shown that there are more than 100 calls per day, coming mostly from nonstudents in the Chicago community. Callers include potential suicides, lonesome individuals in need of company, rape victims, and people who want to establish long-term therapy relationships but feel unable to face another individual with their problems. There have been calls, also, from men who get sexual gratification from hearing a female voice at the other end of the phone. These callers, as well as most of the others, are often encouraged to seek more intensive treatment than the hot-line can offer.

Models of Psychotherapy The form of treatment used by the psychotherapist is guided by the model he or she has of human nature. Thus, the therapist who views people as being controlled by unconscious motives and drives may use a

Freudian method of treatment. The therapist whose view of people is that they are products of external stresses and strains may favor the Adlerians' socially-oriented form of individual psychology or **behavior modification** with its emphasis on controlling stimulus and response variables.

A biological-mechanistic conceptualization of human nature, in which the therapist sees the individual's problems in terms of signs and symptoms of a malfunctioning machine, may result in a preference for physical modes of treatment (that is, drugs or electroshock). The therapist who sees humans as basically healthy organisms whose potential to grow and experience life fully is sometimes not realized may pursue a humanistic or phenomenological strategy such as those of George Kelly, A. H. Maslow, and Carl Rogers.

Approaches to Psychotherapy

17·2 Psychotherapy, broadly defined, includes all forms of treatment aimed at changing personality or behavior. The major part of this section discusses verbal or interview types of interactions between therapists and clients, but some of the more manipulative methods and certain physical forms of treatment will also be presented.

Freudian Psychoanalysis One of Sigmund Freud's important contributions to a view of psychopathology was that individuals repress, or relegate to unconsciousness, their conflicts and their unacceptable and threatening thoughts and impulses. Once in the unconscious, these imponderables become the energy that contributes to distorted perceptions of reality and to symptom development. Let us see how Freud used these and other concepts in psychotherapy, a practice that had its roots in the clinic, where Freud listened to neurotic men and women and formulated his theory of personality.

The major aim of Freudian psychoanalysis is to help the individual gain conscious access to his repressed self so that he will no longer be controlled by unconscious drives, needs, or motives and will be better able to exert conscious control over his life. Since the roots of one's symptoms are presumably found in early childhood, psychoanalysis focuses on childhood relationships and seeks to help the individual achieve emotional understanding about significant early experiences. Toward this end, the analyst's main tools are free association, dream interpretation, transference, and analysis.

Regarding the first of these, Freud laid down a fundamental rule for patients in psychoanalytic therapy: they are to talk about whatever comes to mind without censoring, no matter how painful, trivial, or inane these matters may seem to them. To facilitate free association, the patient relaxes on a couch, with the analyst sitting behind him or her and out of the line of vision, taking notes. When the patient complains that there is nothing left to free-associate about, this too is given a special significance by the analyst. It is interpreted as a symptom of unconscious *resistance* toward the therapist or toward disclosing important material.

This resistance and the contexts within which it occurs also become topics for analysis.

Free association results in a stream of thoughts that, when permitted free rein, provides valuable clues about important wishes and impulses that were repressed while growing up. According to Freud, nothing we say or do is accidental; therefore, even a person's most undisciplined cognitive meanderings have psychological significance. In other words, statements are related in meaningful ways to preceding ones that, in turn, are influenced by prior thinking and actions. This continuous stream of associations adds up, in the sense that it follows logically from, and provides valuable clues about, the individual's total personality.

Freudians also analyze dreams, which they consider the key to the unconscious. The patient's dreams, and his or her feelings about them, are considered especially revealing because he or she can exercise little control over their unfolding. In *The Interpretation of Dreams* (Freud, 1900), Sigmund Freud calls attention to their significance by indicating that dream content stems from the events of the day and represents, often in disguised form, wish-fulfilling expressions of unconscious and unacceptable thoughts.

Transference occurs during psychoanalysis when the patient attributes to the therapist feelings, reactions, animosities, and affections that he or she holds and has held toward influential persons in his or her life. Freud considered this an unusual, but highly significant, feature of the psychotherapeutic relationship. The psychoanalyst structures the situation in a way that almost ensures the occurrence of such a relationship: the professional and social distance from the patient, the position behind the patient during therapy, the interpretation of the patient's seemingly inconsequential remarks and actions—all contribute to the transference. In a sense the therapist becomes a projective object toward whom the patient reacts, albeit unconsciously, as he or she did toward important figures in his or her life. For example, the therapist may be perceived as the patient's mother, spouse, or sibling, usually even becoming the object of the same love or hate the patient has felt toward them.

The development and resolution of the transference is a major part of psychoanalysis because the patient-to-therapist relationship is primarily a product of the patient's repressed distortions and therefore gives the therapist valuable information about basic conflicts and infantile responses. It also affords the analyst opportunities to help the patient both gain awareness of these reactions and discriminate between old conflicts and the new ones directed toward the therapist. One way the therapist facilitates such discrimination is by reacting neutrally, and hence differently from early figures in the patient's life.

But transference can also create difficulties during psychoanalysis. The therapist must guard against *countertransference*—reacting to the patient on the basis of one's own feelings and traits. Through extensive training and with the help of other analysts, the therapist gains a thorough understanding of his or her own motivations and personality in order not to respond to the patient's affections and hostilities with his or her own love and animosity.

Analysis is the psychoanalytic process whereby the therapist helps the patient understand the transference relationship. This personality interpretation is accomplished over an extended period of time during the analytic sessions when the analyst, on the basis of the patient's words and actions, finds occasion to point out how the patient's feelings and conflicts are rooted in his or her past and are not rational reactions to the therapist.

To illustrate how psychoanalytic therapy proceeds, we have selected an excerpt of a case analyzed by Theodor Reik, an orthodox Freudian psychoanalyst (Case Report 17•1). This excerpt, though not a transcript of the dialogue between patient and psychotherapist, furnishes a glimpse of the entire process. The patient, a man in his early thirties, told Reik that he had become increasingly nervous and depressed the previous year and had to interrupt work for a few months. During the early sessions of psychoanalysis, the man gave an autobiographical sketch that extended from childhood to the present crisis. From the beginning, the patient emphasized that he had been lucky because he had an excellent position, that his marriage had been fairly good, and that he loved his children. He also mentioned that his parents had made great sacrifices for his education and that he had been successful in high school and especially in college, where he made social connections that became useful in his later life. The remainder of this patient's analysis is described in Case Report 17•1.

This case illustrates well the analyst's emphasis on the importance of unconscious conflicts and guilt in producing behavioral symptoms. It also demonstrates the typical pattern of **psychoanalysis,** which can be described as follows: Early in the analysis the therapist claims to know what is wrong with the patient. He or she then seeks clinical proof during subsequent sessions, but defers disclosing this knowledge until the patient seems to be emotionally ready to accept these interpretations.

Neo-Freudians and Other Defectors Several schools of psychotherapy being practiced today have their roots in Freudian psychoanalysis. Some of these, such as the developmental theory of Erik Erikson, constitute small but important modifications of the traditional form, but others, as we shall see, were the result of outright defections from the orthodox Freudian camp.

Erik Erikson Erikson's position (1964) is close to Freud's; his eight stages of ego development strongly resemble Freud's psychosexual stages (Chapter 3). Erikson's developmental theory postulates that failure or success in resolving the crisis confronted at each stage results in predictable psychological consequences. Thus, success in early infancy ends in trust, failure in mistrust; success during later infancy in autonomy, failure in self-doubt; and so on, through the eighth stage, late adulthood, in which success or failure may result, respectively, in integrity or despair.

Erikson's popularity on college campuses is due to his recognition of the difficulty some people experience in finding ego **identity,** especially between ages

Case Report 17·1, Psychoanalytic Therapy

The father of a friend had given him a small job in the big manufacturing company in which he had a leading position. A department chief in the company asked him, after a short time in the office, whether he would like to work for him. The young man accepted the offer gratefully and his work was so good that he was promoted. His patron died and was replaced by an older man, who also liked the young, efficient, and well-mannered clerk. He soon became not only the assistant of his new boss but also his confidential adviser. The old man made many complaints about the management of the company and about some of his superiors, including the man who had first helped the patient to get his job. Also, his original benefactor had remained friendly with the ambitious young man and had confided in him, among other things, his growing dissatisfaction with the department chief, the patient's boss. Thus the patient was in an ambiguous situation; he had to listen for hours to complaints and accusations from both sides. Finally, his boss, who was a grumbling and dissatisfied man, was removed from his office to another branch of the company and the young man was asked to take his place.

Now a strange thing happened; slowly, and at first imperceptibly, a change in his attitude took place. He began to doubt his ability to handle the position and became afraid of the great responsibility connected with it. He felt an increasing apprehension and nervousness. . . . He felt increasingly reluctant to go to the office where he had to take over his new position. He was afraid to face the task that awaited him. He stayed away. At the end he refused to leave the house.

While I listened to the patient's report, I felt some hidden emotional connections. . . . It was obvious that the man became ill when a wish that he had nursed for a long time became a reality. He had been very ambitious and had certainly wished to take the place of the old man and thus obtain a prominent position in the company. . . . No doubt, I said to myself, here are powers of conscience operating in the dark.

The patient had wished for a long time that the old man who had been so kind to him would be removed from the position that he wanted for himself. He must have listened to the complaints of the old man and to the expressions of dissatisfaction of his chief with great suspense, and always with the wish that the outcome of the conflict would be that he himself would succeed his boss. And when the old man was finally removed, an unconscious moral reaction set in.

My impression that my patient broke down under the assault of unconscious-guilt-feeling on account of his wishes will have to wait for proof. When I shall tell him much later what I discovered about his own hidden character, he will, I am sure, deny his unconscious conscience got the better of him. Yet he will at the end admit that he must have thought he did not deserve the position. Doesn't this behavior already amount to an unconscious confession of his guilt in thoughts? (From Reik, 1948)

twelve and twenty. This difficulty brings role confusion and with it self-consciousness, distorted sexuality, authority problems, and value confusion, all of which cause anxiety. This anxiety undermines adult security and may lead to mistrust, doubt, guilt, inferiority, isolation, stagnation, and despair.

The role of therapists, according to Erikson (1964, p. 97), is to "become the guardians of lost life stages: ideally speaking, our work of rehabilitation should at least provide a meaningful moratorium, a period of delay in further commitment."

Carl G. Jung (1875–1961). Jung believed that there could be no psychology of consciousness without the recognition of the unconscious, which exists at two levels—the personal and the collective.

Carl Jung's Analytical Psychology Jung was a contemporary of Freud who at first accepted Freud's ideas but later parted company with him and formulated his own theory of personality. Compared with the theories of Freud and Erikson, Jung's *analytical psychology,* as he called it, is mystical; it also deemphasizes sexuality as a central theme. Our brief presentation of this position touches on only a few of its concepts and principles.

For Jung, the **libido** is considered a life energy that originated from the body's processes and that may force the person in either of two directions. The first direction is *introversive* (inner-oriented) and is evident in the person whose world centers on subjective, personal experiences; the second direction is *extroversive* (outgoing) and is manifested by the individual who is more concerned with objects and people.

Another important concept for Jung was the *objective psyche,* which in his early writings he called the **collective unconscious.** It has an autonomous existence independent of a person's subjective being and is the sum total of his or her inherited memory traces. These memories, according to Hall and Lindzey (1970, p. 83), "are not inherited as such; rather we inherit the possibility of reviving experiences of past generations."

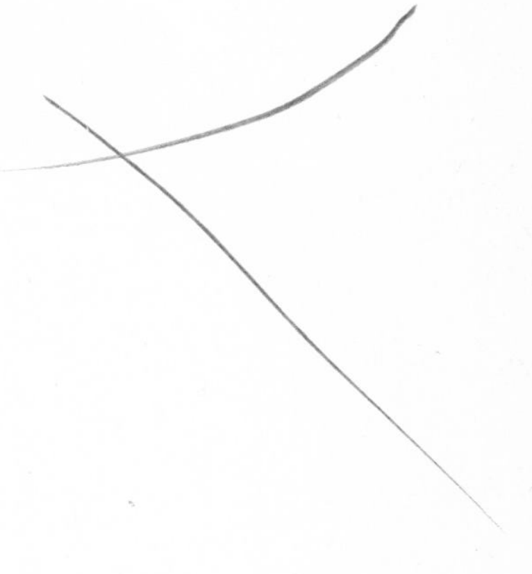

Among the various components of the objective psyche are the **archetypes,** which are like templates stored within each person to produce *images* of things that correspond to one's conscious situation. For example, the archetype of the father creates the image that is then identified with the real father. These archetypes are a storehouse of latent emotions and may be further subdivided into the persona, self, and complexes.

The *persona,* which is the Latin word for "mask," refers to the masks worn by the actors of ancient Greek drama and represents the outer appearance that each individual shows the world. In a sense, it is the individual's response both to society's prescriptions and mores and to his or her own archetypal demands.

Jung defined the *self* as a striving toward an ideal personality; in this sense it is not the real person but rather a motivating force that constantly undergoes modification by the person's conscious and unconscious experiences. And *complexes* according to Jung (1968, p. 188), are each individual's "agglomeration of associations," which are directly involved in his or her becoming neurotic or psychotic:

> A neurosis is a dissociation of personality due to the existence of complexes. To have complexes is in itself normal; but if the complexes are incompatible, that part of the personality which is too contrary to the conscious part becomes split off.

In large part, Jung's theory consists of uncovering the patient's complexes, for he believed that each complex has tensions, energies, and even a personality of its own. A complex can "upset the stomach . . . breathing . . . and heart" (1968, p. 80). His tools for uncovering complexes consisted of interpreting dreams, fantasies, and artistic productions as if they were texts in a remote language that must be studied carefully to be understood.

The Individual Psychology of Alfred Adler Alfred Adler was also a contemporary of Freud and a member of Freud's psychoanalytic circle. He had worked closely with him, even becoming Freud's successor as president of the Vienna Psychoanalytic Society and coeditor of its journal, but then, like several other former associates of Freud, Adler broke away from Freud's unrelenting tutelage. He founded what he called the school of *individual psychology.* Adler's theory of personality and methods of treatment are less well known than those of Freud, but many of its terms and constructs have made their way into the vernacular—**organ inferiority, compensation, lifestyle,** and **feelings of inferiority.**

Adlerian therapy includes three major objectives: (1) understanding the lifestyle of the patient, the specific problem situation, and the significance and meaning of the person's symptoms; (2) explaining the patient to himself or herself in such a way that the person accepts the interpretation, despite the initial negativism and lack of cooperation that are a part of the neurotic personality; and (3) strengthening the patient's social interest by giving him or her the experience of another

Unlike Freudian psychoanalysis, other forms of therapy usually occur with the therapist and patient sitting face to face. The type and amount of verbal interaction depend largely on the particular type of therapy and the individuals involved. (Photograph by National Institute of Mental Health)

Alternative Insight Therapies

THEORIST AND APPROACH	CONCEPTS	GOALS AND TECHNIQUES
Wilhelm Reich (Psychoanalytic)	Blocking of feeling in early childhood causes tension, which remains in the body as muscular rigidity—that is, as *character resistances* and *character armor* (sometimes disclosed in verbalizations or body expressions).	To analyze character resistances and remove the armor by having persons relive traumatic events.
Arthur Janov (Primal therapy; Neo-Freudian)	Primal pain results from denied and suppressed needs and their consequent body tensions.	To remove primal pain by depriving the patient of his defenses. Body expressions and screaming are used to release tensions and to allow the person to feel the original need.
Erich Fromm (Ethical psychoanalysis; Neo-Freudian)	Relatedness to society and the world are essential to psychological well-being.	To bring the person back to society and help him understand the meaning of freedom and life by means of combined psychoanalytic and existential methods.
Harry Stack Sullivan (Interpersonal therapy; Neo-Freudian)	Both personality and psychiatric disorders are interpersonal in origin.	To restore the person's interpersonal relations by analyzing the transference relationships with the therapist.
Viktor Frankl (Logotherapy)	The collective neurosis of our time is loss of meaning in life—the "existential vacuum."	To encourage the patient to expose himself to feared situations ("paradoxical intention") so that it can be demonstrated that the expected results do not occur ("de-reflection").
Albert Ellis (Rational-emotive therapy)	Emotional illness is due to irrational thinking.	To change such thinking, and consequently emotions and behavior, by using rational arguments.
Sidney Jourard (Self-disclosure)	Neuroticism results from a person's using devices to avoid becoming known.	To guide the person back to health by serving as a model and as a genuine teacher.
George A. Kelly (Personal construct counseling)	A person's thinking and behavior are determined by the way he anticipates events—that is, by his personal constructs.	To reconstruct the person's system of constructs, partly through role-playing.
Frederick C. Thorne (Eclectic viewpoint)	Empirical psychological knowledge is integrated into a comprehensive system of theories and techniques.	To teach clients rational, logical problem-solving approaches to living.

person and a feeling of cooperation in the joint task of treatment (Ansbacher and Ansbacher, 1956).

The first of these three objectives involves understanding the occurrence that precipitated the patient's current dilemma. Adlerians try to identify this dilemma, along with the patient's inappropriate responses, by attending carefully to the way in which he or she reports them. Following this general diagnosis, the therapist formulates a special diagnosis by (1) eliciting from the patient behaviors and reports about early childhood recollections, critical childhood disorders, aggravating life conditions (organ inferiorities, pressures in the family, pampering, sibling rivalry, or a neurotic family tradition), in the content of daytime fantasies and nighttime dreams, and (2) carefully examining expressive movements during the therapy sessions.

Explaining the patient to himself or herself, in Adlerian therapy, involves a verbal tour de force, in which the therapist hopes to convince the patient by sheer logic that his or her coping mechanisms are not up to the task of facing life's hardships. But because neurotics are presumed to cling to their faulty lifestyles, Adlerians often resort to overwhelming their patients by correctly predicting behavior that they, the therapists, later witness. In this way, they hope to convince patients that behavior is self-consistent and goal-directed and therefore transparent or predictable and that they, the therapists, are truly expert at understanding such behavior.

The third objective—strengthening social interest—is analogous to the function of the parent, who interprets society to the child. In fact, Adler relegates this task to the mother, and his attitude toward the mothers of neurotics is reflected when he states that if she "fails in this, the task is likely to fall much later to the physician, who is heavily handicapped for it. The mother has the enormous advantage . . . [because] she represents the greatest experience of love and fellowship that the child will ever have" (Ansbacher and Ansbacher, 1956, p. 341).

Perhaps the best way to illustrate how Adlerian therapy works is to let Alfred Adler speak for himself, as he does in Case Report 17•2 when he describes a very pretty girl who had been spoiled by her mother and ill-used by a drunken father. This girl became an actress and had many love affairs, one of which culminated in her becoming the mistress of an elderly married man. This relationship brought her trouble, first because her mother reproached her for her bad judgment, and second, because even though the man loved her, he could not get a divorce from his wife. She then began to suffer from headaches and heart palpitation and became very irritable toward the man.

Humanistic-existential Therapies Humanistic, or existential, therapies generally concentrate on helping the individual to take responsibility for his own life and to realize his potential to be a fully functioning person who is open to experience. Although there may be some discussion of past events as in psychoanalysis, the focus is more often on the here and now.

Case Report 17·2, Adlerian Psychotherapy

The girl's condition was the result of a neurotic method of striving to hasten her marriage, and was not at all ineffective. The married man, who was greatly worried by her continuous headaches, came to see me about my patient, and said he would hurry the divorce and marry her. Treatment of the immediate illness was easy—in fact it would have cleared up without me, for the girl was powerful enough to succeed with the help of her headaches.

I explained to her the connection between her headaches and the competitive attitude with her sister; it was the goal of her childhood not to be surpassed by her younger sister. She felt incapable of obtaining her goal of superiority by normal means, for she was one of those children whose interest has become absorbed in themselves, and who tremble for fear that they may not succeed. She admitted that she cared only for herself and did not like the man she was about to marry.

Her palpitation was due to the fact that she had twice been pregnant and both times had resorted to abortion, when she justified herself to the doctor by saying that her heart was too weak to bear children. It was true that her heart was irritated by tense situations and suppressed anger, but she used this symptom increasingly and exaggerated it to justify her intention never to have children. Self-absorbed women generally show their lack of human and social interest by unwillingness to have children; but sometimes, of course, they desire children for reasons of ambition or for fear of being considered inferior. (From Adler, 1929, 1957)

Carl Rogers and Client-centered Therapy In sharp contrast to the Freudian, Adlerian, and other neo-Freudian approaches is Carl Rogers's client-centered therapy (1951, 1961), which is more in the humanistic-existential tradition. Humanists have turned away from both the traditional medical model of illness and the behaviorist stimulus-response psychology. Instead, humanistic psychology—or third-force psychology, as Maslow called it—focuses on each person as a unique individual with a potential for self-actualization. How the humanist model of human nature differs from the more traditional models can be seen in Carl Rogers's anguish over using the term *client* (1951, p. 7):

> What term shall be used to indicate the person with whom the therapist is dealing? "Patient," "subject," "counselee," "analysand" are terms which have been used. We have increasingly used the term *client*, to the point where we have absorbed it into the label of the "client-centered therapy." It has been chosen because, in spite of its imperfections of dictionary meaning, and derivation, it seems to come closest to conveying the picture of this person as we see it. The client, as the term has acquired its meaning, is one who comes actively and voluntarily to

gain help on a problem, but without any notion of surrendering his own responsibility for the situation. It is because the term has these connotations that we have chosen it, as it avoids the connotation of the sick, or the subject of an experiment, and so on.

Carl R. Rogers (1902–). In addition to creating the concept of client-centered or nondirective therapy, Rogers initiated the recording of therapy interviews for use in research and training.

In contrast to Adler, who views the therapist as the agent mainly responsible for inducing change in the patient's behavior and personality, Rogers places this responsibility squarely on the shoulders of the client. As Rogers sees it, the therapist's task is to create the proper condition for change. This is consonant with his trust in every individual's natural potential for growth, though he recognizes that some people may be temporarily stifled by personal or situational difficulties that await freeing.

A primary objective of Rogerian therapy is to help the client learn to perceive and accept himself or herself without anxious self-evaluation. Presumably, personality difficulties arise from a conflict between a person's two fundamental evaluative processes—those based on self-evaluative tendencies and those based on the values of other persons. Thus the client-centered approach aspires to create an atmosphere during therapy in which the client feels understood (empathic understanding) and accepted as a whole person (unconditional positive regard). Under these circumstances, hopefully, he or she will learn to be minimally critical of himself or herself.

The Rogerian therapist achieves these aims mainly by reflecting the client's feelings. This involves sensing the client's meanings and articulating them as clearly as possible. How this is actually accomplished during the interview is difficult to describe and probably is best exemplified by a transcription from one of Rogers's sessions. For this purpose, we have selected an excerpt from the concluding portion of the thirteenth interview between Rogers and a married woman (Case Report 17•3). This turned out to be her third-from-last session.

Note how in this dialogue the therapist helps the client assume responsibility for her progress by encouraging her to reach her own decisions; the client, rather than her therapist, makes the important interpretations. These differences set off the Rogerian approach from some of the traditional psychotherapies discussed earlier.

A. H. Maslow's Humanistic Psychology Maslow became interested in humanistic psychology during World War II as a result of his disillusionment with human baseness. According to one account (Maddi and Costa, 1972, p. 145), this experience led to his "giving up all his previous studies, finding them insufficiently related to the struggle for human survival that was going on." In order to lift man out of this baseness, he felt, there should be a movement within psychology that emphasized man's greatness and striving to live up to his potential—a psychology of **self-actualization.**

Maslow did not prescribe any specific psychotherapeutic techniques except to say that as "illness becomes more and more severe, it becomes less and less accessible to benefit from need gratification. . . . It is at this point that professional

Case Report 17·3, Client-centered Therapy

Client: I'll tell you how I feel about my coming here. I don't think I have to come twice a week. I would like to come once a week for the time being and see and just talk over my problems once a week. And, then, if everything goes smoothly on the once-a-week deal, why then I think I'm through. The only reason I'm not stopping now, although I feel right now I don't need any more, is that I just want to feel a lasting final few licks, shall we say.

Therapist: You want to feel quite sure that you are really through before you quit.

CL: Or if this is one of these quiet weeks, if it is, why then I'll have to start coming back twice, maybe three times. I hope not.

TH: By and large you feel that you are getting close to the end.

CL: I think so. How does one determine?

TH: Just the way you are determining.

CL: Oh, is that so, just by feeling that you don't have to come as often?

TH: When you are ready to call it quits, why we'll call it quits.

CL: Uh huh, and then no return, uh?

TH: Oh yes, if you feel you want to.

CL: And then I'd have priority on you is that it?

TH: Oh, yes, yes. We don't close the door and lock it, we just say goodbye and if you want to get in touch with me again, why feel free to do so.

CL: I mean, I feel as if I have just about covered almost every phase of my difficulty and, uh, I think one could keep going talking and talking and talking about it, if it weren't doing any good. What I mean to say, if the cure hadn't been started, and I think it has—I sort of have leveled off, quite suddenly it seems to me, because last week, why is it, last Tuesday when I was here I was in a terrible state, this terrible state. I thought of suicide, which I hadn't even thought of for almost a year or so, and yet Tuesday night, maybe its darkest before dawn or something like that, you know, platitudes.

TH: Sometimes it is; (Cl: It is?) sometimes not, I mean, it's interesting.

CL: Yes, but I had really reached a low, and it seems maybe superficial to say that in three or four days I come back and I feel like a different person, but I think maybe I was reaching a certain emotional—setting myself for an emotional revelation, subconscious revelation which I didn't know but that it was just coming to the top like a boil.

(continued)

Case Report 17-3 continued

TH: Getting to the point where you had to do something about the whole business.

CL: Yes, I realized the position, that I had to get it out, and I did, Tuesday night, and it wasn't that I sat down and I said, "Well, Arnold, let's talk it out. . . ." I didn't do that. My feeling of hatred towards him was so intense that I was weak already, really I was so weak—I said something and he misunderstood me. And then I misunderstood him and I said, "Arnold, we just don't meet at all, do we, Arnold?" Then he said, "Well, let's talk" so we sat down and talked. So he took the initiative, and I started to talk to him for a whole hour and a half. Before it opened up I hated him, I couldn't talk, "Oh, he won't understand." "We don't meet on the same level." To myself, "Let's get away from each other. I can't stand to be with you, you irritate me. . ...." Then all of a sudden, I said, "Arnold, do you know that I feel sexually inferior to you," and that did it. The very fact that I could tell him that. Which was, I think that was the very thing, the whole thought to admit, not to admit to myself, because I knew that all the time, but to bring it up so that I could have admitted it to him, which I think was the whole turning point.

TH: To be able to admit what you regarded as your deepest weakness.

CL: Yes.

TH: Just started the ball rolling.

CL: This feeling of sexual inadequacy, but now that he knows it—it isn't important any more. It is like I carried a secret with me, and I wanted somebody to share it and Arnold of all people, and finally he knows about it so I feel better. So I don't feel inadequate.

TH: The worst is known and accepted.

(From Rogers, 1951, pp. 85–87)

(insight) therapy becomes not only necessary but irreplaceable. . . . Free associations, dream interpretation, interpretation of meaning behind everyday behavior, are the major paths by which therapists help the patient to gain conscious insight into himself" (1970, pp. 258–59).

Maslow went beyond the traditional approaches in that he also recommended self-therapy and personal growth groups. Self-therapy has some possibilities if the person learns to know what he or she needs and can then consciously go about satisfying these unmet needs. But this technique has limited usefulness—for example, it cannot be used to treat antisocial personality and neuroses. For these problems, Maslow suggested professional therapy.

Gestalt Therapy The **Gestalt therapy** of Frederick Perls had somewhat different beginnings (1970), although it is also a part of the third force in psychology and shares Rogers's, Maslow's, and Jourard's interest in self-actualization, intimacy, authenticity, and creativity. Just as Maslow was disillusioned about the prospects for human survival, Perls was dismayed by the brutalizing conditions of World War I. But beyond this, Perls's formulations were inspired by his dissatisfactions with the rigid tenets of psychoanalytic libido theory, after the contributions he tried to make to this theory early in his career were rejected.

The emphasis of Gestalt therapy is on the here and now (Wallen, 1970). In contrast to traditional thinkers, Gestaltists concern themselves more with the individual's awareness of present experience than with the past. They argue that whether or not an individual's problems in living stem from early childhood experiences, they can be dealt with in terms of being and relating in the here and now. Thus in Gestalt therapy people are encouraged to specify the changes they desire; and they are assisted, not only in increasing their awareness of how they defeat themselves, but also in experimenting and changing. In Perls's own words (1970, pp. 18–19):

> Especially in therapy, we come to the "sick point," to the point where we are stuck, to the impasse. The impasse occurs where we cannot produce our own support and where environmental support is not forthcoming. Gestalt therapy . . . (helps us) get through the impasse . . . (by) . . . uncovering our own ability, our own eyes, in order to find our potential, to see what is going on, to discover how we can enlarge our lives, to find means at our disposal that will let us cope with a difficult situation.

Gestaltists formulated their therapy around rules and games. The rules are the *principle of the now* ("What is your present awareness?"), *I and thou* ("To whom are you saying this?"), *"it" language* and *"I" language* (change "It is sad" to "I am crying"), *use of the awareness continuum* (the "how" of experience), *no gossiping* ("direct confrontation of feelings"), and *no questions* ("change that question into a statement"). The games are numerous, and an innovative therapist may devise new ones from time to time. Of the dozen or so games listed, the following two are typical (Levitsky and Perls, 1970, pp. 146–49).

> **Unfinished business . . .** is the Gestalt therapy analogue of the perceptual or cognitive incomplete task of Gestalt psychology. Whenever unfinished business (unresolved feelings) is identified, the patient is asked to complete it. Obviously all of us have endless lists of unfinished business in the realm of interpersonal relations, with, for instance, parents, siblings, friends. . . . Resentments are the most common and important kinds of unfinished business.
>
> **Marriage counseling games** The partners face each other and take turns saying sentences beginning with, "I resent you for . . . ," "What I appreciate in your is . . . ," "I spite you by . . . ," "I am compliant by. . . ."

Brief Psychotherapy The conventional and innovative psychotherapies covered so far are time-consuming and expensive. Each session runs about fifty minutes,

The Neglected Client

In an article in the *Black Scholar* (Jones and Jones, 1970), two black psychologists discuss the shortcomings of contemporary counseling for approximately 15 percent of the U.S. population—the blacks. The main problem, according to them, is the economic deprivation of blacks, but the root of the problem may go beyond this.

Even when blacks have the opportunity to be heard, most white middle-class counselors are ill prepared to recognize and deal with them as fellow human beings. The ghetto culture is foreign to these counselors. In a similar vein, Frantz Fanon (1967, pp. 150–51), the noted black psychiatrist from Martinique, said "There has been much talk of psychoanalysis in connection with the Negro . . . but Freud and Adler and even the cosmic Jung did not think of the Negro in all their investigations."

Psychiatrists Grier and Cobbs forcefully bring this point home in their book *The Jesus Bag* (1971), when they suggest that black patients have had little reason over the years to trust healers because they have been singled out by the white therapist's society as a universal victim. It is therefore naive to ask the black client to set aside his defenses and to enter unarmed into the house of his enemy. In their earlier book, *Black Rage* (1968, p. 180) these authors observed:

> In psychotherapy . . . the essential ingredient is the capacity of the therapist to love his patient—to say to him that here is a second chance to organize his inner life, to say that you have a listener and companion who wants you to make it. If you must weep, I'll wipe your tears. . . . I will, in fact, do anything to help you be what you can be—my love for you is of such an order. How many people, black or white, can so open their arms to a suffering black man?

and the average number of sessions, over a two- or three-year period, may be as much as 750 sessions for Freudian psychoanalysis and 200 sessions for most other forms. Such treatment, with its emphasis on insight and self-knowledge, is usually accessible only to the wealthy and to those who have much time to devote to themselves. Clearly it is not geared to handling emergency situations or for the needs of the indigent. For these reasons, and because of federal, state, and local legislation that has encouraged the opening of community mental health centers in urban areas, brief psychotherapy—the so-called fifteen- or twenty-minute hour—has received increased attention from mental health workers (Aguilera et al., 1970; Barten, 1969).

In contrast to long-term psychotherapy with its unhurried pace and detailed exploration, brief therapy quickly focuses on specific, usually crucial, problems to be solved and allows the patient little chance to wander away from this focal point. Its primary, and sometimes only, goals are to abate the patient's symptoms and to restore his or her ability to function adequately.

Toward these ends, the therapist assumes a more active role than in traditional methods. He or she quickly but systematically probes all facets of the patient's situation relating to the problem that led him or her to seek help. The first interview is the most important, for in it the therapist develops his or her theory about the patient's problem. Throughout this session the therapist avoids digressions and focuses only on issues, or on the patient's comments that bear directly on the present problem. During the subsequent five to ten sessions, he or she attempts to help the patient acquire some insight into his or her inability to cope with difficulties, and concentrates on having the patient translate these insights into action.

Because of the brief nature of this method, some writers emphasize the importance of having the patient feel relief as rapidly as possible (Aguilera et al., 1970). Not all patients are capable of benefiting from this treatment. Those who do are usually people whose problem or personality disruption is of recent onset, whose previous adjustment was satisfactory, whose environment is stable, and for whom the degree of precipitating stress was not overwhelming. Brief therapy is not likely to succeed among psychotics or other patients with longstanding illnesses.

Psychotherapy for Couples and Families Sometimes the problem is interpersonal—it exists not within an individual but between people. For example, a couple or a family may have a pattern of communication (or noncommunication) that makes it difficult for individuals to satisfy their needs. Marriage counseling is intended to help couples attain greater understanding of what has gone wrong in their interpersonal relationships and of how they might salvage their marriage, if that is possible. Sometimes an entire family is seen together by a therapist. This makes especially good sense when the child is the client or patient, because it is within the family that each child learns his or her ways of coping with life.

The goals of family therapy consist mainly of fostering greater family understanding of the factors contributing to the problem of the target individual (usually a child). This goal may be achieved by manipulating and changing undesirable environmental conditions or by strengthening each family member's ability to cope with situations in and out of the home.

In most marital and family counseling approaches it is assumed that the root of the problem can be found in unresolved personal conflicts. The way to remedy the problem, then, is to gain insight into, and greater emotional understanding of these conflicts. Behavioral therapists make no such assumptions. Instead they attempt to identify the troublesome stimuli or situations and to modify the reinforcing conditions within the family that sustain maladaptive behavior.

Group Psychotherapy Group psychotherapy, which has been in use for about fifty years, gained increasing recognition immediately after World War II, largely because of the growing demands of large numbers of people for whom individual care was impossible. Like the other therapies covered so far, it involves many orientations and different points of view. Its main objective is to promote the acquisition of insight and self-understanding within the group context. How this is accomplished varies greatly, depending on the orientation of the leader.

Some group therapists follow the classical Freudian or Adlerian model, while others prefer less interpretive approaches. Freudians, for example, conduct themselves as authority or father figures, perceive group members as siblings who act out with one another, and engage freely in the interpretation of feelings. What a patient does and says is treated as transference and is analyzed in terms of his or

As a means of changing behavior and emotions, group therapy involves the individual's adaptation and response to other persons. The persons in the group may be alike or different with respect to age, background, and the type of problem dealt with. (Photograph by National Institute of Mental Health)

her internal dynamics. Adlerians, on the other hand, with their emphasis on social interest eschew internal states and use the group session to promote reorientation, altruism, and healthy interpersonal relationships.

Most group leaders, whatever their orientation, attempt to foster fundamental behavior and personality changes and to investigate reasons for emotional difficulties. All groups provide social stimulation and support for members and encourage them to experiment with relationships with one another. Typically, the group therapist's main responsibility is to stimulate discussion and to ensure that interactions are therapeutic and minimally damaging.

Human Relations Training Many people seek out group experiences not because they feel troubled but because they want to learn to relate better to others or to enhance their own growth. The earliest of such groups, the so-called *T-group* (T for training), had as its main objective the improvement of communication skills. It began just after World War II in response to the needs of educators, business managers, and administrators to learn better ways of coping on their jobs. Within the last decade many people have availed themselves of these groups as vehicles for *human relations training.*

In general, the goals of human relations training differ from those of classical group psychotherapy in that they (1) emphasize the here and now rather than the past or family life, (2) pay more attention to interpersonal competence than to motives for behavior, and (3) stress group processes and member interactions rather than leader-member relationships. With the increased popularization of human relations training there has been a proliferation of *growth centers*, which focus on the enhancement of the total individual.

One such center is the *Esalen Institute*, a nonprofit institution with facilities in Big Sur and San Francisco. It describes itself as a "center exploring the trends in education, religion, philosophy, and the physical and behavioral sciences that emphasize the potentialities and values of human existence." Its methods, sometimes indistinguishable from traditional group therapy, may include a blending of techniques borrowed from psychodrama, art therapy, and interpretive dance as well as yoga, massage, hypnotism, and meditation.

The therapeutic goals of **encounter groups** (as groups for human relations training are sometimes called) are similar to those of the humanistic-existential tradition, especially the client-centered therapy of Carl Rogers and the Gestalt therapy of Frederick Perls. This is evident in the following quote taken from a description of the marathon group (Bach, 1969, pp. 305–306):

> Generally two new modes of acting, feeling, and being emerge during a marathon: (1) transparency of the real self, which (being accepted and reinforced by the peer group) leads to (2) psychological intimacy within the peer group. This sequence from transparency to intimacy is a natural development because what alienates people from one another are the masks they put on, the roles they take, the images they try to create, and many of the games they play.

Much like Gestalt groups, encounter groups attempt to engage participants in a series of games designed to enhance awareness of feelings. These games are also intended to help people become more conscious of their effects on others, to encourage the expression of emotion, and to foster self-understanding and self-acceptance.

One of the concerns commonly expressed about encounter groups, probably because they closely resemble other forms of group therapy, is that they may be dangerous to people who need a form of psychotherapy not offered by these groups. The concern is that some people are not sufficiently buttressed emotionally for the trauma that such encounters may engender. No good evidence of this danger has been produced, however, and most attempts to uncover harmful effects of training groups have failed to be substantiated by research findings. There is in fact some evidence that group participants, rather than being damaged, develop increased openness, greater tolerance for new information, and greater acceptance of human differences (Bunker, 1965; Yalom, 1971).

Behavior Therapy In contrast to the foregoing psychotherapies, behavior therapy relies somewhat less on verbalization, is less concerned with helping patients gain self-understanding or self-acceptance, and is directed more toward removing symptoms than toward restructuring personality. Its origins are also different. Whereas the insight and group methods evolved from clinical practice, behavior therapy grew out of the psychology laboratory. Thus it modifies behavior by applying the

Assertiveness training seeks to help a person learn (1) to express both positive and negative feelings, (2) to let other people know how he or she wants to be treated, and (3) to say yes to one's own desires. More and more women have used this form of behavior therapy to overcome the cultural stereotypes that teach women to subordinate their needs to those of others. (Owen Franken, Stock, Boston)

principles of conditioning stemming from the work of learning theorists such as Pavlov, Thorndike, Watson, and Skinner.

We shall focus here on assertiveness training, which has its roots in Pavlov's classical conditioning schema; on operant (instrumental) behavior modification and token economies, which trace their origins to E. L. Thorndike's and B. F. Skinner's work; and on modeling, which borrows from both classical and operant methods and is the most recent addition to the behavioral approaches.

Assertiveness training, as the name implies, is a form of therapy intended for people whose interpersonal and other behaviors are inhibited by anxiety and who lack appropriate assertive behavior. The therapist's goal in these cases is to augment the elicitation of these previously inhibited responses, with the expectation that each time they appear, there will be reciprocal inhibiting of the anxiety, resulting in some weakening of the anxiety habit (Lazarus, 1971; O'Leary and Wilson, 1975; Wolpe, 1969).

The therapist implements these goals first by asking questions designed to establish how the patient behaves passively in a number of situations ("Suppose that on arriving home after buying an article, you find it slightly damaged. What will you do?") and then by informing the patient that the outward expression of resentment will reciprocally inhibit anxiety. The therapist also points out how the patient's (or others') behavior is maladaptive, and he or she may even argue with the patient until convincing him or her of the logic of becoming more assertive. According to Wolpe and Lazarus (1966, p. 44), "such discourse . . . usually results in enough augmentation of resentment to quell the restraint of fear and permit the emergence of some assertive responses."

The patient is then encouraged, in various real-life situations, to try some of the following types of assertive statements (Wolpe, 1969, pp. 66–67):

Please don't stand in front of me.
I hate your duplicity.
I would rather not say.
Why are you late?
Pardon me—I was here first.
I like you.
I love you.
I admire your tenacity.

Although the idea of trying out these assertive responses in progressively more demanding or stressful real-life situations may be easy for some, not everyone can manage to assert himself or herself without practice. Therefore this training may also involve *behavior rehearsal,* which is a form of role-playing. In these instances, the therapist plays the part of the person who usually evokes anxiety and the patient's role is to assert himself or herself. Wolpe mentions that "a good deal of deconditioning of anxiety frequently takes place during the behavior rehearsal itself" (1969, p. 68). The trick, of course, is to get the inhibition of anxiety to generalize to real-life situations.

Comparison of Insight Therapy and Behavior Therapy

ITEMS FOR COMPARISON	INSIGHT THERAPY	BEHAVIOR THERAPY
Theoretical Bases	Based on depth theories that rely mainly on intrapsychic phenomena.	Based on principles of learning and conditioning that take environment into account.
	Derived from clinical observations.	Derived from laboratory work
	Deductions are confirmed and disconfirmed in the clinical setting.	Basic theory and its deductions are testable in the laboratory.
Diagnosis	Considers symptoms as consequences of intrapsychic and (sometimes) unconscious forces.	Considers symptoms as signs of maladaptive responses due to faulty learning and sustaining environmental conditions.
Treatment	Treatment focuses on the neurotic disorders, with minimal success in removing psychotic symptoms.	Psychotic symptoms as well as those of neurotics are amenable to behavior therapy.
	Treatment of neurotic disorders is usually historically based and techniques involve recall of childhood.	Historical background unimportant; treatment tends to focus on the here and now.
	Cures consist of peeling away defenses, not symptoms.	Cures consist of extinguishing symptoms and eliminating, sustaining, or controlling stimuli.
	Interpretation of behaviors and dreams important.	Analysis of stimulus-response-reinforcement conditions essential.
	Removal of symptoms leads to substitution of new symptoms.	Symptomatic treatment leads to recovery, provided that autonomic as well as skeletal responses are removed.
	Transference and other long-term rapport relationships are essential for curing the neuroses.	Personal relations with therapist not as essential, although sometimes useful.

(Adapted from Eysenck and Rachman, 1965)

Operant Behavior Modification Operant behavior modification accomplishes behavior change in three steps:

1. The therapist makes a thorough analysis of the interaction between the behaving organism and the environment in which the behavior occurs.
2. The therapist brings the consequences of given forms of behavior under his or her control.
3. The therapist transfers this control to the patient (Kanfer and Phillips, 1970).

One application of operant behavior therapy is the treatment of alcoholism, as described in Case Report 17•4. This is the case of a chronic alcoholic (Sulzer, 1965), who often got into trouble while drunk. He frequently vowed to stop drinking but failed to break the habit. He tried traditional psychotherapy without success. **Aversive conditioning** with an emetic was proposed to him, but he rejected it because his job required that he enter taverns and cafes where alcohol is served.

The therapist treating this case was fortunate to enlist the cooperation of two friends the patient was concerned about losing because of his frequent drunken-

Case Report 17•4, Behavior Modification in an Alcoholic

The primary goal of therapy was to reduce or stop the patient's drinking behavior. Solitary drinking did not appear to be a serious problem, because he did not often drink alone. In interviews he seemed concerned about losing the friendship of two men who now found his frequent drunken states so objectionable that they avoided him. Neither friend was a teetotaler, nor did either drink heavily.

The patient contacted his friends, who agreed to the following plan. After working hours they would meet at a conveniently located tavern where the three could drink for a time before going home. The patient was to order only soft beverages. If he ordered or drank hard liquor, the friends would leave immediately. The others could drink anything they wished. This plan was to continue, on a once-a-week basis, for an undetermined period of time. Also, the patient agreed to invite his friends to his home on all occasions that might call for serving alcoholic beverages. They agreed to come and remain only so long as he took no alcohol. They would also invite him to their homes on similar occasions but would not serve him alcohol.

The first planned accompanied drinking session occurred without incident and the patient reported that his initial discomfort quickly disappeared. The bartender, somewhat unexpectedly, served as an additional source of social reinforcement by acting more friendly than he had during the patient's previous visits.

The following day the patient, at the therapist's instructions, planned no business visits to taverns and restricted himself to other eating places not

ness and objectionable behavior. Evidently this cooperation was crucial to the treatment because these friends made it possible to develop social reinforcement for nonalcoholic drinking. The course of his therapy is described in Case Report 17•4, which the reader should examine before continuing.

Careful reading of this case reveals several essential elements of operant behavior therapy: the engineering approach to the study of behavior so that stimulus control is gained, the use of friends as social reinforcers, overt attempts at extinction of undesirable responses, and selective reinforcement of acceptable behaviors. The behavior therapist applied operant conditioning techniques to shape and reinforce more adaptive behavior in and out of the therapeutic environment.

Another variety of behavior therapy that traces its origins to the operant methods of Thorndike and Skinner is the **token economy,** which has been successfully tried in hospitals, where it has been especially effective with schizophrenics. Token-economy procedures were introduced in 1965 by Ayllón and Azrin, who used them in a psychiatric hospital ward, as we described in Chapter 13. They reported that when tokens were distributed as reinforcements for specific chores,

serving hard liquor. Several days later, however, the patient had to visit taverns for business reasons, and on these occasions he drank liquor again, but less than his previous amounts.

On the last day of that week, he contacted his friends to meet him for a drink, which they did. The patient was found to have already had several glasses of liquor when they arrived. The friends were uncertain whether to stay but decided to remain with the patient while he drank. As he sobered up, the patient reported to his friends that he felt quite comfortable and felt little desire to drink with them present. After almost two hours, the group broke up. That was the last day this patient was known to drink any alcoholic beverage.

During this period the therapist met with the patient twice weekly, always expressing approval of reported nondrinking behavior. Also during this time, the patient and his wife considered moving to a somewhat larger apartment in a different neighborhood. The therapist supported the proposed move because most of the patient's neighbors responded to him and his family in a way that strained interpersonal relationships and made sobriety more difficult.

The move was made a little over a month after the beginning of therapy and appeared to have had very favorable consequences. The patient remained sober, and his contacts with new neighbors did not include the kinds of responses he had encountered in his old neighborhood where most people reacted to him with either mild disgust or open disapproval.

(From Sulzer, 1965)

work output increased, but when reinforcements were withheld, work declined drastically. Several investigators using token economies have reported improved self-care behaviors, greater social interaction, and less psychotic behavior (Kazdin and Bootzin, 1972). One report from a West Coast Veterans Administration hospital even linked the initiation of a token-economy program with an increased discharge rate (Atthowe and Krasner, 1968).

Modeling is another form of behavioral therapy that involves both classical and operant conditioning. The chief proponent of modeling is Albert Bandura (Bandura and Walters, 1963; Bandura, 1969a, 1974), who, as we noted in Chapter 16, has argued that imitation, or modeling, may be as fundamental a form of learning as reinforcement. Modeling, which traces its beginnings to the animal experiments on imitation by Miller and Dollard (1941), is also known as **social learning,** *observation learning,* and *vicarious no-trial learning.* It has not yet enjoyed the attention and acceptance of the other behavior therapies and is still largely a research paradigm.

Kanfer and Phillips (1970, pp. 188–89) attempt to show the advantages of modeling over classical and operant conditioning by an example in which someone who has never used chopsticks goes to dinner with friends in a Japanese restaurant. He initiates a trial-and-error learning process, but since none of his available eating responses work, his behavior is "only gradually shaped." Because dropping food in his lap is an aversive conditioned stimulus, he gives up and asks for a fork. Instead, however, he might mentally describe to himself the features of his companions' behavior, modify his own behavior accordingly, and finally ask for instruction. One of his friends would demonstrate the proper technique, and he would then repeat the verbal instructions to himself and carry them out.

Modeling is used in a variety of behavior modification situations, usually in conjunction with other techniques such as **desensitization** of fears. Albert Bandura demonstrated the successful use of this method in a study in which he extinguished children's fear of dogs (Bandura and Menlove, 1968). Forty-eight children with dog phobias were separated into four groups, each of which was treated differently: members of the first group participated in eight sessions, during which they observed a fearless peer model exhibit progressively more fear-evoking interactions with a dog within a pleasant or party context; the second group witnessed the same performance, but in a neutral context; the third group witnessed the dog in a pleasurable setting, but with no peer model; and the fourth group engaged in pleasurable activities without exposure to the dog or peer model. All groups benefited from these procedures in that they showed a reduction in avoidance behavior in the presence of the test dog and an unfamiliar dog a month later, but both modeling conditions led to significantly greater and more stable improvement.

Hypnosis The therapeutic use of hypnosis was first reported in the eighteenth century by Franz Mesmer (1734–1815), who referred to it as animal magnetism. In his medical practice in Vienna, he cured a young woman of hysterical symptoms (convulsions, earaches, toothaches, fainting spells, urine retention, and paralysis) by using magnets. He explained the cure in terms of atmospheric and celestial forces (Mesmer, 1779).

Hypnotism did not gain respectability until the nineteenth century when James Braid (1795–1860), an English physician, coined the terms *hypnosis* and *hypnotism*, attributed hypnotism to suggestion, and asserted that a hypnotized subject was influenced by the operator. The current view of hypnosis, according to T. X. Barber (1974), one of the leading researchers on hypnotic phenomena, is that hypnosis does not differ qualitatively from other states of consciousness. He has proposed a cognitive-behavioral view that regards hypnosis as the product of specific expectancies and attitudes of the person within particular situations.

Hypnosis acquired a place in psychotherapy when Freud and his colleague Josef Breuer began to use it extensively as a psychotherapeutic tool. In 1895 they published *Studien uber Hysteria* (Breuer and Freud, 1895). Subsequently, as is now well known, Freud became disillusioned with the impermanency of hypnotic cures and rejected them as too laborious and ephemeral. In a sense this rejection, plus the low esteem in which experimentally oriented psychologists held this mysterious technique, dealt hypnosis a blow from which it has not yet recovered. However, contemporary experimentally minded psychologists such as T. X. Barber and others have become interested in the phenomenon, and over the past two decades there has been a flurry of activity aimed at understanding its psychotherapeutic possibilities and limitations.

Most depth-oriented therapists recommend using hypnosis only as an adjunctive tool, "for the purpose of facilitating psychotherapy" (Schneck, 1963, p. 169). In this respect hypnosis has been used to facilitate abreaction, or the release of repressed material; to suggest topics about which the patient should dream; to remove an amnesia for particular names and places; to hasten the transference relationship in psychoanalytic therapy; to reassure the patient of the reversibility of his or her condition; and to remove bothersome symptoms and thus focus the patient's attention on relevant areas. Symptoms that have been removed by direct hypnotic or posthypnotic suggestion include headache; neck, shoulder, and back strain; nailbiting; facial tics; some skin disorders or the itching attending them; peptic ulcer (by teaching the patient self-relaxation techniques); and fatty food preferences.

But hypnotherapy, as it is sometimes called, may—like behavior modification—also be viewed as a form of treatment. Many therapists treat people who suffer from habits that can be removed through either hypnosis or behavior therapy. "If the symptom is relieved, and the person is able to function again, then often his self-respect is restored, and he can go about improving his interpersonal relationships in the interests of a better total adjustment" (Wolberg, 1972, p. 229).

In large part, the difference between the adjunctive and the treatment uses of hypnosis depends on one's opinion about what constitutes success and what constitutes failure in psychotherapy. Unless stipulated by specific criteria, the notion of success or failure is meaningless. Gaining insight and restructuring one's personality may not always be as necessary as simply alleviating a symptom.

Biofeedback Techniques that are more closely related to the behavioral approaches than hypnosis, and that have recently been demonstrated to be effective in changing behavior, are the *reward learning,* or so-called biofeedback, methods. Essentially, these methods are designed to provide knowledge of results to subjects learning to control their internal or biological behaviors with the aid of electronic devices. This knowledge, which is the feedback to the organism, serves as a reward to the subject and is usually presented as an auditory or a visual signal.

Alpha-Wave Conditioning In a pioneering demonstration of biofeedback, Joe Kamiya (1962), a psychologist at the University of California Medical School, undertook to train a subject to change his brain-wave activity, particularly his alpha-wave reading (smooth, regular oscillations at a rate of 8 to 13 per second). To accomplish this, he used an operant conditioning approach that consisted of wiring the subject to a remote **electroencephalogram** (**EEG**) recorder and providing him with a **discriminative stimulus** (such as the ringing of a bell) at varying intervals. The subject's task was to guess whether or not he was in alpha at the sound of the bell. After each guess, he was given the correct information. After two or three days the subject guessed correctly on almost all trials, and by the fourth day he was accurate on every trial. Subsequently Kamiya demonstrated that human beings could not only identify alpha but could also learn to produce it on command (Kamiya, 1968) and to produce as much alpha as possible and as little as possible (Nowlis and Kamiya, 1970).

Theoretical and practical questions have been raised about the meaning of alpha control and the widely accepted rationale for using alpha feedback training as a means of teaching individuals to control their anxiety (Orne and Paskewitz, 1975; Lynch et al., 1975). In one study (Orne and Paskewitz, 1975), for example, it was demonstrated that subjects could experience fear as well as the autonomic concomitants of such experiences without associated changes in alpha-wave readings. The data of a second study (Lynch et al., 1975) raise questions about the worth of feedback sessions in teaching persons to control alpha. A third study (Walsh, 1975), however, supports the existence of an "alpha state" and emphasizes the importance of providing subjects with appropriate instructional sets.

Cardiovascular Changes The similarities between biofeedback and conditioning are also apparent in a number of studies in which individuals learn to control their blood pressure, heart rate, and other glandular activities. Especially noteworthy are a series of pioneering studies that originated in Neal Miller's psychological laboratory at Rockefeller University. He and his colleagues demonstrated that almost all of an animal's autonomic responding can be brought under control. In other words, voluntary behavior is not necessarily limited to the movement of the skeletal muscles but can be exercised in the control of the vegetative or autonomic functions (Miller, 1969; Miller and Banuazizi, 1968; Miller et al., 1970). Subsequent attempts to replicate some of these studies, however, have encountered difficulties that cast doubt on some of the earlier findings. It may be, however, that the exaggerated publicity about biofeedback in the popular press is "raising impossible hopes which will inevitably result in a premature disillusionment" (Miller and Dworkin, 1975, p. 96).

Psychotherapeutic Implications One of the major promises of biofeedback research lies in the possibilities it offers for people to help themselves and thus depend less on psychotherapists and others, especially in reducing anxiety, hypertension (usually synonymous with high blood pressure), and tension headaches. If indeed the autonomic nervous system (ANS) can be brought under conscious control, the implications for therapy are considerable, especially in treating the psychophysiological disorders, in which unconscious control is presumed to be exercised by the ANS.

Paul Grim (1971) has lowered anxiety in subjects by self-induced muscle tension and by relaxation with respiration feedback. Relaxation techniques have been reported since the 1930s (Jacobson, 1938), but the addition in Grim's study of a respiration feedback device is new. In this study, Grim used a self-report inventory to assess the anxiety levels of ninety-five nursing students; then, using electronic equipment he had designed to amplify breathing, he trained each student to breathe more and more smoothly until a state of complete relaxation was achieved. When the students again answered the questions on the self-report inventory, their scores were lower, indicating reduced levels of anxiety.

Hypertension causes dizziness and nausea and may culminate in cerebrovascular accidents (strokes) and death. Following the leads of others who have applied operant techniques to modify autonomic functions (Miller et al., 1970), David Shapiro of the Harvard Medical School demonstrated that people can be taught, through operant biofeedback procedures, to raise or lower their blood pressure.

In another clinical study designed to decrease blood pressure, four investigators (Benson et al., 1975) studied fourteen hypertensive patients who had been taught in four consecutive daily lessons to relax by means of *transcendental meditation* (*TM*). The relaxation consists of a mental device (the constant stimulus of a silently repeated sound or word called a mantra), a passive attitude (disregarding all distracting thoughts and constantly redirecting attention to the mantra), decreased muscle tonus (sitting in a comfortable position requiring minimal muscular work), and regular practice (the subject is required to practice the technique for two daily twenty-minute periods).

Repeated measurements of the pretraining blood pressures of the fourteen subjects averaged higher than those obtained from persons with normal blood pressure. After the experimental period of meditation, repeated measures were taken over a thirty-day period and this time the averages showed significant changes in the direction of reduced hypertension.

As a last illustration of therapeutic application we have chosen the work of

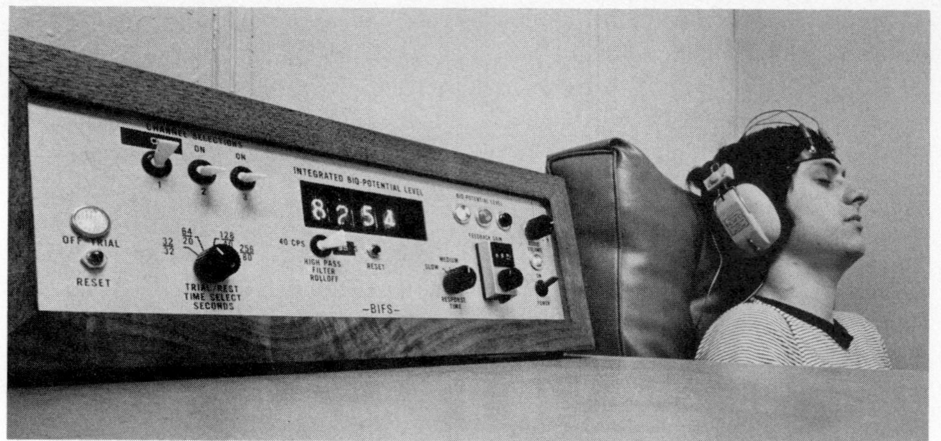

A muscle feedback machine in use. Sensors attached to the forehead record muscle activity while the earphones transmit varying tones to indicate the level of tension in the frontalis muscle group. (Stephen J. Potter)

Budzynski and his associates (1970), who used a feedback-induced muscle relaxation technique to reduce tension headache in five patients over a training period of four to eight weeks. While reclining on a couch in a dimly lighted room, the patient practiced relaxing without feedback during the first two thirty-minute sessions. From the third session on, **electromyographic** (**EMG**) feedback information from activity in the frontalis (forehead) muscle group was given. A high-pitched sound indicated heavy EMG activity, and a low-pitched tone indicated low EMG activity. (The apparatus is shown in Figure 17•1.) The patient was told that the tone follows the tension level in the muscle and was instructed to try to keep the tone low in pitch.

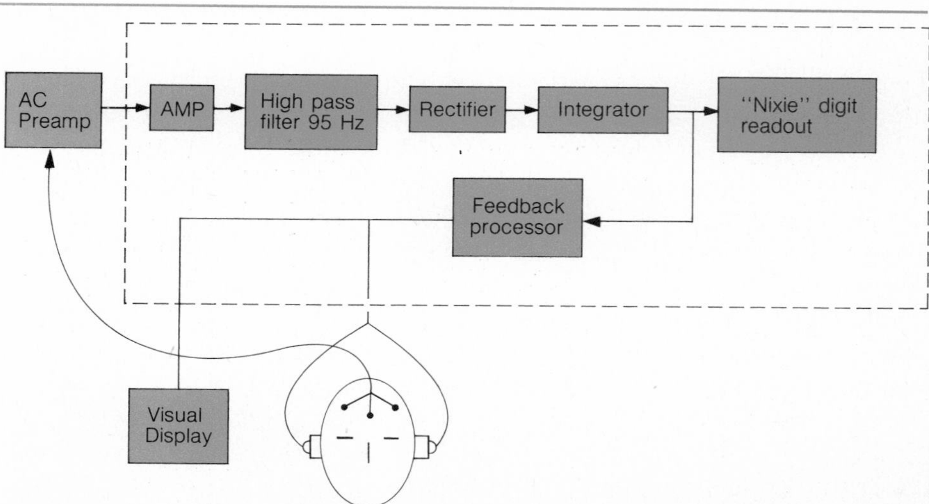

Fig. 17•1 A diagram of the EMG information feedback system designed to reduce tension headaches. (Budzynski et al., 1970)

Effectiveness of Biofeedback Biofeedback seems to be an important discovery, one that may have value in psychological treatment, although many questions must still be answered and many problems solved. When used in conjunction with other psychotherapeutic techniques, biofeedback may be particularly useful with certain patients.

According to Schwartz (1973), even if direct voluntary control of certain bodily functions or patterns of functions proves to have little therapeutic value, biofeedback can still serve to signal that the patient is doing something perhaps harmful to his or her physical or emotional health. Through biofeedback the patient with a visceral or neural disorder may be able to learn new ways of keeping his or her physiological processes within safer limits. Biofeedback is similar to the other psychotherapies in providing corrective feedback.

The Expressive Therapies Special techniques such as dance, art, drama, and games are often used with people who cannot easily verbalize their feelings. These techniques permit them to express their problems or conflicts primarily through action. In a sense, the expressive therapies lay the groundwork for more conventional psychotherapy, although some participants benefit directly from the opportunity for nonverbal self-expression.

We shall briefly discuss play therapy and psychodrama, because they served as early models for many contemporary expressive approaches.

Play Therapy Children often need action-oriented therapy because they do not easily verbalize their conflicts. Through play—the child's primary mode of expression—they may reveal their fears, anxieties, aspirations, feelings, and aggressions. The older the child, of course, the more closely the therapy resembles the talking cure of adults, even though in many instances action or expression still remains the useful catalyst for verbalization.

Depending on the age of the child, various media of play are used. For the younger child they include the standard toys used in his or her home, clay, finger paints, miniature dolls and furniture, as well as punching bags, boxing gloves, and building blocks; older children and adolescents are usually engaged in board games, billiards, or table tennis.

At the outset of therapy, play and action can be valuable icebreakers, because few younger children can sit down and talk their problems over with a total stranger. Throughout therapy, play and action permit children and adolescents to express their most secret wishes and feelings. The aggressive or hostile child, for example, can express animosity by punching or dismembering dolls or dummies, and the frustrated and anxious child can release pent-up emotions by reenacting with dolls numerous scenes that involve family members. Some children attain release by throwing darts, smashing objects, or smearing paint on a canvas or all over themselves.

Depending on his or her theoretical biases, the stage of therapy, and the child's readiness to accept the interpretation, the therapist sometimes interprets these expressions to a child. Regardless of the immediate use made of the material, the therapist has gained important information about the patient that might not have been obtained otherwise.

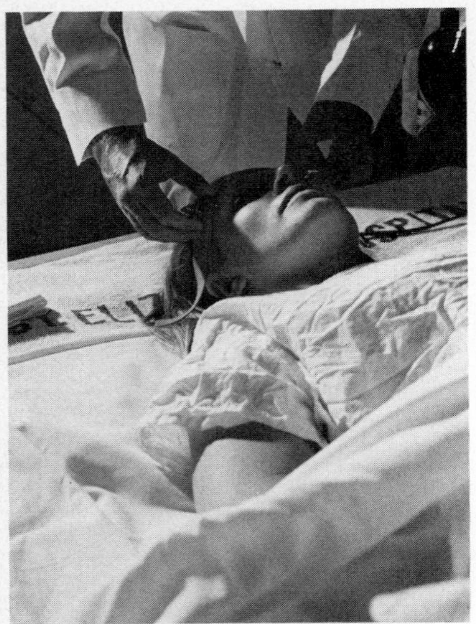

Schizophrenic patients, especially those suffering from depression, mania, or catatonia, are sometimes treated by passing an electric shock through the brain. Afterward the patient does not remember the treatment. (Photograph by National Institute of Mental Health)

Psychodrama In daily life a person has many roles. The same person may play the autocratic leader at work, and the dutiful spouse, the irresponsible spendthrift, or the passive parent at home. **Psychodrama,** invented by J. L. Moreno in 1925, uses role-playing to achieve its goal of helping people act out conscious and unconscious conflicts as well as their feelings and experiences. It seeks to encourage behavior change and greater emotional depth by permitting people to play roles that they cannot perform in their everyday lives.

Whereas play therapy tends to be applied on a one-to-one basis, psychodrama is almost always restricted to group therapy. Roles are enacted on a stage, in front of other group members or an audience, and specially designated and problem-related props and scripts are used.

The patient-audiences, many of whom share the actors' problems and conflicts, can therefore experience the role-playing vicariously (Moreno, 1959).

Somatic Treatment Somatic treatment is also a direct method for inducing behavior change; but it differs in most respects from those already discussed in that it achieves its aim mainly by physical assault on the physiology of the person. These procedures include electroshock therapy (EST) (sometimes also called electroconvulsive therapy or ECT), drug therapy, psychosurgery, and electrical stimulation of the brain (ESB), all of which must be administered by physicians. Often these techniques are used in conjunction with psychotherapy.

Electroshock Therapy (EST) First introduced by the two Italian physicians Cerletti and Bini (1938), electroshock therapy produces convulsions and unconsciousness, as does insulin shock therapy (IST). In EST the patient is first injected with a muscle-immobilizing drug to reduce the danger of self-inflicted harm during the convulsions; then electrical current is applied through two electrodes attached to the temples. Depending on the amount of electrical voltage used (from 65 to 140 volts for about 0.5 second), the resulting seizure resembles an epileptic seizure, either mild (petit mal) or complete (grand mal). EST is usually administered in a series of ten to twelve sessions over a two-week period. When greater amnesia or **regression** is desired (a use of EST that is becoming rare), EST may proceed on a daily (or more frequent) basis.

In the 1930s Meduna introduced the idea of inducing shock to treat severely psychotic patients. He based his theory on two commonly noted observations: patients become less psychotic when they have convulsions, no matter what causes the seizures; and epilepsy and schizophrenia rarely coexist in the same person. Although the validity of these observations is questionable, not much more is known about why the shock therapies reduce the symptoms of schizophrenia. EST has been most effective in treating depression, and its effects on depressed patients last longer than on patients with other psychoses. EST has virtually replaced IST and other shock therapies in the treatment of schizophrenia.

Drug Therapy Until the arrival of the drug therapies in the mid-1950s, EST and other shock therapies were virtually the only treatments for psychosis. Subsequently, the shock therapies came to be considered a thing of the past, a view strongly supported by the pharmaceutical industry. Although the initial enthusiasm that heralded the so-called miracle drugs has waned upon more careful experimentation, many of the available drugs help control various forms of distress. Formerly intractable and uncontrollable patients in hospitals have become manageable and sometimes rational. In fact, the introduction of these drugs has contributed to a steadily decreasing number of hospitalizations, from about 600,000 in 1955 to about half that number in 1976.

In outpatient and inpatient facilities, these drugs are used in combination with one another, or with psychotherapy or behavior modification, as well as with electroshock therapy. The main criticism in recent years has been that many of the psychiatric drugs are too easily available, with the predictable effect that they have been abused. Whereas many people used to try to work out their problems and anxieties or to seek professional help from a clergyman or family physician, the current trend is to depend heavily on antianxiety drugs. On the other hand, drug therapy is cheaper than psychotherapy, behavior modification, or hospitalization. Hence it is within easier reach for most people, rich and poor alike.

Therapeutic drugs are usually categorized according to their uses. The four main types are antianxiety, antipsychotic, antidepressant, and antimanic.

The *antianxiety drugs* are the most widely available and include such well-known trade names as Equanil and Miltown, which have in recent years been replaced in popularity by Valium and Librium. The main therapeutic application of the antianxiety or minor tranquilizing drugs is in the treatment of anxiety, muscular spasms, and tension, any of which may affect most of us or accompany the neuroses and psychophysiological disorders. These tranquilizers, under supervised and prescribed conditions, can also be effective in controlling acute anxiety and delirium tremens. In several well-controlled studies, Rickels (1966) showed their efficacy for the alleviation of neurotic symptoms. But these improvements are often unpredictable, may be due to placebo or suggestibility effects, and depend largely on a combination of the patient's personality and demographic and symptom characteristics. Whatever beneficial effects are derived from the minor tranquilizers, however, seems to be caused by their ability to induce musculoskeletal relaxation. The precise mechanism is not well understood, but some undesirable side effects of abuse are drowsiness; irritability; and, for some of these drugs, even convulsions, coma, and death if the person becomes dependent on them.

Drug Abuse

Psychoactive drugs are chemical substances that alter consciousness. Several principal types of drugs are often used for their psychoactive properties: narcotics, stimulants, depressants, hallucinogens (LSD and marijuana), volatile solvents, as well as numerous approved drugs, including tranquilizers. Abuse of any of these drugs may lead either to unusual physical or psychological sensations or to physiological or psychic dependence.

The so-called hard drugs that relieve pain are called *narcotics.* This category consists largely of the opiates, the best known of which are opium, morphine, heroin, codeine, and methadone. Depending on the individual and the situation, narcotics may produce feelings of serenity, warmth, tranquility, euphoria, nausea, drowsiness, confusion, apathy, lethargy, or even energy and strength.

A few seconds after the injection of a narcotic, the user's face flushes, the pupils constrict, and there is a tingling sensation, particularly in the abdomen. The tingling soon gives way to a feeling of elatedness (the "fix"), which lasts about thirty minutes. The user later drifts into somnolence ("going on the nod"), wakes up, drifts again, daydreaming all the while. These psychoactive effects wear off within about three to four hours, sometimes longer.

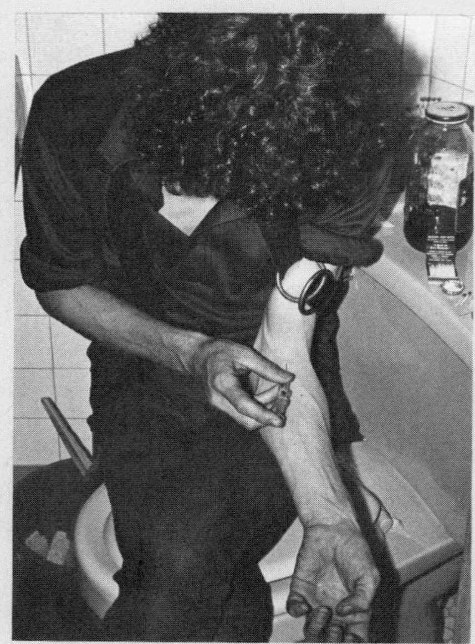

Obtaining a fix. Because of the pronounced danger of addiction, a U.S. law forbids the manufacture or importation of heroin or its salts. (Peter Menzel, Stock, Boston)

Psychic dependence develops when the drug user increasingly turns to narcotics to shut out problems and quell anxieties. Unfortunately, the anguish or misery that existed before taking the drug returns after its effects wear off. Furthermore, the anticipation of the severe withdrawal illness drives the narcotics user to seek out another fix.

The *stimulants* ("uppers"), such as Benzedrine, Dexedrine, and Methedrine (amphetamines), tend to speed up a person's activities, whereas the *depressants* ("downers"), such as Nembutal, Seconal, and Phenobarbital (barbiturates), tend to slow them down. Probably over ten million people in the United States use them legally by prescription, and another half a million individuals (who spend no less than $25 million yearly on amphetamines and barbiturates) obtain them on illicit markets. It has been estimated that about 25 percent of the barbiturates and almost 50 percent of the amphetamines manufactured annually in the United States find their way into illicit outlets.

Few drugs have had so profound an effect on American culture in so short a time as the hallucinogenic (hallucination-producing) drugs, especially lysergic acid diethylamide-25, familiarly known as LSD, acid, sugar, or sugar cube.

LSD is a tasteless, odorless, white powder prepared either synthetically or from ergot, a fungus growth on rye

The *antipsychotic compounds,* formerly known as the major tranquilizers, produce sedation without sleep or confusion and reduce chronic anxiety. The best known of these drugs is Thorazine (marketed under the generic name of chlorpromazine). Clinically, they are often used to reduce excitement, overactivity, and hallucinations in acute schizophrenia; to moderate the paranoid **delusions** of paranoiac and schizophrenic patients; and to attenuate the apathy and withdrawal accompanying other psychotic disorders. Their beneficial effects are believed to be

grain. Since it is difficult to obtain from legitimate sources, LSD is now sold mostly on the black market, where it may appear as sugar cubes mixed with LSD solutions, as powder in capsules, or in vials of solution of 1 cc each for individual doses (selling for from five to ten dollars a dose). In its bootleg form LSD varies widely in quality, dosage, and strength.

Variously called love weed, Indian hay, joy smoke, locoweed, laughing grass, reefer, hashish, hash, weed, or pot, marijuana is the weakest of all stimulant or hallucinogenic drugs. Its technical name is *cannabis indica* or *cannabis sativa,* depending on which part or type of hemp plant it came from, or *cannabis* for short. The hemp plant may be found in the mild climates of Africa, India, Mexico, and the Middle East. The variety grown in the United States is not as potent as the oriental varieties, but the American Indians probably knew and cultivated it for its intoxicating effects.

The short-term physiological effects of marijuana use are few—usually increased pulse rate, reddening of the eyes at the time of use, and dryness of the mouth and throat. Major physiological changes involving, for example, basal metabolism, body temperature, or respiration have not been found. Perhaps most importantly, marijuana has not been directly responsible for deaths caused by overdosage.

There is disagreement regarding the threat of long-term physiological damage from marijuana. Unfortunately, adequate information (particularly on the implications of low dosage, long-term use) is not yet available; but it is generally agreed that marijuana users do not develop a craving or tolerance for it and so are not subject to withdrawal symptoms after its suspension.

The short-term psychological effects of marijuana are numerous. Tests of intellectual and motor performance show impairment, especially at higher dosage levels. The more demanding and complex the task to be performed, the greater the degree of deficit (Clark et al., 1970; Jones et al., 1969; Melges et al., 1970; and Waskow et al., 1970). At extremely high dosages, psychosislike symptoms become increasingly severe. Most users, however, smoke only to the point of obtaining the high they find pleasurable and control the effect. External circumstances of the experience and personal expectations and beliefs about marijuana and its potency also help determine the drug's subjective effects.

A good deal less is known about marijuana's long-term psychological effects, but there have been world-wide reports from time to time indicating that heavy chronic marijuana use causes an *amotivational syndrome,* or a loss of ordinary goal orientation and social indifference (Chopra et al., 1942; Chopra and Chopra, 1957; Christozov, 1965; Indian Hemp Drugs Commission Report, 1893–94, 1969; Roland and Teste, 1958; Warnock 1903). Recent reports of chronic marijuana abuse in America are beginning to associate the drug with a type of social maladjustment characterized by loss of motivation to work, to compete, and to face challenges, as well as with personal slovenliness and avoidance of social interaction (Mirin et al., 1970; Smith, 1968). As with other drugs, however, it is difficult to ascertain whether the unmotivated gravitate toward drugs and find them unusually attractive, or the drugs actually cause loss of motivation.

due to their depressant action on the **hypothalamus** and the **reticular formation** of the brain. These parts of the central nervous system are intimately involved in the reactivity of the autonomic (involuntary) nervous system and arousal of the **cerebral cortex.**

In several well-controlled, large-scale hospital studies that compared the effects of *antipsychotic drugs* and placebos in changing the behavior of schizophrenics, Cole and Davis (1972) found that some of these drugs resulted in clinical improvement. Unfortunately, undesirable side effects were also found. Klein and Davis (1969), for example, list the following: Parkinson's syndrome (tremor, muscular rigidity, drooling), uncoordinated spasmodic body movements, increased heart rate, drowsiness, skin disorders and dermal photosensitivity, liver disease, convulsions, and some fatalities caused by a combination of drug-related effects.

The accidental discovery of such *antidepressant drugs* as Trofanil (generically called imipramine), Nardil (phenelzine), and Elavil (amitriptyline) is typical of the way much of science unfolds. According to one source (Ray, 1972), a new chemical was found in 1952 when preliminary reports suggested that a new drug, *isoniazid*, was effective in treating tuberculosis. When it was used with another drug, *iproniazid*, which is a monoamine oxidase (MAO) inhibitor, the combination was observed to be mood-elevating in tubercular patients. Unfortunately, its clinical efficacy with psychiatric patients was marred by toxic side effects that were as frequent as the successes, and the fatality rate (from liver toxicity) was unacceptable. But the finding that MAO inhibitors favorably affect mood and behavior led researchers to the idea that a noradrenergic substance (an energizer) may interact with chemicals in the brain called catecholamines. This catecholamine hypothesis, stated briefly, suggested that depression can be controlled by increasing the amount of noradrenaline at certain brain sites.

As a result of this research, the tricyclic compounds were developed. They have now replaced the MAO inhibitors for treatment of depression. Trofanil is the trade name of the most commonly used tricyclic drug; studies indicate that it is more effective in moderating the symptoms of depression than a placebo, no treatment, psychotherapy, or EST—although it may not be as effective as EST for the most serious depressions (Nathan and Harris, 1975, p. 242). The main action of antidepressants is as an energizer for depressed persons, but they may be ineffective for day-to-day ups and downs.

The antimanic drug most effective in treatment of the overly elated or euphoric moods of some manic psychotics (people whose psychosis manifests itself in frantic overactivity and a heightened sense of self-importance) is lithium carbonate, which is prescribed by the trade names of Eskalith or Litonate. Since its introduction in 1949, numerous encouraging results have been reported. Its original use was with a chloride compound that proved unsafe, but it was later combined with a carbonate chemical and is now considered reasonably safe and effective with manic patients (Prien et al., 1973) and with some depressed patients (Mendels, 1970).

Psychosurgery Brain surgery has been used for the intractably violent or self-destructive patient. Usually it involves either cutting into or removing portions of the **frontal lobes** (prefrontal lobotomy, lobectomy, or topectomy), or severing the corticothalamic neurons that connect portions of the frontal lobes to the **thalamus.** This surgery has the effect of changing the patient's emotional reactivity, usually decreasing aggressiveness by disconnecting certain nerve bundles.

Although psychosurgery has been reported to calm some patients, its side effects, which sometimes include amnesia and a regression to vegetativeness, are so severe that it must be ruled out except in the most grave situations. It is used only after everything else has failed and only with patients who would otherwise seriously harm others (Greenblatt, 1972).

Electrical Stimulation of the Brain (ESB) Electrical stimulation of the brain, a novel and still experimental approach to manipulating behavior, traces its roots to early work by Galvani (1791), Volta (1800), and DuBois-Reymond (1848–49) on the contraction of frog muscles by means of electrical stimulation. ESB (sometimes also called radio stimulation) had its main breakthrough in the 1930s when Hess (1932) devised a technique for implanting very fine wires within the brains of anesthetized cats to study their behavior. This approach to controlling brain function was refined in the early 1950s by Jose Delgado (1952, 1961), who is currently the chief innovator of ESB. He refined this technique by reducing the size of the electrodes while increasing the number of intracerebral contacts, and by using aseptic precautions during implantations.

ESB has now been used in thousands of animals, and its best-known application was Delgado's demonstration that an angry, attacking bull could be stopped in its tracks by remote radio stimulation. ESB has also been used to stimulate the human brain. This procedure was reported by Delgado (Delgado et al., 1968) in one study in which four severely epileptic subjects, who required the implantation of "stimoceivers" for diagnostic and therapeutic purposes, were constantly monitored by means of electrical implants in the brain. The main objective of recording their intracerebral activity was to identify correlations between electrical patterns and behavior, but Delgado and his co-workers seized upon this occasion to stimulate activity as well as record its occurrence.

According to Delgado, one of the really promising psychotherapeutic applications of ESB is the programming of long-term stimulations. For example, he predicts that someday we will be able to establish two-way radio communication between the brain of a subject and a computer programmed not only to recognize anomalous neuronal activity related to anxiety, depression, rage, or other behavior disturbances, but also to trigger stimulation of specific inhibitory structures that would correct or modify these anomalies and the behaviors they influence.

Evaluation of the Therapies

17·3 How effective are the various approaches to psychotherapy? Are some therapies more useful in treating some problems and other therapies more useful in treating others? How can the individual decide what kind of therapy, if any, will help?

Unfortunately, there are no clear-cut answers to these questions. We have already indicated that the initial enthusiasm for biofeedback was somewhat dampened by the inability of subsequent researchers to replicate earlier findings. Yet we also pointed out that biofeedback can still serve the valuable function of signaling to the therapist and patient that certain changes are appropriate. In regard to the worth of somatic treatments, as we noted, there have been varying reports, and the enthusiastic testimonials by some early users have not always held up under closer scrutiny.

In general, research on the comparative effectiveness of the psychotherapies is beset by three main difficulties: the criterion problem, the placebo effect, and the complexity of the interactive nature of the psychotherapeutic process, which is especially pronounced in group therapy.

The criterion problem boils down to the question "How do we know if and when a person is cured?" You can ask the patient or the therapist, but each has a vested interest in the answer. The patient has spent much time, energy, and probably money on psychotherapy and may report feeling better although objective evidence indicates no improvement. The psychotherapist's testimonial cannot be trusted either, since he or she would like to believe that the patient is better, that he or she is responsible for the improvement, and that the patient's condition would not have improved without him or her.

The *placebo effect*—the therapeutic value of being treated by harmless or ineffective agents that resemble the real thing—can also be a contaminating factor in evaluating therapy. The ability of placebos to heal was dramatically demonstrated in an early study (Volgyesi, 1954), which showed that 70 percent of hospitalized patients with bleeding peptic ulcers were cured by the placebo effect. In this study, a doctor injected patients with distilled water, telling them that it was a beneficial new medicine. A control group, given the same injection by a nurse who said it was an experimental serum of unknown potency showed a remission rate of only 25 percent.

The complex interplay between patient and psychotherapist confronts the prospective researcher with a stream of activity that is difficult to evaluate. Some procedures have to be devised that are comparable to the stop-action of instant-replay techniques of photography and television, and then methods of analysis must be developed.

Despite these difficulties, some evidence is available on the effectiveness of treatment. In general, it suggests that the verbal therapies work and, not surprisingly, that they work best when the therapist is highly experienced (Bergin, 1971; Fiedler, 1950; Kiesler, 1966; Meltzoff and Kornreich, 1970). One early study (Fiedler, 1950) showed that Rogerian, Adlerian, and Freudian psychotherapists are equally effective if they are equally experienced. There were, for example, greater differences between experienced and inexperienced Freudians than between experienced Freudians and experienced therapists of the other schools.

Regarding the effectiveness of the behavioral approaches, the answer again depends largely on whom you ask. Not surprisingly, most behavior therapists claim a high rate of success and compare their techniques favorably with other techniques. These claims, however, are not always supported by solid evidence. A recent book on the topic (Yates, 1975), for example, has pointed to specific problem areas such as smoking and obesity in which behavior therapy has failed. The most favorable outcomes, on the other hand, have been reported for cases in which the main sources of difficulty were specific and easily identifiable behaviors—phobias, tics, obsessive rituals, stuttering, and the like.

What, then, can we say about the value of the various therapies? Obviously, we need more and better designed outcome studies. In the meantime, here are some factors that determine the outcome of therapy according to recent research literature (Luborsky and Spence, 1971):

1. Most patients improve in psychotherapy, but the sicker do not improve as much as the initially healthier.
2. Motivated people and highly anxious ones benefit from psychotherapy.
3. Highly intelligent and achieving patients achieve more in the verbal therapies than the less intelligent and lower achieving ones.
4. The more similar the class and interest backgrounds of therapist and patient, the better the outcome of treatment.
5. A combination of individual and group therapy is better than either one used exclusively.
6. Psychotherapy with drug therapy is somewhat more beneficial than psychotherapy alone, particularly with schizophrenic patients.
7. The longer the duration of treatment, the more favorable the outcome.

The last of these statements needs to be interpreted in the light of two moderating considerations: patients who are not getting what they need drop out sooner; and, as indicated earlier, therapists and patients tend to exaggerate the worth of treatment when they have invested heavily in it.

The Treatment Settings

17·4 Traditionally the main institution for the treatment of behavior pathology has been the mental hospital. In fact, isolating the mentally disturbed from society is as old as history itself. The Bible tells us, for example, that King Nebuchadnezzar of Babylon, whose "mind was so troubled that he could not sleep" (Daniel 2:1) was "banished from the society of men and ate like oxen; his body was drenched by the dew of heaven, until his hair grew long like goats' hair and his nails like eagles' talons" (Daniel 4:33). And "at the end of the appointed time . . . Nebuchadnezzar . . . returned . . . (to his) . . . right mind" (Daniel 4:34).

Among the ancient Egyptians, the care and treatment of mental illness consisted of exorcism—driving out the evil spirits that were presumed to cause the disease. This sacred art was practiced exclusively by priests in temples where those suffering from mental ailments came and invocations were said over them to cast out the evil spirits. Another common practice among the ancients was *trephining*, an operation in which holes were chipped or burred in the skull in order to permit the escape of demons.

Among the early Greeks, as among the Hebrews and Egyptians, behavior devia-

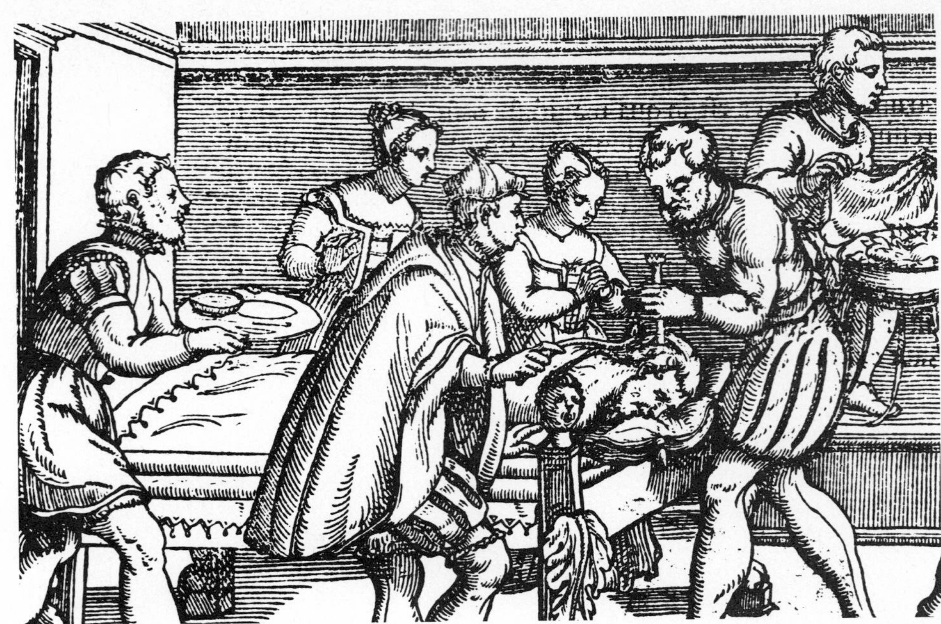

Trephining in a Renaissance clinic. From Croce's *Chirurgiae* . . . , 1573, folio 53b. The operation takes its name from the special instrument used. Called a trephine, it has sawlike edges for cutting out a disk of bone. (National Library of Medicine)

tions were seen as demoniacal visitations (by the goddesses Mania and Lyssa) because of the anger of the gods. In classic mythology the goddess Hera afflicted Hercules with madness because she was jealous of his marriage to the Theban princess Megara. In a rage, Hercules (Schwab, 1936, pp. 165–66)

> became so utterly mad that he tried to murder his cherished nephew Iolaus, and when the boy managed to escape, shot the children that Megara had borne him, imagining that he was aiming his arrows at the giants. It was a long time before his madness left him. But when he realized his terrible mistake, he was bowed down with grief, locked himself into the house, and refused to have anything to do with his fellowmen.

The treatment of the mentally ill during later Greek and Roman times was often characterized by long periods of humanitarian ideas. During the Middle Ages, however, there were equally long periods of return to the practice of witchcraft and exorcism.

In our own country it was not until the nineteenth century that someone began an active campaign for more humane treatment of the mentally ill, and mental hospitals actually came into existence for the poorer people. Dorothea Dix, a wealthy humanitarian social reformer, observed that the emotionally ill were abused and mistreated in the jails and almshouses of Massachusetts. Through her efforts more than thirty state hospitals for the insane were established. Not all authorities on this subject, however, agree that her efforts were beneficial. Ullmann and Krasner (1975, p. 137), for example, accuse her of having introduced into mental hospitals an element of "fault-finding and punishing authority."

In this century, treatment of the mentally ill began to change for the better only after the publication of Clifford Beers's *A Mind That Found Itself* (1908), an autobiographical account of his experiences as a patient in three mental hospitals (two private and one state) in Connecticut, and an indictment of the asylum system. William James, the famous philosopher and psychologist, wrote the introduction to the book, thus exerting his considerable influence on behalf of hospital reform. In the book Beers proposed a program for alleviating the shabby and inhumane conditions, and outlined a plan for establishing a national society that would (1) initiate further reforms in the care and treatment of the mentally ill, (2) disseminate information designed to create a more humane and intelligent attitude toward the mentally ill, (3) encourage and carry on research into the causes and nature of mental disorders, and (4) create more services for treating and preventing mental illness.

In many respects, Beers was half a century ahead of his time. The hospital reforms he proposed are only beginning to take shape. Resources for large-scale dissemination of such information to the public came into being as recently as 1963, and public concern for hospital care for the mentally ill has lagged even further behind these developments. Nevertheless, the mental hospital of today is a far more humane and efficient treatment center than it once was.

The Modern Mental Hospital About one and a half million people in the United States are in mental hospitals. Most of these people were hospitalized because they were so burdened by family and business problems that they could not cope with the routine demands of everyday living. Some are a threat to themselves and others. For patients who are too distraught to look after themselves, the hospital is almost the only place that offers assistance in meeting at least basic needs.

Even today, inpatient services range from the drab low-budget installations of some counties and states to the plush private hospitals of large urban centers. Ideally, the modern, efficiently administered mental hospital provides not only round-the-clock care, but also an environment designed to help patients reestablish the routines of living that were disrupted by their emotional difficulties.

The Realities of Hospitals In mental hospitals many patients feel that they sit out their lives in drab surroundings, sometimes exposed to uninterested (even sadistic) personnel. They complain about the tedium of hospital routine, and say that they feel abandoned by unsympathetic relatives. In his essays on asylums (1961, pp. 151–52), sociologist Erving Goffman describes how a patient in a mental hospital comes to feel deserted by society and deprived of close relationships:

> In the mental hospital, the setting and the house rules press home to the patient that he is, after all, a mental case who has suffered some kind of social collapse on the outside, having failed in some overall way, and here he is of little social weight, being hardly capable of acting like a full-fledged person at all. These humiliations are likely to be most keenly felt by middle-class patients, since their previous condition of life did little to immunize them against such affronts, but all patients feel some downgrading.

Some mental patients are dangerous to themselves and others, and so various means are used to restrain them. This prison aspect of some mental hospitals can contribute to the bad impression people have of them. (Jerry Cooke)

The dehumanizing atmosphere of many mental hospitals, a familiar theme to anyone who has read Ken Kesey's *One Flew over the Cuckoo's Nest* or seen the play or the film, is also pointed up by the Rosenhan studies (described in Chapter 13), in which pseudopatients were readily treated as mentally ill even after they resumed normal behavior (Rosenhan, 1973, p. 257):

> It is clear that we cannot distinguish the sane from the insane in psychiatric hospitals. The hospital itself imposes a special environment in which the meanings of behavior can easily be misunderstood. The consequences to patients hospitalized in such an environment—the powerlessness, depersonalization, segregation, mortification, and self-labeling—seem undoubtedly countertherapeutic.

The Hospital As a Therapeutic Community: An Ideal In recent years many people have thought and written about the kind of place a mental hospital can and should be. From their efforts emerges the concept of the hospital as a therapeutic community. In this community the staff consists of interested and devoted people who encourage patients to communicate with one another and with the staff. In approaching patients, the staff considers what sort of interpersonal experience a patient needs at a particular moment (Stainbrook, 1972). The therapeutic community helps prepare patients for life outside it by allowing them to participate in decisions about their welfare. Since the interior of any hospital can easily clue the patient in to the kind of behavior expected—whether these expectations help promote well-being or stifle it—the physical plant of the therapeutic community should, as much as possible, resemble a home in its openness and the pleasing arrangement of furnishings and the privacy it offers (Kraft, 1966). Some hospital administrations are striving toward these ideals.

Contemporary Alternatives to Hospitals Home treatment, halfway houses, and cooperative retreats are three alternatives to conventional hospitalization. Not all of these alternatives have yet been tried, but each holds some promise as a substitute for the sometimes drab environment of the mental hospital.

Home Treatment The ideal substitute for institutionalization would be to care for the emotionally troubled in the home. Such care, in fact, has been functioning in Amsterdam for approximately thirty years (Weiner et al., 1967) and in the United States for the last twenty years. It involves having professional personnel available twenty-four hours a day to evaluate and treat psychiatric emergencies in the home. Originally set up to alleviate a psychiatric bed shortage, it has been retained and expanded and is now an integral part of the mental health system of some cities. The goal of the service is to treat the patient in the home as soon as a call for help is received. The home visits are usually short; drug therapy is the treatment of choice, and no psychotherapy is administered (Egan and Robinson, 1969).

Such a service is excellent for patients suffering from serious mental illness who

The Right to Treatment

Kenneth Donaldson, a 67-year-old former carpenter, was involuntarily committed by his father to the Florida State Hospital at Chattahoochee in 1957. At the time, a Florida county court judge assured Donaldson that he was being sent to the hospital for medication and psychiatric observation and that he would be out in a few weeks. Diagnosed as **paranoid schizophrenic,** however, Donaldson spent the next fifteen years at Chattahoochee, during which time he made numerous attempts to obtain his release. Finally in 1971 Donaldson was reclassified as mentally healthy and was released.

He immediately filed suit in a Florida Appeals Court, charging violations of his federal civil rights and claiming damages for having been kept in the hospital without receiving adequate treatment. In their defense, some Chattahoochee Hospital doctors claimed that Donaldson received "milieu therapy," but they were unable to prove that there was anything particularly therapeutic to Donaldson about the hospital environment. In fact, according to Donaldson and his attorneys, the hospital was countertherapeutic in that he was confined to a sixty-bed locked hospital ward, was denied ground privileges, and was not permitted to attend occupational therapy. Evidently, Donaldson claimed, the hospital doctors feared that he would try to escape if given ground privileges or that he might learn to use the typewriter in occupational therapy and then prepare legal petitions for his release. Perhaps the most convincing evidence on Donaldson's behalf was that his several unsuccessful attempts at obtaining a release from the hospital qualified him as a troublemaker and as "mentally ill." The doctors appeared to reason that anyone who is confined to a mental hospital must be crazy to try to get out.

Kenneth Donaldson (June 26, 1975) holds a copy of the Supreme Court ruling that states may not confine without treatment patients who present no danger to themselves or others. Donaldson initiated the suit that brought the ruling. (Wide World Photos)

A jury awarded Donaldson $38,500, and in July 1975 this award was upheld by the U.S. Supreme Court, which ruled that a state may not confine anyone involuntarily merely to provide custodial care. If an individual is deprived of freedom for the expressed purpose of treatment, then that individual must be treated. If treatment is not given, the ruling indicates, then the patient must be released unless the state can prove that he is dangerous and cannot function in society.

Even if the Supreme Court ruling and the awarding of damages to Donaldson do not immediately open the doors for the release of other mental patients, they will certainly serve as incentives to hospitals to provide treatment. But this so-called right-to-treatment case raises some questions that will not easily be resolved by court rulings. How can we clearly distinguish between custodial care and treatment? Must patients accept any treatment? Can they refuse treatment, even if their refusal may mean longer hospitalization? Who is to decide what is good treatment? The patient? The doctors? The courts? Society?

will not seek help. Most home treatment plans provide home service teams whose members offer consultation and seminars to community workers and other caretaking agencies (for example, clergy, police, and volunteers), and provide training in community mental health to other mental health professionals. Preliminary research on its treatment effectiveness indicates that it is a feasible alternative to hospitalization for many patients (Weiner et al., 1967, pp. 25–62).

Halfway Houses A second alternative to hospitalization is the halfway house, a transitional living facility that serves as an intermediate stopping point between mental hospital and community. Halfway houses differ from such self-help groups as Alcoholics Anonymous and Synanon in that they do not confine their activities to alcoholism or drug addiction; rather, they deal with all people who have recognized psychiatric problems and take them in as residents during their transitional period, usually just after discharge from the hospital.

The halfway house is typically located within an urban community and provides room and board and a measure of comfort, support, and supervision. It has a democratic, informal, and relaxed atmosphere that, in virtually every aspect of living, permits the resident to assume a far greater degree of autonomy than a hospital does. Although the halfway house does not force the patient into the fixed routine of hospitals, it is like a hospital because it has similar rehabilitative goals and emphasizes the same therapeutic functions. It is also like a boarding house because it offers a greater semblance of family life and demands more participation by its members than hospitals do (Doniger, 1970).

Among the first to propound the idea of a community transitional lodging was the psychologist Fairweather and his colleagues (Fairweather, 1964; Fairweather et al., 1969), who studied traditional hospital treatment procedures and found them largely ineffective. Their idea for reform was based on a Veterans Administration hospital study, which tested the feasibility of forming an autonomous group within the hospital and then moving it to the community as a unit to serve as a bridge to the outside world. Their research showed not only that such a group can be formed, but also that patients within such groups, when compared with those who receive traditional treatment, were more socially active in hospital affairs, displayed higher morale, received more help from and gave more to their fellow patients, and were more optimistic about future employment and marriage. Most important, later community adjustments of former task-group members were superior to those of their traditional-treatment counterparts.

The Cooperative Retreat The third alternative to mental hospitals, the cooperative retreat, is the brain child of a group of social and clinical psychologists—Benjamin and Dorothea Braginsky and Kenneth Ring—who reject the idea that schizophrenics are not competent to conduct their own lives. In *Methods of Madness: The Mental Hospital as a Last Resort* (1969), they proposed that retreat communities be set up as alternatives to mental hospitals and be made available to the public in much the same way that community agencies now serve particular neighborhoods or regions. Under their proposed plan any member of a community could go to the retreat and stay as long as he or she wants, at no cost to him or her, provided there were enough space.

The professional personnel at these cooperative retreats, according to its founders, would be limited to a general medical practitioner and a hotel management expert. In addition, craftsmen, teachers, and artists might be employed to provide a wide range of recreational and occupational activities for the residents. Since these cooperatives are not to be treatment communities, the services of such helping professionals as psychiatrists and clinical psychologists are not anticipated. All activities would be initiated, planned, and executed by the residents rather than by a professional staff. Although similar communities in which the mentally ill cared for one another existed in the fifteenth and sixteenth centuries and were successful then, it is too early to know whether the cooperative is a feasible alternative to mental hospitals in our own time.

Not enough home treatment centers, halfway houses, or cooperatives currently exist to handle the millions who need close care. Therefore, for some time to come, the main mental health care burden will continue to be carried by others. Since the early 1960s that job has been handled within the community mental health center, where every effort is made to reach people who need mental health care but do not need to be hospitalized.

Community Mental Health

17·5 Nicholas Hobbs, a pioneer in community psychology, referred to the community mental health movement as "mental health's third revolution" (Hobbs, 1964, 1969). He saw the three revolutions as follows. The first revolution resulted from the work of Beers, Dix, and others, which was based on the notion that the mentally ill should be treated in a kind and humane way. The second revolution stems from the Freudian preoccupation with intrapsychic phenomena and personality restructuring, and is still very much with us. The third revolution includes not only the *community mental health center* and therapeutic community, home treatment, and halfway houses, but also other services such as day and night hospitals, crisis intervention centers, and nonprofessional psychotherapists.

Mental Health Centers Community mental health centers are a direct outgrowth of the bold new approach outlined by President John F. Kennedy in his message to Congress in February 1963, which led to the passage of the Community Mental Health Centers Act in 1963 and its amendments in 1965 and 1967. This legislation focused the nation's attention on the inadequate care available for treating the mentally ill close to their homes or in their homes; for working with troubled people either directly or through other agencies; for preventing, relieving, or removing conditions leading to mental illness or to unproductive lives; for bringing the principles of mental health to teachers, judges, ministers, employers, and others likely to affect people's lives; for training professionals and nonprofessionals; and for research. Perhaps the greatest tangible benefit from such legislation was the establishment of community mental health services, some of which we discuss below.

The *outpatient service* of the mental health center is the primary and most used facility of the community system. It is the place where most people turn first for help, and it is now uniquely equipped to offer such help in the following five ways (National Clearinghouse for Mental Health Information, 1969):

1. Like the entire center program, outpatient services are easily available to all who live within the center's service area, regardless of their ability to pay or their educational level.
2. The outpatient clinic offers a continuity of care for someone who may be recovering from a stage of illness that required hospitalization.
3. The clinic provides immediate help to those who may be undergoing a short-term crisis.
4. By establishing store-front outposts and traveling teams who go into homes, it extends mental health services to those who would not ordinarily go to a clinic.
5. To carry out the goals of prevention and treatment, the outpatient service helps to operate the center's consultation and education program for community professionals—educators, police, lawyers, physicians, and clergy.

Because outpatient clinics have become not only the largest service but also the key service in the community system, they are also the most extensively used. Two and a half million individuals are now obtaining help in such clinics, including children, adolescents, and adults for whom this service would not be available otherwise.

Community mental health centers have, of course, not done away with the need for hospitals. Psychiatric inpatient care is one of the hospital's essential services; patients are still being referred to public (mainly state) hospitals, especially patients whose disorders are sufficiently serious that they cannot cope with everyday existence on the outside. But now, as an alternative to isolating patients in institutions, several innovative day hospitals and night hospitals exist.

The day hospital offers hospitalization from 9 A.M. until 5 P.M. with the patient taking part in group activities, treatment, and occupational therapy. At night he or she goes home. One of the main advantages of the contemporary day hospital as an alternative to total institutionalization is that patients can maintain their family ties, no longer returning as strangers after long stays in the hospital. Moreover, under the day hospital method, the family itself can become involved in the day-to-day job of bringing the patient back to good health.

The night hospital permits the mentally ill to spend the day at their jobs or other activities and then to go directly to the night center. Like the day center, the night hospital provides part-time hospitalization for those who need occasional respite from the stresses and strains of the work-a-day world. It also offers therapeutic surroundings with a full range of psychiatric treatments. Working patients can thus be involved in an active treatment program without disruption of gainful employment. Like its day hospital counterpart, this arrangement is economical for both patient and institution and avoids some of the drawbacks of full-time hospitalization.

In the past one of the major drawbacks to partial hospitalization was the presumed risk involved in keeping disturbed persons outside a custodial setting; however, the introduction of the tranquilizing drugs in about 1955 has now decreased considerably the dangers involved. Moreover, recent studies have shown that the risks to patient, family, and community are well within the range of tolerance and acceptance (Pasamanick, 1968).

Another arrangement related to the day or night hospital is the sending of mental patients to a general hospital where they can be treated intensively for a week or two and then returned home to convalesce, as they might do if they had any other type of disorder. Such care eliminates much of the stigma associated with mental illness. Moreover, compared with total institutionalization, it is reasonably inexpensive, and part or all of the costs can be defrayed by hospital insurance plans.

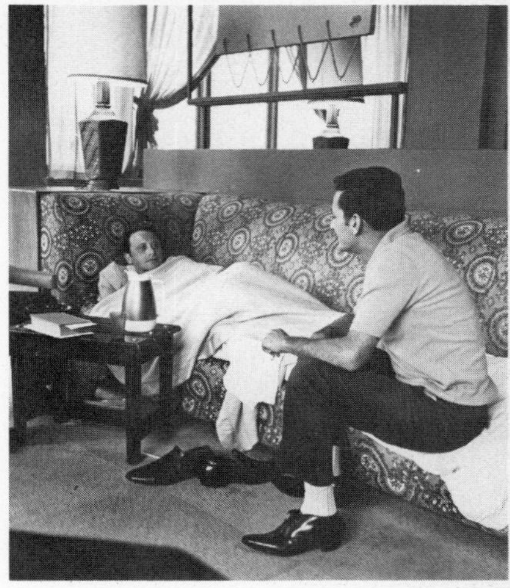

Crisis intervention can be necessary when a person needs help with a drug or alcohol problem. (Robert Foothorap, Jeroboam)

Crisis Intervention Centers In addition to searching for alternatives to traditional inpatient arrangements, psychiatric professionals and others have been looking for novel approaches to meeting the ever-increasing need for outpatient services. Crisis intervention, according to one authority (Parad, 1965), means entering into the life situation of an individual, family, or group to reduce the impact of the stressful event (for example, earthquake, fire, or financial straits) and to utilize the crisis to help the victims solve their present and future problems. In most instances the stationary clinic or center is still the place where such intervention occurs.

Crisis intervention is a logical extension of brief psychotherapy, which evolved from the traditional approaches. While traditional therapies realize their goals (alleviation of symptoms, personality change, enhanced self-image) through an extended, unhurried, and detailed exploration, brief therapy attempts to delineate quickly a specific problem dimension without allowing the patient to digress. Similarly, crisis intervention has as its principal goal the resolution of an individual's immediate crisis and restoration of functioning to at least the level that existed before the crisis. Optimally, of course, given the time and the opportunity, the next goal is to restore functioning above the precrisis level.

One of the earliest crisis intervention centers was the Benjamin Rush Center for Problems of Living, a division of the Los Angeles Psychiatric Service, which opened in January 1962. At the Center, treatment was offered usually the same day it was applied for, but almost always within one week, and there was a maximum treatment period of six visits. Eligibility was open to persons over the age of 13½ in some branches and 17½ at others. The Benjamin Rush Center charges a nominal flat fee for each visit if a person can afford it but, if not, it renders services free. The clinic is open to people living or working in Los Angeles County. Its major treatment emphasis is on specific problems of living, including life crises and psychiatric emergencies. Admission to the center occurs without psychodiagnostic screening; hence people are treated regardless of their psychiatric classification (Aguilera et al, 1970; Morley, 1965).

Another kind of crisis intervention service deals with suicide as its only type of emergency; the first such service was rendered by the Los Angeles Suicide Prevention Center, which opened on September 1, 1958. It now offers around-the-clock, no-waiting, unrestricted-intake, walk-in service to people whose primary problem is suicidal feelings. Its opening was preceded by about ten years of interest in and study about suicide and suicide prevention by its three founders, two psychologists and one psychiatrist—Edwin Shneidman, Norman L. Farberow, and Robert E. Litman. Much of their work was supported by funds awarded by the National Institute of Mental Health, and in large measure the Center grew out of their experience under the research grant.

The Center uses carefully selected, trained, and supervised nonprofessional mental health volunteers whose contribution to its functioning is invaluable. It has two main aims: to educate the public about suicide and to intervene directly to prevent the act of suicide.

Suicide crises are similar to those that occur at other intervention centers. They almost always concern two people, the suicidal person and the significant other. Typically, a telephone worker attempts to ascertain the caller's relation to the other—for example, father, wife, mother, or lover. An interview is arranged, if possible, to see both people at the center. The significant other must be made aware of the situation and, if possible, become involved in the life-saving efforts. In most cases, according to Shneidman and Mandelkorn (1970, p. 137), these "others" show surprise, concern, and willingness to help—at least to some extent; in some cases, however, they must be disregarded or circumvented.

Once the troubled person is at the suicide prevention center, a worker attempts to persuade him or her to see the problem in a broader perspective, or to find a new solution to problems of longer standing. Sometimes, the staff therapist or nonprofessional is able to make arrangements that help the suicidal person overcome seemingly insurmountable obstacles. On other occasions, just setting up an interview with a staff psychiatrist, psychologist, social worker, or volunteer may provide the tension relief needed to ease the critical situation.

Summary

The psychotherapies strive to effect beneficial behavior or personality change. In general, they share a number of common goals: total acceptance of the patient, verbal communication, and a commitment by the client as well as the therapist to strive for change. Psychotherapy takes place in any of a variety of inpatient or outpatient settings and is now accessible to those who are severely disturbed and to persons having difficulty coping with everyday problems.

The therapist, typically, comes from one of three professions—psychiatry, clinical psychology, or psychiatric social work—but could be a trained volunteer or paraprofessional. The form of therapy pursued usually reflects the therapist's model of human nature. Thus, the therapist who views people as unconsciously motivated may subscribe to Freudian psychoanalysis; whereas, if the model is a mechanistic one, the therapist may see problems in terms of the symptoms of a malfunctioning machine in need of repair.

The main treatment models are Freudian psychoanalysis, neo-Freudian and related techniques, and humanistic therapies. The main goal of the Freudians is to make unconscious feelings and needs of persons conscious to them so that they can deal with these emotions and drives. Toward achieving this goal, psychoanalysts use (1) free association, which requires the patient to talk about anything and everything that comes to mind; (2) dream analysis, in which the therapist interprets the patient's dreams and associated feelings; and (3) the analysis of the transference relationship that builds up between the therapist and psychoanalyst. This relationship, in which the patient often responds to the therapist as he or she did toward significant family members, is primarily the product of the patient's repressed feelings and motives.

The neo-Freudians include Erikson, Jung, and Adler. Erikson, whose theory remained closer to Freud's than did the others', is best known for his delineation of the eight stages of ego development and his espousal of the concept of identity and role confusion. Jung's analytical psychology eschews the importance of sex as a central driving force of human beings, and his therapy consists of uncovering the patient's complexes. His tools for accomplishing this, like those of Freud, consisted of interpreting imaginary and dream productions, although Jung did not view these as repressed sexual impulses. Alfred Adler, who—like Jung—parted company with Freud as a result of theoretical and personality differences, formulated an individual psychology that stressed the importance of the influence of social forces in the person's life.

Among the more recent forms of psychotherapy are the humanistic-existential therapies, group approaches, behavior modification, hypnosis, biofeedback, and the expressive therapies. Carl Rogers, A. H. Maslow, and Fritz Perls have been among the more visible practitioners and theorists of the humanistic-existential approach. Rogers placed the main therapeutic responsibility with the client, and this contrasts sharply with doctor-patient approaches of the Freudians and their more recent followers. Maslow, much in the same humanistic tradition, focused primarily on the attributes of the person. And Perls, founder of Gestalt therapy, concentrated on the individual's behavior in the here and now rather than on his or her past experiences.

Several therapies developed in reaction to the time-consuming and expensive nature of one-to-one therapy. Brief psychotherapy more quickly comes to the specific—usually critical—problem. Psychotherapy for couples and families deals with the problems that arise in marriage or family interactions. Group psychotherapy deals with many people at one time and has been made more generally available than any of the foregoing therapies to people seeking to improve their interpersonal competence.

Still more recent forms of treatment than the humanistic-existential and group approaches have been behavior modification, hypnosis, and biofeedback. These methods are less concerned than the others with helping people obtain self-insight and acceptance, and are directed more toward removing symptoms and relieving personal distress. Behavior modification and biofeedback are largely outgrowths of laboratory experiments and learning principles discovered from animal and human studies. Hypnosis, in contrast, was used early in the history of clinical psychotherapy, but fell into disuse as a result of its association with the mystical and occult. Recently, however, its possible psychotherapeutic benefits have undergone important reevaluations.

Special expressive techniques such as dance, art, drama, and games are often used with people who cannot easily verbalize their feelings. These modes permit them to express their problems or conflicts through action.

In sharp contrast to all of the above approaches are the somatic treatments, which are more direct methods for effecting behavior change. These achieve their changes mainly by physical assault. The procedures include electroshock treatment, drugs, psychosurgery, and electrical stimulation of the brain. The first of these is most effective in the treatment of depression. Drug therapy, which was introduced to mental hospitals in the mid-1950s and almost immediately contributed to decreased hospital populations, consists of four main types: antianxiety, antipsychotic, antidepressive, and antimanic drugs. Psychosurgery, a radical form of treatment, has all but fallen into disuse. Electrical brain stimulation is still a highly experimental procedure and is being used only in rare instances.

The treatment settings in which the therapies occur in the United States have evolved considerably from the dungeons that existed at the turn of this century into modern mental hospitals that try to serve as therapeutic communities.

There are several contemporary alternatives to hospitals. One of these is a form of home treatment in which professional personnel evaluate and treat the psychiatrically ill in the patients' homes. Another alternative is the halfway house, which, as the name suggests, is an intermediate stopping point between the hospital and community. Yet another innovative alternative to hospitalization is the cooperative retreat, which would be run by and for mental patients and would be a voluntary facility for people who felt they had to get away temporarily.

Outpatient treatment centers, in contrast to most forms of institutionalization, are geared toward helping persons solve their emotional problems without taking them out of their normal situations. These centers include store-front or walk-in clinics and crisis intervention centers, and are largely responsible for making mental health delivery systems more accessible.

Suggested Readings

Barber, T. X., and Ham, N. W. 1974. *Hypnotic phenomena.* Morristown, N.J.: General Learning Press.

A valuable overview of hypnosis by one of its most prolific and vocal critics.

Bergin, A. E., and Garfield, S. L., eds. 1971. *Handbook of psychotherapy and behavior change: An empirical analysis.* New York: Wiley.

This encyclopedic tome (currently undergoing revision) presents research on the therapies and may be used as a reference book.

Goffman, E. 1961. *Asylums.* New York: Anchor.

This collection of essays emphasizes the role played by mental hospitals in forming mental patients.

Hall, C. S., and Lindzey, G. 1970. *Theories of personality*, 2d ed. New York: Wiley.

This book covers the thinking and research of many leading practitioners of psychotherapy, including Freud, Jung, Adler, Sullivan, Horney, Maslow, and May.

Jones, E. 1953–57. *The life and work of Sigmund Freud*, 3 vols. New York: Basic Books.

Must reading for anyone who wants an in-depth view of the man who charted the course of psychoanalysis and psychotherapy.

Karlins, M., and Andrews, L. M. 1972. *Biofeedback: Turning on the power of your mind.* Philadelphia: Lippincott.

A lucid presentation of a rapidly growing technique.

Latner, J. 1973. *The Gestalt therapy book.* New York: Julian.

This Gestalt therapist presents a well-written guide to the theory, principles, and techniques developed by Fritz Perls.

O'Leary, K. D., and Wilson, G. T. 1975. *Behavior therapy: Application and outcome.* Englewood Cliffs, N.J.: Prentice Hall.

A comprehensive introduction and critique of the uses and abuses of behavior therapy.

Patterson, C. H. 1973. *Theories of counseling and psychotherapy*, 2d ed. New York: Harper & Row.

Written by a practicing, academic-based psychologist, this book covers some of the lesser known therapies (Williamson, Ellis, Rotter, Bordin, Kelly, Grinker, Frankl, and Thorne) as well as better known therapies.

Price, R. H., and Denner, B., eds. 1973. *The making of a mental patient.* New York: Holt, Rinehart & Winston.

Using personal accounts from former mental patients and from experts in the field, this paperback explores reactions to abnormal behavior, commitment proceedings, decisions regarding hospitalization, strategies for coping in the hospital, effects of institutionalization, and the stigma of psychiatric care.

Valenstein, E. S. 1973. *Brain control: A critical examination of brain stimulation and psychosurgery.* New York: Wiley.

After reviewing the sparse and sometimes inadequate research on psychosurgery and brain stimulation, this author discusses the social implications of brain control manipulation and suggests ethical guidelines for its future use.

Yates, A. J. 1975. *Theory and practice in behavior therapy.* New York: Wiley.

This book offers a glimpse at some of behavior therapy's glaring failures such as in treating smoking and obesity.

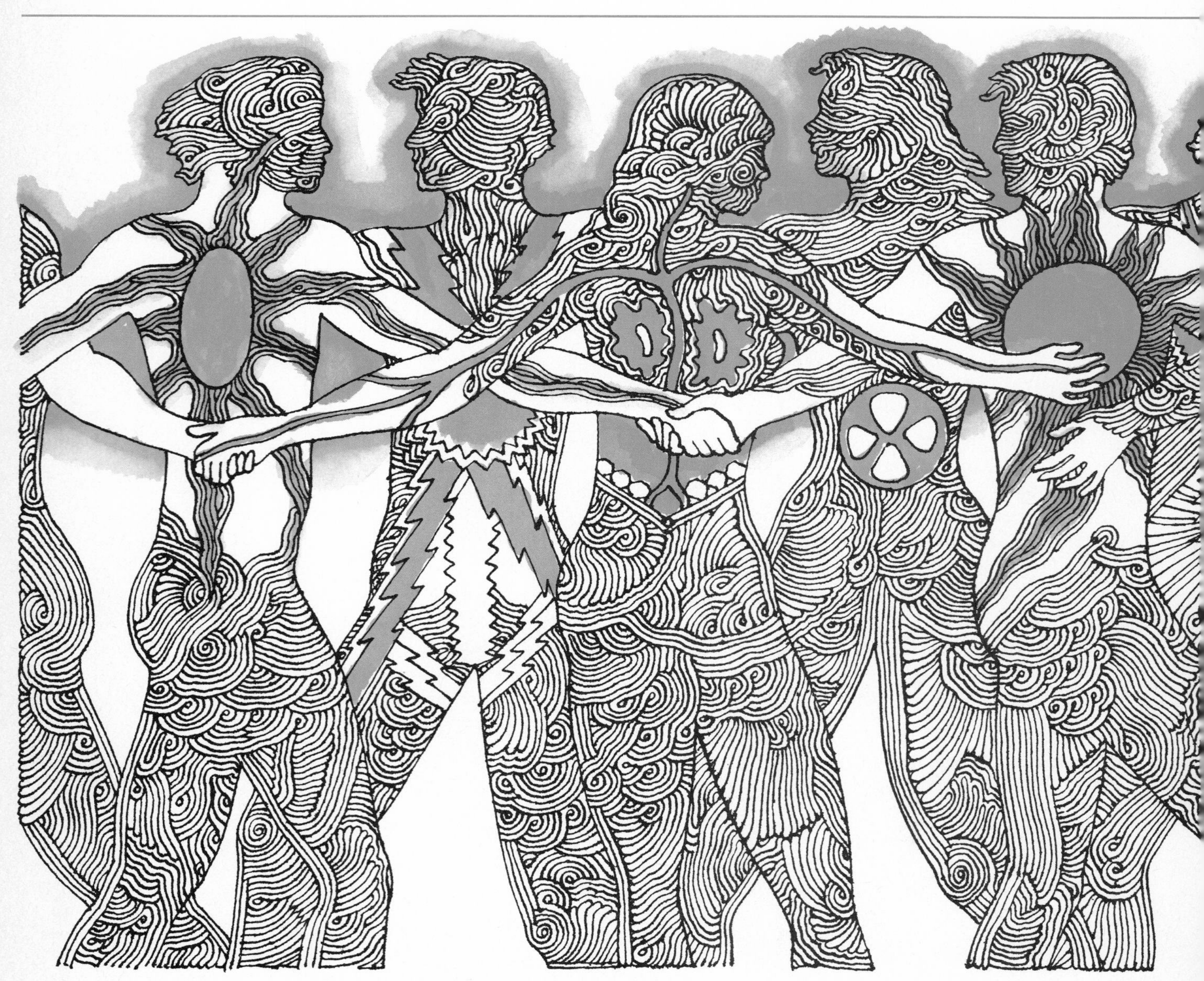

Social Psychology

VI Social psychology is the scientific study of the behavior of individuals in response to their social environment. It examines the ways in which people respond to each other and are affected by the responses of others. It seeks to answer questions such as these:

- ☐ How does a person become aware of and perceive others?
- ☐ How does one learn to modify one's responses with regard to others?
- ☐ How does one evaluate others, learn to like or dislike them, learn to approach them or avoid them?

In some ways, social psychology is much more complex than individual psychology. When an individual responds to the social environment, the environment responds back, and the response from others—indeed the anticipation of that response—affects the individual's behavior.

Through the interaction and interdependence of individuals, larger social structures develop—cliques, groups, teams, organizations, societies, and nations. Each structure has its own goals, which are not always consistent with the goals of individual members. Each structure develops a set of norms, or behavior expectations, that the individual members are pressed to adhere to. Each structure also develops roles, statuses, networks of communication, and leadership assignments.

Some social theorists believe that the group or social organization has properties analogous to the individual organism's: the seat of government (leadership) corresponds to the brain; the communication networks correspond to the neural system; and the persons assigned various functions on behalf of the social organism correspond to the limbs and muscles of the human body. In his classic treatise *Leviathan,* Thomas Hobbes (1651) saw the state as a huge artificial man, created for the protection of the individuals who composed it, but with properties of its own. Although we may be reluctant to accept the analogy of human organism to social organism in its literal form, we nonetheless recognize that social psychology is characterized by the interdependence of persons, of groups, of organizations, and of societies.

Social psychology includes an analysis of the ways in which people become aware of one another and present themselves to others; of the ways in which they form attractions for some and reject others; of the development of common goals and the ways in which people either coordinate their behaviors or compete with one another to reach these goals; of the forms of social structure, the development of roles, communication patterns, status relationships; of the development of attitudes toward persons and objects and the ways in which these attitudes are affected by contact with others; and patterns of interaction, competition and conflict between groups and other social organizations.

We shall consider here only a few aspects of social psychology. In Chapter 18 we shall examine the processes by which persons perceive others and develop impressions of them, attribute causality to their behavior, present themselves to others so that desirable impressions are formed; and evaluate one another. In Chapter 19 we shall examine the processes and methods of interpersonal influence: how people use power bases in affecting the beliefs, attitudes, emotions, and behaviors of others, and the consequences of the use of various power bases. The relationship between individual and group is the focus of Chapter 20: the ways in which the group presses individual members toward uniformity and conformity with group norms; the group basis for self-evaluation of opinions, attitudes, beliefs, and emotions; the occasional situation in which a lone individual affects the judgment of a unanimous majority; the process of groupthink—in which group pressures may lead to risky and sometimes disastrous group decisions; cooperation and competition in group behavior; and the ways in which loss of individuality in a group may lead to immoral group behavior.

Together, these three chapters provide an introduction to a highly complex and rapidly growing field of theory and research—one that has great importance for the future of our society.

Person Perception and Interpersonal Evaluation

18 A few years ago, I rode my bicycle to a small neighborhood grocery store to do some shopping. I had been making repairs on the bicycle, which I parked near the front entrance to the store, and still had on my old clothes, and my hands and forehead were grease-stained. Heavy dark sunglasses were also part of my gear. I did not usually shop at this store, and I felt uncomfortable among the clerks and other customers, most of whom seemed to know one another.

After the clerk rang up my few items, I handed her a twenty-dollar bill. Receiving change for ten dollars, I waited for the remaining ten. A few moments of silence passed. When the clerk finally looked up at me, I hesitantly said, "I believe I gave you a twenty-dollar bill." "No," she said, "it was a ten." I scratched my head incredulously. The lady behind me in line broke the silence. "Yes," she said to the clerk, "I saw it and it was definitely a ten-dollar bill."

Could I have been wrong? I took my change and groceries and walked slowly out the door. Before I could unlock my bicycle, the clerk ran out after me. "I'm sorry," she said, as she handed me a ten-dollar bill, "I found a twenty on top of the stack of tens in the cash register and it must be yours." Close behind her came the other customer. She looked embarrassed, and said, "I'm sorry too. . . . But you know, I was certain that I had seen you give her a ten." "Quite all right," I said, being polite.

But I really didn't think it was all right. As I bicycled off, I wondered what she would have said if she had been testifying before a criminal court and providing critical evidence in a robbery or murder trial. I could not imagine her testifying with any less certainty than that with which she had made her remark to the store clerk. In several classic examples, eyewitness testimony, presumably given in all honesty, has subsequently been proved grossly inaccurate—despite the witness's insistence that the observations were accurate beyond a reasonable doubt.

In eyewitness testimony, the manner in which we observe and perceive others is made particularly explicit. Person perception and impression formation, however, permeate all social interaction, even though we may not be fully aware of these processes at the time. How, then, do we form observations and impressions of others, and what factors account for our accuracy or inaccuracy?

Social Perception As an Active Integrating Process

18•1 In Chapter 8 we observed that perception is an active process. As perceivers, we create meaningful knowledge out of the discrete stimuli we receive—emphasizing some aspects of the stimuli at the expense of others, using our prior experience and expectations to fill in gaps in the information presented, perhaps distorting and selectively emphasizing some stimuli to create a meaningful whole, or *gestalt*.

When I walked into that grocery store, the customers and clerks were undoubtedly going through a process of social perception. It wasn't simply a matter of using their senses to form a perception of me as a discrete physical being. The perceivers attended to some aspects of my physical appearance and behavior more than to others. That I came on a bicycle when most adults travel by car may have suggested that I was different, perhaps a drifter—maybe even financially insolvent or close to it. My sunglasses may have suggested that I wanted to shield my identity. The worn clothing and the grease stains also provided clues that were quickly integrated into a picture of someone who should be watched carefully. There had been some robberies in the neighborhood. Perhaps these occurrences influ-

Even in passing people on the street, we form impressions of them on the basis of their physical appearance and their behavior. (© Roger Lubin 1972, Jeroboam)

enced the way the observers perceived my character. The fact that I was a stranger among a group of people who generally knew one another could also arouse their suspicions.

In a like manner, and usually without being aware of it, we take the discrete bits of information we receive about a person, distorting some, omitting others, and adding items that were not presented to us, and we form an integrated meaningful perception of that person. When Solomon Asch (1946), in some of his classic experiments, presented subjects with the information that a person was "intelligent-skillful-industrious-cold-determined-practical-cautious" and then asked the subjects to tell what this person was like, respondents had no difficulty describing a total person, with unique characteristics, personality, motivations, and interests—their descriptions went far beyond the information given. One subject wrote: "A very ambitious and talented person who would not let anything stand in the way of achieving his goal. Wants his own way. He is determined not to give in, no matter what happens." Such a subject would probably have little difficulty characterizing that person further on an adjective checklist, indicating with some confidence that he was strong (and not weak), important, self-seeking (rather than altruistic), humorless (not humorous), and so on.

The Effects of a Single Trait

18•2 In following up his initial research on person perception and **impression formation**, Asch observed that a single trait or bit of information may have a powerful effect on the ways in which other items of information about a person are organized and interpreted. In the example above, the adjective *cold* appeared to color the meaning of all the other adjectives. If you were told that a woman is cold, what would you think she is like? Might you think of her as also stoic, calculating, humorless, cunning, distant, callous, or having a number of other traits that would tend to make you keep your distance? And what would you think of a person described as warm?

Asch found that when the original string of adjectives was presented, including the word *cold*, the person tended to be rated as ungenerous, unhappy, unstable, humorless, and ruthless. When the word *warm* was substituted (intelligent-skillful-industrious-warm-determined-practical-cautious), the individual was more often rated as generous, happy, good-natured, imaginative, humorous, and humane. Asch further noted that the effects of the central traits *warm* and *cold* seem to go beyond dropping out certain bits of information and adding others: The meanings of other adjectives are changed in the process. A *determined, cold* person may be seen as someone who is stubborn and insists on his own way; a *determined, warm* person may be seen as someone who is earnest and serious in maintaining your friendship (Asch, 1946).

How important is this finding? Does Asch's warm-cold experiment generalize to situations beyond paper-and-pencil descriptions of hypothetical persons? A study by Harold Kelley (1950) supports the effects of the adjectives *warm* and *cold*

Person Perception and Witness Identification

Many suspects in crimes are convicted on the basis of eyewitness testimony. Eyewitnesses are often very certain of the truth of their testimony when they are questioned before the court ("I would recognize that man anywhere"), and such testimony is highly impressive to juries. Yet eyewitness testimony can be extremely unreliable. Often the identification is made on the basis of a few seconds of viewing the culprit, under less than the best visibility, and with the pressures of great stress and sometimes threat to life.

Commonly, the witness becomes more certain of his observations between his first cautious testimony to a police officer and his testimony at a trial. His descriptions of the crime become more complete and exact. Various details about the appearance of the culprit are filled in and made more meaningful and complete. Inconsistencies appear to drop out. Often the details that are filled in fit the witness's expectations about the sort of person who would commit such an act. Racial bias and other sorts of prejudice can, of course, become particularly prominent in these circumstances.

To complicate matters further, the witness may later be asked to pick out a suspect from a photo lineup. Often the photo lineup lends itself to the selection of one photo over the others. In one robbery case the suspect's face was printed larger and darker than the other faces; he was dressed differently; and he was facing right, while the other photos faced to the left. Such bias in a photo lineup does not necessarily indicate an attempt to influence the witness (though this may be done in some cases, perhaps unconsciously, by officers eager for a conviction). The suspect is photographed when he or she has just been brought into the police station—disheveled, frightened, and unprepared for questioning and photographing. The comparison photos are pulled out of the files, and have in many cases been taken when the subjects had been in jail for some time, and were clean-shaven and rested.

In a class at California State University at Hayward, a professor was "assaulted" by a student before a class—141 eyewitnesses. Robert Buckhout (1974) and his associates arranged the incident, made a videotape of the entire sequence, and asked the eyewitnesses to describe the incident. The descriptions were

on perceiving persons in real-life settings. Kelley presented a guest lecturer to a psychology course. Before the lecturer's appearance, students were given sheets of paper that included a brief biographical description of him. They were told that he was a graduate student in social sciences with three semesters of teaching experience, twenty-six years old, a veteran, and married. Further, the sketch read, "People who know him consider him to be a rather (cold, warm) person, industrious, critical, practical, and determined." All students received the same biographical sketch, except that the word *cold* was inserted in half the copies and the word *warm* in the other half. All the students heard the same lecture from the same lecturer.

In a post-lecture questionnaire, the ratings of students supported Asch's original findings. A comparison of the two groups of students revealed that those who had been given the prior expectation that their lecturer was warm were more likely to rate him as considerate, informal, sociable, popular, good-natured, humorous, and humane, and to like him and his lecture. Even more impressive was the students' behavior in later class discussions with the lecturer. These were carefully rated by observers. Fifty-six percent of the students who received the "warm" descriptions

inaccurate in most cases: time was overestimated; the weight of the attacker was overestimated by 14 percent; the attacker's age was overestimated. Seven weeks later, all eyewitnesses were presented with a photo lineup—a series of photographs of six "suspects," including the attacker. Half of the eyewitnesses received an unbiased set of photos in which all of the suspects faced the camera in a similar standard pose and wore a similar facial expression. The other half received the same photo lineup except that suspect No. 5 (the attacker) was presented with his head tilted back at an angle and with a rather distinctive facial expression. When eyewitnesses were told, "One of these men is a suspect in that assault we saw. It is important that you identify him for us," 61 percent chose No. 5. Less than 40 percent did so in the unbiased set of photos. The choice of No. 5 was reduced somewhat when the instructions were, "Do you recognize any of these men?"

In the actual court case mentioned earlier, the judge accepted criticism of the defense counsel that the photo lineup might be biased. He then asked the defense counsel to go to the holding tank, where a number of other suspects for other crimes were being held for trial or questioning, and select six suspects who would stand in the dock with the suspect in the robbery. The eyewitness was now instructed by the judge to completely disregard the earlier identification from the photo lineup. Could he now pick the suspect out from this corporeal (physical) lineup? Again the witness picked out the same suspect and the judge seemed satisfied.

Apparently, the judge did not consider it difficult for a person simply to disregard his earlier perceptions and judgments. Yet data from research on person perception indicate that prior expectations very much influence a person's later perceptual judgments. Biases in identification of suspects in corporeal lineups are also quite evident. In one case in which a witness reported seeing a black person commit a murder, the witness was later presented with a corporeal lineup in which the suspect was the only black. The police justified this lineup on the basis that it was more or less representative of the population in the community, in which very few blacks resided. It was, of course, not surprising that the eyewitness picked the black suspect out of the lineup (*Social Action and the Law Newsletter,* 1975, p. 1).

interacted with him in class discussion, while only 32 percent of those who received the "cold" description did so.

Asch characterized warm and cold as *central traits,* aspects of a person that tend to be particularly powerful in affecting the interpretation of other traits and thus contributing to impression formation. Other traits, of course, can also be central and important in determining how we perceive people. Charles Osgood and his co-workers (Osgood, 1952; Osgood, Suci, and Tannenbaum, 1957) developed a semantic differential technique to determine the meaning people, as well as objects, have for us. The device consists of a series of polar adjective scales. Each scale consists of a pair of adjectives opposite in meaning, with seven blanks between, such as "*warm* ——— ——— ——— ——— ——— ——— ——— *cold.*" The concept to be rated is placed at the top of the page and the respondent indicates with a check mark on each scale how close it is to either end of the scale. By checking the midpoint the respondent may indicate that the adjective pair is irrelevant or that, for example, the concept is equally warm and cold. The method was probably influenced by Asch's early research but elaborated on it considerably.

Osgood and his colleagues determined that we can characterize most objects and people in terms of where they fall on each of three dimensions: (a) an evaluative dimension, represented mainly by the adjective pair *good-bad* (*warm-cold* is highly correlated with *good-bad*); (b) a potency dimension—*strong-weak;* and (c) an activity dimension—*active-passive.* The scale, of course, includes several polar adjectives that correlate with each of the basic three adjective pairs.

In one application of this model Osgood, Suci, and Tannenbaum (1957) found that respondents could characterize major political figures in terms of their location on these three dimensions. Of course, their location would vary with the respondents own political views. For example, applying Osgood's analyses to political figures of the 1970s, a liberal Democrat might characterize Gerald Ford as slightly bad, weak, and passive; Ronald Reagan as bad, strong, and active; and Hubert Humphrey as rather good, weak, and active. A conservative Republican might agree with some of these dimensions for each political figure, but disagree strongly with others. For example, he or she might rate Ronald Reagan as good, strong, and active.

Presumably, then, our perception of a person can be strongly affected if one gives us information that locates the person along the three basic dimensions. Both Asch and Kelley did this, in effect, with respect to one major dimension, the good-bad (warm-cold) dimension—and other adjectives were particularly likely to be affected if they had a high correlation with good-bad. Other information might have altered the ratings of the person along the other two dimensions as well.

Other bits of information, some rather subtle, can sometimes affect our perceptions of others. Harari and McDavid (1973) found that, in evaluating written compositions, fourth- and fifth-grade elementary school teachers are influenced to a surprising degree by the children's first names. A composition attributed to a child named Michael, David, Karen, or Lisa tended to be rated a full letter grade higher than one attributed to Elmer, Hubert, Bertha, or Adele. What image do you have of a child with one of these names? What about names like William (or Bill), Elizabeth (or Betty), Bernard (or Bernie), Catherine (or Katie), Miguel (or Miguelito), Jonathan (or Jonny), or Michelle (or Shelley)? Do your expectations differ for these different names, or for their formal as compared to their familiar forms? Would you respond differently to them?

Male and Female As Central Traits Perhaps some readers insist that they would not respond differently to a person on the basis of name, despite evidence that names do affect how we respond to people. We are often unaware of the subtle ways in which our perceptions of others are determined. In any event, the images activated by *Karen* will almost certainly differ from those activated by *David.* The effects of labeling with female as compared to male names are particularly clear. In the nineteenth century, female authors such as George Sand (Madame Amandine Dudevant) and George Eliot (Mary Anne Evans) decided that their literary works could receive an acceptable reading only if they were published under male pen names.

Several recent studies indicate that labeling a person as female or male affects the evaluation of that person and his or her work. In one study, student subjects were asked to rate a number of articles on a variety of topics—city planning, architecture, dietetics, and law. For some students the author of the article was listed as John McKay, for others it was Joan McKay. Regardless of the area, identical articles were rated more favorably when attributed to John than when attributed to Joan (Goldberg, 1968). When Australian student subjects were asked to explain the academic success of postgraduate students (identified by name only) in a number of occupational specialties (nursing, medicine, teaching), their explanations also varied according to whether the student's name sounded male or female. Male success was explained as due to superior ability, female success to easy course work, good luck, and cheating on examinations (Feather and Simon, 1975). What is perhaps most startling is that the student subjects in both of these studies were women! Other studies suggest that sex bias in ratings is even greater for male raters than for female raters (Deaux, 1976).

The effects of sexual labeling become apparent soon after birth. When you look through the window of a hospital nursery, how many of the babies can you clearly identify as male or female? Without the traditional pink or blue layettes or other identification, you would be hard-pressed to make this differentiation. Yet one study of thirty newborn infants (half of them males, and half females) showed that within the first twenty-four hours the parents were clearly viewing male infants one way and female infants another. Female babies were seen as softer, smaller, finer in features, and less attentive than male babies. The investigators found no physical basis for such differentiation. Male and female babies in this group did not differ significantly in overall birth length or weight, or in measured physical activity or functioning.

Furthermore, within twenty-four hours after the birth of their offspring, parents already were confident that sons resembled their fathers and daughters resembled their mothers. The fathers were more likely to make such differentiations, and thus may be seen as particularly responsible for sex-typing (Rubin, Provenzano, and Luria, 1974).

As we noted in Chapter 5, the effects of sex-typing become more marked as the child matures. Female babies are looked at, talked to, and touched more than males (Lewis, 1972). Girls and boys are encouraged to engage in activities appropriate to members of their sex. By college age, adult men and women have a very clear picture of what to expect from males and females. Females are supposed to be more sensitive, warm, understanding, emotional, intuitive, dependent, and submissive. Males are supposed to be less emotional and more logical, independent, aggressive, and competent. Both males and females have these expectations.

People are also more likely to attribute to themselves the qualities appropriate to their sex. Many mental health workers believe that a healthy adult has the characteristics generally associated with his or her sex. Furthermore, adults of both sexes tend to rate male characteristics as generally more favorable than those attributed to females (Rosenkrantz et al., 1968).

Being "Schizophrenic" As a Central Trait

Few labels have the far-reaching effects of psychodiagnostic labels. Having been labeled insane, schizophrenic, crazy, or manic-depressive, a hospital patient may find it difficult to have the effects of such a label removed, even though he or she behaves in a manner usually considered normal. At least this is the implication of a study involving eight persons generally considered normal (a psychology graduate student, three psychologists, a pediatrician, a psychiatrist, a painter, and a housewife) who got themselves committed to twelve different hospitals. They accomplished this by coming to the admissions desk of a hospital, complaining that they had been hearing voices that seemed to say "empty," "hollow," and "thud."

The patients gave false names to minimize possible effects after the experiment was completed. The pseudopatients who were in the mental health professions also alleged other occupations. Beyond this, however, they answered questions correctly—relationship with siblings, spouse, and children; frustrations and upsets, joys and satisfactions, and so on. On the basis of the interview, the pseudopatients were classified schizophrenic (except for one person who was diagnosed manic-depressive) and admitted to the hospital.

The most disconcerting finding of the Rosenhan study is the circular process involved in diagnostic labeling: Once a person has been diagnosed (labeled) as "schizophrenic," behaviors that would be seen as normal in other people are interpreted as schizophrenic and are then used as evidence to support the diagnostic label. (Robert Foothorap, Jeroboam)

Once on the hospital ward, they all behaved normally in all respects, and no longer reported any of the hallucinatory symptoms. When questioned by ward personnel, they responded that they were feeling just fine. Yet no hospital personnel detected the subterfuge (though a few of the real patients did). Behavior of the pseudopatients was interpreted in ward reports in accordance with the label. One attendant, observing that a pseudopatient was keeping a notebook, wrote in the ward medical chart that the "patient" was "engaging in writing behavior," implying some sort of compulsive activity. The pseudopatients were kept in the hospital for periods of seven to fifty-two days. In several cases it appears that the stay would have been even longer if a spouse or colleague had not intervened.

People who behave in a manner that is not consistent with their sex-role prescription—for example, males who are passive-dependent and females who are aggressive-assertive—are less likely to be popular and are seen as maladjusted, even in this day when sex roles are presumably more flexible (Costrich, Feinstein, and Kidder, 1975). Small wonder, then, that males and females feel pressure to behave in ways that are consistent with sex-role expectations even when they may suffer some financial loss as a result (Bem and Lenney, 1976). Attaching a male or a female label to a person, then, strongly affects how we expect that person to act.

Labeling and Stereotyping Sex roles are just one example of the process of labeling and stereotyping, a process that plays an important role in person perception. In fact, we seldom perceive people as isolated individuals. Rather, we see them as

The effects of labeling on the ways in which information from the pseudopatient was written up by hospital personnel was particularly interesting. One pseudopatient, in response to questions, reported that he had been closer to his mother in early childhood, but in adolescence had become very close to his father. He had at present a close, warm relationship with his wife and children, but occasionally there was friction and exchange of angry words. He had spanked his children only on rare occasions. This could hardly be a very unusual personal history. Yet the hospital report presented this information in phrases such as "A long history of considerable ambivalence in close relationships. . . . Affective stability is absent. His attempts to control emotionality with his wife and children are punctuated by angry outbursts and, in the case of the children, spankings. And while he says that he has several good friends, one senses considerable ambivalence embedded in those relationships also."

Once a person is released from the hospital, is the label of mental illness removed? Is it replaced by the new label *cured?* In no case did this happen. Each pseudopatient was released from the hospital with an only slightly modified label: *schizophrenic, in remission* (Rosenhan, 1973).

In defense of the diagnosticians it should be noted that auditory hallucinations are indeed one indicator of mental illness. In addition, the pseudopatients reported feelings of anxiety when attempting to be admitted to the hospital. Thus, other symptoms of mental illness were present. And finally, it is also a fact that behavior on a mental ward frequently *appears* normal. Thus, some time would have to elapse before a change in behavior, and hence a change in diagnosis, would be perceived.

The hospital staff in this case may also have been reluctant to change the labels of the pseudopatients because no curative treatment had been given. Consider, for example, some cases of physical illness. If an individual has a broken leg and is treated for this problem, the diagnosis changes after the treatment. The leg is no longer called broken. But if a person has a heart attack and merely rests in the hospital as a treatment, the diagnosis after release remains a weak heart. This indicates that the person has a high potential for another heart attack. The label "schizophrenic, in remission" also suggests that the pseudopatient has a high potential for another psychotic episode. Indeed, data support this label inasmuch as individuals previously admitted to a mental hospital have a greater likelihood of reentering the hospital than persons never admitted. In sum, a reasonable argument can be made that the labeling behavior of the diagnostician and the hospital psychiatrists was quite rational and perhaps correct at least in some cases. There are, however, undoubtedly cases in which initial diagnoses are incorrect, or in which a cure has been achieved. In such cases, the persistence of a damaging label is particularly unfortunate.

part of some group or class. Grouping people simplifies the process by which we interact with others. We encounter thousands of people in a lifetime; we may deal with hundreds in a week. How should we respond to them? What should we expect of them? If we can fit a person into a category we think we know something about, then we can feel more secure in thinking we know what to expect. Having labeled someone as male or female, black or white, old or young, warm or cold, rich or poor, we expect of that person the characteristics we attribute to the group.

Perceiving an individual in terms of a class or group instead of as a unique individual is called stereotyping. In one of the earliest studies of stereotyping, Katz and Braly (1933) found that their student respondents considered Jews shrewd and mercenary; Negroes musical, superstitious, and lazy; Germans scientific and industrious; Americans shrewd and materialistic. In later studies of ethnic stereo-

Table 18•1 Fading Social Stereotypes: Five Most Common Adjectives Used by College Students to Describe Americans, Jews, and Negroes in 1933, 1951, 1967

TRAIT	PERCENT CHECKING TRAIT		
	1933	1951	1967
		Americans	
Industrious	48	30	23
Intelligent	47	32	20
Materialistic	33	37	67
Ambitious	33	21	42
Progressive	27	5	17
		Jews	
Shrewd	79	47	30
Mercenary	49	28	15
Industrious	48	29	33
Grasping	34	17	17
Intelligent	29	37	37
		Negroes	
Superstitous	84	41	13
Lazy	75	31	26
Happy-go-lucky	38	17	27
Ignorant	38	24	11
Musical	26	33	47

(Adapted from Karlins, Coffman, and Walters, 1969)

NOTE: When the study was done in 1933, the term in general usage was *Negroes*. Even though *blacks* had replaced *Negroes* by the time the later replications were done, the earlier term was retained to ensure exact comparison between the studies.

typing, students seemed somewhat less willing to lump people into categories, but the stereotyping process was nonetheless evident. There was further evidence that students tended to agree about the characteristics they associated with various ethnic groups, even though the exact nature of the stereotypes had changed (Table 18•1). For example, Jews were seen as less shrewd and mercenary; Negroes as less lazy and less superstitious but more musical; and Americans as less intelligent but more materialistic (Gilbert, 1951; Karlins, Coffman, and Walters, 1969; Brigham, 1971).

There is often some truth in stereotypes. The prominence of blacks among major popular music performers is consistent with the "blacks are musical" stereotype. The number of blacks among major sports figures (well above their percentage of the total population) supports the stereotype that blacks are athletic. The large expenditures by Americans for consumer items (automobiles, televisions, clothing, and the like) as compared to their expenditures for education support the stereotype that Americans are materialistic. Nevertheless, stereotypes tend to exaggerate differences between groups and to blur individual differences. One may not only expect that a given member of a group will fit its stereotype, but also have a false confidence in the accuracy of one's judgment. Negative stereotypes are usually false, but are often used to justify prejudicial attitudes and behaviors.

The danger in labeling and stereotyping is that the label leads us to emphasize or distort certain characteristics of a person so that they fit the stereotype—just as the adjectives in the Asch experiment were reinterpreted and selectively perceived to fit the central trait. A black student may be encouraged to take less demanding academic courses so that he will have more time for track and field practice. A woman student who is interested in doing chemistry research may be influenced to consider a teacher-training program. In these ways, the stereotype and label may indeed mold the individual.

Diagnostic testing, though it may have important uses, may also provide a way of labeling people and forcing them into a mold. In Great Britain, for many years children at age eleven were given an "eleven plus" examination. A difference of only a few points on the examination could lead to two very different educational and career paths. One was a practical education lasting maybe three years and then a life-long job requiring only moderate intellectual skills. The other was schooling through higher education and then an academic or professional career.

Intelligence test scores have been used to label individuals as retarded, borderline, average, superior, or genius. Despite some later attempts to consider the performance of each individual, there is clear evidence that the label itself affects later evaluations of the person. Psychiatric diagnoses can also affect expectations.

The Primacy Effect in Impression Formation

18•3 There are two models of impression formation—how a person develops meaningful and organized impressions of another on the basis of available information. In the interactive model the earliest information received is assumed to influence the interpretation and meaning attached to each bit of information that follows. In the additive model the information is assumed to add up to the same impression, no matter how it is presented.

Asch (1946) offered one test of the interactive model of impression formation by varying the order in which adjective traits were presented to subjects. If the interactive model is accurate, a **primacy effect** should occur—the adjectives presented earliest should have the greatest impact. An additive-learning model, however, might lead us to expect later adjectives to have more impact than earlier ones—a **recency effect**, since the earlier adjectives would not be remembered as well.

Asch gave one group of subjects the following description of a person: intelligent-industrious-impulsive-critical-stubborn-envious. He gave another group the same description in reverse sequence: envious-stubborn-critical-impulsive-industrious-intelligent. As Asch expected, the subjects in his experiment showed a marked primacy effect. Subjects tended to see a person more favorably when the positive adjectives were presented first. They were more likely to dislike the person when the negative adjectives were presented first.

As the first black woman ever elected to Congress or to run for the U.S. presidency, Shirley Chisholm does not fit the stereotype of what blacks or women can or should do. (UPI)

Perhaps the subjects given the *intelligent . . . envious* sequence went through a mental process like this:

Intelligent—bright, clever
Industrious—also hardworking, ambitious, ready to put the cleverness to good use
Impulsive—cannot wait to get on with things; a real doer
Critical—will not accept second-rate work; obviously a person of high standards
Stubborn—sticks to his or her guns, too
Envious—sets sights high; feels uneasy if someone outperforms him or her

Subjects given the *envious . . . intelligent* sequence may have interpreted the description in this manner:

Envious—jealous, petty
Stubborn—hard to get along with; won't cooperate or give an inch
Critical—can't get what he or she wants so puts down others
Impulsive—flies off the handle; shoots from the hip; goes off half-cocked
Industrious—will really work at trying to outdo you
Intelligent—sly and crafty; don't turn your back on this person

Primacy and recency were also studied by Abraham Luchins (1957). Luchins asked his subjects to read the following description:

> After school, Jim left the classroom alone. Leaving the school, he started on his long walk home. The street was brilliantly filled with sunshine. Jim walked down the street on the shady side. Coming down the street toward him, he saw the pretty girl whom he had met the previous evening. Jim crossed the street and entered a candy store. The store was crowded with students, and he noticed a few familiar faces. Jim waited quietly until the clerk caught his eye and then gave his order.

The Pygmalion Effect—Effects of Labeling on Expectations and Performance

How labeling can influence expectations and performance was dramatically demonstrated in a study by Robert Rosenthal and Lenore Jacobson (1968). The study was done in an elementary school in which children were tracked (placed in groups and classes according to their ability). At the beginning of the year the children had been tested on a standard intelligence test. Teachers in eighteen classrooms were told that on the basis of this test certain children had been identified as intellectual bloomers and could be expected to show remarkable improvement during the year. Actually, the students so labeled (about 25 percent of the class) were selected randomly rather than on the basis of the test.

At the end of the year, students labeled as intellectual bloomers received better grades than those not so labeled. Thus, the teachers' expectations of the students did affect their perception of the students' performance. Even more impressive, however, was the effect of labeling on the students' performance on the same intelligence test, which was readministered at the end of the year. Students labeled as intellectual bloomers showed significantly greater improvement than the control group, and this effect even carried over into the next grade level. Rosenthal and Jacobson report that, whereas 19 percent of the control students showed increases in IQ of over 20 points, 47 percent of the intellectual bloomers showed that much improvement. Rosenthal and Jacobson called this influence of teachers over student performance the Pygmalion Effect. Pygmalion was a sculptor in Greek mythology who created from stone a statue of a beautiful woman; following his wishes (and with the assistance of the goddess Aphrodite), the statue became a live companion, Galatea.

The ways in which the teachers' expectations, based on the labeling, alter the students' performance is still a matter of conjecture. It is suggested that perhaps the teacher spends more time and is more patient with the student who is expected to be a bloomer. Perhaps the better grades given to such students provide them with encouragement to work harder. Perhaps the teacher somehow communicates his or her expectations and perception of the student, and the student then believes that he or she is indeed capable of better performance.

The original Rosenthal and Jacobson study was subjected to much methodological criticism, and questions are still raised about the reality of the Pygmalion phenomenon. However, Rosenthal later reviewed these criticisms and answered many of them. In addition, he reviewed a large number of studies by himself and others that were consistent with his original finding. There is also some evidence that the converse effect can also occur—students labeled as poor performers have two strikes against them. Some studies of the learning of word associations indicated that students the teacher has been told are bright learn significantly more rapidly than those labeled as dull, again despite the fact that the labels are assigned randomly (Rosenthal, 1973). An earlier study offered some evidence indicating that children in ghetto schools are particularly likely to perform poorly if they have teachers who are convinced that such children are not capable of learning (Clark, 1963). The implications for education of minority children are very great indeed.

Taking his drink, he sat down at a side table. When he had finished his drink he went home.

Jim left the house to get some stationery. He walked out into the sun-filled street with two of his friends, basking in the sun as he walked. Jim entered the stationery store, which was full of people. Jim talked with an acquaintance while he waited for the clerk to catch his eye. On his way out, he stopped to chat with a school friend who was just coming into the store. Leaving the store, he walked toward school. On his way out he met the girl to whom he had been introduced the night before. They talked for a short while, and then Jim left for school.

Friendly	More friendly than unfriendly	Equally friendly and unfriendly	More unfriendly than friendly	Unfriendly
Forward	More forward than shy	Equally forward and shy	More shy than forward	Shy
Social	More social than unsocial	Equally social and unsocial	More unsocial than social	Unsocial

Fig. 18•1 Scales for rating description of a person. (Luchins, 1957)

Subjects were then asked to check a point on each of the lines in rating scales like those shown in Figure 18•1 to indicate what they thought Jim was like. How would you rate Jim?

If you are like most of the participants in Luchins's study, you probably rated Jim on the unfriendly, shy, unsocial side of the three scales. We are careful to say *probably*, since individual differences and other factors might affect your judgment. However, half of the participants in Luchins's experiment read the same two paragraphs and rated Jim as friendly, forward, and social. Why? Because the paragraphs were presented in reverse order. Note that the first paragraph describes an introverted person, the second an extroverted person. Luchins developed this scenario to test the effect of order of presentation on impression formation.

He first pretested the two halves of the paragraph separately and found that indeed 95 percent of the subjects presented only with the E (extroverted) half rated Jim as very friendly; only 3 percent of those presented only with the I (introverted) half rated him as friendly. For those presented with both halves, the sequence effects were apparent. Seventy-eight percent of those presented with the E-I sequence rated Jim as friendly, as compared to 18 percent of the subjects who received the I-E sequence. Thus, the intitial data were consistent with the earlier studies by Asch.

Luchins, however, wished to determine conditions under which the primacy effect would be reduced and the recency effect made more prominent. He also suggested other factors that might account for the primacy effect. Sometimes the observer may assume that the information received first is more important and should be given greater attention—particularly when that information is part of a written description of behavior. Later information may be discounted as unrepresentative (perhaps in the E-I description Jim is an ordinarily friendly person who was tired at the end of a difficult day and thus tended to avoid people).

Luchins found that he could reduce the primacy effect, or even reverse it, by simply warning subjects that they should suspend their judgments until they had received all the information about Jim. This warning was most effective when it was given halfway through the description—where the content changed from E to I or from I to E. Those of you who read the description and came out with a lower primacy effect, or perhaps a recency effect might have been responding like subjects who had been so warned. Perhaps, also, the effects of earlier material in this chapter alerted you to the dangers of premature judgment.

Luchins also found that he could induce a recency effect by giving his subjects a series of mathematics problems to do between the two halves of the description. Apparently doing the mentally taxing problems interfered with the memory for the initial description, thus assuring that the later content would be given more weight than earlier material (Luchins, 1957).

The implications of primacy effects on judgment are clearer in a study by Jones, Linder, Kiesler, Zanna, and Brehm (1968). In that study, subjects observed students taking a College Entrance Examination Board test and were then asked to rate the students' intelligence. All students got fifteen out of thirty questions right, but some got more of their right answers at the beginning of the test while others got most of the first items wrong and then improved on the later items.

The experimenters began the study with the expectation that there would be a recency effect. Students who did poorly on the first half might reasonably be seen as suddenly getting the hang of things as they showed systematic improvement. They would thus be judged as having superior intelligence. However, in a number of variations of this study, the experimenters found a consistent primacy effect. The subject's initial expectations of the student, formed on the early questions of the test, seemed to lead to labeling that student as either intelligent or unintelligent. The student's later performance had little effect on the subject's perception.

The implications of this primacy effect in impression formation are far-reaching. The elementary-school student who misbehaves at the beginning of the year will be labeled a behavior problem and will have difficulty in overcoming this label. In some schools such a student may be labeled as having MBD (minimal brain dysfunction) or as being HK (hyperkinetic) or EH (educationally handicapped) and may be put on amphetamines by a physician. Here, the primacy effect will be far-reaching.

The college student who gets off to a bad start in a course may be in a much worse position than the student who gets off to a good start, particularly if grading is subjective. Later course work will tend to be graded in accordance with expectations formed at the outset. Obviously, such primacy effects can be overcome. The "late bloomer" label may help. But reversing expectations is not easy. For those involved in evaluating others, an awareness of the dangers of the primacy effect is extremely important.

The Effects of Needs on Impression Formation

18•4 In Chapter 8 we discussed the ways in which a perceiver's motives and needs lead him or her to perceive some aspects of the environment selectively, to avoid perceiving other aspects, and to organize perceptions in accordance with what he or she wishes to perceive. Similarly, when we perceive the behavior of other persons, our needs and motives affect the ways in which we perceive and interpret their behavior. We want to see those we like doing good things. Therefore we are likely to perceive what is consistent with that need and to interpret their actions in a positive light. Yet the same act carried out by someone we do not like tends to be perceived negatively.

In December 1951, just after the end of the football season, students at both Dartmouth and Princeton were shown films of a grudge football game that had been played recently between their two schools. The game was an extremely tense one, with a number of fistfights on the field, key players carried off the field, and additional injuries suffered on both sides. Following the film, the viewers were asked a series of questions about the game. When asked who started the rough play, 86 percent of the Princeton students were convinced that Dartmouth started it, while 53 percent of the Dartmouth students felt that both teams had started it. When asked to check the infractions as they occurred in the film and note who committed them, Dartmouth students saw about an equal number of infractions for both teams (4.3 for Dartmouth, 4.4 for Princeton). Princeton students, however, saw many more infractions by the Dartmouth team (9.8, Dartmouth, as compared to 4.2 for Princeton). Obviously, identical social events are differently perceived according to the motivations and needs of the perceiver (Hastorf and Cantril, 1954).

Were the judges of the Olympic figure-skating competition sometimes biased in favor of their own countries or political allies? Studies have demonstrated that needs and motivations can affect perception—even without the person's conscious awareness of their effect. (United Press International Photo)

Other qualities may also be selectively perceived or distorted according to the needs of the perceiver. Albert Pepitone (1950), in a classic experiment on motivation in person perception, placed high-school students in a situation in which three contest judges would question them on their knowledge of basketball. On the basis of the student's performance the judges could elect to award tickets to a basketball game as a prize. The three judges, actually assistants of the experimenter, followed a script that called for one to be friendly and supportive, another to be neutral, and the third to be highly negative and unfriendly. Students were later asked to rate the judges in terms of how powerful they were. There was a clear tendency for the students to see the friendly judge as most powerful and influential in deciding the winner and the unfriendly judge as least influential.

Furthermore, the degree of motivation also made a difference in perception of the judges. Though the judges followed the same scripts in interviewing all of the students, the students were especially likely to judge the friendly judge as powerful when the prize tickets were to a major university game. The friendly judge was not seen as especially powerful when the prize tickets were to an unimportant high-school game. To see the friendly judge as having more power was, of course, very much in the service of the needs of the students who had a great desire to win the tickets. In a parallel study, Pepitone also found that, when the power of the three judges was the variable, there was a tendency to see the most powerful judge as most friendly.

These two studies support the basic notion that our needs and motivations influence the way we see the behavior and characteristics of others. Obviously, it is this very consideration that leads us to choose as judges or referees in athletic events, persons who would have no clear basis for desiring one side to win rather than the other. International Olympic Games can be a very great problem in this respect. During the 1976 International Winter Olympics, there were numerous charges of bias against judges from both Eastern and Western bloc countries. In many events, such as skiing and slalom races, bias in perception was not a problem, since timing is objective. Judgment of form in ice skating, however, required individual interpretation. When judges from opposing political camps judged the same event, there was often disagreement along national lines.

Were the judges consciously biased, purposely attempting to influence the results? Perhaps. However, experimental evidence cited here as well as in Chapter 8 suggests that such bias may occur despite every attempt by a judge to render a fair decision.

Attributing Causality and Personal Traits

18•5 Thus far, our discussion of person perception has focused on the ways in which the social perceiver meaningfully organizes discrete bits of information about another person—how, on the basis of knowledge about some traits, the perceiver constructs a total picture of the person. Often, however, the perceiver apparently operates very much like a psychologist, observing the other's behavior, and based on this observation, inferring causes, intentions or motivations, and personality traits. The process by which the perceiver infers causality, intention, and personality traits on the basis of observed behavior in a given situation has been called the attribution process. We discussed attribution theory and its origins in the works of Fritz Heider and Kurt Lewin in Chapter 12 in connection with human motivation. We shall now apply attribution analysis to the perception and evaluation of persons. The basic process of attributing traits or dispositions from behavior is clearly outlined by Edward E. Jones and Keith Davis (1965) with a diagram such as that presented in Figure 18•2, which we will follow in our discussion.

The attribution theorist assumes that the perceiver operates very much like a psychologist, with a relatively simple model of human behavior.

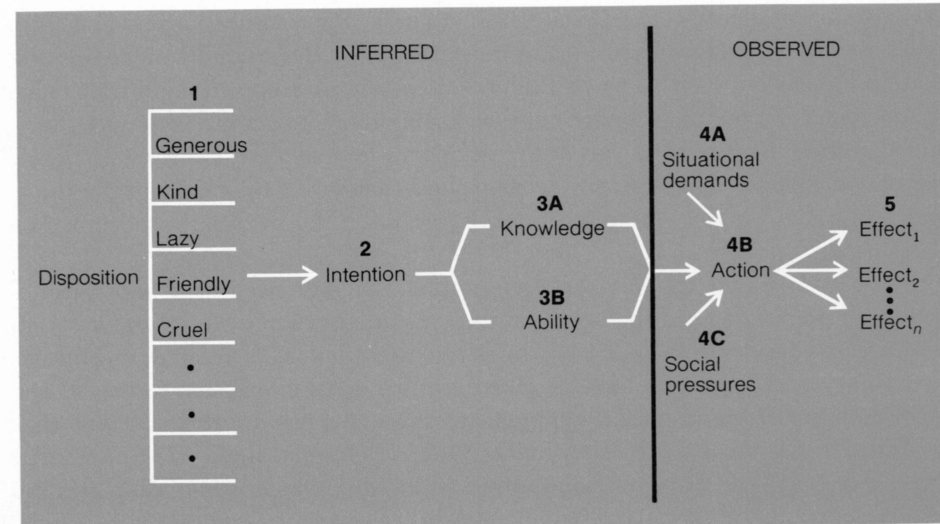

Fig. 18•2 The attribution of dispositions from observed actions. We assume that the actual sequence in behavior moves from left to right. Personal dispositions bring forth intentions. Modified by one's knowledge and ability and later by situational demands and social pressures, these intentions result in certain actions, which in turn have effects. However, we can actually observe only actions and their effects. From that information, we reason backward and make inferences about first knowledge and abilities, then intentions, and finally dispositions. (After Jones and Davis, 1965)

1. A person has certain dispositions to engage in some types of behavior and avoid others: he or she may be generous, kind, lazy, friendly, cruel, or whatever.
2. These dispositions result in certain motivations or intentions. A generous person wants to help people; a lazy person avoids work or effort.
3. Intentions may be limited by knowledge or ability. A person may wish to help someone but not know how or be incapable of doing so.
4. Action may be limited or encouraged by the situation or by the demands of others. A person may be cruel or lazy, unwilling to help others, but when with a group of people who are all helpful and who punish those who are not, that person may help those in need.
5. Action has some effects on oneself or on others. These effects may be good or bad.

The chain of causality, according to this naive theory, runs from 1 through 5. However, the observer can observe directly only the last two elements, not the first three. Thus in attributing dispositions or traits, the observer must move in the reverse order—first observing effects and actions and then drawing inferences from these about knowledge, ability, intentions, and traits.

To illustrate this form of analysis, let us assume that you are a teacher attempting to teach mathematics to a sixth-grade student. You observe this much: The situation (4A) is highly favorable to learning mathematics—pleasant, light, airy room; good math book and exercises; and an excellent teacher eminently capable of teaching mathematics at the sixth-grade level. You want to motivate the student to achieve, and you have the support of the parents in this endeavor (4C). Yet, the student's performance (action) continues at a very low level (4B). Furthermore, because this poor performance is known to your superiors, your reputation is suffering—a very poor effect indeed (5).

These things you can observe. Now you draw some inferences. The student supposedly has the prerequisite knowledge for learning math at this level, and also a reputation for ability to work with abstract concepts; thus knowledge (3A) and ability (3B) suggest that the student should perform better. The only immediately obvious explanation for the poor performance is intention or motivation (2). The student does not do well because he doesn't wish to. Clearly, he has traits (1) that lead to low motivation: laziness and lack of ambition. Since these intentions and dispositions have bad effects for you, you place a negative value on such a student. Thus you as a teacher might attribute dispositions or traits to your student on the basis of observed behavior. (The reader may wish to apply this analysis to our earlier example—in Chapter 12—of the person who steps on your toes in the subway.)

Of course, attributions are often in error. Certain biases in perception and certain preconceptions about the person, as well as lack of information, affect attributions. Are you aware of all of the situational factors that influence the student's performance? Perhaps the room that seems pleasant to you is one where he had an unhappy experience, and so he cannot concentrate there. Are the social pressures to perform well all that strong? Perhaps he does not realize how important this test situation is. Are his knowledge and ability as great as you were told? After all, if he really does not have the knowledge or the ability, you cannot expect him to do well, and the attribution of laziness would be inappropriate.

Thus, you might make an attribution that seems reasonable on the basis of the knowledge available to you, yet the attribution would be in error. In the case described, you would have attributed to the *person* an effect that should more appropriately have been attributed to the *situation* or *environment*. This tendency for observers to underestimate the effects of the situation or environment and incorrectly place the locus of causality in the person is apparently very common (Jones and Nisbett, 1971).

The factors that determine whether acts are attributed to the person or to the situation have received much attention from social psychologists in recent years. We will discuss several considerations that lead us to attribute causality for an act to the actor.

Situational and Role Demands The more strongly a situation or a role motivates a person to perform an act, the less we attribute causality for the act or its effects to the actor. When a situation can explain the behavior, that does not mean, of course, that the situation is responsible—it only makes us less certain of what the actor is really like. Many people who would not rob a bank under ordinary circumstances might do so under threat of death, even if the threat were implied rather than stated. Some would do so even in the absence of that threat. But if the threat was present, as Patricia Hearst claimed in her defense, we are less certain exactly what the person is really like.

In one experiment (Jones, Davis, and Gergen, 1961), when subjects heard a job applicant behaving in a withdrawn, introverted fashion when applying for a job that called for an introverted person, they could not be certain what that person was really like. Similarly, if the job called for an extroverted person and the applicant behaved in a friendly, outgoing manner, the subjects could not be certain whether that person was truly an extrovert. The situational and role demands could account for the behavior. When the behavior was contrary to role and situational demands, subjects were most certain what the applicant was really like: A person who applies for a job that requires an introverted person and behaves in an outgoing, extroverted fashion must indeed be an extrovert.

During Patricia Hearst's trial much was made of an incident in which SLA member William Harris went into a Los Angeles sporting goods store, leaving her alone in a van with grenades, guns, and ammunition. When Harris was held in the store for alleged shoplifting, the prosecution claimed, Hearst could easily have escaped; presumably the situation at that moment freed her to be herself. Instead, she sprayed the store with machine-gun fire, allowing Harris to escape. The defense attempted to establish that she was still not a free agent—that she believed that if she escaped, she would be located and killed by either the SLA or the FBI. Furthermore, the SLA rules of war required that a member assist another soldier being apprehended on penalty of death for failure to do so.

Comparison of Behavior of Others in a Similar Situation One way to determine the impact of situation or role demands on behavior is to observe people in the same or similar situations (Jones and Davis, 1965; Kelley, 1967). Thus, in the 1970–71 trial of Lt. William L. Calley for his part in the 1968 My Lai massacre, much was made of the behavior of other soldiers in the Vietnam War and in other wars.

Not all soldiers in Vietnam acted as Lt. Calley did at My Lai: here a marine carries an invalid from the battle area. (Donald McCullin, © 1968 Magnum Photos)

Consistency of Actor's Present Behavior with Previous Actions Another way we can judge a person's behavior is to compare it with his or her behavior in other situations. If a person behaved similarly under a number of circumstances, then we can reasonably say that this behavior reflects a characteristic of the actor. In both the Calley trial and the Hearst trial the prosecution tried to establish that the defendants had behaved in a consistent fashion in previous circumstances: Calley had a prior history of violence against civilians; Hearst had engaged in a number of acts in support of the SLA prior to the bank robbery for which she was being tried. The defense, in each case, pointed to more acceptable behaviors by the defendants in previous situations.

Effects of the Act Suppose you read that a man left his car parked at the top of a hill and that the car accidentally rolled down the hill, causing some damage. To what extent would you consider the man responsible for what happened? Of course you would want to know more about the car and its condition, whether the man had a history of carelessness, whether the car was parked with its wheels turned toward the curb, and so on. In the absence of any further information, you might consider the man at least somewhat responsible. You would form some preliminary notions about what sort of person he is, about what traits and dispositions would cause someone to be involved in such an accident.

Would you also want to know how much damage and injury was caused as the result of the accident? Perhaps, but consider carefully. Whether the man was really responsible for the car's rolling should not be related to what happened at the bottom of the hill—particularly if the man could not have known what was there. Yet, most people commit this attributional error; they judge responsibility for an act on the basis of the act's effects, particularly when they feel those effects personally.

The car accident episode was actually presented in an experiment by Elaine Walster (1966). Subjects heard several taped versions of the story, all starting with a car rolling downhill. In one version, the car struck a tree part way down the hill, incurring little damage. In a second, the car missed the tree but struck another vehicle, causing considerable damage to it. In a third version, the car rolled still farther down the hill and crashed into a shop, where it seriously injured the

Attribution of Responsibility in the Trials of Lt. Calley and Patricia Hearst

The assignment of responsibility for the commission of an act and the effects of an act is a major point of contention in legal matters. In 1970–71 Lt. William L. Calley was tried for his actions in the My Lai massacre, in which nearly an entire village of unarmed Vietnamese civilians was executed by a U.S. Army contingent under Calley's command. The fact that the violent acts had been carried out by American armed forces was established quite early. However, the American public was sharply divided regarding whether Lt. Calley should be punished for his actions at My Lai.

A number of political commentators had expected that the major basis for this division would be attitudes toward American participation in the Vietnam war: those who objected to U.S. involvement would tend to judge Calley's actions rather harshly. This did not turn out to be the case, however. The major point of disagreement was the extent to which Calley was personally responsible for his action (and thus possessing traits that were reprehensible and punishable) or whether his actions could be attributed to the situation, the circumstances in which he was involved.

These differences in attribution were clearly established in a survey of the attitudes and opinions of a sample of 989 respondents, representing a cross section of the American population (Kelman and Lawrence, 1972). Those who held negative opinions of Calley apparently did so because they tended to play down the importance of the situation in which Calley found himself and to emphasize that he should be held personally responsible for his acts. ("Even a soldier in a combat situation has no right to kill defenseless civilians, and anyone who violates this rule must be brought to trial." "The trial helps to put across the important idea that every man must bear responsibility for his own actions.") Those who were not inclined to condemn Calley felt that way because they tended to emphasize the situation, and to argue that he was under orders from others (subjected to social pressures) and that therefore his actions should not be attributed to his own traits and dispositions. ("It is unfair to send a man to fight in Vietnam and then put him on trial for doing his duty." "The trial used Calley as a scapegoat. One young lieutenant shouldn't be blamed for the failures of his superiors.")

Both the prosecution and the defense in the Calley trial relied heavily on the same sorts of arguments in making their respective cases. The prosecution emphasized that Calley was not under specific orders to carry out a mission such as the My Lai executions, that other soldiers and officers who were under similar conditions did not carry out such activities, that other acts Calley had committed suggested that he had traits and dispositions to perform violent deeds. The defense argued that his orders could be construed as requiring such acts, that he was above all a soldier in a military situation that required obedience, that behaviors that appeared equally vicious after the fact had been carried out by soldiers in Vietnam as well as in other battle circumstances. Apparently, the prosecution arguments were more persuasive, at least with respect to a number of the crimes Calley was accused of, and he was found guilty and sentenced.

A parallel might be noted in the more recent trial of Patricia Hearst for her participation in the Hibernia Bank robbery. Hearst had been kidnapped by members of the Symbionese Liberation Army, held for ransom, and later apparently became a convert to the SLA cause. The point in contention was not her participation in SLA activities but the extent of her responsibility for such participation. Could her behavior be seen as internally caused? Were the circumstances such that she could have refused? Or was she under sufficient threat of death that she had no choice? The question of guilt in her case became even more complicated when it was claimed that she had been brainwashed while a prisoner of the SLA. If so, one might say that she committed the illegal acts of her own free will but if her attitude change was imposed on her by force, is the cause of her behavior internal or external?

shopkeeper and a small child. When subjects were asked the extent of the car owner's responsibility for the damage and blame for the outcome, there was a tendency to see him as more responsible and blameworthy when the accident caused serious damage and less responsible when the damage was slight.

Walster's finding has not always been clearly replicated in other studies. Kelly Shaver (1975) has offered an interesting explanation for the inconsistency in results—what he calls defensive attribution. Shaver says that we are particularly likely to blame the actor if the consequences are serious and, furthermore, if we can see ourselves faced with the same pattern of behaviors. If we often drive in hilly areas and park on steep hills where accidents such as the above can happen, then we are particularly motivated to defend ourselves by saying, "I would never allow something terrible like that to happen. Therefore, if he did allow it to happen, it is clearly his fault and he deserves all the punishment he gets." But if the actor is someone very similar to ourselves, someone whom we can readily identify with because we share certain personality traits, then it is more difficult for us to say that we would never allow something like that to happen, and—again defensively—we may say, "Well, those things just happen from time to time and there is not much anyone can do about it. It is just a matter of chance." We thus make attributional analyses in a way that will be least damaging or threatening to ourselves.

Apparently the court-martial panel (who convicted Lt. Calley of murder in the deaths of Vietnamese citizens and sentenced him to life imprisonment) found him personally responsible for his actions, whereas former President Nixon (who later ordered that Calley be released) thought that the situation was more to blame. (Wide World Photos)

Age and social development are also factors in attributing blame and responsibility according to the effects of an act. The noted Swiss psychologist Jean Piaget (1932) conducted a similar study with children of different ages. These children were presented with two different scenarios:

1. John is called to dinner, and in his hurry, he pushes open a door behind which is a tea cart, breaking fifteen cups.
2. Henri, while trying to get some forbidden jam from the top of a cupboard, knocks down and breaks one cup.

When asked to assess the blame for the act, younger children (under seven) focused almost entirely on the number of cups broken. Breaking fifteen cups is worse than breaking one, and so John is more responsible and should be punished more severely. The effects of the act are more prominent than the intention in determining traits. Older children (nine and over) were much more likely to focus on the intentions. If Henri was trying to sneak off with some forbidden jam and broke a cup in the process, he is more blameworthy and should be punished more severely for his act. John broke more cups but, since he was not aware of the location of the cart, he should not be held responsible.

Moreover, it is not only the effects of the acts that are important in determinig whether the actor is responsible for them, but also the effects of the act *for the observer.* We are more likely to make a personal rather than a situational attribution if we ourselves are harmed by the effects of the act. Presumably, the survivors of My Lai would be much more likely to hold Calley personally responsible, and the shopkeeper or the parent of the child injured by the rolling car would be more likely to say the car owner was personally responsible for the accident (Jones and Davis, 1965).

Attributing Traits, Dispositions, and Moods to Ourselves

18•6 We attribute qualities to ourselves by the same process we use in attributing characteristics to others. The basic analysis presented in Figure 18•2 may thus be reexamined in terms of the ways in which we try to find out about ourselves. There is, of course, an interplay between self-attributions and other-attributions. In our earlier illustration, we asked you to imagine that you are a teacher trying to understand the performance of a student. We suggested that you, as teacher, would begin with the assumption that you are a good teacher, that the student's poor performance cannot be attributed to you. This assumption, of course, need not necessarily be made. You could also conclude that the student is not learning because you are not a good teacher.

Naturally, personal needs enter the picture here. We ordinarily resist attributing failure to ourselves. Our earlier statement that there is a tendency to attribute causality for an act internally (to the person) rather than externally (to the situation) does not hold when we try to understand our own behavior, particularly behavior we might ordinarily not find acceptable. Thus, the interpretation of the same act is different for actor and observer. The actor is more likely to attribute the act to the pressures of the situation, the observer to attribute it to some characteristic of the actor (Jones and Nisbett, 1971). This is more likely to happen in dealing with failure or inappropriate behavior, but it occurs even when the effects are positive.

One reason for this difference in actor and observer attributions may be that the actor has observed himself behaving in a large number of different circumstances, in many situations where his behavior was different from his present behavior. The observer has made few observations of the actor and may even be limited to observing him in this one situation. The tendency for an actor to ascribe causality externally is particularly strong when the effects are negative or generally unacceptable. It has been demonstrated that teachers are more likely to attribute a student's failure to some characteristic of the student (low ability or low motivation), but are more willing to accept for themselves responsibility for the student's success (Beckman, 1970; Johnson, Feigenbaum, and Weiby, 1964).

The Looking-glass Self Sociologists George Herbert Mead (1934) and Charles Horton Cooley (1902) observed long ago that we develop our impressions of ourselves through interaction with others. Cooley suggested that each person serves as a mirror to the others: "each to each a looking glass, reflects the other that doth pass." In attribution terms, he was saying that we assume that some feature in us causes the behavior in the other. Thus if a number of others behave toward us in a manner that suggests we are trustworthy or kind or physically attractive, we may indeed attribute these characteristics to ourselves. Again, the process is not this simple. We do take into account the situation, our knowledge about the others and their possible motivations (for example, are they being ingratiating or are they prejudiced?) and temper our interpretation of their responses accordingly.

Dissonance Reduction and Self-perception Daryl J. Bem (1967) and Harold H. Kelley (1967) have pointed out the importance of self-perception in the attribution of qualities to oneself. We observe our own behavior and may then draw conclusions about ourselves: "How mean I was to my best friend today. I must be a nasty person." "After all that studying, I messed up on that exam. Could it be that I'm a bit stupid?" "That was awfully nice of me, helping that elderly man across the street when I was in a hurry. I guess I must be a rather thoughtful person at heart." To be sure, the process may be less explicit, but apparently we often do make such attributions to ourselves.

Bem (1972) has suggested that a number of studies of **cognitive dissonance** can be interpreted in this light. (Recall our discussion of cognitive dissonance in Chapter 12.) If a woman continues to smoke even though she knows that smoking leads to lung cancer, she may draw certain conclusions about herself: she must really enjoy smoking, or she must be a weak person who cannot resist temptation. On the other hand, if she gives up smoking, despite some awareness that she got a lot of satisfaction from smoking, she may conclude that she is a person with will power or that she has now become convinced of the dangers of smoking.

Recall also Festinger and Carlsmith's classic study (1959) of cognitive dissonance and forced compliance (Chapter 12), in which subjects were inveigled into lying to an innocent "student," telling her that an extremely boring task was actually quite interesting. Festinger and Carlsmith found that subjects who were paid \$20 for lying to the student did not change their beliefs about the task. In a later questionnaire, they continued to say that the task was boring. But those paid only \$1 seemed to have convinced themselves. In their later responses, they said the task was actually rather interesting.

According to cognitive dissonance theory, the subjects in the \$20 condition experienced little dissonance between their behavior (saying the task is interesting for \$20) and their beliefs (that the task was really very boring). The \$20 reward allowed them to accept this inconsistency as only apparent. The \$1 reward, however, did not allow such justification, and the dissonance became all the more disconcerting for the subjects. They thus reduced dissonance by changing their evaluation of the task.

The self-perception analysis of this experiment adds several nuances to the dissonance explanation, and allows us to relate the experiment to attribution theory. The \$20 reward becomes one of the situational determinants of the person's behavior (step 4A in Figure 18•2): sometimes the rewards are high enough to allow us to behave in a manner that is inconsistent with our beliefs.

Social Comparison and Self-evaluation The behavior of subjects in the Festinger-Carlsmith study can be viewed as similar to that of the job applicant who is really introverted but who behaves in an extroverted fashion in an interview for a job that requires extroversion. Let's carry the attribution and self-perception analysis further. In attempting to evaluate himself, the job applicant may also assess the extent to which his behavior is determined by situational demands. To do this, he observes what others do in the same job interview.

This point is illustrated in an experiment by Stanley Morse and Kenneth Gergen (1970) in which male undergraduate applicants were interviewed for a very attractive and lucrative summer job. Part of the application required the respondents to fill out a questionnaire that measured their self-esteem. The interview was conducted in the presence of another applicant for the job (actually a confederate of the experimenter), and the appearance and behavior of the second applicant were varied in two experimental conditions. Some subjects found themselves with a well-dressed, carefully groomed applicant who carried an attache case and appeared suave and well-mannered; other subjects saw an applicant who wore an old sweatshirt, torn trousers, and no socks, and who seemed dazed and ill-mannered. Presumably, the dress and behavior of the subjects were typical of undergraduates—somewhere between Mr. Clean and Mr. Dirty.

It is reasonable to assume that most subjects believed that an applicant for a job is expected to be reasonably well-groomed and well-mannered. So when a subject saw Mr. Clean, he might well think, "Obviously, he has the right idea. If you really want a job, you should dress and behave appropriately. Compared to him I must look like a slob. I must really be a rather inadequate person." But if he sees Mr. Dirty, he might instead think, "Perhaps one usually is expected to look sharp for a job interview, but that must not be so important in this case, judging from the way that fellow looks and behaves. By comparison, I look pretty good, I must really be a rather neat, competent person."

Whether the thought processes of the subjects followed exactly the pattern we have described we cannot know, but the data from the self-esteem questionnaire clearly indicate that subjects in the "Mr. Clean" condition were much more likely to rate themselves as ignorant, sloppy, and inferior, and less attractive than those in the "Mr. Dirty" condition. Our perceptions of ourselves can be very much affected by comparison with another, and by evaluation of situational demands.

Self-perception and Emotions A major controversy in psychology late in the nineteenth century revolved around the way in which people experience emotions. William James (and simultaneously Carl Lange) offered a rather novel analysis of emotional experience. James presented his theory quite vividly: "Common sense says, we lose our fortunes, are sorry and weep; we meet a bear, are frightened and run; we are insulted by a rival, are angry and strike." Instead, James suggested "We feel sorry because we cry, angry because we strike, afraid because we tremble" (James, 1890). The James-Lange theory of emotion then argued that the bodily changes occurred directly in response to the exciting event, and that the experience of these physiological changes was the emotion. The behavioral biology of emotions is discussed in Chapter 25. Here we shall discuss a much more recent social psychological analysis, first suggested by Stanley Schachter and his co-workers

(Schachter and Singer, 1962), which helps place the analysis of emotional experience in the context of attribution and self-perception theory.

In their ground-breaking study, Schachter and Singer injected their subjects with epinephrine (or adrenaline), a drug that stimulates the **sympathetic nervous system**, causing increased perspiration, faster heartbeat, more rapid breathing, and other physiological sensations that normally accompany emotional experiences. Some subjects were carefully informed of the sorts of physiological changes that would occur as the result of the drug. Other subjects were not told what physiological changes to expect. Still others were misinformed. A control group received an injection of saline solution instead of epinephrine.

Just before the injection could take effect, all subjects were presented with situations that would ordinarily lead to emotional responses: another student (actually a confederate) waiting in the room with the subject would begin to behave in a rather extreme fashion. In one variation, the confederate became very playful, began to throw paper airplanes, doodled, twirled a hula hoop, and generally behaved in ways that seemed to suggest happiness, indeed euphoria. In another variation, the confederate began to show anger and irritation at the experimental procedure, finally tearing his experimental questionnaire into shreds and angrily stomping out of the room. The experimenters had stationed observers in an adjacent room, where they could watch the subjects through a one-way mirror and see the extent to which the subjects began to show the emotional behaviors of the confederate. They also gave the subjects questionnaires in which they were asked to assess their own emotional state.

Perhaps some suicide attempts could be averted if people on certain medications were aware of the psychological effects of these medications and could thus properly attribute the cause of a mood such as depression and not turn this symptom against themselves. (United Press International Photo)

It had already been established that epinephrine leads to physiological changes suggesting emotional experience. But which emotion would be experienced? In earlier research a variety of emotions was reported following the injection. In this experiment it was expected that the emotion experienced and reported would be determined by the situation and by the behavior of the confederate. A euphoric confederate would prompt euphoric experience and behavior in the subject. And, essentially, that expectation was fulfilled—for those subjects who had not been informed about the effects the injection would have on them. The subjects who had been informed could explain their sensations.

The results of the experiment were dramatic, as shown in Table 18•2. Subjects who were not informed about the effects of the epinephrine, or who were misinformed, tended to show and experience emotions matching the behavior of the confederate: anger when he was angry, euphoria when he was euphoric. This did not happen with subjects who were given a placebo (saline solution) or who received epinephrine and were correctly informed of its effects.

Although some criticisms (Leventhal, 1974) of the Schachter and Singer study have been made, extensions of the theory have led to further supportive evidence in other contexts. For example, male subjects who are shown pictures of female nudes and given false feedback about their heartbeats will feel they are most aroused by photos seen while their heart rate changed dramatically and to rate these photos as most attractive (Valins, 1966).

Table 18·2 Euphoric Behavior and Angry Behavior as a Function of Behavior of Partner, Type of Injection Received, and Knowledge of Effects of Injection

EXPERIMENTAL CONDITION: FORM OF INJECTION	EUPHORIC BEHAVIOR WITH EUPHORIC PARTNER	ANGRY BEHAVIOR WITH ANGRY PARTNER
Epinephrine, not informed about effects	18.28	+2.28
Epinephrine, informed about effects	12.72	−0.18
Placebo	16.00	+0.79

NOTE: Data from experiment by Schachter and Singer (1962), based on ratings by observers. Different scales were used to measure euphoric and angry behavior, but in each case the higher the scores, the greater the indication of emotion.

The evidence from these studies has important implications for understanding behavior and mental health. At a time when various types of medication are being prescribed, and when the physiological and emotional side effects are not always clear to the patient (and sometimes not even to the physician), an unexplained physio-emotional change may have serious consequences. Would we be as angry at the driver who cuts in front of us if we were aware that our increased heart rate, breathing, and sweating were really caused by a medication we had just taken? Is it conceivable that suicides have resulted from the depressant side-effects of a tablet taken to suppress a cold, and that the patient, being unaware of these side effects, examines his life situation and focuses on the aspects that would justify a depressed state?

Perhaps the same sorts of effects might be produced by bodily changes that occur naturally. Karen Paige (1973), reviewing the literature on menstruation, reports higher morbidity rates and greater incidence of pathological behavior during the premenses and menses: crimes by women are more likely to occur during these phases; there is much more depression; and the suicide rate increases dramatically. She attributes these effects to our society's negative attitudes toward menstruation. However, there is reason to believe that these effects are magnified by the reluctance of women to attribute their psychophysiological experience to the menstrual process (Koeske and Koeske, 1975). The several studies available offer convincing arguments for keeping people informed, not only of the psychophysiological effects of medication, but of bodily changes that accompany menstruation, puberty, aging, traveling at high altitudes, and other common events in our lives.

Summary

Our interaction with others is characterized by attempts to understand what other people are like and, through observing them, what we ourselves are like. Sometimes we are aware of this process of self- and other-evaluation, but it is such an integral part of social interaction that ordinarily it occurs without our conscious awareness. The perception of others is an active, integrating process, in which the bits of information we receive are organized into a meaningful pattern or gestalt. Discrepant information is often ignored, or somehow reinterpreted so that it fits in with the consistent pattern.

Some pieces of information become more important than others, and give different meanings to the less important aspects of behavior we perceive. Warm and cold are such central traits; we hear that someone is a warm, contemplative person and the word *contemplative* does not have the same meaning to us that it would have if the person were described as a cold, contemplative person. These central traits affect not only the way we perceive others, but the way we interact with them. Strong-weak and active-passive are other central traits. In addition, there are important and influential labels that affect how we perceive others. We perceive a person quite differently depending on whether that person is female or male—not only in seeing the obvious physical traits, but also in interpretations of behaviors. The effects of the male and female label begin at birth and affect our perceptions of others and ourselves throughout our lives. We also use other labels that turn out to be highly influential. Our expectations differ from one racial or national group to another, and we behave quite differently toward someone who is labeled mentally ill. This tendency to perceive individuals in terms of their group labels while ignoring individual differences is called stereotyping.

Each new bit of information we acquire about a person is affected by the information we have received previously. The tendency to give greater weight to first impressions is called the primacy effect and it is particularly common in impression formation. An opposing recency effect may occur, particularly if there is a time interval between successive bits of information or if we are forewarned or sensitized against giving too much weight to first impressions. Our impressions of others are also affected by our needs and desires. We sometimes selectively perceive and distort information we receive about others to fit what we would like to see.

An important aspect of impression formation is the manner in which we attribute causality and responsibility for actions or effects. The ways in which we draw conclusions about a person's basic traits or dispositions from his behavior and the circumstances in which it occurs are called the attribution process. Generally, we observe a person's actions and their effects, and the circumstances under which these occur; then we draw inferences about the person's efforts, abilities, and (from these) basic traits and dispositions. A basic analysis in attribution focuses on whether actions are attributed internally to the person or externally to the circumstances. Thus, in making attributions about the person, we consider (1) the situational and role demands, the pressures from others; (2) how that person's behavior compares with that of others in similar situations; (3) the consistency of the person's behavior with his previous behaviors; and (4) the effects of the action. The more severe the effects, the more likely we are to attribute the cause internally to the person, rather than externally to the situation.

We follow a similar process in attributing traits and dispositions to ourselves, attempting to interpret our behavior in relation to the circumstances in which it occurs. There is, however, a greater tendency to attribute the behavior of others internally, to their traits and dispositions, while attributing our own behavior to the situation, especially if the effects are bad. In evaluating our behavior, we are likely to observe how others are behaving in similar circumstances. In this way we get additional clues about whether our behavior reflects what we are or whether it reflects the situation in which we are behaving. This process of evaluating and attempting to understand ourselves is evident beyond the basic analysis of traits or dispositions. We also evaluate our emotions by observing how we behave, and seeing whether the situation contributes to our behavior.

Suggested Readings

Cook, M. 1971. *Interpersonal perception.* Baltimore, Md.: Penguin.

Reviews perception of others; stereotyping; and impression formation as applied to psychiatric diagnosis, job interviews and selection, and bias in social workers' case reports.

Deaux, K. 1976. *The behavior of women and men.* Monterey, Cal.: Brooks/Cole.

Includes several chapters on stereotypes of men and women in personality traits, performance evaluation, and self-perception. Other chapters deal with success and failure striving, communication styles, altruism, aggression, bases of attraction, and interaction strategies.

Hastorf, A. H.; Schneider, D. J.; and Polefka, J. 1970. *Person perception.* Reading, Mass.: Addison-Wesley.

Brief and concise discussion of basic issues in person perception, accuracy, impression formation, attribution theory, and the effects of person perception on interpersonal behavior.

Jones, J. 1972. *Prejudice and racism.* Reading, Mass.: Addison-Wesley.

Analysis of prejudice from a psychological, sociological, and historical perspective. While firmly basing his study on theory and research, the author does not hide his personal feelings regarding the inequities of racism.

Raven, B. H., and Rubin, J. Z. 1976. *Social psychology: People in groups.* New York: Wiley.

Presents in greater detail the material presented in this text in Chapters 18 through 20 and may be used as a follow-up. Also includes chapters on the person alone; liking, disliking, friendship, and aggression; interdependence of persons; structure of groups; leadership; and conflict, harmony, and tension between groups.

Ruble, D. N.; Frieze, I.; and Parsons, J. (eds.) 1976. Sex-typed behavior: Persistence and change. *Journal of Social Issues* 32: Whole No. 2.

Series of articles by active contributors to research and theory on sex-role stereotyping. These articles cover sex differences and attributions in achievement, sex-role attitudes of black women, uses of social power and sex roles, and the inhibiting effects of sex-role conflict.

Shaver, K. G. 1975. *An introduction to attribution processes.* Cambridge, Mass.: Winthrop.

A well-organized, interestingly written review of research and theory regarding the ways in which individuals attribute characteristics, traits, and intentions to others as well as to themselves.

The Psychological Dynamics of Interpersonal Influence

19 How does a teacher influence a student to solve a math problem by a new method? How does a psychotherapist alter the behavior or beliefs of a client? How does a parent influence a child to cut the grass, practice the piano, or choose a particular vocation? How does a wife influence her husband to do household tasks not traditionally perceived as part of a husband's role? How does a police officer influence a motorist to follow traffic regulations? Indeed, how do people generally influence the attitudes, beliefs, emotions, and behaviors of others?

Throughout the ages, people have been interested in and concerned about the ways in which they influence the behavior of others and the ways in which they are influenced by others. We shall examine some theories of social influence in this chapter.

Social Influence and Social Development

19·1 From birth on, a person is influenced by others. Through understanding the ways in which a child is dependent on others we can gain insight into the ways in which influence occurs. Socialization (see Chapter 5) is, of course, a social influence process. A common theme in theories of socialization is the child's social dependence on others for the satisfaction of basic and secondary needs. In one social-psychological analysis of socialization, a distinction is made between effect dependence and information dependence (Jones and Gerard, 1967). *Effect dependence* exists when a person relies on another for the direct satisfaction of needs. The child is dependent on adults for food, warmth, shelter, avoidance of pain, and contact comfort. Later this dependence extends to satisfaction of secondary needs—approval, love, and acceptance—which, though initially less basic, can affect the health and even the life of the individual.

Effect dependence leads to immediate control by means of

rewards and punishments. By promising rewards or by threatening to withhold rewards or impose punishments, the parent can powerfully influence the child's behavior. The child also learns to control the parent's behavior with smiles, kind words, or desirable action or with tears, screams, or frowns—behaviors the parent finds either rewarding or painful.

But the dependence of a child on the parent is not limited solely to the mediation of rewards and punishments. The child is also dependent on the parent for many kinds of information about the environment, including meanings that may be assigned to that environment, behaviors that will prove satisfying or harmful, and knowledge of what is right or wrong, helpful or harmful, healthy or unhealthy. When can one touch an oven without being burned? How can one walk in the rain without getting wet? What can one eat without getting sick? How does one tie one's shoes? This form of social dependence is called *information dependence*.

Though information dependence probably becomes prominent slightly later in the child's development than effect dependence, dependence on others for knowledge about the world and how to relate to it may become more significant than the rewards and punishments that those others mediate. These two forms of dependence show themselves in a number of complex ways in which people influence each other.

Social Influence and the Bases of Social Power

19·2 We shall define **social influence** as any change in a person's cognitions, attitudes, behavior, or emotions that has its origins in another person or group. We shall call the person or group exerting the influence the **influencing agent**, and the recipient of that influence the **target** person. The influencing agent's potential ability to influence the target is called the **social power** of the influencing agent over the target.

Often we have the power to influence another, but we do not use it. Thus, as social power is potential influence, social influence is kinetic (or activated) power.

Social power comes from resources that the influencing agent has, and these resources we refer to as the *bases of social power*. These resources can be related to effect dependence and information dependence, as we shall see later. We shall discuss here six bases of social power, which appear to include most of the resources that make social influence possible (French and Raven, 1959; Raven, 1974a).

Suppose a mother who has discovered that her young son has begun to smoke is determined to change his smoking behavior and possibly also his attitudes toward smoking. What methods might she use?

1. She may marshal evidence about the harmful effects of smoking and convince him that it will indeed injure his health. This is *informational power*.
2. She may offer him a reward if he quits smoking, such as an increase in his allowance or a camping trip. This is *reward power*.
3. She may threaten either to punish her son physically or to withhold his allowance. This is *coercive power*.

4. She may tell him that she has learned from experience and from knowledge of physiology what the effects of smoking are and that he should therefore take her advice on this matter. This is *expert power.*
5. She may point out to him that *she* does not smoke, and she may hope that the son identifies with her enough to want to behave and believe as she does. This is *referent power.*
6. She may say that since she is his mother, she has responsibility for guiding his behavior, and that he should feel obliged to obey her. This is *legitimate power.*

Which of these six bases of social power do you think might be most effective in changing the son's behavior? Which would lead to both behavior and attitude change? Which would lead to the most long-lasting change? Which requires *continued* dependence on the influencing agent?

Parents' referent power can work both for and against them. (American Cancer Society)

Power and Dependence We began our discussion by stressing that social influence begins with dependence of a person on an influencing agent for satisfaction of needs or for information. Now we add that sometimes the *change* that results continues to be dependent on the agent and sometimes it becomes independent of the agent. Fritz Heider (1958, pp. 4–5) illustrates this point vividly with an analogy—a description of two ways in which a hand can move a ball across a table (Figure 19•1):

> In one case, a ball is pushed so that it rolls across a plane. In another case, the ball is guided by a hand and its movements are dependent at each moment on the movement of the hand. . . . In the first case, an influence from the outside is

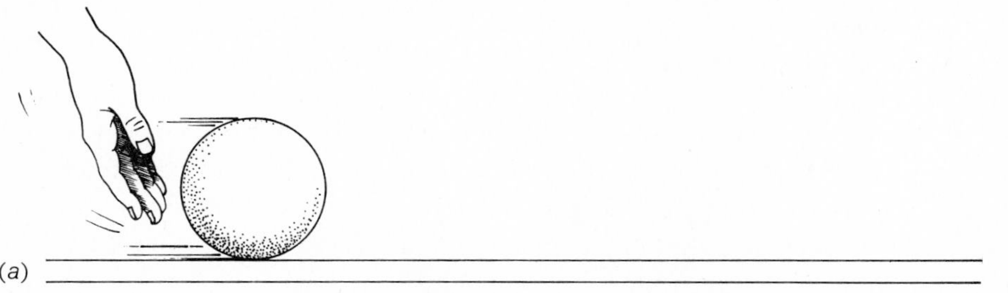

Fig. 19•1 The unguided and guided ball. Fritz Helder illustrates the distinction between change that becomes independent of an influencing agent and change that continues to be dependent on the agent. This analogy carries over to our analysis of socially independent influence, which results from informational power, and socially dependent influence, which results from reward, coercion, expertise, reference, or legitimacy.

active once. . . . In another case, when the ball is guided during the whole movement, the course of events is continually influenced from the outside.

In our example of the mother and the son who smokes, the mother might well be concerned about whether the changed behavior of her son would be socially dependent on her or would become independent of her. If the son were asked why he no longer smokes, she would prefer that he truthfully respond that he no longer likes smoking and has no desire to smoke. Such a change would be socially independent of the influencing agent, the mother.

The other five bases of social power would lead, at least initially, to socially dependent change. The son whose mother wants him to stop smoking would answer that he no longer smokes because "my mother offered me a camping trip," or "my mother threatened to cut my allowance," or "my mother knows best," or "I admire my mother and want to do as she does," or "my mother has the right to ask me to stop smoking." In these five instances, the son's changed behavior is dependent on the mother in the same way the movement of the guided ball continues to be dependent on the hand.

Influence That Becomes Independent of the Agent: Informational Influence Informational influence results from the content of the communication from the agent, and it generally involves cognitive change—a new perception of the situation. The mother who successfully uses informational power in getting her son to stop smoking will probably have to produce several arguments: smoking leads to cancer, smoking can shorten life expectancy, smoking is costly, and so on. In effect, the use of informational power, sometimes called **persuasion**, involves restructuring the target's perceptions of a situation; tying changes in behavior to the target's values, beliefs, and attitudes; and pointing out how the change would lead either toward desired ends or goals or away from unwanted results. There is a vast literature detailing the ways in which information can be used to produce lasting change in attitudes, beliefs, and behavior.

Informational influence, obviously, has many advantages for the influencing agent, since the changes that result are no longer dependent on the agent and thus appear to be more stable and permanent than those produced by other means of influence. The use of informational influence is consistent with many of our values, which stress individuality and freedom of decision. The philosophy of education espoused by John Dewey (1916), Jerome Bruner (1968), and many others stresses the value of informational influence in education. Changes in the beliefs and behaviors of students, after all, should result from the students' understanding, and should not continue to depend on the source (the teacher or the textbook). A student who follows a particular procedure in solving a math or chemistry problem simply because he is concerned about getting a good grade, or because he accepts the teacher's expertise, will be at a disadvantage when he leaves the classroom and must function on his own.

Informational Influence Through Emphasizing Inconsistencies

One of the most common means of informational influence involves creating cognitive dissonance—making the target aware of inconsistencies among beliefs, attitudes, values, and behaviors. Students who oppose permitting Communist speakers to address the public might change their attitudes when they realize that such prohibition is counter to freedom of speech (Rosenberg, 1956). Students who tend to favor racial segregation in housing might adopt more favorable attitudes toward integration when confronted with the inconsistency between segregation and values such as equality of opportunity, promoting American prestige abroad, and being broad-minded and worldly wise (Carlson, 1956).

Changes in attitudes or behaviors through awareness of inconsistency do not always come easily. A change in one attitude may create inconsistency with others. Carlson found, in fact, that the change in attitudes toward desegregation in housing occurred for those with moderate attitudes, but not for those who were extremely negative. Furthermore, there is evidence that changes in expressed attitude are much easier to obtain than changes in behavior (McGuire, 1969).

In light of this evidence, then, Milton Rokeach's research (1971) on attitude and value consistency is particularly interesting. Rokeach and his co-workers presented groups of college students with eighteen values that he had previously determined to be basic, and asked each student to rank them from most to least important or preferred. Among these values, students tended to rank freedom as very high and equality much lower. Rokeach then made some subjects aware of the inconsistency in this ordering: "I see that you think your own freedom is pretty important. You must think that your own freedom is more important than the freedom of others, since you rank equality as much lower."

These students were also shown correlations, obtained from other students, between the ranking of these values and attitudes toward civil rights—persons who rank freedom high and equality low are especially likely to be unsympathetic to civil rights. The interpretation was made that people who are concerned about their own freedom but unconcerned about the freedom and opportunities of others are especially likely to want to deny equal opportunities and rights to others. Many of the students were evidently disturbed by the inconsistency, and indicated dissatisfaction with their rankings of the values.

Three to five months later, these students ranked equality higher than before and also indicated more favorable attitudes toward civil rights issues. These changes were especially evident for students who had said they were dissatisfied with their rankings. Even more dramatic were changes in behavior. Students who had been confronted with their inconsistency were more likely to respond to a mail appeal to join and provide financial support for the National Association for the Advancement of Colored People. They were also more likely to enroll in ethnic studies courses.

One might speculate that the changed rankings on the questionnaires were merely an attempt to give the experimenters the results they wanted. However, the NAACP solicitation came by mail some time later and could not reasonably be associated with the research; similarly, enrollment in the ethnic studies courses occurred later in a setting quite separate from the research. Furthermore, fifteen to seventeen months after the testing, students were solicited to renew their memberships in the NAACP, and those who had been confronted with their inconsistency tended to respond favorably.

Rokeach compared the results from subjects in the inconsistency condition to a control group of subjects who receive the initial tests at the same time but who were not confronted with the inconsistencies. This group showed no change in rankings or attitudes, and were less likely to respond favorably to the NAACP or to enroll in ethnic studies programs.

The Rokeach experiments offer strong indications of the possibility of informational influence on attitudes, values, and behaviors through confrontation with inconsistencies.

Of course, informational influence may be dependent on a general background of knowledge previously available to the student. (Similarly, Heider's independent rolling ball is still dependent on other factors in its environment—inertia, friction, gravity, and so on.) Sometimes a teacher must rely on dependent forms of social influence such as expertise to influence a student, even while hoping that eventually the student will develop a cognitive background within which informational influence will be possible.

Socially Dependent Influence That Requires Surveillance: Reward and Coercive Influence All social influence involves rewards or punishments in some form, but reward influence and coercive influence specifically require that the rewards and punishments be *mediated* by the influencing agent. The agent determines whether the reward or the punishment will be given. Any change in the target obtained by reward power or coercive power is dependent on the influencing agent.

Reward power is involved in an offer of better grades for doing a term paper, a promotion promised to a worker who does his job in the prescribed manner, a promise to a neighbor to care for her dog while she is on vacation if she will look after your plants while you are away. Coercive power can involve the threat of a failing grade if an assignment is not turned in on time, a threat of demotion or dismissal for not following proper procedures on the job, a threat to a neighbor that you will call the police if she does not control her dog's barking. These are rather obvious forms of reward and coercion, but there are more subtle personal forms that involve personal approval or disapproval by the influencing agent. Liking, approval, love, and agreement can be powerful sources of reward, just as disliking, disapproval, hatred, and disagreement can be effective means of coercion.

Sometimes the same influence attempt by an influencing agent will be perceived by one target as reward power and by another as coercive power. For example, when a supervisor announces to workers that their promotions depend on whether they meet their quotas, one worker may interpret this as coercion (a threat to withhold promotion), and another may interpret it as reward (a promise to recommend promotion). Such differences in interpretation may be due to the personalities of the workers or to their prior interaction with the supervisor. Whatever the reason, the effects of the influence attempt are different for the two workers.

A major drawback of both reward and coercive power is that surveillance is necessary for their effectiveness. A motorist who obeys the 55-mph speed law solely because of the coercive power of the police will not obey unless he suspects that he might be observed by the police. The son whose sole reason for not smoking is fear of a reprimand will smoke in a place where he is certain his mother cannot observe him.

Although surveillance is crucial in using either reward power or coercive power, evidence indicates that surveillance is more easily done when reward power is used, because the target finds it advantageous to call attention to compliance. The target who is threatened with punishment may try to hide his or her degree of compliance or noncompliance to avoid any possibility of punishment. Thus, an automobile assembly supervisor who uses coercion to make certain that workers test the tightness of each bolt on the engine block must have someone watch them and double-check the work before the hood is in place. Such continued surveillance may not be as important when reward is used (Ring and Kelley, 1963).

Reward power and coercive power may operate differently in two other ways:

1. Evidence indicates that the threat of punishment necessary in coercive power may lead the target to dislike the agent, thus making continued influence more difficult. Reward is more likely to lead to a more positive personal relationship between agent and target (Rubin and Lewicki, 1973; Kipnis, 1958; Horai et al.; 1970).
2. Coercive power, with its general negative tone, may lead the target to escape or avoid the situation entirely, if possible, and get out of the agent's range. The professor who continually threatens his students with failing marks if they do not turn in assignments on time may soon find that students avoid taking his class.

Thus, when an influencing agent can choose the manner in which his influence attempt is presented, he would do well to choose a presentation that suggests reward rather than punishment. A professor can promise better grades if students complete their assignments, rather than threaten poor grades for those who do not. A supervisor can promise to write a recommendation for promotion rather than threaten to withhold such a recommendation.

Socially Dependent Influence That Does Not Require Surveillance Three other bases of social power—expertness, reference, and legitimacy—also result in social influence that is dependent on the influencing agent. However, these bases are dependent on the influencing agent to a lesser degree than reward and coercion because surveillance is not necessary. In each case, dependence is evident: "I stopped smoking because (a) Mom knows what she's talking about (expertness); (b) Mom doesn't smoke (reference); (c) Mom has a right to demand it (legitimacy)." All three of these probably develop as forms of information dependence (which we defined earlier as a dependence on others to know what is wise or what to do, or to exercise control) but through a process of development, the information per se becomes secondary and the target complies on the basis of faith, respect, or admiration for the agent.

Expert Influence Expert influence exists when the target changes because of the attribution—usually based on faith—of superior knowledge or ability to the influencing agent. The mother who asks her son to stop smoking because "I have studied the medical evidence, and therefore I know what is best in this case" is attempting to use her expert power. She does not actually present the data she has acquired from her studies, but expects the son to take her superior knowledge on faith.

The changed behavior continues to be dependent on the agent. (Indeed, in some cases, experts who wish to maintain their expert power and the dependence that goes with it—for example, investment counselors—avoid explaining the basis for their advice, lest the recipient use it to form independent judgments in the future.) However, surveillance is not necessary for maintenance of the change. We can think of many examples of expert power—the physician advising a patient; the teacher who says "Solve the problem in this way. I can't explain why, but it will work"; or the person who gives you directions in the unfamiliar town you are driving through.

Referent Influence When the target changes because he identifies with the agent and evaluates himself by comparison with the agent, referent influence is at work. Often we adopt opinions, attitudes, or behaviors because we gain satisfaction from our similarity to others.

Referent influence is particularly evident among teen-agers, who tend to look to each other to determine how to dress, talk, or play; which movie to see; or which courses to study. Sometimes, the agent may be quite distant—a boy may gain satisfaction from eating the same breakfast cereal as his favorite baseball star, or a girl may affect the hairstyle or dress of her favorite actress or pop singer.

Legitimate Influence The key concepts in legitimate influence are *ought, should,* and other words or phrases suggesting obligation or duty. "I am supposed to do as she asks. After all, she has the authority to ask me to do some things." Legitimate power grows out of the target's acceptance of a role-structural relationship with the influencing agent. Where this power is fully effective (as it often is in industrial, business, or military organizations), the target feels compelled to do as the superior asks, without question, merely because the agent is superior.

Someone had blundered?
Theirs not to make reply,
Theirs not to reason why,
Theirs but to do and die.

. . .

Into the jaws of death,
Into the mouth of hell
Rode the six hundred.

—Alfred, Lord Tennyson, *The Charge of the Light Brigade* (1854)
(Photo Courtesy of the National Army Museum)

Referent Influence and Aggressive Behavior

How often have we heard parents explain the unruly behavior of their child as the result of getting in with a bad bunch of children? Such explanations can sometimes be a convenient way to shift to others responsibility for unacceptable behavior. However, research by Albert Bandura and his co-workers offers strong support for the notion that aggressive behavior of children and adolescents can result from imitating, or modeling, the behavior of others with whom they identify—what we have been calling referent influence (Bandura, 1973; Bandura, Ross, and Ross, 1961).

In the initial investigations the subjects were nursery-school children who observed an adult engage in agressive behavior and shouts with a large inflated doll ("Sock him in the nose . . . hit him down . . . throw him in the air . . . kick him. . . POW . . ."). After the adult left the room, the children were observed through a one-way window as they followed the aggressive behavior of the adult, even adding a few innovations, such as stabbing the doll or shooting it with a toy gun. In a control condition, where the adult played with construction pieces, subsequent aggressive behavior by the children was not likely.

Children generally identify with adults in situations such as this and apparently use them as models or referents for their own behavior. Perhaps some degree of expert power was also involved: the children attribute superior knowledge to the adult, and assume that adults know best what to do in a particular situation. But referent influence becomes clear in the finding that boys are more likely to imitate the adult male model, whereas girls are more likely to imitate the adult female model (Bandura, Ross, and Ross, 1961).

Bandura, Ross, and Ross demonstrated that a child who observes an adult behaving aggressively will tend to behave that way also. (Courtesy of Albert Bandura)

In a later study, Bandura (1965) found that a child who had observed an aggressive model would be less likely to show imitative aggression if there was some suggestion that he might be punished for aggressive behavior. Thus the referent influence of the aggressive model could be offset by the coercive power of the experimenter. The deterrent effect of coercion did not have long-lasting effects, however. Once the child was free to behave without threat of punishment, the aggressive behavior was exhibited. This relationship between coercive power and referent power may have interesting implications for child-rearing practices.

It has been found that parents who punish aggressive behavior in the home are likely to have children who are particularly aggressive in school (Sears, Maccoby, and Levin, 1957). A parent who uses punishment in the home can inhibit aggressive behavior, but the very act of punishment provides a model for the child. Though inclined to imitate the parent's aggression, the child inhibits such behavior in the home, for fear of punishment. Out of sight of the coercive parent, the child engages in aggressive behavior toward other children.

Particularly in battle situations, the military demands that a soldier accept the legitimate power of his superior officers even if he doubts the wisdom of the requested behavior. In the press of battle, there may not be time for explanations or for surveillance of individual soldiers. Thus there seems to be a logical basis for the use of legitimate power rather than informational power or coercive power. Much of basic training focuses on establishing the legitimate power of superior officers. Trainees are forced to do ridiculous things (like digging holes and then filling them up), to go through rigorous parade drills, or to stand at strict attention for long periods. However, there are times when a subordinate must think for himself and question the wisdom of an order from a superior. Articles in military journals argue this point from time to time, without resolution.

The Legitimate Power of the Experimenter Suppose you have responded to a classified advertisement offering $4.50 for one hour's participation in a study on learning. You appear at the university laboratory and are greeted by the experimenter (looking very much like the typical university scientist in his lab coat) and another subject, a pleasant-looking middle-age man. You are told that this is a study of the effects of punishment on learning. A drawing of lots determines that you will be the teacher and the other subject the learner. To facilitate his learning of word associations, you (the teacher) will shock him each time he makes an error. You watch the learner as he is strapped into a chair in the other room and electrodes are attached to his arm. (He mentions that he once had a heart problem, and that he hopes the shocks will not affect it.) You get a slight sample of the shock yourself to give you an idea of what it is like (it is clearly unpleasant), and the experimenter explains that the shocks can be extremely painful, but will cause no permanent tissue damage.

Now the apparatus is explained to you. You have in front of you a panel (Figure 19•2a) on which several switches are labeled in 15-volt increments from 15 ("light shock") through 375 ("Danger: severe shock") to 450 ("XXXX"). Each time the learner makes an error, you will give him a shock, starting at 15 volts and increasing the voltage after each subsequent error.

At first the learner answers correctly, but then he makes an error—buzz—a 15-volt shock. Then he makes another—30 volts. Then 45 volts, 60, 75, 90, and so on. At 150 volts, the learner demands to be let out of the experiment. At 180 volts he cries out that he can no longer stand the pain. At 300 volts he screams and makes no further response. You look at the experimenter, who tells you that you must go on. You are to treat a nonresponse as an error.

Would you continue the experiment until the experimenter told you it was completed? If not, at what point would you refuse to go on? Please consider these questions carefully before proceeding.

What we have described is an experiment actually carried out at Yale University by Stanley Milgram (1963, 1974) (Figure 19•2). In his first experiment, Milgram studied the compliance behavior of forty male adults who had responded to an ad in a New Haven paper. They varied in age from twenty to fifty and included postal clerks, high-school teachers, salesmen, engineers, and laborers. Education level varied from elementary school to doctorates and professional degrees.

Milgram described the essentials of his experiment to a number of Yale students, colleagues, and psychiatrists, and then asked them to predict how far typical

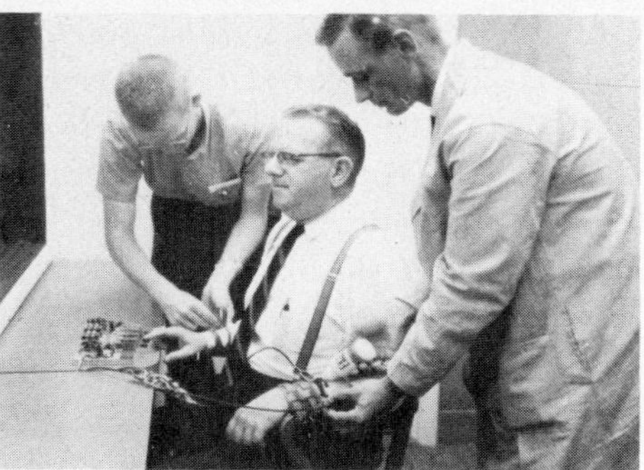

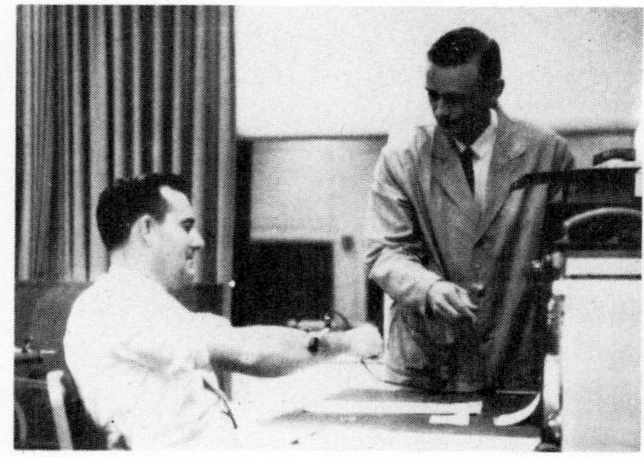

Fig. 19•2 Milgram's study of legitimate power of the experimenter. (*a*) The control panel indicating shock levels, which ranged from 15 volts ("light shock") through 375 ("Danger: severe shock") to 450 volts ("XXXX"). The panel had been carefully designed by a scientific instruments manufacturer. (*b*) The "learner" is strapped into his chair in an adjacent room (with the assistance of the subject), and the experimenter (in lab coat) attaches electrodes with electrode paste to learner's arm. (*c*) One subject refuses to continue shocking the "learner." (*d*) After the experiment, the subject is introduced to the "learner," who, it is explained, is actually a confederate and did not really receive any shocks. (Copyright 1965 by Stanley Milgram. From the film *Obedience*, distributed by the New York University Film Library)

American subjects would go in shocking the "learner" in this situation. Though there was some variation in responses, most agreed that the "teachers" would be unlikely to go very far in shocking the "learner."

Results of Milgram's first experiment are presented in Table 19•1. As we can see, the degree of compliance is startling: Twenty-six of the forty "teachers" went all the way to the highest level of shock—beyond the point marked "danger: severe shock."

The results are typical of those obtained by Milgram in several other replications and variations of this study, and by others who have repeated the study in other settings. Of course, all of the subjects in the experiment were "teachers" (Milgram had arranged the lot drawing to assure this). The "learner" was really an accomplice of the experimenter, who always behaved in a prescribed fashion. In fact, to ensure careful control of the experimental situation, the voice of the "learner" was tape-recorded, and the same tape played back to each "teacher" at the appropriate shock level. The filmed behavior of the "teachers" and their responses during and after the experiment clearly indicate that they were not aware that the "learner" was actually an accomplice. The "teachers" showed considerable conflict and stress as they increased the shock level at each error. They were obviously relieved when the experiment was explained to them afterward and a smiling "learner" came out to shake their hands.

Table 19·1 Levels of Shocks Administered by Subjects in Milgram (1963) Obedience Experiment ($N = 40$)

VERBAL DESIGNATION AND VOLTAGE INDICATION	NUMBER OF SUBJECTS FOR WHOM THIS WAS MAXIMUM SHOCK
Slight Shock	
15	0
30	0
45	0
60	0
Moderate Shock	
75	0
90	0
105	0
120	0
Strong Shock	
135	0
150	0
165	0
180	0
Very Strong Shock	
195	0
210	0
225	0
240	0
Intense Shock	
255	0
270	0
285	0
300	5
Extreme Intensity Shock	
315	4
330	2
345	1
360	1
Danger: Severe Shock	
375	1
390	0
405	0
420	0
XXXX	
435	0
450	26

Milgram carried out his first study at a time when the trial of Adolf Eichmann was being widely discussed. Eichmann was tried in Jerusalem for his operation of Nazi death camps in which hundreds of thousands of Jews, Gypsies, and other people were gassed and incinerated. Eichmann insisted he was simply a soldier following the orders of his superiors, and thus should not be held accountable for his actions. (See the discussion of attribution theory and responsibility in Chapter 18.) Milgram wished to determine the extent to which legitimate power could be used to get people to commit acts ordinarily contrary to accepted moral codes. The results were startling, even to Milgram.

Note that the subjects complied with the experimenter's instructions without any real threat of punishment (what could the experimenter do to those who did not comply?) or promise of reward. The small sum of $4.50 was given to the subject on arrival and it was indicated that he or she could keep it regardless of what followed. Evidently the acceptance of the structural relationship between subject and experimenter was enough to establish the legitimate power of the experimenter—subjects apparently feel that by agreeing to their subject role they are accepting the experimenter's right to prescribe behaviors for them within a broad range, and that they are obliged to comply. Later Milgram carried out several variations of the experiment, to establish the conditions of compliance more clearly:

1. *Evidence of expertise of the experimenter.* The original experiment was conducted in Yale University laboratories with professional-looking instrument panels and an experimenter who looked the part, complete with coat and professional bearing. Perhaps the entire setting contributed to the subject's attribution of expert power to the experimenter. To test this, Milgram repeated the study in Bridgeport, Connecticut, some distance from Yale, in a dingy rented office, with less professional-looking equipment and an experimenter dressed like a student and giving the impression of less expertise. This time 48 percent complied completely. This finding suggests that some appearance of expertise might have been involved in the original study, when 65 percent complied completely.
2. *Closeness of the victim.* Apparently, compliance was enhanced when the "learner" was in another room out of sight. If the "learner" could not even be heard, the amount of shocking increased still further. But the degree of shocking decreased as the subject was moved closer to the victim. It was less if the "learner" could be both seen and heard, still less if the "learner" sat beside the teacher, and least if the subject had to touch the victim or press his hand against the electrode. Thus, being close to the victim creates some restraints against administering punishment on command.
3. *Closeness of the experimenter.* The legitimate power of the experimenter seems to increase with physical closeness of the experimenter to the subject. There is less obedience if the experimenter is in another room, or if commands are presented in a tape-recorded message.

In Nazi concentration camps such as this one (left) at Nordhausen, Jews, Slavs, Poles, Gypsies, and other people were executed and incinerated. The death toll was estimated at over six million. Generally believed to be director of the Nazi plan for extermination of undesirables, Karl Adolf Eichmann (in bullet-proof booth) at his 1961 trial in Jerusalem pleaded: "I have regrets and condemnation for the extermination of the Jewish people which was ordered by the German rulers, but . . . I was only receiving and carrying out orders. . . . When there is no responsibility, there can be no guilt" (*Time*, January 14, 1961). (Wide World Photos)

4. *Behavior of others.* The behavior of other subjects can affect that of the "teacher." If others are present and they encourage him to shock the "learner," he will be more likely to do so. If he sees another subject refuse to shock a "learner," he will also be more willing to refuse. Thus the referent power of other subjects can be used either to enhance or to mitigate the experimenter's power.

Many experiments have shown the great degree to which subjects comply with the experimenter's commands. In one such study (Orne and Evans, 1965), subjects were induced by the experimenter to grasp what appeared to be a dangerous reptile, to plunge a hand into concentrated acid, and to throw a glass of acid at an experimenter's assistant. (The subject was indeed given a glass of powerful acid, and the effects of the acid demonstrated, but the glass was replaced by one containing a harmless solution when the subject was not looking.)

Aside from the moral implications of such behaviors, the evidence of the legitimate power of the experimenter has raised questions about the validity of a number of psychological experiments. To what extent are experimental results a function of the subject's anticipation of what the experimenter wants, and his or her desire to comply with the legitimate requests of the experimenter (Rosenthal, 1966)?

Ethical Considerations in the Obedience Experiment

Lest there be doubt that the Milgram Obedience Experiment was accepted as real by the subjects, Milgram offered some vivid accounts of the behavior of some of the "teachers" who presented severe shock to a fellow subject. In describing one subject, he writes:

> I observed a mature and initially poised businessman enter the laboratory smiling and confident. Within twenty minutes he was reduced to a twitching, stuttering wreck, who was approaching a point of nervous collapse. He constantly pulled on his earlobe, and twisted his hands. At one point, he pushed his fist into his forehead and muttered: "Oh, God, let's stop it." And yet he continued to respond to every word of the experimenter and obeyed to the end. (Milgram, 1963, p. 377)

Milgram also describes sweating, trembling, biting of lips, groans, digging of fingernails into flesh, nervous laughing fits. After the post-experimental interview, steps were taken to "assure that the subject would leave the laboratory in a state of well-being. A friendly reconciliation was arranged between subject and the victim, and an effort was made to reduce any tensions that arose as a result of the experiment."

Nevertheless, ethical objections have been raised. In a critical article, Diana Baumrind (1964) wondered "what sort of procedures could dissipate the type of emotional disturbance described." She argued that the experiment must have led to loss of dignity, self-esteem, and trust, and probably to guilt and some psychological malaise on the part of the subjects. In addition, she asked whether such research might damage the public image of psychology.

In response, Milgram pointed out that in the wake of the actions by Nazi leaders and their underlings during World War II, the recent trials of soldiers and officers for their behavior during the Vietnam War, and innumerable other crimes against humanity committed under orders, we need to try to understand such situations to forestall other such events. Milgram reported that 84 percent of his subjects indicated that they were pleased that they had had the chance to participate in the study, and 75 percent said that they definitely felt that such research should be carried out. A Yale psychiatrist who examined a number of subjects at various times later insists that there was no sign of continued harmful psychological effects.

Yet the topic continues to be discussed by psychologists and others. The American Psychological Association has published a statement in its *Ethical Principles in the Conduct of Research with Human Participants* (1973), which reads:

> **Principle 1** In planning a study the investigator has the personal responsibility to make a careful evaluation of its ethical acceptability, taking into account these Principles for research with human beings. To the extent that this appraisal, weighing scientific and humane values, suggests a deviation from any Principle, the investigator incurs an increasingly serious obligation to seek ethical advice and to observe more stringent safeguards to protect the rights of the human research participant.
>
> **Principle 4** Openness and honesty are essential characteristics of the relationship between investigator and research participant. When the methodological requirements of a study necessitate concealment or deception, the investigator is required to ensure the participant's understanding of the reasons for this action and to restore the quality of the relationship with the investigator.
>
> **Principle 7** The ethical investigator protects participants from physical and mental discomfort, harm and danger. If the risk of such consequences exists, the investigator is required to inform the participant of that fact, secure consent before proceeding, and take all possible measures to minimize distress. A research procedure may not be used if it is likely to cause serious and lasting harm to participants.

Does Milgram's study meet these criteria? The consensus seems to be that it does, but disagreement continues. In attempting to safeguard against unjustified and improper damage to experimental subjects, most universities today have committees on research with human subjects that review research plans and determine whether the research is ethically justifiable.

Other Forms of Legitimate Power Obviously, legitimate power does not depend on formal organizational structure. Any accepted structural relationship wherein one person is obliged to accept another's influence can be seen as a legitimate power relationship. If someone does a favor for you, you may feel obliged to respond to a request to return the favor (Regan, 1971; Goranson and Berkowitz, 1966). If you have harmed someone, even unintentionally, he can legitimately ask you to do something for him to help make up for it (Freedman, Wallington, and Bless, 1967). In traditional male-female relationships, members of one sex were seen as having a legitimate right to expect a member of the other sex to comply with certain wishes—for example, a woman could legitimately expect a man to open a door for her. Of course, with changing conceptions of sex roles, such legitimate sex-related power relationships are gradually passing away.

One interesting form of legitimate power is the legitimate power of the powerless. In most societies, it is considered appropriate for a person who needs help to demand and expect it from someone more fortunate. A blind person can legitimately ask a sighted person for help crossing the street, and the sighted person feels obliged to comply. A child can legitimately ask an adult to help tie a shoe or button a coat. A study conducted in Israel focused on the form of legitimate power Israelis used in attempting to influence bureaucrats (for example, in asking for medical attention at the medical service even though the person asking had forgotten his medical card.) Elihu Katz and Brenda Danet (1966) found that Israelis of American and European origin were more likely to use the more formal kind of legitimate power ("I am a member of this organization and I have a right to expect you, a functionary, to do this for me"). Israelis of Middle Eastern and African origin were more likely to use the legitimate power of the powerless ("Please, I am helpless in this and you are in a position to help me; you must do so").

Can One Have Negative Power?

19·3 In our analysis of social influence and the bases of social power, we have focused on changes in the target that bring him or her into line with the beliefs, attitudes, behaviors, and desires of the influencing agent. Our definitions of influence and power do not, however, preclude the possibility of induced changes that increase the discrepancy between agent and target. Such negative changes are particularly evident with referent and expert power. When you are undecided about how to vote in an election, you may vote against a particular candidate because he or she was supported by a newspaper you detested or distrusted. Another case in point is the boy who refuses to wear green jeans to school because a boy he hates always wears green jeans. In the 1976 primary campaign, the campaign managers for candidate George Wallace urged voters not to vote for his opponent Jimmy Carter on the grounds that the former supporters of Senator George McGovern were now voting for Carter.

Thus, both referent power and expert power may exert negative influence:

> "I don't like Sally. I don't want to be like her. So whatever she says, does, or believes, I want to do the opposite."
>
> "I don't trust Jim. He probably knows more than I do, but if he asks me to do something, it is probably because it will benefit him and possibly hurt me. Therefore my best bet is to do the opposite."

Negative expert influence is evident when a used-car salesman says, "Take my word for it, this 1972 Ford is a much better car for you than that 1973 Chevrolet," and you wonder what he stands to gain if you make that choice.

In one test of negative referent influence, eighty persons of various ages and backgrounds who happened to be sitting on park benches in New York's Washington Square were asked their opinions on social issues. Another person sitting nearby (an accomplice of the experimenters) listened in on the respondent's statements and disagreed with them and insulted him: "ridiculous . . . terribly confused . . . obviously wrong . . . no one believes that . . ." and so on. When the respondent was interviewed again slightly later, without the accomplice present, he became more extreme in the opinions he had originally held. In other words, his responses shifted even more strongly away from those presumably held by the accomplice.

For comparison, the experimenters did some interviews with the accomplice either sitting quietly on the bench without commenting, or attempting persuasion without insult. In neither of these conditions was there a significant change in the respondent's opinion (Abelson and Miller, 1967).

In a test of negative expert influence, subjects were given a statement arguing that a steel shortage plaguing the country at that time was due to excessive labor union demands. When that statement was attributed to a columnist who was closely associated with the steel industry (and who would have a personal vested interest in having people believe that the unions and not industry were to blame), subjects tended to disagree with the statement. The same statement attributed to an objective source led to positive changes (agreement with the statement). A change in opinion opposed to that advocated in a communication has been called a boomerang effect (Hovland and Weiss, 1952).

Interaction Among Power Bases

19•4 We have been describing power bases as if they were independent of one another. Ordinarily, however, an influence attempt involves two or more bases of power. The mother who wants her son to stop smoking may offer him a reward, but at the same time implicitly invoke her legitimate power as a mother, and her referent power as a model for his behavior. Indeed, she may not be aware of the power bases she is invoking.

In a classic study of social power relationships in a hospital setting it was found that the power basis the doctor thought he was using to influence nurses was not the one the nurses thought he was using. Whereas he may have thought she was complying with his requests out of respect for his superior knowledge or expertise the nurse may have complied because of his legitimate power or possibly his coercive power (Stanton and Schwartz, 1954). Many tensions in work situations probably stem from such discrepancies in perceptions of power bases.

It would seem that to be most effective in influencing someone, the more bases of power employed the better. However, such a strategy might not always be best. We have already pointed out that coercive power can lead the target to reject the agent personally—we do not usually like people as much if they are threatening to punish us. And since we tend to disidentify with people we dislike, the use of coercive power undermines referent power. Coercive power might also weaken other bases of power. The target might reasonably ask, "If my supervisor really had the right to ask me to do this, he would not be threatening me so much." As one experiment has demonstrated, coercive power may lead to even less compliance than legitimate power, once the possibility of surveillance is removed (Raven and French, 1958).

The relationship between expert and referent power is also an interesting one. The creation of a situation that leads to increased expert power (the superiority of the agent with respect to the target) can reduce referent power (which is more likely if the target feels some similarity or bond with the agent). Teachers sometimes recognize this dilemma—they would like to have their students feel a mutual friendly relationship with them, but worry lest this lead students to disrespect the teachers' expertise. Supervisors sometimes wonder whether establishing a referent relationship would undermine their legitimate power.

The main point here is that a combination of power bases does not operate additively, and indeed one basis of power may diminish the effectiveness of another when the two are used simultaneously.

Enhancing Social Power

19•5 There are several ways to enhance social power.

Emphasizing the Power Bases In attempting to influence others, we may use the power basis that seems most appropriate at the moment without thinking much about it. Sometimes however, the influence process involves a planned strategy, in which we first set the stage for influence and then make the actual influence attempt. An agent who wants to enhance his or her expert power would do well to let the target know just how expert he or she is. A doctor or a lawyer can display diplomas and other certificates of competence prominently throughout the office. (It also helps to display a number of impressive books on one's bookshelves.)

An agent who wishes to use referent power may set the stage by claiming to have much in common with the target. For example, a Presidential candidate campaigning in Illinois will point out that he was born in Illinois. In Texas he may

Expert and Referent Power and Reported Reception of ESP Images

Bertram Raven, Helge Mansson, and Edwin Anthony (1962) investigated the ways in which a group can influence an individual's belief in extrasensory perception and the person's reported reception of ESP images. Prior to the experiment, experimenters measured the subjects' belief in the possibility of extrasensory perception.

Female subjects participated in the study in groups of four, each member seated in a separate booth where she could not see the others. The group was told that someone in an adjacent room, who claimed to be an effective ESP sender, would attempt to send to the subject the image of a star. There was, of course, no sender in the other room. Each subject would attempt to receive the image and to indicate her success or failure by pushing a button marked "receive" or one marked "not receive." The subjects would respond consecutively, in a sequence determined by lot, and each subject's response would be indicated to the others on a light panel in each booth.

Actually, the light signals were controlled by the experimenter, and the lot gave each subject the impression that she was last. Subjects were given thirty trials, on twenty-three of which each subject was given the impression that the other three had received an ESP image. In the first phase of the experiment, group pressures clearly appeared to increase the number of reported receptions of ESP images and also to lead to a higher belief in the existence of ESP than when the responses were made without any indication of the other subjects' responses.

In the second phase of the experiment, seventy-two additional subjects participated in essentially the same situation, except that now expert and referent influence of the co-participants were manipulated simultaneously, through the experimenter's verbal instructions regarding the perceptual ability of the co-participants. Subjects were each given the impression that the three others had been tested extensively in a perceptual laboratory. Twenty-four subjects (in a high attributed ability condition) were told that their partners had been found to have unusually keen and reliable perceptual skills; twenty-four (in the moderate ability condition) were given to understand that the others were average in this skill—not too different from the subject; twenty-four others (in a negative attributed ability condition) were told that the other three were highly unreliable perceivers.

It was expected that these verbal manipulations would vary both the expert and the referent power of

say he is really a Texan, since he spent his childhood there. In New York, he may suddenly become a New Yorker, since his parents came from New York and often talked about their home state.

A beggar enhances his legitimate power of helplessness by first emphasizing his extreme need and his inability to help himself.

Personal reward and personal coercive power can be enhanced by any of a number of means that make the agent's approval desirable and disapproval painful for the target. The agent emphasizes his or her own positive qualities and desirability. An ambitious salesperson often finds out quite a bit about what his or her prospective client likes in people. Does the client like people who are forceful or gentle, casual or formal? And emphasizing a similar religious outlook or political view increases both personal reward and personal coercive power as well as referent power. The various devices of ingratiation and favor-doing discussed below also increase the value of one's approval. Another device found effective, particularly with children, is the withholding of social contact and opportunity for approval. In two studies in nursery schools, it was found that children were

the group. Co-participants who were seen as high in attributed ability would have great expertise power but lower referent power. Co-participants with average ability would have higher referent power, but less expert power. Co-participants in the low-ability condition would be low in both power bases.

It was predicted that expert power would be more likely to affect belief in ESP, while referent power would be more likely to affect behavior. That is, when we want to know what is really true, then we look to experts, yet we look to others like us to help us decide how we should behave. The results, as indicated in Table 19A-1, are in line with these predictions. Subjects were most likely to report receiving ESP images when they were grouped with similar others who reported receiving images. They were most likely to increase their belief in ESP, if—by their behavior—three others who were expert perceivers appeared to believe in ESP. Participants with low ability had little influence on either belief or behavior.

Table 19A·1 Number of Subjects Reporting Reception of ESP Images and Changing Beliefs

	HIGH ATTRIBUTED ABILITY	MODERATE ATTRIBUTED ABILITY	NEGATIVE ATTRIBUTED ABILITY
NUMBER REPORTING RECEIVING ESP IMAGES	8	15	7
Change in Belief in ESP			
Increased	13	5	5
No change	2	2	2
Decreased	9	17	17
N	24	24	24

In the high-attributed-ability condition, the same expert power that increased the agents' influence on belief appears to have decreased their influence on behavior. Does this seem reasonable? Perhaps we can think of examples in which this occurs. A minister, priest, or rabbi, who is seen as an expert on religion and morality, tries to persuade his parishioners to be more accepting of other religious or ethnic groups. Is he successful? He does influence them to believe that they *should* be more open-minded, that acceptance of others is morally right. Yet the parishioner may think "our minister is so unusual a person that I cannot expect to live up to his standards." Perhaps such a parishioner's behavior would be influenced more by the tolerant and understanding behavior of other parishioners.

more likely to change their behavior in response to personal reward ("good," "fine," "good one,") after they had waited alone for twenty minutes. The effects of approval were reduced if during a preceding period the child had twenty minutes of intensive play with the adult, during which the adult approved of the child's behavior repeatedly (Gewirtz and Baer, 1958 a, b).

Reducing Power of Opposing Influencing Agents Sometimes an influencing agent tries to change a person's attitude or behavior that is already under the influence of another influencing agent. In this case, the attitude or behavior can be more effectively changed if the other agent's influence is diminished. To do this, the agent may go through the various power bases the opposing agent may have utilized and attempt to weaken them or even to make them negative.

Is the opposing agent using reward power? Show that the reward is not all that great. Is it coercive power? Then prove that the punishment cannot be effectively administered. Legitimacy? Explain that the agent does not have the right to expect the compliance sought and that the target is under no obligation. Expert? Cast doubt on how much the agent knows. Referent? Show that the agent is someone that no respectable person would want to identify with. Informational? Show that the logic in the opposing argument is faulty, or that the information is incomplete or false. Indeed, any means that may be used to isolate the target from the opposing agent, physically or psychologically, or both, increases the possibilities of counterinfluence.

Creating a Proper Scene or Mood The teen-ager who wants to ask his or her parents for something may sometimes consciously soften them up, or get them in the right mood. The agent is often aware that the target is more likely to comply at some times than at others. If the target has had a good day, has had a successful experience, or is otherwise in a good mood, he or she may be more susceptible to a request. There is indeed evidence that people are more readily influenced by a persuasive communication if it is presented while the target is eating peanuts and drinking a soft drink. This is true even when the donor of the food and beverage has carefully dissociated himself from the persuasive message. Comparison subjects not given the peanuts and soft drink were less readily influenced, and influence was reduced further if the message was read while the room was permeated with an unpleasant odor (Janis, Kaye, and Kirschner, 1965).

Although one might reasonably expect a persuasive communication to be less effective if it is presented while the recipient is distracted, distractions sometimes seem to increase influenceability. In one such study different forms of distraction were introduced while messages were presented. Some subjects were shown sexually provoking slides (positive distraction), some were shown slides of scenery (neutral distraction), and some were shown medical slides of dismembered and burned human limbs (negative distraction). Positive distraction appeared to increase influence, whereas negative distraction reduced it (Zimbardo, Ebbeson, and Fraser, 1968, as reported in Zimbardo and Ebbeson, 1970).

In explaining these results, students of attitude change say that when a target reads or hears a message designed to change his or her opinion, the content has a positive effect (toward the change desired by the agent), but the target also mobilizes counterarguments that have a negative effect. The strong negative distraction reduces the ability of the target to concentrate on the content of the message, diminishing the message's positive impact. A neutral or positive distraction keeps the target from concentrating on his or her counterarguments, thus making the message more powerful.

This same reasoning may explain why a person may be more influenceable if he or she is tired, weak, or otherwise unprepared to deal with an influence message. Salesmen commonly speak about means of reducing sales resistance, and apparently believe that a tired person (or one who is less alert following a few alchoholic drinks) is easily persuaded to buy.

Ingratiation and Social Influence One of the best-selling books of the 1930s and the decades following was Dale Carnegie's *How to Win Friends and Influence*

People (1936). Carnegie's advice was as simple as it was manipulative—if you want to influence people, you should first get them to like you. He then proceeded to give a number of illustrations to show how this could be accomplished, but his major advice was, "Dole out praise lavishly." You can also get people to like you by agreeing with them. You don't even have to believe that your target's acts are praiseworthy, or that his or her opinions are correct.

Later Edward E. Jones and a number of other social psychologists experimentally investigated what they called ingratiation (the tactics people use to get others to like them). They found that many of the techniques suggested by Carnegie could be effective, with certain limitations (Jones, 1964). A major limitation is that the ingratiating device must not be obviously manipulative (Jones, 1964; Deutsch and Solomon, 1959). We tend to reject obvious flattery and the attempts of "yes-men" to be ingratiating. However, the agent may reduce the target's suspicion by praising the target to a third person, in a manner that allows the target to believe he is overhearing a conversation and that the agent's praise is not meant for the target's hearing. One factor that works in the ingratiator's favor is the general desire we all have to be praiseworthy and to be right in our opinions. This desire can be exploited effectively by praise or agreement that might appear ingratiating to an objective observer.

Ingratiation works as an influence device through increasing the agent's personal reward and coercive power. If we especially like someone, his or her approval is all the more rewarding to us, and his or her disapproval all the more punishing. Thus ingratiation, when effective, has the effect of building up the agent's resources for reward and punishment, and thereby increasing his or her power. Ingratiation may also increase referent power—we want to be like, or be in agreement with, people we like and who generally agree with us.

Favor-doing and Social Influence At airports and outside theaters, many of us have encountered young men and women offering candy, a book, or some other small token. It is a gift, they say, and is without obligation. If we accept, they proceed to tell us about the value of their religious sect, and later ask us to join, or at least to give them something to help them in their good work. These young missionaries have discovered a power-enhancing device that has also been demonstrated in social psychological research. We are more ready to accept influence from others who have done us a favor.

Favor-doing does not lead to reward power in the usual sense. The reward is given before the influence attempt, and is not contingent on the influence being accepted. Favor-doing is probably effective in at least two ways:

1. It invokes a reciprocity norm (Gouldner, 1960) that basically requires us to do unto others as they have done unto us. Even if the agent says we are not obligated, we nonetheless feel obliged to do something in return. Thus, favor-doing may enhance a form of legitimate power.
2. It may also lead to a form of ingratiation. We naturally like others who have

done things for us, and thus favor-doing may enhance personal reward and referent power.

The effectiveness of favor-doing as a power-enhancing device has been demonstrated in a number of studies (Berkowitz and Daniels, 1964; Goranson and Berkowitz, 1966). In one study (Regan, 1971) college students participated in pairs, but in separate rooms, rating and judging a series of pictures. At a break in the experiment, one of the subjects (actually an accomplice of the experimenter) asked to be excused briefly. He returned shortly afterward. In some experimental conditions, the accomplice simply returned to the room. In others, he came back carrying two soft drinks, saying, "I asked the experimenter if I could get something to drink and he said it was okay, so I brought a drink for you also." The subject accepted the drink and the study resumed.

Various persons (such as members of some religious sects) utilize the psychologically sound technique of prefacing an influence attempt with a gift. (Owen Franken, Stock, Boston)

At a later break, the accomplice was heard asking the experimenter whether he might send a note to the subject, and when given permission sent a message asking the subject to buy some raffle tickets to help build a new high-school gym. The data clearly support the hypothesis that favor-doing enhances power. Subjects who had received the favor bought nearly twice as many raffle tickets as those who did not receive a favor.

In a similar study done earlier by Jack Brehm and Ann Cole (1966), the subject was asked to give his first impression of another subject in what was described as an important psychological experiment. Again, at a break, and before the actual ratings began, the other subject (an accomplice) asked to be excused, and returned —sometimes with a soft drink for the real subject and sometimes empty-handed. Later the accomplice asked the subject for help in carrying out very dull tasks. Can you predict the condition ("soda" or "no soda") in which the subject would be more likely to help the accomplice? Consider this experiment carefully before answering.

If you predicted that, as in the first experiment, helping would be more likely in the "soda" condition, you were wrong. Brehm and Cole found that subjects were *less* likely to help when they had first been given a favor, and this result was in keeping with their hypothesis. A major difference in the experiments was that here there was a suggestion that the subject would have to be objective in rating the other person, and that meant being independent in his judgments. The experimenters suggest that the favor was seen as a threat to the subject's independence and freedom. Brehm (1966) used the term *reactance* to refer to counterinfluence behaviors (negative influence due to the person's concern about restriction of freedom).

Thus favor-doing can have a negative effect when the favor appears to reduce the recipients' freedom of action. Also, favor-doing, like ingratiation, is ineffective, or even negatively effective, in enhancing power when the motives of the favor-doer are clearly suspect. Perhaps the airport missionaries increase their effectiveness by emphasizing that the gift is a gift of love and does not carry any obligation, even if they privately hope that it does.

Effective Use of Guilt Dan Greenburg (1964), in his witty tongue-in-cheek booklet *How To Be a Jewish Mother*, states his basic principle quite early: "Underlying all techniques of Jewish Motherhood is the ability to plant, cultivate, and harvest guilt. Control guilt and you control the child. . . . Let your child hear you sigh every day; if you don't know what he's done to make you suffer, *he* will."

The use of **guilt** as an influence-enhancing device is not limited to Jewish mothers, of course, or to mothers in general. It is common folk wisdom that people feel a need to expiate guilt. Furthermore, several experiments have demonstrated that a person who believes she or he has harmed someone, or otherwise transgressed is more likely to accede to a request. One of these uses a device similar to Milgram's obedience study. The "teacher" again was asked to encourage learning in a second subject, who was an accomplice of the experimenter. Half of the "teachers" did this by (persumably) shocking the "learner" for errors (but at a somewhat lower presumed level of shock than in the Milgram experiment). The other half merely signaled errors with a buzzer. After the learning part of the study, the "learner" casually asked the "teacher" to make a number of telephone calls to help in a campaign to save California's redwood forests. As in Milgram's experiment the subjects experienced considerable guilt after shocking the "learner." The data were consistent with the guilt-and-compliance hypothesis—75 percent of the subjects who had delivered shocks agreed to the request, while only 25 percent of those who had merely given a buzzer signal did so.

Of course, compliance might have been due to sympathy or compassion for the "learner" who received the shock. The experimenters controlled for this possible interpretation by introducing a condition in which the subject saw the "learner" getting shocked but did not administer the shocks himself. In that condition, the amount of compliance was about the same as in the buzzer condition (Carlsmith and Gross, 1969).

Parallel experiments have demonstrated the same basic phenomenon. In one experiment, guilt was induced by surreptitiously rigging a table so that it fell down, scattering data cards all over the floor. Some subjects were led to believe that their clumsiness was responsible, while it was clear to others that they were not responsible (Freedman, Wallington, and Bless, 1967). In another study, guilt was induced by having a confederate tell the subject what the experiment was about while they were waiting. The experimenter then entered, told the subjects it was extremely important that they not know about the experiment beforehand, and asked if they knew anything about it. The subjects almost invariably denied such knowledge, thus lying to the experimenter and experiencing some guilt about it. In both cases, the subject who felt guilty was more likely to accede to the experimenter's request to volunteer additional hours of experimentation (Freedman, Wallington, and Bless, 1967).

Why does guilt lead to increased compliance? First, it may lead to increased legitimacy—a form of the reciprocity norm we mentioned earlier. Just as we feel obliged to do something for someone who has done something for us, we also feel that a person we have harmed has a legitimate right to ask us for something and that we are obliged to comply. An additional possibility is that our doing harm to someone, or transgressing, is damaging to our self-image, and atonement functions to repair that image.

Influence by Gradations By our definitions, an agent's social power is demonstrated by his or her ability to influence a target. We shall now go one step further, and add that effective influence (influence that does what you want it to) may in fact further increase that power. There is evidence that after we have influenced someone, we will be seen as more powerful, both by the target and by observers. It follows further that an influence attempt that fails reduces the agent's social power (unless, of course, the target feels guilty for failing to comply and then feels obliged to comply with future requests).

The agent can soften up the target by first asking him or her to do something relatively innocuous, then making a greater demand, and then a still greater demand. This device of influence by gradations was described many years ago by Jerome Frank. He first asked subjects to eat dry soda crackers, and when they stopped asked them to eat still more. His legitimate power as experimenter was such that he could induce them to eat an amazing number of soda crackers. When they reached what appeared to be their absolute limit, they refused to eat any more. Frank would then try influencing by gradations: "Would you at least pick up a cracker? Now smell it. Now touch it to your lips. Taste it. Now would you eat it?" Frank found that by this method he could get subjects to eat many more soda crackers (Frank, 1944). The technique is somewhat similar to the procedure called **shaping** in instrumental conditioning theory (Chapter 10). Social psychologists, however, assume that the influence-by-gradations method involves more of a cognitive process, which we will discuss later.

Jonathan Freedman and Scott Fraser (1966) have also called this method of influence the "foot-in-the-door technique," borrowing from the parlance of door-to-door salesmen. They conducted two studies that demonstrated its effectiveness. The basic procedure was to call people and ask them to comply with a small request, then call again about three days later with a larger request.

In the first study, the target was asked to answer a few simple questions about his or her use of household products; the large request was to allow a group of six men to come to the house and conduct a sizeable inventory of household products and their use, at some inconvenience to the resident. In the second study, householders were first asked to put up a small sign in front of their house or sign a petition to keep California beautiful; the larger request was to pose in front of their house a huge unattractive "Drive Carefully" sign. With very few exceptions, the householders readily agreed to the small request—to answer a few questions about household products or to put up a small sign. In both studies, a comparison group was approached with the larger request immediately, without having first received the smaller request. Both studies yielded similar results: successful influence with the smaller request more than tripled the amount of compliance with the larger request.

Several possible reasons might explain the effectiveness of the foot-in-the-door technique. It may lead to greater attribution of power to the agent, since he has been successful in the first instance. This does not explain all of the results, however, since in their second study Freedman and Fraser employed different influencing agents for the small and large request and yet got a significant foot-in-the-door effect. A second possibility is that the target's self-image changes—after complying with the small request, the target thinks, "I must be a generous, cooperative, civic-minded person" and is thus more ready to comply with a further request.

The findings are also consistent with theory and research that we will describe next. The changed behavior following the first influence leads to secondary effects: a reevaluation by the person of his or her attitudes, beliefs, and behaviors, so as to reduce dissonance and inconsistency.

Secondary Effects Following Social Influence

19·6 We stated earlier that the exercise of informational power leads most immediately to changes in the target that are independent of the agent, whereas the other bases of power lead to changes that in some way are dependent on the agent. Clearly, however, we can all think of changes due to reward, coercion, legitimacy, expertise, and reference that *subsequently* become independent of the agent. The young man who was influenced to give up smoking by the mother who threatened punishment or promised reward may *later* decide that he does not like smoking after all and continue his abstinence even away from mother. The changes in private attitude and belief following dependent forms of power result from certain secondary changes:

1. New information or perceptions may become available to the target as the result of his or her changed behavior.
2. The target may change his or her perception of the influencing agent.
3. The target, finding that his behavior is inconsistent with his beliefs or attitudes, changes those beliefs or attitudes to make them consistent with the behavior.

New Information Resulting from Social Influence We all learn from what we do. Each act teaches us something new about our world and ourselves. We also learn new things from acts that have been forced on us, or that we have been persuaded to perform. Examples of second-order changes are common. A teacher relying on expert power tells a student to work a math problem a certain way; the student can't see why until she has done it several times and sees that it really works. A parent invoking reward or coercion power insists that a child try some

It remains to be seen what behavior and attitude changes will result from the integration of schools through busing. (Shelly Katz, Black Star)

spinach, which looks unappetizing. The child tastes it and learns that it tastes much better than it looks. For many years, major-league baseball managers would not allow black athletes on their teams because they felt certain that this would destroy their team's *esprit de corps*. Finally, they were forced to hire their first black player (Jackie Robinson), and within a few years, baseball players could scarcely believe that any opposition had ever existed.

In this way, then, following effective use of one of the dependent power bases, the target may begin to see things differently, and privately accept the change—it works like informational power, except that the information has resulted secondarily. Such secondary change is so obvious that few social psychologists have paid much attention to it.

New Perceptions of the Influencing Agent The use of one power base by an agent may affect some of his other power bases. If the agent chooses to use coercion, the threat of punishment makes the target like him or her less, diminishing some of the other power bases, such as personal reward, referent, and expert. It also follows that after the use of other power bases, such as reward, referent, or expert, the agent may be liked more, and whatever act he advocates will be evaluated more favorably. The mother who effectively invokes referent and reward power in getting her son to stop smoking may be appreciated, and some of the positive affect attached to the mother may then carry over to the act itself. There is indeed a tendency to associate a reward received from a person with the act that has been advocated.

Dissonance Reduction and Changes in Self-perception Following Compliance

The basic notion of dissonance theory is that a person feels some discomfort or uneasiness if his cognitions are inconsistent. Recall the example we gave in Chapter 12 of the woman who was smoking even though she knew that smoking might lead to lung cancer. The person then tends to change either her behavior (give up smoking), or her cognitions (decide that smoking is not really that dangerous; or, even if it is dangerous, one lives only once and the many other satisfactions connected with it outweigh the dangers).

In Chapter 12, we discussed the concept of conflict in choices between alternatives. It is reasonable to assume, according to Leon Festinger (1957), that following the resolution of any conflict, dissonance is almost inevitable. Why? Because after a decision, the many cognitive elements favoring the rejected alternative are all initially present, as are the many cognitive elements opposed to the selected alternative.

Suppose a woman student from a midwestern university has been accepted for medical school at a rather good midwestern university and an excellent west coast university. She is in conflict over which to choose. The midwest school is close to home, has an excellent biochemistry department, and has lower fees; but its reputation is lower, the teaching hospital is mediocre, and the climate is severe. The west coast school has a better overall reputation and an excellent medical laboratory, as well as a much better climate; but its biochemistry program leaves much to be desired, its fees are much higher, and it is far from home and friends. After some agonizing the student chooses the west coast school. Now the conflict is resolved, but dissonance is initially very high. "Why am I moving so far away from home to a school with high fees and a poor biochemistry department," the student may ask, "when I could have been closer, paid less, and acquired a good biochem background?" Dissonance theory predicts that over time, these elements will change so as to support her decision—the biochem program at the west coast school begins to seem better, the cost and location seem less important, and so on.

Social influence also presents a conflict situation. The very fact that social influence is involved implies that the target was not prepared to engage in the influenced activity without the influence. When the mother threatens her son (who enjoys smoking) with punishment if he does not give up smoking, he may initially experience considerable conflict: "Should I give up an activity that I enjoy, or accept a punishment that I find painful?" The amount of conflict depends, of course, on the intensity of his desire to smoke and the severity of the punishment. Let us assume that the desire to smoke is strong. Presumably, if the punishment is small (say, a wrist slap), there will be little conflict and the son will continue to smoke. If the punishment is very large (permanent denial of the family car, or complete disinheritance), then again the conflict may not be very great, and the son will give up smoking. Conflict would be greatest somewhere between the extremes, at a point at which the incentives to change the behavior (stemming from the threats or promises of the influencing agent) would be approximately equal to the desires by the target to continue in the same behavior. Presumably he would have the greatest hesitation before deciding (Figure 19•3).

What about dissonance after decision? Presumably it would follow the same pattern. Dissonance would be low at either extreme. At the high punishment end (point *d* on Figure 19•3), the son would comply, without any real dissonance after decision. ("Why did I comply? Because if I hadn't, the world would have fallen in on me.") At the low punishment end (point *a*), there would similarly be little dissonance after decision.

At point *c*, just past the breaking point, the son eventually would comply and then ask, "Why did I give up smoking? It isn't as if the punishment were all that great." And at this point, Festinger says, there is a particularly strong tendency to say, "It wasn't just that. Smoking is a dirty, dangerous, expensive, terrible habit. I only wonder why I didn't give it up earlier." Festinger also suggests that such a reformed nonsmoker would be especially likely to try to persuade others to give up smoking.

At point *b* the punishment is not quite great enough to induce the son to give up smoking. He finally rejects the influence and receives the punishment, which is quite painful. "Why did I get myself in such a mess?" he asks. "Because smoking is really very satisfying and relaxing. And what is more I think I will go out and get a few more cartons right now." Within a very small range of punishment levels some targets radically change their opinions in the direction influenced, and independent change results, while at a point slightly lower the target maintains his behavior or shows a boomerang effect, becoming even more convinced that his

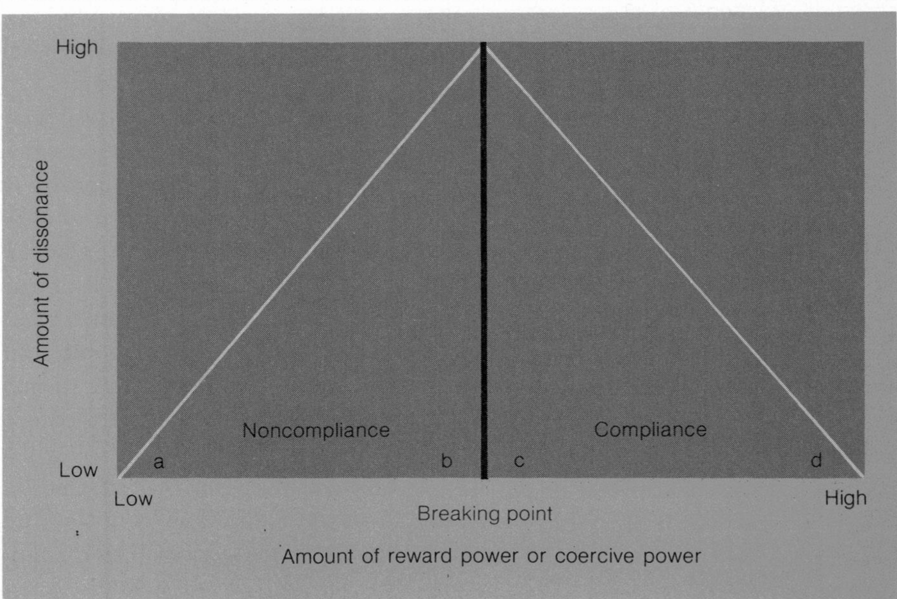

Fig. 19•3 Festinger dissonance model. (Festinger, 1957)

original views were correct. This, then, is the forced-compliance theory we alluded to earlier. It has stimulated a tremendous amount of social psychological research.

If we now reexamine the Festinger and Carlsmith study (1959) in which subjects were given either $20 or $1 to tell a naive female "subject" that a boring task was in fact enjoyable (Chapters 11 and 18), we can see that the experimenters were using varying degrees of reward power—subjects in the $20 condition were at point *d,* subjects in the $1 condition at point *c.* The subjects who were paid $1 experienced greater dissonance and were more likely to bring their attitudes in line with their behavior.

Of course, dissonance-reduction is not limited to coercive power or reward power. Presumably variation in the use of any power basis could lead to variation in the conflict before compliance or noncompliance and in the dissonance afterward. One of the more interesting dissonance studies apparently used a combination of legitimate, referent, and personal reward power. That experiment, conducted by Ewart Smith (1961) and later developed further by Philip Zimbardo and his associates (Zimbardo, Weisenberg, Firestone, and Levy, 1965), focused on the responses of male army reservists and ROTC students who were asked to eat fried grasshoppers as part of a survival training course. Some of the reluctant reservists were asked to do this by a likable, easygoing, and pleasant officer. The others were ordered to do so by a stiff, formal, generally unpleasant officer. Legitimate power was presumably equal in both cases, but the pleasant officer had an apparent advantage in referent power and probably personal reward (his approval was desirable) as well. The advantage, however, was only apparent. Both officers were equally able to get the men to eat the undesirable food, but those who faced the unpopular officer were particularly likely to indicate later that they *liked* the grasshoppers. They evidently needed to justify their behavior—and they did so by convincing themselves that grasshoppers weren't that bad after all.

The reason so much research has been done on cognitive dissonance and forced compliance is that it seems to conflict with common sense. We might ordinarily expect someone to enjoy an unpleasant task more if given a huge reward for doing it. The enjoyment or anticipated enjoyment of the reward would carry over to the act itself and to the attitude associated with the act. Some studies have indeed found such an effect. For example, Milton Rosenberg (in an experiment using Ohio State students) arranged to have each subject wait in a room for an experiment to commence. While the subject waited, a graduate student—apparently not associated with the Rosenberg study—asked the subject to write an essay arguing that the Big Ten Champion Ohio State football team should not be allowed to play in the Rose Bowl (a position counter to the attitudes of virtually all Ohio State students). For writing the essay, some students were offered 50¢, some $1, and some $5.

Then the subjects reported to Rosenberg for the actual experiment, which involved, among other things, a measure of attitude toward allowing the OSU team to play in the Rose Bowl. Rosenberg found that as the reward increased, the corresponding attitude change also increased. He suggested that students in the Festinger and Carlsmith study were made suspicious by the great amount of money

Can You Legislate Beliefs and Feelings?

A common objection to legislation designed to bring about social change (for example, civil rights laws) is that "you can't legislate people's hearts and minds." Imposing penalties for certain behaviors involves coercive power, and so surveillance must be in force at all times. Do we really want a society like that?

We do have evidence, however, that attitudes change following legislation or other legal action. Frequent surveys of opinions about school desegregation in the South indicate that there has been a steady increase in acceptance of desegregation since the 1954 Supreme Court ruling that forbade racially segregated schools. Another example is provided by a study of how legislation establishing medicare, a program of federally supported health insurance for people over sixty-five, affected physicians' attitudes and beliefs.

When medicare was considered by Congress in 1965, the opposition of the medical profession was considerable. Physicians and medical associations lobbied, campaigned, wrote letters to newspapers, gave speeches. They pointed out that medicare would lead to imposition of a federal bureaucracy on the medical profession, that it would force physicians to spend their time on paper work instead of treating patients, that it would destroy the personal approach to medicine, that there would be widespread boycotts and physicians giving up their practices, that there would be shortages of medical care, and so on. Even if Congress successfully imposed medicare on them, physicians supposedly would never accept it and would comply, if at all, only under threat of legal action.

John Colombotos, a sociologist, decided to test the extent to which physicians would maintain their attitudes following such legislation (Colombotos, 1969). Some 1205 physicians were interviewed in New York State. The first interviews were conducted in 1964 and early in 1965 (before the legislation was passed); a subsample of 676 were reinterviewed in mid-1966 (after the law was passed, but before it officially went into effect); and a remaining 331 physicians were reinterviewed early in 1967 (after the legislation had been implemented for several months). The question that was most indicative of attitudes toward medicare was "What is your opinion about the bill that would provide for compulsory health insurance through social security to cover hospital costs for those over sixty-five—are you in favor of such a plan, or are you opposed to it?" The responses are represented in Table 19B•1. Evidently the physicians' attitudes became dramatically more favorable as soon as legislation was passed, and continued to become more favorable after the legislation was implemented.

What form of secondary influence was operating? Were the physicians responding to the legitimate power of their elected congressional body? Did they read the law only after it was passed, and thus see that it was not as objectionable as they had originally thought? Did they reduce dissonance after passage—first deciding that they would have to comply with it and then trying to justify their compliance by looking for favorable aspects of the law? The basis for the change in attitudes is not clear from this field investigation. What is clear is that attitudes changed following legal action and that there was behavioral compliance. Despite widespread threats of boycott and early retirement, virtually all of the physicians did in fact comply with the law.

Table 19B•1 Attitudes of Physicians toward Medicare before Passage of Legislation, after Passage, and after Implementation

ATTITUDE	BEFORE PASSAGE	AFTER PASSAGE	AFTER IMPLEMENTATION
Favor	38%	70%	81%
Oppose	54%	26%	19%
Don't know, no answer	8%	5%	—
	100%	101%	100%

($20), and were thus put on their guard to hold firm to their position (Rosenberg, 1965).

Other studies have demonstrated that such suspicion reduces the dissonance effect, but that the original finding can be obtained even when the possibility of suspicion on the part of subjects is reduced. A number of factors tend to increase the likelihood of dissonance and attitude change after forced compliance when there is a lower rather than a higher incentive. The tendency to change attitudes is greater when (1) the target feels that he has a true choice; (2) the target feels that his action has real implications for himself as well as others (for example, if the Ohio student feels that his essay might in fact determine whether OSU goes to the Rose Bowl); (3) the target's counterattitudinal behavior is made public—the essay will be published in the local papers, or otherwise circulated to a wide audience; (4) the target feels personally responsible for the consequences of his action; (5) the target puts something of himself into the counterattitudinal behavior (he will change more if he is actively involved in writing the essay or improvises in the reading of a counterattitudinal statement, rather than merely repeating what someone else has written) (Carlsmith, Collins, and Helmreich, 1966; Collins, 1973).

In Chapter 18, we indicated that some of the phenomena dealt with under the general framework of forced compliance and dissonance reduction could also be considered fruitfully in terms of attribution theory. The attribution theorist would say that the army reservist who ate grasshoppers was examining his own behavior and trying to understand it, as were the students who were paid to describe the experiment falsely. In the high-dissonance conditions ($1 and the nice officer) the target cannot attribute his behavior to external factors, and thus must look internally. Though there have been some disputes between dissonance theorists in interpreting these experiments, the basic predictions tend to be the same, and the two approaches (dissonance theory and attribution theory) to interpreting forced compliance do not seem grossly incompatible.

Brainwashing or Coercive Persuasion

19•7 The term *brainwashing* was taken from the Chinese *hsi mao*, literally "wash brain," and was used particularly in reference to Chinese Communist "thought control" or "ideological molding" programs. The Chinese thought-reform programs were developed as the Communists began to control substantial areas of China in the 1930s, and these programs became widespread after the Communists completely took over China in the 1940s. These programs were justified on the grounds that the masses, who had not been educated in a Communist society, must somehow be cleansed of their bourgeois attitudes and ideology. Peasants and small merchants especially were candidates for brainwashing programs, since they were likely to resist indoctrination (simple informational or expert power). Yet the desired end even of brainwashing was reeducation and rehabilitation—private acceptance of the new ideas that would be independent of the influencing agents.

Engineering False Confessions

It has been estimated that 80 percent of crimes are solved through the suspect's confession during police interrogation. Considering the costs of criminal trials for defendants as well as for the state, perhaps one should applaud this shortcut in the legal process However, we occasionally hear that a suspect who was convicted on the basis of his confession, and never repudiated it, was subsequently found innocent when the real culprit admitted having committed the crime—and the new confession was supported by unmistakable evidence.

In the days when the third degree with its rubber hoses and other means of torture was used with some frequency, confessions were often clearly the result of coercive power—and often, when the coercive power of the interrogator was removed, the suspect repudiated his confession. Today there are many more safeguards against strong-arm methods in interrogation (although these methods are apparently still used on occasion) and perhaps, paradoxically, that is exactly why we now hear of more cases in which false confessions were not repudiated.

Philip Zimbardo (1970) has suggested that as harsher methods have been proscribed, police interrogators have developed softer, more subtle methods, which make it less clear to the suspect that his confession is externally caused. He wonders why he has confessed and sometimes convinces himself that since his confession was not made under obvious duress, perhaps it has some truth in it.

A major manual used by police interrogators, in fact, suggests subtle techniques for obtaining confessions (Inbau and Reid, 1962). These techniques are consistent with a number of devices we have described for enhancing power. They include creating a proper scene or mood. Interview the suspect when he is tired, and thus more susceptible to influence—after he has been in the holding tank without sleep. Interrogators can work in shifts so that they are fresh and rested while the prisoner is tired. Interview the suspect in an unfamiliar room, in a straight chair that does not permit relaxation or rest. A bright light focused on the suspect's face also helps. An interrogator should compliment the suspect in any way possible, be sympathetic, say that he understands why the suspect may have been involved in this situation. Of course, the interrogator dwells on anything that may make the suspect feel guilty.

Sometimes a "Mutt and Jeff" method is used. Mutt is very forceful, and may indeed use or threaten physical punishment. Jeff then replaces him, behaving in a friendly fashion, saying that something must be done about Mutt, but unfortunately he is too strong. Jeff will try to protect the suspect if the suspect will be cooperative (favor-doing). Using just the right amounts of pressure and threat is important. And the suspect should be encouraged to write out his confession, with the officer helping him with details where possible—but it is important that the suspect feel that the confession is really coming from him. He will thus be less likely to repudiate it later.

Similar interrogation processes have been used in other settings. Some of the devices for obtaining confessions from Soviet citizens in the famous purge trials of the 1930s came to light after the fall of Stalin, revealing some of the same interrogation techniques. These techniques were also used by the Chinese Communists, with civilians after the communist takeover (Lifton, 1963), and with American servicemen captured during the Korean War (Schein, 1961).

Later the same techniques, with apparent improvements and modifications, were used with Western civilians who remained in the People's Republic of China (Lifton, 1963) and with American and other United Nations military personnel captured in the Korean war (Schein, 1961). In Edgar Schein's first complete analysis of the phenomenon, he preferred the term *coercive persuasion,* to brainwashing and defined it as a systematic use of coercive power to produce independent change (Schein, 1961). The methods actually used were derived from theories of social influence that are available to us, particularly as described earlier in our sections on power enhancement and the secondary effects of social power.

More recently, the term *brainwashing* has acquired a broader colloquial usage in which it may refer to all sorts of social influence processes. There are allegations that mass-media campaigns brainwash the American public into accepting certain political candidates, or that consumers are brainwashed by advertising campaigns. After a visit to American troops in Vietnam, former Governor George Romney complained that the military had brainwashed him into supporting a lost cause. The term hints at some sort of magical quality, but "a person can no more wash another's brain with coercion or conversation than he can make him bleed with a cutting remark" (Szasz, 1976).

Patricia Hearst (1972), student. (Wide World Photos)

The Patty Hearst Case Few events in recent years have aroused as much interest and controversy as the kidnapping, "conversion," arrest, and conviction of newspaper heiress Patricia Hearst. Most of the controversy surrounds two issues: (1) Was Patty brainwashed? (2) To what extent was she responsible for her actions?

Patty's appearance and behavior before she was kidnapped in February 1974 did not seem unusual or remarkable. She dressed like other Berkeley undergraduates; she was politically inactive; she had spent several months buying china, glassware, and other necessities in preparation for her forthcoming marriage.

Shortly after she was carried screaming from her apartment, her abductors identified themselves as the Symbionese Liberation Army (SLA). Their communiques, full of militant radical rhetoric, demanded that the Hearsts distribute millions of dollars worth of food to the poor. A large amount of food was distributed. Then a taped message arrived in which Patty criticized her father for both the quantity and the quality of the food distributed. More food was distributed.

Two months after she had been kidnapped, Patty declared in a second taped message that she had joined the SLA. Calling herself Tania, she also denounced American society in general, called her parents pigs and her former fiance a sexist, and denied in advance any suggestion that she might have been brainwashed. In a photograph sent with the tape, she posed before the SLA emblem, wearing battle dress and holding a submachine gun. Patty's parents refused to believe this was their daughter speaking: "We've had her twenty years and they've had her only sixty days, and I don't believe she's going to change her philosophy that quickly."

In April a San Francisco bank was robbed by several people who identified themselves as members of the SLA. One of them proclaimed she was Tania, threatened a bank guard, and appeared prominently in the videotape made by the bank's camera, holding a carbine in her left hand. When there was some speculation that Tania's gun might not have been loaded or that she was acting under duress, another tape surfaced in which she insisted that her gun was loaded and that no one had intentionally pointed a gun at her.

Patricia Hearst (April, 1974), bank robber? (Wide World Photos)

Shortly thereafter, SLA member William Harris was caught allegedly shoplifting in Los Angeles, and Tania covered his and Emily Harris's escape with several bursts of automatic fire, emptying one carbine and then picking up another. Abandoning their van, the Harrises commandeered another, kidnapping the driver. Tania identified herself to the driver.

Later Los Angeles police surrounded the SLA hideout and laid siege to it, firing several hundred rounds with automatic weapons and lobbing in tear gas cannisters, one of which set fire to the house. Six people inside the house died in the holocaust, and until the bodies were identified, many of the people who had watched the fiery shootout on television wondered whether Tania was one of them. In another part of Los Angeles, Tania and the Harrises had also watched the episode on television.

Another tape appeared, in which Tania agonized over the loss of life, identified one of the dead—William Wolfe—as her lover, and vowed that their deaths would not be in vain. Nothing more was heard from Tania until she and the Harrises were arrested in the fall of 1975 in the San Francisco apartment where she had been living under the name of Pearl. At her booking she gave a clenched-fist salute to newsmen and listed her occupation as "urban guerrilla—self-employed." In jail her attitudes seemed to change again, and she let it be known that she now preferred to be called Patty.

During Patty's trial for the bank robbery in San Francisco, defense lawyer F. Lee Bailey argued that she had acted under threat of death (an extreme exercise of coercive power). He produced witnesses who testified that the SLA had threatened the lives of people it opposed, and evidence that some of those threats had been carried out. Patty testified that she had been in constant fear for her life and had acted as she did only because she was certain any false move would mean her death. James Browning, the prosecuting attorney, countered with notes in Patty's handwriting reviewing robbery plans, methods for making time bombs out of pop-up toasters, and basic revolutionary theory. He argued that Patty could have escaped on numerous occasions, and that her behavior such as at the time of the shoplift or at the time of her arrest were not consistent with the claim of duress.

Bailey's second line of defense was that Patty was a victim of coercive persuasion, more popularly known as brainwashing. He brought forth prominent experts in psychiatry, including Robert Lifton, author of the previously cited volume on Chinese brainwashing of civilians; Louis J. West, chairman of the UCLA Psychiatry Department; and Martin Orne, University of Pennsylvania professor of psychiatry, whom we cited in the discussion of extreme legitimate power. The defendant also testified. In many cases her testimony was corroborated by that of other witnesses and by evidence. We shall summarize their testimony here and interpret it according to theories of social power and influence,—not in defense of Patty Hearst, but to illustrate the devices for enhancing social power and the secondary effects following social influence (both of these topics were discussed earlier) and to illustrate the manner in which coercive persuasion might operate.

Emphasizing the Power Bases The SLA captors quickly emphasized to their captive that she was completely under their control (coercive power). She was manacled, blindfolded, and locked in a closet, and was dependent on them for satisfaction of her basic needs—food, water, warmth, light, companionship, even carrying out bodily functions. After some time they would open the door occasionally to let in some air, which then became an important source of reward power. The social isolation was powerful in establishing a need for social contact with and approval of her only available companions (referent power) as in the study by Gewirtz and Baer (1958a, b) cited earlier. They also emphasized their omniscience—their thorough knowledge of her background (expert power)—and began to emphasize their legitimate power as the true revolutionaries destined to overcome the fascist society oppressing the masses.

Reducing Power of Opposing Influencing Agents By completely isolating Patty from the rest of the world, the SLA managed to control all information from outside sources. They could then provide her with whatever information they wished and in whatever form. They soon convinced her that her parents did not really care whether she lived or died, since they were slow to provide the food for the poor that was demanded. Her captors also suggested that there was a government conspiracy to refrain from rescuing her, and that, to make the SLA look bad, the FBI and other law enforcement officials would probably kill her if she was captured, while making it appear that she had been murdered by the SLA.

Creating a Proper Scene or Mood To diminish any attempts at psychological resistance, Patty was placed under great physical strain. The long period in the cramped closet with little air and no light was exhausting. There was the continual blaring of martial music, the noise of clicking carbines, and being called out at odd hours of the day and night, which would tire her further and make it all the more difficult to resist influence.

Ingratiation and Favor-doing Only after some time in captivity was Patty allowed to come out occasionally and talk with her captors. It was then that they presented themselves in a more favorable light. They emphasized their selflessness, their devotion to the cause of oppressed people everywhere. As the captors extended further privileges—an opportunity to bathe with less restriction, permission to be outside the closet for longer and longer periods, the chance to participate in discussions—these were probably seen as favors extended to a prisoner of war by an army that need not grant favors or special treatment. It is not unlikely that Patty felt gratitude for the improved treatment and felt an obligation to do something for her captors in return.

Effective Use of Guilt Both Lifton (1963) and Schein (1961) discuss at some length the various ways in which guilt is used in the Chinese thought-reform programs. It

Tania (April, 1974), Symbionese Liberation Army soldier. (Wide World Photos)

appears that guilt was also used extensively by the SLA captors. Patty was forced to examine her former life as a child and heiress of a wealthy capitalist family. She had been living off the fat of the land while poor people in her own country and throughout the world were starving. What had she done with her life thus far that was meaningful and that would contribute to the welfare of others? Now was her chance to do something to atone for her sins and those of her family.

Influence by Gradations Once their power was clearly established, the SLA began to influence Patty's behaviors and attitudes, gradually making more extreme requests and demands. First, she was questioned about her family and background, and the information was used in preparing the tape scripts. The first tape in which Patty's voice was heard was rather innocuous. It used some of the information she had provided and merely asked her parents to be more cooperative in meeting ransom demands. Had she written it? Probably not, but reading it represented some degree of compliance.

She next posed for a picture in SLA uniform, submachine gun in hand, SLA color banner in the background—a picture that was later widely circulated. The second tape was more extreme and identified her clearly with the SLA. The fact that this tape was widely read outside further increased her commitment to her changed patterns of behavior. The attacks on her family, her fiance, and the society at large, of course, represented even greater compliance with the SLA position. There was then participation in SLA military drills, instruction in use of weapons, discussion of plans to rob banks. Then there was the act for which she was charged: participation in the bank robbery. Now, turning back would be difficult indeed and the events that followed only strengthened her identification with her new comrades.

New Perceptions Following Influence Following each successive act of compliance, Patty began to see things she had not seen previously. During political discussions with her SLA captors, she began to see more and more of what seemed like a logical revolutionary position. As she worked with them, she began to see some of the exhilaration that goes with having a clear purpose, a socially desirable goal. As the result of her role in the bank robbery, she began to see the police circulars describing her as possibly dangerous and to fear and even hate the sources of authority she had formerly respected.

Dissonance Reduction and New Perceptions of Self It is reasonable to suppose that each act of compliance was preceded by much conflict and followed by much dissonance. How can one justify to oneself having recorded a vitriolic attack on one's parents, family, and fiance? If the SLA followed procedures that had apparently been used by the Chinese in thought-control programs, they probably asked her to read the message several times, making certain that she read it with feeling. It would have been more dissonance-producing if she had in fact written and prepared the statement herself. (UC Berkeley psychologist Margaret Singer has stated that she believes the messages were in fact written by SLA theoreticians.) If she did not write the statement, it is at least likely that she contributed some substance and form to it. The fact that her statement and actions would be made public would further increase dissonance. Certainly, her actions had important implications for herself as well as for others. It thus appears that her successive actions must have created much dissonance and led her to change her attitudes and opinions to conform with her behaviors.

Patty Hearst (January, 1976), awaiting trial. On April 12, 1976, she was convicted of bank robbery and given a temporary sentence (thirty years) until medical evaluations could be made and studied. On September 24, the sentence was revised to seven years. (United Press International Photo)

Patty's perception of herself, following self-perception and attribution theory, would have changed to help her account for her behavior, especially as she was given more and more apparent choice over how and when to comply. Perhaps the most critical decision occurred when General Cinque told her that she could now choose either to throw her lot in with the SLA and become a full member or return to her family. Her court testimony gives some indication of the uncertainty involved in either alternative. Cinque had earlier told her that she could not leave the SLA alive, since she would jeopardize them by doing so. Yet now he suggested that she might do so without being executed—but there was some ambiguity on this point.

If Patty left, however, she feared that she might be killed by the FBI. But here also there was uncertainty. And what were her prospects of being happy with the SLA? She had by this time had a great deal of support from the group, had developed romantic attachments, and had felt like one of them—yet joining them would go against everything she had grown up with. She finally decided to remain with them, and the extreme conflict before the decision must have contributed to great dissonance afterward and a need to reexamine herself. Surely the person she had known as Patty Hearst could not really be part of the Symbionese Liberation Army; her significant change in self-perception was accompanied by the taking on of her new name, Tania.

Coercion vs. Coercive Persuasion The defense position seemed to have a degree of inconsistency to it, which one might have expected the prosecution to seize upon. If purely coercive power were involved in Patty-Tania's actions, as F. Lee Bailey claimed throughout his presentation, then her actions were never really voluntary. She had robbed the bank for fear of ultimate punishment and felt no personal commitment to it. However, the coercive-persuasion defense, to which the psychiatric expert witnesses testified most convincingly, contended that through secondary effects of influence she had indeed accepted her actions as her own at the time she was committing them. The defense seemed to be trying to have it both ways.

Apparently the jury focused on the main defense and after an unexpectedly brief deliberation found the defendant guilty. In explaining the verdict, some jurors pointed out that they could not buy the defense argument that Tania had committed the bank robbery involuntarily, solely to save her life. The evidence to the contrary seemed too strong.

Would the defense have been more effective if it had been based solely on the coercive-persuasion argument? Bailey later said he thought this would not have won an acquittal. It has never before been used as a defense in a civilian trial—though it was used to acquit some American military personnel accused of collaborating with the enemy during the Korean and Southeast Asian wars.

The next question, which will undoubtedly be discussed further in legal circles, is whether coercive persuasion should be an acceptable defense for the commission of criminal acts. We here return to our discussion of attribution of responsibility for actions. Behavior carried out under severe threat tends to be seen as externally caused; thus the actor is not seen as responsible. But coercive persuasion implies choice on the part of the actor *at the time the act is committed,* even though the actor's mental state at the time of the act is affected by external factors prior to the act.

Psychiatrist Thomas Szasz argues strongly against the acceptability of a coercive-persuasion defense. Whether or not Patty Hearst was brainwashed into committing her act, he says, is a meaningless question. "Asking it is an intellectual and moral cop-out; answering it is psychiatric prostitution; and believing the answer is self-deception" (Szasz, 1976). He goes on to argue that if we are to judge this behavior as due to coercive persuasion, can we then hold that any action that might be influenced by others is also excusable—a person who commits a robbery because he wanted to go along with his delinquent companions, a person who accepts a bribe because he has seen others he respects doing so, and so on.

That abuse of the coercive-persuasion defense is dangerous to our system of justice is all too evident. The question remains, however, whether a relatively naive person who is inveigled into committing an unacceptable act through a highly sophisticated use of social influence techniques can still be held fully responsible for his or her actions and if not, what safeguards we can erect to avoid abuse of such a legal defense.

Summary

Social influence is defined as a change in one person (the target of influence) that has its origins in another person or group (the influencing agent). Social power is the potential ability of an agent to influence a target.

Social influence and social power are outgrowths of our dependence on others. We are dependent on others for need satisfaction (effect dependence) and knowledge about the world (information dependence).

There are six primary bases of social power: information, reward, coercion (threat of punishment), expertise, reference (identification of the target with the agent), and legitimacy. Social influence through the use of informational power becomes most immediately independent of the influencing agent, since the target ties the changed behavior to the content itself (he or she knows why the change in behavior is intrinsically valuable), rather than continuing to relate it to the agent. An important method of informational influence is making the target aware of inconsistencies in his or her behaviors, values, attitudes, or beliefs. Informational influence also tends to be the most stable of the six bases of social influence.

Reward and coercive influence are initially very dependent on the influencing agent. It is particularly important that the target believe the agent can maintain surveillance and know whether or not conformity is taking place. Surveillance is easier with reward power than with coercive power, since the target wants the agent to know that he or she has complied; reward power also leads to more positive relationships between agent and target.

Expert, referent, and legitimate power also lead to change that is dependent on the agent, but surveillance by the agent is not necessary for the change to occur and continue. Both expert and referent power have negative as well as positive forms; that is, sometimes we do exactly the opposite of what is requested if we believe the agent is using superior knowledge to manipulate us in ways that are not in our best interests; sometimes we want to disidentify and adopt contrary behavior. Legitimate power takes several forms—formal legitimacy, which comes from organizational structure; legitimacy of obligation to someone who has done something for us; and the legitimate power of the helpless and powerless. Legitimate power can take ominous forms, as shown in the cases of Adolf Eichmann and William Calley.

The different bases of power may complement one another when used in combination, or they may oppose one another. For example, increased use of referent power may reduce expert power, and vice versa.

Social power may be enhanced by a number of different devices. These include emphasizing the bases of power, diminishing the effectiveness of opposing influencing agents, creating a proper scene or mood, ingratiation, favor-doing, using guilt, and influencing the target in small gradations (similar to the shaping of behavior described by learning theorists).

Often social power has secondary effects, with the result that initially dependent patterns of change become independent: (1) a target may have access to new information and new perceptions merely on the basis of his influenced behavior; (2) he may get a different view of the influencing agent; and (3) the changed behavior may be inconsistent with prior attitudes and beliefs. The last kind of secondary change has been studied extensively, under the title of "forced compliance." Change in belief or attitude following influence seems to be most likely when the amount of influence (particularly reward or threatened punishment) is about equal to the forces against the changed behavior—the situation is most likely to lead to conflict before decision. Efforts at such dissonance reduction after forced compliance are likely to be especially strong if the target feels that he or she (1) has a real choice, (2) has taken counterattitudinal action that has important practical implications, (3) is responsible for the consequences, and (4) has a personal investment in the counterattitudinal behavior.

Coercive persuasion (popularly called brainwashing is an application of the basic principles of social influence theory. Coercive persuasion is the engineering of private acceptance of change through the initial use of coercion. The process has been described in the Chinese Communist throught-control programs for Chinese and foreign civilians and in dealing with prisoners of war. However, it probably occurs in many other situations as well, though less formally. Coercive persuasion analysis was one of the defense arguments in the Hearst case. The extent to which illegal behavior can be excused on the basis of its being perpetrated as the result of coercive persuasion is a serious legal and moral issue.

Suggested Readings

Brehm, J. 1972. *Loss of freedom: A theory of psychological reactance.* Morristown, N.J.: General Learning Press.

A brief review of Brehm's theory of reactance. Examines the factors that lead persons to avoid influence that appears to undermine their perception of themselves as free agents.

Collins, B. E. ed., 1973. *Public and private conformity: Competing explanations by improvisation, cognitive dissonance, and attribution theories.* Andover, Mass.: Warner Modular Publications.

Collection of reprinted articles with commentary, which is presented as a dialogue between competing theorists and researchers regarding the bases for changes in opinion and attitude following forced compliance.

Deutscher, I. 1973. *What we say/what we do: Sentiments and acts.* Glenview, Ill.: Scott, Foresman.

Concentrates particularly on consistency and inconsistency between attitudes and behavior, summarizing classical articles from sociological and psychological literature. Applies these analyses to social problems such as drinking, cheating on examinations, racial attitudes and behavior, and immorality.

Goffman, E. 1971. *Strategic interaction.* Philadelphia: University of Pennsylvania.

Fascinating analysis of the ways in which we manipulate others, drawing from the analogy of an espionage game in which each person tries to manipulate and outguess other people. Analysis is applied to the Cuban missile crisis, male-female dating relations, bargaining, and other interesting day-to-day interpersonal strategies.

Jones, E. E., and Wortman, C. 1973. *Ingratiation: An attributional approach.* Morristown, N.J.: General Learning Press.

Analysis of the illicit devices that a person uses to curry favor and gain his own ends.

Milgram, S. 1975. *Obedience to authority,* New York: Harper.

Presents a series of studies elaborating on Milgram's well-known study of extreme obedient behavior, as described in this text.

The Dynamics of Interaction between Individual and Group

20 Russia was a devastated country in the years following the ravages of World War I, the overthrow of the czarist regime, and the October revolution that produced the soviet state. Many children were separated from their families or were orphaned because of the war or the famine that ensued. These *bezprizorniki* (pronounced bez-pree-ZOR-nee-kee, literally "uncared-fors") were left without guidance or provisions. They fended for themselves, roaming the countryside in bands like wolf packs, bringing terror to the occasional traveler or isolated farmer. In 1921 they numbered an estimated 7 million.

Soviet officials at first branded the *bezprizorniki* as hooligans, or young counter-revolutionaries, and tried to end their violence and thievery through harsh repression. When that failed, an attempt was made to gather them together into colonies and to rehabilitate them. Initially this approach was no more successful than other programs to rehabilitate delinquents that have been tried in many countries, including our own.

Anton Semyonovich Makarenko (pronounced M'-KAR-yen-koh), a young man trained to teach in secondary schools, was assigned to one of these colonies near Poltava. The dilapidated and ransacked facility there had formerly housed delinquents. His experiences in that colony are told in this sensitive and moving account, *The Road to Life* (Makarenko, 1955).

When the first *bezprizorniki* arrived, Makarenko greeted them with an idealistic speech about their new life. The newcomers paid scant attention, whispered to one another, and exchanged sardonic glances. They listened to his other proposals with courteous indifference, and then simply ignored his requests to perform chores in the colony. Makarenko and his staff worked hard, chopping wood, clearing paths, and looking after the farm, hoping to set an example (referent influence) for their charges.

The *bezprizorniki*, however, looked at their dedication with disdain. The attitude of the young men toward their teachers crystallized into habitual insolence and frank hooliganism, as they told dirty stories in front of the women teachers, threw their plates about the dining room, and made jeering comments while playing with knives. Some of the young men would sneak out of the colony at night, and neighboring villagers began to complain of being attacked and robbed. Makarenko procured a revolver for his own protection and began to despair of accomplishing anything in the colony.

Finally a breakthrough came. When a big strapping fellow named Zadorov refused to chop some wood, Makarenko, bursting with long-repressed frustration and indignation, hit him. Zadorov lost his balance and fell against a stove, and Makarenko hit him again. Then, grabbing a poker, he turned to his other charges and warned, "Either you all go this minute to work in the woods, or you leave the colony, and to hell with you."

Makarenko's violent act was contrary to his own best judgment and to his idealistic convictions. It was contrary also to the rules of the Department of Education. Yet, to the amazement of Makarenko and his colleagues, the young men went off to work and for the first time showed respect for the authorities in the colony. Why? Makarenko suggests several reasons.

Perhaps overpowering one of their own informal leaders—someone strongly opposed to the authorities of the camp—had some effect. The threat of being sent to a camp for juvenile delinquents or forced to fend for themselves in the countryside again was clearly powerful. Makarenko felt also that seeing him lose his temper and respond to frustration may have led to a degree of **identification** with him (referent influence) that his earlier words of reconciliation and understanding could not accomplish. At the same time Makarenko realized that he could not continue to rule the camp by threat and coercive power. Nor could he continue to use referent power through the identification of the young men with him. Eventually his charges must collectively influence and rehabilitate one another.

To facilitate this process, he sought ways of fostering a sense of common identity and mutual sharing. Monitors were appointed for each dormitory, and dormitories were compared for cleanliness, productivity, and other qualities. Teams were organized to go into the forests and apprehend anyone illegally chopping down trees.

When some of the colonists showed signs of drunkenness, they were asked to explain themselves before the group, including Makarenko. They admitted that they had bought *samagon* (Russian "moonshine") from nearby peasants. The colonists, after obtaining official approval, formed raiding parties who surprised the offending peasants and destroyed their stills. These acts further strengthened their group identity and their identification with legal authorities.

Later, the colonists were organized into permanent detachments, each with responsibility for a particular task such as shoe repair, plowing, or woodchopping. These detachments sometimes competed with one another to see which one could contribute the most to the welfare of the community. But to forestall restricted group identification and possible negative interpersonal effects of such competition, the colony also organized detachments for short-term tasks. The membership of a temporary detachment consisted of one representative from each of several permanent detachments.

Eventually, the sullen, antisocial, hostile collection of *bezprizorniki* was forged into a model colony, the Gorki colony (named after author Maxim Gorki), which served as the basis for many similar rehabilitation programs. In addition, the Gorki colony became recognized as a model agricultural settlement, and it developed a rich cultural component. Members of detachments presented plays in a reconstructed theater, and local villagers eagerly attended these events. Makarenko's antagonist, Zadorov, later became a successful engineer, and many other graduates also achieved success.

How widely the procedures developed by Makarenko can be implemented in other societies and situations remains to be demonstrated. However, the major theme of *The Road to Life* is the effectiveness of a group in positively influencing individual behavior, a topic we will explore in this chapter. Through cooperation, competition, and the operation of group norms, the group can have tremendous power in influencing its individual members. Under other circumstances, the group can also liberate an individual from norms or standards that normally limit his behavior—resulting sometimes in greater experience of freedom, and sometimes in acts that would ordinarily be considered immoral.

Pressures Toward Uniformity in Groups

20·1 In research and observations on behavior in groups, it is frequently observed that members of a group tend to adopt similar attitudes, beliefs, opinions, and judgments, and generally to behave similarly. This seems particularly true of groups whose members identify closely with one another, and in which the members thus exert referent power on one another. Teen-agers seem to copy the dress, speech, and mannerisms of other teen-agers. Such tendencies toward uniformity in behavior also occur in casual groups, as can be clearly demonstrated in an age-old prank. On a busy sidewalk or plaza, a few participants look up at a certain place, stare at it, and perhaps also point to it. Gradually more and more passersby stop and look up at that same place, though they have no idea what they should be seeing.

This tendency toward uniform behavior among passersby was carefully studied in New York City by Stanley Milgram, Leonard Bickman, and Leonard Berkowitz (1969). At a busy place on the sidewalk one or more (up to fifteen) confederates would, at a signal, simultaneously look up at the experimenter's window and continue to stare at that point for sixty seconds. Data were gathered from 1424 pedestrians who unwittingly served as subjects in that experiment. Milgram, Bickman, and Berkowitz found that the number of pedestrians who stopped and looked up at the window was very much a function of the number of confederates who did so. With only one confederate, 42 percent of the pedestrians who passed during that minute looked up, and 4 percent stopped walking while doing so. With fifteen confederates, 86 percent of the pedestrians looked up at the window, and 40 per-

Pressures toward uniformity are felt even in casual groups such as passersby on a city street. (Elizabeth Hamlin, Stock, Boston)

cent stopped. Clearly, the group effect on individual pedestrians increased with the size of the group.

Group Norms and Pressures Toward Uniformity in Group Judgment Muzafer Sherif has been a major exponent of the notion that groups develop unique properties beyond those contributed by their individual members. He has argued that when individuals interact with one another, particularly in situations that are unclear or ambiguous, they tend to develop mutually accepted standards of behavior, belief, attitude, dress, and the like (Sherif, 1935, 1936). These common standards, or group norms, tend to persist and to provide direction for the individual members, who then feel pressure to conform to them. In order to demonstrate this phenomenon in a laboratory setting, Sherif developed a clever experimental device.

Sherif began his study with individual judgments of movement. A lone subject was seated in a darkened room, a pinpoint of light appeared for two seconds, and the subject was asked to judge how many inches the light had moved during that time. The light then appeared again and again, for a large number of trials. The subjects differed considerably in their initial judgments; some said that the light moved an inch, some as much as fifteen inches. In fact, the light had not moved at all.

As we learned in Chapter 8, we normally perceive the movement of an object in terms of its spatial relationship to other objects. If we see a ball rapidly changing its location with respect to a background of trees, houses, and telephone poles, which maintain their relationship to one another, we perceive the ball as moving, and can estimate its degree of movement relative to the other objects. If we see a pinpoint of light in an otherwise dark room, we have no real background against which to judge it. If asked how far it moves in a given period of time, we may guess wildly, since even a stationary light appears to move. This apparent movement has been called the autokinetic (self-movement) effect. In Sherif's study, it was, of course, heightened by the experimenter-created expectancy: By asking the subjects to estimate *how much* the light moved, the experimenter was implying that it *did* move.

Sherif observed that a subject would typically give widely varying estimates of movement on successive trials—seventeen inches, three inches, five inches, twelve inches—but that as the trials went on, there was a gradual stabilization of estimates. By the 100th trial, a subject might settle on an estimate of about eight inches, and concentrate most judgments around that distance. Sherif suggested that in the absence of other physical objects to use as a reference, the subject's previous estimates served as a background or frame of reference, against which to make new judgments. Thus, we might say an individual norm developed as a guide for future behavior.

Now, suppose two or three subjects who had made a hundred judgments on their own were placed in a room together. Each would have stabilized his or her estimates around a different individual norm (say, two inches, five inches, and eight inches) and would initially give a similar estimate in a group situation. However, these estimates would soon tend to converge. Usually the more extreme estimates would move toward a central, but not necessarily average, point. After a number of group judgments, a group norm would be established (say, six inches) and thereafter all members of the group would give estimates close to that figure.

In a later study, new groups were composed of members who had no prior experience judging the light. In this condition convergence toward the norm was noticeably more rapid. Without previous individual norms to guide their judgments, subjects more rapidly converged toward the group norm, whereas subjects who had had individual trials initially experienced conflicting pressures between their individual norms and the group norms.

Can you now predict what would happen if you took one subject from each of three groups that had previously judged the autokinetic phenomenon and placed them in a new group? Sherif conducted such an experiment, and found that the members of the new group eventually converged toward a norm, but the rate of convergence was much slower than in naive groups. The three group members were now experiencing group-norm conflict—the pressures from their previous group norms working in opposition to the developing norm of their new group.

This simple experimental situation exemplifies many of the group-norm pressures commonly experienced in real life. If we observe children in a new nursery school or kindergarten class playing on the playground, we can see many differences in the sorts of games they play and in their manner of interaction. Gradually, however, they develop common norms for their behavior, and carry these over to new classes. In military training camps, the young men reporting for basic training often come from varying geographical regions, from urban and rural areas, and from different social class backgrounds. Initially, they may experience conflicting

In any group (such as one composed of children who live in the same neighborhood or who go to the same school) a group norm gradually develops and shapes the behavior of the group members. (Mitchell Payne, Jeroboam)

pressures from differing group norms involving speech, mannerisms, vocabulary, food preferences, treatment of property, and so on. Eventually, group norms develop that may cause problems for the young men when they return to civilian life.

In short, as Sherif points out, when a group of individuals is brought together into a new situation, there may be initial disagreements, but gradually a group norm develops that provides a guide for the group members. Furthermore, there are pressures on the individual members to adhere to the group norm. We shall now address ourselves to these pressures.

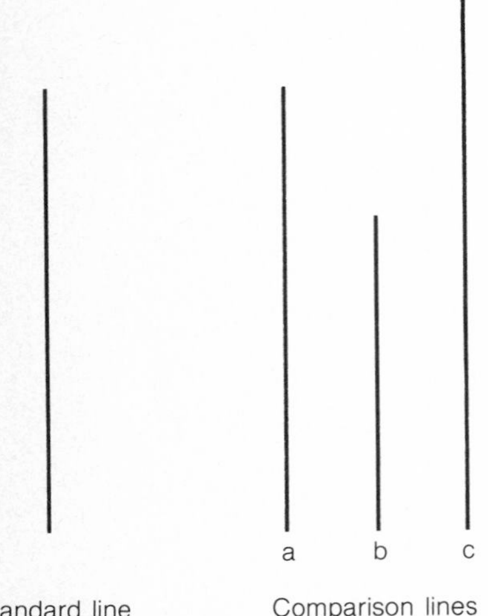

Fig. 20•1 Example showing lines in the same proportions as those used in Asch's study of group effects on judgments.

Group Pressures on Individual Members In Sherif's studies, the subjects in the group experiment were presented with a situation that was ambiguous for each of the members, and in which the members were about equally committed to a given judgment. To understand the degree of group pressures on a member who deviates from a norm, it would be useful to examine a less ambiguous situation, one in which the majority makes a judgment clearly counter to that of a lone deviant. This was the situation examined experimentally by Solomon Asch and a number of other investigators who followed his lead (Asch, 1956).

Try to imagine yourself in the situation of one of Asch's subjects. You arrive at the experiment and are seated next to the last of the twenty subjects, all in a row. This is to be a study of line judgment. The experimenter presents each member of the group with a card on which are a standard line and three comparison lines labeled "a," "b," and "c." The experimenter then asks which of the three comparison lines is closest in length to the standard. Responding in numerical order, each subject chooses "a." A different card is presented, and each subject chooses "b," which does indeed appear to you to be the same length as the standard. After several such uneventful trials, a card with lines in the same proportions as those shown in Figure 20•1 is presented. The first eighteen subjects choose "c." It is now your turn. How would you respond?

Simulating a Microculture

In Sherif's original experiment (Sherif, 1935) on group judgment of the movement of a pinpoint of light, the subjects were naive and inexperienced at this sort of task, and there was a general tendency for the initially variable judgments to converge toward a central estimate. On occasion, one subject would adopt a relatively extreme judgment and the others would converge toward it. A confederate instructed to hold his ground stubbornly could similarly influence the others so that their judgment moved toward his.

In a later experiment, Robert Jacobs and Donald T. Campbell (1961) wished to see how long the influence of such an assertive "subject" could continue in successive generations of groups. They assembled three subjects, one of whom was a confederate who was to hold to a judgment of around 15 inches. Jacobs and Campbell found that, over a series of thirty trials, the group settled on a norm much closer to 15 inches than would ordinarily be the case. (They had previously found that movement estimates by naive subjects generally converge toward a group norm around 3.5 inches.)

The confederate was then replaced by a naive subject and the process continued for another thirty trials. The normative judgment came down only a little. On each of the next two series of thirty trials, one of the original naive members of the group was replaced by a new member, finally leaving an entirely new group generation. But the effect of the confederate still showed. Even in the fifth group generation the group judgments continued to be significantly higher than those in groups that had not had any contact (direct or indirect) with an extremist member. Only after the confederate's group had been completely replaced six times were the effects of the confederate dissipated.

How long ago was the first West Point graduation at which a newly graduated cadet threw his hat into the air? However long ago it was, all such cadets now revel in the tradition. (U.S. Army Photograph)

The findings from this study were qualified somewhat by Weick and Gilfillan (1971). Their groups, rather than attempting to judge movement of an ambiguous stimulus, were given a task to solve that could be handled either by an easier strategy or by a more difficult strategy. The experimenters had planted a confederate in each group who argued vigorously for a predetermined strategy—either the easier one or the more difficult one. In these newly created groups the confederate was generally successful in persuading the others to accept the strategy he proposed. However, the permanence of his influence depended on which strategy he proposed. The effects of a domineering confederate who influenced the group toward the more difficult strategy were dissipated over a few group generations; an influence toward an easier strategy tended to continue indefinitely.

Have you ever joined a new club or moved into a new neighborhood where the people had some behavior or ritual whose purpose you could not understand? Perhaps it was a peculiar greeting, a method of running a meeting, or a norm about when to hang out laundry. That different form of behavior was probably initiated by some influential person or group, perhaps long before. You and your friends may have modes of behavior that you take for granted, but that might seem unusual to a new person coming into your group. It has been pointed out that the personnel of the U.S. Navy are completely replaced every thirty years, but some patterns of behavior that may have been established during the Revolutionary War still persist.

Occasionally some historian locates the origin of a peculiar form of behavior, but the traditional norm is followed even when no one is aware of its origin. For example, in our society, different groups or organizations customarily refer to a toilet by different terms: army—*latrine,* navy—*head,* circus—*donnicker,* prison—*bucket,* or *tin throne,* hospitals and business establishments—*lavatory,* and in other groups or settings a variety of other terms are used—*john, crapper, altar, washroom, rest room, water closet,* and so on. It is reasonable to believe that at some time a particularly influential member of one of these groups or organizations first used his favorite word for toilet and that that usage long outlived its originator.

Of course, the subjects who gave such flagrantly incorrect answers in Asch's experiment were all confederates following a prearranged script. The nineteenth subject was the only naive subject in the group. Asch had expected that in contrast to the Sherif autokinetic study, very few subjects would be affected even by a unanimously incorrect response from nineteen subjects. Asch used cards in which the comparison lines varied noticeably in length—as would lines that measured 5 inches, 4 inches, and 6¼ inches, for example—and the standard line was always the same length as one of the comparison lines. Given an unambiguous judgmental task, everyone *should* respond correctly.

Asch had pretested his cards and found that when naive subjects were given the task on their own, very few made any errors in judgment. Yet, to his astonishment, one-third of the naive subjects in this experiment made a patently erroneous response at least 50 percent of the time when they had first heard a unanimous majority make that response. Only 25 percent of his subjects remained completely unaffected by the unanimous group error.

Did it take a unanimous majority as large as nineteen to get the effect? In tests with groups of various sizes, Asch found some slight group effect even with one other member and a bit more with two. But the majority effect was at its maximum when the erroneous majority had just three members and did not increase in groups of four to twenty members.

Following each experimental session, Asch carefully interviewed the subjects. Some of the subjects who refused to go along with the erroneous majority were confident in their judgment, and incredulous at the mistaken majority. Other subjects who maintained their independence later admitted that they were far from confident of the validity of their perceptions. Why did the yielders allow themselves to be so grossly influenced?

Their explanations varied, and are in some ways consistent with our analysis of social power in Chapter 19. On the trials in which they gave the same response as the erroneous majority, a few naive subjects said that they actually saw the lines the way they reported them—for example, that the 6¼-inch line looked as long as the 5-inch line. Such a response would indicate informational influence.

The largest number of the yielders reported various forms of socially dependent influence that do not require surveillance: *expert* ("I think a majority is usually right" or "There's a greater probability of eight being right than one"); *legitimate* ("After all, the majority rules"); *referent* ("You always like to go along with the group and be like everyone else" or "I felt the need to conform. . . . It was more pleasant to agree than to disagree").

A somewhat smaller number showed the forms of socially dependent influence that require surveillance, apparently fearing that they might be ridiculed or rejected by others *(coercion)* or hoping that they would be treated more favorably if they went along with the group *(reward)*. That coercion and reward were indeed involved was demonstrated later in several experiments, including a more carefully controlled study by Deutsch and Gerard (1955). In that study it was found that the degree of **conformity** to the majority declined significantly (but far from completely) when subjects were seated in booths and the identity of the individual respondents was kept secret.

The lone subjects who were concerned about the responses of the others to their deviant responses may have had good reason for their concern. Asch, in a follow-up study, reversed his initial experimental procedure. Instead of having a confederate majority and a lone naive subject, he now had a naive majority of sixteen and one lone confederate. The confederate (No. 15) gave the same erroneous responses the confederate majority had given in the initial experiment. The responses of the subjects were vividly described by Asch:

> At the outset they greeted the estimates of the dissenter with incredulity. On the later trials there were smiles and impromptu comments. As the experiment progressed, contagious and, in some instances, uncontrolled laughter swept the group. At one point, as the group reported their correct estimates, the sudden impact of the single wrong response appeared so droll that the experimenter, who had created the situation, was seized with an irrepressible tendency to join in the laughter. (Asch, 1952, pp. 479–80)

Conformity to the group norm may be due to fear of punishment or to hope for reward. In this parade review (as in many situations where the group has a common goal or purpose) being out of step would also be disturbing to both the individual and the group. (U.S. Army Photograph)

Pressures Toward Uniformity and Social Comparison Thus far, we have seen that an individual often feels pressed to conform to a group norm. Such conformity may be due to the fear of punishment or hope for rewards from the group. But often it appears that the lack of uniformity in a group is disturbing, not only to the lone deviant member but to the group as a whole. Why, then, do we experience pressures toward uniformity?

Leon Festinger examined this question in several important theoretical papers (Festinger, 1950; Festinger, 1954). Obviously, he says, pressure toward uniformity may arise when such uniformity is necessary for the attainment of a common goal. A work group must have some agreement about how a job should be done if it is to work as a coordinated unit; an athletic team must have some uniformity of opinion about strategy.

Less obvious, however, is our need to feel that we are correct in our opinions, beliefs, attitudes, behaviors, and even emotions. In Sherif's study of pressures toward uniformity in the autokinetic effect, this need was illustrated with particular clarity. We are continually evaluating ourselves, sometimes without explicit awareness, attempting to determine whether we are thinking and behaving appropriately.

If we have some physical basis for checking ourselves out, we are less likely to look to others. If Sherif had conducted his experiment in broad daylight, with the subjects asked to estimate the movement of the flashlight in a room with all sorts of physical frames of reference (the wall, the chairs, table, and so on), it is unlikely that subjects would have been as concerned about the estimates of their fellow subjects—unless they unanimously made an estimate that was different from the subject's (as in the Asch experiment). The pressure toward uniformity that Sherif's subjects felt resulted from their dependence on this social basis for reality. Sometimes people have other means for evaluating the correctness of their behavior, opinion, belief, or emotion. We may sometimes turn toward our own previous experience or knowledge (as Sherif's subjects, who had already made the autokinetic judgments on their own for 100 trials, did. We may sometimes turn toward tradition: "How have people handled things like this in the past?" But when these bases for self-evaluation are not available to us, we are especially likely to turn toward other people who are present and faced with a similar situation.

Responses to Pressures Toward Uniformity What happens, then, when we find ourselves with a group of people who appear to differ from us in their opinions, beliefs, emotions, or behaviors? Festinger said that when we are faced with such a situation, we initially experience some uneasiness or tension (he later used the term **cognitive dissonance,** a concept we have already discussed at several points in this text). Suppose, for example, we tend to favor John C. Throckmorton for president and we are in a group that considers Throckmorton completely unacceptable. There are several ways we can reduce our tension.

1. Change our opinion. ("Maybe Throckmorton is not such a good candidate after all.")
2. Influence or persuade the others. ("Throckmorton is the person you should support.")
3. Reject the others as bases for comparison. ("These people don't know about politics," or "They are blinded by their own selfish needs.")
4. Distort our perception of the situation. ("I don't think they are as opposed to Throckmorton as their words imply—in fact, they may be putting me on, and I think they really like Throckmorton.")
5. Minimize or reduce the importance or relevance of the problem. ("I don't really care about our disagreement about Throckmorton—it is not that important anyway," or "This is a social group, not a political group, and so our disagreement is not important to our relationship.")

What determines which of these methods we will use when we experience pressure toward uniformity? A considerable amount of research has been directed toward this question. We will state a few general findings here.

Personality and General Self-confidence Persons low in self-esteem, intelligence, and self-confidence are especially likely to change their opinions when they differ from others. Those with higher self-confidence and self-esteem are more likely either to try to influence others or to reject them.

Also likely to change their own opinions are persons with authoritarian and rigid personalities or who have difficulty accepting ambiguity (Costanzo, 1970; Crutchfield, 1955; Hovland, Janis, and Kelley, 1953; Janis, 1954; Hovland and Janis, 1959). An authoritarian personality tends to be submissive to those in authority, though domineering toward subordinates. A rigid personality tends to hold on to beliefs, attitudes, and behaviors despite new experiences that argue for change. Authoritarianism and rigidity go hand in hand with an unwillingness to accept ambiguity, to want to see things as clear cut, black or white, true or false (Adorno,

Using Others to Evaluate Our Emotions

Perhaps we can readily think of instances in which we have compared ourselves to others in order to evaluate the appropriateness of our opinions, attitudes, or performance. It is less obvious that we also use similar others to evaluate our emotions. Children who are waiting to be vaccinated may talk to one another and look at one another to see whether they are appropriately frightened by the prospect. Students seem especially likely to talk to one another and compare themselves to one another before they take critical examinations. They may want to determine whether they are properly prepared or whether they studied the right topics, but there is some reason to suspect that they also want to see whether they themselves are appropriately fearful.

Stanley Schachter carried out an experiment to test whether fear does indeed serve as a basis for affiliation, and whether social comparison would lead to such affiliation. Subjects in the experiment, female Minnesota undergraduates, were greeted by a so-called Dr. Gregor Zilstein of the University of Minnesota Medical School's Department of Neurology and Psychiatry, who told them that they would be taking part in a study of the effects of electric shocks. To subjects in the high-anxiety condition, he said: "I must be completely honest with you. . . . These shocks will hurt; they will be painful . . . but, of course, they will do no permanent damage. . . ." The appearance of the apparatus in the room was indeed frightening to anyone in the high-anxiety condition. Subjects in the low-anxiety condition were told, "Do not let the word *shock* trouble you. I assure you that what you feel will not be painful in any way. It will resemble a tickle or a tingle rather than something unpleasant."

While the equipment was presumably being prepared for the experiment, subjects were asked to wait in an adjoining room. They were, however, given a choice: They could wait in a room alone with some reading material to occupy them; or they could wait in a room with other subjects who were also waiting for the experiment. (Since it was this choice that Schachter was interested in, the experiment ended at this point, after the choice was made and before the waiting period actually began. No shocks were administered.)

As Schachter predicted, the subjects in the high-anxiety condition preferred to wait with others (63 percent made that choice). Those in the low-anxiety condition were less likely to want to wait with others (33 percent). Why? There could be a number of explanations: perhaps waiting with others could help to pass the time and thus take one's mind off the fearful events to come; or perhaps they could jointly plan a way to escape from the situation; or perhaps someone could tell the others more about the experiment.

Schachter did not reject the possibility that these factors might operate to some extent under some conditions. However, through a series of experimental variations, he systematically eliminated them as necessary factors in this experiment. Eliminating the possibility of talking or planning, for example, did not eliminate the tendency to affiliate with others when in the high-anxiety condition. Also, subjects in the high-anxiety condition were not as desirous of waiting with others if these others were waiting to see a professor about an examination. They preferred to wait with others who were expecting a similar fate.

These results confirmed Schachter's original hypothesis. When threatened and frightened, people affiliate with others in order to compare themselves to the others and to find out whether their emotional reaction to the situation is appropriate. In such conditions, then, it is not simply that "misery loves company," but that "misery loves similarly miserable company." Schachter's basic findings have been replicated in several later studies, which involved not only fear of shock, but also intense noise, hunger, and altered glucose level of blood (Schachter, 1959; Zimbardo and Formica, 1963; MacDonald, 1970; Wrightsman, 1960).

Does the presence of others reduce anxiety? Not necessarily. In studies that followed the Schachter experimental paradigm, subjects actually waited together in anticipation of a painful experience. Measures of anxiety levels before and after the waiting period indicated that there was a convergence toward a group norm—reminiscent of Sherif's findings on the autokinetic effect. Some subjects increased their anxiety level, some reduced it, but the final state indicated greater similarity in anxiety level among the group members (Wrightsman, 1960; Schachter,1959).

Frenkel-Brunswik, et al., 1950). Apparently, when the authoritarian, rigid, ambiguity-fearing person encounters a majority opinion with which he or she differs, there is a tendency to conform to the authority of the group and to accept the group opinion, thus reducing the ambiguity that results from disagreement with the group. What seemed like a rigid opinion then becomes quite brittle.

Cultural Factors It has been suggested that cultures differ in their emphasis on conformity and uniformity. David Riesman (1950) presented evidence that some cultures are particularly conformist, not tolerant of differences. In such societies individual members are other-directed and use others as a basis for evaluating themselves. In some other societies individuals are inner-directed, and not as concerned with what others think or do. They look within themselves for the logical basis of their thoughts and actions. In still others individuals are tradition-directed. They are less concerned with what others do now, looking instead to the way things have been done in the past.

A study by Stanley Milgram, using a procedure similar to Asch's, found that Norwegians (whose society is generally homogeneous) are likely to conform when they find themselves differing from a unanimous majority, while the French (whose society is more varied and heterogeneous) are likely to reject the erroneous majority (Milgram, 1961). Another study found that the collective ideological orientation in the Soviet Union leads children to conform to peer pressure, while such conformity is much less likely among children in Israel. The same study found that in Israel children in the cooperative rural communities (kibbutzim), where group identity is stressed, were more conformist than those in individual family settings (Shouval et al., 1975).

Amount of Disagreement and Unanimity in Group If the disagreement is small, it can more easily be overlooked and dismissed as irrelevant or unimportant. A small disagreement also makes it easier to change one's opinion. If the disagreement is larger, and if there is a sizable majority, the pressure on the deviant to change is especially great. (In the Asch experiment, a majority of three or larger resulted in great pressure on the lone deviant to change, even though the judgment task was unambiguous.) A deviant faced with a large and unanimous majority, moreover, does not feel able to persuade the majority to change. He may, however, reject the entire group as a basis for comparison, as quite a few of Asch's subjects did. In one version of the Asch experiment it was found that even in a large group if just one other person (a confederate) agrees with the naive deviant, then the number of subjects who agree with the majority goes down dramatically.

Ambiguity of Object of Disagreement People are more likely to change their opinions if the object of disagreement is unclear or ambiguous, as a complicated issue or a physical stimulus might be. An ambiguous object of disagreement also increases the possibility of distorting the amount of disagreement. When the point of disagreement is less ambiguous and when there are external bases of support (an opinion about which there is a lot of clear evidence, or the judgment of lengths of lines that are sharp and clear), there is less change and a greater likelihood of either influencing or rejecting others.

Relevance of Disagreement to Group Functioning We are less likely to reject a group majority opinion or to minimize its importance if the point of disagreement is clearly relevant to the group functioning and group goals. Thus, as members of a political club, we can easily ignore or reject as unimportant a disagreement about the relative merits of one automobile over another, but not a disagreement about the relative merits of one candidate over another.

Attractiveness to Others and Identification with Them When we feel some affiliation with others, we are less likely to reject them, and more likely either to attempt to influence them, to change our opinion toward them, or to minimize the discrepancy (Collins and Raven, 1969; Back, 1951).

Social Comparison and Abilities Festinger expanded his theory of social comparison processes to the analysis of abilities. Just as we want to feel that our beliefs, attitudes, judgments, and emotions are correct, we also want to feel that we have a proper evaluation of our abilities. Are we performing adequately, in terms of the resources available to us? Did we really do as well on an examination as we should? Is our tennis game what it should be? If we have some independent means of gauging our abilities, or if we have had enough experience that we feel confident we know where we stand, then we are relatively unconcerned about how others do.

But often we do not know how to evaluate our abilities, or something happens to shake us up. We may receive an unusually poor grade, or do unusually well in a game against a quite good opponent, or apply for a fellowship that is crucial to our career plans. In such circumstances, we are especially likely to look to others in order to evaluate ourselves. When the grades for the first exam in a course are posted, we probably look first at our own grade and then at the grades of others—but not just any others. We look at the grades of the classmates we consider roughly similar to us academically, those to whom we can compare ourselves. A golfer who wants to know how well he is doing would not learn much from comparing himself with someone either much more capable or much less capable than he.

Festinger points out that we normally compare our abilities (in contrast to opinions) to those of someone just a bit better than we are. When we find such a person, the possible responses are similar to those we can use when we encounter a difference in opinion. If we are concerned about the discrepancy, we can change by trying to improve our performance. We can try to influence the person to change—as by disrupting the person's performance (for example, coughing just as our golfing opponent is preparing to make a difficult putt) (Festinger, 1954; Wheeler, Shaver, et al., 1969). We can reject the person as really quite different and not an appropriate person for comparison. We can distort our perception of the difference or minimize the importance of the difference.

Can a Minority Influence a Majority?

Most research on conformity has focused on the influence of the group on the deviant member, particularly the pressures on the deviant to change toward the group norm. Ordinarily, it is assumed, a minority member has much greater difficulty influencing the majority, unless he is in a position of leadership or has considerable reward, coercive, expert, or legitimate power. Nevertheless, one series of studies (Sherif, 1936; Jacobs and Campbell, 1961) has shown that an assertive, lone, minority person *can* have an impact on the majority—particularly in an ambiguous situation. Two persistent minority members should have an even greater impact.

A French social research team conducted a series of studies on the effects of a two-person minority on a group color-judgment task. Groups of six female subjects with normal vision were presented with a series of thirty-six color slides and asked to identify aloud the color of each slide. In pretests the slides had been found to fall clearly within the blue range of the color spectrum. The two confederates in the group, following prior instructions, consistently announced firmly that the slides were green. The influence of the minority was clear: 32 percent of the naive subjects were influenced to report that at least four of the slides were green.

The degree to which four subjects could be swayed by two persistent deviants in a relatively unambiguous judgment was surprising. Even more surprising was the effect on the independents who refused to be swayed by the erroneous but apparently confident minority. Did their stalwart behavior stem from a self-confident, critical attitude? Further research indicates that it did not.

These supposedly independent subjects took part in a separate study later, conducted by a different experimenter, in which they sat in separate booths and were asked to name the colors of a series of sixteen disks (rather than slides). The disks were in the blue-green range of the color spectrum. The independent subjects, despite their earlier resistance to consistent pressure to rate blue slides as green, were now more likely to rate the blue-green disks as more greenish on the color spectrum. Apparently the minority pressure had succeeded in changing their views of the color spectrum. What had appeared to be independence and refusal to bow to the persistent minority now seemed to be a form of dependence—a concern about looking bad before fellow members of their own majority when making a public judgment. Once they were given an opportunity to make a private judgment, the real effects of the persistent minority became more evident (Faucheux and Moscovici, 1967; Moscovici, Lage, and Naffrechoux, 1969).

Have you ever been to a meeting of a political club at which a dynamic speaker attempted to persuade the members that their majority position was incorrect? Ordinarily, such a speaker appears to be unsuccessful. Members of the club attack his position and few concede that his position has any real merit—at least during the meeting. But what happens after the meeting? A sleeper effect may occur that results in some changed but undisclosed opinions.

Pressures on the Majority to Maintain Uniformity: Responses to Deviance
Our discussion has indicated that a group member who finds himself or herself different from other members of the group experiences discomfort and feels pressure to restore uniformity. The majority members of the group also feel such pressure. For example, a group of employees may feel pressure from a worker who works more rapidly than the rest; a small community may feel pressure from a member whose sexual practices are contrary to those generally believed correct; a social group may feel pressure from a person whose religion differs markedly from that of others in the group. When the majority perceive the deviance as threatening to

their beliefs about what is correct or proper, they respond in ways that parallel the responses used by a deviant individual.

Majority Change Toward Deviant On occasion the majority may be swayed by a firm and convincing minority member—especially if the person is in a position of leadership or is highly respected for other reasons. A popular leader who retires to a small community may differ from his neighbors in many ways, but if he is held up as an ideal, others may be affected by him, rather than the reverse.

Change in the majority toward the deviant is ordinarily unlikely, however. Part of the reason for this is that change in one group member toward the deviant's position would decrease (not increase) uniformity. The member who conforms to the deviant will experience pressures from the group.

Influencing the Deviant The group ordinarily attempts to influence the deviant to change his behavior, belief, or attitude toward the group norm. We can all recall instances in which a deviant member (the lone Democrat in a group of Republicans; the lone pro-abortionist in a group of anti-abortionists) was subjected to a barrage of persuasive arguments from the other group members.

Rejection of Deviant If influencing the deviant proves to be difficult, the group rejects the deviant as a basis for social comparison. By designating the deviant member as a queer, a freak, a jock, or by some other pejorative term, they need no longer concern themselves so much with the fact that the person is different from them.

Often such rejection of the deviant as a basis for social comparison is accompanied by personal rejection and by punishment. One of the harshest punishments meted out by British workers to a deviant worker is called "sending them to Coventry": complete social isolation of the deviant worker and the family except for contacts that are absolutely necessary for the job. The effects on the deviant can be devastating. Similar punishments have been meted out by Mennonites and members of other religious sects to members of the community who deviate from traditional religious practices.

Distortion of Perception and Minimization of Relevance These may occur when the object of disagreement is ambiguous or when the matter is of marginal importance to the group.

Factors That Determine Which Devices Are Used by Groups These factors parallel those used by the individual deviant to restore uniformity. Personality and cultural factors play important roles. There is some indication that people who live in cities—where there is generally more heterogeneity—are more likely to dismiss deviance as irrelevant or unimportant. Thus a homosexual is more likely to be accepted in a large urban setting than in a small village (Milgram, 1970). The greater the unanimity and uniformity within the group, the greater the group pressure on the individual to conform. Obviously the more relevant the topic of disagreement to the group, the greater the pressure of the group to restore uniformity. And the greater the cohesiveness of the group, the greater the pressure toward uniformity.

An Experimental Study of Deviation and Rejection in Groups In an early test of Festinger's theory, Stanley Schachter (1951) set up a series of boys' clubs, with eight to ten members in each. On the basis of their initial preference, some of the boys were assigned to a club that was involved in activities they liked, while some were told that their first choice was not available. This device allowed Schachter to vary the cohesiveness of the clubs.

At the first club meeting, the members were asked to discuss a juvenile delinquency case and say how they thought the delinquent should be treated. Sometimes the case was presented as highly relevant to the total activities of the club; sometimes it was presented as a one-time occurrence that was not relevant to the club's overall activities. Within each club, there were three confederates, each of whom behaved according to a prearranged plan. A *deviant* took a position strongly opposed to the majority and maintained it throughout. A *mode* took the opinion held by the majority and stuck with it. A *slider* initially took a deviant position and then gradually moved toward the majority opinion.

In keeping with his hypotheses, Schachter found that the club members were especially likely to reject the deviant member personally and assign him to unpopular jobs. The slider and the mode were generally preferred and were assigned to more prestigious positions. As predicted, this tendency to reject the deviant and to accept the mode and the slider was especially strong in clubs that were highly cohesive and when the topic of disagreement was relevant to the club's functioning. It was much less true in clubs that were not cohesive and when the topic of disagreement was not as relevant.

The communications of the club members were monitored and Schachter found parallel data here. Initially, the club members communicated more to the deviant and to the slider (who was initially deviant). These communications were indicative of attempts at persuasion. Such initial communications to the deviant were especially likely in the high-cohesive relevant clubs. But as the discussion proceeded, these clubs were especially likely to cease communication to the deviant—a change that paralleled their members' personal rejection of the deviant. The tendency to communicate intensively to the deviant at the beginning and to greatly diminish communications later was less evident in the low-cohesive irrelevant clubs.

Perhaps similar findings apply to a family whose son or daughter comes home from college with different attitudes or behaviors. Often such deviance from the family norm is met by aggressive attempts to convince the wayward member that his or her attitudes or behaviors are wrong. When this proves ineffective, the family may stop communicating on this issue, or may personally reject the deviant. According to the theory of social comparison proposed by Festinger and Schachter, such a two-step reaction to the deviant would be more likely in a family that is very cohesive than in one that is not.

Group Decisions and Social Change

20·2 The pressures toward uniformity that characterize groups can often serve as a source of resistance to change and progress. Innovation by a member, suggestions for improved operations, and plans for elimination of practices that may have served a useful purpose at one time but are no longer appropriate tend to be resisted by a group. However, Kurt Lewin believed that the group norms that may normally cause resistance to change can sometimes be harnessed to facilitate change. (Though this point was not explicitly developed in Makarenko's *The Road to Life*, it is clear that his approach to the *bezprizorniki* involved replacing older norms through the development of new group norms—and that group decisions made on the basis of discussion were very much a part of his procedures.)

Using Group Norms for Social Change During World War II, there was a scarcity of many kinds of meat, but supplies of organ meats (for example, sweetbreads, kidneys, lungs, and brain) were plentiful. Organ meats, which are prepared as delicacies in some countries, were generally unacceptable to Americans. How could this be changed?

An obvious method would be an information campaign, using various media to appeal to patriotism and to point out that organ meats are nutritious and can be prepared in a way that makes them tasty. Such campaigns were attempted by some U.S. governmental agencies, but without much success. Lewin suggested that group norms might mitigate against the change. Families, as groups, would frown on the eating of organ meats. In addition, a housewife who used them might have to contend with the disapproval not only of her family, but also of her friends and neighbors. The answer, then, would be to change the group norm.

Lewin and his co-workers conducted a series of studies with housewives who were members of Red Cross units. He arranged for two different experimental conditions at meetings of these groups. In some groups a speaker gave what appeared to be a convincing lecture on the value of using organ meats. In other groups, a discussion leader made the same information available, but encouraged the women to examine the evidence collectively, discuss it, and arrive at a group decision. Lewin was confident that when the evidence was presented in the latter way and properly discussed, the group would decide to use more organ meats.

This turned out to be a correct assumption. When the meat choices of the housewives were compared later, it seemed clear that the group discussion and decision had been especially effective in increasing the use of organ meats: 32 percent of the housewives in the discussion group condition had used these meats, while only 3 percent of the women in the lecture condition had done so. Later studies showed that group decision could also persuade homemakers to serve more milk, orange juice, and cod liver oil and persuade college students to eat more whole-wheat bread (Lewin, 1943, 1952). A follow-up experiment indicated that it was the group decision rather than the discussion that had been particularly effective in implementing the change in the group (Bennett, 1955).

Group Participation and Decisions in Industry These experiments by Lewin and his followers suggested wider possibilities for social change (Lewin, 1947). That group norms greatly affected the level of production in industrial settings had already been observed. A classic study at the Hawthorne Works of the Western Electric Company (Roethlisberger and Dickson, 1939) showed that simply separating a group of workers from the rest of the factory could lead to the development of group morale and new norms of productivity. It was also observed that workers who deviated from the group norms—producing at either a much higher or a much lower rate—would be subject to pressures from their fellow workers toward conformity.

Lester Coch and John R. P. French, Jr., repeated the essentials of Lewin's experiments in a pajama factory. They observed that when the work routine was changed somewhat, productivity declined substantially. This was, of course, expected, but since the new method was not intrinsically more difficult, the workers might be expected to increase their level of production once the new method was learned. This, however, was not the case. Furthermore, it was observed that when a worker attempted to increase production toward the earlier level, other group members exerted pressures (such as derogatory remarks and other indications of disapproval) to bring the worker into line.

Following Lewin's strategy, Coch and French then presented workers with evidence from industrial engineers that a higher level of production was possible. Some workers' groups were given the data by management and the appropriate rate of production was announced. Other groups, having been presented with the data, were encouraged to discuss them and to arrive jointly at an appropriate production rate. Coch and French found that in the latter case the new production norm that was established through participation and decision by the workers was in fact accepted by the workers, and productivity level soon exceeded the earlier level. The group with no worker participation in setting the norm apparently did not accept the suggested norm, and never recovered their earlier rate of production (Coch and French, 1948).

The applicability of these findings does have some limitations, however. Apparently, the effects of group norms in increasing levels of productivity depend on the workers accepting the legitimacy of such group participation. Where workers consider norms handed down from management appropriate and work group decisions inappropriate, the Coch and French findings do not apply (French, Israel, and Ås, 1960). Furthermore, workers may suspect management of using the group process to manipulate workers for its own purposes. In such cases, also, group participation in setting norms fails to increase productivity. Only when management truly accepts the idea of worker participation—even to the point of accepting the workers' right to make decisions counter to management's initial position—will the Coch and French effect occur (Katz and Kahn, 1966).

Pressures on Members to Exceed the Group Norm

20•3 Having examined a number of situations in which there are pressures on group members toward uniformity, we must now consider the not infrequent case in which members feel pressed to exceed the norm. One obvious example of such pressures is the classroom in which grading is done on a curve with a fixed percentage receiving A's, B's, and so on. Another example occurs in industry or in sales groups, when prizes or bonuses are offered to those who produce or sell the most.

Pressures from Cooperation and Competition Cooperation in a group and the members' acceptance of common goals may increase the level of activity and the quality of the group product. It has been observed that when there is real acceptance of the group and its goals, members may be more motivated by the potential gains for their group as a whole than by their own gains as individuals (Zander and Wolfe, 1964; Zander, 1971). Members then share their knowledge and help each other, thus increasing each other's effectiveness.

There is also evidence that competition may raise the level of activity in a group as each person attempts to exceed the others. However, under certain circumstances the competition among group members may have negative effects on morale and cohesiveness. Furthermore, when the work of the group can benefit from coordination and sharing of activity, the competition among members may actually reduce productivity (Deutsch, 1949; Raven and Eachus, 1963; Thomas, 1957; Collins and Raven, 1969). This occurs because members are unwilling to share information or otherwise assist their fellow members, since helping a fellow member only decreases one's own chances of winning the reward.

Makarenko (1955) was able to use an interesting combination of cooperation and competition in order to increase the activity of the work teams in the Gorki colony. Individuals within work teams were encouraged to compete with one another in contributing to the productivity of their work team. The competition was in terms of greatest contribution to the team product. The detachments were also sometimes in competition with one another to contribute the most to the welfare of the colony. Similar devices have been used in the kibbutzim of Israel (Raven and Leff, 1965).

Makarenko's approach has been applied widely in the modern Soviet educational system. In the Soviet classroom, students sit in rows, and each row has a separate group identity. The members of a row are given individual grades, merits, and

Group Decisions and Accident Reduction in a Japanese Shipyard

Under the direction of Jyuji Misumi, a group of Japanese social psychologists recently applied the group decision approach to reducing accident rates in a large Nagasaki shipyard (Misumi, 1974). As a result of the postwar educational boom in Japan, most of the young workers in the shipyard had completed high school, whereas the older supervisors had at best a junior high school education. Presumably, this imbalance in educational level reduced the supervisors' expert and legitimate power as well as their referent power. In this case, using group pressures from the worker peer groups seemed particularly appropriate as a means of improving work conditions.

The program developed by the social psychology project team was as follows:

1. Each work team was divided into small groups with two to eight members. These groups were encouraged to meet together to discuss safety problems, with the help of the social psychologists.
2. The suggestions for accident reduction presented by the various groups were consolidated by the project team and presented to the various groups for further discussion and decision. Foremen and other high-ranking supervisors were not present at these discussions, so that the decisions would emanate from the group.
3. Each group arrived at a specific set of safety-related decisions. Some decisions applied to specific work operations—for example, periodically checking the firmness of the hooks for heavy lifting and of the buttresses that held heavy parts in place and then indicating whether the particular equipment was in good order. Other decisions were related to group procedure, such as agreeing to hold a group meeting at the end of each work day to consider safety procedures.
4. Each worker agreed to decide on something specific that he could do to promote safety. He committed himself to his chosen safety resolution by pasting a reminder of it inside his work helmet.
5. The groups agreed to meet for fifty minutes before work each Friday to discuss how well each worker had followed the decisions of the group during the week and, if necessary, to evaluate earlier decisions.

With very few exceptions, the individual workers tended to comply with these decisions. The group meetings by the 4000 workers meant that many work hours were unavailable for production, yet production did not decrease. Indeed, it appears to have increased during the period of the study. Even more dramatic was the reduction in accidents—67 percent in a five-year period (Figure 20A·1).

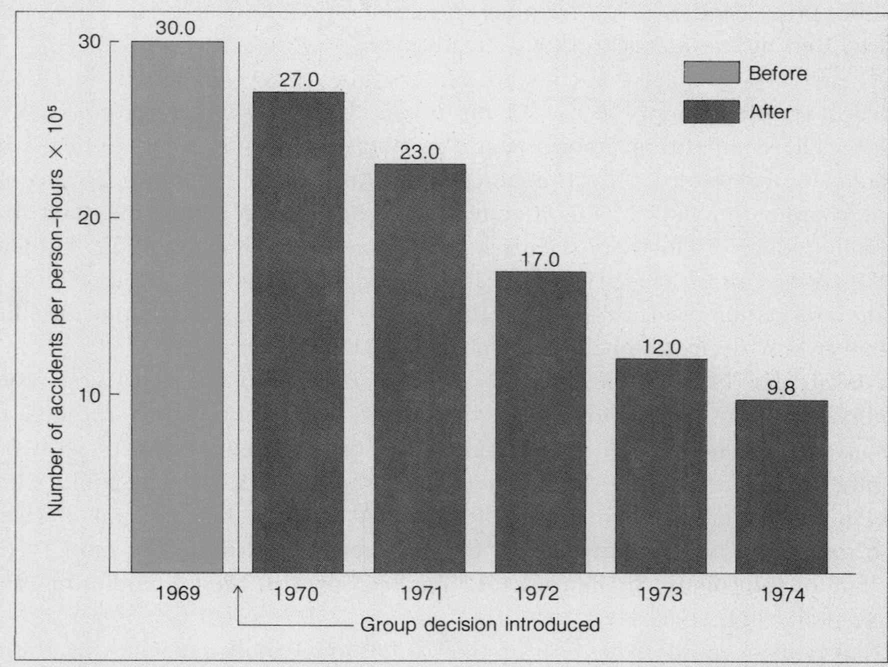

Fig. 20A·1 Accident rate before and after group decision was introduced in a Nagasaki shipyard. (Misumi, 1974)

demerits for educational activities, good citizenship, and the like, but the row is also rated, for each row is in competition with the other rows. Members of each row are encouraged to compete in terms of contributing to the score of that row.

Rows are thus encouraged to compete with one another to see which row will receive the highest marks. At the same time, however, rows are cooperating, since their collective scores determine the rating of the entire classroom. Similarly, classrooms compete with one another, but cooperate in helping the school to compete with other schools, and so on. Thus a member of a row who does not perform well will be criticized for his individual work, and will also be told that he has let his row down. A student who does very well will be commended not only as an individual, but also for his contribution to the group effort. Thus, one is rewarded for exceeding the group norm. At the same time, members of the row are criticized if they allow one of their members to fall behind.

Urie Bronfenbrenner, an American developmental psychologist who has studied the modern Soviet classroom, observes that, as a result of such group pressures, little groups of children can be seen after class, coaching one of their members who is having difficulty. Thus there is some reason to believe that the combination of pressures to compete and cooperate for a common goal can improve the effectiveness of the group learning process. One might wonder, however, whether there is a point at which a student may feel overwhelmed by the tremendous pressures imposed by the group, classroom, and the teacher (Bronfenbrenner, 1962).

The Risky Shift A pharmaceutical company has developed a new birth-control pill. The results of research using it on animals and on a few humans show that the pill is unusually effective. However, there is some question about its safety. In the tests there were a few instances of cancerous growths following use of the pill, and some members of the research staff recommend further testing.

The board of directors of the company now is faced with a decision. Should it put the new pill on the market, thus getting the jump on a number of other companies who are testing a similar product? If they do, there could be tremendous profits, but if the pill were to prove unsafe, users would suffer greatly and the losses would be tremendous. The alternative is to stick to the product the firm currently has on the market, which is making an acceptable but not impressive profit, but whose safety has been clearly substantiated.

The individual positions of the board members will probably vary. Our earlier discussion of group norms suggests that after the group meeting to resolve their differences, those most strongly opposed to immediate marketing of the new pill will become less opposed and those most strongly in favor will become less so: the group will settle on a middle position. However, there is some indication that the final group decision in situations such as this will not be an average of the original individual decisions. Instead, it appears that the group decision may be more risky than the combination of the initial individual decisions. This tendency for individuals in groups, under certain specified circumstances, to make more risky decisions than they would on their own has been called the **risky shift**.

The first experimental evidence for the risky shift was presented by James Stoner (1961) in a study that used a Choice Dilemmas Questionnaire or CDQ (Kogan and Wallach, 1964). The CDQ presents the subjects with a number of hypothetical choice dilemmas in which they must choose between a relatively safe pattern of behavior with small rewards and a dangerous pattern with the possibility of high gains. For example, an electrical engineer can take a very attractive job with little security or stay in his present job, which has security but is otherwise only moderately attractive; a college senior must choose between an outstanding graduate school where there is a good chance that he will flunk after one year, and a mediocre school where he will be sure to complete his studies; a prisoner of war in a Nazi POW camp may survive the war in the generally unappealing conditions of the camp or risk death in escaping to freedom.

Stoner first gave twelve such items to groups of subjects individually, then brought them together to discuss the items and make a group decision. In most of the items the members made more risky choices in the group situation than they had made on their own.

At first, social psychologists were skeptical of Stoner's results. Perhaps they were peculiar to the male MIT management students who served as his subjects, or to the particular test items he used. However, the study was repeated with some variations: in other settings, with females, with grade-school children, in other countries, with industrial workers, with professionals, and with others. The risky shift still appeared (Dion, Baron, and Miller, 1972; Raven and Rubin, 1976). Furthermore, though the risky shift occurs most clearly in the CDQ, with its hypothetical situations, there is evidence that it also occurs in real-life choices that have important actual implications, such as giving advice in a student counseling situation (Malamuth, 1975) and in casino gambling (Blascovich, Ginsburg, and Veach, 1975).

To explain the risky shift, some have suggested that in the group discussion a risky leader may have an especially important role. Others say that perhaps the individual feels less personal responsibility in a group and is more willing to take a risky position since the negative effects can be partially attributed to others. Still others have suggested that during the discussion the individuals become more familiar with what the alternatives really mean. None of these has received clear support as sufficient conditions for a risky shift (Raven and Rubin, 1976).

The most convincing explanation is that the risky shift occurs where riskiness is a value, a desirable characteristic to have, and where caution is viewed with disfavor. Under such conditions, each person wants to make certain that he is not *less* risky than the average person and, preferably, at least somewhat more risky. It has, in fact, been demonstrated that Ugandans (in whose society caution rather than risk is highly valued) tend to show a conservative shift in the group (Carlson and David, 1971).

Group Values and Runaway Norms If the value hypothesis correctly explains the risky shift, then there should also be a group shift toward more extremity in many other choice situations. This has, in fact, been demonstrated. In a study with French student subjects, at a time when there was a general national value attached to the prestige of former President Charles de Gaulle, groups of students shifted toward a more positive attitude toward de Gaulle than would be indicated by their prior private opinions. When there was a national trend to denigrate the United States, attitudes toward the United States became more negative following group discussion (Moscovici and Zavalloni, 1969). There are also studies that indicate greater group polarization (a shift toward extremity) in racial views (Myers and Bishop, 1970), altruism (Schroeder, 1973), and legal attitudes (Cvetkovich and Baumgardner, 1973). Perhaps any value a group holds strongly is likely to lead to competition among its members. Each person wants at least to be up to the value standard of the group, and possibly a bit above it.

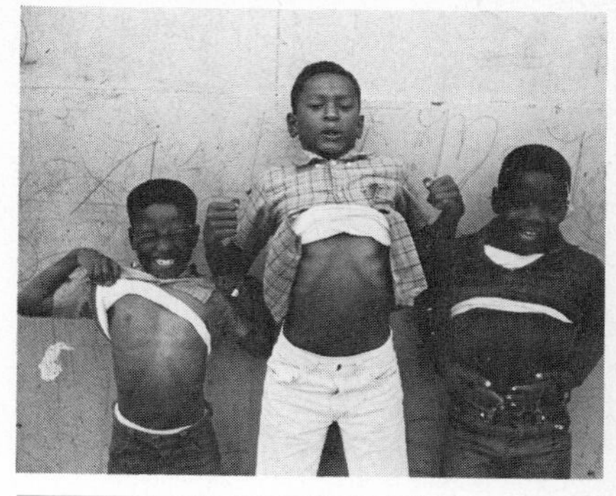

Young boys who value strength and toughness may try to surpass one another in these qualities. (Ken Graves, Jeroboam)

In a study that used a form of the Sherif autokinetic effect, it was found that the group members showed a group change toward estimates of greater movement if it was suggested that seeing more movement was indicative of intellectual promise (Baron and Roper, 1976). In a monastery, where piety is highly valued, each monk may attempt to be the most devout. Where generosity is valued, each person may make a special effort to be more generous than the others. In a motorcycle gang, where speed is valued, each may attempt to go faster than the others. As one overtakes another, that rider may in turn become someone who must be surpassed.

This tendency for a group to strive to excel its own prior standards has been called a *runaway norm* (Raven and Rubin, 1976). It has been suggested that just such a runaway norm may have contributed to the series of events in the Nixon administration that culminated in the Watergate burglary, the breaking into the files of a psychiatrist's office, and many other activities that were so reprehensible as to lead to the Nixon administration's downfall. The norm among the members of President Nixon's inner circle was to be loyal, tough, and unscrupulous in dealing with the administration's enemies. Those who had a reputation for softness were either dismissed or given diminished status. Thus each unscrupulous act led others to try to surpass it in daring and aggressiveness (Raven, 1974b).

Group Pressures Toward Nonuniformity: Social Roles

20·4 Sociologists have long observed that groups tend to be differentiated into positions, and that differing behaviors, beliefs, and attitudes are expected of the people who occupy these positions. For example, males are often expected to behave differently from females. Fathers are expected to behave differently from mothers, sons, or daughters. Teachers are expected to behave differently from students. These differing behaviors are called social roles.

It may seem paradoxical to observe that the nonuniformity that results from role differentiation in a group is really a result of pressure toward uniformity. The members of a group develop agreement on how the group should be structured or differentiated into positions. There is also agreement on the sorts of behaviors expected for these positions. But the expected behaviors—the roles themselves—

Group Decisions and Groupthink

Sometimes several outstanding individuals, all experts in their fields, can arrive at a group decision that is truly disastrous. One such failure in the group process occurred when the advisory council assembled by President John F. Kennedy (a group that included experienced administrators, top experts in foreign policy, brilliant economists, experts in Latin American affairs, and military savants) decided to approve an invasion of Cuba (actually manned by Cuban emigrés), with hidden U.S. military support. The Bay of Pigs invasion was quickly stopped by Castro's forces, and the U.S. role was exposed, to our worldwide humiliation. Several advisors, such as Harvard professor Arthur M. Schlesinger, Jr., later wondered publicly how such a brilliant group could have arrived at such a stupid decision.

Irving L. Janis (1972) studied this and similar fiascoes, and argued that the failure could be attributed to what he called *groupthink:* a deterioration of mental efficiency, reality testing, and moral judgment (among members of a group) which results from in-group pressure. Often we hear of poor group decisions that result from low cohesiveness in a group, with members fighting, competing, bickering, and otherwise undermining one another. However, Janis offers convincing evidence that groupthink is more likely to occur in highly cohesive groups, and that cohesiveness itself contributes to the poor group decision. High cohesiveness leads members into several illusions or delusions, all based on the assumption that their group is outstanding:

1. *Illusion of superior morality and invulnerability.* The group thinks that it is superior, morally as well as intellectually, and that therefore it can win against any opponent. (Certainly, Castro and his advisors were no match for the United States.)
2. *Illusion of unanimity.* The assumption is that if this is a highly cohesive group, its members will agree with one another. (The Kennedy advisory group operated in what one member called "a curious atmosphere of assumed consensus.")
3. *Suppression of personal doubts and pressures toward uniformity.* Members are afraid to take issue with what they assume to be the group consensus. Certainly one does not want to be attacked by members of a group one respects. (In the President's advisory council the members assumed that if such an outstanding group considered an invasion of Cuba appropriate, then their own doubts must be unjustified.)
4. *Self-appointed mindguards.* Whenever one of the members begins to take issue with the direction in which the group is moving, the mindguards take issue with him and point out how wrong he is. (A few council members who were more hawkish than the others stepped forward as informal preservers of the group position.)

differ according to position. A person who occupies a position and does not behave in accordance with the role prescribed for that position experiences the same pressures toward conformity as does a deviant from other group norms. The failure to behave in accordance with a role expectation is just as threatening to the social reality of the other group members as an opinion that differs from that held by the group.

As we mentioned in Chapter 18, sex roles are particularly well defined in our society. Males are expected to be dominant, aggressive, competent, and unemotional. Females are expected to be emotional, expressive, intuitive, dependent, and submissive. Both adult males and adult females appear to agree that these behaviors should be followed by males and females, respectively. Males believe

5. *Docility fostered by suave leadership.* Even if members have doubts about the group, they cannot express doubts against their leader. (President Kennedy's popularity served only to further subdue the doubters.)

Groupthink may also have been operative in the following situations: the 1941 decision by U.S. Pacific chiefs of staff to ignore warnings that the Japanese might launch an attack at Pearl Harbor; the decision by President Truman's staff to allow General McArthur to launch his attack into North Korea; the decisions by the Israeli chiefs of staff to ignore warnings of a joint Arab surprise attack in the Yom Kippur War of 1973; the decision by the German firm Grüenthal Chemie to market the tranquilizer thalidomide (which had not been thoroughly tested and which later led to death and deformity for thousands of infants); the decision by the executives of the Ford Motor Company to launch the Edsel, which could not possibly compete in the automobile market.

How can a group guard against groupthink? President Kennedy apparently learned from the Bay of Pigs disaster. Later, when the Soviet Union secretly established missile bases in Cuba, his advisory team dealt with the matter much more wisely and effectively. The techniques for avoiding groupthink include the following:

The 1958 Edsel may be one example of the failure of group decision processes—perhaps because of the phenomenon called groupthink. (Collections of Greenfield Village and Henry Ford Museum, Dearborn, Michigan)

1. One member should be appointed critical evaluator—a position that encourages that person to play devil's advocate, attacking the group decisions without fear of punishment.
2. The leader should avoid taking a position himself, so as not to impose that position on the group.
3. Independent evaluative groups should continually evaluate the decisions of the major decision-making group.
4. The policy-making group should break up into subgroups, which would each arrive at their own independent decisions, and then reconvene to compare positions.
5. Group members should be encouraged to discuss their group deliberations with colleagues outside the advisory group and get independent evaluations.
6. Outside independent experts should be brought in from time to time to give their impartial judgments.
7. After reaching preliminary decisions, the group should have a separate meeting at which each member should be encouraged to take issue with the decision and to express any doubts.

One can only hope that major governmental policy-making groups will take heed of Janis's suggestions, and so avoid some national disasters in the future.

that they do indeed follow male roles and females believe that they follow female roles. Although male roles are considered more desirable and indicative of better adjustment, psychiatrists believe that those who do not conform to their sex role are somehow maladjusted. Society at large stigmatizes and otherwise punishes the male who displays female behaviors and the female who displays male behaviors (Rosenkrantz et al., 1968; Broverman et al, 1970).

What happens when a person occupies two positions with differing role requirements? A woman who occupies an executive role faces certain problems. As an executive, she is expected to be dominant, decisive, forceful, and otherwise to behave in ways that are inconsistent with the traditional female role. To avoid such role conflict, talented women in the past tended to avoid occupational positions that were in conflict with their female roles, thus not fully making use of their resources.

There is some evidence that sex roles are changing, with greater freedom of expression for both males and females (Frieze, Johnson, et al., 1976). Two social psychologists, Sandra and Daryl Bem, advocate an androgynous society, in which the differentiation of many of the characteristic male and female role patterns would be blurred. They report, with considerable personal satisfaction, that they have been able to reallocate male and female roles within their own family in a manner that has given each a greater feeling of freedom and opportunity for self-expression (Bem and Bem, 1970).

Liberation of Group Members from Constraints

20·5 In most of the discussion so far we have emphasized the ways in which groups impose pressure on members to behave in particular ways. To round out the picture, we should also recognize that groups sometimes free individuals from constraints. Such group liberation of the individual can manifest itself in three ways.

1. *Presentation of alternative norms* is a means whereby one group can provide an alternative standard that an individual may use in resisting pressure from another group. A teen-ager whose family has stern, traditional, norms may turn to a peer group that provides alternative norms emphasizing freedom. Another teen-ager, whose clique at school requires behavior that is at variance with his or her personal moral standards, may turn to a church teen group that provides support and a means of resisting the school clique.
2. *Diffusion of responsibility* is another means by which a group may free an individual from pressures to behave in a particular manner. Sometimes we can avoid doing a required act and reduce any guilt we may have for that avoidance by convincing ourselves that others could just as easily have done it. For example, when people are being called upon to reduce energy consumption, a lone person leaving a classroom at night is likely to turn off the lights on the way out. A group of people leaving at the same time would be less likely to do so. Each group member assumes that someone else can take care of the lights. Or we can commit a generally unacceptable act as part of a group and then say that the responsibility was the group's rather than our own.
3. *De-individuation* is a group process that may overlap diffusion of responsibility. In de-individuation, the individual member merges his or her identity into the group—at least at the times the group act is being committed. An unacceptable act is then attributed to the group, and the individual member experiences no social pressure as an individual.

Though no less important, the use of alternative norms as a means of group liberation is perhaps the most obvious of the three and will not be discussed here in detail. Let us now examine diffusion of responsibility and de-individuation.

Diffusion of Responsibility in Groups On March 13, 1964, the *New York Times* reported the tragic death of Kitty Genovese, a resident of Queens, New York. The incident was so shocking as to stimulate innumerable Sunday morning sermons and an even greater number of studies by social psychologists:

> For more than half an hour, thirty-eight respectable law-abiding citizens in Queens watched a killer stalk and stab a woman in three separate attacks in Kew Gardens. Twice the sound of the resident's voices and the sudden glow of their bedroom lights interrupted him and frightened him off. Each time he returned, sought her out, and stabbed her again. Not one person telephoned the police during the assault. One witness called the police after the woman was dead.

Though this episode was especially dramatic, it is hardly unique. Similar accounts appear in the papers from time to time. The point that many commentators found difficult to comprehend was that thirty-eight witnesses were present, and none attempted to help. Paradoxically, according to two social psychologists, the presence of a large number of witnesses actually reduced the likelihood of Ms. Genovese getting help (Darley and Latané, 1968). To test their hypothesis, they devised a laboratory experiment.

A man who makes traditional distinctions between women's work and men's work might be willing to buy groceries but not to prepare the meal or to clean up afterward. (Gabor Demjen, Stock, Boston)

An undergraduate student, who believed that he was participating in a study of communication, was placed in a room alone with an intercom system through which he could presumably communicate with subjects in other rooms. Depending on the experimental condition, the subject was part of a two-person, three-person, or six-person group. The members of the group were to use the intercom to discuss personal problems associated with college life. The intercoms were hooked up so that when one person spoke, the others could not. Each member of the group identified himself and on the second round of communication, each began to tell something about himself. The first speaker in the second round of communication began:

> "I-er-um-I think I-I need-er-if-if-could-err-er-somebody er-er-er-er-er give me a little-er-give me a little help here because-er-I-er-I'm-er-er-h-h-having a-a-a-real problem-er-right now and I-er-if somebody could help me out it would-it-would-er-er s-s-sure be-sure be good . . . because-er-there-er-er-a cause I-er-uh-I've got a-a- one of the-er sei-------er-er-things coming on and and-and I could really-er-use some help so if somebody would-er-give me a little h-help-uh-er-er-er-er-c-could somebody-er-er help-er-uh-uh-uh (choking sounds). . . . I'm gonna die-er-er-I'm . . . gonna die-er-help-er er-seizure (chokes, then quiet)."

The voice of the victim was actually recorded and made to simulate an epileptic seizure. Darley and Latané were interested in seeing how quickly the subject would rush out of his experimental room to try to give aid to the victim. As we can see in Figure 20•2, the effects of group size are dramatic. In the two-person group, where the subject was alone with the victim, every one of the subjects went to offer assistance, and 85 percent of the subjects left their rooms while the seizure was in progress. In the three-person group, the delay in helping was quite noticeable, with only 62 percent running out to aid while the seizure was going on, and a number not going to aid the victim at all. In the six-person group, only 31 percent went to help during the seizure; 38 percent did not leave their rooms.

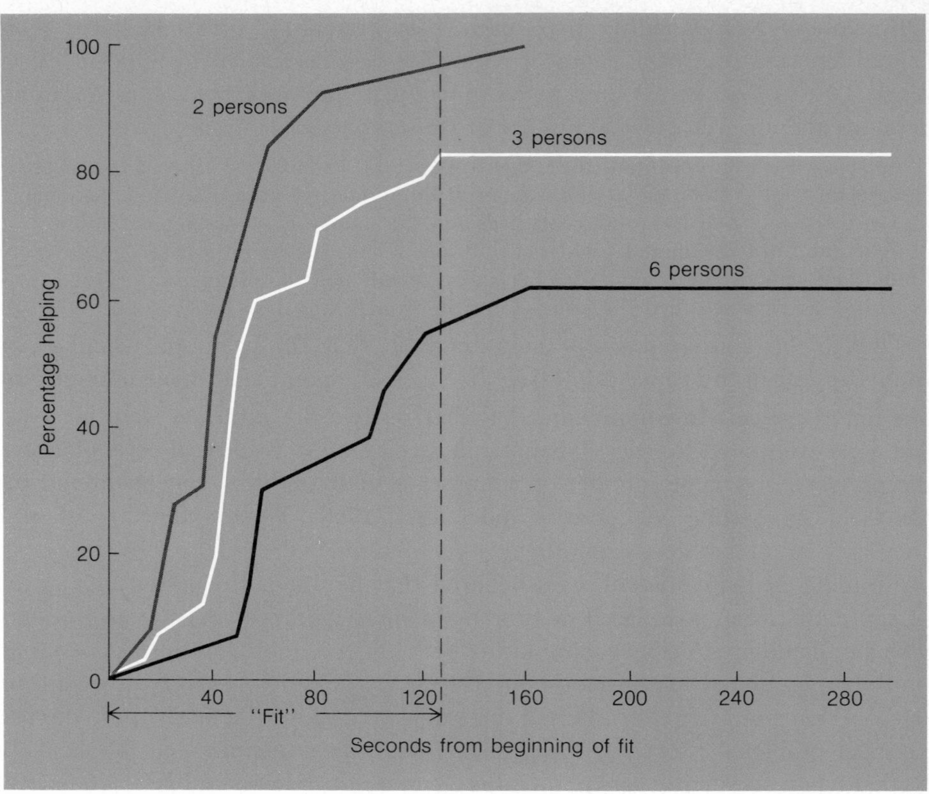

Fig. 20•2 Cumulative distributions of helping responses. (From Darley and Latané, 1968)

Later studies on helping behavior listed many other variables that might contribute to a decision to help others in an emergency: the helping behavior of others who serve as models, the favorable or unfavorable characteristics of the person in need of help, the extent to which help appears to be needed, and the possible dangers or costs of helping (Staub, 1974; Macaulay and Berkowitz, 1970). However, Darley and Latané emphasized the importance of diffusion of responsibility and diffusion of guilt in groups. In effect, the potential helper who is in the company of others may say, "It is no more my responsibility than the others. They could help as well as I, so why should I put myself out and possibly expose myself to danger?" "If I don't help, and the victim dies or is seriously harmed, then I cannot be blamed much. The blame belongs to all of us equally."

Diffusion of responsibility may apply in many other circumstances. Latané and Darley (1968) found that a subject in an experimental room who suddenly smells smoke is more likely to report it if alone than if others are present. A similar effect occurs in tipping in restaurants—the larger the number of diners dining together, the less the average tip left by each person (see Figure 20•3, Freeman, Walker, et al., 1975). We have also suggested that diffusion of responsibility may account for groups taking more risky positions than individuals, but the evidence on this point is not as clear-cut.

Whether or not they used the terms explicitly, people who conduct campaigns for charity, against pollution, against waste of energy resources, or against littering realize that diffusion of responsibility and diffusion of guilt are major factors causing people to avoid doing what they know should be done. Charity campaigns stress that each person's contribution is critical—and sometimes attempt to make this more personal by direct individual involvement. For example, a program for war orphans may use a foster parents campaign in which each contributor is made to feel responsible for one child.

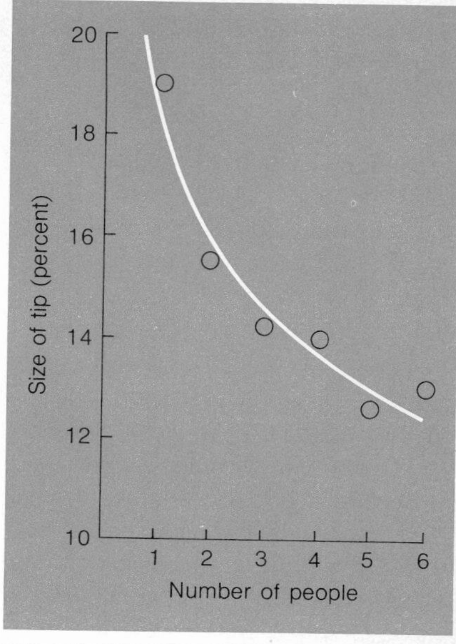

Fig. 20·3 Size of the tip left at a restaurant as a function of the number of people eating together at the same table. (Freeman, Walker et al., 1975)

De-individuation in Groups and Reduction in Constraints It has long been observed that people in crowds or mobs may behave in ways that would be morally repugnant to each participant individually (LeBon, 1896). It has been observed that many a lynch mob included among its members otherwise staid, religious, and generally nonviolent pillars of the community. This point was illustrated dramatically in Walter V. Clark's fictionalized account of *The Ox Bow Incident* (1943). In explanation, it is suggested that people of "high moral character," whose hostile or antisocial impulses are restrained by a moral code, may in some circumstances indulge their "natural" behavioral tendencies, provided that they can submerge their individual identities in a larger group identity. This loss of individual identity in a group is called *de-individuation.*

In an initial test of the de-individuation hypothesis, Leon Festinger, Albert Pepitone, and Theodore Newcomb (1952) arranged for groups of four to seven students to discuss hostility toward their parents. It was assumed that such hostility may appear in the natural course of development, but that expression of hostility is restrained by generally accepted codes. Festinger, Pepitone, and Newcomb found that, with some encouragement, the students would express hostile attitudes, but that some groups were more hostile in their expression than others. A willingness to express hostility was indeed related to de-individuation, which was measured by asking students to remember who made what statements. (An inability later to correctly attribute statements made in a group was seen as an indication of de-individuation.) Furthermore, a post-experimental questionnaire indicated that subjects in groups that were de-individuated and in which hostility was more willingly expressed were also more likely to say that they found the group experience enjoyable. The reduction of restraints then appeared to provide some satisfaction for the participants.

This anti-smoking poster emphasizes personal responsibility for the consequences of smoking, making it more difficult for the smoker to assume that smoking is a problem that only other smokers need deal with. (American Cancer Society)

Since it was correlational, the Festinger, Pepitone, and Newcomb study could not satisfactorily determine the direction of causation. Perhaps the expression of hostility led to de-individuation rather than vice versa. However, the effects of de-individuation have been represented in several other studies. In one study, female subjects in one experimental condition were asked to wear their best clothes (which clearly differentiated one subject from another), they wore name tags, addressed one another by first names, and generally emphasized their individual identities. In the contrasting de-individuated condition, the subjects were dressed in baggy lab coats with no name tags, no name identifications, and with individual

De-individuation and Aggression in Simulated Prisons

In their simulation of a prison environment, Philip Zimbardo, Craig Haney, and Curtis Banks provide a particularly dramatic example of the ways in which group situations can bring about extreme behavior. To recruit applicants, they used a newspaper ad offering $15 per day for participation in a two-week study of prisons. From the many applicants screened and tested, eighteen young men were selected as being normal, healthy, and free of significant signs of psychological disturbance. They were told that some of them would participate as prisoners and some as guards, and interestingly enough most expressed a preference for the role of prisoner. The assignments were in fact random—nine prisoners and nine guards.

The prisoners were "arrested" by the Palo Alto police, handcuffed, searched, and brought to the "Stanford County Jail" in the basement of the Stanford University psychology department. After being undressed and "deloused," they were given simulated prison garb (loose-fitting smocks) and a simulated prison haircut (a nylon stocking over their hair), and a symbolic chain was locked to their ankles. After being given the prison orientation, they were locked in their cells. Of course, the research team was aware that prisoners do not ordinarily wear smocks, nylon stocking caps, or chains. However, they were interested in simulating the degradation, humiliation, and loss of identity that usually accompany imprisonment.

Each of the guards was issued a khaki uniform, sunglasses to cover his eyes, and three items to carry while on duty—a club, a whistle, and cell keys. The guards were told that they were not to use physical violence against the prisoners. Guards worked three at a time in three eight-hour shifts.

In the simulated prison, the guards had complete control over the prisoners, including deciding when (and if) prisoners could get out to use the toilet, when and where prisoners could smoke, and whether talking was permitted. They could also call the prisoners out for bedcheck.

Though the men were assigned randomly to the role of prisoner or guard, and presumably did not differ initially, the role assignments soon made for very distinct patterns of behavior and apparent personality differences. The prisoners became increasingly subservient, and some showed signs of psychological disturbance (one prisoner was finally released after his behavior began to seem bizarre). Guards became increasingly authoritarian and brutal. They would call the prisoners out of bed in the middle of the night and ask them to repeat their prison numbers over and over. They forced the prisoners to do pushups (sometimes putting their feet on the backs of the prisoners while they did so). They denied them toilet privilege, and even restricted the frequency with which they could empty their "slop buckets" so that the prison began to smell.

At the same time, the prisoners began to behave like prisoners, becoming passive, subservient, and occasionally rebellious (there was one major demonstration by prisoners that was quickly and brutally subdued by the guards). In later interviews, it was difficult for the prisoners to believe they had behaved that way—but even more difficult for the guards to believe their own behavior. Even the experimenter, who played the role of the chief prison administrator, and the student who played the role of warden, were quickly caught up in their roles, and behaved with what later seemed to them to be a lack of sympathy for the prisoners and a concern about maintaining law and order.

Finally, the experimenters felt that the study should be brought to a close—because it became clear to them that it was no longer simply an experiment, but something too closely approximating a prison, with its severe brutality. And how long did it take to reach such a state? Only five days—on the sixth day the experiment was halted.

What accounted for such extreme behavior? The effects of the roles of prisoner and guard were obviously powerful. It also appears that the de-individuation of the guards permitted them to engage in behaviors they might otherwise find unacceptable. Furthermore, a norm of firmness and brutality seemed to develop. When a group of guards adopt the position that it is crucial to maintain law and order, that softness with prisoners does not pay, that a guard who is lax is "chicken" or unfit to do his duty, each guard may try to outdo the other in brutality (Haney, Banks, and Zimbardo, 1973).

identities blurred. Subjects in both conditions were asked to discuss pornographic literature. The de-individuated subjects were more free and lively in their discussion and used more obscene words (Singer, Brush, and Lublin, 1965).

In an experiment in which subjects shocked one another (presumably to study empathy), subjects who were dressed in smocks with hoods, and whose individual identities were disguised were more likely to administer heavy shocks to others, as compared to subjects in an individualized condition (Zimbardo, 1969). (Actually no shocks were administered, but a confederate acted as though she were receiving painful shocks.)

It is not unreasonable to assume that soldiers (whose battle dress reduces their individual identities), police, Ku Klux Klansmen, and people who can merge into large crowds or mobs and lose identity may thereby feel more free to engage in behaviors they might otherwise consider morally repugnant.

Summary

From birth on, a person is continually interacting with, being influenced by, and exerting influence on groups. Much of the influence process in groups can be seen in terms of pressures toward uniformity. Individual members of groups tend to behave similarly, and to have similar attitudes, beliefs, values, judgments, and emotions.

In Muzafer Sherif's classic experiment on the autokinetic effect, subjects tended to converge to a common judgment in estimating the movement of a point of light. Though pressures toward uniformity may be especially clear when a group is judging an ambiguous stimulus, it has been shown that such pressures toward conformity with a group judgment occur even when unambiguous judgments are involved, as in the estimation of lengths of lines. The means by which a unanimous group majority imposes the group norm on an individual correspond to the basis of power discussed in Chapter 19—threat of punishment, promise of reward, reference, legitimacy, expertise, and persuasion.

Pressures toward uniformity in groups sometimes arise from the necessity for agreement in order to achieve a common goal. However, a major factor in pressures toward uniformity is the need for social comparison. Each person wishes to believe that he or she is behaving, thinking, or performing properly or experiencing appropriate emotions.

Comparison with others provides one means for evaluating oneself—though at times other means, such as reference to clear physical evidence, appeal to one's prior knowledge and experience, or comparison with traditions, are available. If these alternative means of self-evaluation are not available, the person is especially likely to use other people for such purposes, and pressures toward uniformity within a group are especially evident.

A person in disagreement with a group norm may use various ways to restore uniformity with the group: changing one's opinion or attitude to bring it closer to the group's, influencing or persuading others to change, rejecting other people as inappropriate for comparison, misperceiving the disagreement so that it is interpreted as agreement, or minimizing the importance or relevance of the disagreement. Which of these devices is used depends on several factors: personality and self-confidence; cultural factors; the amount of disagreement and degree of unanimity in the group; degree of ambiguity of the object of disagreement; relevance of the disagreement to group functioning; and degree of cohesiveness of the group, attraction toward the group, and identification with it. The same pressures toward uniformity and social comparison processes also occur in evaluating one's abilities, except that in this case the person looks toward others who are slightly superior to himself or herself.

Pressures toward uniformity also affect the majority of a group when a member of that group deviates from the group norm. In such instances, it is unlikely that the majority will respond by conforming to a lone deviant, though that may happen if the deviant is prestigious, powerful, persuasive, or in a leadership position. If the object of disagreement is ambiguous, or of borderline relevance to the group, the majority may distort the degree or importance of deviance or overlook the discrepancy as insignificant. More probably, however, the group will attempt to influence the deviant member to change toward the group, by persuasion or, in some cases, by threat of punishment. If persuasion is ineffective, the group may reject the deviant member, both personally and as a basis for comparison. Highly cohesive groups are especially likely to experience pressures toward uniformity, and are therefore more likely to communicate with, and attempt to influence the deviant. Such groups are also more likely to reject the deviant if persuasion is ineffective.

The effects of group norms can be so powerful that it is sometimes easier to change the behavior of a group as a whole than that of each person individually. It has been demonstrated that social change can be brought about through group discussion and group decision. The group decision then serves as a norm that affects all of the individual members. In some cases, high cohesiveness and pressures toward uniformity may lead to poor group decisions, sometimes with disastrous consequences.

Groups may pressure individual members to try to exceed the group average or norm. Groups sometimes explicitly or implicitly foster competition among group members, encouraging them to show that they are bolder, riskier, more courageous, more zealous in helping the group toward its goals. Such pressures can lead to a runaway norm, an escalation in which each member tries to appear bolder, tougher, or more hostile toward an enemy of the group. Intergroup conflict can sometimes result from such runaway norms.

Though groups generally impose pressures on individual members, a group can also sometimes liberate a member from pressures from other groups, or from an adherence to certain social codes. There is evidence that individuals are less likely to help a person in need if other persons are present. The group thus provides for diffusion of responsibility or diffusion of guilt. Sometimes groups allow for de-individuation, in which each person loses his or her individual identity in a group. An individual then feels less concerned about adhering to generally accepted moral codes. The violent behavior of mobs, of police in police raids, of prison guards, and of soldiers can sometimes be explained in terms of de-individuation.

Suggested Readings

Darley, J., and Darley, S. A. 1973. *Conformity and deviation.* Morristown, N. J.: General Learning Press.

Brief account that supplements our discussion of conformity and deviation.

Davis, J. H. 1969. *Group performance.* Reading, Mass.: Addison-Wesley.

Examines the process by which individuals become members of performing groups. Sections focus on audience effects on individual behavior; effects of coaction; group problem-solving, learning, and decision making; effects of group size and composition; and the operation of group norms.

Freedman, J., and Doob, A. 1968. *Deviancy: The psychology of being different.* New York: Academic Press.

Reviews evidence indicating the ways in which the conformist punishes and behaves hostilely toward the deviant, and the resulting tendencies of deviants to affiliate with each other. Applications to analysis of drug culture, counterculture, and prison society.

Janis, I. L. 1972. *Victims of groupthink: A psychological study of foreign-policy decisions and fiascoes.* Boston: Houghton-Mifflin.

Fascinating application of group theory and research to national policy-making. Includes a study of group process in the Bay of Pigs invasion, the Cuban missile crisis, the Pearl Harbor defense plan, and the Marshall Plan.

Kiesler, C., and Kiesler, S. B. 1969. *Conformity.* Reading, Mass.: Addison-Wesley.

Brief, but thorough introduction to the analysis of conformity and deviation, with particular attention to public and private conformity and deviation.

Ulmer, S. S. 1971. *Courts as small and not so small groups.* Morristown, N. J.: General Learning Press.

Applies research from the small group literature to analysis of collegial court decisions, including effects of group structure, seating location, risky shifts, and leadership.

Two Approaches to Animal Behavior: Ethology and Psychology

21 Animal behavior has for a long time been investigated by two groups that have assumed different models of animal nature, applied different research methods, and obtained different and sometimes conflicting results. Psychologists in a wide variety of subdisciplines of psychology have studied animals, but the study of animal behavior has been the province of the comparative psychologist. Traditionally, **comparative psychology** has been defined as the study of the behavior of animals, and particular attention has been given to comparing animal behavior to human behavior.

Zoologists, in a subdiscipline of zoology called ethology, have also studied animal behavior. **Ethology** has been defined by workers in that field as the biological study of behavior (Tinbergen, 1951, 1969). In general, ethologists have been particularly concerned about the function of behavior in the life of the animal in its natural environment.

Psychologists have tended to emphasize the influence of environmental factors on behavior and consequently have stressed the importance of learning. They have also looked for and found some basic principles of behavior that apparently apply across animal species. We have touched on these principles at various places in this book—in Chapter 1, when we discussed the growth of behaviorism as one branch of psychology, in Chapters 3, 5, and 18, when we discussed social learning theory, in Chapters 3, 13, and 17, when we discussed behavior modification; in Chapter 13, when we discussed the application of Skinner's theories to human personality; and most notably in Chapter 10, when we considered learning in terms of conditioning. To the extent that behaviorists have studied animals to arrive at their basic principles of behavior, behaviorist psychology overlaps comparative psychology.

Especially in the formative years of ethology, ethologists tended to emphasize instinctive (innate) behaviors and the importance of evolution. In general, ethologists have been concerned with differences rather than similarities among animals, since different animals presumably inherited different genes and evolved along different evolutionary pathways in different environments.

Both psychologists and ethologists have attempted to study animal behavior objectively. They have confined their attention to the gross body movements of the animal that can be studied and confirmed by other observers. Both groups have avoided postulating mental events (such as thoughts and insight) as the causes of animal behavior. Since both groups have claimed to study objective animal behavior, it may seem surprising that their models, methods, and results have been so different. In this chapter we shall discuss these differences, the reasons for them, and the movement toward a synthesis of these two approaches.

Why Study Animals?

21·1 As we noted in Chapter 3, animal experiments can be useful in studying the developmental and physiological aspects of psychology. By using animals, investigators can conduct certain kinds of experiments such as measuring the influence of genetic makeup or of certain hormones and drugs on behavior. From experiments on rats, for example, endocrinologists have learned some basic principles of hormonal action that help us understand how the endocrine system functions in humans.

A particular animal behavior can be studied for several different reasons. We might seek to find out its cause. What stimulus variables in the environment have precipitated the behavior we are studying? What internal factors (such as hormones, or deficient or excessive functioning of brain areas) influence this behavior? Getting answers to these questions commonly involves laboratory experiments in which all influencing variables except one are held constant so that the investigator can determine that variable's influence on behavior.

We can seek to find out what function the observed behavior has in the organism's natural environment. In certain animals, for example, aggressive behavior sometimes seems to function to allow the animal to establish a territory and to keep other animals outside the boundaries.

Still another reason for studying animal behavior is to find out the evolutionary significance of a behavior. To some extent, behavior is influenced by genetic heritage. Indeed, many features of our anatomy (such as brain size, which we will discuss in Chapter 22) and physiology (such as reproductive processes) can be seen as modifications of the anatomy and physiology of our primate ancestors. We may therefore inquire into the possibility that behavior itself has evolved.

Although animal behavior is important in its own right, investigators often study animal behavior in order to find out about human behavior. One area of recent popular interest in applying information from animal studies is aggression. Humans seem to be the only animal species whose social interactions sometimes result in the injury and death of other members of the species. Is this aggression instinctive, as books such as *On Aggression* (Lorenz, 1966), *The Territorial Imperative* (Ardrey,

An Ethologist Looks at Human Aggression

Aggressive behavior within a species is common, but only rarely does it result in the opponent's death. Why are humans an exception to this rule?

Tinbergen (1968) speculates that the destructive aspects of human aggressive behavior may be due to a culture's influence on behavior combined with a biological heritage of aggression. Aggression in animals serves some very useful purposes. For example, if one member of a territorial species wanders into the territory of another, an aggressive encounter may result. This usually involves the emission of aggressive signals such as biting, pushing, and vocalizing, and the withdrawal of the intruder with little or no physical damage to the participants.

In Tinbergen's view, an animal in an aggressive encounter is actually in a state of motivational conflict. It is driven to attack, but it is also driven to flee. He believes that the balance between the instinctive urges toward attack and avoidance underlies the defense of territorial boundaries and the establishment of social hierarchies. Some animals acting individually or in pairs defend territories against intruders, but humans and other primates defend territorial boundaries as a group. Thus, social hierarchies and territorial defense are combined.

If we have inherited some of these behavior patterns, what has gone wrong? Why do we kill instead of merely signaling? Tinbergen feels that the cultural heritage of humans has upset the balance between attack and avoidance. Soldiers going into battle are taught that fleeing is an indication of cowardice and will be severely punished. Facing the enemy may be less traumatic than the punishments and social disgrace meted out to the deserter. The innate urge to flee may be countermanded by the culturally initiated mandate to fight.

A second way of preventing injury in an aggressive encounter is for one animal to emit appeasement or capitulation behaviors, which cause the antagonist to stop the attack. Usually the submissive animal assumes a position in which it is highly vulnerable to attack (Figure 21A·1). Such appeasement postures may be forbidden by our culture, which demands that we be brave, persistent, and domineering in physical combat. Not only do we fail to make appeasement gestures, but modern weaponry may place us at such a distance from our adversary that we cannot see these signals if they are made. The men who drop bombs from airplanes or fire artillery shells several miles do not see the ultimate effect of these weapons. People may be able to kill at a distance even though they could not in face-to-face combat.

Tinbergen raises the question of extent to which education can counteract what he considers our inherited urge for aggression. He speculates that Lorenz (1966) and other ethologists are probably correct in stating that the elimination of aggressive behavior through education may be a difficult or impossible task, and that aggressive behavior will probably become more common as population density increases and as we deplete the resources of the planet. Instead, he suggests that tendencies toward aggressive behavior be redirected into socially useful enterprises such as scientific research, the space program, or national endeavors such as Holland's endless fight against the sea. He notes that in animal societies and in human societies, strong group cohesiveness exists when the group is united against an outside enemy.

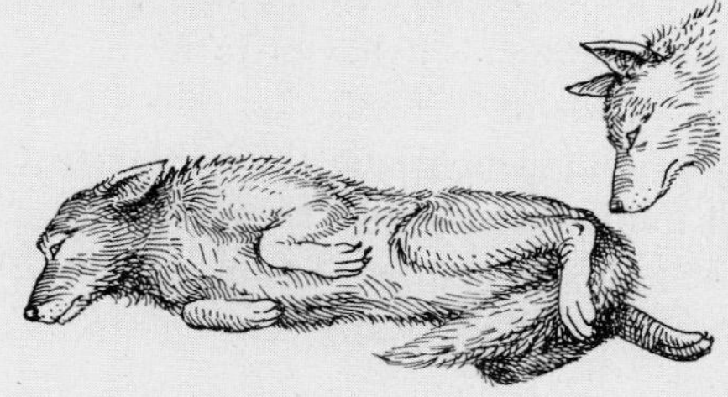

(*a*)

(*b*)

Fig. 21A·1 (*a*) Passive submission postures in the wolf. The inferior wolf is lying on its side with ears directed back and tail placed between its legs. The superior wolf is investigating the genital region of the inferior wolf. (*b*) Submission posture combined with begging for food (dog lying on side) in Eskimo dogs. (Schenkel, 1967)

1966), and *The Naked Ape* (Morris, 1968), would have us believe? Can aggression be environmentally controlled, as B. F. Skinner (1948, 1971) contends? Answers to these questions are still forthcoming, as the work of ethologists and psychologists merges together.

Historical Perspective on the Link Between Animal Behavior and Human Behavior

21·2 For many centuries, philosophers and scientists have tried to understand the causes of behavior. Their efforts have produced several different models of animal nature, which have influenced the orientation and development of both psychology and ethology. Those who pursue their inquiry within the theoretical framework of a Cartesian model (the model proposed by Descartes), for example, are likely to perceive the animals they study almost as machines. Those whose assumptions derive from a Darwinian model are likely to perceive animals as organisms that have evolved by natural selection. These investigators try to understand an animal's behavior by studying its evolutionary history and the environment in which it lives.

We shall sketch here the history of these two major models of animal nature that guide inquiry into the behavior of humans and other animals. Underlying these different paths of inquiry is the attempt to determine whether animal behavior can tell us anything significant about human behavior.

Descartes: The Animal As a Machine In the early seventeenth century the French mathematician and philosopher René Descartes proposed the theory of reflexology, which postulates that all animal behavior results from simple reflex mechanisms that are activated by external stimuli. Descartes compared these reflex mechanisms to the action of mechanical statues common in landscaped gardens of the wealthy in France during his time. These statues were set in motion by water pressure from hydraulic systems that were activated by pressure on foot switches hidden in the garden paths. For example, a visitor stepping on a foot switch might cause a statue of Diana bathing to hide in the bushes. If the visitor followed the statue, he or she might be challenged by Neptune brandishing a trident and then assaulted by a surge of water from a sea monster (Skinner, 1931).

Descartes postulated that all animals, including humans, are reflex machines guided by external stimuli but with one basic difference between the behavior of humans and that of other animals: human behavior is also guided by mental events. He believed that in the human, the nonmaterial mind interacts with the material body by means of the **pineal body,** a small unpaired structure about in the center of the brain. Therefore, according to Descartes's theory, studies of animal behavior are not relevant to human behavior because there are influences on human behavior (mental events) that are absent in other animals.

Darwin: The Animal As a Rational Being The publication of the *Origin of Species* in 1859 was a momentous event in the study of animal behavior. In proposing that one animal species evolves from another, Darwin implied that animal species should be considered not as unique entities but as related organisms in a continuing thread of life. This **continuity hypothesis** resulted in two basic trends in animal behavior studies.

One of these trends was that investigators began to scrutinize human behavior for signs of instinctual determinants. Because human beings evolved from animals that are assumed to possess **instincts,** these investigators assumed that humans must also possess instincts, some of which may even be the same as those of animals. Social scientists began to catalog instincts for observable human behaviors. The lists of instincts grew longer and longer, some containing as many as 1500 instincts, including the instinct for what they called philoprogenitiveness but we might simply call sex. By the 1920s, it became obvious that the practice of constructing instinct lists was of questionable value for at least two reasons: anthropologists were showing that behavior differs dramatically from culture to culture, and behaviorist psychologists were showing that learning is an important determinant (according to some, the only determinant) of behavior.

The other trend in animal behavior studies was that investigators began to scrutinize animal behavior for signs of intelligence, specifically reasoning ability, a characteristic formerly assumed to be exclusively human. Eventually, learning was studied in many different forms of organisms in an attempt to gauge their levels of intelligence.

Darwin may have impeded the growth of a scientific approach to the study of animal behavior by encouraging the publication of anecdotal accounts (many of which were unverified or inaccurate) of animals supposedly expressing such human-

This lithograph from the early 1900s satirizes the attempt then being made by some people to train animals as if they possessed human intelligence. (The Bettmann Archive)

Are Human Facial Expressions Innate?

Charles Darwin (1872) argued that human facial expressions are inherited—that they are unlearned components of our animal heritage perhaps little modified by human culture. He assumed, for example, that human baring of the teeth in contempt is related to the baring of the teeth by a snarling carnivore before it bites its prey.

A universalistic approach is one, such as Darwin's, that stresses the importance of innate factors. In this view, facial expressions are pancultural, since learning has little effect on them. A relativistic view of facial expression stresses the importance of learning and suggests that the language of facial expression is different in different cultures.

How do we determine which view is correct? At least two approaches have been taken: (1) to examine facial expression in children born blind and deaf and (2) to look for similarities of facial expression in humans living in different cultures. Blind and deaf-blind children have been observed to display remarkably normal facial expressions, at least at certain ages (Freedman, 1964; Eibl-Eibesfeldt, 1970). These observations have been interpreted as evidence of a universalistic explanation of facial expressions.

Paul Ekman (1971) assumes that basic facial expressions such as smiling result from certain muscle groups of the face being stimulated in a pattern that the individual does not have to learn. However, he also believes that cultural factors play a role in determining which stimuli elicit the facial responses, how the responses are displayed (what Ekman calls display rules), and the effect of the facial expressions on other people. The display rules are thought to prescribe how we should intensify, deintensify, neutralize, or mask the innate facial expressions. For example, middle-class, white, urban adult males in the United States are taught to refrain from showing sadness and fear in public places. When two corporate executives meet after one has been promoted and the other has been passed over, both are smiling even though one is very happy and one is very sad (Ekman, 1971).

Ekman and Friesen (1975) constructed an atlas of the human face. By combining the results of cross-cultural studies, some theories about emotion, and a knowledge of facial muscles, they specified the muscles that take part in the expression of each of six basic emotions—surprise, fear, disgust, anger, happiness, and sadness. Models were told to recreate these facial movements, which were then photographed for the atlas.

like emotions as suspicion, jealousy, humor, wonder, and curiosity. In one of his own anecdotes, Darwin described the behavior of an affectionate baboon who stole puppies and kittens and carried them around. When one of the kittens happened to scratch the baboon, apparently inflicting pain, the baboon bit off the kitten's claws. Darwin labeled that act as expressing anger and as demonstrating reasoning ability. Reading human emotions or values into the behavior of other animals is a practice referred to by social scientists as *anthropomorphism.* As we learned in Chapter 1, many books on animal behavior were crammed with such anecdotes, supposedly illustrating the intellectual powers of animals.

Thorndike: Learning As Trial and Error Edward Thorndike's (1911) studies of cats in puzzle boxes (discussed in Chapters 1 and 10) showed that the cats did not suddenly discover the solution to the puzzle by reasoning or by insight, as the tellers of anthropomorphic anecdotes supposed. Instead, the cats seemed to learn to escape from the puzzle box by repeatedly making errors and by gradually strengthening the connection between making a particular response and gaining

FEAR

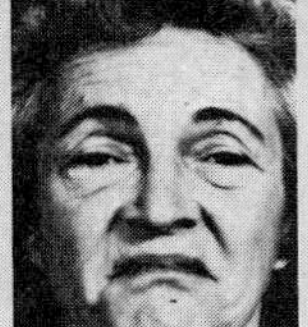
DISGUST

HAPPINESS

ANGER

Table 21C·1 Percentage Agreement in How Photograph Was Judged Across Cultures

EMOTION	UNITED STATES (N = 99)	BRAZIL (N = 40)	CHILE (N = 119)	ARGEN-TINA (N = 168)	JAPAN (N = 29)
Fear	85%	67%	68%	54%	66%
Disgust	92%	97%	92%	92%	90%
Happiness	97%	95%	95%	98%	100%
Anger	67%	90%	94%	90%	90%

(Ekman and Friesen, 1975, p. 25) (Photos courtesy of Silvan Tomkins and Paul Ekman. © Ed. Gallob.)

Table 21C·1 shows examples of photographs chosen by Ekman and Friesen as clear examples of these emotions. These pictures were shown to people of five different literate cultures: United States, Brazil, Chile, Argentina, and Japan. The facial signals for these four emotions were interpreted similarly by the majority of the different peoples. Ekman stressed that the appropriate emotion for these faces may have been similarly interpreted because the subjects came from literate countries where they also had access to movies and television. Perhaps the uniformity of pancultural responses to these pictures indicates the influence of education and not the innate nature of facial expression.

For a better answer, Ekman and Friesen (1975) gave the pictures to natives of New Guinea, some from the Fore culture and some from the Dani culture. These peoples have just recently been "discovered." Some had a little schooling but none had been exposed to a caucasian teacher. In a test with pictures depicting all six emotions, the New Guineans matched pictures and words for happiness, sadness, disgust, and surprise, but some confused fear and anger. Thus these natives with their stone-age culture were, in general, interpreting facial expressions in the same way as caucasian Americans. This suggests that human facial behavior rests on a foundation of unlearned responses.

access to the food outside the box. The correct response might be pulling a string or pushing a pedal, but the cats often engaged in ineffectual behaviors such as attempting to squeeze between the slats of the puzzle box, biting, scratching, pawing, and vocalizing.

Observers of animal behavior had also believed that cats have well-developed powers of imitation. Instead, Thorndike found that watching another cat figure out how to escape from the puzzle box did not improve a cat's performance when placed in the puzzle box itself. The mystique of the animal mind was called into question.

Thorndike's work led him to conclude that the ability to learn has evolutionary significance: human dominance in the world is due not to superior speed and strength or to sharp claws and teeth, but to the ability to learn, store, and convey information. Thorndike was therefore interested not only in how animals learn but also in how they differ in learning ability. Although he expected to find that different species learned in different ways, he found that crabs, fish, turtles, dogs, cats, and human infants all seem to learn in essentially the same manner, albeit at different rates. One outcome of Thorndike's failure to find species differences in learning has been that psychologists studying learning have concentrated on a few species, such as the domestic rat, that were thought to be representative of other species.

Lorenz: Emphasis on Genetically Programmed Behavior Konrad Lorenz (1965), one of the founders of ethology, has contended that animal behavior (such as aggression) is strongly influenced by genes. This notion shows the influence of Darwin's work, especially the concept of **natural selection,** according to which only the fittest survive. Lorenz believes that the influence of environment on animal behavior is slight and that even human behavior is strongly influenced by instinct. Lorenz has stipulated that although both human and animal behavior can be modified by learning, it is appropriate to study the instinctive components of various types of behavior before we study how learning can modify these behaviors.

Lorenz has stressed the need to study animal behavior, not in the artificial context of the laboratory, but in the animal's natural environment. He has studied a particular aspect of animal behavior as a feature that fits in with the other behavior patterns of the animal, helps it to survive and reproduce in its particular environment, and may have served some function in the evolution of the species.

Skinner: Emphasis on Learned Behavior Although most psychologists who study animal behavior would be classified as behaviorists, B. F. Skinner has been called a radical behaviorist. He has modified the Cartesian model of human nature as a machine by eliminating any reference to mental activity and adding a very strong emphasis on learning. According to Skinner, there is no need to speculate about what goes on inside animals or humans, since only behavior is observable. In fact, Skinner ridicules concepts of what he calls an inner man. He has stressed the profound importance of the environment in shaping behavior and has de-emphasized genetic determinants of behavior (Skinner, 1971).

Although Skinner's radical behaviorism has not been accepted by the majority of psychologists, present-day psychology has been strongly influenced by a more moderate behaviorism. Until recently, psychology has been notable for both its lack of concern with genetic differences in behavior and its tendency to study very few animals in an attempt to find general principles of behavior.

Studying Animal Behavior

21·3 In our discussion of developmental psychology, personality, and abnormal behavior, we have repeatedly confronted the nature-nurture controversy. How much do heredity and environment interact in affecting behavior? This issue faces students of animal behavior also. Some think that environment is the primary influence on animal behavior, whereas others believe that behavior is primarily genetically determined.

Animal Behavior from the Psychologists' Perspective As we saw in Chapter 1, for approximately thirty years (including the last two decades of the nineteenth century), many pioneers in the field of psychology struggled to create a science of the human mind. To do this, they used human subjects trained to describe in detail what they experienced while the mind was presumed to be in operation. Eventually it became apparent that such subjective data alone could not provide the basis for a science of psychology. Many psychologists then turned to the study of behavior. These so-called behaviorists believed that to be a science, psychology must be based on the objective data that could be obtained by observing behavior.

Ivan Pavlov's procedures for studying conditioning in dogs suggested to behaviorists such as B. F. Skinner a means for obtaining objective data from observing behavior. *(Sovfoto)*

Obtaining Objective Data The historical setting we have just described had a profound influence on the study of animal behavior by the psychologist. Apart from the clinical work being done in psychodynamic psychology, psychology became basically a laboratory study of behavior. The laboratory approach is an *interventionist* approach—one in which the investigator carefully structures the environment, manipulating one variable at a time and holding others constant. The investigator can then determine whether the **independent variable** (the one being manipulated) actually influences behavior and, if so, in what ways the behavior changes.

As we saw in Chapter 10, the Russian physiologist Ivan Pavlov studied in detail such questions as whether the order and timing in which stimuli are presented are important in **conditioning**. He chose his stimuli arbitrarily, assuming that the animal could form new reflexes in response to the stimuli and that these reflexes would be adaptive (that is, they would fit the environmental conditions). Pavlov showed that a neutral stimulus such as a metronome click could be used to condition saliva flow, even though, in nature, the metronome click is unlikely to be associated with food.

Pavlov's work had a significant influence on early behaviorists such as John B. Watson. Skinner, too, claimed that Pavlov's work had given him an important clue for research on behavior: control your conditions and you will see order. Although Skinner was impressed with the idea that behavior could be reduced to a simple element (for example, a **reflex**), he was concerned that the type of conditioning demonstrated by Pavlov applied only to conditioned reflexes, a limited segment of an animal's learning capabilities.

Deemphasizing Heredity and Instinct The study of both hereditary influences on behavior and the concept of instinct became virtually extinct in early twentieth-century psychology. Many psychologists claimed that behaviors that appeared to be unlearned would, if properly analyzed over the developmental history of the organism, be seen to be influenced by the environment.

As part of this debate, Zing Yang Kuo (1932) suggested that the ability of the chick to peck at objects on the day it hatches should not be attributed to instinct. Although the behavior seems to emerge intact without benefit of learning, it may be critically influenced by experience previous to hatching. To test this hypothesis, Kuo removed sections of shell from fertile chicken eggs and studied the development of behavior in the chick embryo. He found that the heartbeat, which appears early in the life of the embryo, forces the chick's head up and may result in the swallowing of a small amount of fluid. This involuntary head-tossing and swallowing may be the experiential basis necessary for the development of the pecking and eating behavior of the newly hatched chick. Studies such as this cast doubt on the presumed instinctual bases of certain kinds of behavior.

Behavior Control In several experiments using **reinforcement,** Skinner clearly demonstrated the power of the environment to control behavior. Skinner reinforced the desired response (such as a bar press or a key peck) with a stimulus (such as food for a hungry animal) only when the animal produced the requisite number of responses. Thus, when demand levels were high, animals were induced to produce hundreds of responses in order to obtain a single reinforcement. By this method, pigeons have been trained to play table tennis (Skinner, 1956), to steer a bomb toward the silhouette of a battleship (Skinner, 1960), and to inspect gelatin capsules in a pharmaceutical company (Verhave, 1966).

In Skinner's view, behavior is shaped by two factors: the reinforcement contingencies in the environment and the subject's history of being reinforced. Therefore, if we know what variables influence a behavior and in which direction they influence it, we should be able to control that behavior. For example, a baby's crying that is caused by fluctuations in room temperature can be reduced by raising the baby in a temperature-controlled "air crib" such as Skinner devised. Skinner also claimed that productivity of workers can be greatly increased if they are reinforced with praise (or with whatever is appropriate reinforcement) when they make a "correct" (as determined by the person who controls the reinforcement schedule) response.

Animal Behavior from the Ethologists' Perspective The history of ethology before the 1920s is somewhat difficult to trace. Darwin's writings (1859, 1871, 1872) contained much that would today be classified as ethology. Darwin suggested that an animal's behaivor should be considered from the same perspective as its anatomical structures, which probably have some adaptive significance and are clearly products of the animal's evolutionary history. Darwin is not considered the founder of modern ethology primarily because he lacked followers to capitalize on his insights.

In the 1920s Konrad Lorenz of Vienna began to publish his observations on animal behavior. Lorenz had considerable first-hand knowledge of animal behavior and was interested in making detailed observations of what animals did in natural or seminatural environments. A few years later, Niko Tinbergen joined the effort and the two collaborated on several studies. The result was the emergence of ethology—the biological study of behavior.

Appetitive and Consummatory Behavior Ethologists stress two important categories of behavior—appetitive and consummatory. *Appetitive behavior* is flexible and is influenced by learning and by the demands of the environment. Perhaps the most important characteristic of appetitive behavior is that it sets up the animal for the performance of *consummatory behavior*, which is stereotyped, species-specific, and probably not influenced by learning. In their normal habitat, animals engage in appetitive behavior until they encounter a *sign stimulus*, which serves to release the consummatory behavior. Animal behavior seems adapted to the environment because certain stimuli within the broad range of stimuli available to the organism release a particular behavior in the same way that a key releases a lock.

For example, Lorenz (1939) has stated that the common tick is "prewired" to respond to particular stimuli by implanting itself in the skin of a human or other animal. These stimuli are a 37°C temperature and the presence of butyric acid—two stimuli provided by the bodies of human beings and some other animals, but not by plants or inanimate objects. In this example the appetitive behavior has not been clearly identified.

Konrad Lorenz is largely responsible for initiating the study of animals in natural and seminatural environments. Here he is shown with a group of hand-reared greylag geese. (Photo H. Kacher)

Action-Specific Energy Lorenz postulated a buildup of a hypothetical substance, *action-specific energy*, as the motivation for consummatory behavior. Lorenz described the action-specific energy as accumulating much as water flows into a reservoir. If a sign stimulus is encountered in the environment, that energy is released and is consumed by the execution of behavior. If no sign stimulus is encountered, then a particular consummatory behavior may be released out of its usual context and appear without any apparent stimulus (**vacuum activity**). Following the release of the behavior, a time might be required to accumulate more energy before the behavior could occur again. This concept of energy being spontaneously released with no external stimulus is one of the main points of contention in Lorenz's theory of innate aggression.

Lorenz was influenced by E. von Holst's pioneering work (1939) on locomotion in fishes. Von Holst severed the fish's spinal cord from its brain, making it impossible for the brain to influence swimming movements. He then placed the fish in a holder that restrained its body but allowed free movement of dorsal, pectoral, and tail fins. The various fins showed rhythmic beating even though the spinal cord was disconnected from the brain and no rhythmic stimuli were present in the fish's environment. Furthermore, each ray of each fin, although beating in the same rhythm, was slightly out of phase, so that the beat spread across the fin in a regular manner.

Von Holst concluded that the rhythmic beat of the fins must be under the control of endogenous signals generated by the nerve cells in the spinal cord. This finding implies that movements can be influenced by internal factors as well as by external factors. Animals do not behave only when prodded into action by environmental stimuli.

Function of Behavior Lorenz and Tinbergen have been greatly concerned with the function of behavior in the natural environment. They ask "What is the significance of a particular behavior in the life of the organism?" To answer this question, they have sought to determine the nature of an animal's habitat and the types of behavior patterns it exhibits there, particularly behaviors relating to self-preservation and to reproduction. Indeed, the starting point of ethology was the attempt to describe animal behavior as it occurs in the natural environment, perhaps when there has been minimal opportunity for learning. Behaviors that may look haphazard and unpredictable when casually observed may appear orderly and comprehensible after enough effort has been made to observe them accurately in the environment in which they evolved.

Evolution of Behavior Lorenz and Tinbergen have been concerned with the question: How did the behavior under observation evolve into its present form? Since we have virtually no fossilized record of behavior to analyze, we must compare the behavior patterns of related species and estimate how these behavior patterns changed over the course of evolutionary development.

Natural selection can produce evolutionary change in animal structure or behavior only if it can operate on genetically determined characteristics. Therefore, study of the evolution of behavior has centered on behavior patterns that are assumed to be inherited and are rather uniform within a species. Change produced by the environment—such as learning—cannot be inherited and cannot produce evolutionary change.

Since ethologists stressed the study of the evolution of inherited behavior patterns and since the various animals they studied evolved along slightly different pathways, it seemed reasonable to assume that, among animals, differences in behavior stand out more than similarities.

Choice of an Animal to Study

21·4 One's orientation and purpose in studying animal behavior will, of course, dictate the choice of animal for experimentation or observation. There are approximately one million described species of animals. (Undescribed species may total another one or two million.) Of this total, 96 percent are invertebrates (animals without backbones) and 4 percent are vertebrates (animals with backbones).

Many of the well-known mammalian species appear in various strains that may differ behaviorally. Strains are subgroups of a species that develop distinctive characteristics because of inbreeding within the strain, yet can breed with other strains of the same species. Some strains have been domesticated over the centuries and some, such as certain rat and mouse strains, have been highly inbred. In mice, more than 200 mutations have been reported and have been preserved by consistent mating of brothers and sisters until that mouse strain is believed to be isogenic—that is, until every member of the strain has exactly the same genes as every other member (Green, 1968). In rats, several generations of domestication can influence anatomy as well as behavior.

Choice of Animals by Psychologists F.A. Beach (1950) tabulated the species used in psychological research, as they were reported in articles published in the *Journal of Comparative and Physiological Psychology* and its predecessors during the first half of this century (Table 21•1). His tabulation showed that, before World War I, a broad variety of animals were studied, including invertebrates and many vertebrates other than mammals—a trend possibly indicating attempts to measure the degree of intelligence of animals presumed to be on various rungs of the evolutionary ladder. In the 1930s a stable trend developed, with approximately 60 percent of the studies using the rat as the experimental subject. At the same time, mammals other than the rat were studied somewhat, but invertebrate research dropped to a low level.

Table 21•1 shows that the trend toward concentration on the rat as a typical research animal held stable between the 1940s and the 1960s. In Beach's analysis, the types of problems researched were also tabulated. He found that throughout the 1930s and 1940s learning was the single most important topic of experimentation (Figure 21•1).

Table 21•1 Percentage of Studies Reported in *Journal of Comparative and Physiological Psychology* Dealing with Various Kinds of Animals

ANIMALS	1947–49[1]	1956–58[2]	1960–66[3]
Rats	67%	62%	58%
Other mammals	24	30	33
Other vertebrates	15	5	7
All nonvertebrates	4	3	2

1. (Beach, 1950)
2. (Dukes, 1960)
3. (Kutscher, unpublished)

Concentration on the Rat The domestic rat has played a prominent role in psychological research almost from the beginning. At the very end of the nineteenth century, rats were first used in three different laboratories (Lockard, 1968) for studying maze learning. The choice was a happy one. It soon became evident that rats quickly learn to find their way through a maze, gradually eliminating errors—just as they quickly learn their way through the cellars and walls of houses. The rat generally breeds well in captivity; becomes gentle with handling; is physically

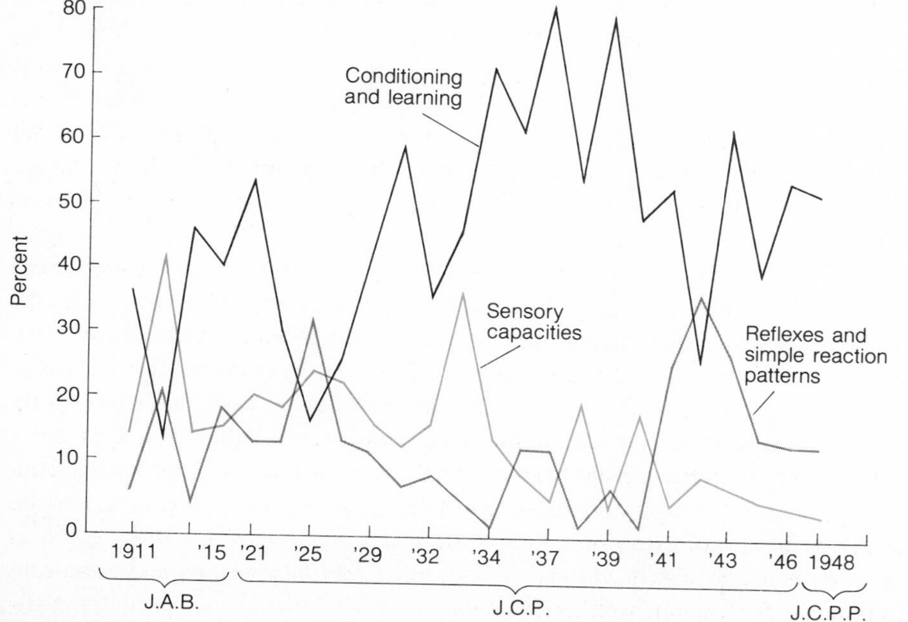

Fig. 21•1 Relative distribution of topics of articles published in the *Journal of Comparative and Physiological Psychology* and its forebears, *Journal of Comparative Psychology* and *Journal of Animal Behavior.* Note the attention given to conditioning and learning. (Beach, 1950)

B. F. Skinner has chosen to work extensively with pigeons in his conditioning experiments. (Ken Heyman)

vigorous; is an active, alert animal; and usually shows a high level of exploratory behavior, which enables it to learn well.

Rats have long been bred in captivity. In the nineteenth century in England and France, rats were trapped to be used in the sport of rat baiting. A terrier was placed in a pit containing many rats and spectators wagered on how long it would take the dog to kill all of them (Lockard, 1968). This tradition, with selective breeding for desirable characteristics such as *albinism* (lack of pigmentation), may have produced the stock for twentieth century research animals.

H. D. King (1939) and his associates attempted to reenact the domestication process by bringing wild Norway rats into the laboratory and breeding them in captivity. After twenty-five generations, the brain, thyroid, and adrenal glands of these rats decreased in weight, their bodies became fatter and showed an accelerated growth rate, and their fertility increased resulting in more litters. These domesticated rats lost much of their viciousness and fear of humans and made little effort to escape when the cage door was left open.

Results of Specialization in Particular Animals Psychologists in general have tended to work with a few species that are assumed to be representative of others, first rats and—to a lesser extent—pigeons, monkeys, and dogs. Such specialization has aided research in various fields. From experiments on rats, for example, endocrinologists have established an important data base on hormone function. There are some species differences in endocrine function, but the similarities seem to be much more important.

In **genetics,** the fruit fly *Drosophila melanogaster* is probably the most widely used animal subject. Indeed, it almost seems custom-made for research on **genes.** It reproduces rapidly, with only twelve days elapsing between laying of the egg and the emergence of the adult insect. The cells contain only four **chromosomes** (cells of most laboratory mammals contain about twenty) and each chromosome pair is distinctly shaped and readily recognizable. *D. melanogaster* mutates profusely. The giant chromosomes found in its salivary glands are so large that genes can actually be located on them (Schmidt-Nielsen, 1967). As far as we know, genetic principles of *D. melanogaster* do not differ in any important respect from those of mammals.

In neurophysiology, extensive research has focused on the giant squid's **axon** (Brink, 1951), a portion of the giant nerve cell that plays a prominent role in the squid's jet-propulsion mechanism (its ability to rapidly shoot a jet of water out behind it and thus move through the water). The axon of this nerve cell is so large that microelectrodes can actually be placed inside it for measurements of electrochemical events during the passage of a **nerve impulse.** The squid axon does differ in certain respects from mammalian axons, but many basic physiological properties of the membranes of axons are the same in both kinds of animal. The problems have simply been easier to study in the squid.

Skinner's *Behavior of Organisms* (1938) was based on experimentation on rats. *Schedules of Reinforcement* (Ferster and Skinner, 1957) was based entirely on the behavior of pigeons, but nowhere in the book is doubt expressed concerning the generality of the principles of behavior discovered. In fact, it is probably in instrumental conditioning that we find the fewest differences among a variety of birds and mammals.

Figure 21•2 shows cumulative response records made by three different animals, a pigeon, a rat, and a monkey. There is no significant difference between them.

> Pigeon, rat, monkey, which is which? It doesn't matter. Of course, these three species have behavioral repertoires which are as different as their anatomies. But once you have allowed for differences in ways in which they act upon the environment, what remains of their behavior shows astonishingly similar properties. (Skinner, 1956)

Skinner claims that similar curves have been generated by mice, cats, dogs, and human children. If he is correct, studying instrumental conditioning in many species would be unnecessary.

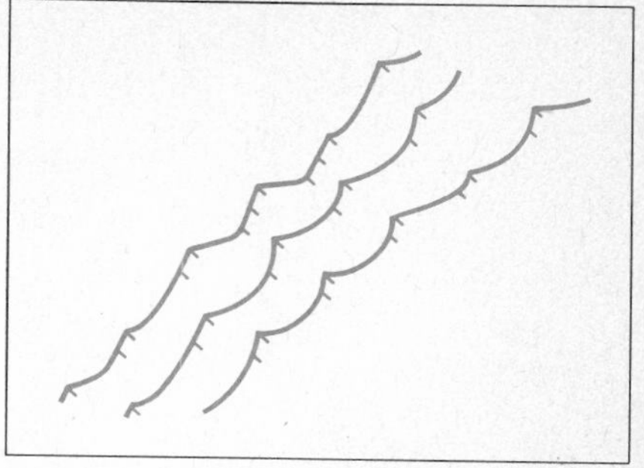

Fig. 21•2 Cumulative response curves for a rat, a pigeon, and a monkey responding on a complex schedule of reinforcement. During the fixed-ratio segment of the schedule, a specific number of responses are required before reinforcement is given. On the fixed-interval schedule segments, the animal must wait a certain time before receiving reinforcement. Typically, on this schedule responses are emitted at low rates in the early part of the interval and then at higher rates immediately before the next reinforcement, thus producing a scalloped response curve. (Skinner, 1956)

Choice of Animals by Ethologists In the 1960s a survey of *Behaviour,* a British journal that publishes papers with an ethological perspective, showed that ethologists have a strong interest first in birds and then in arthropods (mostly insects), and somewhat less of an interest in mammals and fishes. In view of their emphasis on species differences in behavior, it is not surprising that ethologists have studied a variety of animals. If we assume that, during the course of their evolution, animals have been influenced by different selection pressures and have become adapted to different environments, it is reasonable that we should find species differences in behavior. Many ethologists caution against generalizing findings on the behavior of one species to the behavior of other species because behavior patterns may have diverged (as body types did) during the course of evolution.

Although observations of behavior have been made on many species, certain animals (such as the herring gull and the stickleback fish) have received much attention—usually as a temporary expedient in order to provide a background of information for later comparative work. Tinbergen set out to do comparative work on gull behavior, but found that he first had to concentrate on only a few species (the herring gull, the black-headed gull, and the kittiwake) in order to learn some of the fundamental behavior patterns. When an observer begins to observe a flock of gulls, the birds look alike and the behaviors seem disorderly and insignificant. Gradually the patient observer learns to recognize the individual birds and the various patterns of the behaviors as well as the manner in which these behaviors influence the behavior of other species.

21•5 Controversies Between Psychologists and Ethologists

The potential for conflict between these two approaches should be obvious by now. It is not surprising that, given their diverse points of intellectual origin, these two dedicated and capable groups of workers should arrive at different theoretical outlooks and research strategies.

In studying great apes in the East African jungles, Jane Goodall not only has observed them from afar, but also has won their confidence enough to interact with them in friendly ways. (© National Geographic Society)

Where to Study Behavior Applying the laboratory approach of physics and chemistry, psychologists stress controlling all variables so that the influence of the one under study may be clearly seen. In so doing, they usually create an environment unlike any found in nature. In the ethologist's opinion, behavior in artificial environments cannot be safely extrapolated to behavior in natural environments and only the latter is really significant.

How Much to Intervene The experimental, laboratory approach of the psychologist is, of course, an interventionist approach. In the laboratory, environmental restrictions are imposed and only the behaviors left open to the animal are studied. According to ethologists, however, the observer should be as unobtrusive as possible, perhaps hiding in a blind, or viewing the behavior through field glasses. The early ethological work was thus basically descriptive, not experimental. Such an approach pays a price, however, because the observer is never sure what variables are acting and interacting in the environment and influencing the animal's behavior at any moment. According to Tinbergen (1965):

> The naturalist knows perhaps better than any other zoologist how immensely complex are the relationships between an animal and its environment, how numerous and severe are the pressures the environment exerts, the challenges the animal has to meet in order to survive, but also to contribute substantially to future generations.

Which Behavior to Study Psychologists have sometimes asked what behaviors the animal can be made to produce, whereas ethologists have often been concerned with finding what behaviors the animal normally exhibits in its environment. Getting pigeons to steer bombs toward battleships or inspect gelatin capsules in pharmaceutical companies are certainly impressive accomplishments of behavioral technology, but they may tell us little about behaviors that influence the animal's survival in nature.

The Importance of Learning Most psychologists, many of whom had a strong environmentalist and behaviorist orientation, stressed the importance of learning in the shaping of behavior. Arguing over the definition of instinctive behavior, behaviorists have pointed out that it is logically not possible to prove that a behavior pattern has never been influenced by learning or altered by environmental factors (Beach, 1955). Behaviorists looked for and found environmental influences on behavior.

Many ethologists stressed the study of innate behavior patterns, which they assumed to be unlearned. They considered it crucial to catalog the animal's behavioral repertoire before the animal was exposed to learning opportunities. Lorenz (1965) has argued that ethologists should begin the study of behavior when it first appears in the lifespan of the organism and should not try to see what environmental influences might have influenced the behavior before it actually appeared. Following this strategy, Lorenz noted many behaviors that appeared to be uninfluenced by learning.

One psychologist (Beach, 1955) pointed out that the classification of behavior into learned and innate may date back to twelfth-century theological teachings that tried to draw a clear difference between man and beast. Human behavior was said to be guided by reasoning (which implied learning), and animal behavior was allegedly guided by inherited instinctive urges.

Some psychologists have argued that classifying behavior into mutually exclusive learned and innate categories tells us nothing useful about the behavior and may inhibit research on factors (such as maternal care or complexity of the environment) during early life that control its development and expression. They have argued that we need **ontogenetic** studies—studies of the development of the behavior over the lifespan of the organism, in order to fully understand the environmental effects on it.

Modern Synthesis of Psychology and Ethology

21·6 We have sketched the development of the psychological and ethological approaches to animal behavior in order to emphasize the strengths of each. Currently both psychologists and ethologists are reassessing their positions and attempting to form a synthesis of the two viewpoints. The controversies between them have stimulated attempts to clarify issues and refine terminology and have produced changes in orientation and methodology in both disciplines.

Changes in the Psychologists' Approach Perhaps the most significant change in the psychologists' approach in recent years has been the gradual affirmation that general laws of animal behavior may not be as easy to discover as was once thought. Species differences in physiological mechanisms and in behavior resulting from the action of these mechanisms may be real and very important. Some of the evidence for this view comes not from broad comparative studies involving many organisms, as one might expect, but from more sophisticated studies of the rat.

Species Differences in Behaviors That Can Be Conditioned Recent experimental findings have challenged the notion that, provided the experiment is properly conducted, any conditioned stimulus (CS) and any unconditioned stimulus (US) can be paired, and any response can be strengthened by presentation of any reinforcing stimulus. It now appears that the animal brings to the experimental session certain predetermined response characteristics and possibly certain predispositions to learn (Seligman, 1970).

As described in Chapter 10, avoidance conditioning involves learning that a particular stimulus (the CS) signals the onset of something unpleasant (the US) and then learning how to avoid the US. In an active avoidance experiment, the animal must do something in order to avoid the US, whereas in a passive avoidance experiment, the animal learns to do nothing in order to avoid the US. Rats readily learn certain kinds of avoidance conditioning. They can easily be trained to run

The Ventromedial Hypothalamus and the Search for General Principles of Brain Function

Can work on animal brains tell us anything about the function of the human brain? In research on the brain areas that control feeding behavior, the answer seems to be yes.

When small areas of the rat ventromedial **hypothalamus** are destroyed, thus creating a brain lesion, hyperphagia (overeating) occurs. During the dynamic phase of hyperphagia, food intake and body weight increase enormously. During the subsequent static or obese phase of this abnormal eating behavior, food intake declines somewhat but remains above the intake level of the control rats; body weight is maintained at a higher level than before surgery. The animal acts as though the regulatory mechanism controlling its body weight has been reset, but not totally turned off (Teitelbaum, 1955).

The original studies of hyperphagia showed that the animal with brain lesions did not simply become voracious. Instead, obese rats were more reluctant than normal rats to do activities to get food—such as pressing a bar, pulling a weight, or lifting a heavy lid (Miller et al., 1950). In another experiment, obese rats almost ceased to eat a quinine-adulterated diet that the normal and dynamic hyperphagic rats ate in the same amount as the standard diet (Teitelbaum, 1955). When the diet was sweetened with dextrose, obese rats consumed about twice as much of the food as did normal rats. Thus, hyperphagia is specific to particular kinds of foods that presumably are highly palatable. Some investigators have called this condition finickiness.

There is considerable evidence that obese humans (with no known brain damage) are very similar to rats with hypothalamic damage in the ventromedial area. In one study (Hashim and Van Itallie, 1965), obese and normal humans were taken off their normal diets and eating routines and were given a bland liquid diet dispensed by machine. Thus food was divested of its taste, aroma, and textural characteristics, along with the social amenities that normally accompany eating. The normal individuals took enough of this new diet to maintain body weight, but the obese individuals consumed only a fraction of their normal caloric intake and lost weight. Even when they were allowed to drink from cups instead of from the mechanical dispenser, caloric intake was only about 25 percent of what it was on the normal diet.

Stanley Schachter (1971) has made an extensive analysis of obese humans and rats made obese by means of hypothalamic lesions. He found that in both organisms, compared to normal-weight individuals, the obese eat more food per day (the definition of hyperphagia), eat fewer meals per day, eat more per meal, and eat faster. They eat more "good" tasting food and less "bad" tasting food. They are more emotional and generally less active. In both rats and humans the obese do not work hard to get food, although large amounts of food are ingested if it is readily available.

Schachter suggests that in intact (unoperated) rats and normal-weight humans, food intake is controlled to a large extent by internal cues (such as blood sugar, tissue needs, and stomach emptying) with taste of food playing a somewhat less important role. The lean rat or human eats until internal cues shut off food intake. For the obese rat or human, internal cues may be ignored and taste may play the decisive role in control of eating. If it tastes good, it is ingested in large amounts. If it tastes even slightly bad, it is rejected.

In hibernating animals the ventromedial hypothalamus may serve another function besides controlling daily food intake. Hibernators must enter hibernation with large amounts of body fat to sustain them. In the fall, behavior of the animal about to hibernate is very much like that of the rat with a ventromedial lesion and the obese human. They all develop hyperphagia along with finickiness, resist doing work required to get food, and accumulate body fat. It is possible that in all three cases the ventromedial hypothalamus is functioning at a reduced level.

down a runway to avoid shock (Miller, 1941), but it is very difficult to condition a rat to press a bar to avoid shock (Seligman, 1970). This failure is particularly surprising since rats can easily be trained to press a bar to secure food, water, light, heat, and even a sex partner. However, in the typical passive avoidance situation, rats sometimes learn to avoid shock in a single trial.

How are we to explain these differences in the rat's ability to learn how to avoid —either actively or passively—an unpleasant stimulus? One explanation (Bolles, 1970) is that avoidance responses similar to those made to threats in nature are easiest to learn. Wild rats typically run or freeze when threatened. Both responses are adaptive in certain situations. Running may remove the animal from whatever is threatening it, and freezing may make the animal undetectable in its environment. Perhaps only in the laboratory is a bar-pressing response an efficient way to deal with a threat. Some of the rats that do learn to bar-press to avoid shock do so in a very peculiar manner—they rise above the bar, freeze, and fall on the bar. Thus their behavior is more like freezing than pressing.

Species Differences in Reactions to Stimuli M. E. P. Seligman tells an anecdote that is appropriate here as an example of human behavior that corroborates a large body of research on animals (Seligman and Hager, 1972). After dining with his wife at a restaurant where he had one of his favorite foods, béarnaise sauce, he attended a performance of *Tristan und Isolde*. Later that evening he became ill with gastrointestinal flu, and subsequently he developed an aversion to béarnaise sauce. He did not acquire an aversion to other stimuli in the environment on that evening such as the white plates in the restaurant, *Tristan und Isolde*, or his wife.

How can illness cause taste aversion? It seems to be a matter of classical conditioning. A neutral stimulus, (CS), such as the sauce, is paired with illness (US) and vomiting (UR). After one exposure this pairing yields an aversion (CR) to the CS.

Recent experiments in conditioned aversion show that not every stimulus can be used as a CS. In one experiment (Garcia and Koelling, 1966) where rats were overexposed to X rays in order to produce illness later, the clicking of an electrical relay sounded while they were drinking saccharin water. Thus they were given "noisy and sweet" water before they became ill. The radiation illness apparently takes about one hour to develop. Later the rats were tested with the noisy stimulus alone and then with the sweet stimulus alone. When given the noise alone while drinking water, they showed no aversion to drinking, and drank as much as they had on a test prior to the X-ray exposure. The noise had no disruptive effects even though it had been present immediately before the illness. When offered saccharin water, the rats were reluctant to drink. Evidently the saccharin had become associated with the illness but the noise had not.

In a companion experiment, rats were given an electric shock while drinking "noisy and sweet" water. On subsequent tests, the drinking of "noisy" water was inhibited, but the drinking of sweet water was not. This means that the rats could learn to associate noise with shock and taste with illness, but could not associate the taste with shock or noise with illness.

According to one interpretation (Seligman, 1970), an animal may be prepared to make a particular kind of association. In such cases, classical conditioning requires very few trials. When an animal is unprepared for a particular association, conditioning may require many trials. When an animal is *contraprepared* (meaning that certain associations are very difficult or perhaps even impossible to form), even a large number of trials may fail to establish a CR. Animals may be prepared to form associations between taste and illness, unprepared to form associations between noise and shock, and contraprepared to form associations between taste and shock.

Another problem in interpreting conditioned aversion experiments is that the interval between the CS (taste) and the US (illness) may be an hour or more and yet successful conditioning occurs. In other types of conditioning, CS-US intervals longer than a few seconds do not permit conditioning. Perhaps the animal is prepared to form taste-illness associations even if the illness-producing food was eaten long before the illness began. The adaptiveness of such a response is obvious. If an animal eats a novel food and becomes ill, future avoidance of that food is adaptive. A common problem in attempting to poison wild rats is that if the poison does not kill the rats on the first exposure, they may never eat the same kind of poisoned food again. Even though Seligman understands all these facts, he still cannot eat béarnaise sauce.

Although studies such as these have been done only with rats, it seems likely that other animals have different patterns of preparedness for conditioning. For example, the bobwhite quail, like the rat, can learn to avoid water made sour by the addition of acid when this flavored water is followed by the induction of illness (Wilcoxon et al., 1971). Unlike the rat, however, the quail shows an aversion to added coloring as well as to added taste. For many birds, taste may play a minor role compared to visual cues, since food (for example, seeds) may be encased in a shell. Only when it reaches their crop is the food material broken down enough to release potential taste cues. Furthermore, food must be recognized from a distance and may be taken quickly.

The subjects of conditioning experiments do not fit a *tabula rasa* ("blank slate") model of a creature in whom *any* learning associations can be formed by stimulus presentations. The state of preparedness of each animal dictates the kinds of associations possible and the degree of difficulty involved in making those associations.

Changes in the Ethologists' Approach Ethologists are making considerable use of controlled experimental situations to better evaluate the influence of certain variables on behavior. They have begun to make sophisticated analyses of the interaction of environmental stimuli with physiological processes inside the animal as they attempt to understand the causal events bridging stimulus and response. Ethologists are also making more use of statistical procedures to quantify and evaluate their observations.

Environmental Effects on Behavior and Physiology Many ethologists have agreed with T. C. Schneirla (1956) and other psychologists that more attention should be devoted to the ontogeny of behavior—that is, to the development of behavior over the organism's lifespan. Behaviors previously considered instinctive are now known to be influenced by environmental stimuli and may even involve learning. For example, male stickleback fish raised in isolation from the time of hatching show normal sexual and social behavior when they are exposed to adult sticklebacks for the first time: they court females and mate with them and they attack males that intrude on their territory. Although learning does not seem to be required for the first performance of these behaviors, their normal development may result from some event such as the fish seeing its own reflection in the glass wall of its tank (Schneirla, 1956).

Even the functioning of a physiological system may depend for its adequate development on appropriate environmental stimulation. For example, the rods in the eye of the frog do not develop normally unless they are exposed to light during the tadpole stage (Knoll, 1956).

Becoming Physiologically Sophisticated Classical ethologists have sometimes been criticized for being physiologically naive. Specifically, they have been accused of postulating events and mechanisms inside the organism that are unsupported by observation or seem contrary to what we know about animal physiology. For example, Lorenz has postulated the existence of a mechanism by means of which action-specific energy accumulates inside an organism and is released when the organism encounters a sign stimulus. Lorenz's model for this mechanism is a reservoir filled with fluid that is released when an appropriate stimulus makes contact with a drain mechanism. However, nothing we know about the physiology of the mammalian nervous system fits this description.

Tinbergen (1951) proposed that ethologists deal seriously with physiological mechanisms. The few who have heeded his advice have made great strides in some research areas, such as reproductive behaviors. Behaviors such as pair formation, courtship, copulation, nest-building, egg-laying, incubation, and the feeding of the young must appear at the appropriate time and in the appropriate sequence for successful reproduction to occur. Figure 21•3 shows the interactions (both known and probable) of factors that influence these behaviors in canaries (Hinde, 1970).

During spring, light striking the female canary's retina produces nerve impulses that are transmitted to the brain, eventually influencing the **hypothalamus,** which secretes chemicals (releasing factors) that enter the bloodstream, move to the anterior pituitary, and control the release of hormones from that gland. The anterior pituitary releases or increases output of gonadotrophins, pituitary hormones, which enter the bloodstream and go to the ovaries, causing them and associated sex structures to increase in size. Also, the ovaries secrete estrogen and the secondary sex hormones prolactin and progesterone. The estrogen, along with the external stimulus of the male canary, precipitates copulatory behavior. Estro-

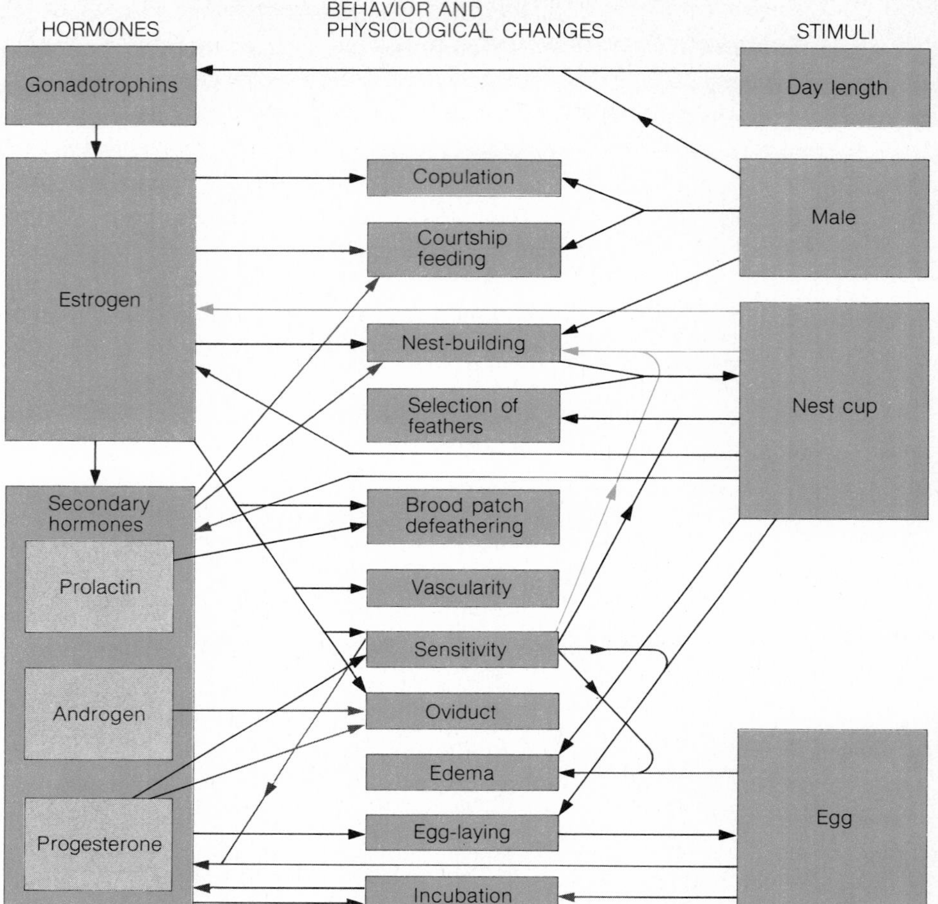

Fig. 21·3 The comprehensive analysis of the interaction of hormone production and external stimuli in the production of behavior can lead to a complicated system of interacting variables. The black lines indicate that one factor causes something to happen. The yellow lines indicate that one factor inhibits the action of another. The gray lines indicate probable relationships that have yet to be firmly established. (Hinde, 1970)

gen also influences nest-building, which requires gathering and forming nesting materials into a cup shape. The newly defeathered and swollen brood patch of the female canary apparently causes her to seek softer nesting materials such as feathers. Thus, as she approaches egg-laying, she creates a more adequate environment for the development of the young.

The behaviors of incubating eggs and feeding the young have not yet been analyzed, but they too are probably affected by a complex web of interacting variables.

The Future of Research in Animal Behavior

21·7 What lies ahead in the field of animal behavior? Probably we shall see more synthesis of the findings and methodology of the psychologists and the ethologists. Animal behavior will probably be viewed in a wider perspective as we inquire into its causation, its function in the habitat, and its evolutionary development.

In addition, the rapid strides being made in such areas as the physiology of brain function, endocrine action, renal function, cardiovascular events, neurotransmitters, and the chemical basis of memory should provide additional insights into an understanding of the physiological substrates of animal behavior. Some of the concepts of psychologists and ethologists regarding physiological mechanisms of behavior have been understandably vague because physiologists have not clarified certain critical functions—for example, precisely how a hormone acts on nerve cells—or because physiologists have not asked the questions that will provide answers needed to understand behavior.

Finally, we shall probably see even more attention paid to discovering what animal behavior can tell us about human behavior. We are probably past the stage of uncritically extrapolating results from animal experiments to explain human behavior.

Summary

The study of animal behavior is a scientifically respectable enterprise, but there has been much uncertainty about how to interpret the information gained. Many psychologists have viewed the study of certain animals, such as the rat, as a convenient basis for obtaining general rules of animal behavior. Ethologists have stressed studying animal behavior to find out why some living organisms are able to exist in particular environments while others cannot.

Some psychologists have modeled their method after physics and chemistry, while ethologists have used the methods of natural history. This dichotomy of approaches to animal behavior, with different historical antecedents, has provided some lively controversy.

Psychologists have shown that under well-controlled environmental conditions in which reinforcements are given only when the animal successfully makes particular responses, very complex behaviors can be performed by animals.

Ethologists have generally emphasized species differences, genetic determination, instinctive behavior (in contrast to learned behavior), the function of behavior in the environment, and the possible evolutionary development of behavior. In general, field observations in the animal's habitat have played a major role in ethology, although more recently seminatural environments and even unnatural laboratory settings have been used.

Ethologists, as well as some psychologists, have stressed the need to turn their attention to the study of human behavior, particularly aggressive behavior. Some psychologists have emphasized the cultural determinants of human behavior and stressed the importance of controlling the environment so that humans do not learn to be aggressive. Ethologists have given particular attention to our animal heritage and to the hypothesis that we have inherited aggressive behavior from our evolutionary forebears much as we have inherited the shapes of our bones and teeth.

In recent years, we have begun to see a synthesis of the two viewpoints. Psychologists have begun to take seriously the problem of species differences in behavior and the possibility that studies on a single "representative" animal such as the rat may not actually tell us enough about general rules of behavior for all organisms. Ethologists have begun to give serious consideration to the physiological mechanisms underlying behavior. The previous controversies have been beneficial to both sides in helping to clarify the problem areas and helping us to understand the strengths and weaknesses of the various methodological approaches.

Suggested Readings

Eibl-Eibesfeldt, T. 1970. *Ethology: The biology of behavior.* New York: Holt, Rinehart, and Winston.

This textbook, written by an ethologist, emphasizes the instinctive components of behavior. The author also shows how the methodology developed in the study of animal behavior might be used in the study of human behavior.

Ekman, P., and Friesen, W. V. 1975. *Unmasking the face.* Englewood Cliffs, N.J.: Prentice-Hall.

A highly readable book about an extensive program of research on human facial expressions.

Lorenz, K. 1966. *On aggression.* London: Methuen.

An international best seller by one of the founders of modern ethology.

Morris, D. 1968. *Naked ape: A zoologist's study of the human animal.* New York: McGraw-Hill.

A highly readable attempt to study human behavior by using the principles of study worked out with animal behavior.

Schacter, S. 1971. Some extraordinary facts about obese humans and rats. *American psychologist* 26: 129–44.

In one of the few comprehensive attempts at a comparative study, Schacter shows that obese humans act very much like brain-damaged rats that subsequently become obese.

Seligmann, M. E. P., and Hager, L. L., eds. 1972. *Biological boundaries of learning.* New York: Appleton-Century-Crofts.

A collection of scholarly papers noteworthy because they show how modern psychologists have come to think that species differences may be important in learning.

Skinner, B. F. 1971. *Beyond freedom and dignity.* New York: Knopf.

This book is the ultimate in extrapolating from animal behavior to human behavior. When we control human behavior through reinforcement, as we should do Skinner argues, notions such as freedom and dignity become superfluous.

Brain Evolution and Behavior Evolution

22 In Chapter 21 we stressed the importance of viewing behavior in an evolutionary perspective. In this chapter we shall consider methods for doing this, as well as the difficulties that can be encountered. We shall emphasize two lines of inquiry:

1. What trends can we see in the evolution of brains in animals, including humans?
2. What trends are evident in the evolution of behavior? It is quite possible that some of these trends can be related to brain development.

The Study of Evolution and Its Relevance to Behavior

22·1 In tracing the evolution of structures, such as bones or teeth, there may be a fossil record with which to document evolutionary changes. Commonly there are gaps in the record, however, and we are forced to speculate. When we study the evolution of the brain, we face the problem of inadequate fossil evidence, since brains are soft tissue and seldom fossilize before they have decomposed. Some skulls did fossilize, however, and have endured to the present.

When we try to trace the evolution of behavior patterns, we are challenged by the fact that, except for a few fossilized footprints and worm burrows, we have no fossil evidence of behavior and therefore must use comparative studies of the behavior of living forms to make inferences about the evolution of behavior.

How Animal Life Is Believed to Have Evolved Environmental conditions capable of supporting multicellular life probably came into existence 600 to 1200 million years ago. Evidence that multicellular life did appear on the earth at least 500 million years ago has been found in fossilized rocks.

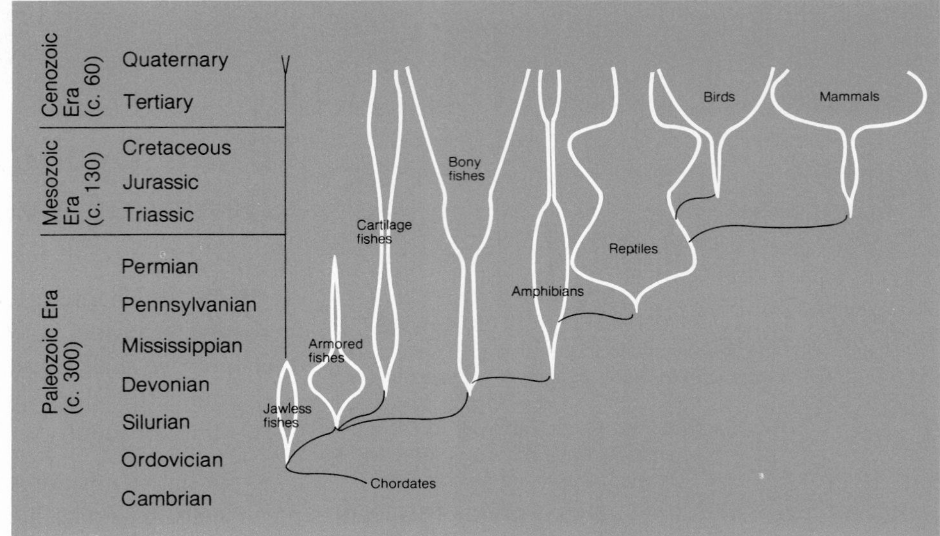

Fig. 22•1 A highly simplified scheme depicting the evolution of vertebrates. The horizontal variations in the width of the configuration for each class represent the changing number of species existing at a particular time. The numbers in parentheses give the estimated duration of each geologic era in millions of years. (Adapted from Simpson, 1949)

Eventually a wide diversity of life forms appeared in the ancient oceans (Figure 22•1). Sharklike animals with skeletons of cartilage evolved; they were followed by bony fish, some of whom successfully migrated into fresh water.

The land was devoid of life for a long time, although both vertebrates and invertebrates thrived in the water. The appearance of amphibians (which probably evolved from animals similar to our modern-day lung fish) was a giant step in evolution. Amphibians such as frogs are able to function both in water and on land. They are, however, only moderately successful as land animals because they must remain close to water in order to reproduce. (Amphibian eggs are laid in the water, where they develop into aquatic forms such as tadpoles.)

Another important step in the evolution of land animals was the development of the reptilian amniotic egg, which provided nourishment for the embryo on land and prevented it from drying out even in warm and dry environments. Modern-day reptiles may seem to have modest learning abilities and limited behavioral repertoires, but reptiles served a very important role in evolution as precursors of the birds—animals that developed feathers and usable wings approximately 150 million years ago (Figure 22•2).

Reptiles also gave rise to mammals; this in turn led to the high level of brain complexity and organization seen in humans. This last life form has been highly successful, adapting to virtually every climate and ecological niche in the world and reproducing at a high rate.

How Do We Study Evolutionary Development? There are two basic ways to study the evolutionary development of a particular characteristic. We can study either (1) the fossil record, to learn how that characteristic appeared at different stages in evolutionary history or (2) various living creatures to see the contemporary form of the characteristic.

The study of a particular characteristic in living creatures can involve either closely related animals or animals specially selected with reference to the characteristic. When we study closely related animals, we can look for similarities and differences in the characteristic—similarities because of the close genetic kinship and differences because each form has adapted to a particular ecological niche. When we study specially selected animals, we can compare those that have a certain characteristic with those that do not, or we can assess the effects of the characteristic in animals that have it to varying degrees. For example, some anatomists claim that bird brains have no **neocortex** (the type of brain tissue believed necessary for a high level of learning and adaptive behavior). Mammals do have a neocortex, but in widely varying amounts. We could thus inquire into the behavioral importance of neocortical evolution by studying a variety of carefully selected living animals.

Because fossil records are incomplete for soft tissues such as the brain and the circulatory system, evolution of structural changes must be studied by comparing living forms. Many years ago, college biology majors and premedical students commonly took a course in comparative anatomy in which they studied various systems (such as the circulatory system and the nervous system) in frogs, mud-puppies, and cats, because these three life forms were thought to represent distinct stages of evolutionary complexity and perhaps stages in the evolutionary development of these systems. Such a practice may be a useful teaching device, but we must remember that cats did not evolve from present-day mud-puppies, which, in turn, did not evolve from present-day frogs. In fact, no living species has evolved from any other living species, although two species may have a common ancestor.

The evolutionary history of the horse is well known and demonstrates the existence of trends in evolutionary history and the use of the fossil record to document that history (Figure 22•3). Specialists in the paleontology of the horse have expended much effort in studying and arranging the fossilized remains of horses in an attempt to show the evolutionary pathways by which the horse reached its present status. An early ancestor of the modern horse was a small animal that is believed to have walked on feet having five toes. Apparently, during the last 65 million years, four toes on each foot became mere vestiges, and the horse came to walk on only one toe. The reduction in number of toes was accompanied by a general increase in the size of the animal. The horse achieved its present size during the last few million years.

There has been much speculation about the selection pressures that favored the development of a large one-toed horse. Such a horse may have been less vulnerable to predators, especially if it lived in open country where speed could be used. Perhaps the one-toed hoof added speed and hence had survival advantage.

Fig. 22•2 The study of evolution has traditionally included attempts to find the missing links that mark the evolutionary transition from one life form to another. The fossil animal *Archaeopteryx* appears to be a transition form between reptiles and birds. The teeth, claws, and bones (especially in the long tail) are reptilelike, but impressions of feathers also were found in the fossil remains. (National Museums of Canada)

Homology and Analogy Soon after Darwin's work appeared, many people began to assess animal behavior in terms of the **phylogenetic** history of the animal. The

Types of fossil horses found in the western United States			
Period	Epoch	Forefoot	Hind foot
Age of Man (Quaternary)	Recent	 One toe Splints of 2d and 4th digits	 One toe Splints of 2d and 4th digits
	Pleistocene		
Age of Mammals (Tertiary)	Pliocene		
	Miocene	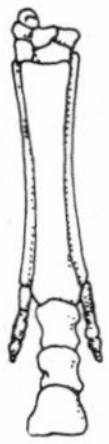 Three toes Side toes not touching the ground	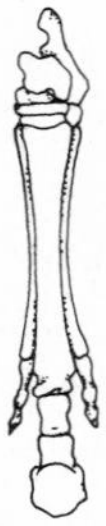 Three toes Side toes not touching the ground
	Oligocene	 Three toes Side toes touching the ground Splint of 5th digit	 Three toes Side toes touching the ground
	Eocene	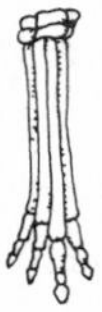 Four toes	 Three toes Splints of 1st and 5th digit
	Paleocene	Hypothetical ancestors with five toes on each foot	
Age of Reptiles	Cretaceous Jurassic Triassic		

Fig. 22•3 Although mutations produce random changes in organisms, certain trends in structure have been observed, possibly because of long-lasting selection pressures exerted by the environment. The evolution of the horse's foot shows definite trends in structural change. (Hanson, 1972)

phylogeny of an animal is its history of development from related species, usually traced over very long periods of time. Closely related animals were expected to show similar behavioral patterns, although any pattern might evolve somewhat differently in various animals. The same similarities exist in anatomical structure. For example, in Figure 22•4 we can see many similarities in the bone structure

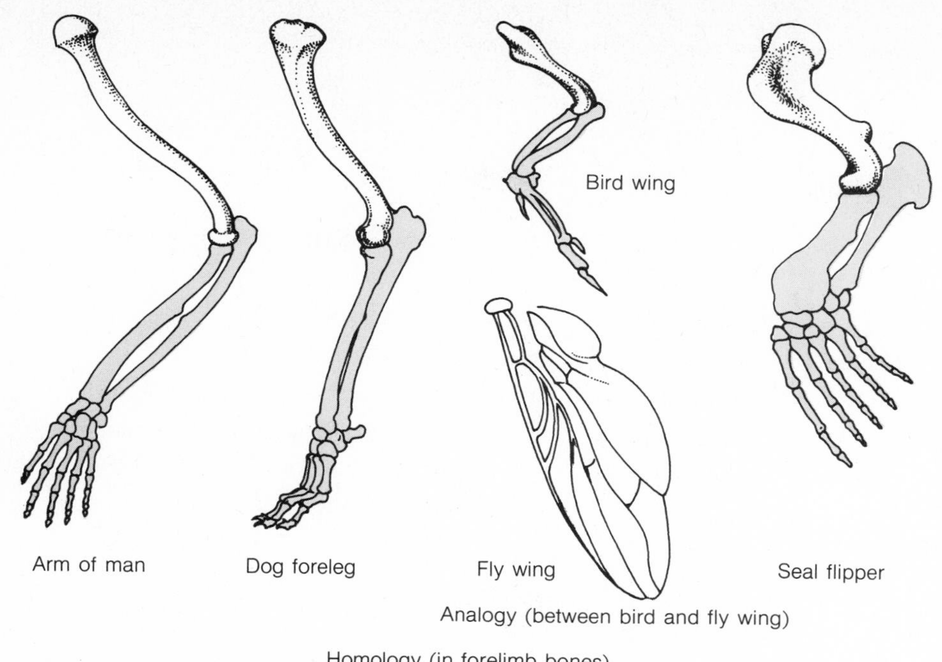

Fig. 22·4 The forelimbs of the four vertebrates depicted are composed of *homologous* bones, each of which is believed to have evolved from the same bone in a common ancestral form. Each forelimb has become specialized for a different kind of behavior. Although the fly wing and the bird wing both make flight possible, the two forms are *analogous* but not homologous, because the two structures have no common evolutionary heritage. (Wilson et al., 1973)

of various forelimbs (man, dog, bird, and seal). When a particular bone appears in all these life forms, it is said to be homologous, meaning that the bone can be traced to precisely the same bone in some ancestral life form. Nevertheless, the bone appears in slightly different shapes in these life forms, indicating evolutionary divergence.

The fly wing and the bird wing have some superficial similarities, but their evolutionary origins are distinct. They are said to be analogous, not homologous, and are the product of evolutionary convergence.

The early anatomists were impressed by the similiarities they saw in bone structure and in other characteristics of organisms; evolutionary theory explained these similarities. Bone structures are similar because the organisms evolved from similar ancestral forms. The differences are due to adaptation of the various forms to different environments. The paddlelike flipper of the seal enables it to adjust to an existence including both land and sea. The foreleg of the dog enables it to live successfully on dry land and to run down fast-moving prey.

Two Theories That Relate Behavior to Evolution Two theories of evolution have left an imprint on the study of animal behavior, including that of humans. Jean Lamarck's theory has been generally rejected, yet it still seems to influence some of the work done in comparative psychology in the twentieth century, particularly in ranking animals on a scale of intelligence. Charles Darwin's theory was generally accepted and provides the best model for the comparative study of behavior.

Classification Schemes

The beginning student in biology may look upon the animal kingdom as a buzzing mass of confusion, but closer inspection reveals some order in the relationships of the 1 million or so species described. For example, because of certain characteristics, the species *Homo sapiens* belongs to a genus *(Homo),* family *(Hominidae),* order *(Primates),* class *(Mammalia),* and phylum *(Chordata)* as well as to other subdivisions (Table 22A·1).

Carolus Linnaeus, an eighteenth-century Swedish botanist, is regarded as the originator of modern scientific classification of plants and animals. His classification, however, was often based on superficial resemblances and external characteristics. A bat, for example, was classed as a bird because it seemed birdlike in shape and behavior; a whale was classed as a fish because it seemed fishlike in shape and habitat. When Charles Darwin imparted a firm foundation to evolutionary theory over 100 years ago, classification came to be based on common evolutionary descent. In this system, bats and whales are classed as mammals not only because they have similar characteristics, but also because these traits are homologous, being derived from common ancestors.

An important inference is made from the fact that there are at present very few marine mammals compared with the number of living land mammals. We assume that marine mammals such as the whale have evolved from a stock of land mammals and that land mammals did not evolve from marine mammals.

Table 22A·1 Classification of Humans in the Animal Kingdom

CLASSIFICATION	NAME	CRITERIA
Kingdom	Animal	They are living forms not classified as plants.
Phylum	Chordates	They have an embryonic elastic rod of cells as part of the internal skeleton.
Subphylum	Vertebrates	Their adults have a vertebral column.
Superclass	Tetrapods	They are four-limbed.
Class	Mammals	Their young are suckled.
Subclass	Theria	Their young are liveborn.
Intraclass	Eutheria	They do not have pouches like kangaroos.
Order	Primates	They have flat nails, among other special traits.
Suborder	Anthropoidea	They are tailless and either semierect or erect.
Family	Hominidae	They are erect and have large brains.
Genus	Homo	They have modern brain structure and the largest relative brain size.
Species	sapiens	They are the only living species of the genus.

(Lerner, 1968, p. 18)

Lamarck: Behavior Alters Inheritance Lamarck saw life as a single evolutionary ladder ascending from simple, one-celled life forms through the more complex, many-celled life forms to the most complex life form—humans. He thought that if an animal became extinct, its place on the ladder of life would soon be filled because of the ascending evolution of a less complex species.

How do animals adapt to their environment, or ecological niche? The long neck of the giraffe, for example, enables it to browse on the leaves of trees, a food source not systematically used by other animals in the same environment. Lamarck thought that at some time in the past, ancestors of the present-day giraffe began to stretch their necks to eat tree leaves, lengthening their neck muscles and bones, and that these acquired characteristics (eating leaves off trees and longer necks) were somehow passed on to their offspring. The offspring, in turn, stretched even farther, until long-necked giraffes evolved. At each level of the evolutionary ladder, special anatomical characteristics appear as a result of animals emitting certain kinds of behavior that satisfy specific demands of the environment.

Lamarck's theory seemed to provide two important guidelines for the study of evolution. First, the level of complexity reached during evolution was simply a function of the animal's position on the "Great Ladder of Life." He provided a one-dimensional yardstick for assessing the stages of evolutionary development reached.

Second, he accounted for the cause of trends in evolutionary development. The environment in which an animal lives induces the animal to behave in a certain fashion (for example, stretching its neck). These behaviors and attendant changes in structure are then inherited and influence future generations of animals living in that same environment.

Lamarck's theory was ultimately rejected primarily because (1) fossil evidence indicated that there were many parallel lines of evolution, not a single line, and (2) the study of genetics has shown that acquired characteristics (changes in the animal during its lifetime) cannot be inherited.

Darwin observed the many varieties of finches on the Galapagos Islands, off the coast of Peru (the mainland has only one species—the seed-eating ground finch). He attributed these differences to the different selective pressures exerted by the ecological situations where the finches settled on the islands. Six species remained as ground finches—mostly seed-eating, though one adapted to feeding on the prickly pear cactus—while eight species became tree finches, some of which are insectivores. The species are differentiated primarily by their beak shape and size. (Courtesy of the American Museum of Natural History)

Darwin: Inheritance Selects Behavior Charles Darwin spent five years (1831–1836) sailing around the world on the H.M.S. *Beagle*. As ship's naturalist, his mission was to study the flora, fauna, and geologic features of the lands encountered during the journey. Both Darwin's collections of rocks, animals, and plants and his voluminous journals of observations provided the documenting evidence for the theory of evolution he proposed more than twenty years later.

The types of animals Darwin saw on the islands off the coast of South America varied slightly from island to island, but they all seemed to have distinct South American characteristics. To account for these differences and similarities, Darwin (1859) hypothesized that one species can evolve into another. He did not completely reject Lamarck's theory that changes within animal types come about through behavior; but he proposed another possibility, the theory of **natural selection,** based on principles of population growth stated by Thomas Malthus, a British economist.

Malthus wrote that animals have the ability to reproduce to a population level well beyond that for which the environment can provide food, thus resulting in fierce competition for sustenance. Darwin was well informed about the nature of animal populations and quickly surmised that animals particularly well suited to a certain environment survive at the expense of less well-suited animals. For example, a change in the shape of its bill might enable a bird to exploit a food source more effectively. A cockroach that could run faster than other cockroaches might well survive longer than the others and therefore be more likely to reproduce.

Darwin was also well aware that reproduction is vital. The life forms that have the most reproductive success become dominant; natural selection favors their survival. For example, in the case of giraffes, although giraffes with necks of various lengths continually appear, the environment maintains selection pressures favoring long-necked individuals. Behaviors that enable organisms to survive until they are sexually mature and then to pass their genes on to the next generation are truly adaptive.

Darwin saw evolution as essentially a blind process. He did not have the benefit of the findings of modern **genetics,** yet he understood that somehow changes in structures must arise spontaneously. We now know that such changes can be produced by random genetic **mutations** (a relatively permanent change in the genetic material). For example, a mutation producing larger bones is just as likely to occur as one producing smaller bones. The selection pressures of the environment decide which mutation, if either, survives. Most mutations are lethal and mutant life forms die either before birth or before they become capable of reproduction. Such mutations are lost from the gene pool. Evolutionary change results because mutations sometimes confer survival advantages on the mutant organism.

For example, some strains of insects have developed immunity—a genetic mutation—to certain insecticides. A resistant strain of insect can thus develop and reproduce in an environment in which other strains die out, and so the genes supplying the survival trait increase in frequency in the gene pool. Similarly, as genes favoring long necks increased in the gene pool, giraffes assumed their present configuration.

Evolution of the Brain

22·2 We do not know the details of either gross or microscopic anatomy of the brains of fossil animals. The few natural casts of the brain cavity that have been unearthed have told us little about details of the brain. However, by filling the brain cavity of a complete fossil skull with material such as sand, we can estimate the volume and weight of the brain that once filled the cavity.

As in trying to answer questions about the evolution of behavior, we can examine fossil animals and living representatives of now-extinct animals that are believed to have played an essential role in evolution. From these studies we find certain trends in the evolution of the brain:

1. Brain weight tends to increase relative to body weight.
2. Primitive vertebrates, it is estimated, had enough nerve cells (**neurons**) in the brain to run the body. During the course of evolution there has been an increase in numbers of nerve cells above the basic amount.
3. There has been a selective increase in certain areas of the brain, especially the **neocortex.**

Students of evolution conclude that these brain changes have in some way made possible the diversity of learning ability found in higher primates, especially human beings.

Relationship of Brain Weight to Body Weight For many years a small group of biologists have worked on the problem of the size of the parts of an animal in relation to the size of the whole animal. The study of these relationships is called allometry. Allometric data have shown that if the logs of the weights of a particular type of organ from various animals are plotted against the logs of the weights of the bodies from which the organs came, a straight-line function results. In other words, the more a body weighs, the more an organ from that body weighs. We could also call this a positive correlation.

H. J. Jerison (1969) plotted the log of the brain weight of a variety of vertebrates against the log of their body weights. As shown in Figure 22•5, the straight-line function holds, but it is not of the same magnitude for mammals and birds as for reptiles and fishes. For any given body weight, mammals and birds tend to have larger brains than reptiles and fishes. That is to say, the formula for deriving the relationship between brain size and body weight differs in different animal classes.

By measuring the brain cavities of fossil animals, Jerison was able to study how brain size may have changed over evolutionary history. To discover whether mammalian brain size changed relative to body during the course of evolution, Jerison (1961) plotted log brain weight against log body weight for fossil mammals from the Eocene period (40 to 60 million years ago) and from the Oligocene period (28 to 33 million years ago) and for mammals now living. For all three groups, log brain weight was related to log body weight in straight-line functions having identical slopes. However, during the course of mammalian evolution the straight

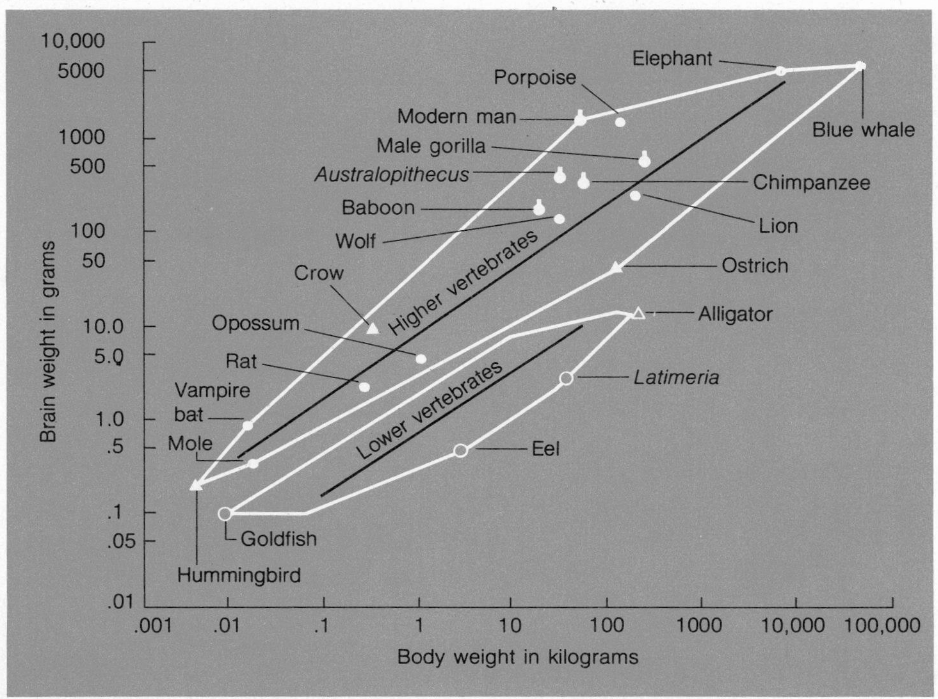

Fig. 22•5 The relationship between brain weight and body weight in higher vertebrates (mammals and birds) and lower vertebrates (reptiles and fish). The white lines enclose the data points, and the black lines indicate the best fit for the data points. (Jerison, 1969)

line moved upward on the graph, indicating an evolutionary trend for brain size to increase relative to body weight.

Jerison (1969) also measured the size of the brain case in fossilized dinosaur skulls. He then attempted to estimate the body weight of these animals from scale models and other available information. When he plotted log brain weight against log body weight, the resulting straight-line function formed an extension of the function line for living reptiles. This evidence means that dinosaur brains were not unusually small, but were exactly the size we would expect for a reptile of that body weight.

Increase in brain size is probably most noticeable in human evolution, and considerable functional importance has been attached to this finding. Figure 22•6 illustrates differences in brain size and skull shape in the living gorilla, in *Homo sapiens* and in two types of fossil man. Note that the gorilla's brain case makes up a relatively small part of the skull, which shows massive brow ridges and a sloping forehead. The *Australopithecus africanus* skull belongs to a type of early human who lived approximately 600,000 to 2 million years ago. His mean, or average, brain size was slightly less, and his body size very much less, than those of a gorilla. *Homo erectus*, represented by forms such as *Peking man* and *Java man*, lived between 500,000 and 1 million years ago. The skull shape is similar to that of the modern human, although the brain is slightly smaller.

Sometime in the last 100,000 years (a short time in the evolutionary history of life), the human skull attained its present shape and the human brain its present size—approximately 1300 milliliters (ml). On an evolutionary time scale, the increase in human brain size has been explosive. It is tempting to speculate that

Fig. 22•6 Comparison of skull morphology and cranial capacity for the gorilla and for three types of human. These forms are not necessarily in a direct line of evolutionary descent, but they do illustrate some of the phases that have appeared in human evolution. (Pilbeam, 1972)

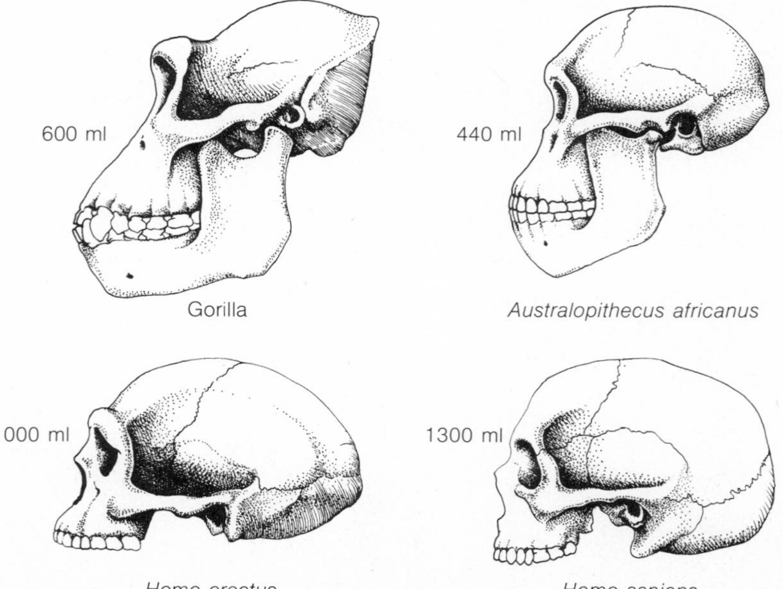

the intellectual capacities of humans are related to this extraordinary increase in amount of brain tissue.

Surplus Neurons and Learning Ability Jerison (1963, 1969) has also studied a variety of living mammals in order to estimate the number of neurons in the brain required to carry on the basic functions of integrating sensory information and controlling body movements and activities of the viscera (internal organs such as heart and kidneys). From determinations of number of neurons in the brains of primitive mammals (for example, insectivores such as the tree shrew) Jerison expected to be able to estimate how many neurons would be needed to run the body in advanced mammals such as primates.

He found that many primates have more neurons than he estimated were needed to run the body; he called this surplus "extra" neurons. The modern human has over 8 million surplus neurons, while gorillas and chimpanzees have about 3 million. Figure 22•7 shows a clear trend for the number of surplus neurons to increase as the size of the brain increases.

The superiority of primate learning performance over that of other animals, and of human learning performance over that of other primates, is often attributed to the huge increase in tissue (made up of neurons) of the **cerebrum**—specifically the *cortex*, which is the thin outer covering of the cerebrum. Figure 22•8 shows several brains that differ in complexity. (This series of animals does not represent

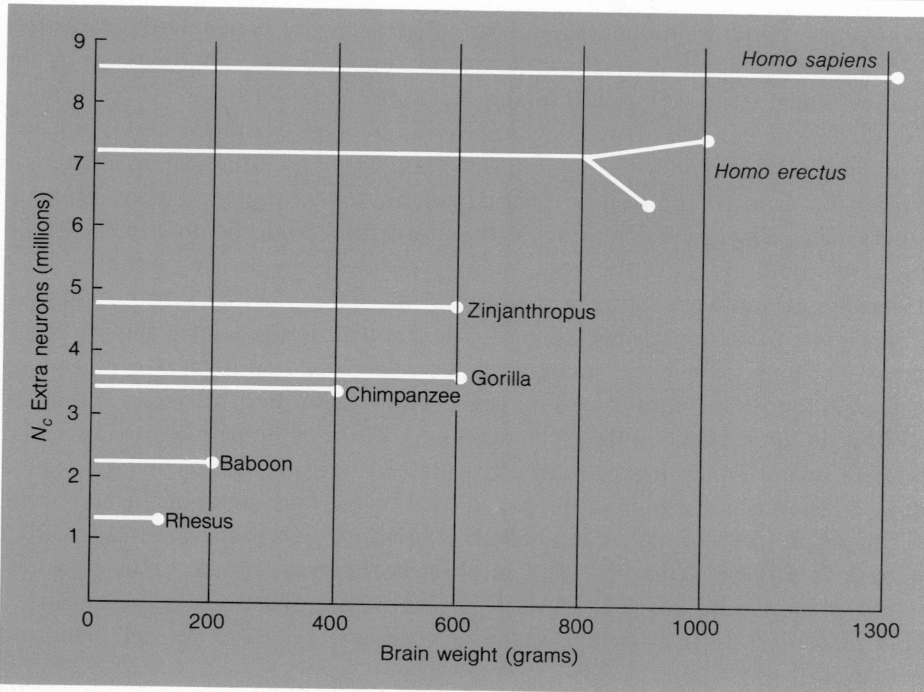

Fig. 22•7 The number of extra neurons possessed by the brains of various life forms. To calculate these, Jerison first estimated both the total number of neurons in the brain of each animal and the hypothetical number of neurons required to run the body. (After Jerison, 1963)

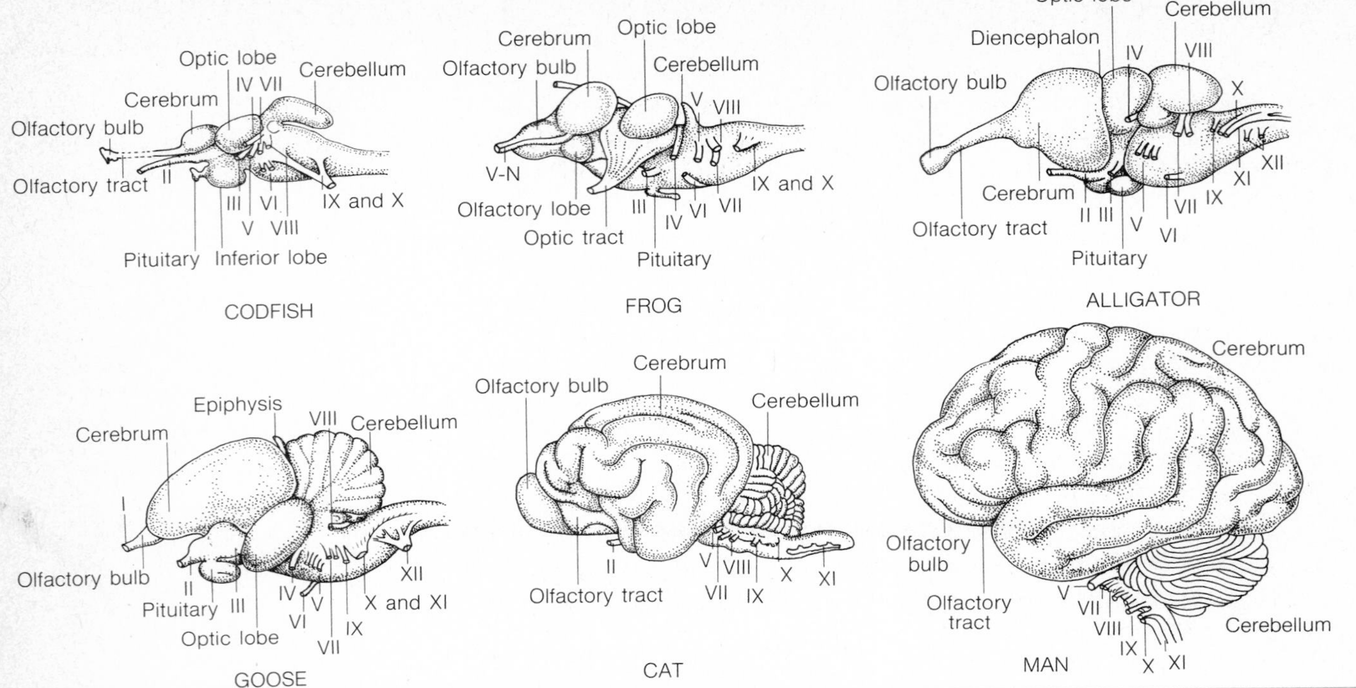

Fig. 22·8 Representative vertebrate brains (not drawn to scale). Structures such as the cerebrum and cerebellum appear in each form, even though the various life forms have evolved along very different pathways. (Truex and Carpenter, 1964)

a phylogenetic descent.) At one extreme is the human brain, which is characterized by a proportionately immense cerebrum that is highly convoluted (intricately folded), because of an abundance of cortical tissue. At the other extreme is the codfish, which has a very small, smooth cerebrum.

When brains of insectivores such as tree shrews are examined and compared with human brains and with the supposed brain size of hypothetical insectivores as large as humans, certain trends in basic brain anatomy become obvious. Humans have smaller olfactory bulbs (which carry information from the nose to the brain) than we would expect if they were simply oversized insectivores, but they have 156 times as much neocortex as we would expect (Stephan and Andy, 1969).

There are some remarkable similarities in brain structure among the life forms shown in Figure 22·8, even though they have developed on distinct evolutionary pathways for a few hundred million years. The codfish, frog, alligator, and goose all have an optic lobe (visible in the drawings), which is the part of the brain that receives neural inputs from the eye. In cats and humans, the optic lobe (called optic tectum) is not seen because it is covered by the large lobes of the cerebrum. All these animals also have a cerebellum. This structure's shape differs somewhat in each animal, but it has the same location in the brain and, as far as we know, serves to coordinate and refine muscle activity. Brain structures seem to show a kind of conservatism in nature. Once something develops, it appears over and over again.

Evolution of Behavior

22•3 Students of the evolution of behavior have proceeded in ways similar to those of paleontologists interested in the evolution of structure. They have looked for similarities and differences in behavior that would dictate whether an animal should be classified in one category or another. They have also compared these categories with categories based on structural similarities and differences, and they have searched for transitional forms of behavior.

Research on the evolution of behavior has concentrated on three questions: Are homologous behavior patterns similar in animals that are closely related phylogenetically? How does the behavior enable an animal to survive in the environment? What trends are apparent in the evolution of behavior?

Homologous Behavior Patterns Lacking fossil evidence, the student of the evolution of behavior must turn to a comparative study of living forms to try to identify homologous behavior. The student must look for similar forms of behavior and attempt to determine whether they occur under similar situations, are triggered by similar stimuli, and result from similar motivations. Just as the comparative anatomist finds structural similarities among closely related species, so the comparative psychologist can expect to find corresponding behavioral similarities among closely related species. In fact, the closer the relationship between two species, the more similar their structures and behaviors should be.

Figure 22•9 shows a simplified phylogenetic tree of the even-toed ungulates (hoofed mammals). The animals on the right side of the figure are ruminants (cud-chewing animals), those on the left are not. Cud-chewing behavior and the anatomical characteristics that accompany it emerged in one line of evolutionary development, but not in the other. We expect to find more anatomical and behavioral similarities between giraffes and deer than between giraffes and hippopotamuses when the appropriate observations are made.

As the paleontologist studies bones (such as the horse's foot presented in Figure 22•3) in order to piece together an animal's evolutionary history, so the student of behavioral evolution searches for units of behavior from which to draw conclusions about how an animal's behavior evolved. Niko Tinbergen (1959) chose to study gulls because they are monophyletic (coming from a common line of descent) and so are likely to have behavioral as well as anatomical similarities. Figure 22•10 shows four behavioral units he found in the meeting ceremony of the herring gull. Behaviors such as these are virtually identical in all members of the same species.

The behavioral units shown in Figure 22•10 are called display behaviors. Display behaviors are species-specific and somewhat stereotyped behaviors that usually occur in a particular situation, such as during the approach of another bird. These behaviors seem to have signal value, meaning that they convey information to other birds. Tinbergen believes that display behaviors may have evolved from other types of behavior. For example, if one bird were to run from the other, it might first turn its head (facing-away behavior) in the direction it will run. It may not

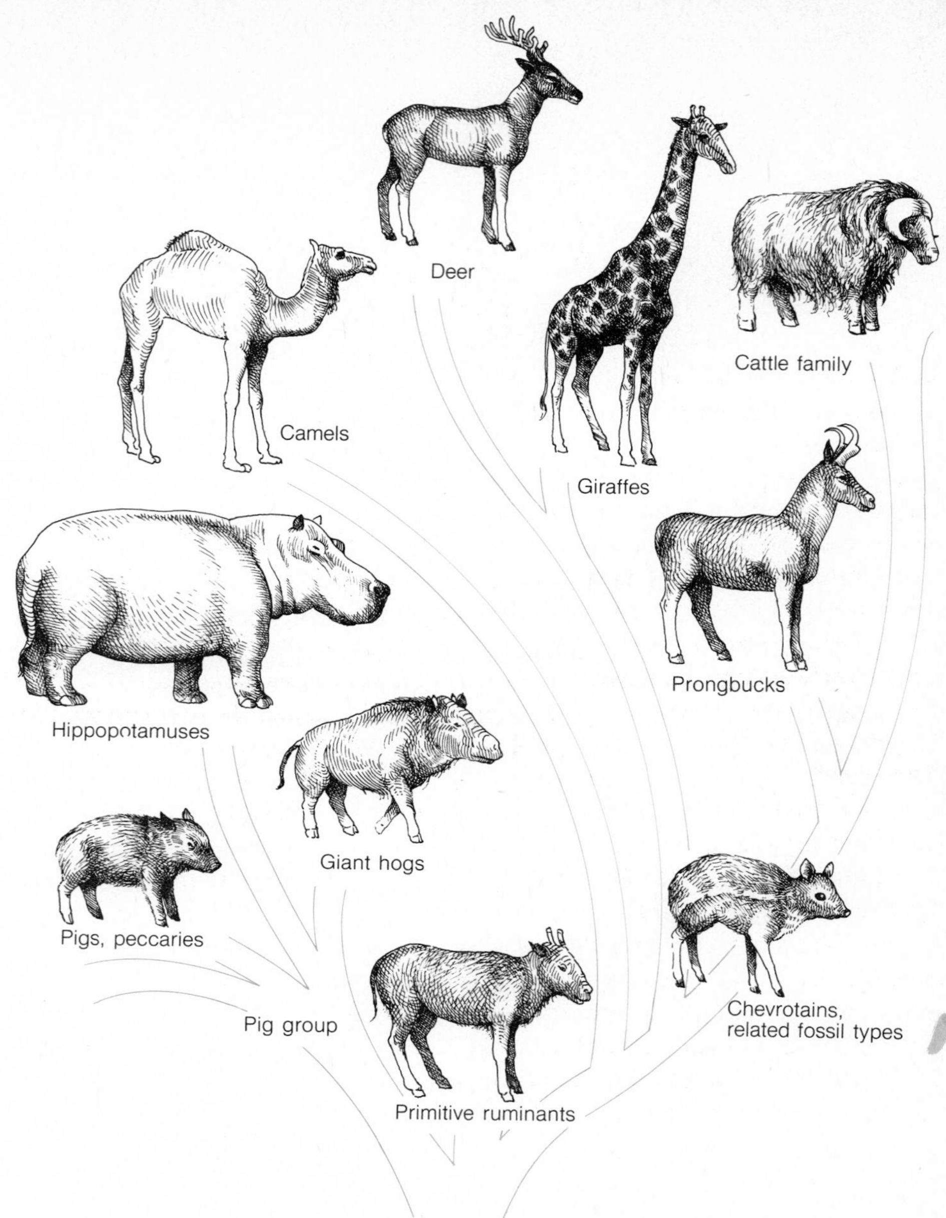

Fig. 22•9 A phylogenetic tree of the even-toed ungulates, the artiodactyls. This classification is based on anatomical as well as behavioral evidence. The animals on the right are ruminants (cud-chewing animals), but the pig group on the left is not. (Romer, 1971)

actually run away because the social behavior of gulls seems to consist of two urges: an urge to approach and interact with another bird and an urge to flee (Tinbergen, 1963).

Figure 22•11 shows facing-away behaviors in several types of gulls. The behavior is somewhat different for each species and may have become adapted to somewhat different situations by evolutionary divergence, although the behaviors all sprang from the same evolutionary origin.

Tinbergen considers these behavior patterns homologous, just as the forelimb bones shown in Figure 22•4 are homologous. Thus, when evolutionary behavioral adaptations are peeled away, the basic units of gull behavior emerge.

Survival Value of Behavior As we have seen, various species of gulls do show similarities in basic behavior patterns. Sometimes the variations in form seem to fit the environment in which the animal lives. For example, the kittiwake gull nests and rears its young high up on narrow cliffside ledges, while other gulls nest on the beach. The kittiwake shows gull-like behavior patterns, but these patterns seem strikingly modified for life in a very small space remote from predators (Cullen, 1957).

Kittiwake Behavior Kittiwake adults are remarkably tame and unresponsive to the intrusion of humans or other potential predators. In contrast, the herring gull and the black-headed gull both nest on the beach, issue alarm calls, and often attack intruders. Young herring gulls are mobile and move about the nesting area, often mingling with the young of other nesting pairs. Kittiwake young, however, are immobile and remain in their nests. If herring gull eggs are placed in kittiwake nests, the eggs hatch normally and the young are accepted by the parents, but the young herring gulls come to grief by wandering over the precipice of the cliff. Herring gull chicks are camouflaged from predators with down of a buff ground color and a pattern of irregular dots, but the down of kittiwake young has a conspicuous silver sheen.

Beach-living gulls usually build simple nests from a small amount of vegetation that they collect. Kittiwake gulls bring mud to the steep cliffs and tramp it down to make a platform, thus creating more nesting space. Their young do not exhibit the characteristic pumping (up and down) movement of the head used by other gulls to attract their parents to come and feed them. Kittiwake parents do not need to be attracted to the nest, since they have no place else to land but on the nest. Beach-living gulls must learn to recognize their young, which wander around and often become interspersed with the young of other birds. Kittiwake young, however, do not leave the nest, and so their parents do not need to learn to recognize their young from among the young of other parents. Behavior patterns, like anatomy and physiology, seem appropriate to the animal's ecological niche.

Significance of Eggshell Removal Within the first few hours after the hatching of a black-headed gull chick, the parent bird grasps the broken eggshell in its beak, flies or walks to a place outside the nest, and drops the eggshell. Tinbergen and his co-workers (1962) were interested in the evolutionary significance of this relatively simple behavior, which can be completed in seconds, is done only a few times each season, and is not a universal behavior among gulls. Kittiwake gull eggshells

Fig. 22•10 The meeting ceremony of the herring gull: (*a*) oblique call of male, (*b*) mew call, (*c*) choking, (*d*) facing away. Behaviors such as these are virtually identical in all members of the same species. (Tinbergen, 1959)

Fig. 22·11 Examples of a homologous behavior (facing away) in three species of gulls. (*a*) Lower bird faces away while other bird jabs (kittiwake); (*b*) bird on left faces away while other bird adopts aggressive upright stance (common gull); (*c*) both female (left) and male face away (black-headed gull). Presumably the species variations in this behavior are due to a slightly different evolutionary history for each species. (Tinbergen, 1959)

are not removed from the nest but are usually trampled or kicked out of the nest during the normal course of activity.

Tinbergen demonstrated from careful observation and experimentation that eggshell removal by the black-headed gull has adaptive significance. Gull eggs are normally camouflaged, but the camouflage pattern is compromised after hatching and so the eggshell is more easily seen by predators. The kittiwake gull, on its cliffside nesting site, has no predators, but the beach-nesting black-headed gull has several, including other black-headed gulls. In addition, herring gulls sometimes steal black-headed gull eggs, and carrion crows and foxes may come looking for food.

Why isn't the eggshell removed immediately after hatching? Tinbergen speculated that eggshell removal is a compromise behavior that seems to provide maximum protection for the young. If the parent were to leave the nest to remove the eggshell immediately after an egg hatched, the wet newborn chick would be vulnerable to being swallowed by other black-headed gulls nesting nearby. Once the chick dries, however, it becomes harder to swallow, and its dry down provides some protective coloration.

Tinbergen assumed that the antipredator behaviors of the black-headed gull evolved under certain selection pressures from the environment. If there is too much disparity between the behavior of an animal and the demands of the environment, that animal will perish.

Trends in the Evolution of Behavior What kinds of selection pressures are exerted during the evolution of behavioral capabilities? Improvement in learning ability ought to be favored—this would mean improvement not only in speed of learning, but also in the type of learning the animal is capable of. E. L. Thorndike (1911) studied various kinds of animals and concluded that although they may differ in speed of learning or in what they learn, the basic principles of learning and possibly the basic learning mechanisms are the same for all animals.

Reversal Learning and Probability Learning M. E. Bitterman (1965), who has made some noteworthy comparative studies of particular kinds of learning, compared the learning abilities of fish and rats on two basic types of learning problems: reversal learning and probability learning. Bitterman found reason to question Thorndike's conclusions.

In **reversal learning** experiments the subject learns to make a response to one of two stimuli. One stimulus is designated as correct and is reinforced 100 percent of the time. When this response is well learned, the experimenter reinforces only the other stimulus. The subject must then learn to stop responding to the previously correct stimulus and respond to the new one. As soon as the subject reaches the required **criterion level of performance,** the problem is reversed again. (See Figure 22•12 for the apparatus used to train fish.)

Rats, monkeys, and pigeons make fewer and fewer errors in learning successive reversals to criterion levels. These animals seem to be learning something about the problem itself. Fish learn to reverse each time they are required to, but they do not show any improvement during successive reversals.

Improvement in reversal learning seems to be superior to lack of improvement because this response enables the subject to learn more rapidly-which situations produce **reinforcement.** In the life of an animal in the wild, food may be present for only a short time in any one place, and then the animal must find a new food source or starve.

In **probability learning** experiments, each stimulus is reinforced, according to a random schedule of reinforcement, a certain percentage of the time. Although subjects cannot learn when a particular target will be reinforced, they apparently can learn something about the ratio of reinforcement for each target.

The beaks of the birds and their behavior are adapted to each other and to their needs. The curved bill of the parakeet is good for cracking seeds, for gouging out chunks of fruit, and for climbing. The shoebill has a flat, serrated beak that aids in holding frogs. The rufous hornbill can use his beak to protect himself against marauding monkeys and snakes. (San Diego Zoo Photos)

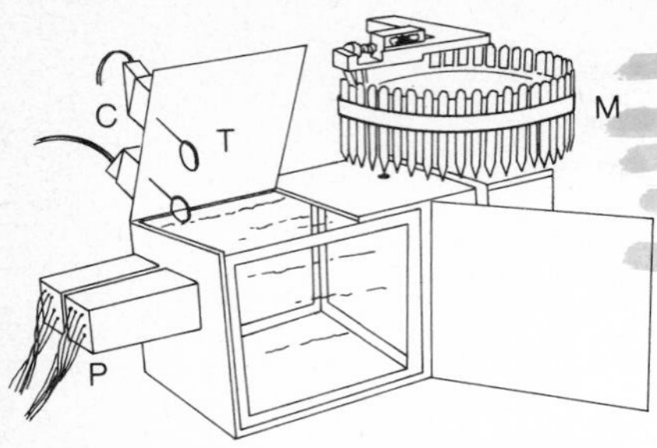

Fig. 22•12 The experimental apparatus used by Bitterman to study learning in fish. When the fish presses on the correct target (T), the magazine (M) dispenses a live worm into the water. Phonograph cartridges (C) hold the targets and register contacts with them. The projectors (P) enable the experimenter to project a color onto the target. (Bitterman, 1965)

Fish tend to respond on about 70 percent of the trials to the target that is reinforced 70 percent of the time (Fig. 22•13). Bitterman calls this behavior pattern *probability matching.* Rats and monkeys tend to respond on nearly all of the trials to the target that is reinforced 70 percent of the time, a response pattern Bitterman calls *probability maximizing.* If you were the subject, what would you do? A little arithmetic should convince you that maximizing is the better strategy because it provides the greater chance for reward:

Probability Matching

$(.70 \times .70) + (.30 \times .30) = .58$ probability of reward

Probability Maximizing

$(1.00 \times .70) = .70$ probability of reward

Probability maximizing seems to be a more advanced type of behavior than probability matching because it results in more reinforcement.

Bitterman concentrated on qualitative rather than quantitative differences in learning ability. He assumed that animals differ in speed of learning and concentrated his efforts on discovering whether some animals are capable of a particular kind of learning. For example, the fish Bitterman studied appeared unable to improve in reversal learning even though hundreds of trials were run.

The results of Bitterman's experiments are shown in Table 22•1; the response patterns are labeled as ratlike and fishlike, and the animals are also arranged in an order corresponding roughly to the conventional scale of complexity. (Where there were no data, no entries were made, but entries were made where—as in the

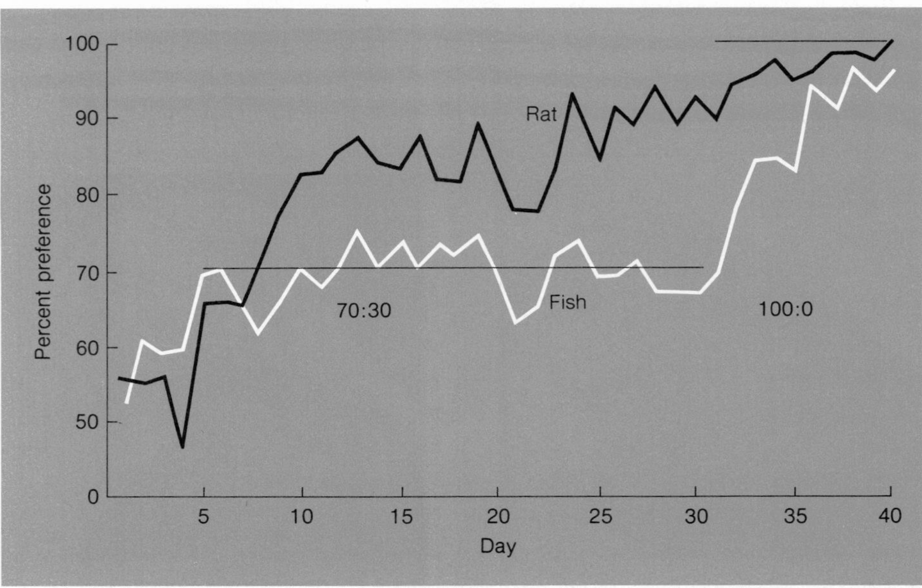

Fig. 22•13 An example of *maximizing* behavior (rat) and *matching* behavior (fish) in a visual probability task. (Bitterman, 1965)

case of the turtle—data were incomplete.) Bitterman implies that ratlike responses are superior to fishlike responses and are an evolutionary development in higher animals.

Bitterman anticipated two major criticisms of this work: (1) that only a small sample of available species were used, and (2) that the listing of animals in an assumed increasing order of complexity is too simple and, in terms of phylogenetic development, clearly incorrect (Hodos and Campbell, 1969).

> The uncontaminated linear order which now appears in the table, while undeniably esthetic, is rather embarrassing from the standpoint of the far-from-linear evolutionary relationships among the species studied; nonlinearities are perhaps to be expected as the behavioral categories are refined and as the range of tests is broadened. (Bitterman, 1965, p. 409)

In the eleven years since the table was published (largely for illustrative purposes), there have been some changes in the findings, as Bitterman expected. In particular, under a limited set of conditions, goldfish and mouthbreeders do show progressive improvement in reversal, although the changes take a rather specialized form. Furthermore, turtles have been found to show progressive improvement in reversal learning on visual as well as spatial problems (Bitterman, 1975).

Nevertheless, Bitterman's work has produced irrefutable evidence that animals do differ in how they learn. The problem is to relate these differences to the level of evolutionary complexity.

Learning Sets As we learned in Chapter 10, a learning set is a condition of being prepared to learn in a particular way. Having solved several problems of the same general type, many animals behave as though they have learned the principle underlying the problems.

Harry Harlow (1949) studied the formation of learning sets. In this task the subject is presented with two objects on a tray and must discover which object

Table 22·1 Behavior of a Variety of Animals in Four Classes of Problems That Differentiate Ratlike and Fishlike Behavior

	SPATIAL PROBLEMS		VISUAL PROBLEMS	
ANIMAL	REVERSAL	PROBABILITY	REVERSAL	PROBABILITY
Monkey	R	R	R	R
Rat	R	R	R	R
Pigeon	R	R	R	F
Turtle	R	R	F	F
Decorticated rat	R	R	F	F
Fish	F	F	F	F
Cockroach	F	F	—	—
Earthworm	F	—	—	—

NOTE: F (fishlike) indicates random probability matching and failure of progressive improvement in habit reversal. R (ratlike) indicates maximizing or nonrandom probability matching and progressive improvement in habit reversal. Transitional regions are connected by the stepped line. The brackets group animals that have not yet been differentiated by these problems. (Bitterman, 1965, p. 408)

The Desert Environment As an Example of Selection Pressures

Few environments are as apparently hostile to life as the desert. Daytime air temperatures sometimes reach 120°F., with much higher temperatures at the ground surface. The extreme heat, burning sun, and low humidity promote excessive loss of body fluids though perspiration, which helps to regulate body temperature. Water is often sparsely distributed in the desert, and there are few plants to use for food, moisture, or shade. Many types of animal life that thrive in nondesert conditions would perish in the desert, which makes strong, easily identifiable demands on organisms. What structures or behaviors have evolved in desert-living animals in order for them to survive and reproduce?

The pack rat, or wood rat *(Neotoma),* a common rodent in many nondesert environments, can survive the rigors of desert existence, even though it must maintain a sizable water intake and is less tolerant of water deprivation than the common laboratory rat. One reason for the pack rat's survival in the desert is that it is nocturnal, or active at night, when desert temperatures are much lower. During the day the pack rat lies, covered with debris, in a shallow nest, in the shade of a mesquite bush or a cactus, where temperatures are lower than on the surrounding desert surface. The pack rat's most important adaptation to desert life seems to be its ability to get food and moisture from cacti in spite of their spines. (Cacti are 90 percent water, and can provide both food and water in the dry season, when other food sources fail.) In addition, the pack rat is among the few animals able to ingest and excrete the oxalic acid contained in cacti. These behavioral, anatomical, and metabolic modifications enable the pack rat to inhabit an environment in which few other animals can survive.

The pack rat can survive in the desert because of its behavioral, anatomical, and metabolic adaptations to the heat and lack of water. (San Diego Zoo Photo by Ron Garrison)

Perhaps the most dramatic example of adaptation to a desert environment is the camel, the standard beast of burden in many desert countries (Schmidt-Nielsen et al., 1956). Although the camel's hump is a distinctive physical feature, it does not play a major role in helping the camel adapt to the temperature extremes and water scarcity characteristic of the desert. Unlike most other mammals, the camel does not try to maintain its body temperature at a particular level. Rather, it allows its temperature to rise during the day as it absorbs and stores heat. At night when the desert cools, the camel radiates heat and its body temperature goes down. Similarly, the camel is able to tolerate losing large amounts of body water (approximately as much as a quarter of its body weight) and to drink that much within a relatively short time when water is available—two very useful abilities in an environment in which water sources are few and far between. Even during a maximal loss of body fluid, the camel loses relatively little water from its blood.

Such special features of desert animals probably appeared through natural selection over a long period of time, while animals without these features gradually lost out in the contest to survive and to reproduce there.

conceals a morsel of food. Since on the first trial of each learning problem, the animal has no way to know which stimulus object is correct, we expect performance to be only about 50 percent correct. On the second trial, however, since the correct answer remains the same, animals with highly proficient learning sets may perform at close to 100 percent, while animals who are not forming learning sets still have an expected error rate of 50 percent. Harlow found that over the course of hundreds of learning trials involving various problems, some animals not only learn to solve each individual problem, but also learn some general principles.

Figure 22•14 shows a family of smooth curves for performance on trial 2 of a learning-set problem. Figure 22•15 shows a simplified family tree for some of these animals. Some speculative interpretations can be made from comparison of these two figures. The higher primates—humans and the great apes (gorillas and chimpanzees)—show the highest level of performance in forming learning sets and are also the most closely related primates phylogenetically. Among the lower primates, the Old World monkeys (rhesus and mangabey) perform at an intermediate level, and the New World monkeys (spider, cebus, and squirrel) perform at a lower level. The marmoset, which is thought to be one of the most primitive monkeys, also performs learning sets at a relatively low level. The tree shrew, an insectivore that is sometimes considered similar to an ancestor of the primates, was tested over several hundred trials and seems unable to form learning sets. The laboratory rat, which is capable of learning many things, is relatively incapable of forming learning sets, but the pigeon performs very well on this task.

Thus there is some indication that learning ability is higher in animals that have evolved to a high level of complexity, particularly those—such as humans and apes—having a large brain with abundant neocortex.

In Harlow's study of learning sets, the monkey chooses either of two objects, one of which conceals some food. On the basis of the first trial, some animals quickly learn either to stay with the correct response (if they chose correctly the first time) or to switch to the other response (if they were wrong the first time). Animals who are not learning how to learn continue to choose in a random manner and to be correct only 50 percent of the time. (H. F. Harlow, University of Wisconsin Primate Laboratory)

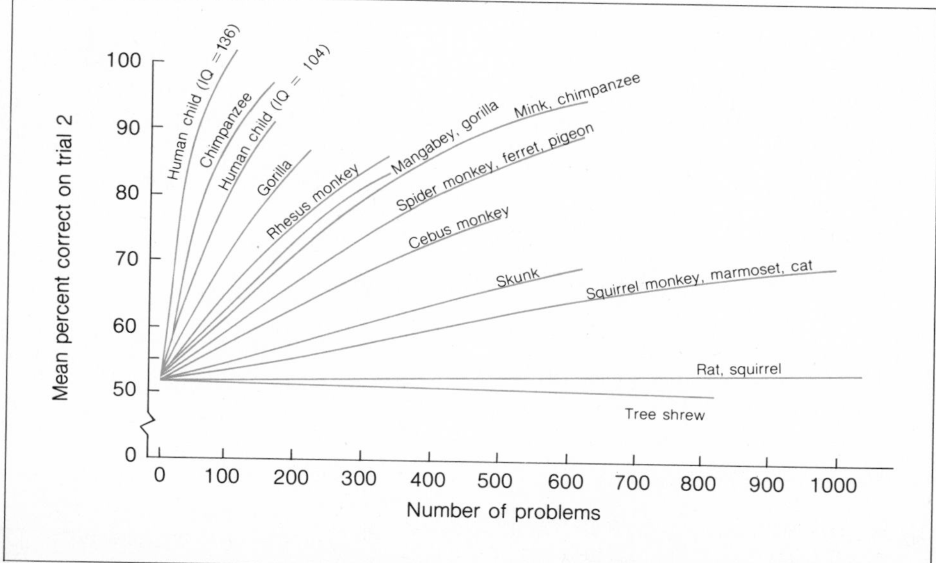

Fig. 22•14 The approximate rate of development of learning sets in mammals. This rate is sometimes roughly equated with the level of evolutionary development. (Hodos, 1970)

Fig. 22·15 A family tree of the primates. From insectivores (such as the tree shrew) to humans there is a relative increase in the size and complexity of the brain. (Romer, 1971)

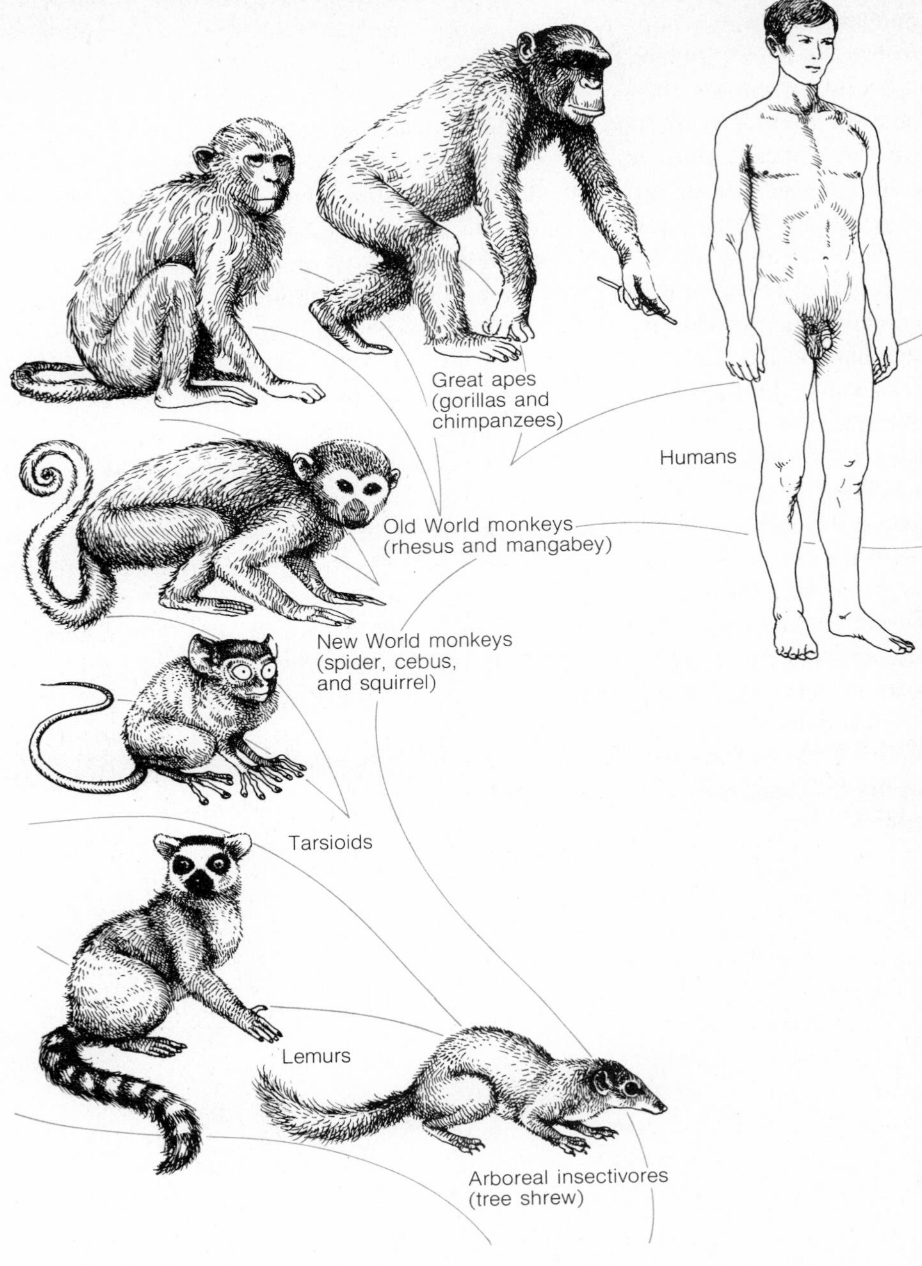

Summary

Structures or behaviors in living animals that presumably evolved from a common structure or behavior in a common ancestor are called homologous. Structures or behaviors of living organisms that are highly similar but have evolved separately in different lines of evolutionary development are called analogous. Differentiating between homologies and analogies is one of the major problems in the study of evolution and is particularly difficult in the study of behavior.

Jean Lamarck proposed that animals evolved in a straight-line manner. Less complex types thus developed into more complex types over time. Lamarck's theory has proved incorrect, yet there is a tendency to speak loosely of higher and lower animals or to look for levels of intelligence as though animals could be grouped on a Great Ladder of Life. Charles Darwin's theory and the subsequent research it generated have established that animal evolution proceeded along many separate pathways of development. Living animals are perched on their own branch of the evolutionary tree. No living animal has evolved from any other living animal.

In studying the evolution of anatomical structures, we can gather fossil remains of homologous structures in extinct animals and also observe structures of closely related species to determine the various forms these structures have taken. When studying the evolution of the brain, however, we really know only size (weight or volume) of the brain of the fossil animals and very little about the anatomy of those brains. For living and fossil animals, there is a relationship between brain size and body weight, though the exact formula differs in different animal classes. For example, mammals and birds have a larger brain per unit of body weight than reptiles and fishes. Living mammals have larger brains per unit body weight than extinct mammals. In the evolution of humans there has been a relatively rapid increase in brain size, which may account for our extraordinary intellectual ability.

The study of the evolution of behavior gets virtually no help from the fossil record, but must rely instead on a study of homologous behaviors in living forms. In herring gulls, for example, display behaviors, such as those involved in threat or greeting, seem to be highly similar in related gulls with differences possibly attributable to the different environments in which the animals evolved. In the kittiwake gull, behaviors are suitable for nesting on a cliff ledge, while the herring gull's behaviors are suitable for nesting on the beach.

Certain evolutionary trends in learning ability are discernible. It is possible that more complex animals are capable of showing improvement in reversal learning whereas less complex animals are not. In the formation of learning sets, certain mammals, such as humans and apes, learn rapidly, while other mammals, such as the rat, cannot learn from learning sets at all. It is possible that superior learning ability may relate to the number of neurons an animal has over and above the number required to run its body.

Suggested Readings

Bitterman, M. E. 1975. The comparative analysis of learning. *Science* 188: 699–709.
A summary of years of work on species differences in learning.

Cullen, E. 1957. Adaptations in the kittiwake to cliff nesting. *Ibis* 99: 275–302.
One of the most widely cited papers on the evolution of behavior, particularly in regard to how behavior fits the environmental niche of the animal.

Jerison, H. J. 1969. Brain evolution and dinosaur brains. *American Naturalist* 103: 575–88.

A fascinating study of a very difficult problem, the study of the evolution of the brain.

Schmidt-Nielsen, K. 1964. *Desert animals.* Oxford: Oxford University Press.

While concentrating on the match between environment and the physiological capabilities of animals, this book also deals with behavioral adaptations to a hostile environment.

Tinbergen, N. 1959. Comparative studies of the behaviour of gulls (Laridae): A progress report. *Behaviour* 15: 1–81.

In this paper, now a classic, the author attempts to develop the methodology for dealing with the evolution of behavior.

Genetics and Behavior

23 An organism's observable anatomical, behavioral and physiological characteristics determine its **phenotype.** These observable characteristics result from three factors: **genotype** (the genetic information an organism inherits from its parents), the environmental forces the organism encounters during its lifetime, and the interaction of its genotype with environment. A particular environmental force may affect an animal of one genotype quite differently from an animal of another genotype. Although recent research studies emphasize the importance of these genotype-environment interactions, it is difficult to quantify the influence of the genotype, the environment, and the interaction between the two on the shaping of behavior, without the techniques of modern **genetics.**

The first notable studies of genetics were done by Gregor Mendel, whose paper on the inheritance of certain characteristics in garden peas was published in 1866. Although Mendel's reports of this and other experiments were convincing, his work was virtually ignored until the early twentieth century, when Thomas Hunt Morgan began a series of extensive breeding experiments using the fruit fly *Drosophila melanogaster.* Morgan's studies established the laws of genetic inheritance. By 1913, it was known which locations on the **chromosomes** were responsible for determining certain traits. In 1915, Morgan, Sturtevant, Muller, and Bridges published *The Mechanism of Mendelian Heredity,* which outlined most of the major principles of modern genetics.

Application of the principles of genetics to the study of behavior has provided psychologists with a methodology for systematically and quantitatively studying the genetic and environmental factors that determine behavior and that influence its evolutionary development. In this chapter, we shall discuss some of this work.

Some Basic Principles of Genetics

23•1 The development and maintenance of an organism is possible only because that organism has the ability to store, retrieve, and utilize the genetic information vital to cell structure and function. This genetic information is carried by **genes** located on chromosomes inside the organism's cells. When a cell is not dividing, there is a threadlike chromatin material inside the cell nucleus. When a cell divides, the chromatin organizes into pairs of homologous chromosomes, which are held together by a connection called a centromere (Figure 23•1). Because chroma-

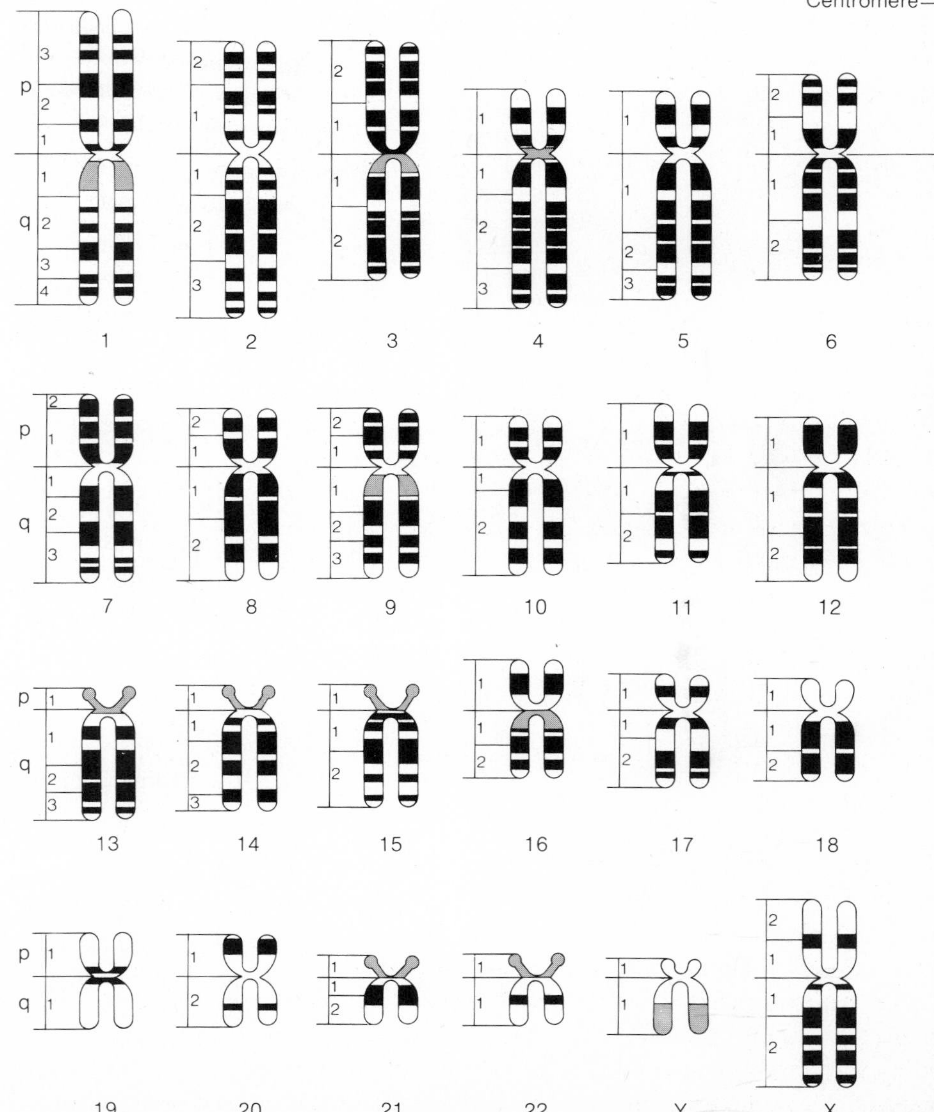

Fig. 23•1 The 23 pairs of chromosomes in humans. When chromosomes are treated with special stains, each pair absorbs the stain in a unique pattern and can thus be easily identified. The twenty-third pair of chromosomes contains the sex chromosomes, X and Y. (Rowley, 1974)

tin and chromosomes readily absorb certain stains, they may be clearly seen under a high-powered microscope.

A gene is the unit of heredity. It is located at a particular place on a chromosome and is predominantly involved in the determination of a single trait, perhaps by influencing the formation and structure of a single enzyme. Genes are composed of giant molecules of the organic substance **deoxyribonucleic acid (DNA).** These molecules have complex structures. The precise order in which the chemical components are assembled to make up these molecules carries the genetic code. A gene cannot be seen by looking through a microscope. Its presence, position, and function must be inferred from the results of careful breeding experiments.

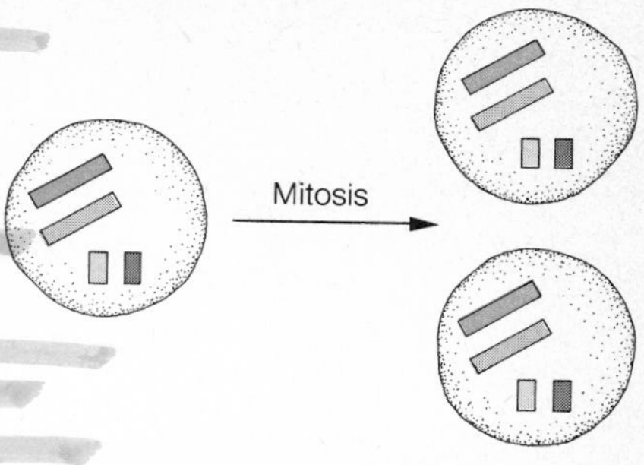

Fig. 23•2 Mitosis. During this process cells of the body reproduce themselves precisely.

Reproduction and Biological Diversity Although it is possible to discover how many chromosomes a particular animal possesses, the number of genes has not been determined accurately for any organism. An animal may have thousands of genes—humans may have as many as 100,000. But the presence or absence of only one gene at one particular locus (place) on a chromosome can profoundly affect an animal's behavior, probably by controlling a critical step in a biochemical pathway.

At conception, an organism such as a mammal is a fertilized egg (*zygote*)—a single cell whose particular genotype is made up of equal contributions of genes from each parent. The information contained in this zygote influences hair type, eye and skin pigmentation, body structure and size, and many other traits that develop during the organism's lifetime. When the cell divides to form two new cells, the chromosomes duplicate themselves exactly and so the new cells are identical to the "parent" cell in every respect. All the cells of the body contain the same genetic material (DNA) in their chromosomes and thus have the same genotype, although various cells serve different bodily functions. This process of cell division is called **mitosis** (Figure 23•2). It occurs continuously in the life of an organism as mature cells wear out, die, and are replaced.

Reproduction of a species involves a type of cell division called **meiosis,** during which the chromosomes divide and one chromosome of each pair is passed on to the sex cell, or **gamete** (egg or sperm). Theoretically, the number of different types of gametes that can be formed from one parent is 2^n, where n is the number of chromosome pairs in the parent organism. For example, each parent cell in Figure 23•3 contains 2 chromosome pairs and can produce 2^2, or 4, gametes.

Human beings have 23 chromosome pairs, including the sex chromosomes. Therefore, each human parent can produce 2^{23} or 8,388,608 different kinds of gametes, any one of which can combine with any one of the other parent's 8,388,608 gametes to form a zygote. If chromosomes were passed on intact from parent to offspring, the chromosome might be considered as the unit of heredity rather than the gene. Actually, chromosomes sometimes break, and segments at precisely the same location are exchanged between chromosomes within a homologous pair during meiosis. It is therefore possible that certain genes might start out on one chromosome and end up on another. This ability to cross over, break,

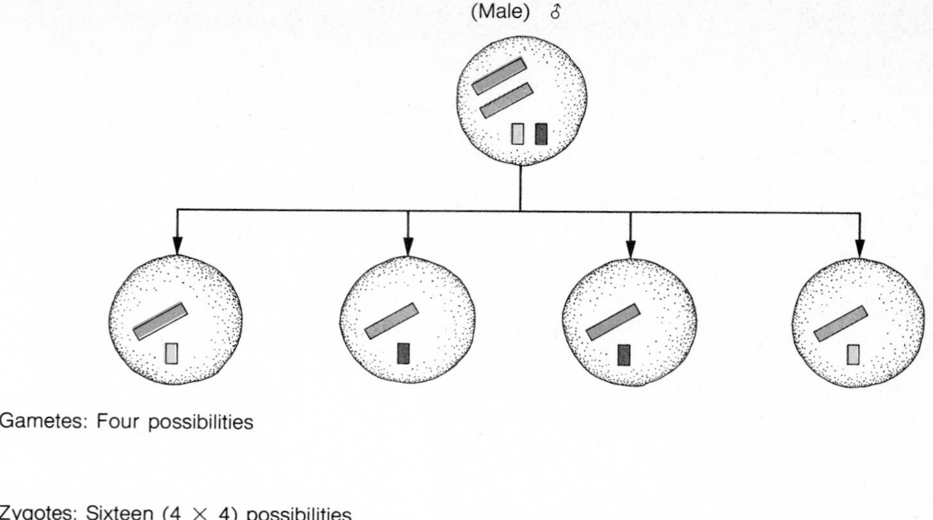

Zygotes: Sixteen (4 × 4) possibilities

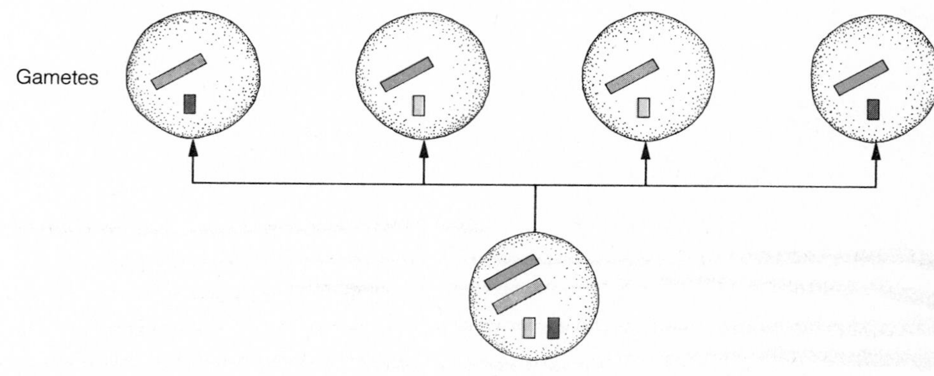

Fig. 23·3 Meiosis. During this process the sex cells (gametes) are formed.

and rejoin (synapse) increases the possibility of diversity. C. Stern (1949) estimated that a human couple could theoretically produce 20^{24} different zygote genotypes (this is more than the number of people who have ever lived), thus providing abundant diversity upon which **natural selection** can operate and playing an important role in the process of evolution.

How Genes Work Each gene on one member of a chromosome pair corresponds in location and function to a specific gene on the other member of the chromosome pair. At a particular locus a gene may appear in two or more (sometimes as many as 200) different forms, or **alleles.** The genotype of the animal is determined by which alleles it inherits. The interaction of these alleles determines which traits appear in the developing organism. For example, genes for blue eyes and genes for brown eyes are alleles whose particular DNA codes determine eye color by controlling the biochemical pathways that lead to the formation of pigment in the iris.

Although the DNA in the chromosomes never leaves the cell nucleus, it is stimulated at certain times to produce a particular form of **ribonucleic acid (RNA)** according to the information contained in the DNA molecule. This messenger RNA leaves the nucleus and enters other structures within the cell, where it forms the template (pattern) for constructing a particular molecule required for a bodily function.

The fruit fly *Drosophila melanogaster* is a popular subject for genetic research because it has a short gestation period and only four pairs of chromosomes, which are extraordinarily large in the salivary glands and the intestine and are thus easily seen microscopically (Figure 23•4). Figure 23•5 represents a map of *D. melanogaster's* chromosomes showing where some of the genes are located. This information was obtained from detailed records of hundreds of breeding experiments rather than from microscopic examination, which shows only light and dark banding of DNA in the chromosomes rather than actual genes. Sometimes the bands on a section of a chromosome can be seen to uncoil and form puffs. It is believed that

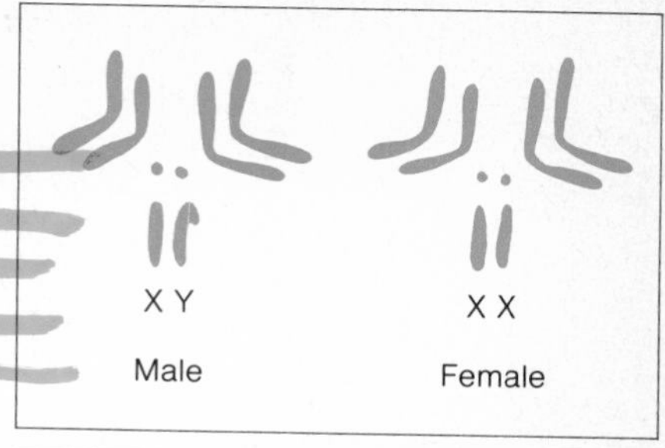

Fig. 23•4 *Drosophila melanogaster's* four pairs of chromosomes. Note the X and Y chromosomes of the male and the two X chromosomes of the female. (Ehrman and Parsons, 1976)

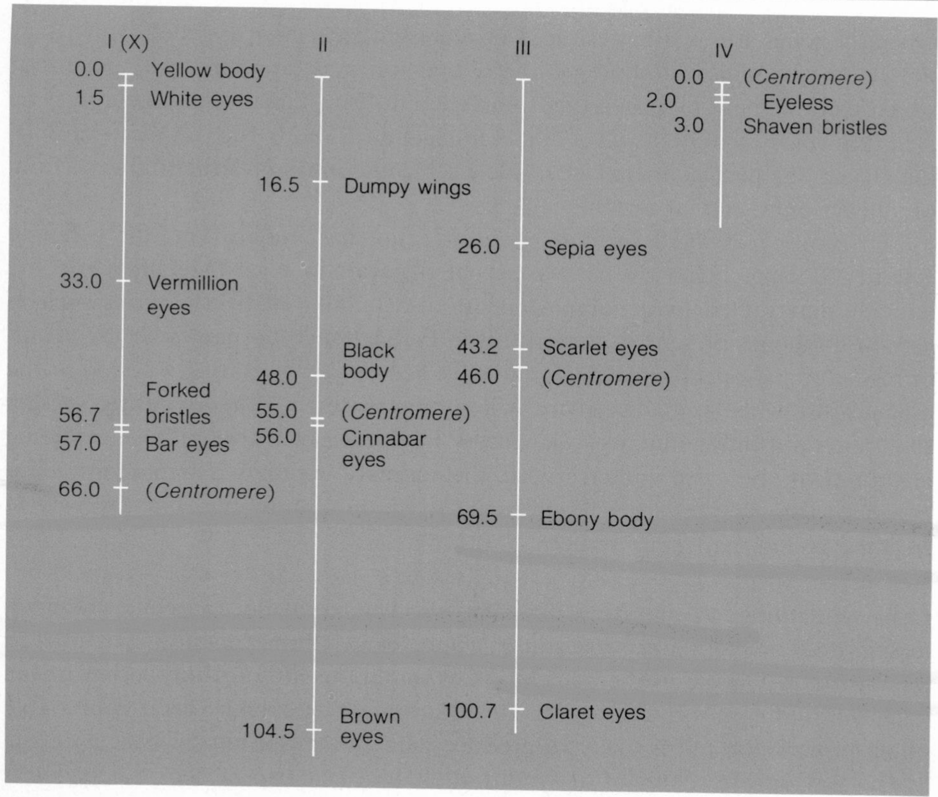

Fig. 23•5 The loci of several common genes (represented by the horizontal lines) and the four chromosome pairs (represented by the vertical lines) of *D. melanogaster* as determined from the results of breeding experiments. (Ehrman and Parsons, 1976, after Bridges and Brehme, 1944, and other sources)

The genetic mutation that produced this three-legged horse (Turnersville, Texas, 1937) lacks survival advantage, and so three-leggedness is not likely to become a common trait among horses. (Photography Collections, Humanities Research Center, University of Texas)

when this happens, the DNA of the gene at that locus on the chromosome is forming messenger RNA. When the rate of RNA synthesis diminishes, the puffs recede. Puffs appear at other places in the chromosomes at other times, probably indicating that other genes are then producing RNA.

These observations indicate that genes are not continuously active but are switched on and off by some mechanism. It is also reasonable to believe that a gene's action may be influenced by the amount of product, perhaps an enzyme, that the particular gene causes to be synthesized. Presumably, a large amount of product may inhibit the process and a small amount may allow it to proceed. But how is the action of a gene controlled? How do the various cells of a single organism function so differently and assume so many forms and yet contain precisely the same DNA? Genes that direct the formation of hemoglobin, for example exist in the nuclei of all the cells of the body but function only in the bone-marrow cells; genes that stimulate the production of a particular **hormone** exist in the nuclei of all the cells of the body but function only in the **endocrine** gland cells. Apparently only 10 to 20 percent of an organism's genes are active at one time in making an RNA template.

Genes that produce proteins are known as structural genes. These genes are believed to be turned on and off by operator genes, each of which is probably located close to its corresponding structural gene on the same chromosome. Operator genes are in turn activated or repressed by regulator genes, which may not be on the same chromosome as the operator gene and structural gene, but which control them by generating some chemical substance. The regulator gene is in turn controlled by the level of certain chemicals inside the cell. For example, high levels of a particular enzyme inside a cell could inhibit a structural gene from producing more of that enzyme.

The concept of regulator and operator genes has implications for behavior genetics. Certain behaviors such as sexual behavior in mice (McGill, 1970) are strongly determined by genotype but are also influenced by chemicals such as certain hormones present in the organism. Perhaps such hormones act by means of regulator and operator genes to influence genetic action during a period in the animal's life when sexual behavior is appropriate. Such a theory clearly implies that genes not only influence behavior by interacting with the animal's external environment, but also interact with the animal's internal environment. This theory implies that a gene's action is not fixed and continuous, but can vary in response to internal circumstances.

Gene Mutations A mutation is produced when an allele, for some unknown reason, does not reproduce itself in the normal way during meiosis, but instead produces a new allele in the gamete. Most mutations are probably lethal to the organism that carries them. If such an organism survives, however, it is probably physically inferior and is likely to produce defective offspring.

The first known report of a mutant allele was made in 80 B.C., when it was observed that some mice move in a peculiar waltzing pattern rather than in a

Genetic Regulations in Fly Molting

The process of regulation of the action of a particular gene by substances inside the cell is illustrated by the molting process of certain flies as they emerge from the pupa phase and enter the imago (adult) phase (Thiessen, 1972). The insect changes from a wormlike form into a fully developed adult, a process that must involve considerable protein formation and use of genetic information because the organism changes its structure completely. Furthermore, certain genes are called into action only at this time in the organism's life.

The fly's process of changing from one phase to another seems to operate in the following manner (Figure 23A·1). Neurons in the insect brain produce a substance called ecdysiotropic hormone, which moves down the axons of these neurons and into storage in the corpus cardiacum (a neural structure attached to the brain). At molting time, the ecdysiotropic hormone is released and carried to the insect's prothoracic gland where the molting hormone ecdysone is released to act on certain loci of chromosomes I and IV.

Probably regulator and operator genes are involved in this process. Within fifteen to thirty minutes after ecdysone is released, puffs appear at a particular locus on chromosome I, indicating that active production of RNA is in progress. Somewhat later, a puff appears on chromosome IV. When the molt is complete, these puffs disappear, indicating that the genes at those loci are quiescent. Apparently, therefore, the genes necessary for molting are called into action precisely when they are needed.

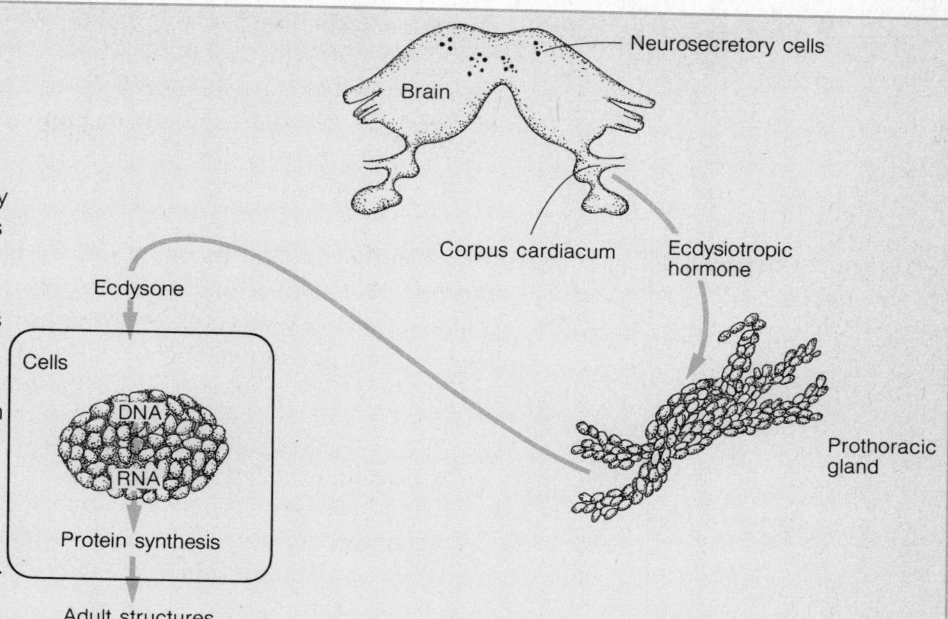

Fig. 23A·1 Schematic diagram of molting in flies. (Adapted from Hoar, 1966)

straight line. Not until this century was the genetic basis for this malfunction understood as the action of a particular mutant allele on the nervous system in mice. Geneticists have calculated that the discovery of "waltzer," was made 10,245 mouse generations ago, a span of time equivalent to 204,900 years of human life (Lindzey and Thiessen, 1970). At least eighty other neurological mutants have been identified in mice, many of which have been given descriptive names such as ducky, twirler, jittery, pirouette, and jumpy. Twirler, for example, results from malfunction of the vestibular system and the cerebellum, which controls body coordination by precisely inhibiting and coordinating muscle activity in response to information from the vestibular system. Without the action of the cerebellum, muscle activity would be jerky and uneven.

Scientists study these mutants and their effects on behavior in order to improve our understanding of neurological malfunctions in humans. It is believed that each of these defects is produced because the mutant allele blocks the formation of a particular enzyme or results in the formation of an inappropriate enzyme.

Behaviors Influenced by Single Alleles

23•2 Many behavioral traits are influenced by several genes at various loci on different chromosomes and can be studied only if sophisticated mathematical techniques are used. However, behaviors such as phenylketonuria and Huntington's chorea in humans, and audiogenic seizure proneness in mice, result from a single mutant allele. The genetic basis for these behaviors is as follows:

1. Only two alleles, which we will call A_1 and A_2, can appear at a particular locus on each homologous chromosome.
2. If an animal were to have the same allele at this locus on each chromosome, its genotype must be either A_1A_1 or A_2A_2. Such an animal is therefore homozygous at this locus and will exhibit the phenotype produced by the allele it possesses.
3. If the animal were to have two different genes at this locus, its genotype must be A_1A_2. This animal is heterozygous and the phenotype it exhibits will depend on how these alleles interact.
   a. If A_1 is **dominant** over A_2, then the phenotype will be the same for both A_1A_1 and A_1A_2 genotypes.
   b. If A_1 is **recessive,** then the phenotype for A_1A_1 will be different from that for A_1A_2.

The examples that follow illustrate how some dominant and recessive genes affect behavior.

Phenylketonuria Phenylketonuria (PKU) was discovered in the 1930s, when phenylpyruvic acid was identified in the urine of affected individuals (Bonner, 1961). This disease occurs in about one in 10,000 individuals but appears more commonly among brothers and sisters and in the offspring of consanguineous marriages—marriages between persons who have a common ancestor, such as cousins, an uncle and a niece, or an aunt and a nephew.

The defect is apparently due to a single recessive mutant gene that apparently has no DNA code for synthesizing the enzyme needed to convert the amino acid phenylalanine (present in a normal diet) into the amino acid tyrosine, which is important as a precursor of several chemical substances that are essential for normal development and function of the nervous system. Since tyrosine is also present in the diet, this defect may appear harmless. However, dietary phenylalanine can be converted to phenylpyruvic acid, a substance that has deleterious effects when it accumulates in the body. The diet of phenylketonuric individuals must therefore contain levels of phenylalanine high enough to meet the metabolic needs of the individual but low enough to prevent dangerous buildup of phenylpyruvic acid.

In order for an infant to have phenylketonuria, it must inherit two identical defective genes—one from each parent. About one parent in fifty carries this defective gene but appears to be normal. The chances of two carrier parents producing a phenylketonuric child are one in four.

Prevention of mental retardation from phenylketonuria depends on early detection and treatment. Both the blood and urine of PKU individuals contain abnormally high amounts of phenylalanine and its degradation products, which can be detected by simple chemical tests. One or more of these tests have been done routinely for several years on all infants born under medical supervision, and so mental retardation no longer occurs in most phenylketonuric infants.

After twelve hours without food, carriers of PKU have high levels of phenylalanine in their blood and exhibit low tolerance to injected phenylalanine—two characteristics that can easily be detected by chemical tests. The information that such tests provide can assist a couple in making a decision about whether to have a child of their own.

Huntington's Chorea Most deleterious genes are recessive as are those in phenylketonuria, and can be passed on to an offspring by a heterozygous parent who is phenotypically normal. Such genes can remain in the gene pool for a long time without being eliminated by natural selection. When a deleterious gene is dominant, the organisms that are homozygous or heterozygous for the trait are physically inferior to normal individuals and may be hindered from generating progeny, thus failing to pass along these genes. An example of a deleterious condition resulting from a dominant gene is Huntington's chorea. This invariably fatal human disorder produces distinct behavioral changes in which the muscles twitch in an involuntary, although sometimes well-coordinated, manner. (*Chorea* is derived from the Greek work for "dance.") The affected individual commonly loses intellectual function, develops insanity, becomes ataxic (unable to move), and ultimately dies.

The dominant allele responsible for this condition is designated *H*. Because it is assumed that the homozygous dominant condition *HH* would be lethal in utero or very early life, individuals carrying this trait are probably heterozygous (*Hh*). The majority of the population is therefore homozygous recessive for the normal condition (*hh*).

The gene for this disorder was brought to the United States from Suffolk, England, by three men who were deported in 1830 because of their unusual behavior. These men married in the United States and produced offspring. Presently the incidence of the disorder is one in 25,000.

Since this is a dominant and ultimately lethal gene, how have the genes for Huntington's chorea survived in the population? Apparently the survival of this condition is due to its delayed onset. The mean age for its appearance is thirty-five, representing a range of fifteen to sixty-five years of age. Therefore, an individual may produce progeny before the disordered gene manifests itself. The offspring of an afflicted parent have a theoretical 50 percent chance of getting or escaping the malady, depending on whether they inherit the recessive normal allele or the dominant chorea allele (Ehrman and Parsons, 1976).

Audiogenic-seizure Proneness in Mice The mode of inheritance of phenylketonuria and Huntington's chorea has been determined by studying the family trees of afflicted individuals. In studies with animals, however, we can conduct precisely controlled breeding experiments in order to determine how a trait is inherited. This technique is particularly useful when the trait being studied in experimental animals is related to a human trait. Seizures, for example, are a common medical problem in humans and result from nervous system abnormalities. From studies of seizure behavior in animals, we can learn about the level of excitability of the nervous system and about the factors that influence this level. This knowledge is especially important because many drugs alter the brain's excitability level.

A seizure trait in mice that has been studied extensively in the laboratory is proneness to audiogenic seizures. When an affected mouse is exposed to a loud sound stimulus, its muscles contract and relax alternately, thus producing a twitching, convulsive movement. In studying this behavior, R. L. Collins and J. L. Fuller (1968) placed mice one at a time into a sound-deadening box that contained a loud bell. The experimenters then activated the bell for one minute and noted whether or not an audiogenic seizure occurred. By controlled breeding of the two mouse strains they studied, Collins and Fuller discovered that audiogenic-seizure behavior depends on two allelic genes: *Asp* (normal, or audiogenic-seizure resistant) and *asp* (audiogenic-seizure prone.) *Asp* is dominant over *asp*, and so the audiogenic-seizure-resistant phenotype results from either of two genotypes: *AspAsp* or *Aspasp*. The audiogenic-seizure-prone phenotype results only from the homozygous recessive genotype *aspasp*. Thus this trait is inherited similarly to phenylketonuria in humans.

The inheritance of audiogenic-seizure proneness in mice is represented in Figure 23•6. One of the parent strains shown is phenotypically audiogenic-seizure prone, and must therefore have the two recessive genes *aspasp*. The other parent strain has two dominant genes *AspAsp* for resistance to audiogenic seizures (normal). All the first generation offspring (F_1) produced by breeding these two parent strains have the heterozygous genotype *Aspasp* and are phenotypically normal. When the F_1 animals are bred to each other to produce the F_2 generation, the genes are reassorted or segregated, and three different gene combinations occur. Homozygous dominant (*AspAsp*) and heterozygous (*Aspasp*) animals are all phenotypically seizure resistant; homozygous recessive (*aspasp*) animals are phenotypically seizure-prone. Theoretically, two *Aspasp* animals will be produced for one *AspAsp* and one *aspasp*, and so the ratio of seizure resistance to seizure proneness in the F_2 generation is 3 to 1.

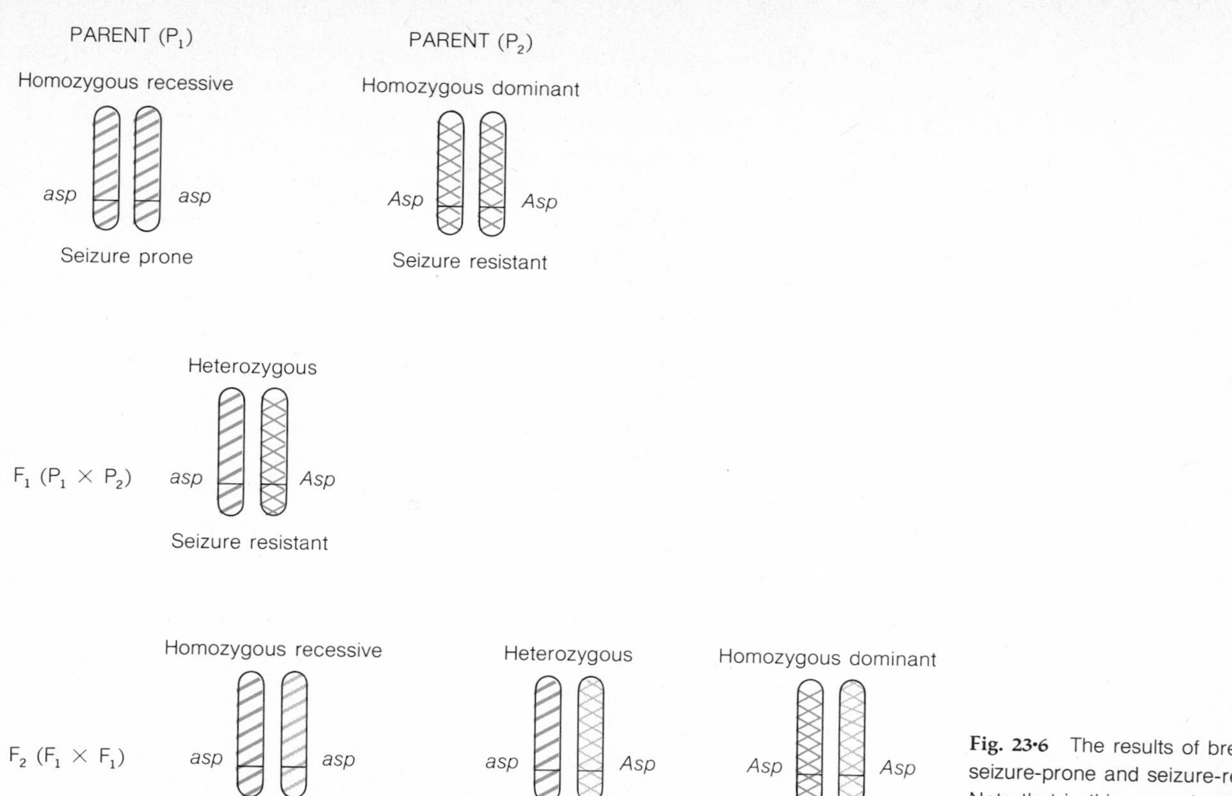

Fig. 23·6 The results of breeding seizure-prone and seizure-resistant mice. Note that in this example, all the F_1 mice are isogenic (have the same genotype).

In addition to identifying both the recessive allele responsible for audiogenic seizure proneness in mice and the mechanism by which the allele is inherited, Collins and Fuller have identified the chromosome and the approximate locus at which the *Asp-asp* allele is found. As yet, we have such precise information for no other behavior.

Genotype and Fitness

23·3 Darwin's theory of natural selection is often called a theory of the survival of the fittest, because organisms that are better able than other organisms both to withstand the selection pressures of a particular environment and to reproduce, usually attain numerical superiority over less fit organisms. For example, the bacterium *Escherichia coli (E. coli)* thrives in many chemical environments but not in those containing the antibiotic drug streptomycin, which usually kills all but a few of the *E. coli* bacteria present. If the surviving bacteria reproduce, their offspring may be streptomycin resistant. The drug does not induce this resistance in the *E. coli* bacteria; it selects for it.

Resistance to streptomycin occurs in approximately one out of 10 million *E. coli* bacteria and is probably due to a mutant gene. This allele may occur only infrequently among *E. coli* in most chemical environments, but it may become the only surviving allele in environments containing streptomycin.

Although there is an apparent relationship between fitness and the inheritance of behavior traits, fitness can be defined only in relation to a particular environment. For example, the mutant *E. coli* is the least fit strain in the bacterium's normal chemical environment, but it is the most fit strain in a streptomycin environment. The expanding human population on earth attests to our biological fitness for our environment. However, if the world's land masses were suddenly covered with shallow seas, the oyster would be more fit than we.

Hygienic Behavior in Bees Traits that improve reproduction in all its phases, from sexual behavior of the parents to care of the young, should theoretically confer some fitness on the offspring. This process is illustrated in W. C. Rothenbuhler's (1964) studies of the resistance of honeybees to American foulbrood, a contagious disease that attacks and kills bee larvae. Bees that are genetically susceptible to the disease leave their diseased larvae in the capped cells of the honeycomb, apparently making it possible for the infection to spread. Bees that are resistant to foulbrood demonstrate hygienic behavior by uncapping the honeycomb cells that contain the diseased larvae and removing these larvae from the hive. This hygienic behavior apparently confers fitness by reducing the chance that the infection will spread throughout the beehive, which may contain as many as 60,000 individuals and is the center of intense social activity—including frequent body contact during the dancing of the bees and frequent transfer of stomach contents from bee to bee.

Rothenbuhler determined that the bees' hygienic behavior results from two pairs of recessive alleles, each at a different chromosomal locus. One recessive allele controls uncapping the cells; the other controls removing the diseased larvae. To demonstrate complete hygienic behavior, a bee must be homozygous recessive at both loci. If this were the only genotype in a bee colony, both forms of hygienic behavior would be exhibited by every bee.

Rothenbuhler also noted that hygienic bees are generally more active and sting more than other bees. During the course of an experiment, he made ninety-eight visits to colonies of unhygienic bees and received only one sting. In ninety-eight visits to colonies of hygienic bees, however, he received 143 stings.

Nesting Behavior in Birds In birds, the survival of the young usually depends on the efficiency with which the parents build the nest. We might therefore expect nest-building to be under some genetic control, especially since the construction of some nests seems complex and stereotyped. Furthermore, bird nests often show such marked species specificity that the species of bird can be identified from the nest it builds.

Imprinting: How Does a Duck Know Who It Is?

Early experience is critically important even in birds. When a bird follows another bird or when it shows mating behavior, it usually expresses these behaviors toward a member of its own species. These behaviors are therefore probably adaptive. How does a bird learn what species it is? How does it learn to follow its mother?

Apparently birds inherit a little "teaching machine" that is ready to teach the animal its identity. Konrad Lorenz (1965) has maintained that much of a duckling's behavior is innate (unlearned) and is rigidly controlled by environmental stimuli. However, the innate behavior is incomplete and contains breaks in continuity that must be filled by learning. For example, to follow may be innate, but the duckling must learn whom to follow. In real life, the object it learns to follow is its own mother.

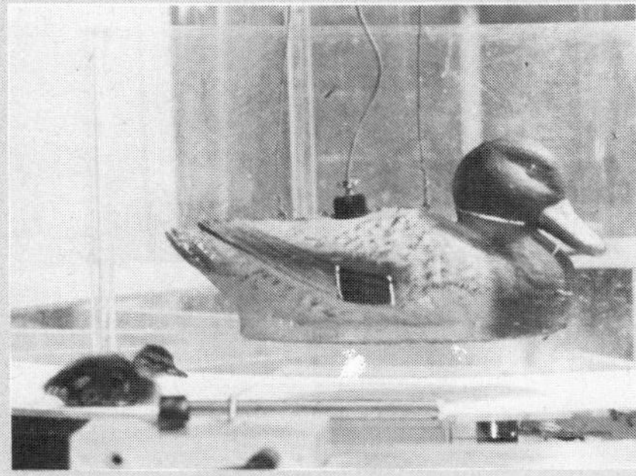

Fig. 23B•1 Imprinting a duckling. (Courtesy of Eckhard B. Hess)

In the laboratory, ducklings can be taught to follow almost anything—a tomato-juice can, an electric train, an experimenter, a papier-mâché model. The procedure by whicn a duckling forms an attachment to another organism or object and thus learns who it is is called **imprinting.** The duckling in Figure 23B•1 is apparently being taught that it is a papier-mâché mallard. The duckling may or may not be a mallard, but it is not papier-mâché. Furthermore, it is being taught to follow a male duck instead of a female.

A duckling used in an imprinting experiment hatches in a cardboard box, where it is unable to see any environmental stimuli other than the inside of the box. The duckling may then be shown a male decoy model that can move and utter a human rendition of *"gock, gock."* To test to see whether the imprinting was effective, the duckling is later shown the male model paired with a real female mallard that moves and makes real mallard sounds. Imprinted ducklings choose the decoy over the live duck.

Pairs of lovebirds will breed and raise their young in captivity, and they usually form lifelong pair bonds within a few hours. W. C. Dilger (1962) selected two types of lovebirds (peach-faced lovebirds and Fischer's lovebirds) to study in the laboratory, where he provided some of the stimuli normally found in the birds' natural environment. Some typical behavior patterns of two kinds of lovebirds are shown in Figure 23•7. During the courtship feeding engaged in by peach-faced lovebirds, the male feeds the female. These birds carry nesting materials such as bark and leaves, several strips at a time, by tucking them into their upraised plumage. Their completed nests are shaped like a well.

Dilger considers the behavior of Fischer's lovebirds to represent a more advanced stage of evolution than that of peach-faced lovebirds. Their courtship feeding is somewhat more elaborate, and they carry nesting materials one piece at a time in their beaks. Their nests are elaborately constructed and have a roof and a tunnel entrance.

The complexity and rigidity of the behaviors of these two varieties of lovebirds suggest a genetic basis, and the evidence provided by breeding experiments supports this position. For example, when peach-faced lovebirds were mated with

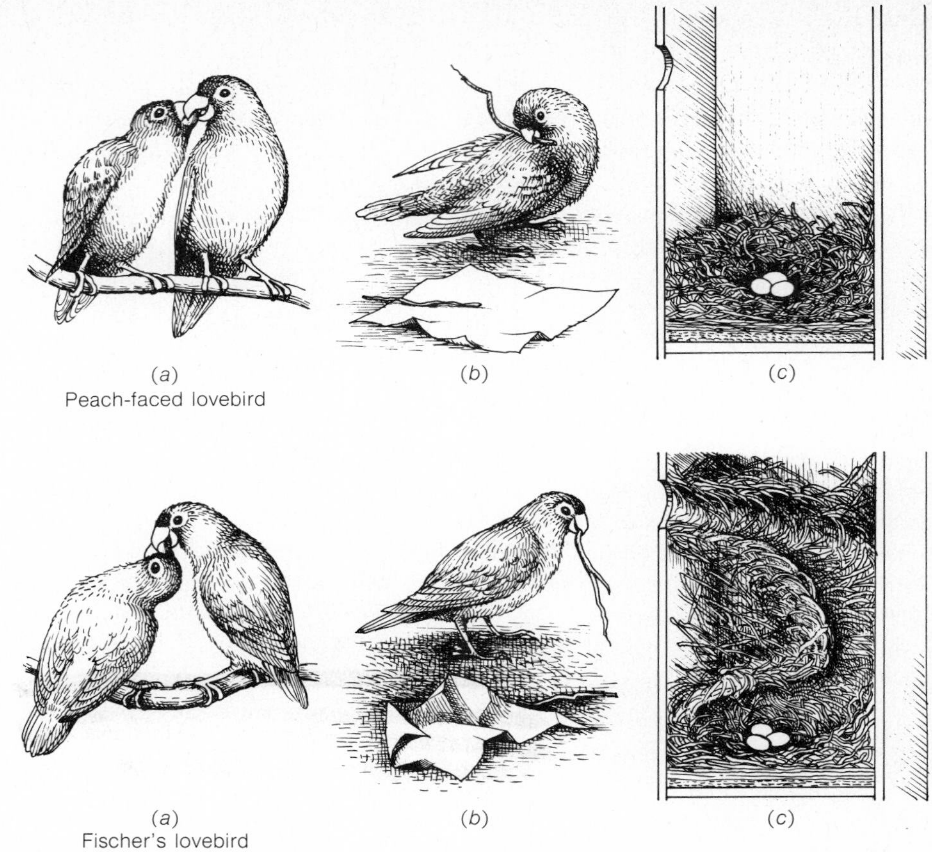

Fig. 23·7 The courtship and nesting behavior of lovebirds. (Dilger, 1962)

Fischer's lovebirds, the hybrid F_1 generation exhibited some very interesting behavioral characteristics that were apparent composites of the behaviors of both parents. The hybrid offspring cut strips of nesting material without difficulty, but when they tried to transport it to the nest, they seemed unable to decide whether to carry the material in the beak or to tuck it into the feathers. They were successful in getting the materials to the nest only when they carried them in the beak—a procedure which they used only about 6 percent of the time. On other occasions, they raised the feathers and made elaborate tucking motions, but the materials invariably fell out on the way to the nest.

The transportation of nesting material by tucking was markedly resistant to learning even though it invariably resulted in failure. After two months, the birds still exhibited tucking behavior nearly 60 percent of the time. After three years, nesting material was usually carried in the beak and attempts to tuck it into the plumage became infrequent; when tucking behavior was exhibited, it was more efficient than before. Unfortunately, the F_1 generation turned out to be sterile, thus precluding further breeding experiments to study the genetic basis of behavior in these lovebirds.

Inbreeding Depression We have seen that meiosis provides enormously diversified genotypes. In fact, the fitness of an organism depends on this diversity. Factors such as inbreeding that reduce genotypic diversity usually produce organisms that are less fit than organisms produced by factors such as outbreeding that encourage diversity. (*Inbreeding* is the mating of organisms that have common ancestors; *outbreeding* is the mating of unrelated organisms.)

The detrimental effects of inbreeding are called inbreeding depression. These effects can be clearly identified in the human population. For example, the death rate among children in the general population below the age of ten years is 24 per 1000. The death rate is more than three times higher among the offspring of cousin marriages—81 per 1000 (Thiessen, 1972).

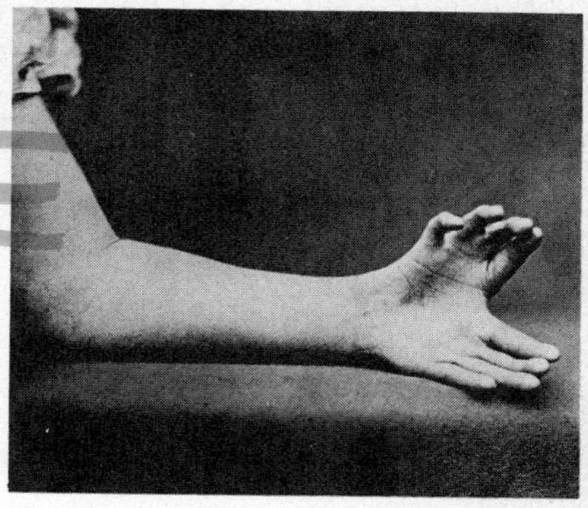

Genetic defects such as this eight-fingered hand (c. 1862) are far more likely to occur in the offspring of consanguineous marriages than in the general population. (From an original in the possession of the Royal Society of Medicine)

W. J. Schull and J. V. Neel (1965) studied 1500 Japanese children who were the offspring of marriages between first cousins, and an equal number of children of parents with no common ancestry. Both groups were matched as closely as possible for socioeconomic variables. Children of first-cousin marriages were inferior to children of unrelated couples on seventeen developmental, physiological, and behavioral measures. They walked and talked later, scored lower on verbal and performance items on intelligence tests, and scored lower on tests of language in school. In another study, Adams and Neel (1967) found that offspring of brother-sister and father-daughter matings had a higher incidence of defects such as mental retardation, bilateral cleft palate, and premature death. In fact, rare genetic defects are seen only in consanguineous matings. It is interesting to note that most societies have strict taboos against sexual relations between close relatives (incest). Whatever the cultural basis for these taboos, they are apparently biologically necessary to the survival of a fit human species.

Difficulties have been encountered in the laboratory during attempts to develop inbred mouse strains, a task usually accomplished by mating brothers and sisters over at least twenty generations. It is probable that for every inbred mouse strain currently maintained for research purposes, ten strains were originated. For example, when D. S. Falconer (1960) attempted to develop twenty inbred mouse strains, nineteen of the lines became extinct before the twentieth generation was reached. Extinction occurs for many reasons: lack of fertility, failure of females to care for young, infanticide, high susceptibility to disease, diminished litter size, reduced body weights, and the appearance of a deleterious and sometimes lethal defect that is extremely rare in the general population, but common in the inbred line.

Most deleterious traits result from recessive genes (Bruell, 1964a). If these traits came from a dominant gene, they would appear frequently in the population, would decrease fitness in every organism bearing the gene, would be infrequently reproduced, and would eventually be eliminated from the gene pool. A recessive gene, however, can be carried without being expressed and can thus be passed around the population undetected. When related organisms reproduce, genes transmitted to the offspring come from only a small sample of the gene pool. As long as inbreeding continues, a large portion of the gene pool is excluded from transmission to future generations. This factor, in addition to the ancestral genetic similarity of the mating partners, dramatically increases the chances for the offspring to be homozygous for the recessive trait, thus leading to an increase in the frequency of its appearance and to deleterious effects.

Intermediate Inheritance If we breed a mouse with a high level of serum cholesterol to an unrelated mouse with a low level of serum cholesterol and then measure the level of serum cholesterol in the F_1 generation, we will find the offspring's cholesterol level to be approximately halfway between the cholesterol levels of the two parents (Bruell, 1963). Such a halfway point is called midparent; it represents the intermediate inheritance of a trait by the offspring. Intermediate inheritance is common for traits that are controlled by many alleles. As each parent contributes some dominant and some recessive alleles for the trait to the offspring, the resulting phenotype must result from some kind of summation of the inherited alleles. Midparent results have also been obtained from comparing hematocrit values for parental strains of mice and their offspring (Bruell, 1964a). (Hematocrit values represent the percentage of the whole blood volume occupied by the blood cells after centrifugation in a special graduated tube called a hematocrit.)

Hybrid Vigor Sometimes crossing two parental strains results in a condition called hybrid vigor, which is in one sense the opposite of inbreeding depression. Hybrid vigor is the appearance of a trait in the offspring in a more extreme form than it appears in either parent. For example, if we mate parents of two different inbred mouse strains, the offspring would be hybrids and might be hardier, faster growing, and (when adults) larger than the parents.

In studying hybrid vigor, Collins (1964) tested inbred mouse strains and hybridized crosses in a shock-avoidance task. At the beginning of each trial, a buzzer was sounded and was followed 2.5 seconds later by a tone, which was itself followed 2.5 seconds later by a shock. To avoid the shock, the mice had to respond to the buzzer and the tone by leaping across a pit containing a grid floor charged with electricity.

Collins's subjects were from five inbred mouse strains and from the offspring of all possible mating combinations of the five inbred strains. When two strains were bred, reciprocal crosses were formed by breeding a female of one strain with a male from the second strain, and then breeding a male from the first strain with a female from the second strain. In most cases the performance of the offspring (F_1) was superior to that of either parent, thus demonstrating hybrid vigor. Similar results were obtained in studies of wheel-running tasks (Bruell, 1964b) and exploratory activity (Bruell, 1964a).

Although the phenomenon of hybrid vigor was observed long ago by animal breeders and botanists, its genetic basis is not yet completely understood. However, a possible explanation is that deleterious alleles are recessive and that hybrids such as randomly bred (outbred) laboratory mice are often heterozygous for these alleles. They carry them while showing no ill effects. For example, if one parent mouse has the genotype *AA:bb* and the other parent has the genotype *aa:BB*, then each parent is homozygous for a recessive allel, which will diminish the biological vigor of that physiological or behavioral trait. All mice in the F_1 generation, however, would be heterozygous at both loci and have the genotype *Aa:Bb*. The dominant genes produce vigorous expression of both traits so that the offspring should be more fit than either parent.

Speculation suggests that traits showing hybrid vigor have been acted on by natural selection and that activity and learning ability may be such traits. Traits that have not been acted on by natural selection show intermediate inheritance (Bruell, 1964a). Breeding experiments might therefore be useful in identifying the behavioral traits that have been influenced by natural selection.

Natural Selection Although Darwin (1859, 1871) was unaware of the principles of genetic transmission, he observed that selection pressures in the environment determine which animals survive to pass along their hereditary material to future generations. He noted that in some animal species, conspicuous coloration of the male plays a role in attracting a mate. In other species, the males fight for a breeding territory and even for a mate. Because, for example, phenotypes for conspicuous coloration or for fighting strength probably provide a selection advantage, the genes underlying these traits should increase in frequency within the population. Genes underlying inconspicuous coloration or fighting-weakness phenotypes will be lost from the gene pool if the carrier of these genes is prevented from reproducing. Darwin called this process of selecting for mating characteristics *sexual selection.*

As the preceding example shows, natural selection favors one gene over another in a particular environment by operating on phenotype rather than on the genotype itself. If a gene pool contains genes for fleet-footedness and genes for slow-footedness, for example, slow-footed animals will survive for a while and reproduce. However, predators will catch more slow-footed animals than fleet-footed ones, and so the number of slow-footed animals will gradually decrease and genes for slow-footedness will eventually disappear from the gene pool. If the animals themselves are predators, the fleet-footed ones will get more food than the slow-footed ones, and thus be favored to survive.

Applying Genetics to Studying Behavior in the Laboratory

23·4 Despite the biologically deleterious effects of inbreeding, at least 200 inbred mouse strains are currently used in biomedical and behavioral research projects. Many of these strains have been maintained since the 1920s and 1930s. The parent mice used by Collins and Fuller (1968) to study audiogenic seizures were from inbred strains, and the inbred C57BL/6 mouse strain is widely used in the laboratory to study aging, alcohol intake and metabolism, tissue culture, air pollution, hematology, cancer chemotherapy, radiation, and nutrition (Green, 1968).

There are two basic reasons for using inbred strains despite the difficulties involved in developing and maintaining them. First, the inbred strains are believed to be isogenic—that is, every animal within the strain has exactly the same genotype as every other animal except for sex differences. Therefore, behavioral differences among animals of the same strain should be due to environmental rather than genetic variables. Second, inbreeding may permanently fix certain rare alleles so that they can be studied over a long period of time.

For example, a mutant allele called moth-eaten has been identified in mice. The first moth-eaten mouse was noticed in a litter of normal mice because of its disheveled fur. Study showed that this mouse lacked a certain white blood cell needed for immunity to disease. Because the body's immune system plays a role in cancer, the moth-eaten mouse strain has been developed and maintained for use in cancer research (Shultz, 1976). (If it were not deliberately bred and maintained, however, the moth-eaten mutant would probably disappear from the gene pool because a defect in the immune system probably represents a defect in fitness that would ultimately be lethal.) Other mutant inbred mouse strains develop diseases such as muscular dystrophy and diabetes and are thus useful in studying these diseases experimentally.

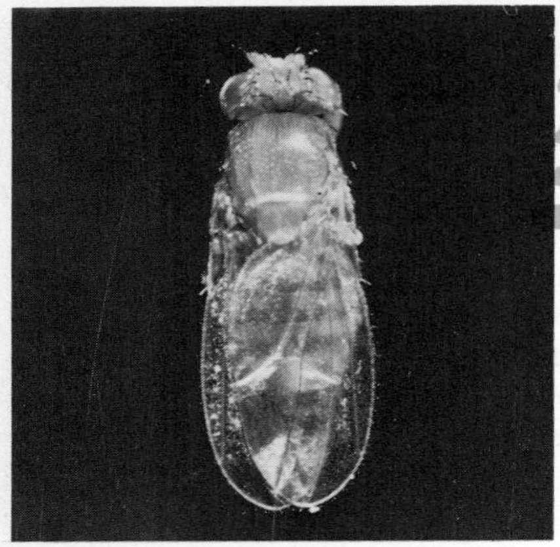

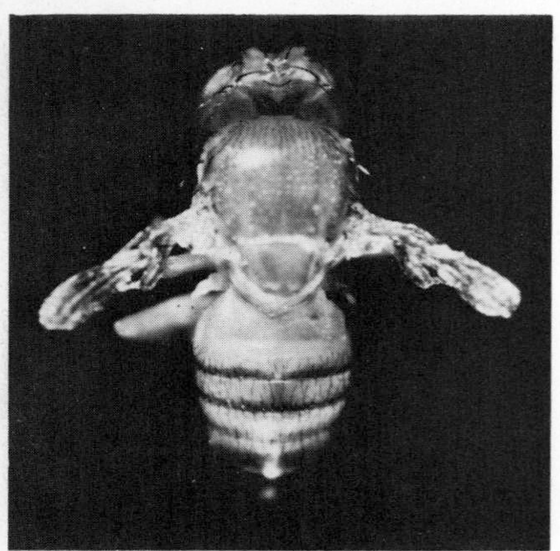

Selective breeding of *Drosophila* (top) can produce variations such as curved wings (middle) or vestigial wings (bottom). (Courtesy Carolina Biological Supply Company)

Selective Breeding The judicious use of selective breeding to determine the genetic characteristics of the research subjects permits the investigator to study questions that cannot be examined in any other manner. In a selective-breeding procedure, the geneticist does on a vastly compressed time scale what selection pressures do during the course of evolution. The geneticist selects the trait to perpetuate and allows only the animals who possess that trait to breed and transmit their genes. The behavior geneticist, unlike natural selection, commonly selects animals for breeding that are either high or low on a particular trait so that both extremes of that trait can be produced. The geneticist may also maintain a random-breeding line in which no selection criteria are applied, to see whether the mean level of a trait's expression changes spontaneously.

The process of selective breeding for a particular trait can best be illustrated by the breeding experiments of W. R. Thompson (1954), who studied the inheritance of learning abilities in rats. He trained rats in a Hebb-Williams maze, which contains movable barriers between a start box and a food receptacle in opposite corners. In order to reach the food, a hungry rat had to learn the path around the barriers. Thompson used six warm-up trials to reduce the rat's emotionality in the maze. He then presented twelve problems, followed by twelve problems that were mirror images of the first twelve.

There were significant individual differences. Some rats learned much more rapidly than others. Thompson then bred the dull rats (that made many errors) to other dull rats, and the bright ones (that made few errors) to other bright rats. In the first generation (F_1), very little selective-breeding effect was seen in maze-learning (Figure 23•8). By the third generation (F_3), selective breeding had a statistically significant impact on the number of errors made by the offspring of dull rats compared to the offspring of bright rats. By the sixth generation, the error scores for the two breeding populations were distinctly different.

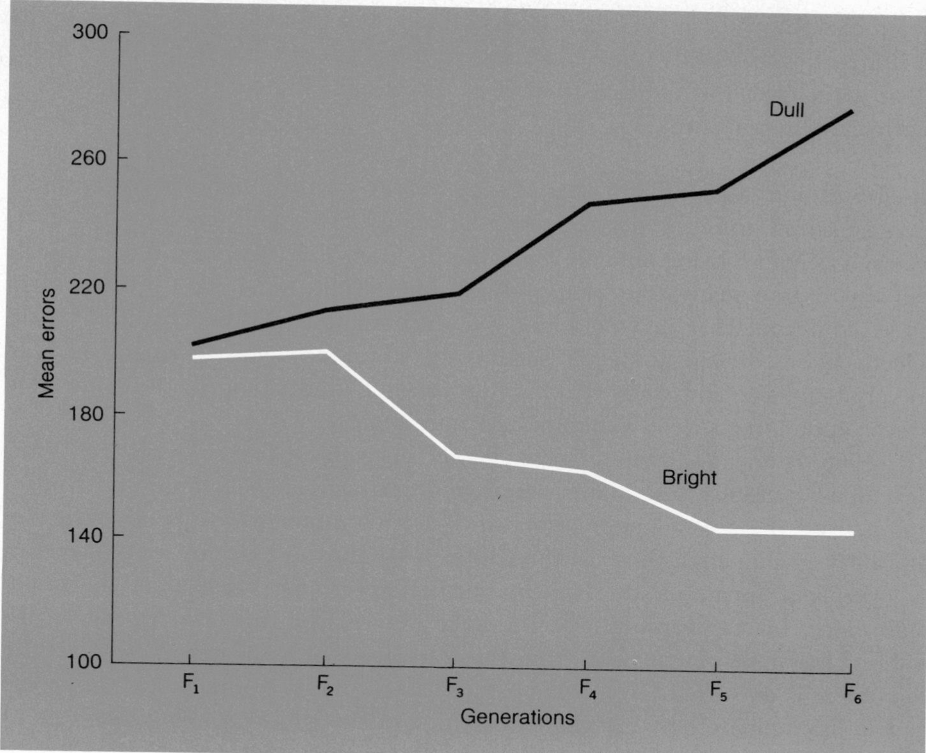

Fig. 23·8 The results of selective breeding for maze-learning in a Hebb-Williams maze. Note that within six generations, two distinct lines have been produced. (Thompson, 1954)

Thompson selected rats making many errors and rats making few errors to contribute their genes to their respective gene pools, thereby selecting for the abilities measured by a Hebb-Williams maze and allowing other genes to be lost. It is important to realize that rats who learn mazes rapidly do not necessarily show superior performance on other types of learning problems—their brightness is restricted to maze learning. In Thompson's experiments the influence of genotype is magnified because it was manipulated and the environment was held constant.

Maze-learning in rats, along with all other forms of behavior, is controlled jointly by the heredity passed on to the animal in its DNA and by the environment in which the animal is raised. In a selective breeding experiment, the environment is held as constant as possible for all animals and the assortment of genes is regulated. By observing the phenotypes (in this example, learning ability) and breeding only the animals exhibiting the phenotype's extremes, we can demonstrate a genetic influence on learning. Probably learning behavior is influenced by multiple alleles, some of which may improve performance and some diminish it.

In Thompson's original breeding population, the genes were randomly distributed because reproduction in the animal colony had not yet been selectively controlled to produce a desired behavior. When bright rats were bred to other bright rats, the random reassortment of the genes for brightness ceased and they began to accumulate in the bright strain. However, as we shall see later, the results of this particular selective breeding may fail to appear in behavior if the environment is changed; this indicates that these genotypic differences are specific to a particular environment.

Brain Size and Learning In Chapter 22, we saw that the brain size may affect an organism's learning ability and reasoning ability. If we wish to study this effect, we can easily find living animals that differ in brain size. However, these animals will also differ in many other characteristics, that will be unrelated to the problem under study but that may confound the experimental results. Therefore, if we selectively breed a single species (such as the laboratory mouse), we may be able to vary brain size and study its effect on learning ability, and at the same time keep confounding species variables to a minimum.

In 1966, Wimer and Prater selectively bred mice on the basis of brain size. They developed a strain whose brains were significantly larger than those of a control group from the general population, and another strain whose brains were significantly smaller than those of the controls. When these strains were placed in an open-field apparatus, the large-brain mice were more active than the small-brain mice. In one learning task, the mice were placed in a T-maze filled with water. Their task was to swim from the start point at the base of the T to the top of the T, one arm of which was painted black, and the other white. The mice had to discriminate between the black arm and the white arm to gain access to a ladder that provided a means of escape from the maze. Large-brained mice learned this maze faster than the small-brained mice.

Other experiments on mice bred for brain size support Wimer and Prater's finding that brain size affects activity and learning. In an experiment comparing large-brained mice to mice of normal brain size, large-brained mice were more active in an open-field apparatus (Wimer, Roderick, and Wimer, 1969). Large-brained mice were better at learning to be active to avoid a shock punishment (active avoidance), but they were worse in learning to be inactive to avoid a shock (passive avoidance). In another study, M. F. Elias (1969) found large-brained mice to be superior to small-brained mice in reversal learning. These studies support Jerison's theory (1963) that the evolutionary enlargement of the human brain made possible our high level of learning ability.

Alcohol Consumption in Mice In the hope of explaining the effects of alcohol consumption on human behavior, alcohol intake has been studied in mice (Rodgers, 1966). In a typical alcohol-preference experiment, mice are placed in individual cages containing a tube of water and a tube of alcohol solution (usually 10 percent ethanol in water, which is equivalent to 20 proof). The amount of alcohol solution consumed is divided by the total fluid intake from both tubes in order to determine the preference ratio. If the preference ratio is 0.50, the mouse is drinking from the alcohol tube and from the water tube in precisely the same amount and no preference is being shown. A ratio above 0.50 indicates a preference for alcohol.

Figure 23•9 shows the results of an alcohol preference experiment done on nineteen inbred mouse strains. The C57BL/6J mouse strain and all but one of the related C57 strains show a distinct preference for alcohol. This consistency among strains that have a common ancestry (such as C57 and C58 strains) is particularly remarkable because the C57 and C58 sublines have been maintained as separate breeding stock since 1921 and the C57 sublines have been separated since the mid 1930s. The A and DBA strains indicate aversion to alcohol by drinking nearly all of their daily fluid intake from the water bottle. A few strains show an intermediate level of preference.

Inheritance of Alcohol Preference After identifying differences among strains in a behavioral trait, such as alcohol preference, breeding experiments can be done to discover how the trait is inherited. In one such breeding program, the high-alcohol-preference C57BL/Crgl strain was crossed with the low-alcohol-preference A/Crgl strain (Rodgers and McClearn, 1962). (Note that although these strains are inbred, Figure 23•9 shows some variability in alcohol-preference scores of the individual mice.) The preference scores for the F_1 generation fell generally between those of the two parents, indicating that alcohol preference is inherited in an intermediate fashion.

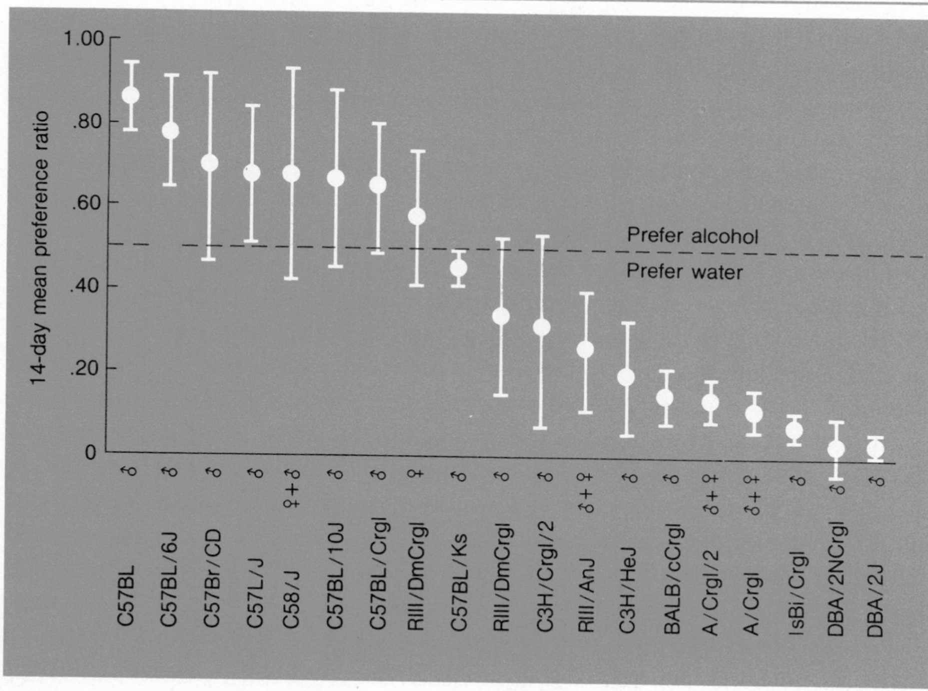

Fig. 23•9 Alcohol preference scores of inbred mouse strains. The dots represent the average preference score for each strain; the extremes of each vertical line represent the range within which the individual scores fell. The sex of the mice studied is indicated along the X-axis (♀ for female, ♂ for male). (Rodgers, 1966)

The absence of evidence for hybrid vigor suggests that alcohol preference is not acted on by natural selection. The various mating crosses done in this and similar breeding programs indicate that more than one pair of alleles is involved in determining alcohol preference but that the number is probably not large (Rodgers, 1966).

Physiology of Alcohol Preference Although we know that alcohol preference in mice is largely influenced by genotype, we should like to know the precise mechanism by which a particular configuration of DNA leads to high alcohol intake in the C57BL mouse strains, while the DBA mouse strains consume only small amounts of alcohol before totally rejecting it (Eriksson and Pikkarainen, 1968). Female C57BL mice may consume almost 90 percent of their total fluid intake as 10 percent alcohol, and males, almost 70 percent. What physiological mechanisms mediate these differences and how do they differ in the two strains? Organisms do not inherit behaviors, organs, or even enzymes. They inherit DNA in the genes. This genetic DNA produces substances such as enzymes, which affect metabolic processes and even behaviors such as alcohol preference. Perhaps C57 mice drink more alcohol than other strains because they have more enzymes to metabolize it.

In one study, alcohol preference was measured in several mouse strains; then the mice were sacrificed and their livers analyzed for *alcohol dehydrogenase*, an enzyme involved in alcohol metabolism (Rodgers et al., 1963). In general, there was a positive relationship between these two measures: strains that had high alcohol preference scores generally had high levels of alcohol dehydrogenase in their livers, and strains low in alcohol preference had low alcohol dehydrogenase levels. These results were confirmed by a study in which C57BL mice with high alcohol intakes had consistently higher liver alcohol dehydrogenase levels than DBA/2 mice with low alcohol intakes (McClearn et al.; 1964).

When they were forced to drink an alcohol solution because no other fluid was given, both mouse strains showed an increase in alcohol dehydrogenase in the liver. When these mice were forced to drink alcohol and then the alcohol was withdrawn for three weeks and replaced with water, liver alcohol dehydrogenase levels fell to the level found in animals that had never drunk alcohol. However, C57BL mice still had a higher level of alcohol dehydrogenase than did DBA/2 mice. These studies suggest that some functional relationship exists between alcohol preference and intake and some enzymes needed for alcohol metabolism.

It is still not clear how alcohol and its metabolites signal the brain to reject or accept alcohol. One possibility is that the respiratory and circulatory poison *acetaldehyde* (which alcohol breaks down into) builds up in the bloodstream and inhibits alcohol preference behavior. Although acetaldehyde is normally broken down into nontoxic substances by the enzyme *acetaldehyde dehydrogenase*, perhaps so much of it is formed by the metabolism of ingested alcohol that it cannot all be degraded. The excess acetaldehyde may therefore inhibit further alcohol intake in some way. However, if an animal's system contains large amounts of acetaldehyde dehydrogenase, the acetaldehyde formed from alcohol metabolism would not build up in the animal's bloodstream.

This theory is supported by a study by Sheppard, Albersheim, and McClearn (1970), where an alcohol-preferring strain (C57BL) was compared to an alcohol-rejecting strain (DBA/2). The livers of C57BL mice contained more acetaldehyde dehydrogenase than did those of the DBA/2 mice, thus allowing acetaldehyde levels to be higher in the blood streams of the DBA/2 mice. The F_1 mice fell between the two parent groups in alcohol preference and in acetaldehyde dehydrogenase levels. When the C57BL and DBA/2 strains were each injected with the same amount of alcohol, acetaldehyde built up in the blood of the DBA/2 mice more rapidly than in the C57BL mice, and remained at a higher level for at least four hours after the injection.

Although the theory the preceding study supports is not borne out by every study of alcohol preference (Rodgers, 1966) and many of the questions remain unanswered, this study represents a good example of attempts to define the physiological basis for an inherited behavior. We know that many physiological links connect DNA and behavior, and that some of those links involve enzyme systems by which genes act on phenotypes. Someday we may know why animals that inherit slightly different DNA configurations behave differently even though they are reared under apparently identical conditions.

Interaction of Heredity with Environment

23·5 By breeding animals selectively, behavior geneticists can use genotype as an independent variable in their experiments. Genotype differs from other independent variables in psychological experiments because it is regulated before the animal is born and cannot be changed during the course of an experiment. However, genotype does not invariably determine how an animal will act in a particular stimulus situation. Instead, the animal's genotype will interact with external variables (such as the type of environment in which the animal is reared) in order to produce a behavior. In other words, behavior cannot be controlled simply by controlling the genes passed onto offspring from their parents. Indeed, many of the experiments we have discussed show that genotype can make a strong contribution to behavior *when animals are reared under the same conditions.* However, when these conditions are varied, behavior may be so strongly influenced as to obscure some of the genetic differences that would be obvious in a uniform environment.

Both genetic and environmental factors shape behavior. Failure to consider their interaction may result in either misunderstanding the influence of an environmental variable because of the choice of genotype, or misunderstanding the influence of genotype on behavior because of the choice of a particular environment. The importance of considering both of these aspects is illustrated in the discussions that follow.

The restricted environment (top) and the enriched environment (middle) separated by a partition (bottom) as used in the Cooper and Zubek studies on how environment influences maze-bright and maze-dull rats. (Photographs courtesy of R. M. Cooper)

Environmental Enrichment and Food Seeking N. D. Henderson (1970) studied the influence of environmental enrichment on six inbred mouse strains and on all thirty F_1 crosses possible (reciprocal crosses were made). He attempted to select for study a behavior that was biologically relevant to what the animal might do in its natural environment and that might be influenced by environmental enrichment. He raised animals in two environments: (1) standard semitransparent mouse cages containing no additional equipment, and (2) cages that were enriched with a small maze, steel tubing, wire-mesh ramps, a hollow log, and some rocks. At six weeks of age, both groups of mice were tested on a simple food seeking task. When they were hungry, the mice were placed in a large enclosure that contained food on a platform high on one wall. In order to reach the platform containing the food, the mice had to climb a narrow wire-mesh ladder, run along a narrow ramp, and cross a series of waterpipes. At first all of the mice engaged in futile jumping. The time that elapsed from the first exposure to the food to the solution of the problem (gaining access to the food) represented the learning score for each mouse.

As Figure 23•10 shows, there is no simple answer to the question "How does being reared in an enriched environment affect performance on a task that requires use of skills acquired in that environment?" For three strains of mice in the experiment, being reared in an enriched environment improved performance (lowered the time required to solve the problem). For the three other strains, however, enrichment had no apparent effect on performance. This study suggests, therefore, that the effect of enrichment depends on (interacts with) the genotype of the animal being enriched.

Before we can answer the question "How do the various strains differ in performance on this task?" we must specify the type of rearing environment. We can see in Figure 23•10 that when the C3H/He and RF mice are reared in the standard environment, their performances are virtually indistinguishable. When they are reared in the enriched environment, however, the C3H/He strain is clearly superior in performance. Henderson cautioned that the standard-cage environment may mask some differences between strains that we would otherwise see. It is also important to note that, in general, hybrid offspring performed better than their inbred parents, thus indicating hybrid vigor and suggesting that the behavior may have been influenced by natural selection (Bruell, 1964a).

Environmental Influences on Maze-bright and Maze-dull Rats We saw previously that the behavioral ability to perform a maze-learning task seems to be remarkably well controlled by heredity—within only six generations of selective breeding, distinct lines of maze-bright and maze-dull rats were produced (Thompson, 1954). This is an interesting finding, especially in view of the controversy regarding heredity and intelligence in humans (Jensen, 1969), which we discussed in Chapter 4. Apparently, however, genetically bright and genetically dull rats differ in learning ability only if they are raised in a standard laboratory environment.

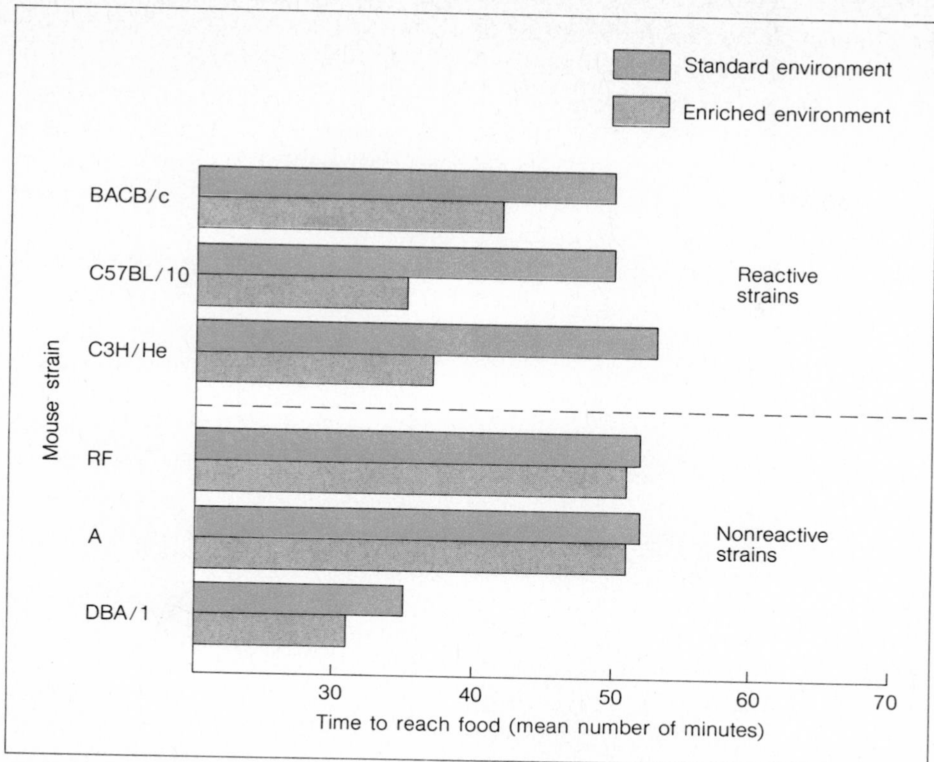

Fig. 23·10 The effect on task performance of rearing six inbred mouse strains in standard or enriched environments. The environmental variable improved performance in three of the six strains. (After Henderson, 1970)

In studies by R. Cooper and J. Zubek (1958), mixed populations of selectively bred bright and dull rats were raised under special environmental conditions. Although the cages were alike in size and in mesh construction, the so-called restricted environment contained only a food box and a water pan whereas the enriched environment contained also ramps, mirrors, swings, marbles, tunnels, bells, and other such objects that could be easily moved in the cage. In addition, the two environments were separated by a partition—painted gray on the "restricted" side and white with designs in black and luminous colors on the "enriched" side. The rats lived in these special environments from weaning (twenty-five days of age) until they were sixty-five days old, when they were tested in a Hebb-Williams maze.

The results of Cooper and Zubek's experiment (Table 23·1) show that if maze-bright and maze-dull rats are tested only in an enriched environment or only in a restricted environment, the different genetic backgrounds appear not to affect maze performance. Indeed, if these had been the only environments used, the original breeding experiment would probably not have been done. Only under the normal laboratory environment were genetic differences reflected in maze performance.

Table 23·1 Mean Error Scores for Maze-Bright and Maze-Dull Rats Raised in Different Environments

RATS	ENRICHED ENVIRON-MENT	NORMAL ENVIRON-MENT	RESTRICTED ENVIRON-MENT
Bright	111	117	170
Dull	120	164	170

(Cooper and Zubek, 1958)

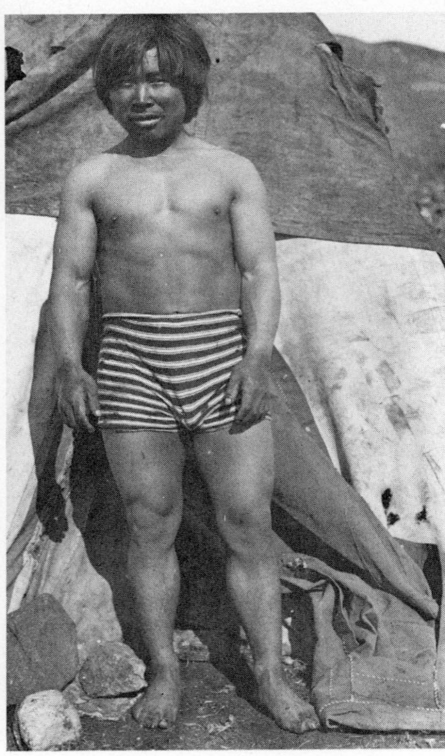

A Masai warrior has a different phenotype from that of an Eskimo because their genotypes differ, the environments where they live differ, and their genotypes interact differently with their environments. (Left: Afrique Photo; right: Courtesy of the American Museum of Natural History)

An organism's genotype does not produce a phenotype in a vacuum but in an environment that contains some degree of complexity (various stimuli). Neither the effects of an environment nor the effects of heredity can be understood in isolation but must be considered as a system where an organism's genotypes interact with environmental factors to produce that organism's phenotypes.

Testosterone and Sexual Behavior Male and female guinea pigs display different sexual behaviors. For example, a female in heat displays lordosis, a behavior in which the back is arched and pelvis raised. Males exhibit a more complex series of sexual behaviors ending in mounting a female and ejaculating.

Are their sex differences dependent on heredity or on environment? From the standpoint of heredity, the answer appears to be simple. Females have two X chromosomes, and males have one X and one Y chromosome. Therefore, the information contained in the Y chromosome programs the sex differences that differentiate males and females. Experimental research has shown, however, that anatomical, physiological, and behavioral sex differences are strongly influenced by the environment in some interesting ways.

W. C. Young (1965) injected pregnant guinea pigs with testosterone (a male sex hormone) approximately thirty to thirty-five days after conception. As a result,

Cyclic Sexual Behavior: What Sex Is the Hypothalamus?

In mammals, the anterior pituitary gland of both females and males secretes hormones that enter the bloodstream and stimulate sex organs in turn to release hormones. In females, the two major ovarian hormones estrogen and progesterone influence the reproductive cycle, whereas in males the testicular hormone testosterone does not follow a cycle—at least not so obvious a one.

In a female rat, for example, an estrous cycle is completed every four to five days. During the estrous cycle, the size of the uterus changes, ovulation occurs, and the female rat goes into heat (behavioral estrus), during which period she demonstrates lordosis and is receptive to the male. These events in the estrous cycle and the accompanying cyclic release of estrogen and progesterone are controlled by the cyclic release of certain hormones from the anterior pituitary gland. In a male rat, however, these cycles do not exist. Apparently, the anterior pituitary gland puts out a constant amount of the hormone that induces a steady output of testosterone from the testes.

Why is the female hormone system cyclic, while the male system is not? Apparently, some of the sex differences of male and female nervous systems appear during a critical period in the development of the organism. The **hypothalamus** controls the function of the anterior pituitary gland and its output of hormones. Therefore, the hypothalamus and the parts of the nervous system that influence its function must become sexually differentiated.

Surgical experiments indicate that the anterior pituitary glands of male and female rats are apparently interchangeable. If the anterior pituitary gland from a male rat is placed under the hypothalamus of a female, the male pituitary gland will support normal cycling behavior in the female. The locus of cycling behavior appears to be a sexually differentiated hypothalamus.

several changes were produced in the anatomy and behavior of the offspring. The males were not affected, but the females were masculinized. In some cases the females so resembled the males anatomically at birth that the sexes were indistinguishable. When the masculinized females grew into adults, they exhibited fewer female sexual behaviors such as lordosis, and more male behaviors such as mounting other females. Subsequent manipulation of sex hormone levels did not result in more typical female behavior. Young therefore concluded that exposure to testosterone before birth had influenced the development of the females' nervous systems.

Summary

Behavior genetics is the study of how the behavior of an organism is influenced by the genes contributed to it by its two parents. An organism does not inherit behavior but rather, inherits genetic material (DNA) contained in chromosomes. The DNA molecules influence the development of the body's structure, function, and behavior by complex chemical events that probably involve basic enzyme systems. An organism's genotype is determined by the genes it possesses at each locus on its chromosomes, which exist in pairs. Some genotypes can be determined from breeding experiments in which the breeding history of animals is carefully controlled and the outward characteristics (phenotype) are carefully observed.

Because genes are reassorted during meiosis (the type of cell division that produces sex cells during reproduction), two parents may theoretically produce a tremendous number of different genotypes in their offspring. The greater the number of chromosomes in an organism, the greater their possible combinations and diversity.

The fruit fly *Drosophila melanogaster* has been widely studied in genetics because it has only four pairs of chromosomes and these chromosomes are very large in some of *D. melanogaster's* tissues. Many of *D. melanogaster's* genes have been identified at particular loci on the chromosomes.

Genes probably influence phenotype by producing a particular enzyme. It now appears that the action of these structural genes is controlled by operator and regulator genes that switch gene action on or off, depending on environmental conditions.

Some behaviors are believed to be dependent on a single allele (gene). A single recessive allele is responsible for a biochemical defect in humans called phenylketonuria, which results from a missing enzyme and causes mental retardation. Huntington's chorea in humans and audiogenic seizures in mice are also dependent on a single allele, but their physiological basis is not known.

Only inherited traits can be acted on by evolutionary pressures. Environmentally produced changes cannot be inherited. Certain inherited traits such as hygienic behavior in bees and nest building in birds seem to be related to survival. In order to survive the selection pressures of the environment, an organism must possess some degree of fitness. Genotype apparently plays some role in determining phenotypic fitness, which is also related to biological diversity. But the genotype may react differently in different environments in the production of the phenotype.

Inbreeding is likely to preserve physical deformities that might be rare in an outbreeding population. Inbred organisms may be inferior to outbred organisms in behavioral capabilities. Outbreeding often results in animals that are vigorous physically and behaviorally (hybrid vigor).

In spite of the problems of inbreeding depression, inbred mouse strains have been widely used in studying behavioral genetics and some medical problems that beset humans. Inbreeding provides breeding stock of known genotype from which we can discover the mode of inheritance of certain behavioral traits and their physiological basis. For example, the inheritance of alcohol preference may depend on the level of certain enzymes involved in alcohol metabolism.

Another way to study the genetics of a behavioral trait is to breed selective strains that are high and low in a particular trait. For example, mice have been selectively bred for brain size and for maze-learning ability. Selective breeding makes possible experiments that can be done in no other way because the constitutional characteristics of the experimental subjects are shaped before the experiment begins—even before the experimental subjects are born.

Although controlled breeding can produce behavior differences in research animals, we must remember that an animal's phenotype is the product of genotype and its interaction with the environment. In most of the successful demonstrations of the power of genotype to shape behavior, environmental influences have been held constant. Sometimes changing the environment causes genetically determined differences in behavior to disappear.

Suggested Readings

Asimov, I. 1962. *The genetic code.* New York: Orion Press.

A clear account of the basic principles of the molecular aspects of genetics.

Lindzey, G., and Thiessen, D. D. 1970. *Contributions to behavior-genetic analysis.* New York: Irvington.

Summaries of research programs in several important areas of behavior genetics of the mouse.

Manosevitz, M.; Lindzey, G.; and Thiessen, D. D.; eds. 1969. *Behavior genetics: Method and research.* New York: Appleton-Century-Crofts.

A comprehensive collection of previously published articles of research techniques and findings in behavior genetics.

McClearn, G. E.; and DeFries, J. C. 1973. *Introduction to behavioral genetics.* San Francisco: W. H. Freeman.

A compact, useful, basic textbook in behavior genetics.

Thiessen, D. D. 1972. *Gene organization and behavior.* New York: Random House.

A short, clear, basic textbook in behavior genetics.

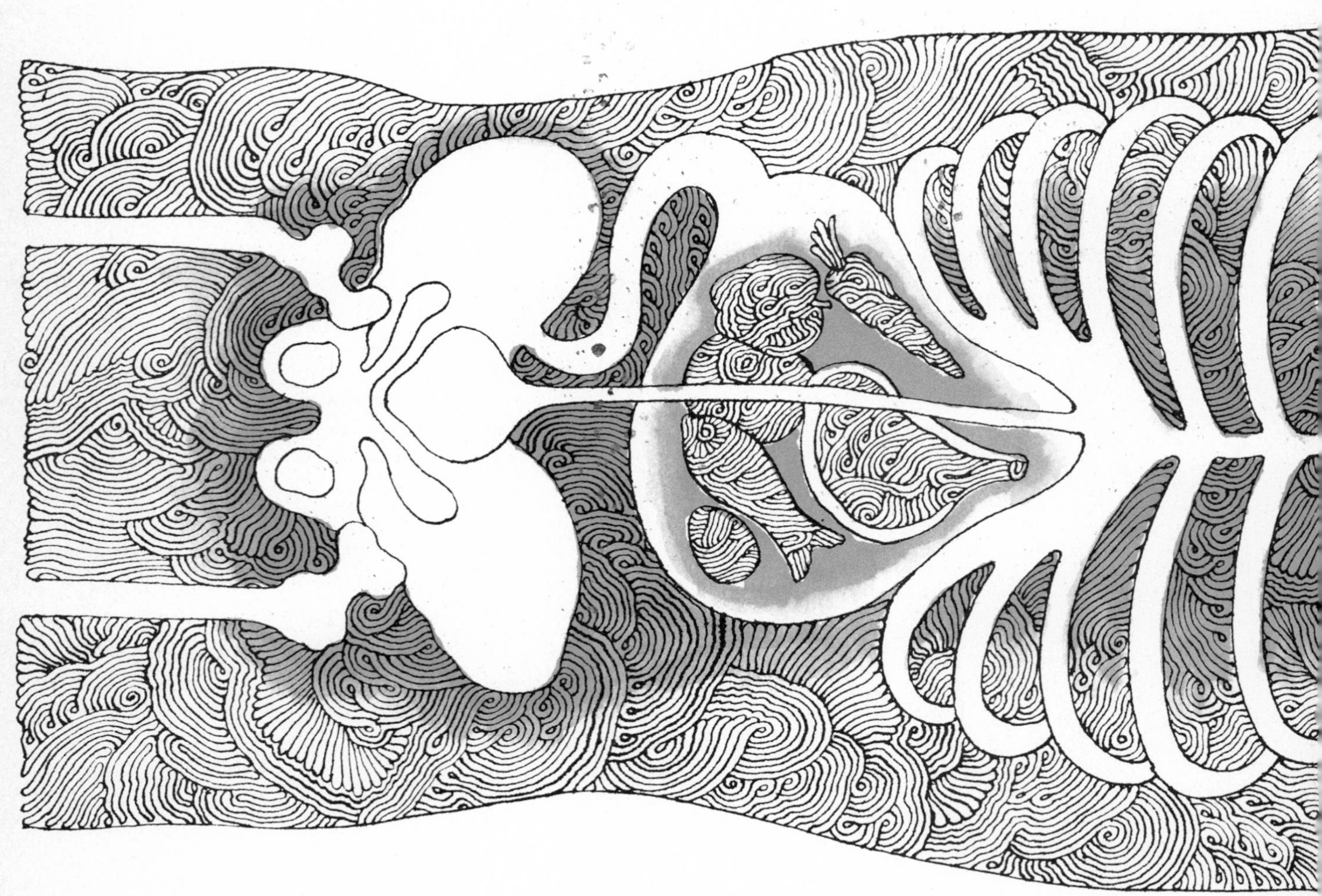

Biological Psychology

VIII

Biological psychology is concerned with the brain processes involved in activities such as thinking, emotions, and perceiving. The brain controls behavior, and behavior and experience can change the structure and function of the brain. These changes can be momentary or they may last a lifetime.

Our goal in this part is to reduce ideas derived from the study of behavior to ideas about the biological functions of the brain. In other words, we seek to understand behavior in terms of the workings of the brain. Our explanations of behavior will thus consist of answers to such questions as: "What are the elements of the brain and what are their properties?" and "How could functions, such as learning, be accomplished with these elements?"

In all but the simplest cases, we cannot give a complete explanation of behavior in terms of biological functions, both because these functions are extremely complex and because they are still being discovered. There are several different levels or methods of analyzing the brain and its functions. The anatomist examines the sizes, shapes and arrangements of the components of the brain. The physiologist studies the ways that communication occurs within the brain and the functions of cells in the brain. The clinical neurologist examines behavior impairment that is caused by disease or injury of the brain. Each approach to the relationship between brain and behavior provides a slightly different look at the areas of research that comprise biological psychology.

Communication in the Brain

24 In this chapter we will examine how the brain is structured, how it develops, what the elements of the brain are, and how brain signals are generated and transmitted. With this basic knowledge of the structure and functions of the brain we will be able to consider some of the ways in which the brain receives and integrates information and determines patterns of movements.

Gross Organization of the Nervous System

24•1 The nervous system extends throughout the entire body. It can be divided into two parts: the **central nervous system** and the **peripheral nervous system** (Figure 24•1). The central nervous system consists of the brain and spinal cord. It is encased by the bone of the skull and the backbone (vertebral column). The peripheral nervous system connects the central nervous system to the rest of the body. It is found outside the skull and vertebral column and is connected to muscles, organs, and sensory receptors. Our primary concern in this chapter is the brain.

In addition to the direct influence of the nervous system on the muscles and organs of the body, behavior is also controlled by chemicals known as **hormones** that are secreted by other organs of the body. Hormones circulate throughout the body and control bodily functions such as growth and reactions to stress.

When discussing the structure of the brain, we will consider first its gross parts (as seen by ordinary observation) and then the cellular elements that form the gross parts of the brain (seen by microscopic observation of thin sections of the brain). Some of the labels used to identify particular brain regions may seem strange. They often come from Greek or Latin words for common objects, shapes, or forms—for example, amygdala ("almond"), pons ("a bridge"), colliculus ("little hill")—or from the family name of the anatomist who initially described that particular area of the brain.

DAN

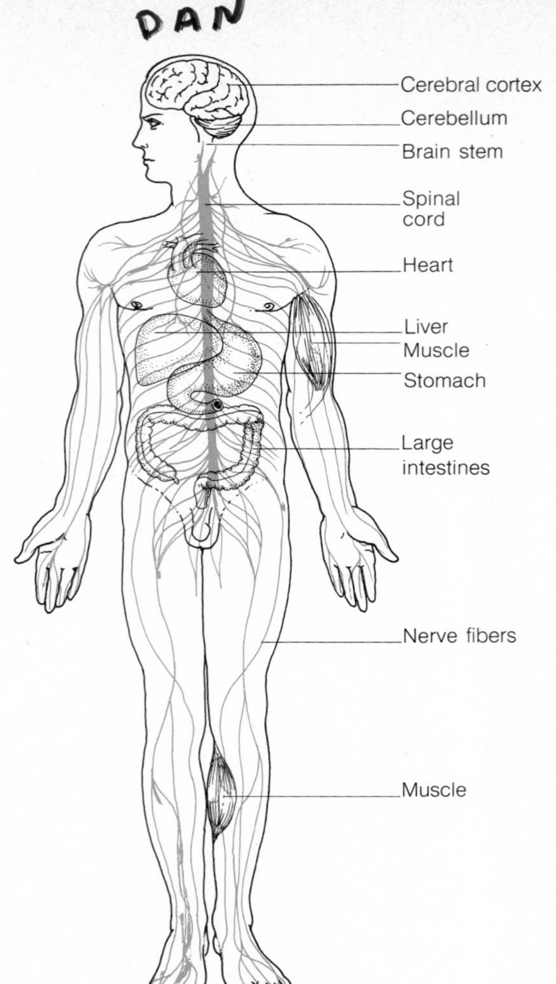

Fig. 24•1 The *central nervous system* consists of the brain and the spinal cord. The spinal cord is connected to the brain and has input and output connections with the rest of the body. The peripheral nervous system (colored yellow in this drawing) consists of bundles of axons (an axon is a part of a nerve cell) referred to as nerves and groups of nerve cells that are situated outside the brain and spinal cord. The nerves of the peripheral nervous system carry sensory information to the brain and spinal cord, and they transmit control information from the brain and spinal cord to the muscles and organs of the body. The parts of the peripheral nervous system that are involved in the control of such automatic functions as heartbeat and digestion are called the autonomic nervous system. Those parts concerned with voluntary muscle movements and with most sensory input are called the somatic nervous system. (Adapted from Goss, 1973; Dawson, 1974)

Gross Parts of the Brain As we saw in Chapter 22, the human brain, when removed from its skull, has a characteristic shape that distinguishes it from the brains of other species (see Figure 22•8). Clues as to the function of a part of the brain may often be derived from comparing the size or complexity of that part of the brain in animals with different behavioral capabilities.

Figure 24•2 shows various views of the human brain. Like the rest of the body, the brain may be divided into a left and a right half with similar structures in each half. If we look at the brain from the top or the bottom, we see that it is divided into two hemispheres. These are called the **cerebral hemispheres.** Some parts of the brain are inside these hemispheres while others are arranged along the middle of the brain.

We may define six major parts of the brain (Figure 24•3): the cerebral cortex, the basal ganglia, the thalamus, the hypothalamus, the cerebellum, and the brain

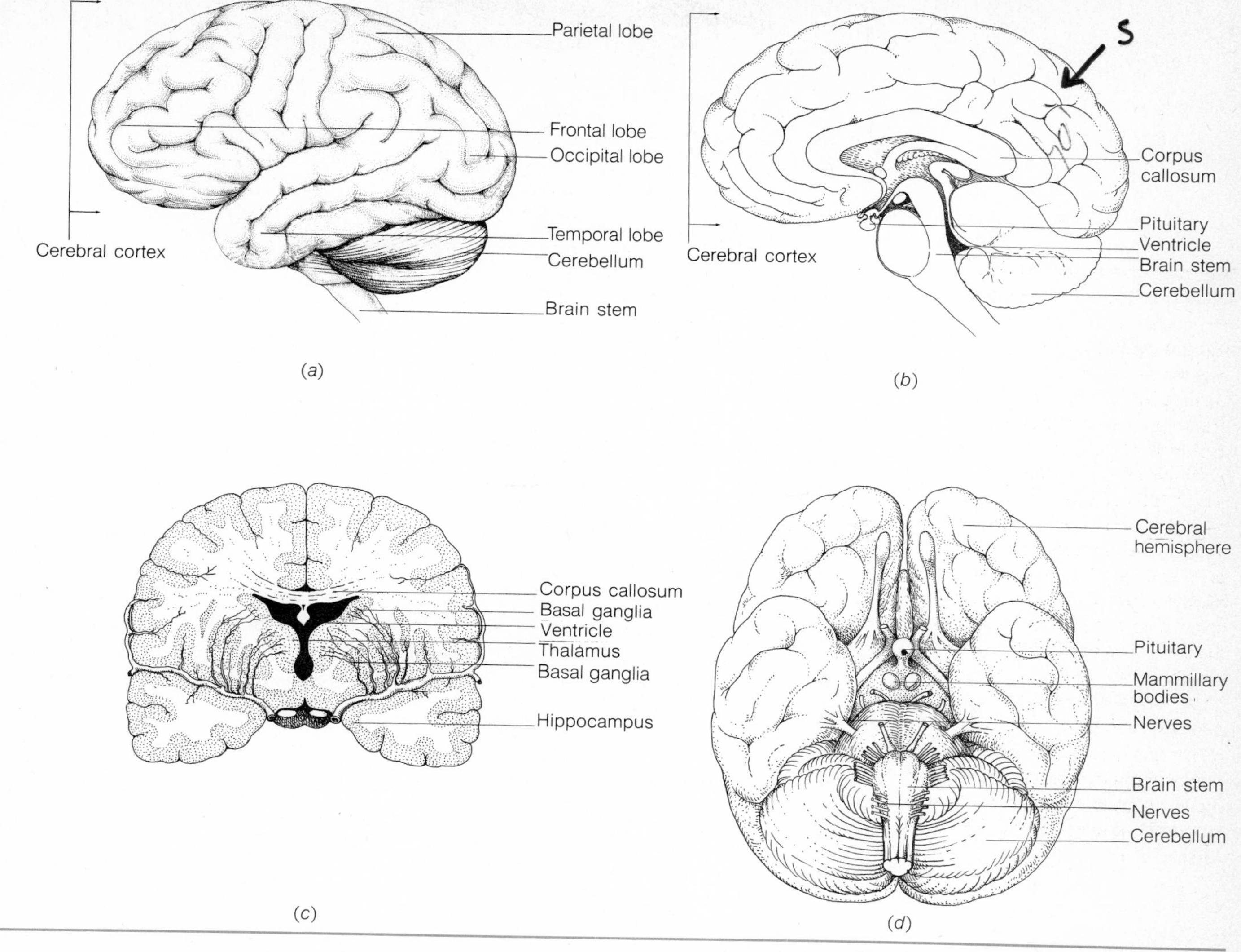

Fig. 24·2 Four views of the human brain. (*a*) A lateral (side) view showing the cerebral cortex (note its deep folds) and cerebellum. (*b*) A medial (middle) view showing the ventricles and some other structures. (*c*) If we cut the brain along a plane parallel to the face, we can see some of the structures that are beneath the cerebral cortex in each hemisphere. (*d*) A bottom view of the brain showing where some of the nerve fibers carrying information to and from the brain emerge. (Adapted from Milner, 1970; Goss, 1973; and Netter, 1962)

stem. The **cerebral cortex** consists of the outer layers of each of the cerebral hemispheres. In humans, the cerebral cortex is extensively folded, whereas in some mammals it is fairly smooth (as we saw in Chapter 22, Figure 22·8). The **basal ganglia** are located below the cortex in each of the cerebral hemispheres. The **thalamus** is centered around the middle of the brain. The **hypothalamus** lies below the thalamus at the base of the brain. The **cerebellum** is behind the cerebral hemispheres. The **brain stem** is behind the thalamus and below the cerebellum but connected to both of them.

The cerebral cortex and thalamus are involved in the processing of complex sensory information and the control of voluntary muscle movements. The basal ganglia may be involved in the elaboration and control of muscle movements.

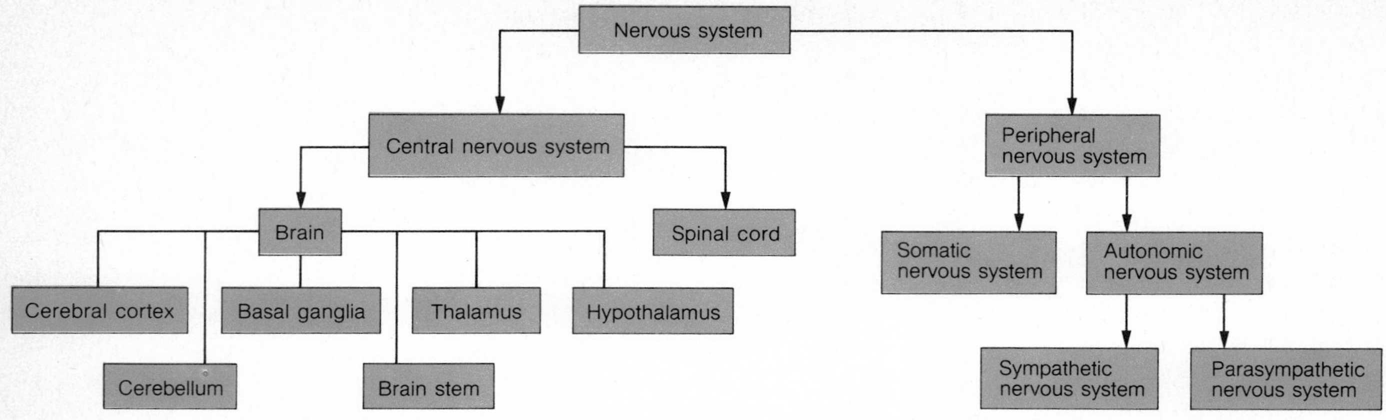

Fig. 24•3 Major components of the nervous system. The sympathetic and parasympathetic divisions of the autonomic nervous system will be discussed in Chapter 25.

The cerebellum governs such things as balance and smooth movements of limbs. The hypothalamus and brain stem are important in the regulation of basic bodily functions.

When we ascribe certain functions to different parts of the brain, we must remember three things. First, particular functions may involve many brain areas working together. Second, while it is convenient to discuss such broad functions as learning and perception as if they were separate categories of behavior, there are not necessarily separate parts of the brain that correspond to these processes. And finally, an area of the brain may be responsible for many more functions than we have suggested.

The entire brain is surrounded by protective coverings called the *meninges*, and floats inside the skull in fluid called the *cerebrospinal fluid*. This fluid also circulates in chambers inside the brain called *ventricles*, and exchanges materials such as nutrients and waste products with certain parts of the brain. The meninges, cerebrospinal fluid, and ventricles cushion the brain against injury from both ordinary and accidental movement of head and body.

The Cellular Level The brain of an adult human contains from 10 to 20 billion cells. These cells vary widely in size and shape and are arranged in distinctive collections or assemblies known as brain regions or nuclei. This is another use of the word *nucleus* in addition to the one you are familiar with as describing a part of a cell. The major divisions of the brain described in the preceding section may often be further divided into nuclei.

Although there is great structural diversity among the billions of cells in the brain, brain cells fall into two classes: **nerve cells** and **glial cells.** These two classes of cells can be seen when brain tissue is sliced very thinly and examined under a microscope. Figure 24•4 (in color section) shows two of the many shapes nerve cells may have.

Nerve Cells All nerve cells consist of (1) a *cell body* region containing a nucleus that directs the metabolic machinery of the cell; (2) *dendrites,* which are extensions that branch off of the cell body (they frequently resemble a tree); and (3) an *axon,* which is a single, thin cylindrical extension from the cell body (Figure 24•5). The cone-shaped area close to the cell body where the axon originates is known as the *axon hillock.* Beyond the axon hillock, the axon is tubular; in most vertebrates its diameter ranges from 0.5 to 20 microns.

Numerous branches are evident at the end of an axon. These branches terminate on other nerve cells. The region where nerve cells connect is called a **synapse** (Figure 24•6). Each synapse consists of (1) a *presynaptic terminal,* which is frequently a kind of swelling at the end of a branch of the axon, (2) a *postsynaptic area,* which is usually a specialized part of either a dendrite or the cell body and (3) a *synaptic cleft* or separation (from 20 to 40 nanometers wide) between these two elements. The cell body and dendrites of any nerve cell in the brain are studded with many such synapses; a single nerve cell may have from 50 to 100,000 of them.

We would like to know more about the intricate molecular structure of the synapse, about how synaptic connections form during development, and about how the structure of the synapse changes with use. Research on these topics may provide the basis for understanding how the brain works and how experience modifies brain function.

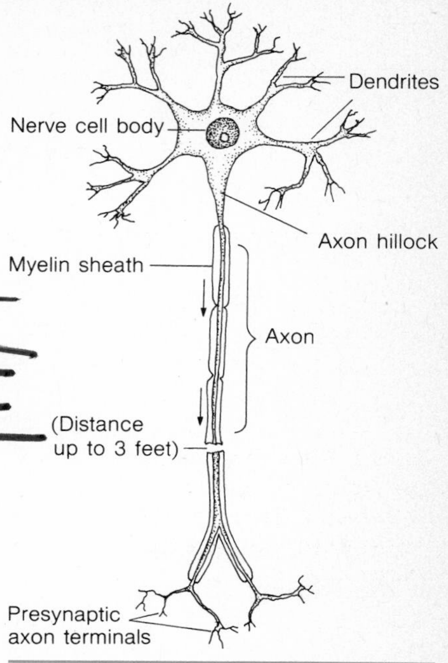

Fig. 24•5 An outline of a nerve cell. Dendrites receive inputs. The axon transmits activity away from the cell body to the axon terminals. The cell body contains a nucleus that directs the metabolic machinery of the cell. The differences in shapes of nerve cells are mostly due to differences in the shape of their dendrites and the size of their cell bodies. (From Thompson, 1967)

Glial Cells Glial cells are distributed throughout the brain. In many regions they are far more numerous than nerve cells. Glial cells are thought to be involved in separating nerve cells, in transporting nutrients to and from the vascular system (the arteries, capillaries, and veins) of the brain, and in providing a foundation or framework on which nerve cells may grow and organize.

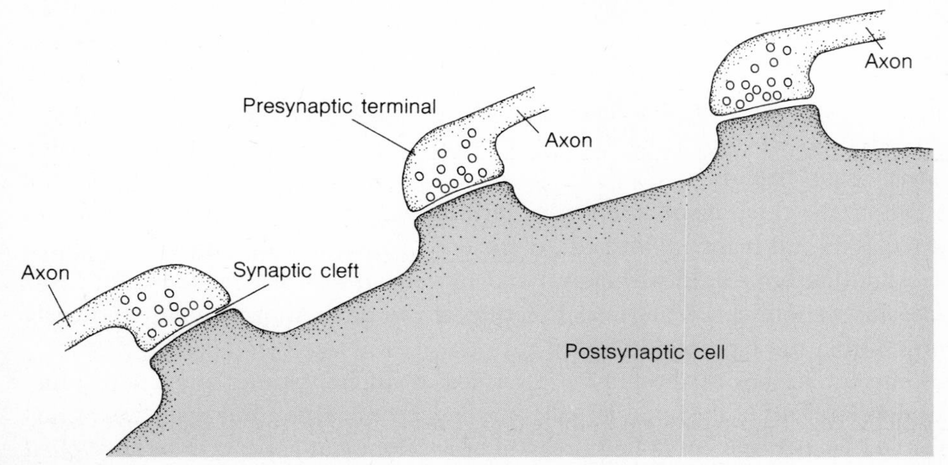

Fig. 24•6 Basic components of the synapse. A branch of the axon ends in a slight bulge known as the presynaptic terminal. The presynaptic terminal is separated from the next nerve cell (the postsynaptic cell) by a narrow gap called the synaptic cleft. Bodies within the presynaptic terminal (drawn here as circles) contain a chemical that can influence the postsynaptic cell at certain points (called receptor sites), thus allowing nerve cells to communicate.

Axons are frequently embedded in a sheath formed by glial cells. This sheath material, called **myelin,** provides a kind of electrical insulation. The functional effect of this insulation is to enable nerve signals to travel faster.

Cellular Composition of Brain Regions Any brain region is composed of nerve and glial cells arranged in distinctive ways. In many brain regions, these assemblies of cells form layers called a *laminar arrangement.* Figure 24•7 (in color section) shows the arrangement of cells in four different areas of the brain.

The ways in which nerve cells are assembled and connected determine the ways in which information is processed in particular brain regions. The perceptual strategies we discussed in Chapter 8 describe processes that are carried out by the distinctive arrangements of nerve cells in the brain, and the signals that travel in these arrangements of cells.

Growth and Development of the Nervous System

24•2 As we saw in Chapters 3 through 6, the extensive behavior changes that occur during the course of life from birth to old age, are orderly and sequential. This regularity of behavior development is especially evident in the development of movements during infancy and early childhood. Some of the motor reflexes of infancy (Figure 24•8) disappear as the infant grows, but may reappear later in life, perhaps following brain injury. The regularity of motor development is characteristic of a broad range of behaviors, including the acquisition of language and thought; this suggests an underlying orderliness and regularity in the maturation of the brain.

What changes occur in the brain's organization as it grows and develops? At the very beginning of fetal life, the rapid cell division of the fertilized egg results in a ball-like cluster of cells. Part of this cluster then spreads out into the shape of a plate that soon consists of several layers (Figure 24•9). One of these layers, called the *ectoderm,* is the beginning of the nervous system. Its cells form a tube along the length of the *embryo* and divide repeatedly to form the precursors of nerve and glial cells. At this stage, these cells have no axons or dendrites and are called *neuroblasts.* The neuroblasts migrate away from the tube and slowly arrange themselves in clusters of cell groups that begin to take on the characteristic appearance of the various brain regions.

During the three months following fertilization of the egg, the major outlines of the body and brain are formed. At the end of that period, the fetus is capable of exhibiting both head withdrawal and movement at every joint. Figure 24•10 (in color section) shows an overall picture of the progression of brain and body form during the fetal period.

Different regions of the brain are formed at different times and rates during the development of the *fetus.* Usually, the larger cells of the adult brain are formed first and smaller cells later. This program of development appears to be controlled by intrinsic, genetic mechanisms such as we discussed in Chapter 23. By the time

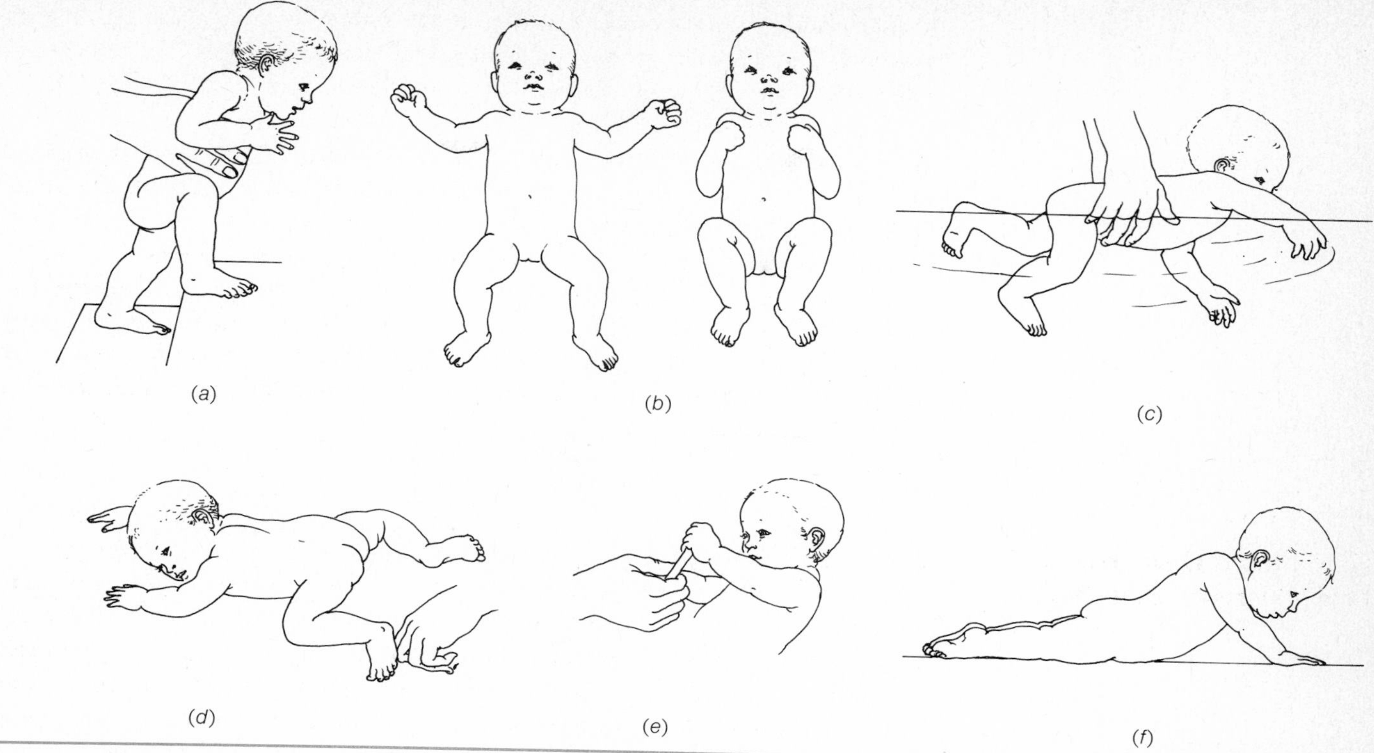

Fig. 24•8 Some reflexes seen in most human infants at birth or within a month thereafter. (*a*) Walking reflex is elicited (until age three months) when the infant is held in an upright position. (*b*) Moro reflex (until age four months): the arms and legs are drawn up as in an embrace when there is a loud noise or sudden motion. (*c*) Swimming reflex is elicited (until age four months) when the infant is exposed to water. (*d*) Crawling reflex appears (until age nine months) when pressure is applied to the bottoms of the feet. (*e*) Palmar reflex (until age nine months): the infant grasps an object placed in the hand. (*f*) Supporting reflex: arms extend as hands touch a level surface. (From Cratty, 1970)

of birth, nearly all of the nerve cells have appeared. In fact, more nerve cells are formed during fetal life than survive to birth.

At birth, the human brain weighs 350 grams; by adulthood, it weighs 1300 to 1500 grams. (Female brains generally weigh less than male brains simply because the average body weight of females is less than that of males.) Various cellular processes such as myelinization result in the vast difference between birth and adult brain weights. In myelinization many of the axons in the brain develop a covering of myelin. This process takes place at different rates throughout the brain, even into the third and fourth decades of life. Although some myelinization occurs before birth, it is more intensive after birth.

The greatest changes that take place in the brain's nerve cells from birth to maturity occur in the dendrites, which increase vastly in length and complexity and in the number of synapses they contain. A graph showing the rapid increase in the number of synapses in cerebral cortex of a rat is shown in Figure 24•11. The brain is especially sensitive to environmental influences during this period of rapid growth.

Factors Affecting Nervous System Development Factors that guide the growth of the nervous system are still being discovered. The early formation of the characteristic structure of the brain seems to be programmed by genetic information,

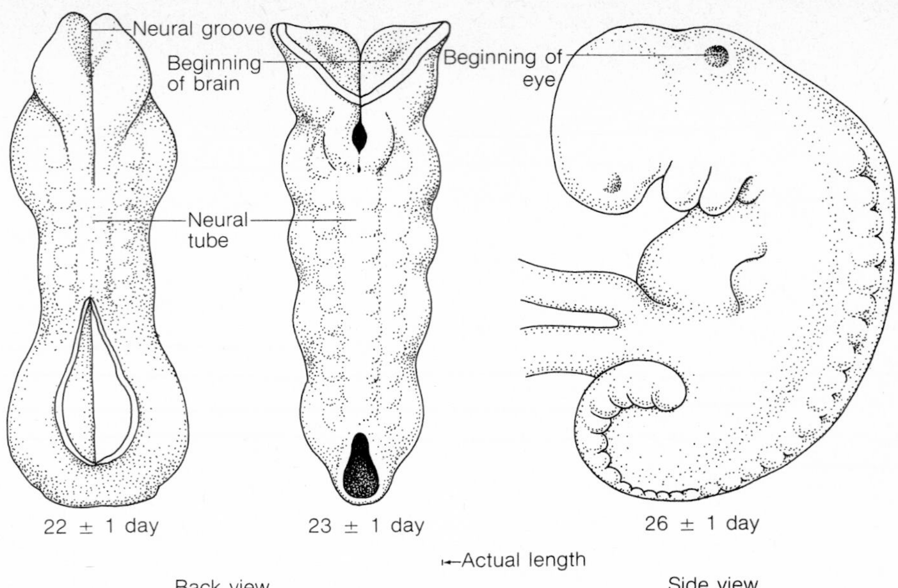

Fig. 24·9 Early in the development of a human embryo, cells in the ectoderm form a tube (the neural tube) that is the beginning of the brain and spinal cord. Before long the fetus may exhibit movements and sensitivities, indicating a working nervous system. (Adapted from Moore, 1974)

but early experience may also have an impact. Various factors can disastrously influence brain development, altering behavioral capabilities and even producing mental retardation. Some of these factors include disturbances of the fetal environment, complications of the birth process, and certain early postnatal influences.

Genetic Factors If a brain is to form and mature normally, its developmental processes must be controlled by normal genetic mechanisms. Abnormal genetic mechanisms underlie many forms of mental retardation and are inherited in various ways. In some cases, a developmental abnormality is due to a mutant **gene** or genes that may be carried by one or both parents.

The most obvious and potentially catastrophic disorders of nervous system development result when both parents carry the same harmful mutant gene. The abnormalities that can result in the offspring are usually *metabolic disorders*, some of which involve the absence of an **enzyme** that controls a critical biochemical step in the synthesis or degradation of an important chemical substance.

The metabolic disorder *phenylketonuria*, for example, is genetically controlled. As we saw in Chapter 23, this disorder results from the buildup of excess phenylpyruvic acid in the body because the enzyme needed to metabolize phenylalanine (which is present in a normal diet) is missing due to a gene defect. Brain changes produced by this state include smaller brain size and less myelinization of nerve fibers. This abnormality occurs only if the dietary intake of phenylalanine is high. If the disorder is diagnosed early enough, brain damage can be prevented by putting the patient on a special diet low in phenylalanine.

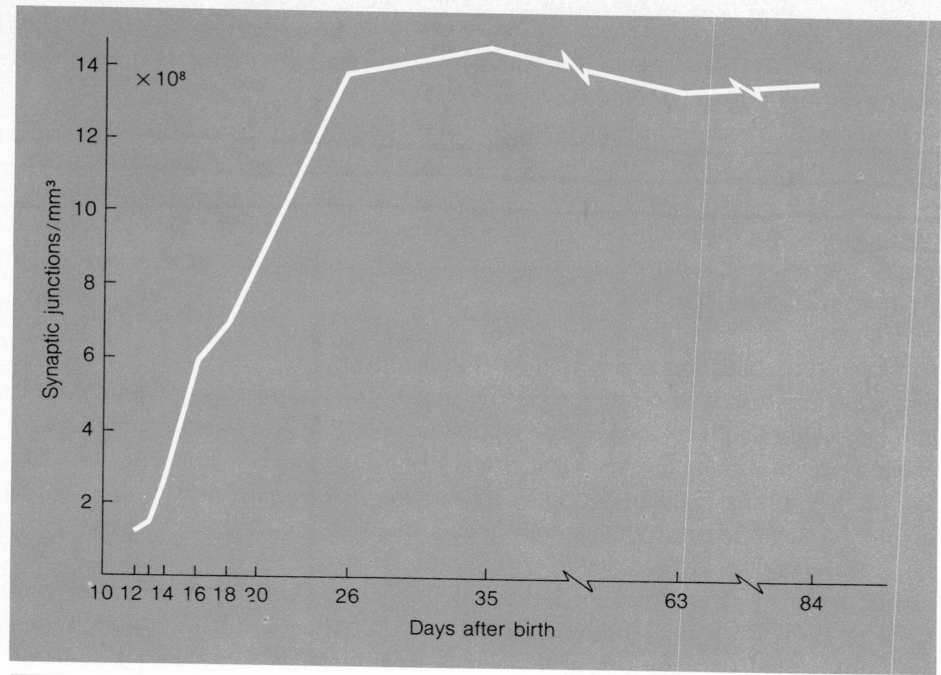

Fig. 24·11 The number of synapses per cubic millimeter in the cerebral cortex of a rat at various ages after birth. Synapses were counted with the aid of an electron microscope. (From Aghajanian and Bloom, 1967)

Early Experience Although many features of brain development seem to be guided by intrinsic, genetic mechanisms, some research studies suggest that early experience can modify the structural properties of the brain. The experiments of D. Krech, M. Rosenzweig, E. Bennett, and M. Diamond over the past twenty years show that environmental enrichment increases the structural development of rat brains (this has been summarized most recently by Rosenzweig and Bennett, 1976). In these experiments, one group of rat litter mates was reared individually in isolated cages (impoverished environment), while another group of litter mates grew up among other rats in a large community cage (enriched environment) containing many objects that could be used as toys. The rats raised in the enriched environment had deeper and heavier brain cortexes, a greater number of glial cells, and longer dendrites on some of their cortical cells than the rats raised in the impoverished environment.

Gerbils were also used in experiments to show the effects of an enriched environment. (Courtesy E. L. Bennett and Mark R. Rosenzweig)

Experiments that limit sensory experience early in life provide further evidence of the impact of experience on the development of the nervous system. Blakemore (1974) and others (such as Hirsch and Spinelli, whose work was discussed in Chapter 8) raised kittens from birth in environments that allowed them to see only certain visual features (only vertical stripes, for example). When the cortical areas involved in vision were examined in these animals, they were found to have developed many cells that responded best to the type of visual features they had grown

Apparatus used in an experiment (Blakemore, 1974) to determine whether early experience affects perception by modifying brain structure. The kitten was exposed to vertical stripes for a few hours every day and spent the rest of the day in the dark. The cortex of a cat raised this way is more responsive to vertical lines than is the cortex of a cat raised in a normal environment.

up seeing. Hence, in an animal exposed to vertical stripes, early in life, there were many nerve cells that responded best to vertical stripes later in life. It is as though early exposure organizes the connections in the brain.

The results of such experiments suggest that (1) early selective visual experience affects the structure and function of certain cortical cells and (2) these modifications occur only during certain critical periods of development (much as **imprinting** does). These controversial experiments suggest that experience may determine whether an existing synapse will function normally and even whether a particular synapse will be formed at all.

Maternal Virus Infection Maternal infections during pregnancy can have strong effects on the organization of the central nervous system of the developing fetus and may cause handicaps (including mental retardation) and sensory impairments (such as deafness). In recent years, the relationship between viral infections of the mother during pregnancy (especially *rubella*, or German measles) and childhood neurological handicaps have been identified.

The connection between *rubella* virus infection during pregnancy and fetal malformation became apparent following a large-scale *rubella* epidemic in Australia in 1941. Both the studies conducted at that time and subsequent studies have established that the risk of fetal malformation or of spontaneous abortion was particularly great if the mother's *rubella* infection occurred during the first three months of pregnancy. In a 1964 study involving 6000 pregnant women, 10 percent of the children born to women who had symptoms of German measles during the first three months of pregnancy had neurological dysfunctions at birth. Of the pregnant women who were exposed to the *rubella* virus but had no symptoms, 0.6 percent gave birth to neurologically handicapped infants.

The anatomical basis for the neurological handicaps evident in children who have been affected by prenatal *rubella* infection include abnormalities of the blood vessels of the brain and so blood flow is impaired. The brain weight deficiency observed in affected children probably results from the ability of the *rubella* virus to prevent cell proliferation during critical embryological periods. Hearing loss that appears to involve the mechanisms of the inner ear is a common handicap of these children.

Other maternal virus infections such as chicken pox, measles, and smallpox can produce in humans severe developmental consequences similar to those caused by *rubella*, although the incidence of brain malformation in these cases is less.

Complications in the Birth Process: Birth Asphyxia If certain complications occur in the uterus or during the birth process, the supply of oxygen to the developing brain is severely diminished or even temporarily cut off. The resulting oxygen deprivation usually causes brain damage and deters normal brain development. Some episodes of oxygen deprivation result from an obstruction in the umbilical cord, from disease in the placenta that encloses and supports the fetus, or from separation of the umbilical cord from the placenta during birth.

The results of oxygen deprivation can be seen in certain behavior responses of the newborn infant. These responses are measured on the *Apgar scale* and include crying intensity and the presence or absence of crying at birth. Children who have been oxygen-deprived have poorer scores on the Apgar scale than do children whose prenatal development and birth have been uncomplicated. Experimental studies using monkeys show that birth asphyxia causes marked structural changes in the brain, including degeneration of brain cells.

Malnutrition Although inadequate nutrition during adulthood seems not to affect brain structure, malnutrition during prenatal and postnatal brain development can slow or stop myelinization and dendrite development and can reduce the number of nerve cells formed. In human beings, the impact of malnutrition on brain structure is greatest during the periods of maximal brain growth that occur during late gestation and the first few months after birth (Dobbing and Smart, 1974).

An indirect assessment of the impact of malnutrition on brain size is available in measurements of head circumference of children. Many studies show that early malnutrition may result in permanent reduction of head circumference, which in turn suggests that the brain has not developed to normal size (Figure 24•12). Some data suggest that brain changes due to early malnutrition may be related to reduced intellectual capacities as assessed by IQ tests. Since adequate sensory stimulation is also necessary for brain development and since early malnutrition frequently occurs in environments where adequate sensory stimulation

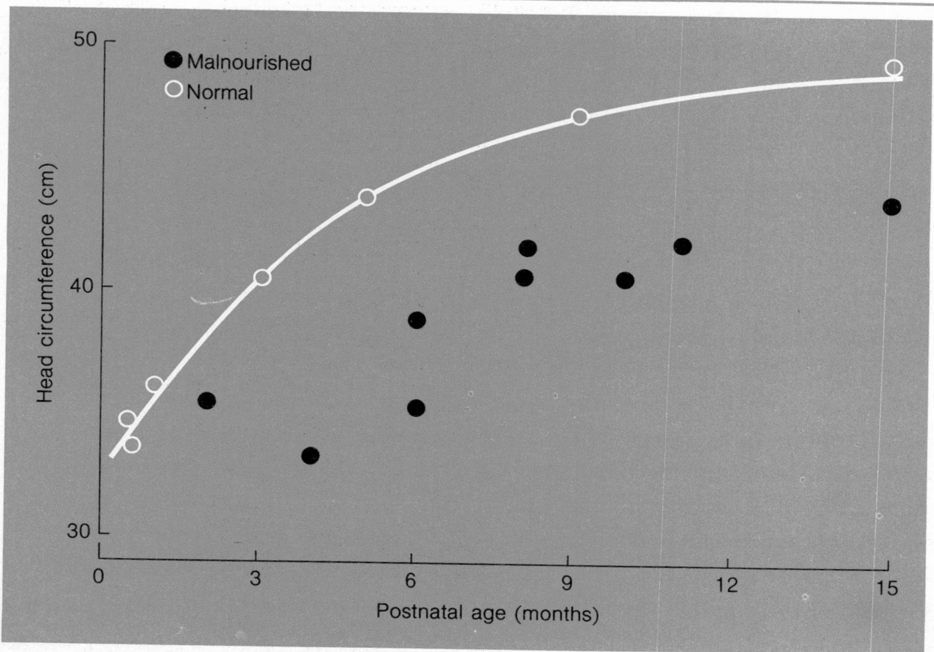

Fig. 24•12 Head circumference in normal and malnourished children. (Winick and Rosso, 1969)

is not available, it is difficult to attribute reduced IQ performance directly to malnutrition.

Hormone Imbalance Hormones are chemicals that are secreted into the bloodstream by the brain and other organs of the body. They direct and regulate activities such as growth and rate of bodily activity. Difficulties may arise if a hormone level is too high or too low. For example, let us consider the effects of an imbalance of thyroid hormone, the hormone regulating growth and *metabolism.*

Inadequate thyroid hormone (hypothyroidism) causes a general slowing of nerve cell development in the brain, which can result in cretinism, a form of mental retardation. Experimental studies in rats have shown that the number of synapses in the cerebellum can be influenced by too much or too little thyroid hormone (Nicholson and Altman, 1972). Too much thyroid hormone (hyperthyroidism) causes cellular proliferation to stop prematurely, thus limiting the total number of nerve cells in the brain. These effects may result from the impact of this hormone on metabolic events associated with protein synthesis.

Environmental Toxins and Brain Development Some of the chemical products and developments of modern industrialized society exert insidious and extremely destructive effects on brain structure; frequently these effects can lead to permanent behavior dysfunctions. These toxin-induced destructive effects can have a particularly strong impact on young children since some toxins can modify brain structure at significant developmental periods.

Some well-known examples of these potentially destructive processes have resulted from heavy metal poisoning due to exposure to mercury or lead. Lead-containing paint is still found on the walls and woodwork in some old houses, although it is no longer manufactured. Because it has a sweet taste, this paint is often chewed from old furniture and woodwork by young children, whose nervous systems may become irreversibly damaged.

Brain Regrowth Following Injury

24·3 Is there any evidence of brain regrowth following injury? This is a vital question because many people sustain brain injuries from accidents or from diseases such as paralytic stroke, in which the flow of blood to the brain is impaired. Unlike some other organs of the body, the brain does not make nerve cells after the age of one to two years. (Glial cells, however, are produced throughout life.)

When an axon outside the brain in the peripheral nervous system is cut, it is removed from the metabolic machinery of the nerve cell to which it was attached, and is absorbed by the body. The stub remaining on the nerve cell slowly regrows; sprouts appear at the tip of the stub, and they seem to follow paths similar to the path of the original axon. In some cases, however, scar tissue formed as a result of the injury can block the path of the regrowing axon.

For many years, it was thought that the process of axonal regrowth characteristic of the peripheral nervous system did not occur in the brain. However, new microscopic techniques present a much clearer picture of nerve components in the brain and it appears that some axons do regrow following injury. Regrowth of dendrites may also occur after some forms of injury. It has not yet been demonstrated, however, whether this regrowth forms a basis for behavioral compensation after a brain injury. If methods can be developed to stimulate and control regrowth of injured brain regions in humans, a potent aid in the behavioral rehabilitation of brain-injured persons may become available.

Brain Signals

24·4 We have learned that nerve cells have areas specialized for inputs (postsynaptic areas on dendrites and cell body) and outputs (the axon and the presynaptic membrane) of signals between nerve cells, and that the nervous system consists of highly organized groups of interconnected nerve cells. To understand how nerve cells produce behavior, it is not sufficient to know how they are interconnected. We must also know how signals are generated, transmitted, elaborated, integrated, and analyzed by nerve cells and groups of nerve cells. These signals play upon the structure of the nervous system to produce movements, thoughts, and emotions and to analyze stimulus information.

While brain signals involve both chemical and electrical events, we often observe only the electrical events. In some models of the nervous system, we imagine that the transmission and processing of electrical signals are the only events of interest. Thus when we speak of "circuits" in the brain, we mean connected groups of nerve cells in which electrical signals are generated, transmitted, and analyzed.

Nerve cells are unique in that they have the capacity to generate and conduct excited states, thus providing the signals that transmit and process information in the brain. These signals are transmitted along the nerve cell, and at its terminals (ends of the axon) they produce changes that communicate some of the features of the nerve cell's excited state to other nerve cells.

Excited states are complex physiochemical events. Two principal classes of excited states form the signal repertoire of nervous system communications: (1) *nerve impulses* (spikes) are pulselike events that last from 0.5 to 2.0 milliseconds and are transmitted as in a chain reaction along an axon at speeds from less than 1 meter per second to over 100 meters per second; (2) *graded events* (slow potentials) are local changes in the magnitude of a nerve cell's electrical potential. They occur postsynaptically and may trigger a nerve impulse in the postsynaptic cell body. These changes are called graded because their size is directly related to the size of the stimulus producing them. Therefore, the local graded potentials produced by many stimuli may sum to produce an overall shift in the resting membrane potential of the postsynaptic cell. This is in contrast to the nerve impulse, in that the intensity of a stimulus can change the frequency of a nerve impulse, but not its amplitude (size).

The Resting Membrane Potential The surface of the nerve cell is a *membrane* that separates the inside of the cell (intracellular space) from the area outside it (extracellular space). This membrane has selective properties in that it separates electrically charged particles called ions. As a consequence of this ability, there is a difference in electrical potential across the membrane. This difference ranges from −60 to −90 millivolts.

Figure 24•13 shows how this potential can be measured. When both electrodes are situated in the extracellular region, there is no potential difference. As one electrode moves through the cell membrane, a sudden drop in potential is registered on the meter. This potential difference is called the *resting membrane potential.* Many other kinds of cells have a resting membrane potential, but only the nerve cell has the ability to change its potential as a way of signaling and processing information. *Depolarization* refers to a reduction of the membrane potential (toward zero), while *hyperpolarization* refers to an increase in membrane potential.

Transmission of the Nerve Impulse Along Axons Suppose that at one end of an axon we were to place two wires connected to an electrical stimulator and at the other end of the axon we had a pair of electrodes that measure the membrane potential (Figure 24•14). If the electrical stimulus depolarizes the axon by approximately 15 millivolts (changing the membrane potential from −70 mv to −55 mv), then the recording electrodes report rapid depolarization: the membrane potential briefly jumps to an amplitude of +30 millivolts. The duration of this change is about 1 to 2 milliseconds; it is known as the nerve impulse. The nerve impulse is an active, sudden change in the membrane rather than a mere reflection of the stimulus. If we apply a more intense electrical stimulus, several of these impulses —each similar in form, amplitude, and duration—will occur in rapid succession. Therefore, increasing stimulus intensity to the axon changes the frequency of the nerve impulses but not their amplitude. If we gradually decrease stimulus intensity, we will find a critical threshold, or level, below which a nerve impulse does not occur.

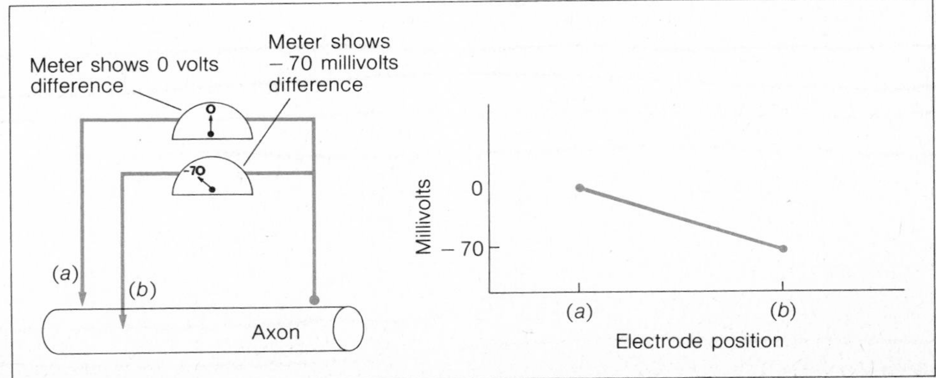

Fig. 24•13 Measurement of the resting membrane potential. If both measuring electrodes are outside the axon (*a*), there is no difference in voltage between them. However, if one electrode is inside (*b*), a difference of −60 to −90 millivolts is measured. This difference in potential from the inside of the cell to the outside is termed the resting membrane potential.

Fig. 24·4 Nerve cells from the cerebral cortex (*a*) and the cerebellum (*b*), each with outline drawings showing the major parts of nerve cells. (Arnold Leiman)

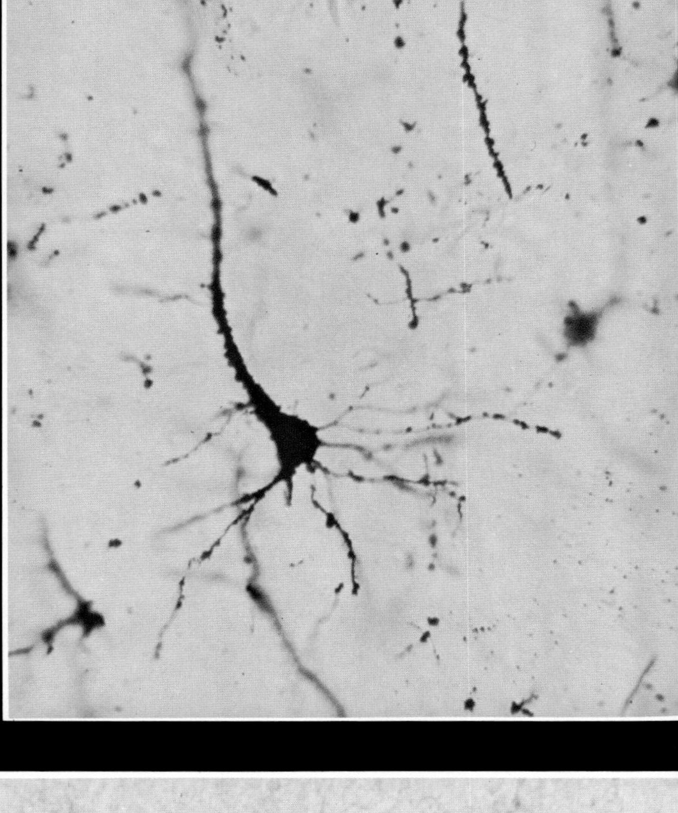

(*a*)

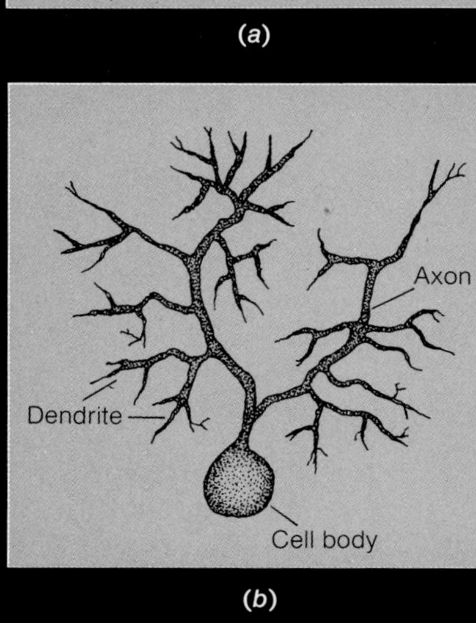

(*b*)

(*a*)

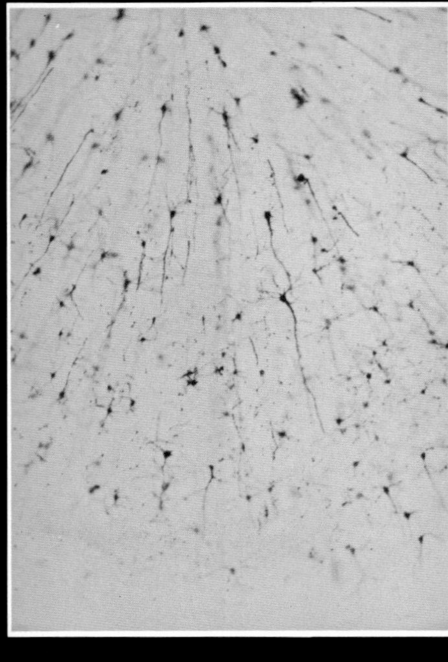

(*b*)

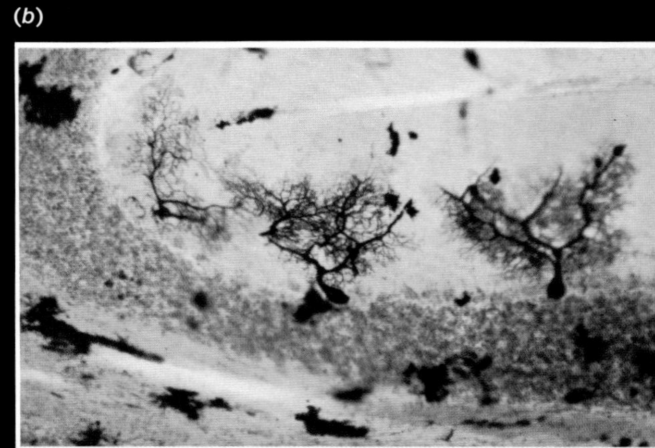

(*c*)

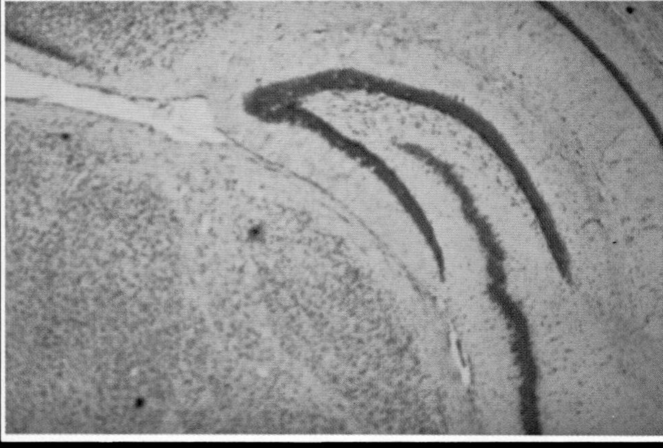

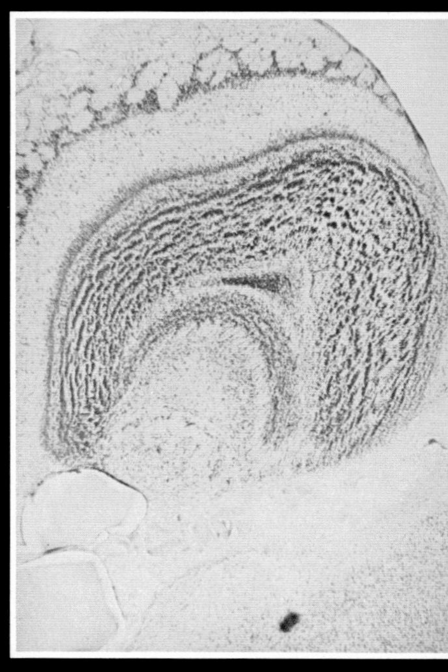

(*d*)

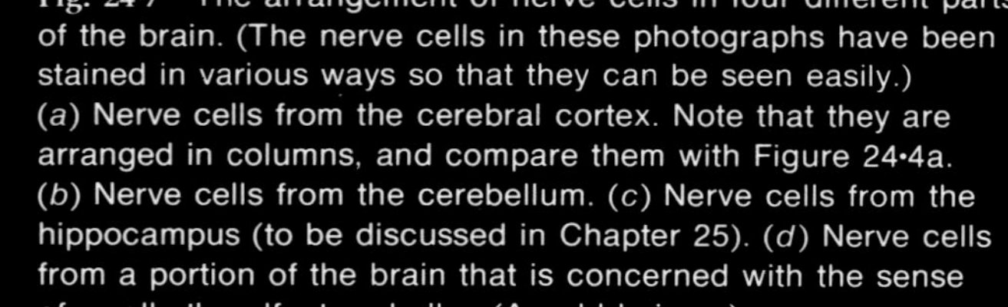

Fig. 24·7 The arrangement of nerve cells in four different parts of the brain. (The nerve cells in these photographs have been stained in various ways so that they can be seen easily.) (*a*) Nerve cells from the cerebral cortex. Note that they are arranged in columns, and compare them with Figure 24·4a. (*b*) Nerve cells from the cerebellum. (*c*) Nerve cells from the hippocampus (to be discussed in Chapter 25). (*d*) Nerve cells from a portion of the brain that is concerned with the sense of smell—the olfactory bulbs. (Arnold Leiman)

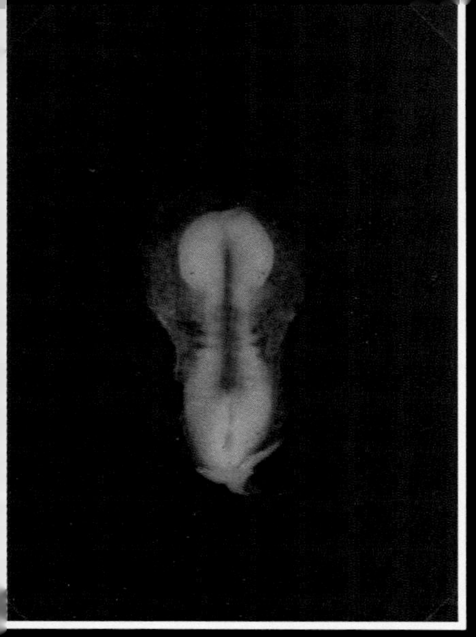

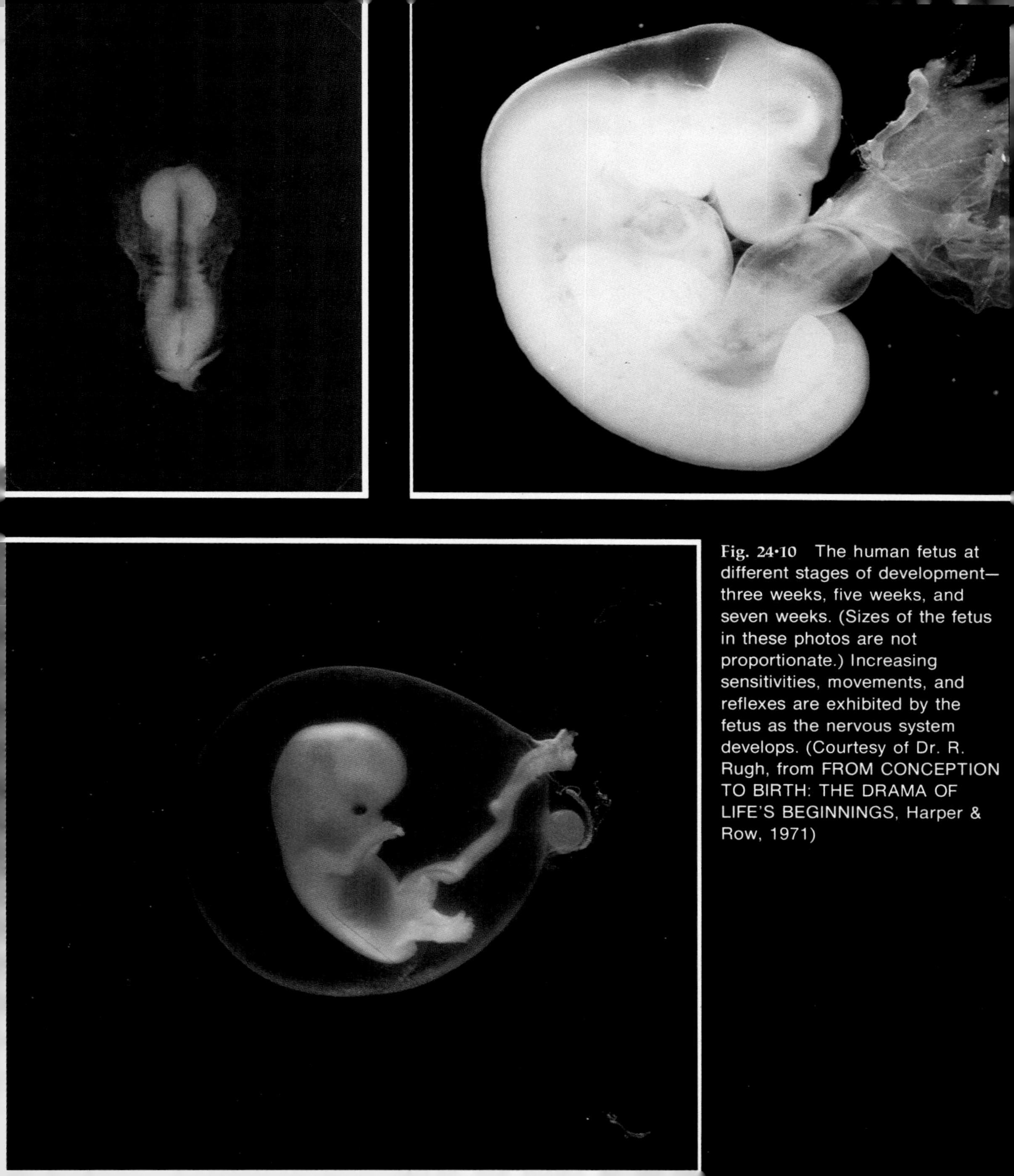

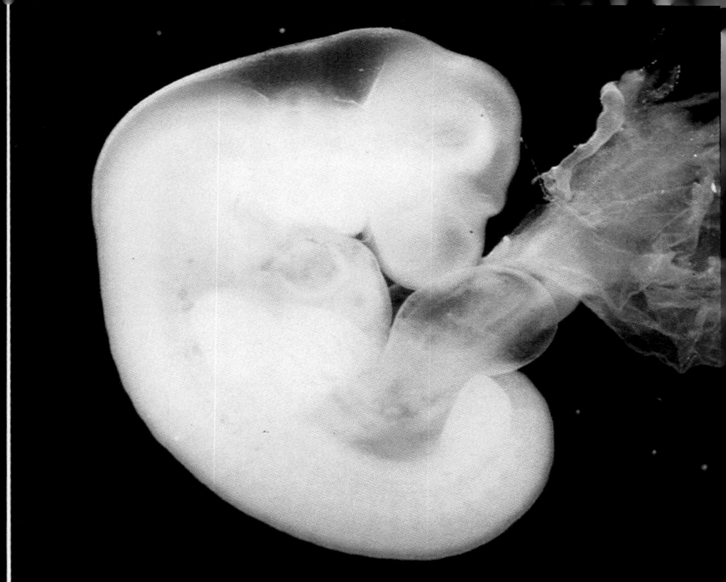

Fig. 24•10 The human fetus at different stages of development—three weeks, five weeks, and seven weeks. (Sizes of the fetus in these photos are not proportionate.) Increasing sensitivities, movements, and reflexes are exhibited by the fetus as the nervous system develops. (Courtesy of Dr. R. Rugh, from FROM CONCEPTION TO BIRTH: THE DRAMA OF LIFE'S BEGINNINGS, Harper & Row, 1971)

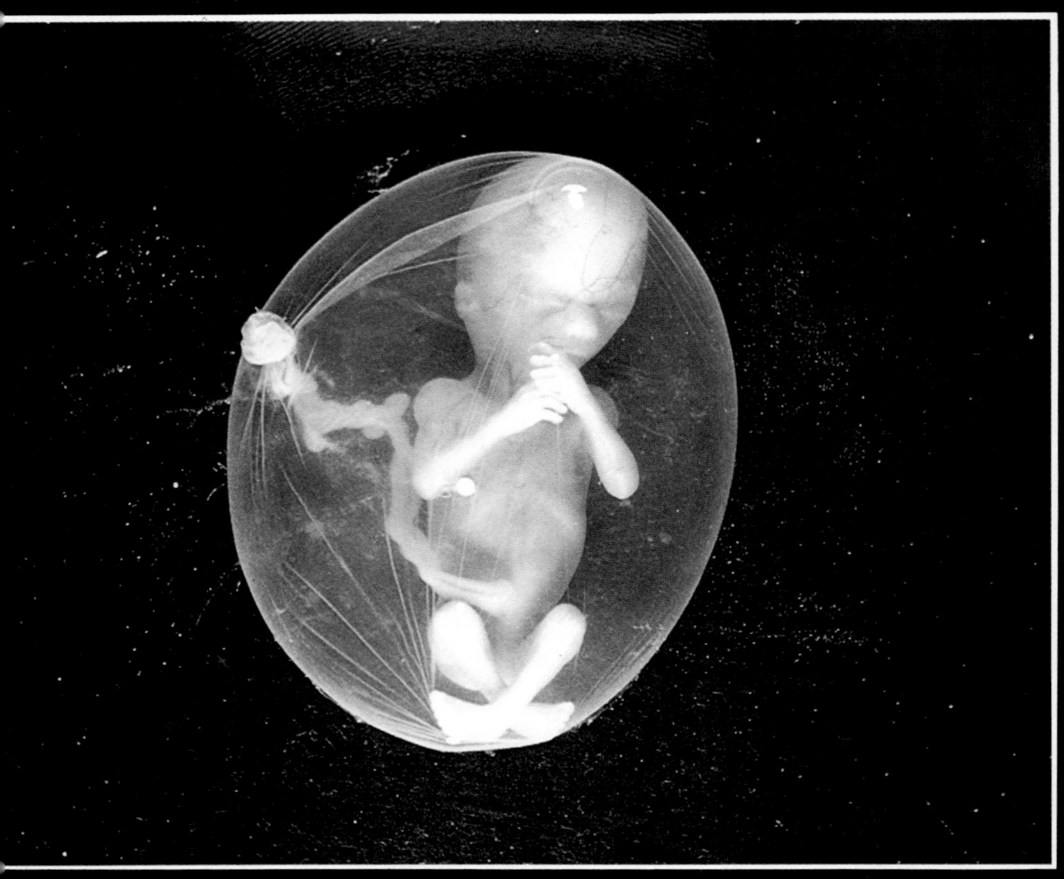

g. 24·10 continued The human fetus at
ree months. (Courtesy of Dr. R. Rugh,
om FROM CONCEPTION TO BIRTH:
HE DRAMA OF LIFE'S BEGINNINGS,
arper & Row, 1971)

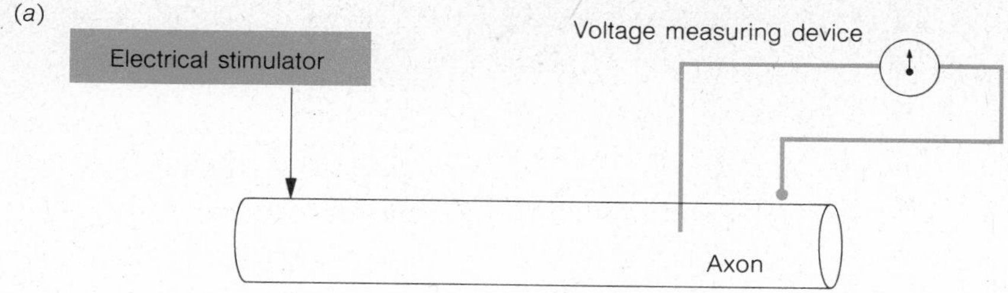

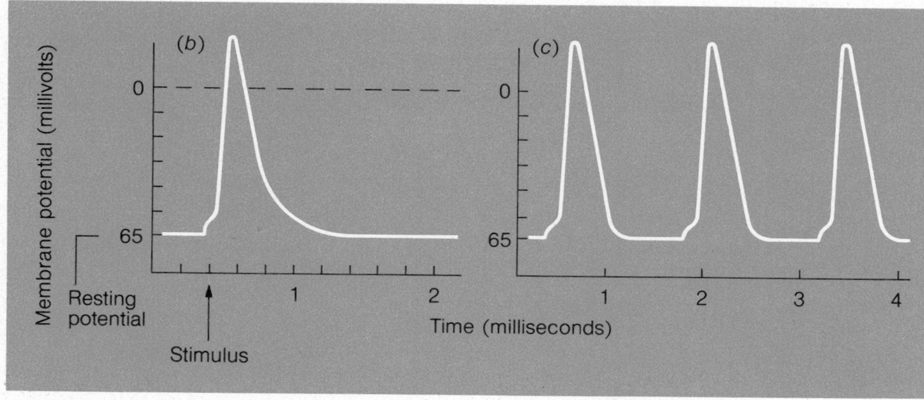

Fig. 24•14 (*a*) If a depolarizing stimulus is applied (by the electrical stimulator) to one end of an axon, then a short time later we can record a transient change in the membrane potential at the other end of the axon. This change is a rapid depolarization and subsequent hyperpolarization, and is called the spike potential. (*b*) The characteristic shape of the spike potential as a function of time. (*c*) If we increase the intensity of the stimulus, the number of spikes recorded at the other end of the axon increases, but their size and shape remain the same.

Suppose we were to record membrane potentials along the axon at varying distances from the stimulating electrode (Figure 24•15). If we employ an electrical stimulus above threshold level, a nerve impulse will appear at successive positions on the axon. Therefore, the nerve impulse does not instantly appear at all locations, but travels at a finite velocity (varying from less than 1 meter per second to over 100 meters per second, depending on the size and structure of a particular axon) down the axon. Increasing stimulus intensity does not change this velocity.

Why does a nerve impulse initiated at one position on an axon travel down its length? In essence, the nerve impulse is regenerated at successive places along the axon. Once the impulse begins, an electrical circuit is formed between the region where the nerve impulse is occurring (the active region) and adjacent regions. Electrical currents from the active region extend to the adjacent regions and modify the cell membrane there so that the nerve impulse can be produced in the adjacent regions. The nerve impulse travels from one position to the next in much the same way as an explosive chain reaction travels. For example, if we placed a series of dynamite sticks close together in a row and ignited the first stick, the resulting explosion would set off the next dynamite stick and so forth in succession. The explosion of each stick would be sufficient to cause the same event to occur in its closest neighbor.

In the axon, the flow of current from a region of the nerve impulse is analogous to the heat released by an explosion of a dynamite stick. Transmission along the axon involves a process in which the nerve impulse is regenerated in successive

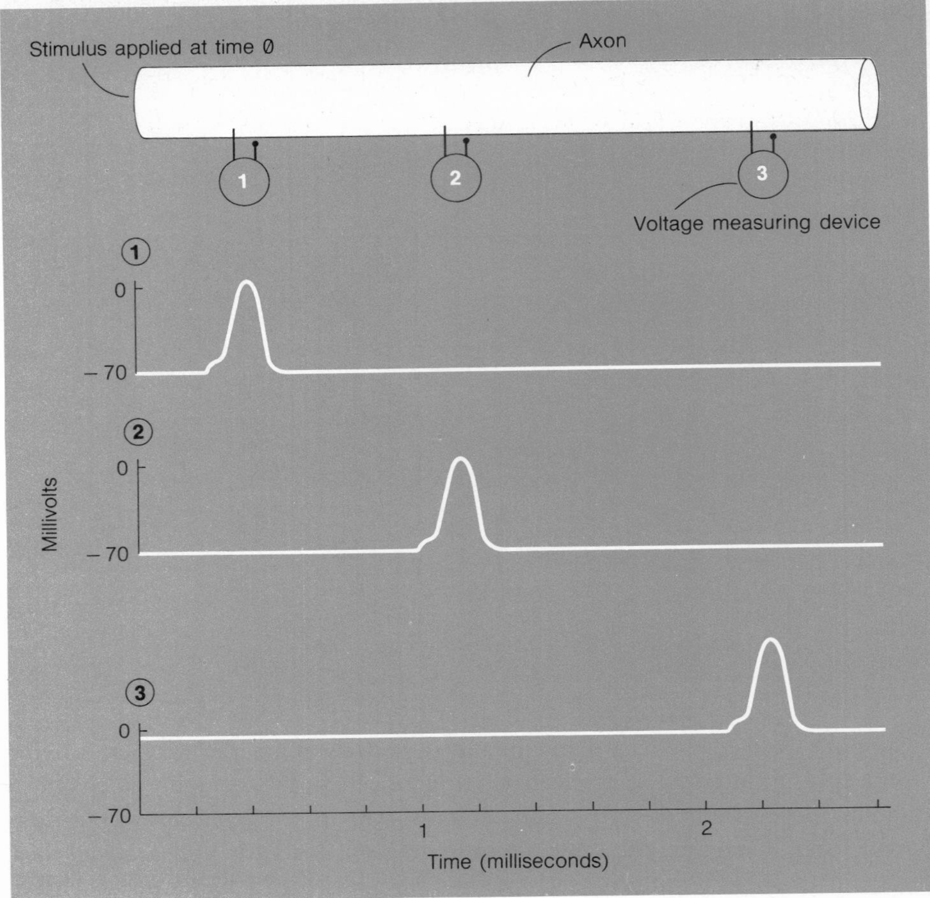

Fig. 24·15 If we stimulate one end of an axon and record the time when the spike impulse occurs at various points along the axon, we find that the nerve impulse (spike) is propagated along the axon at a constant velocity. This velocity depends only on the physical nature of the axon, not on the intensity of the initiating stimulus. The shape of the nerve impulse remains fairly constant.

segments of the axon. The process of nerve impulse transmission is extremely efficient. Unlike the explosion of dynamite, however, the axon is not consumed or burned up.

After a nerve impulse has been set off, there is a time, called the *refractory period*, during which the axon cannot be excited. This period, which may last several milliseconds, limits the number of nerve impulses that can be produced in the axon in a given period of time. Although the nerve impulse can travel in either direction along the axon, the refractory period prevents the nerve impulse from traveling back to the area through which it has just passed. Thus, once started, a nerve impulse travels in one direction, and does not continuously produce other nerve impulses.

Since nerve impulses have an all-or-nothing property, the intensity of the stimulus causing them must be encoded in various time patterns. For example, the intensity of a stimulus could be coded by the frequency of nerve impulses per unit of time.

Transmission Across Synapses A nerve cell receives input from axons of numerous other nerve cells by way of synapses located on the surface of its cell body and on its dendrites. Communication of nerve impulses between nerve cells can occur either by electrical transmission (common among invertebrates) or by chemical transmission (common among higher vertebrates).

Electrical Transmission at Synapses At some synapses, the presynaptic terminal and the postsynaptic surface are only about 2 to 4 nanometers (nm) apart. In these synapses there is an electrical coupling between the presynaptic and postsynaptic surfaces. As a consequence, current flow associated with nerve impulses in the presynaptic axon terminal can travel across the narrow synapse cleft to the postsynaptic surface. Transmission across this synapse is similar to transmission along the axon, but transmission occurs only in one direction—into the postsynaptic cell. These synapses function with little time delay and are frequently part of the neural circuits that mediate escape behavior in simple invertebrates.

Chemical Transmission at Synapses The largest class of synapses in both invertebrate and vertebrate nervous systems involves chemical transmission across synaptic clefts of 20 to 30 nanometers. In Figure 24•16, which shows the principal components of a chemical synapse as viewed through an electron microscope, we can see that the presynaptic terminal (usually an axon ending) contains numerous *synaptic vesicles*—small spherical objects that contain a chemical called a *synaptic transmitter.* A single presynaptic terminal contains thousands of these vesicles. There are many different kinds of synaptic transmitters among the nerve cells of the brain.

The sequence of steps in the chemical processes that occur at a typical synapse are as follows:

1. The synaptic transmitter substance is synthesized and stored in vesicles inside the axon terminals. This process involves the uptake of precursors (the chemical substances used in transmitter synthesis), and enzymes that control the particular synthetic process. Some synthesized transmitter may be stored at some synapses, while the rest remains in vesicles ready for release.
2. Through a series of steps that are as yet unknown, nerve impulses cause the vesicles to abut the presynaptic terminal membrane and to release their transmitter into the synaptic cleft. This process involves the uptake of calcium ions into the presynaptic terminal; hence transmitter release can be blocked if the concentration of extracellular calcium ions is low.
3. The released transmitter travels across the synaptic cleft and attaches to receptor sites on the postsynaptic membrane surface where it produces a change in the permeability of some ions, which results in a change in membrane potential.
4. Transmitter action terminates in any of several ways—different synapses may have different termination mechanisms. At some synapses, where the transmitter substance is *acetylcholine* (nerve-muscle junctions and junctions be-

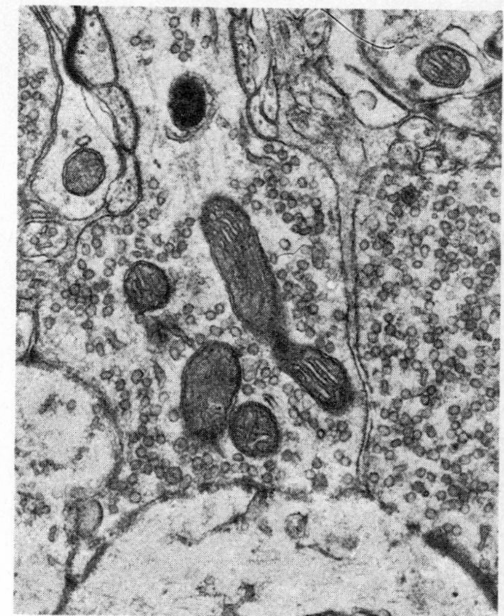

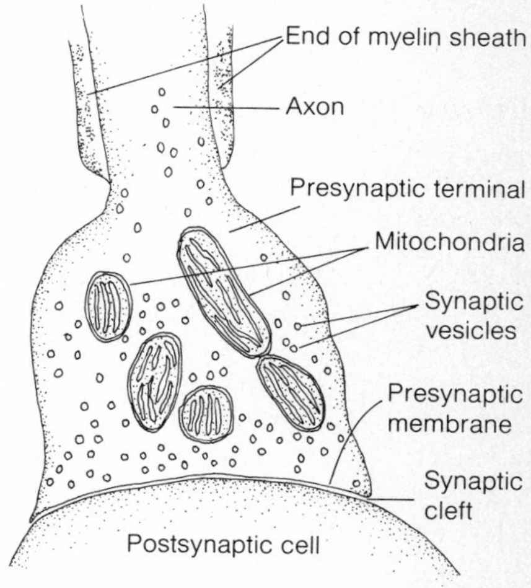

Fig. 24•16 A synapse, both as photographed under high magnification and as diagramed. The large structures in the presynaptic terminal are mitochondria, which are involved in cellular metabolism. A large number of synaptic vesicles can be seen. These vesicles can merge with the presynaptic membrane, discharging their load of transmitter into the synaptic cleft. The transmitter attaches to receptor sites on the postsynaptic cell and changes the resting potential of the postsynaptic cell, producing an IPSP or EPSP. (Photo by Henry J. Ralston, III, M.D., University of California, San Francisco)

Electrical Potentials from the Human Brain

In the early part of the twentieth century, with the beginning of the development of sensitive electronic recording techniques, attempts were made to record brain electrical activity. Using electrodes attached to the scalp of humans, psychiatrist Hans Berger (1929) noted rhythmic waves occurring at about a frequency of 10 per second. These electrical potentials were called alpha waves. Berger found them to be especially evident when the subject was in a relaxed, waking state with the eyes closed.

Many years passed before the scientific community agreed that the rhythmic waves observed from electrodes attached to the scalp are indeed derived from brain cells. Since 1940, the field of electroencephalography has used brain-wave recording such as Berger's to study the physiology of the nervous system. Table 24A·1 lists the types of waves found in human **electroencephalograms** and the arousal states they characterize.

What is the nature of these waves? Intensive study of how these wave processes are related to the electrical properties of single nerve cells suggests that EEG waves represent sums of the excitatory and inhibitory postsynaptic potentials at the numerous synapses in the brain. This sum of neural activity is seen at the scalp as potentials that may be as low as 10 to 20 millionths of a volt in amplitude.

Table 24A·1 Types of Waves and Rhythms in the Human Electroencephalogram and Their Approximate Specifications

TYPE OF WAVE OR RHYTHM	FREQUENCY PER SECOND (RANGE)	PERCENT OF TIME PRESENT	CONDITION WHEN PRESENT	NORMAL OR DISEASED
Alpha	8–12[a]	5–100	Awake, relaxed; eyes closed	Normal
Beta	18–30	5–100	Awake; no movement	Normal
Gamma	30–50	5–100	Awake	Normal—sleep deprived
Delta	0.5–4	Variable	Asleep	Normal
	0.5–4	Variable	Awake	Diseased
Theta	5–7	Variable	Awake; emotion or stress	Normal and diseased
Sleep spindles	12–14	Variable	Sleep onset	Normal

[a]Lower for infants and young children.
(From Lindsley and Wicke, 1974)

tween some brain cells), the synaptic action is terminated by the enzyme *acetylcholinesterase,* which breaks down this transmitter. The action of other transmitters is terminated by a reuptake mechanism whereby the transmitter is reabsorbed into the presynaptic terminal. Or a transmitter could diffuse away from the synapse, thereby terminating its action.

When the transmitter reaches the receptor site on the postsynaptic membrane surface, it combines with other substances to produce changes in the permeability of the membrane to electrical ions and thereby alters the membrane potential. If depolarization results, the events occurring at the receptor site are called *excitatory postsynaptic potentials* (EPSP); if hyperpolarization occurs, these events are called *inhibitory postsynaptic potentials* (IPSP). Synaptic potentials, in contrast to the all-or-nothing character of axonal nerve impulses, are graded—their amplitude is proportional to the amount of released transmitter. The magnitude of a

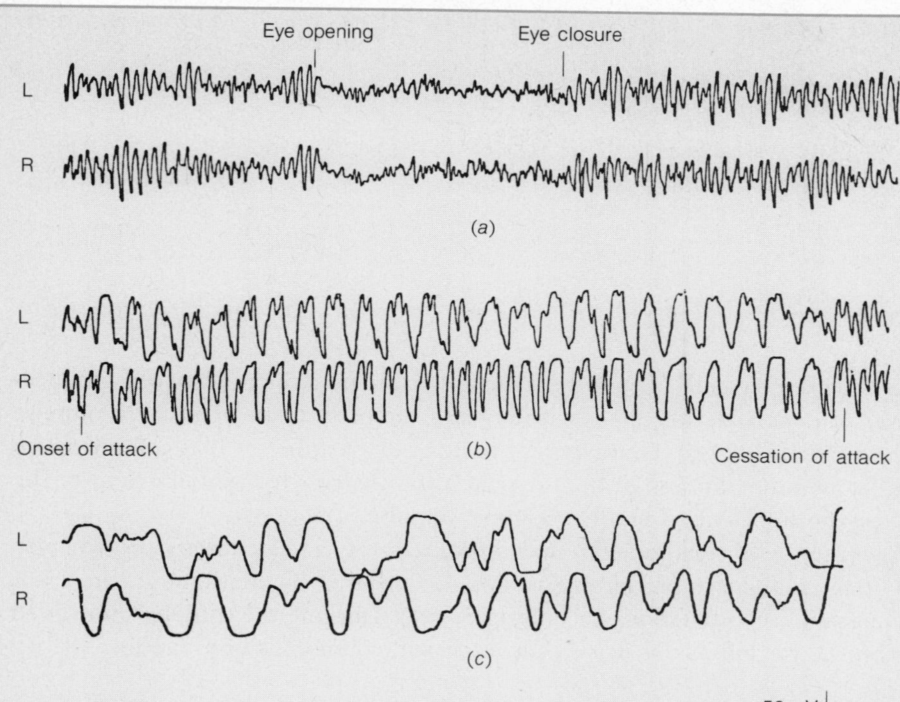

Fig. 24A·1 Examples of EEG recordings. The labels "L" and "R" on the pairs of waveforms refer to records taken from the left and right cerebral hemispheres, respectively.

(*a*) A normal adult electroencephalogram showing the effects of opening and closing the eyes. Eye opening is associated with a blocking or suppression of the alpha rhythm (the large amplitude waves with a frequency of about 10 waves per second) and the appearance of low-voltage, fast activity (beta rhythm). When the eyes close, there is a return of the alpha rhythm.

(*b*) The electroencephalogram during a petit mal epileptic seizure in a nineteen-year old male. This person had frequent seizures, characterized by a blank stare, flickering of the eyelids, and a failure to respond to instructions. The EEG recording shows large, slow waves of about three per second during the attack.

(*c*) The electroencephalogram made by a four-year-old boy with brain damage from acute viral encephalitis. The EEG recording shows a dominant activity of slow waves (one to two cycles per second), despite attempts to awaken the child. (From Curtis, Jacobson, and Marcus, 1972)

EEG recordings are especially important in the study of seizure activity and epilepsy. The intense synchronized activity of nerve cells that occurs during a seizure can be compared to a sudden storm. The use of EEG recordings as a diagnostic tool in medicine has made a significant contribution to early diagnosis and treatment of seizure disorders in human beings. Normal and abnormal brain wave patterns are shown in Figure 24A·1.

synaptic potential falls off as the distance from the synaptic region increases.

If the magnitude of the summed excitatory postsynaptic potentials is sufficiently large (10 millivolts or more of depolarization), it may initiate a nerve impulse (spike). Spike initiation in the postsynaptic cell occurs in the region at the beginning of the axon known as the axon hillock.

Summation of synaptic events is illustrated in Figure 24·17, which shows several active synapses on a nerve cell. The amount of transmitter released by each presynaptic terminal determines the amplitude of the postsynaptic potential at each postsynaptic surface. If nerve impulses arrive rapidly at a presynaptic terminal, successive postsynaptic potentials may build up. This is called *temporal summation.* In general, excitatory postsynaptic potentials from many synapses are needed before the threshold for production of a nerve impulse in the axonal hillock is reached. In this sense, the nerve cell integrates information.

Spatial summation occurs when postsynaptic potentials are summed across

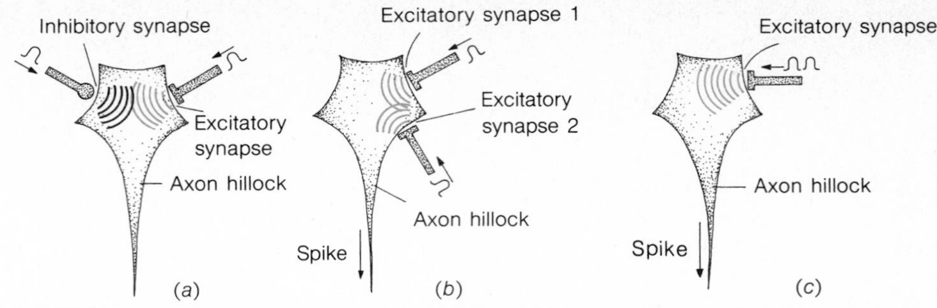

Fig. 24•17 In these schematic drawings, excitatory postsynaptic potentials are in yellow and inhibitory postsynaptic potentials are in black. These potentials are graded activity, which decreases in amplitude as it travels out into the cell body.

(*a*) Excitatory and inhibitory events interact (sum) in the cell body. If the sum of this activity is greater than the cell's threshold, a nerve impulse (spike) will be initiated at the axon hillock.

(*b*) Spatial summation. Each excitatory input alone is insufficient to initiate a nerve impulse. But when both inputs are active, their summed activity is great enough to initiate a nerve impulse.

(*c*) Since it takes a few milliseconds for the postsynaptic activity produced by one synapse to disappear, it is possible that activity at different times at the same synapse can sum and trigger a nerve impulse.

many synapses on a cell. Typically, a single synapse on a brain nerve cell produces a level of depolarization that is inadequate for production of a nerve impulse in the axon of that cell. However, if a number of synapses on that cell are active at the same time, the sum of their depolarizations across the spatial extent of the cell may be sufficient to produce a nerve impulse.

The examples in Figure 24•18 show how excitatory and inhibitory postsynaptic potentials combine to produce nerve impulse patterns. These examples are a few of the possible combinations for only a few cells. Imagine the complex and varied possibilities for billions of nerve cells, each with thousands of synapses!

Ionic Basis of Neural Activity The mechanisms that are the basis for the initiation and propagation of nerve impulses and synaptic potentials involve the distribution and movement of ions. We have previously noted that there is a potential difference across the membrane of nerve cells and that this condition implies a separation of charges across the membrane. How does this state arise? The basic factor related to the membrane potential of nerve cells is that the intracellular and extracellular environments of nerve cells differ in their concentration of various types of ions.

When the nerve cell is at rest, potassium ion concentration is high inside the cell and low outside it, and sodium ion concentration is high outside the cell and low inside it. These concentration differences reflect the fact that under resting conditions the nerve cell membrane is differentially permeable to these ions and sodium is virtually excluded from the cell. Perhaps there are pores in the membrane that select or allow ion passage according to size. These ion concentration differences result in the establishment of the resting membrane potential.

Changes in the permeability of the cell membrane to sodium and potassium ions underlie the generation of the action potential or synaptic potentials. When depolarization of the axon membrane is produced by an artificial electrical stimulus or by the summation of synaptic potentials, the permeability of the membrane to sodium ions suddenly changes and the positively charged sodium ions enter the axon—rapidly since they are at a higher concentration outside than inside. The movement of these ions into the axon results in a rapid shift in the membrane potential that is evident as the rising phase of the nerve impulse. The

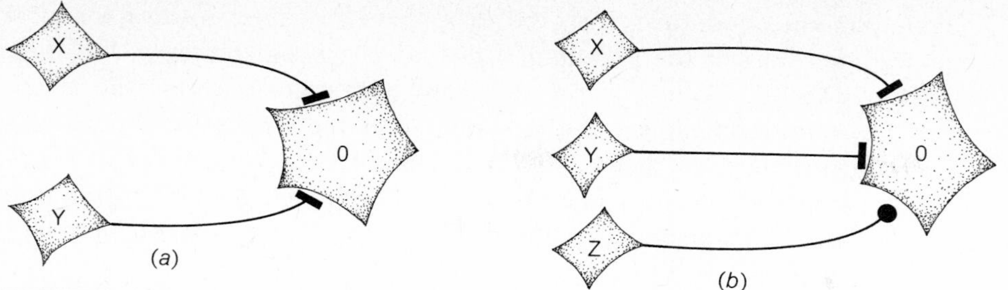

Fig. 24•18 Examples of computation in the nervous system. Nerve cells (labeled x, y, z) synapse onto an output nerve cell (labeled 0). We represent an excitatory synapse by —┫ and an inhibitory synapse by —●. In (*a*) 0 produces an output *only* if a and b are active simultaneously. This corresponds to the logic function "x and y." In (*b*) x and y must be active to produce an output, but in addition, the inhibitory nerve cell, z, must not be active. This corresponds to the logic function "x and y and not z."

return to the level of the resting potential involves an outward movement of potassium ions at which time some active mechanism pumps sodium ions out of the cell and the resting potential of the membrane is restored. Once the nerve impulse is initiated at a point on the axon, the current flow from this point changes the permeability to sodium ion of an adjacent region, and the process of sodium ion movement from outside to inside the cell is repeated along the axon.

The ionic mechanisms of synaptic transmission are more complex. The release of the synaptic transmitter produces postsynaptic membrane changes in permeability to various ions. These changes in turn increase (hyperpolarize) the postsynaptic membrane (an IPSP) or depolarize it (an EPSP).

24•5 Effects of Drugs on the Nervous System

Throughout history, human beings have searched for chemical agents that could relieve pain (analgesics), change mood or emotions (stimulants or depressants), or aid in hunting (neurotoxins). In many cultures, such chemical agents were amply provided by the leaves, fruits, seeds, and roots of various plants and trees. In some cases, knowledge of past use of some plant or extract has fostered contemporary drug investigation into the potential beneficial effects of the active ingredient. The development during the past twenty-five years of drugs that modify behavior has generated intense interest in how drugs act on the nervous system. We do know that drugs can affect the nervous system by acting directly on the processes at the cell membranes or by altering any of the neurochemical steps that occur at synapses.

There is no single classification scheme that encompasses the entire range of uses for drugs that affect the nervous system. Some can be classified under several categories. One system of classifying these drugs is presented in Table 24•1.

Drugs That Affect Membrane Permeability: Neurotoxins Some drugs act as poisons (*neurotoxins*) by interfering with the ionic activity of the nerve membrane. Many marine animals contain such poisonous substances. In some cases, the neurotoxin is introduced by a bite or a spine; in others, the neurotoxin may become apparent only if the whole creature is eaten.

Because it contains the neurotoxin tetrodotoxin, the pufferfish is less than nourishing. (New York Zoological Society Photo)

The substance tetrodotoxin is a good example of a neurotoxin. It is found in the ovaries and liver of the pufferfish, a fact which discourages other fish from eating the pufferfish. When placed on axons, tetrodotoxin blocks the action potential without changing the resting potential or the resting membrane resistance. Its action on neural membranes seems restricted to an interference with the mechanisms controlling the increase in sodium conductance that is produced when the axonal membrane is stimulated. The axons of animals that produce tetrodotoxin are resistant to its action.

The neurotoxin batrachotoxin, which is found in the skin secretions of a South American frog, produces a marked increase in axonal membrane permeability to sodium ions and thus leads to fatal convulsions. The inhabitants of Colombian rain forests used to use it on the darts for their blow guns to ensure the deaths of animals felled by the darts.

Many less exotic, commonly used drugs affect membrane interactions. Aspirin and similar pain suppressants appear to act on neural mechanisms by increasing potassium ion permeability and decreasing chloride permeability, so that the membrane potential is increased.

Drugs That Affect Synaptic Chemical Processes Most of the drugs that modify brain activity have an effect on some step in the chemical processes that occur at a synapse and thus inhibit or facilitate synaptic action. Drug action at synapses can (1) interfere with transmitter synthesis, (2) block transmitter release, (3) interfere with transmitter breakdown after release, and (4) block postsynaptic effects (*postjunctional block*).

For example, the botulism toxin, which may be produced by bacteria that can live and develop under anerobic (oxygen-free) conditions, prevents the release of transmitter molecules in *cholinergic synapses* (synapses that use acetylcholine as a transmitter). Since many synapses and the nerve-muscle junction use acetylcholine, the effects of this toxin are frequently complete respiratory paralysis and subsequent death.

Toxic effects are also caused by some nerve gases and by insecticides (such as parathion) that prolong the action of acetylcholine by acting on acetylcholinesterase, thereby interfering with transmitter destruction.

This class of drugs may also be beneficial in the treatment of some diseases in which either inadequate amounts of acetylcholine are released or there is difficulty in releasing acetylcholine. One such disease is *myasthenia gravis*, characterized by a ready fatiguability of skeletal muscles that can advance to paralysis. Treatment of such diseases may involve anticholinesterases (drugs that interfere with acetylcholinesterase) that will prolong the action of released acetylcholine.

At synapses where acetylcholine is the transmitter, synaptic activity can be blocked by some substances that act at the postsynaptic receptor surfaces. This blocking action is characteristic of the drug *curare*, which was once used by South American Indians to fell prey. It causes paralysis by blocking the postsynaptic action of acetylcholine.

Table 24·1 A Classification of Drugs Affecting the Nervous System

I. Drugs used in the treatment of emotional disorders
    A. Antipsychotics
    B. Antianxiety drugs
    C. Antidepressants

II. Psychogenic–hallucinogenic drugs

III. Stimulants

IV. Sedatives and hypnotics

V. Analgesics (pain relievers)

VI. Local anesthetics

VII. General anesthetics

VIII. Paralytic drugs

IX. Anticonvulsants

Chemical Models of Schizophrenia

Not long ago, approximately 50 percent of the hospital beds in this country were occupied by psychiatric patients. This use of hospital facilities reflected a huge toll in terms of personal anguish and social cost. Most of these hospitalized psychiatric patients suffered from the psychosis schizophrenia. (The psychiatric portrait of this disease was presented in Chapter 16.)

Speculation about the causes of schizophrenia has ranged from notions about possession by demons to the view that some kind of toxic substance is responsible for the condition. Treatment of schizophrenia has also ranged widely, including a variety of elixirs, high doses of vitamins, psychosurgery, and electroshock. In the 1950s the advent of the drug chlorpromazine changed the treatment of schizophrenia and resulted in a major reduction in the patient population of psychiatric hospitals.

Chlorpromazine belongs to the class of drugs called phenothiazines. Some investigators have suggested that drugs of this class act on the fundamental mechanisms of schizophrenia. Cellular studies of how these drugs act show that they block postsynaptic receptor sites for the transmitter dopamine, reducing the possibility that terminals using dopamine as a transmitter can exert a postsynaptic effect.

Researchers have long sought an experimental model of schizophrenia. Early interest in hallucinogens such as LSD was partially based on the hope that these drugs could produce temporary psychoses that could be used as experimental models of schizophrenia. However, many aspects of the psychoses associated with the commonly used hallucinogens are different from those of schizophrenia. For example, hallucinogens induce symptoms of delirium, disorientation, and confusion that trained observers can readily distinguish from schizophrenia. Furthermore, schizophrenics who have been given hallucinogens have reported effects that differ markedly from the cognitive, perceptual, and emotional states they customarily experience.

Solomon Snyder (1972) has shown that a psychotic state associated with the use of amphetamines comes close to being a model of schizophrenia. Sometimes persons addicted to amphetamines will progressively increase their daily drug consumption, even reaching 100 times the original dosage, and some individuals who ingest such quantities over prolonged periods develop a paranoid state similar to paranoid schizophrenia. These symptoms usually disappear a few days or weeks after withdrawal of the drug. The most effective antidote to amphetamine is chlorpromazine.

Drugs that interfere with or potentiate (accentuate) the action of the *biogenic amines* (a large group of transmitter substances including such transmitters as *serotonin, norepinephrine,* and *dopamine*) often produce changes in mood or emotional responsiveness. Such drugs include tranquilizing drugs, antidepressant drugs, and hallucinogens such as LSD. The problems resulting from use and abuse of these drugs have stimulated intensive research on the biogenic amine transmitters.

A general theory of mood or emotions and biogenic amines has been proposed by J. Schildkraut and Seymour Kety (1967) at Harvard Medical School. They argue that drugs that inhibit the amount of *catecholamines* (a class of biogenic amines that includes dopamine and norepinephrine) produce sedation or depression, and that drugs that facilitate the release of norepinephrine or dopamine produce excitement and are frequently mood elevators (Table 24•2). Figure 24•19 shows how some of the drugs that act at *adrenergic synapses* (synapses where the transmitter is norepinephrine) affect the levels of norepinephrine.

Table 24·2 Summary of the pharmacological observations compatible with the catecholamine hypothesis of affective disorders

DRUG	EFFECTS ON MOOD IN HUMANS	EFFECTS ON BEHAVIOR IN ANIMALS	EFFECTS ON CATECHOLAMINES IN BRAIN (ANIMALS)
Reserpine	Sedation Depression (in some patients)	Sedation	Depletion (intracellular deamination and inactivation)
Tetrabenazine	Sedation Depression (in some patients)	Sedation	Depletion (intracellular deamination and inactivation)
Amphetamine	Stimulant	Stimulant Excitement	Releases norepinephrine (? onto receptors) Inhibits cellular uptake (and inactivation) of norepinephrine
Monoamine oxidase inhibitors	Antidepressant	Excitement Prevents and reverses reserpine-induced sedation	Increases levels
Imipramine	Antidepressant	Prevents reserpine-induced sedation Potentiation of amphetamine effects	Inhibits cellular uptake (and inactivation) of norepinephrine ? Potentiates action of norepinephrine (as in periphery)
Lithium salts	Treatment of mania		? Increases intracellular deamination of norepinephrine ? Decreases norepinephrine available at receptors
α-Methylparatyrosine	Sedation (transient) with hypomania upon withdrawal	Sedation (in some studies)	Inhibits synthesis

(From Schildkraut and Kety, 1967)

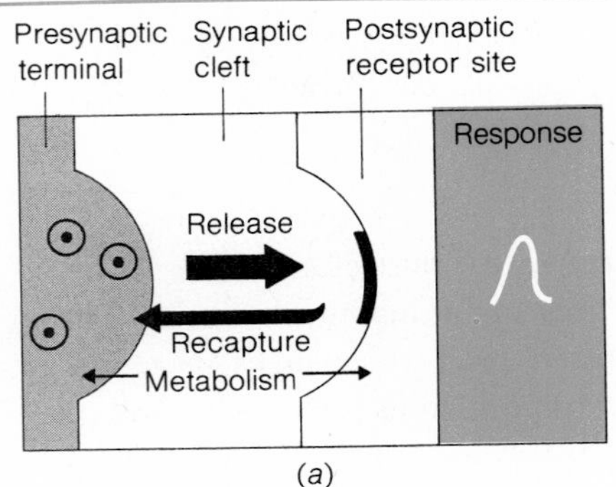

(*a*)

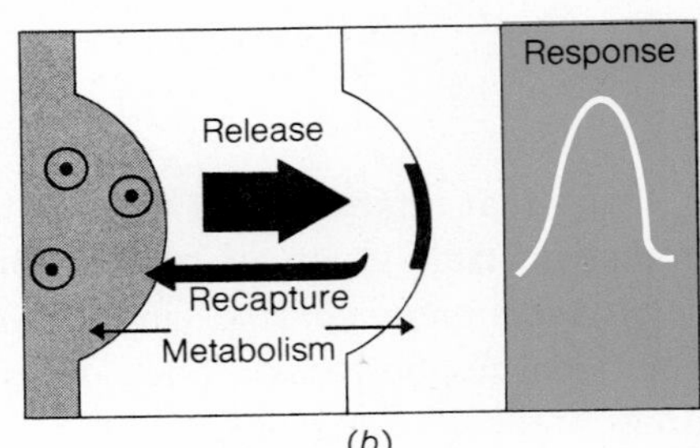

(*b*)

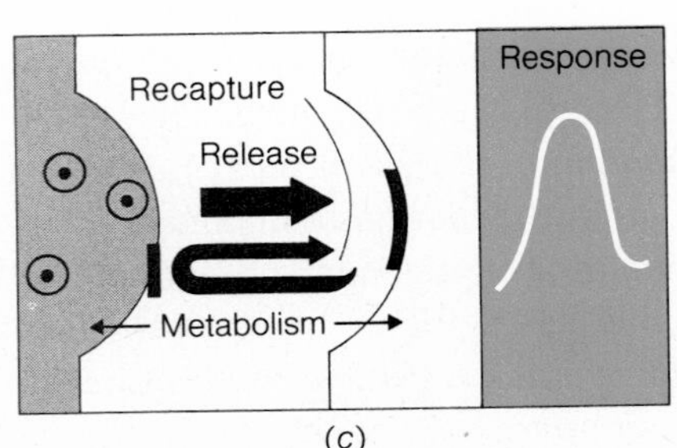

(*c*)

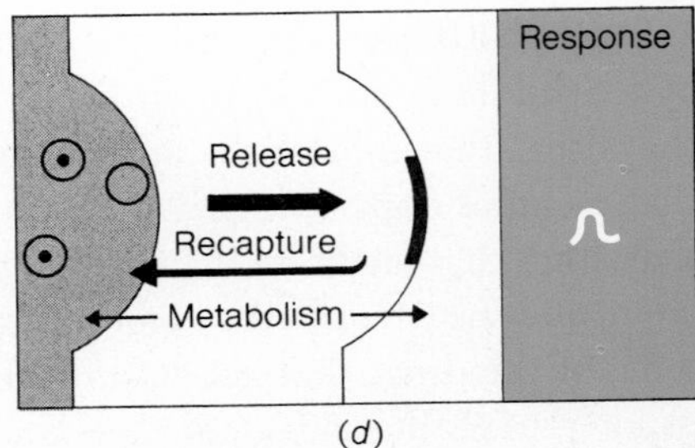

(*d*)

Fig. 24·19 (*a*) Normal release, recapture and metabolism of norepinephrine at an adrenergic synapse (a synapse that uses norepinephrine as a transmitter). The curve represents the normal response of a postsynaptic cell. Amphetamine (an antidepressant) increases the availability of norepinephrine at the synapse either by promoting the release of norepinephrine (*b*) or by blocking recapture (*c*). (*d*) Reserpine (which reduces blood pressure and may induce depression) reduces the response by depleting the norepinephrine in storage. (From Axelrod, 1974)

Communication and Hormones

24•6 Rapid communication in the nervous system involves both transmission of nerve impulses along axons and integration of synaptic potentials produced by the release of transmitter substances to axon terminals. The time involved in these processes is in the range of milliseconds. A much slower form of communication within the brain and with the body involves the action of hormones. The time scale of this communication is frequently measured in terms of hours or days.

Hormones are chemical substances secreted into the blood stream by the **endocrine glands** (Figure 24•20). Hormones affect the functions of our organs and cellular processes and the coordination and integration of our behaviors. Table 24•3 lists some mammalian hormones, where they are produced in the body, and some of their principal effects. The target organs are quite extensive since some fundamental cellular processes are controlled or influenced by hormonal secretions.

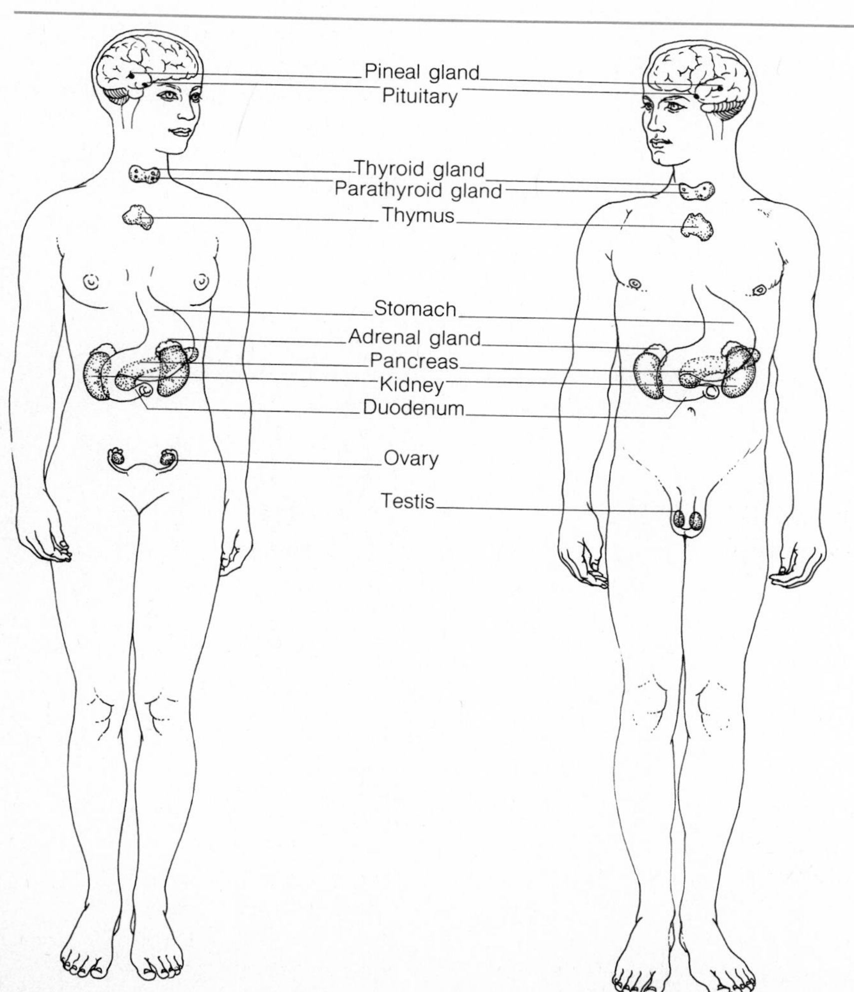

Fig. 24•20 Position of the endocrine glands in the human body. An endocrine gland is any structure that secretes a hormone. Many of these structures (such as the stomach) have other functions besides secreting hormones.

Table 24.3 Important Mammalian Hormones

SOURCE	HORMONE	PRINCIPAL EFFECTS
Pyloric mucosa of stomach	Gastrin	Stimulates secretion of gastric juice
Mucosa of duodenum	Secretin	Stimulates secretion of pancreatic juice
	Cholecystokinin	Stimulates release of bile by gallbladder
	Enterogastrone	Inhibits secretion of gastric juice
Damaged tissues	Histamine	Increases capillary permeability
Pancreas	Insulin	Stimulates glycogen formation and storage; stimulates carbohydrate oxidation; inhibits formation of new glucose
	Glucagon	Stimulates conversion of glycogen into glucose
Kidney plus blood	Hypertensin	Stimulates vasoconstriction, causing rise in blood pressure
Testes	Testosterone	Stimulates development and maintenance of male secondary sexual characteristics and behavior
Ovaries	Estrogen	Stimulates development and maintenance of female secondary sexual characteristics and behavior
	Progesterone	Stimulates female secondary sexual characteristics and behavior, and maintains pregnancy
Thyroid	Thyroxin, triiodothyronine	Stimulate oxidative metabolism
	Calcitonin	Prevents excessive rise in blood calcium
Parathyroids	Parathormone	Regulates calcium-phosphate metabolism
Thymus	Thymosin	Stimulates immunologic competence in lymphoid tissues
Adrenal medulla	Adrenalin	Stimulates syndrome of reactions commonly termed ''fight or flight''
	Noradrenalin	Stimulates reactions similar to those produced by adrenalin, but causes more vasoconstriction and is less effective in conversion of glycogen into glucose.

(From Keeton, 1972)

Table 24.3 Important Mammalian Hormones (*continued*)

SOURCE	HORMONE	PRINCIPAL EFFECTS
Adrenal cortex	Glucocorticoids (corticosterone, cortisone, hydrocortisone, etc.)	Inhibit incorporation of amino acids into muscles; stimulate formation (largely from noncarbohydrate sources) and storage of glycogen; help maintain normal blood-sugar level
	Mineralocorticoids (aldosterone, deoxycorticosterone, etc.)	Regulate sodium-potassium metabolism
	Cortical sex hormones (adrenosterone, etc.)	Stimulate secondary sexual characteristics, particularly those of the male
Hypothalamus	Releasing factors	Regulate hormone secretion by anterior pituitary
	Oxytocin, vasopressin	*See* Posterior pituitary
Anterior pituitary	Growth hormone	Stimulates growth
	Thyrotrophic hormone	Stimulates the thyroid
	Adrenocorticotrophic hormone (ACTH)	Stimulates the adrenal cortex
	Follicle-stimulating hormone (FSH)	Stimulates growth of ovarian follicles and of seminiferous tubules of the testes
	Luteinizing hormone (LH)	Stimulates conversion of follicles into corpora lutea; stimulates secretion of sex hormones by ovaries and testes
	Prolactin	Stimulates milk secretion by mammary glands
	Melanocyte-stimulating hormone	Controls cutaneous pigmentation in lower vertebrates
Posterior pituitary (storage organ for hormones apparently produced by hypothalamus)	Oxytocin	Stimulates contraction of uterine muscles; stimulates release of milk by mammary glands
	Vasopressin	Stimulates increased water reabsorption by kidneys; stimulates constriction of blood vessels (and other smooth muscle)
Pineal	Melatonin	May help regulate pituitary, perhaps by regulating hypothalamic releasing centers

A giant or a dwarf can result from malfunctions of the pituitary gland. (Circus World Museum, Baraboo, Wisconsin)

The **pituitary gland** is the endocrine gland that plays the most important role in hormonal processes. It is found at the base of the skull and is connected to the hypothalamus by the pituitary stalk. The human pituitary gland weighs about 0.5 grams; it is divided into two lobes—the *anterior pituitary* (the adenohypophysis) and the *posterior pituitary* (the neurohypophysis). The anterior pituitary lobe secretes several different hormones, some of which control the output of other endocrine glands (Table 24•3). For example, *adrenocorticotrophic hormone*—released by the anterior pituitary lobe—affects the endocrine activity of the adrenal cortex. (The secretions of the **adrenal gland** control an amazing variety of physiological reactions, including the metabolism of carbohydrate and of protein, and the salt-and-water balance in the body.) Similarly, *thyrotrophic hormone*—released by the anterior pituitary lobe—stimulates the production and secretion of thyroid hormones, which in turn inhibit the further pituitary release of thyrotrophic hormone. This kind of feedback control characterizes the regulation among many of the endocrine glands.

The impact of hormones on behavior is especially apparent in patients whose endocrine glands release either excessive or insufficient amounts of hormones. For example, when the pituitary gland fails to manufacture and release normal amounts of growth hormone, dwarfism results; an oversupply of growth hormone results in gigantism. Surgical removal of specific endocrine glands in animals produces experimental models of these hormone-secretion abnormalities.

Sensory Communication to the Brain

24•7 For any organism, the representation (or encoding) of some of the physical characteristics of its internal and external worlds is dependent on the detection of stimuli and on the communication to the brain of information about these stimuli. In Chapter 7 we discussed many aspects of the sensory receptors for the visual, auditory, gustatory, olfactory, skin, and kinesthetic senses.

There are two common physiological problems in the detection of environmental stimuli and in the transmission of information about them. First, how is the stimulus detected by the sense receptor? Second, how is the information that is present in the stimulus coded and represented in the sensory paths to the brain and within the brain? In this section we will consider answers to these questions.

Sensory Mechanisms The picture of the world provided by sensory input to the brain is not an exact reflection of the world. Rather, the sensory systems of an organism are selective, reacting to or emphasizing some aspects of impinging stimuli and ignoring or remaining insensitive to other aspects. Humans, for example, cannot detect electrical fields, but some fish can. Some nonprimate mammals, (like dogs and cats) are far more capable of detecting odors than humans are but have little ability to distinguish color. Bats can detect sound frequencies several times higher than those humans can detect—an ability that enables bats to orient themselves and to detect prey.

For any organism, the picture of the external world selected by its sensory mechanisms is an important determinant of its adaptive success or failure—that is, whether it survives or not. The selective nature of an organism's sensory equipment reflects the path along which it has evolved. This selectiveness to stimuli is possible because of the development of distinctive sensory receptors and specialized properties of brain processing.

There are certain cells that are specialized for detection of certain kinds of energy, chemicals, motion, and the like. These cells, called receptor cells, must translate the incoming information into the language of the brain—into nerve impulses and graded potentials. On the basis of incoming information, electrical activity (called the receptor potential) is initiated in receptor cells. This electrical activity is similar to the excitatory and inhibitory postsynaptic potentials described earlier. The receptor potential may in turn initiate a nerve impulse, or affect the membrane potential of nearby nerve cells. Let us look at this process as it applies to the eye.

The ears of the horseshoe bat are one of the many variations in ears that have developed in bats since they depend on their hearing to find food and to avoid collisions, although they can see fairly well. (J. H. D. Hooper)

In the retina of the eye there are receptor cells (cones) specialized for detection of color and receptor cells (rods) specialized for detection of low light levels. Light impinging on the cones and rods changes the structure of molecules inside these cells. This chemical change in turn affects the cell membrane causing a hyperpolarizing shift (the receptor potential) in the membrane potential. This shift is transmitted to other cells and eventually gives rise to spike activity that transmits information from the retina to the brain.

Other receptors—for example, some of those in the skin—may simply be the dendrites of sensory cells (free nerve endings). In the case of the sense of touch, mechanical pressure may serve to open channels in the cell membrane that are specific to various ions, thus giving rise to the receptor potential.

Many receptors are closely associated with structures such as eyelids, ears, and noses that concentrate energy and can be used to influence the effectiveness of a stimulus. For example, we can open and close our eyes, turn our heads to hear better, sniff, and so on. In a way, the brain is controlling the effectiveness of the sensory organ involved. This form of control by the brain is an example of efferent control, and is common in sensory systems. The term *efferent* means away from a particular nervous system structure, whereas *afferent* means toward a nervous system structure. Thus an afferent pathway is one that brings information into the brain. Besides controlling the direction of the eyes and similar external changes, the brain may send efferent signals that change the sensitivity of the actual receptor cells or their closely associated cells, and thus modulate the afferent flow of information.

Representation of Information in Inputs to the Brain There are several aspects of stimulus inputs that must be represented by brain activity. These include stimulus intensity, stimulus location, stimulus identity, and stimulus history. In this discussion we will deal with general principles operating in all sensory systems that are involved in the representation of these dimensions. While we have a fairly clear idea as to how sensory information is gathered by receptors and encoded in the brain, we still know little about how such information affects behavior. Certainly the basic principles we will discuss here will be used in the final explanation of behavior in terms of neural activity.

Stimulus Intensity The simplest way of representing stimulus intensity is by the rate at which nerve cells fire (produce nerve impulses); the nerve cell firing rate increases with increments in stimulus intensity. However, in many sensory systems, the organism can respond to a far greater range of stimulus intensities than could be encoded by the firing of a single nerve cell. Another way for the nervous system to represent stimulus intensity in spite of the limited range of a single nerve cell is to activate varying numbers of nerve cells; a stronger stimulus will be encoded by activating more nerve cells than are activated for a weaker stimulus.

A further refinement of this way of representing stimulus intensity is apparent in sensory systems that have elements with different thresholds for activation. In this kind of system, high-threshold elements will code (fire selectively) for high-intensity stimuli and low-threshold elements will code for low-intensity stimuli.

Stimulus Location How do we know the position of stimuli in our environment? In some sensory systems the position of a stimulus is encoded by which nerve fiber is activated and which portion of the brain this fiber is connected to. For example, the position of a skin stimulus is encoded in terms of which peripheral fiber is activated and the location of active brain cells (Figure 24·21). This is an example of topographic mapping of a sensory surface onto the cells of the brain;

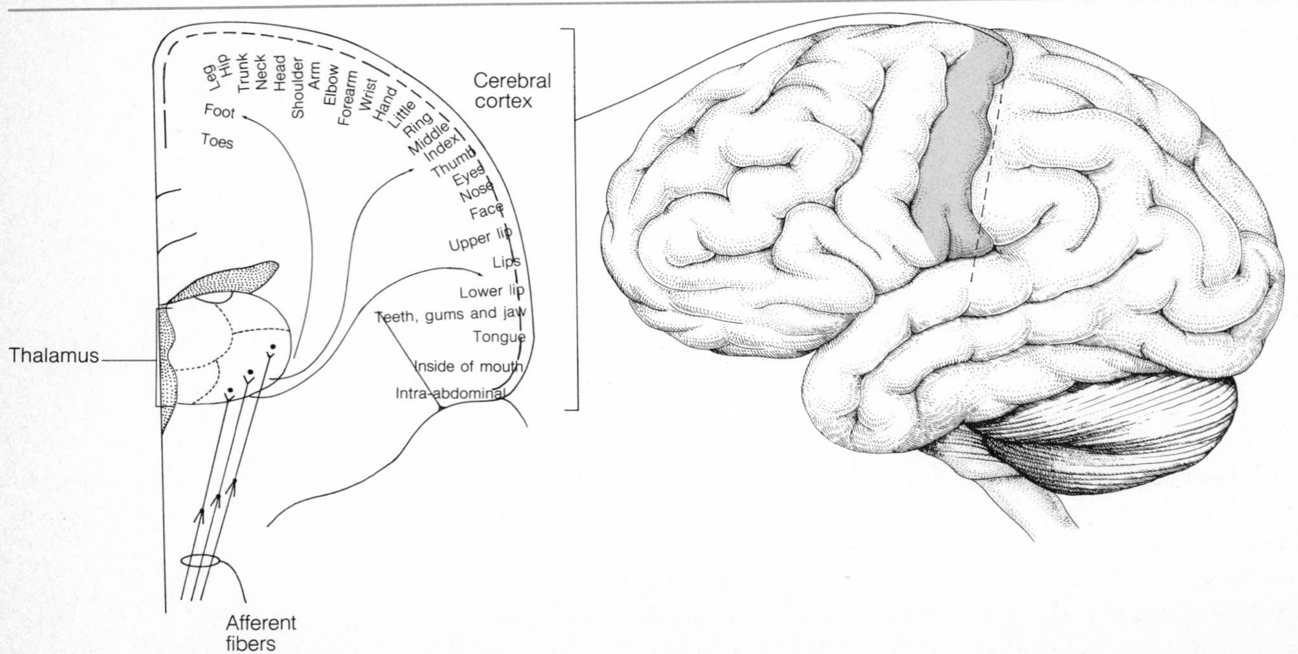

Fig. 24·21 Cross section of the left cerebral hemisphere (taken at the dotted line on brain in the lower part of the figure) showing the relationship between the location on the surface of the skin of a touch and the cells in the cerebral cortex that respond to that touch. Note that parts of the body, such as the lips, which are very sensitive to touch, have a larger portion of the cortex devoted to them. The afferent fibers for these sensations are indicated by lines coming up through the thalamus to the cortex. (Penfield and Roberts, 1959).

that is, each position or location in the outside world or body surface activates a specific position or location in the brain.

There are some sensory systems in which location of a stimulus source is possible without a mapping mechanism. In the auditory and olfactory systems stimulus location is determined by the nervous system in one of two ways: by making successive comparisons or by simultaneously comparing the right and left sides of the body. Successive comparisons are best illustrated by attempting to locate a sound with one ear. If the sound is very brief, sound localization is virtually impossible. However, it is possible to locate the position of sounds of longer duration by using head movements and relating head position and maximal sound intensity.

Simultaneous comparisons for the representation of stimulus localization are also evident in brain mechanisms that mediate sound localization. At a neural level, there are cells that compare inputs from the right and left ears. This computation enables a localization of the sound.

A feat of sensorimotor integration. (Ted Streshinsky)

Stimulus Identity If a stimulus is delivered to a skin surface, how does the nervous system identify this event as touch, pain, pressure, cold, or warmth? If a sound is presented, how is frequency represented? Stimulus identity is commonly handled by nerve cell specialization. Each kind of stimulus activates different specialized cells, as we have seen in Chapter 7.

The view of specialization of nerve cells of receptors and brain pathways with respect to specialized categories within a particular sensory system encounters some difficulties in skin sensation. At some body surfaces (such as the cornea of the eye) there is only one type of receptor (free nerve ending), although a variety of sensations (touch, pain, and pressure) can be felt. This suggests that in some cases stimulus identity may be encoded by the pattern of nerve activity from a receptor rather than by the kind of receptor being stimulated or its location.

Stimulus History The detection of novelty or familiarity with respect to sensory inputs to the brain involves both sensory adaptation (discussed in Chapters 7 and 10) and a feature of learning called habituation (discussed in Chapters 4 and 10). **Adaptation** refers to the decreased output of a receptor as a function of continued stimulation. Some receptors adapt quickly to long-lasting stimuli and others adapt more slowly. **Habituation** refers to a decrease, in response to repeated stimulation, that is a product of changes in the brain and spinal cord. Synaptic processes are involved rather than changes in peripheral receptor mechanisms.

Brain Communication to the Muscles

24·8 Walking, running, dancing, playing a musical instrument, speaking, writing —all these acts pose a similar problem. How does a nervous system determine the temporal ordering of muscle movements displayed in such acts? Mechanisms in the brain and spinal cord must be able to select the appropriate muscles and guide the degree of excitation of these muscles. This basic problem was discussed by Karl

Lashley (1951) in a now classic paper called "The Problem of the Serial Order of Behavior." Using examples from the analysis of speech, Lashley showed that the brain uses some program or internal model to generate sequential muscle activity rather than having discrete speech units, each of which acts successively as the stimulus for the next. In speech, as with other motor movements, both internal programs and listening to what we say guides our production of movement.

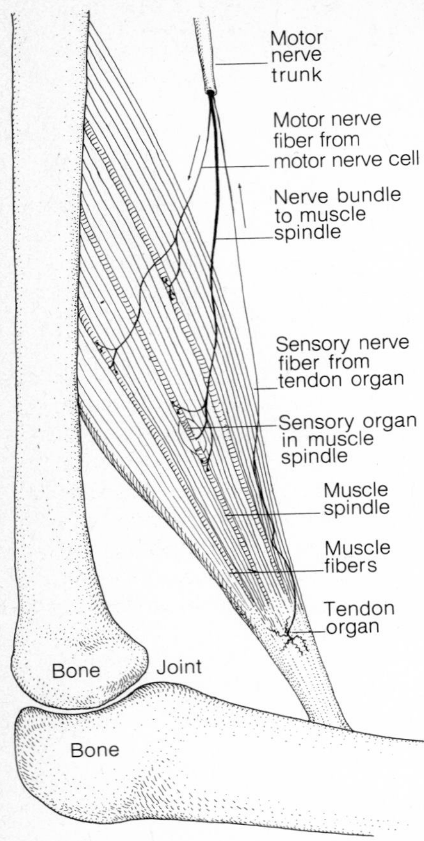

Fig. 24•22 A muscle contains many individual muscle fibers that can only shorten and are ordered to do so by the activity of motor nerve cells. Within the muscle are also sense organs. The tendon organ senses force, while the muscle spindle contains a sense organ that senses the length of the muscle. This information is used to exactly control the position (length) and force of muscles. This diagram does not show the various elements of a muscle in correct size proportion.

Relationships Among Muscles, Bones, and Nerves The only movement a muscle can make by itself is to shorten. Its structure and nerve connections accomplish this action. For example, when the biceps muscle (connected to the forearm bone) contracts, the forearm bends at the elbow. Contraction of the triceps muscle produces the opposite movement—extension of the arm. This process illustrates the antagonistic, or reciprocal, manner in which muscles are commonly paired around joints. As one muscle shortens, the opposite muscle passively lengthens. The smooth functioning of movements requires that excitation of one muscle be paired with relief from excitation (inhibition) of the reciprocal (antagonistic) muscle.

Sensory Elements in Muscle A muscle contains sensory elements that respond to changes in its length (Figure 24•22). The *stretch reflex circuit*, which enables the arm to maintain a load, is fundamental to neural control of movement. For example, when a biceps muscle is stretched as the result of a load such as a lifted weight, sensory receptors in the muscle are excited, and send nerve impulses to the spinal cord. In the spinal cord the axons carrying these impulses form synapses with motor nerve cells (cells that control a muscle) and impulses travel back to the biceps muscle along the axons of these motor nerve cells. These impulses cause the muscle to shorten, balancing the load-imposed stretch of the muscle (Figure 24•23). Impulses from the spindles of the stretched muscle also inhibit the spinal motor nerve cells serving the antagonistic muscle, preventing it from interfering with the shortening of the stretched muscle.

If the sensory elements of the stretch reflex circuit are cut, the usual consequence is paralysis of the affected limb.

The Spinal Cord Many basic muscle movements are produced by nerve cells in the spinal cord, rather than by nerve cells in the brain. Therefore, faster responses can be made in emergency situations (as in pulling the hand away from a hot object). Furthermore, the nerve cells in the spinal cord can free the brain from controlling some of the details of muscle movements. Thus, the stretch reflex

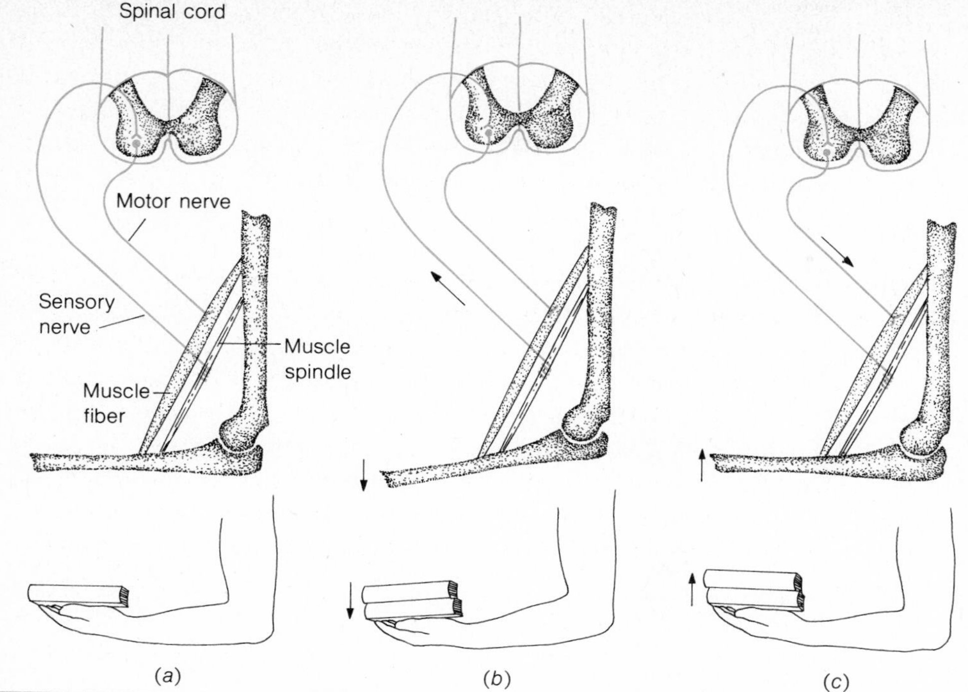

Fig. 24·23 A highly schematic representation of the events involved in a stretch reflex, which occurs when a muscle is engaged in a steady contraction under voluntary control. (*a*) The elbow flexes against a load by the action of the biceps muscle. (*b*) If we increase the load, the muscle is stretched and the arm moves down. This stretching causes the sensor organs in the muscle to send (upward arrow) nerve impulses to the spinal cord, where they impinge on a motor nerve cell at a synapse and excite it. (*c*) Motor impulses are sent (downward arrow) to the stretched muscle, where they cause it to contract and restore the arm to its original position. (From Merton, 1972)

helps maintain a limb's position once it is set by the brain, regardless of changes in the load on the limb. These local behavior circuits are called **reflexes.** We have already seen an example of a reflex in the feedback control of muscle length with changing loads.

If the connections between the brain and the spinal cord are cut, a surprising number of behaviors (such as emptying of the bladder) remain; apparently they are mediated by the nerve cells of the spinal cord. Such behaviors become evident after a recovery period (spinal shock period), which may last a few hours in cats and dogs and many months for humans. However, all voluntary movement is lost, as is sensation from the region below the cut.

It has been possible to gain some understanding of the basic organization of spinal nerve cells with respect to basic movements by studying the reflexes and movements that remain in animals whose spinal cords have been cut (Figure 24·24). For example, stimulation of the toe pads in such an animal results in abrupt withdrawal of the stimulated limb. Other behaviors, such as bladder emptying and some copulatory behavior, still exist. Thus, some very basic properties of movement appear to be "wired in" to the organization of the spinal cord.

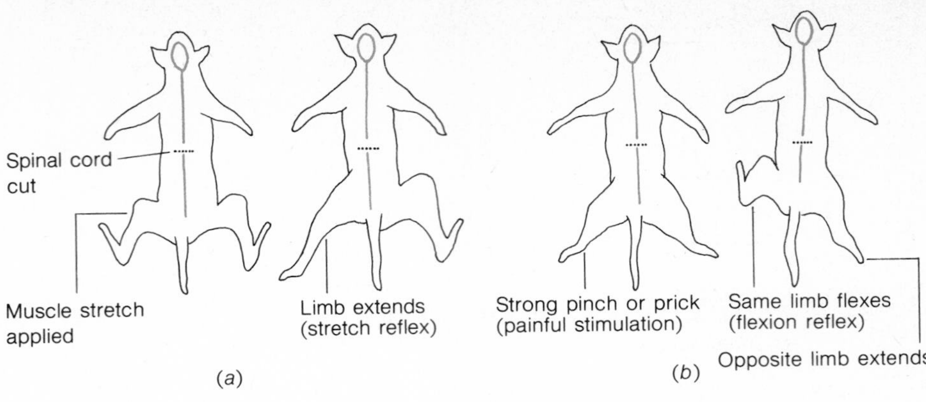

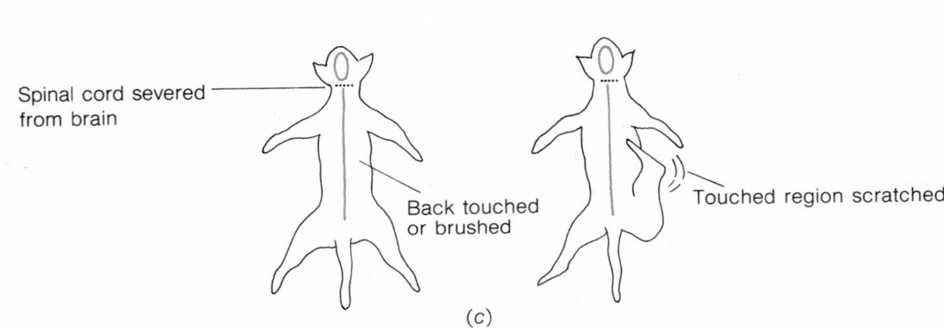

Fig. 24•24 Examples of reflexes that remain in a cat after the spinal cord has been cut. Stretching a muscle produces a reflex shortening of that muscle. When a painful stimulus is applied to the paw, the stimulated leg withdraws while the opposite leg extends. Touching the back initiates scratching. These examples show the wide range and complexity of sensory and motor activity mediated by the spinal cord alone. (From Thompson, 1967)

Motor Control in the Brain

24•9 There are numerous brain structures involved in the control of movements. A variety of fiber tracts extend from these structures to the motor nerve cells in the brain and spinal cord. The motor nerve cells in turn control the muscles.

For convenience, we can divide the brain structures involved in the control of movement and their related fiber tracts into three systems: the pyramidal system, the extrapyramidal system, and the cerebellum. Figure 24•25 schematically shows these structures and their pathways to the motor nerve cells.

The Pyramidal System The pyramidal system consists of cells in regions of the cerebral cortex and the axons from these cells (the *pyramidal tract*) that travel down to the spinal cord motor nerve cells. Where in the cortex are these cells and what kinds of movements do they control?

In the late nineteenth century, several experimenters showed that electrical stimulation of some regions of the cerebral cortex could produce bodily movements, particularly flexion of the limbs. From these early findings and from the findings of similar recent experiments maps have been constructed showing where in the cerebral cortex electrical stimulation can affect movement. A particularly important cortical region is the *motor cortex* (Figure 24•26). The largest region

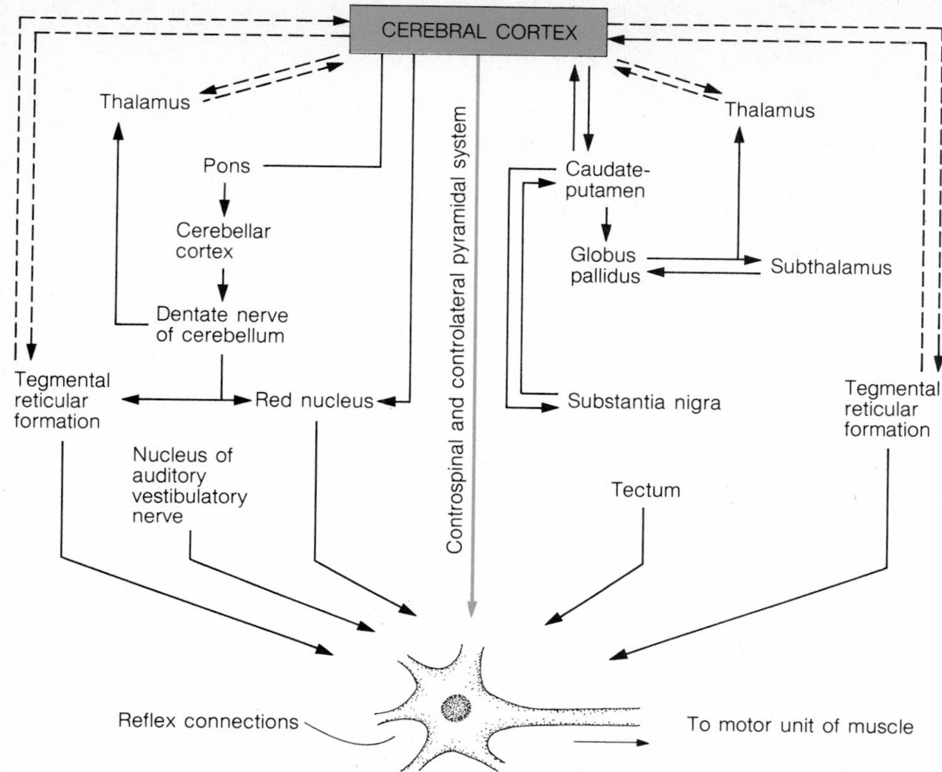

Fig. 24·25 Some of the many brain areas involved in the control of movement and the pathways from these areas to the motor nerve cells that actually control the muscles. Selective damage to any of these areas may allow us to disentangle the various components of movement control. (From Ranson and Clark, 1959)

of motor cortex controls hand movements—the most elaborate and complex movements made by humans and other primates. Thus the area of cortex devoted to a particular part of the body is proportional to the complexity of movement possible in that area. Recent studies show that colonies of cells in the motor cortex are related to particular muscle groups and that they are arranged in columns; this organization is similar to that for the cortical cells in the sensory systems.

Clinical observation and motor cortex stimulation studies suggest that the pyramidal system provides the executive mechanisms for voluntary movements. Voluntary movements are those movements we can consciously control, as opposed to such involuntary movements as heartbeat.

Some investigators have proposed a different role for the pyramidal system. The neuropsychologist Arnold Towe (1971) has suggested that the motor cortex monitors the progress of movements by analyzing sensory information, but does not initiate movements. Rather, it controls the excitability of organized groups of cells in other brain locations (the brain stem, for example). Towe has emphasized that the pyramidal system came rather late in evolutionary development. Among existing vertebrates, only mammals have a pyramidal system, yet many nonmammalian vertebrates (such as birds and fish) display a vast range of elaborate

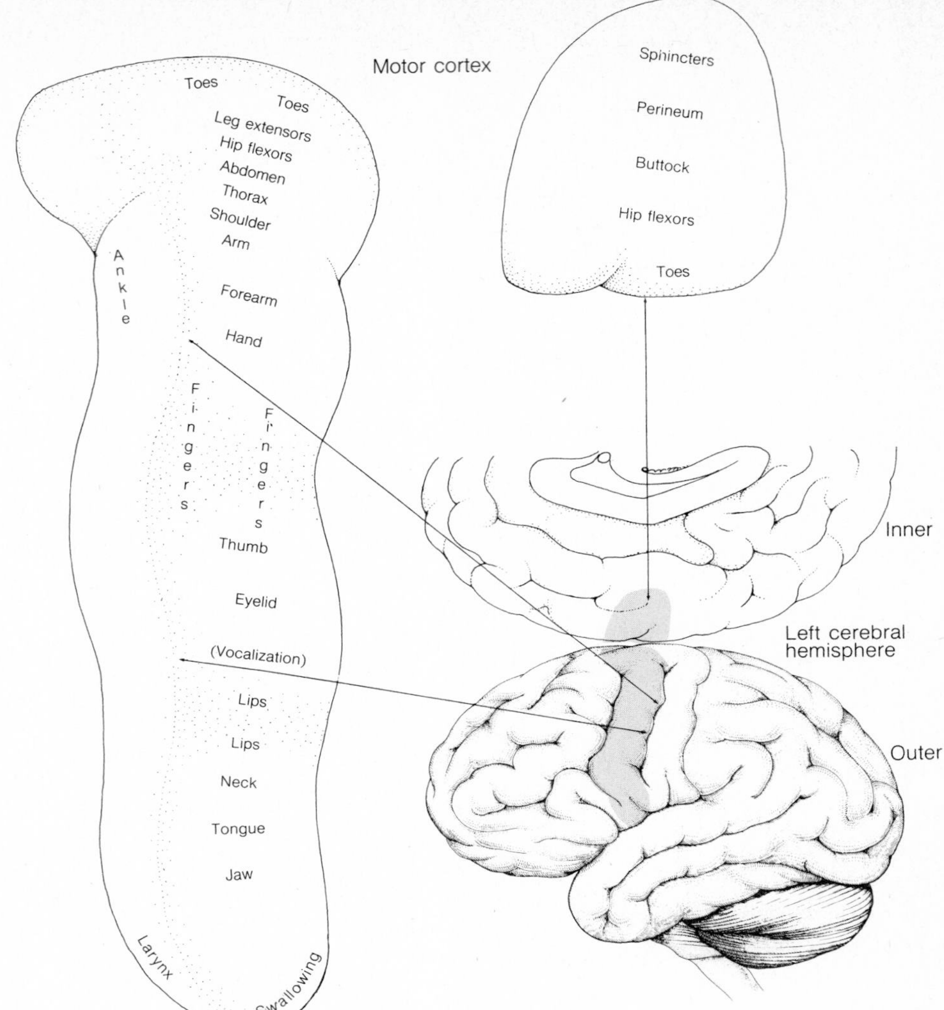

Fig. 24•26 The motor cortex in humans (in color here) is folded over at the top of each cerebral hemisphere and continues down the inside of the hemisphere. This schematic drawing shows which parts of the motor cortex control which parts of the body. The finer the control of movement needed in a body part (such as the tongue), the larger the portion of cortex devoted to that part. (From Krieg, 1966)

movement patterns. Furthermore, cutting the pyramidal tract does not prevent limb movements.

What is the relationship between the firing of nerve cells in the motor cortex and the velocity, force, and length of a movement? E. V. Evarts (1973) recorded impulses from pyramidal tract motor nerve cells in monkeys while they made certain trained limb movements (Figure 24•27). Evarts found that pyramidal tract motor nerve cells discharge prior to a movement, and that the firing rate of some cells is related to the force generated by the movement. The final position of a limb is less obviously related to motor nerve cell firing patterns. In general, the right half of the brain is connected to the left half of the body, and vice versa. Thus, damage to the pyramidal system such as is produced by strokes commonly

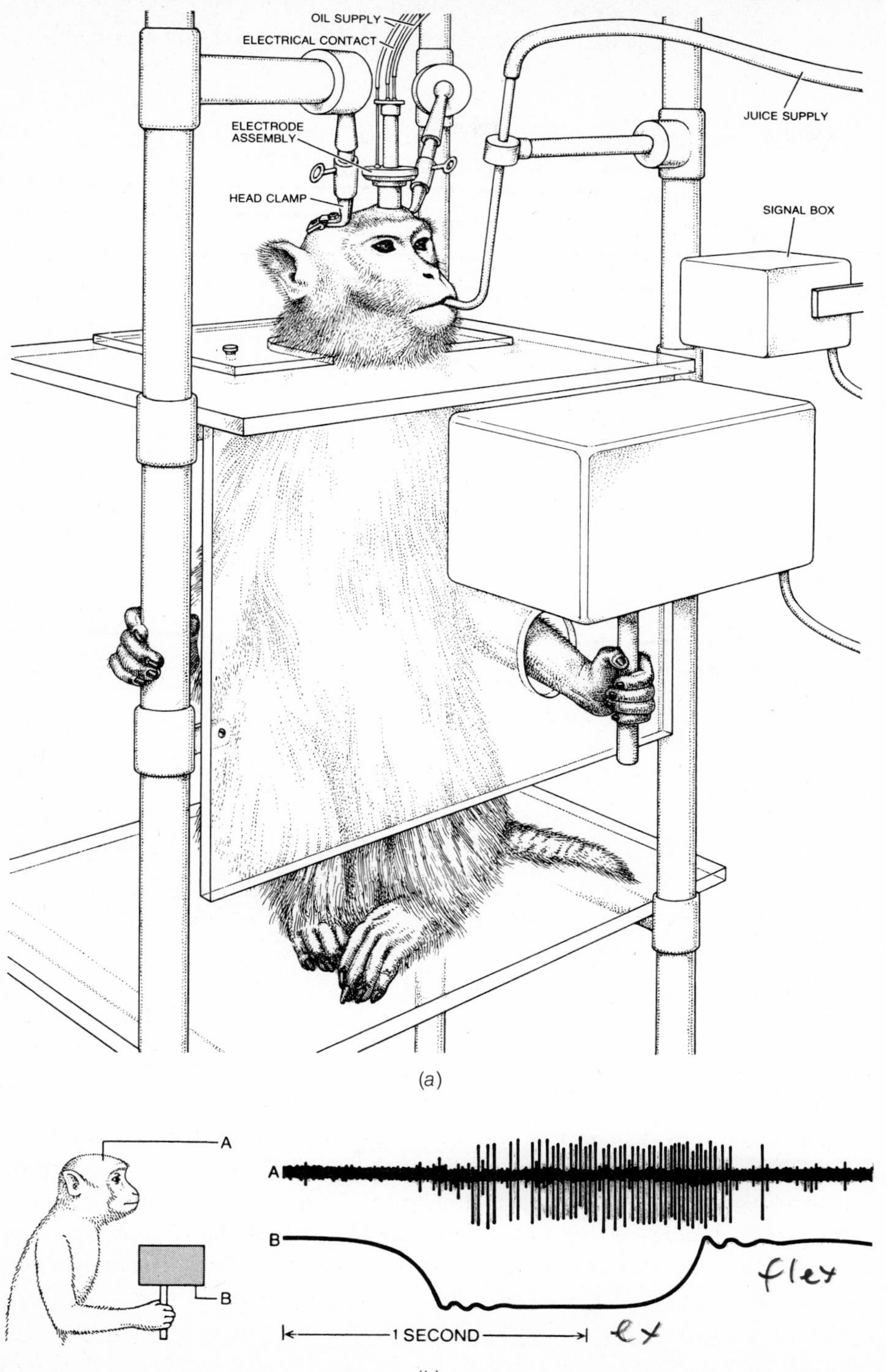

Fig. 24·27 The apparatus used by E. V. Evarts (1973) to record the activity of single nerve cells in the areas of the cerebral cortex that are involved in muscle control. (*a*) The monkey's head is painlessly immobilized so that the microelectrode in the brain does not change position during the experiment. The monkey has been trained to move the vertical rod by flexing its wrist when a light in the signal box comes on. If it makes the required movement within a specified time, it receives a reward of fruit juice through the tube in its mouth. (*b*) When trace *B* is at its lowest, the wrist is extended. When the trace is at its highest, the wrist is flexed or bent forward. Recordings from a single nerve cell in the motor cortex (*A*) during the movements show that the cell was active during flexion but not during extension. The nerve cell in the motor cortex (*A*) is active before the flexion of the muscles (*B*). (From Evarts, 1973)

results in partial muscle paralysis on the side of the body opposite the injured brain hemisphere. Stroke damage is particularly evident in the fine motor control of the hands.

The Extrapyramidal System The extrapyramidal system consists primarily of the basal ganglia located in the cerebral hemispheres and some closely related major brain stem nuclei (substantia nigra and red nucleus). Lesions in these regions of human brains produce movement impairments different from those produced by interruption of pyramidal system connections.

Human disease processes that involve the basal ganglia and related extrapyramidal nuclei are characterized by increased movement, especially involuntary movements such as tremor (rhythmic repetitive movements), chorea (tics and jerks), and ballism (violent movements of the limbs). Tremor frequently results from alternating contractions of reciprocal muscles. There are three forms of tremor: (1) resting tremor, which occurs when the affected limb is fully supported; (2) postural tremor, which occurs when the affected subject attempts to maintain a posture, such as an extended arm or leg; and (3) intention tremor, which occurs during voluntary movement.

Resting tremor (usually with a frequency of five to six tremors per second) is characteristic of *Parkinson's disease*, the most common human disease involving the basal ganglia. This disease may also produce slow twisting motions of the hand and foot and can affect movements of the eyelids and tongue. In recent years, great advances have been made in the treatment of this disorder. Parkinson's disease patients are deficient in the synaptic transmitter dopamine. When they are given a substance (L-Dopa) from which dopamine can easily be made by the body, there is relief of tremor and other symptoms such as muscle rigidity. Symptoms similar to Parkinson's disease may occur with the use of certain tranquilizers (particularly the *phenothiazines*, the most famous of which is the drug *chlorpromazine*). These substances act either by interfering with the storage of dopamine or by blocking postsynaptic receptor sites at synapses where dopamine is the synaptic transmitter.

Choreic movements (chorea) are uncontrollable, brief, and forceful. They seem like strange exaggerations of normal movements, and may include jerking movements of the fingers, facial grimace, or dancelike movements of the feet. *Huntington's chorea* is a genetic disorder characterized by these unusual movements and profound deterioration in mental processes. In some of these patients, a marked loss of brain nerve cells in a nucleus of the basal ganglia has been found. *Ballism* involves an uncontrollable, violent flailing of the limbs (Figure 24•28). The movement is sudden and usually involves one side of the body (hemiballismus). Lesions in the *subthalamic nucleus* region can produce this syndrome in human beings and monkeys.

Apparently, one of the major functions of the extrapyramidal system is to inhibit the contraction of muscles that are not needed in a movement. Diseases,

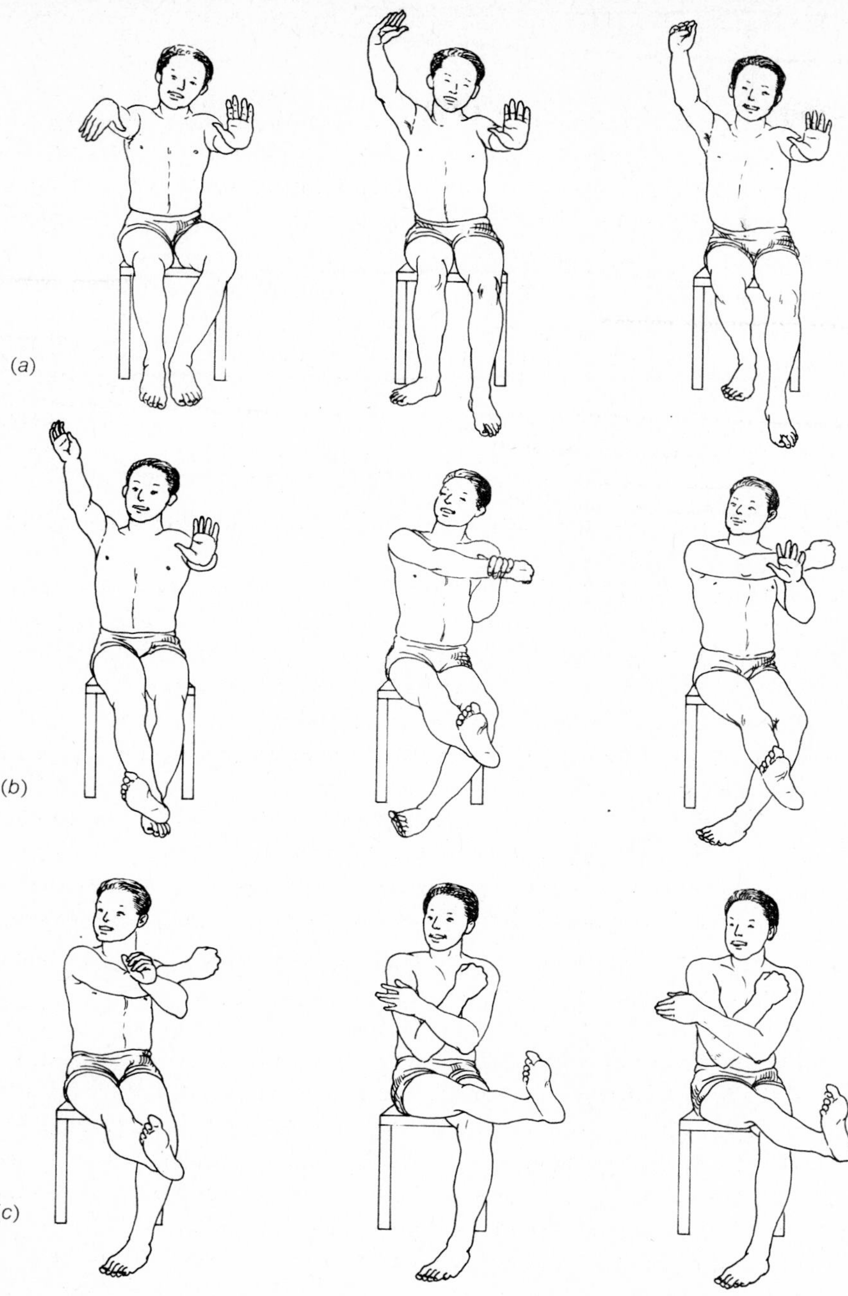

Fig. 24·28 Ballism affecting the right side of the body. (*a*) Following the order to lift both arms, the affected right arm is raised with delay and overshoots. (*b*) Then forceful movements of the right arm and right leg suddenly begin, and the right hand closes into a fist. (*c*) After the right arm is caught with the left, it goes into a sudden extension together with the right leg. During these ballistic movements, there is forced laughing. All the movements last less than two seconds. Pictures are drawn from a motion picture. (From Jung and Hassler, 1960)

such as Parkinson's disease, interfere with this inhibition, and the afflicted person performs a variety of involuntary movements.

The Cerebellum In vertebrates, the cerebellum consists of a many-folded sheet of nerve cells (see Figure 22•8). Its size varies among vertebrates according to the range and complexity of their movements. For example, the cerebellum is larger in fish with extensive locomotor behavior than in sedentary fish.

Inputs to the cerebellum come from other motor areas of the brain and from sensory sources. Both the pyramidal and extrapyramidal systems send impulses to the cerebellar cortex. Thus, the cerebellum receives information from systems that both monitor and execute movements. This relationship suggests that the cerebellum has a role in feedback control of movements since this form of control involves comparison of information about intended movements and the position or state of muscles at any instant. This comparison provides a basis for correcting movements. Such a control mechanism is characteristic of goal-directed behavior, such as reaching for an object.

Disorders of the cerebellar cortex are characterized by difficulty in making smooth, even movements and in starting and stopping movements. These impairments include the following:

1. Irregularity in the direction, extent, and rate of movement, as manifested by a tendency to sway and fall, especially while walking or maintaining balance.
2. Inability to perform rapidly alternating movements.
3. Tremors during a movement or during maintenance of a posture, and irregular jerks toward the end of a movement.
4. To-and-fro movements of the eyes during attempts to fixate on an object, and changes in the characteristic voluntary eye movements.
5. Disordered speech, either slurred or broken into explosive bursts.
6. Weakness and fatigue of a limb, as in the inability to maintain a grip.

The type of impairment a patient has depends on the portion of the cerebellum damaged. Damage to the cerebellum can be caused by tumors, infections, and toxins such as alcohol, lead, and DDT. There are also hereditary defects of the cerebellum.

The nature of the various disorders of the motor systems and the location of the damaged tissue provide major clues in unravelling the operation of the motor system. We have seen that even the simplest movement may involve the participation of many different systems in the brain.

Summary

The structure of the nervous system derives from the organization of nerve and glial cells. While individual nerve cells may vary in form, they share the same basic components—dendrites, cell body, and axon. The synapse is the junction between two nerve cells and is important in drug effects and in normal information-processing activities of the brain.

Brain regions are identified or described by their gross shape or by the cellular patterns seen with microscopic observation. The development of the nervous system proceeds according to a genetic program, but experience, toxins, and other agents can modify development. Although the development of the nervous system extends over many years, the most intense changes take place prenatally and during the first two to three postnatal years. Prominent postnatal events include further formation of dendrites and synapses, myelinization of axons, and an increase in glial cells. The nervous system is especially sensitive to disruptive effects during periods of rapid growth.

The basis of the information-handling capacity of the nervous system is the ability of neurons to generate nerve impulses (spikes) and graded potentials. Nerve impulses are used to encode and transmit information over distances, whereas graded potentials interact locally to allow nerve cells to process information.

Motor movements arise from activity generated in a variety of brain areas including the cerebral cortex, the basal ganglia, the brain stem, and the cerebellum. The type of movement disorder produced by damage at any of these sites provides clues to their role in the control of movement.

It is tempting to imagine a sensory input controlling a motor movement in a rather direct fashion. Actually, this occurs only in the simplest cases of spinal reflexes. In all other cases, the generation of behavior is exceedingly complex. Even the simplest movement requires the coordinated activity of many brain areas.

Suggested Readings

Eccles, J. C. 1972. *The understanding of the brain.* New York: McGraw-Hill.

A Nobel laureate's look at brain functioning from the cellular view, including a consideration of the ways in which the brain works in complex behavior.

Gardner, E. 1975. *Fundamentals of neurology: A psychophysiological approach.* 6th ed. Philadelphia: W. B. Saunders.

An introduction to the anatomy of the human brain, with particular consideration of clinical brain syndromes.

Kuffler, S. W., and Nicholls, J. G. 1976. *From neuron to brain.* Sunderland, Mass.: Sinauer.

A comprehensive current discussion of the basic properties of signals in nervous systems.

Thompson, R. F. 1975. *Introduction to physiological psychology.* New York: Harper and Row.

A comprehensive textbook covering the entire field of biological psychology.

Winick, M. 1976. *Malnutrition and brain development.* New York: Oxford University Press.

An examination of the social and biological consequences of malnutrition during the period of brain organization.

Behavioral Biology

25 In Chapter 24, we discussed the basic structural and functional properties of the brain and the general rules governing brain processing of sensory inputs and determination of movements. In this chapter we extend our discussion to the more complex problems in the field of behavioral biology. These problems include the brain mechanisms involved in learning and memory, the mediation of language and speech, the nature of sleep and arousal, the brain processes concerned with internally regulated states such as eating, and the neural control of emotions. Progress on these problems is slow, for these are some of the major riddles of human existence. However, intensive work by many scientists has begun to yield answers about the brain activities involved in complex behaviors.

Behavioral Biology of Learning and Memory

25•1 As we saw in Chapter 10, learning is the process of changing behavior as a result of experience. We can say that memory is the retention of that change. From the simplest animals to humans, some form of learning and memory is evident. The ability to modify behavior as a result of experience means that some aspects of brain function and structure are changed, perhaps permanently. The nature of these changes is currently a mystery, but a variety of imaginative theories have been proposed to explain the biological substrates of learning and memory (Table 25•1).

Frequently investigators have proceeded on the assumption that a single type of brain change may form the basis of learning and memory. However, the diversity of forms of learning suggests that from a neurobiological perspective, learning and memory may involve many different mechanisms. In this sense, the brain may contain an array of different memory devices.

Table 25·1 Some Mechanisms That May Underlie Learning and Memory and Where They Occur

MECHANISM	LOCATION
Facilitation of synapses with successful use	Synapses
Axon terminals swell during activity	Synapses
Destruction of synapses	Synapses
Directed growth of nerve processes and creation of synapses	Synapses and whole nerve cell
Glial Storage	Glial cells
Residual excitation in nerve cells	Groups of nerve cells
Coherence of activity in populations of nerve cells	Groups of nerve cells
Neural holograms	Groups of nerve cells

(Adapted from Leiman and Christian, 1973, Table 6-1, p. 127)

What Are the Biological Questions Regarding Learning and Memory? Although experimental work in the area of learning and memory has tested many theories, using a variety of techniques, animals, and types of learning, the basic biological questions can be succinctly stated as "Where?" and "How?"

"Where?" deals with the places or regions in the brain that are or might be involved in the acquisition, storage, and retrieval of information. Specific experimental questions include: Are memories stored in particular regions of the brain and not in others? Are memories stored as changes in the molecular structure of chemicals in brain cells? Can learning produce changes at synapses?

"How?" deals with neurochemical, neuroanatomical, and neurophysiological mechanisms or processes involved in learning and memory. Specific questions include: How is information distributed to various brain areas involved in learning and memory? How do the brain areas involved in learning and memory change as a result of experience? What changes in the structure of synapses occur with use? What chemical processes in the cell are involved with memory?

Many scientists believe that learning and memory are fundamental puzzles in the biology of behavior. We will examine a few of the neurobiological approaches to learning and memory.

Biological Analysis of Differences Between Short-term and Long-term Memory In Chapter 8, we introduced the theory that (1) information such as stimuli and the responses made to them are held in short-term memory for periods of seconds to minutes, and (2) this information may be lost unless it is stored in long-term memory, which is virtually nonerasable. According to this theory, events in short-term memory are somehow selected and stored in long-term memory. This process of transferring information from short-term memory to long-term memory is called memory consolidation.

Some of the first evidence for the distinction between short- and long-term memory and the time required for memory consolidation came from the study of head injuries in humans. It has been commonly observed that persons who lose consciousness following a blow to the head may not be able to recall the events immediately prior to that trauma. They have a **retrograde amnesia** (loss of memory for events before a trauma) that may extend back in time for a period of minutes to many hours. This blank period—especially the few minutes before trauma—remains forever inaccessible, resisting the efforts of psychoanalysis, hypnosis, drugs, and other treatments designed to facilitate recall. To explain this type of memory failure, it is generally hypothesized that events are held in a short-term storage mechanism that involves dynamic brain processes such as the residual excitation of nerve cells or neural activity circulating in loops of interconnected nerve cells. The impact of trauma on such a mechanism is to destroy the dynamic activity or perhaps to "jam" it.

Many researchers have used animals in experiments exploring memory consolidation. These experiments involve various disruptive agents, including anesthesia, convulsions induced by drugs or electrical stimulation of the brain, and the injection into the brain of substances that interfere with metabolic processes necessary for maintenance of electrical excitability of nerve cells. In a typical experiment, animals are exposed to a brief learning experience and then the treatment that disrupts brain functioning is administered. Some animals receive this treatment immediately after the learning experience, some 15 seconds later, some 30 seconds, and so on up to an interval of perhaps one or two hours. The next day, the animals in the various experimental conditions are tested for retention of what was learned. With a long delay between learning and the disruptive treatment, animals show good retention; that is, they have formed an enduring memory. With a short delay, animals may show no evidence of memory formation. These experiments indicate that consolidation of learning into permanent memory requires a certain period of time.

The time required for memory consolidation varies from seconds to many minutes (Figure 25•1). This variation may reflect the existence of diverse forms of short-term memory processes. For example, consolidation times for motor learning may differ from those for verbal learning. The neural signals (either electrical or chemical) that lead to the activation of permanent storage are unknown.

Biological Aspects of Learning and Memory in Humans: Amnesic Syndromes and Brain Injury Accidents, diseases, aging processes, and neurosurgical treatments in humans can lead to dramatic changes in learning and memory processes. Studies of such people can provide information about the role of the particular brain regions in the processes of information storage and retrieval and may eventually contribute to the development of rehabilitative programs for brain-injured persons.

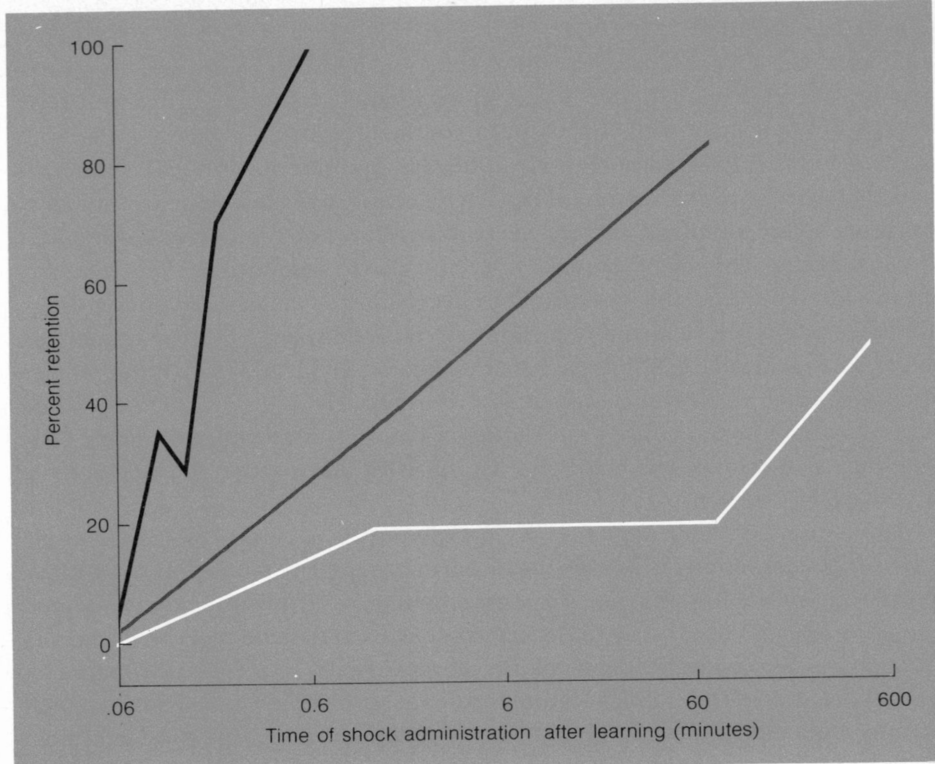

Fig. 25·1 The three curves come from experiments using different kinds of learning situations. In all experiments, the sooner after learning that a disruptive shock is given, the less the animal retains. The variation in the curves suggests that memory consolidation proceeds at different rates for different kinds of learning situations. (Adapted from Chorover, 1976)

Transient Global Amnesia The rare person who forgets everything about himself or his surroundings is usually regarded as suffering hysterical amnesia, a form of amnesia that results from stressful personal conflicts. However, there are people who have an extensive memory loss that cannot be explained as hysterical amnesia. Such persons seem to have a neurological rather than a psychiatric disorder and are referred to as suffering from transient global amnesia. These cases primarily involve middle-age and older patients who suddenly suffer a memory loss (typically this occurs after strong physical exertion) that may last from minutes to hours. The following case description is adapted from a paper by K. W. G. Heathfield, P. B. Croft, and M. Swash (1973).

> The principal of a technical college was seen five days after an episode of amnesia that had occurred on his sixtieth birthday. He had been chopping wood for two hours on a warm day when he suddenly lost his memory. He repeatedly asked his wife where he was and what he was doing. His speech and behavior were otherwise normal. His wife called their family physician who confirmed the memory loss, which extended back for several years. Toward the end of the doctor's visit the patient's memory began to return. Memories for a period of two hours before the episode remained permanently lost.

There were no other abnormal findings during or after the episode. An EEG (electroencephalogram) recorded sixteen days later showed an excess of diffuse low voltage theta brain waves, but no focal abnormality. He returned to work and noticed no aftereffect. During the next six years he had no recurrence and he retained a good memory throughout that time.

Heathfield, Croft, and Swash point out that the retrograde amnesia gradually shortens with recovery, although the events of the trauma and those immediately before it seem to be lost from memory. This transient global amnesia may arise from a trauma due to change in blood flow in the brain, especially in the temporal lobes.

The Temporal Lobes and Anterograde Amnesia The temporal lobes and associated brain regions (including the *hippocampus* and the *medial dorsal thalamic nuclei*) appear to be involved in human memory. Their involvement is especially evident in some human cases that are characterized by inability to form new memories (*anterograde amnesia*).

Few clinical reports in the neurological literature are as dramatic and poignant as the case of H.M., who suffered a remarkable change in memory functioning following the bilateral (in both hemispheres) removal of portions of the *temporal lobes* (Figure 25•2). He had a twenty-year history of disabling epileptic seizures (from the age of seven) and this surgical procedure was successfully performed in an effort to remove the brain regions believed to be responsible for the patient's seizure activity. (Surgery of this sort has proven remarkably effective in achieving this goal in patients for whom drug therapy measures have been ineffective.)

In the twenty-odd years following his surgery, H.M. has been virtually unable to remember events that have occurred following his surgery. He has also lost the memory of some events that occurred prior to the surgery. He cannot recall experiences after surgery, including names, faces, and where he lives. He is especially unable to remember verbal material, but shows some capacity for motor learning. This memory impairment occurs without generalized confusion or fuzziness. His immediate memory capability and speech and language capabilities are intact, and he scores high on conventional IQ tests. He says, "Every day is alone in itself, whatever enjoyment I've had, and whatever sorrow I've had," and "Right now, I'm wondering. Have I done or said anything amiss? You see, at this moment everything looks clear to me, but what happened just before? That's what worries me. It's like waking from a dream; I just don't remember" (B. Milner, 1959). H.M. was operated on at the age of twenty-seven and has been studied since that time by Dr. Brenda Milner of the Montreal Neurological Institute.

Destruction of parts of the brain due to infections and metabolic impairments can also lead to memory disorders in humans. *Korsakoff's syndrome* is a disorder characterized by an anterograde amnesia. The syndrome arises from a thiamine deficiency and is strongly associated with destruction of the *mammillary bodies,* two rounded protuberances at the base of the brain (Figure 25•2). Tumors that impinge on this brain region may produce a similar memory failure (Kahn and

Fig. 25·2 In this drawing of the underside of the brain, part of the left temporal lobe and the hippocampus have been removed (area between dotted lines). Removal of these areas on both sides of the brain produced the anterograde amnesia seen in the patient H.M. Below this figure are drawings of the brain made at a plane perpendicular to the top view and at the locations indicated by the labeled, dotted lines. The right side is intact, but the left side shows what the brain looked like after the removal of the tissue. The two mammillary bodies shown in the top drawing are also important in memory mechanisms. (From B. Milner, 1959)

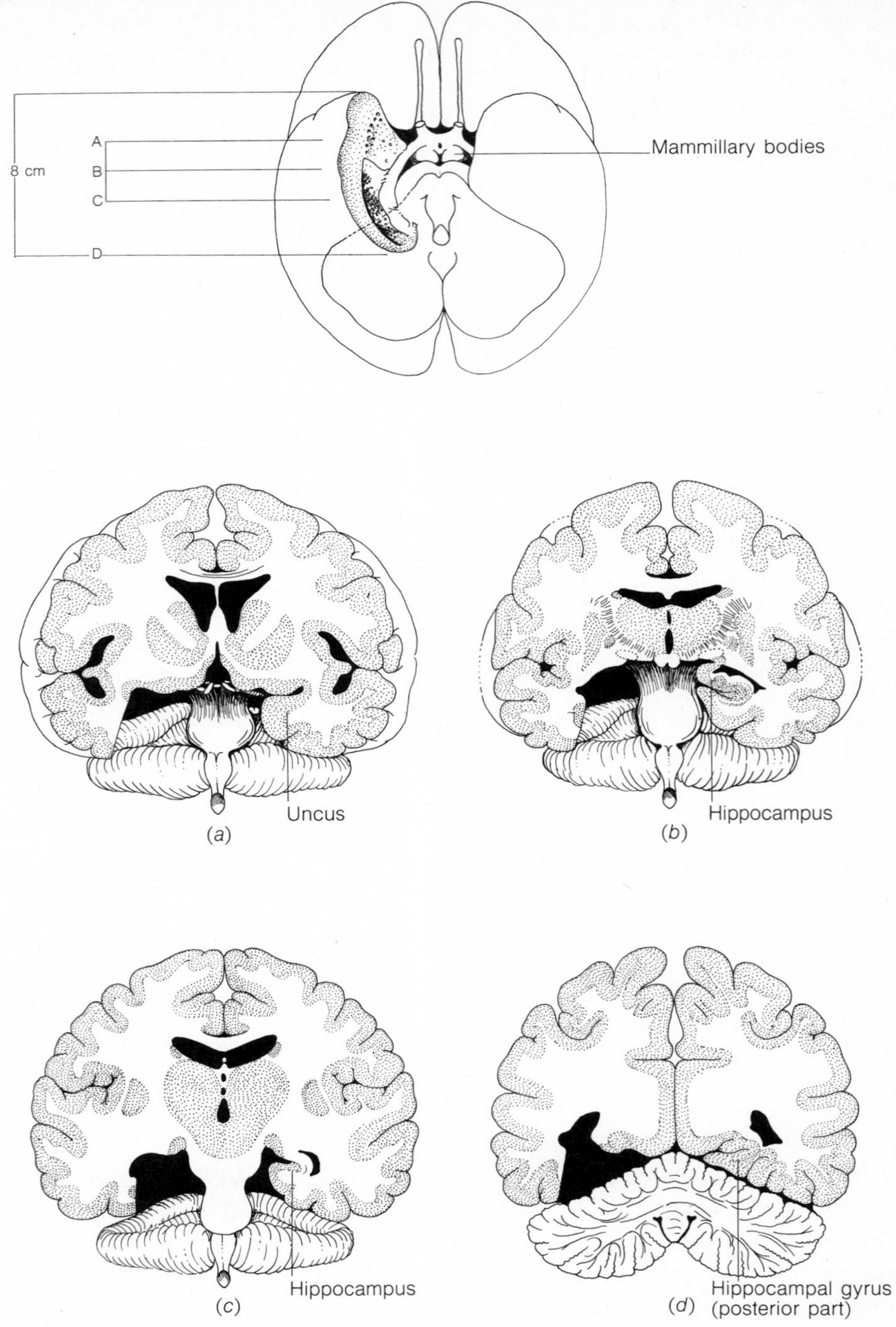

Crosby, 1972). Korsakoff's syndrome is frequently seen in chronic alcoholics who fail to eat properly because they derive most of their caloric input from alcohol and thus develop a thiamine deficiency.

Starr and Phillips (1970) described a case of severe memory impairment following a viral infection of the brain in which the temporal lobes were especially damaged. The patient showed good immediate recall of verbal items and good retention of events that had occurred many years before his illness, but could not establish new long-term memories. A detailed analysis of his remaining memory abilities indicated that he could store some memories. It may be that amnesic cases of this kind can store information but cannot recall it. Starr and Phillips emphasized that this memory disorder was greater for certain kinds of tasks, such as verbal rather than motor learning. This again suggests that there may be a variety of learning and memory mechanisms in the brain.

Brain Chemistry Approaches to Learning and Memory Advances in biochemical genetics during the past twenty-five years have resulted in a growing understanding of the mechanisms of inheritance. We know that the large **deoxyribonucleic acid molecules (DNA)** found in the chromosomes of cells control the inherited characteristics (including some behavior patterns) of all species (see Chapters 22 and 23). The information encoded in the DNA molecule is a form of species memory; is it possible that an individual's experience could be similarly encoded at a molecular level? Perhaps in a molecule similar to DNA? The possibility that memories are encoded as some sort of chemical change in cells has inspired a variety of experiments. Some approaches to the relation of brain chemistry and memory are:

1. Research on changes in the levels or synthesis rates of cellular chemicals as a function of learning experiences.
2. Research on the effects on learning and memory of altering the concentration or synthesis of particular chemicals (for example, proteins) in the cell.
3. Research on the possibility of transfer of memory from one animal to another by extracting brain-component chemicals from a trained animal and injecting them into an untrained animal.

In Sweden, Holger Hydén (1967) has perfected techniques for measuring the quantities of **ribonucleic acids (RNA)** and proteins in nerve cells. After animals had learned a task, Hydén dissected nerve cells out of various regions in their brains and measured changes in the quantities of these chemicals they contained. For example, some animals were required to retrieve food with their nonpreferred paw (many animals prefer to do certain tasks with a certain paw). When the animals had learned to use that paw, protein levels in nerve cells from their hippocampi were examined and compared with the protein levels in nerve cells from the hippocampi of untrained animals. Hydén noted that learning this task had apparently produced an increase in the synthesis of a particular protein in the trained animals. Similar changes have been described by this group of experimenters when the learning involved a form of sensory conditioning.

Biochemical experiments involving imprinting in chicks (see Chapter 22) have provided another approach to correlating molecular changes with learning (Horn, Rose, and Bateson, 1973). Imprinting with a visual stimulus (such as a flashing light) produced changes in the amount of RNA and protein synthesized.

Experiments such as these demonstrate that nervous system activity influences metabolism of RNA and protein; other experiments have also demonstrated that there are links between cell metabolism and synaptic activity. However, it is not clear that these changes are due to learning. Numerous organismic variables, such as arousal or stress, apparently influence nerve cell metabolism and may accompany learning processes. Thus it is difficult to ascribe changes such as Hydén found only to the effects of learning. Scientific research is a long way from demonstrating the existence of *memory molecules*.

Cellular chemical events related to learning have also been examined using drugs that modify the metabolism of RNA and protein. In these experiments, animals are trained to perform a response after being given a drug (such as an antibiotic) that inhibits the synthesis of RNA or protein. If the establishment of long-term memory is dependent on the synthesis of protein or RNA, then these drugs should impair memory. The results of studies using various antibiotics have allowed us to conclude that (1) well-established long-term memories are extremely resistant to chemical destruction by these drugs, and (2) newly established memories are dependent on protein synthesis since administration of these drugs at the time of training can inhibit the formation of long-term memories (Flood and Jarvik, 1976).

The behavioral data derived from formal experiments and from informal intuitions indicate that once consolidation has occurred, a memory can be extremely stable. The permanence of memory has led investigators in the direction of searching for enduring molecular changes, either at the level of the structural appearance of nerve cells or at the level of molecules that may have stability. Such questions may be premature since more broad questions about the circuitry and neurophysiology of learning have yet to be answered.

Neurophysiological Studies of Learning and Memory Wherever the changes produced by experience are wrought in the brain, the events that lead to these changes are the electrical responses of nerve cells: graded events and nerve impulses. These activities are necessary preludes to any enduring structural or biochemical changes.

Current neurophysiological experiments on learning use simple animals such as the aplysia (a marine snail) and the crayfish, whose nervous systems are composed of comparatively few nerve cells. The collections of nerve cells (ganglia) in both the aplysia and the crayfish contain some large nerve cells that can be individually identified. This makes it possible to trace the pattern of nerve cell connections in these animals. By examining the cellular changes that accompany learning in such simple animals, scientists hope to discover fundamental rules about memory operations that are applicable to all creatures. After all, the basic mechanisms of axonal transmission and synaptic interactions at a cellular level appear to be similar in all animals, from the simplest to the most complex.

Many of the neurophysiological studies of learning and memory in the aplysia and the crayfish have examined habituation. **Habituation** involves learning not to respond to a repetition of a stimulus that has no consequences for the animal. It is characterized by a declining response to repeated presentations of the same stimulus. This decrease in response is not due to muscle fatigue nor to adaptation of a receptor; the response will still occur when a novel stimulus is presented. Thus, habituation tunes the nervous system to respond to novel stimuli—stimuli that are not predictable because of prior repetition. Studies of habituation in simple animals have focused on stereotyped, species-typical defensive or escape behaviors. For example, prodding the abdomen of a crayfish produces vigorous flexion of its tail, which swiftly propels the animal in a dart-like manner away from the stimulus. Repeating this stimulation results in a waning of this response (Figure 25•3). Under some circumstances, such habituation can be shown to last for days. Presentation of a novel stimulus (for example, prodding with a different force) usually results in restoration of the habituated escape response.

The circuitry mediating this escape response can be described in detail, because there are so few elements in the nervous system. In fact, both the escape and habituation behaviors can be displayed by an abdominal region removed from the rest of the animal. Once the connections are known, attempts can be made to locate the sites of the neural changes that produce habituation at a cellular level. Studies involving both the tail-flexion response in crayfish and a defensive reflex in aplysia emphasize that habituation is attributable to changes in the pre-

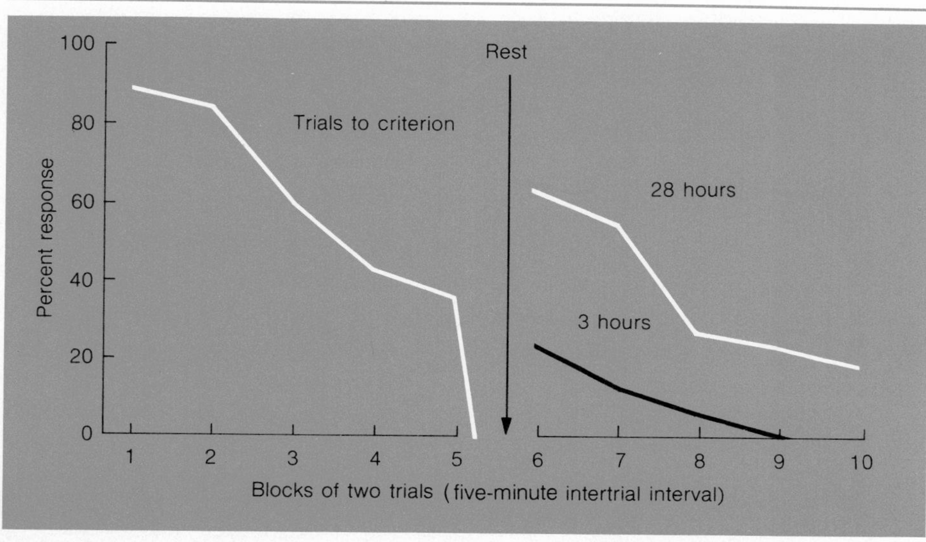

Fig. 25•3 Habituation of tail-flexion response. Left: Mean percentage of trials on which tail flips occurred in rested animals in response to taps to the side of the abdomen. Trials to criterion consisted of taps at one per minute in blocks of ten separated by ten-minute rests until completion of a block without any responses (mean trials to criterion was 20). Right: Responses after rests of the stated duration. (Adapted from Wine and Krasne, 1972 and from Wine, Krasne, and Chen, 1975)

synaptic part of the synapse (Zucker, Kennedy, and Selverston, 1971; Krasne, 1976).

Habituation has also been studied in animals whose spinal cords have been cut. In Chapter 24 we noted that cutting the spinal cord isolates the spinal cord from the brain, and that the isolated spinal cord can still display various simple reflex behaviors. One such simple reflex is the withdrawal of a limb from an intense stimulus. Thompson and his colleagues (1973), among others, have shown that repetitive elicitation of this reflex leads to habituation of the response. Figure 25•4 shows the response of one kind of nerve cell within the spinal cord to repeated stim-

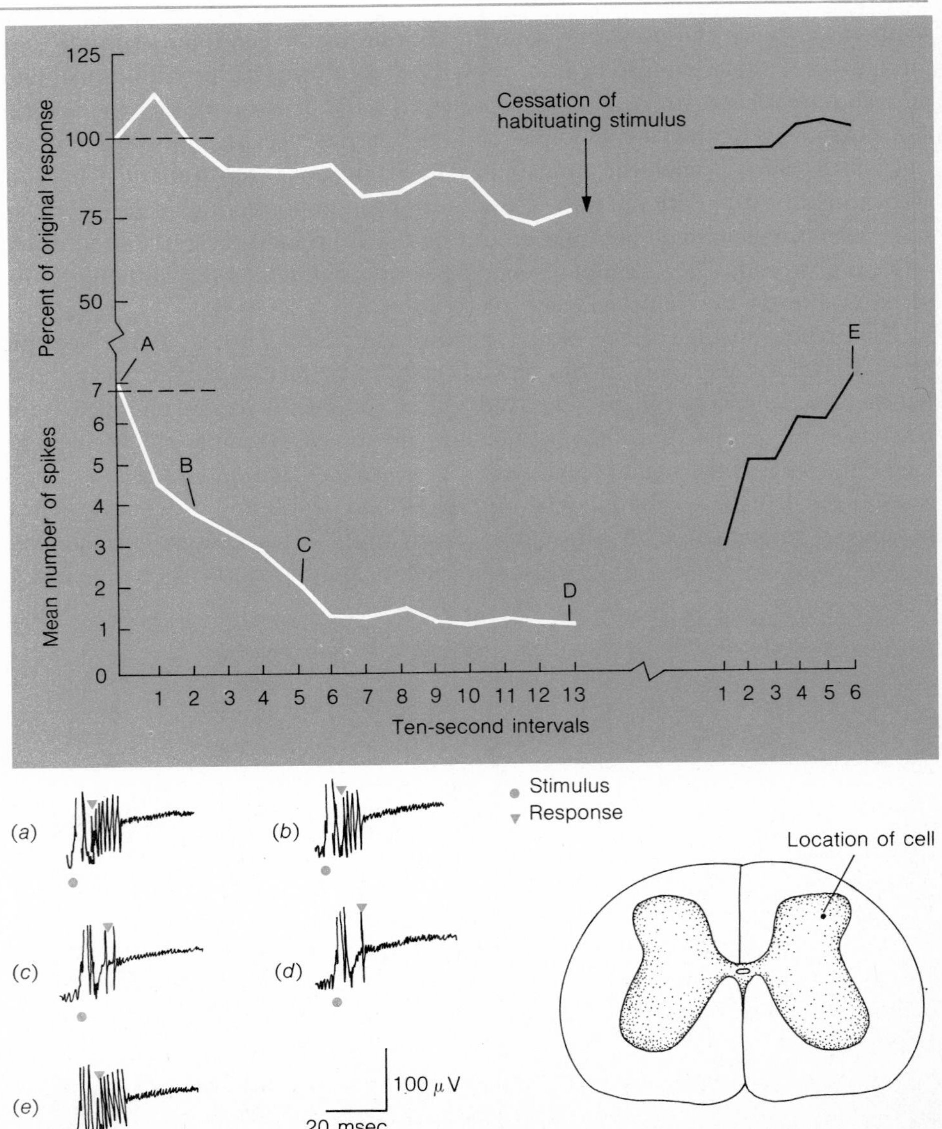

Fig. 25•4 An example of a nerve cell in the spinal cord that appears to mediate habituation. The white curve in the upper graph represents the amplitude of a reflex response; the white curve in the lower graph represents the rate of nerve cell firing to a repeated stimulus (at a rate of two stimuli per second). The black curves represent the amplitude of the reflex and the firing rate of the nerve cell after the habituating stimulus has been stopped, allowing the habituated response to recover.

Below these graphs are tracings showing the nerve impulses generated by this nerve cell at various times during the experiment, as indicated by the capital letters. To the right of these tracings is a schematic cross section of half the spinal cord, which shows the location of the cell from which these data were taken. (Adapted from Groves and Thompson, 1973)

ulation. This class of nerve cells, which shows a decreased discharge when the stimulus is repeated, may be responsible for habituation of the flexion reflex. Again, a change in the activity of presynaptic terminals seems to be responsible for the habituation.

Learning and Memory in Populations of Nerve Cells The brain of complex animals is composed of billions of nerve cells. In studies of learning and memory only a very small set of these cells can be sampled. Some investigators argue that, in order to get a more comprehensive picture of the processes involved in learning and memory, it is necessary to use methods that provide some indication of the spatial and temporal processes that occur across many neural elements. By way of analogy, a large group of people, each holding either a black or a white placard, can form words or pictures when they raise or lower the cards according to some plan. Perhaps you have seen such displays at football games. However, if you were to look at only one card you would not see the message the entire group is communicating—"WIN," for example. Similarly, we may not see the relation between the activity of a single nerve cell and learning and memory, but we might see a relation when large groups of nerve cells are observed.

Electrodes can be used to record the activity of a large number of neurons. Unlike smaller electrodes used to record the activity of a single nerve cell (see Figure 24•27, for example), these larger electrodes can only record the sum of the activity of a large number of nerve cells. The potentials thus recorded are called gross potentials. The **electroencephalogram (EEG)** recorded at the human scalp is an example of such a gross potential.

E. R. John (1972) recorded the gross potentials that were generated during discrimination learning at different places in an animal's brain. Before the animal learned to discriminate one stimulus from other stimuli, very few areas in the brain responded to the stimulus. After learning, electrical activity specific to the stimuli used in the discrimination appears at a wide variety of brain regions, including the thalamus and various parts of the cerebral cortex (Figure 25•5). This suggests that learning involves changes in a large number of nerve cells at a variety of brain regions. Perhaps each nerve cell changes only a slight bit, and the activity of a large group of nerve cells is necessary to produce a memory.

We have seen that there are many conjectures about the mechanisms of learning and memory. Some theories argue that memory involves the development of new molecules or increased concentrations of the molecules found in cells. Some theories emphasize changes in the structure of synapses as a function of use; such changes might facilitate further transmission through the synapses. Some theories suggest that learning and memory might involve the construction of new synapses or growth of dendrites. Other theories have argued that glial cells may store memory.

At another level of analysis, perhaps specific brain regions store memories, or perhaps memories are somehow distributed throughout the brain. Indeed, the many possible mechanisms and locations of learning and memory suggest that

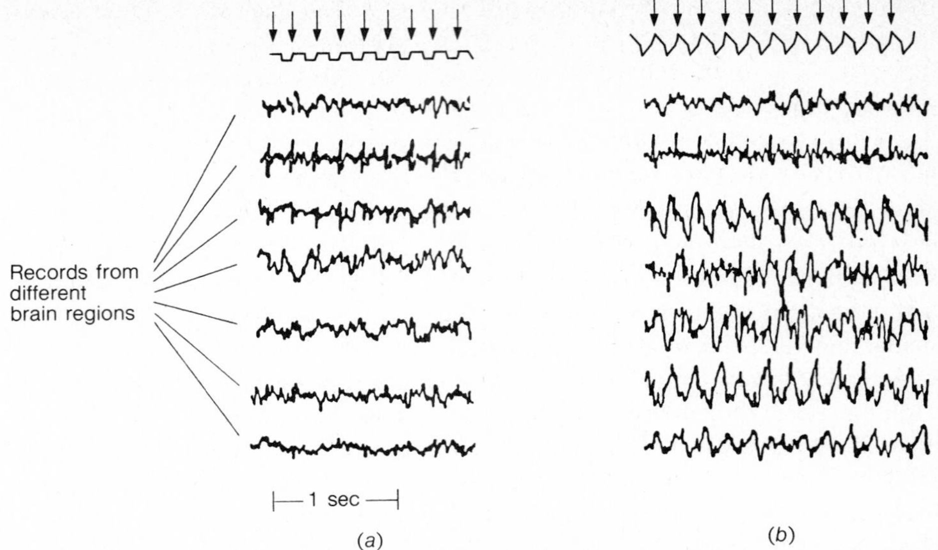

Fig. 25•5 EEG recordings of responses to a visual stimulus that is presented at times indicated by the arrows.
(*a*) Before the animal has learned to discriminate the visual stimulus, only a few brain locations show a response to it.
(*b*) After the animal learns the visual discrimination, many more brain areas respond to the stimulus. (Adapted from John, 1972)

the brain can store information in many different ways. For example, the retention of verbal material may involve a neural storage mechanism that is quite unlike the mechanism for storage of emotional memories. At present, there is insufficient evidence available on which to base selection of one view as *the* mechanism of learning and memory.

Behavioral Biology of Language

25•2 Human language is composed of a set of sounds and symbols that have distinct meanings. These elements are arranged in sequences according to rules. Anyone who knows the sounds, symbols, and rules of a particular language can generate sentences. Many scientists see language as the essence of human experience—indeed, life without language in one form or another seems inconceivable.

All languages have similar elements, and language is learned in a similar fashion by all children (see Chapter 4). These aspects of language suggest that the abilities fundamental to production of language may be inherent in the biological structure of our brains. In this section we will examine some of the approaches and ideas that have characterized attempts to uncover the biological bases of human language.

Evolution of Language By examining fossils and studying monkeys that are closely related to humans, we can gain some insight into when language appeared and into the kinds of behaviors and brain structures from which language arose. The use of sound for communication often has advantages over the use of other sensory channels. For example, it makes communication possible at night, or in other situations in which the animals involved cannot see each other. The development of spoken communication clearly has survival value.

On the basis of his studies of the probable shape and length of the vocal tract of archaelogical specimens, A. M. Liberman (1974) has suggested that the speech production capability of *Homo sapiens* is perhaps only 50,000 years old. He further argues that the vocal tracts in human infants and in nonhuman primates (monkeys) are shaped so that they cannot produce all the sounds that speech requires. Other archaelogical studies have attempted to infer brain size from skull fragments of different geological eras. Brain size with respect to body weight may correlate with intelligence, and the use of language requires a certain level of intelligence.

The chatter (calls) of nonhuman primates has been intensively examined in both field and laboratory studies. Detlev Ploog and his collaborators at the Max Planck Institute in Munich (see Jürgens and Ploog, 1970) have studied the vocal behavior of squirrel monkeys, cataloging the calls they produce and the communication properties of those sounds in a social context. Their calls include shrieking, quacking, chirping, growling, and yapping sounds. Direct electrical stimulation of some regions of a squirrel monkey's brain can elicit some of these calls, but stimulation of the cerebral cortex generally fails to elicit vocal behavior. Other investigators have shown that removal of parts of the cerebral cortex of nonhuman primates has little effect on vocalization behavior. Removal or damage of cerebral cortex in humans can dramatically affect language.

Throughout history, people have tried to teach various animals how to talk. In most cases, if any communication occurred, it was because the person involved improved his or her meowing, grunting, or barking, rather than because the animal produced sounds of human speech. In order to speak like a human, an animal must have not only a certain level of intelligence, but also a vocal apparatus similar to that of a human.

Since both the vocal tracts and the basic vocal repertoires of modern nonhuman primates are different from those of humans, scientists have given up attempting to train animals to produce human speech. Rather, they have asked whether nonhuman primates can be taught forms of communication that have features similar to human language, including the ability symbolically to represent objects in the environment and to manipulate these symbols.

The Gardners at the University of Nevada have been successful in getting chimpanzees to acquire a gesture type of language called signing—the sign language of deaf humans. These animals have learned many signs and are able to use them spontaneously and to generate new sentences using sequences of these signs. Ann and David Premack (1972) have used another approach in examining cognitive capabilities of chimpanzees that may be related to language. They teach chimpanzees a language based on an assortment of colored chips (symbols) that can adhere to a magnetic board. After extensive training, the chimpanzees can manipulate these chips in ways that reflect an acquired ability to form sentences and to note various logical classifications.

Thus, while nonhuman primates (at least those as intelligent as the chimpanzee) do not have a vocal system, they do have a capacity for learning language. Neurological studies of such animals may provide an experimental approach to understanding brain mechanisms related to human language.

Neurological Aspects of Language: Hemispheric Specialization and Cerebral Dominance In humans, many gross structural features of the right and left cerebral hemispheres are similar, but their functions are quite different. This is reflected in the fact that we can do many things (such as writing) better with one hand than with the other. Most people use the right hand for writing. You will remember that the right side of the body is connected to the left half of the brain, and vice versa. Therefore, the left half of the brain in most people may be specialized for writing—and perhaps for other functions in language.

It is traditional to call the half of the brain that may be specialized for language the dominant hemisphere. This suggests that one side of the brain is always in control. However, a broader perspective is that the two hemispheres are specialized for controlling different behaviors—for some functions the left cerebral hemisphere is dominant, and for others the right hemisphere is dominant.

The differential properties of the cerebral hemispheres are best illustrated in a series of studies by Roger Sperry and his collaborators at California Institute of Technology. These experiments involved a small group of human patients who underwent a surgical procedure designed to provide some relief from frequent, disabling epileptic seizures. In these patients, epileptic activity initiated in one hemisphere spread to the other hemisphere via the *corpus callosum*, the large bundle of fibers that connects the two hemispheres (see Figure 24•2). Surgically cutting the corpus callosum appreciably reduces the frequency and severity of the patient's seizures.

Earlier studies by other investigators showed that this relief from seizures was not accompanied by any apparent changes in brain function as assessed by general behavior testing methods such as IQ tests. But the corpus callosum in humans is a huge bundle of over one million axons, and it seemed strange that the principal connection between the cerebral hemispheres could be cut without producing detectable changes in behaviors.

Using more sensitive behavioral techniques, Sperry reexamined these patients. Some of the behavioral procedures for testing these patients are shown in Figure 25•6. Stimuli can be directed to either hemisphere by presenting them in different places in the visual field or in different places on the surface of the body. For example, objects the patient feels with the left hand result in activity in nerve cells of the sensory regions in the right hemisphere. Since the corpus callosum is cut in these patients, most of the information sent to one half of the brain cannot travel to the other half. By controlling stimuli in this fashion, the experimenter can present stimuli selectively to one hemisphere or the other and thus test the capabilities of each hemisphere.

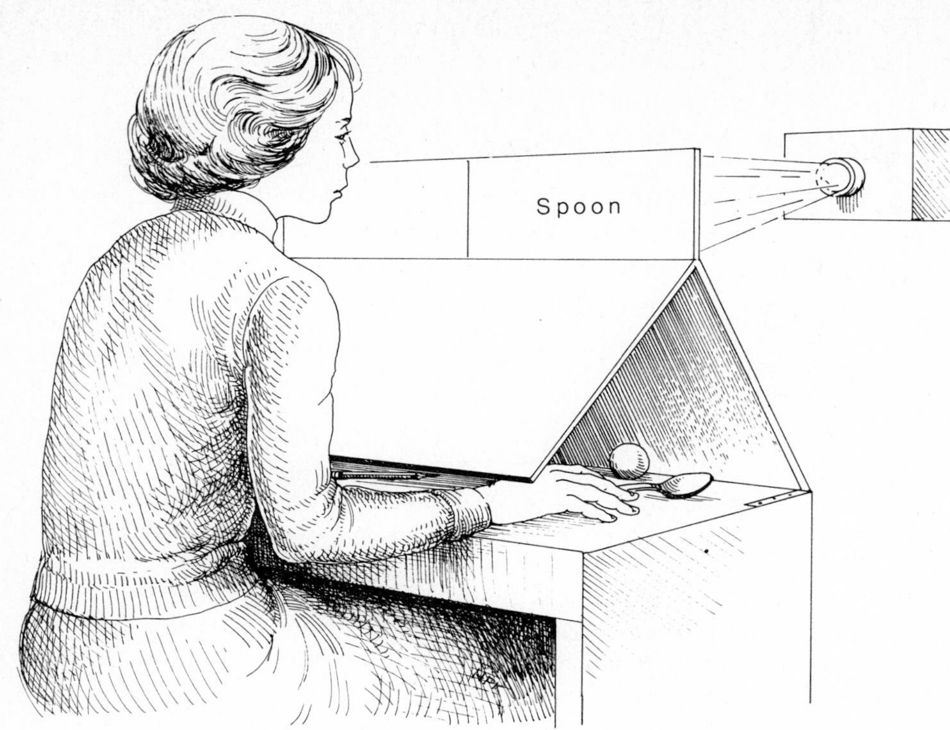

Fig. 25·6 The experimental situation used to test the abilities of each hemisphere in a patient whose corpus callosum has been cut. When the patient's gaze is fixated on a dot marking the center of the projection screen, the experimenter flashes a word or a picture of an object on the screen, to one side of the dot or to the other. This visual stimulus goes only to the half of the brain that is on the side opposite the side where the word or picture was flashed. The word *spoon* shown here will be sent to the left cerebral hemisphere. (See Figure 7·7 in Chapter 7 for a diagram of the visual pathways into the brain.)

Below the projection screen there is a shield that prevents the patient from observing her hands. The experimenter then places objects (such as a spoon or an apple) in either of the patient's hands. The patient must identify the objects on the basis of touch alone. (Adapted from Sperry and Gazzaniga, 1967, and Thompson, 1975)

Sperry's studies showed that words projected into the left hemisphere (that is, the stimuli were presented in the right part of the visual field) can be read easily and communicated verbally. No such linguistic capabilities were evident when the information was directed to the right hemisphere. More recently Zaidel (1973), a colleague of Sperry's, has shown that the right hemisphere has a small amount of linguistic ability. For example, it can recognize simple words. In general, the vocabulary and grammatic capabilities of the right hemisphere are far less developed than they are in the left hemisphere. On the other hand, the right hemisphere was superior on tasks involving spatial relations.

Studies of patients whose corpus callosums have been cut (referred to as *split-brain* humans) have provided the inspiration for intensive examination of functional dissimilarities between the cerebral hemispheres in humans. Some of the functions suggested for each hemisphere are listed in Table 25·2. Some researchers (among them, Galin, 1974) have emphasized that there is a basic difference in the mode of thinking of the right and left hemispheres, not merely a functional duplication.

Table 25·2 Functions Controlled by the Left and Right Hemispheres of the Cerebral Cortex

LEFT HEMISPHERE	RIGHT HEMISPHERE
Propositionizing	Visual imagery
Linguistic	Visual or kinesthetic
Storage	Executive
Symbolic or propositional	Visual or imaginative
Eduction of relations	Eduction of correlates
Verbal	Perceptual or nonverbal
Discrete	Diffuse
Symbolic	Visuospatial
Linguistic	Preverbal
Verbal	Visuospatial
Logical or analytic	Synthetic perceptual

(Adapted from Bogen, 1969)

Brain Injury and Language Most of our understanding of the relationship of brain mechanisms and language is derived from observation of language impair-

The Left-handed

From studying skull fractures of animals preyed upon by ancient man, anthropologists speculate that left-handedness goes back a long time into prehistory. Throughout history, many unusual attributes have been ascribed to the left-handed person—from the possession of an evil personality to a diffuse form of cerebral cortex organization. Indeed, the English term *sinistral* ("left-handed") comes from the same Latin root as the word *sinister!*

Left-handed people comprise a small percentage of human populations. Table 25A·1 shows the distribution of left-handedness in a large population of school-age children (Hardyck, Petrinovich, and Goldman, 1976). A figure of around 10 percent is commonly reported, although this percentage may be lower in parts of the world where teachers actively discourage left-handedness.

Table 25A·1 Distribution of Handedness by Sex in 7688 School Children

HANDEDNESS	BOYS $N = 3960$	GIRLS $N = 3728$	TOTAL $N = 7688$
Right	3543 (89.5)	3404 (91.3)	6947 (90.4)
Left	417 (10.5)	324 (8.7)	741 (9.6)

NOTE: Percentages by sex are given in parentheses. (Hardyck, Petrinovich, and Goldman, 1976)

Many studies have sought to show cognitive and emotional differences between left- and right-handed humans, the implication being that these groups differ in cerebral cortex organization. Some studies (using relatively small samples of subjects) have shown a link between left-handedness and cognitive deficits. Such data tend to be contradictory, perhaps because of simplistic views of handedness. Some individuals are ambidextrous—at least with regard to some tasks—or alternate their hand preference from task to task.

Hardyck, Petrinovich, and Goldman undertook a large-scale study of handedness and cognitive performance. They examined over 7000 children in grades 1 through 6 for school achievement, intellectual ability, motivation, socioeconomic level, and the like. In a detailed analysis of the resultant data, they clearly showed that left-handed children did not differ from right-handed children on any measure of cognitive performance.

ments following brain injury due to accidents, diseases, or strokes. A problem involved in studying such injury is the difficulty of ascertaining how localized the damage is. Nevertheless, there are some common syndromes of language impairment that appear to be related to distinct brain regions. In approximately 90 to 95 percent of the cases of language disorders due to brain injury, language disorders (called aphasia) are most dramatically evident if the damage is to the left cerebral hemisphere but not if it is to the right cerebral hemisphere. The reverse is true for the remaining 5 to 10 percent of the cases.

The form of language disorder depends on the region of injury. Figure 25·7 shows two areas in the left cerebral cortex where damage affects language ability. Damage to the shaded region of cortex nearest the front of the brain (Broca's area) results in marked speech impairment. In this disorder, called *Broca's aphasia*, the patient has difficulty producing words (even with considerable prompting and other forms of assistance), uses nouns more frequently than verbs, and makes errors in grammar. Although speech production is severely impaired, such patients can often write words correctly and can readily understand written and spoken language. This motor impairment of speech is, perhaps, somewhat understandable since this region is quite close to motor cortex. In studies of the effects of electrical

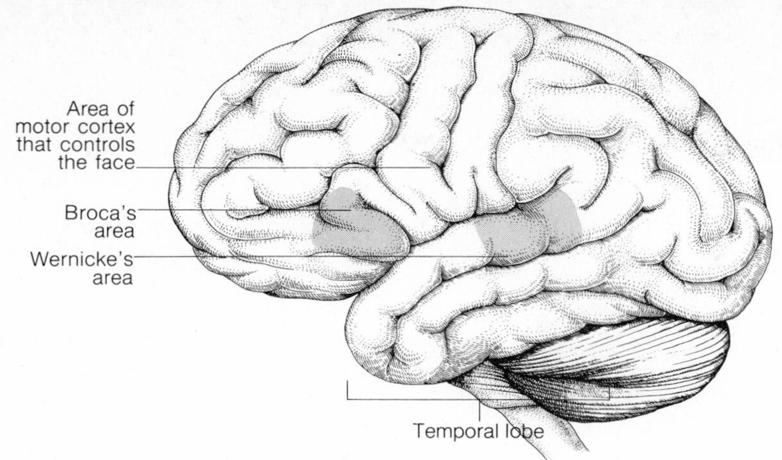

Fig. 25•7 Side view of the human cerebral cortex showing two of the more important brain areas involved in language. Broca's area is near the regions of cortex that are involved in the motor control of the muscles of the lips, jaw, tongue, soft palate, and vocal cords, and may control these motor brain areas. Damage to Broca's area disrupts the production (but not comprehension) of speech.

Wernicke's area is near the portions of the brain involved in the processing of auditory information. Damage to this area disrupts the comprehension of speech and results in speech with little content.

stimulation of this area, Wilder Penfield and Lamar Roberts (1959) showed that excitation of this region can arrest ongoing speech (Figure 25•8).

In contrast to this syndrome, injury to the shaded region of cortex near the middle of the brain in Figure 25•7 (temporal lobe) produces a marked, enduring deficit in language comprehension. In this form of aphasia, called *Wernicke's aphasia,* speech appears effortless and fluent, but it is frequently composed of gibberish and many unusual forms of language usage. The region of cortex where injury produces this deficit has come to be known as Wernicke's area.

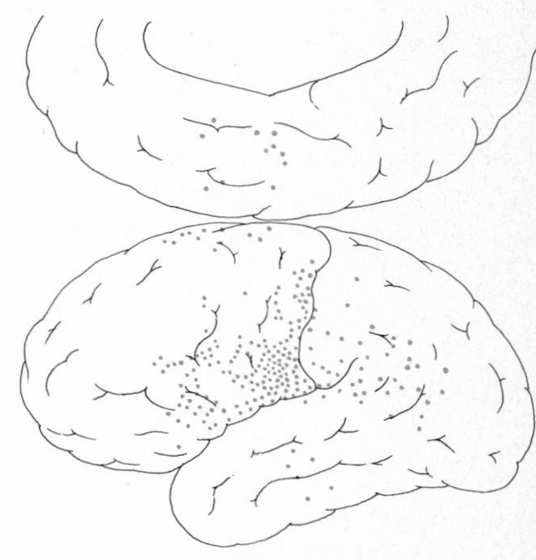

Fig. 25•8 Complete arrest of speech occurred when the brain was stimulated at the points shown. This stimulation may have interfered with speech mechanisms or with the motor control of the vocal apparatus. (From Penfield and Roberts, 1959)

Anatomical and Physiological Basis of Hemispheric Differences The search for the biological basis of hemispheric differences has included both anatomical and neurophysiological studies. Emerging research suggests that the two hemispheres have a slightly different form. In a study of adult temporal lobes, Geschwind and Levitsky (1968) at the Harvard Medical School found that in 65 percent of the brains examined, a region of the cerebral cortex known as the *planum temporale* was larger in the left hemisphere than in the right hemisphere. In 11 percent the right side was larger. The region examined (temporal lobes) includes part of Wernicke's area. Presumably, the difference in the size of the area reflects the specialization (dominance) of one cerebral hemisphere for language. This difference in cortical size is even more evident at birth. It appeared in 86 percent of the infant brains examined. This evidence suggests an intrinsic basis for *cerebral dominance* in language, since the asymmetry appears before any environmental reinforcement of dominance can occur.

Another approach to the assessment of functional differences in the brain involves recording the gross potentials produced by the brain in response to sounds. Figure 25•9 shows some of the gross potentials recorded in an experiment of this type. The potentials produced by language-related sounds are greater in amplitude in the left hemisphere than in the right hemisphere. Furthermore, electrical activ-

Fig. 25•9 (*a*) Distinctive electrical potentials are seen over Broca's area in the left hemisphere when subjects produce words (in this case a word with the letter *p* in it). These large potentials are not seen in the right side of the brain. (*b*) In the control part of the experiment, the subject was asked to spit, because spitting requires many of the same muscle movements as speech does. In this case, the brain potentials are similar on both sides of the brain. Thus the difference in brain activity seen in (*a*) is probably related to the brain mechanisms involved in speech rather than to some details of the muscle movements involved in speech. (From McAdam and Whitaker, 1971)

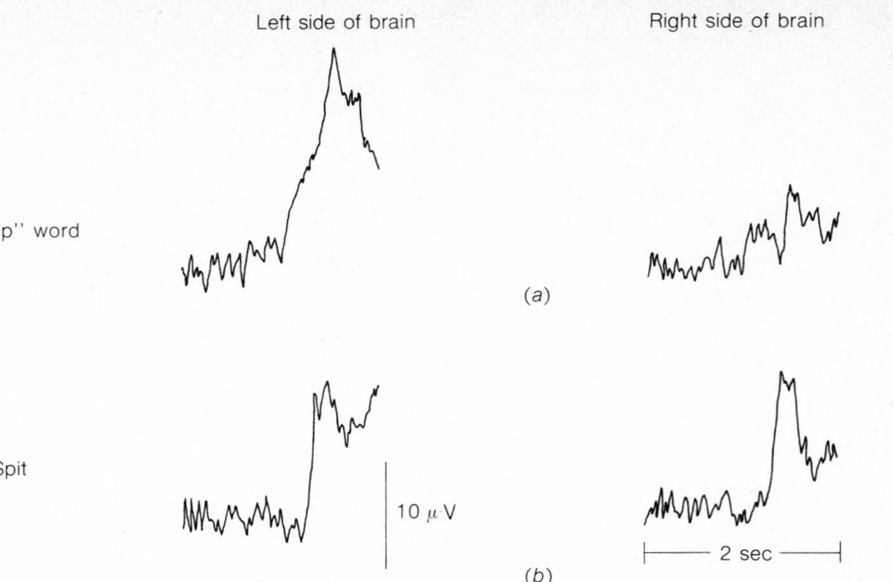

ity over Broca's area in the left hemisphere shows a significant change prior to speech production.

In sum, most of these studies suggest that the neural mechanisms for language reside in the left hemisphere of the brain and that separate brain areas are devoted to such things as understanding and producing speech.

Behavioral Biology of Sleep and Waking

25•3 One-third of human existence is spent asleep. Until recently, our knowledge of this vast slice of life was limited to the intuitions and sentiments of poets, lovers, and psychiatrists. In the last decade, however, research in this area by physiologists, neuroanatomists, and psychologists has focused on the behaviors of sleep and the mechanisms that control its onset, duration, and cycles. It has been discovered that sleep is an elaborate sequence of states. This view of sleep has developed as a result of intensive studies of the frequency and amplitude of electrical waves in the brains of sleeping humans and other sleeping animals.

The examination of EEG recordings from humans during a typical night of sleep reveals five sleep stages (illustrated in Figure 25•10).

Stage 1 *Alpha activity*, which is a wave form that is apparent during relaxed periods, disappears as the person gets drowsy.

Stage 2 Wave forms known as *spindles* become evident.

Stage 3 Slow waves (two or three per second) are mixed in with the spindles.

Stage 4 Spindles disappear; there is a continuous train of high-amplitude slow waves.

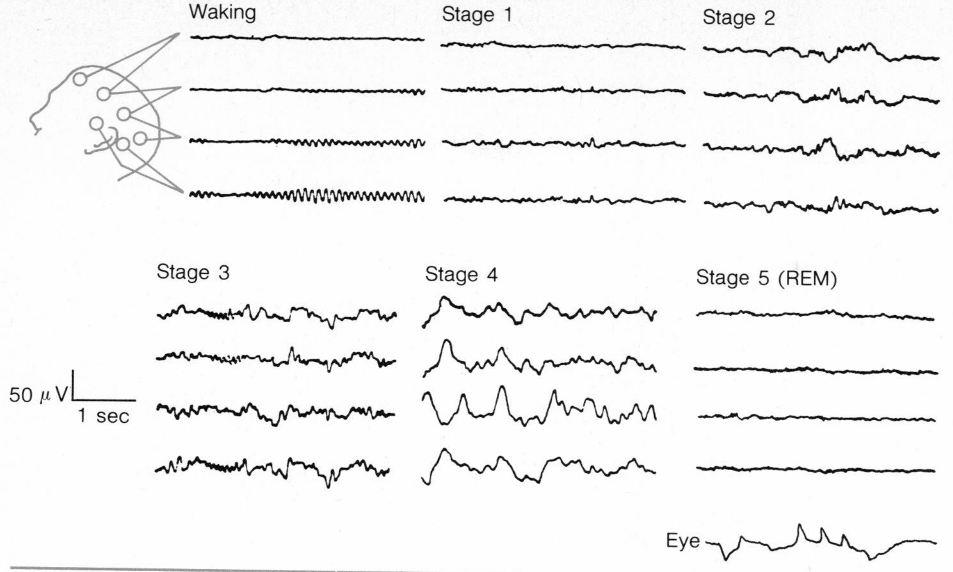

Fig. 25•10 Brain waves during waking and sleep. Waking: low-voltage, high-frequency waves accompanied by alpha waves in the posterior (back) end of the brain. Stage 1 (drowsing): alpha waves disappear. Stage 2: wave forms known as spindles appear. Stage 3: slow waves (two to three per second) appear and are mixed with spindles. Stage 4 (deep sleep): spindles disappear and slow waves increase. Stage 5, (REM, or paradoxical, sleep): a return of low-voltage, high-frequency waves accompanied by jerky, rapid eye movements (bottom record shows eye movements) and a loss of tension in postural muscles. (Adapted from Stevens, 1973)

Stage 5 Low-voltage, high-frequency waves appear; there is a loss of muscular tension accompanied by jerky movement of the eyes. This stage of sleep is known as *REM* (*rapid eye movement*) sleep because of its characteristic eye movements.

The REM stage of sleep is also known as *paradoxical sleep*, because the frequency and amplitude of the brain waves are similar to those made when the person is awake. Dreams with vivid perceptual imagery most commonly occur during this stage of sleep—it is as if the brain is somehow awake but disconnected from activity.

These sleep states alternate during a night's sleep. As Figure 25•11 shows, stages 3 and 4 are prominent during the early hours of sleep. Stage 5 (REM or paradoxical sleep) is especially evident during the latter half of a night's sleep. Each sleep cycle lasts from 90 to 110 minutes and contains episodes of all five sleep stages. REM sleep occupies about 20 to 25 percent of human sleep time.

Comparisons among various mammals show characteristic differences in sleep behavior. Generally, smaller animals with high metabolic rates spend a large percentage of their daily life asleep (80 to 90 percent for the bat) and have short sleep cycles (ten minutes for the laboratory rat). The only animal that fails to show REM sleep is the spiny anteater, an ancient, egg-laying mammal.

The characteristics of sleep-waking cycles change during the course of life. Nearly all mammalian infants show a high percentage of total daily sleep and REM sleep. REM sleep occupies 50 percent of the total sleep time of full-term infants during the first two weeks of life (Figure 25•12). A daily rhythm of sleeping and waking is not established until an infant is several weeks old, and unlike adults, human infants can go directly from a waking state to REM sleep. Waking-state

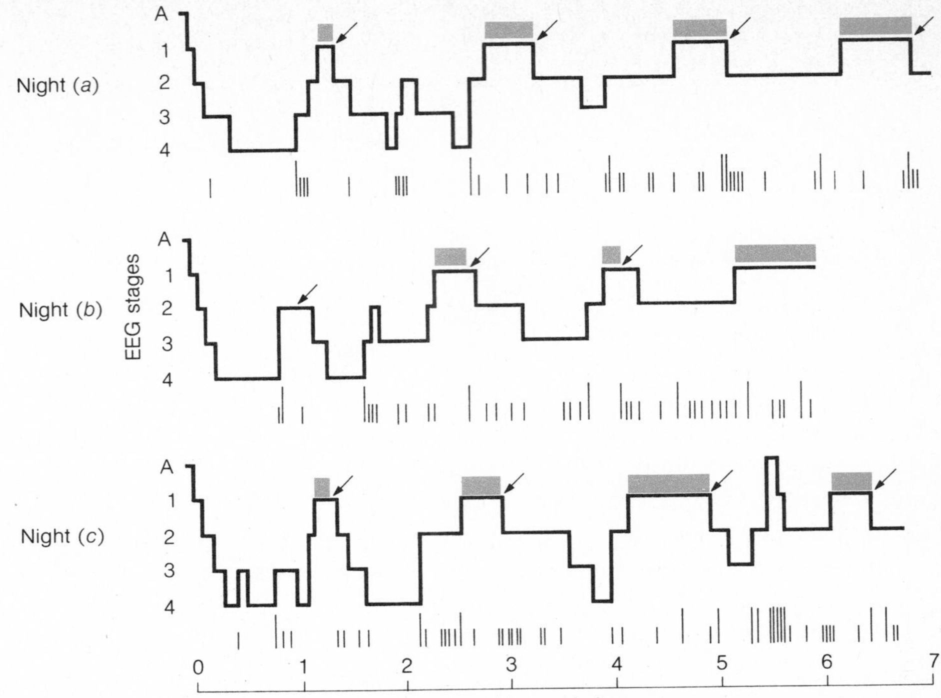

Fig. 25·11 The cyclic variations in the stages of sleep during three nights. Numbers on the left indicate the stages of sleep; the letter *A* indicates the awake state. Colored bars indicate periods of REM sleep. The arrows indicate the end of a sleep cycle as measured from the end of one REM period to the end of the next. The vertical lines indicate the occurrence and intensity of body movement. (Adapted from Dement and Kleitman, 1957)

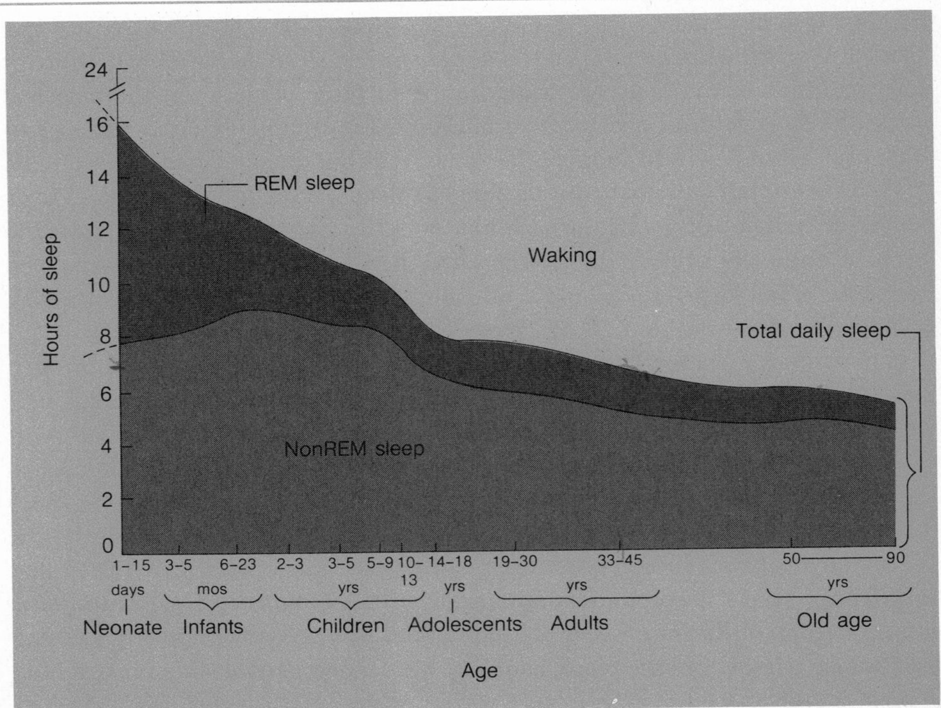

Fig. 25·12 Changes with age in total amount of daily sleep and the proportion of sleep time spent in REM sleep. Note the rapid decrease in REM sleep in the early years. (From Roffwarg, Mouzio, and Dement, 1966)

alpha waves appear in human infants when they are four months old, after which alpha-wave frequency continues to increase until about age twenty-one. Stage 4 sleep declines as the human adult ages; at age sixty it occupies 55 percent less sleep time than at age twenty.

Sleep Deprivation For one reason or another many of us sometimes go to bed later or get up earlier than we might like. Not surprisingly such experiences leave us tired. But do the processes that regulate sleep keep track of sleep losses and compensate for them on subsequent nights of uninterrupted sleep? The answer is yes, to some extent.

The characteristics of sleep compensation mechanisms can be seen in the case of a young man who deprived himself of sleep for 264 hours (eleven days). This self-designated subject came to the attention of investigators as a result of media coverage of the man's intention to set a new record for the *Guinness Book of Records.* EEG studies were done on "recovery nights" following the period of sleep deprivation to assess whatever compensatory processes might occur. Recovery of stage 4 sleep loss was apparent particularly on the first recovery night and occurred at the expense of stage 2 sleep. REM sleep recovery was apparent on the second recovery night; overall, REM sleep came closer to having its debt paid off than did the slow-wave sleep stages. This phenomenon of increased REM sleep after a period of sleep deprivation is known as REM rebound.

Early studies of sleep deprivation showed dramatically that prolonged sleep loss is hazardous to the psyche. Some researchers noted psychotic behavior in their subjects after several days of sleep deprivation; there were even schizophrenic episodes in some subjects after prolonged sleeplessness. More recent studies, however, show that the results of sleep deprivation depend on personality factors. Psychotic states resulting from sleep deprivation are rare, although other behaviors, such as inability to sustain attention, irritability, and episodes of disorientation, are common.

Sleep Disorders in Humans Fitful sleep is occasional for some people and a regular occurrence for others. For people who habitually lose sleep because of tension and worry, sleep becomes a focus of intense concern. During the last decade, research on the basic mechanisms of sleep has contributed to our understanding of the biology of sleep.

Insomnia, or the inability to fall asleep, is the most common form of disordered sleep. Studies in sleep laboratories of people who routinely experience insomnia show that although chronic insomniacs report an inability to sleep, their EEGs during the course of a night indicate that they experience sleep states. Furthermore, these subjects are moderately unresponsive to stimuli during a recorded sleep state. Quantitative assessments of these EEGs show less REM and more stage 2 sleep than "good" sleepers exhibit. No differences between insomniacs and good sleepers are evident in regard to sleep stages 3 and 4.

Both sleeping pills and drugs such as alcohol and antihistamines can exert marked effects on sleep by suppressing REM sleep. Initial doses of some drugs suppress REM sleep, but as use of the drug continues, REM sleep returns.

Chronic use of a bedtime sleeping pill can lead to a marked reduction in REM sleep and to a decrease in stages 3 and 4 of slow-wave sleep. A. Kales and J. Kales's studies (1974) of sleeping-pill insomnia show that abrupt withdrawal of sleeping pills leads to a sudden and striking increase in the amount of REM sleep. During this period, patients report disturbed sleep with intense dreams. To attenuate the effects of this REM rebound, the Kaleses recommend slow withdrawal from habitual use of sleeping pills.

William Dement and his collaborators (see Mitler et al., 1975) have reported a sleep-loss syndrome, called *sleep apnea*, that apparently involves the basic neural mechanisms controlling respiration. Persons afflicted with this sleep disorder awaken frequently during the night, because the neural mechanisms that control breathing break down during sleep, respiration stops, and the resultant loss of oxygen triggers arousal.

Another sleep disorder, *narcolepsy*, is a disease characterized by sudden attacks of sleep at any time during the day. EEGs show that persons afflicted with this disorder go from a state of wakefulness immediately into REM sleep.

Brain Mechanisms of Sleep and Arousal What brain mechanisms govern the onset, maintenance, and termination of sleep? As yet, no single hypothesis successfully deals with this question, but some interesting theories have been proposed.

For many years, it was thought that sleep is caused by the accumulation in the brain and body of a sleep-producing substance called a *hypnogen*. The existence of such a substance was proposed by Pieron in 1913 on the basis of his experiments in which cerebrospinal fluid from fatigued dogs was injected into rested animals who subsequently went to sleep. In some experiments after Pieron's, animals were injected with filtered blood drawn from animals in which sleep had been induced by thalamic stimulation. In other experiments, the vascular systems of two animals were surgically linked together. In both cases, the exchange of blood containing a hypnogen was believed to be responsible for the observed similarity in the animal's sleep patterns. Some critics of this conclusion pointed out that human Siamese twins may not sleep at the same time. This criticism may not be valid because many Siamese twins do not share vascular systems.

An important theory was proposed by the Belgian neurophysiologist F. Bremer (1935), who studied EEGs of cortical electrical activity in cats after various neural pathways had been surgically interrupted. In one experimental group in which the brain stem had been isolated from the spinal cord, the EEGs showed arousal (waking) and sleep states. However, if the cut was made at the upper end of the brain stem, the EEGs showed only persistent sleep states that could not be interrupted even by strong stimuli. Bremer suggested that a cut made at the upper end of the brain stem isolated the brain from most sensory information, and the brain was therefore never aroused from sleep. A cut made at the lower end of the brain stem allowed sensory information to enter the brain and thus produce arousal.

In the late 1940s, Bremer's work was reinterpreted by Magoun, Lindsley, and Moruzzi (see Magoun, 1958) on the basis of their experiments involving the extensive central core of the brain stem called the **reticular formation** (Figure 25•13). Three kinds of observations suggested that the reticular formation is involved in maintaining arousal, and therefore sleep results from a decline of activity in this region.

By stimulating this region electrically, these scientists produced rapid arousal (waking) in sleeping animals. Damage to this region, however, caused the animals to become comatose. The animals were not comatose if all sensory input to the brain stem was eliminated (by cutting sensory pathways) and the reticular formation was not damaged.

These results suggested that the sleep and arousal effects noted by Bremer were caused by interference with an arousal or activating system within the brain stem. This system includes parts of the reticular formation. In Bremer's experiments, cutting the brain stem where it joined the spinal cord left the reticular formation connected to the brain, so normal sleep and wakefulness were seen. When the brain stem is cut near the brain, the reticular formation is disconnected from the brain and the animal becomes comatose.

These conclusions initiated a continuing series of experiments on factors that control the arousal mechanisms of the reticular formation. Current studies implicate only certain portions of the reticular formation in the maintenance of arousal. In addition, other brain areas besides the reticular formation may be involved in various aspects of arousal.

The areas of the reticular formation that are involved in arousal are located in the more rostral (head end) regions of the brain stem. The activity of these aroused regions may be inhibited by areas in the caudal (tail end) of the brain stem. If the brain stem is transected between these two areas (Figure 25•14), the animal shows persistent wakefulness (for example, nine-day periods), as the rostral, arousing areas are no longer inhibited by more caudal areas.

Experiments by M. Jouvet (1972) implicated other brain regions in the control of arousal mechanisms. One of these regions is the *raphé nucleus*, which is a system of nerve cells located in the middle of the brain stem. These nerve cells release the synaptic transmitter serotonin that apparently initiates slow-wave sleep by inhibiting the release of another synaptic transmitter (norepinephrine) from nerve cells in another brain stem area called the *locus coeruleus*. The locus coeruleus nerve cells are responsible for some aspects of REM sleep and arousal.

Since serotonin inhibits the nerve cells in the locus coeruleus, changing the level of serotonin in the brain can influence sleep and wakefulness. For example, when a substance called PCPA is injected into cats, serotonin levels are reduced and the cats become insomniac. Raising serotonin levels by injecting the cats with chemicals from which serotonin is synthesized results in the return of slow-wave sleep.

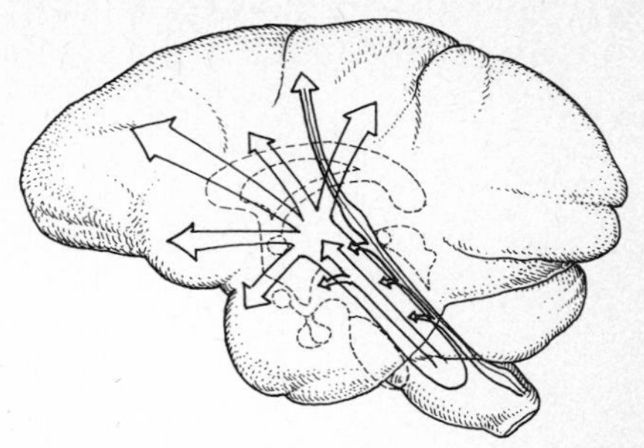

Fig. 25•13 An X-ray view of a monkey brain, showing the location of the reticular formation in the brain stem. Arrows from the top of this formation indicate the influence it has on the cerebral cortex and other parts of the brain. Arrows entering it indicate afferent (sensory) pathways. (From Magoun, 1954)

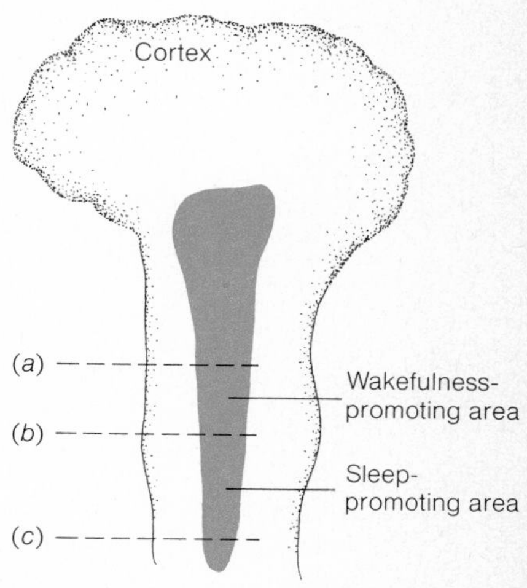

Fig. 25•14 Schematic view of the reticular formation. If the brain stem is cut at point *A*, permanent sleep results. When the brain stem is cut at *C*, animals show normal sleep and waking cycles. A cut at *B* produces persistent wakefulness since the inhibitory influence from the sleep-promoting area is no longer present.

Jouvet suggests that an interaction between the serotonin-containing raphé nucleus nerve cells and the locus coeruleus nerve cells may control sleep cycles. As slow-wave sleep progresses, the level of serotonin decreases, and the locus coeruleus initiates REM sleep. Activity of the locus coeruleus nerve cells may also stimulate the uptake of serotonin by the raphé nucleus nerve cells. The interaction between these two brain areas causes slow-wave and REM sleep to alternate until the level of serotonin released is low enough to allow a return of the waking state. When serotonin again reaches a critical level, the consequent inhibition of the arousal mechanisms causes sleep.

In addition to the raphé nucleus, some brain regions (including the thalamus) apparently effect the onset and maintenance of slow-wave sleep. In cats, when these regions are stimulated electrically, sleep behavior occurs. Apparently many brain regions are capable of inducing sleep and deactivating arousal mechanisms. However, the forms of interaction among these regions have yet to be defined.

What's Sleep For? Our common experience suggests that the biological roles of sleep can readily be described, but research evidence does not support a simple explanation. Sleep is commonly thought to have a restorative function whereby whatever resources have been expended or depleted as a result of activity or arousal are recovered. This theory is difficult to corroborate because (1) any recovery processes that take place at the level of nerve cell metabolism are difficult to measure or to identify, and (2) during REM sleep many body processes are quite active. For example, EEGs show apparent arousal of the brain, and heart rate and blood pressure increase. These activities seem incompatible with a recovery process. Perhaps recovery processes occur, but only during slow-wave sleep, and REM sleep has a biological function of its own.

Another theory suggests that the biological role of sleep is to conserve metabolic energy. Perhaps sleep prevents energy exhaustion by providing a period of inactivity or rest—that is, we sleep to avoid making demands on our energy capabilities that would be made and could not be met if we remained awake. For example, small animals with high metabolic rates sleep a great deal during a single day. If they were to remain in an arousal state for long periods, the demands of arousal in addition to the demands of their arousal metabolism might be too much for their bodily system to meet.

Behavioral Biology of Emotions

25·4 Love, hate, fear, and anger commonly denote internal states we call feelings or emotions. Emotions can be captured by painters, sculptors, dancers, musicians, and writers, but they frequently elude the scientist seeking to understand their biological states. Therefore, the emotions selected for biological study are usually those readily reflected in obvious behavioral expression—that is, states of aggression or defense elicited by aversive stimulation. States of affection or pleasure have been less commonly studied. The principal features of emotional expression that have been studied are changes in heart rate, blood pressure, perspiration, and stomach activity. These are also the measures of emotional reactivity commonly employed in lie detector tests.

Visceral organs such as the heart, stomach, intestines, and body responses such as sweating and changes in pupil size are controlled by the autonomic nervous system (see Figure 24•3). In some respects this system mediates these organs in much the same way as the spinal cord's motor nerve cells interact with the skeletal muscles. The **autonomic nervous system** has two divisions: the *sympathetic nervous system* and the *parasympathetic nervous system* (Figure 25•15).

The sympathetic system consists of clusters of nerve cells (ganglia) that lie in a chain formation outside the spinal cord and are connected to it. These ganglia generally have an activating effect—for example, they increase heart and respiration rate and activate sweat glands.

The parasympathetic system consists of ganglia of nerve cells in the brain stem and lower parts (sacral region) of the spinal cord; these cells connect to ganglia that are adjacent to the visceral organs. These ganglia in turn synapse on the same organs that are controlled by the sympathetic system and frequently have effects opposite to those of the sympathetic ganglia—for example, slowing the heart rate.

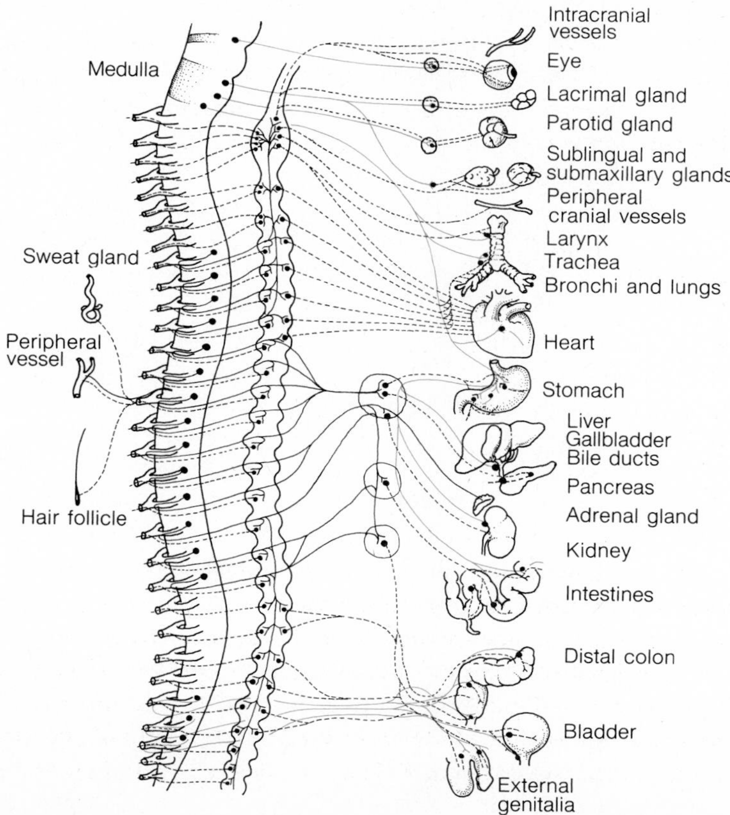

Fig. 25•15 The autonomic nervous system and the organs they control. In this schematic drawing, the parasympathetic system is drawn in color. Note that most organs receive inputs from both sympathetic and parasympathetic fibers. (From Netter, 1962)

Electrical Stimulation of "Pleasure" Areas in the Brain

In the early 1950s James Olds and Peter Milner (1953) showed that rats would learn to press a bar to receive electrical stimulation of certain brain regions (Figure 25B·1). The direct electrical stimulation of these brain areas in part resembles the impact of conventional rewards such as food (for the hungry rat) or water (for the thirsty rat).

Perhaps stimulation of these parts of the brain is pleasurable or rewarding for the animal. A rat will press a bar many thousands of times in a row to receive electrical stimulation of these brain areas. The hypothalamus and medial forebrain bundle are especially effective brain areas for reinforcing behaviors by direct electrical stimulation of the brain.

Fig. 25B·1 When the rat presses the bar, a small amount of electric current is delivered to certain areas of its brain via the wire that hangs from the ceiling.

Together, these two systems control the glands and visceral organs and maintain a balanced internal state (**homeostasis**).

Changes in the organs that are controlled by the autonomic nervous system can be measured readily. Their responses to stress and emotion-provoking stimuli have been the subjects of many studies. In one such study, John I. Lacey (1967) has shown that in humans the pattern of visceral response is a distinctive, individual attribute that can be identified very early in life. For example, under the same stress conditions, one individual may respond with changes in heart rate while another might respond with changes in gastric activity. Lacey called this apparently enduring characteristic *autonomic response stereotypy.* His data suggest that the breakdown of autonomically controlled viscera due to the stresses of life (as with stomach ulcers) may reflect a distinctive autonomic reactivity set up early in life. In other words, emotions are distinctively expressed by the viscera.

The automatic, reflexive properties of the autonomic nervous system do not preclude the possibility of learning to control the autonomic nervous system. **Biofeedback** is one of the techniques central to the study of learning control of the autonomic nervous system. In a biofeedback experiment, the state of a visceral function is measured, and this information is conveyed to the person on whom the measurement is being made. Suppose, for example, that the subject's blood pressure is extremely high. The blood pressure cannot be directly controlled because the subject has no way of knowing its level at a given moment. However, monitoring the subject's blood pressure, the experimenter can tell him or her what it is and when it has decreased to some level set by the experimenter. The subject is then encouraged to maintain this lowered level—perhaps by continuing to think relaxing thoughts. In short, the subject is provided feedback of information on biological states, so that he or she can understand the consequences of activities that influence those states. This procedure is a form of operant conditioning (described in Chapter 10). Many such biofeedback experiments have demonstrated that modifications in visceral behavior and in the forms of electrical activity in the central nervous system can be learned. Biofeedback techniques may be useful in therapy for some autonomic dysfunctions.

The Brain and Emotions The role of various brain structures in emotional responses has been studied by observing the effects on emotional responses either of direct electrical stimulation of the brain or of brain lesions. In these experiments, particular attention has been directed toward analysis of rage and fear responses since these are readily apparent and are rather stereotyped and species-specific.

Various aspects of the behaviors involved in rage or attack can be evoked by stimulating different areas of the brain, including portions of the hypothalamus and the brain stem. Many of these areas are anatomically connected, and the resulting circuit is called the circuit of Papez, after Jaime W. Papez (1937), who first described it. Stimulation of various points in this circuit causes various forms of attacking or defensive behaviors—a fight-or-flight reaction.

The many observations of elicited rage in nonhumans have been related to human violence in a provocative book by Mark and Ervin (1970). They argue that violence in some humans may arise from brain disease in structures associated with portions of the brain, and they present several human cases in which violent behavior appears to be related to epileptic seizures in the temporal lobes.

Summary

Complex behaviors such as learning, memory, language, sleep, and emotions can be explained in terms of the functions of various parts of the brain. Despite remarkable progress, we are far from a complete understanding of the biological substrates of complex behaviors.

Learning involves acquiring new information; memory involves the recording of that information by structural or functional changes at some level of the brain. A variety of clinical and experimental data suggest that information is initially stored in a short-term memory that can be easily disrupted. The process of memory consolidation transfers information from short-term memory to a virtually non-erasable long-term memory.

The biological changes that underlie memory may occur at a chemical level within the nerve cell or at the synapses between nerve cells, or they may be a function of the changes in activity of a large group of nerve cells. There is evidence that there may be a variety of memory mechanisms.

Animals, such as the aplysia and the crayfish, that have simple nervous systems are used by scientists to trace the circuits involved in learning and to localize the changes underlying memory. Habituation, a simple form of learning, has been extensively investigated in these animals.

While language is considered to be a human ability, the beginnings of language can be seen in the calls of higher primates (monkeys); in addition, chimpanzees have been taught to use sign language. Areas of the cerebral cortex are important in human language: Broca's area is involved in the production of speech and Wernicke's area in the understanding of speech.

Language is one of the many behaviors controlled by one cerebral hemisphere or the other. Experiments involving patients whose corpus callosums have been cut clearly demonstrate the different functions that are controlled by each cerebral hemisphere.

There are five stages of sleep. These can be detected by monitoring the frequency and amplitude of brain electrical activity during sleep. During REM sleep the brain appears to be awake and active, yet the sleeper is deeply asleep and perhaps dreaming. The reticular formation in the brain stem is especially implicated in the control of sleep and wakefulness. Animals with damage to this area become comatose. A feedback relationship between various nuclei in the reticular formation may govern the cycles of sleep and waking.

The study of emotions has concentrated on emotions, such as rage and fear, that produce obvious visceral and behavioral reactions. The viscera are controlled primarily by the autonomic nervous system. While the activities of the viscera are not normally under conscious control, the technique of biofeedback may allow for some conscious control. Biofeedback is a possible therapy for disorders such as high blood pressure.

Suggested Readings

Dimond, S. 1972. *The double brain*. Baltimore: Williams & Wilkins.

A thorough discussion of the functional differences between the hemispheres of the human brain.

Hartmann, E. L. 1973. *The functions of sleep*. New Haven: Yale University Press.

A discussion of some of the basic biological and psychological properties of sleep states and theoretical models of the functional roles of sleep.

Lenneberg, E. H. 1967. *Biological foundations of language*. New York: Wiley.

A broad look at the evolutionary and neurological data relating to language in humans.

Mark, R. 1974. *Memory and nerve cell connections: Criticisms and contributions from developmental neurophysiology*. New York: Oxford University Press.

A look at biological memory from the perspective of nervous system development.

Rosenzweig, M. R., and Bennett, E. L., eds. 1976. *Neural mechanisms of learning and memory.* Cambridge, Mass.: MIT Press.

A broad contemporary look at experimental tactics and accomplishments in the study of the neurobiology of memory.

Thompson, R. F. 1975. *Introduction to physiological psychology.* New York: Harper and Row.

A comprehensive textbook covering the entire field of biological psychology.

Glossary

The terms in this list are used in Chapters 24 and 25. They are important to one's understanding of these chapters, but most of them are not used in other chapters of this book. As in other chapters, boldface terms in the text are defined in the glossary-index at the back of the book.

acetylcholine An organic chemical found in nerve cells. When released, it serves as a synaptic transmitter to propagate nerve impulses and initiate muscle contractions.

acetylcholinesterase An enzyme that terminates the action of the synaptic transmitter acetylcholine.

adrenergic synapses Synapses where the transmitter is norepinephrine. (See Figure 24•19).

adrenocorticotrophic hormone (ACTH) A hormone secreted by the anterior pituitary, often in response to stressful situations. It controls the endocrine activity of the adrenal cortex.

alpha activity Rhythmic electrical activity, with a frequency of 8 to 12 Hz, recorded from the brain during relaxed periods. (See Table 24A•1.)

amphetamine Central nervous system stimulant such as benzedrine and dexedrine, which are addictive. Amphetamines may achieve their effect by potentiating the release of the neurotransmitter norepinephrine. (See Table 24•2.)

anterior pituitary (adenohypophysis) The anterior lobe of the pituitary gland. It secretes several hormones (such as ACTH), many of which stimulate the output of other endocrine glands (such as the adrenal cortex).

Apgar scale A scale developed by Dr. Virginia Apgar (1953) for evaluating an infant at birth on the following dimensions: heart rate, respiration, muscle tone, reflex irritability, and color. On a scale from 0 to 10, an infant scoring below 5 is in need of medical attention.

asphyxia Lack of adequate oxygen, which may cause brain damage and, if untreated, death by suffocation.

autonomic response stereotypy The individual, enduring visceral response to stress that is manifested very early in life. Some people typically respond to stress with a speeded-up heartbeat, others with stomach cramps, and so on.

axon A fiber arising from the nerve cell body, and connecting that nerve cell with other nerve cells, muscles, or glands. Axons carry information away from the cell body by transmitting nerve impulses (spikes).

axon hillock The initial portion of the axon, which arises out of the nerve cell body. Nerve impulses (spikes) are normally initiated at the axon hillock, because this area of the axon has the lowest threshold for producing a nerve impulse.

ballism A severe chorea, characterized by violent, rapid, uncontrolled movements of the limbs. Hemiballism is ballism affecting only one side of the body. Ballism is often seen after damage to the basal ganglia. (See Figure 24•28).

biogenic amines Nitrogen-containing organic compounds (including catecholamine, dopamine, serotonin and norepinephrine), which are transmitters or may affect synaptic transmitters.

Broca's aphasia Impairment of speech production resulting from damage to a portion of the frontal cortex (third frontal gyrus) of the brain. Named after Paul Broca (1861).

catecholamines A class of biogenic amines (including dopamine and norepinephrine) that act as transmitters. Inhibition of these substances may produce sedation or depression. (See Table 24•2.)

cell body The body of the nerve cell, containing the nucleus (which regulates some activities of the nerve cell) and from which arise the axon and dendrites.

cerebral dominance A term used to explain phenomena such as handedness, reflecting an asymmetry of function between the two cerebral hemispheres. One hemisphere may "dominate" some functions such as speech, while the other may "dominate" motor coordination.

cerebrospinal fluid A fluid that circulates around and through the brain and spinal cord, providing nutrients, absorbing vibrations, and removing waste material.

chlorpromazine (thorazine) A drug that has a tranquilizing effect.

cholinergic synapses Synapses in the brain and nerve-muscle junctions at which acetylcholine is the synaptic transmitter.

corpus callosum The large bundle of nerve fibers connecting the two cerebral hemispheres. (See Figure 24•2.)

delta waves Slow, brain electrical activity consisting of high amplitude waves. This type of activity usually occurs during stage 4 sleep. (See Figure 24A•1.)

dendrite The extension of the cell body of a nerve cell that tapers from the nucleus and conveys impulses to the cell body. (See Figure 24•5.)

depolarization The reduction of an electrical potential toward zero, as during transmission of a nerve impulse. (See Figure 24•14.)

dopamine A biogenic amine that is a transmitter in the central nervous system.

ectoderm The layer of tissue in the embryo from which the nervous system develops. (See Figure 24•19.)

embryo The earliest stage of human development, from conception through about six to twelve weeks thereafter.

epilepsy Nervous system malfunction primarily characterized by the uncontrolled activity of large groups of neural elements. This produces seizures, which may be either severe (grand mal) or mild (petit mal).

EPSP (excitatory postsynaptic potentials) A depolarizing shift in a neuron's membrane potential due to transmitters impinging on its receptor sites. (See Figure 24•17.)

fetus The developing embryo from about six weeks through birth. (See Figure 24•10.)

graded events (slow potentials) The shifts in the electrical potential of a nerve cell due to release of transmitters from other nerve cells. These shifts are summed (see spatial and temporal summation), and may trigger an action potential (spike) in the nerve cells.

hippocampus The portion of the brain located in the medial portion of the temporal lobe. Apparently functions in retention of recent memory and in motor learning. (See Figure 25•2.)

Huntington's chorea A hereditary disorder involving the basal ganglia, which is characterized by chorea (rapid, jerky movements), speech difficulties, and progressive deterioration of mental processes such as thinking and reasoning. This disorder appears only in adults. Named after George Huntington (1850–1916), an American physician who first described the disorder.

hyperpolarization An increase in electrical potential away from zero. (See Figure 24•14.)

hypnogen A sleep-producing substance that was presumed to accumulate in the brain and body.

IPSP (inhibitory postsynaptic potentials) Generally, a hyperpolarizing shift in a neuron's membrane potential due to transmitters impinging on its receptor sites. (See Figure 24•17.)

Korsakoff's syndrome Brain damage due to dietary deficiency such as occurs in severe alcoholism. An interesting symptom is the loss of memory for recent events. Named after S. S. Korsakoff (1889).

laminar arrangement Arranged in layers. This is a characteristic arrangement for nerve cells in the central nervous system. Thus cerebral cortex has a laminar arrangement, as it consists of six layers of nerve cells.

locus coeruleus Catecholaminergic (catecholamine-producing) cells located in the floor of the fourth ventricle; probably involved in the regulation of REM sleep.

mammillary bodies Two rounded projections located in the floor of the posterior hypothalamus. They are part of the limbic system and may play a part in emotion. (See Figure 25•2.)

medial dorsal thalamic nuclei One of several nuclei located in the thalamus; projects to frontal lobes.

membrane A thin covering that serves to separate one body part from another. May selectively allow certain fluids or chemicals to pass from one area to another.

memory molecules An abstract concept representing the notion that memory may reside in the peculiar chemical composition of some substance such as DNA or RNA.

meninges Protective membranes that cover the brain.

metabolic disorders Abnormalities (such as diabetes or phenylketonuria) that are due to defects in metabolism. If these abnormalities are congenital, body and/or brain development may be affected.

metabolism The broad term for the physiological processes responsible for building (anabolism) and destroying (catabolism) chemical compounds in the body.

motor cortex The portion of the cerebral cortex just anterior to the central fissure; responsible for some aspects of body movements. (See Figure 24•26.)

narcolepsy A disease in which the patient may rapidly fall asleep at any time —day or night. EEG recording shows a transition directly to REM sleep from wakefulness.

neuroblasts Precursors of nerve and glial cells formed by the ectoderm in the embryo.

neurotoxins Chemicals such as tetrodotoxin that block the functions of nerve cells.

nerve impulse (spike) A pulse-like electrical event that lasts from 0.5 to 2.0 milliseconds and travels along an axon. (Contrast *graded events.*) (See Figure 24•14.)

norepinephrine (noradrenalin) A catecholamine similar to epinephrine (adrenalin). Used as a transmitter by the peripheral sympathetic nervous system and perhaps in the central nervous system. Released as a hormone by the adrenal medulla in response to "fight or flight" situations. (See Figure 24•19.)

paradoxical sleep (stage 5 sleep) A sleep state characterized by an activated EEG pattern, rapid eye movements (REM), and loss of muscle tone. Called paradoxical because the brain appears to be awake while animal is deep in sleep.

parasympathetic nervous system One subdivision of the autonomic nervous system; generally encourages conservation and restoration of bodily resources (e.g., activates digestion). (Contrast *sympathetic nervous system.* See Figure 25•15.)

Parkinson's disease A disease involving insufficient dopamine in the basal ganglia; it is characterized by rigidity of movement and by tremors that are worse when the patient is not making voluntary movements. Dopamine replacement therapy may provide relief.

phenothiazines Tranquilizers such as chlorpromazine (thorazine), which reduce aggressive outbursts and agitation in psychotic patients.

phenylketonuria A genetically determined metabolic disorder in which the enzyme needed to metabolize the amino acid phenylalanine is absent. The resultant buildup of phenylpyruvic acid leads to mental retardation and early death. A diet free of phenylalanine can prevent this.

planum temporale An area of the temporal lobes of the cerebral cortex. It includes part of Wernicke'a area (understanding of speech), and is usually larger in the left hemisphere than in the right.

posterior pituitary (neurohypophysis) The posterior lobe of the pituitary gland. It produces two hormones. One regulates water exchange and the other causes contractions of the uterus and lactation.

postjunctional block A blocking of synaptic transmission by interference with postsynaptic receptor sites.

postsynaptic area The part of a dendrite or cell body that forms a synapse with the axon of another nerve cell. Usually contains receptors sensitive to transmitters. (See Figure 24•6.)

presynaptic terminal The small swelling on part of an axon that forms a synapse with another nerve cell (the postsynaptic cell). One axon may form many thousands of terminals. (See Figure 24•6.)

pyramidal tract A group of nerve fibers from the cerebral cortex that extend through the medulla down to the spinal cord. These fibers presumably mediate voluntary control over skeletal muscles, although other theories have been proposed.

raphé nucleus A system of neurons located in the midline of the brain stem. The nerve cells contain serotonin and apparently initiate slow-wave sleep.

refractory period The period after a nerve impulse during which the axon is inexcitable. This characteristic of nerve cells limits the number of impulses produced in a given time period.

REM (rapid eye movements) The characteristic rapid eye movements occurring during stage 5 (paradoxical) sleep. Often used synonymously with stage 5 sleep.

resting membrane potential The potential across a resting (i.e., no synaptic stimulation is impinging) nerve cell's membrane of -60 to -90 millivolts. It occurs because of the difference in ion concentrations on either side of the membrane. (See Figure 24•13.)

serotonin (5-hydroxytryptamine) A biogenic amine derived from tryptophan (an amino acid) that acts as a transmitter in the central nervous system.

sleep apnea A sleep disorder in which cessation of respiration occurs due to faulty neural mechanisms controlling breathing. The lack of oxygen triggers arousal and resumption of breathing.

spatial summation The summation of neural excitation from the many spatially separate synapses on a nerve cell. (See Figure 24•17.)

spindles A characteristic pattern of brain electrical activity produced during the second stage of sleep. They are called spindles because the brain waves gradually increase in amplitude and then gradually decline. (See Figure 25•10.)

split-brain studies Studies of animals whose corpus callosums have been severed, thus disconnecting the two cerebral hemispheres.

stretch reflex circuit The neural feedback circuit between the sensory muscle spindles of a particular muscle, the spinal cord, and the axons of the motor nerves of that same muscle. The circuit operates to cause a stretched muscle to shorten, and inhibits antagonistic nerve impulses that would interfere with the shortening. (See Figure 24•23.)

subthalamic nucleus A part of the extrapyramidal system lying below the thalamus. Damage to this system may produce sudden violent tossing of the limbs (ballism).

sympathetic nervous system The division of the autonomic nervous system generally involved in visceral activation. (Contrast *parasympathetic nervous system.*) (See Figure 25•15).)

synapse A junction between two nerve cells, in which a presynaptic terminal of one nerve cell is in close enough contact with the postsynaptic membrane of another so that chemical and/or electrical transmission of information can occur. (See Figure 24•16.)

synaptic transmitter Any one of a number of chemicals (such as acetylcholine) that are released from one nerve cell to transmit information to a second nerve cell. They attach to receptor sites on the second nerve cell (postsynaptic cell) and alter its membrane potential.

synaptic vesicles Small packages containing a synaptic transmitter; found in presynaptic terminals. (See Figure 24•16.)

temporal lobe The portion of the cerebral cortex lying below the lateral fissure. Areas of it are involved in memory function and understanding language. (See Figure 25•7.)

temporal summation The summation of neural excitation over time.

thyrotrophic hormone A hormone secreted by the anterior pituitary. It controls the endocrine activity of the thyroid.

tryptophan An amino acid that is the precursor of serotonin.

ventricles Fluid-filled chambers within the brain that provide channels for the continuous flow of cerebrospinal fluid (a nutrient-providing fluid). (See Figure 24•2.)

Wernicke's aphasia Impairment of language comprehension due to damage to Wernicke's area (a region of the temporal lobes) in the brain.

Appendix A: Statistics

Statistics play a necessary role in evaluating and reporting the results of psychological research. A researcher uses psychological measurement to record observations in the form of numerical data. Statistics are used to organize the observations, to summarize or indicate the main characteristics, and frequently, to make inferences or generalizations about a larger set of observations (a **population**) from a subset of these observations (a **sample**).

Statistics are necessary because observations collected under identical conditions vary not only from individual to individual, but also within an individual from time to time. If everybody in an experiment got exactly the same score, there would be no need for statistical analysis. But because scores differ, it is necessary to determine representative or summary values for a set of scores.

Statistics are appropriate for the purpose because observations or data in psychological research are usually in a quantitative form. A measure of performance might be a score for an individual, such as the number of correct answers or the number of errors made on a test. It might be a rating—a numerical value assigned to an individual to show his or her ranking relative to a comparative group. It might be a frequency count for an entire group of individuals, such as a count of the number of people who made no errors, those who made one error, and those who made more than one error.

This appendix introduces some basic statistical concepts, then uses some of the formulas and calculations of statistics in an example problem. We have already met most of these concepts in Chapter 2 and elsewhere in the book, but here we will see how they can actually be calculated.

Basic Statistical Analysis

When many individuals have been measured, there is usually duplication of scores. Often the first step in examining quantitative observations is to organize the data into a form known as a **frequency distribution.** A frequency distribution is constructed by listing the scores from the highest to the lowest and then tabulating the frequency with which each of these values occurs. When the scores are collected under different conditions or from different groups of subjects, frequencies are usually tabulated separately for each group in order to make comparisons between the different distributions. The reorganized data can be presented either in a frequency distribution table or in a frequency polygon, the graphic equivalent of the table. The polygon in Figure 1 graphically presents the data supplied in Table 1. The sides of the polygon, the so-called curves, are really a series of straight lines connecting the values plotted.

Although frequency distributions allow gross comparisons between two or more sets of data, they are not the most efficient way of communicating experimental results. The second step, then, is to calculate additional summary measures—single values that characterize important aspects of the data. Usually there are two characteristics of interest to a researcher. First, how well did the group as a whole perform? Second, how consistent or similar was the performance of each group?

The first of these characteristics is assessed by a measure of central tendency, a single value that represents overall group performance. There are actually three measures of central tendency. The **mode** is the most frequently occurring score or value. The **median** is the middle value of a distribution, that is, the value above and below which an equal number of scores appears. The **mean,** better known as the arithmetic average, is obtained by summing all the scores and dividing the sum by the number of scores. The mean, median, and mode are identified in Figure 1.

Table 1 Frequency Distribution for Fifteen Scores

SCORE	*f*
8	2
7	1
6	1
5	2
4	1
3	1
2	7
Total	15

Which measure is the best? In most cases, the mean is the best measure of central tendency. Its value, unlike the others, is determined by the specific value of each score in the distribution. Changing the value of any one score would automatically change the value of the mean, but not necessarily the values of the median or mode. The median is particularly insensitive to extreme scores in a distribution. For example, raising one score in Figure 1 from 8 to 23 would not affect the value of the median, but it would change the mean from 4 to 5. This characteristic of the median makes it very useful for describing distributions in which a few scores differ greatly from the rest of the scores. Using the median, you simply ignore the extreme cases. The mode is the least sensitive of the measures of central tendency, since its value is totally unaffected by the values of any score other than that of the score that appears most frequently. However, the mode is frequently used to summarize nonnumerical data where the median and mean are impossible to determine. In the normal distribution, the mean, median, and mode all fall together in the center of the bell-shaped curve. An unbalanced distribution, such as the one in Figure 1, is called a skewed distribution.

The second main characteristic of data to be summarized is the amount of variability in the scores. Measures of variability indicate how similar or homogeneous the scores in a distribution are to one another. Again there are three measures. The *range* is obtained by subtracting the lowest score from the highest score. In Figure 1, for example, the range is 6. The *average deviation* from the mean is obtained by first subtracting the mean from each score—ignoring the sign (+ or −) of the difference—and then taking the average of these differences. (The absolute values must be used because the algebraic sum of deviations from the mean is always zero.) The third and most frequently encountered measure of variability is the **standard deviation.** It is also based on the difference between the individual scores and the mean, but the negative values are eliminated by squaring each of the differences. The standard deviation, then, is the square root of the average (mean) of these squared deviations. In Table 2 the standard deviation is computed for the set of scores used in Figure 1.

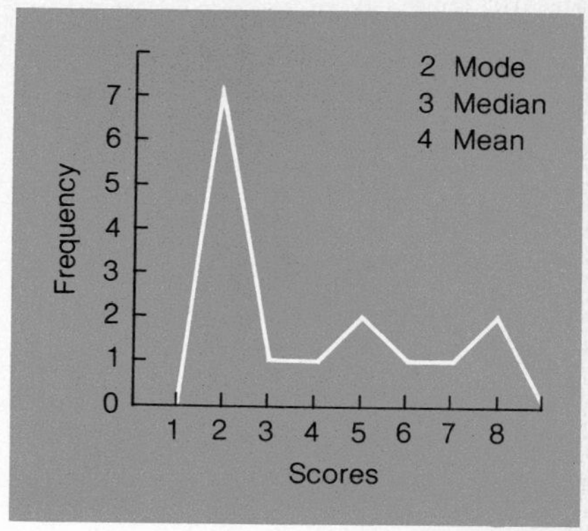

Fig. 1 A frequency polygon showing fifteen scores.

Although all three measures can show differences in the scatter of scores, they vary in their usefulness. The range, being dependent upon only two scores—the highest and lowest—which may or may not be representative of the rest of the data, provides at best a rough measure of variability. The average deviation is adequate as a summary measure for describing actual data, and in fact, has an advantage over the standard deviation in being both easier to calculate and easier to interpret. In spite of these advantages, the standard deviation is the most frequently used measure of variability because it alone has the mathematical properties that allow it to be combined with other summary measures. Because of these properties, the standard deviation can be used to compare scores in two or more different distributions, to quantify the relationship between different sets of data, and to make estimates of variability both of sets of scores larger than the sample and of the values of summary statistics calculated on different samples. The standard deviation serves many functions other than simple description.

Table 2 Computation of Standard Deviation for Fifteen Scores

SCORE	DIFFERENCE BETWEEN SCORE AND MEAN	SQUARED DIFFERENCE
2	2 − 4 = 2*	$2^2 = 4$
2	2 − 4 = 2	$2^2 = 4$
2	2 − 4 = 2	$2^2 = 4$
2	2 − 4 = 2	$2^2 = 4$
2	2 − 4 = 2	$2^2 = 4$
2	2 − 4 = 2	$2^2 = 4$
2	2 − 4 = 2	$2^2 = 4$
3	3 − 4 = 1	$1^2 = 1$
4	4 − 4 = 0	$0^2 = 0$
5	5 − 4 = 1	$1^2 = 1$
5	5 − 4 = 1	$1^2 = 1$
6	6 − 4 = 2	$2^2 = 4$
7	7 − 4 = 3	$3^2 = 9$
8	8 − 4 = 4	$4^2 = 16$
8	8 − 4 = 4	$4^2 = 16$

Sum of squared differences = 76

Average squared difference $= \frac{76}{15} = 5.07$

Square root of average squared difference $= \sqrt{5.07}$

$= 2.25$ standard deviation

*Disregard the minus sign.

After calculating one or more measures of central tendency and variability, what is the next step in statistical analysis? When the data consists of two test scores for each subject, a logical question would be whether performance on one test is related in any consistent fashion to performance on the second test. Do subjects who do well in one test also tend to do well on the second test? A good way to determine whether this type of relationship exists is to plot the scores in what is called a scatterplot. In a scatterplot, the scores on one test are represented on the horizontal axis of a graph, and the scores on a second test on the vertical axis. Each point in the graph indicates the two scores of a single subject because it is the point of intersection of the scores of those two tests.

Some idealized scatterplots are shown in Figure 2. If the points fall in a straight line that is positively sloped (extending from the lower left corner to the upper right corner as in scatterplot *a*), the relationship between scores is known as a perfect positive relationship. Every increase of five points on one task is associated with a consistent increase of ten points on the second. Scatterplot *b* in Figure 2 shows a perfect negative relationship; the points again fit a straight line, but the straight line is negatively sloped (extending from the upper left corner to the lower right corner). Here an increase of five points on one task is associated with a con-

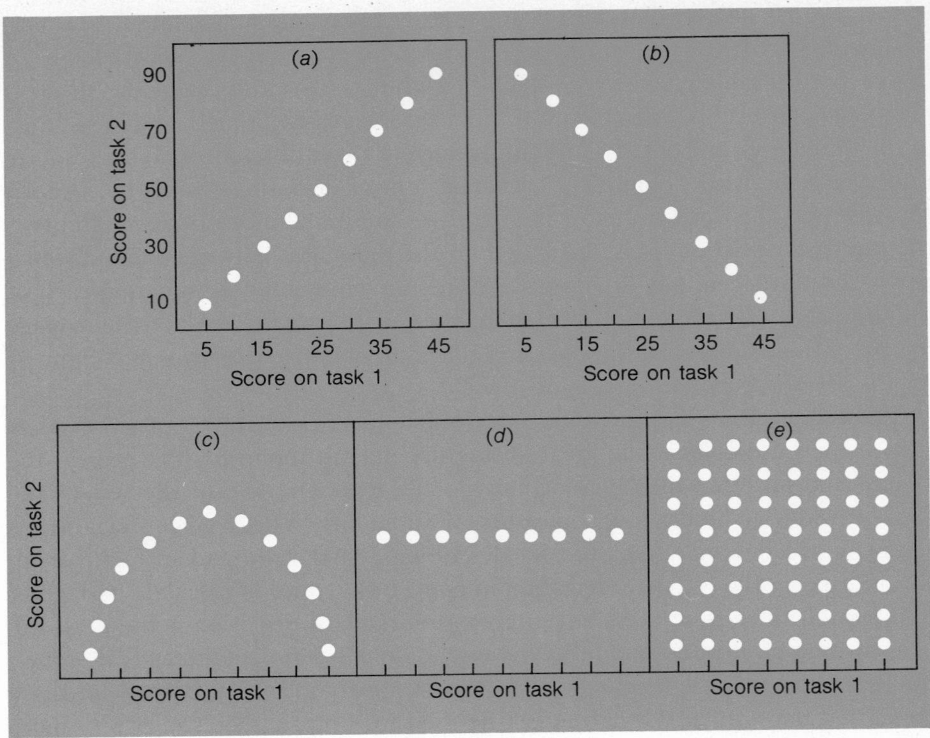

Fig. 2 Idealized scatterplots showing a perfect positive correlation (*a*), a perfect negative correlation (*b*), and zero correlations (*c, d, e*).

sistent decrease of ten points on the other task. In scatterplots *c, d,* and *e,* there is no consistent relationship between the scores on the two tasks. In *c,* as the scores on the first task increase, scores on the second task first increase but then decrease. In *d,* the scores on the second task stay the same regardless of changes in the first task scores, and in *e,* all possible scores on the second task are associated with all possible scores on the first. It would be rare to find relationships like these in any real set of data.

Luckily we need not rely on an eyeball analysis of a scatterplot to indicate the amount of relationship between two variables. A statistic is available for exactly quantifying the direction and amount of linear relationship between pairs of scores in a scatterplot. This statistic is known as the coefficient of correlation or simply the **correlation.** Values of the correlation can vary from 0, indicating no consistent relationship, upward to +1.00 or downward to −1.00, indicating a perfect positive or negative relationship respectively. In psychological research, correlations of plus or minus .5 or more are usually considered to be relatively strong; those between .3 and .5 are moderate, and those below .3 are low.

Although high scores on one variable are by definition associated with low scores on the other in a negative correlation, good performance on one task is not necessarily assoicated with poor performance on the other. A high score does not always reflect good performance, as can be seen if one measure were number of errors or time needed to complete a task. With measures like these, the lower the score, the better the performance.

A correlation should not be taken as an indication of a causal relationship between the two variables under consideration. We cannot say whether variable A affects variable B, or whether B affects A, or whether a third variable, C, affects both A and B. Correlation indicates only the presence of a relationship, not the cause of the relationship.

After the main characteristics of one or more sets of data have been summarized, we want to know whether the results permit generalization. Can we infer that the characteristics of data collected from a limited number, or sample, of subjects will be the same as those from the complete set, or population, of possible subjects? This is the basic question of statistical inference. It is an extremely important question since it is seldom if ever possible to observe an entire population, which might include thousands or even millions of subjects.

Inferences about the characteristics of a population from the data of a single sample can never be made with absolute certainty. A sample, by definition, contains fewer than all possible subjects. A second sample drawn from the same population could consist of entirely different subjects, as might a third, a fourth, and so on. With different subjects in successive samples, the means, standard deviations, and other statistics calculated on the sample data will probably vary. When the values of these statistics vary from sample to sample, it is impossible to say that the characteristics of any one sample reflect the characteristics of the entire population.

Under certain conditions, however, it is possible to use the data from a single sample to make estimates of the values of these statistics for the entire population, and to make these estimates with a known margin of error. The estimate consists of a range of values, known as the confidence interval, within which the true value of some population statistic (the mean, for example) can be expected to fall. The condition that must be met in order to make these inferences is the random selection of subjects. With random sampling, each member of the population at large has an equal opportunity of being included in the sample. Values of statistics calculated on samples drawn at random from a given population have a known probability of occurrence. This probability enables the researcher to make estimates of the values of population statistics from sample data with a known margin of error.

Estimating the value of a population statistic is not the only type of statistical inference. More often, in fact, investigators wish to know whether a particular set of scores on subjects in an experimental group reflect a major change caused by the experiment, or whether the differences between scores for the experimental and control groups occurred simply by chance. This type of inference is known as **hypothesis testing,** since the investigator tests a hypothesis about a population by using one or more samples drawn at random from that population.

Here is an example to illustrate the steps taken in testing a statistical hypothesis. Suppose we wish to test the hypothesis that students who study with a new introductory psychology text will do better on a comprehensive exam than students who study an older text. We might randomly select forty students from the population of introductory psychology students and then randomly assign half of these students to the new-text condition and half to the old-text condition. Students in the two groups are treated identically: they are to learn psychology solely from the assigned text, and at the end of a fixed period of time, take a common comprehensive exam. The grades on this common exam are the scores we will use to test our hypothesis.

Assume that we found a difference in means between the scores of the two groups. A question now is whether the difference in means is due to the two different texts—and, therefore, would occur if we were to test all possible introductory psychology students in this experiment—or whether it occurred in our sample just by the chance selection of the individuals in the two test groups.

The first step is to assume that this difference between means would not occur if the whole population were to be tested. In effect, we would be asserting that the **independent variable** (which text is used) has no effect on test performance. This assumption is known as the *null hypothesis*, and it is this hypothesis that is subjected to test. If our null hypothesis proves to be true, then the difference between means that we found with our sample must have occurred simply by chance.

The next question to ask is, what is the probability of finding a difference as large as we did with our samples simply by chance? If subjects were randomly selected, it is possible to determine the probability of getting a mean difference this large or larger by chance alone. Calculations will be based on the size of our samples and on the standard deviation within each sample.

Once we know the probability, it is time to make a decision. If there is a low probability of getting mean differences of that size simply by chance, we reject the possibility that only chance factors are operating. We would conclude that the sample difference must reflect a real difference in the amount of learning derived from each of the two textbooks. On the other hand, if we get a sample difference that has high probability of occurrence simply by chance, we are left with the possibility that the independent variable (the type of text) has no effect.

A difference between means with a probability of chance occurrence that is low enough to reject the null hypothesis is referred to by statisticians as a *significant difference*. The criterion used in deciding whether or not the probability is sufficiently low is called the level of significance. In psychological research it is common practice to use one of two criteria, the 5 percent or the 1 percent level of significance. Using the former, a difference expected only 5 percent of the time or less by chance alone would be called significant and lead to the rejection of the null hypothesis. The second criterion is more stringent since it requires a difference between means that would occur only 1 percent of the time or less by chance to reject the null hypothesis.

It is possible to determine the probability of occurrence of the values of statistics calculated on samples drawn randomly from the population because the values of such statistics tend to be distributed in known ways. Many statistics, as well as many raw scores, tend to approximate what is known as the normal distribution. This distribution, depicted graphically in Figure 3, is a theoretical frequency distribution with a characteristic bell-shaped form. As you can see, values in the middle occur with the greatest frequency, and values at the extremes (very high or very low) occur only rarely. Values in the normal distribution are described in terms of how many standard deviations they lie above or below the mean, the middle value in this distribution. For example, if the mean is 100 and the standard deviation is 15, we know that a value of 115 is one standard deviation above the mean and that a value of 70 lies two standard deviations below the mean.

What is more important about the normal distribution is that we can make relatively precise statements about the frequency of occurrence of different raw scores. For example, 68 percent of the values lie within one standard deviation from the mean—34 percent above and 34 percent below; 95 percent lie within two standard deviations; and 99 percent lie within three standard deviations. Other frequencies can be similarly determined from the standard normal curve table, which is available in almost any introductory statistics book. If we know both that a particular type of sample statistic is normally distributed and how far in standard deviation units a specific value of this statistic lies above or below the mean of the distribution, we can easily determine from this table the expected frequency or probability with which this value or one larger should occur.

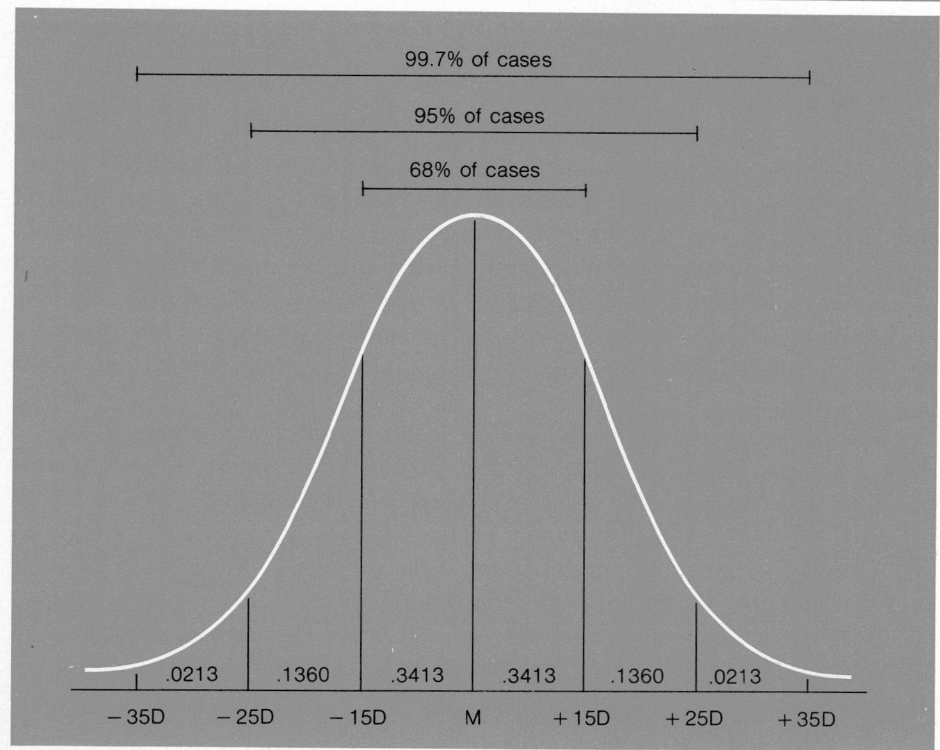

Fig. 3 Relative frequency of cases contained within certain limits in the normal distribution.

To use the normal curve in testing a statistical hypothesis, only one thing is changed. The mean of the distribution of our scores is a hypothesized value rather than a known value. We obtain the probability of getting a particular sample result, assuming that our raw scores are normally distributed around the mean. The probability taken from the normal curve table is then compared with a particular level of significance to see whether our assumption is warranted.

The normal distribution is certainly not the only type of distribution used in making statistical inferences. Different kinds of distributions, such as the *t*-distribution, the *F*-distribution, and the χ^2 (chi-square)-distribution, and many others are available when the normal distribution is not appropriate. The choice of which distribution to use for comparison depends on such factors as the type of statistical hypothesis being tested, the number of samples used, the size of the samples, and what kinds of assumptions one is willing to make about the populations from which the samples are selected. Although the characteristics of many of these distributions differ considerably from those of the normal curve, these distributions are all theoretical frequency distributions, and hence, like the normal curve, enable us to make statements about the probability of specific sample results.

The Calculation of Statistics: An Example

Many students dislike taking multiple-choice exams. One of the most frequently heard complaints is against multiple-choice questions that include "none of the above" as one of the incorrect alternatives. The usual criticism is that the mere presence of this alternative makes a student less confident about choosing one of the positively stated alternatives and hence more likely to change from the correct answer to the incorrect "none of the above."

A professor of psychology decided to test the **validity** of this complaint for the students in her class. She reasoned that if this complaint were true, then students should do better on questions that do not have "none of the above" as an incorrect alternative. When constructing a midterm for one of her classes, she chose twenty multiple-choice questions, all of which had five positively stated alternatives, and which she knew from previous tests were of approximately equal difficulty. She placed the twenty questions in a box, shook it, and then drew out ten questions. For each of these questions, designated as X questions, she changed one of the four incorrect alternatives to "none of the above" and made it the fifth alternative. The remaining ten questions, designated as *Y* questions, were changed only to ensure that the fifth alternative was also incorrect. The twenty questions were presented in an unsystematic order on the test, which was administered to fifteen students.

In scoring the test, the professor counted the number of X questions correctly answered and the number of *Y* questions correctly answered for each student. Her basic data, then, consisted of fifteen pairs of scores, the first of the pair an X score and the second a *Y* score. Listed in the same order as in her grade book, the pairs of scores for the fifteen students were 2, 7; 3, 9; 2, 7; 6, 10; 5, 9; 7, 9; 2, 8; 5, 7; 2, 5; 8, 10; 8, 10; 2, 7; 2, 6; 2, 7; 4, 9.

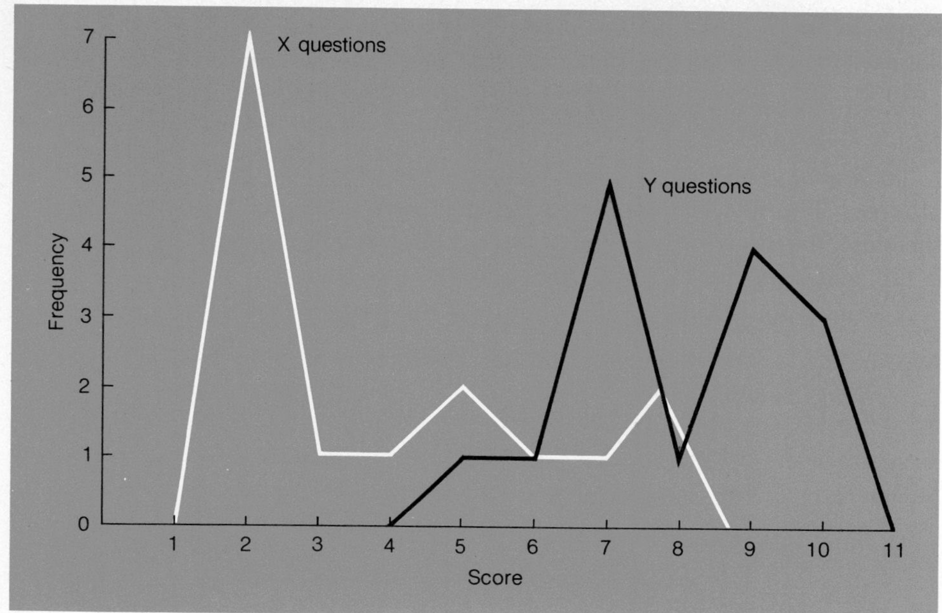

Fig. 4 Frequency polygon showing the distribution of scores for the two types of questions.

Organizing Data An initial step in summarizing the main characteristics of the data is to organize them into a frequency distribution (Table 3). To do this:

1. List the possible scores from the highest to the lowest actually observed (as in the left column of Table 3).
2. Determine the frequency with which each of the scores occurred for the X questions (f_X).
3. Determine the frequency with which each of the scores occurred for the Y questions (f_Y).

The data can be presented either in table form or in graphic form, the frequency polygon. For easy comparison, the polygon in Figure 5 shows the frequency of scores for both groups of questions. The scores are indicated on the horizontal axis, and the frequencies on the vertical axis. It is easy to see that students did better on the *Y* questions than on the X questions. Specifically, there were more low than high scores on the X questions, and more high than low scores on the *Y* questions.

Table 3 Frequency Distributions of Possible Scores on Two Types of Questions

SCORE	f_X	f_Y
10	0	3
9	0	4
8	2	1
7	1	5
6	1	1
5	2	1
4	1	0
3	1	0
2	7	0
Total	15	15

Central Tendency A measure of central tendency would be used to represent the level of performance for each type of question.

The mode (the most frequently appearing score) for the X questions is 2 (which occurred 7 times) and for the *Y* questions, 7 (which occurred 5 times).

To determine the value of the median, list the scores in order from lowest to highest. The median is the middle score—3 for the X questions and 8 for the *Y* questions.

X questions: 2, 2, 2, 2, 2, 2, 2, **3**, 4, 5, 5, 6, 7, 8, 8
Y questions: 5, 6, 7, 7, 7, 7, 7, **8**, 9, 9, 9, 9, 10, 10, 10

(For an even number of observations, the median is the average of the two middle scores.)

To determine the value of the mean, sum the scores and divide by the number of scores. The sum of scores on the X questions is 60, and there are 15 scores; therefore, the mean for the X questions is 4. The sum of scores on the Y questions is 120, and there are 15 scores; therefore, the mean is 8.

A formula for calculating the mean uses the following symbols:

M_X (or M_Y): the mean of the X (or Y) scores

ΣX (or ΣY): the sum of the X (or Y) scores (The symbol Σ means to add up all of the values following it.)

N_X (or N_Y): the number of X (or Y) scores

The formulas therefore would be:

$$M_X = \frac{\Sigma X}{N_X} \text{ and } M_Y = \frac{\Sigma Y}{N_Y}$$

All three measures of central tendency show that the students performed better on the Y questions than on the X questions, which included "none of the above."

Variability The measures of variability indicate how much dispersion or scatter there is among the values of scores. There are three measures—the range, the average deviation, and the standard deviation.

The range, obtained by subtracting the lowest score from the highest score, is 6 for the X questions ($8 - 2 = 6$) and 5 for the Y questions ($10 - 5 = 5$).

To determine the average deviation, subtract the mean from each of the scores —disregarding the sign or direction of the difference—and then average these differences. The average of these absolute differences is the average deviation.

Arranged in order from the lowest to the highest scores, the absolute differences between the X scores and their mean, 4, are 2, 2, 2, 2, 2, 2, 2, 1, 0, 1, 1, 2, 3, 4, 4. The sum of these differences, indicated by $\Sigma|X - M_X|$, is 30. (The two parallel lines around $X - M_X$ indicate that absolute as opposed to algebraic differences are being used.) Therefore the average deviation is:

$$\frac{\Sigma|X - M_X|}{N_X} = \frac{30}{15} = 2.0$$

Similarly, for the Y scores, the absolute differences are 3, 2, 1, 1, 1, 1, 1, 0, 1, 1, 1, 1, 2, 2, 2, and the average deviation is:

$$\frac{\Sigma|Y - M_Y|}{N_Y} = \frac{20}{15} = 1.33$$

The third measure, the standard deviation (S. D.), is obtained for the X scores by applying the following formula:

$$S.D._X = \frac{\sqrt{\Sigma(X - M_X)^2}}{N}$$

The formula is shorthand for the following steps:

1. Subtract the mean from each of the scores: $X - M_X$
   $-2, -2, -2, -2, -2, -2, -2, -1, 0, 1, 1, 2, 3, 4, 4$
2. Square the differences: $(X - M_X)^2$
   $4, 4, 4, 4, 4, 4, 4, 1, 0, 1, 1, 4, 9, 16, 16$
3. Sum the squared differences:

   $$\Sigma(X - M_X)^2 = 76$$

4. Find the average squared difference:

   $$\frac{\Sigma(X - M_X)^2}{N_X} = \frac{76}{15} = 5.07$$

5. Take the square root of the average squared difference:

   $$S.D._X = \sqrt{5.07} = 2.25$$

Applying the same steps to calculate $S.D._Y$,

1. $-3, -2, -1, -1, -1, -1, -1, 0, 1, 1, 1, 1, 2, 2, 2$
2. $9, 4, 1, 1, 1, 1, 1, 0, 1, 1, 1, 1, 4, 4, 4$
3. $\Sigma(Y - M_Y)^2 = 34$
4. $\frac{\Sigma(Y - M_Y)^2}{N_Y} = \frac{34}{15} = 2.27$
5. $S.D._Y = \sqrt{2.27} = 1.51$

All three measures indicate greater variability for X scores than for Y scores; that is, the X scores differ more from one another than do the Y scores.

Correlation In our example, each student has a score on the X questions and a score on the Y questions. To determine whether there is any consistent relationship between performance on the two tasks, we can calculate the value of the correlation coefficient.

The correlation coefficient r can be calculated by using the following equation:

$$r = \frac{\frac{\Sigma XY}{N_P} - M_X M_Y}{S.D._X S.D._Y}$$

Table 4 Computation of t-value

X	Y	D	D^2
2	7	5	25
3	9	6	36
2	7	5	25
6	10	4	16
5	9	4	16
7	9	2	4
2	8	6	36
5	7	2	4
2	5	3	9
8	10	2	4
8	10	2	4
2	7	5	25
2	6	4	16
2	7	5	25
4	9	5	25

$\Sigma D = 60$
$\Sigma D^2 = 270$
$N_D = 15$
$M_D = 4$

$$t = \frac{4}{\sqrt{\dfrac{270 - [(60)^2/15]}{15 - 1}}} = \frac{4}{\sqrt{\dfrac{270 - (3600/15)}{14}}} = \frac{4}{\sqrt{\dfrac{270 - 240}{14}}} = \frac{4}{\sqrt{\dfrac{30}{14}}} = \frac{4}{1.46} = 2.74$$

We have already calculated the values of the means, M_X and M_Y, and the values of the standard deviations, S.D.$_X$ and S.D.$_Y$. Those values can be substituted in the equation.

The symbol N_p stands for the number of *pairs* of observations. In our example, there are 15 pairs of scores.

The only new value to be calculated is ΣXY. To obtain this value, multiply each X score by the corresponding Y score for each student, and then sum these values. For our data,

$$\begin{aligned}\Sigma XY &= 2(7) + 3(9) + 2(7) + 6(10) + 5(9) + 7(9) + 2(8) + 5(7) + 2(5) \\ &\quad + 8(10) + 8(10) + 2(7) + 2(6) + 2(7) + 4(9) \\ &= 520\end{aligned}$$

and

$$r = \frac{\dfrac{520}{15} - (4)(8)}{2.25(1.51)} = \frac{34.67 - 32}{3.40} = \frac{2.67}{3.40} = .78$$

A correlation of .78, which is considered very high, indicates a strong relationship between performance on the two types of questions. This result shows that students with the higher scores on X questions also tended to get higher scores on Y questions, and students with lower scores on X questions also tended to get the lower scores on Y questions.

Statistical Inferences Having found a difference between the mean number of correct answers for X and Y questions (4 as opposed to 8), we might ask whether it represents a true difference between the two types of questions or whether it occurred simply by chance—the basic question of statistical inference.

The null hypothesis is that there is no true difference in difficulty between the two types of questions. In other words, the hypothesis we would like to reject is that the performance on the X type of question would be just as good on the average as that on the Y type of question if we were to examine the whole population of psychology students. If this hypothesis is correct, on the other hand, the difference of 4 we found between the two means in our sample must have occurred simply by chance. The next step then is to determine how likely it would be to find a difference of 4 or larger between means in our sample if there were no difference between means in the population.

To answer this question, we shall calculate a new statistic, t, for our sample data. We will then be able to use the t-distribution table in order to make statements of the probability of our sample result. The t-distribution is used here because we do not know any of the values of the population statistics, but instead have to estimate them from sample data, and because the sample size is quite small.

The t-value for our data can be calculated by substituting into the following equation:

$$t = \frac{M_D}{\frac{\Sigma D^2 - [(\Sigma D)^2/N_D]}{N_D - 1}}$$

The symbol D stands for the algebraic difference between an X score and a Y score for each student, obtained by subtracting X from Y. M_D refers to the mean of these difference scores; ΣD^2 refers to the sum of the squared difference scores; $(\Sigma D)^2$ refers to the square of the sum of the difference scores; and N_D refers to the number of difference scores. The basic steps are shown in Table 4.

A t-value as large as, or larger than, 2.74 would be expected by chance only 16 times out of 1000 (.016). Since this probability is considerably lower than the 5 percent level of significance, we can assert with some confidence that the null hypothesis is false. We would thus conclude that there really is a difference in difficulty between the two types of questions.

Appendix B: The Metric System of Measurement

Selected Elements of the Metric System of Measurement

UNIT	SYMBOL	VALUE
Length Units		
kilometer	km	1,000 meters
meter	m	base unit*
decimeter	dm	0.1 meter
centimeter	cm	0.01 meter
millimeter	mm	0.001 meter
Mass Units		
kilogram	kg	base unit*
gram	g	0.001 kilogram
decigram	dg	0.10 gram
centigram	cg	0.01 gram
milligram	mg	0.001 gram

UNIT	SYMBOL	VALUE
Volume Units		
cubic meter	m^3	derived unit†
cubic decimeter	dm^3	0.1 cubic meter
cubic centimeter	cm^3	0.01 cubic meter
cubic millimeter	mm^3	0.001 cubic meter
Capacity		
liter‡	l	accepted unit§
deciliter	dl	0.10 liter
centiliter	cl	0.01 liter
milliliter	ml	0.001 liter
Area		
square kilometer	km^2	1,000,000 square meters
square meter	m^2	derived unit†
square centimeter	cm^2	0.0001 square meter

NOTE: Because the United States is a signatory to the Treaty of the Metre (1875), the specific metric system we are converting to is the International System of Units (usually abbreviated SI after its French name, *Le Système International d'Unités*) established in 1960 at the eleventh General Conference on Weights and Measures (usually abbreviated CGPM after its French name, *Conférence Générale des Poids et Mesures*) in order to standardize international usage. According to SI, *mitre* and *litre* are the only accepted spellings for those units. However, we have maintained in this book the customary American spellings. Also, there are no periods after symbols for the units of measure since they are considered by SI to be symbols rather than abbreviations.

*A base unit is a unit of measure that has only one characteristic.

†A derived unit is a unit of measure that has at least two characteristics, such as length and width. It is formed by multiplying a base unit by itself or by multiplying or dividing a base unit by one or more other units.

‡*Liter* is a special name for a cubic decimeter of liquid, and the cubic decimeter is a subunit of the derived unit of volume, the cubic meter.

§An accepted unit outside SI that the CGPM has accepted for use along with SI because the unit is widely used. Hour and degree (of angle) are other such units.

Prefixes for Basic Metric Units

MULTIPLES				SUBDIVISIONS			
Prefix	Symbol	Power of 10	Equivalent	Prefix	Symbol	Power of 10	Equivalent
tera-	T	10^{12}	trillion	deci-	d	10^{-1}	tenth part
giga-	G	10^{9}	billion	centi-	c	10^{-2}	hundredth part
mega-	M	10^{6}	million	milli-	m	10^{-3}	thousandth part
kilo-	k	10^{3}	thousand	micro-	μ	10^{-6}	millionth part
hecto-	h	10^{2}	hundred	nano-	n	10^{-9}	billionth part
deka-	da	10^{1}	ten	pico-	p	10^{-12}	trillionth part

NOTE: All the prefixes used to designate multiples in SI are Greek in origin, and all the prefixes used to designate subdivisions are derived from Latin.

Conversion Tables

INCH FRACTIONS TO METRIC

Inches	Centimeters	Inches	Centimeters
1/32	0.079	1/2	1.27
1/16	0.159	9/16	1.429
1/8	0.318	5/8	1.588
3/16	0.476	3/4	1.905
1/4	0.635	13/16	2.064
5/16	0.794	7/8	2.222
3/8	0.953	15/16	2.381
7/16	1.111	1	2.54

INCH DECIMALS TO METRIC

Inches	Millimeters	Inches	Millimeters
0.001	0.025	0.06	1.524
0.002	0.051	0.07	1.778
0.003	0.076	0.08	2.032
0.004	0.102	0.09	2.286
0.005	0.127	0.1	2.54
0.006	0.152	0.2	5.08
0.007	0.178	0.3	7.62
0.008	0.203	0.4	10.16
0.009	0.229	0.5	12.70
0.01	0.254	0.6	15.24
0.02	0.508	0.7	17.78
0.03	0.762	0.8	20.32
0.04	1.016	0.9	22.86
0.05	1.27	1	25.4

WHOLE INCHES TO METRIC

Inches	Centimeters	Inches	Centimeters
1	2.54	7	17.78
2	5.08	8	20.32
3	7.62	9	22.86
4	10.16	10	25.4
5	12.7	11	27.94
6	15.24	12	30.48

FEET TO METRIC

Feet	Centimeters	Feet	Meters
1	30.48	4	1.219
2	60.96	5	1.524
3	91.44	6	1.829
		7	2.134
		8	2.438
		9	2.743
		10	3.048

MILES TO METRIC

Miles	Kilometers	Miles	Kilometers
1	1.609	6	9.656
2	3.219	7	11.265
3	4.828	8	12.875
4	6.437	9	14.484
5	8.047	10	16.09

OUNCES (WEIGHT) TO METRIC

Ounces	Kilograms	Ounces	Kilograms
1	0.028	9	0.255
2	0.057	10	0.284
3	0.085	11	0.312
4	0.113	12	0.340
5	0.142	13	0.369
6	0.170	14	0.397
7	0.198	15	0.425
8	0.227	16	0.454

POUNDS TO METRIC

Pounds	Kilograms	Pounds	Kilograms
1	0.454	6	2.722
2	0.907	7	3.175
3	1.361	8	3.629
4	1.814	9	4.082
5	2.268	10	4.536

OUNCES (LIQUID) TO METRIC

Ounces	Liters	Ounces	Liters
1	0.03	17	0.503
2	0.059	18	0.532
3	0.089	19	0.562
4	0.118	20	0.591
5	0.148	21	0.621
6	0.177	22	0.651
7	0.207	23	0.680
8	0.237	24	0.710
9	0.266	25	0.739
10	0.296	26	0.769
11	0.325	27	0.798
12	0.355	28	0.828
13	0.384	29	0.858
14	0.414	30	0.887
15	0.444	31	0.917
16	0.473	32	0.946

(Acknowledgments continued from page iv of front matter)

Tables 16•1, 16•2, 16•3, 16•4, 16•5 Earlier versions appeared in ESSENTIALS OF ABNORMAL PSYCHOLOGY. Copyright © 1974 by Benjamin Kleinmuntz. By permission of Harper & Row, Publishers.

Page 571 Table adapted from *The Causes and Cures of Neurosis* by H. J. Eysenck and S. Rachman. © 1965 Knapp, San Diego. Used by permission of the publisher and Routledge & Kegan Paul Ltd.

Table 18•1 Adapted from "On the fading of social stereotypes: Studies in three generations of college students" by M. Karlins, T. L. Coffman, and G. Walters in *Journal of Personality and Social Psychology,* 1969, 13:1–16. *Copyright 1969 by the American Psychological Association. Reprinted by permission.* **18•2** Adapted from "Cognitive, social, and physiological determinants of emotional state" by S. Schachter and J. E. Singer in *Psychological Review,* 1962, 69:379–99. *Copyright 1962 by the American Psychological Association. Reprinted by permission.*

Table 19•1 Adapted from "Behavioral study of obedience" by S. Milgram in *Journal of Abnormal and Social Psychology,* 1963, 67:371–78. *Copyright 1963 by the American Psychological Association. Reprinted by permission.* **19B•1** Adapted from "Physicians and medicare: A before-after study of the effects of legislation on attitudes" by J. Colombotos in *American Sociological Review,* 1969, 34:318–34. © 1969 American Sociological Association. Used by permission of the publisher and author.

Table 21C•1 Reprinted from Paul Ekman and Wallace V. Friesen, UNMASKING THE FACE: A Guide to Recognizing Emotions from Facial Clues, © 1975, p. 25. Prentice-Hall, Inc. Reproduced by permission of Prentice-Hall, Inc., Englewood Cliffs, New Jersey.

Table 22•1 Adapted from "Phyletic differences in learning" by M. E. Bitterman in *American Psychologist,* 1965, 20: 396–410. *Copyright 1965 by the American Psychological Association. Reprinted by permission.*

Table 24•2 Reprinted from "Biogenic amines and emotion" by J. J. Schildkraut and S. S. Kety in *Science,* 156(7 April 1967):21–30. Copyright 1967 by the American Association for the Advancement of Science. Used by permission of the publisher and J. J. Schildkraut. **24•3** Reprinted from BIOLOGICAL SCIENCE, Second Edition, by William T. Keeton. By permission of W. W. Norton & Company, Inc. Copyright © 1972, 1967 by W. W. Norton & Company, Inc. **24A•1** Reprinted from "The electroencephalogram: Autonomous electrical activity in man and animals" by D. B. Lindsley and J. D. Wicke in R. F. Thompson and M. Patterson (eds.) *Bioelectric Recording Techniques,* 1974. © 1974 Academic Press, Inc. Used by permission of the publisher and D. B. Lindsley.

Table 25•1 Adapted from "Electrophysiological analysis of learning and memory" by A. L. Leiman and C. N. Christian in J. A. Deutsch (ed.) *The Physiological Basis of Memory.* © 1973 Academic Press, Inc. Used by permission of the publisher and J. A. Deutsch. **25•2** Adapted from "The other side of the brain; an appositional mind" by J. E. Bogen in *Bulletin of the Los Angeles Neurological Society,* July 1969, 34:135–62. © 1969 Los Angeles Neurological Society. Used by permission of the publisher and author. **25A•1** Reprinted from "Left-handedness and cognitive deficit" by C. Hardyck, L. F. Petrinovich, and R. D. Goldman in *Cortex,* in press.

Fig. 1•1 Adapted from *Great Experiments in Psychology* by H. Garrett. © 1951 Appleton-Century-Crofts, Inc. Used by permission of the estate of Henry E. Garrett.

Fig. 2•1 From CHILD PSYCHOLOGY by G. G. Thompson (Boston: Houghton Mifflin Company, 1962). Reprinted by permission of the publisher. **2B•1** Adapted from "The Growth and Decline of Intelligence: A Study of a Homogeneous Group between the Ages of Ten and Sixty" in *Genetic Psychology Monographs,* 1933, 13:223–298. © 1933 The Journal Press. Used by permission of the publisher.

Fig. 3A•1, 3A•2 Adapted from "Physical Maturing among Boys as Related to Behavior" in *Journal of Educational Psychology,* 1950, 41:129–48. *Copyright 1950 by the American Psychological Association. Reprinted by permission.* **3•1, 3•2** Adapted from "The Physical and Mental Growth of Girls and Boys Age Six to Nineteen in Relation to Age at Maximum Growth" in *Monographs of the Society for Research in Child Development,* 1939, 4(Serial No. 22). © 1939 The Society for Research in Child Development, Inc. Used by permission of the publisher. **3•3** Adapted from "Physical Changes in Adolescence" by W. W. Greulich in *43rd Yearbook of the National Society of Study of Education, Part I,* 1944. © 1944 by National Society for Study of Education. Used by permission of the society. **3•4** Adapted from "Effects of restricted opportunity for tactual, kinesthetic, and manipulative experience on the behavior of a chimpanzee" by H. Nissen, K. Chow, and J. Semmes in *American Journal of Psychology,* 1951, 64:485–507. © 1951 University of Illinois Press. Used by permission of the publisher.

Photo, p. 74 Reprinted from "Pattern vision in newborn infants" by R. L. Fantz in *Science,* 140(April 1963):296–97. Copyright 1963 by American Association for the Advancement of Science. Used by permission of the publisher and author.

Fig. 4•1 From "The origin of form perception" by Robert L. Fantz. Copyright © by Scientific American, Inc. All rights reserved. **4•2** Reprinted from "How adults and children search and recognize pictures" by Norman H. Mackworth and J. S. Bruner in *Human Development,* 1970, 13:149–77. © 1970 S Karger AG, Basil. Used by permission of the publisher and Norman H. Mackworth. **4•3** Reprinted from "The development of perception in the preschool child" in Paul H. Mussen (ed.) *European Research in Cognitive Development, Monographs of the Society for Research in Child Development,* 1965, 30(Serial No. 100). © 1965 The Society for Research in Child Development, Inc. Used by permission of the publisher. **4•4** Reprinted from "A facial dimension in visual discrimination by human infants" by R. A. Haaf and R. Q. Bell in *Child Development,* 1967, 38:893–99. © 1967 The Society for Research in Child Development. Used by permission of the publisher and R. A. Haaf. **4•5** Adapted from "An investigation of the auditory analysis in neonates and young children" by A. J. Bronshtein and E. P. Petrova, translated (from Russian) and reprinted in Y. Brackbill and G. G. Thompson (eds.) *Behavior in infancy and early childhood: A book of readings,* 1967. © 1967 The Free Press. Used by permission of the publisher. **4•6** Adapted from "The sequential patterning of prone progression in the human infant" by Louise Bates Ames in *Genetic Psychology Monographs,* 1937, 19:409–60. © 1937 The Journal Press. Used by permission of the publisher and author. **4•7** Adapted from "The development of motor abilities during the first three years" by N. Bayley in *Monographs of the Society for Research in Child Development,* 1935, 1. © 1935 The Society for Research in Child Development. Used by permission of the publisher and author. **4•9** Adapted from "Learning in the first year of life" by L. P. Lipsitt in L. P. Lipsitt and C. C. Spiker (eds.) *Advances in Child Development and Behavior,* vol. 1, 1963. © 1963 Academic Press, Inc. Used by permission of the publisher and L. P. Lipsitt. **4•11** Adapted from "Conditioned head turning in human newborns" by E. R. Siqueland and L. P. Lipsitt in *Journal of Experimental Child Psychology,* 1966, 3:356–76. © 1966 Academic Press, Inc. Used by permission of the publisher and authors. **4•12** Adapted from "Experimental studies of appetitional behavior in human newborns" by H. Papoušek in H. W. Stevenson, E. H. Hess, and H. L. Rheingold (eds.) *Early behavior: Comparative and developmental approaches,* 1967. © 1967 John Wiley & Sons, Inc. Used by permission of the publisher. **4•13** Adapted from "Vertical and horizontal processes in problem solving" by H. Kendler and T. Kendler in *Psychological Review,* 1962, 69:1–16. *Copyright 1962 by The American Psychological Association. Reprinted by permission.* **4A•1** Reprinted from "Reflection-impulsivity and reading ability in primary grade children" by Jerome Kagan in *Child Development,* 1965, 36:609–28. © 1965 The Society for Research in Child Development, Inc. Used by permission of the publisher and author. **4•14** From *Of Children: An Introduction to Child Development* by Guy R. Lefrançois. © 1973 by Wadsworth Publishing Company, Inc., Belmont, California 94002. Reprinted by permission of the publisher. **4•15** From "Developmental studies of figurative perception" by David Elkind in L. P. Lipsitt and H. W. Reese (eds.) *Advances in Child Development and Behavior,* vol. 4, 1969. © 1969 Academic Press, Inc. Used by permission of the publisher and author. **4•16** From WORD, Vol. 14 (1958) page 150. Reprinted by permission of Johnson Reprint Corporation. **4•17** Reprinted with permission of Macmillan Publishing Co., Inc. from "The first sentences of child and chimpanzee" by Roger Brown in Roger Brown (ed.) *Psycholinguistics: Selected Papers,* 1970. Copyright © 1970 by The Free Press, a Division of Macmillan Publishing Co., Inc. **4•19** Adapted from "Differential growth of mental abilities" by L. L. Thurstone in *Science,* 121 (April 1955):627. Copyright 1955 by the American Association for the Advancement of Science. Used by permission of the publisher and author. **4•20** Adapted from *The Structure of Human Abilities* by P. E. Vernon. © 1960 Methuen & Co., Ltd. Used by permission of the publisher. **4•21** Adapted from "Genetics and intelligence: A review" by L. Erlenmeyer-Kimling and L. F. Jarvik in *Science,* 142(December 1963):1477–79. Copyright 1963 by the American Association for the Advancement of Science. Used by permission of the publisher and L. Erlenmeyer-Kimling. **4B•1** Copyright © 1963 by Harcourt Brace Jovanovich, Inc. and reproduced with their permission from CHILDREN'S DRAWINGS AS MEASURES OF INTELLECTUAL MATURITY by Dale B. Harris.

Fig. 5•3 Adapted from "The development of social attachments in infancy" by H. R. Schaffer and G. E. Emerson in *Monographs of the Society for Research in Child Development,* 1964, 29 (Serial No. 94). © 1964 The Society for Research in Child Development, Inc. Used by permission of the publisher and H. R. Schaffer. **5•4** Redrawn from "Consequences of Different Kinds of Parental Discipline," by Wesley C. Becker in REVIEW OF CHILD DEVELOPMENT RESEARCH, edited by Martin L. Hoffman & Lois W. Hoffman, © 1964 Russell Sage Foundation. **5•5** Adapted from "Father-fantasies and father-typing in father-separated children" by G. R. Bach in *Child Development,* 1946, 17:63–80. © 1946 The Society for Research in Child Development, Inc. Used by permission of the publisher. **5•6** Adapted from "Stage and sequence: The cognitive-developmental approach to socialization" by L. Kohlberg in David Goslin (ed.) *Handbook of Socialization Theory and Research,* 1969. © 1969 Rand McNally & Co. **5A•1** Adapted from Arthur T. Jersild and Frances B. Holmes, *Children's Fears.* (New York: Teachers College Press, 1935), p. 230. **5•7** Adapted from "A cognitive developmental analysis of children's sex-role concepts and attitudes" by L. Kohlberg in Eleanor E. Maccoby (ed.) *The Development of Sex Differences,* 1966. © 1966 by the Board of Trustees of the Leland Stanford Junior University. **5B•1** Adapted from *Sociometry in Group Relations: A Work Guide for Teachers* by J. J. Jennings. © 1948 American Council on Education. Used by permission of the publisher.

Fig. 6•1 From S. L. Pressey & R. G. Kuhlen, PSYCHOLOGICAL DEVELOPMENT THROUGH THE LIFE SPAN, Harper & Row, 1957. After H. E. Jones and H. S. Conrad, "The growth and decline of intelligence: A study of a homogeneous group between the ages of 10 and 60," *Genetic Psychology Monographs,* 1933, 13:223–98; C. C. and W. R. Miles, "The correlation of intelligence scores and chronological age from early to late maturity," *American Journal of Psychology,* 1932, 44:44–78; and D. Wechsler, *The Measurement of Adult Intelligence* (3rd ed.), Baltimore, Williams & Wilkins, 1955. **6A•1** Adapted from "The creative years in science and literature" by H. Lehman in *Scientific Monthly,* 43 (August 1936): 151–62. Copyright 1936 by the American Association for the Advancement of Science. Used by permission of the publisher. **6•2** Adapted from "Structure of the self-concept from adolescence through old age" by R. H. Monge in *Experimental Aging Research,* 1976, 2. © 1976 Experimental Aging Research. Used by permission of the publisher.

Fig. 7•1, 7•4, 7•6 From AN INTRODUCTION TO PSYCHOLOGY by Ralph Norman Haber and Aharon H. Fried. Copyright © 1975 by Holt, Rinehart and Winston. Reprinted by permission of Holt, Rinehart and Winston. **7•2, 7•8, 7B•1** From THE PSYCHOLOGY OF VISUAL PERCEPTION by Ralph Norman Haber and Maurice Hershenson. Copyright © 1973 by Holt, Rinehart and Winston, Inc. Reprinted by permission of Holt, Rinehart and Winston. **7•5** Adapted from "Organization of the primate retina: Electron microscopy" by J. E. Dowling and B. B. Boycott in *Proceedings of the Royal Society (London),* 1966, Series B,166:80–111. © 1966 Royal Society. Used by permission of the publisher. **7•7** Adapted from *Fundamentals of Neurology,* 6th ed. by E. Gardner. © 1975 W. B. Saunders Company. Used by permission of the publisher and author. **7•10** Adapted from "Vision: II. The nature of the photoreceptor process" by S. Hecht in C. Murchison (ed.) *A Handbook of General Experimental Psychology,* [1934] 1969. © 1969 Russell & Russell, Publishers. Used by permission of the publisher. **7•12** Adapted from "Eye movements in relation to retinal action" by R. W. Ditchburn in *Optica Acta,* 1955, 1:171–76. © 1955 Taylor & Francis, Ltd. Used by permission of the publisher. **7•15** From PSYCHOLOGY: ITS PRINCIPLES AND MEANINGS by Lyle E. Bourne, Jr. and Bruce R. Ekstrand. Copyright © 1973 by The Dryden Press, A Division of Holt, Rinehart and Winston. Adapted by permission of Holt, Rinehart and Winston. **7•21** From THE EXPERIMENTAL PSYCHOLOGY OF SENSORY BEHAVIOR by John F. Corso. Copyright © 1967 by Holt, Rinehart and Winston, Inc. Reprinted by permission of Holt, Rinehart and Winston. **7•23** Beasley, W. C.: Figure 20, p. 353 from READINGS IN EXPERIMENTAL PSYCHOLOGY edited by Willard Lee Valentine, Harper & Row, 1931. **7•24, 7•25, 7•26** From Roger Brown and Richard J. Herrnstein, PSYCHOLOGY, p. 348. Copyright © 1975 by Little, Brown and Company. Reprinted by permission. **7•29** Adapted from "Studying the senses of taste and smell" by C. Pfaffmann in T. G. Andrews (ed.) *Methods of Psychology,* 1948. © 1948 John Wiley & Sons, Inc. Used by permission of the publisher. **7•30** Adapted from "Observations on the neurohistological basis of cutaneous pain" by H. H. Wollard, G. Weddell, and J. A. Harpman in *Journal of Anatomy,* 1940, 74:413–40. © 1940 Anatomical Society of Great Britain and Ireland. Used by permission of Cambridge University Press, W. B. Saunders Company, and E. Gardner. **7•31** From BIOLOGY, Fourth Edition by Willis H. Johnson, Louis E. Delanney, Thomas A. Cole, and Austin E. Brooks. Copyright © 1966, 1972 by Holt, Rinehart and Winston, Inc. Reprinted by permission of Holt, Rinehart and Winston. **7•32** From *Reflex Activity of the Spinal Cord,* by R. S. Creed, D. Denny-Brown, et al. published by the Oxford University Press.

Fig. 8•1, 8•14, 8•15 Adapted from THE PERCEPTION OF THE VISUAL WORLD by James J. Gibson. Copyright © 1950. Used by permission of Houghton Mifflin Co. **8•3, 8•5, 8•7, 8•9, 8•25** From THE PSYCHOLOGY OF VISUAL PERCEPTION by Ralph Norman Haber and Maurice Hershenson. Copyright © 1973 by Holt, Rinehart and Winston, Inc. Reprinted by permission of Holt, Rinehart and Winston. **8•11** From Roger Brown and Richard J. Herrnstein, PSYCHOLOGY, p. 385. Copyright © 1975 by Little, Brown and Company. Reprinted by permission. **8•12** Julian E. Hochberg, PERCEPTION, © 1964, pp. 38, 41. Reproduced by permission of Prentice-Hall, Inc., Englewood Cliffs, New Jersey. **8•13** From B. Julesz, Binocular Depth Perception without Familiarity Cues, *Science* 145(24 July 1964):356–62. Copyright 1964 by the American Association for the Advancement of Science. Used by permission of the publisher and author. **8•16** From THE SENSES CONSIDERED AS PERCEPTUAL SYSTEMS by James J. Gibson. Copyright © 1966. Used by permission of Houghton Mifflin Co. **8•17** Reprinted with permission from P. L. Latour, "Visual threshold during eye movements," *Vision Research,* 1962, 2:261–262. © 1962, Pergamon Press Ltd. **8•18** Adapted from *Perception and Motion* by K. U. Smith and W. M. Smith. © 1962 W. B. Saunders Co. Used by permission of K. U. Smith. **8•20** Reprinted from "Visual scanning of triangles by the human newborn" by P. Salapatek and W. Kessen in *Journal of Experimental Child Psychology,* 1966, 3:155–67. © 1966 Academic Press, Inc. Used by permission of the publisher and P. Salapatek. **8•22** Adapted from *Ames Demonstrations in Perception* by W. H. Ittelson, [1952] 1968. © 1952, 1968 Hafner Press. Used by permission of the author. **8•23, 8•32** Reprinted from *Eye Movements and Vision* by A. L. Yarbus. © 1967 Plenum Publishing Corporation. Used by permission of the publisher. **8•24** Excerpted from "Decision time without reaction time: Experiments in visual scanning" by U. Neisser in *American Journal of Psychology,* 1963, 76:376–85. © 1963 The University of Illinois Press. Used by permission of the publisher. **8•28** From "Pictorial Perception and Culture" by Jan B. Deregowski. Copyright © by Scientific American, Inc. All rights reserved. **8•29** Reprinted from "Age in the development of closure ability in children" by C. M. Mooney in *Canadian Journal of Psychology,* 1957, 11:219–26. © 1957 Canadian Psychological Association. Used by permission of the publisher and author. **8B•1** Adapted from "The information available in brief visual presentations" by G. Sperling in *Psychological Monographs,* 1960, 74(Whole No. 498):11. *Copyright 1960 by the American Psychological Association. Reprinted by permission.* **8•31** Reprinted with permission from G. Sperling, "A model for visual memory tasks," *Human Factors,* 1963, 5:19–31. © 1963, Pergamon Press Ltd.

Fig. 9•1 Adapted from "Distinctive features of learning in the higher animal" by D. O. Hebb in J. F. Delafresnaye (ed.) *Brain Mechanisms and Learning,* 1961. © 1961 Blackwell Scientific Publications Ltd. Used by permission of the publisher and author. **9•2,** Adapted from "Hierarchical retrieval schemes in the recall of categorized word lists by G. H. Bower, M. C. Clark, A. M. Lesgold, and D. Winzenz in *Journal of Verbal Learning and Verbal Behavior,* 1969, 8:323–43. © 1969 Academic Press, Inc. Used by permission of the publisher and G. H. Bower. **9•3** Adapted from "The 'similarity' factor in retroaction" by E. S. Robinson in *American Journal of Psychology,* 1927, 39:297–312. © 1927 The University of Illinois Press. Used by permission of the publisher. **9•4** Adapted from "Interference and forgetting" by Benton J. Underwood in *Psychological Review,* 1957, 64:49–60. *Copyright 1957 by the American Psychological Association. Reprinted by permission.* **9•6** Reprinted from "The fate of primary memory items in free recall" by F. I. M. Craik in *Journal of Verbal Learning and Verbal Behavior,* 1970, 9:143–148. Copyright © 1970 Academic Press, Inc. Used by permission of the publisher and author. **9•7** Adapted from "Recall for words as a function of semantic, graphic, and syntactic orienting tasks" by T. S. Hyde and J. J. Jenkins in *Journal of Verbal Learning and Verbal Behavior,* 1973, 12:471–80. © 1973 Academic Press, Inc. Used by permission of the publisher and T. S. Hyde.

Fig. 10•1 Adapted from "The effects of the introduction of reward upon the maze performance of rats" by Hugh C. Blodgett in *University of California Publications in Psychology,* 1929, 4:113–34. Copyright © 1929 by The Regents of the University of California. reprinted by permission of the University of California Press. **10•3** Adapted from "The generalization of conditioned responses: I. The sensory generalization of conditioned responses with varying frequencies of tone" by Carl Iver Hovland in *Journal of General Psychology,* 1937, 17:125–48. © 1937 The Journal Press. Used by permission of the publisher. **10•4** Adapted from "Differential conditioning and intensity of the UCS" by W. N. Runquist, K. W. Spence, and D. W. Stubbs in *Journal of Experimental Psychology,* 1958, 55:51–55. *Copyright 1958 by the American Psychological Association. Reprinted by permission.* **10.5** Adapted from "Wavelength generalization after discrimination learning with and without errors by H. S. Terrace in *Science* 144(3 April 1964):78–80. Copyright 1964 by the American Association for the Advancement of Science. Used by permission of the publisher and author. **10A•1** Adapted from "Traumatic avoidance learning: The outcomes of several extinction procedures with dogs" by R. L. Solomon, L. J. Kamin, and L. C. Wynne in *Journal of Abnormal and Social Psychology,* 1953, 48:291–302. *Copyright 1953 by the American Psychological Association. Reprinted by permission.* **10•8** Adapted from "Effects of non-random intermittent reinforcement schedules in human eyelid conditioning" by W. F. Prokasy, R. A. Carlton, and J. D. Higgins in *Journal of Experimental Psychology,* 1967, 74:282–88. *Copyright 1967 by the American Psychological Association. Reprinted by permission.*

Fig. 11•2 Adapted from "The associative basis of the creative process" by S. A. Mednick in *Psychological Review,* 1962, 69: 220–32. *Copyright 1962 by the American Psychological Association. Reprinted by permission.* **11•4** Adapted from "Retrieval time from semantic memory" by A. M. Collins and M. R. Quillian in *Journal of Verbal Learning and Verbal Behavior,* 1969, 8:240–47. © 1969 Academic Press, Inc. Used by permission of the publisher and A. M. Collins.

Fig. 12•2 Adapted from "Behavior potentiality as a joint function of the amount of training and the degree of hunger at the time of extinction" by C. T. Perin in *Journal of Experimental Psychology,* 1942, 30:93–113. *Copyright 1942 by the American Psychological Association. Reprinted by permission.* **12•3** Adapted from "Behavior theory and selective learning" by K. W. Spence in M. R. Jones (ed.) *Nebraska Symposium on Motivation,* 1958, vol. 6:73–107. © 1958 University of Nebraska Press. Used by permission of the publisher. **12•4** Weiner, Bernard, THEORIES OF MOTIVATION: From Mechanism to Cognition, © 1972 by Rand McNally College Publishing Company, Chicago, figure 2–1, page 30. **12•6** Adapted from "Values expressed in American children's readers: 1800–1950." by R. de Charms and G. H. Moeller in *Journal of Abnormal and Social Psychology,* 1962, 64:136–42. *Copyright 1962 by the American Psychological Association. Reprinted by permission.*

Fig. 14•4 Adapted from "Behavior therapy in the home: Amelioration of problem parent-child relations with the parent in a therapeutic role" by R. P. Hawkins, R. F. Peterson, E. Schweid, and S. W. Bijou in *Journal of Experimental Child Psychology,* 1966, 4:99–107. © 1966 Academic Press, Inc. Used by permission of the publisher and R. P. Hawkins. **14•7** Reprinted from *Hidden Figures Test* by S. Messick. © 1962 Educational Testing Service. Used by permission of the publisher.

Fig. 15•1 Adapted from "Steepness of approach and avoidance gradients in humans as a function of experience: Theory and experiment" by S. Epstein and W. D. Fenz in *Journal of Experimental Psychology,* 1965, 70:1–12. *Copyright 1965 by the American Psychological Association.* Reprinted by permission. **15•2** Adapted from "Reduction of postoperative pain by encouragement and instruction of patients" by L. Egbert, G. Battit, C. Welch, and M. Bartlett in *New England Journal of Medicine,* 1964, 270:825–27. © 1964 Massachusetts Medical Society. Used by permission of the publisher. **15•6** Adapted from "The short circuiting of threat by experimentally altering cognitive appraisal" by R. S. Lazarus and E. Alfert in *Journal of Abnormal and Social Psychology,* 1964, 69:195–205. *Copyright 1964 by the American Psychological Association. Reprinted by permission.* **15•7** Adapted from *Social Change and Prejudice* by B. Bettelheim and M. Janowitz. Copyright © 1964 The Free Press of Glencoe, a Division of The Macmillan Company. Used by permission of the publisher and authors. **15•8** Adapted from "The mechanism of vision: I. A method for rapid analysis of pattern vision in the rat" by K. S. Lashley in *The Pedagogical Seminary and Journal of Genetic Psychology,* 1930, 37:453–60. © 1930 The Journal Press. Used by permission of the publisher. **15•9** Adapted from "Motivational properties of frustration: III. Relation of frustration effect to antedating goal factors" by A. Amsel and W. Hancock in *Journal of Experimental Psychology,* 1957, 53:126–31. *Copyright 1957 by the American Psychological Association. Reprinted by permission.*

Fig. 17•1 Adapted from "Feedback-induced muscle relaxation: Application to tension headache" by T. Budzynski, J. Stoyva, and C. Adler in *Journal of Behavior Therapy and Experimental Psychiatry,* 1970, 1:205–11. © 1970, Pergamon Press Ltd. Used by permission of the publisher.

Fig. 18•1 Adapted from "Experimental attempts to minimize the impact of first impressions" by A. S. Luchins in C. I. Hovland (ed.) *The Order of Presentation in Persuasion,* 1957. © 1957 Yale University Press. Used by permission of the publisher. **18•2** Adapted from "From acts to dispositions: The attribution process in person perception" by E. E. Jones and K. E. Davis in L. Berkowitz (ed.) *Advances in Experimental Social Psychology,* vol. 2, 1965. © 1965 Academic Press, Inc. Used by permission of the publisher and E. E. Jones.

Fig. 19•3 Adapted from *A Theory of Cognitive Dissonance* by L. Festinger. © 1957 Row, Peterson & Company. Used by permission of the author.

Fig. 20•2 Adapted from "Bystander intervention in emergencies: Diffusion of responsibility" by J. M. Darley and B. Latané in *Journal of Personality and Social Psychology,* 1968, 8(4):377–83. © 1968 Society for Personality and Social Psychology, a division of the American Psychological Association. Used by permission of the publisher and authors. **20•3** Adapted from "Diffusion of responsibility and restaurant tipping: Cheaper by the bunch" by S. Freeman, M. R. Walker, R. Borden, and B. Latané in *Personality and Social Psychology Bulletin,* 1975, 1:584–87. © 1975 Society for Personality and Social Psychology, a division of the American Psychological Association. Used by permission of the publisher and B. Latané. **20A•1** Adapted from "Action research on the development of leadership, decision making processes, and organizational performance in a Japanese shipyard," 1974, paper presented at the 18th International Congress of Applied Psychology, Montreal, Canada by J. Misumi. © 1974 J. Misumi. Used by permission of the author.

21A•1 Adapted from "Submission: Its features and functions in the wolf and dog" by R. Schenckel in *American Zoologist,* 1967, 7:319–29. © 1967 American Society of Zoologists. Used by permission of the publisher.

Fig. 21•1 Adapted from "The snark was a boojum" by F. A. Beach in *American Psychologist,* 1950, 5:115–24. *Copyright 1950 by the American Psychological Association. Reprinted by permission.* **21•2** Adapted from "A case history in scientific method" by B. F. Skinner in *American Psychologist,* 1956, 11:221–33. *Copyright 1956 by the American Psychological Association. Reprinted by permission.* **21•3** Adapted from *Animal Behavior: A Synthesis of Ethology and Comparative Psychology* by R. A. Hinde. © 1970 McGraw-Hill Book Company. Used by permission of the publisher.

Fig. 22•1 Adapted from *The Meaning of Evolution* by G. G. Simpson. © 1949 Yale University Press. Used by permission of the publisher. **22•3** Adapted from *Animal Diversity* by E. D. Hanson. © 1972 Prentice-Hall, Inc. Used by permission of the publisher. **22.4** Adapted from *Life on Earth* by E. O. Wilson, T. Eisner, W. R. Briggs, R. E. Dickerson, R. L. Metzenberg, R. D. O'Brien, M. Susman, and W. F. Boggs. © 1973 Sinauer Associates, Inc. Used by permission of the publisher. **22•5** Adapted from "Brain evolution and dinosaur brains" by H. J. Jerison in *American Naturalist,* 1969, 103:575–88. © 1969 The University of Chicago Press. Used by permission of the publisher. **22•6** Reprinted with permission of Macmillan Publishing Co., Inc. from *The Ascent of Man* by David Pilbeam. Copyright 1972 by David R. Pilbeam. **22•7** Adapted from "Interpreting the evolution of the brain" by H. J. Jerison in *Human Biology,* 1963, 35:263–91. © 1963 Society for the Study of Human Biology. Used by permission of the publisher. **22•8** Adapted from *Human Neuroanatomy,* 6th ed., by R. G. Truex and M. B. Carpenter. © 1969 The Williams & Wilkins Co., Baltimore. Used by permission of the publisher and M. B. Carpenter. **22•9, 22•15** Adapted from *The Vertebrate Story,* rev. ed. by A. S. Romer. © 1971 The University of Chicago Press. Used by permission of the publisher. **22•10, 22•11** Adapted from "Comparative studies of the behaviour of gulls (*Laridae*): A progress report" by N. Tinbergen in *Behaviour,* 1959, 15:1–81. © 1959 *Behaviour.* Used by permission of the publisher. **22•12, 22•13** Adapted from "Phyletic differences in learning" by M. E. Bitterman in *American Psychologist,* 1965, 20:396–410. *Copyright 1965 by the American Psychological Association. Reprinted by permission.* **22•14** Adapted from "Comparative study of brain and behavior" by W. Hodos in F. O. Schmitt (ed.) *The Neurosciences.* © 1970 The Rockefeller University Press. Used by permission of the publisher and author.

Fig. 23•1 From Paris Conference (1971): Standardization in Human Cytogenetics. In Birth Defects: Orig. Art. Ser., (ed.) D. Bergsma. Published by The National Foundation—March of Dimes, White Plains, N.Y., Vol. VIII, No. 7, 1972. **23•4, 23•5** Adapted from *The Genetics of Behavior* by L. Ehrman and P. A. Parsons. © 1976 Sinauer Associates, Inc. Used by permission of the publisher. **23•7** From "The behavior of lovebirds" by William C. Dilger. Copyright © 1962 by Scientific American, Inc. All rights reserved. **23•8** Adapted from "The inheritance and development of intelligence" by W. R. Thompson in *Proceedings of the Association for Research in Nervous and Mental Disease,* 1954, 33:209–231. © 1954 Association for Research in Nervous and Mental Disease, Inc. Used by permission of the publisher. **23•9** Adapted from "Factors underlying differences in alcohol preference among inbred strains of mice" by D. A. Rodgers in *Psychosomatic Medicine,* 1966, 28:498–513. © 1966 American Psychosomatic Society. Used by permission of American Elsevier Publishing Co. **23•10** Adapted from "Genetic influences on the behavior of mice can be obscured by laboratory rearing" by N. D. Henderson in *Journal of Comparative and Physiological Psychology,* 1970, 72:505–11. *Copyright 1970 by the American Psychological Association, Reprinted by permission.*

Fig. 24•2 Adapted from *Gray's Anatomy,* 29th American ed., Charles Goss (ed.) © 1973 Lea & Febiger. Used by permission of the publisher; from PHYSIOLOGICAL PSYCHOLOGY by Peter M. Milner. Copyright © 1970 Holt, Rinehart and Winston, Inc. Reprinted by permission of Holt, Rinehart and Winston; adapted from an original painting by Frank H. Netter, M. D. for THE CIBA COLLECTION OF MEDICAL ILLUSTRATIONS published by CIBA-GEIGY Corporation. **24•5** From INTRODUCTION TO PHYSIOLOGICAL PSYCHOLOGY by Richard F. Thompson, Fig. "a" 3.15 (p. 93). Harper & Row. 1975. By permission of the publisher. **24•8** Adapted from *Perceptual and Motor Development in Infants and Children* by Bryant J. Cratty. © 1970 The Macmillan Company. Used by permission of the author. **24•9** Adapted from *Before We are Born: Basic Embryology and Birth Defects* by K. Moore. © 1974 W. B. Saunders Company. Used by permission of the publisher and author. **24•11** Adapted from "The formation of synaptic functions in developing rat brain: A quantitative electron microscopic study" by G. K. Aghajanian and F. E. Bloom in *Brain Research,* 1967, 6:716–27. © 1967 Elsevier/North-Holland Biomedical Press. Used by permission of the publisher. **24•12** Adapted from "Head circumference and cellular growth of the brain in normal and marasmic children" by M. Winick and P. Rosso in *Journal of Pediatrics,* 1969, 74:774–78. © 1969 The C. V. Mosby Company. Used by permission of the publisher and M. Winick. **24•19** From "Neurotransmitters" by Julius Axelrod. Copyright © by Scientific American, Inc. All rights reserved. **24•23** From "How We Control the Contraction of Our Muscles" by P. A. Merton. Copyright © by Scientific American, Inc. All rights reserved **24•24** From FOUNDATIONS OF PHYSIOLOGICAL PSYCHOLOGY by Richard F. Thompson, Fig. 12.6 (p. 371). Harper & Row, 1967. By permission of the publisher. **24•25** Adapted from *The Anatomy of the Nervous System* by S. W. Ranson and S. L. Clark. © 1959 W. B. Saunders Company. Used by permission of the publisher. **24•26** Adapted from *Functional Neuroanatomy,* 3d ed. by W. J. S. Krieg. © 1966 by Brain Books. Used by permission of the publisher. **24•27** From "Brain Mechanisms in Movement" by Edward V. Evarts. Copyright © by Scientific American, Inc. All rights reserved. **24•28** Adapted from "The extrapyramidal motor system" by Richard Jung and Ralph Hassler in *Handbook of Physiology,* vol. 2, 1960. © 1960 American Physiological Society. Used by permission of the publisher and Richard Jung. **24A•1** Adapted from *An Introduction to the Neurosciences* by B. A. Curtis, S. Jacobson, and E. M. Marcus. © 1972 W. B. Saunders Company. Used by permission of the publisher and B. A. Curtis. **Photo, p. 796** Reprinted from "Developmental factors in the formation of feature extracting neurons" by C. Blakemore in F. O. Schmitt and F. G. Worden (eds.) *The Neurosciences: Third Study Program.* © 1974 The MIT Press. Used by permission of C. Blakemore.

Fig. 25•1 Adapted from "An experimental critique of 'consolidation studies' and an alternative 'model-system' approach to the biophysiology of memory" by S. Chorover in M. R. Rosenzweig and E. L. Bennett (eds.) *The Neural Mechanisms of Learning and Memory,* 1976. © 1976 The M.I.T. Press. Used by permission of the publisher. **25•2** Adapted from "The memory defect in bilateral hippocampal lesions" by B. Milner in *Psychiatric Research Reports,* 1959, 11:43–52. © 1959 American Psychiatric Association. Used by permission of the publisher. **25•3** Adapted from "The organization of escape behavior in the crayfish" by J. J. Wine and F. B. Krasne in *Journal of Experimental Biology,* 1972, 56:1–18. © 1972 Cambridge University Press; and from "Habituation and inhibition of the crayfish lateral giant fibre escape response" by J. J. Wine, F. B. Krasne, and L. Chen in *Journal of Experimental Biology,* 1975, 62:771–82. © 1975 Cambridge University Press. Used by permission of the publisher. **25•4** Adapted from "A dual-process theory of habituation: Neural mechanisms" by P. M. Groves and R. F. Thompson in H. V. S. Peeke and M. J. Herz (eds.) *Habituation; II. Electrophysiological Substrates,* 1973. © 1973 Academic Press, Inc. Used by permission of the publisher and P. M. Groves. **25•5** Adapted from "Switchboard versus Statistical Theories of Learning and Memory" by E. R. John in *Science,* 177(8 September 1972):850–64. Copyright 1972 by the American Association for the Advancement of Science. Used by permission of the publisher and author. **25•6** From INTRODUCTION TO PHYSIOLOGICAL PSYCHOLOGY by Richard F. Thompson, Fig. 3.4 (p. 73). Harper & Row, 1975. By permission of the publisher; and adapted from "Language following surgical disconnection of the hemispheres" by R. W. Sperry and M. S. Gazzaniga in F. L. Darley (ed.) *Brain Mechanisms Underlying Speech and Language,* 1967. © 1967 Academic Press, Inc. Used by permission of the publisher and editor. **25•8** Adapted from *Speech and Brain Mechanisms* by Wilder Penfield and Lamar Roberts. © 1959 Princeton University Press. Used by permission of the publisher. **25•9** Adapted from "Language production: electroencephalographic localization in the normal human brain" by D. McAdam and H. Whitaker in *Science,* 172(30 April 1971):499–502. Copyright 1971 by the American Association for the Advancement of Science. Used by permission of the publisher and D. McAdam. **25•10** Adapted from "The electroencephalogram: Human recordings" by Janis Stevens in R. F. Thompson and M. Patterson (eds.) *Bioelectric Recording Techniques,* 1974. © 1974 Academic Press, Inc. Used by permission of the publisher and R. F. Thompson. **25•11** Adapted from "Cyclic variations in EEG during sleep and their relation to eye movements, body motility, and dreaming" by W. Dement and N. Kleitman in *Electroencephalography and Clinical Neurology,* 1957, 9:673–90. © 1957 Elsevier/North-Holland Biomedical Press. Used by permission of the publisher and W. Dement. **25•12** Adapted from "Ontogenetic development of the human sleep-dream cycle" by H. P. Roffwarg, J. N. Mouzio, and W. C. Dement in *Science,* 152(29 April 1966):604–19. Copyright 1966 by The American Association for the Advancement of Science. Used by permission of the publisher and H. P. Roffwarg. **25•13** From Homans, John. A TEXTBOOK OF SURGERY, 6th Ed., 1945. Courtesy of Charles C. Thomas, Publisher, Springfield, Illinois. **25•15** Adapted from an original painting by Frank H. Netter, M.D. for THE CIBA COLLECTION OF MEDICAL ILLUSTRATIONS published by CIBA-GEIGY Corporation.

References

Text references are indicated by the boldface numbers

Abelson, R. P., and Miller, J. C. 1967. Negative persuasion via personal insult. *Journal of Experimental Social Psychology* 3:321–33. **646**

Adams, M. S., and Neel, J. V. 1967. Children of incest. *Pediatrics* 40:55–62. **769.**

Adler, A. 1917. *Study of organ inferiority and its physical compensation.* New York: Nervous and Mental Diseases Publishing. **541**

Adler, A. 1927. *Practice and theory of individual psychology.* New York: Harcourt Brace Jovanovich. **541**

Adler, A. 1929, 1957. *The science of living.* New York: Greenberg. **561**

Adorno, T. W.; Frenkel-Brunswik, E.; Levinson, D. J.; and Sanford, R. N. 1950. *The authoritarian personality: Studies in prejudice.* New York: Harper & Row. **682**

Aghajanian, G. K., and Bloom, F. E. 1967. The formation of synaptic junctions in developing rat brain: A quantitative electron microscopic study. *Brain Research* 6:716–27. **795**

Aguilera, C. C.; Messick, J. M.; and Farrell, M. S. 1970. *Crisis intervention: Theory and methodology.* St. Louis: Mosby. **566, 567, 595**

Ahammer, I. M., and Baltes, P. B. 1972. Objective versus perceived age differences in personality: How do adolescents, adults, and older people view themselves and each other? *Journal of Gerontology* 27:46–51. **163**

Ainsworth, M. D. S. 1972. Attachment and dependency: A comparison. In J. Gewirtz (ed.), *Attachment and dependency.* Washington, D.C.; Winston. **60**

Ainsworth, M. D. S.; Bell, S. M. V.; and Slayton, D. J. 1971. Individual differences in strange situation behavior of one-year-olds. In H. R. Schaffer (ed.), *The origins of human social relations.* London: Academic Press. **118**

Ainsworth, M. D. S. and Wittig, B. A. 1969. Attachment and exploratory behavior of one-year-olds in a strange situation. In B. M. Fors (ed.), *Determinants of infant behavior,* vol. 4. London: Methuen. **118**

Alexander, F. 1950. *Psychosomatic medicine: Its principles and applications.* New York: W. W. Norton. **511, 537**

Allport, G. W. 1966. Traits revisited. *American Psychologist* 21:1–10. **417**

American Psychiatric Association. 1968. *Diagnostic and statistical manual of mental disorders* (DSM 11). Washington, D.C.: American Psychiatric Association. **503, 509, 512, 513, 516, 523, 524**

American Psychological Association. 1973. *Ethical principles in the conduct of research with human participants.* Washington, D.C.: American Psychological Association. **644**

Ames, A. Jr. 1955. An interpretative manual for the demonstration in the psychology research center. Princeton: Princeton University Press. **266**

Ames, L. B. 1937. The sequential patterning of prone progression in the human infant. *Genetic Psychology Monographs* 19:409–60. **78, 79**

Amir, M. 1972. The role of the victim in sex offenses. In H. L. P. Resnick and M. E. Wolfgang (eds.), *Sexual behaviors: Social, clinical, and legal aspects.* Boston: Little, Brown. Pp. 121–67. **531**

Amoore, J. G. 1970. *Molecular basis of odor.* Springfield, Ill.: Charles C. Thomas. **232**

Amsel, A. 1958. The role of frustrative non-reward in non-continuous reward situations. *Psychological Bulletin* 55:102–19. **494**

Amsel, A., and Hancock, W. 1957. Motivational properties of frustration: III. Relation of frustration effect to antedating goal factors. *Journal of Experimental Psychology* 53:126–31. **494, 495**

Anderson, J., and Bower, G. H. 1973. *Human associative memory.* New York: Halsted Press. **380**

Ansbacher, H. L., and Ansbacher, R. R., eds. 1956. *The individual psychology of Alfred Adler.* New York: Harper & Row. **560**

Apgar, V. 1953. A proposal for a new method of evaluation of the newborn infant. *Anesthesia and Analgesia* 32:260–67. **857**

Ardrey, R. 1966. *The territorial imperative.* New York: Atheneum. **708**

Arenberg, D. 1968. Concept problem solving in young and old adults. *Journal of Gerontology* 18:165–68. **155**

Arkoff, A. 1957. Resolution of approach-approach and avoidance-avoidance conflicts. *Journal of Abnormal and Social Psychology* 55:402–404. **482**

Aronson, E., and Mills, J. 1959. The effect of severity of initiation on liking for a group. *Journal of Abnormal and Social Psychology* 59:177–81. **401**

Asch, S. E. 1946. Forming impressions of personality. *Journal of Abnormal and Social Psychology* 41:258–90. **605, 613**

Asch, S. E. 1952. *Social psychology.* Englewood Cliffs, N.J.: Prentice-Hall. **679**

Asch, S. E. 1956. Studies of independence and conformity: I. A minority of one against a unanimous majority. *Psychological Monographs* 70 (9, Whole No. 416). **676**

Astor, G. 1974. The charge is rape. Chicago: Playboy Press. **529, 530**

Atkinson, J. W. 1964. *An introduction to motivation.* Princeton, N.J.: Van Nostrand. **405**

Atthowe, J. M., Jr., and Krasner, L. 1968. A preliminary report on the application of contingent reinforcement procedures (token economy) on a "chronic" psychiatric ward. *Journal of Abnormal Psychology* 73:37–43. **574**

Ayllón, T., and Azrin, N. H. 1965. The measurement and reinforcement of behavior of psychotics. *Journal of the Experimental Analysis of Behavior* 8:357–83. **433, 573**

Axelrod, J. 1974. Neurotransmitters. *Scientific American* 230 (6): 58–71. **810**

Babrick, H. P.; Babrick, P. O.; and Wittlinger, R. P. 1975. Fifty years of memory for names and faces: A cross-sectional approach. *Journal of Experimental Psychology; General* 104: 54–75. **318**

Bach, G. R. 1946. Father-fantasies and father-typing in father-separated children. *Child Development* 17:63–80. **123, 124**

Bach, G. R. 1969. The marathon group: Intensive practice of intimate interaction. In H. M. Ruitenbeek (ed.), *Group therapy today: Styles, methods and techniques.* Chicago: Aldine. Pp. 301–309. **569**

Bachman, J. G. 1970. *Youth in transition.* Ann Arbor: Institute for Social Research, University of Michigan. **540**

Back, K. W. 1951. Influence through social communication. *Journal of Abnormal and Social Psychology* 46:9–23. **683**

Baer, P. E. 1972. Cognitive changes in aging. In C. M. Gaitz (ed.), *Aging and the brain.* New York: Plenum Press. **161**

Baldwin, A. L.; Kalhorn, J.; and Breese, F. H. 1945. Patterns of parent behavior. *Psychological Monographs* 58 (3, Whole No. 268). **119, 120, 540**

Baldwin, A. L.; Kalhorn, J.; and Breese, F. H. 1949. The appraisal of parent behavior. *Psychological Monographs* 63 (4, Whole No. 299). **119, 540**

Baltes, P. B.; Schaie, K. W.; and Nardi, A. H. 1971. Age and experimental mortality in a seven-year longitudinal study of cognitive behavior. *Developmental Psychology* 5:18–26. **154**

Bandura, A. 1965. Influence of model's reinforcement contingencies on the acquisition of imitative responses. *Journal of Personality and Social Psychology* 1:589–95. **135, 639**

Bandura, A. 1969a. *Principles of behavior modification.* New York: Holt, Rinehart & Winston. **134, 574**

Bandura, A. 1969b. Social learning theory of identificatory processes. In D. Goslin (ed.), *Handbook of socialization theory and research.* Chicago: Rand McNally. Pp. 213–62. **54, 134**

Bandura. A. 1973. *Aggression: A social learning analysis.* Englewood Cliffs, N.J.: Prentice-Hall. **535, 540, 639**

Bandura, A. 1974. Behavior theory and the models of man. *American Psychologist* 29:859–69. **574**

Bandura, A. and Menlove, F. L. 1968. Factors determining vicarious extinction of avoidance behavior through symbolic modeling. *Journal of Personality and Social Psychology* 8:99–108. **574**

Bandura, A.; Ross, D.; and Ross, S. A. 1961. Transmission of aggression through imitation of aggressive models. *Journal of Abnormal and Social Psychology* 63:575–82. **639**

Bandura, A., and Walters, R. H. 1963. *Social learning and personality development.* New York: Holt, Rinehart & Winston. **134, 574**

Bannister, D., and Fransella, F. 1971. *Inquiring man.* Baltimore: Penguin Books. **467**

Barber, T. X. 1974. *Hypnotic phenomena.* Morristown, N.J.: General Learning Press. **575**

Barker, R. C.; Dembo, T.; and Lewin, K. 1943. Frustration and regression. In R. G. Barker, J. S. Kounin, and H. F. Wright (eds.), *Child behavior and development.* New York: McGraw-Hill. Pp. 441–58. **493**

Barnes, J. M., and Underwood, B. J. 1959. Fate of first-list associations in transfer theory. *Journal of Experimental Psychology* 58:97–105. **358**

Baron, R. S., and Roper, G. 1976. Reaffirmation of social comparison views of choice shifts: Averaging and extremity effects in an autokinetic situation. *Journal of Personality and Social Psychology* 33:521–30. **693**

Barron, F. 1957. Originality in relation to personality and intellect. *Journal of Personality* 25:730–42. **366**

Barron, F. 1965. The psychology of creativity. In *New Directions in Psychology,* vol. II. New York: Holt, Rinehart & Winston. **366**

Barten, H. H. 1969. The coming age of the brief psychotherapies. In L. Bellak and H. H. Barten (eds.), *Progress in community mental health,* vol. 1. New York: Grune & Stratton. Pp. 93–122. **566**

Bartlett, F. C. 1932. *Remembering: A study in experimental and social psychology.* New York: Cambridge University Press. **312**

Baumrind, D. 1964. Some thoughts on ethics of research: After reading Milgram's "Behavioral Study of Obedience." *American Psychologist* 19:421–23. **644**

Bayley, N. 1935. The development of motor abilities during the first three years. *Monographs of the Society for Research in Child Development* (No. 1). **78, 80**

Bayley, N. 1969. *Bayley scales of infant development: Brith to two years.* New York: Psychological Corporation. **99**

Beach, F. A. 1950. The snark was a boojum. *American Psychologist* 5:115–24. **719**

Beach, F. A. 1955. The descent of instinct. *Psychological Review* 62:401–10. **393, 722, 723**

Beach, F. A. 1958. Neural and chemical regulation of behavior. In H. F. Harlow and C. N. Wolsey (eds.), *Biological and biochemical basis of behavior.* Madison: University of Wisconsin Press. **136**

Beasley, W. C. 1931. Discriminations based on varying the relative amplitudes of four frequencies in combination. In W. L. Valentine (ed.), *Readings in experimental psychology.* New York: Harper & Row. Pp. 350–54. **221**

Beaumont, W. 1833 (1902). *Experiments and observations on the gastric juice and the physiology of digestion.* New York: Dover. **511**

Becker, W. C. 1964. Consequences of different kinds of parental discipline. In M. L. Hoffman and L. W. Hoffman (eds.), *Review of child development research,* vol. 1. New York: Russell Sage Foundation. pp. 169–208. **120, 121**

Beckman, L. J. 1970. Effects of students' performance on teachers' and observers' attributions of causality. *Journal of Educational Psychology* 61:76–82. **410, 624**

Beers, C. W. 1908 (1948). *A mind that found itself.* New York: Doubleday. **589**

Beidler, L. M. 1961. Biophysical approaches to taste. *American Scientist* 49:421–31. **231**

Békésy, G. von. 1960. *Experiments in hearing.* New York: McGraw-Hill. **223**

Békésy, G. von. 1964. Sweetness produced electrically on the tongue and its relation to taste theories. *Journal of Applied Physiology* 19:1105–13. **231**

Békésy, G. von. 1966. Taste theories and the chemical stimulation of single papillae. *Journal of Applied Physiology* 21:1–9. **231**

Bem, D. J. 1967. Self-perception: An alternative interpretation of cognitive dissonance phenomena. *Psychological Review* 74:183–200. **625**

Bem, D. J. 1972. Self-perception theory. In L. Berkowitz (ed.), *Advances in experimental social psychology,* vol. 6. New York: Academic Press. **390, 625**

Bem, D. J., and Allen, A. 1974. On predicting some of the people some of the time. *Psychological Review* 82:506–20. **452**

Bem, S. L., and Bem, D. J. 1970. Case study of a nonconscious ideology: Training the woman to know her place. In D. J. Bem (ed.), *Beliefs, attitudes, and human affairs.* Monterey, Calif.: Brooks/Cole. **696**

Bem, S. L., and Lenney, E. 1976. Sex typing and the avoidance of cross-sex behavior. *Journal of Personality and Social Psychology* 33:48–54. **610**

Benedict, R. 1954. Continuities and discontinuities in cultural conditioning. In W. E. Martin and C. B. Stendler (eds.), *Readings in child development.* New York: Harcourt Brace. **143**

Bennett, E. B. 1955. Discussion, decision, commitment, and consensus in group decision. *Human Relations* 8:251–73. **688**

Benson, H.; Rosner, B. A.; Marzetta, B. R.; and Klemchuk, H. M. 1975. Decreased blood pressure in pharmacologically treated hypertensive patients who regularly elicited the relaxation response. In L. V. DiCara, T. X. Barber, J. Kamiya, N. E. Miller, D. Shapiro, and J. Stoyva (eds.), *Biofeedback and self-control: 1974.* Chicago: Aldine. pp. 341–50. **577**

Berger, H. 1929. Uber das Electrenkephalogramm des Menschen. *Archiv fur Psychiatrie und Nervenkrankheiten* 87:527–70. **804**

Bergin, A. E. 1971. The evaluation of therapeutic outcomes. In A. E. Bergin and S. L. Garfield (eds.), *Handbook of psychotherapy and behavior change: An empirical analysis.* New York: Wiley. Pp. 217–70. **586**

Berko, J. 1958. The child's learning of English morphology. *Word* 14:150–77. **95, 96**

Berkowitz, L., and Daniels, L. R. 1964. Affecting the salience of the social responsibility norm: Effects of past help on the response to dependency relationships. *Journal of Abnormal and Social Psychology* 68:275–81. **652**

Berlyne, D. E. 1960. *Conflict, arousal, and curiosity.* New York: McGraw-Hill. **399**

Bettelheim, B., and Janowitz, M. 1950. *Dynamics of prejudice.* New York: Harper & Row. **491, 492**

Bettelheim, B., and Janowitz, M. 1964. *Social change and prejudice.* New York: Free Press. **492**

Binet, A., and Simon, T. 1908, 1916. *The development of intelligence in children.* Vineland, N.J.: Publication of the Training School. **99**

Birren, J. E. 1964. *The psychology of aging.* Englewood Cliffs, N.J.: Prentice-Hall. **57**

Birren, J. E., and Botwinick, J. 1955. Age differences in finger, jaw, and foot reaction time to auditory stimuli. *Journal of Gerontology* 10:429–32. **157**

Birren, J. E., and Morris, D. F. 1961. Analysis of the WAIS subtests in relation to age and education. *Journal of Gerontology* 16:363–39. **161**

Bitterman, M. E. 1965. Phyletic differences in learning. *American Psychologist* 20:396–410. **747, 748, 749**

Bitterman, M. E. 1975. The comparative analysis of learning. *Science* 188: 699–709. **749**

Blakemore, C. 1974. Developmental factors in the formation of feature extracting neurons. In F. O. Schmitt and F. G. Worden (eds.), *The neurosciences: Third study program.* Cambridge, Mass.: MIT Press. **795, 796**

Blascovich, J.; Ginsburg, G. P.; and Veach, T. L. 1975. A pluralistic explanation of choice shifts on the risk dimension. *Journal of Personality and Social Psychology* 31:422–29. **692**

Block, J. 1961. *The Q-sort method in personality assessment and psychiatric research.* Springfield, Ill.: Charles C. Thomas. **470**

Blodgett, H. C. 1929. The effects of the introduction of reward upon the maze performance of rats. *University of California Publications in Psychology* 4:113–34. **324**

Bloom, L. 1970. *Language development: Form and function in emerging grammars.* Cambridge, Mass.: MIT Press. **98, 99**

Bogen, J. E. 1969. The other side of the brain; an appositional mind. *Bulletin of the Los Angeles Neurological Society* 34:135–62. **843**

Bolles, R. C. 1970. Species-specific defense reactions and avoidance learning. *Psychological Review* 77:32–48. **725**

Bolles, R. C. 1972. The avoidance learning problem. In G. H. Bower (ed.), *The psychology of learning and motivation,* vol. 6. New York: Academic Press. **338**

Bonar, H. S. 1942. High school pupils list their anxieties. *School Review* 50:512–15. **151**

Bonner, D. M. 1961. *Heredity.* Englewood Cliffs, N.J.: Prentice-Hall. **762**

Boring, E. G. 1957. *A history of experimental psychology.* 2d ed. New York: Appleton-Century-Crofts. **13, 14**

Börnstein, W. S. 1940. Cortical representation of taste in man and monkey: II. The localization of the cortical taste area in man and a method of measuring impairment of taste in man. *Yale Journal of Biological Medicine* 13:133–56. **230**

Botwinick, J. 1971. Sensory-set factors in age difference in reaction time. *Journal of Genetic Psychology* 119:241–49. **157**

Botwinick, J. 1973. *Aging and behavior.* New York: Springer. **155, 158, 159, 175**

Botwinick, J., and Storandt, M. 1973. The role of speed of performance in cognitive functioning. Unpublished. **158**

Bower, G. H.; Clark, M. C.; Lesgold, A. M.; and Winzenz, D. 1969. Hierarchical retrieval schemes in the recall of categorized word lists. *Journal of Verbal Learning and Verbal Behavior* 8:323–43. **303, 304**

Bower, G. H., and Holyoak, K. 1973. Encoding and recognition memory for natural sounds. *Journal of Experimental Psychology* 101:360–66. **318**

Bower, G. H., and Winzenz, D. 1969. Group structure, coding and memory for digit series. *Journal of Experimental Psychology* 80, part 2:1–17. **303**

Bower, T. G. R. 1964. Discrimination of depth in premotor infants. *Psychonomic Science* 1:368. **264**

Bower, T. G. R. 1975. Infant perception of the third dimension and object concept development. In L. B. Cohen and P. Salapatek (eds.), *Infant perception: From sensation to cognition* vol. 2. New York: Academic Press. Pp. 33–49. **263**

Bowlby, J. 1958. The nature of the child's tie to his mother. *International Journal of Psychoanalysis* 39:35. **114**

Bowlby, J. 1969. *Attachment and loss: Attachment.* New York: Basic Books. **114**

Bowlby, J. 1973. *Attachment and loss: Separation.* New York: Basic Books. **114, 118**

Brady, J. V.; Porter, R. W.; Conrad, D. G.; and Mason, J. W. 1958. Avoidance behavior and the development of gastroduodenal ulcers. *Journal of Experimental Analysis of Behavior* 1:69–72. **511**

Braginsky, B. M.; Braginsky, D. D.; and Ring, K. 1969. *Methods of madness: The mental hospital as a last resort.* New York: Holt, Rinehart & Winston. **592**

Braine, M. D. S. 1963. The ontogeny of English phrase structure: The first phrase. *Language* 39:1–14. **98**

Brehm, J. W. 1962. Motivational effects of cognitive dissonance. In M. R. Jones (ed.), *Nebraska symposium on motivation,* vol. 10. Lincoln: University of Nebraska Press. pp. 51–77. **401**

Brehm, J. W. 1966. *A theory of psychological reactance.* New York: Academic Press. **652**

Brehm, J. W., and Cole, A. H. 1966. Effect of favor which reduces freedom. *Journal of Personality and Psychology* 3:420–26. **652**

Breland, K., and Breland, M. 1961. The misbehavior of organisms. *American Psychologist* 16:681–84. **338**

Bremer, F. 1935. Cerveau isolé et physiologie du sommeil. *Société de biologie comptes rendus* 118:1235–41. **850**

Breuer, J., and Freud, S. 1895 (1955). *Studien uber Hysterie.* London: Hogarth. **424, 575**

Brian, C. R., and Goodenough, F. L. 1929. The relative potency of color and form perception at various ages. *Journal of Experimental Psychology* 12:197–213. **82**

Bridges, C. G., and Brehme, K. 1944. *The mutations of Drosophila melanogaster.* Carnegie Institution Publication No. 552. Washington, D.C.: Carnegie Institution. **759**

Brigham, J. C. 1971. Ethnic stereotypes. *Psychological Bulletin* 76:15–38. **612**

Brink, F. 1951. Synaptic mechanisms. In S. S. Stevens, (ed.), *Handbook of experimental psychology.* New York: Wiley. pp. 50–93. **720**

Brogden, W. J. 1939. Sensory preconditioning. *Journal of Experimental Psychology* 25:323–32. **331**

Bronfenbrenner, U. 1962. Soviet studies of personality development and socialization. In R. Bauer (ed.), *Some views of Soviet psychology.* Washington, D.C.: American Psychological Association. **691**

Bronshtein, A. J., and Petrova, E. P. 1952. Issledovanie zvukovogo analizatora novorozhdennykh i detei rannego grudnogo vozrasta (An investigation of the auditory analysis in neonates and young infants) 2:333–43. Translated and reprinted in Y. Brackbill and G. G. Thompson (eds.), *Behavior in infancy and early childhood: A book of readings.* 1967. New York: Free Press. **76, 77**

Broverman, I. K.; Vogel, S. R.; Broverman, D. K.; Clarkson, F. E.; and Rosenkrantz, P. S. 1972. Sex-role stereotypes: A current appraisal. *Journal of Social Issues* 28:63. **139**

Broverman, I. K., et al. 1970. Sex-role stereotypes and clinical judgments of mental health. *Journal of Consulting and Clinical Psychology* 34:1–7. **695**

Brown, J. S. 1957. Principles of intrapersonal conflict. *Conflict Resolution* 1:135–54. **478**

Brown, R. 1970. The first sentences of child and chimpanzee. In R. Brown (ed.), *Psycholinguistics: Selected papers.* New York: Free Press. **95, 97**

Brown, R. 1973. *A first language, the early stages.* Cambridge: Harvard University Press. **98**

Brown, R., and Bellugi, U. 1964. Three processes in the acquisition of syntax. *Harvard Educational Review* 34:133–51. **98**

Brown, R., and Herrnstein, R. J. 1975. *Psychology.* Boston: Little, Brown. **221, 222, 224, 251**

Brown, R., and McNeill, D. 1966. The tip of the tongue phenomenon. *Journal of Verbal Learning and Verbal Behavior* 5:325–37. **311**

Bruch, H. 1970. Eating disorders in adolescence. In J. Zubin and A. M. Freedman (eds.), *The psychopathology of adolescence.* New York: Grune & Stratton. pp. 181–97. **523**

Bruell, J. H. 1963. Additive inheritance of serum cholesterol level in mice. *Science* 142:1664–65. **770**

Bruell, J. H. 1964a. Inheritance of behavioral and physiological characters of mice and the problem of heterosis. *American Zoologist* 4:125–38. **769, 770, 771, 778**

Bruell, J. H. 1964b. Heterotic inheritance of wheelrunning in mice. *Journal of Comparative and Physiological Psychology* 58:159–63. **770**

Bruner, J. S. 1964. The course of cognitive growth. *American Psychologist* 19:1–15. **49**

Bruner, J. S. 1968. *Toward a theory of instruction.* New York: W. W. Norton. **634**

Bruner, J. S.; Goodnow, J. J.; and Austin, G. A. 1956. *A study of thinking.* New York: Wiley. **368**

Bruner, J. S., and Postman, L. 1949. On the perception of incongruity: A paradigm. *Journal of Personality* 18:206–23. **266**

Bruno, F. J. 1972. *The story of psychology.* New York: Holt, Rinehart & Winston. **13, 16**

Bryne, D. 1974. *An introduction to personality.* 2d ed. Englewood Cliffs, N.J.: Prentice-Hall. **470**

Buckout, R. 1974. Eyewitness testimony. *Scientific American* 231:23–31. **606**

Budzynski, T.; Stoyva, J.; and Adler, C. 1970. Feedback-induced muscle relaxation: Application to tension headache. *Journal of Behavior Therapy and Experimental Psychiatry* 1:205–11. **578**

Bunker, D. R. 1965. Individual applications of laboratory training. *Journal of Applied Behavioral Science* 1:131–48. **569**

Buss, A. H. 1966. *Psychopathology.* New York: Wiley. **501, 543**

Busse, E. W., and Pfeiffer, E. 1969. Functional psychiatric disorders in old age. In E. W. Busse and E. Pfeiffer (eds.), *Behavior adaptation in later life.* Boston: Little, Brown. **175**

Busse, E. W., and Reckless, J. B. 1961. Psychiatric management of the aged. *Journal of the American Medical Association* 175:645–48. **175**

Cameron, N. 1963. *Personality development and psychopathology: A dynamic approach.* Boston: Houghton Mifflin. **526**

Campbell, E. Q. 1969. Adolescent socialization. In D. A. Goslin (ed.), *Handbook of socialization theory and research.* Chicago: Rand McNally. **143**

Cannon, W. B. 1929. *Bodily changes in pain, hunger, fear, and rage.* 2d ed. New York: Appleton. **511**

Capretta, P. J. 1967. *A history of psychology in outline from its origins to the present.* New York: Delta. **10**

Carey, S. T., and Lockhart, R. S. 1973. Encoding differences in recognition and recall. *Memory and Cognition* 1:297–300. **302**

Carlsmith, J. M.; Collins, B. E.; and Helmreich, R. L. 1966. Studies in forced compliance: I. The effect of pressure for compliance on attitude change produced by face-to-face role playing and anonymous essay writing. *Journal of Personality and Social Psychology* 4:1–13. **661**

Carlsmith, J. M., and Gross, A. E. 1969. Some effects of guilt on compliance. *Journal of Personality and Social Psychology* 11:232–39. **653**

Carlson, E. R. 1956. Attitude change through modification of attitude structure. *Journal of Abnormal and Social Psychology* 52:256–61. **635**

Carlson, J. A., and Davis, C. M. 1971. Cultural values and the risky shift: A cross-cultural test in Uganda and the United States. *Journal of Personality and Social Psychology* 20:392–99. **692**

Carmichael, L. 1926. The developmen of behavior in vertebrates experimentally removed from the influence of external stimulation. *Psychological Review* 33:51–58. **58**

Carmichael, L. H.; Hogan, P.; and Walter, A. A. 1932. An experimental study of the effect of language on the reproduction of visually perceived forms. *Journal of Experimental Psychology* 15:78–86. **313**

Carnegie, D. 1936. *How to win friends and influence people.* New York: Simon & Schuster. **650**

Carnegie, D. 1937. *Public speaking and influencing men in business.* New York: Association Press. **306**

Carson, R. C. 1969. *Interaction concepts of personality.* Chicago: Aldine. **503**

Cartwright, D. 1974. *Introduction to personality.* Chicago: Rand McNally. **468**

Cates, J. 1970. Psychology's manpower: Report on the national register of scientific and technical personnel. *American Psycholgist* 25:254–63. **9**

Cattell, P. 1940. *The measurement of intelligence of infants and young children.* New York: Psychological Corporation. **99**

Cattell, R. B. 1963. Theory of fluid and crystallized intelligence: A critical experiment. *Journal of Educational Psychology* 54: 1–22. **161**

Cerletti, U., and Bini, L. 1938. L'electroshock. *Archives General Neurologica Psichiatrie Psicoanalyt* 19:266–75. **580**

Champney, H. 1941. The variables of parent behavior. *Child Development* 12:131–66. **119**

Chomsky, N. A. 1957. *Syntactic structures.* The Hague: Mouton. **95, 98**

Chomsky, N. A. 1968. *Language and mind.* New York: Harcourt Brace Jovanovich. **98**

Chopra, I. C., and Chopra, R. N. 1957. The use of the cannabis drugs in India. *U.N. Bulletin on Narcotics* 9(1):4–29. **583**

Chopra, R. N.; Chopra, G. S.; and Chopra, I. C. 1942. Cannabis sativa in relation to mental diseases and crime in India. *Indian Journal of Medical Research* 30(1): 155–71. **583**

Chorover, S. 1976. An experimental critique of "consolidation studies" and an alternative "model-system" approach to the biophysiology of memory. In M. R. Rosenzweig and E. L. Bennett (eds.), *The neural mechanisms of learning and memory.* Cambridge, Mass.: MIT Press. **832**

Christozov, C. 1965. L'Aspect marocain de l'intoxication cannabique d'âpres des études sur des malades mentaux chroniques: Premiére partie et deuxième partie. *Maroc Medical* 44:630–42, 866–900. **583**

Clark, K. B. 1963. Educational stimulation of racially disadvantaged children. In A. H. Passow (ed.), *Education in depressed areas.* New York: Bureau of Publications, Teachers College, Columbia University. **614**

Clark, L. D.; Hughes, R.; and Nakashima, E. N. 1970. Behavioral effects of marihuana: Experimental studies. *Archives of General Psychiatry* 23:193–98. **583**

Clark, W. V. T. 1943. *The Ox Bow incident.* New York: New American Library. **699**

Cleaver. E. 1968. *Soul on ice.* New York: Dell Publishing. **529**

Cleckley, H. 1959. Psychopathic states. In B. Arieti (ed.), *American handbook of psychiatry.* New York: Basic Books. pp. 567–88. **524**

Cleckley, H. 1964. *The mask of sanity.* 4th ed. St. Louis: Mosby. **524**

Clemes, S. 1964. Repression and hypnotic amnesia. *Journal of Abnormal and Social Psychology* 69:62–69. **490**

Coch, L., and French, J. R. P., Jr. 1948. Overcoming resistance to change. *Human relations* 1:512–32. **688**

Cohen, B. H. 1966. The some-or-none characteristics of coding behavior. *Journal of Verbal Learning and Verbal Behavior* 5:182–87. **303**

Cole, J. O., and Davis, J. M. 1972. Antidepressant drugs. In A. M. Freedman and H. I. Kaplan (eds.), *Treating mental illness: Aspects of modern therapy.* New York: Atheneum. pp. 310–35. **583**

Coleman, J. C. 1976. *Abnormal psychology and modern life,* 5th ed. Glenview, Ill.: Scott, Foresman. **516, 533**

Collins, A. M. and Quillian, M. R. 1969. Retrieval time from semantic memory. *Journal of Verbal Learning and Verbal Behavior* 8:240–47. **379**

Collins, B. E., ed. 1973. *Public and private conformity: Competing explanations by improvisation, cognitive dissonance, and attribution theories.* Andover, Mass.: Warner Modular Publications. **661**

Collins, B. E., and Raven, B. H. 1969. Group structure: Attraction, coalitions, communication, and power. In G. Lindzey and E. Aronson (eds.), *The handbook of social psychology,* 2d ed., vol. 4. Reading, Mass.: Addison-Wesley. **683, 689**

Collins, R. L. 1964. Inheritance of avoidance conditioning in mice: A diallele study. *Science* 143:1188–90. **770**

Collins, R. L., and Fuller, J. L. 1968. Audiogenic seizure prone (asp)—a gene affecting behavior in linkage group VIII of the mouse. *Science* 162:1137–39. **764, 771**

Colombotos, J. 1969. Physicians and medicare: A before-after study of the effects of legislation on attitudes. *American Sociological Review* 34:318–34. **660**

Conger, J. J. 1973. *Adolescence and youth.* New York: Harper & Row. **147, 148**

Cooley, C. H. 1902. *Human nature and the social order.* New York: Scribner. **624**

Cooper, R. M., and Zubek, J. P. 1958. Effects of enriched and restricted early environments on the learning ability of bright and dull rats. *Canadian Journal of Psychology* 12:159–64. **779**

Coopersmith, S. 1967. *The antecedents of self-esteem.* San Francisco: W. H. Freeman. **146**

Correnti, S. 1965. A comparison of behaviorism and psychoanalysis with existentialism. *Journal of Existentialism* 5:379–88. **15**

Corso, J. F. 1967. *The experimental psychology of sensory behavior.* New York: Holt, Rinehart & Winston. **219**

Costanzo, P. R. 1970. Conformity development as a function of self-blame. *Journal of Personality and Social Psychology* 14:366–74. **680**

Costrich, N.; Feinstein, J.; and Kidder, L. 1975. When stereotypes hurt: Three studies of penalties for sex-role reversals. *Journal of Experimental Social Psychology* 11:520–30. **610**

Craik, F. I. M. 1970. The fate of primary memory items in free recall. *Journal of Verbal Learning and Verbal Behavior* 9:143–48. **320**

Craik, F. I. M., and Lockhart, R. S. 1972. Levels of processing: A framework for memory research. *Journal of Verbal Learning and Verbal Behavior* 11:671–84. **309**

Craik, F. I. M., and Tulving, E. 1975. Depth of processing and retention of words in episodic memory. *Journal of Experimental Psychology: General* 104:268–94. **309**

Cratty, B. J. 1970. *Perceptual and motor development in infants and children.* New York: Macmillan. **793**

Creed, R. S.; Denny-Brown, E.; et al. 1972. *Reflex activity of the spinal cord.* New York: Oxford University Press. **235**

Cronbach, L. J., and Meehl, P. E. 1955. Construct validity in psychological tests. *Psychological Bulletin* 52:281–302. **453**

Crutchfield, R. S. 1955. Conformity and character. *American Psychologist* 10:191–99. **680**

Cullen, E. 1957. Adaptations in the kittiwake to cliff nesting. *Ibis.* 99:275–302. **745**

Cumming, E., and Henry, W. H. 1961. *Growing old.* New York: Basic Books. **57, 165**

Curtis, B. A.; Jacobson, S.; and Marcus, E. M. 1972. An introduction to the neurosciences. Philadelphia: W. B. Saunders. **805**

Cvetkovich, G., and Baumgardner, S. R. 1973. Attitude polarization: The relative influence of discussion group structure and reference group norms. *Journal of Personality and Social Psychology* 26:159–65. **693**

Darley, J. M., and Latané, B. 1968. Bystander intervention in emergencies: Diffusion of responsibility. *Journal of Personality and Social Psychology* 8:377–83. **697, 698**

Darwin, C. 1859 (1962). *Origin of species.* New York: Macmillan. **10, 710, 716 737, 771**

Darwin, C. 1871. *The descent of man and selection in relation to sex.* New York: Modern Library. **716, 771**

Darwin, C. 1872 (1965). *The expression of the emotions in man and animals.* Chicago: University of Chicago Press. **712, 716**

Darwin, C. 1877. A biographical sketch of an infant. *Mind* 7:285–94. **26, 58**

Dawson, H. 1974. *Basic human anatomy.* 2d ed. New York: Appleton-Century-Crofts. **788**

Deaux, K. 1976. *The behavior of men and women.* Monterey, Calif.: Brooks/Cole. **609**

de Charms, R., and Moeller, G. H. 1962. Values expressed in American children's readers: 1800–1950. *Journal of Abnormal and Social Psychology,* 64:136–42. **408**

Deci, E. L. 1975. *Intrinsic motivation.* New York: Plenum Press. **399**

Deese, J. 1962. On the structure of associative meaning. *Psychological Review* 69:161–75. **378**

Deese, J. 1970. *Psycholinguistics.* Boston: Allyn & Bacon. **375**

Delgado, J. M. R. 1952. Permanent implantation of multilead electrodes in the brain. *Yale Journal of Biological Medicine* 24:351–58. **585**

Delgado, J. M. R. 1961. Chronic implantation of intracerebral electrodes in animals. In D. E. Sheer (ed.), *Electrical stimulation of the brain.* Austin: University of Texas Press. pp. 25–36. **585**

Delgado, J. M. R.; Mark, V.; Sweet, W.; Ervin, F.; Weiss, G.; Bach-Rita, G.; and Hagiwara, R. 1968. Intracerebral radio stimulation and recording in completely free patients. *Journal of Nervous and Mental Disease* 147:329–40. **585**

Dement, W., and Kleitman, N. 1957. Cyclic variations in EEG during sleep and their relation to eye movements, body motility, and dreaming. *Electroencephalography and Clinical Neurology* 9:673–90. **848**

Deregowski, J. B. 1972. Pictorial perception and culture. *Scientific American* 227:82–88. **279, 281**

Deutsch, F., and Nadell, R. 1946. Psychosomatic aspects of dermatology with special consideration of allergic phenomena. *Nervous Child* 5:339–64. **510**

Deutsch, M. 1949. An experimental study of the effects of cooperation and competition upon group process. *Human Relations* 2:199–231 **689**

Deutsch, M., and Gerard, H. B. 1955. A study of normative and informational social influences upon individual judgment. *Journal of Abnormal and Social Psychology* 51:629–36. **678**

Deutsch, M., and Solomon, L. 1959. Reactions to evaluations by others as influenced by self-evaluations. *Sociometry* 22:93–112. **651**

Dewey, J. 1916. *Democracy and education.* New York: Macmillan. **634**

DiCaprio, N. S. 1974. *Personality theories: Guides to Living.* Philadelphia: W. B. Saunders. **443, 444, 445**

Dilger, W. C. 1962. The behavior of lovebirds. *Scientific American* 206:89–98. **767, 768**

Dion, K. L.; Baron, R. S.; and Miller, N. E. 1972. Why do groups make riskier decisions than individuals? In L. Berkowitz (ed.), *Advances in experimental social psychology,* vol. 5. New York: Academic Press. **692**

Ditchburn, R. W. 1955. Eye movements in relation to retinal action. *Optica Acta* 1:171–76. **209**

Dobbing, J., and Smart, J. L. 1974. Vulnerability of developing brain and behavior. *British Medical Bulletin* 30:164–68. **797**

Dohrenwend, B. P., and Dohrenwend, B. S. 1969. *Social status and psychological disorder: A causal inquiry.* New York: Wiley. **536**

Dollard, J., and Miller, N. E. 1950. *Personality and psychotherapy: An analysis in terms of learning, thinking, and culture.* New York: McGraw-Hill. **533**

Doniger, J. 1970. Is a halfway house therapeutic?—The Woodley House. In E. R. Sinett and A. D. Sachson (eds.), *Transitional facilities in the rehabilitation of the emotionally disturbed.* Lawrence: University of Kansas Press. pp. 63–71. **592**

Doppelt, J. E., and Wallace, W. L. 1955. Standardization of the Wechsler Adult Intelligence Scale for older persons. *Journal of Abnormal and Social Psychology* 51:312–30. **161**

Douvan, E., and Adelson, J. 1966. *The adolescent experience.* New York: Wiley. **144**

Dowling, J. E., and Boycott, B. B. 1966. Organization of the primate retina: Electron microscopy. *Proceedings of the Royal Society (London)* (Series B) 166:80–111. **198**

DuBois-Reymond, E. 1848–49. Untersuchungen über thierische Elektricität, vols. 1 and 2. Berlin: Reimer. **585**

Dukes. W. F. 1960. The snark revisited. *American Psychologist* 15:157. **719**

Duncker, K. 1945. On problem solving. *Psychological Monographs* 58 (Whole No. 270). **365**

Dunphy, D. C. 1963. The social structure of urban adolescent peer groups. *Sociometry* 26:230–46. **148**

Dusek, J. 1975. Do teachers bias children's learning? *Review of Educational Research* 45:661–84. **123**

Dzendolet, E., and Meiselman, H. L. 1967. Gustatory quality changes as a function of solution concentration. *Perception and Psychophysics* 2:29–33. **230**

Eaton, J. W., and Weil, R. J. 1955. *Culture and mental disorders: A comparative study of the Hutterites and other populations.* New York: Free Press. **536**

Ebbinghaus, H. 1885 (1964). *Memory.* New York: Dover. **297**

Egan, M. H., and Robinson, O. L. 1969. Home treatment of severely disturbed children and families. In A. J. Bindman and A. D. Spiegel (eds.), *Perspectives in community mental health.* Chicago: Aldine. pp. 538–44. **590**

Egbert, L.; Battit, G.; Welch, C.; and Bartlett, M. 1964. Reduction of postoperative pain by encouragement and instruction of patients. *New England Journal of Medicine* 270:825–27. **476, 477**

Ehrenwald, J. 1960. Neurosis in the family. *Archives of General Psychiatry* 3:232–42. **536**

Ehrman, L., and Parsons, P. A. 1976. *The genetics of behavior.* Sunderland, Mass.: Sinauer. **759, 764**

Eibl-Eibesfeldt, I. 1970. *Ethology: The biology of behavior.* New York: Holt, Rinehart & Winston. **712**

Eisdorfer, C.; Burse, E. W.; and Cohen, L. D. 1959. The WAIS performance of an aged sample: The relationship between verbal and performance IQs. *Journal of Gerontology* 14:197–201. **161**

Eisdorfer, C., and Wilkie, F. 1973. Intellectual change with advancing age. In L. F. Jarvik, C. Eisdorfer, and J. E. Blum (eds.), *Intellectual functioning in adults.* New York: Springer **161**

Eisenberg, R. B.; Coursin, D. B.; and Rupp, N. R. 1966. Habituation to an acoustic pattern as an index of differences among human neonates. *Journal of Auditory Research* 6:239–48. **76**

Ekman, P. 1971. Universals and cultural differences in facial expression of emotions. *Nebraska Symposium on Motivation* 19:207–83. **712**

Ekman, P., and Friesen, W. V. 1975. *Unmasking the face.* Englewood Cliffs, N.J.: Prentice-Hall. **712, 713**

Elder, G. H., Jr. 1962. Structural variations in the child-rearing relationship. *Sociometry* 25:241–62. **145, 146**

Elder. G. H., Jr. 1963. Parental power legitimation and its effect on the adolescent. *Sociometry* 26:50–65. **145, 147**

Elder, G. H., Jr. 1968. Parent-youth relations in cross-national perspective. *Social Science Quarterly* 49:216–28. **144, 145**

Elder, G. H., Jr. 1971. *Adolescent socialization and personality development.* Chicago: Rand McNally. **145**

Elias, M. F. 1969. Differences in spatial discrimination reversal learning for mice genetically selected for high brain weight and unselected controls. *Perceptual and Motor Skills* 28:707–12. **774**

Elkind, D. 1969. Developmental studies of figurative perception. In L. P. Lipsitt and H. W. Reese (eds.), *Advances in child development and behavior,* vol. 4. New York: Academic Press. **93**

Ellis, A. 1962. *Reason and emotion in psychotherapy.* New York: Lyle Stuart. **559**

Engen, T. 1961. Direct scaling of odor intensity. *Reports from the psychological laboratories, The University of Stockholm,* 106. **232**

Engen. T. 1964. Psychophysical scaling of odor intensity and quality. *Annual of the New York Academy of Science* 116:504–16. **232**

Engen. T.; Kuisma, T. E.; and Eimas, P. D. 1973. Short-term memory of odors. *Journal of Experimental Psychology* 99:222–25. **319**

Engel, T.; Lipsitt, L. P.; and Kaye, H. 1963. Olfactory responses and adaptation in the human neonate. *Journal of Comparative and Physiological Psychology* 56:73–77. **84**

Epstein, A. W. 1973. The relationship of altered brain states to sexual psycopathology. In J. Zubin and J. Money (eds.), *Contemporary sexual behavior: Critical issues in the 1970s.* Baltimore: Johns Hopkins University Press. Pp. 297–310. **544**

Epstein, S., and Fenz, W. D. 1965. Steepness of approach and avoidance gradients in humans as a function of experience: Theory and experiment. *Journal of Experimental Psychology* 70:1–12. **474, 476**

Erdelyi, M. H. 1974. A new look at the new look. *Psychological Review* 81:1–25. **273**

Erdelyi, M. H. 1976. Has Ebbinghaus decayed with time? Unpublished research. **290**

Erdelyi, M. H., and Becker, J. 1974. Hyperamnesia for pictures. Incremental memory for pictures but not for words in multiple recall trials. *Cognitive Psychology* 6:159–72. **290**

Erikson, E. H. 1950. *Childhood and society.* New York: W. W. Norton. **53, 162**

Erikson, E. H. 1959. Identity and the life cycle: Selected papers. *Psychological Issues Monograph Series I,* No. 1. New York: International Universities Press. **144**

Erikson, E. H. 1964. *Insight and responsibility.* New York: W. W. Norton. **555, 557**

Erikson, E. 1968. *Identity, youth, and crisis.* New York: W. W. Norton. **53**

Eriksson, K., and Pikkarainen, P. H. 1968. Differences between the sexes in voluntary alcohol consumption and liver ADH-activity in inbred strains of mice. *Metabolism* 17:1037–42. **776**

Erlenmeyer-Kimling, L., and Jarvik, L. F. 1963. Genetics and intelligence: A Review. *Science* 142:1477–79. **108**

Ervin, S. J., Jr. 1965. Why Senate hearings on psychological tests in government. *American Psychologist* 20:879–80. **471**

Estes, W. K. 1944. An experimental study of punishment. *Psychological Monographs* 57, No. 263. **122**

Evarts, E. V. 1973. Brain mechanisms in movement. *Scientific American* 229(1):96–103. **822, 823**

Eysenck, H. J. 1960. Classification and the problem of diagnosis. In H. J. Eysenck (ed.), *Handbook of abnormal psychology.* London: Pitman. Pp. 1–31. **503**

Eysenck, H. J., and Rachman, S. 1965. *The causes and cures of neurosis.* San Diego: Knapp. **571**

Fairweather, G. W., ed. 1964. *Social psychology in treating mental illness: An experimental approach.* New York: Wiley. **592**

Fairweather, G. W.; Sanders, D. H.; Maynard, H.; and Cressler, D. L. 1969. *Community life for the mentally ill: An alternative to institutional care.* Chicago: Aldine. **592**

Falconer, D. S. 1960. *Quantitative genetics.* New York: Ronald Press. **769**

Fanon, F. 1967. *Black skin, white masks.* New York: Grove Press. **566**

Fantz, R. L. 1961. The origin of form perception. *Scientific American* 204:66–72. **73, 74**

Frantz, R. L. 1963. Pattern vision in newborn infants. *Science* 140:296–97 **73, 74**

Faucheux, C., and Moscovici, S. 1967. Le style de comportement d'une minorité et son influence sur les réponses d'une majorité. *Bulletin du Centre d'Etudes et Recherches Psychologiques* 16:337–60. **684**

Feather, N. T., and Simon, J. G. 1975. Reactions to male and female success and failure in sex-linked occupations: Impressions of personality, causal attributions, and perceived likelihood of different consequences. *Journal of Personality and Social Psychology* 31:20–31. **609**

Fechner, G. 1860 (1966). *Elements of Psychophysics.* English edition edited by H. E. Adler, D. H. Howes, and E. G. Boring. New York: Holt, Rinehart & Winston. **189**

Ferracuti, F. 1972. Incest between father and daughter. In H. L. P. Resnick and M. E. Wolfgang (eds.), *Sexual behaviors: Social, clinical and legal aspects.* Boston: Little, Brown. Pp. 169–83. **527, 528**

Ferster, C. B. and Skinner, B. F. 1957. *Schedules of reinforcement.* New York: Appleton-Century-Crofts. **720**

Feshback, S. 1964. The function of aggression and the regulation of aggressive drive. *Psychological Review* 71:257–72. **405**

Festinger, L. 1950. Informal social communication. *Psychological Review* 57:271–92. **679**

Festinger, L. 1954. A theory of social comparison processes. *Human Relations* 2:117–40. **679, 683**

Festinger, L. 1957. *A theory of cognitive dissonance.* Evanston, Ill.: Row, Peterson. **400, 657, 658**

Festinger, L., and Carlsmith, J. M. 1959. Cognitive consequences of forced compliance. *Journal of Abnormal and Social Psychology* 58:203–10. **400, 625, 659**

Festinger, L.; Pepitone, A.; and Newcomb, T. 1952. Some consequences of de-individuation in a group. *Journal of Abnormal and Social Psychology* 47:382–39. **699**

Fiedler, F. E. 1950. A comparison of therapeutic relations in psychoanalytic nondirective and Adlerian therapy. *Journal of Consulting Psychology* 14: 436–55. **586**

Flavell, J. 1963. *The developmental psychology of Jean Piaget.* New York: Van Nostrand. **93, 127**

Flood, J. E., and Jarvik, M. E. 1976. Drug influences on learning and memory. In M. R. Rosenzweig and E. L. Bennett (eds.), *Neural mechanisms of learning and memory.* Cambridge, Mass.: MIT Press. **836**

Fortune, R. 1932. Incest. In *Encyclopedia of the social sciences,* vol. 7. New York: Macmillan. Pp. 620 ff. **528**

Frank, J. D. 1944. Experimental studies of personal pressure and resistance: I. Experimental production of resistance. *Journal of General Psychology* 30: 23–41. **654**

Frankl, V. E. 1962. *Man's search for meaning.* Boston: Beacon. **559**

Freedman, D. G. 1964. Smiling in blind infants and the issue of innate vs. acquired. *Journal of Child Psychology and Psychiatry* 5:171–84. **48, 712**

Freedman, J., and Haber, R. N. 1974. One reason why we rarely forget a face. *Bulletin of the Psychonomic Society* 3:107–109. **281**

Freedman, J. L., and Fraser, S. C. 1966. Compliance without pressure: The foot-in-the-door technique. *Journal of Personality and Social Psychology* 4:195–202. **654**

Freedman, J. L.; Wallington, S. A.; and Bless, E. 1967. Compliance without pressure: The effect of guilt. *Journal of Personality and Social Psychology* 7:177–24. **645, 653**

Freeman, S.; Walker, M. R.; Borden, R.; and Latané, B. 1975. Diffusion of responsibility and restaurant tipping: Cheaper by the bunch. *Personality and Social Psychology Bulletin* 1:584–87. **698, 699**

French, J. R. P., Jr.; Israel, J.; and Ås, D. 1960. An experiment on participation in a Norwegian factory: Interpersonal dimensions of decision-making. *Human Relations* 13:3–20. **688**

French, J. R. P., Jr., and Raven, B. H. 1959. The bases of social power. In D. Cartwright (ed.), *Studies in social power.* Ann Arbor: Institute for Social Research, University of Michigan. **632**

Frenkel-Brunswik, E. 1949. Intolerance of ambiguity as an emotional and perceptual personality variable. *Journal of Personality* 18:108–43. **171**

Freud, S. 1900 (1967). *The interpretation of dreams.* J. Strachey, tr. New York: Avon. **426, 554**

Freud, S. 1904 (1971). *Psychopathology of everyday life.* New York: W. W. Norton. **421**

Freud, S. 1923 (1962). *Ego and the id.* J. Strachey, ed. J. Riviere, tr. New York: W. W. Norton. **51, 421**

Freud, S. 1933 (1966). *Complete introductory lectures on psychoanalysis.* J. Strachey, ed. and tr. New York: W. W. Norton. **425, 487–88**

Frey, M. von, and Kiesow, F. 1899. Uber die Function der Tastkorperchen. *Zeitschrift fur Psychologie* 20:126–263. **232, 234**

Friedman, M. 1969. The general causes of coronary artery disease. In M. Friedman (ed.), *The pathogenesis of coronary artery disease.* New York: McGraw-Hill. **176**

Frieze, I.; Johnson, P.; Parsons, J. E.; Ruble, D. N.; and Zellman, G. L., eds. 1976. *Women and sex roles: A social psychological perspective.* New York: W. W. Norton. **696**

Fromm, E. 1968. *The revolution of hope.* New York: Harper & Row. **559**

Galanter, E. H. 1962. Contemporary psychophysics. In *New Directions in Psychology I.* New York: Holt, Rinehart & Winston. **190**

Galin, D. 1974. Implications for psychiatry of left and right cerebral specialization. *Archives of General Psychiatry* 31 (4):572. **843**

Galvani, L. 1791. De viribus electricitatis in motu musculari: commentarius. *Proceedings Academie de Bologna* 7:363–418. **585**

Garcia, J., and Koelling, R. A. 1966. Relation of cue to consequence in avoidance learning, *Psychonomic Science* 4:123–24. **725**

Gardner, E. 1975. *Fundamentals of neurology.* 6th ed. Philadelphia: W. B. Saunders. **202, 233**

Gardner, E. F., and Thompson, G. G. 1956. *Social relations and morale in small groups.* New York: Appleton-Century-Crofts. **151**

Garmezy, N. 1974. Children at risk: The search for the antecedents of schizophrenia. Part II: Ongoing research programs, issues, and intervention. *Schizophrenia Bulletin* 9:55–125. DHEW Publication No. (ADM) 75–145. National Institute of Mental Health. **539**

Garrett, H. 1951. *Great experiments in psychology.* New York: Appleton-Century-Crofts. **4, 27**

Gelman, R. 1969. Conservation acquisition: A problem of learning to attend to relevant attributes. *Journal of Experimental Child Psychology* 7:167–87. **95**

Geschwind, N., and Levitsky, W. 1968. Human brain: Left-right asymmetries in temporal speech region. *Science* 161:186–87. **845**

Gesell, A. 1928. *Infancy and human growth.* New York: Macmillan. **99**

Gesell, A. 1954. The ontogenesis of infant behavior. In L. Carmichael (ed.), *Manual of child psychology,* 2d ed. New York: Wiley. **66, 78**

Gewirtz, J. L., and Baer, D. M. 1958a. Deprivation and satiation of social reinforcers as drive conditions. *Journal of Abnormal and Social Psychology* 57:165–72. **649, 665**

Gewirtz, J. L., and Baer, D. M. 1958b. The effect of brief social deprivation on behaviors for a social reinforcer. *Journal of Abnormal and Social Psychology* 56:49–56. **649, 665**

Gibson, E. J. 1969. *Principles of perceptual learning and development.* New York: Appleton-Century-Crofts. **277**

Gibson, J. J. 1950. *The perception of the visual world.* Boston: Houghton Mifflin. **240, 253, 256**

Gibson, J. J. 1966. *The senses considered as perceptual systems.* Boston: Houghton Mifflin. **257**

Gilbert, G. M. 1951. Stereotype persistence and change among college students. *Journal of Abnormal and Social Psychology* 46:245–54. **612**

Gill, M. M. 1959. The present state of psychoanalytic theory. *Journal of Abnormal and Social Psychology* 58:1–8. **428**

Glanzer, M., and Clark, W. H. 1963. Accuracy of perceptual recall: An analysis of organization. *Journal of Verbal Learning and Verbal Behavior* 1:289–99. **382**
Glucksberg, S. 1962. The influence of strength of drive on functional fixedness and perceptual recognition. *Journal of Experimental Psychology* 63:36–51. **360**
Goffman, E. 1961. *Asylums: Essays on the social situation of mental patients and other inmates.* New York: Anchor. **589**
Gold, M., and Douvan, E. 1969. *Adolescent development.* Boston: Allyn & Bacon. **144, 145**
Goldberg, P. A. 1968. Are women prejudiced against women? *Transaction* April:28–30. **609**
Goldfarb, W. 1941. An investigation of reaction time in older adults and its relationship to certain observed mental test patterns. Teachers College, Columbia University, Contributions to Education, No. 831, New York. **158**
Goodenough, F. L. 1926. *Measurement of intelligence by drawings.* Yonkers, N.Y.: World Book. **109**
Goranson, R. E., and Berkowitz, L. 1966. Reciprocity and responsibility reactions to prior help. *Journal of Personality and Social Psychology* 3:227–32. **645, 652**
Goss, C. M. ed. 1973. *Gray's anatomy.* Philadelphia: Lea & Febiger. **788, 789**
Gottesman, I. I., and Shields, J. 1966. Schizophrenia in twins: Sixteen years' consecutive admissions to a psychiatric clinic. *British Journal of Psychiatry* 112:809–18. **539**
Gottesman, I. I., and Shields, J. 1972. *Schizophrenia and genetics: A twin study vantage point.* New York: Academic Press. **539**
Götz, A., and Jacoby, L. L. 1974. Encoding and retrieval processes in long-term retention. *Journal of Experimental Psychology* 102:291–97. **320**
Gouldner, A. W. 1960. The norm of reciprocity: A preliminary statement. American Sociological Review 25:161–78. **651**
Green, E. L. 1968. *Handbook on genetically standardized JAX mice.* Bar Harbor, Me.: Jackson Laboratory. **718, 771**
Greenblatt, M. 1972. Psychosurgery. In A. M. Freedman and H. I. Kaplan (eds.), *Treating mental illness: Aspects of modern therapy.* New York: Atheneum. Pp. 372–81. **585**
Greenburg, D. 1964. *How to be a Jewish mother.* Los Angeles: Price, Stern & Sloan. **653**
Greulich, W. W. 1944. Physical changes in adolescence. In *43d Yearbook of the National Society of Study of Education, Part I.* **65**
Grier, W. H., and Cobbs, P. M. 1968. *Black rage.* New York: Basic Books. **500, 566**
Grier, W. H., and Cobbs, P. M. 1971. The Jesus bag. New York: Bantam. **566**
Grim, P. 1971. Anxiety change produced by self-induced muscle tension and by relaxation with respiration feedback. *Behavior Therapy* 2:11–17. **577**
Grings, W. W.; Carlin, S.; and Appley, M. 1962. Set suggestion and conditioning. *Journal of Experimental Psychology* 63:417–22. **352**
Groves, P. M., and Thompson, R. F. 1973. A dual-process theory of habituation: Neural mechanisms. In H. V. S. Peeke and M. J. Herz (eds.), *Habituation: II Electrophysiological substrates.* New York: Academic Press. **838**
Gurland, B. J. 1973. A broad clinical assessment of psychopathology in the aged. In C. Eisdorfer and M. P. Lawton (eds.), *The psychology of adult development and aging.* Washington, D.C.: American Psychological Association. **173**
Gustavson, C.; Kelly, D. J.; Sweeny, M.; and Garcia, J. 1976. Prey-lithium aversions: I. Coyotes and wolves. In press. **338**
Gutman, G. M. 1966. A note on the MPI: Age and sex differences in extroversion and neuroticism in a Canadian sample. *British Journal of Social and Clinical Psychology* 5:128–29. **171**
Haaf, R. A., and Bell, R. Q. 1967. A facial dimension in visual discrimination by human infants. *Child Development* 38:893–99. **75, 76**
Haber, R. N.; Haber, L. R.; and Rosenberg, K. 1976. Word length and word shape as peripherally perceived information in reading. Unpublished research. **294**
Haber, R. N., and Fried, A. H. 1975. *An introduction to psychology.* New York: Holt, Rinehart & Winston. **197, 201, 251**
Haber, R. N., and Hershenson, M. 1973. *The psychology of visual perception.* New York: Holt, Rinehart & Winston. **193, 196, 203, 204, 207, 242, 244, 245, 247, 276**
Haber, R. N., and Standing, L. G. 1969. Direct measures of short-term visual storage. *Quarterly Journal of Experimental Psychology* 21:43–59. **284**
Haith, M. M. 1976. Visual competence in early infancy. In R. Held, H. Leibowitz, and H. L. Teuber (eds.), *Handbook of sensory physiology,* vol. 8. New York: Springer Verlag. **263**
Hall, C. S., and Lindzey, G. 1970. *Theories of personality.* 2d ed. New York: Wiley. **557**
Hall, G. S. 1916. *Adolescence.* 2 vols. Norwood, Pa.: Norwood Editions. **142**
Hall, G. S. 1922. *Senescence, the last half of life.* Norwood, Pa.: Norwood Editions. **47**
Halverson, H. M. 1937. Studies of the grasping responses of early infancy: I. *Journal of Genetic Psychology* 51:371–92. **77**
Haney, C.; Banks, W. C.; and Zimbardo, P. G. 1973. Interpersonal dynamics in a simulated prison. *International Journal of Criminology and Penology* 1:69–97. **700**
Hanson, E. D. 1972. *Animal diversity.* Englewood Cliffs, N.J.: Prentice-Hall. **734**
Harari, H., and McDavid, J. W. 1973. Teachers' expectations and name stereotypes. *Journal of Educational Psychology* 65:222–25. **608**
Hardyck, C.; Petrinovich, L. F.; and Goldman, R. D. 1976. Left-handedness and cognitive deficit. *Cortex.* In press. **844**
Hare, R. D. 1970. *Psychopathy: theory and research.* New York: Wiley. **524, 543**
Harlow, H. F. 1949. The function of learning sets. *Psychological Review* 56:51–65. **749**
Harlow, H. F. 1953. Motivation as a factor in the acquisition of new responses. In M. R. Jones (ed.), *Nebraska symposium on motivation.* Lincoln: University of Nebraska Press. Pp. 24–49. **399**
Harlow, H. F. 1959. Love in infant monkeys. *Scientific American* 202:68–74. **58, 114, 115, 116**
Harlow, H. F., and Harlow, M. K. 1966. Learning to love. *American Scientist* 54:244–72. **114**
Harris, D. B. 1963. *Children's drawings as measures of intellectual maturity.* New York: Harcourt, Brace, and World. **109**
Hartline, H. K. 1949. Inhibition of activity of visual receptors by illuminating nearby retinal elements in the *Limulus* eye. *Federation Proceedings* 8:69–112. **200**
Hartup, W. W., and Lempers, J. 1973. A problem in life-span development: The interactional analysis of family attachments. In P. B. Baltes and K. W. Schaie (eds.), *Life-span developmental psychology: Personality and socialization.* New York: Academic Press. Pp. 235–52. **119**
Harvey, O. J.; Hunt, D. E.; and Schroder, H. M. 1961. *Conceptual systems and personality organization.* New York: Wiley. **467**
Hashim, S. A., and Van Itallie, T. B. 1965. Studies in normal and obese subjects with a monitored food dispensing device. *Annals of the New York Academy of Sciences* 131:654–61. **724**
Hastorf, A. H., and Cantril, H. 1954. They saw a game: A case study. *Journal of Abnormal and Social Psychology* 49:129–34. **617**
Havighurst, R. J.; Neugarten, B. L.; and Tobin, S. S. 1968. Disengagement and patterns of aging. In B. Neugarten (ed.), *Middle age and aging.* Chicago: University of Chicago Press. **166**
Hawkins, R. P.; Peterson, R. F.; Schweid, E.; and Bijou, S. W. 1966. Behavior therapy in the home: Amelioration of problem parent-child relations with the parent in a therapeutic role. *Journal of Experimental Child Psychology* 4:99–107. **462, 463**
Healy, W.; Bronner, A. F.; and Bowers, A. M. 1958. The structure and meaning of psychoanalysis. New York: Knopf. **52**
Heathfield, K. W. Y.; Croft, P. B.; and Swash, M. 1973. The syndrome of transient global amnesia. *Brain* 96:729–36. **832**
Hebb, D. O. 1949. *The organization of behavior.* New York: Wiley. **132**
Hebb, D. O. 1961. Distinctive features of learning in the higher animal. In J. F. Delafresnaye (ed.), *Brain mechanisms and learning.* Oxford: Blackwell Scientific Publications. **299**
Hebb, D. O. 1972. *A textbook of psychology.* 3d ed. Philadelphia: W. B. Saunders. **351**
Hecht, S. 1934 (1969). Vision: II. The nature of the photoreceptor process. In C. Murchison (ed.), *A handbook of general experimental psychology.* New York: Russell & Russell. **206**
Heilbrun, A. B., Jr. 1973. *Aversive maternal control: A theory of schizophrenic development.* New York: Wiley. **540**
Heider, F. 1958. *The psychology of interpersonal relations.* New York: Wiley. **408, 633**

Held, R., and Hein, A. V. 1958. Adaptation of disarranged hand-eye coordination contigent upon re-afferent stimulation. *Perceptual and Motor Skills* 8:87–90. **259**

Helmholtz, H. von. 1856–1866. *Treatise on physiological optics.* Gloucester, Mass.: Peter Smith. **223**

Henderson, N. D. 1970. Genetic influences on the behavior of mice can be obscured by laboratory rearing. *Journal of Comparative Physiological Psychology* 72:505–11. **778, 779**

Henle, M. 1944. The influence of valence on substitution. *Journal of Psychology* 17:11–19. **404**

Hering, E. 1870 (1964). *Outline of a theory of the light sense.* Cambridge, Mass.: Harvard University Press. **215**

Hess, R. D., and Shipman, V. 1957. Cognitive elements in maternal behavior. In J. P. Hill (ed.), *Minnesota symposia on child psychology,* vol. 1. Minneapolis: University of Minnesota Press. **94**

Hess, W. R. 1932. *Bertrage zur Physiologie d. Hirnstammes.* Leipzig: George Thieme. **585**

Hetherington, E. M., and Parke, R. D. 1975. *Child psychology.* New York: McGraw-Hill. **89**

Hickey, T.; Hickey, L.; and Kalish, R. 1968. Children's perceptions of the elderly. *Journal of Genetic Psychology* 112:227–35. **162, 163**

Hickey, T., and Kalish, R. 1968. Young people's perceptions of adults. *Journal of Gerontology* 23:216–19. **163**

Hilgard, E. R.; Atkinson, R. C.; and Atkinson, R. L. 1975. *Introduction to psychology.* 6th ed. New York: Harcourt Brace Jovanovich. **192, 220**

Hinde, R. A. 1970. *Animal behavior: A synthesis of ethology and comparative psychology.* New York: McGraw-Hill. **727, 728**

Hirsch, H. V. B., and Spinelli, D. N. 1970. Visual experience modifies distribution of horizontally and vertically oriented receptive fields in cats. *Science* 168:869–71. **260**

Hoar, W. S. 1966. *General and comparative physiology.* Englewood Cliffs, N.J.: Prentice-Hall. **761**

Hobbs, N. 1964. Mental health's third revolution. *American Journal of Orthopsychiatry* 34:822–33. **593**

Hobbs, N. 1969. Mental Health's third revolution. In A. J. Bindman and A. D. Spiegel (eds.), *Perspectives in community mental health.* Chicago: Aldine. Pp. 29–40. **593**

Hochberg, J. E. 1964. *Perception.* Englewood Cliffs, N.J.: Prentice-Hall. **251**

Hochberg, J. E., and Brooks, V. 1962. Pictorial recognition as an unlearned ability: A study of one child's performance. *American Journal of Psychology* 75:624–28. **279**

Hodos, W. 1970. Comparative study of brain and behavior. In F. O. Schmitt, (ed.), *The neurosciences.* New York: Rockefeller University Press. **751**

Hodos, W., and Campbell, C. B. G. 1969. Scala naturae: Why there is no theory in comparative psychology. *Psychological Review* 76:337–50. **749**

Hoffman, M. L. 1975. Moral internalization, parental power, and the nature of parent-child interaction. *Developmental Psychology* 11:228–39. **126**

Hoffman, M. L. 1970. Moral development. In P. H. Mussen (ed.), *Carmichael's manual of child psychology,* vol. 2, 3d ed. New York: Wiley. **123, 126, 128**

Hoffman, M. L., and Salzstein, H. D. 1967. Parent discipline and the child's moral development. *Journal of Personality and Social Psychology* 5:45–57. **122**

Hofstaetter, P. R. 1954. The changing composition of "intelligence": A study in T-technique. *Journal of Genetic Psychology* 85:159–64. **105**

Holmes, T. H., and Rahe, R. H. 1967. The social readjustment rating scale. *Journal of Psychosomatic Research* 11:213–18. **475**

Holmes, T. H., and Wolff, H. G. 1950. Life situations and backache. In *Life and stress and bodily disease: Proceedings of the Association for Research in Nervous and Mental Diseases,* vol. 29. Baltimore: Williams & Wilkins: Pp. 750–72. **510**

Holmes, T. S., and Holmes, T. H. 1970. Short-term intrusions into the life-style routine. *Journal of Psychosomatic Research* 14:121–32. **475**

Holst, E. von. 1939. Die relative Koordination als Phänomen und als Methode zentralnervoser Funktionsanalyse. *Ergebnisse der Physiologie* 42:228–305. **717**

Holst, E. von. 1954. Relations among the central nervous system and the peripheral organs. *British Journal of Animal Behavior* 2:89–94. **248**

Holt, E. B. 1931. *Animal drive and the learning process, an essay toward radical empiricism,* vol. 1. New York: Holt. **393**

Honzik, M. P. 1957. Developmental studies of parent-child resemblance in intelligence. *Child Development* 28:215–28. **108**

Honzik, M. P.; Macfarlane, J. W.; and Allen, L. 1948. The stability of mental test performance. *Journal of Experimental Education* 17:309–24. **100**

Horai, J.; Haber, I.; Tedeschi, J. T.; and Smith, R. B. 1970. It's not what you say, it's how you do it: A study of threats and promises. *Proceedings of the 78th Annual Convention of the American Psychological Association.* 5:393–94. **637**

Horn, G.; Rose, S. P.; and Bateson, P. P. 1973. Monocular imprinting and regional incorporation of tritrated uracil into the brains of intact and "split-brain" chicks. *Brain Research* 56:227–37. **836**

Horrocks, J. E. 1962. *The psychology of adolescence: Behavior and development.* 2d ed. Boston: Houghton Mifflin. **64**

Horrocks, J. E., and Thompson, G. G. 1946. A study of the friendship fluctuations of rural boys and girls. *Journal of Genetic Psychology* 69:189–98. **150**

Hovland, C. I. 1937. The generalization of conditioned responses: I. The sensory generalization of conditioned responses with varying frequencies of tone. *Journal of General Psychology* 17:125–48. **330**

Hovland, C. I., and Janis, I. L., eds. 1959. *Personality and persuasibility.* New Haven: Yale University Press. **680**

Hovland, C. I.; Janis, I. L.; and Kelley, H. H. 1953. *Communication and persuasion.* New Haven: Yale University Press. **680**

Hovland, C. I., and Weiss, W. 1952. The influence of source credibility on communication effectiveness. *Public Opinion Quarterly* 15:635–50. **646**

Hulicka, I. M. 1967. Age differences in retention as a function of interference. *Journal of Gerontology* 22:180–84. **155**

Hull, C. L. 1943. *Principles of behavior.* New York: Appleton-Century-Crofts. **393**

Hull, C. L. 1951 *Essentials of behavior.* New Haven, Conn.: Yale University Press. **393**

Hunt, J. McV. 1961. *Intelligence and experience.* New York: Ronald Press. **75, 87**

Hyde, T. S., and Jenkins, J. J. 1973. Recall for words as a function of semantic, graphic and syntactic orienting tasks. *Journal of Verbal Learning and Verbal Behavior* 12:471–80. **321**

Hydén, H. 1967. RNA in brain cells. In G. C. Quarton, T. Melnechuk, and F. O. Schmitt (eds.), *The neurosciences.* Cambridge, Mass.: MIT Press. **835**

Inbau, F. and Reid, J. E. 1962. *Criminal interrogations and confessions.* Baltimore: Williams & Wilkins. **662**

Indian Hemp Drugs Commission Report, 1893–94. 1969. *Marihuana* (introduction by J. Kaplan). Silver Spring, Md.: Thomas Jefferson Publishing. **583**

Ittelson, W. H. 1952 (1968). *Ames demonstrations in perception.* New York: Hafner. **267**

Ivanov-Smolensky, A. G. 1933. *Metodika issledovaniya uslovykh reflexosov u cheloveka.* Moscow: Medgiz (Medical State Press). **332**

Jacobs, R. C., and Campbell, D. T. 1961. The perpetuation of an arbitrary tradition through several generations of a laboratory microculture. *Journal of Abnormal and Social Psychology* 62:649–58. **677, 684**

Jacobson, E. 1938. *Progressive relaxation.* Chicago: University of Chicago Press. **577**

James, W. 1890. *The principles of psychology.* New York: Holt. **262, 626**

Janis, I. L. 1954. Personality correlates of susceptibility to persuasion. *Journal of Personality* 22:504–18. **680**

Janis, I. L. 1958. *Psychological stress.* New York: Wiley. **476**

Janis, I. L. 1972. *Victims of groupthink: A psychological study of foreign-policy decisions and fiascos.* Boston: Houghton Mifflin. **694**

Janis, I. L.; Kaye, D.; and Kirschner, P. 1965. Facilitating effects of "eating-while-reading" on responsiveness to persuasive communications. *Journal of Personality and Social Psychology* 1:183–86. **650**

Janov, A. 1970. *The primal scream—primal therapy: The cure for neurosis.* New York: Dell. **559**

Jeffrey, W. 1968. The orienting reflex and attention in cognitive development. *Psychological Review* 75:323–34. **73, 86**

Jenkins, R. I. 1966. Psychiatric syndromes in children and their relation to family background. *American Journal of Orthopsychiatry* 36:405–57. **536**

Jennings, J. J. 1948. *Sociometry in group relations: A work guide for teachers.* Washington, D.C.: American Council on Education. **149**

Jensen, A. R. 1964. The Rorschach technique: A re-evaluation. *Acta Psychologica* 22:60–70. **460**

Jensen, A. R. 1969. How much can we boost IQ and scholastic achievement? Harvard Educational Review 39:1–123. **107, 778**

Jerison, H. J. 1961. Quantitative analysis of evolution of the brain in mammals. *Science* 133:1012–14. **739**

Jerison, H. J. 1963. Interpreting the evolution of the brain. *Human Biology* 35:263–91. **741, 774**

Jerison, H. J. 1969. Brain evolution and dinosaur brains. *American Naturalist* 103:575–88. **739, 740, 741**

Jersild, A. 1954. Emotional development. In L. Carmichael (ed.), *Manual of child psychology*. New York: Wiley. **132**

Jersild, A., and Holmes, F. 1935. *Children's fears*. New York: Teachers College Press. **133**

John, E. R. 1972. Switchboard versus statistical theories of learning and memory. *Science* 177:850–64. **839, 840**

Johnson, D. M. 1972. *Systematic introduction to the psychology of thinking*. New York: Harper & Row. **363**

Johnson, M. M. 1963. Sex-role learning in the nuclear family. *Child Development* 34:319–33. **140**

Johnson, T. J.; Feigenbaum, R.; and Weiby, M. 1964. Some determinants and consequences of the teacher's perception of causality. *Journal of Educational Psychology* 55:237–46. **624**

Johnson, W. H.; Delanney, L. E.; Cole, T. A.; and Brooks, A. E. 1972. *Biology*. 4th ed. New York: Holt, Rinehart & Winston. **234**

Jones, E. E. 1964. *Ingratiation*. New York: Appleton-Century-Crofts. **651**

Jones, E. E., and Davis, K. E. 1965. From acts to dispositions: The attribution process in person perception. In L. Berkowitz (ed.), *Advances in experimental social psychology*, vol. 2 New York: Academic Press. **618, 621, 624**

Jones, E. E.; Davis, K. E.; and Gergen, K. J. 1961. Role playing variations and their informational value for person perception. *Journal of Abnormal and Social Psychology* 63:302–10. **620**

Jones, E. E., and Gerard, H. B. 1967. *Foundations of social psychology*. New York: Wiley. **631**

Jones, E. E., and Nisbett, R. E. 1971. *The actor and observer: Divergent perceptions of the causes of behavior*. Morristown, N.J.: General Learning Press. **409, 452, 620, 624**

Jones, H. E., and Conrad, H. S. 1933. The growth and decline of intelligence: A study of a homogeneous group between the ages of ten to sixty. *Genetic Psychology Monograph* 13:223–98. **32, 159**

Jones, K. L.: Shainberg, L. W.; and Byer, C. O. 1969. *Drugs and alcohol*. New York: Harper & Row. **583**

Jones, M. C., and Bayley, N. 1950. Physical maturing among boys as related to behavior. *Journal of Educational Psychology* 41:129–48. **54, 55**

Jones, M. H., and Jones, M. C. 1970. The neglected client. *The Black Scholar* 5:35–42. **566**

Jones, R. A.; Linder, D. E.; Kiesler, C. A.; Zanna, M.; and Brehm, J. W. 1968. Internal states or external stimuli: Observers' attitude judgments and the dissonance-theory-self-persuasion controversy. *Journal of Experimental Social Psychology* 4:247–69. **616**

Jost, H., and Sontag, L. W. 1944. The genetic factor in autonomic nervous system function. *Psychosomatic Medicine* 6:303–10. **124**

Jourard, S. M. 1971. *The transparent self*. 2d ed. New York: Van Nostrand Reinhold. **559**

Jouvet, M. 1972. The role of monoamines and acetylcholine-containing neurons in the regulation of the sleep-waking cycle. *Ergebnisse der Physiologie* 64: 166–307. **851**

Julesz, B. 1964. Binocular depth perception without familiarity cues. *Science* 145:356–62. **251, 252**

Jung, C. G. 1968. *Analytical psychology: Its theory and practice*. New York: Vintage Books. **557, 558**

Jung, R., and Hassler, R. 1960. The extrapyramidal motor system. In *Handbook of physiology*, vol. 2. Washington, D.C.: American Physiological Society. **825**

Jürgens, U., and Ploog, D. 1970. Cerebral representation of vocalization in the squirrel monkey. *Experimental Brain Research* 10:532–54. **841**

Kagan, J. 1965. Reflection-impulsivity and reading ability in primary grade children. *Child Development* 36:609–28. **88**

Kagan, J.; Henker, B. A.; Hen-Tov, A.; Levine, J.; and Lewis, M. 1966. Infants' differential reactions to familiar and distorted faces. *Child Development* 37:519–32. **75**

Kagan, J.; Sontag, L. W.; Baker, C. T.; and Nelson, V. L. 1958. Personality and IQ change. *Journal of Abnormal and Social Psychology* 56:261–66. **100**

Kahn, E. A., and Crosby, E. C. 1972. Korsakoff's syndrome associated with surgical lesions involving the mammillary bodies. *Neurology* 22:117–25. **833**

Kales, A., and Kales, J. 1974. Sleep disorders: Recent findings in the diagnosis and treatment of disturbed sleep. *New England Journal of Medicine* 290: 487–99. **850**

Kalish, R. 1975. *Late adulthood: Perspectives on human development*. Monterey, Calif.: Brooks/Cole. **163, 165**

Kamiya, J. 1962. Conditional discrimination on the EEG alpha rhythm in humans. Paper presented at the April meeting of the Western Psychological Association. **576**

Kamiya, J. 1968. Conscious control of brain waves. *Psychology Today* 1(11): 56–60. **576**

Kanfer, F. H., and Phillips, J. 1970. *Learning foundations of behavior therapy*. New York: Wiley. **503, 572, 574**

Kanner, L., and Eisenberg, L. 1957. Early infantile autism, 1943–1955. *Psychiatric Research Reports* 7:55–66. **542**

Kaplan, H. B., and Pokorny, A. D. 1970. Aging and self-attitude: A conditional relationship. *Aging and Human Development* 1:241–50. **171**

Karlins, M.; Coffman, T. L.; and Walters, G. 1969. On the fading of social stereotypes: Studies in three generations of college students. *Journal of Personality and Social Psychology* 13:1–16. **612**

Karpman, B. 1961. The structure of neurosis: With special differentials between neurosis, psychosis, homosexuality, alcoholism, psychopathy, and criminality. *Archives of Criminal Psychodynamics* 4:599–646. **524**

Kastenbaum, R., and Aisenberg, R. 1972. *The psychology of death*. New York: Springer. **177**

Katz, D., and Braly, K. W. 1933. Racial stereotypes of one hundred college students. *Journal of Abnormal and Social Psychology* 28:280–90. **611**

Katz, D., and Kahn, R. L. 1966. *The social psychology of organizations*. New York: Wiley. **689**

Katz, E., and Danet, B. 1966. Petitions and persuasive appeals: A study of official-client relations. *American Sociological Review* 31:811–22. **645**

Kazdin, A. E., and Bootzin, R. R. 1972. The token economy: An evaluative review. *Journal of Applied Behavioral Analysis* 5:343–72. **574**

Keeton, W. T. 1972. *Biological science*. New York: W. W. Norton. **812–13**

Kelley, H. H. 1950. The warm-cold variable in first impressions of persons. *Journal of Personality* 18:431–39. **605**

Kelley, H. H. 1967. Attribution theory in social psychology. In D. Levine (ed.), *Nebraska symposium on motivation*, vol. 15. Lincoln: University of Nebraska Press. **409, 621, 625**

Kelly, G. A. 1955. *The psychology of personal constructs*. New York: W. W. Norton. **436, 466, 559**

Kelly, G. A. 1960. Man's construction of his alternatives. In G. Lindzey (ed.), *Assessment of human motives*. New York: Grove Press. **438**

Kelly, G. A. 1963. *A theory of personality*. New York: W. W. Norton. **436**

Kelman, H. C., and Lawrence, L. H. 1972. Assignment of responsibility in the case of Lt. Calley: Preliminary report on a national survey. *Journal of Social Issues* 28:177–212. **622**

Kendler, H. H., and Kendler, T. S. 1962. Vertical and horizontal processes in problem solving. *Psychological Review* 69:1–16. **85**

Kepecs, J. G., and Robin, M. 1950. Life situations, emotions, and atopic dermatitis. In *Life stress and bodily diseases: Proceedings of the Association for Research in Nervous and Mental Diseases*, vol. 29. Baltimore: Williams & Wilkins. Pp. 1010–15. **510**

Kesey, K. 1962. *One flew over the cuckoo's nest*. New York: Viking. **590**

Kiesler, D. J. 1966. Some myths of psychotherapy research and the search for a paradigm. *Psychological Bulletin* 64:114–20. **586**

Kimble, G. A. 1961. *Hilgard and Marquis' conditioning and learning*. New York: Appleton-Century-Crofts. **330**

King, H. D. 1939. Life processes in gray Norway rats during fourteen years in captivity. *American Anatomical Memoirs* 17. **720**

Kingsley, R. D., and Hall, V. C. 1967. Training conservation through the use of learning sets. *Child Development* 38:1111–26. **95**

Kinsey, A. C., and Gebhard, P. H. 1953. *Sexual behavior in the human female*. Philadelphia: W. B. Saunders. **524, 531**

Kinsey, A. C.; Pomeroy, W. B.; and Martin, C. E. 1948. *Sexual behavior in the human male*. Philadelphia: W. B. Saunders. **524, 531**

Kipnis, D. 1958. The effects of leadership style and leadership power upon the inducement of attitude change. *Journal of Abnormal and Social Psychology* 57:173–80. **637**

Kiritz, S., and Moos, R. 1974. Physiological effects of social environments. *Psychosomatic Medicine* 36:96–114. **180**

Kirk, R. E. 1968. *Experimental design: Procedures for the behavioral sciences.* Belmont, Calif.: Brooks/Cole. **25**

Klein, D. F., and Davis, J. M. 1969. *Diagnosis and drug treatment of psychiatric disorders.* Baltimore: Williams & Wilkins. **584**

Kleinmuntz, B. 1974. *Essentials of abnormal psychology.* New York: Harper & Row. **502, 504, 506, 513, 520, 521, 525, 526, 527, 539**

Knoll, M. D. 1956. Über die Entwicklung einiger Functionen im Auge des Grasfrosches. *Zeitschrift für vergleich Physiologie* 38:219–37. **727**

Koeske, R. K., and Koeske, G. F. 1975. An attributional approach to moods and the menstrual cycle. *Journal of Personality and Social Psychology* 31: 473–78. **628**

Kogan, N., and Wallach, M. A. 1964. *Risk-taking: A study in cognition and personality.* New York: Holt, Rinehart & Winston. **692**

Kohlberg, L. 1963. The development of children's orientations toward a moral order: I. Sequence in the development of moral thought. *Vita Humana* 6: 1–33. **128**

Kohlberg L. 1964. Development of moral character and ideology. In M. L. Hoffman and L. W. Hoffman (eds.), *Review of child development research,* vol. 1. New York: Russell Sage Foundation. **53, 128, 129, 130**

Kohlberg, L. 1966. A cognitive-developmental analysis of children's sex-role concepts and attitudes. In E. E. Maccoby (ed.), *The development of sex differences.* Stanford: Stanford University Press. Pp. 82–173. **53, 140, 142**

Kohlberg, L. 1969. Stage and sequence: The cognitive-developmental approach to socialization. In D. Goslin (ed.), *Handbook of Socialization Theory and Research.* Chicago: Rand McNally. Pp. 347–480. **126, 128, 130, 131, 133**

Kohlberg, L., and Zigler, E. 1967. The impact of cognitive maturity upon the development of sex-role attitudes in the years four to eight. *Genetic Psychology Monographs* 75:84–165. **140, 141**

Köhler, I. 1964. *The formation and transformation of the perceptual world.* New York: International Universities Press. **258**

Köhler, W. 1925. *The mentality of apes.* New York: Harcourt Brace. **353**

Korchin, S. J., and Basowitz, L. 1957. Age differences in verbal learning. *Journal of Abnormal and Social Psychology* 54:64–69. **156**

Kraft, A. M. 1966. The therapeutic community. In S. Arieti (ed.), *American handbook of psychiatry,* vol. 3. New York: Basic Books. Pp. 542–51. **590**

Krasne, F. 1976. Invertebrate systems as a means of gaining insight into the nature of learning and memory. In M. R. Rosenzweig and E. L. Bennett (eds.), *Neural mechanisms of learning and memory.* Cambridge, Mass.: MIT Press. **838**

Kretschmer, E. 1925. *Physique and character.* London: Routledge & Kegan Paul. **450**

Krieg, W. J. S. 1966. *Functional neuroanatomy.* 3d ed. Evanston, Ill.: Brain Books. **822**

Kuenne, M. R. 1946. Experimental investigation of the relations of language to transposition behavior in young children. *Journal of Experimental Psychology* 36:471–90. **60, 61, 85**

Kuhlen, R. B., and Lee, B. J. 1943. Personality characteristics and social acceptability in adolescence. *Journal of Educational Psychology* 34:321–40. **150**

Kuo, Z. Y. 1932. Ontogeny of embryonic behavior in aves: IV. The influence of embryonic movements upon the behavior after hatching. *Journal of Comparative Psychology* 14:109–22. **715**

Lacey, J. I. 1967. Somatic response patterning and stress: Some revisions of activation theory. In M. H. Appley and R. Trumbull (eds.), *Psychological stress.* New York: Appleton-Century-Crofts. **854**

Lancaster, E. 1958. *The final face of Eve.* New York: McGraw-Hill. **509**

Langer, J. 1969. *Theories of Development.* New York: Holt, Rinehart & Winston. **43**

Lashley, K. S. 1930. The mechanism of vision: I. A method for rapid analysis of pattern vision in the rat. *Journal of Genetic Psychology* 37:453–60. **493**

Lashley, K. S. 1951. The problem of serial order in behavior. In L. A. Jeffress, (ed.), *Cerebral mechanisms in behavior, the Hixon symposium.* New York: Wiley. **818**

Latané, B., and Darley, J. M. 1968. Group inhibition of bystander intervention in emergencies. *Journal of Personality and Social Psychology* 10:215–21. **698**

Latour, P. L. 1962. Visual threshold during eye movements. *Vision Research* 2:261–62. **256, 258**

Lazarus, A. A. 1971. *Behavior therapy and beyond.* New York: McGraw-Hill. **570**

Lazarus, R. S. 1966. *Psychological stress and the coping process.* New York: McGraw-Hill. **474, 498**

Lazarus, R. S. 1968. Emotions and adaptation: Conceptual and empirical relations. In W. A. Arnold (ed.), *Nebraska symposium on motivation.* Lincoln: University of Nebraska Press. **489**

Lazarus, R. S., and Alfert, E. 1964. The short circuiting of threat by experimentally altering cognitive appraisal. *Journal of Abnormal and Social Psychology* 69:195–205. **491**

LeBon, G. 1896 (1974). *Psychology of peoples.* New York: Arno Press. **699**

Lee, L. C. 1971. The concomitant development of cognitive and moral codes of thought: A test of selected deductions from Piaget's theory. *Genetic Psychology Monographs* 83:93–146. **133**

Lefrançois, G. R. 1973. *Of children: An introduction to child development.* Belmont, Calif.: Wadsworth. **92**

Lehman, H. C. 1936. The creative years in science and literature. *Scientific Monthly* 43:151–62. **160**

Leiman, A. L., and Christian, C. N. 1973. Electrophysiological analysis of learning and memory. In J. A. Deutsch (ed.), *The physiological basis of memory.* New York: Academic Press. Pp. 125–73. **830**

Lenneberg, E. H. 1967. *Biological foundations of language.* New York: Wiley. **95, 96**

Lerner, I. M. 1968. *Heredity, evolution, and society.* San Francisco: W. H. Freeman. **736**

Leventhal, H. 1974. Emotions: A basic problem in social psychology. In C. Nemeth (ed.), *Social psychology: Classic and contemporary integrations.* Chicago: Rand McNally. **627**

LeVine, R. 1959. Gusii sex offenses: A study in social control. *American Anthropologist* 61:6. **530**

Levitsky, A., and Perls, F. 1970. The rules and games of Gestalt therapy. In J. Fagan and I. L. Shepherd (eds.), *Gestalt therapy now: Theory, techniques, applications.* New York: Harper & Row. Pp. 140–49. **565**

Lewin, K. 1935. *A dynamic theory of personality.* New York: McGraw-Hill. **404, 405, 478**

Lewin, K. 1936. *Principles of topological psychology.* New York: McGraw-Hill. **478**

Lewin, K. 1943. Forces behind food habits and methods of change. *Bulletin of the National Research Council.* 108:35–65. **688**

Lewin, K. 1947. Frontiers in group dynamics: 1. Concept, method, and reality in social science: Social equilibria and social change. *Human Relations* 1:5–41. **688**

Lewin, K. 1948. *Resolving social conflicts.* New York: Harper. **143**

Lewin, K. 1951. *Field theory in social science.* New York: Harper. **478**

Lewin, K. 1952. Group decision and social change. In S. E. Swanson, T. M. Newcomb, and E. L. Hartley (eds.), *Readings in social psychology,* 2d ed. New York: Holt. **688**

Lewis, M. 1972. Culture and gender roles: There's no unisex in the nursery. *Psychology Today* 5:54–58. **609**

Liberman, A. M. 1974. The specialization of the language hemisphere. In F. O. Schmitt and F. J. Worden (eds.), *The neurosciences: Third study program.* Cambridge, Mass.: MIT Press. **841**

Liebert, R. M., and Spiegler, M. D. 1974. *Personality: Strategies for the study of man.* Homewood, Ill.: Dorsey Press. **455, 460**

Lifton, R. J. 1963. *Thought reform and the psychology of totalism.* New York: W. W. Norton. **662, 665**

Lindsley, D. B., and Wicke, J. D. 1974. The electroencephalogram: Autonomous electrical activity in man and animals. In R. F. Thompson and M. Patterson (eds.), *Bioelectric recording techniques.* New York: Academic Press. **804**

Lindzey, G., and Thiessen, D. D. 1970. *Contributions to behavior-genetic analysis.* New York: Appleton-Century-Crofts. **761**

Lipsitt, L. P. 1963. Learning in the first year of life. In L. P. Lipsitt and C. C. Spiker (eds.), *Advances in child development and behavior,* vol. 1. New York: Academic Press. **81, 82**

Lockard, R. B. 1968. The albino rat: A defensible choice or a bad habit? *American Psychologist* 23:734–42. **719, 720**

Lorenz, K. 1939 (1973). The comparative study of behavior. In K. Lorenz and

P. Leyhausen (eds.), *Motivation of human and animal behavior: An ethological view.* New York: Van Nostrand Reinhold. **717**

Lorenz, K. 1965. *Evolution and modification of behavior.* Chicago: University of Chicago Press. **23, 714, 722, 767**

Lorenz, K. 1966. *On aggression.* New York: Harcourt Brace Jovanovich. **708, 709**

Lowenthal, M. F., and Haven, C. 1968. Interaction and adaptation: Intimacy as a critical variable. *American Sociological Review* 33:20–30. **168**

Luborsky, L., and Spence, D. P. 1971. Quantitative research on psychoanalytic therapy. In A. E. Bergin and S. L. Garfield (eds.), *Handbook of psychotherapy and behavior change: An empirical analysis.* New York: Wiley. Pp. 408–33. **587**

Luchins, A. S. 1957. Experimental attempts to minimize the impact of first impressions. In C. I. Hovland (ed.), *The order of presentation in persuasion.* New Haven: Yale University Press. **613, 615, 616**

Lykken, D. T. 1957. A study of anxiety in the sociopathic personality. *Journal of Abnormal and Social Psychology* 55:6–10. **542, 543**

Lynch, J. J.; Paskewitz, D. A.; and Orne, M. T. 1975. Some factors in feedback control of human alpha rhythm. In L. V. DiCara, T. X. Barber, J. Kamiya, N. E. Miller, D. Shapiro, and J. Stoyva (eds.), *Biofeedback and self-control: 1974.* Chicago: Aldine. Pp. 341–50. **576**

McAdam, D., and Whitaker, H. 1971. Language production: Electroencephalographic localization in the normal human brain. *Science* 172:499–502. **846**

Macaulay, J., and Berkowitz, L., eds. 1970. *Altruism and helping behavior.* New York: Academic Press. **698**

McCandless, B. R. 1970. *Adolescents: Behavior and development.* Hinsdale, Ill.: Dryden Press. **144**

McClearn, G. E.; Bennett, E. L.; Hebert, M.; Kakihana, R.; and Schlesinger, K. 1964. Alcohol dehydrogenase activity and previous ethanol consumption in mice. *Nature* 203:793–94. **776**

McClelland, D. C. 1961. *The achieving society.* Princeton, N.J.: Van Nostrand. **407**

McClelland, D. C.; Atkinson, J. W.; Clark, R. A.; and Lowell, E. L. 1953. *The achievement motive.* New York: Appleton-Century-Crofts. **456, 457**

Maccoby, E. E., and Jacklin, C. N. 1974. *The psychology of sex differences.* Stanford: Stanford University Press. **137, 138, 140**

McCord, W., and McCord, J. 1964. *The psychopath: An essay on the criminal mind.* New York: Van Nostrand Reinhold. **524**

MacDonald, A. P. 1970. Anxiety, affiliation, and social isolation. *Developmental Psychology* 3:242–54. **681**

McGill, T. E. 1970. Genetic analysis of male sexual behavior. In G. Lindzey and D. D. Thiessen (eds.), *Contributions to behavior-genetic analysis.* New York: Appleton-Century-Crofts. Pp. 57–88. **760**

McGraw, M. B. 1935. *Growth: A study of Johnny and Jimmy.* New York: Appleton-Century-Crofts. **66, 77**

McGraw, M. B. 1941. Development of neuromuscular mechanisms as reflected in the crawling and creeping behavior of the human infant. *Journal of Genetic Psychology* 58:83–111. **78**

McGuire, W. J. 1969. The nature of attitudes and attitude change. In G. Lindzey and E. Aronson (eds.), *The handbook of social psychology,* vol. 3, 2d ed. Reading, Mass.: Addison-Wesley. Pp. 136–314. **635**

MacKinnon, D. W. 1962. The nature and nurture of creative talent. *American Psychologist* 17:484–95. **366**

Mackworth, N. H., and Bruner, J. S. 1970. How adults and children search and recognize pictures. *Human Development* 13:149–77. **75**

Mackworth, N. H., and Morandi, A. J. 1967. The gaze selects informative details within pictures. *Perception and Psychophysics* 2:547–52. **265, 266**

MacLean, P. D. 1973. New findings on brain functions and sociosexual behavior. In J. Zubin and R. Money (eds.), *Contemporary sexual behavior: Critical issues in the 1970s.* Baltimore: Johns Hopkins University Press. Pp. 53–74. **544**

McNeill, D. 1970. The development of language. In P. H. Mussen (ed.), *Carmichael's manual of child psychology.* New York: Wiley. **95, 97**

Maddi, S. R., and Costa, P. T. 1972. *Humanism in personology: Allport, Maslow and Murray.* Chicago: Aldine-Atherton. **562**

Maddox, G. 1963. Activity and morale: A longitudinal study of selected subjects. *Social Forces* 42: 195–204. **166**

Magoun, H. W. 1954. The ascending reticular system and wakefulness. In J. F. Delafresnaye (ed.), *Brain mechanisms and consciousness.* Springfield, Ill.: Charles C. Thomas. **851**

Magoun, H. W. 1958. *The waking brain.* Springfield, Ill.: Charles C. Thomas. **851**

Maher, B. A. 1966. *Principles of psychopathology.* New York: McGraw-Hill. **537**

Maher, B. A. 1970. *Introduction to research in psychopathology.* New York: McGraw-Hill. **503**

Mahl, G. F. 1953. Physiological changes during chronic fear. *Annals of the New York Academy of Sciences* 56:240–52. **511**

Maier, N. R. F. 1949. *Frustration: The study of behavior without a goal.* New York: McGraw-Hill. **492**

Makarenko, A. S. 1955. *The road to life: An epic of education.* 3 vols. Moscow: Foreign Languages Publishing House. **671, 673, 687, 689**

Malamuth, N. M. 1975. A systematic analysis of the relationship between group shifts and characteristics of choice dilemmas questionnaire. Ph.D. dissertation, University of California, Los Angeles. **692**

Malinowski, B. 1927. *Sex and repression in savage society.* New York: Harcourt Brace Jovanovich. **528**

Maltzman, I. 1966. Awareness: Cognitive psychology vs. behaviorism. *Journal of Experimental Research in Personality* 1:161–65. **432**

Mark, V. H., and Ervin, F. R. 1970. *Violence and the brain.* New York: Harper & Row. **855**

Maslow, A. H. 1954, 1970. *Motivation and personality.* New York: Harper & Row. **443, 501, 564**

Maslow, A. H. 1972. *The farther reaches of human nature.* New York: Viking Press. **443**

Massaro, D. 1970. Retroactive interference in short-term recognition memory for pitch. *Journal of Experimental Psychology* 83:32–39. **318**

Masters, W. H., and Johnson, V. E. 1970. *Human sexual inadequacy.* Boston: Little, Brown. **531**

Mead, G. H. 1934. *Mind, self, and society.* Chicago, Ill.: University of Chicago Press. **624**

Mead, M. 1950. *Coming of age in Samoa.* New York: New American Library. **143**

Mead, M. 1953. *Growing up in New Guinea.* New York: New American Library. **143**

Mednick, S. A. 1962. The associative basis of the creative process. *Psychological Review* 69:220–32. **363, 364**

Meehl, P. E. 1954. *Clinical versus statistical prediction.* Minneapolis: University of Minnesota Press. **456**

Meehl, P. E. 1962. Schizotaxia, schizotypy, schizophrenia. *American Psychologist* 17:827–38. **538**

Meehl, P. E. *Psychodiagnosis: Selected papers.* Minneapolis: University of Minnesota Press. **503**

Mehler, J. 1963. Some effects of grammatical transformations on the recall of English sentences. *Journal of Verbal Learning and Verbal Behavior* 2:346–51. **377**

Meisels, M. M., and Cantor, F. M. 1971–72. A note on the generation gap. *Adolescence* 6:523–30. **147**

Meissner, G. 1859. Untersuchungen über en Tastsinn. *Zeitschrift für Rationelle Medicin* 7:92–118. **232**

Meissner, W. W. 1965. Parental interaction of the adolescent boy. *Journal of Genetic Psychology* 107:225–33. **147**

Melges, F. T.; Tinklenberg, J. R.; Hollister, L. E.; and Gillespie, H. K. 1970. Marihuana and temporal disintegration. *Science* 168(3935):1118–20. **583**

Meltzoff, J., and Kornreich, M. 1970. *Research in psychotherapy.* New York: Atherton. **586**

Mendel, G. 1866 (1965). *Experiments in plant hybridization.* Cambridge, Mass.: Harvard University Press. **755**

Mendels, J. 1970. *Concepts of depression.* New York: Wiley. **584**

Menninger, K. A. 1958. *Theory of psychoanalytic technique.* New York: Basic Books. **550**

Merrill, B. 1946. A measurement of mother-child interaction. *Journal of Abnormal and Social Psychology* 41:185–89. **126**

Merton, P. A. 1972. How we control the contraction of our muscles. *Scientific American* 226(5):30–37. **819**

Mesmer, F. A. (1770) 1957. *Memoir of F. A. Mesmer, doctor of medicine, on his discoveries.* J. Eden, tr. Mount Vernon, N.Y.: Eden Press. **575**

Messick, S. 1962. *Hidden figures test.* Princeton, N.J.: Educational Testing Service. **469**

Meyer, W. J. 1959. Relationships between social need strivings and the development of heterosexual affiliations. *Journal of Abnormal and Social Psychology* 59:51–57. **148**

Meyer, W. J., and Bendig, A. W. 1961. A longitudinal study of the Primary Mental Abilities Test. *Journal of Educational Psychology* 52:50–60. **105**

Miles, C. C., and Miles, W. R. 1932. The correlation of intelligence scores and chronological age from early to late maturity. *American Journal of Psychology* 44:44–78. **159**

Milgram, S. 1961. Nationality and conformity. *Scientific American* 205: 45–51. **682**

Milgram, S. 1963. Behavioral study of obedience. *Journal of Abnormal and Social Psychology* 67:371–78. **640, 642, 644**

Milgram, S. 1970. The experience of living in cities. *Science* 167, 1461–68. **685**

Milgram, S. 1974. *Obedience to authority: An experimental view.* New York: Harper & Row. **640**

Milgram, S.; Bickman, L.; and Berkowitz, L. 1969. Note on the drawing power of crowds of different size. *Journal of Personality and Social Psychology* 13:79–82. **673**

Miller, G. A. 1956. The magical number seven, plus or minus two. *Psychological Review* 63:81–97. **287**

Miller, N. E. 1941. An experimental investigation of acquired drives. *Psychological Bulletin* 38:534–35. **725**

Miller, N. E. 1944. Experimental studies on conflict. In J. McV. Hunt (ed.), *Personality and the behavioral disorders,* vol. 1. New York: Ronald Press. Pp. 431–65. **483**

Miller, N. E. 1948. Studies of fear as an acquirable drive: I. Fear as motivation and fear-reduction as reinforcement in the learning of new responses. *Journal of Experimental Psychology* 38:89–101. **396**

Miller, N. E. 1951. Learnable drives and rewards. In S. S. Stevens (ed.), *Handbook of experimental psychology.* New York: Wiley. Pp. 435–72. **396**

Miller, N. E. 1959. Liberalization of basic S-R concepts: Extensions to conflict behavior, motivation, and social learning. In S. Koch (ed.), *Psychology: A study of a science,* vol. 2. New York: McGraw-Hill. Pp. 196–292. **483**

Miller, N. E. 1969. Learning of visceral and glandular responses. *Science* 163:434–35. **577**

Miller, N. E.; Bailey, C. J.; and Stevenson, J. A. F. 1950. Decreased "hunger" but increased food intake resulting from hypothalamic lesions. *Science* 112: 256–59. **724**

Miller, N. E., and Banuazizi, A. 1968. Instrumental learning by curarized rats of a specific visceral response, intestinal or cardiac. *Journal of Comparative and Physiological Psychology* 65:1–7. **577**

Miller, N. E., and Bugelski, R. 1948. Minor studies of aggression: II. The influence of frustrations imposed by the in-group on attitudes expressed toward out-groups. *Journal of Psychology* 25:437–42. **492**

Miller, N. E.; DiCara, L. V.; Solomon, H.; Weiss, J. M.; and Dworkin, B. 1970. Learned modifications of autonomic functions: A review of some new data. *Circulation Research,* Supplement 1, 26:1–3; 27:1–11. Reprinted in L. V. DiCara, T. X. Barber, J. Kamiya, N. E. Miller, D. Shapiro, and J. Stoyva (eds.), *Biofeedback and self-control: 1970.* Chicago: Aldine. Pp. 351–59. **577**

Miller, N. E., and Dollard, J. 1941. *Social learning and imitation.* New Haven: Yale University Press. **574**

Miller, N. E., and Dworkin, B. 1975. Visceral learning. Recent difficulties with curarized rats and significant problems for human research. In L. V. DiCara, T. X. Barber, J. Kamiya, N. E. Miller, D. Shapiro, and J. Stoyva, (eds.), *Biofeedback and self control: 1974.* Chicago: Aldine. Pp. 13–103. **577**

Millon, T., and Millon, R. 1974. *Abnormal behavior and personality.* Philadelphia: W. B. Saunders. **503, 523**

Milner, B. 1959. The memory defect in bilateral hippocampal lesions. *Psychiatric Research Reports* 11:43–52. **833, 834**

Milner, P. M. 1970. *Physiological psychology.* New York: Holt, Rinehart & Winston. **789**

Mirin, S. M.; Shapiro, L. M.; Meyer, R. E.; Pillard, R. C.; and Fisher, S. 1970. Casual versus heavy use of marijuana: A redefinition of the marijuana problem. Paper presented at the 123d annual meeting of the American Psychiatric Association, San Francisco. **583**

Mischel, W. 1966. A social learning view of sex differences in behavior. In E. E. Maccoby (ed.), *The development of sex differences.* Stanford: Stanford University Press. 56–81. **138**

Mischel, W. 1968. *Personality and assessment.* New York: Wiley. **452**

Mischel, W. 1969. Continuity and change in personality. *American Psychologist,* 24:1012–18. **452**

Misumi, J. 1974. Action research on the development of leadership, decision-making processes, and organizational performance in a Japanese shipyard. Paper presented at the 18th International Congress of Applied Psychology, Montreal. **690**

Mitler, M. M.; Guilleminault, C.; Orem, J.; Zarcone, V. P.; and Dement, W. C. 1975. Sleeplessness, sleep attacks and things that go wrong in the night. *Psychology Today:* 45–50. **850**

Moncrieff, R. W. 1944. *The chemical senses.* New York: Wiley. **232**

Money, J., and Ehrhardt, A. A. 1972. *Man and woman, boy and girl.* Baltimore: Johns Hopkins University Press. **136**

Monge, R. H. 1976. Structure of the self-concept from adolescence through old age. *Experimental Aging Research* 2. **171, 174**

Monge, R. H. and Gardner, E. F. 1972. *A Program of Research in Adult Differences in Cognitive Performance and Learning: Backgrounds for Adult Education and Vocational Retraining.* Final Report, U.S. Office of Education, Grant No. OEG 1-7-061963-0149. **66**

Monge, R. H., and Hultsch, D. 1971. Paired-associate learning as a function of adult age and the length of the anticipation and inspection intervals. *Journal of Gerontology* 26:157–62. **157**

Mooney, C. M. 1957. Age in the development of closure ability in children. *Canadian Journal of Psychology* 11:219–26 **281**

Mooney, R. 1942. Surveying high-school students' problems by means of a problem check list. *Educational Research Bulletin* 21:57–69. **151**

Moore, K. L. 1974. *Before we are born: Basic embryology and birth defects.* Philadelphia: W. B. Saunders. **794**

Moreno, J. L. 1953. *Who shall survive?* New York: Beacon House. **149**

Moreno, J. L. 1959. Psychodrama. In S. Arieti (ed.), *American handbook of psychiatry,* vol. 2. New York: Basic Books. Pp. 1375–96. **580**

Morgan, C. L. 1894. *An introduction to comparative psychology.* London. **10**

Morgan, T. H.; Sturtevant, A. H.; Muller, H. J.; and Bridges, C. B. 1915 (1972). *The mechanism of Mendelian heredity.* New York: Johnson Reprint Corp. **755**

Morley, W. E. 1965. Treatment of the patient in crisis. *Western Medicine* 3:77–86. **595**

Morris, D. 1968. *Naked ape.* New York: McGraw-Hill. **710**

Morse, S. J., and Gergen, K. J. 1970. Social comparison, self-consistency, and the concept of self. *Journal of Personality and Social Psychology* 16:148–56. **626**

Moscovici, S.; Lage, E.; and Naffrechoux, M. 1969. Influence of a consistent minority on the responses of a majority in a color perception task. *Sociometry* 32:148–56. **684**

Moscovici, S., and Zavalloni, M. 1969. The group as a polarizer of attitudes. *Journal of Personality and Social Psychology* 12:125–35. **693**

Moss, H. 1967. Sex, age, and state as determinants of mother-infant interaction. *Merrill-Palmer Quarterly* 13:19–36. **125**

Mowrer, O. H. 1947. On the dual nature of learning—A reinterpretation of conditioning and problem solving. *Harvard Educational Review* 17:102–48. **343**

Munns, M. 1971. Is there really a generation gap? *Adolescence* 6:197–206. **147**

Murray, H. A. 1943. *Thematic apperception test.* Cambridge, Mass.: Harvard University Press. **455**

Mussen, P. H.; Conger, J. J.; and Kagan, J. 1974. *Child development and personality.* 4th ed. New York: Harper & Row. **150, 517, 540, 541**

Myers, D. G., and Bishop, G. D. 1970. Discussion effects on racial attitudes. *Science* 169:778–79. **693**

Nathan, P. E., and Harris, S. L. 1975. *Psychopathology and society.* New York: McGraw-Hill. **584**

National Clearinghouse for Mental Health Information. 1969. *Outpatient services: A service of the community mental health center.* Public Health Service Publication No. 1578. Washington, D.C.: U.S. Government Printing Office. **593**

National Institute of Mental Health. 1973. *Utilization of mental health facilities, 1971: Analytical and special study reports.* DHEW Publication No. NIH 74-657. Washington, D.C.: U.S. Government Printing Office. **532**

National Institute of Mental Health. 1975. *The cost of mental illness, 1971.* DHEW Publication No. 76-265. Washington, D.C.: U.S. Government Printing Office. **532**

Neisser, U. 1963. Decision time without reaction time: Experiments in visual scanning. *American Journal of Psychology* 76:376–85. **270, 271, 285**

Netter, F. 1962. *The Ciba collection of medical illustrations*, vol. 1, The nervous system. Summit, N.J.: Ciba Pharmaceutical Co. **789, 853**

Neugarten, B. L., and Datan, N. 1973. Sociological perspectives on the life cycle. In P. B. Baltes and K. W. Schaie (eds.), *Life-span developmental psychology: Personality and socialization*. New York: Academic Press. **57, 58, 164**

Neugarten, B. L.; Havighurst, R. J.; and Tobin, S. S. 1968. Personality and patterns of aging. In B. L. Neugarten (ed.), *Middle age and aging*. Chicago: University of Chicago Press. Pp. 173–79 **166, 167, 168**

Neugarten, B. L.; Moore, J. W.; and Lowe, J. C. 1965. Age norms, age constraints, and adult socialization. *American Journal of Sociology* 70:710–17. **164, 165**

Neugarten, B. L.; Wood, V.; Kraines, R. J., and Loomis, B. 1968. Women's attitudes toward the menopause. In B. L. Neugarten (ed.), *Middle age and aging*. Chicago: University of Chicago Press. Pp. 196–200. **170**

Newell, A., and Simon H. C. 1963. GPS: A program that simulates human thought. In E. A. Feigenbaum and J. Feldman (eds.), *Computers and Thought*. New York: McGraw-Hill. **370, 371**

Newell, A.; Simon, H. C.; and Shaw, J. C. 1960. Report on a general problem-solving problem. *Proceedings of International Conference on Information Processing*. Paris: UNESCO. **370**

Newton, I. 1672 (1971). A new theory of light and color. *Philosophical Transactions for the Royal Society of London*. In D. T. Whiteside and M. A. Hoskin (eds.), *Mathematical papers of Isaac Newton*, vol. 3, 1670–1673. Cambridge: Cambridge University Press. **214**

Nicholson, J. L., and Altman, J. 1972. Synaptogenesis in the rat cerebellum: Effects of early hypo- and hyperthyroidism. *Science* 176:530–32. **798**

Nickel, T. W. 1974. The attribution of intention as a critical factor in the relation between frustration and aggression. *Journal of Personality* 42:482–92. **408**

Nissen, H.; Chow, K.; and Semmes, J. 1951. Effects of restricted opportunity for tactual, kinesthetic, and manipulative experience on the behavior of a chimpanzee. *American Journal of Psychology* 64:485–507. **68**

Norbeck, E.; Price-Williams, D.; and McCord, W. M., eds. 1968. *The study of personality: an interdisciplinary appraisal*. New York: Holt, Rinehart & Winston. **536**

Nowlis, D. P., and Kamiya, J. 1970. The control of electroencephalographic alpha rhythms through auditory feedback and the associated mental activity. *Psychophysiology* 6:476–84. **576**

O'Bryan, K. G., and Boersma, F. J. 1971. Eye movements, perceptual activity, and conservation development. *Journal of Experimental Child Psychology* 12:157–69. **92**

Olds, J., and Milner, P. 1954. Positive reinforcement produced by electrical stimulation of septal area and other regions of rat brain. *Journal of Comparative and Physiological Psychology* 47:419–27. **854**

O'Leary, K. D., and Wilson, G. T. 1975. *Behavior therapy: Application and outcome*. Englewood Cliffs, N.J.: Prentice-Hall. **570**

Opler, M. K. 1959. Cultural differences in mental disorders: An Italian and Irish contrast the schizophrenias—U.S.A. In M. K. Opler (ed.), *Cultures and mental health: Cross-cultural studies*. New York: Macmillan. Pp. 425–42. **536**

Orne, M. T. 1962. On the social psychology of the psychological experiment. *American Psychologist* 17:776–83. **436**

Orne, M. T., and Evans, F. J. 1965. Social control in the psychological experiment: Antisocial behavior and hypnosis. *Journal of Personality and Social Psychology* 1:189–200. **643**

Orne, M. T., and Paskewitz, D. A. 1975. Aversive situational effects on alpha feedback training. In L. V. DiCara, T. X. Barber, J. Kamiya, N. E. Miller, D. Shapiro, and J. Stoyva, (eds.), *Biofeedback and self-control: 1974*. Chicago: Aldine. Pp. 336–40. **576**

Ornitz, E. M., and Ritvo, E. R. 1968. Perceptual inconsistency in early infantile autism. *Archives of General Psychiatry* 18:76–98. **542**

Osgood, C. E. 1952. The nature and measurement of meaning. *Psychological Bulletin* 49:197–237. **397, 607**

Osgood, C. E.; Suci, G. J.; and Tannebaum, P. H. 1957. *The measurement of meaning*. Urbana, Ill.: University of Illinois Press. **607, 608**

Osofosky, J., and O'Connell, E. 1972. Parent-child interaction: Daughters' effects upon mothers' and fathers' behaviors. *Developmental Psychology* 7:157–68. **46, 126**

Owens, W. A., Jr. 1963. Age and mental abilities: A longitudinal study. *Genetic Psychology Monographs* 48:3–54. **161**

Paige, K. 1973. Women learn to sing the menstrual blues. *Psychology Today* 7(4):41–46. **628**

Paivio, A. 1971. *Imagery and verbal processes*. New York: Holt, Rinehart & Winston. **316**

Papez, J. W. 1937. A proposed mechanism of emotion. *Archives of Neurology and Psychiatry* 38:725–43. **855**

Papoušek, H. 1967a. Conditioning during postnatal development. In Y. Brackbill and G. G. Thompson (eds.), *Behavior in infancy and early childhood: A book of readings*. New York: Free Press. **83**

Papoušek, H. 1967b. Experimental studies of appetitional behavior in human newborns. In H. W. Stevenson, E. H. Hess, and H. L. Rheingold (eds.), *Early behavior: Comparative and developmental approaches*. New York: Wiley. **83, 84**

Parad, H. J. 1975. Introduction. In H. J. Parad (ed.), *Crisis intervention: Selected readings*. New York: Family Service Association of America. Pp. 1–4. **595**

Parke, R. D., and Walters, R. H. 1967. Some factors influencing the efficacy of punishment training for inducing response inhibition. *Monographs of the Society for Research in Child Development* 32 (Serial No. 109). **135**

Parsons, T. 1954. The incest taboo in relation to social structure and the socialization of the child. *British Journal of Sociology* 2:101. **528**

Pasamanick, B. 1968. The community care of schizophrenics. In R. Williams, and L. D. Ozarin (eds.), *Community mental health*. San Francisco: Jossey-Bass. Pp. 394–415. **595**

Pavlov, I. P. N. D. *Selected works*. Koshtoyants, Kh. S. (ed.), Moscow: Foreign Language Publishing House. **13**

Pavlov, I. P. 1927. *Conditioned reflexes*. New York: Dover. **72, 511**

Penfield, W., and Roberts, L. 1959. *Speech and brain mechanisms*. Princeton, N.J.: Princeton University Press. **816, 845**

Pepitone, A. 1950. Motivational effects in social perceptions. *Human relations* 3:57–76. **617**

Perin, C. T. 1942. Behavior potentiality as a joint function of the amount of training and the degree of hunger at the time of extinction. *Journal of Experimental Psychology* 30:93–113 **394**

Perls, F. S. Four Lectures. 1970. In J. Fagan and I. L. Shepherd (eds.), *Gestalt therapy now: Theory, techniques, applications*. New York: Harper & Row. Pp. 14–38. **565**

Pfaffmann, C. 1948. Studying the senses of taste and smell. In T. G. Andrews (ed.), *Methods of psychology*. New York: Wiley. **231**

Pfaffmann, C. 1960. The pleasures of sensation. *Psychological Review* 67:253–68. **231**

Phares, E. J. 1972. *Locus of control*. Morristown, N.J.: General Learning Press. **465**

Piaget, J. 1932 (1948). *The moral judgment of the child*. Glencoe, Ill.: Free Press. **127, 623**

Piaget, J. 1950. *The psychology of intelligence*. London: Routledge and Kegan Paul. **49, 87**

Piaget, J. 1951. *Play, dreams, and imitation in childhood*. New York: W. W. Norton. **87**

Piaget, J. 1972. Intellectual evolution from adolescence to adulthood. *Human Development* 15:1–12. **95**

Pieron, H. 1913. Le Problème physiologique du sommeil. Paris: Masson. **850**

Pilbeam, D. 1972. *The ascent of man*. New York: Macmillan. **740**

Plog. S. C., and Edgerton, R. B., eds. 1969. *Changing perspectives in mental illness*. New York: Holt, Rinehart & Winston. **536**

Premack, A. J., and Premack, D. 1972. Teaching language to an ape. *Scientific American* 227(4):92–99. **841**

Pressey, S. L., and Kuhlen, R. G. 1957. *Psychological development through the life span*. New York: Harper & Row. **159, 171**

Prien, R. F.; Clett, C. J.; and Caffey, E. M. 1973. *A comparison of lithium carbonate and imipramine in the prevention of affective episodes in recurrent affective illness*. Perry Point, Md.: Central Neuropsychiatric Laboratory, Veterans Administration. **584**

Prince, M. 1906 (1969). *Dissociation of a personality*. New York: Greenwood. **509**

Prokasy, W. F.; Carlton, R. A.; and Higgins, J. D. 1967. Effects of non-random intermittent reinforcement schedules in human eyelid conditioning. *Journal of Experimental Psychology* 74:282–88. **351**

Proshansky, H.; Ittelson, W.; and Rivlin, A. 1970. *Environmental psychology: Man and his physical setting*. New York: Holt, Rinehart & Winston. **179**

Radke, M. J. 1946. The relation of parental authority to children's behavior and attitudes. *University of Minnesota Child Welfare Monograph* no. 22. **123**

Ranson, S. W., and Clark, S. L. 1959. *The anatomy of the nervous system.* Philadelphia: W. B. Saunders. **821**

Raven, B. H. 1974a. The comparative analysis of power and power preference. In J. R. Tedeschi (ed.), *Power and influence.* New York: Aldine-Atherton. **632**

Raven, B. H. 1974b. The Nixon group. *Journal of Social Issues* 29(4):297–320. **693**

Raven, B. H., and Eachus, H. T. 1963. Cooperation and competition in means-interdependent triads. *Journal of Abnormal and Social Psychology* 67:307–16. **689**

Raven, B. H., and French, J. R. P., Jr. 1958. Legitimate power and observability in social influence. *Sociometry* 21:83–97. **647**

Raven, B. H., and Leff, W. F. 1965. The effect of partner's behavior and culture upon strategy in a two-person game. *Scripta Hierosolymitana* 14:148–55. **689**

Raven, B. H.; Mansson, H. H.; and Anthony, E. July 1962. *The effects of attributed ability upon expert and referent influence* Tech. Rep. No. 10, Nonr 233(54). Los Angeles: University of California, Los Angeles. **648**

Raven, B. H., and Rubin, J. Z. 1976. *Social psychology: People in groups.* New York: Wiley. **692, 693**

Ray, O. S. 1972. *Drugs, society, and human behavior.* St. Louis: Mosby. **584**

Razran, G. H. S. 1933. Conditioned responses in children: A behavioral and quantitative review of experimental studies. *Archives of Psychology* 23(148): 120. **85**

Reese, H. W. 1962. Verbal mediation as a function of age level. *Psychological Bulletin* 59:502–509. **86**

Reese, H. W., and Lipsitt, L. P., eds. 1970. *Experimental child psychology.* New York: Academic Press. **58, 84**

Regan, D. 1971. Effects of favor and liking on compliance. *Journal of Experimental Social Psychology* 7:627–39. **645, 652**

Reich, W. 1960. *Selected writings.* New York: Farrar, Straus & Giroux. **559**

Reik. T. 1948. *Listening with the third ear.* New York: Farrar, Straus & Giroux. **550, 556**

Reitan, R. M. 1971. Sensorimotor functions in brain-damaged and normal children of early school age. *Perceptual and Motor Skills* 33:655–64. **33**

Revusky, S., and Garcia, J. 1970. Learned associations over long delays. In G. H. Bower (ed.), *The psychology of learning and motivation,* vol. 4. New York: Academic Press. **338**

Rickels, K. 1966. Drugs in the treatment of neurotic anxiety. In P. Solomon, *Psychiatric drugs.* New York: Grune & Stratton. Pp. 225–38. **581**

Riegel, K. F. 1973. Dialectic operations: The final period of cognitive development. *Human Development,* 16, 346–70. **95**

Riegel, K. F.; Riegel, R. M.; and Meyer, G. 1967. A study of the drop-out rates in longitudinal research on aging and the prediction of death. *Journal of Personality and Social Psychology* 4:342–48. **154**

Riesen, A. H. 1947. The development of visual perception in man and chimpanzee. *Science* 106:107–108. **58, 68**

Riesman, D. 1950. *The lonely crowd.* New Haven: Yale University Press. **682**

Rimland, B. 1964. *Infantile autism.* New York: Appleton-Century-Crofts. **542**

Ring, K., and Kelley, H. H. 1963. A comparison of augmentation and reduction as modes of influence. *Journal of Abnormal and Social Psychology* 66:95–102. **637**

Robins, L. N. 1966. *Deviant children grown up.* Baltimore: Williams & Wilkins. **543**

Robinson, E. S. 1927. The "similarity" factor in retroaction. *American Journal of Psychology* 39:297–312. **310**

Rodgers, D. A. 1966. Factors underlying differences in alcohol preference among inbred strains of mice. *Psychosomatic Medicine* 28:498–513. **774, 775, 776, 777**

Rodgers, D. A., and McClearn, G. E. 1962. Alcohol preference of mice. In E. L. Bliss (ed.), *Roots of behavior.* New York: Harper & Row. **775**

Rodgers, D. A.; McClearn, G. E.; Bennett, E. L.; and Hebert, M. 1963. Alcohol preference as a function of its caloric utility in mice. *Journal of Comparative and Physiological Psychology* 56:666–72. **776**

Roethlisberger, F. J., and Dickson, W. J. 1939. *Management and the worker.* Cambridge: Harvard University Press. **688**

Roffwarg, H. P.; Mouzio, J. N.; and Dement, W. C. 1966. Ontogenetic development of the human sleep-dream cycle. *Science* 152:604–19. **848**

Rogers, C. R. 1951. *Client-centered therapy: Its current practice, implications, and theory.* Boston: Houghton Mifflin. **561, 563–64**

Rogers, C. R. 1959. A theory of therapy, personality, and interpersonal relationships, as developed in the client-centered framework. In S. Koch (ed.), *Psychology: A study of a science,* vol. 3. New York: McGraw-Hill. Pp. 184–256. **442**

Rogers, C. R. 1961. *On becoming a person.* Boston: Houghton Mifflin. **442, 561**

Rogers, C. R., and Dymond, R. F., eds. 1954. *Psychotherapy and personality change: Co-ordinated studies in the client-centered approach.* Chicago: University of Chicago Press. **470**

Rokeach, M. 1971. Long-range experimental modification of values, attitudes, and behavior. *American Psychologist* 22:453–59. **635**

Roland, J. L., and Teste, M. 1958. Le cannabisme au Maroc. *Maroc-Medical* 387:694–703. Also appears under Benabud, A. 1957. Psychopathological aspects of the cannabis situation in Morocco: Statistical data for 1956. *U.N. Bulletin on Narcotics* 9(4):1–16. **583**

Romanes, G. J. 1882 (1970). *Animal intelligence.* London: Gregg International Publishers, Ltd. **10, 11, 26**

Romer, A. S. 1971. *The vertebrate story.* Chicago: University of Chicago Press. **744, 752**

Rorschach, H. 1942. *Psychodiagnostics.* Bern: Hans Huber. **459**

Rosen, E.; Fox, R. E.; and Gregory, I. 1972. *Abnormal psychology.* 2d ed. Philadelphia: W. B. Saunders. **545**

Rosenberg, M. 1965. *Society and the adolescent self-image.* Princeton, N.J.: Princeton University Press. **146**

Rosenberg, M. J. 1956. Cognitive structure and attitudinal affect. *Journal of Abnormal and Social Psychology* 53:367–72. **635**

Rosenberg, M. J. 1965. When dissonance fails: On eliminating evaluation apprehension from attitude measurement. *Journal of Personality and Social Psychology* 1:28–42. **661**

Rosenhan, D. L. 1973. On being sane in insane places. *Science* 179:250–58. **437, 503, 591, 611**

Rosenkrantz, P., et al. 1968. Sex-role stereotypes and self-concepts in college students. *Journal of Consulting and Clinical Psychology* 32:287–95. **609, 695**

Rosenthal, R. 1966. *Experimenter effects in behavioral research.* New York: Appleton-Century-Crofts. **643**

Rosenthal, R. 1973. *On the social psychology of the self-fulfilling prophecy: Further evidence for Pygmalion effects and their mediating mechanisms.* New York: MSS Modular Publications. **614**

Rosenthal, R., and Jacobson, L. 1966. Teachers' expectancies: Determinants of pupils' IQ gains. *Psychological Reports* 19:115–18. **614**

Rosenzweig, M. R., and Bennett, E. L. 1976. Enriched environments: Facts, factors, fantasies. In J. McGaugh and L. Petrinovich (eds.), *Knowing, thinking, and believing.* New York: Plenum Press. **795**

Ross, L. E. 1961. Eyelid conditioning as a tool in psychological research. In W. F. Prokasy (ed.), *Classical conditioning.* New York: Appleton-Century-Crofts. **352**

Rothenbuhler, W. C. 1964. Behavior genetics of nest cleaning in honey bees: IV. Responses of F_1 and backcross generations to disease-killed brood. *American Zoologist* 4:111–23. **766**

Rotter, J. B. 1966. Generalized expectancies of internal versus external control of reinforcement. *Psychological Monographs* 80(1), Whole No. 609):1–28. **464**

Rowley, J. D. 1974. Identification of human chromosomes. In J. J. Yunis (ed.), *Human chromosome methodology.* New York: Academic Press. **756**

Rubin, J. Z., and Lewicki, R. J. 1973. A three-factor experimental analysis of interpersonal influence. *Journal of Applied Social Psychology* 3:240–57. **637**

Rubin, J. A.; Provenzano, F. J.; and Luria, Z. 1974. The eye of the beholder: Parents' views on sex of newborns. *American Journal of Orthopsychiatry* 44:512–19. **609**

Ruch, F. L. 1934. The differentiative effects of age upon human learning. *Journal of General Psychology* 11:261–85. **155, 156**

Ruch, F. L., and Zimbardo, P. 1971. *Psychology and life.* Glenview, Ill.: Scott, Foresman. **97**

Runquist, W. N. 1957. Retention of verbal associates as a function of strength. *Journal of Experimental Psychology* 54:369–74. **309**

Runquist, W. N.; Spence, K. W.; and Stubbs, D. W. 1958. Differential conditioning and intensity of the UCS. *Journal of Experimental Psychology* 55:51–55. **331**

Salapatek, P., and Kessen, W. 1966. Visual scanning of triangle by the human newborn. *Journal of Experimental Child Psychology* 3:155–67. **74, 263**

Sarbin, T. R. 1942. A contribution to the study of actuarial and individual methods of predictions. *American Journal of Sociology* 48:593–602. **456**

Saul, L. J., and Bernstein, C. 1941. The emotional setting of some attacks of urticaria. *Psychosomatic Medicine* 3:351–69. **510**

Schachter, S. 1951. Deviation, rejections, and communication. *Journal of Abnormal and Social Psychology* 46:190–207. **686**

Schachter, S. 1959. *The psychology of affiliation.* Stanford: Stanford University Press. **681**

Schachter, S. 1971. Some extraordinary facts about obese humans and rats. *American Psychologist* 26:129–44. **724**

Schachter, S., and Singer, J. E. 1962. Cognitive, social and physiological determinants of emotional state. *Psychological Review* 69:379–99. **627, 628**

Schaffer, H. R., and Emerson, G. E. 1964. The development of social attachments in infancy. *Monographs of the Society for Research in Child Development* 29(Serial No. 94):5–77. **114, 116, 117**

Schein, E. H. 1961. *Coercive persuasion: A socio-psychological analysis of the "brainwashing" of American civilian prisoners by the Chinese communists.* New York: W. W. Norton. **662, 663, 665**

Schenkel, R. 1967. Submission: Its features and functions in the wolf and dog. *American Zoologist* 7:319–29. **709**

Schildkraut, J. J., and Kety, S. S. 1967. Biogenic amines and emotion. *Science* 156:21–30. **809, 810**

Schmidt-Nielsen, K. 1967. The unusual animal, or to expect the unexpected. *Federation Proceedings* 26:981–86. **720**

Schmidt-Nielsen, K.; Schmidt-Nielson, B.; Houpt, T. R.; and Jarnum, S. A. 1956. Water balance of the camel. *American Journal of Physiology* 185:185–94. **750**

Schneck, J. M. 1963. Hypnosis in psychiatry. In J. M. Schneck (ed.), *Hypnosis in modern medicine.* Springfield, Ill.: Charles C. Thomas. Pp. 169–203. **575**

Schneirla, T. C. 1956. Interrelationships of the "innate" and the "acquired" in instinctive behavior. In *L'instinct dans le comportement des animaux et de l'homme.* Paris: Masson. Pp. 387–452. **727**

Schroeder, H. E. 1973. The risky shift as a general choice shift. *Journal of Personality and Social Psychology* 27, 297–300. **693**

Schull, W. J., and Neel, J. V. 1965. *The effects of inbreeding on Japanese children.* New York: Harper & Row. **769**

Schwab, G. 1936. *Gods and heroes: Myths and epics of ancient Greece.* New York: Pantheon. **588**

Schwartz, A. N. 1975. Planning microenvironments for the aged. In D. S. Woodruff and J. E. Birren (eds.), *Aging: Scientific perspectives and social issues.* New York: Van Nostrand. **179**

Schwartz, G. E. 1973. Biofeedback and therapy: Some theroetical and practical issues. *American Psychologist* 28:666–73. **579**

Sears, R. R.; Maccoby, E. E.; and Levin, H. 1957. *Patterns of child rearing* New York: Harper & Row. **518, 519, 639**

Seligman, M. E. P. 1970. Laws of learning. *Psychological Review* 77:406–18. **723, 726**

Seligman, M. E. P. 1975. *Helplessness: On depression, development and death.* San Francisco: W. H. Freeman. **410, 505, 512**

Seligman, M. E. P., and Hager, J. L., eds. 1972. *Biological boundaries of learning.* New York: Appleton-Century-Crofts. **725**

Selye, H. 1950. *The physiology and pathology of exposure to stress.* Montreal: Acta. **538**

Selye, H. 1956. *The stress of life.* New York: McGraw-Hill. **474, 538**

Shakow, D., and Rapaport, D. 1964. *The influence of Freud on American psychology.* Cleveland: World. **10**

Shanas, E.; Townsend, P.; Wedderburn, D.; Friis, H.; Millhof, D.; and Stehouwer, J., eds. 1968. *Old people in three industrial societies.* New York: Atherton. **168**

Shaver, K. G. 1975. *An introduction to attribution processes.* Cambridge, Mass.: Winthrop. **623**

Sheldon, W. H., and Stevens, S. S. 1942. *The varieties of temperament.* New York: Harper & Row. **450**

Sheppard, J. R.; Albersheim, P.; and McClearn, G. 1970. Aldehyde dehydrogenase and ethanol preference in mice. *Journal of Biological Chemistry* 245:2876–82. **777**

Sherif, M. 1935. A study of some social factors in perception. *Archives of Psychology* 27 (187). **674, 677**

Sherif, M. 1936. *The psychology of social norms.* New York: Harper & Row. **674, 684**

Sherman, M., and Key, D. B. 1932. The intelligence of isolated mountain children. *Child Development* 3:279–90. **100**

Shirley, M. M. 1931. *The first two years: A study of twenty-five babies,* vol. I. Minneapolis: University of Minnesota Press. **78**

Shneidman, E. S., and Mandelkorn, P. 1970. How to prevent suicide. In E. S. Shneidman, N. L. Farberow, and R. E. Litman (eds.), *The psychology of suicide.* New York: Science House. Pp. 125–43. **596**

Shouval, R.; Venaki, S. K.; Bronfenbrenner, U.; Devereaux, E. C.; and Kiely, E. 1975. Anomalous reactions to social pressure of Israeli and Soviet children raised in family versus collective settings. *Journal of Personality and Social Psychology* 32:477–89. **682**

Shultz, L. D. 1976. The "motheaten" condition. *Publication of Jackson Laboratory.* 23:3–4. **772**

Shuttleworth, F. K. 1939. The physical and mental growth of girls and boys age six to nineteen in relation to age at maximum growth. *Monographs of the Society for Research in Child Development* 4 (Serial No. 22):248–49. **63, 64, 65**

Simpson, G. G. 1949. *The meaning of evolution.* New Haven: Yale University Press. **732**

Sines, J. O.; Cleeland, C.; and Adkins, J. 1963. The behavior of normal and stomach lesion susceptible rats in several learning situations. *Journal of Genetic Psychology* 102:91–94. **512**

Singer, J. E.; Brush, C. A.; and Lublin, S. C. 1965. Some aspects of deindividuation: Identification and conformity. *Journal of Experimental Social Psychology* 1:356–78. **701**

Siqueland, E. R., and Lipsitt, L. P. 1966. Conditioned head turning in human newborns. *Journal of Experimental Child Psychology* 3:356–76. **82, 83**

Skeels, H. M. 1966. Adult status of children with contrasting early life experiences. *Monographs of the Society for Research in Child Development* 31 (Serial No. 105). **108, 110**

Skinner, B. F. 1931. The concept of the reflex in the description of behavior. *Journal of General Psychology* 5:427–58. **710**

Skinner, B. F. 1938. *The behavior of organisms.* New York: Appleton-Century-Crofts. **347, 720**

Skinner, B. F. 1948. *Walden Two.* New York: Macmillan. **30, 347, 710**

Skinner, B. F. 1953. *Science and human behavior.* New York: Macmillan. **30, 533**

Skinner, B. F. 1956. A case history in scientific method. *American Psychologist* 11:221–33. **716, 721**

Skinner, B. F. 1960. Pigeons in a pelican. *American Psychologist* 15:28–37. **343, 716**

Skinner, B. F. 1971. *Beyond freedom and dignity.* New York: Knopf. **30, 347, 433, 710, 714**

Skodak, M., and Skeels, H. M. 1949. A final follow-up study of one hundred adopted children. *Journal of Genetic Psychology* 66:21–58. **108**

Smiley, S. S. 1972. Optional shift behavior as a function of dimensional preference and relative arc similarity. *Journal of Experimental Child Psychology* 14:313–22. **82**

Smith, D. E. 1968. Acute and chronic toxicity of marijuana, *Journal of Psychedelic Drugs* 2:37–41. **583**

Smith, E. E. 1961. The power of dissonance techniques. *Public Opinion Quarterly* 25:626–39. **659**

Smith, K. U., and Smith, W. M. 1962. *Perception and motion: An analysis of space-structured behavior.* Philadelphia: W. B. Saunders. **259**

Smith, M. E. 1926. An investigation of the development of the sentence and the extent of vocabulary in young children. *University of Iowa Studies in Child Welfare* 3 (5). **97**

Snyder, S. H. 1972. Catecholamines in the brain as mediators of amphetamine psychosis. *Archives of General Psychiatry* 27:169–79. **809**

Social Action and the Law Newsletter, 1975, 2:1. **607**

Solomon, R. L.,; Kamin, L. J.; and Wynne, L. C. 1953. Traumatic avoidance learning: The outcomes of several extinction procedures with dogs. *Journal of Abnormal and Social Psychology* 48:291–302. **345**

Solomon, R. L., and Postman, L. 1952. Frequency of usage as a determinant of recognition thresholds for words. *Journal of Experimental Psychology* 43:195–201. **266**

Spearman, C. 1927. *The abilities of man.* New York: Macmillan. **101**

Spelt, D. K. 1948. The conditioning of the human fetus in utero. *Journal of Experimental Psychology* 38:375–76. **81**

Spence, K. W. 1957. The empirical basis and theoretical structure of psychology. *Philosophy of Science* 24:97–108. **22**

Spence, K. W. 1958. Behavior theory and selective learning. In M. R. Jones (ed.), *Nebraska symposium on motivation*, vol. 6. Lincoln: University of Nebraska Press. Pp. 73–107. **395, 396**

Spence, K. W.; Farber, I. E., and McFann, H. H. 1956. The relation of anxiety (drive) to performance in competitional and noncompetitional paired-associates learning. *Journal of Experimental Psychology* 52:296–305. **398**

Sperling, G. 1960. The information available in brief visual presentations. *Psychological Monographs* 74 (Whole No. 498):11. **282**

Sperling, G. 1963. A model for visual memory tasks. *Human Factors* 5:19–31. **286, 287**

Sperry, R. W., and Gazzaniga, M. S. 1967. Language following surgical disconnection of the hemispheres. In F. L. Darley (ed.), *Brain mechanisms underlying speech and language.* New York: Grune & Stratton. **843**

Spielberger, C. D. 1962. The role of awareness in verbal conditioning. In C. W. Eriksen (ed.), *Behavior and awareness.* Durham: Duke University Press. Pp. 73–101. **432**

Spitz, R. A., and Wolf, K. M. 1946. The smiling response: A contribution to the ontogenesis of social relations. *Genetic Psychology Monographs* 34:57–125. **263**

Stainbrook, E. 1972. The hospital as a therapeutic community. In A. M. Freedman and H. I. Kaplan (eds.), *Treating mental illness: Aspects of modern therapy.* New York: Atheneum. Pp. 385–94. **590**

Standing, L.; Conezio, J.; and Haber, R. N. 1970. Perception and memory for pictures: Single trial learning of 2500 visual stimuli. *Psychonomic Society* 19:73–74. **280**

Stanton, A. H., and Schwartz, M. S. 1954. *The mental hospital.* New York: Basic books. **647**

Starr, A., and Phillips, M. I. 1970. Verbal and motor memory in the amnestic syndrome. *Neuropsychologia* 8:75–88. **835**

Staub, E. 1974. Helping a distressed person: Social, personality, and stimulus determinants. In L. Berkowitz (ed.), *Advances in experimental social psychology.* New York: Academic Press. **698**

Steinschneider, A. 1967. Developmental psychobiology. In Y. Brackbill (ed.), *Infancy and Early Childhood.* New York: Free Press. **72**

Stephen, H., and Andy, O. J. 1969. Quantitative comparative neuroanatomy of primates: An attempt at phylogenetic interpretation. *Annals of the New York Academy of Science* 167:370–87. **742**

Stephenson, W. 1953. *The study of behavior.* Chicago: University of Chicago Press. **469**

Stern, C. 1949. *Principles of human genetics.* San Francisco: W. H. Freeman. **758**

Stevens, J. 1973. The electroencephalogram: Human recordings. In R. F. Thompson and M. Patterson (eds.), *Bioelectric recording techniques.* New York: Academic Press. **847**

Stevens, S. S. 1951. Mathematics, measurement, and psychophysics. In S. S. Stevens (ed.), *Handbook of experimental psychology.* New York: Wiley. **34**

Stevens, S. S. 1957. On the psychophysical law. *Psychological Review* 64:153–81. **193**

Stoner, J. A. F. 1961. A comparison of individual and group decisions involving risk. Master's thesis, Sloan School of Management, MIT. **692**

Streib, G. F. 1965. Are the aged a minority group? In A. W. Gouldner and S. M. Miller (eds.), *Applied sociology.* New York: Free Press. **165**

Streib, G. F. 1956. Morale of the retired. *Social Problems* 3:270–76. **169**

Streib, G. F. 1958. Family patterns in retirement. *Journal of Social Problems* 14:46–60. **168**

Suchman, R. G., and Trabasso, R. 1966. Color and poem preference in young children. *Journal of Experimental Child Psychology* 3:177–87. **82**

Sullivan, H. S. 1953. *The interpersonal theory of psychiatry.* New York: W. W. Norton. **559**

Sulzer, E. S. 1965. Behavior modification in adult psychiatric patients. In L. P. Ullmann and L. Krasner (eds.), *Case studies in behavior modification.* New York: Holt, Rinehart & Winston. Pp. 196–99. **572, 573**

Sundberg, N. D.; Tyler, L. E.; and Taplin, J. R. 1973. *Clinical psychology: Expanding horizons.* 2d ed. New York: Appleton-Century-Crofts. **550**

Sussman, M. B. 1965. Relationships of adult children with their parents in the United States. In E. Shanas and G. Streib (eds.), *Social structure and the family: Generational relations.* Englewood Cliffs, N.J.: Prentice-Hall. **168**

Swets, J. A.; Tanner, W. P., Jr.; and Birdsall, T. G. 1961. Decision processes in perception. *Psychological Review* 68:301–40. **191**

Swift, E. J. 1910. Relearning a skillful act: An experimental study in neuromuscular memory. *Psychological Bulletin* 7:17–19. **319**

Szasz, T. 1970. *The manufacture of madness: A comparative study of the Inquisition.* New York: Harper & Row. **503**

Szasz, T. 1976. Some call it brainwashing. *New Republic* 174:10–12. **663, 668**

Taffel, C. 1955. Anxiety and conditioning of verbal behavior. *Journal of Abnormal and Social Psychology* 51:496–501. **432**

Taylor, C. W., and Barron, F., eds. 1963. *Scientific creativity: Its recognition and development.* New York: Wiley. **366**

Taylor, J. S. 1953. A personality scale of manifest anxiety. *Journal of Abnormal and Social Psychology* 48:285–90. **397**

Teitelbaum, P. 1955. Sensory control of hypothalamic hyperphagia. *Journal of Comparative and Physiological Psychology* 48:156–63. **724**

Terman, L. M. 1925. *The mental and physical traits of a thousand gifted children.* Stanford: Stanford University Press. **103**

Terman, L. M. 1938. *Psychological factors in marital happiness.* New York: McGraw-Hill. **169**

Terman, L. M., and Miles, C. C. 1936. *Sex and personality.* New York: McGraw-Hill. **173**

Terrace, H. S. 1964. Wavelength generalization after discrimination learning with and without erros. *Science* 144:78–80. **339**

Thiessen, D. D. 1972. *Gene organization and behavior.* New York: Random House. **761, 769**

Thigpen, C. H., and Cleckley, H. M. 1954. A case of multiple personality. *Journal of Abnormal and Social Psychology* 49:135–51. **509**

Thigpen, C. H., and Cleckley, H. M. 1957. *The three faces of Eve.* New York: McGraw-Hill. **509**

Thomas, E. J. 1957. Effects of facilitative role interdependence on group functioning. *Human Relations* 10:347–66. **689**

Thompson, G. G. 1944. The social and emotional development of preschool children under two types of educational programs. *Psychological Monographs* 56 (Whole No. 5). **47**

Thompson, G. G. 1962. *Child psychology.* Boston: Houghton Mifflin. **22, 123, 148**

Thompson, G. G., and Horrocks, J. E. 1947. A study of the friendship fluctuations of urban boys and girls. *Journal of Genetic Psychology* 70:53–63. **150**

Thompson, R. F. 1967. *Foundations of physiological psychology.* New York: Harper & Row. **791, 820**

Thompson, R. F. 1975. *Introduction to physiological psychology.* New York: Harper & Row. **843**

Thompson, R. F.; Groves, P. M.; Teyler, T. J.; and Roemer, R. A. 1973. A dual-process theory of habituation: Theory and behavior. In H. V. S. Peeke and M. J. Herz (eds.), *Habituation.* New York: Academic Press. **838**

Thompson, W. R. 1954. The inheritance and development of intelligence. *Proceedings of the Association for Research in Nervous and Mental Disease* 33:209–31. **772, 773, 778**

Thomson, D. M., and Tulving, E. 1970. Associative encoding and retrieval: Weak and strong cues. *Journal of Experimental Psychology* 86:255–62. **301**

Thorndike, E. L. 1911 (1965). *Animal intelligence.* New York: Macmillan. **27, 712, 747**

Thorndike, E. L., and Woodworth, R. S. 1901. The influence of improvement in one mental function upon the efficiency of other functions (I); II. The estimation of magnitudes; III. Functions involving attention, observation, and discrimination. *Psychological Review* 8:247–61, 384–95, 553–64. **356, 357**

Thorne, F. C. 1950. *Principles of personality counseling.* Brandon, Vt.: Journal of Clinical Psychology Press. **559**

Thorpe, J. G.; Schmidt, E.; Brown, P. T.; and Castell, D. 1964. Aversion-relief therapy: A new method for general application. *Behavior Research and Therapy* 2:71–82. **545**

Thurstone, L. L. 1946. Theories of intelligence. *Scientific Monthly* 62:101–12. **101**

Thurstone, L. L. 1955. Differential growth of mental abilities. *Science* 121:627. **34, 104, 105**

Tighe, L. S., and Tighe, T. J. 1965. Overtraining and discrimination shift behavior in children. *Psychonomic Science* 2:365–66. **86**

Tinbergen, N. 1951. *The study of instinct.* London: Oxford. **707, 727**

Tinbergen, N. 1959. Comparative studies of the behaviour of gulls (*Laridae*): A progress report. *Behaviour* 15:1–81. **743, 745, 746**

Tinbergen, N. 1963. *The herring gull's world.* London: Collins. **744**

Tinbergen, N. 1965. Behavior and natural selection. In J. A. Moore (ed.), *Ideas in evolution and behavior.* New York: Natural History Press. Pp. 519–44. **744**
Tinbergen, N. 1968. On war and peace in animals and man. *Science* 160: 1411–18. **709**
Tinbergen, N. 1969. Ethology. In R. Harre (ed.), *Scientific thought 1900–1960.* Oxford: Clarendon Press. Pp. 238–68. **707**
Tinbergen, N.; Broekhuysen, J.; Feekes, F.; Houton, J. C. W.; Kruuk, H.; and Szulc, E. 1962. Egg shell removal by the black-headed gull *Larus ridibundus L.*: A behaviour component of camouflage. *Behaviour* 19:74–117. **745**
Titchener, E. B. 1896. *An outline of psychology.* New York: Macmillan. **12**
Towe, A. 1961. Central control of movement. *Neuroscience Research Program Bulletin* 9:1–170. **821**
Troll, L. E. 1971. The family of later life: A decade review. *Journal of Marriage and the Family* 33:263–90. **168**
Truex, R. G., and Carpenter, M. B. 1969. *Human neuroanatomy.* 6th ed. Baltimore: Williams & Wilkins. **742**
Tulving, E., and Osler, S. 1968. Effectiveness of retrieval cues in memory for words. *Journal of Experimental Psychology* 77:593–601. **301**
Tulving, E., and Thomson, D. M. 1973. Encoding specificity and retrieval. *Psychological Review* 80:352–73. **301**
Turiel, E. 1966. An experimental test of the sequentiality of developmental states in the child's moral judgments. *Journal of Personality and Social Psychology* 3:611–18. **131**
Turiel, E., and Rothman, G. R. 1972. The influence of reasoning on behavioral choices at different stages of moral development. *Child Development* 43:741–56. **131**
Tversky, A., and Kahneman, D. 1974. Judgment under uncertainty: Heuristics and biases. *Science* 185:1124–31. **437**
Ullman, L. P., and Krasner, L. 1975. *A psychological approach to abnormal behavior.* 2d ed. Englewood Cliffs, N.J.: Prentice-Hall. **503, 543, 588**
Underwood, B. J. 1949. *Experimental psychology.* 1st ed. Appleton-Century-Crofts. **358**
Underwood, B. J. 1957. Interference and forgetting. *Psychological Review* 64:49–60. **311**
Valins, S. 1966. Cognitive effects of false heart-rate feedback. *Journal of Personality and Social Psychology* 4:400–408. **627**
Verhave, T. 1966. The pigeon as a quality control inspector. *American Psychologist* 21:109–15. **716**
Vernon, P. E. 1960. *The structure of human abilities.* London: Methuen. **106**
Volgyesi, F. A. 1954. "School for patients," hypnosis-therapy and psychoprophylaxis. *British Journal of Medical Hypnotism* 5:8–17. **586**
Volta, A. 1800. On the electricity excited by the mere contact of conducting substances of different kinds. *Philosophical Transactions* 90:403–31. **585**
Wallen, R. 1970. Gestalt therapy and Gestalt psychology. In J. Fagan and I. L. Shepherd (eds.), *Gestalt therapy now: Theory, techniques, applications.* New York: Harper & Row. Pp. 8–13. **565**
Walsh, D. H. 1975. Interactive effects of alpha. In L. V. DiCara, T. X. Barber, J. Kamiya, N. E. Miller, D. Shapiro, and J. Stoyva (eds.), *Biofeedback and self-control: 1974.* Chicago: Aldine. Pp. 341–50. **576**
Walster, E. 1966. Assignment of responsibility for an accident. *Journal of Personality and Social Psychology* 3:73–79. **621**
Walters, R. H.; Leat, M.; and Mezei, L. 1963. Inhibition and disinhibition of responses through empathetic learning. *Canadian Journal of Psychology* 17:235–43. **135**
Walters, R. H.; Parke, R. D.; and Cane, V. A. 1965. Timing of punishment and the observations of consequences to others as determinants of response inhibition. *Journal of Experimental Child Psychology* 2:10–30. **135**
Warnock, J. 1903. Insanity from hasheesh. *Journal of Mental Sciences* 49:96–110. **583**
Waskow, I. E.; Olsson, J. E.; Salzman, C.; and Katz, M. M. 1970. Psychological effects of tetrahydrocannabinol. *Archives of General Psychiatry* 22(2):97–107. **583**
Watson, J. B. 1924a. *Behaviorism.* New York: Peoples Institute. **440**
Watson, J. B. 1924b. *Psychology from the standpoint of a behaviorist.* Philadelphia: J. B. Lippincott. **380**
Watson, J. B., and Rayner, M. 1920. Conditioned emotional reactions. *Journal of Experimental Psychology* 3:1–14. **328**
Watson, R. I. 1971. *The great psychologists.* 3d ed. Philadelphia: J. B. Lippincott. **5, 12, 15, 16**
Weber, E. H. 1912. Concerning touch. In B. Rand (ed.), *The classical psychologists.* Gloucester, Mass.: Peter Smith. **190**
Wechsler, D. 1955. *The measurement and appraisal of adult intelligence.* Baltimore: Williams & Wilkins. **101, 159**
Weick, K. E., and Gilfillan, D. P. 1971. Fate of arbitrary norms in a laboratory microculture. *Journal of Personality and Social Psychology* 17:179–91. **677**
Weinberg, K. S. 1955. *Incest behavior.* New York: Citadel. **527**
Weiner, B. 1966. The effects of motivation on the availability and retrieval of memory traces. *Psychological Bulletin* 65:24–37. **488**
Weiner, B. 1972. *Theories of motivation: From mechanism to cognition.* Chicago: Rand McNally. **397**
Weiner, B., and Kukla, A. 1970. An attributional analysis of achievement motivation. *Journal of Personality and Social Psychology* 15:1–20. **411**
Weiner, B., and Sierad, J. 1975. Misattribution for failure and the enhancement of achievement strivings. *Journal of Personality and Social Psychology* 31:415–21. **410**
Weiner, I. B. 1962. Father-daughter incest: A clinical report. *Psychiatric Quarterly* 26:607. **527, 528**
Weiner, L.; Becker, A.; and Friedman, T. T. 1967. *Home treatment: Spearhead of community psychiatry.* Pittsburgh: University of Pittsburgh Press. **590, 591**
Weiss, J. M. 1968. Effects of coping response on stress. *Journal of Comparative and Physiological Psychology* 65:251–60. **512**
Weiss, J. M. 1970. Somatic effects of predictable and unpredictable shock. *Psychosomatic Medicine* 32:397–409. **512**
Weiss, J. M. 1971. Effects of coping behavior in different warning signal conditions on stress pathology in rats. *Journal of Comparative and Physiological Psychology* 77:1–13. **512**
Werner, H. 1948. *Comparative psychology of mental development.* New York: International Universities Press. **50**
Werner, H. 1957. The concept of development from a comparative and organismic point of view. In D. B. Harris (ed.), *The concept of development.* Minneapolis: University of Minnesota Press. **50**
Werner, H., and Kaplan, B. 1950. The acquisition of word meanings: A developmental study. *Monograph of the Society for Research in Child Development* 15 (Serial No. 51). **372**
Wertheimer, Max. 1923. Untersuchungen zur Lehre von der Gestalt. *Psychologishe Forschung* 4:301–303. Translated by Don Cantor for Herrnstein, R. J., and Boring, E. G. 1965. *A source book in the history of psychology.* Cambridge: Harvard University Press. **12**
Westermarck, E. 1934. *Three essays on sex and marriage.* New York: Macmillan. **528**
Wever, E. G. 1949. *Theory of hearing.* New York: Wiley. **223**
Wheatstone, C. 1838. Contributions to the physiology of vision. *Philosophical Transactions of the Royal Society of London* 142:371–94. **251**
Wheeler, L.; Shaver, K. G.; Jones, R. A.; Goethals, G. R.; Cooper, J.; Robinson, J. E.; Gruder, C. L.; and Butzine, K. W. 1969. Factors determining choice of a comparison other. *Journal of Experimental Social Psychology* 5:219–32. **683**
White, R. W. 1959. Motivation reconsidered: The concept of competence. *Psychological Review,* 66:297–333. **428**
White, S. H. 1965. Evidence for a hierarchical arrangement of learning processes. In L. P. Lipsitt and C. C. Spiker (eds.), *Advances in child behavior and development,* vol. 2. New York: Academic Press. **85, 87, 106**
Whorf, B. L. 1956. *Language, thought, and reality.* New York: Wiley. **381**
Wilcoxon, H. C.; Dragoin, W. B.; and Kral, P. A. 1971. Illness-induced aversions in rat and quail: Relative salience of visual and gustatory cues. *Science* 171:826–29. **726**
Wilson, E. O.; Eisner, T.; Briggs, W. R.; Dickerson, R. E.; Metzenberg, R. L.; O'Brien, R. D.; Susman, M.; and Boggs, W. F. 1973. *Life on earth.* Stamford, Conn.: Sinauer. **735**
Wimer, C., and Prater, L. 1966. Some behavioral differences in mice genetically selected for high and low brain weight. *Psychological Reports* 19:675–81. **774**
Wimer, C.; Roderick, T. H.; and Wimer, R. E. 1969. Behavioral differences in mice genetically selected for brain weight. *Psychological Reports* 25:363–68. **774**
Wine, J. J., and Krasne, F. B. 1972. The organization of escape behavior in the crayfish. *Journal of Experimental Biology* 56:1–18. **837**
Wine, J. J.; Krasne, F. B.; and Chen, L. 1975. Habituation and inhibition of the crayfish lateral giant fibre escape response. *Journal of Experimental Biology* 62:771–82. **837**

Winick, M., and Rosso, P. 1969. Head circumference and cellular growth of the brain in normal and marasmic children. *Journal of Pediatrics* 74:774–78. **797**

Witkin, H. A.; Dyk, R. B.; Faterson, H. F.; Goodenough, D. R.; and Karp, S. A. 1962. *Psychological differentiation.* New York: Wiley. **468**

Wittkower, E. D., and Dubreuil, G. 1968. Cultural factors in mental illness. In E. Norbeck, D. Price-Williams, and W. M McCord (eds.), *The study of personality: An interdisciplinary appraisal.* New York: Holt, Rinehart & Winston. Pp. 279–95. **536**

Wolberg, L. R. 1972. *Hypnosis: Is it for you?* New York: Harcourt Brace Jovanovich. **575**

Wolf, S. 1965. The expectations of society. *Journal of Medical Education* 40:3. **511**

Wolf, S., and Goodell, H. 1968. *Harold G. Wolff's stress and disease.* Springfield, Ill.: Charles C. Thomas. **511**

Wolpe, P. 1969. *The practice of behavior therapy.* New York: Pergamon. **570**

Wolpe, P., and Lazarus, A. A. 1966. *Behavior therapy techniques: A guide to the treatment of neuroses.* New York: Pergamon. **570**

Woollard, H. H.; Weddell, G.; and Harpman, J. A. 1940. Observations on the neurohistological basis of cutaneous pain. *Journal of Anatomy* 74:413–40. **233**

Wright, J. 1974. Reflection impulsivity and information processing from three to nine years of age. Paper presented at American Psychological Association meeting. **88**

Wrightsman, L. S., Jr. 1960. Effects of waiting with others on changes in level of felt anxiety. *Journal of Abnormal and Social Psychology* 61:216–22. **681**

Yalom, I. D. 1971. Report in *Frontiers of Psychiatry: Roche Report* 1, No. 14. **569**

Yankelovich, D. 1969. *Generations apart.* New York: CBS News. **147**

Yarbus, A. L. 1967. *Eye movements and vision.* New York: Plenum Press. **269, 270, 292**

Yates, Aubrey J. 1975. *Theory and practice in behavior therapy.* New York: Wiley. **586**

Yates, F. A. 1966. *The art of memory.* London: Routledge and Kegan Paul. **305**

Young, T. 1807 (1971). On the theory of light and colours. In *Course of lectures on natural philosophy and the mechanical arts,* vol. 2. New York: Johnson Reprint Corp. **214**

Young, W. C. 1965. The organization of sexual behavior by hormonal action during the prenatal and larval periods in vertebrates. In F. A. Beach (ed.), *Sex and behavior.* New York: Wiley. **780**

Zaidel, E. 1973. Linguistic competence and related fucntions in the right hemisphere of man following cerebral commissurotomy and hemispherectomy. Ph.D. thesis, California Institute of Technology. **843**

Zander, A. F. 1971. *Motives and goals in groups.* New York: Academic Press. **689**

Zander, A. F., and Wolfe, D. 1964. Administrative rewards and coordination among committee members. *Administrative Science Quarterly* 9:50–69. **689**

Zaporozhets, A. V. 1965. The development of perception in the preschool child. In P. Mussen (ed.), *European research in cognitive development. Monographs of the Society for Research in Child Development* 30 (Serial No. 100). **75**

Zeaman, D., and House, B. J. 1963. The role of attention in retardate discrimination learning. In N. R. Ellis (ed.), *Handbook of mental deficiency.* New York: McGraw-Hill. **33, 86**

Zigler, E. F., and Harter, S. 1969. The socialization of the mentally retarded. In D. A. Goslin (ed.), *Handbook of socialization theory and research.* Chicago: Rand McNally. **33**

Zigler, E. 1963. Metatheoretical issues in developmental psychology. In M. H. Marx (ed.), *Theories in contemporary psychology.* New York: Macmillan. Pp. 341–69. **43**

Zimbardo, P. 1969. The human choice: Individuation, reason, and order versus de-individuation, impulse, and chaos. In W. J. Arnold and D. Levine (eds.), *Nebraska symposium on motivation.* Lincoln: University of Nebraska Press. Pp. 237–308. **701**

Zimbardo, P. 1970. The psychology of police confessions. In J. V. McConnell (ed.), *Readings in social psychology today.* Del Mar, Calif.: CRM Books, Pp. 102–107. **662**

Zimbardo, P.; Ebbeson, E.; and Fraser, S. 1968. *Emotional persuasion: Arousal state as a distractor.* Stanford: Stanford University Press. **650**

Zimbardo, P., and Ebbeson, E. 1970. *Influencing attitudes and changing behavior.* Reading, Mass.: Addison-Wesley. **650**

Zimbardo, P., and Formica, R. 1963. Emotional comparison and self-esteem as determinants of affiliation. *Journal of Personality* 31:141–62. **681**

Zimbardo, P.; Weisenberg, M.; Firestone, I.; and Levy, B. 1965. Communicator effectiveness in producing public conformity and private attitude change. *Journal of Personality* 33:233–55. **659**

Zinberg, N. E., and Kaufman, I. 1963. Cultural and personality factors associated with aging: An introduction. In N. E. Zinberg and I. Kaufman (eds.), *Normal psychology of the aging process.* New York: International Universities Press. **175**

Zitrin, A.; Dement, W. C.; and Barchas, J. D. 1973. Brain serotonin and male sexual behavior. In J. Zubin and J. Money (eds), *Contemporary sexual behavior: Critical issues in the 1970s.* Baltimore: Johns Hopkins University Press. Pp. 297–310. **544**

Zubek, J. P., and Solberg, P. A. 1954. *Human development.* New York: McGraw-Hill. **133**

Zucker, R. S.; Kennedy, D.; and Selverston, A. I. 1971. Neuronal circuit mediating escape responses in crayfish. *Science* 173:645–49. **838**

Name Index

Glossary and Subject Index

William J. Meyer, author of Chapter 2 on research methods and Chapters 3 through 6 on developmental psychology

Professor of psychology and director of the Doctoral Training Program in developmental psychology, Syracuse University
Ph.D., developmental psychology, Syracuse University, 1957
Advisor to a project evaluating the effectiveness of Project Follow Through
Research interests: learning and performance, cognitive development, children's friendships
Author: *Developmental Psychology* (Prentice-Hall, 1965) and *Studies of Childhood and Adolescence* (Ginn, 1967)

Ralph Norman Haber, author of Chapter 7 on sensation and Chapter 8 on perception

Professor of psychology, visual science and education, University of Rochester
Ph.D., psychology, Stanford University, 1957
Research interests: perception, vision, memory, motivation and emotion, computer applications and programming
Author: *Contemporary Theory and Research on Visual Perception* (Holt, 1968); *Information Processing Approaches to Visual Perception* (Holt, 1969)
Coauthor: *The Psychology of Visual Perception* (Holt, 1973); *Introduction to Psychology* (Holt, 1975)

Willard Runquist, coauthor of Chapter 9 on memory, Chapter 10 on learning, and Chapter 11 on cognition

Professor of psychology, University of Alberta
Ph.D., Northwestern University, 1956
Postdoctoral fellow with Kenneth Spence, University of Iowa
On board of directors, Canadian Psychological Association
Member of Psychological Research Grants Committee, National Research Council of Canada
Author of over seventy articles in Canadian and U.S. journals

Peggy A. Runquist, coauthor of Chapter 9 on memory, Chapter 10 on learning, and Chapter 11 on cognition; author of appendix on statistics

Assistant professor of psychology, University of Alberta
Ph.D., University of Alberta, 1971
Author of many journal articles

Bernard Weiner, author of Chapter 12 on motivation and Chapters 13 through 15 on the person

Professor of psychology, UCLA
Ph.D., personality psychology, University of Michigan, 1963
Research interests: personality traits and processes, behavior correction, social perception and motivation, and emotion
Author: *Theories of Motivation: From Mechanism to Cognition* (Rand McNally, 1972); *Success and Failure in Education: Motivators of Performance* (Ernst Klett, 1975)
Coauthor: *Attribution: Perceiving the Causes of Behavior* (General Learning Press, 1972)
Editor: *Achievement Motivation and Attribution Theory* (General Learning Press, 1974); *Cognitive Views of Human Motivation* (Academic Press, 1975)

Benjamin Kleinmuntz, author of Chapters 16 and 17 on abnormal behavior

Professor and director of clinical training, University of Illinois, Chicago Circle
Ph.D., clinical psychology, University of Minnesota, 1958
Research interests: psychodiagnosis, psychometrics, inventories and rating scales, personality assessment, psychopathology
Author: *Essentials of Abnormal Psychology* (Harper & Row, 1974) and numerous articles

Bertram H. Raven, author of Chapters 18 through 20 on social psychology

Professor of psychology, UCLA, and director or the Doctoral Training Program in personality and social psychology
Ph.D., social psychology, University of Michigan, 1953
Visiting professor: University of Nijmegen, Netherlands (Fulbright Scholar), Hebrew University in Jerusalem (Guggenheim Fellow), and London School of Economics (NIMH Special Fellow)
Research interests: social influence and group problem solving (laboratory studies) and social power relationships in field settings
Coauthor: *Social Psychology: People in Groups* (Wiley, 1976)
General editor: *Journal of Social Issues*

Charles L. Kutscher, author of Chapters 21 through 23 on comparative psychology

Professor of psychology, Syracuse University
Ph.D., physiological psychology, University of Illinois, 1962
Research interests: physiology of motivation, especially the internal factors that control drinking
Author: *Readings in Comparative Studies of Animal Behavior* (Xerox, 1971) and many articles

Arnold Leiman, author of Chapters 24 and 25 on biological psychology

Associate professor of psychology, University of California, Berkeley
Ph.D., psychology and brain research, University of Rochester
Research interests: sensory physiology and development of the nervous system
Author of twenty journal articles in fields such as electrophysiology of learning and memory, auditory neurophysiology, and nervous system tissue culture
Coauthor: chapter in *The Physiological Basis of Memory* (Academic Press, 1973) and chapter in *Annual Review of Psychology* 1968 (Annual Reviews, 1968)

This book was set by Applied Typographic Systems, Mountain View, California. The text typefaces combine 10-point Illumna and 10-point Vega Light, with display lines in Elegante Semibold.

Sponsoring Editor	Michael Zamczyk
Project Editor	Gretchen Hargis
Designer	Janet Bollow
Photo Research	Judith Chaffin, Brenn Lea Pearson, Faye Reddecliff
Permissions Editor	Judith Chaffin
Illustrator	Patrick Maloney
Technical Illustrators	Barbara Hack and Heather Kortebein
Cover Photograph	Tom Tracy

7890/54321